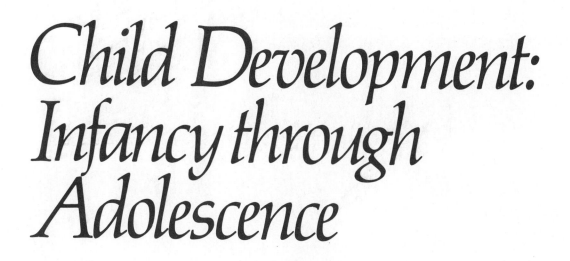

*Child Development:
Infancy through
Adolescence*

JOHN WILEY & SONS
New York   Chichester   Brisbane   Toronto   Singapore

Child Development: Infancy through Adolescence

Alison Clarke-Stewart
University of California at Irvine

Susan Friedman

*To all the children and parents
who offered us a slice
of their lives*

COVER PAINTING: **Martin A. Lowenfish at 4 yrs old**
INTERIOR AND COVER DESIGN: **Dawn L. Stanley**
PHOTO EDITOR: **Safra Nimrod**
COPY EDITOR: **Priscilla Todd**
PRODUCTION MANAGER: **Robin Besofsky**
TECHNICAL ART AND ILLUSTRATION: **Blaise Zito
Associates, Inc.**

Library of Congress Cataloging in Publication Data:

Clarke-Stewart, Alison, 1943–
  Child development.

  Includes bibliographies and indexes.
  1. Child development.   I. Friedman, Susan,
1947–   II. Title.   [DNLM: 1. Child Development.
WS 105 C613c]
RJ131.C567   1987   155.4   86-32570
ISBN 0-471-84493-4
Printed in the United States of America
10 9 8 7 6 5 4 3 2

Preface

This book has grown from a second fruitful collaboration between Alison, a developmental psychologist, and Susan, a writer. From the beginning, we have had two goals: to present the latest and best in theory, research, history, and ideas about how children develop, from conception through adolescence; and to present some of this information in portraits of real children. The parents and children whose words create the slice-of-life examples throughout this book are all real people, although Susan has given them fictional names to protect their privacy. The children represent a wide range of personalities, temperaments, and abilities, and their parents represent a wide range of philosophies of child rearing.

We have tried to tell the story of children's development comprehensively and cogently, to come up with a book that is engrossing, easy to read, and accessible to psychology majors and nonmajors alike. We have based it on a thorough combing of books and journals for the most recent and reliable research on genetics, brain growth and development, perceptual development, language, memory, and information processing, self-concept and identity, social bonds and attachment, the role of fathers, special stresses on families (divorce, mothers' work, living with handicaps, etc.), learning and behavior problems, and the developments special to adolescence such as scientific and logical thought, egocentrism, and psychosocial maturity.

In writing this book, we've gone through a bit of consciousness raising ourselves and have included fathers, not just mothers, in descriptions of children's development, because more and more fathers today take an active part in caring for their children. (When research participants were mothers exclusively, the text reflects this fact.) From chapter to chapter, we've also alternated the sex of ''the'' child—*he* learns so and so; *she* reaches for such and such—to avoid sexism.

The book is organized into six main parts. The first part describes the history and methods of the study of child development. The second part describes the workings of heredity and prenatal development. Each of Parts Three through Six is divided into separate chapters on physical, cognitive, and social and emotional development. Within this traditional structure, the parts follow children's development from infancy, through early and middle childhood, and into adolescence.

The organization, structure, readability, and absorbing interest of the text, we hope, make it easy to learn and to teach from. As teachers, we have taken pains to create a pedagogically effective book. Chapters are organized chronologically, but teachers also can readily use the book in courses arranged topically just by assigning chapters or parts of chapters in a topical order. To allow this, we have deliberately avoided overlap between chapters and have provided cross-references where necessary. Each chapter includes theory, research findings, and apt examples from real children's lives. We also have included focus boxes on subjects of special importance or interest. Key terms appear in bold type, and each chapter offers a summary and a list of suggested readings.

Acknowledgments

Like raising children, writing a book takes endless time and the support of many caring people. We deeply thank the parents and children who took the time to talk to us about their lives. A number of reviewers helped us to create a better teaching and learning tool: Doran French, University of Wisconsin; Suzanne Getz, Penn State University; Lila Gleitman, University of Pennsylvania; William S. Hall, University of Maryland; Elaine Justice, Old Dominion University; Frank Kessel, University of Houston; Linda Lavine, State University of New York at Cortland; Margaret Matthaei, San Antonio College; Carolyn Mebert, University of New Hampshire; M. C. Pugmire-Stoy, Ricks College; Dean Richards, University of California; Robert Siegler, Carnegie-Mellon University; Connie Steele, Texas Tech University; Ellen Strommen, Michigan State University; Ross Thompson, Nebraska University; Cynthia Whitfield, C. Whitfield Consulting.

We thank our editors at Wiley, Carol Luitjens, who encouraged us to write a book that would ''tell the story,'' and Warren Abraham, who has brought it all to fruition. Priscilla Todd kept her eagle eye on the editing of the manuscript, and Robin Besofsky, Dawn Stanley, and Safra Nimrod have marshaled it through the long production process. Sharon Hamill, a graduate student at UCI, treked to the library innumerable times in search of elusive references and never came back empty handed. We appreciate her good spirits and dedicated determination.

To our own children, to Christopher and Andrew, and to Harris, we say, thanks, as always, for being there.

Irvine, California   ALISON CLARKE-STEWART

New Haven, Connecticut   SUSAN FRIEDMAN

Contents

Foundations

chapter one

History and theories

The child before the science of child psychology

Today we largely take for granted the fact that infants and children look, speak, think, and play differently from older people. We believe that infancy and childhood unfold in gradual stages of development and that the standards for adults' and children's behavior differ greatly. "Don't be too hard on him," the doting grandparent insists, "He's only a child." Today children are sent to school and prohibited by law from working. Their families cherish the milestones of their development—the first steps, the first words, the early finger paintings and homemade cards—and tolerate many of their youthful displays of temper.

But only a few centuries ago, children as young as 6 were sent from home as servants or apprentice laborers. They were dressed as adults, expected to work like adults, and in many ways were treated like adults. Discipline was sometimes harsh, and children were expected to conform as early as possible to proper standards of behavior. Many children in the 16th, 17th, and early 18th centuries in the United States and England were treated in ways that today seem cruel and inhumane (Aries, 1962; Piers, 1978). Children were thought to need training in correct behavior, rather like domestic animals. Some parents punished their children severely, in the belief that a child's will had to be broken if society were not to be thrown into disorder. Puritan parents could be especially strict, for they believed that children were born as sinful creatures with devilish wills. Only hard work and strict limits would lead to salvation. Happiness was looked upon as ungodly. In extreme cases, children might be beaten or even killed for breaking rules.

Not all children were treated harshly, though. Many parents treated their children kindly and lovingly (Pollock, 1983). Most parents resorted to physical discipline only when milder measures had failed. Brutal, battering parents were rare. Even in the 1500s, educated parents understood that children are different from adults, that they play, and need adults' protection, discipline, and education. Parents' diaries reveal close family bonds, as they tell of mothers sitting through the night at a sick child's side and of children coming freely to their fathers for help with problems.

Even so, today's notion of childhood as a unique period of innocence, joy, and gradual development is new. Textbooks on child development are youngsters themselves, born of the relatively new philosophy that children are worthy of systematic study. Today we devote careful attention and scientific study to children's development, things that were not done in past centuries. How did we arrive at this point?

Philosophical roots: Locke and Rousseau

In the 18th century, scholars first recognized children as fitting subjects of intellectual interest. John Locke (1632–1704), a physician and philosopher, proposed that early experiences deeply influence later life. Children are not born as sinful creatures, he suggested. Instead, the infant is born as a blank slate, or *tabula rasa*, on which experiences in life write their story. Through interactions with people in the environment, each child develops his or her unique character and abilities. Because childhood is a formative period, Locke suggested, it merits the careful attention of adults. By encouraging their children's curiosity and answering their questions, parents would encourage their children to develop into rational, attentive, and affectionate people. Such careful parents would not have to resort to punishment. Locke believed that individual children were born with differences in intelligence and temperament, but he emphasized the role of learning and the importance of the parent as a rational teacher of a receptive child. Locke rejected the idea, popular during his lifetime, that children are born with knowledge. In modern terms, Locke saw **nurture**, or external forces, as the driving force in development.

A second philosopher, Jean-Jacques Rousseau (1712-1778), also challenged accepted beliefs about children. But whereas Locke emphasized the influence of nurture on development, Rousseau emphasized the importance of **nature**, or internal forces. Rousseau argued that children are not simply inferior adults or ignorant students. Children, Rousseau believed, are born with their own individual natures, and adults must not expunge this individuality in a quest for reason or social order. Adult knowledge, he argued, cannot and should not be poured into a child like water into a pitcher. To Rousseau, children were active, testing, self-willed explorers of their world, who should be allowed to grow with little pressure from their parents. Through a process of natural unfolding, children would reach the point where they could reason logically. Only then, late in childhood, should adults begin to reason with and actively teach children.

These two philosophers can be considered the first direct ancestors of the psychology of child development. They were the first scholars to write about the importance and uniqueness of the period of childhood, and in their differences of opinion brought to the field of developmental psychology one of its central issues—the question of whether nature or nurture is primarily responsible for shaping development.

The scientific forefather: Darwin

The next ancestor of developmental psychology appeared a century after Rousseau, when Charles Darwin (1809–1882) upset accepted beliefs with his theory of evolution. With this theory Darwin radically changed the way that scientists thought about the development of species, of societies, and of human beings. The idea of development was central to Darwin's *Origin of Species*, published in 1859, and for a half century after this treatise was published, scientists looked for developmental changes in and across different species. Development over the human life cycle—from a watery existence before birth, to crawling and creeping, and into maturity—they believed, would recapture the evolution of the human species from water-dwelling forms, through lower animals, to the primates, and finally *homo sapiens*. It was said that **ontogeny**—the development of the individual—repeats **phylogeny**—the development of the species. Studying one would reveal truths about the other. Scientists began searching for these truths by documenting the genesis of behaviors in the development of children. As it turned out, they were mistaken in their belief that ontogeny repeats phylogeny. But even so, these scientists were responsible for making the study of children's development into a science.

Darwin himself kept a baby journal in which he recorded the visible changes in his eldest child, Doddy, from the time he was born. Thus, Darwin not only introduced a theoretical rationale for a scientific approach to studying children's behavior, he also introduced a useful technique for gathering data.

The early 20th century: child psychology as a fledgling science

G. Stanley Hall was the first psychologist to study children and adolescents systematically.

G. Stanley Hall: childhood recollections

G. Stanley Hall (1844–1924) brought Darwin's wide-ranging curiosity and naturalist's outlook to the study of human behavior for its own sake. He was the first psychologist to take an interest in studying children and adolescents. Out of this interest, he carried out many studies in the 1880s and 1890s, including "The Contents of Children's Minds," "The Story of a Sand Pile," and "A Study of Dolls." These were enthusiastic, spirited, though scientifically undisciplined attempts to fathom children's development. Hall administered more than 100 such studies, yet he is criticized for not having had a clear theory of development and for not having conducted experiments or systematic observations. His method was simply to ask adults about what they did as children or what their own children did. This survey method was an improvement over the loose narrative recording methods in vogue at that time.

Perhaps it was the breadth of Hall's interests, at a time when psychology was forming itself into firmly identifiable schools of thought, that limited the influence of this psychological forefather of developmental psychology. Hall was a generalist at a time when specialists took all the laurels. He was an intuitive, passionate enthusiast at a time when dispassionate, precise measurement and observation were the rule. Nevertheless, by the beginning of the 20th century, through the influence of Hall and his contemporaries, the study of children, or "child study," had been established as a legitimate discipline. A journal for research on children had been launched, societies to observe children had been formed, and a series of biographical studies focusing on the childhood years appeared. Still, the field lacked tools with which to gather objective and quantifiable data. Its only methods of study were descriptive observations, in which children were regarded rather like trees or plants, and questionnaires, which were used to call forth recollections of childhood from adults.

Binet and Simon: the first IQ test

It was in France soon thereafter that child study acquired an important scientific tool. Alfred Binet (1857–1911) and Théophile Simon (1873–1961) devised the first standardized test of intelligence. Binet and Simon's efforts were prompted by the French government's need to find and separately educate children of low intelligence. Until Binet and Simon devised their intelligence test, educators had unscientifically categorized children into fuzzy categories such as "moron," "idiot," or "imbecile." But Binet and Simon's intelligence test was more precise. It started with easy questions and ended with difficult ones, and in between it covered the range of mental abilities from perception to reasoning. After testing many children of all different ages in the same, standardized fashion, Binet and Simon calculated age **norms** for the test, that is, the number of questions that most children of a particular chronological age could answer correctly. Individual children's test scores then could be measured against clear, quantifiable standards. Thus, this test gave psychologists an objective tool for the study of children's intelligence.

Arnold Gesell: natural blooming

Arnold Lucius Gesell (1880–1961) also systematically observed children at different ages. He observed and photographed them unobtrusively, through a one-way window (see photo at the beginning of chapter 2), a method that developmental psychologists still use today. The information about children's development that Gesell collected through his observations also is used today. His timetables detailing when most children reach certain milestones of development, published in *An Atlas of Infant Behavior* (1934) and *Infant and Child in the Culture of Today* (1943), are still widely available and are referred to by parents and pediatricians to chart children's growth and progress. These observations and developmental timetables were used by Gesell himself, however, not just to get information about how adequately individual children were developing but to support his firm belief that development is **maturational**.

Like Rousseau, Gesell conceived of development as a process of natural unfolding on the stage of environment. Development, he suggested, is the result of inherited factors, rooted in anatomy and physiology. It requires no pressure from the external environment. Thus, for example, mechanical walkers or walking lessons are neither helpful nor harmful, for when children's bodies are ready, they begin to walk (see Figure 1.1). Similarly, when children are ready, they begin to talk, to tell stories, and to read. According to

*Figure 1.1 Motor development in infancy is **maturational**. Although different infants reach motor milestones at slightly different ages, all infants, regardless of their ethnicity, social class, or temperament, reach them in the same order. The bottom of each bar in the graph indicates the age at which 25 percent of the infants tested could perform the behavior. The top indicates the age at which 90 percent could perform it.*

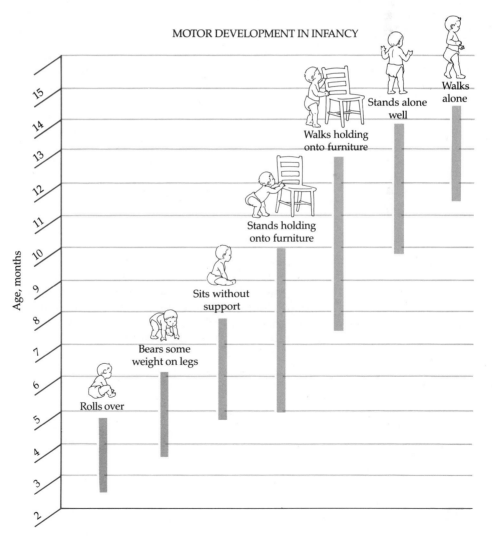

MOTOR DEVELOPMENT IN INFANCY

Walks alone

Stands alone well

Walks holding onto furniture

Stands holding onto furniture

Sits without support

Bears some weight on legs

Rolls over

Age, months

Gesell, children develop a bit like plants. Parents plant and tend them, but whether the plant turns out to be a hardy wildflower or a delicate rose is determined by the child's inheritance, not by the parents' care.

John Watson: the birth of behaviorism

An entirely different view of development issued from Gesell's contemporary, John Broadus Watson (1878–1958). For Watson, raising children was more like building a house than planting a garden. Parents and others "construct" children out of learned behaviors, habits, skills, and feelings. To explain how they do so, Watson turned to the ideas of **classical conditioning** presented by Ivan Pavlov (1849–1936) in his work with dogs. Watson demonstrated that children could be taught to fear neutral objects by pairing them with a scary or aversive stimulus, just as Pavlov had gotten dogs to salivate when they heard a sound that had been paired repeatedly with the presentation of food. In a demonstration of this principle, Watson placed an infant on a table in front of him. Watson's assistant then took the baby's familiar tame rabbit out of its box and handed it to the baby.

> He starts to reach for it. But just as his hands touch it I bang the steel bar behind his head. He whimpers and cries and shows fear. Then I wait awhile. I give him his blocks to play with. He quiets down and soon becomes busy with them. Again my assistant shows him the rabbit. This time he reacts to it quite slowly. He doesn't plunge his hands out as quickly and eagerly as before. Finally he does touch it gingerly. Again I strike the steel bar behind his head. Again I get a pronounced fear response. Then I let him quiet down. He plays with his blocks. Again the assistant brings in the rabbit. This time something new develops. No longer do I have to rap the steel bar behind his head to bring out fear. He shows fear at the sight of the rabbit. He makes the same reaction to it that he makes to the sound of the steel bar. He begins to cry and turn away the moment he sees it (Watson, 1928, pp. 52–53).

Watson's success in changing children's behavior led him to take a strong pro-nurture position on development. He asserted firmly that environmental conditioning brings about the child's learning and development and laid upon parents complete responsibility for their children's behavior:

> All we have to start with in building a human being is a lively squirming bit of flesh, capable of making a few simple responses such as movements of the hands and arms and fingers and toes, crying and smiling, making certain sounds with its throat. . . . Parents take this raw material and begin to fashion it in ways to suit themselves. This means that parents, whether they know it or not, start intensive training of the child at birth (Watson, 1928, pp. 45-46).

Watson's ideas about parents' responsibilities were unrealistic. Children are not just the products of their parents' training. Despite his controlled demonstrations, Watson's suggestions came more from his personal philosophy than from empirical study.

But Watson did contribute an experimental method to the scientific study of children. Until Watson came on the scene, psychologists had done much of their research by asking their subjects to report on their subjective experiences, a method known as introspection. Watson criticized introspection as unverifiable and as clearly inappropriate for child or animal subjects. Wanting to establish psychology as a purely objective branch of natural science, Watson (1913) proposed that psychologists study only *observable* be-

John Broadus Watson sought to make psychology an objective science by giving it one direction and one method, the observation of behavior.

havior and that their theoretical goal be simply the prediction and control of behavior. This approach, which Watson aptly named **behaviorism**, was a far cry not only from the impressionistic work of the introspectionists but from the naturalistic research of Darwin, Hall, and Gesell.

focus *John Watson: no coddling allowed*

John Watson had radical ideas about raising children according to behaviorist principles. One of his pet peeves was mothers who showed their children too much love.

> Loves are home made, built in. The child *sees* the mother's face when she pets it. Soon, *the mere sight of the mother's face* calls out the love response. . . .So with her footsteps, the sight of the mother's clothes, of her photograph. All too soon the child gets shot through with too many of these love reactions (Watson, 1928, p. 75).

The problem with "love reactions," he believed, was that they smothered a child's initiative and spontaneity. Watson asked mothers to

> . . . remember when you are tempted to pet your child that mother love is a dangerous instrument. An instrument which may inflict a never healing wound, a wound which may make infancy unhappy, adolescence a nightmare, an instrument which may wreck your adult son or daughter's vocational future and their chances for marital happiness (Watson, 1928, p. 87).

Parents, Watson argued, should behave like strict executives in an efficiently organized household. Like others of the day, Watson was concerned with "scientific management." The home, like the factory or the office, was to be managed efficiently, economically, and precisely. Like a model worker, an infant was to obey rules and to perform on time. Children were to be regulated and scheduled from their very first days. Feedings should be given the infant every four hours. As Watson wrote in a Children's Bureau pamphlet to mothers, *Are You Training Your Child to Be Happy*? (1930),

> – *Begin when he is born.*
> – Feed him at exactly the same hours every day.
> – Let him sleep after each feeding.
> – Do not feed him just because he cries.
> – Let him wait until the right time.
> – If you make him wait, his stomach will begin to wait.
> – His mind will learn that he will not get things by crying.

Toilet training, Watson believed, should begin when the infant is 1 to 3 months old. (Today's parents usually are advised to wait until a child acts "ready" for toilet training, somewhere between the ages of 2 and 3 years.) By aggressively administering enemas and by scheduling the infant for sessions on the potty, mothers were to eliminate dirty diapers in the early months. Watson's advice sounds harsh to us today, although his goals are those of conscientious parents everywhere: to raise productive, independent, and responsible members of society.

Sigmund Freud: innocence lost

A third, very different theory of how children develop was proposed by Sigmund Freud (1856–1939), a physician from Vienna. When Freud published his *Three Contributions to the Sexual Theory* (1905), he shocked his Victorian audience right down to their lace pantaloons. He claimed that children are born with the beginnings of sexual feelings, a belief that was not popular in the sexually repressive society of the day.

> Childhood was looked upon as "innocent" and free from the lusts of sex, and the fight with the "demon of sensuality" was not thought to begin until the troubled age of puberty. Such occasional sexual activities as it had been impossible to overlook in children were put down as signs of degeneracy and premature depravity or as a curious freak of nature (Freud, 1935, p. 58).

Freud, however, asserted that sexuality starts at the beginning of life, and because of it childhood is dramatic, complicated, and full of psychological conflict.

The sexual experiences of childhood, moreover, lay the foundation for adult behavior. Thus the infant's pleasure in nursing at the mother's breast foreshadows adult pleasure in kissing, sucking, and licking. Events connected with early oral pleasures (or deprivations) foreshadow adult habits like overeating, heavy drinking, or smoking. Freud was the first of developmental psychology's forebears to stress so clearly the connections between childhood and adult behavior. He saw a unifying thread to a person's development from birth to death. Early experiences, he believed, leave an unconscious mark in a person's memory. They are "unconscious" because a person forgets or represses them, and they are, therefore, unavailable to ordinary, conscious thought. Only through dreams, jokes, slips of the tongue, and other windows to the unconscious can a person retrieve unconscious ideas. Yet these unconscious ideas shape development.

In earliest infancy, the ideas and experiences that are most important center in the infant's mouth. In this **oral stage**, Freud believed, the infant focuses on the pleasures of sucking and taking in food with mouth and tongue. In this period, the mother must not frustrate the infant's impulses to suck and mouth objects. In the second year of life, the child focuses on the conflict between keeping things in and letting them go, between asserting his or her selfhood and will—"No, it's mine!"—and acting on generous impulses—"Here, Mommy." How the mother negotiates the conflicts of toilet

Sigmund Freud dramatized the links between the physical pleasures of the infant and the sexual satisfactions of the adult.

training in this **anal stage**, Freud believed, shapes the child's concepts of self and others. During the **phallic stage**—in the next three years—the child develops an especially strong desire for the parent of the opposite sex. A boy wants to replace his father in his mother's affections, a conflict Freud called **Oedipal**, after Oedipus, the character in Greek myth who killed his father and married his mother. A girl wants to replace her mother in her father's affection, a desire called by Freud the **Electra conflict**, after another mythical Greek character. Said one not untypical 5-year-old girl, rather cruelly, to her mother, ''I hope that you die before Daddy does. Then I will marry him.'' At this stage, boys begin announcing, ''I'm going to marry Mommy,'' and children may try to maneuver themselves into their parents' bed. Children resolve their Oedipal and Electra conflicts by the end of this period, according to Freud, by identifying with their same-sex parent and thereby possessing their opposite-sex parent vicariously. After the phallic stage comes the quieter **latency period** of middle childhood, during which, Freud theorized, sexual feelings go underground and children immerse themselves in school and community activities. Finally, with puberty, the adult sexuality of the **genital stage** begins.

Freud suggested the existence of three mental structures within each individual. The first structure is the powerful, pleasure-seeking, instinctual **id**. It drives children—and adults—to want and desire, to yearn for satisfaction and pleasure. In infants' cries for food and attention—and smiles when parents deliver—and in the barrage of the toddler's ''I want cookie,'' ''Dat *my* bike!'' and ''No nap,'' we hear early echoes from the id. The **ego** is the mental structure that emerges with the rapid expansion of memory. It coexists, not always peacefully, with the id. Ego development helps children to control their impulses, to bury some ideas in the unconscious, and to allow others to bubble to the surface. Ego is realistic self-interest, and it governs the choice of realistic goals and realistic strategies for maximizing pleasure and coping with stress. In the preschooler's transparent attempts to get what he or she wants—''I love you, Nana. What did you bring me?''—we see evidence of the ego. The rules and inhibitions laid down by parents—''Brush your teeth before bedtime''—and culture—''Do unto others. . . .'' are internalized in the third mental structure, the **superego**. Informally called a ''conscience,'' the superego helps children to obey rules, follow ethical principles, and get along with others.

With his sweeping ideas about child development, Freud influenced later thinking in psychology. Although not all his ideas have been accepted by the scientific community, some have been, and these have become part of the way we all think about children today. For example, we now believe that children have irrational and hidden motives, that they express sexual and emotional impulses, that their lust for pleasure often puts them at loggerheads with their parents' and others' needs for order, control, and reason, and that how children resolve internal and external conflicts affects their lives as adults. To a large extent, these beliefs started with Freud.

The middle 20th century: theories of child development

Dollard, Miller, Sears: social learning theorists

Despite Freud's influence on the field of psychology, from 1930 to 1960 it was learning theory that dominated mainstream American psychology. American psychologists went beyond the principles of classical conditioning that Pavlov

focus *Behavior modification*

Parents have long known that rewarding a child's behavior will cause it to recur. It doesn't take too many bedtime pleas for "one more glass of water, p'eeze" for parents to grump, "No more!" B.F. Skinner, an influential behaviorist, carefully raised his daughter according to principles of operant learning. Here Skinner describes his 9-month-old daughter sitting on his lap at nightfall:

> The room grew dark, and I turned on a table lamp beside the chair. She smiled brightly, and it occurred to me that I could use the light as a reinforcer. I turned it off and waited. When she lifted her left hand slightly, I quickly turned the light on and off. Almost immediately she lifted her hand again, and I turned the light on and off again. In a few moments she was lifting her arm in a wide arc "to turn on the light" (Skinner, 1979, p. 293).

Skinner later toilet trained his daughter with a potty chair that played a song whenever she urinated into it.

Operant learning techniques have been used to solve serious developmental problems, too. Children who are socially isolated and who barely speak have been trained to communicate. First they are rewarded for uttering any sound, then for words, then phrases, and finally for short sentences. Psychologists also have modified children's violent aggression with behavior modification techniques. They may reward the children, first, with tangible prizes like candies and stickers for cooperating and sharing. Later they may reward them with tokens like check marks or poker chips that are redeemable for toys, gum, or comic books. In addition, they may punish aggressive behavior with a brief time-out period such as five minutes alone in a room. After several weeks, children consistently given this treatment are usually cooperative, at least in the setting in which they have been reinforced. These are just a few examples of the many kinds of behavior problems that have been modified through reinforcement applied systematically, conscientiously, and consistently.

and Watson had explored. Their experiments showed that stimuli regularly associated with **primary (biological) drives** that are basic to human survival, including hunger and thirst, themselves became the objects of **secondary**, or **learned drives**. John Dollard, Neal Miller, and Robert Sears applied this principle of learning to children's development. For example, they conceived of an infant's attachment to the mother as a secondary drive, learned through association with the infant's primary hunger drive. They suggested that the infant learns to seek the mother's love and attention because she gives food and comfort and alleviates pain. With the principles of primary and secondary drives as their guide, Dollard, Miller, and Sears proposed a theory of development based on learning theory.

Baer, Bijou, Gewirtz: operant learning theorists

Another group of psychologists also tried to explain children's development in terms of learning. Psychologists following the lead of B. F. Skinner, such as Sidney Bijou, Donald Baer, and Jacob Gewirtz, applied principles from **operant learning theory** to the study of children. The principles that they adapted were those of **operant conditioning**. Skinner had demonstrated that people (and animals) keep acting in ways that are rewarded by pleasant consequences and stop acting in ways that are punished by unpleasant consequences. Bijou, Baer, and Gewirtz demonstrated that children's social behavior can be shaped by the **reinforcement** or **punishment** of their actions. Gewirtz (Gewirtz and Boyd, 1977b), for example, analyzed interactions between mothers and infants, showing that a mother's smiles and encouragement are reinforced by her infant's smiles, gurgles, and movements, while the latter, in turn, are strengthened by the smiles and movements of the mother. Operant learning theory had the virtue of being easy to demonstrate, especially in a tightly controlled setting. The effectiveness of reinforcement to change the frequency of children's behaviors—saying ''yes,'' paying attention, and so forth—was amply demonstrated in many **behavior modification** experiments in laboratories, schools, and homes.

Bandura, Walters, Mischel: observational learning

Yet children seem to learn many things in the absence of obvious reinforcement. They imitate their parents and others without getting tangible rewards—the 3-year-old copies the way her mother's hands gesture as she speaks, and the 4-year-old stomps into his room and slams the door just like his older brother does. Why? A third group of learning theorists, including Albert Bandura, Richard Walters, and Walter Mischel, proposed a theory of observational learning to account for this kind of learning. They suggested that children watch and listen to how others behave and then imitate them. Children, according to this theory, need no obvious reward for copying, say, the way that parents push the shopping cart, brush their hair, hold their forks, or button their shirts, or for copying the way that other children speak, or blow bubbles with their drinking straws, or laugh at bathroom jokes.

Bandura conducted research in the laboratory to observe systematically the conditions under which imitation flourishes. There he found that children were most likely to imitate adults who were nurturant, powerful, affectionate, and who possessed things that the children wanted. At home, he suggested, children imitate their parents because their parents have these very qualities. According to observational learning theorists, the fact that parents are loving and powerful in their children's eyes is enough to motivate the children to imitate them. Parents need not resort to bribes of cuddly dolls or shiny red trucks to get the children to use toilets instead of diapers and spoons instead of fingers.

These three groups of learning theorists—espousing social learning, operant learning, and observational learning—kept alive Locke and Watson's pro-nurture view of development from the 1930s to the 1960s. They reflected the dominant American view, in psychology and in much of American society, of people's perfectibility, controllability, and changeability. But a number of other theories of development drew small but growing followings over this period as well.

research focus

Imitating a model

According to observational-learning theorists, children learn by imitating the behavior of parents, other children, film and television characters. To test the degree of children's willingness to imitate, Albert Bandura and his co-workers (Bandura, Ross, and Ross, 1963) showed 3- and 4-year-old children a film of a person acting aggressively and watched to see whether the aggressive acts would be imitated. The children were divided into four groups of 24; half of each group were boys, half girls.

The experimenters showed half of the children in the first group a man, the other half a woman, punching, hammering, hitting, and yelling at a large rubber clown. They showed another group a movie of the same adults carrying out their aggressive acts. They showed a third group of children a cartoon in which a cat punched, hit, and hammered the clown. The fourth group of children was exposed to no aggressive model at all. At this point, all of the children were allowed to play briefly with some attractive toys and then deliberately frustrated by having the toys removed. Finally, the children were allowed to play with a set of toys that included a large rubber clown. The question: would the children punch and hit the clown?

They certainly did. The children imitated the aggressive behavior that they had seen. Compared with the children who hadn't seen any aggression, the children who had seen it acted far more aggressively. Girls were more likely to imitate the female model, boys the male model. The cartoon prompted the greatest number of aggressive acts, but the filmed and the live adult model did their share as well of prompting aggression in the children.

These scenes from films of Bandura's research demonstrate how children imitate exactly the attacks of an adult model on a Bobo doll.

John Bowlby focused the attention of researchers and policymakers on the importance for healthy development of having a strong relationship with mother in the first years of life.

Erik Erikson has been a major contributor to our understanding of the psychological crises occurring in childhood, adolescence, and adulthood.

Tinbergen, Lorenz, Bowlby: the ethological approach

One such theory was **ethology**, the study of how animals behave in their natural habitats. Ethology stands in clear contrast to behaviorism, with its emphasis on how behavior may be modified by external forces in artificial environments. Ethology has much in common with the naturalistic approaches of Darwin and Gesell. One of the principles of animal behavior demonstrated by ethologists Niko Tinbergen and Konrad Lorenz, which later was picked up by developmental psychologists, was that animals are born with predispositions to learn particular forms of behavior during **critical periods** of their lives. Soon after they hatch, for example, ducklings begin to follow the nearest large moving object they see. This phenomenon is called **imprinting**. Under ordinary circumstances, ducklings imprint on their mothers and follow them about—a biological mechanism that helps keep the ducklings safely near their source of food and care. Under unusual circumstances, however, hatchlings might imprint on something else—a person or a large red ball, for example.

Influenced by the ethological approach, John Bowlby, a British psychoanalyst, explored the question of whether human children also become attached to their mothers or other people during a critical period in infancy. Bowlby analyzed the process through which infants develop deep and loving relationships with their mothers. Human infants, like hatchlings, need to stay close to their mothers to survive. The forms of behavior that infants are born with, like crying, grasping, clinging, and, later, following, help them to stay close to their mothers. From this physical closeness, children develop emotional bonds to their mothers. Bowlby stressed the dangers to children's development if their caretakers are numerous or unstable, emotionally or physically distant, insensitive or inattentive. His theory strongly influenced thinking about social and emotional development and was important in changing practices in orphanages and other residential institutions for children. It presented a very different view of the development of an infant's relationship with the mother from those proposed by learning theorists. For them, the infant is reinforced for interacting with the mother or develops a relationship with her because she satisfies the need for food. It is also different from that proposed by Freud, in which the relationship of mother and infant revolves around the sensual satisfaction of sucking. Bowlby studied the same issues as Freud and followed for some distance in his footsteps, but he was influenced by other theoretical approaches and other data and ultimately came up with his own unique theory of social development. The same is true of the next developmental theorist we discuss.

Erik Erikson: a psychosocial integration

Erik Erikson is a psychologist who first studied child psychotherapy in Vienna with Anna Freud, Sigmund Freud's eminent daughter. With this training he devised a way of interpreting children's behavior by watching them play with dolls and other toys rich in possible psychological meanings. Erikson then moved to the United States, where he did clinical interviews and therapy with such diverse groups as Northwest Indians, Harvard students, soldiers, and civil rights volunteers. Out of this varied background, Erikson expanded Freud's theory of **psychosexual development** and developed his own theory of **psychosocial development**.

Unlike Freud's, Erikson's theory of human development covered the whole life span (see Table 1.1). Erikson stressed social and cultural aspects of development, not just sexual ones, as Freud had done. Erikson proposed that the way in which individuals cope with their social experiences shapes their lives. Individuals, he suggested, cross eight different crisis points over the course of their lives. At each crisis, people are vulnerable to developing negative feelings like guilt, inferiority, or isolation. But they also stand poised to enlarge and deepen their personalities to encompass positive feelings like trust, intimacy, generativity, and integrity. In each crisis period, the ''inner laws of development'' create possibilities, which are shaped by the people and the social institutions—schools, church, judicial system, and so on—that

Table 1.1
Developmental progression

Age	Freud's stages	Erikson's crises
1st year	*Oral Stage* Infants obtain pleasure through stimulation of the mouth, as they suck and bite.	*Trust versus Mistrust* Infants learn to trust, or mistrust, that their needs will be met by the world, especially by the mother.
2nd year	*Anal Stage* Children obtain pleasure through exercise of the anal musculature during elimination or retention.	*Autonomy versus Shame, Doubt* Children learn to exercise will, to make choices, to control themselves; or they become uncertain and doubt that they can do things by themselves.
3rd to 5th year	*Phallic (Oedipal) Stage* Children develop sexual curiosity and obtain pleasure through masturbation. They have sexual fantasies about the parent of the opposite sex and guilt about their fantasies.	*Initiative versus Guilt* Children learn to initiate activities and enjoy their accomplishments, acquiring direction and purpose. If they are not allowed initiative, they feel guilty for their attempts at independence.
6th year through puberty	*Latency Period* Children's sexual urges are submerged; they put their energies into acquiring cultural skills.	*Industry versus Inferiority* Children develop a sense of industry and curiosity and are eager to learn; or they feel inferior and lose interest in the tasks before them.
Adolescence	*Genital Stage* Adolescents have adult heterosexual desires and seek to satisfy them.	*Identity versus Role Confusion* Adolescents come to see themselves as unique and integrated people with an ideology; or they become confused about what they want out of life.
Early adulthood		*Intimacy versus Isolation* Young people become able to commit themselves to another person; or they develop a sense of isolation and feel they have no one in the world but themselves.
Middle age		*Generativity versus Stagnation* Adults are willing to have and care for children, to devote themselves to their work and the common good; or they become self-centered and inactive.
Old age		*Integrity versus Despair* Older people enter a period of reflection, becoming assured that their lives have been meaningful, and they grow ready to face death with acceptance and dignity; or they despair for their unaccomplished goals, failures, and ill-spent lives.

fill or frustrate the person's needs. Although some parts of one's personality may be predetermined, the resolution of each phase of personality development is worked out within specific social situations.

In infancy, for example, the infant learns to trust or mistrust that his needs for food, warmth, and comfort will be met by the people around him. How reliably and responsively a mother attends to the infant's needs affects not only the relationship between the two but the more general attitude the infant forms toward the world. This attitude affects how well the infant deals with the next important crisis, when as a toddler he must deal with his earliest expressions of independence. Whether the toddler resolves this second crisis with self-control or with uncertainty and shame depends on how his parents respond to his attempts at independence—whether they respond with tolerance and support or with impatience and anger. The resolution of this second crisis in turn affects the child's ability to meet the next crisis, and so on.

Erikson, like Freud, saw development as occurring in distinct *stages* during a person's lifetime. He suggested that what happened in one stage was qualitatively different from what happened before or after, and developments in one stage built on those in earlier stages. All people progress through the stages in the same order, although not necessarily at the same rate. In normal development, people go forward through the stages, not backward.

This view of development as occurring in stages is different from the view held by learning theorists, who saw development as gradual, cumulative, and continuous. It is a view expressed strongly by the next theorist we discuss.

Jean Piaget: master theorist

Jean Piaget (1896–1980) was perhaps the one single theorist with the greatest effect on modern developmental psychology. Systematically and intensively observing children—his own three included—over his entire lifetime, Piaget developed and tested the fullest existing explanation of how human thought develops from infancy to adulthood. Trained in biology to observe expertly, Piaget watched, recorded, and sometimes intervened in the behavior of his

By observing children in their ordinary activities and by asking them probing questions, Swiss psychologist Jean Piaget was able to construct a theory of how children's minds develop.

focus   *Jean Piaget in his own words*

INTERVIEWER: It is clear that coming out of your background. . . when you suddenly ran over and started with live children, you were no longer sitting in an armchair, you were no longer working with animals or theorems, you were beginning to do things with children. How did your colleagues react to you? Didn't they think this was a rather strange way for an armchair philosopher or laboratory scientist to start behaving?

PIAGET: My colleagues were disturbed. An old botanist friend of mind said, "You, you are lost to science." But then he had me tell him what I was doing, and he became all excited, and said, "Oh, if I were only a psychologist. . .!"

INTERVIEWER: Dr. Piaget, in American psychology we find learning and learning theory of great interest, particularly learning as a function of external reinforcement as Skinner has emphasized. . . . You do not focus on learning as obviously as many American psychologists do. . .

PIAGET: We have to redefine learning. We have to think of it differently. First of all, learning depends upon the stage of development. . . . And development is not simply the sum total of what the individual has learned. Secondly, in thinking of reinforcements, we must not think only of external reinforcements but of internal reinforcements, through self-regulation. . . .

INTERVIEWER: . . . Would you say that. . .natural curiosity is in fact the important thing in the process of human development?

PIAGET: Yes, yes. But it is a curiosity which goes through various steps, in the sense that whenever one problem is solved, new problems are opened up. These are new avenues for curiosity. We have to follow this development of problems. We should not allow children a completely free rein on the one hand, nor channel them too narrowly on the other hand. . . . Implicit curiosity keeps growing and flourishing. . . . Once when one of my children was in his playpen—this was when he was at the sensorimotor level, well before any language—I held out an object to him horizontally, so that if he simply tried to pull it towards himself, it was blocked by the rails of the playpen. He tried various positions, and finally got it in, but he got it in by chance, and he wasn't satisfied. He put it back outside the playpen and tried to do it again, and continued until he understood how he had to turn it to get it through the rails. He wasn't satisfied just to succeed. He wasn't satisfied until he understood how it worked (Evans, 1973, pp. 67-71).

young subjects. Here is an example of an observation he made on the crying of a newborn:

> Obs. 1: On the very night after his birth, T was wakened by the babies in the nearby cots and began to cry in chorus with them. At 0;0 (3)[1] he was drowsy, but not actually asleep, when one of the other babies began to wail; he himself thereupon began to cry. At 0;0 (4) and 0;0 (6) he again

---

[1] In Piaget's shorthand, this represents the age 0 years, 0 months, and 3 days.

began to whimper, and started to cry in earnest when I tried to imitate his interrupted whimpering. A mere whistle failed to produce any reaction (Piaget, 1962, p. 7).

Similar records were made as Piaget watched infants look for toys hidden under pillows, watched children pour water from one glass into another, asked children the rules to their games, and listened carefully as they revealed their reasoning. From such carefully recorded observations, Piaget wove hypotheses, tested them repeatedly, and then joined them into a comprehensive theory of the stages of cognitive development. In Piaget's theory, children are born ready to adapt to and to learn from the world. They do not have to be taught deliberately to crawl or to walk or, later, that objects obey certain physical laws and people obey moral rules. Whereas Locke, Watson, and the learning theorists believed that knowledge was imposed on the child from outside, and Rousseau and Gesell believed that abilities were inborn, Piaget set these two beliefs into balance. To him, children construct knowledge as they mentally organize information from the environment. Infants and children actively participate in their own development. They manipulate and explore their world, guided by their ''mental structures'' or mental representations of how things work. Qualitative changes in these mental structures occur for all children as they make shifts in their organization of knowledge in a particular order of stages (see Table 1.2).

Although Piaget's theory of cognitive development is in part already being replaced by other theories, Piaget's careful and systematic observations have provided the most vivid and detailed picture so far of the developing cognitive capacities of the child. The notions he proposed offered important insights into children's thinking and reshaped how developmental psychologists thought about intellectual development, about the active way in which children approach learning, and about the interaction of nature and nurture. Piaget was a brilliant observer of children, and his work was instrumental in showing adults how to consider children's thought on *children's* terms. The broad distinctions he made among stages of development from infancy through childhood continue to be useful for describing children's thought. There is no question that Piaget's work changed the way that people think about thinking and the ways in which they talk about the influence of nature and nurture.

Table 1.2
Piaget's stages of cognitive development

Stage	Activities and achievements
Sensorimotor Birth to 2 years	Infants discover aspects of the world through their sensory impressions, motor activities, and coordination of the two.
Preoperational 2 to 7 years	Children cannot yet think by operations, by manipulating and transforming information in basic and logical ways. They can think in images and symbols and form mental representations of objects and events.
Concrete Operational 7 to 11 years	Children can understand logical principles that apply to concrete, external objects.
Formal Operational Over 11 years	Adolescents and adults can think abstractly. Their thinking is no longer constrained by the givens of the immediate situation but can work in probabilities and possibilities.

Trends in the study of child development in the 1970s

The 1970s saw a number of changes in the study of child development that were to some extent inspired by Piaget's work. One change was an intensified search for the origins of development—which was Piaget's goal as well. Sophisticated research methods and medical techniques pushed back the frontiers of understanding to earliest infancy and even beyond, to events before birth. Following from Piaget's recognition of the infant as an active initiator and learner rather than a helpless creature buffeted by random events, developmental researchers focused their attention on demonstrating the amazing competence of infants. Today we understand that infants initiate contact and influence their surroundings from the moment of birth. They cry and look, vocalize and smile, manipulate objects, hold their parents' attention, and place their personal stamp on interactions. One infant gallops toward every new object and physical feat, throwing herself into learning to roll over, creep, and walk. Another moves only his eyes and hands as he stares dreamily at shapes and colors. Let a stranger approach, and he hides his face in Mother's shoulder. One result of seeing infants as active participants has been an interest in individual differences in infants' temperaments—bold explorer, shy dreamer—and how these differences in temperament affect parents and others. How do the relationships of the adventurous, active baby, who energetically explores for hours on end, differ from those of the quiet baby, who sleeps or plays in one spot most of the day, for example? This is one of the questions that developmental researchers today are exploring.

A related focus of research is the question of how strongly infants' early experiences determine their later development. Researchers in the 1970s suggested that the effects of early experience, although important, were not permanent or irreversible, as many psychologists in the 1960s, influenced by Freud, Erikson, and Bowlby, had believed. They found, for example, that when young children who had been deprived of stimulation were adopted into rich family lives, they generally caught up to children who had enjoyed advantages from the start. Today, most developmental psychologists take a

Infants are active and competent beings who place their personal stamp on interactions with the people and things in their small world, a fact that was not properly appreciated by psychologists until the 1970s.

moderate position on the issue of early experience, asking to what extent and under what conditions early experience is reversible. They are more likely to talk about the interaction of nature and nurture than to make strong claims for the effect of either one alone and to analyze aspects of development according to whether they are more resistant or more vulnerable to effects of the environment.

Another major shift after Piaget's work became known in the United States in the early 1960s was a marked trend toward studying children's cognition. Developmental psychologists investigated how children perceive form and depth, how they learn language, what they understand about rules, ideas, and principles. Even developmental psychologists who were primarily interested in children's social and emotional development felt the influence of this trend. They integrated the methods, theory, and findings of research on cognitive development with the study of social and emotional events and began to explore the domain of children's ''social cognition''—knowledge about the social world.

Theories in perspective

Theories are important because they provide frameworks for ideas and information. They offer general rules and principles that help to organize empirical results. They give scientists something to hang their facts and findings on. Theories form the trunk and major branches; hypotheses and data, the smaller branches and twigs of scientific knowledge. In developmental psychology, each of the theories we have discussed serves this function. Each enriches our understanding of the complexities of human development. Each sheds light on the processes of development and helps to organize facts and hypotheses. Of course not all the theories we have presented can be correct. Which one is right? The truth is that no one theory is all right or all wrong. All the theories that we have discussed have been tried and found wanting in some respect, if only because they don't cover everything we know about development. Yet each also has contributed to our knowledge in long-lasting ways.

From Freud's psychosexual theory we have retained the ideas that unconscious motives affect behavior in subtle, complicated ways, that people's needs, impulses, and problems change as they get older, and that extreme experiences in the first few years of life can leave an indelible mark on later psychological development. From learning theory we have retained the idea that children's actions can be controlled by the manipulation of reward and punishment and by the actions of models whom they can imitate. From Gesell's maturational theory we have retained the notion that there is a biological current underlying normal growth; development is not imposed totally from without. From Piaget's theory of cognitive development we have learned that infants and children are not passive receivers of experience but are, instead, active builders of their own knowledge. As the field of developmental psychology develops, it is encouraging to see that our explanations of development are growing less extreme and simplistic, more subtle and eclectic, as elements from a variety of theories—old and new—are absorbed and integrated.

New theoretical approaches

Developmental psychologists today are not limited to the theories we have described—maturational, psychosexual, psychosocial, learning, cognitive. Researchers in the 1980s are also influenced strongly by new theoretical ap-

proaches—information processing, dialectical, life span, ecological, and sociobiological—and by new versions of the old theories—neobehavioristic, neo-
Freudian, and neo-Piagetian.

Information processing

Information processing is an approach to understanding human behavior
and development that came in with computers. People, like computers, take
in information and remember it. How they do so is the central question in the
information-processing approach. The roots of the information-processing
approach are in the fields of computer science, communications theory, and
linguistics. From computer science came the recognition that people and
computers are both manipulators of symbols. From communications theory
came the notions of information coding and channel capacity. From linguistics
came information about how people build and use grammars. The information-processing approach—like computers—quickly became popular in the
1970s and now dominates the field of cognitive psychology.

Developmental psychologists who take an information-processing approach study how information is processed and remembered by people of
different ages. Do 2-year-olds remember less efficiently than 8-year-olds? Do
preschoolers tell more disorganized stories than older children? If so, why?
Information processers suggest that young children do not think as well as
older children because they have not yet learned strategies for deploying their
mental processes efficiently and because they have accumulated less knowledge. The information-processing approach has proved useful in the study of
cognitive development as researchers have uncovered both strengths and
weaknesses in Piaget's theory. The results of their investigations will be
discussed in later chapters on cognitive development.

Dialectical approach

To psychologists who take a **dialectical view**, human development is a process
of continual change. All development evolves out of a state of imbalance.
Upheaval and disequilibrium are utterly necessary. Stability and calm are
merely temporary stepping-stones in the turbulent stream of human development, as a person achieves temporary syntheses between opposing positions.
The child emerging from the tantrums and stubbornness of the toddler period
with a degree of self-control and amiability, only to plunge headlong into
vacillation between "Me a baby, Mommy" and "Me do it *myself*, Mommy. Me
a big boy," illustrates this disequilibrium. Psychologists with a dialectical
view do not ask how people achieve tranquility and find answers. These were
the questions that Piaget asked. His stages of development represent cognitive equilibrium. Psychologists with a dialectical view ask how people create
problems and raise questions (Riegel, 1976). The dialectical approach is opening new windows and producing new ideas for developmental psychologists
interested in processes such as problem solving, communication, and language.

Life span approach

In the past, developmental psychologists studying children tended to see
developmental change as leading in a single direction, toward a single end
point—maturity. They viewed childhood and adolescence as periods of developmental growth and gain, adulthood as static, and old age as a period of
loss and decline. Developmental psychologists taking a **life span** approach
suggest that developmental psychologists consider all human change, from
the very beginning to the very end of life, to be development. They stress the

potential for growth during adulthood and old age (and conversely, for decline during childhood or adolescence). The life span approach has broadened the horizons of developmental psychology.

Life span developmental psychologists also have demonstrated the importance of broad historical contexts within which people develop. Children who grew up during the Great Depression have, as adults, different values from those who were young in the complacent 1950s, life span researchers have shown. Children who receive the benefits of computer education in elementary school likely will have different cognitive strategies from those whose math curriculum centered on Jolly Numbers workbooks. Life span developmental psychologists take major social and technological historical changes into account when they describe the development of individuals and groups over the life span.

Ecological approach

Developmental psychologists who take an **ecological** approach consider how children accommodate to the environments in which they grow and live. They are interested in how settings and contexts influence behavior and development. According to Urie Bronfenbrenner, a prime spokesman for this approach, the settings or environments in which children grow up can be viewed as systems, which exist simultaneously at various levels. The **microsystem** is composed of the network of ties between children and their immediate settings such as school or family. The **mesosystem** is composed of the network of ties among major settings in the child's life. For example, the mesosystem for an American 12-year-old might include ties among family, school, friends, church, and camp. The **macrosystem** is composed not of settings that directly affect a child, but of broad, general, institutional patterns in the culture such as the legal, political, social, educational, and economic systems.

Ecological psychologists systematically study these systems within which the child develops. Like the ecologist in the natural sciences who investigates the life and times of the porpoise by studying all the nearby sea creatures and the human boaters and hunters and water polluters who make up the porpoise's world, the ecological psychologist examines factors at many different levels in the human environment. For instance, he or she might investigate the social class of the children under study, their family's composition, and the type of day-care center or nursery school they were attending and then would look for complex patterns of interactions between the children's development and these aspects of their environments.

Sociobiology

According to sociobiologists, behavior has a genetic basis. **Sociobiology** is a modern extension of the naturist positions of Rousseau, Darwin, Gesell, and Lorenz. Sociobiologists like Harvard's Edward Wilson, an entomologist, and Robert Trivers, a biologist, have suggested that social behavior, like physical traits, is the direct product of evolution and, furthermore, that the behavior that improves the chances of a person's genes being reproduced will be passed on genetically to the next generation. Some developmental psychologists have found that the sociobiological approach sheds light on important questions about child development, such as why there are inborn differences between the sexes, how children's social groups are organized into dominance hierarchies, what the bases of the attachment between parents and children are, and how and why parents invest their time and energy in caring for their offspring. In the long run, how useful sociobiology will prove for understanding human development remains an open question, but it is a theory that is likely to influence the field of child development in the 1980s and to enrich traditional psychological theories.

New versions of old theories

Erikson's psychosocial theory of development, as we pointed out, was a revision and extension of Freud's psychosexual theory. In the last decade, revisions of learning theory and of Piaget's cognitive developmental theory also have appeared. Bandura (1980), for example, incorporated cognitive elements into social learning theory and stressed the role of thinking in children's learning. Children are more likely to imitate a model, for example, if they think that imitation is what is desired. Their actions also are influenced by their self-perceptions—their judgments about how effective they are likely to be in a situation. These self-perceptions are based on past successes, evaluations by other people, and observations of other people's performance. In another revision of social learning theory, Mark Lepper (1983) incorporated another cognitive element, children's understanding of why they are doing something. When children believe that external forces rather than their own internal motivations are making them do something, their intrinsic interest in doing it declines. These revisions of learning theory might be classified as **neobehavioristic**.

There are also **neo-Piagetian** theories—theories that are based on Piaget's structural theory of cognitive development but go beyond it. Theories by Juan Pascual-Leone (1980), Robbie Case (1985), and Kurt Fischer (1980) fall into this category. These theorists retain Piaget's idea that development occurs in stages, but they change the specifics. According to Pascual-Leone and Case, each higher stage is based on the child's ability to store more items in short-term working memory and to perform familiar cognitive activities automatically. According to Fischer, abilities develop in three tiers: sensorimotor skills, representational skills, and abstract skills. Each tier can be broken down into increasingly complex levels. As children master specific skills, they build upon and transfer skills from one domain to another. Development is gradual, and people attain relatively different degrees of proficiency within levels. Only in the skills that they are called on to perfect most consistently do people reach their highest possible level. The rule, not the exception, thus is for people to achieve unevenly within levels and to be at different levels for different skills.

These neo-behaviorists and neo-Piagetian theories represent developmental psychologists' best efforts to integrate new data into old theoretical frameworks. With all these new theoretical approaches—information processing, dialectical, ecological, life span, sociobiological, neobehavioristic, **neo-Freudian**, and neo-Piagetian—our understanding of development undoubtedly will continue to grow and develop through the next decades as it has grown and developed since the beginning of the century.

Social influences on the study of child development

Over the years, the study of child development has been influenced by more than abstract theoretical concerns. Developmental psychologists have wanted to know more than how to describe and explain development; they also have wanted to control, change, and improve development. The field of child development has been influenced by people's desire to find answers to impor-

In the 1980s, when the mothers of so many young children work outside the home, a major social concern has been to provide these children with good day care and a major research concern has been to study the effects of day care on children's development.

tant social problems and concerns. For example, developmental psychologists were instrumental in setting up and studying kindergartens early in this century, because they wanted to provide young children with good environments for learning. They became interested in studying children's nutrition, growth, and dental development when, during World War I, thousands of presumably healthy young men, given enlistment physical examinations, showed evidence of shockingly poor nutrition and tooth decay. They began important longitudinal studies of development from infancy to adulthood—the Fels Longitudinal Study, the Berkeley Growth Study, the Berkeley Guidance Study, and the New York Longitudinal Study—because they were concerned about the practical problems of child rearing. They conducted valuable studies of how early environment affects the long-term social, academic, and psychological growth of children from various ethnic backgrounds, after widespread alarm about black children's performance in school was voiced in the 1960s. They did important research on sex differences as a result of the wave of feminism in the 1970s. More recently the research of developmental psychologists has included investigations of such practical problems as how children's development is affected by television, day care, mothers' working, and divorce, and how to predict, prevent, and treat children's autism, hyperactivity, learning disabilities, and depression.

What developmental psychologists study

What are the questions—both theoretical and practical—that most interest today's developmental psychologists?

What is development?

The most basic underlying question for developmental psychologists, obviously, is "What is development?" The answer, though, is not as obvious as the question. Developmental psychologists must try to distinguish development—and more specifically, human development—from all other kinds of change, like learning, forgetting, brain damage, and drug effects. "Development" implies that the change is systematic, not random; that it is perma-

25

nent, not temporary; that it is progressive, not regressive—it goes forward not backward; that it is steady, not fluctuating; that it occurs over some period of time within a person's lifetime, not in an hour or over two generations; that it occurs for all people, not just a few; and perhaps most centrally, that it is related to a person's increasing age and experience.

The nature of developmental change

The next obvious question for developmental psychologists is how abilities and behavior, language and emotions, moral understanding and gender roles, social skills and sympathy change as people get older. What can a 4-year-old do and say that a 2-year-old cannot? How is the moral reasoning of an adolescent different from that of a 10-year-old or a 30-year-old? At what age can children first count, speak, tie their shoes? An important question is whether the changes in any particular trait, ability, or behavior are continuous—increasing gradually and steadily over time, as learning theorists like Watson or Skinner suggested—or discontinuous—occurring in sudden spurts or stages, as Piaget proposed. To developmental psychologists, this issue is central. A related question is whether the rate and the pattern of development are the same for everyone. Do children who start out low on some ability remain at the bottom of their peer group, or do they later bob to the top, surpassing even their precocious peers? Do children who start out more competent than others stay that way, developing at a constant rate, or do they go through periods when their abilities develop less quickly and their age-mates are able to catch up?

To make judgments about continuity, developmental psychologists must face the problem of recognizing continuity when it happens. Unlike physical growth—"every day and every way getting bigger and better"—psychological growth involves changes in *form*. The question for developmental psychologists then is how to recognize what different behaviors mean at different ages. Take crying, for example. Does an infant's crying mean the same as an adolescent's crying, because the overt behavior—tears, grimaces, sobs—is obviously similar, or does the infant's crying reflect a difficult temperament and mean the same as rulebreaking and rebelliousness in an adolescent? Developmental psychologists try to trace the threads of continuity in intellect, social actions, and personality as they answer questions about the nature of developmental change.

Domains of development

Another kind of question that interests developmental psychologists is how development in different areas of human functioning fits together. Typically, the field of developmental psychology is divided into three separate domains:

- physical development, including body changes and motor development;
- cognitive development, including thought and language; and
- social-emotional development, including personality and relations with other people.

But people are whole beings, and their behavior is not sharply divided into three neat categories. Development involves interconnected changes across all domains. As the infant eats and gains weight (physical domain), she smiles and coos at her parents (social-emotional domain), who then talk to her and stimulate her hearing (cognitive domain) and give her opportunities to develop skills like grasping a spoon (physical domain), while at the same time allowing her to explore the smells and textures of her food (cognitive domain) as they beam fondly at the mess she is making (social-emotional domain)—

and so on. To study the development of the whole child, developmental psychologists ask questions that cross domains. For example, "How does feeling sad or having a physical handicap affect children's learning?" "How does learning to crawl affect infants' social opportunities?" "How does knowing a second language affect adolescents' thinking and interacting with others?"

Causes of development

The last general research question for developmental psychologists is "What causes development?" In the past, as we have seen, scientists interested in the causes of human development often cast their questions in extreme forms. Is development a product of inborn, internal forces—"nature"—or is it a product of environmental, external forces—"nurture"? Do people inherit intelligence, or does intelligence develop through personal experiences? Do people inherit their physical size and shape, their moral tendencies, their love of music, or do these qualities develop as a result of environmental influences? More recently, extreme positions of nature versus nurture have softened. Psychologists now ask more subtle questions about how internal and external forces work *together* to produce an individual's development. How are inherited aspects of a person's intelligence, morality, musicality, physical size and shape, they ask, influenced by environmental conditions? What are the limits of these environmental influences? How do inherited characteristics themselves influence the environment? How do the relative influences of heredity and environment change with age?

In even more subtle questions, developmental psychologists ask about the internal mechanisms of development. How do transitions between developmental levels of functioning actually take place? What makes the child's mind leap—or creep—to the realization that objects are permanent, that mothers and fathers are worth pursuing, that words stand for things, or that you can't put square pegs into round holes?

Looking forward

Developmental psychology is a lively and important field of research and study. Developmental psychologists study questions that are intellectually challenging and pragmatically useful. They have much to teach—and much to learn.

Development is a complex journey, with winding paths, sharp curves, critical turning points, and many roads not taken. Developmental psychologists are now quite knowledgeable about many of the *facts* of development: they know what newborns can see and hear, when babies start to walk and talk, whether preschoolers can run and read, and what changes puberty brings. They are getting better at predicting the direction that a person will take on the developmental journey—whether he or she will do well in school, be active and fidgety, cheat on tests, feel insecure in strange situations, or beat up the teacher. They are learning more and more about the *processes* of development, about how people learn new habits, incorporate new information, form new relationships, and about how these depend on inherited traits, past experiences, and present circumstances. Still, there is much to learn.

Future developmental psychologists will be less content to describe the developmental landscape and more concerned with explaining what underlies it. They will probe the connections between brain and behavior, hormones and health, inheritance and intelligence, culture and child care. They will search for evidence to support their theoretical constructs, and in their search for developmental continuities, they will integrate knowledge from different domains of development with knowledge gained from other areas of psychology as well as from fields like genetics, physiology, neurology, and anthropology.

Developmental psychology is a fascinating, fertile field, one that is well worth your cultivation. You will get your introduction to it in this book, as you go from the very beginning of human life through the end of adolescence, seeing along the way the issues, facts, theories, and questions about how children develop.

This book reflects our view of the state of the art in developmental psychology. Much space in the book is given to descriptions of children's abilities and behavior at different ages—what children can do at 2 months, 2 years, and 12 years. These are the fundamental data of developmental psychology and provide a necessary basis for understanding human development. But where possible we have also discussed theoretical explanations of what these abilities and behavior mean. There is no single theoretical framework tying together the different chapters of the book, because, as yet, there is no single theory tying together all the data in developmental psychology. Human development is extremely complex—more complex than the best of our theories. We have discussed aspects of different theories where they seem most important—either because, historically, they inspired the research or because, currently, they seem to explain it. We have in some places related data to traditional theories—behaviorism, Freudian, Piagetian—but the thrust of the book comes more from contemporary theoretical approaches—neo-behaviorist, neo-Freudian, neo-Piagetian, ecological, information processing. Our view of theory is eclectic and integrative. Our view of development is also eclectic and integrative. We see development as interactive, characterized by both continuities and discontinuities, involving both overt behavior and underlying structures, subject to multiple internal and external forces which jointly give rise to a variety of developmental trajectories and outcomes.

Summary

1. The study of child development is a product of the 20th century, although its philosophical roots extend back to John Locke's and Jean Jacques Rousseau's ideas about human nature. G. Stanley Hall founded the study of child development in the United States. Binet and Simon devised the first objective, standardized test of children's intelligence. Three powerful theories of development were proposed by Gesell (maturational), Watson (behaviorist), and Freud (psychoanalytic).

2. During the middle of the 20th century, American psychology was dominated by learning theory. Social learning theorists applied principles of primary and secondary drives to development. Operant learning theorists used a mechanistic learning theory to explain social behavior, proposing that it is a series of responses that can be increased by reinforcement. Observational-learning psychologists suggested that children learn social behavior by observing and imitating others, without external reinforcement. Erik Erikson introduced his theory of human development as a series of crises over the whole life span. Jean Piaget elaborated an interactionist theory of children's cognitive development that remains influential today.

3. Recent trends in the study of child development have included the study of ever younger infants, the belief that infants are active and competent,

and a questioning of the belief that early experience affects development irreversibly and permanently.

4. In the 1980s, new approaches likely to influence the study of child development are information processing, dialectical, life span, ecological, sociobiological, neobehavioristic, neo-Freudian, and neo-Piagetian.

Key Terms

nurture	genital stage	psychosexual development
nature	id	psychosocial development
ontogeny	ego	information processing
phylogeny	superego	dialectical
norm	primary (biological) drive	life span
maturational	learned (secondary) drive	ecological
classical conditioning	operant learning theory	microsystem
behaviorism	operant conditioning	mesosystem
oral stage	reinforcement	macrosystem
anal stage	punishment	sociobiology
phallic stage	behavior modification	neobehavioristic
Oedipal conflict	ethology	neo-Piagetian
Electra conflict	critical period	neo-Freudian
latency period	imprinting	

Suggested readings

ARIÈS, PHILIPPE. *Centuries of Childhood.* New York: Random House (Vintage Books), 1962. The metamorphosis of the concept of childhood from the Middle Ages to the present view of childhood as a distinct phase of life, traced through paintings, diaries, school curricula, and the history of games.

GINSBURG, HERBERT, and OPPER, SYLVIA. *Piaget's Theory of Intellectual Development* (2nd ed.). Englewood Cliffs, N.J.: Prentice-Hall, 1979. An explanation of Piaget's theory and helpful examples of each stage of cognitive development, in words any undergraduate can understand.

HALL, CALVIN. *A Primer of Freudian Psychology.* New York: New American Library, 1979. Delivers what it promises, an understandable overview of Freud's enormous output, for those who are starting to examine his ideas.

KAGAN, JEROME. *The Nature of the Child.* New York: Basic Books, 1984. An elegantly written discussion of historical and contemporary views of the child which shows how ideas have changed over the years.

KESSEN, WILLIAM. *The Child.* New York: Wiley, 1965. Readings selected from 1200 years of Western writing about children, connected by comments tracing the history of child study.

MILLER, PATRICIA. *Theories of Developmental Psychology.* New York: W. H. Freeman, 1983. A good overview of the major theories in child development: Piagetian, Freudian, psychosocial, social learning, information processing, ethological.

SOMMERVILLE, J. *The Rise and Fall of Childhood.* Beverly Hills, Calif.: Sage, 1982. A concise history of childhood throughout civilization.

chapter two
Methods

Many studies, many methods

A study of dolls (1896)

G. Stanley Hall, the first psychologist to study children, believed that a study of children's play with dolls would be important to the young and growing field of child psychology. He believed this, he said, because dolls were so popular among children, ''so nearly universal among both savage and civilized peoples,'' and because playing with dolls showed children's instincts at work. He therefore designed a series of questions about children's experiences with their dolls and circulated them among some 800 teachers and parents. He received 648 completed questionnaires—a good return by any standard.

Hall began to codify and categorize the thousands of pages his subjects had returned. There were no computers in 1896, no courses in statistics. Hall was charting new territory as he worked with the returned questionnaires. He first described:

> ***"Material of which Dolls Are Made, Substitutes, and Proxies"***
> Of 845 children, with 989 preferences, between the ages of three and twelve, 191 preferred wax dolls; 163, paper dolls; 153, china dolls; 144, rag dolls; 116, bisque dolls; 83, china and cloth dolls; 69, rubber dolls; 12, china and kid [leather] dolls; 11, pasteboard dolls; 7, plaster of paris dolls; 6, wood dolls; 3, knit dolls; while a few each preferred papier-maché, clay, glass, cotton, tin, celluloid, French, Japanese, brownie, Chinese, sailor, negro, Eskimo dolls, etc. (Ellis and Hall, 1896, cited in Kessen, 1965, p. 153).

Hall believed that nothing illustrated the ''doll instinct'' and the ''vigor of the animistic fancy'' so well as the kinds of doll substitutes children made. He then listed these substitutes:

> Pillows were treated as dolls by 39 children, who often tied strings around the middle of the pillow, using a shawl for the skirt; sticks, sometimes dressed in flowers, leaves, and twisted grass were used by 29; bottles, filled with different-colored water and called different people, some with doll-head corks, by 24; cob or ear of corn (red ears favored, corn silk for the hair, a daisy perhaps serving for a hat) by 19; dogs by 18; cats and kittens by 15 (Kessen, 1965, p. 154).

Rudimentary as his methods were, out of Hall's ''statistical'' descriptions emerged a detailed picture of children's play and preferences late in the Victorian era.

> In our returns curly hair is preferred to straight; red cheeks are a special point of beauty, as are red knees in fewer cases. Boy dolls are only about one-twelfth of all, and it is remarkable how few dolls are babies rather than little adults. . . . Out of 579 answers . . . 88 mentioned preference for blue eyes; 27, for brown eyes; and 8, for black eyes. As to hair preferences 118 mention light hair; 62, curly hair; 27, dark hair; 8, real hair; and 5, red hair (Kessen, 1965, p. 157).

The doll study included sections on feeding and disciplining dolls, on dolls' sleep, illnesses, names, hygiene, families, and accessories. Hall noted that there seemed to be no ''law of relationship''—what today's researcher might term a correlation—between the size of a doll and the size or age of its child-owner. He took up the question of sex differences, too, and whether boys did or should play with dolls. Boys, he found, ''are naturally fond of and should play with dolls.'' Hall believed it was unfortunate that doll play was considered right for girls rather than boys. Although one must beware of making boys effeminate, Hall said, he was nevertheless convinced that "on the whole, more play with girl dolls by boys would tend to make them more sympathetic with girls as children, if not more tender with their wives and with women later" (Kessen, 1965, p. 160).

In this example of one of the earliest studies of children's development, Hall was not guided by a theoretical framework or question in designing his research. His statistical analyses were of the simplest sort, and he was not beyond speculating freely about what he thought his findings implied.

A study of feeding and thumb-sucking in infants (1950)

In Robert Sears and George Wise's study of feeding and thumb-sucking in infants, the theoretical basis of the research was clear and explicit: social learning theory. Sears and Wise set out to test whether infants develop a secondary, or learned, drive of sucking because sucking is consistently associated with the primary goal of food. They predicted that they would find that infants who had sucked more, that is, who had been weaned from breast or bottle to a cup at a later age, would have a stronger sucking drive. They predicted that these infants would have been more disturbed when their mothers began to wean them and would have been more likely to suck their thumbs.

Sears and Wise contacted the families of 80 children who were private patients of a Kansas City pediatrician. At the time of the study, which was spring 1946, the 80 children ranged in age from 2 to 10 years old. They came from 75 different families, of which most were middle class, Protestant, and headed by a working father and a mother who stayed at home to care for her children. All the children studied were normal, healthy members of stable families.

The study consisted of a series of interviews of mothers who had been asked in a preliminary letter to participate in a study of normal child development. Proceeding from an eight-page mimeographed questionnaire, the interviewer, a man, spent roughly an hour asking about the children's general health and development, sleeping and eating habits, toilet training, social relationships, level of activity, nervous habits, temperament, and sexual development (see Table 2.2). The interviewer was careful not to stress feeding habits over other aspects of the children's histories, and he "adopted an objective but interested and sympathetic attitude." Sears and Wise were aware of the limitations inherent in such a plan. First, the interviewer could not record the mothers' comments verbatim, so the language of the answers was sometimes that of the interviewer. (Psychologists did not use tape recorders in 1946.) Second, the researchers had to depend on the mothers' inevitably subjective interpretations of their children's behavior. Third, they had to rely on mothers' memories of events, and human memory is never infallible.

Sears and Wise broke their data down into subsets to test their prediction. First they divided the 80 children into groups according to how long they had fed by sucking. A group of 10 were weaned to a cup by the age of 2 weeks. A middle group of 18 were weaned between 2 weeks and 3 months. The "late" group of 52 children were weaned after 4 months of age. Sears and Wise then established a scale that assigned a numerical value to the degree of frustration each child was reported to have shown in reaction to weaning. As had been predicted, their results showed that the longer a child had been fed by sucking, the more disturbed the child had been at weaning. But when they tested whether thumb-sucking was related to the strength of the child's sucking drive, they found only a weak relation.

Sears and Wise's study was clearly more "scientific" than Hall's. They were guided by a specific theoretical question, they used somewhat more complex statistics, and they kept closer to the evidence in interpreting their findings.

A study of television's effects on children's behavior (1973)

By 1973, the science of studying children was more advanced. In that year, Lynette Friedrich and Aletha Huston Stein of Pennsylvania State University published a study of how young children were affected by television. Friedrich and Huston Stein took pains to describe the theoretical background of their work, especially their debt to the influential work of Albert Bandura. Bandura, as we have seen, had theorized that children learn simply by observing. It was Friedrich and Huston Stein's intent to study such learning in a "naturalistic" rather than in a "contrived" setting. Their subjects were 97 children—52 boys, 45 girls—between 3 and 5 years old. They were all attending a summer nursery school. For the first three weeks, the psychologists simply observed the children's behavior. During the next four weeks, they showed the children television programs with aggressive, prosocial, or neutral content. Within each of two classrooms, children were divided into an Aggressive Condition, in which they saw aggressive "Batman" and "Superman" cartoons; a Prosocial Condition, in which they saw "Mr. Rogers" episodes, emphasizing friendship, sharing, accepting rules, controlling aggression, and the like; and a Neutral Condition, in which they saw films that were neither aggressive nor prosocial. The third two weeks of the study were used for evaluating any effects of the television viewing. The psychologists observed the children's behavior, gave them intelligence tests, tested their knowledge of the programs' content and interviewed their mothers.

Children in the Aggressive Condition were found to be less able to tolerate delay than they had been before seeing the aggressive films. Also, if they were children who already had been relatively aggressive, they acted even more aggressively after watching the aggressive films. The children in the Prosocial Condition persisted longer at tasks, followed rules, and tolerated delays better. The children's behavior at home also changed.

Friedrich and Huston Stein's study was exemplary in modern research on developmental psychology. It was carefully controlled, theoretically and practically informative, and based on appropriate methods of collecting and analyzing evidence. Theirs is not the only research approach used in developmental psychology today, however.

A study of mothers' influence on their infants' play (1980)

Quite a different approach was taken by another team of researchers from Pennsylvania State University, Jay Belsky, Mary Kay Goode, and Robert Most. These researchers tried to show how mothers influence their children's play. They proposed that by directing the infant's attention to objects around the house, the mother teaches the infant how to focus his or her own attention.

In the first phase of the study, eight infants at each of the ages of 9, 12, 15, and 18 months were observed as they interacted with their mothers. All the mothers were their infant's primary caregiver; all but four were middle class. A researcher made two 45-minute visits to the family's house at a time when the infant was expected to be awake and alert and when the father was at work. Mothers were told to go about their usual household routine. The researcher then observed the mother's behavior by looking for six kinds of attention-focusing acts:

1. Pointing: when the mother pointed to an object or moved something so that the infant could get to it
2. Demonstrating: when the mother showed the infant how to do something
3. Moving: when the mother physically moved the infant's hands through the motions of an activity
4. Instructing
5. Highlighting: when the mother described an object's unique property
6. Naming objects

The infant's play and exploration also were observed and coded into categories, such as manipulating objects, putting objects together, using an object appropriately, and playing imaginatively with an object.

The findings were much as the researchers had predicted. Infants who displayed the greatest competence while exploring objects had mothers who most often focused their attention on objects in the environment. The researchers further analyzed their results to conclude that physical, rather than spoken, promptings were more effective in focusing infants' attention and in shaping their play.

The second part of the study was an experiment. Sixteen infants were randomly assigned to either an experimental condition or a control condition. The groups were matched for the infants' sex and birth order and for the parents' education. Mothers and infants in both groups were visited once a week for three weeks. Mothers in the experimental group were not told that they were part of an experiment for fear of biasing their behavior. They were just told that the observer would stop writing from time to time to ''share his observations'' with the mother. In fact, the observer tried to influence the mother's behavior by making her conscious of the times when she focused her baby's attention on an object. The observer might remark how interesting it was that the mother was pointing to an object or highlighting it for the baby. Each of the eight mothers in the experimental condition received between 37 and 49 such pointed interventions in the three visits. Mothers in the control condition did not receive any such interventions. The observers' notes on the infants' behavior were later coded by someone who did not know the purpose of the study. The coders scored the notes for the same kinds of play and exploration as had been coded in the first part of the study.

As they had predicted, the researchers found that compared to those in the control group, the mothers in the experimental condition more often focused their infants' attention on objects. Furthermore, the infants in the experimental condition engaged in more competent play than their control group counterparts at a follow-up visit two months later.

This is another exemplary modern study. It combines important theoretical and practical concerns, careful observations, and two approaches to research—observing children and mothers as they interacted naturally at home and intervening experimentally to change their interaction patterns.

There are many more models of research, but this sampling of four studies presents a picture of the variety of research methods that are possible and preferable in developmental psychology. In this chapter we will go through the steps involved in designing, setting up, and conducting any study of children's development. This information will help you to understand and appreciate the discussions of research in the later chapters of this book.

The scientific method

In Chapter 1, we traced the evolution of the study of child development from a philosophy into a science. Today, as our four example studies show, the study of development is strictly scientific. The studies we now rely on are those that are based on the **scientific method**.

- In these studies, the researcher usually begins with a specific **hypothesis**. ''Infants have temperamental characteristics that are evident from the moment they are born.'' ''Prenatal growth can be hindered by mothers' smoking.'' ''Ice cream is an effective reward.'' A hypothesis is a hunch, guess, or prediction about the world. It may grow out of a chance observation, intuition, the findings of another study, or it may be based on a formal theory. Entire theories never can be tested in a single study; they are meant to be broken down into specific, testable hypotheses. The most valuable theories are those that lead to a coherent set of testable hypotheses. In areas with no existing theory or previous study, a researcher may begin with curiosity and a question: ''Do infants have different temperaments when they are born, and if so, how long do they persist?'' ''Does cigarette smoking during pregnancy damage a developing fetus?'' ''Does promising children ice cream make it more likely that they will sit still during class?''

- The hypothesis or question then is tested against reality. Reality in scientific studies takes the form of objective facts and evidence—**data**—that are systematically collected. For the hypotheses stated, relevant data would include the regularity with which a number of different infants ate and slept and how much they cried; the occurrence of birth defects in infants of smoking and nonsmoking mothers; the length of time that children sat still under different conditions.

- These data are then analyzed statistically so that the researcher can determine whether they support or disconfirm the original hypothesis.

- Finally, the study may be repeated, with different subjects, different procedures, or by different researchers. If subsequent studies produce results that confirm those from the original study, then the hypothesis and the theory from which it was derived are strengthened.

Research designs

To design a study that conforms to the scientific method, the researcher must make a series of choices. There is no single ''right'' research method. For one thing, there are different research designs to choose from. Some designs are more apt than others for particular purposes. But the choice that the researcher makes depends on more than the research question under investigation. It also depends on the resources available and on the researcher's stamina, taste, and judgment.

Longitudinal versus cross-sectional

To answer questions about the course and continuity of development, researchers must study people at different ages. But there are two basic ways of doing this. In a **longitudinal research design**, a sample of children is followed over an extended period, as they get older. In a **cross-sectional research**

design, separate samples of children of different ages are studied. In the cross-sectional study, the subjects are chosen carefully so that the children in the different age samples are as nearly alike as possible in all ways other than age. They are of the same sex, social class, physical health, and so on. From the differences observed between the samples, then, the researchers can infer how behavior changes as a result of increasing age. But they must make their inferences cautiously, because their samples may have differed in ways that they did not realize. The reason that a group of 9-year-olds is more advanced than a group of 6-year-olds, for example, may be that the 6-year-olds have all gone through a stressful infancy because war was declared soon after they were born or that the 9-year-olds all had participated in an enriching pre-school program or have taken nutritional supplements. Having comparable samples at different ages is essential in cross-sectional research. If researchers are careful about selecting their samples, cross-sectional research has the advantage of producing at least a rough outline of developmental change more quickly than longitudinal research. Most of the research reported in this book is cross-sectional.

Longitudinal research takes the long view. It yields answers about growth curves and patterns of change with age. It sheds light on continuities and discontinuities in development, showing, for instance, whether the development of independence from Mother takes place gradually and regularly or in spurts, dips, and plateaus, or whether bright 6-month-olds are still leading the pack of 2-year-olds, 6-year-olds, and college applicants on IQ tests. A longitudinal design is the only way of answering whether individual children's IQ test scores are stable over time, whether difficult babies become difficult children, whether underweight newborns are still small for their age years later—because the same children are studied at different ages.

But the longitudinal design also has weaknesses. Imagine that you want to study the relation between age and intelligence for boys and girls from birth to maturity. The cross-sectional strategy is to choose a large sample of boys and girls, say 100 at each age from 6 months to 21 years, and give them all intelligence tests. The longitudinal strategy is to test the same small sample of, say, 100 boys and girls, repeatedly from 6 months until they turn 21. The longitudinal approach is not only slow—taking a full 21 years—but risky. Some of the subjects will move away, and some will drop out of the study. Those who drop out may differ in some way from those who remain in the study, and their absence may bias the study's results. The dropouts may be the least intelligent or the most intelligent. Also, after years of taking tests, the subjects in the longitudinal sample will show **practice effects**. They will have grown so used to taking intelligence tests that the test results will be affected, and so the researcher will have to compensate for that effect as well. Finally, even after making all these adjustments, the researcher still will have to be cautious in generalizing about the findings. Because only one **cohort** (children born in the same year) was followed, the researcher cannot generalize to children who grew up during a different historical epoch. Their experiences and consequently their patterns of development may have been unique. Longitudinal research has its drawbacks; it is laborious and time-consuming, but, as one authority suggests, "It exerts a calming influence on the tendency to make simple what is very complicated in child development" (Kessen, 1960, p. 50).

The best research design for assessing development includes elements from both longitudinal and cross-sectional strategies: the researcher studies several different-aged samples longitudinally over a period of years (see Figure 2.1). This **cohort sequential research design** has the advantages of being relatively short in duration (for subjects and researchers), of including more than a single historical cohort, and of charting individuals' development over time.

CROSS-SECTIONAL
DESIGN

Grade 2

Grade 5

Grade 7

In a cross-sectional research design, the researcher studies groups of children who are of different ages, like the children in these three classes. This design reveals overall age-related changes, but not individual patterns of development.

LONGITUDINAL
DESIGN

Age 7

Age 9

Age 11

Age 13

Age 15

In a longitudinal research design, the researcher studies individual children, over time, as they develop. The main drawback in this design is having to wait for the children to grow older. The main advantage of the design is that it reveals individual patterns of development, as seen in these three children.

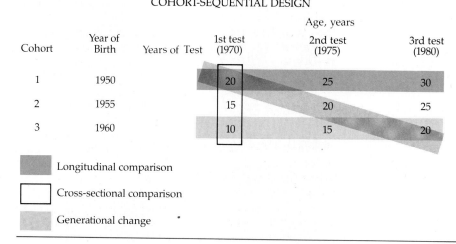

COHORT-SEQUENTIAL DESIGN

Cohort	Year of Birth	Years of Test	Age, years 1st test (1970)	2nd test (1975)	3rd test (1980)
1	1950		20	25	30
2	1955		15	20	25
3	1960		10	15	20

Longitudinal comparison

Cross-sectional comparison

Generational change

Figure 2.1 The cohort-sequential design combines elements of longitudinal and cross-sectional designs and also yields information about differences between generations or cohorts of subjects.

Another choice in designing a study is between correlation and experiment. Researchers interested in finding out what causes development must choose one of these two designs.

In a **correlational design**, researchers look but don't touch. They measure relations among things without trying to intervene. If they are interested in studying the development of children's social skills, for example, they might observe children from rich and poor families and determine whether rich children are more sociable than poor children. They might observe children of mothers who are themselves extremely sociable and compare them with the children of mothers who are less sociable. In correlational research, researchers do not manipulate children's behavior. Instead, they systematically observe its occurrence in different groups of children or in children in different situations. Identical twins may be compared to fraternal twins; adopted children may be compared to those raised by their biological parents. Children in one culture or social class may be compared to those in another. In one example of a correlational observational study, Jerome Kagan and Steven Tulkin (1971) observed child rearing of 60 mothers from two different socioeconomic groups. A trained observer visited each home twice, for about two hours. The observer noted for each five-second interval whether the mother kissed, held, tickled, bounced, or talked to the baby and whether the baby played, looked, or made a positive or negative vocalization to the mother (see Table 2.4). Middle-class mothers, the researchers found, were more likely than lower-class mothers to talk to and entertain their infants; their infants were more likely to be quiet when their mothers talked and to vocalize after they stopped.

Researchers who choose a correlational design may start out with a single, diverse group rather than two groups of children. Belsky and his associates used this kind of correlational design in the first part of the study of mother–child interaction described earlier (''A Study of Mothers' Influence on Their Infants' Play'').

The correlational design has been especially useful for studying the effects of deprivation on children's development. Ethically, researchers cannot deprive children of things they need. But they can look for children who are lacking a particular kind of experience and then compare them with other children who are not. Observations of children in orphanages and other institutions have been used to study how deprivation affects development.

The correlational design yields valuable information about development in different environments. It is the design chosen by researchers who take an ecological approach to studying development. But this method of research has its limitations. One limitation is that a researcher often cannot measure or control all of the variables in the environment under study. Children in different cultures, different social classes, or different families have experiences that differ in many ways, not just in the ways that researchers know about and measure. It is hard to determine which of these ways might be responsible for the differences observed in the children's behavior. Even more serious, it is impossible to separate cause and effect in a correlational study. The researcher cannot know, for example, whether parents are influencing children or children are influencing parents. Any observed association between the two only demonstrates that the behavior of parents and children is *related*. To solve this problem of cause and effect, researchers often intervene directly in children's environments, providing "causes," of which they then measure the "effects." The way that they do this is by using an experiment.

In an **experimental design**, researchers do touch; they actually manipulate environments and look at the effects of their manipulations on children's behavior. An experimenter may read special books to children, reinforce children for playing with blocks, or show children a movie. The children who receive the special treatment are the experimental group. The **control group** consists of children who are not treated specially. Children are assigned to one group or the other at *random*. The researchers then assess the effects of their manipulation on the experimental group's behavior by seeing how the behavior of children in this group changes in comparison with the behavior of

To study the effects of the environment on children's development, researchers can intervene directly in the children's lives by setting up experimental programs and watching how the children who attend the programs develop.

children in the control group. Thus they know whether their manipulation caused a difference in children's behavior.

In a true experimental design, it is essential that there be a control group to which subjects are randomly assigned. In one study, long considered a classic demonstration of the powerful effects of environment on intelligence (Skeels, 1966), for example, no randomly assigned control group was used, and the classic results now seem in tatters. In the study, researchers found that 13 children who were removed from an institution and placed in adoptive families (supposedly the experimental group) increased dramatically in their IQ scores, whereas the IQ scores of children who stayed in the orphanage (supposedly a control group) dropped. Unfortunately, however, children had not been randomly assigned to stay in the orphanage or to be placed in an adoptive home. The children who stayed therefore were not really a control group; those adopted were not really an experimental group. The children were selected either to stay or to be adopted by their adoptive parents and the orphanage staff. Later investigation revealed that the children who stayed in the orphanage had had the lowest IQ scores in the orphanage to begin with—the results of poor genetic endowment and disease (two were born with syphilis, for example), and that the adopted children were more capable and attractive from the start (Longstreth, 1981). Therefore, the original investigator's conclusion that adoption alone produced the difference of some 75 IQ points observed between the two groups was not proved by the study. A true experiment must have a true control group.

Even with a control group, the experimental design has limitations. Often it is neither practical nor ethical to use children as experimental subjects. Children must not be subjected to extreme changes in environment, for example. In such cases, researchers sometimes can use cats, rats, or primates as experimental subjects. There is always a danger in applying research findings on development in animals to human beings, of course, but sometimes the effort is worth making. In carefully constructed animal experiments, cause and effect can be shown precisely enough to justify tentative generalizations to human behavior. The work of Harry and Margaret Harlow and their associates at the University of Wisconsin (for example, Harlow and Griffin, 1965; Harlow and Zimmerman, 1959) provides a good example of experiments on animals to study development. These researchers performed many experiments with rhesus monkeys, depriving infant monkeys of social contacts for various periods of time, watching to see how mothers and infants reacted when they were separated, seeing how monkeys behaved when their only contact was with a wire mesh ''mother'' or a terrycloth ''mother,'' and so on. These experiments with monkeys provided important hypotheses for researchers to follow in work on human children. Animal research is valuable because it allows for extreme and well-controlled manipulations of the environment.

In experiments with children, researchers are limited not only in how extreme their manipulations may be but in how long their experiments may last. Researchers therefore often have measured only the immediate effects of relatively brief manipulations of children's behavior. In the observational-learning study by Bandura described earlier, for example, children in the experimental groups watched an adult or a cartoon character kick, punch, and throw a rubber Bobo doll and then were left alone with the Bobo doll, all within a brief period of time.

Recently researchers have expanded experimental designs beyond this short time frame. For example, they have trained parents to give children the experimental treatment. It is not ethical to ask parents to act aggressively toward, to hit, or to punish their children for the sake of an experiment. So what researchers have done instead is to train some parents—the experimental

Research on animal subjects allows investigators to set up conditions that would be unethical with human subjects. In this study, the young monkey hugs the terry cloth ''mother'' that he is being raised with and ignores a cold, wire ''mother,'' even though she offers milk.

group—to be *less* aggressive toward their children, while other parents—the randomly chosen control group—continue to use their normal level of physical punishment with their children. Such training programs for parents represent a broader form of experiment, in which **interventions** are carried out over longer periods of time. They also take place not in the laboratory but in children's natural environments.

Other studies in which the traditional experiment has been extended in time and taken out of the laboratory include Friedrich and Huston Stein's study of the effects of aggressive and prosocial films on young children's behavior in the natural environment of the nursery school and Belsky and his associates' study of mother–infant interaction at home. The latter study is unusual because it combined both correlational and experimental designs. The advantage of using both correlation and experiment flexibly and in combination was clear in that study, and this research strategy is likely to be used by more and more researchers in the future.

Table 2.1 summarizes the pros and cons of different research designs.

Collecting data

Once researchers have chosen their research design, they must decide how they will collect the data they need to test their hypothesis or answer their research questions.

Naturalistic versus structured observations

Researchers may choose to focus on children's naturally occurring, unconstrained, and spontaneous behavior as they play freely at home or at nursery school. Developmental psychologists taking an ethological approach would do this kind of **naturalistic observation**. So might a behaviorist who wanted to document naturally occurring reinforcement patterns. In contrast, a researcher might choose to observe children's behavior in constrained situations set up by the researcher—such as presenting a new toy, an unfamiliar peer, or a tape recording of a baby crying, for example. These observations would be more **structured**. In a correlational research design, data often are collected in

Table 2.1
Pros and cons of research designs

Design	Pros	Cons
Longitudinal: Same sample observed at different ages.	Shows developmental curves for individuals or groups. Shows temporal sequences of events.	Expensive, time consuming. Subjects may drop out during course of study.
Cross-sectional: Different samples observed at different ages.	Gives view of average developmental changes with age.	Does not indicate individual growth curves. Does not indicate temporal relations.
Experimental: Controlled treatment given to subjects selected at random.	Effects of known, specified, controlled treatment can be determined.	Questionable whether findings apply to situations outside the often artificial one of the experiment. Treatment is usually short term.
Correlational: Subjects observed without researcher intervening.	Shows behavior and relationships as they occur in real life.	Cannot be used to determine cause and effect.

naturalistic observations. In experiments, data often are collected in structured observations. But structured observations also may be used in correlational research, just as naturalistic observations may be used in experiments.

In naturalistic observations, researchers try hard not to influence the behavior of the children they are studying. Some observations can be done without the children's knowledge and without any intrusion into their activities. These might be done in a public park or supermarket. But these observations tap only public behavior. Usually psychologists are interested in how children behave in their private lives at home or in school. As we saw in Chapter 1, Arnold Gesell introduced the one-way window, through which the observer can see without being seen, as a means for observers to watch children without interfering with their activities. Unfortunately, not many homes—or even schools—come equipped with one-way windows. Researchers doing naturalistic observation in these settings, therefore, must make every effort to fade inconspicuously into the woodwork. One way to do this is to take as little equipment as possible into the home or classroom. In most settings, cameras and lights and tripods would stand out, and so observers resort to notebooks and clipboards or small handheld video cameras. In a few studies, observers have hidden themselves and their equipment in small, portable booths that they took to the homes. But most often observers just sit quietly in a corner of the room out of the way. They are careful not to initiate interactions with the child they are observing—no waving, winking, or saying "Whatcha doin'?" They keep their eyes on their papers or camera. If the child approaches them, they try to discourage curious attention by acting bland, boring, and unresponsive. Another way to be unobtrusive is to work alone. Bevies of adults carrying clipboards are harder to ignore than one silent person in the corner. To minimize conspicuousness, researchers often choose observers who are as much like the children's parents or teachers as possible.

In the naturalistic observation pictured on the left, an observer collects data on nursery school children's play by sitting quietly and taking notes. In the playroom observation on the right, the observer views toddlers and parents through a one-way window.

To keep to a minimum the stress that being observed inevitably creates, observers try to put children, their parents, and teachers at ease before the observation begins. They may spend some hours or days in the setting to let the children get used to their presence. They describe their purpose to the parents or teachers in the least threatening way possible, emphasizing the fact that they are not judges or experts making an evaluation, but that they are just gathering information about how children usually play or interact.

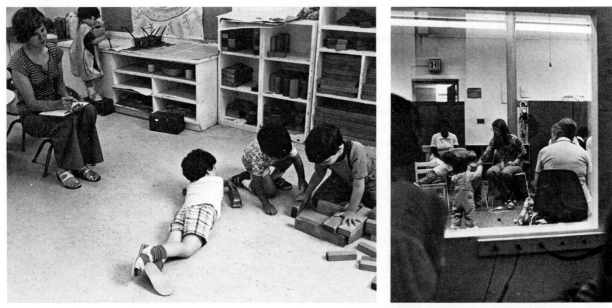

Despite all these precautions, being observed inevitably affects the "target," and when people are aware that they are being observed, they may act more stiffly, shyly, self-consciously, politely, and positively. Even so it is unlikely that they can or will disguise completely their usual ways of behaving just to put on a good show for the observer. After the first few visits from an observer, a parent or teacher usually begins to act in his or her customary ways. Frederick Wiseman, maker of dramatically revealing documentary films of people in schools and other institutions, described the effect of being observed well when he suggested that the stress of being observed may lead people to modify their behavior, but this modification is likely to be in the direction of increasing their most familiar and comfortable kinds of behavior, not bringing out new or unusual behavior. This familiar behavior, of course, is just what the observer is interested in.

An alternative to observations by unfamiliar people is for parents, teachers, babysitters, and other familiar people to record children's activities. Charles Darwin, you recall, observed and wrote about his son Doddy's behavior. Darwin, of course, was a trained observer as well as a parent. Not all parents are so capable—or so objective. Nevertheless, most parents can be guided and trained to make useful observations of their children's actions. Researchers have used this strategy successfully in investigations of very young children's spontaneous expressions of sympathy (Zahn-Waxler and Radke-Yarrow, 1979; Zahn-Waxler, Radke-Yarrow, and King, 1979) and recall (Ashmead and Perlmutter, 1980), for example. Because these kinds of behavior crop up infrequently in young children and are most likely to occur in comfortable surroundings, an unfamiliar observer might have to spend hours waiting for a single instance. Having parents collect the data is the more efficient strategy for this kind of research. Parents might be less reliable and desirable as observers of their *own* actions, however. The temptation to consciously or unconsciously distort the facts would be stronger, and focusing attention on their own actions could lead parents to change their behavior.

One further strategy for collecting data naturalistically is to "bug" children's rooms with audio or video recorders. One mother who wanted to study her 2-year-old's private monologues after she had tucked him in for the night set up a tape recorder in his room (Weir, 1962). If she had stayed in the room with him, he might have talked *to* her rather than rambling freely on his own. This method of tape-recording children's (and their parents') talk has been used occasionally by other researchers, too. Freda Rebelsky and Cheryl Hanks (1971), for example, hooked microphones to 10-month-old infants and found that their fathers spoke to them an average of only 37 seconds a day. Barbara Tizard (Tizard, Carmichael, Hughes, and Pinkerton, 1980) sewed microphones into nursery school children's shirts or dresses to record their private conversations with other children and with teachers. In the future, video technology is likely to be used to observe children unobtrusively.

Only naturalistic observation can tell us about children's "real lives," "typical activities," and "normal encounters." This is their unique advantage. More structured observations have the advantages of giving researchers more control over the situation and of giving them a chance to look at how different people behave in a single, standard situation. It is all very well to know that children attending day-care centers act differently there from the way that children reared exclusively at home act at home, for example. But it is also important to find out whether day-care children act the same as home-reared children when they are in an unfamiliar room, given a set of unfamiliar toys, and introduced to an unfamiliar child or adult. Only then can developmental psychologists make general statements about how putting children in day care or keeping them at home affects their behavior.

Structured observations offer such standard situations. They also can be more efficient than naturalistic observation for producing particular kinds of data. Why wait around the playground to observe children's cooperation and competition, for instance, when you can structure games, contests, races, and problems that will elicit these kinds of behavior in a half-hour session? Structured situations let researchers focus effectively on just the behavior they are interested in.

Like naturalistic observations, structured observations raise concerns about the intrusiveness of observers and their equipment. Although behavior in structured observations is more constrained than in naturalistic observations, the researcher still wants children to feel comfortable and not to act as if they are under the lens of "the professor." But structured observations provoke other concerns as well. Researchers must try to make the setting itself comfortable and unthreatening, so they convert university classrooms and laboratories into "living rooms," furnished with rocking chairs and fireplaces, and camouflage their one-way windows behind stylish window blinds or partially drawn drapes.

Structured observations do not necessarily have to be done in laboratory settings, however. It is possible to structure observations of children's activities at home or at school—in their natural, everyday settings—by giving children specific tasks. There may even be advantages to carrying out structured observations in these natural settings, where children are more comfortable. Recently, researchers demonstrated that when children were asked to do the same thing—remember to take the cupcakes out of the oven—at home and in a laboratory setting, they used more sophisticated memory strategies and were less anxious and cautious at home (Ceci and Bronfenbrenner, 1985). Whether researchers choose to do their structured observations at home or in the laboratory, however, they must be careful to control all aspects of the environment. More than a few researchers have been dismayed to find that the infants they were observing ignored the attractive toys they had been provided with and spent all their time scrutinizing the nest of electric wires hooked up to the camera, studying the dustballs on the windowsill, or huddling in the corner to escape the blast from the air conditioner. Researchers using structured observations need to make the whole situation—the room, the temperature, the furniture, the noise, the toys, the parent's behavior, the observer's instructions—identical for all subjects and focused on the task at hand.

Observers watch a child from behind a one-way window in a structured laboratory play situation. The situation is set up to maximize the likelihood of seeing aggressive behavior.

When these concerns are met, structured observations can yield important information. The assessments of infants' and toddlers' abilities, in which the child is shown blocks, a red ring, pictures, or a broken doll, represent one kind of structured observation that has been very revealing. Another is the so-called "strange situation," in which the relationships of infants and mothers are assessed with a series of carefully choreographed, standardized sequences of separations and reunions. Data from many such structured observations are included in our current knowledge of child development.

One limitation of *both* naturalistic and structured observations is that they must focus on children's and adults' *overt* behavior—what can be seen, heard, recorded, and quantified. Researchers must take care not to project their own points of view and attitudes onto their research subjects, but record their observations of behavior systematically and objectively. They must be careful in inferring what their subjects are thinking, feeling, or intending from how they behave. The traditional method for finding out what people are thinking is to *ask* them, by using interviews and questionnaires.

Interviews and questionnaires

With interviews and questionnaires, researchers actively probe children's and adults' ideas, thoughts, abilities, and motives. Their data come in the form of words rather than observed actions. Especially with children, interviewers have to work sensitively and skillfully in order to get true indications of their subjects' abilities without misinterpreting or distorting the responses they are given. Jean Piaget was one such skilled interviewer of children. Here he interviews a 6-year-old on his thoughts about lying.

PIAGET: Do you know what a lie is?

CLAI: It's when you say what isn't true.

PIAGET: 2 + 2 = 5. Is that a lie?

CLAI: Yes, it's a lie.

PIAGET: Why?

CLAI: Because it's not right.

PIAGET: The boy who said 2 + 2 = 5, did he know it was wrong, or did he just make a mistake?

CLAI: He made a mistake.

PIAGET: Then, if he made a mistake, did he tell a lie or not?

CLAI: Yes, he told a lie.

PIAGET: A bad one or not?

CLAI: Not very bad.

PIAGET: You see this gentleman? (Piaget points to a graduate-student assistant.)

CLAI: Yes.

PIAGET: How old do you think he is?

CLAI: 30 years old.

PIAGET: I would say 28. (The student says he is 36.)

PIAGET: Have we both told a lie?

CLAI: Yes, that's a lie.

PIAGET: A bad one?

CLAI: Not too bad.

PIAGET: Which is the worst, yours or mine, or are they both the same?

CLAI: Yours is the worst, because the difference is biggest.

PIAGET: Is it a lie, or did we just make a mistake?

CLAI: We made a mistake.

PIAGET: Is it still a lie, or not?

CLAI: Yes, it's a lie. (Piaget, 1932, p. 140).

Not all interviewers are so skillful or as patient as Piaget. They run the risk of asking leading questions, not probing responses deeply enough, not establishing rapport with their young subjects, and not interviewing all subjects in the same way. Interviewers can avoid some of these risks by using interviews and questionnaires that are prepared ahead of time. With practice, they can also learn to ask the same questions of all subjects in the same even-handed way. Prepared and practiced interviews have been used many times to probe parents' attitudes and knowledge and to get information from them about children's development. In Sears and Wise's study of thumb-sucking, for example, researchers used structured interviews with mothers to investigate the relations between child rearing and infants' behavior (see Table 2.2). Countless interviews and questionnaires, given to parents, teachers, and children, have been used to collect data about child development. With young children themselves, however, unless the interview is very simple, short, and specific, interviewers often need the flexibility to follow the unpredictable, creative twists that their subjects introduce. In these cases a less structured interview is called for.

Table 2.2
Questions from Sears and Wise's interview

1. Now let's go back to the beginning. Can you remember how things were when you found you were pregnant with X?
   a. Was he planned for?
   b. Was it a good time to have a baby?
   c. How did you feel during the pregnancy?
   d. How did the delivery go?
   e. How much change did it make in your life when X came along?
   f. How did you feel about this pregnancy in relation to your others?

2. Did you have help after the baby came?
   a. How much did your husband help to care for X?

3. How was he fed, breast or bottle?
   a. Why did you decide to do it that way?
   b. What kind of a feeding schedule did you have?

4. When did you start weaning?
   a. How did you decide what was the right time?
   b. How did you go about it?
   c. How did X react?
   d. How long did it take?

5. What about X's eating now—is he a good eater?
   a. Have there ever been any feeding problems?
   b. What have you done about teaching him table manners?
   c. Do you insist he eat what's on his plate or just as much as he wants?

6. Can you remember any special habits X had as a baby, like rocking or thumb-sucking?
   a. Does he have any now?
   b. What have you done about them?

SOURCE: Sears, Rau, and Alpert, 1965, pp. 265–266.

With older children and adults, researchers can often use paper and pencil questionnaires, which subjects fill out themselves. Compared to in-person interviews, this method has both advantages and disadvantages. Its advantages lie in its standardization of responses, its protection of subjects' anonymity, and its economy of administration (an entire class of children can fill out a carefully constructed questionnaire at one time under the supervision of the teacher or a research assistant). Its disadvantages are its lack of flexibility, its dependence on subjects' abilities to understand written questions, and its ineffectiveness for probing sensitive topics.

No matter how well prepared, sensitive, and flexible the interviewer is, no matter how carefully crafted the questionnaire, moreover, interviews and questionnaires have one limitation that resides not within the researcher or the instrument but within the subject. Whether intentionally or not, people may distort or misreport what they tell the interviewer or put down on the questionnaire. Young children may not remember events well or describe them accurately. Parents often misremember even such seemingly obvious facts as the age at which their children first walked or spoke. The possible solutions to this problem include asking only straightforward questions about objective happenings, not requiring or allowing reporters to make complicated subjective interpretations of their own or others' actions, and asking about things that happened in the recent, not the distant, past. There are also ways of wording questions so that subjects do not think that there is only one clearly desirable answer and feel impelled to give it rather than the truth. "Do you beat you child?" is *not* a subtle question. Researchers might do better with something more on these lines: "Children often are difficult to discipline, as I'm sure you realize only too well. Here are some stories about problems that children present. Please tell me how you might handle problems like these if they happened with your child. . . ."

Tests

One quick way to collect data about children's development is to give the children standardized tests—IQ tests, personality tests, tests of perceptual abilities, and the like. These tests are widely available and offer researchers easily and objectively collected data to compare with the results of other researchers. When choosing a test, the researcher must be concerned with whether it is valid. **Validity** is the indication of how accurately a test measures what it is supposed to measure. If a thermometer registers 212 degrees Fahrenheit when it is placed in boiling water at sea level and registers 32 degrees Fahrenheit when the water is frozen, it is a valid instrument for measuring temperature. The measurement of psychological traits and abilities is more elusive.

True validity indicates how well a test conforms to the best scientific idea of the underlying trait or construct being measured—intelligence, self-esteem, social maturity, achievement motivation, and so on. But true validity is a theoretical concept, not empirically measurable. Therefore other measures of validity are used as approximations of true validity. A test may be considered valid, for one thing, if its items fairly represent the relevant body of knowledge. For example, the validity of a math test is high if the items have to do with arithmetic and algebra; the validity is low if the items have to do with the mating behavior of killer bees. Another measure of validity is a test's ability to predict success on a second variable supposedly related to the ability being tested. For example, if academic success is believed to depend on intelligence, we would expect people who get good grades to score higher on IQ tests. A third measure of validity is how well a test correlates with another established

One relatively easy way to get information about children's development is to administer standard tests. In the Peabody Picture Vocabulary Test, a child is asked to point to the appropriate pictures as the tester names objects. Testing a child alone allows the examiner to establish rapport and to detect special circumstances–sleepiness, nervousness, and the like—that might affect his or her performance.

test. The validity of any newly devised intelligence test, for example, is usually determined by how highly individuals' scores on it correlate with their scores on established tests like the one devised by Binet and Simon. In choosing a test, a researcher must balance concerns about validity against the desire for innovation and the willingness to take risks. The best solution is for the researcher to use more than one test or measure of a trait.

The pros and cons of different methods of collecting data are summarized in Table 2.3.

Recording and coding the data

Once researchers have decided on their methods of collecting data, they must decide how to record and code the data. Researchers can choose from a wide variety of techniques for recording data—from writing a narrative account of

Table 2.3
Pros and cons of data collection methods

Method	Pros	Cons
Structured Observation: Behavior observed in a standard, contrived situation.	Data from different subjects can be compared. Data not restricted to preestablished test responses.	Does not get at underlying attitudes. Not known whether observations can be generalized to other situations.
Naturalistic Observation: Spontaneous behavior observed in familiar environment.	Provides information about behavior in the real world. Offers description of activities, behavior, interactions.	Settings for different subjects are not comparable. Does not assess maximum performance possible. Some kinds of abilities may not be observable.
Questionnaire or Test: Same assessment given to all subjects.	Data from different subjects can be compared. Individual's performance can be compared to norms.	Data limited to preestablished responses.
Interview: Questions posed to children, parents, teachers.	Quick way to get information. Only way to assess conscious intentions and attitudes.	Interviewees are biased, not accurate reporters of past events or their own behavior.

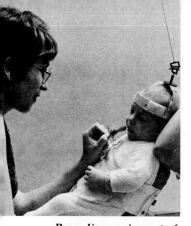

Recording equipment of various kinds is useful for studying infants' perceptual abilities. By sucking on the nipple, the baby in the study controls a light display. The equipment records the baby's sucking and head turning and when the light display comes on and goes off.

interaction in a notebook, to pressing a computer key every time the subject does something, to making a clinical judgment about how warm a person is, to marking checks on a list at each occurrence of a kiss, smile, caress, or word of praise. Checking whether a subject passed or failed each item on a test is perhaps the easiest way of recording data. At the other extreme, during an interview or an observation, researchers may have to use cameras or tape recorders to catch everything that is happening. Mechanical devices for recording data, like electroencephalographs, electrocardiographs, spectrographs, and stabilimeters are also available for assessing brain waves, heart rates, vocalization patterns, and activity levels. Each of these techniques produces useful information. The choice of which one to use depends on the researcher's desire for detail and on the time and money available.

Turning this recorded information into data that can be analyzed, then, requires coding it into categories or numbers: how often a behavior was observed in two hours; how intense, or loud, or loving the behavior was; how many test answers were correct; and so on. Some of this coding can be done on the spot, if researchers are very experienced and use established checklists, tests, or rating scales (see Table 2.4). In other cases, observers turn detailed notes, taken during the observation or interview, into ratings, descriptions, or scales after the fact. When the observations are filmed or videotaped, researchers can go back and pore over their records to find each significant

Table 2.4
Observation categories and coding for mother-infant interaction

1. *Location:* Distance of mother from infant, scored each time it changes.
   a. Face to face.
   b. Within two feet (within arm's distance).
   c. More than two feet away.
2. *Physical contact.*
   a. Kiss: Mother's lips touch child.
   b. Hold: Mother supports child's weight—mother carries child, child sits on mother's lap, etc.
   c. Active physical contact: Mother tickles child, bounces child on lap, throws child in air, etc.
3. *Prohibitions:* Mother interferes with or stops an act of the child's that has begun.
   a. Verbal: Negative command (for example, ''stop that'' or ''don't do that'').
   b. Physical: Mother stops child's motor activity or takes object from child. (To control for possible differences in infants' activity levels, which could result in some infants receiving more prohibitions than others, the researchers computed a ratio in which the total number of maternal prohibitions was divided by the number of five-second intervals in which the infant was either walking or crawling. Another possible bias was that infants moving around on the floor would have more opportunities to engage in behaviors that might be prohibited; thus, a second ratio was computed in which the total number of maternal prohibitions was divided by the amount of time that the infant was free to crawl or walk on the floor.)
4. *Maternal vocalization:* Mother says words to child. (This category was analyzed separately for each location in category 1.)
5. *Keeping infant busy:* Mother provides activity for child.
   a. Entertain: Mother holds attention of child by nonverbal sounds, body movements such as peekaboo, or the use of a toy—such as shaking a rattle. If words were used with an entertainment behavior, category 4 was also scored.
   b. Give object: Mother gives child an object and makes no effort to hold child's attention.

SOURCE: Tulkin and Kagan, 1972.

glance, raised eyebrow, and fleeting smile. Once again, whether the researcher codes every possible minute behavior or settles on broader ratings or categories is a personal choice. There are advantages and disadvantages to both methods. The first method gives more objective and detailed information, but it takes more time and may be more superficial. The second method gives more clinical and global information, but it may be more subjectively biased. (We discuss the problem of bias in the next section.)

Problems in doing a study

Sampling

Not only do researchers have to decide how much detail they should record and how many acts of behavior they should code, but they also must decide how many subjects they should study. If they study too few children—fewer than, say, 25—they run the risk that chance or individual variations among the children will bias their results. By limiting themselves to a few subjects, researchers also can detect only the strongest statistical relations among the variables they are studying. With only 15 subjects, for example, researchers have less than one chance in four of detecting a moderately strong correlation of .30. (Correlations are discussed later in this chapter.)

The nature of the research question and the chosen methods of collecting data serve as guidelines for determining the adequate number of subjects in a study. If the researcher collects extensive data on each child, then there is some justification for including fewer subjects. Detailed **case studies** of one or a few subjects can give information that more superficial measures on a large sample of subjects do not. Studying in painstaking detail how a few infants learn language or interact with their mothers has led researchers to important insights into development. Studying children who are unique in some way also has contributed invaluable understanding—whether it be a 4-year-old expert on dinosaurs or a child raised in extreme deprivation. A case study of one girl, Genie, for example, who grew up in almost total isolation until she was rescued at age 13, has provided unique information about the limits of language development (Curtiss, 1977).

These photos illustrate the usefulness of a case study for finding out about human development, here the long-term effects of early experience. Monica was born with a malformation that required her to be fed by a stomach tube when she was an infant. As a young child, Monica fed her doll without holding it. Later, as a mother, Monica did not hold her own infant in her arms during feeding.

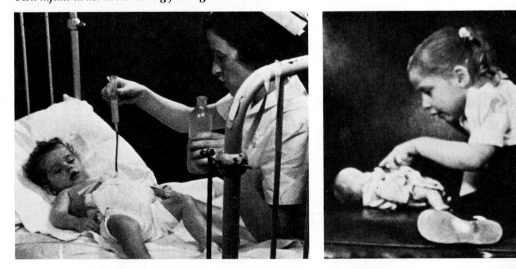

Under ordinary circumstances, however, researchers do not encounter such cases. Instead, they study large numbers of children so that they can make statements about children's development *in general*. Besides studying a large number of children, researchers try to choose children who will represent the entire population in which they are interested. A **representative sample** of American infants, for example, would include infants from all racial and religious groups and from all social classes, in the same proportions as the general population. If samples are not representative, the results obtained from them may not apply to the general population or be consistent with what other researchers have found. The results of one early study (Shirley, 1933) of the ages at which infants reached certain milestones of motor development—sitting, creeping, walking—for example, do not agree with findings from more recent studies. This sample included only white, Minnesota-born, infants of northern European ancestry; no black, Asian, or Hispanic infants were included. Researchers often find that a single group of subjects cannot aid them in answering all their questions. For that reason, having several groups of subjects is an advantage, and when the findings are the same for more than one group, the researchers can be confident that their findings are **robust**.

Researcher bias

Another problem that researchers must guard against as they collect data is that their own biases do not creep in and influence their results. This problem is most likely to crop up when the person collecting the data is aware of the hypothesis being tested and very much wants it to "work." Researchers' expectations then can color their observations and taint what should be neutral and bias-free. Even without knowingly intending to bias results, if they know what the hypothesis is, researchers can exert a subtle influence on their subjects' behavior. An example of how biases work is offered by an experiment in which a neurologist named Henry Head in 1903 underwent surgery to cut and rejoin a nerve in his arm, temporarily numbing a patch of skin on the back of his hand (Miller, 1978). Head reported that feeling returned to the numbed patch in two stages. But although the same operation has since been performed several times, no one has gotten this result. Why not? Presumably because Head was trying to prove a hypothesis about the human nervous system, to which he was firmly committed, and his belief unconsciously shaped his sensations so that they confirmed the hypothesis. More recently, a group of developmental psychologists (Goren, Sarty, and Wu, 1975) claimed to have demonstrated that infants prefer to look at pictures of human faces rather than at pictures of other, equally complex figures. Other researchers repeating the study did not get the same results. They suggested that the first group had unwittingly biased their results by holding the infants on their laps while they looked at the pictures and turning the infants slightly toward the face pictures. It is essential that such sources of bias be eliminated from research.

To protect against bias, researchers collecting data must be "blind" to the subject's condition. They must not know to which group—experimental or control, middle class or lower class, day care or home reared—subjects belong. That way they will not consciously or unconsciously distort either the subjects' behavior or their own record of that behavior. In a **double-blind study**, neither subjects nor data collectors know who is in the experimental and control groups. Thus the nurse in a double-blind study of mothers' and infants' nutrition, for example, does not know which of the cans she gives to each mother are filled with a protein and calorie supplement and which are filled with a placebo, and neither do the mothers. To protect against researcher bias, in well-designed studies people other than the designer of the

Unbiased research can be replicated. Other people, looking at the same behavior, must agree that the child was feeding himself or herself, or grasping, or stacking toys, or smiling, and so on.

research act as observers, experimenters, or interviewers. Two or more independent observers also may observe the same child, and this will help to cancel out personal biases. Observers, moreover, can be given instructions that are so detailed and specific that it would be hard for them to bias observations (short of outright cheating).

Reliability and replicability

One way that researchers demonstrate that their results are not biased is to show that their observations are **reliable** and their results **replicable**. Observations cannot be unique to one observer. Other people, looking at the same behavior, must agree that the child was smiling, or acting fearful, or building towers with blocks, that the parent was loving or demanding, and so on. The observations must be, as far as possible, objective reflections of reality. For this reason, it is customary for more than one observer, rater, or tester to collect data in a study. Before the observers begin, they are trained until they agree on the meaning of the observational categories or interview responses. Then, from time to time, their agreement is checked. The degree to which they agree is one indication of reliability. Another indication is the extent to which several observations of a single child are comparable. Researchers want to find out about children's typical activities—what Kristy usually does, not just what Kristy did from 9 to 10 o'clock one Sunday morning—and so they must spend enough time observing Kristy at different times of day and on different days to be able to make general summaries of Kristy's behavior. Tests, interviews, and questionnaires, too, like observations, are reliable if they yield essentially the same results when given to a person at different, closely spaced times.

When reliability is high, it is more likely that the results of the study will be replicated, if another researcher or the same researcher at a different time and with different subjects repeats the study. **Replicability** is another important criterion of scientific research.

Analyzing data

Once data have been collected and coded, they must be analyzed. For detailed case studies, a richly vivid clinical description may be enough. But for most studies, the analysis of data is done statistically—these days, usually with the help of a computer. Several different kinds of analysis are possible.

Descriptive analysis

If the researchers simply want to describe children's behavior, they can analyze the frequencies or levels of the children's behavior—the frequencies of
smiles, sniffles, and sentences beginning with "I," incidents of helping, or
levels of height, health, intelligence, or sociability. One very simple way to
analyze such descriptive data is to sum up the occurrence of behaviors for the
sample as a whole. Hall did this in his study of dolls, for example. When data
are quantitiative and form an **interval scale**, researchers can calculate the
mean or average frequency or level for the sample. "The average income for
the families studied was $20,000 per year." "The average number of 'I'
utterances made by each child observed was 14." Even more informatively,
researchers can calculate mean levels or frequencies for different groups in the
study: boys and girls, blacks and whites, rich and poor children, 2-, 4-, and
6-year-olds. "The average IQ score for boys was 100, for girls, 102." "The
average number of questions was 10 for 2-year-olds and 40 for 4-year-
olds.""Half of the 6-year-olds and 70 percent of the 8-year-olds passed the
test." Perhaps best of all for descriptive purposes, researchers can analyze
their data graphically. They can plot a graph that represents the test scores of
each child in the sample or the number of times each child in the sample
laughed, hugged, or poked. Usually, for a large sample, these scores and
frequencies form a normal, or bell-shaped, curve (Figure 2.2). When data form
a curve of this shape, they are said to form a **normal distribution**. At the tails
of the curve are a relatively small number of very high and very low scores,
and in the middle are a large number of intermediate scores. The same
number of people have scores above the peak of the curve as below it. The bell-
shaped curve illustrates the fact that most people's scores—for height, weight,
or intelligence, for example—cluster around the mean, or norm. Relatively few
people are extremely short or tall, thin or fat, mentally retarded or gifted. On
a normal curve of IQ scores (see Figure 12.1), for example, the mean is 100
points. The same number of people have scores between 90 and 100 and
between 100 and 110, between 80 and 90 and between 110 and 120. But more
people have scores between 90 and 110, a range of 20 IQ points, than between
70 and 90 or 110 and 130 points, which are also ranges of 20 IQ points.

Finding a normal curve in their data tells researchers that their sample is
large enough and representative enough so that they may proceed with
further statistical analyses, most of which require that the data to be analyzed

NORMAL CURVE

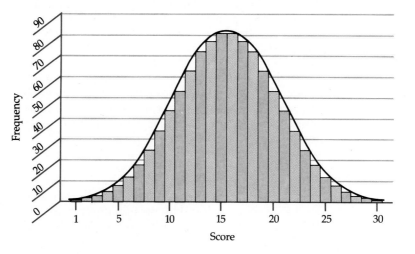

*Figure 2.2 When the
number of children re-
ceiving each score from 1
to 30 is plotted, it forms
a symmetrical normal,
or bell-shaped, curve.*

DEVELOPMENTAL
CURVES

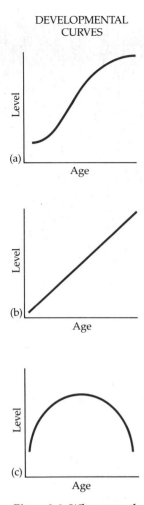

(a)

(b)

(c)

Figure 2.3 When growth or development over time is plotted, it usually takes one of these three shapes: (a) an S-shaped curve, in which development increases gradually and then levels off; (b) a straight line, in which development continues to increase; or (c) an inverted U-shaped curve, in which development first increases and then declines.

be normally distributed. It also allows them to predict how tall, smart, or heavy children in the general population will be. It allows them to tell parents whether their child is exceptionally bright or slow, sociable or shy, and so on. For developmental psychologists, however, the more interesting graphic analysis shows how the levels or frequencies of children's behavior change with age. This analysis requires them to plot a **growth curve**, by recording mean scores of children at different ages. Growth curves take one of three basic shapes. An ability or behavior may increase in an S-shaped curve, in which the increase occurs rapidly over a certain period of time—the ''formative period''—and then slows down and perhaps stops (Figure 2.3a). Height and verbal intelligence, for example, follow this general curve. Alternatively, an ability or behavior may keep increasing or decreasing steadily in a straight line (Figure 2.3b). This kind of growth is not likely to continue across the entire life span, however. Most abilities eventually reach a plateau. People do not keep getting bigger and better every day and every way all their lives. Finding a straight line usually reflects the fact that researchers have included just one part of the life span—the verbal ability or height of 2- to 12-year-olds, for example. Some behaviors or abilities increase first, hit a peak, and then decrease as a person gets older (Figure 2.3c). Perceptual and motor abilities are two kinds of behavior that fit such an ''inverted U''-shaped curve.

Significant differences

When subjects can be divided into different groups—experimental versus control group, black versus white children, 2-year-olds versus 6-year-olds, children who live in apartments versus children who live in houses, and so on—the researchers usually want to report not just what the mean or average scores for the groups are, but whether there are **statistically significant** differences between these mean scores. Differences are statistically significant when they are so large that they are not likely to have occurred by accident, or by chance. Researchers usually set an acceptable probability level of something occurring by chance at 5 percent; that is, if an event has less than a 5 percent chance (one chance in 20) of having happened by sheer coincidence, it is considered statistically significant. There are standard statistical tests for determining how likely any given difference is to have occurred by chance. These tests take into consideration the number of subjects in the study, the size of the difference between the groups, and the variability among the subjects within the groups. Analyzing the data for significant differences tells researchers whether the differences they observed—that boys are taller than girls, for example—reflect *real* differences in human development and behavior or appear because the researchers happened to pick a sample with a few extremely tall boys or a few extremely short girls.

Statistical Relations

For some questions, researchers want to know not about differences between groups, but about how individual children's behavior is related to their particular background, age, experience, or abilities. To learn about these relations, researchers usually use some form of the statistical analysis of **correlation**. A correlation reflects the degree to which two variables are related, that is, the degree to which two variables increase or decrease together. It is indicated by a number ranging from −1.0 to +1.0, or it can be plotted on a graph. In a perfect positive correlation (correlation coefficient = +1.0), the child who scores highest on one variable also scores highest on the other; the child who scores second highest on one variable also scores second highest on the other; and so on. A perfect correlation is illustrated in Figure 2.4a. In a

PERFECT CORRELATIONS

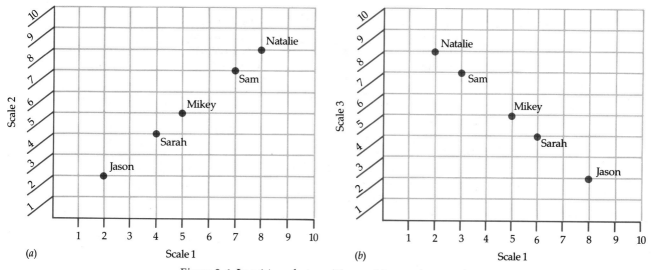

Figure 2.4 In a (a) perfect positive or (b) negative correlation, subjects fall in exactly the same rank order on both of the scales.

perfect negative correlation (correlation coefficient = −1.0; see Figure 2.4b), the two variables are inversely related: the child scoring highest on one variable scores lowest on the other variable, the child scoring second highest on the first variable scores second lowest on the other, and so on.

In the real world, it is extremely unusual to find perfect correlations, positive or negative. Usually there is some degree of association, but it is not perfect. Children who score above the mean in intelligence might be likely to score above the mean in sociability, for instance, or children whose mothers are above average in intelligence will be likely to be above average in intelligence. Just how closely the rankings on the two variables match is reflected in correlation coefficients that range between .99 and − .99 (see Figure 2.5).

There are statistical tests to establish whether the level of correlation observed is significantly greater than zero. Whether a particular correlation coefficient is statistically significant depends on how large it is and on how many subjects were included in the analysis. When there are only a few subjects in the sample, the correlation coefficient must be quite high (for example, for a sample of 15 subjects, a correlation coefficient must be larger than .50 to be significantly greater than zero). With a large sample, a much smaller coefficient is significant (for example, for a sample of 400, a coefficient of .10 is significant). The researcher can look up any correlation coefficient in a statistical table to see whether it is significant.

Interpreting results

After all the decisions about the design of the research have been made and the data have been collected and analyzed, there remains a final, critical task: the results must be interpreted. The researcher must explain just what the results *mean*. Interpreting results is no easy task. The relations discovered among the variables may point in different directions, or they may be confusing or inconsistent. They may not clearly confirm or disconfirm the researcher's hypotheses. More insidious, even when the results are consistent,

CORRELATION
SCATTERPLOTS

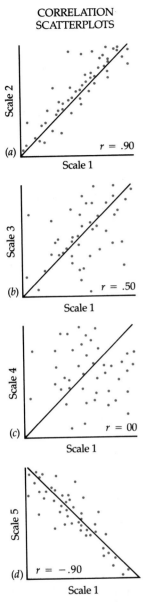

Figure 2.5 Scatter plots of four correlations, ranging from .90 to −.90.

researchers must be careful not to succumb to the temptation to overinterpret their findings. They must be careful not to draw more sweeping conclusions than are justified. Researchers must not suggest that their results apply more broadly than they do, or generalize to all children when they have studied only a sample of Head Start children from North Carolina, or generalize to all parents when they have observed only middle-class moms in Peoria. They should not tout a correlation of .15 as exceptionally important. Even if that .15 is statistically significant, because 500 children were observed, .15 is still not impressive in absolute size. It does not explain much about what is happening. (To be precise, it explains only 2 percent of the variation observed in the other variable.) Similarly, researchers should not make headlines over an IQ difference of 5 points, which, with a large sample, is statistically significant but in real life is inconsequential. They should not lead people to think that their findings will predict the behavior of an individual child. Statistical analyses apply only to groups of children and reflect only probabilities of occurrence.

Most important, researchers must not claim that one variable *caused* another when they have documented only that the two are *correlated*. No matter how high a correlation is, it does not mean that one variable is causing the other, only that the two are related. Finding a strong correlation between intelligence and sociability does not mean that children are sociable *because* they are intelligent. (Both may be a function of age, for instance.) Finding a high negative correlation between children's intelligence and their mothers' punitiveness does not prove that punishing children *makes* them less intelligent. Less intelligent children may elicit more punishment from their mothers, or less intelligent mothers may be more punitive toward their children, for instance. Getting a highly significant correlation between parents' and children's IQ scores does not necessarily mean that intelligence is transmitted genetically. More intelligent parents may provide a more stimulating environment for their children, and this may cause their children to do better on IQ tests. Finally, finding *no* significant correlation between two variables does not necessarily mean that one variable is *not* influencing the other. One variable may cause another, but *more* of it does not cause *more* of the other. For example, some baby talk, or vitamin C, or play with toys may be necessary for infants to develop intellectually, but using *more* baby talk, vitamin C, or toys will not make babies more intelligent.

In the real world of complex human development, causes and effects are seldom clear-cut. Effects may operate in both directions at once, and causes may be many. By repeatedly measuring and seeing which variable changes first and which next, researchers can chart causes and effects more clearly. With more sophisticated statistical analyses, researchers can rule out some causal paths as implausible. But some causal questions are likely to remain unanswered, and researchers always must be cautious in interpreting their results.

Ethics of doing research on children

As they design their studies and choose their research methods, researchers also must be concerned with the *ethics* of doing research on children. Clearly, researchers must not treat children cruelly or callously for the sake of scientific discovery. But what are the ethical limits on researchers? Is it ethical for a child to be shown a violent movie so that researchers can study the effects of filmed violence on aggression? Is it ethical to subject children to the stress of their mother's absence or of the sound of a baby crying helplessly to study the development of social relationships and empathy? Is it ethical to test babies' perception by having shapes loom down on them and then veer away only at the last moment? Clearly, researchers should not lie to subjects about the research or its possibly harmful effects. But how much deception is acceptable? Is it ethical to record mothers and children interacting without their knowledge? Is it ethical for a child to be told that she is making a picture for another ''sick child,'' when the researcher is actually studying children's generosity under varying conditions?

Ethical questions about scientific research have been raised more and more insistently in recent years. University committees now must approve researchers' plans to make sure that children's and other subjects' rights are not violated. These committees must be satisfied that the research will do no harm to the subjects, that it will not subject them to events that are significantly different from those they might encounter in their daily lives, and that it offers potential benefits to science or society. They must be satisfied as well that children and their parents will have given their ''informed consent'' to the procedures—that they will know in advance what to expect and will have consented to participate on the basis of their understanding. Some old investigations, done in the 1930s, '40s, and '50s, probably would not be approved by a human subjects committee today. In one investigation, for example, 11-day-old infants were submerged facedown in water to see whether they would swim (McGraw, 1939/1967). Some struggled, clutched for support, gasped for breath. In another investigation, two infants were reared in relative isolation so that researchers could study the effects of such a practice on certain activities (Dennis, 1938, 1941). The ethics of these research designs seem unacceptable to us now, in the 1980s.

Children are inexperienced and vulnerable, and researchers must take extra care in using them as research subjects. The issue of whether children actually are competent to give informed consent has been hotly debated. Some people insist that because adults are larger and more powerful than children, children easily—*too* easily—can be swayed by them. To protect children, the American Psychological Association (1968) has set ethical standards for research on child development; they include the following:

1. Even the youngest child has rights that supersede those of an investigator. Children must not be coerced, and they must be given the opportunity to refuse to participate and to withdraw from the study at any time.

2. No investigator may hurt a child psychologically or physically.

3. Parents must give their consent in writing to any investigation involving their children, and they must be given accurate information about the study before they do so.

4. Children's identities must be concealed and their confidences respected.

5. Money and gifts to children do not override any ethical standards.

6. Professors of developmental psychology should inform their students about these ethical standards of conduct in research on children.

Summary

1. Current knowledge about children's development has emerged from studies that follow the scientific method. Such studies begin with a specific hypothesis or question that is then tested against reality.

2. To study the course and continuity of human development, researchers study people at different ages. One way they do this is longitudinally—following a sample of subjects for an extended period; another way is cross-sectionally—observing separate samples of subjects of different ages. Researchers may overcome the limitations of these two research designs by studying a number of overlapping age samples longitudinally.

3. Researchers can choose between correlational and experimental research designs. In a correlational design, researchers do not manipulate children's behavior; they observe its occurrence systematically in different children and in different settings and look for relations between the behavior and other factors. In contrast, when they conduct an experiment, researchers actually manipulate environments and look at how these affect children's behavior. Research that combines correlation and experiment may offer the best of both designs.

4. Observations may take place in children's natural settings or in constrained settings where the researchers can better control what happens. Different settings—home, nursery school, unfamiliar laboratory, hospital—all may influence children's behavior in different ways. Naturalistic observation provides insight into children's ''real lives'' and typical activities. Structured observations give researchers the chance to see how different children behave in a single, standard setting.

5. Observations focus on children's overt behavior. Interviews, tests, and questionnaires probe what they think and feel—their ideas, thoughts, abilities, and motives.

6. Researchers must decide how much data to amass and how many subjects to study. Their aim is to study large enough numbers of children and children who are representative of the entire population so that they can use their data to make general statements about children's development.

7. Researchers must take care that their own biases do not influence their results. Testing, observations, and interviews should be conducted by research assistants who do not know to which group subjects belong or the hypothesis of the study. Results must be objective, reliable, and replicable.

8. Researchers usually analyze average or mean differences between groups' behavior and test whether these differences are statistically significant, that is, whether they are large enough so that they are unlikely to have occurred by chance. Correlations are statistical measurements of how two variables increase or decrease in relation to one another.

9. In interpreting their data, researchers must take care not to infer too much, for example, claiming causes when they have documented only correlations.

10. Conducting research with children binds developmental psychologists to strict ethical standards. Research must not cause harm to children, parents must give informed consent ahead of time, research must be confidential, and children's rights to refuse to participate must be respected.

Key terms

scientific method	experimental design	double-blind study
hypothesis	control group	reliability
data	interventions	replicability
longitudinal research design	naturalistic observation	interval scale
cross-sectional research design	structured observation	mean
practice effects	validity	normal distribution
cohort	case study	growth curve
cohort-sequential research design	representative sample	statistical significance
correlational design	robust	correlation

Suggested readings

COOK, R. and CAMPBELL, DONALD. *Quasi-experimentation*. Boston: Houghton-Mifflin, 1979. A discussion of research strategies on important social issues.

HOGARTH, ROBIN (Editor). *Question Framing and Response Consistency*. San Francisco: Jossey-Bass, 1982. A collection of articles by researchers in the behavioral and social sciences about research that uses interviews and questionnaires.

KIMMEL, ALLEN (Editor). *Ethics of Human Subject Research*. San Francisco: Jossey-Bass, 1981. An important and thorny issue—ethics of research—is discussed from a number of different perspectives.

REIS, HARRY (Editor). *Naturalistic Approaches to Studying Social Interaction*. San Francisco: Jossey-Bass, 1983. One in a series of paperback books on methodology in the social and behavioral sciences. This one describes six different observational methods.

RICHARZ, ANN. *Understanding Children through Observation*. St. Paul: West Publishing, 1980. A guide to practical observations of infants and children, with specific suggestions for research topics and recording forms.

SACKETT, GENE (Editor). *Observing Behavior (Vols. 1 and 2)*. Baltimore: University Park Press, 1978. An advanced discussion of direct behavioral observation methods.

SILVERMAN, IRWIN (Editor). *Generalizing from Laboratory to Real Life.* San Francisco: Jossey-Bass, 1981. Another volume in the series on methodology in the social and behavioral sciences. This one discusses the scope of laboratory observations.

PART TWO

Beginnings

chapter three
Heredity

When I was pregnant with Sam, our first child, I believed that heredity contributed the basic physical elements—eye color, body type, the shape of nose and fingers, and the like. Environment, I thought, contributed the rest. Parents—the baby's environment—molded their malleable little creature to fit their patterns of life. It was parents who formed a baby's habits of sleeping and eating and who could make the baby an anxious, nervous wreck or a charming, outgoing pleasure. It was parents who created sleeping problems and feeding problems. I guess that I believed that heredity controlled development before birth and that then environment took over. Well, wake up and smell the coffee, Mother!

My pleasant fantasy lasted until about 60 seconds after Sam was born. He opened his eyes and looked around the delivery room with a calm, friendly, and curious expression on his face—not a malleable lump, but a fully formed little person.

In temperament, Sam has continued to be calm, friendly, curious, and from the first minute, exceptionally alert. This boy notices everything. He sleeps when *he* needs to. When he was two weeks old, he stayed awake for 11 hours straight with no signs of flagging. Sam nursed when *he* was hungry, not by any schedule we imposed—and I was going to be the mother who scheduled my baby's feedings so that the rest of life could go on undisturbed.

I know that we've had *some* influence on Sam's development. He's thriving because of the nourishment and love he gets from his family. But Sam certainly has cleared up my naïve assumptions about heredity and environment.

Nature–nurture interaction

As Sam taught his mother, children are products of both heredity and environment. In times past, as we saw in Chapter 1, those who studied children's development usually thought that people developed according to the dictates of *either* environment—''nurture''—*or* heredity—''nature.'' But today, behavioral scientists know that nature and nurture, heredity and environment, both contribute continually and inseparably to a person's development. They are beginning to understand how very complex this process really is.

The **genotype** is all of a person's genetic inheritance. But the actual **expression** of the genotype as a person's visible characteristics and behavior is called the **phenotype**. The phenotype depends not only on the person's genetic inheritance but on all the environmental forces that affect the person from the moment of conception. Even if we knew a baby's genotype, we still would not be able to predict with certainty how the person would turn out. From the moment of conception, many possibilities are open to each unique human being.

Skin color is a good example to illustrate how genes and environment both contribute to development. Skin color depends on various genes—including those that produce melanin, a pigment that makes skin look dark or fair, and those that block the production of melanin, like the gene for albinism. The amount of sunlight affects how fully these genes are expressed. In regions with little sun, people born with genes for dark skin will have relatively light skin, because the genotype will not be fully expressed. But people with genes for dark skin who live in the tropics, where the sunlight is strong and continuous, will have dark skin. Their environment fosters the full expression of their skin color genotype.

Just as sunlight in the environment interacts with genes to determine skin color, stimulation in the environment interacts with genes to determine intelligence. For a child's genetically inherited intelligence to be expressed fully, the child needs loving interest and stimulating attention from adults. The amount of stimulation a child receives may actually alter the child's brain chemistry (Vandenberg, 1968). Thus the intelligence of a child who grows up in an enriched environment, with lots of toys and talk and teaching, is likely to be expressed more fully than the intelligence of a child who grows up in an impoverished environment.

In short, the expression of a person's genetic inheritance is influenced both by genotypic patterns and by factors in the environment (see Figure 3.1). The genotype determines many of the person's basic characteristics and capacities, limits and potentials. The environment helps to determine the direction and speed of the person's development. Scientists have proposed several models to represent the complex relations between genotype and environment, between nature and nurture.

Models of gene–environment interaction

The **reaction range** model (Gottesman, 1963) shows how genotypes and phenotypes are related in different environments. In Figure 3.2, for example, Alice and Laura are twin sisters with identical genotypes who are adopted at birth into different families. Alice's adoptive parents dote on her, talk to and praise her, buy her books and puzzles, and send her to an excellent school. But Laura's adoptive parents ignore, punish, and thwart her, barely letting her attend school at all. Because the twins are reared in such different environments, their abilities also turn out to be different, despite their identical genotypes. At age 15, Alice scores 120 on an IQ test; Laura scores only 90. Thus the reaction range model shows how different phenotypes can develop from the same genotype in different environments. The model also illustrates the contrasting case: similar environments lead to more similar phenotypes among children with different genotypes. In Figure 3.2 Fred has a genotype for lower intelligence. Paul has one for higher intelligence. But Fred is given special attention, lessons, and schooling, whereas Paul is given just ordinary attention. Consequently, both turn out to have IQs of 100.

GENOTYPE-ENVIRONMENT INTERACTION

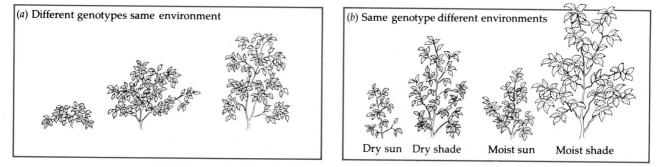

Figure 3.1 The plants in the picture on the left were grown under identical conditions. They look different because the genotype of each is unique. In contrast, the plants in the picture on the right all grew from cuttings of one plant. They look different because they were grown under quite different environmental conditions.

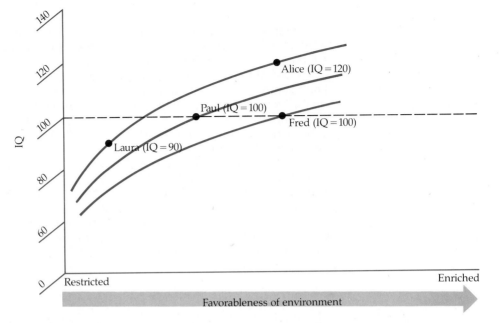

Figure 3.2 Each genotype for IQ has a reaction range of expression, depending on the favorableness of the environment. In this illustration, twins Alice and Laura have the same genotype but are raised in different environments and therefore have different IQ scores (90 and 120). Brothers Paul and Fred have different genotypes but are raised in similar environments and therefore get the same IQ scores (100).

Not all human characteristics have the same reaction range as intelligence, however.

> Just after his third birthday, Sam visited the pediatrician for a routine checkup. As he chatted with Sam and Sam's father, the pediatrician charted Sam's height (41 inches) and weight (38 pounds). "What are you feeding this child?" the pediatrician joked. "He's off the charts."
>
> "Iron filings," Sam's father replied. "He eats more than I do."
>
> "You're tall yourself," the pediatrician said, "so it stands to reason that Sam will be too."

Since he was just a few weeks old, Sam's height has been in at least the 95th percentile for his age. Like his father and his grandfathers, Sam is going to be tall. Height is one characteristic that is under fairly strict genetic control. Other human characteristics—like intelligence and sociability—are more susceptible to variations in the environment and have larger reaction ranges (see Figure 3.3).

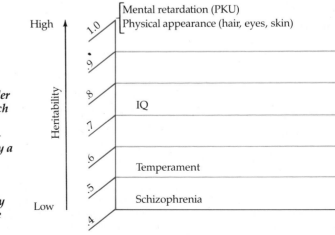

Figure 3.3 Some aspects of development are fully under the control of genetics. Eye and hair color are two such physical traits. They are relatively unaffected by environmental factors. But IQ is more vulnerable to environmental effects, and temperament may be equally a product of environment and heredity. Schizophrenia may have only a 40 percent inherited basis and may owe its expression more to environmental than to genetic causes. Thus although environment and heredity both contribute to human development, their relative influence on particular traits varies widely.

68

Characteristics under tight genetic control are said to be highly "**ca-nalized.**" This term comes from a model of genetic–environmental interaction proposed by Conrad Waddington (1957) (see Figure 3.4). In this model, as a child develops, his or her genotype for a particular trait may be thought of as a ball rolling down the slopes and valleys of a three-dimensional landscape. If the valley floor is broad and its slopes are shallow, the ball can be thrown off course—derailed from the normal developmental path—by environmental conditions. The genotype for the trait is not well protected from environmental forces. But if the valley is deep, with a narrow floor and steep, protective walls, the "winds" of the environment are less likely to blow the ball off course. Even if the ball is displaced by a strong wind, it is likely to regain its course. This pathway along the deep valley is highly "canalized" and well protected from environmental forces. Even if some childhood illness interferes with Sam's growth for a time, for example, he is likely to make up the lost height when he recovers. But his youthful gregariousness—what his mother calls his "animal high spirits"—may well be moderated under the demands of teachers and others who expect him to concentrate on studying and to blend with his classmates.

To add to the complexity of interaction between genes and environments, not only are there differences in canalization for different traits, but the degree of canalization for the same trait may change as the child gets older. In general, during a child's first few years, it seems, the valleys are deep and narrow, and development is highly canalized. Human infants follow the same path of development as they have for hundreds of generations. But later on, the degree of canalization of these characteristics diminishes and differences in environment grow increasingly influential.

On a beautiful Sunday morning, 2½-year-old Sam and his parents joined friends and their 8-year-old son at the children's section of the Bronx Zoo. Timmy, the 8-year-old, was fascinated by the animals. He knew about snakes and owls from school books. He peppered his father with questions about the elephants. Timmy's teacher later reported that the zoo had made quite an impression on Timmy. He had done almost nothing but eat and sleep snakes ever since. At home, too, Timmy drew snakes; asked for books about snakes; and became an instant snake expert. But the zoo had made very little impression on Sam. The animals could have danced on their heads, and Sam wouldn't have noticed. The only thing Sam was interested in was Timmy, his idol.

Figure 3.4 **This adaptation of Waddington's (1962) landscape model of interaction between heredity and environment shows the hypothetical development of three different kinds of characteristics. Physical appearance, here height, is highly canalized—under strict genetic control. Social behavior, here sociability, is much less canalized and more susceptible to environmental influences. Intellectual development, here mathematical ability, is highly canalized in the early years but less so later.**

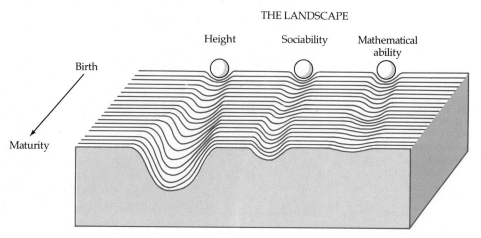

The zoo trip may well have been formative for Timmy, influencing the course of his mental development. For Sam, the zoo was just another setting for watching Timmy. Children experience different environments differently at different ages.

Mothers' and children's IQs

"How do genes and the environment contribute to children's intellectual development?" was the question asked by a team of investigators from the Frank Porter Graham Center at the University of North Carolina (Yeates, MacPhee, Campbell, and Ramey, 1983). They followed 112 children from birth to age 4 and tested their IQs at intervals. They also observed the children's home environments to see the kinds of stimulation available there, and they gave IQ tests to the children's mothers to try to estimate the children's inherited intelligence levels.

Their results showed that as the children grew older, their IQ scores were increasingly well predicted by the combination of their mothers' IQ scores and the ratings of their home environments. As 2-year-olds, 11 percent of the variation in the children's IQs could be predicted by this combination of genetics and environment. As 4-year-olds, 29 percent could be predicted. But the relative importance of genetics and environment changed. For 2-year-olds, the mother's IQ was more highly related to the infant's IQ than the home environment was. Knowing how stimulating the home was added nothing to the researchers' ability to predict the infant's intelligence. But for 4-year-olds, the stimulation of the home environment was the main predictor. The mother's IQ added nothing to the prediction.

This study supports the view that after infancy, as the child begins to explore the world, a shift occurs in the relative importance of inheritance and environment for intellectual development. By the time the child is 4 years old, the study results suggest, home environment is as important as genotype in predicting IQ.

As children leave infancy and begin to explore the world, the stimulation in their environment becomes increasingly important in the development of their intelligence. By the time children are 4 years old, their environment weighs equally with their genotype in predicting their IQ scores.

Finally, there is one more wrinkle of complexity in the interaction of genes and environment. Not only does the environment affect the expression of a person's genotype, but the person's genotype affects the environment. Sandra Scarr and Kathleen McCartney (1983) proposed that in essence people make their own environments. They do so in two ways. First, their genotype evokes a particular response from the environment. Active, happy babies, for example, evoke more social reactions from their caregivers than expressionless babies. A bright, curious child evokes more interesting interactions than a dull, withdrawn one. Second, a person actively seeks the environment that he or she finds stimulating and compatible. The child who loves music learns to play an instrument. The girl who is gifted at languages studies anthropology or journalism. The boy with high visual-spatial ability becomes a pilot or a mechanic. This kind of active ''niche picking'' increases as children get older. Young children, who have less control over their environments, do less ''niche picking'' than adolescents. Adolescents make important choices on their own, choices that are in keeping with their own talents and inclinations, their genotypes.

It is clear that to understand how children develop, we need to examine both genetic and environmental influences and their interaction. In this chapter, we start at the beginning of that process, with the story of genetics.

Genetic building blocks

DNA and RNA

As children get older, they increasingly pick their own activities, and in doing so, they are drawn to aspects of their surroundings that mesh with their genetic inheritance.

Each human cell contains 46 **chromosomes** in its nucleus. Each long and thin chromosome is made up of over 1000 **genes**, strung out like a chain. The genes are made of molecules of **deoxyribonucleic acid (DNA)**. The long DNA molecule (Figure 3.5) is made of two strands of alternating sugar and phosphate molecules attached to nitrogen bases—adenine, cytosine, guanine, and thymine—which are twisted around each other and connected by rungs in the shape of a laddered spiral. During normal cell division, or **mitosis**, the DNA, which is packed tightly into the nucleus of the cell, ''unzips,'' breaking its rungs and forming two separate strands. The nitrogen bases in each of these strands then pick up complementary nitrogen bases that are loose in the cell nucleus, making a new laddered spiral identical to the first. Thymine picks up adenine, adenine picks up thymine, guanine picks up cytosine, and cytosine picks up guanine. In this fashion all 46 chromosomes of the cell reproduce themselves. Then the two sets of 46 chromosomes move to different sides of the cell, a barrier forms between them, and the cell divides into two identical daughter cells.

The DNA in each human cell contains the chemical instructions for building a complete human being. It provides the instructions for creating a new member of the human species with basic human characteristics like limbs, head, and hair rather than fins or feathers; and it provides the instructions for creating a new individual with his or her own unique combination of characteristics like eye color, intelligence, height, and blood type. The particular order in which the molecules making up the DNA are arranged is the genetic code for these individual characteristics. A person's genotype, thus, is like a blueprint. To get from blueprint to human being, information in the DNA molecules is transcribed into molecules of **ribonucleic acid (RNA)**. These RNA molecules take the information from the DNA into the cytoplasm of the cell, which contains the raw material for making protein. Out of the proteins made according to the instructions from the RNA, the many functioning parts and capacities of each human being develop.

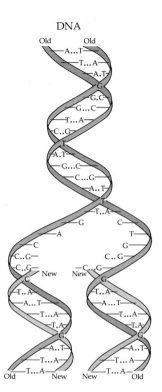

Figure 3.5 *Two strands of sugar, phosphate, and nitrogen molecules—adenine (A), thymine (T), guanine (G), and cytosine (C)—intertwine. They form a double helix, which is the structure of the DNA molecule. When a DNA molecule reproduces itself, the two strands of the double helix separate, and each serves as the template for the synthesis of a complementary strand (Watson, 1976).*

Meiosis

For a new human being to be created, a special kind of cell division, **meiosis**, must occur (see Figure 3.6). Germ cells in the reproductive organs, the **testes** and **ovaries**, divide by meiosis to form **sperm** cells and **ova**. In this process, the chromosomes of the germ cells line up side by side in **homologous**, or parallel, pairs, one chromosome originally being from the person's mother and one from the person's father. While they are lined up, each chromosome doubles. At this stage, any of the four strands of a homologous pair may break. If two strands from different chromosomes break at the same point, **crossover** may take place, and pieces of the strands then join in a new combination. After the genetic material is exchanged, the paired and doubled chromosomes separate and separate again, as their cells divide and divide again, leaving sperm and ovum with only half the number of chromosomes that the other cells of the body contain. At **conception**, when the 23 chromosomes in the man's sperm cell join the 23 chromosomes in the woman's ovum, the number of chromosomes in the new cell, or **zygote**, is 46.

Chromosomes

Of the 46 chromosomes in each zygote, 44 (22 pairs) are **autosomes**, and it is these that carry most of the genetic code for the development of intelligence, height, eye color, and the like. The other pair of chromosomes determines whether the new human being is male or female. If the zygote contains two **X chromosomes**, a female develops. If the zygote contains one X and one **Y chromosome**, a male develops. Every zygote inherits an X chromosome from the mother, because all of her body's cells contain two X chromosomes, and so each of her ova contains one X chromosome. Because men's body cells contain

MEIOSIS

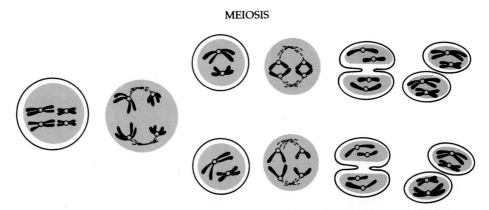

Figure 3.6 The process of cell division in testes and ovaries is called **meiosis.** *The first step in the process is for the chromosomes in each germ cell to line up in 23 homologous, or parallel, pairs. One chromosome of each pair is originally from each parent. Next, the chromosomes double, then separate and separate again, leaving the four resulting sperm or ova with only 23 chromosomes each.*

an X and a Y chromosome, the father's sperm cells each contain *either* an X *or* a Y chromosome. Whether the infant turns out to be a boy or a girl therefore is determined by the sex chromosome in the sperm.

Inheritance of physical characteristics

Sam has his mother's head—her dark skin, white teeth, brown eyes, and shiny hair—and his father's body—his height, lankiness, and metabolism. ''Every time he turns,'' his mother says, ''I see a glimmer of myself, my sister, my parents, and my grandparents. The curve of his cheeks reminds me of Sam's father and grandfather. The shape of his eyes reminds his grandmother of her own mother's eyes. It's easy to lose yourself in the looking glass of your child.''

Natalie is quiet and dark-haired. Plump, short, and slow-moving, like her father's mother, Natalie rarely runs at full tilt or jumps from high places. She has her father's dark, wavy hair and her mother's clear white skin. Everyone who sees her remarks on how much Natalie looks like her father when he was her age. In fact, when she saw a snapshot of her father as a toddler, she insisted that it was a picture of herself. Like both of her parents, Natalie has unusually beautiful light blue eyes. When her mother was pregnant, she knew one thing for sure about her developing child: he or she would have light blue eyes.

Hair and skin color, height and weight, eye color and shape are among the physical characteristics coded in genes located on the autosomal chromosomes. The probability of a person's inheriting curly hair or of growing to over six feet, for example, can be predicted with some certainty from knowing the hair type or height of the person's parents and grandparents. Natalie's mother was right in predicting Natalie's blue eyes. All the children born to her and her husband would inherit their striking blue eyes. Blue eyes are inherited through a simple pattern of genetic inheritance. Blue eye color is a **recessive** characteristic: A person has blue eyes only when both chromosomes in the pair carrying the gene for eye color carry the blue-eye gene. Brown eye color is a **dominant** characteristic: A person with brown eyes needs only one brown-

Although body weight is an inherited physical characteristic, it is influenced by environmental factors such as diet and exercise.

eye gene in the pair. Thus, if both parents have blue eyes, they can contribute only blue-eye genes to their child, and that child will have blue eyes. If both parents have brown eyes, the chance that their child will have blue eyes cannot exceed 25 percent (see Figure 3.7). This simple pattern of inheritance is followed not only for eye color, but for various other physical traits as well. For example, curly hair is dominant over straight hair, prominent noses over smaller noses, thick lips over thin, cleft chins over smooth, and shortness over tallness. But most physical characteristics follow more complicated patterns that involve more than one gene. They are **polygenic**. Predicting polygenic characteristics in a new human being, even knowing the parents' characteristics, is difficult.

Although these physical characteristics are inherited, extremes of environment—diet, health, living conditions, and the like—can affect their expression. As we have seen already, skin color is affected by the amount of available sunlight. Severe malnutrition gives African children thin reddish hair, even though they have inherited genes for thick dark hair. Body weight, especially in females, although an inherited characteristic, is influenced by diet. (So Natalie, who has always tended to plumpness, should be steered to snacks of apples and celery sticks rather than cookies and candies to keep her from gaining too much weight.) Second-generation Japanese-Americans, who eat the rich diet available in this country, are, on the average, taller than their parents who grew up in Japan.

Because of the complexities of inheritance patterns, the infinity of possible genetic combinations, and the fact that phenotypes are affected by the environment, we will never be able to predict with complete certainty before birth what any particular child will look like. True, we may know from observing the parents that a child is likely to be short and to have brown eyes,

Figure 3.7 This chart illustrates the process by which eye color is inherited by a child. When both parents have blue eyes, the child is certain to have blue eyes. When both parents have brown eyes, the child has only a 6 percent chance of having blue eyes. When one parent has blue eyes and the other has brown, the child has a 25 percent chance of having blue eyes.

INHERITANCE OF EYE COLOR

One parent's eye color	+	Other parent's eye color	→	Baby's eye color							Chance of baby's having Blue eyes	Chance of baby's having Brown eyes
bb		BB		bB	or	bB	or	bB	or	bB	0%	100%
		bb		bb	or	bb	or	bb	or	bb	100%	0%
		Bb		bB	or	bb	or	bB	or	bb	50%	50%
Bb		BB		BB	or	BB	or	bB	or	bB	0%	100%
		bb		Bb	or	Bb	or	bb	or	bb	50%	50%
		Bb		BB	or	Bb	or	bB	or	bb	25%	75%
BB		Bb		BB	or	Bb	or	BB	or	Bb	0%	100%
		bb		Bb	or	Bb	or	Bb	or	Bb	0%	100%
		BB		BB	or	BB	or	BB	or	BB	0%	100%

Genotype: B = Brown gene   b = blue gene

Phenotype: BB = Brown eyes   Bb = brown eyes   bb = blue eyes fair skin, and wavy hair. We may know from tests done prenatally that a fetus is male or female or carrying genes or chromosomes for certain specific disorders. But we still are far from being able to read the whole genetic code and even farther from knowing the extent of environmental effects. Genetic research is one of the most exciting fields in science today, and new discoveries about how genes work roll off the presses every month. But the more we find out, it seems, the more complex the picture becomes. Geneticists have found out, for example, that genes are not always static in their regulation of behavior. They may jump or split, creating complex changes in systems of genes. They may turn on and off at different points in development. Even though great strides are being made in the understanding of genetic transmission, some mystery in an individual's physical development will undoubtedly always remain.

Inheritance of Behavioral Traits

The mystery increases when we leave physical characteristics and look at the development of behavioral characteristics. Behavioral characteristics are even more susceptible to environmental influences than physical characteristics are. They are also more difficult to dissect so neatly into identifiable pieces like noses, lips, and eyes. What is more, behavioral characteristics all seem to be polygenic. Geneticists have not yet identified a single gene that produces variation in a single behavioral trait. They do not even know of a complex behavior that is entirely under genetic influence. Only rarely can more than half of the variability of an observed behavioral trait be traced to genetic influence (Plomin, 1983). Thus, although the principles of genetics are extremely important to students of human development, it will be some time before we can specify how human chemistry affects complex human behavior. We may observe that a child like Natalie is calm, shy, and musical, but we are far from being able to identify the genetic bases for these traits. What we do know about the inheritance of behavioral characteristics we have learned through indirect methods like studying twins and family trees.

Methods of study

Twin studies

Sir Francis Galton, Charles Darwin's cousin, led scientists to one ingenious method for studying the heritability of behavioral characteristics. Galton realized that identical twins, who by definition have the same genotype, would give scientists a window through which to observe the contributions of environment and heredity. Since he made that suggestion, twin studies have been an important source of information about the relative contributions of environment and heredity to human behavior.

A pair of twins is either "identical," technically called **monozygotic (MZ)**—single-egg—twins or "fraternal," **dizygotic (DZ)**—double-egg—twins. Identical twins develop from one fertilized egg by mitosis and therefore have exactly the same genotype. Early in development, the contents of the single egg divide into two embryos. In the uterus, the two embryos usually are enclosed within a single fetal membrane, although sometimes the identical embryos migrate separately into the uterus and attach at different points. Fraternal twins develop when two ova are released and fertilized by separate sperm at the same moment of conception. These two embryos have genotypes no more alike than those of any two brothers and sisters. They may look alike or not, be of the same sex or not.

Psychologists study twins by comparing the similarity, or **concordance**, of identical twins with the similarity of fraternal twins. Differences between identical twins can be laid directly to differences in environment. Differences between fraternal twins can be laid to differences in both environment and heredity. Comparing similarities between pairs of fraternal and identical twins suggests whether a characteristic is inherited.

Unfortunately, twin studies have limitations. They do not allow researchers to separate the effects of environment totally from the effects of heredity. For example, identical twins look so much alike that they may be treated more alike than fraternal twins are.

> My husband still has trouble telling our 13-year-old identical twin sons apart. Like most everybody else, he treats them like a single creature called, "You boys," as in "Will you boys please turn down that record player?"

Identical twins may also spend more time together, making their environments more nearly alike than those of fraternal twins. To overcome these limitations, psychologists have tried to find identical twins who have grown up in different families. The assumption is that such twins' similarities arise from heredity and their differences from factors in the environments in which they are raised. In fact, even before birth, the twins' environments may differ. They may have different access to their mother's blood supply; or one of them may suffer oxygen deprivation during delivery. Some twins are mirror images of each other. The consequences of this may be minor, such as differences in handedness, or they may be major, such as differences in dominant brain hemispheres with associated differences in general cognitive or personality styles. But even if these cases could be eliminated from the studies, the biggest problem with this approach is finding identical twins who have been raised apart. Fewer than 200 sets of identical twins raised in different families have been found and studied in the past half century. Of these, only three sets were reared apart in completely different environments and had no contact with each other from birth (Farber, 1981).

Family trees

Researchers also study the inheritance of characteristics by analyzing their presence or absence among members of entire families. One famous

Monozygotic twins (front), having identical genotypes, are identical in appearance and abilities. Dizygotic twins (back) can be as unlike as any two brothers or sisters.

THE NOTORIOUS "KALLIKAKS"

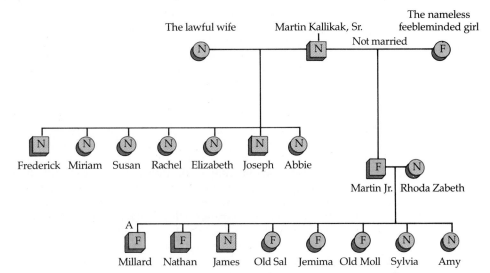

Figure 3.8 **The study of the notorious "Kallikaks" was an early use of a family tree for tracing genetic influences on development. This family tree shows that in the judgment of their townsfolk, Martin's legitimate sons and daughters were normal (N), but illegitimate Martin, Jr., was feebleminded (F) like his mother, and so were a number of the grandchildren (Goddard, 1912).**

family-tree study focused on a family named by the investigator the "Kallikaks" (Goddard, 1912; see Figure 3.8). "Kallikak" is a combination of the Greek words for "good," *kalos*, and for "bad," *kakos*. Martin Kallikak, a soldier in the Revolutionary War, so it was claimed, fathered an illegitimate son by a retarded tavern maid. Of the five generations and 480 descendants of the maid, many were drunks, prostitutes, thieves, felons, and ne'er-do-wells. Some 143 descendants were considered retarded. But Martin Kallikak also married a wife of "good stock." Of the 496 descendants of this marriage, most were landowners, merchants, and teachers. One was reported to be "sexually loose," and two had "appetite for strong drink." Although this example may be more interesting than scientific, carefully done family-tree studies can yield important information about heredity. The open question, of course, is to what extent differences in rearing and environment interact with the differences in inheritance to produce lines of descendants with different characteristics.

In another type of family-tree study, investigators trace the relatives of individuals with a particular trait or disorder. If the incidence of the trait among first-degree relatives—parents, children, brothers and sisters—is higher than among second-degree relatives—aunts and uncles, nieces and nephews, cousins—the trait can be presumed to have at least some genetic basis. The limitation of this method is that the environments of first degree relatives also are likely to be more similar than the environments of second-degree relatives. Thus, although this method is useful for tracing the inheritance of traits *not* affected by the environment, it does not separate the contributions of environment and heredity for traits that *are* affected by the environment.

Adopted children

Another method of studying heredity involves adopted children. In one kind of adoption study, researchers compare the behavioral characteristics of adopted children with those of their biological and their adoptive parents. If the adopted children resemble their adoptive parents more than they resemble their biological parents, the resemblance is presumed to stem from environmental factors. Comparisons also can be made between the adopted children and their biological siblings who are raised by their natural parents. In one old study, Marie Skodak and Harold Skeels (1949) studied children of retarded mothers, who had stayed with their mothers or who had been adopted by parents with normal IQs. The average IQ of the adopted children was higher than the average IQ of the children who had stayed with their retarded mothers. This finding suggested that the home environment affects the development of children's intelligence. But the average IQ of the adopted children of retarded mothers was lower than the average IQ of adopted children whose mothers were not retarded. This finding suggested that genetic endowment also plays a role. This study clearly showed that both heredity and environment contribute to development.

More recently, efforts to study the contributions of heredity and environment in adopted and nonadopted children have gotten more complex. In the Colorado Adoption Project (Plomin, Loehlin, and DeFries, 1985), for example, researchers have compared the correlations between development and environmental stimulation for children in adoptive families with those of children in natural families. The correlations usually are higher in the natural families, leading the researchers to suggest that genetic factors not only contribute directly to children's development, but also mediate the effects of the environment on development.

Even though it has not been possible to trace behavior patterns directly to specific genes, these indirect methods—twin studies, family-tree studies, and adoption studies—have allowed developmental psychologists to determine whether heredity contributes to the development of particular abilities, behavior patterns, and behavior problems. In the future, researchers may use these methods to determine how and to what extent heredity actually contributes.

Experimental intervention

Twin studies, family trees, and adoption are methods used by behavior geneticists to study genetic bases of behavior. An alternative approach to studying nature–nurture interaction is to study the effect of the environment on development, by trying to change children's development experimentally. This is the method of experimental developmental psychology. The researcher assigns children to an experimental treatment—extra stimulation, increased discipline, more toys—or to a control condition in which they receive no extraordinary treatment. Then he or she assesses the effects of the experimental intervention. This method has been used most frequently by researchers to try to change children's intelligence levels. Unfortunately, this method, like the others, has limitations. There are both practical and ethical problems in intervening in children's lives in ways that are as extreme as one needs to test fully the limits of environmental effects on development.

Personality and temperament

Personality is the typical and consistent way in which a person acts and approaches the world. Sam is friendly, cheerful, and boisterous. His father calls him "sensitive but low-strung." Natalie is quiet, passive, and shy. Other children are aggressive, greedy, blundering, high-strung, demonstrative, tentative, or anxious. **Temperament** is an infant's natural disposition or style of activity—the infant's "personality." Sam's mother mentioned that in the hospital delivery room, Sam was already calm and curious. Natalie's parents found her disposed to be quiet and passive right from the start. In a longitudinal study of children's temperaments from infancy to adolescence, Alexander Thomas, Stella Chess, and Herbert Birch (1968) found that children's temperaments appeared early and seemed to be quite stable throughout the children's early years. They surmised from this that temperament has some genetic basis. One aspect of temperament that seems to be inherited is activity level and the behavioral characteristics associated with it—being fidgety, impatient, ''on the go'' or quiet, sedentary, and still. Although some people have criticized this study (we discuss these criticisms in Chapter 7), its findings are supported by evidence from twin studies, which also suggests that activity level has a genetic component: activity level is more concordant in identical than in fraternal twins.

Sociability is another aspect of temperament and personality that appears to be partly inherited. Longitudinal studies of children from birth to maturity and studies of twins and adopted children suggest that people inherit the inclination to be friendly and outgoing or shy and withdrawn. Sociable Sam shouts hello and makes friends with the mail carrier, the neighbors, the neighbors' dogs, and every soul who walks, jogs, or runs past his front door. Natalie rarely speaks above a whisper and smiles a shy hello even to people she knows well.

Also inherited may be tendencies to be empathic, nurturant, and altruistic, adaptable, dominant, assertive and self-confident; conforming; or depressed (Daniels and Plomin, 1985; Goldsmith, 1983; Matheny and Dolan, 1975; Rushton, 1984; Vandenberg, 1968). In her comprehensive review of studies of identical twins raised apart, Susan Farber (1981) concluded that the evidence of similarities was most convincing for the following personality traits: characteristic mood, emotional expressiveness, pattern of anxiety, and styles of talking, laughing, and moving. Intriguing case studies of the very few identical twins and triplets who have been reared apart since infancy hint that inheritance may govern even more specific traits.

Studies of the similarities of identical twins suggest that there is a genetic basis for abilities, intelligence, temperament, sociability, interests, and mental illness.

This does not mean, however, that the die of personality is cast with the genes. Children with identical temperaments do not always develop in identical ways. Identical twins do not always act alike. What happens to the dispositions found in infancy and the personality styles found in childhood depends to a large extent on children's interactions with their parents and other people. For example, two of the infants in the longitudinal study by Thomas, Chess, and Birch were twins adopted into different families that were similar socially and financially. As newborns, the infant girls had similar temperaments. They slept on very irregular schedules, and they cried a lot when they weren't sleeping and were hard to console. These were temperamentally cranky, or "difficult," infants. The parents in one of the adoptive families pleasantly checked their daughter for cold or wetness each night when she woke up and then, if nothing was wrong, left her alone. She soon stopped waking up at night. The parents in the other family responded to their daughter's nightly crying by picking her up, fussing over her, and feeding her. When she was 27 months old, this child had become so difficult to manage that the parents sought counseling. Two different families' styles had fostered two patterns of development.

focus   *Twins reared apart*

In 1981, Robert Shafran went to college in New York State, and strange things began happening to him. Other students called, "Hi, Eddy," a young woman whom he didn't know kissed him on the lips, and a fellow insisted that he was a dead ringer for Eddy Garland. His curiosity aroused, Robert looked at pictures of Eddy. He was astonished at how similar they looked. Robert got in touch with Eddy, and the facts of their births emerged. The monozygotic brothers were born 27 minutes apart and had been adopted when they were 6 months old. They found that their IQs were the same, that they liked the same music, food, and sports. Pictures of the reunited brothers appeared in newspapers and happened to be spotted by a family named Kellman. David Kellman, it turned out, was their third identical brother. As his adoptive mother said of the triplets, "They talk the same. The laugh the same. They hold their cigarettes the same—it's uncanny" (*New York Times*, September 19 and 23, 1981).

In another remarkable case, twins George and Millan were separated immediately after birth and adopted into different families. They, too, met for the first time when they were 19 years old. When they met, they looked so much alike that neighbors mistook one for the other. Both were handsome; both were athletic. Both had won boxing championships, and both were artistically inclined. Millan was musical; George worked as a commercial artist. They even had cavities in the same teeth. On personality tests, their scores were nearly identical. Within a few months of each other, George and Millan developed a rare crippling spine disease. In both twins, the disease responded to treatment. Only on social views, consistent with their different adoptive backgrounds, did the twins differ.

In yet another case, identical twin Oskar Stohr stayed in Europe with his mother while his brother, Jack Yule, went to Trinidad with their father. The boys were raised in different religions, spoke different languages, and had different kinds of schooling. But when they met each other at age 47, they

Intelligence

There is also evidence from twin, family-tree, and adoption studies that intelligence and the abilities making up intelligence, such as comprehension of words and fluency of speech, mathematical and spatial abilities, reasoning, and memory, are to some extent genetically influenced. After reviewing many studies, conducted over the course of half a century and comprising 30,000 correlations, Loise Erlenmeyer-Kimling and Lissy Jarvik (1963) concluded that the closer the family relationship, the more similar people's IQs (see Figure 3.9). In their review, the concordance between IQ scores averaged .49 for brothers and sisters, .53 for fraternal twins raised together, and .87 for identical twins raised together—making a strong case for the contribution of genetics to IQ.

But, as we have already suggested, environment also affects intelligence. When identical twins were raised apart, the correlation between their IQ scores was only .75 (or even lower, according to an analysis of these cases by Farber [1981]). To what extent does environment affect the expression of intelligence? Overall intelligence seems to be rather deeply canalized. The difference in IQ scores that can be produced by differences in normal environment is only about 25 IQ points, by one estimate (Scarr–Salapatek, 1975).

both spoke quickly, angered easily, and shared the same quirky habits, like flushing the toilet before they used it and fiddling with other people's rubber bands (Chen, 1979). Heredity, it seems, may extend even to the most minute of human characteristics.

These informal reports are only suggestive, and there are other possible explanations for the coincidences observed. For one thing, when many characteristics are examined, some are likely to be identical in a pair of twins just by chance. For another, the twins' environments might have been more alike than reporters realized. We need more research before we can state the extent and scope of genetic influence.

When these triplets, who had been separated in infancy, discovered one another as young men, they found that they shared more than physical appearance. They smiled and talked in the same way, had similar food preferences, and listened to the same kind of music. They had identical IQs, smoked too much, and held their cigarettes the same way.

THE INHERITANCE OF INTELLIGENCE

Figure 3.9 The contribution of heredity to intelligence is shown by comparing the correlations of IQ scores for unrelated individuals, siblings, fraternal (DZ) twins, and identical (MZ) twins, raised together (colored bars). The contribution of environment is suggested by the difference between these correlations and those of children raised in different homes (white bars) (Erlenmeyer-Kimling and Jarvik, 1963).

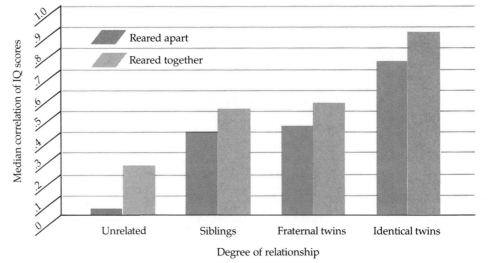

In one study, Sandra Scarr and Richard Weinberg (1983) studied the intelligence levels of black children adopted into white families. In their Transracial Adoption Study, adoptive parents and their biological children scored somewhat above average on intelligence tests appropriate for their ages. Black children adopted into these families also scored somewhat above average. Those adopted before they turned 1 year old scored 110 on IQ tests, about 20 points higher than comparable children from the black community. Environment was not all-powerful, however. Correlations of the IQ scores of the children, their biological, and their adoptive parents showed that the children's intelligence scores were related both to their biological parents' scores (heredity) and their adoptive parents' scores (environment). Based on these correlations, the investigators concluded that 40 to 70 percent of the IQ variation they found in these children arose from genetic factors.

Specific abilities may respond more to environmental factors. Two investigators (Mather and Black, 1984) studied the language skills of fraternal and identical twins. They found that twins' understanding of word meanings had a hereditary basis, but how children actually spoke was influence by environmental factors.

The environment may affect children's development of intelligence in many different ways. Sometimes children passively receive stimulation from the environment. They are most likely to do this in infancy and early childhood as they are bathed in sounds and sights that keep their senses alert and developing. As they get older, children actively select some of their stimulation from the environment. They watch and listen to "Sesame Street" and tune out background sounds like their parents chatting with a neighbor. This selected stimulation also contributes to children's development of intelligence. Third, the environment gives children the chance to act on it—to play with blocks and toys, books and ball—and thus to be influenced by it. Finally, the environment gives children chances to participate actively in conversations and exchanges, to interact with adults who listen, respond, give feedback, and teach little lessons. This, too, affects the development of language and intelligence.

The degree to which the environment influences the expression of intelligence or language, of course, also depends on how extreme the environmental conditions are. Never talking to a baby, for example, would impair the *research focus* *Louisville twin study*

By comparing the mental development of identical and fraternal twins in the Louisville Twin Study, Ronald Wilson (1983) uncovered important facts about the genetic basis of intelligence. The twins in this study were tested more than a dozen times between the ages of 3 months and 15 years. These tests showed that bursts and pauses in intellectual development were closely synchronized in twins, especially in identical twins (see Figure 3.10). In infancy, the twins' scores bobbed up and down, and concordances between fraternal and identical twins were essentially the same. But from the age of 1½ years onward, the concordance between identical twins' scores was markedly higher than that between fraternal twins', and it continued to increase as the twins got older. (The concordance for identical twins was about .80 at 1½ years and about .90 at 15 years.) Concordances between fraternal twins, in contrast, declined steadily after the children reached 3 years of age, until the concordance at age 15 was only about .50.

Wilson also studied the twins' home environments to see how well their physical and emotional surroundings were promoting their intellectual development. In infancy, the relation between the twins' mental development and their home environments was weak. But by age 2, the relation was stronger, and from age 3 onward, the relation was quite strong. As Wilson noted, it is always difficult to separate the effects of environment and heredity, because parents furnish their children with both. Even so, he concluded, his study suggests that the principal link between parents' and children's intelligence is genetic and that environment intensifies the effects of heredity. Intelligence may have genetic roots, but it is also susceptible to environmental forces.

baby's intellectual development far more severely than, say, not teaching nursery rhymes. Furthermore, never talking to a baby during the period when speech ordinarily develops would be far more harmful to the baby's intellectual development than not talking to a teenager, for *when* an environmental factor is encountered is also crucial.

Inheritance of disorders

Ask any expectant parent what kind of baby he or she wants, and you are likely to hear, ''I don't care, just as long as it's healthy.'' In most cases, their wish comes true. But occasionally problems arise because of abnormal chromosome numbers or structures or because of defect-producing genes.

Sex-related disorders

There are two kinds of problem related to the sex chromosomes. One is an abnormality in the number of chromosomes in the zygote. When sexual reproduction goes normally, as we have described, the human ovum carries an X sex chromosome, and the sperm that merges with it carries either another X or a Y chromosome. But when meiosis goes wrong, an embryo may develop with too many, too few, or broken pieces of sex chromosomes. Noticeable sex-chromosome abnormalities appear once in every 200 births (Reed, 1975).

In some cases, a sperm carries both X and Y chromosomes. When one of these sperm fertilizes a normal ovum, the resulting XXY male has **Klinefel-**

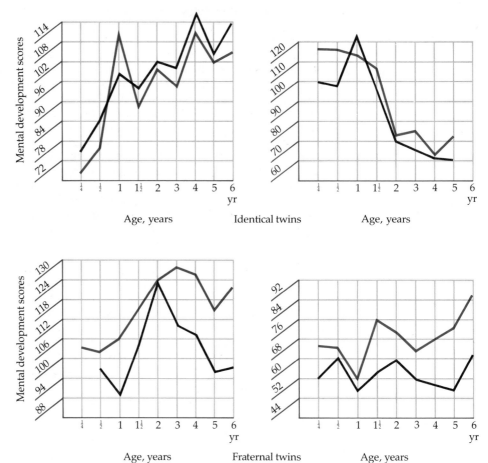

Figure 3.10 Trends in IQ scores during early childhood for two identical twins (top) and two fraternal twins (bottom) show the greater similarity of developmental patterns in identical twins (Wilson, 1978).

ter's syndrome. He is sterile because he has no functioning testes; he may develop small breasts. Some males with Klinefelter's syndrome have low intelligence. In other cases, the sperm carries no sex chromosomes. When such a sperm fertilizes a normal ovum, a single-X female is born with **Turner's syndrome**. She is short, has a broad neck, and lacks all or most of the female internal reproductive organs and secondary sex characteristics. Many women with Turner's syndrome do poorly on tests of spatial and perceptual reasoning and have psychological problems but normal verbal skills.

Sometimes a sperm carries two X or two Y sex chromosomes. When a sperm carrying two Y chromosomes fertilizes a normal ovum, a male with the **XYY syndrome** is born. This syndrome is associated with tallness, adolescent acne, abnormal genitals, and limited intelligence. It was once thought that XYY males were prone to violence, because a disproportionate number appeared in prisons. A closer examination, however, showed that most XYY males do not get into trouble with the law, and those who do are not inherently violence prone, but their limited intelligence made it likely that when they did commit crimes, they would be caught (Witkin et al., 1976). Some psychologists have suggested that boys with the XYY syndrome are likely to develop behavior problems and should get therapy. Yet it is also possible that by singling out such boys for treatment, an expectation on the part of parents or others might actually induce behavior problems. The solution to the problem is not clear.

A second kind of sex-related congenital problem involves disorders that come from defect-producing genes located on the sex chromosomes. **Sex-linked** defect-producing genes usually are recessive and carried on the X chromosome. Because males have only one X chromosome, they are more susceptible to these disorders. Whenever their single X chromosome contains the disorder, it will be expressed, because there is no corresponding normal dominant gene from the Y chromosome. For a female to exhibit a sex-linked disorder, she must inherit the defective gene from *both* parents. If a female inherits a harmful recessive gene from just one parent, she has a second X chromosome with a parallel gene to counteract the expression of the recessive gene. Hemophilia (lack of blood-clotting factors), color blindness, and baldness are sex-linked defects that appear almost exclusively in males. Girls may carry one gene for hemophilia without being bleeders, but boys who inherit the gene for hemophilia will have the disease. Chances are that half of the daughters of mothers who carry the gene for hemophilia will themselves be carriers, but half of the sons will be hemophilic.

Physical defects

As with the sex chromosomes, when something goes wrong during meiosis and the zygote ends up with more or fewer than 22 pairs of autosomal chromosomes, problems may ensue. When chromosome pair 21 does not separate, and the zygote has 47 instead of 46 chromosomes, the child suffers from **Down's syndrome**. These children have retarded mental and motor development, broad and flat faces, eyes slanted upward and a prolonged fold along the inner corner of the eye, straight and thin hair, short feet and hands, and heart defects.

As women get older, they face increasingly greater risks of bearing a child with Down's syndrome. Women under 30 bear only one Down's syndrome child in 3000. But women between 30 and 34 bear 1 in 600; women between 35 and 39, 1 in 280; women 40 to 44, 1 in 80; and women over 44 bear Down's syndrome babies once in every 40 births (Apgar and Beck, 1974). One possible explanation for this increasing risk is based on the fact that women are born with all the ova they will ever have (although in immature form). Because women's germ cells are exposed to environmental hazards, viruses,

Down's syndrome results when the zygote has an extra chromosome 21. Children with this disorder have retarded mental and motor development and distinctive facial features.

and even emotional stress from the time of their birth, this long period of exposure increases the risk that chromosome pairs will not separate during meiosis. But in up to one-third of the cases of Down's syndrome, the man and not the woman contributes the extra chromosome (Magenis, Overton, Chamberlin, Brady, and Louvrien, 1977).

Other physical disorders arise when harmful genes are passed on from parents to their children. **Sickle-cell anemia** is a painful and sometimes life-threatening disease found among American blacks. About 10 percent of American blacks are carriers of the sickle-cell gene. That is, they have one sickle-cell gene and one normal gene for blood cell shape. They inherited the sickle-cell trait from their African ancestors. In Africa, where malaria was a common and deadly disease, people whose blood cells formed a sickle shape were likelier than others to survive an attack of malaria. The sickle-cell trait thus was adaptive, and people who had a sickle-cell gene were likely to survive to the age of sexual maturity and thus to pass on the gene to their children. But transported to North America, where there is no malaria, the sickle-cell trait is maladaptive. In people with the sickle-cell trait, when the level of oxygen is low, the red blood cells become sickle-shaped and clump together, blocking the flow of blood through the person's small blood vessels. Depending on the location and extent of the blockage, the disease causes circulatory problems, pain, or death. People with the sickle-cell trait must be protected from conditions that reduce the oxygen in their blood, such as illness, strenuous exercise, and high altitude.

Phenylketonuria (PKU) is a metabolic disorder that is also genetically based. Infants who receive the genes for this recessive trait from both parents cannot make phenylalanine hydroxylase, an enzyme necessary for digestion. They therefore cannot digest the phenylalanine in many foods, including milk. This amino acid then accumulates and prevents normal brain development. The infants are irritable and hyperactive. One-third have seizures. As children, they are mentally retarded. But this disease now can be controlled. Once a newborn has consumed milk for about a week, an excess of the undigested phenylalanine can be detected in a blood test. Infants for whom the disorder is detected at this early age are given milk substitutes. Later they eat a special diet that contains only the smallest necessary amount of phenylalanine. They stay on this restricted diet until brain development is complete, at the end of adolescence.

Although this diet limits the abnormalities that phenylalanine buildup causes, it cannot prevent all ill effects. Infants and children with PKU are prone to emotional and learning disorders that their brothers and sisters without PKU do not have (Berman and Ford, 1970; Dodson, Kushida, Williamson, and Friedman, 1976; Steinhausen, 1974). Parents' reactions to their children with PKU may contribute to the development of these problems (Kopp and Parmelee, 1979). Anxious over children whose mental and physical development is threatened if the prescribed diet is not suitable or not followed, parents may be overprotective or rejecting.

These are just a few examples of genetically transmitted physical disorders. Others are listed in Table 3.1. Virtually all diseases (cancer, arthritis, diabetes, multiple sclerosis) seem to have *some* genetic component, but the links are less clear than in the disorders we have discussed.

Behavior disorders

Certain of children's behavior problems, such as sleepwalking, car sickness, bed-wetting, constipation, and nail-biting, also seem to have a genetic component, for the concordances are higher among identical than fraternal twins (Bakwin, 1970, 1971a, 1971b, 1971c, 1971d). More seriously, **schizophrenia**, a

Table 3.1
Common genetic disorders

Disorder	Course	Pattern of Inheritance	Frequency	Detection in carriers	Detection in fetus
Cystic fibrosis: enzyme deficiency that causes mucus to obstruct breathing and digestion	fatal	recessive	1 in 20 whites are carriers; 1 in 1000 infants afflicted	likely	likely
Diabetes: pancreas doesn't produce insulin	moderately serious to fatal; insulin plus diet offer some protection	recessive	1 in 2500 children; higher in Native Americans	no	no
Hemophilia: blood lacks clotting factor	clotting factor can be injected; internal bleeding may cripple or kill	X-linked	1 in 1000 males	yes	yes
Huntington's chorea: brain and body begin wasting away in adulthood	fatal	X-linked	rare	yes	likely
Hydrocephalus: water in brain	mental retardation or death; surgery can sometimes alleviate	multiple genes	1 in 100 infants	no	only in the most serious cases
Muscular dystrophy: umbrella term for 13 disorders that destroy muscles	muscle wasting; sometimes fatal	some X-linked, some recessive, some multiple genes	100,000 Americans	some	some
Spina bifida: lower spine not closed over	crippling or death	multiple genes	3 in 1000 infants	no	yes
Phenylketonuria (PKU): protein not metabolized normally	mental retardation	recessive	1 in 15,000 infants	no	yes
Pyloric stenosis: intestinal blockage	death, if not corrected surgically	multiple genes	1 in 200 males 1 in 1000 females	no	no
Sickle-cell anemia: abnormal red blood cells	pain, heart and kidney disease, death	recessive	1 in 400 black infants; 1 in 10 blacks are carriers; 1 in 20 Hispanics are carriers	yes	yes
Tay-Sachs disease: wasting of nervous system	fatal	recessive	1 in 30 Jews are carriers	yes	yes

mental illness characterized by jumbled thoughts and speech, hallucinations, and delusions, appears to have a genetic base. Children of schizophrenic parents are 15 times likelier to have schizophrenia as adults than are adults in the population at large. Even if they are adopted into normal families, these children are likely to become schizophrenic (Rosenthal, 1970). Identical twins are concordant for schizophrenia four times as often as fraternal twins. Relatively few identical twin siblings of schizophrenics are found to be normal. Most of the twins who do not have schizophrenia have symptoms that border on it. These "schizoid" people are suspicious and rigid of thought, suffer panic attacks, and grow afraid in the face of ordinary challenges.

Another disorder that has genetic roots is **dyslexia**, a difficulty in reading and spelling that affects people of normal intelligence who have no emotional disturbances or known neurological or sensory handicaps. Some form of dyslexia is estimated to affect as many as 10 percent of school-age children. Studies of twins and other relatives have shown that some forms of dyslexia have a strong hereditary basis (Decker and DeFries, 1981; DeFries and Baker, 1983). Among identical twins, the concordance rate for dyslexic reading disability is over 90 percent. Among fraternal twins, the concordance is about 30 percent. Siblings and parents of dyslexics are also poorer readers than relatives of unaffected children. In families of dyslexic children, over 60 percent of the stability in the children's reading scores over a period of years can be attributed to heredity, compared to less than 1 percent of the stability of normal children's reading scores.

Genetic counseling

Sam's parents are American Jews of Russian, Polish, and German descent. They knew that they might be carriers of an illness that is invariably fatal to children, **Tay-Sachs disease**. This disorder afflicts Jews of Eastern European descent. When Sam's mother learned that she was pregnant, her doctor suggested that her husband have a blood test to find out whether he was a Tay-Sachs carrier. (This blood test is not performed on pregnant women. If Sam's father were found to be a carrier, the tests for his pregnant wife would be more complicated.) Because Tay-Sachs is a recessive trait, only one parent need be free of the trait to ensure that his or her children will not inherit the disease.

"When it was time to phone the doctor for the test results," Sam's mother recalls, "I was so frightened that I was trembling. When I was growing up, I had known of a young girl who had died of Tay-Sachs. It was a horror for her family. Tay-Sachs attacks the baby's nervous system, and it slowly loses all function. The baby can't smile, can't sit up, can't focus its eyes. It dies by inches. Some families have Tay-Sachs children institutionalized. Some nurse them at home. These babies go from being beautiful and normal to helpless in a couple of years. Finally, they stop breathing.

"Waiting for the doctor to get on the phone, I just prayed. *If* we were carriers and *if* our baby had Tay-Sachs, I would definitely have an abortion. Why bring a child into the world only to watch it die? Anyway, the doctor got on the phone. He said that we were safe. I went limp from relief."

When people suspect that they might transmit a genetic disorder to their children, they can seek the advice of genetic counselors even before they get pregnant. Someday, genetic counseling may become a routine aspect of family planning. But today special circumstances should alert prospective parents to seek such counseling. These circumstances include the following:

1. The couple already has a child with a disorder that might be of genetic origin.
2. The woman has had several miscarriages.
3. The couple has relatives with a genetic problem.

4. Husband and wife are blood relatives or come from the same genetic stock.

5. The woman is over 35.

Diabetes, cystic fibrosis, clubfoot, cleft palate, Down's syndrome, spina bifida, Tay-Sachs, sickle-cell anemia, hemophilia, PKU—all these are genetic abnormalities that can be detected before a baby is born. Some can be identified through tests of the mother's blood. Others can be identified through tests of the amniotic fluid surrounding the developing fetus, in a procedure called **amniocentesis**. During amniocentesis, a doctor first locates the fetus with **ultrasound**, in which high-frequency sound waves bounce off the contours of the fetus and form a detailed picture on a video screen. The doctor then draws amniotic fluid through a needle inserted into the mother's abdomen and uterus, without touching the fetus. The amniotic fluid is cultured for a month and the cells are then examined for the presence of any genetic abnormalities. The problem for prospective parents is what to do if, at this point, the tests reveal the presence of a disorder. Unfortunately, amniocentesis cannot be performed until the 14th or 15th week of pregnancy, because only then is there enough amniotic fluid to sample, and the process then takes another four weeks to complete. Parents who learn that the fetus does have a genetic defect must decide whether to end a five-month pregnancy, when the fetus is already perceptibly moving in the uterus, and the pregnancy is too far advanced for simple, safe abortion techniques.

A newer test, which can be performed as early as the 10th week of pregnancy, offers advantages to parents who want to know about—and, if necessary, do something about—their developing child's genetic condition. More and more hospitals are performing **chorionic villus biopsies**, in which a sample of chorionic villus is snipped or suctioned through the mother's cervix. Chorionic villi are tiny protrusions of the chorion, the membrane that surrounds the fetus and eventually forms part of the placenta. The tissue sample is larger and the results of analyzing it are quicker than with amnio-

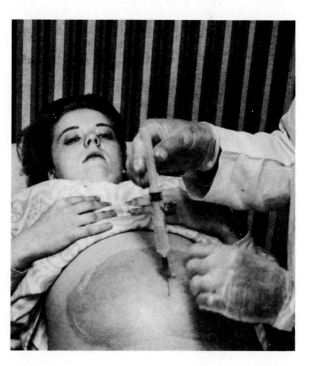

In amniocentesis a syringeful of amniotic fluid is removed during the woman's fourth month of pregnancy. The chemical contents of the fluid are analyzed for evidence of certain diseases, or cells sloughed off from the fetus are cultured and later checked for chromosomal abnormalities.

focus *A critical decision*

Ten weeks pregnant with their second child, Michelle Robertson and her husband, Corey, met with a genetic counselor at the teaching hospital near their home. Although their first child, a daughter, seemed healthy, Michelle didn't want to ''press her luck,'' as she put it. Her own first cousin had died in his early 20s of sickle-cell anemia, after long years of pain, hospital stays, and crises. Now her brother's 5-year-old son was showing signs of the disease. He had kidney problems and frequent infections. Michelle suspected that she and perhaps her husband were carriers of sickle-cell trait. Several weeks before, the Robertsons had had a first visit with the genetic counselor. She had taken a complete history and blood samples.

Today, at their second visit, the Robertsons would learn whether they were carriers. If they were carriers, they had decided that Michelle would have a relatively new test, a chorionic villus biopsy. The biopsy would tell them whether the fetus was male or female and whether it would be a carrier or a victim of sickle-cell anemia.

The counselor's news was mixed. Both Michelle and Corey carried the recessive gene for sickle-cell anemia. ''What that means,'' the counselor explained, drawing arrows on a family-tree diagram, ''is that this baby has one chance in four of having inherited the gene from each of you and therefore of having sickle-cell anemia. But the baby also may *not* have inherited the recessive gene from either of you, or it may have inherited the sickle-cell gene from only one of you, making it only a carrier—as you both are.''

''I guess this means we go ahead with the biopsy. Can it tell us how sick the baby will be if the baby has inherited the disease?'' Corey asked.

''No. We can't tell that ahead of time, I'm afraid,'' the counselor answered. ''But if the fetus does have sickle-cell anemia, you have the option of ending the pregnancy. Some couples end the pregnancy and try again. Others decide to adopt. Others decide not to have children.''

''No,'' Michelle sighed, ''I don't think I could have an abortion.''

''You'll have time to decide how you want to proceed once the biopsy results are in. We can talk more then about your options, if you want,'' the counselor suggested.

''Well, we've got some thinking to do,'' Michelle answered. ''But if worse does come to worst, at least we'll have some time to prepare ourselves mentally.'' The tests for sickle-cell anemia make it possible for parents to know for certain whether their fetus is affected with the sickle-cell trait. For other genetic conditions, however, parents can be told only the odds. Odds can be less than comforting when lives hang in the balance.

People who know that they risk transmitting a genetic disorder to their offspring face difficult decisions. For them, the decision to have a child may be more complicated than usual. Often their questions lead only to more questions; answers may be scarce indeed (see Figure 3.11). How serious is the genetic condition? Does it kill (like Tay-Sachs)? Does it cause mental retardation (like PKU and hydrocephalus) or other severely limiting conditions? Can surgery correct the condition (as with clubfoot)? Can drugs control it (as with hemophilia and diabetes)? What will be the child's and the family's actual quality of life?

centesis. Although chorionic villi biopsies also have risks, eventually they may allow scientists to detect any of the 3800 diseases and disorders for which genetics may be responsible (Schmeck, 1983).

THE DECISION TO HAVE A BABY

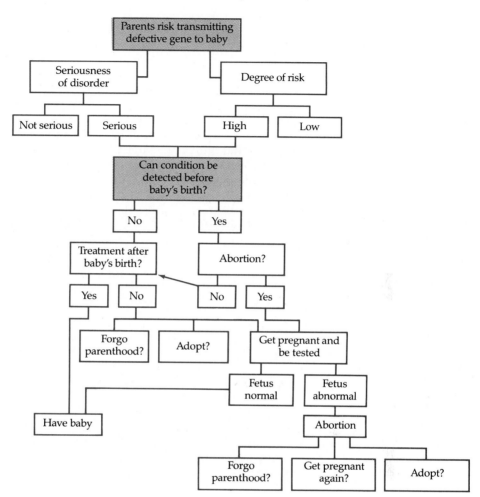

*Figure 3.11 **Parents facing the possibility of transmitting a genetic disorder to their baby are confronted with a number of decisions—and, in some cases, difficult uncertainties. For each fact and option provided by genetic counselors, prospective parents supply their own decisions. Couples vary greatly in their willingness to undergo abortion, to care for a disabled child, or to take the sometimes heroic measures that treatment entails.***

Geneticists today are using discoveries in the field of molecular biology to identify and detect the genetic conditions that lead to these disorders. Right now they can identify the specific DNA defect that causes more than a dozen inherited disorders including sickle-cell disease, Tay-Sachs disease, Huntington's disease, heart disease, and congenital emphysema. Rapid progress is being made, and the locations of new genes are being mapped all the time. Geneticists predict that they will be able to identify most of the known genetic disorders by 1990. Eventually, they will be able to draw genetic profiles to identify people at risk. Then women with the profile for breast cancer will know to have frequent diagnostic breast scans, and people with the profile for skin cancer will know to use sun blockers. Ultimately, scientists hope to cure genetic diseases by snipping out and replacing defective genes. Meanwhile, prevention continues to be the best and safest course.

Summary

1. Both environment and heredity contribute to the development of each human being. The genotype is an individual's genetic inheritance. Its expression in visible characteristics and behavioral patterns is the individual's phenotype. Some human characteristics are the outcome of single genes; most are affected by many different genes.

2. The chemical instructions of heredity are transmitted by deoxyribonucleic acid (DNA). All an individual's thousands of genes, which lie on the 46 human chromosomes, are made of DNA. The DNA molecule is shaped like a spiral ladder. It can reproduce itself and thereby transmit genetic material from parents' germ cells to a new individual.

3. Chromosomes within the germ cells divide by the process of meiosis. Each sperm or ovum is left with 23 chromosomes. When sperm and ovum unite at conception, the number of chromosomes is doubled to 46, the normal number for human body cells.

4. The sex chromosomes determine an individual's sex. An ovum always contains an X chromosome. If it is fertilized by an X-chromosome-bearing sperm, a female results. If it is fertilized by a Y-chromosome-bearing sperm, a male results. The autosomes supply most of the genetic information for the inheritance of physical and behavioral characteristics.

5. The inheritance of behavioral characteristics is complex and polygenic. By studying the presence of certain behavioral characteristics in fraternal versus identical twins, in adopted children and their adoptive and biological parents, and in family trees, researchers try to find out whether behavioral characteristics are inherited. Intelligence, activity level, sociability, and schizophrenia are partly inherited.

6. In genetic counseling, tests of blood and fetal cells are used to detect inherited disorders and to provide prospective parents with information upon which to decide whether to prevent or prepare for the birth of a defective child.

Key terms

genotype
expression
phenotype
reaction range
canalized
chromosomes
genes
deoxyribonucleic acid (DNA)
mitosis
ribonucleic acid (RNA)
meiosis
testes
ovaries
sperm
ova

homologous
crossover
conception
zygote
autosomes
X chromosome
Y chromosome
recessive
dominant
polygenic
monozygotic (MZ)
dizygotic (DZ)
concordance
personality

temperament
Klinefelter's syndrome
Turner's syndrome
XYY syndrome
sex-linked
Down's syndrome
sickle-cell anemia
phenylketonuria (PKU)
schizophrenia
dyslexia
Tay-Sachs disease
amniocentesis
ultrasound
chorionic villus biopsy

Suggested readings

APGAR, VIRGINIA, and BECK, JOAN. *Is My Baby All Right?* New York: Pocket Books, 1974. The major congenital problems carefully explained, with personal accounts to humanize the complex medical and psychological impact of birth defects.

FARBER, SUSAN. *Identical Twins Reared Apart: a Reanalysis*. New York: Basic Books, 1981. A comprehensive review of all existing studies of twins raised apart, in which the author tries to track down the evidence for genetic effects on intelligence and personality.

LEWONTIN, RICHARD. *Human Diversity*. New York: W. H. Freeman, 1982. A scholarly treatment of human variety and its basis in evolution, heredity, and environment, including an up-to-date overview of the nature of genetic mechanisms.

WATSON, JAMES D. *The Double Helix*. New York: New American Library, 1968. A thrilling suspense story of the competition to unlock the secret of life by discovering the structure of DNA. One of the few lively descriptions of the scientific community.

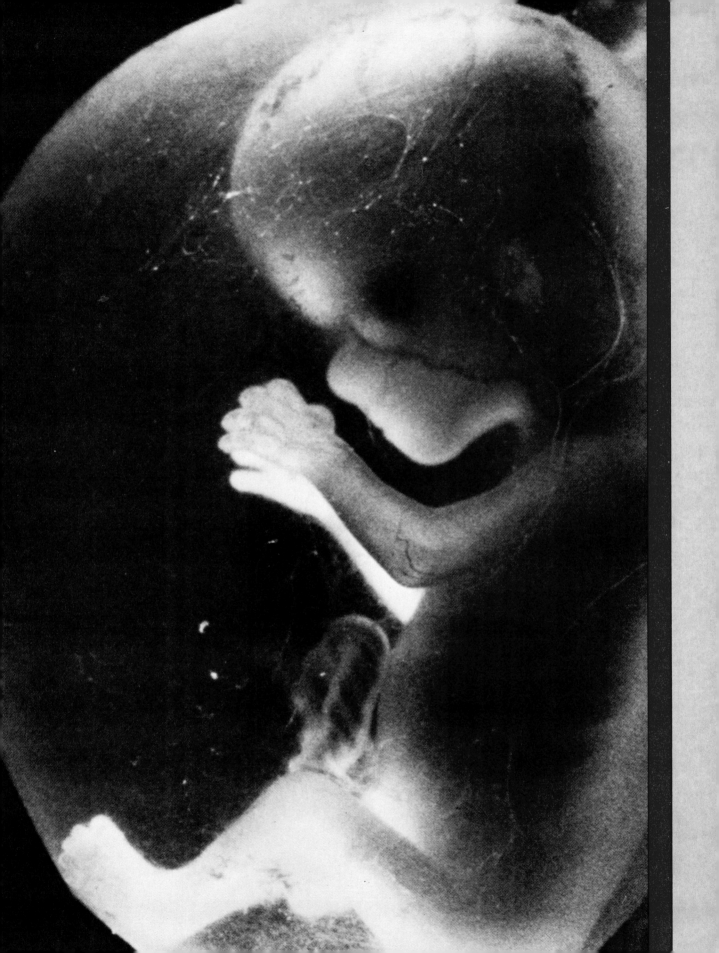

chapter four
Prenatal development and birth

Beginning new life

The conception of a child is the moment that a new life begins—the beginning of cells dividing and multiplying so that in mere months an infant is ready to greet the world. Skin and skeleton, limbs and organs, hair and nails, muscles and reflexes take form in these months before birth. Conception also begins a new stage of life for the man and the woman whose sperm and ovum have united. The parents-to-be take on roles and embark on a relationship like no other. They cannot divorce themselves from the growing fetus, take a vacation from their 24-hour-a-day connection to it, or postpone the day of its arrival. They, too, go through developmental changes as the birth of the infant grows closer. In this chapter we will describe the development in the fetus and parents during the eventful nine months of pregnancy and prenatal growth.

The parents' choices

Not so long ago, couples were expected to have large broods. Parents seen walking with their "only two" children raised comments—unflattering ones. Even as recently as the late 1960s, reference books listed information about "childlessness" under "sterility"—for the assumption was that people without children suffered from a medical malady. Whereas in the 1950s, 1 couple in 100 did not have children, by the early 1980s, that figure had risen to 10 childless couples in 100—some voluntarily and some involuntarily. Today, for many people in our culture, parenthood has become a matter of choices. To a large extent, couples choose whether, when, and how many children to have.

These choices are never simple. Even the most deliberate choice about whether to have children inevitably is a mixture of rational and irrational elements, biological and psychological forces, practical and emotional realities, conscious and unconscious thoughts. Some reasons for having children are poor: to escape from life at home with parents; to have someone little to dress up and play with; to get back at parents, boyfriend, or spouse; to try to save a shaky marriage; to satisfy the wishes of spouse or parents; to prove that one is a real man or woman; or to ward off fears of a lonely old age and empty death. The decision to have a child is sounder if it is based on a feeling of being ready to take on the responsibilities of having an infant; being financially and psychologically prepared for the joys and strains of parenthood; and wanting a child to love and nurture and watch grow to adulthood.

> We were both from families with lots of kids, and even when we were still dating we talked about wanting a house full of kids. It seemed to both of us the natural way for families to be. We've got three wonderful kids, and although it would be nice to have more, I think we've got all we can take care of right now.

The number of children couples have is now, for many of them, a matter of deliberate decision.

I was in my 30s, my career was launched, and I knew that I was mature enough to welcome a new person into our lives. My husband felt pretty much the same way. He wanted a child he could do all sorts of wonderful things with—go to baseball games, see movies, cook supper, go to the beach.

The major reason for the trend toward deliberately planned children is simple: better contraception. Contraceptives have been available for centuries. Pitch, animal earwax, oxgall, and elephant dung all have been touted for their abilities to prevent conception. But more appealing and more effective contraceptives became available only in the mid-1800s, when the rubber-manufacturing process was perfected. Then, middle-class people could approach their pharmacists for rubber diaphragms and condoms. Here is an 1885 letter (with the original spelling) from one woman in Ohio to her sister in North Dakota, imparting important news about a vaginal diaphragm, or *pessary*:

> ''You want to know of a sure preventative [to pregnancy]. Well plague take it. The best way is for you to sleep in one bed and your Man in another.. . .
>
> ''Well now [there is] the thing. . . . I do not know whether you can get them out there. They are called Pessairre or female prevenative if you don't want to ask for a 'pisser' just ask for a female prevenative. They cost one dollar when Sis got hers it was before any of us went to Dak[ota] The directions are with it'' (Schlissel, 1982, pp. 109-110).

But not until the mid-1900s did the more reliable methods of contraception—birth control pills and intrauterine devices (IUDs)—become available and widely used.

In addition to better contraception, recent social pressures have made many women question whether or when to become parents. The majority of women now need, want, and hold jobs. They want to fulfill themselves through their work and may want to postpone or, in some cases, altogether avoid the demands of an infant. Yet even now, the internal and external pressures on young adults to have children remain strong. Some religious groups forbid the use of contraception or abortion. Many employers grow suspicious of employees who do not start families. Parents push subtly (or not so subtly) for grandchildren, and other adults wonder what their childless friends are waiting for. Women themselves may feel as if a biological clock is ticking off their childbearing years. The decision to have a child is complex, often conflicted, and probably unique for every couple.

The choice of when to have a child is also complex. Many couples today postpone childbearing until they are financially and socially settled.

> Peter was born when I was in my late 30s. By then my career was established, I could support a baby, and I had the emotional reserves to spare that I hadn't had when I was trying to make a place for myself professionally. It was also time to have a baby before the hourglass simply ran out.

Yet many other couples rush into parenthood, either unintentionally or because they let nature take its course.

> After we got married, we didn't plan or not plan. We did what came naturally. Had three babies in five years.

There are pros and cons to either choice. The couple whose first child appears when they are 20-year-old students, newcomers to marriage, and perhaps near strangers to each other, may be staggered by parenthood. But as still energetic 40-year-olds, these same parents have launched the child into the world and can face their own middle age relatively free of child care. In contrast, the couple whose first child arrives as they approach 35 or 40 faces a middle age of active child care. But they have had perhaps two decades as adults to weave a marriage and careers that will embrace that much wanted child.

Couples are also beginning to have a say about the sex of the child they will conceive. Couples now can increase the odds of conceiving a boy or a girl because of the physical differences between X-chromosome-bearing sperm (which produce girls) and Y-chromosome-bearing sperm (which produce boys). For one thing, the X chromosome is much larger than the Y chromosome. As a result, the X-chromosome-bearing sperm is fatter, slower swimming, and somewhat hardier than the slimmer, swifter, and shorter lived Y-chromosome-bearing sperm. In one method of tipping the scales, the action of centrifugal force on a container of sperm separates the heavier X-bearing sperm from the lighter Y-bearing sperm, and a woman then is artificially inseminated with predominantly one kind of sperm. In another method, doctors make use of the fact that X- and Y-bearing sperm have different surface electrical charges to separate them, attracting the Y-bearing sperm to a positively charged pole and then drawing them off for artificial insemination. At home, a couple can increase their chances of conceiving a son from about 53 percent to about 65 percent if they take the following steps: before sexual intercourse, the woman douches with a baking soda solution; the couple has intercourse right when the woman is ovulating; and during intercourse the woman reaches orgasm. These measures make the vagina less acidic and therefore less dangerous for the delicate Y-bearing sperm which, being faster moving, is then likely to reach the ovum first. Couples can increase their chances of having a daughter from about 47 to about 54 percent if they do the following: the woman first douches with a vinegar solution; the couple has intercourse the day before ovulation; and during intercourse the woman does not reach orgasm. These measures kill off some of the Y-bearing sperm and increase the chances for the slower X-bearing sperm to reach the ovum first.

Parents' choices about having children are many and increasingly complex, as technology offers new levels of control over conception and opens new possibilities of reproduction.

Conception

All pregnancies begin when sperm and egg unite. Roughly 14 days before her menstrual period, a woman **ovulates**, and a mature egg, or ovum, is released from one of her ovaries. The ovaries contain thousands of immature ova, called **oocytes** (which have been present since the woman's birth), but usually only one mature egg is released (ovulated) each cycle into the fringed ends of one of the two **fallopian tubes**. These microscopically thin tubes are lined with thousands of waving cilia (see Figure 4.1), which move the ovum toward the **uterus**. During sexual intercourse, a man ejaculates millions of sperm, or **spermatozoa**, his reproductive cells. These sperm are produced in the testes, then mixed with seminal fluid and ejaculated. Each cubic inch of ejaculated semen may contain over 300 million swimming sperm. Out of the millions of sperm that are ejaculated into the woman's vagina and that swim through the **cervix** and into the uterus, only one will merge with the mature ovum in the fallopian tube. Why then are there so many sperm? The millions of sperm ejaculated are insurance that a few hundred will actually near the ripe ovum. Most sperm swim into the wrong fallopian tube or get lost in the vagina or uterus. Sperm live for only 48 hours or so after ejaculation, and the ovum is receptive for only 12 to 24 hours. Conception, therefore, is limited to a 72-hour period in each menstrual cycle. During this brief period, the environment in

CONCEPTION

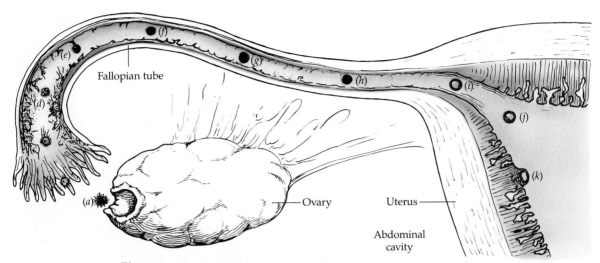

Figure 4.1 *The story of conception is this:* **(a)** *an ovary releases an ovum into the abdominal cavity.* **(b)** *The waving movements of millions of cilia on the fringed ends of the fallopian tube draw in the ovum.* **(c)** *The ovum begins the second stage of meiosis.* **(d)** *When a sperm penetrates the ovum, it stimulates it to complete meiosis.* **(e)** *Chromosomes from sperm and ovum mingle.* **(f)** *The chromosomes go through mitosis.* **(g)** *The fertilized ovum, the zygote, divides.* **(h, i)** *The zygote divides repeatedly as it moves through the fallopian tube and* **(j)** *into the uterus.* **(k)** *On the seventh day the sphere of cells attaches to the uterine wall (Grobstein, 1979).*

the female reproductive tract is especially ''friendly.'' The rest of the time it is too acidic for sperm to survive. At ovulation, too, the mucous plug in the cervix, which protects the uterus from infection, is thinner and easier for sperm to swim through.

Although the design is grand, the elements of conception are tiny. The ovum is tinier than the period at the end of this sentence, and the sperm is tinier still. Its oval head, midpiece, and tail measure only $1/500$ of an inch. It has been estimated that the ova that have produced all the people in the world would fit into a single shoebox, and the sperm would fit into a thimble. The fallopian tube is four inches long and no wider than a hair.

Conception often is imagined as a gender-stereotyped event, during which the egg sits passively as sperm eagerly cluster around, looking for a way to enter. It is thought of as more like an old fraternity mixer than what it really is: the meeting of an active sperm with an equally active—liberated— egg. Now that electron microscopes have let observers follow the minute events of conception, we are beginning to appreciate the egg's contribution (Schatten and Schatten, 1983). True, the sperm does make the first move. As the front-running sperm makes contact with the egg, a long filament shoots out, molecule by molecule, from the head of the sperm and harpoons the egg. Then the touch of the filament sets the egg in motion. Tiny extensions on its surface reach up and embrace the sperm's head and tail. The sperm, now entwined in the egg's tiny villi, injects calcium ions into the egg. These instantly cause a chemical reaction that changes the electrical charge of the egg's external membrane from negative to positive, and this repels all other sperm. The block lasts for about half a minute, by which time the egg has secreted proteins to form a tough outer covering that rises to enclose the privileged first sperm. The sperm then pushes farther into the center of the egg, and as the sperm's beating tail propels it toward the center of the egg, the

(a)

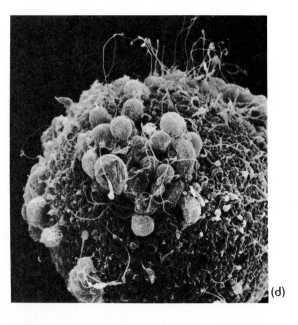

(d)

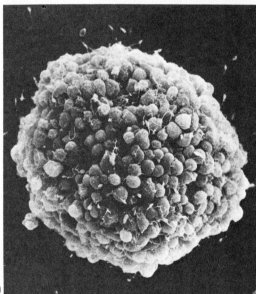

(b)

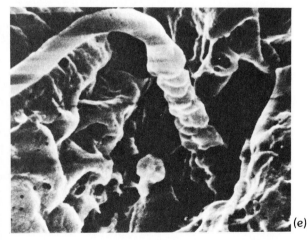

(e)

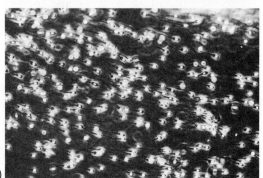

(c)

(a) *The ovum, only a fraction of a millimeter in size, is about to be drawn into a fallopian tube.* **(b)** *The ovum divides and becomes surrounded by nutritional cells.* **(c)** *Meanwhile, an army of sperm swim through the glassy, fluid mucus at the entrance to the cervix.* **(d)** *As the head of one of the sperm succeeds in penetrating the cell membranes of the ovum, the surface of the egg changes and seals it off from further entry.* **(e)** *The chosen sperm enters the ovum and merges with the egg nucleus. Fertilization has been accomplished.*

nucleus of the egg rushes toward it. In less than one minute, the nucleus crosses the egg. The nuclei of egg and sperm meet and move together to the center of the egg. In the sperm's nucleus are the 23 chromosomes that bear one-half of the genetic instructions for building a new human being. The other 23 chromosomes are contained within the ovum. Substances in the egg activate the sperm's chromosomes so that they can merge with those of the egg. The now fertilized ovum contains pairs of chromosomes, one half from each parent. It is now a zygote which, with amazing speed, will develop into a complex, billion-celled human being.

Fertility

But things do not always go smoothly. Not everyone who decides to have a baby conceives easily.

> We have been trying to conceive for six years now. We've tried everything. People say that we should go ahead and adopt, but I want *our own* baby, not someone else's.

> With Mikey and Erica, I think I was pregnant within an hour of our decision to put away the diaphragm.

Lucky couples, like Mikey and Erica's parents—one third of those who are trying—do conceive in their first month. Half of the couples who are trying conceive by the third month, three-quarters by the sixth month. But some couples—one in six—cannot conceive a child. After a year of regular sexual intercourse without contraception, these couples are diagnosed as being infertile. Many then begin a sometimes slow and painful course of treatment.

> I was 32 and we had been married for two years when we decided to start our family. It was amazing how nervous we both were. After so much time worrying that I might get pregnant, it felt strange to suddenly reverse course. We had planned to have our baby in the spring, because that would fit best with our vacation plans and job leaves. But the months came and went; still no baby. I began to worry. My husband acted unconcerned. We decided to have intercourse more often, to vary our positions. Finally, I made an appointment with my gynecologist. She performed some preliminary tests and then referred us to fertility specialists. We seemed to fit the infertility "profile" to a T. We had postponed pregnancy until my fertility had begun to fall off with age. After four years of tests, temperature taking, surgery, and countless visits to doctors, I finally got pregnant. Those years were an ordeal that no one should have to go through.

The problem of **infertility** facing this couple has become increasingly common in the past 20 years. There are many causes of infertility. One cause is the postponement of parenthood into a woman's middle or late 30s, because fertility drops off sharply after the age of 30. A Yale University study of women over 35 who had not had children showed that they needed an average of over two years to conceive, rather than the usual six months (*Time*, September 10, 1984). In another study, only about half of the women over 35 *ever* conceived (Federation CECOS, Schwartz, and Mayaux, 1982). Stress is another cause of infertility; more than one woman has found herself missing menstrual periods during stressful times at home or the office. Another cause is sexually transmitted **pelvic inflammatory disease (PID)**, which leaves scars on the woman's fallopian tubes, ovaries, and uterus. Half of the cases of PID result from **chlamydia**, a sexually transmitted disease that only recently has been detectable through a simple laboratory test. Another quarter of the cases of PID result from gonorrhea, a disease that may create no symptoms (in women especially) and that may defy treatment. IUDs also have come to light recently as a cause of infertility. Some women who have had prolonged exposure to toxic chemicals become infertile. Being underweight is another cause of infertility. One irony in the fitness wave that has washed over this country is that when some women exercise strenuously, they lose too much body fat to support the hormones necessary for menstrual cycling, and they cannot conceive. A condition called **endometriosis**, the appearance of uterine tissue in places besides the uterus, such as the ovaries or fallopian tubes, is yet another cause of infertility in women. Various physiological problems, too, can cause a woman to be infertile. Ovaries may not release mature ova, fallopian tubes may be blocked, cervical mucus may prove impenetrable to sperm, fertilized ova may not implant or remain implanted in the uterine wall.

But women account for just 60 percent of all infertility problems. The other 40 percent of infertility problems reside with men. Sperm may be too few, abnormally shaped, or weak swimmers. Blocked ducts may fail to deliver sperm into the urethra leading out of the body, and varicose veins in the testicles may interfere with sperm production. Men's fertility also declines with age.

So many factors can operate to prevent normal conception that it sometimes seems a miracle that anyone is born! Infertility can be a devastating problem. It can undermine a couple's sexual and personal relationship. It can undermine their self-esteem and confidence in their masculinity and femininity. It tears away at friendships, careers, and even at savings accounts. Clearly, infertility has high personal and social costs. But nearly all cases of infertility are diagnosed, and about half ultimately are cured. One established solution for infertility is surgery to tie off varicose veins in a man's testicles or to unblock a woman's fallopian tubes. The microsurgery to open fallopian tubes is very delicate and succeeds only about half the time. Surgery and drugs can help to control endometriosis. Drugs also can help some men with low sperm counts or abnormally shaped sperm. Another method for dealing with infertility is **artificial insemination**. Artificial insemination has been practiced throughout this century and now accounts for some 20,000 births every year (Fleming, 1980). It is a simple, painless procedure in which a syringe is used to deposit semen at the entrance to the woman's uterus. A man's semen can be collected and pooled if the concentration of sperm is low. An anonymous donor's semen can be used if a man cannot produce normal sperm in enough quantity. Semen also can be frozen for years and retain potency. Some men take advantage of this and deposit sperm in "sperm banks" for later use. These sperm bank depositors include men planning to be surgically sterilized, men facing chemotherapy, which may damage their sperm's genetic content, and men who want to make their sperm available to women who need artificial insemination.

Alternative reproduction

Adopting an infant, a traditional alternative for infertile couples, is now so difficult that some couples resort to other means of having a child. Few healthy infants are available for adoption, and the wait for them is long—over five years in many cases. Many couples therefore are turning to methods of **alternative reproduction**. These methods are designed to bypass a woman's blocked or damaged fallopian tubes.

One method of alternative reproduction is **in vitro fertilization**, the creation of the so-called **test-tube baby**. Louise Joy Brown, the first test-tube

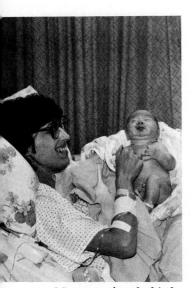

Moments after the birth, surrogate mother Elizabeth Kane holds her baby for the first and only time, as his adoptive mother looks on.

baby, was delivered in England in 1978. Since then, over 1000 other test tube babies have been born. Clinics that treat infertile couples with in vitro fertilization (literally "in glass," that is, in a glass laboratory dish) have been established all over the world, and with the increase in infertility, it is likely that still others will appear. In this procedure, the mother first takes fertility drugs to ripen several of her ova. (The chances of a successful pregnancy are higher if more than one ovum is recovered.) Doctors recover the ripe ova by **laparoscopy**, surgery during which general anesthesia is given, small incisions are made in the woman's navel and at the base of her abdomen, and a telescope and fiber-optic illuminator—the "laparoscope"—are introduced through the incisions. The ripe ova are removed by vacuum suction and incubated in a glass dish for three hours or so. Then a few drops of concentrated semen are added to the dish, and a number of the ova are fertilized. Within 36 hours, each fertilized egg begins to divide. When each zygote consists of eight cells, the doctor inserts them into the woman's uterus. From this point, the pregnancy can proceed normally, as the zygotes attach to the wall of the uterus and continue to grow. (One result of inserting up to nine zygotes, the usual procedure, has been a relatively large number of "test-tube" twins, triplets, and quadruplets. To reduce the chance of these multiple births, some doctors now insert only four zygotes.)

A second method of alternative reproduction is **surrogate mothering**. In this procedure, a fertile woman is hired by a couple in which the wife is infertile. The surrogate mother then is artificially inseminated with the husband's sperm and carries the resulting fetus to term. After she gives birth, she turns the baby over to the couple. **Ovum transfer** is a third method of alternative reproduction. In this procedure, a fertilized ovum is removed from a donor woman's uterus and implanted into the uterus of the infertile woman. Donors are given thorough physical and psychological examinations, and their genes are checked for abnormalities. After a suitable donor has been found, doctors use drugs to synchronize her menstrual cycle with that of the woman who will be the recipient. When the donor ovulates, she is artificially inseminated with sperm from the infertile woman's husband. Five days later, the fertilized egg, or zygote, reaches the uterus and can be removed to the uterus of the infertile woman, whose own body is at the same receptive point in her menstrual cycle. The zygote implants itself in her uterus, and the pregnancy continues normally. In 1984, the first American child resulting from an ovum transfer was born in Long Beach, California. In 1986 the implantation of a frozen fertilized ovum resulted in a successful birth. Compared to "old fashioned" reproduction, these alternative methods are used only rarely. But they are becoming more common—and more ingenious—as time passes.

Prenatal development

The prenatal period begins with conception and ends with birth. During these nine months, the development of one fertilized cell into a complete human infant seems wondrous. Yet for each infant, development proceeds according to a master blueprint. Body parts and functions develop at roughly the same rates and in the same order for all infants (Figure 4.2).

When I was pregnant with what turned out to be Sam, I loved to look at pictures of fetuses at various points of development. Then I'd announce at dinnertime, "Well, the baby just got fingers and toes," or "This is the week for the chambers of the heart to develop.'' When the organs all were forming in the first weeks, I often felt scared that something might go wrong.

We have been given a peek at this development in the womb by such modern marvels as photo optics.

Stages of prenatal development

The months of pregnancy can be divided into three stages. The first, the **germinal stage**, begins when the ovum is fertilized and ends some two weeks later, when the zygote attaches to the wall of the uterus. The second, the **embryonic stage**, lasts from the second through the eighth week of pregnancy. During this period, the organs form. The third, the **fetal stage**, lasts until birth and is the period when the fetus grows in size and gains function in its organs and muscles.

Germinal stage
Between the first and 14th days after conception, the fertilized egg first divides into two identical cells, then doubles to four, eight, and so on. Cell division by mitosis begins within 36 hours after fertilization and continues ever more rapidly. Sixty hours after fertilization, a mulberry-shaped, 12- or 16-celled **morula** is floating in the mother-to-be's fallopian tube (see Figure 4.3). Each cell has until this point been **totipotent**. Separated from the others, any

It took away half of what I was and replaced it with a blank space. I want to know about my background, my medical history, but I also want to know precisely what he had in mind when he was a donor (Andrews, 1984, p. 22).

A case in France illustrates some of the legal quandaries created when men donate their sperm to a sperm bank in the knowledge that they have a terminal disease. In this case, after the man's death, his widow sued to be artificially impregnated with her dead husband's sperm. The sperm bank refused on the grounds that the husband had left no clear instructions about the disposition of the sperm and therefore that his widow had no right to them. Lawyers debated whether the sperm were more like a transplanted organ or a piece of property. The widow's lawyer argued that the sperm deposit implied a contract, and the court agreed.

Surrogate motherhood raises equally unsettling issues. The College of Obstetrics and Gynecology has asked doctors to check especially carefully into the psychological and physical fitness of possible surrogates and of the infertile couples who might use a surrogate. Most state laws do not directly cover surrogate motherhood. But in many cases, old laws are still on the books. Those banning payment to a woman who gives a child up for adoption are common, yet should they be used against surrogate mothers? How should the law distinguish between paying a woman for carrying a child and paying her for the child? How should the law deal with the surrogate mother— impregnated by a donor-father's sperm—who refuses to relinquish her infant after it is born? Do unmarried women have the same rights to the services of surrogates as married women do? These are some of the complex and unanswered questions raised by alternative reproduction.

As biological technology speeds ahead of custom and law, we can all too easily find ourselves pitched into a brave new world.

---

cell can develop into a whole human infant—one way in which identical twins get their start in life. By the time the morula has formed, the cells are no longer totipotent. Those on the inside of the "berry" are large, those on the outside, small. Specialization has begun.

Floating slowly through the fallopian tube, the morula gently descends to rest on the uterine wall about four days after fertilization. The rounded **blastula**, as it is now called, is composed of over 100 cells, with fluid at its center. Within a few days the blastula has developed into a **blastocyst**, a more thoroughly specialized and organized sphere of cells. At one side are larger cells forming the embryonic disk, which will turn into the embryo and, later, the fetus. The smaller, outer cells will form themselves into a life-support system for the fetus made up of an outer membrane, the **chorion**, the inner "bag of waters" or **amnion**, the **placenta**, and the yolk sac.

Having floated in the uterus for a day or so, the blastocyst settles down in one spot. Rather like a space capsule that touches down on the moon's surface, the embryo has "landed." The uterine lining is rich with blood, spongy, and receptive to the blastocyst. The outer cells of the blastocyst project tiny roots, or **villi**, directly into the mother's blood vessels as the blastocyst burrows ever more deeply—**implants** itself—into the uterine wall. Nearly half of all blastocysts are abnormal and do not implant themselves in the uterine wall (Roberts and Lowe, 1975). But for those blastocysts that do implant, the cell wall of the uterus then closes the opening through which the blastocyst has burrowed. Implantation is complete.

PRENATAL MILESTONES

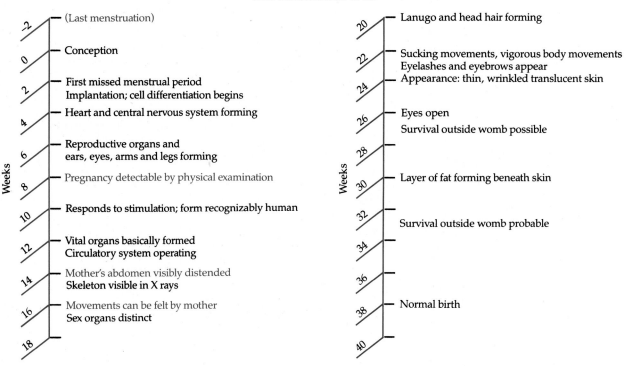

Figure 4.2 **This chart shows the timing of milestones in prenatal development for infant and mother.**

Embryonic stage

Two weeks after conception, the embryonic disk has folded and formed the distinct layers of cells called an **embryo**. From the outer layer of cells, or **ectoderm**, a bulge called the **primitive streak** forms—the primitive tissue from which brain, spinal cord, nerves, sense organs, and skin will form. From the inner layer of cells, or **endoderm**, will form the lining of the gut, salivary glands, pancreas, liver, heart, lungs, and respiratory system. From a soon-to-develop middle layer of cells, the **mesoderm**, will form cartilage and bone, muscles, blood vessels, heart, and kidneys.

The embryo's life-support system already has begun to form. Amniotic fluid is filling the amnion and making a warm cushion that protects the embryo against injury or shock. The yolk sac is generating blood cells and the germ cells that will someday let this tiny embryo itself be a mother or father. The placenta, the source of nutrients and oxygen for the fetus, is beginning to function. The placenta—like the astronaut's support system—breathes, digests, and excretes for the multiplying cells of the embryo. It is connected to the embryo through the pulsating **umbilical cord**. Along the cord's ropy length, a vein carries oxygen, sugars, fats, rudimentary proteins, and minerals to the embryo while two arteries carry waste products, carbon dioxide, and urea from the embryo, eventually to be disposed of by the mother's lungs and kidneys. Through the placenta, the mother's and embryo's blood vessels are brought into close contact. The bloodstreams of mother and embryo do not actually mix, but oxygen, nutrients, and wastes pass between them through the thin capillary walls of the embryo. The placenta screens out some harmful substances, including most bacteria, but viruses, gases, and many drugs pass through the placenta from mother to embryo.

SIZE OF THE GROWING FETUS

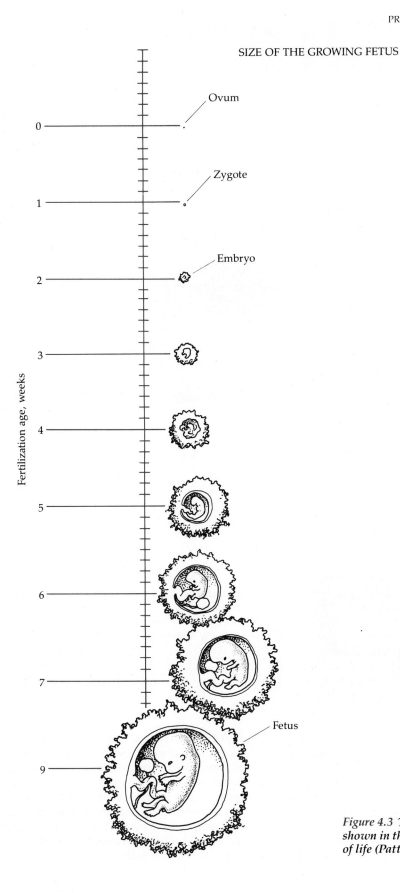

Ovum

Zygote

Embryo

Fetus

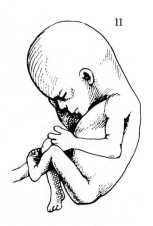

11

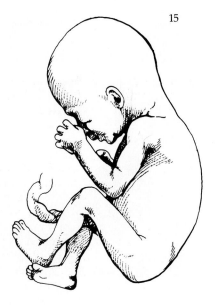

15

Figure 4.3 The ovum, zygote, embryo, and fetus are shown in their actual sizes during the first 15 weeks of life (Patten, 1968).

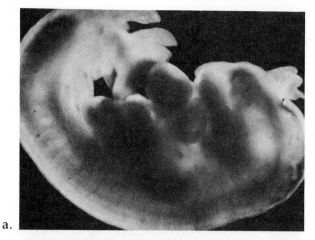

a.

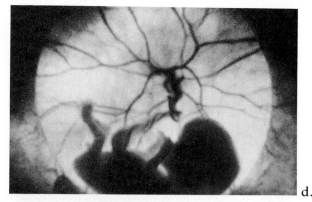

d.

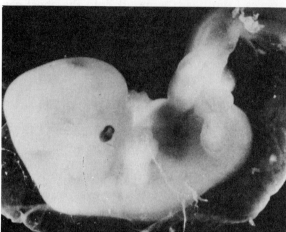

b.

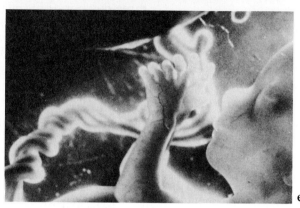

e.

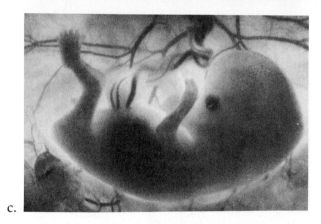

c.

(a) *Almost 30 days old and about 4 millimeters in length, this embryo already has the buds that will become arms and legs.* (b) *At 6 weeks the embryo has a definite head, and the retinas of the eyes have formed. The embryo looks much less like a tadpole and more like a human being.* (c) *Face, nose, and mouth are distinguishable at 11 weeks, and the muscles have formed.* (d) *At 3 months the muscles go into action and the fetus actually moves.* (e) *Nourishing blood flows to this 4-month-old fetus at the rate of 0.25 liter per minute.*

Third and fourth weeks. In the third and fourth weeks after conception, the cells of the pea-sized embryo multiply rapidly and organize themselves into functional units. The groove that runs along the primitive streak forms a tube and then develops into foundations of the brain, spinal cord, nervous system, and eyes. The heart develops first into a tube and then into a chambered pump. A system for digesting food and kidney-like structures begin to form. All these developments take place according to a master plan, by which development starts at the head and moves to the tail, in **cephalocaudal** order. First the head, then the trunk, and then the lower extremities develop. The

108

plan also calls for development to proceed **proximodistally**, from the midline of the body—spine, heart, face—outward to the shoulders, arms and legs, hands and feet.

> *Second month.* I was never so tired in my whole life as I was during my second month of pregnancy. The midwife said that it was because of hormones, but I think it was because my baby was developing so fast. I'd tease my husband, "Hey, I can't make dinner tonight. This baby's got me busy making his *brain*!"

During the second month of prenatal life, new physical structures develop with astonishing speed from the foundations laid in the first month. During a three-day period at the beginning of this month, for example, buds for arms, legs, and the visual system all take form. During the month, the stomach and esophagus form; the heart moves from near the mouth into the chest cavity and a valve is created that separates its upper and lower segments. Nerves grow and form connections between brain, nose, and eyes. Primitive ovaries and testes form.

A photograph of the translucent embryo at the end of the embryonic period shows a creature that looks like a human being. Its face has eyes, nose, mouth, and lips, ears and jaw in the proper places. Its hands have fingers and thumbs, its legs, knees, ankles, feet and tiny toes. With a powerful microscope, one can see whether the embryo is a boy or a girl. Cartilage, the flexible material of the adult human's ear, begins to be replaced by bone in the center of the long arm and leg bones in a process called **ossification**. This process marks the beginning of the third and final phase of prenatal development.

The embryonic stage is a critical period when organs and body structures must form if development is to proceed normally. If heart, eyes, and lungs do not appear now, they never will. If the round buds at the end of the arms and legs do not form themselves into finger and toes, they never will. The embryonic cells are also particularly susceptibile to their environment during this stage of development, which poses both grave risk and great biological advantage. The risk is that the embryo is vulnerable to abnormal development if it is exposed during this critical period to radiation, toxins, or infection. The advantage is that the embryo is also very responsive to chemical messages from genes and other cells that organize the sequence of specialized cell development. The embryonic cells can respond readily to the message of the DNA molecules in each cell and to the blueprint for interaction between specialized systems of the body.

Fetal stage

During the fetal stage, which lasts from the end of the second month of prenatal life until birth, the structures and systems that have developed grow in size and in efficiency.

Third month. Nine weeks into its prenatal existence, the fetus is an inch long, weighs one-tenth of an ounce, and has a disproportionately large—but entirely human-looking—head. The appearance of the fetus, with its large head, mysterious eyes, and perfect innocence, has long fascinated people and captured their imaginations. In movies like *E.T.* and *Close Encounters of the Third Kind*, for instance, the wonderful alien creatures who befriend earthlings look much like fetuses. In the third month after conception, the fetus's eyelids form and are sealed shut. The roof of the mouth closes. The fetus digests amniotic fluid, excretes urine from functioning kidneys, and breathes fluid in and out of its lungs. A male fetus develops a penis. Nerves connect to muscles, and the fetus begins to make reflexive kicking, darting, and dodging movements. In a few weeks, the fetus can kick and turn his or her feet. Toes now curl, fists form, thumb opposes to fingers, head turns, mouth opens and closes and swallows, and the fetus can even suck his or her thumb. Earlier the fetus responded to stimulation with the whole body. Now the fetus can move and respond with specific parts. Stroke a hand, and the arm moves. Touch an eyelid, and the eye squints. The fetus also can move spontaneously, and he or she already has a distinct level of activity.

Fourth month. During the fourth month, the fetus grows more quickly than in any other month: from 3½ inches and 1 ounce to 6 inches and 4 ounces. Now the mother can feel the **quickening**, the first perceptible movements of the stronger, larger fetus kicking against her abdomen.

> I first felt a faint tap-tap-tapping of the baby in the 16th week. "So soon?" my mother asked. We should have known then that this was going to be one very active baby.

> When I felt Sam bumping around inside me, I sometimes pictured him as swimming in a pool and kicking against the sides when he changed directions.

Stronger neck muscles and a bonier skeleton help support the fetus's ever more human-looking head. Finger- and footprints have formed on the tiny touchpads of palms and soles. The eyes sense light. A female fetus develops inner and outer genitals—uterus, vagina, clitoris, and associated structures. Meanwhile, the placenta has begun to produce most of the hormones that prepare the mother's body for producing milk and the infection-fighting substances to protect the fetus.

Fifth month. During the fifth month, the fetus grows to 1 foot in length and a weight of 1 pound. The mother typically begins to "show" her pregnancy during this month as the abdominal walls expand outward to accommodate the developing baby. The fetus's sweat glands, eyelashes and brows, and hair on the head all form. **Lanugo**, a downy hair, begins to grow over most of the body. Like the astronaut freed from gravity, the fetus bounds and turns in the fluid-filled uterus. The mother feels periods of quietness—as the fetus sleeps or rests—between periods of waking activity. The fetus sheds old cells and develops new ones. These dead skin cells mix with fat from the oil glands and cover the body with a protective cream called **vernix**. Vernix keeps the fetus's skin supple as it floats in mineral-rich amniotic fluid—very "hard water" indeed.

Sixth month. During the sixth month, the fetus's eyelids first open, and the eyes can look up, down, and to the sides. The intestines descend into the abdomen. Cartilage continues to turn into bone. Development of the six layers of cells in the cerebral cortex—that part of the brain responsible in adults for complex conscious thought—is completed. The fetus can reflexively grasp, breathe, swallow, hiccough, and taste.

> One morning I was awakened from sleep by violent, rhythmic movements at the base of my abdomen. For a minute I was terrified, but then I realized that the baby had the hiccoughs!

One ingenious obstetrician treated a patient who had too much amniotic fluid by injecting a sweetener into the amnion. The fetus promptly swallowed some of the fluid, absorbed it, and passed it to the mother for her to excrete (reported in Montagu, 1962).

The 6-month fetus is still a vulnerable creature, barely equipped to survive outside the womb. The fetus has not yet gotten immunities from the mother's system. A fetus may breathe regularly for up to 24 hours at a time, but is still so immature that infants born at this stage will not survive without intensive medical care. Lacking fat under the sensitive skin, the fetus needs to be kept warm.

The relatively new medical specialty, **neonatology**, care of newborns (neonates), has greatly increased the chances of survival for fetuses born prematurely. Today, many 6-month fetuses survive and have a fair chance at functioning normally because of the intensive medical care provided by neonatologists. **Fetology** is the even newer medical specialty devoted to treating problems in fetuses before birth. Blood transfusions, the insertion of drainage tubes into kidneys, brains, and collapsed lungs, and surgical repairs on urinary tracts all have been performed on fetuses while still in their mothers' uteruses. One fetus with **hydrocephaly**, excess fluid in the brain, for example, had his brain surgically punctured and drained before he was born. When he was born, he showed no hydrocephaly and no signs of the surgery. In another case, doctors successfully drained the fluid from a fetus's collapsed lung. It is likely that fetologists will be called on to treat more and more selected cases in the future. Perhaps 1 in 400 to 500 fetuses may be candidates for surgery *in utero* (Kotulak, 1981).

Seventh month. At the beginning of the seventh month after conception, the fetus weighs about 2 pounds and has organs mature enough to offer a 50–50 chance of surviving outside the womb if birth comes prematurely and intensive care is provided. The fetus's brain now can regulate breathing, body temperature, and swallowing. It contains trillions of connected nerve cells, specialized into sections devoted to hearing, seeing, smelling, vocalizing, and moving. Many reflexes, including sucking and grasping, are established. During the seventh month, the testes of most male fetuses begin to descend into the scrotum from the abdominal cavity, where, protected from the body's internal temperature, the sperm produced after puberty will be able to survive. The ova of the female fetus already are formed in the ovaries.

Eighth month. In the eighth month of prenatal development, the fetus's body prepares for life outside of the uterus. For fetuses weighing 3 pounds or more, the chances of survival outside the uterus increase to 85 percent. The lungs are still immature, the **alveoli**, or tiny air sacs in them, not prepared to turn oxygen into carbon dioxide. The fetus's digestive and immune systems are also immature. But under the skin, a vital layer of insulating fat is laid down. This fat increases the fetus's chances of survival outside the womb.

In the eighth month, nerve cells in the brain develop branches and neurotransmitters so that messages can be passed from nerve to nerve. At this point, the nerve cells begin to function (see Figure 4.4). As a result, in the eighth month, the fetus begins to lurch, roll, startle, or lift his or her head in response to a loud or sharp noise. The fetus can be soothed by the mother's heartbeat and rhythmic walk and aroused into vigorous kicking by the sounds of a piano, television, even a dishwasher.

Apparently, the fetus at this age can also learn. Studies of learning by fetuses were first carried out over 40 years ago. In one such study (Sontag and Newbery, 1940), a loud noise was made repeatedly outside the uterus. At first the fetus responded with a quickened heartbeat, but after hearing the noise a number of times, the fetus stopped reacting, apparently having learned to ignore the noise. In a second study (Spelt, 1948), a fetus was subjected to a loud and startling noise and at the same time to vibrations. After about 20 trials, the fetus startled upon feeling the vibrations without the noise. Apparently, this fetus had learned the connection between the vibrations and the noise. Unfortunately, these early studies did not separate the reactions of the mother from those of the fetus, and so the results are difficult to interpret. They have, however, gained support from recent research with both animals and humans (Kolata, 1984). In one recent study, for example, Anthony De-

PRENATAL BRAIN GROWTH

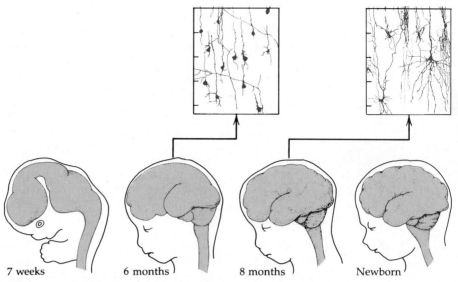

7 weeks   6 months   8 months   Newborn

Figure 4.4 The tubelike early brain matures through a series of bends. Areas of the brain enlarge, and the cerebral hemispheres grow over the cerebellum and other regions. Although the main outlines of the brain are established by the sixth month, the surface convolutions, which greatly increase the area and volume of the cortex, do not appear until the eighth month. At the same time, inside, as the sections from the visual cortex show, branches that allow the relay of impulses between nerve cells increase greatly in number and length (Grobstein, 1979).

Casper and his associates (Spence and DeCasper, 1982) showed that newborn infants prefer hearing their mother read a nursery rhyme that she has read aloud twice a day during the last six weeks of pregnancy to one that she has never read before. This finding suggests that the infants had learned to recognize the cadences of the nursery rhymes read to them in utero.

It also suggests that fetuses can hear voices while they are in the uterus. In one study of the sounds that penetrate the uterus (Armitage, Baldwin, and Vince, 1980), hydrophones implanted in the uteri of two pregnant ewes revealed that loud sounds—like shouts and bangs—could be heard clearly. Normal conversational tones from outside the uterus were somewhat dulled. Sounds from inside the ewes, of drinking, eating, swallowing, and heavy breathing were also audible, although heartbeats were not. The researchers concluded that in the fluid environment of the uterus, fetal sheep can hear sounds from both inside and outside of the mother. When hydrophones were placed in the amniotic sac of human mothers (Querleu and Rennard, 1981), speech sounded audible but muffled. It must be heard over the ambient noise, which is as loud as the noise in a factory (Aslin et al., 1983). But even if speech is muffled, in another study, speech sounds made outside the mother's abdomen while she was in labor elicited more marked change in the infant's heart rate than did pure tones (Macfarlane, 1977). These studies demonstrate that sounds do penetrate the uterus and affect the fetus. The question of how clearly the fetus actually *hears*—with its ears full of amniotic fluid—has not been settled yet, however. A related question that also has not been settled is whether pregnant women who expose their fetuses to classical music and stimulating language routines actually give the infants a head start at learning.

Ninth month. Because Sam was facing forward rather than backward, like most babies, he wedged his toes under my ribcage in a thoroughly

Pregnancy is a time when moodiness and anxiety are common and the mother-to-be feels fear and concern for herself and for the developing fetus.

uncomfortable maneuver. So I would push his toe down, and he would snap it right back.

In the home stretch, with just a few weeks before birth, the average fetus is 20 inches long and weighs 7 pounds. Now growth finally slows down. If it didn't, the infant would weigh 200 pounds at age 1! Crowded into the uterus now, the fetus folds up into a ball and squirms a bit, moving only hands, feet, and head. A heavy head makes most fetuses settle head-down, with skull wedged into the mother's pelvic girdle. As the fetus settles in, the mother feels a ''lightening.'' The bulge in her abdomen is lower. She feels less pressure on her diaphragm and lungs. The formerly spongy placenta toughens, and immunities—against measles, mumps, whooping cough, and other illnesses the mother has been exposed to—pass from mother to fetus. As labor begins, the placenta releases the hormone **oxytocin**. It prepares the mother's body to make milk and ushers in the birth process. In 266 days, a single cell has grown into a unique human infant, ready for life outside of the womb.

How pregnancy affects parents

During the nine prenatal months when so much is happening to the fetus, the expectant parents, too, go through changes. Nearly all expectant parents go through a period of emotional flux, when mood and anticipation run high one moment and low the next. Not surprisingly, pregnancy has been termed a ''maturational crisis'' (Bibring, Dwyer, Huntington, and Valenstein, 1961), a time for psychological growth and adjustment.

Emotional strains

Most pregnant women, research has shown, feel vulnerable, sensitive, and in need of support (Leifer, 1977; Shereshefsky and Yarrow, 1973). They are moody at times and worry about the health and well-being of the developing fetus. Few expectant mothers develop severe emotional problems, however, especially if they are well adjusted and looking forward to the ''blessed event.'' Well adjusted women are more likely to worry about the health of their fetus than about their own health, and they are likely to grow more confident and sure of themselves as the pregnancy progresses. Women who are emotionally unstable even before they conceive, whose pregnancies are unplanned or unwanted, and whose relationships with the father are shaky are more likely to develop strong anxieties about themselves during their pregnancy. In both expectant parents, the pregnancy may revive childhood conflicts and anxieties. Some expectant parents abstain from sexual intercourse during the last months of the pregnancy, afraid that they will harm the fetus during intercourse and orgasm. Sexual abstinence can put yet another strain on the relationship between expectant parents. Affectionate and cooperative couples can most successfully navigate the sexual difficulties and emotional strains brought on by impending parenthood.

As the stresses and strains of pregnancy are better recognized, expectant fathers and mothers stand a better chance of getting meaningful help. In the Soviet Union, prenatal psychological screening and therapy are standard procedures. In England a doctor has devised a way of screening women who may need extra support during their pregnancies (Horsley, 1972). In this country, researchers have found that counseling can help fathers and mothers to adjust to their new families during and after pregnancy (Shereshefsy and Yarrow, 1973). Despite the symptoms, strains, and worries of pregnancy, most women and men ultimately bring themselves into harmony with their developing child and their impending parenthood.

focus   *Expectant fathers*

Expectant fathers may feel some of the same symptoms as pregnant women. This sympathetic syndrome has been called **couvade**, from the French word meaning to hatch or brood. The term was first applied in 1865 by Sir Edward Burnett Tylor, a cultural anthropologist. Among some peoples, he witnessed a ritual in which fathers took to their beds as their wives went into labor and complained woefully of their own physical pains of childbirth. Such couvade rituals have been practiced all over the world for hundreds of years. Chinese fathers practiced couvade rituals in the 18th century, fathers in Japan and India did so in the 19th century. In the Americas, Indians from California, the West Indies, and South America practiced couvade rituals. Couvade also has been reported in Zaire, the Balearic Islands, and the Baltic states.

What about expectant fathers in our own culture, where there are no special rites? Here, couvade is not a ritual but an unintentional and unconscious reaction to a woman's pregnancy. In one study of 327 expectant fathers, one quarter experienced couvade symptoms in the forms of poor appetite, toothache, nausea, and illness (Trethowan and Conlon, 1965). In another study (Shereshefsky and Yarrow, 1973), two-thirds of the expectant fathers reported feeling nausea, backache, or other physical maladies common to pregnant women. When 200 white, lower-middle class expectant mothers were asked about their husbands' health, 41 percent of them reported that their husbands had developed symptoms during the pregnancy (Munroe and Munroe, 1971).

In the last study, fathers with more couvade symptoms were less likely to have completed high school. They made more ''female'' drawings—with rounded forms rather than ''male'' expanded, projected forms—on a picture completion test. Their taste in television programs—for medical dramas and family stories in which social relationships were important—coincided with

Physical strains

> I was so sick to my stomach during the first three months that I was pregnant with Sam that one night I showed up at the dinner table with a blanket over my head and managed to get down one spoonful of plain boiled rice.

Pregnancy brings with it physical strains as well as psychological ones. For one thing, in the early months, biochemical changes lower women's threshold to nausea and vomiting. Some psychologists have speculated that women who are anxious about their pregnancies are more vulnerable to nausea, but this speculation has never been proved. It makes sense, however, that anxiety can magnify the physical discomforts of pregnancy. For another thing, the early months of pregnancy bring fatigue.

> When I was first pregnant with Tim, I couldn't do much work because I was so tired. I'd close my office door and take an hour's nap with my face on my desk. At night when I got home, I slept some more. Was I ever relieved when I started to feel better.

Pregnant women also may crave or abhor certain foods, a tendency that is likely to be physiological in origin but aggravated by psychological reactions. Because the sense of taste is dulled during pregnancy, some women crave strong-tasting—sharp, sour, salty, or spicy—foods. Between one-third women's taste more than with the taste of the symptom-free fathers, who preferred more violent shows. Although they did less housework, fathers with symptoms did more baby care and made more family decisions. A significant number of men with symptoms reported that their fathers had been absent during their childhoods. In sum, it seems that expectant fathers who experience symptoms of couvade are likely to have more ''feminine'' and child-oriented interests, values, and identifications. They allow themselves to share their wife's pregnancy empathically and anxiously, rather than denying or intellectualizing it away.

It comes as no surprise that the psychological strains on expectant parents should translate themselves into the common physical symptoms of stress. Jerrold Lee Shapiro, who has interviewed many expectant fathers, maintains:

> Men have serious fears about birth and fatherhood that simply go unaddressed. . . . There is great pressure on the expectant father to participate as his wife's coach and supporter in the delivery room, but little attention is paid to the emotional and psychological aspects of his becoming a father. . . . Men go through as many emotional changes and experiences as women during pregnancy and childbirth (Hillinger, 1984, p. 14).

From his survey of 156 expectant fathers, Shapiro concludes that many find childbirth exhilarating but waiting stressful indeed. Every father interviewed worried that his child might be born brain-damaged. They worried about providing for the child financially and about being replaced by the child in their wives' affections. Although in our culture we do not ritualize and formally recognize their feelings, significant numbers of expectant fathers nonetheless suffer psychosomatic symptoms. Clearly, fathers, too, feel the stress and strain of impending parenthood.

and two-thirds of pregnant women apparently suffer from cravings or aversions to certain foods.

A more extreme physical strain comes to some women: **toxemia** is a potentially life-threatening condition during pregnancy in which a woman retains fluid, vomits, gains weight rapidly, and has high blood pressure. If toxemia is unchecked, a woman may have seizures, enter a coma, and die. No one knows the cause of toxemia. As with nausea, people are divided in their opinions about whether its cause is psychological or physiological.

Adjustment to pregnancy

One way of looking at pregnancy is to see it as a period of development when a woman responds to an unfolding series of demands (Gloger-Tippelt, 1983). These demands are biological, social, and psychological. During the first trimester of pregnancy, a woman may experience sudden and dramatic disruptions in her accustomed ways of feeling and acting. The first disruptions of a woman's system are hormonal and physiological. Menstruation stops, and the woman may feel tired and nauseated, have sensitive breasts, and need to urinate often. She also may find elements of her identity threatened. She may feel psychological disruptions in her sense of maturity (''I'm a woman now, not a girl''), her sense of responsibility (''I will have to be a good mother''), her sexual identity (''How do I balance being a lover and a mother?''), her work identity (''Should I leave my job to stay home with the baby?''), and her sense of creativity and power (''I have created life''). She may also feel disruptions in her social relationships with her partner, friends, relatives, and employer. When the risk of miscarriage and many of the physical discomforts diminish, this phase ends.

In the second phase of pregnancy, many of the unpleasant symptoms like nausea and fatigue give way to relief and satisfaction. Obstetrical devices make it possible to hear the fetus's heartbeat or to see it by means of ultrasound, and these signs reassure the mother-to-be. Most women by now have committed themselves to, and feel familiar with, their pregnancy. Increasingly then, the woman becomes focused on the rapidly developing fetus. The fetus begins to signal his or her presence with movements and kicking. The fetus becomes a living presence rather than the symptom or abstraction it had been earlier in the pregnancy. Anxieties tend to be at low ebb, and the pregnant woman is likely to start making the practical arrangements in her education, work, and relationships that ready her for active motherhood. Now that she looks pregnant, the mother-to-be evokes certain predictable responses from others.

> People were so friendly to me when I was pregnant. They'd smile, or they'd give me their place in line, or they'd offer me a seat. Some people tapped my belly. One woman said she tapped it for good luck. Little kids stared. Several little boys informed me that they had babies growing in *their* tummies.

> When I was pregnant with Sam, the lady next door wouldn't let me wash the windows of the house, the people at the corner store wouldn't let me carry my own groceries to the car, and the guy who cut my hair told me it was bad luck to raise my arms over my shoulders.

By the eighth month and final phase of pregnancy, her large abdomen, the heavy baby settled in her pelvis, and the increased demands on her circulation and digestion can make a pregnant woman uncomfortable during sleep, eating, and moving around in general. Psychologically, the woman faces imminent birth. She may worry about pain, helplessness, losing self-control, or even about losing her partner, dying, or bearing a deformed child. Now is when she is likely to gather information about childbirth, to enroll in prepared childbirth classes, and to engage with her partner in relaxation exercises. She may also actively prepare for the new arrival by buying clothes and equipment, by learning about feeding, furniture, and the like.

> We put off buying baby furniture or clothes until my last month. I was superstitious about buying them any earlier than that, but also the baby wasn't real enough to either one of us until very late in my pregnancy.

Socially, the woman anticipates and prepares for the birth with others in her life. She may leave her job and increase her visits to the doctor.

How the prenatal environment affects the fetus

The developing fetus may be affected by any substance that can pass through the placenta and into the bloodstream. Whatever a pregnant woman eats or drinks, whatever drugs she takes, whatever she breathes in may be transmitted to the fetus. Whether she is well nourished or not, whether she is generally healthy or ill, whether she is serene or anxious, whether she is exposed to radiation or other harmful substances all may affect the development of her fetus. Figure 4.5 illustrates just some of the many environmental conditions that affect the newborn infant.

A German woman gathers fuel into a baby carriage. Researchers have found that the number of infants born with malformations, which was high in Germany during World War II, was even higher after the war. The question remains whether stress, malnutrition, scant medical care, or some other factor caused the increase.

FACTORS AFFECTING THE NEWBORN

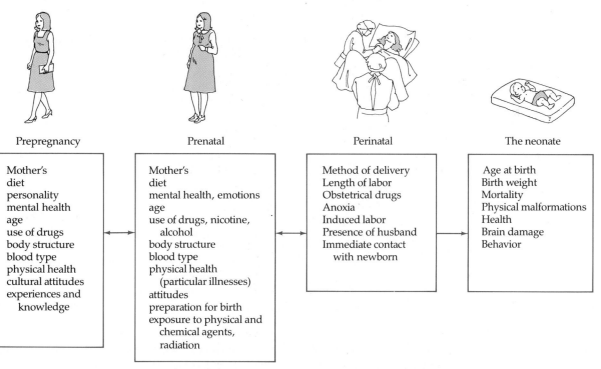

Prepregnancy	Prenatal	Perinatal	The neonate

Mother's
diet
personality
mental health
age
use of drugs
body structure
blood type
physical health
cultural attitudes
experiences and
    knowledge
	Mother's
	diet
	mental health, emotions
	age
	use of drugs, nicotine,
	    alcohol
	body structure
	blood type
	physical health
	    (particular illnesses)
	attitudes
	preparation for birth
	exposure to physical and
	    chemical agents,
	    radiation
		Method of delivery
		Length of labor
		Obstetrical drugs
		Anoxia
		Induced labor
		Presence of husband
		Immediate contact
		    with newborn
			Age at birth
			Birth weight
			Mortality
			Physical malformations
			Health
			Brain damage
			Behavior

Figure 4.5 This illustration shows some of the factors that may influence an infant's earliest health and development. Even before conception, the mother's health, age, nature, and attitudes affect the infant. Events occurring through the nine months of prenatal development, the conditions and method of the delivery and birth, and the condition of the newborn also all influence health and development.

117

The mother's emotional state

When a pregnant woman feels continued anxiety, distress, trauma, or extreme fear or grief, her body reacts with profound, involuntary changes. Heart and respiration rates and secretions of glands all respond to emotional turmoil. If a pregnant woman is fearful, for example, her brain may signal her adrenal glands to secrete the hormone cortisone. When cortisone enters her bloodstream, it can direct blood flow toward her own internal organs, effectively diverting blood away from the fetus and reducing the amount of oxygen the fetus gets. Although the chemical effects of pregnant women's emotions can be traced by blood tests, it is less easy to assess how these changes affect the fetus's behavior. An experiment in which pregnant women are deliberately subjected to stress and their unborn infants examined cannot be justified ethically. Although studies with rats have shown that prenatal stress affects the later behavior of the offspring (Ward, 1972), these results do not necessarily apply to human beings.

One way to examine the effects of emotional stress on human prenatal development is to do longitudinal studies on the course of many pregnancies and identify those in which stress occurs naturally. In one longitudinal study, from 1930 to 1950, investigators followed the pregnancies of a large number of women, eight of whom experienced severe stress during their pregnancies (Sontag, 1940, 1944). The fetuses of these women were many times more active, sometimes moving several hundred percent more than they had before the stress began. These active fetuses weighed less at birth and were likely to have stomach and feeding problems. As infants, they were advanced in motor development over other infants their age, but they were also more restless, cranky, and sensitive to noise, and they vomited, cried, and had diarrhea more often.

Another strategy for studying the effects of prenatal stress is to chart how frequently malformations occur in entire populations as they undergo periods of stress. Researchers have studied the rates of German and British infants born with malformations during the events leading up to, during, and after World War II, for example (Stott, 1971; see Figure 4.6). The rate of malformations in German infants was high in 1933, the year Hitler came to power, high again in the war years, and finally rose dramatically after the war, from two per thousand in 1945 to eight per thousand in 1949. The rate of malformations in Britain was highest during the years of heaviest German bombing and declined throughout the rest of the war and postwar period. Unfortunately, psychologists can only speculate about the reasons for the observed increases, because many factors might have been at work. Was the increase in the year that Hitler took power a psychological reaction? Was the German postwar increase a result of malnutrition and scant medical care or the psychological injury of defeat? Was the British increase during the bombing blitz a result of stress or of overwork, cold, and insomnia? This research strategy thus leaves open as many questions as it answers.

A third strategy is to correlate the incidence of malformations in infants with the incidence of stressful events that occurred while their mothers were pregnant—divorce, moving to a new house or community, or death in the family. By using this strategy, investigators have found that prenatal stress predicts a condition called **pyloric stenosis**, in which infants are born with a narrowed stomach opening (Revill and Dodge, 1978). In another study, Finnish researchers (Huttunen and Niskanen, 1978) found that children whose fathers had died during the babies' prenatal period had more psychological and behavior problems than infants whose fathers died during the babies' first year of life.

Another way in which the mother's emotional state may affect the fetus is by causing a spontaneous abortion, or miscarriage. In one study, pregnant

STRESS AND FETAL MALFORMATIONS

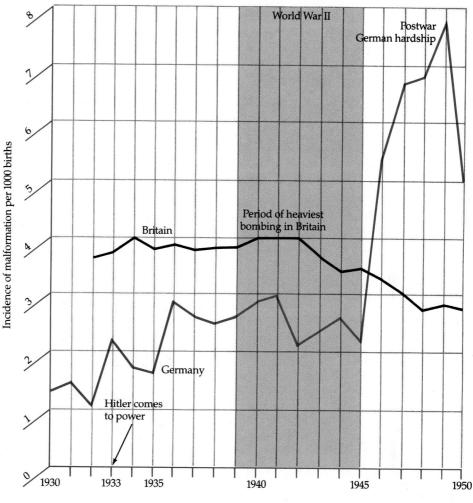

Figure 4.6 Stress during pregnancy is likely to be translated into increases in infant malformations, although no one can know for certain whether psychological or physiological events are responsible. This graph shows the rates of birth malformations in German and British infants during the years of the World War II period (Stott, 1971).

women who had suffered at least three spontaneous abortions were found to be significantly more tense and anxious than pregnant women who had never had a spontaneous abortion (Grimm, 1962). But we cannot tell whether the emotions of these women predisposed them to miscarry or whether their histories of miscarriages made them so anxious that they miscarried again. In a second step in this study, some of the women who had miscarried received counseling during their next pregnancies. Their anxieties were calmed, and they carried their pregnancies to term.

There are many possible sources of stress on the pregnant woman in our society (Table 4.1). Taking the results of all these studies together suggests that pregnant women's extremely stressful emotions do influence their infants' prenatal development. Further research is needed, however, before we will be able to predict the likelihood, the exact nature, or the extent of these effects.

Illness

The effects of pregnant women's illnesses on their fetuses have been documented more clearly. Two chronic conditions that pose perhaps the greatest danger to the developing infant are **diabetes** and **Rh incompatibility**. Diabetes causes the mother's blood sugar level to rise, and many diabetic women

Table 4.1
Factors causing stress during pregnancy

- Pregnancy unplanned
- Baby unwanted
- First baby
- Older sibling still an infant
- Large family
- Not enough money
- Not enough food
- No prenatal care
- Physical strains
- Fear of childbirth
- Pending loss of job, school, or autonomy
- Mother works throughout pregnancy
- Baby expected to be malformed
- Mother younger than 18
- Mother older than 35

take the hormone insulin to lower their blood sugar. Both high blood sugar and insulin increase the chance that the mother will miscarry or that the baby will be overweight, have physical and neurological problems, or be stillborn. In one study of diabetic and nondiabetic mothers conducted by Michael Yogman and his associates (Yogman, Cole, Als, and Lester, 1982), infants of diabetic mothers looked at objects less readily and were less alert. Their eye movements were jerky, and they had trouble looking at a human face. They had poor head control when pulled into a sitting position, they trembled, and their skin color changed rapidly to a deep red or mottling. They were less responsive and more difficult to care for. As many of their parents said, the babies were ''hard to get to know.'' On successive days, the test scores of the comparison group improved, but those of the diabetic group got worse.

The Rh factor is a protein in the red blood cells of about 85 percent of the population. When a fetus's blood contains the Rh protein and the mother's blood does not, Rh incompatibility occurs. If any Rh positive blood from the fetus enters the mother's Rh negative blood—perhaps during the process of birth itself—the mother's system forms antibodies to the Rh factor. Problems therefore are unlikely to affect a firstborn child, but the red blood cells of fetuses during later pregnancies are subject to attack by the antibodies of the now sensitized Rh negative mother. The possible consequences to the infant include jaundice, premature birth, stillbirth, and brain damage. Some affected infants require blood transfusions immediately after birth or even before if they are to survive. In most cases, however, the Rh negative mother is given an injection of Rh immune globulin (RhoGam) right after each delivery, miscarriage, or abortion, to prevent her immune system from creating antibodies to the Rh factor.

> We had been quite lucky with our three children. I had been given RhoGam, and all of them were born healthy. But when I got pregnant—by accident—with our fourth child, we ran into problems. She needed three complete transfusions right after delivery, and we weren't sure she was going to make it. But make it she did, thank heavens.

Acute infectious diseases caught by pregnant women also affect the fetus. German measles, or **rubella**, is particularly dangerous. Following the

German measles epidemic of 1964–1965 in the United States, 30,000 fetuses and newborns died, and 20,000 were born blind, deaf, mentally retarded, or with heart defects. Although having German measles does no harm in the first two weeks of pregnancy, in the following two weeks, when organs are forming in the embryo, it harms one-half of the embryos whose mothers contract it. After that the risk diminishes. During the second month of pregnancy, German measles harms only 22 percent, and during the third month, only 6 to 8 percent of the fetuses whose mothers get the disease. Women of childbearing age can be tested for immunity to German measles; almost 85 percent in the United States are immune. Those who are not immune should be vaccinated 6 months or longer before getting pregnant.

Nutrition

> "What do you eat for breakfast?" the midwife asked me when I was pregnant.
>
> "I usually have toast," I answered.
>
> "And what's on the toast?" she pressed on.
>
> "Butter," I confessed, suspecting that this was the wrong answer.
>
> "*Butter*? Butter has no protein. Use peanut butter, or melted cheese, but make sure you get protein. Protein, protein, protein! That baby needs protein!"
>
> (I got the picture.)

Whether a woman is well or poorly nourished before, during, and after pregnancy also affects the fetus's development. Because pregnancy itself places so many demands on her system, a woman should be well nourished as she begins her pregnancy. It is very difficult to overcome nutritional deficiencies during pregnancy, a time when caloric needs increase by about 20 percent, when the needs for protein and riboflavin increase by 45 percent, and the need for vitamin C increases 100 percent. A pregnant woman needs to eat about 2000 wisely chosen calories a day.

So important is nutrition to fetal development that children conceived during the cool autumn and winter weather—when their mothers eat heartier, protein-rich roasts and stews—are heavier, healthier, more likely to go to college and to appear in *Who's Who in America* than children conceived in warmer weather—when their mothers are more likely to skip heavy meals in favor of fruit and salads. Likewise, more mentally retarded children are conceived in spring and summer than in winter, and the hotter the summer, the likelier this is to be. Children for whom the 8th to 12th weeks of prenatal development, when the brain is developing most rapidly, coincided with the hottest months were found to be the most severely retarded of a sample of retarded patients in one Columbus, Ohio, study (Knobloch and Pasamanick, 1966). Infants conceived during periods of famine also may have impaired intelligence (Montagu, 1962). Newborn infants of chronically malnourished mothers lag in motor and neurological development. They suffer from malnutrition themselves, weigh less, and have lighter and less protein-dense placentas than normal infants (Bhatia, Katiyar, and Agarwal, 1979).

Not only do general nutritional or protein deficiencies affect prenatal development, but so do deficiencies in specific vitamins and minerals. Early in this century, this link was demonstrated when a large number of Swiss infants were born severely mentally retarded. The cause of their retardation was traced to a lack of iodine in the soil of their native regions. Without iodine in the diets of their pregnant mothers, the fetuses' thyroid glands did not develop normally. The effects were mental retardation, stunted growth, and deafness. Once iodine was given to adults in the area, the problems disappeared (Montagu, 1962).

When pregnant women's diets are improved, their infants' health improves as well. In one wartime study (Ebbs, Brown, Tisdall, Moyle, and Bell, 1942), one group of pregnant women stuck to their normal deficient diets while another randomly chosen group was given a diet containing extra vitamins, minerals, protein, and calories. Of the mothers in the malnourished group, 12 percent miscarried or had stillbirths, and 8 percent delivered prematurely. Of the mothers in the improved-diet group, there were no miscarriages or stillbirths, and only 2 percent had premature births. Their labors were an average of five hours shorter, and the infants had fewer major and minor illnesses in their first six months.

A generation or two ago, physicians warned pregnant women against gaining more than 10 or 15 pounds during their pregnancies. The belief was that a higher weight gain might cause toxemia.

> When I was pregnant with Sam's father, I gained 12 pounds. That was all they allowed us in those days. Some women asked for diet pills to curb their appetites. Heaven knows what that did to their babies.

But physicians today realize that women who gain too *little* weight may have stillbirths or infants that are too small. They advise women to gain at least 24 pounds during the course of a pregnancy (see Figure 4.7), and women who begin their pregnancies overweight are cautioned against trying to reduce until after their babies are born.

Mother's age

Although most adolescent girls can get pregnant in their early teens and woman remain fertile for 40 years or so, the years between 22 and 29 are physiologically the best time to have a baby. In this prime time, both mothers and infants are more likely to survive and to go through pregnancy and

WEIGHT GAIN AVERAGE PREGNANCY
(TOTAL: 24 lb)

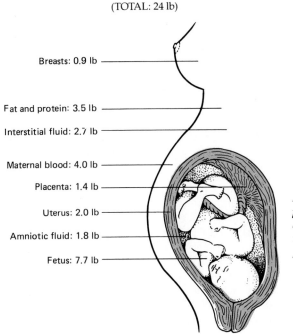

Breasts: 0.9 lb

Fat and protein: 3.5 lb

Interstitial fluid: 2.7 lb

Maternal blood: 4.0 lb

Placenta: 1.4 lb

Uterus: 2.0 lb

Amniotic fluid: 1.8 lb

Fetus: 7.7 lb

Figure 4.7 Of the 24 pounds of weight gained during a normal pregnancy, only about 3½ pounds are stored as fat and protein. The rest acts as a buffer against the stresses of the period after birth (Newton and Modahl, 1978).

delivery free of complications. Yet social trends have increased the number of births to women both older and younger than this prime age range. Risks to older women include difficulties in conceiving and delivering and an increased probability of having a child with Down's syndrome. Another consequence is an increased likelihood that the child will have problems in developing fine-motor skills (Gillberg, Rasmussen, and Wahlstrom, 1982).

Teenage pregnancy is also risky. Physically immature, and often psychologically unprepared for pregnancy, many teenage mothers have long labors and premature deliveries; their infants are often underweight and may not survive their first year. Many factors contribute: a teenager's uterus is immature, her body is still growing, she may be poorly nourished, and she may lack prenatal medical care. This powerful combination of disadvantages makes early childbearing as dangerous to mother and child as late childbearing.

Compared to the mother's age, the father's age seems to put his child at less of disadvantage. Older men may contribute the extra twenty-first chromosome that causes Down's syndrome. They may also father children who are dwarfed, because of a mutation called **achondroplasia**, a cartilage disorder (Evans and Hall, 1975). But although the risk of fathering a child with a genetic mutation increases between the ages of 30 and 60, even after 60 the risk is less than 1 in 100.

Mother's work

Today, the majority of women of childbearing age hold jobs that take them outside their homes. Many women work through their pregnancies, right up to the time of delivery. Does a pregnant woman's work affect her health or that of her fetus? It may well do so. In a survey of 7700 pregnancies, it was found that women who continued working in their third trimester bore infants who weighed from 5 to 14 ounces less than infants born to women who remained at home (Naeye and Peters, 1982). The weight deficit was greatest when the mother herself was underweight or had high blood pressure. The women whose jobs required them to stand for long periods when they were in their third trimester had fetuses who were most severely underweight, probably because the blood supply to these mothers' uteri and placentas was poor. Of course, these risks are just statistical probabilities. Many women work throughout their pregnancies without ill effects to their babies. The decision about how long to continue working has to be based on a variety of factors like the woman's health, the kind of work she does, and the leave policy where she works.

Parity

The number of children a woman already has borne, her **parity**, also affects the course of pregnancy and prenatal development. It takes a woman's endocrine system some four years to return to its previous level after a pregnancy (Maccoby, Doering, Jacklin, and Kraemer, 1979). Any infant born sooner than that may be at a disadvantage. Beyond this period needed for recuperation, later-born infants seem to have a better prenatal environment than firstborns. Blood circulation to the placenta is richer after a first, "practice-session" pregnancy. Many later-borns are heavier at birth and suffer from fewer malformations and birth complications. Many women have easier labors and deliveries of later-born children. Said one mother,

> With my second child, my labor was about one-third as long as it had been with my first. It was as if my body had learned "the route." It somehow cooperated with the contractions rather than fighting them, as

it had done the first time. I recovered faster, too. Everything about the second time was easier.

But the advantages of the first ''practice session'' are lost if later births follow either too quickly or too late.

External factors

Although the uterus is a protected environment for the fetus—with its warm fluid to cushion shocks and its layers of membrane and abdominal muscle—it is not impervious to the external environment. Through the placenta, the fetus is affected by whatever the pregnant mother eats, drinks, smokes, or breathes. Certain substances are now known to cross the placental barrier and to cause physical deformities and behavioral disorders in the fetus. More are being discovered all the time. **Teratology** is the study of structural and functional deformities in children. It takes its name from the Greek word *teras*, meaning ''monster'' or ''marvel.'' The goal of teratologists is to trace the causes of deformities and to anticipate risks to prenatal development. Teratologists point out the critical periods in prenatal development and the external factors—**teratogens**—that may interfere with normal development. Unless they cause a **mutation** in the genes, teratogens affect only the individual fetus and are not passed on to his or her own children, should there be any.

In the sections that follow, we will describe some of the most important of these teratogens.

When this 7-year-old's mother was pregnant, she took an antinausea drug for morning sickness. Her son was born without hands or arms, and his legs are short because he has no thighs. Yet he feeds himself, colors, draws, writes, and plays several instruments with his feet.

Drugs

Until 1961, people did not know that chemicals could cross the placenta and damage the fetus (Wilson, 1977). That was the year after large numbers of infants were born without arms or legs, a condition called **phocomelia** (seal limbs). Their mothers, it turned out, had taken the drug thalidomide to quell the nausea of early pregnancy, and it had prevented the normal development of the fetuses' limbs. Before the connection between the drug and the deformity was made, 10,000 infants with phocomelia were born, of whom one half have survived to adulthood. The thalidomide disaster made scientists and laypeople alert to the previously unsuspected dangers that drugs may pose to the developing fetus.

Even so, until 1969, some pregnant women were given the hormone **diethylstilbestrol (DES)** to prevent miscarriage. Sixty percent of these women's daughters developed abnormal vaginal tissues and cervical structures (Elliot, 1979). Some of their sons developed abnormal testicular structures that cause sterility (Cosgrove and Henderson, 1977).

Still, pregnant women continue to take drugs every day. One study showed that women took an average of ten drugs, not even counting vitamins, iron, caffeine, nicotine, and alcohol (Hill, 1973). Over half took aspirin or other painkillers, diuretics, or antihistamines; one-third took sedatives; one-fifth took hormones. Most hormones, sedatives, antibiotics (tetracycline, streptomycin, etc.), tranquilizers (Valium, Thorazine, etc.), and anticoagulants now are known to have potentially harmful effects on the embryo or fetus.

Street drugs also can hinder fetal development. Pregnant women who are addicted to cocaine, heroin, or methadone pass their addiction on to their fetuses, who are born addicted and must go through withdrawal after birth. Many of these infants are born prematurely, underweight, and irritable

(Householder, Hatcher, Burns, and Chasnoff, 1982; Ostrea and Chavez, 1979; Strauss, Lessen-Firestone, Starr, and Ostrea, 1975; Jeremy and Hans, 1985). They are tense, fussy, resist cuddling, and sleep irregularly. At the age of 1 year, their motor and cognitive development still may be lagging.

Drugs hit the fetus as hard as they do for two reasons: first, because a small amount of a drug for an adult is a huge amount for the tiny fetus; and second, because liver enzymes, necessary for breaking down drugs, do not develop until after birth. The drugs therefore stay in the body of the fetus. Women may stop taking drugs when they find out that they are pregnant, but many do not even realize that they *are* pregnant until the embryo already has been damaged. Tranquilizers, street drugs, and birth control pills all can cause deafness, cleft palate, heart and joint defects, arm and leg defects, neurological and behavior disorders that may show up at birth or later. Drugs taken in combination may have even more disastrous effects on a fetus than one drug taken alone (Wilson and Fraser, 1977). Total abstinence from all drugs that are not absolutely necessary for her own health is the best policy for any pregnant woman.

Smoking

> When I got the news that I was pregnant, I reacted by treating myself to my last cigarette. Mikey and Erica's babysitter smoked all the way through her pregnancy. I spoke to her one time about the harm it does to the baby, but she said she was too nervous to quit.

With every drag on a cigarette, pregnant smokers bathe their own and their fetuses' systems in toxic substances. Pregnant smokers have 28 percent more miscarriages, stillbirths, and newborn deaths. During the last trimester of pregnancy, their fetuses gain an average of 6 fewer ounces than those of nonsmokers. Fetuses whose fathers smoke are also at risk for low birth weight (Ericson, Kallen, and Westerholm, 1979; Evans, Newcombe, and Campbell, 1979; Frazier, Davis, Goldstein, and Goldberg, 1961; Himmelberger, Brown, and Cohen, 1978; Jacobson, Fein, Jacobson, Schwartz, and Dowler, 1984; Niswander and Gordon, 1972).

How does cigarette smoking stunt the fetus's growth? In one study, pregnant women smoked two cigarettes for 10 minutes each, and their blood was sampled every 2½ minutes (Quigley, Sheehan, Wilkes, and Yen, 1979). The smoking quickly raised the women's blood pressure and pulse rate. It replaced the oxygen in their blood with carboxyhemoglobin, a gas from the carbon monoxide in the smoke. The mothers' blood levels of epinephrine and norepinephrine also rose. These chemicals narrow the blood vessels in the placenta, cutting the nutrients available to the fetus and reducing its intake of oxygen in a second way. After their mothers had smoked for 7½ minutes, the heart rates of the fetuses rose and continued rising to an average of 23 beats per minute. The result of all these physiological changes, particularly the fetus's deprivation of the oxygen that is so necessary for prenatal growth, is to increase the likelihood that the fetus will be abnormally small and have other defects as well.

It is also possible that some of the harmful effects of smoking are psychological in nature. If an expectant mother smokes because she is anxious, the direct effect of the smoking may be compounded by the indirect effect of her anxiety (Yerushalmy, 1971, 1972). Even so, pregnant women may find it easier to stop smoking than to stop feeling anxious, and doing so can definitely benefit the baby. In a large study of the 17,000 infants born between March 3 and March 8, 1958, in Great Britain, mothers who had cut their smoking to five cigarettes a day or fewer gave birth to infants who were nearly as heavy as those of nonsmokers (Butler, Goldstein, and Ross, 1972).

Are there long-term harmful effects on children if their parents smoke during pregnancy? The evidence here is not so clear. Some researchers indeed have found that these children continue to be small and are likely to do poorly in school and on tests of attention and orientation as well (Butler and Goldstein, 1973; Fogelman, 1980; Streissguth et al., 1984). Other researchers have not found significant physical or intellectual effects (Hardy and Mellits, 1972; Lefkowitz, 1981). Those infants who survive the prenatal and neonatal periods may not have major problems later. To some extent what happens depends, on the overall quality of their lives as children. Nevertheless, some minority of children are impaired. The risk is not worth taking. Pregnant women—and their partners—should stop smoking and stay out of smoke-filled rooms.

Alcohol

> A woman who is one of my patients had a baby right around the same time as I had Natalie. The poor baby had fetal alcohol syndrome. The mother said she drank a six-pack of beer every night after work while she was pregnant. Why? She'd always drunk that much before, and no one had told her it was too much.

No one knows exactly how much alcohol during pregnancy is *too* much, but heavy drinkers run a 17 percent risk of having a stillborn baby and a 44 percent chance of having one that is deformed. The **fetal alcohol sydrome** was identified in 1973 among infants born to pregnant women who drank heavily (Jones, Smith, Ulleland, and Streissguth, 1973). A similar syndrome was later observed in infants born to pregnant women who smoked marijuana (Hingson et al., 1982). Infants with fetal alcohol syndrome are born short for their weight and do not go through a normal period of catch-up growth after birth. They are mentally retarded and slow in motor development, and they may also suffer from defects of the eye, heart, joints, arms, or legs. Many have small skulls and a distinctive look to their face: eyes spaced far apart, flat nose, and underdeveloped upper jaw. It has been estimated that as many as 20 percent of the children in mental retardation centers suffer from fetal alcohol syndrome (Rawat, 1982).

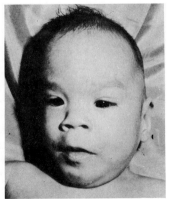

When a pregnant woman drinks 12 ounces of beer or 1.5 ounces of liquor, the fetus receives a full and debilitating adult dose of alcohol. Continued drinking during pregnancy can affect a baby's intelligence and appearance.

Alcohol affects the fetus directly. Alcohol crosses the placenta and, like other drugs, because the fetus's liver is immature, remains in its system for a long time. In one experiment with pregnant women, all of whom drank on occasion, half the subjects got an ounce of 80-proof vodka in diet ginger ale, and half got only ginger ale (Fox et al., 1978). All the women were between 37 and 39 weeks pregnant. In all the women who drank the vodka, the fetus stopped breathing at some point between 3 and 30 minutes later. Many of the fetuses did not breathe for over half an hour. As mothers' blood alcohol levels dropped, the fetuses' breathing picked up again. Because fetuses are so sensitive to alcohol, even small amounts may cause abnormalities in development. During the last three months of pregnancy, when the fetus's brain is developing, alcohol may be extremely dangerous. One study of almost 3500 embryos aborted during the first three months of pregnancy showed that mothers who drank had embryos with no more abnormalities than mothers who did not drink (Matsunaga and Shiota, 1981). In other words, the effects of alcohol, like smoking, are most severe later in pregnancy. Mothers who drink heavily but who can cut down their alcohol intake during the last three months of pregnancy bear significantly fewer babies who are abnormally small (Rosett, Weiner, Zuckerman, McKinlay, and Edelin, 1980). Fully 27 percent of the babies born to heavy drinkers who drank throughout their pregnancies had a head circumference below the 10th percentile, but only 4 percent did when mothers cut down on their drinking in the last three months of pregnancy. Similarly, 45 percent of babies born to heavy drinkers were low in birth weight, compared to 8 percent born to mothers who cut down in the last three months.

When fetal alcohol syndrome was first described, doctors thought that pregnant women could drink moderately without harming the fetus. But they have since come to revise this idea. There may be no safe level of alcohol intake during pregnancy. In a study of moderate drinkers, women who drank an average of 2 ounces of 100-proof alcohol a day, 12 percent of the babies showed one or more signs of fetal alcohol syndrome. Only two of the babies born to a comparison group of women who drank little or no alcohol showed these signs (Hanson, 1977). The amount of alcohol the pregnant women drank seemed to correspond roughly with the rate of abnormalities in their babies—a rate that went as high as 50 to 75 percent in heavy drinkers. Other studies support this finding—that the more alcohol pregnant women drink, the more likely their infants are to be sluggish, inattentive, and slow to learn (Jacobson et al., 1984; Richardson and Day, 1986; Streissguth, Barr, and Martin, 1983). These deficiencies continue for at least the first four years (Streissguth et al., 1984). For this reason, doctors now advise pregnant women to avoid drinking any alcohol.

But even this may not solve the problem completely. Recent evidence suggests that some effects of alcohol drunk *before* pregnancy may persist, even if women cut down during pregnancy. In one study, the intelligence level of 1-year-olds born to heavier drinkers (3 or more drinks on occasion) was 12 points lower than that of infants born to equally intelligent light drinkers—even though all the mothers had stopped drinking while they were pregnant (O'Connor and Brill, 1984). This study needs to be replicated. In the meantime, all women in their childbearing years would be well advised to be cautious about their drinking.

Radiation

I had a dental checkup very early in my pregnancy with Sam. So when the hygienist asked if they could take X rays, I said no, because I was pregnant. She wrote ''pregnant'' across the front of my chart. I guess I was being pretty careful.

The radiation from X rays and other sources can cause harmful mutations in genetic material. It can cause mutations of chromosomes in the unripe ova stored in a female's ovaries or in the sperm-producing cells in a male's testes. For this reason, unless they are absolutely necessary, X rays of the lower abdomen and pelvis should be avoided in the childbearing years and earlier. When a woman is pregnant, exposure to radiation before the zygote implants in the uterine lining is likely to end the pregnancy. If the zygote survives, however, it is likely to be normal. But exposure to radiation after implantation affects development in a variety of ways. If an embryo is exposed to radiation, it is likely to develop deformities of the central nervous system that kill it soon after birth. If a fetus is exposed to radiation, it may later develop malignant tumors or leukemia or have stunted growth (see Table 4.2). Extreme doses of radiation, from radiation therapy or atomic explosion, cause **microcephaly** (small skull size), mental retardation, Down's syndrome, hydrocephaly, defects of skull formation, or death (Joffe, 1969). Radiation fallout in the air and ground around us may also, according to some investigators, raise the rates of malformations (Joffe, 1969). Other investigators disagree, saying that natural radiation levels in most parts of the world are not high enough to harm fetuses' development (Brent, 1977). Atomic waste buried under land or water and accidents at nuclear power plants are more likely to pose hazards to fetal development.

Chemical hazards

As more and more women continue to work through their pregnancies, the environmental hazards to which their fetuses are exposed increase. Women who work in textile plants are exposed to dust, dyes, mothproofing chemicals, and flame retardants. Women who work in laboratories are exposed to radiation, bacteria, powerful solvents, and chemicals that cause cancer. Even women who stay home are exposed to some hazards.

> When I was pregnant with Mikey, I closed all the windows when my neighbors had their trees sprayed for bugs. When the smog was especially bad, I stayed inside and turned on the air conditioner. I really didn't want to take any chances.

Potentially dangerous chemicals float through the air we breathe, the water we drink, and the food we eat. Pesticides sprayed on vegetation and the toxic chemicals dumped underground in many states are suspected of causing miscarriages, stillbirths, and birth defects. Benzene (a solvent used in cleaning), carbon monoxide (in cigarette smoke and automobile exhaust), carbon disulfide, hydrocarbons, lead and mercury (in food), and vinyl chloride (a plastic) are just a few of the everyday substances known to affect fetal development. The latest question is what Nutrasweet, a common sugar substitute, does to the developing fetus. Pregnancy is a time to be especially careful about exposure to chemicals.

> When I was pregnant with Kristy, I got fanatical about what I would eat and drink—only natural foods and bottled water.

Keeping safe

The best insurance against problems during pregnancy is to have regular checkups with a qualified obstetrician throughout pregnancy. Once a woman knows that she is pregnant, she can avoid the medicines, radiation, and other substances that might harm the fetus. Some problems, such as a blocked urinary tract, Rh disease, or too much fluid in the fetus's brain, require a physician's diagnosis and treatment. Regular checkups ensure that the preg-

Table 4.2
Some maternal conditions endangering the child

Mother's condition or behavior	Possible effect on embryo, fetus, or newborn
Incompatibility of maternal and fetal blood	Jaundice, anemia, death
Viral infection (rubella, mumps, hepatitis, influenza, etc.)	Malformations, fetal death, prematurity, retarded fetal growth, disorders and infection in the newborn
Malnutrition	Retarded fetal growth, malformations, less developed brain, greater vulnerability to disease
Thalidomide	Hearing defects, deformed limbs, death
Excessive vitamin A	Cleft palate, congenital anomalies
Analgesics	Respiratory depression
Aspirin in large doses	Respiratory depression, bleeding
Anesthetics or barbiturates	Respiratory depression
Tetracycline	Inhibition of bone growth, discolored teeth
Streptomycin	Hearing loss
Drug addiction	Growth deficiency, withdrawal syndrome, respiratory depression, death
Heavy smoking	Retarded fetal growth, increased fetal heart rate, prematurity
Alcohol drinking	Growth deficiency, developmental lag
X ray	Malformations, cancer

SOURCE: Adapted from Carole Lotito Blair and Elizabeth Meehan Salerno, *The Expanding Family: Childbearing.* Boston: Little, Brown & Co., 1976, Table 12.2. Copyright © 1976, by Carole L. Blair and Elizabeth M. Salerno.

nant woman will know what and how much to eat and will have necessary vitamin supplements. Regularly checking blood pressure, weight, and urine ensures that any toxemia or other complication that develops can be dealt with promptly and effectively. At the end of pregnancy, if a problem is suspected, fetal monitors and sonograms can provide information that helps the doctor and parents to decide how best to manage the delivery.

Prenatal vulnerability

Although the teratogens we have discussed sometimes cause death or severe malformations, damage is not inevitable. Human beings have a **self-righting tendency**, a tendency to develop normally under all but the most damaging conditions. Even when exposed to possible harm, most fetuses develop normally. Despite all of the harmful substances to which fetuses may be exposed in our modern world—viruses and bacteria, junk food and alcohol, drugs and radiation—only 3 to 6 percent of the babies born today suffer actual malformations (Heinomen, Slone, and Shapiro, 1976). In addition to this self-righting tendency, a ''self-cleansing tendency'' operates to eliminate severely malformed fetuses by spontaneous abortion in the first three months of prental development.

When damage from a harmful substance does occur, it may range from slight to fatal. The severity of the effect rests on three factors:

1. *The constitution of the fetus*: Different fetuses react differently to the same teratogen. One might die, one might survive with severe malformations, and a third might have only a slight malformation.

2. *When exposure occurs*: The same teratogen affects a zygote, an embryo, and a fetus differently. Before cells are differentiated, exposure to a toxin is likely to kill the organism. After cells are differentiated, during the embryonic period, damage affects specific organs or systems at the particular time they are being formed (see Figure 4.8). In the fetal period, the toxin is most likely to affect behavior or intelligence.

3. *The amount of exposure*: The more extreme the exposure to the teratogen, the more severe are its effects. Evidence from pregnant women who lived through the atomic bombings of Hiroshima and Nagasaki shows, for example, that no women who were within a mile of the center of the bombing bore live infants. Three-quarters of those who were 1 to 4 miles from the center miscarried, had stillbirths, or bore severely malformed infants. The infants of women farther away suffered mental and physical retardation and abnormal skull size (Joffe, 1969; Wilson, 1977).

Thus the timing and amount of exposure to a teratogen, in combination with the individual's constitution, all operate together to determine the extent of the damage.

Figure 4.8 This chart shows critical periods in the prenatal development of organs. In the embryonic period, the likelihood of structural malformation is greatest (dark color), because organs are being formed. After organs are formed, the likelihood of structural defects declines (light color) (Moore, 1977).

CRITICAL PERIODS IN PRENATAL DEVELOPMENT

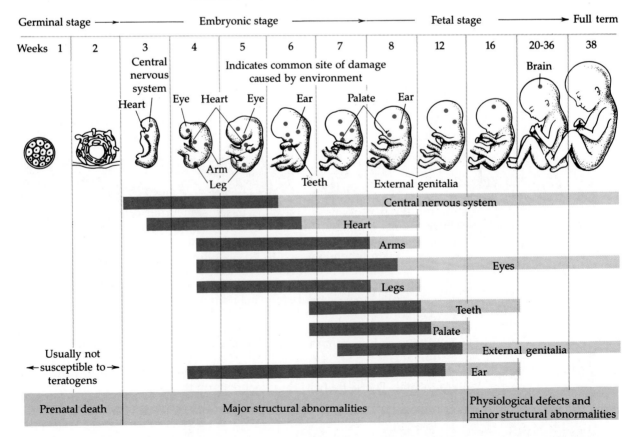

Delivery and birth

Labor

For nine months, the mother has carried, protected, and thought about the creature developing within her. Now the big moment finally has arrived. Filled with anticipation and curiosity—and at least a little anxiety—she prepares for her moment of truth, her first glimpse of the intimate stranger. She begins the hard work that will end in the birth of the infant. For many mothers, **labor** begins at night, when the mother feels her uterine muscles contracting. These contractions, which are usually about 15 to 20 minutes apart and last for 15 to 60 seconds each, stretch the cervix—the opening to the uterus through which the fetus will pass into the vagina and, from there, into the outside world. The cervix gradually opens from 0.2 inch to 4 inches. As labor intensifies, the uterus contracts more intensely every two to five minutes, and these powerful contractions open the cervix the last inch. When the cervix has opened, the infant's body—in most cases, the top of the skull—begins to push through into the vagina. This stage of labor lasts an average of 14 hours for a first baby, 8 hours for later ones, although there are wide individual variations.

> I listened with envy as a friend described her labor. After the contractions started, she called her husband and went outside to bring in the cat. That done, she waited a few minutes for her husband to arrive and then drove with him to the hospital. By the time they got there, she was so fully dilated that the nurse had her do breathing exercises to try to slow things down until the doctor could get there. The baby was born half an hour later. My labor lasted 37 hours!

The means of delivery affects the parents' experience of birth. **(a)** *In the traditional hospital delivery room, childbirth becomes one kind of experience.* **(b)** *In a home, or a homelike birthing center, birth may seem somewhat different.* **(c)** *A cesarean delivery is still another kind of experience for parents.*

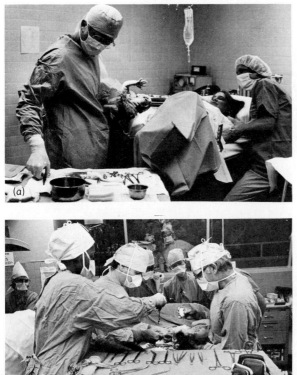

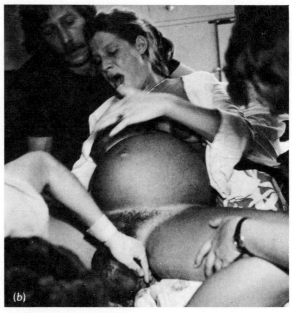

The second stage of labor begins once the crown of the infant's head appears at the vagina and does not recede with each contraction—a point called, naturally enough, **crowning**. Crowning is an exciting time.

> Once Sam's head crowned, I could feel a rush pass through everyone in the room. ''Brown hair! It's got brown hair,'' my husband told me almost incredulously. ''It's time to push now,'' the midwife told me. ''Push that baby out.'' Pushing was such a relief after the intense contractions I had been having that it was actually almost pleasant.

During the second stage of labor, which lasts between half an hour and two hours, contractions wash over the laboring woman every minute or two and last for a minute each. With each wave, she may feel a profound urge to breathe deeply, tense her muscles, and push the baby out.

> I wasn't prepared for the overwhelming urge to push. It felt as unstoppable as vomiting when you're nauseated and your stomach has just turned over.

To turn the infant's head so that it is facing the mother's back and to guide the infant's head through the vagina, the doctor may use forceps or a vacuum device. The doctor may also give the woman an **episiotomy**, a small incision at the entrance to the vagina so that the surrounding tissues will not tear. The area is naturally numbed by the pressure of the infant's head, though some doctors also use a local anesthetic.

After the infant's head is out of the vagina, the doctor turns it sideways and the shoulders and body slide out quickly (see Figure 4.9). When the umbilical cord hits the air, a jelly-like substance inside it makes it swell and the blood vessels tighten. More contractions separate the placenta and other membranes from the uterus and push them out through the birth canal as the **afterbirth**.

> Giving birth was so different from what I had expected. It was less bloody, more painful, and more exhilarating. It was *much* more beautiful. I was surprised at how beautiful the umbilical cord was—all translucent and pearly gray.

Changing attitudes toward childbirth

The final outcome of any successful birth is a normal infant and intact mother. But the social conventions and attitudes with which people surround the biological events of childbirth transform its meaning from one culture and one historical era to another.

> My grandparents were all born at home between the 1890s and 1910 or so, some with a midwife and others with a doctor in attendance. My parents were born in the hospital, their mothers under general anesthesia. As one of my grandmothers said, ''I didn't want to know what happened. I wanted to wake up 24 hours later and have someone bring me a nice clean baby.'' My mother gave birth to me in a hospital, too. My father wasn't allowed in with her. She said she inhaled some kind of ''gas'' for pain and was in and out of consciousness. When I had Sam, my husband coached me all the way through labor. I had no painkillers, but I was attended by an obstetrician and a nurse–midwife. The whole routine was set up to make us feel comfortable and together.

Until the 1500s, all mothers delivered their infants at home. Midwives attended them, and doctors were called only for complicated cases that midwives felt unprepared to handle. Over the course of two hundred years, however, doctors learned more about anatomy and physiology. In the mid-1700s, obstetrics became an important part of a doctor's medical training. In large cities, medical students and midwives learned at recently established maternity clinics and wards how to deliver the infants of poor and unmarried mothers and those whose deliveries were not expected to be straightforward.

The women who delivered their infants in the maternity wards of hospitals, however, suffered a horrendously high death rate. Nearly one in every four died of **childbed fever**. The medical students who attended them used to go from dissecting dead bodies to delivering infants, carrying on their unwashed hands the germs that caused this disease. After a Viennese physician, Ignaz Semmelweis, recognized the problem in the early 1840s and introduced the practice of hand washing before attending a laboring woman, the rate of childbed fever fell. Around this time as well, doctors first began using **anesthesia** for their surgical and obstetrical patients. Chloroform was favored by

STAGES OF CHILDBIRTH

The first stage of labor

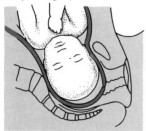 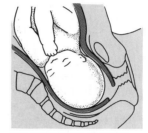 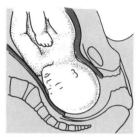

In early labor, where effacement, or thinning, has occurred and the cervix is starting to dilate.

The continuation of dilation of the cervix.

Approaching full dilation of the cervix.

The second stage of labor

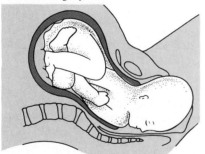 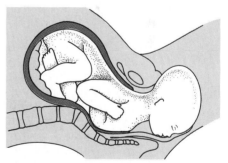

Face down, the baby's head is pressed against the perineum, which gradually stretches, widening the vaginal opening.

The baby's skull extends as it sweeps up over the perineum. The top of the skull and then the brow emerge first.

*Figure 4.9 **The first stage of childbirth begins with effacement and continues to the full dilation of the cervix. During the second stage of labor, the fetus pushes through the cervix and vagina and is born.***

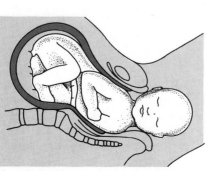 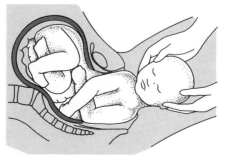

Once the head is born, the shoulders rotate in the pelvis, turning the head to left or right.

The top shoulder is born first, after which the rest of the body slides out easily.

James Young Simpson, a Scottish physician, for dulling pain. Women began asking for something to reduce their pain during childbirth, but clergymen said that anesthesia interfered with God's wish that, after the expulsion from the Garden of Eden, women bear children in sorrow (Genesis 3:16). This argument lost power in 1853 when Queen Victoria of England gratefully bore her eighth child under chloroform.

By the end of World War I, women giving birth in hospitals were routinely afforded the benefits of cleanliness, the sterilization of gowns and instruments, and optional anesthesia. By that time, doctors also knew how to transfuse blood. Hospital births came to seem safer and less painful than home births. Nearly all mothers were given general anesthesia. Nearly all fathers were banished to waiting rooms.

Around this time, an English obstetrician, Grantly Dick-Read, began to wonder whether a laboring woman's feelings of fear and helplessness might not intensify her tension and pain during childbirth. In his *Childbirth Without Pain*, Dick-Read (1933) suggested that a woman who was made less fearful would feel less pain as well. His prescription for **natural childbirth** was made up of a set of facts about labor and delivery plus a set of exercises to strengthen muscles, enhance relaxation, and control breathing. Dick-Read's idea was that although women in labor might still need small doses of painkillers, their informed and practiced behavior during labor would help them minimize pain and the need for drugs to control it. Some women took advantage of Dick-Read's suggestions, but natural childbirth did not grow really popular until another obstetrician discovered its possibilities.

Fernand Lamaze, a French doctor, visited Leningrad in 1951 and saw unmedicated women going through labor with an entirely different approach from that of the French women he was used to. Pregnant women in Russia, he discovered, learned to concentrate on their breathing and muscle tension so that they worked with rather than against the natural contractions of labor. Lamaze imported the method to France. There he trained people to coach laboring women so they could regulate their breathing, relax, and concentrate on the work to be done. Soon the method was imported to the United States. Here, in the six weekly classes that begin in the mother's seventh month of pregnancy, the husband (or another relative or friend) is trained to coach and monitor the woman and to support her physically and emotionally during childbirth. Now every year in this country, over 500,000 couples take a Lamaze training course, usually taught by a trained nurse or physiotherapist. A recent survey of 400 hospitals throughout the country showed that Lamaze preparation was widespread (Wideman and Singer, 1984). Virtually all the hospitals allowed fathers into labor and delivery rooms, and almost all obstetricians recommended Lamaze training to their patients. In over 70 percent of the hospitals, more than half of the women—from all regions, cities, income levels, and ethnic backgrounds—had Lamaze preparation. The numbers increase every year. Some hospitals have converted space into homelike birthing rooms, where unmedicated women can labor, deliver, and recover in the same place, and where they and their labor partner have a degree of comfort and privacy.

How effective is Lamaze training? In one study comparing women who had taken Lamaze classes and women who had medicated deliveries without this preparation, the researchers found that although the women did not differ significantly in their levels of anxiety, those who had taken the course felt more positively about their pregnancies, needed less pain medication, remembered their labors as less painful, and felt better about themselves (Tanzer and Block, 1976). All the women who had experienced childbirth as rapturous or ecstatic were in the natural childbirth group.

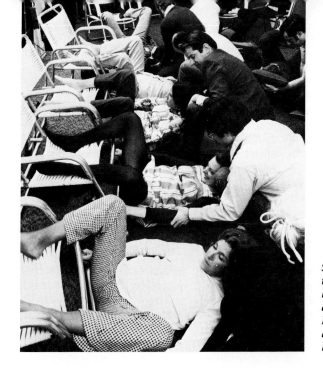

Some research suggests that training in the Lamaze method leads to fewer birth defects and complications. In this Lamaze class pregnant women and their partners practice for labor and delivery.

Another, larger study compared 500 pregnant women trained in the Lamaze method with 500 women not so trained (Hughey, McElin, and Young, 1978). Members of the two groups were matched according to age, race, number of previous pregnancies, and level of education. Women who had taken Lamaze classes had one-third the number of cases of toxemia, one-half the number of premature deliveries, and one-fourth the number of surgical deliveries. Their babies were less likely to have fetal distress and more likely to survive. It was not only the Lamaze training that made the difference between the two groups, of course, because the Lamaze-trained group was self-selected and probably had other psychological and physical advantages over the other group that the researchers could not control for. The study also did not establish precisely what about the Lamaze method worked so well— information about childbirth, breathing exercises, the presence of a supportive coach, or some other component. A more recent study has shown that women who felt that they were in control of their labor coped better with childbirth than those who accepted pain medication (Entwisle and Doering, 1981). Control, it seems, is more important than relief from pain in helping women to cope with the physical and psychological stresses of childbirth. In another study, women accompanied by a supportive partner during labor and delivery experienced fewer problems in childbirth, labored for less time, were more alert after delivery, and interacted more with their newborns than mothers without such support (Sosa, Kennell, Klaus, Robertson, and Urrutia, 1980). The fathers, too, may benefit from their involvement. For many fathers, witnessing their child's birth is a ''peak experience,'' as it is for many mothers. Said one father:

> All of the Lamaze classes, all of the reading I did, all of the talking to other fathers didn't prepare me for the world-altering magnificence of my son's birth. I cried, my wife cried, the baby cried—even the obstetrician cried for joy. I swear, it felt as if the air pressure somehow changed at that moment, and it's never been the same since. Before Sam was born, I was always ambivalent about everything and everyone. That changed the minute he was born.

The most recent innovation in delivery procedures comes from another French obstetrician, Frederick Leboyer. Leboyer felt that the conventional

135

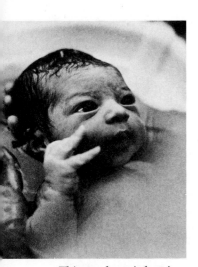

This newborn infant is being gently lowered into a warm bath similar to the amniotic waters he has just left. French obstetrician Frederick Leboyer recommended this practice to ease the infant's transition from womb to room.

methods of delivery were unnecessarily harsh and violent for the infant. He decided to do away with the bright lights, the clanking instruments, and the quick cut of the umbilical cord, to stop dangling infants upside down and slapping them on the buttocks right after birth. In Leboyer's method of **gentle birth**, the transition from soft, warm, dimly lit, muffled womb is eased with soft lights, quiet voices, a warm room, and gentle handling. Immediately after birth, the newborn is placed on the mother's abdomen and its back gently massaged. In this way, amniotic fluid is expelled from the windpipe. After a few little cries, the baby breathes naturally, and only after the umbilical cord stops pulsing is it cut. The baby is then gently raised upright and carried to a warm bath and, from there, to a warm diaper. Leboyer (1975) found that infants handled with such gentleness and respect radiated contentment.

Does the Leboyer method really make a difference? Systematic studies are scant. One French investigator (Rapoport in Salter, 1978), found that 120 8-month to 4-year-olds delivered by the Leboyer method were free of sleeping and emotional problems, had highly developed interests in people and things, and were socially well adapted. Their scores on a test of infant adaptiveness were above average. But the study lacked an all-important control group of infants delivered in the usual way. In a study in which a group of 17 infants delivered by traditional hospital methods was compared with 20 delivered by the Leboyer method, it was found that the infants differed significantly in their first 15 minutes (Oliver and Oliver, 1978). The traditionally delivered group showed more physical tension, blinking, sucking, trembling, and shuddering. The Leboyer-delivered infants were more relaxed, opened their eyes more, and made more soft sounds. In their baths, they relaxed their muscles, opened their eyes, moved around, and did not cry. But did these effects last beyond the period soon after birth? One investigator who followed newborns delivered by the Leboyer method for their first three months found that the effects were relatively short-lived (Sorrells-Jones, 1983).

Medication during childbirth

On the issue of medication for pain during childbirth, pregnant women seem to divide themselves into two camps. Said two women from the same Lamaze class:

> I intend to get through the whole delivery without a drop of medication. I'll resist anyone who tells me otherwise. I want to experience the whole event, and I want my baby to, too.

> Half jokingly, I asked my obstetrician if I could have an epidural from my first trimester on. If the pain gets bad, I'll be glad for some relief. I hate pain.

Of all the women who give birth in hospitals in the United States, it is estimated that 95 percent accept some form of pain medication (Brackbill, 1979). This is a mixed blessing. Although these drugs relieve the mother's pain, they also pass into the fetus's bloodstream and reduce its oxygen supply. In consequence, some infants are born too weak to breathe on their own and may suffer from a lack of oxygen to their brain. Drugs can also depress the newborn's attentiveness and vigor of sucking (Brazelton, 1961). Even a local, **epidural anesthesia**, which numbs the mother between chest and knees, slows the newborn's motor abilities somewhat, especially the ability to control the head when the infant is pulled into a sitting position (Scanlon, Brown, Weiss, and Alper, 1974). More severe effects are observed when the mother is given more and stronger drugs (Lester, Als, and Brazelton, 1982).

research focus

Gentle birth

Leboyer's gentle birth method is supposed to benefit babies in many ways. Advocates believe that gentle birth makes babies more quietly alert, socially responsive, and less irritable than other babies, and that it improves mothers' reactions to their babies and their experience of childbirth in general. Jean Sorrells-Jones, (1983), at the University of Chicago, decided to test these beliefs. She chose a group of 40 mothers and babies and randomly assigned half to a Leboyer gentle birth group and half to a control group that experienced the usual hospital delivery. Most of the mothers were poor, black, and single. None had participated in prepared childbirth training, none received anesthesia, and all the babies were healthy firstborns. The mothers were told late in labor which type of delivery they would receive; as it turned out, they were so thoroughly engaged in laboring that none perceived anything unusual about her delivery. None had heard about the philosophy of gentle birth beforehand. The hypothesis that mothers who experienced gentle birth would describe their labor and delivery more positively than the mothers in the control group was not borne out.

Sorrells-Jones collected six separate sets of data from the two groups of mothers and babies. In the delivery room, she observed for 17 minutes after each birth. Then she assessed each baby two and three days after birth for reflexes and behavior. She interviewed each mother two and three days after delivery for her reactions to her experience and for her perceptions of her baby. She observed each mother feeding her baby between two and three days after delivery. At six weeks, psychologists who did not know to which group any baby belonged administered tests of infant development.

The results showed that newborns in the gentle birth group did, as advocates claimed, have more periods of quiet alertness than the other babies. But, contrary to their claims, the gentle birth babies were not less irritable or more sociable. Mothers of the gentle birth group did not perceive their babies more positively than the other mothers, and they did not engage in more looking or touching with their babies. At 6 and 12 weeks, the babies did not differ appreciably on tests of intellectual and motor development. Sorrells-Jones concluded that any differences between the two groups did not last beyond the period immediately following delivery. Of course, as she said, any method of childbirth that produces quiet and alert babies is worthy of support.

Not all these effects disappear right away. Before birth, the placenta can cleanse the fetus's system of some drugs. But when the umbilical cord is cut, the level of a drug in the newborn's bloodstream is 70 percent that of the mother, and as we have seen, the newborn's internal organs are inefficient at cleansing its system of drugs. For at least four weeks after birth, newborns of medicated mothers tend to see somewhat more poorly and to lag slightly behind newborns of unmedicated mothers in muscular and neural development (Brackbill, 1979).

How might these effects of medication affect the course of an infant's development? Understandably, this is a question to which parents and obstetricians would very much like the answer. But the answer is not easy to come by. Because so many different factors affect the newborn's progress, it is difficult for investigators to isolate specific causes of long lasting effects. But newborns whose mothers have been heavily medicated during childbirth generally interact differently with their mothers and other people from newborns whose mothers have not been medicated. In one study, for example, newborns whose mothers had been more heavily medicated during childbirth opened their eyes significantly less while they were nursing and responded less to sounds than newborns of less medicated or unmedicated mothers (Brown et al., 1975). If these early behaviors harden into patterns of interaction, the relationship between infant and parents may suffer.

> When Jason was born, he did not breathe right away because of the anesthesia I had been given a few minutes before. Someone was supposed to be waiting right there with a stimulant for the baby just in case he wasn't breathing. But no one was there, and it took a minute or more until they finally got him breathing. He was sluggish and hard to get started sucking. He'd drop off to sleep and then wake up hungry in just a little while. It was hard to get in tune with his needs. He was also very irritable.

Anesthesia also increases the risks for the mother. Five percent of the women who die during childbirth die from anesthesia, and another 5 percent die from the complications it creates (Hellman and Pritchard, 1971). Nevertheless, fewer than 20 in every 100,000 women die from giving birth, and recent improvements in drugs mean that more mothers and babies will emerge safely from childbirth.

Birth complications

If labor does not begin spontaneously at around 38 weeks of pregnancy, or if it does not proceed quickly and smoothly enough once it does begin, labor may be **induced** by one of several different methods. One way to induce labor is to break open the membranes that hold the fetus and placenta. This quick, painless procedure, performed through the vagina and cervix, causes uterine contractions to begin or to pick up strength. Another way to induce labor is to give the pregnant woman a drug like oxytocin, a hormone that stimulates uterine contractions. Although induction technically refers to medical intervention that begins labor, the intervention may continue so that it produces a **speeded labor**.

> My contractions had been coming irregularly for 36 hours, and the doctor was worried that I was getting too tired. She had an intravenous line started for pitocin—a drug that makes the contractions faster and harder—and things really started moving along then. They monitored the strength of the contractions so that they didn't get *too* strong. Kristy was born four hours later.

Except in certain clear-cut instances—when induction will save the life of mother or child—when and why to induce labor are matters of judgment for the obstetrician. Some obstetricians induce the majority of their patients; some induce very few. The gray area is large, and the pros and cons of induced labor always must be weighed. In favor of induction, of course, is its use to save the life of or reduce the risk of damage to mother or child. Medication can speed along the contractions and dilation of a woman and fetus who are in danger of exhaustion from a long labor. Some people also argue in favor of induction because a mother can be well rested and well prepared for birth, with her stomach empty of food. Others argue against it, noting that babies of oxytocin-induced mothers run a higher risk of jaundice, that induced labor requires more painkillers than normal labor, that more babies need special medical care and separation from their mother after an induced labor (Macfarlane, 1977).

Another birth complication that affects the course of labor and delivery is the baby's position in the uterus. Normally, the crown of the baby's skull presents first through the vagina. Shoulders, trunk, and legs follow. This position offers the baby the best chances for navigating the anatomical obstacles of the birth passage. Some babies, however, present in a **breech position**, with their buttocks first. Breech babies are in danger because they may begin to breathe when their bottom is delivered but their head remains in the uterus. In such a case, they may suffocate or contract a serious respiratory infection. In other cases, the breech baby cannot pass through the birth opening and must be delivered by a surgical procedure, **cesarean section**.

Breech babies, twins, very large babies, and those showing unusual distress during prenatal development or delivery all may require cesarean sections. But sometimes this surgery is performed because physicians want a more convenient schedule or are being cautious about the possibility of malpractice suits. The number of cesarean deliveries increased from 5 percent in 1968 to 16 percent in 1978 (Donovan, 1977; Hausknecht and Heilman, 1978). Prospective parents should ask about any unusual procedures that are suggested. Cesarean births increase risks to mothers and infants. Women take longer to recover and are less likely to survive a cesarean than a vaginal delivery (Evrard and Gold, 1977). Interaction between mothers and infants born by cesarean birth also may be less active, vigorous, and positive in the first year (Pedersen, Zaslow, Cain, and Anderson, 1981).

Premature births

> After a long bout of infertility and a very difficult pregnancy, a friend of ours had a tiny baby girl in just the sixth month of pregnancy. She weighed only 1½ pounds, and for a long time no one expected her to survive. But she turned out to be a real little fighter, and she did make it. Now she's a bouncy 2-year-old.

Babies born after pregnancies that last between 35 and 40 weeks after conception are **full-term babies**. Babies born earlier than this are called **preterm babies**. Those born later are called **postterm babies**.[1] Of all the complications of birth in this country, prematurity is the most common, affecting about 7 percent of all newborns.

Why are babies born prematurely? There are many possible reasons, and we have mentioned a number of them already. Mothers who are very young, fatigued, poorly nourished, or in poor health are likely to deliver prematurely; mothers who smoke, take drugs, have uterine problems, infections, toxemias, or who get no prenatal care are also likely to deliver prematurely. Many of the women who deliver prematurely are poor and without financial or social resources. In one-half of all cases of preterm births in this country, there is no known cause (Annis, 1978).

The number of preterm babies who survive has increased, and the severity of the problems they face has declined greatly in this century and continues to do so. Although most babies born after fewer than 26 weeks of prenatal development are too young to survive, some do make it. There are no hard and fast rules, and a preterm baby's chances depend heavily on the available medical care. Now at the best hospitals, almost all preterm babies weighing over 3½ pounds survive; 80 to 85 percent of preterm infants weigh-

---

[1]Some babies are "small for dates," that is, born at full term but underweight. They are discussed in Chapter 5.

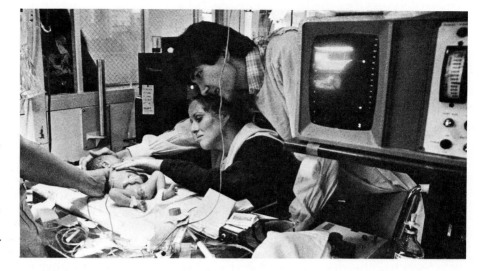

The complicated equipment that helps premature infants to survive can also be intimidating to new parents. Many hospitals try to help parents overcome their fears and, most important, begin touching and caring for their infants while they are still in intensive care.

ing between 2½ and 3½ pounds survive; and so do 50 to 60 percent of those weighing only 1½ to 2¼ pounds. In the last few years alone, the survival rate of infants weighing between 1 and 2 pounds has risen from 20 to 40 percent. About 10 percent of the babies born prematurely have serious problems, like blindness, mental retardation, neurological problems, or cerebral palsy. Another 15 percent have moderately severe problems, and 75 percent—the majority—have no serious problems, if they have good hospital care (Goldberg and DiVitto, 1983; Kopp, 1983). Their development may be somewhat delayed, however. Even calculating the age of these children from conception rather than from birth, prematurely born infants compared with full-term babies are, on the average, somewhat delayed in early motor development. This delay may be the result of the relative inactivity imposed by a bed in an intensive care nursery compared with the uterine swimming pool. As for intellectual development, 85 percent of prematurely born infants are in the normal range, but on the average their IQ scores are somewhat lower, at least during the first few years of life, than those of full-term infants (Goldberg and DiVitto, 1983).

Boys seem more vulnerable to the problems associated with prematurity than girls. One study of preterm and full-term babies, all of whom were born to poor black mothers, showed that at 13 months of age, the preterm boys scored significantly lower on tests of motor development and intelligence than preterm girls of the same birth weight, although there was no comparable difference between boys and girls born at normal weight (Braine, Heimer, Wortis, and Freedman, 1966). The slight lag that boys have in neurological development is apparently magnified into a noticeable problem by the stress of a premature birth.

In the hospital, preterm babies' physical functions are carefully charted. Their heart rates, breathing rates, blood pressure, blood sugar, and urine, among other indicators, are all monitored. Placed in sterile **incubators**, the tiny preterm babies automatically are provided with warmth, oxygen, and humidity. Pumps deliver nutrients and fluids to the babies through tubes to the stomach. Many preterm babies cannot breathe alone, because their lungs are too immature to produce surfactin, a substance necessary for the lungs to use oxygen. They are therefore placed on ventilators. In some hospitals also, doctors are testing artificial surfactant, made from animal tissue, that can be sprayed into babies' lungs at birth.

The hospital incubators in which premature babies are placed are descendants of those designed in Paris early in this century and publicized at fairs and expositions here and abroad. (At the 1932 Chicago World's Fair, these "child hatcheries" attracted more paying customers than any exhibit except Sally Rand, the fan dancer!) The first American hospital to care for preterm infants was opened in Chicago in 1923. Doctors then believed that overfeeding would kill these little babies and prescribed a regimen of virtual starvation:

13th hour: 1 teaspoon boiled water

15th hour: 1½ teaspoons boiled water

17th hour: 1 teaspoon breast milk

19th hour: 2 teaspoons water

21st hour: 1½ teaspoons milk

23rd hour: 2½ teaspoons water

Quite obviously, this regimen does not meet the infant's nutritional needs, and it was soon modified. The next 40 years saw few other changes in the treatment of preterm infants. In the 1960s, however, better equipment for detecting physical problems, tubes for feeding, new drugs, new surgical techniques, and finer needles for injections were developed. Regional hospitals came to specialize in neonatal intensive care for preterm infants. Neonatologists refined their methods. They learned that an excess of oxygen given to preterm babies on ventilators, for example, causes blindness. Unfortunately, many preterm babies still go blind, and neonatologists are searching for other causes—such as bright lights—and other cures—such as freezing the edges of the **retina**, that part of the eye that changes light into nerve signals to the brain (Kolata, 1986).

Today neonatologists are concerned not only with the physical survival of the preterm infant, but also with the quality of later development. They are concerned that preterm babies not develop problems from their treatment in the intensive care nursery. There, the tiny, scrawny babies lie attached to tubes and wires in their incubators. Without fat beneath the skin, they do not look like the plump, cute creatures to which parents or nurses are accustomed. Their heads may be covered with cotton stocking caps to conserve heat; their eyes may be blindfolded. Intimidating equipment monitors heart rate, respiration, temperature, blood gases, and helps the baby to breathe, feed, and fight infection or jaundice. The intensive care unit is noisy: 60 to 80 decibels (which is louder than a typical business office). Fluorescent lights burn day and night. The babies are handled often for tests and medical care, but most of these contacts are brief and unpleasant for the baby. It is hard for parents to feel at home in such a stressful place, even if they live nearby. Many live far away. All these factors mean that the hospitalized preterm infant rarely gets the same kind of loving care that the normal term infant does.

Now that people who work in hospitals know about these problems, they have begun to make intensive care nurseries more human. When this happens, premature infants gain weight faster and do better on tests of motor and visual responses to stimulation (Goldberg and DiVitto, 1983). It has been shown to benefit babies if the hospital nursery is made more like the womb— with tape-recordings of mothers' heartbeats, a rocking hammock lined with warm, soft sheepskin, or a waterbed—or more like home, with lots of loving handling and bright, attractive mobiles over the incubators. In one recent study, for example, massaging and moving premature babies' arms and legs for 45 minutes a day while they were in the intensive care unit resulted in a 47 percent greater weight gain, significantly more time awake and active, and more mature behavior (Scafidi et al., 1986). In fact, the infants who were given the treatment could leave the hospital six days earlier than those who were not. Another approach to making the intensive care unit more like home is to

focus   *Bears for babies*

The central nervous system of babies born prematurely is too immature to regulate their breathing reliably, and so nurses and doctors in newborn intensive care nurseries have looked for artificial ways to regulate these babies' breathing. Most recently, Evelyn Thoman, a Connecticut psychologist, has invented a "breathing" bear (Turkington, 1984). The blue plush bear is placed in the baby's crib and connected to a pump outside of the crib that makes it "breathe" regularly and rhythmically. The tempo at which the bear is set to breathe is patterned after the baby's own rate of breathing during sleep. Many people assume that these tiny babies are passive, but they are actually more mobile than full-term babies. They can get around, especially when they are on their tummies or sides. They can cuddle against the bear, and they do. When the baby finds the bear and cuddles against it, the baby soon begins to breathe in time with the bear's breathing. In this way, the baby's breathing is stabilized. When the baby is breathing regularly, it is likely to sleep regularly and to cry less—benefits not only for the baby but for the nursery as well.

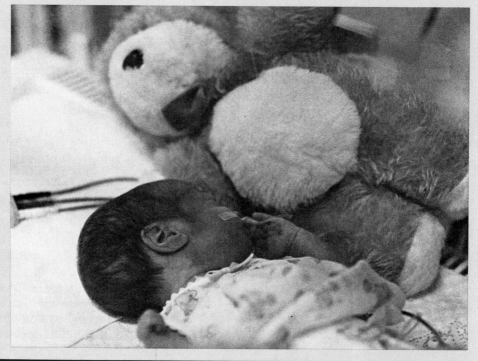

A mechanical "breathing" bear is set to breathe in the tempo of the sleeping infant. Once in contact with the regularly breathing bear, the infant begins to breathe more regularly too.

get parents more involved with their babies. When parents take part in discussion groups with other parents of premature babies, they visit more, feel more comfortable, and better understand the problems that their tiny preterm babies face.

Now that many preterm babies survive, some of them with defects, we face the difficult ethical issue of how to weigh the *value* of life against the *quality* of life. Who is to decide, and how is the decision to be made about what treatment, if any, is best for preterm babies? In many cases, doctors do not know whether a preterm baby who survives will be defective. Yet doctors do exert control over preterm babies' chances of survival when they put them on respirators, perform surgery, and administer other medical procedures—or they do not. The complexities of this ethical issue came to a head over the last few years in several "Baby Doe" cases, when infants born with severe defects were allowed by their parents and doctors to die. When these cases became known to the public, the parents and doctors involved were sued. As a result, the federal government instituted regulations specifying that all infants must be treated, regardless of the doctors' prognosis and the parents' wishes, and regardless, too, of the infant's probable quality of life. Only infants who were in irreversible comas or terminally ill, the regulation stated, should be allowed to die. Most recently, in June 1986, the Supreme Court of the United States struck down these federal regulations that imposed treatment without parents' consent. Today we are left to grapple with difficult ethical issues—even as we rejoice over the increasing number of lives that are saved.

Summary

1. During sexual intercourse around the time of ovulation, sperm from the man enter the woman's vagina, swim into the uterus and up the fallopian tubes, where one penetrates the ovum and merges its genetic material with the ovum's.

2. Infertility affects about 15 percent of the couples trying to have children. Many of them can be helped to have children through surgery, drugs, artificial insemination, in vitro fertilization, ovum transfer, or surrogate mothering. About 40 percent of the cases of infertility are attributed to the man, particularly to the quantity or quality of the sperm. About 60 percent are attributed to the woman, particularly to a failure to ovulate or blocked or damaged fallopian tubes.

3. Conception marks the beginning of pregnancy and prenatal development; birth marks its end. In the earliest stage of prenatal development, the germinal stage, the fertilized egg divides into cells, which form a sphere, and implants itself in the lining of the uterus. In the embryonic stage, from 2 weeks to 2 months after conception, organ systems form. In the fetal stage, which lasts from 2 months until birth, the organs grow and physical functions develop.

4. Pregnancy brings changes and adjustments to both expectant parents. Both may feel emotional and physical strains. A pregnant woman proceeds through a succession of social, physical, and psychological adjustments in preparation for childbirth and motherhood.

5. The development of the fetus is affected by the mother's emotional state, health, diet, age, number of previous pregnancies, and exposure to drugs, radiation, and other environmental hazards.

6. Environmental substances affect prenatal development by causing genes to mutate, by interfering with normal cell division, or by delaying or distorting growth. These effects range from mild to lethal, their severity depending on the timing and dosage of the exposure and the constitution of the individual fetus.

7. Prenatal development is protected by a self-righting tendency, which means that it proceeds normally except under the most adverse conditions. It also is protected by a self-cleansing tendency, which means that severely abnormal embryos and fetuses are miscarried.

8. At some time around the end of the ninth month of pregnancy, labor begins. In the first stage, strong contractions of the uterine muscles thin and open the cervix. In the second stage, the baby is pushed out of the uterus, usually head first. In the third stage, uterine contractions deliver the afterbirth—placenta and membranes. Labor may be induced or speeded up if it does not begin on its own or its pace seems, to a doctor, too slow for the safety of mother or child.

9. Attitudes toward childbirth vary from one culture and one historical era to another. Today in our culture, many people favor natural births during which the mother actively participates by controlling her breathing and relaxing. In many such births, the father or another labor coach is present at the delivery. Some people also favor ''gentle birth'' into a warm, dimly lit room, with calm procedures designed to relax infant and parents. The effects of gentle births may not last beyond a few hours. But the amount and type of medication that women are given during childbirth does affect their newborns.

10. Births are complicated when labor is late in starting or lasts longer than average, when the baby's position in the uterus is unusual, or when the mother's pelvis is too narrow for the baby to pass through. In these cases, the doctor may perform a surgical cesarean section.

11. The most common birth complication is prematurity. Premature birth is associated with conditions that are especially common among poor women. Most preterm babies can be saved with good hospital care, and the majority suffer no serious permanent handicaps, although their development may be somewhat delayed. In efforts to reduce these delays, hospital staff have tried to humanize the stressful, noisy atmosphere of the intensive care nurseries where preterm babies are cared for.

Key terms

ovulate
oocyte
fallopian tube
uterus
spermatozoa
cervix
infertility
pelvic inflammatory disease (PID)
chlamydia
endometriosis
artificial insemination
alternative reproduction
in vitro fertilization
test-tube baby
laparoscopy
surrogate mothering
ovum transfer
germinal stage
embryonic stage
fetal stage
morula
totipotent

blastula
blastocyst
chorion
amnion
placenta
villi
implant
embryo
ectoderm
primitive streak
endoderm
mesoderm
umbilical cord
cephalocaudal
proximodistal
ossification
quickening
lanugo
vernix
neonatology
fetology
hydrocephaly

alveoli
oxytocin
couvade
toxemia
pyloric stenosis
diabetes
Rh incompatibilty
rubella
achondroplasia
parity
teratology
teratogen
mutation
phocomelia
diethylstilbestrol (DES)
fetal alcohol syndrome
microcephaly
cesarean section
self-righting tendency
labor
crowning
episiotomy

afterbirth
childbed fever
anesthesia
natural childbirth
gentle birth

epidural anesthesia
induced labor
speeded labor
breech position
full-term babies

preterm babies
postterm babies
incubator
retina

Suggested readings

ANNIS, LINDA F. *The Child before Birth*. Ithaca, N.Y.: Cornell University Press, 1978. A thorough and clearly written presentation of the prenatal physical development of the child, with explanations of Rh disease and other possible prenatal complications.

COREA, GENA. *The Mother Machine*. New York: Harper and Row, 1986. A powerful examination of the damaging and frightening implications of new reproductive technologies—artificial insemination, ovum transfer, in vitro fertilization, surrogate mothering, and sex determination.

GOLDBERG, SUSAN, and DiVITTO, BARBARA A. *Born Too Soon: Preterm Birth and Early Development*. San Francisco: W. H. Freeman, 1983. An up-to-date consideration of significant aspects of preterm infants' development, including methods of caring for them and aiding their development.

GUTTMACHER, ALAN. *Pregnancy, Birth and Family Planning*. New York: Signet, 1984. Written for expectant parents—facts and reassurance from a medical authority.

MACFARLANE, AIDAN. *The Psychology of Childbirth*. Cambridge, MA: Harvard University Press, 1977. A warm and revealing account of the feelings of expectant parents before and during childbirth.

NILSSON, LENNART. A *Child Is Born: the Drama of Life before Birth*, with text by A. Ingelman-Sundberg and C. Wirsen. New York: Dell, 1981. Remarkable photographs taken in the womb between conception and birth.

SHAPIRO, HOWARD. *The Pregnancy Book for Today's Woman*. New York: Consumers Union, 1984. Sound advice about nutrition, drugs, and hazards to the expectant mother.

PART THREE

Infancy

chapter five

Physical and perceptual development

An infant's first month is an exciting, exhausting, exhilarating time. Contrary to parents' expectations—fed on baby food advertisements—their tiny infant is not exactly the clear-eyed, rosy-cheeked, smiling moppet that they fantasized about during pregnancy. No, the real infant squawks, and snores, and sneezes. When they lay the baby gently in the crib for a quiet nap, all they hear from their pip-squeak is a barrage of wheezes and wails. A helpless creature who can't even support its own head somehow has the entire household at attention. The eyes that parents want to gaze into are usually shut tight in sleep or squinting from crying spells, and when they do open, the infant seems to look everywhere but *at* the poor parents. Smiles come and go for no reason that anyone can decipher. But when they do come, they are so thoroughly enchanting that Mother and Dad will work for *days* just to get another one.

This fascinating, puzzling, habit-forming infant is also exceptionally vulnerable in this first month of life. More people die in the first month of life than at any other time before old age. Newborns who weigh at least five pounds and have developed for at least 28 weeks (out of the normal full-term 38) in their mother's uterus have the best chances of surviving this risky first month. Newborn girls have better chances of surviving than newborn boys, and newborn blacks have better chances of survival than newborn whites of comparable weight and gestational age. They are probably less vulnerable to environmental assaults because physiologically they are more mature.

The stress to the newborn of emerging from the warm and watery protection of the uterus is so great that doctors and nurses who attend the birth use a quick and simple test to judge the baby's condition. The **Apgar test**, developed by Dr. Virginia Apgar in 1953, is used in delivery rooms all over the United States and in other countries. At one minute and again at five minutes after birth, the newborn is scored on heart rate, respiration, muscle tone, reflex irritability, and color (see Table 5.1). For each category, the newborn receives a 0, 1, or 2. The healthiest babies get a total score of between 7 and 10 points. These babies have hearts beating strongly over 100 times a minute, lusty cries, firm muscle tone, and skin tinged pink rather than ashen. Tickled on the soles of their feet, they quickly cry, cough, or sneeze. About 90 percent of the babies born in the United States pass their first test, the Apgar, with flying colors (a 7 or better).

I had heard of the Apgar, but I was still surprised when the delivery room nurse told us that Natalie had a 9 at one minute and a 10 at five

Table 5.1
Baby's first test: the Apgar scoring system

Sign	Score		
	0	1	2
Heart rate	Absent	Slow (<100)	>100
Respiratory effort	Absent	Weak cry; hyper-ventilation	Good; strong cry
Muscle tone	Limp	Some flexion of extremities	Good flexion
Reflex irritability (response to skin stimulation of feet)	No response	Grimace	Coughing, sneezing, crying
Color	Entire body blue or pale	Body pink, extremities blue	Entire body pink

minutes. Naturally, I immediately wanted to know why she hadn't gotten a 10 the first time. Her hands and feet were bluish, as it turned out.

Those who score 4 or below need immediate medical attention if they are to survive.

Jason didn't breathe right away after he was born, probably because I had been given some Demerol only a few minutes before that. He was limp and blue. The doctor and nurses got very quiet and intense as they tried to start him breathing. I heard the nurse murmur, ''Still not breathing'' what seemed hours later but was only a minute or two. They worked on him, and he sort of spluttered and fussed. Then his whole body transformed from a pasty gray to a healthy pink. His first Apgar was a 3, but his second was a 7.

Tasks for the newborn

With birth, an infant moves from one kind of environment—the dim, warm, protected liquid of the uterus, where breathing and feeding are automatic—into a radically different environment—the bright, noisy, cool, and airy world, where for the first time the infant must breathe and feed on his or her own. Within moments of birth, each newborn must abandon one system of respiration—the placenta—and make functional another—the lungs. Until that sudden indrawing of air into the lungs occurs, the baby's life is in doubt. If the baby is to live, it must begin breathing air within minutes after emerging from the birth canal. That first breath will come—to pinken the infant's body and to thrill the parents who themselves wait with bated breath—only after mucus and amniotic fluid have cleared the lungs. Some of the fluid is squeezed out through the infant's mouth and nose by pressure in the birth canal during birth itself. Some escapes by gravity if the infant is held upside down. Some may be suctioned by a waiting nurse. Some evaporates or is absorbed into the infant's bloodstream. Once into breathable air, and even before the umbilical cord is clamped, the newborn begins to snort, snuffle and sneeze, trying to clear the air passages and to inflate the thousands of air sacs in the lungs.

As the umbilical cord is exposed to the cool air, to sponging, and to handling, it ceases pulsing and constricts. The doctor clamps and cuts it, and the flow of blood from the placenta stops. The infant's own circulatory system now must function on its own. Blood flow in the infant's heart at this point actually changes directions. As blood begins to flow for the first time to the infant's lungs, the pressure in the chambers of the heart alters. Pressure increases in the left atrium and closes a valve. Now the infant's blood begins to flow through the heart from left to right rather than from right to left, as it had before birth. This critical change may plunge the infant's blood pressure downward and race the heartbeat to 140 counts a minute. For even the healthiest of infants, it may take ten days for blood pressure to stabilize.

After nine months in the tropical heat of the uterus—98.6 degrees Fahrenheit—the newborn also must adjust to the cooler, changeable temperatures of the outside world. Most newborns have only a thin layer of fat under their delicate skin, and their temperatures may drop as much as 5 degrees right after birth.

As soon as Sam was born, the nurse laid him on my stomach, dressed in a little cotton cap to conserve his body heat. A while later, the nurse put him under red warming lights. Finally, when he was wheeled into my room on the maternity ward, he was swaddled in several cotton blankets and sleeping peacefully inside what looked like a toaster oven! Alarmed, I asked what was wrong. The nurse calmly told me that Sam was having trouble regulating his temperature and that the warmer would help him. By the next day, he was out of the toaster and doing fine on his own.

Most infants' temperatures stabilize within eight hours or so after birth.

Not only must newborns breathe and warm themselves, but they must also begin drinking, digesting, and excreting. Healthy newborns can suck and swallow, taking in an ounce or two of liquid every two hours or so during their first days. Their bowels first excrete a tarry waste left over from fluid and cells swallowed in the uterus. Soon their stomachs and intestines begin to secrete the substances necessary for digesting nutrients.

With birth, the newborn's protection from germs in the sterile uterus comes to an end. Now the infant's vulnerable system is assaulted by all the microorganisms—harmless and harmful alike—that live in our world—in Father's sneezes, on Grandma's hands, in an unsterilized bottle of formula, or hanging around the diaper pail. Many newborns seem to lose ground for a time, as their unpracticed immune systems fight to create antibodies to a flood of bacteria and viruses. Although newborns receive immunities to some diseases from their mothers before birth and after, through the mother's breast milk, their immature immune systems must nonetheless take on a host of invaders.

Risks to infants

Although newborns are most vulnerable during the first month, the whole first year poses special risks. Prematurity, slow growth before birth, disease after birth, respiratory problems, malnutrition, poor medical care, poverty, neglect, even a mother's poor health all take their toll on infants during the vulnerable first year. In general, the mortality rate for black infants is twice as high as it is for white infants in the first year of life, probably because of these factors. In the United States, the survival rate for infants of all races has been increasing (Table 5.2). But it is still lower than the rate in many other nations that have more widely available health services.

Low birth weight

Look at a row of new babies in their hospital cribs, and you will see a varied assortment of sizes, shapes, weights, and degrees of physical maturity. One little peanut may weigh as little as 5½ pounds. The string bean in the next crib weighs 7 pounds stretched out to a long 22 inches. Next door is a hefty 10 pounder who looks to the unpracticed eye more like 3 *months* old than 3 days. The average newborn weighs a few ounces over 7 pounds and extends 20 inches from head to heel. Some variation in birth weight is normal. But at the extremes—newborns who weigh under 6 pounds or over 10 pounds—there can be problems.

As we saw in Chapter 4, prematurity is a common cause of dangerously low birth weight. But some full-term babies also are underweight. These babies are called **small for gestational age** or **small for dates**. The various reasons they are small—mothers' smoking, poor nutrition, poor prenatal care, and so forth—also were discussed in Chapter 4. Like premies, these babies are vulnerable to a range of risks. At one extreme, the risks are deadly: stillbirth or death soon after birth. Serious but not deadly risks include cerebral palsy, epilepsy, and brain damage of other sorts. Many small-for-dates babies,

Table 5.2
Infant mortality rates in developed countries[a]

Country	1979	1980	1981	1982	1983
Finland, Japan	7.8	7.6	6.8	6.5	6.3
Sweden	7.5	6.9	6.9	6.8	7.0
Denmark	8.8	8.4	7.9	8.2	8.0
Netherlands	8.7	8.6	8.3	8.3	8.4
Canada, France	10.5	10.3	9.6	9.2	9.0
Australia	11.4	10.7	10.0	10.3	10.0
England	12.9	12.1	11.1	11.0	10.2
Singapore	13.2	11.7	10.7	10.7	10.5
United States	12.9	12.6	11.8	11.3	10.9[b]
Belgium	11.2	11.0	11.6	11.7	11.3
Greece	18.7	17.9	16.3	14.3	14.0
Puerto Rico, Cuba	19.6	19.3	18.6	18.0	16.3
Hungary, Poland	23.0	22.2	20.8	20.0	19.1
Yugoslavia	32.7	31.4	30.7	29.9	31.7

[a]Figures show rate of deaths of infants under 1 year per 1000 live births.

[b]The 1984 rate for the United States was 10.5.

SOURCE: *Demographic Yearbook.* New York: United Nations, 1983.

especially if they were under 3½ pounds, have lower than average intelligence (Wiener, 1962; Wilson, 1985). Others have normal IQs but develop minor or temporary problems in school or in learning.

Low birth weight rarely acts in isolation. Its harmful effects intensify when it combines with other risks to development. Such risks may be biological, such as poor central nervous system functioning; or they may be environmental, such as oxygen starvation during birth, crowded, chaotic living conditions, unresponsive or uninvolved parents, unsafe or unstimulating play spaces. When small-for-dates babies are born into families with these problems, they are likely to perform increasingly poorly on IQ tests as they get older, but the performance of those born into families with more educational and economic resources improves with age (Wilson, 1985).

The effects of low birth weight combined with biological and environmental risks were demonstrated in a study conducted by a team of researchers in London (Harvey, Prince, Bunton, Parkinson, and Campbell, 1982; Parkinson, Wallis, and Harvey, 1981). One index of biological risk that the researchers used was a smaller than normal fetal skull size (skull size giving some indication of fetal brain development). Low birth weight children whose skull growth had slowed early in prenatal development (before 26 weeks), the researchers found, had delayed development and problems in balancing and coordinating their movements. They scored significantly lower than children of normal birth weight on tests of reading, language, reasoning, handwriting, number, perception, motor, and memory. Teachers were likely to say that these children often were absent from school and had trouble communicating with peers and teachers and doing their schoolwork. Low-birth-weight infants whose skull size had been normal until late in prenatal development did not generally exhibit these problems. A second biological factor related to how low-birth-weight babies developed was sex. Recall that boys are less likely than girls to survive the first month because they are more vulnerable to environmental assaults. Low-birth-weight infants are particularly vulnerable, and in this study low-birth-weight boys had more severe learning problems than low-birth-weight girls. The index of environmental risk used in the study was socioeconomic status (SES). Low-birth-weight children from families with low SES scored significantly lower on the tests than low-birth-weight babies from families with high SES. Low SES, with its associated poorer nutrition and stimulation, apparently aggravated the risks for low-birth-weight infants. A number of girls from the low-birth-weight, small-skull group whose families were of high SES, in contrast, were doing quite well at school. These findings suggest that sex and social class may override the effects of low birth weight. In sum, it is clear that low birth weight puts an infant at risk for serious problems, but just how serious those problems turn out to be depends on other conditions—both biological and environmental. Major efforts are now underway in this country to develop programs that will provide the environmental support and stimulation that will help low-birth-weight infants develop normally.

Sudden infant death syndrome (SIDS)

Some babies are born with vulnerabilities that are not immediately obvious but have tragic consequences. In the United States, some 5,000 to 10,000 babies die suddenly and unexpectedly each year after suffering few, if any, symptoms. These babies go to sleep, apparently well, and never wake up. They are victims of **sudden infant death syndrome (SIDS)**, or crib death—every new parent's nightmare. Found mostly in 2- to 6-month olds, SIDS may strike as early as at two weeks but rarely occurs after one year. SIDS is the major cause of infant death after the first month. Many researchers have struggled to identify the causes and correlates of SIDS (Duffty and Bryan, 1982; Haddad, Walsh, Leistner, Grodin, and Mellins, 1981; Kahn and Blum, 1982; Lipsitt, McCullagh, Reilly, Smith, and Sturner, 1981; see Table 5.3). To summarize their results: SIDS peaks in the winter and spring (Figure 5.1) and, in about 60 percent of cases, afflicts infants who have mild upper respiratory infections, especially those who have been given phenothiazine for their colds. SIDS is associated with low Apgar scores, low birth weight, premature birth, and jaundice soon after birth. Many mothers of SIDS infants have suffered anemia or flu during their pregnancies, have smoked, have had little prenatal care, or have experienced a rapid second stage of labor. They are likely to be young and poor. Most SIDS infants have grown slowly after birth

Table 5.3
The SIDS scenario

Mother is likely to be:	poor
	adolescent
	smoker
	anemic during pregnancy
Baby is likely to be:	premature
	underweight
	male
	poor sleeper
	bottle-fed
	suffering from a cold and a stuffy nose
Time is likely to be:	winter or spring
Place is likely to be:	at high altitude
Problem is likely to be:	defective respiratory system

INCIDENCE OF SUDDEN INFANT DEATH SYNDROME

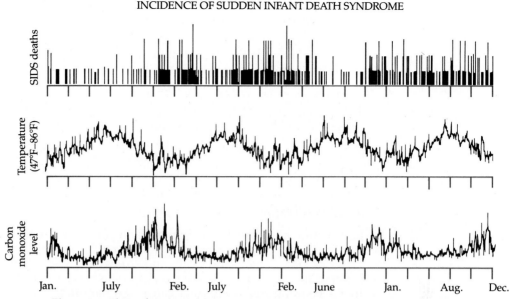

Figure 5.1 **Plots of daily incidence of SIDS in Los Angeles County between January 1974 and December 1977. Notice that low temperature and high carbon monoxide levels during the winter months tended to coincide with increases in SIDS (Hoppenbrouwers et al., 1981).**

and have been slow to develop long periods of quiet sleep. SIDS occurs more often at high altitudes and in cities.

Those factors are the correlates, but what actually causes SIDS? One theory links SIDS with an imbalance of the hormone triiodothyronine (T-3) (Tilden and Chacon, 1981). Another theory is that infants who die of SIDS have blocked airways and constricted vocal tracts, the sounds of which can be detected in a characteristic cry. Breathing abnormalities during sleep are the most common characteristic associated with SIDS. Normally, a respiratory control center in the brain regulates breathing during sleep. As the amount of carbon dioxide in the blood rises, a person breathes in more oxygen in response. Several researchers have suggested that SIDS may be related to faulty chemical regulation of breathing. One researcher has found that the respiratory control center does not operate properly in SIDS infants (Hunt, 1982). The blood levels of carbon dioxide in these infants rise, but the infants do not compensate by breathing in more oxygen. Eventually, they stop breathing. This researcher advocates early detection of abnormal breathing patterns during sleep and administration of the drug theophylline. This drug, which resembles caffeine, stimulates the breathing reflex. Other researchers suggest that parents be taught how to monitor their infant's breathing at home, with a device that sounds an alarm when the infant's breathing is interrupted, a condition called **apnea**. Every infant goes through apneas, both asleep and awake, but infants at risk for SIDS may not begin breathing again on their own. The alarm alerts parents, who can take measures to help the infant start breathing again.

> When Ted was just a few days old and still in the hospital nursery, he had several incidents when he just stopped breathing. They ran every test in the world on him, but they couldn't find a definite cause for the problem. When we left the hospital, the pediatrician showed us how to hook Ted up to an apparatus for his crib that sounds an alarm if he stops breathing while he's asleep. It's happened several times, although the

doctor thinks that in time Ted'll outgrow the problem. I'll tell you, it's really scary to live with this hanging over your baby's head.

One alternative—for parents to sleep with their infant—has been proposed by anthropologist James McKenna (1985). For nearly all of human history, infants have slept in close physical contact with their mothers for the first year of life or beyond. Today it is only Westernized humans who sleep separately from their infants. Infants born with weaknesses in their breathing might be helped by hearing the sounds of their mothers' steady breathing (as premature infants are helped by the breathing bears described in Chapter 4, Focus: Bears for Babies). McKenna is testing this proposal by comparing the breathing patterns of parents and infants as they sleep either together or apart.

Malnutrition

Both before and after birth, human beings need nourishment if their bodies and minds are to grow and thrive—calories for energy, protein for building, vitamins and minerals for health and strength. A good deal of prenatal care is devoted to a pregnant woman's diet, because it has been amply documented that a good and balanced diet can make the difference between health and illness in both mother and child. After birth, infants who are severely malnourished may suffer a form of starvation called **marasmus**. These infants barely grow. Their muscles atrophy. If they live, they are unresponsive and never catch up to adequately nourished children. They learn less and, later, perform poorly on intelligence and psychological tests.

Such extreme malnourishment is uncommon in this country. But in a world where starvation threatens to wipe out whole groups of people—as it now does in the barren regions of northern Africa—it is critical that we understand all the factors that contribute to disease, death, and developmental delay by starvation. Why, for instance, in countries where malnutrition is common do some children suffer more than others? A study of a Mexican farming village showed that a mother's health was the single most important determinant of an infant's nutrition and growth (Cravioto, Birch, DeLicardie, Rosales, and Vega, 1969). Another determinant was family size: an infant with more brothers and sisters, who themselves needed food, got less to eat; an infant with lots of productive adults in the family got more.

One of the best predictors of infants' growth and health is whether they are breast-fed by their mothers or get a commercial formula from a bottle. Mother's milk is specially suited to human infants. It is clean and digestible and confers immunities on the vulnerable infant. Sometimes called ''nature's vaccine,'' mother's milk protects infants against allergies, diarrhea, upper respiratory infections, and other illnesses. Soon after birth and for two to four days thereafter, **colostrum** is secreted from the mother's breasts. It is a clear liquid, rich in protein, from which infants receive white blood cells that destroy bacteria and viruses and produce antibodies. It also carries a sugar that helps the infant's gut to fight disease—a nutrient that can mean the difference between life and death to infants in areas where food is scarce and disease common.

Mother's milk helps infants not only to gain weight faster in their first month but to avoid obesity later on (Neuman and Alpaugh, 1976). Why is this so? For one thing, breast-feeding mothers do not urge their infants to take more to drink. Their infants simply suck until they are sated, whether they take one ounce or four ounces at a feeding. They are therefore not overfed. For another thing, breast-fed infants are more active than formula-fed infants. They wake up more often at night and move about more often when they are

Infants with marasmus, a form of starvation, barely grow, are unresponsive, and, if they live, learn less than adequately nourished infants.

A mother's milk protects infants against allergies, diarrhea, respiratory infections, and helps them to gain weight. Breast feeding also brings mother and infant into frequent close contact.

awake (Bernal and Richards, 1969). This activity level also helps keep them thin. Of course, it is also possible that mothers who breast-feed have other attitudes that later keep them from overfeeding their children, and this, too, contributes to the children's later leanness (Weil, 1975).

While they are breast feeding, mothers have to eat properly. One group of researchers studied nursing mothers in rural Taiwan (Joos, Pollitt, Mueller, and Albright, 1983). These women usually ate rice, sweet potatoes, and other vegetables, but little animal protein. The researchers wanted to find out whether supplementing the mothers' diet right after pregnancy, when they were breast feeding, would benefit their children's growth and development. Half of 300 breast-feeding women were randomly assigned to receive a high-calorie protein supplement plus vitamins and minerals. They began taking the supplement three weeks after childbirth. The others received a **placebo**, which provided a few extra calories plus a vitamin and mineral pill. Tests of the babies' motor and intellectual abilities showed that although overall mental scores of infants in the treatment group were not significantly higher than those in the control group, overall motor scores were higher. Infants whose mothers had received the supplement could sit, stand, and bring two objects together in front of them (an indicator of neurological maturity) at younger ages than infants whose mothers continued eating deficient diets. These results show that nutrition does affect development—even when that nutrition takes a somewhat indirect route through the mother's system to the infant's.

But it is not only essential nutrients that reach the infant through the mother's milk. Harmful substances do too. Breast milk carries chemicals, alcohol, and nicotine to the developing infant. These substances can have the same harmful effects right after birth as they did when transmitted by the mother before birth. Alcoholic nursing mothers may even transmit an alcohol syndrome to their newborns, or so animal research suggests, because the newborn's brain is still developing (Rawat, 1982). In the United States, nursing mothers have been warned not to eat freshwater fish like whitefish and trout, which may carry industrial pollutants like polychlorinated biphenyls (PCBs). But, as we have pointed out, as long as the pollutants can be avoided, mother's milk has many advantages for infants. Some public health experts consider breast feeding always to be desirable but, in poor families, to be necessary for infants' survival (Jelliffe and Jelliffe, 1982). Although prepared formula can offer an infant adequate nutrition, many pediatricians urge new mothers to consider breast feeding for its nutritional and immunizing advantages. And although bottle feedings also can be times of close and loving contact between parents and infants, breast feeding by necessity brings mother and infant into close and frequent physical contact. Breast feeding may be physically and psychologically rewarding for both mother and infant and so perpetuate itself and lead to continued close contact.

Despite its advantages, only about one-half of the mothers of newborns in this country decide to nurse. Why? Many working women find breast feeding incompatible with the demands of their jobs. Few employers offer women places where they can nurse. In fact, in some places women may be fired if they insist on nursing during working hours.

> Just after Sam was born, the newspapers were full of stories about a fire fighter who had been let go for nursing her baby at the fire station when she was on her breaks. I was grateful that I never ran into any problems like that.

Other women cite inconvenience, discomfort, embarrassment, worries about having enough milk, and just plain distaste as reasons for not nursing. Attitudes toward nursing in public also may deter mothers from nursing.

When our third baby was born, my husband and I occasionally went out to a restaurant just to have some time to talk. I was nursing the baby then, so he came along too. At one restaurant, the captain came over and asked me please to nurse the baby in the ladies' room. I had covered up with a shawl, but apparently some customer had complained. That was a real nuisance.

The most important thing may be for mothers to feed their infants as they wish—bottle feeding without guilt or breast feeding without embarrassment.

Failure to thrive

Wise parents know—and researchers confirm—that if infants are to grow and thrive, they need loving attention no less than they need milk. Leave an infant in a disorganized home, with a caregiver who is unresponsive and who ignores or restricts the infant's activities, and you have set the stage for trouble. For under conditions like these, infants are likely to stop growing, to lose weight, and to fall behind other infants in reaching important developmental milestones like sitting up, creeping, or walking. Often when infants suffering from this condition, called **failure to thrive**, are examined, no organic cause is apparent. A sequence something like the following has been proposed as a model of how failure to thrive develops (Bradley, Casey, and Wortham, 1984). First, the pattern of interaction between parents and infant is not harmonious. The parents are unresponsive and unaccepting of the infant. The infant, too, may be difficult or unresponsive. Then, the parents fail to provide the infant with needed nurturance. They do not feed the infant enough, and the infant often is left hungry, dirty, wet, and unattended. Finally, miserable, under great stress, apathetic, and isolated, the infant begins to develop hormonal and cellular abnormalities. Normal growth and signs of responsiveness wither.

In one instance, an emaciated 8-month-old girl was brought to a Boston hospital. Unlike a normal 8-month-old, she could not sit up alone, and she did not respond when people talked to her. With good medical attention, she began to gain weight, to play, even to smile. She left the hospital but returned within two months—scrawny, dirty, smelly, restless, and apathetic. This time, the hospital treated the mother as well as the child. The mother had no husband, four children, little money, and few friends or relatives. She was given dental care for her badly neglected teeth, medicine for a chronic urinary infection, and regular counseling from a social worker. Her older two children were placed in a nursery school. A homemaker and a public health nurse visited her at home every day. The mother's depression began to lift, and she found energy for nurturing her baby. Now the baby began to gain weight, to grow taller, and to develop normally for her age. When she was 5 years old, the little girl was still doing well (Newberger, Newberger, and Harper, 1976). It is clearly in everyone's best humanitarian and economic interests that interventions come as early as possible in such cases.

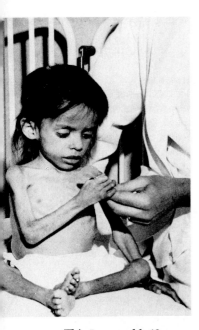

This 5-year-old, 13-pound girl failed to thrive because her parents were unable to give her the attention and nutrition she needed.

Physical Growth

When we brought Jason home from the hospital, Kristy met us at the front door and said, "But his skin doesn't fit." Later it was hard to remember how skinny he'd been.

The vast majority of infants, in this country at least, are born healthy, hungry, and energetic. They slurp their milk so noisily that it gladdens even a hovering grandma's heart. The wrinkled and wizened newborn fills out within a matter of weeks into a plump, round-cheeked, dimpled little charmer who increasingly resembles those idealized portraits on the cereal packages. Tissues and organs already formed before birth continue to develop and enlarge.

Brain growth

The infant's central nervous system continues to mature according to an internal timetable that is affected very little by the infant's environment. Brain wave records of 6-week-old infants born after 28 weeks in the womb are almost identical to those of infants born after 34 weeks and tested immediately, even though the 6-week-olds have been exposed to as many weeks of sights, sounds, human contact, and handling (Dreyfus-Brisac, 1975).

Brain activity in the first month of life occurs primarily in the sensorimotor cortex, brain stem, and cerebellum. The first brain cells to function are those in the primary motor area that control arms and trunk. By the time the infant is 3 to 4 months of age, brain activity in the cerebral cortex is common. At this point, the infant's cortex has enough mature cells to direct voluntary movements of the arms, and primary sensory areas of the cortex also develop. First touch and then vision and hearing are affected. Brain activity resembling that seen in adults, which occurs predominantly in the frontal cortex and association areas, takes place by about 7 months. Then infants can integrate sights, sounds, and voluntary movements as they reach for a ball, examine toys, and react to strangers (Conel, 1939–1967; Chugani and Phelps, 1986).

Body growth

The average American newborn, as we have seen, weighs in at 7½ pounds. What determines how much a baby weighs at birth? The size of the parents is one factor. The mother's size exerts a **restraining effect** on the size of the developing fetus. Thus even if the father is large, the size of the mother's uterus and pelvis restrains the fetus's growth to a size that her body can usually sustain and push through the birth canal.

> My sister and I look much alike, and we're exactly the same build, height, and weight. I'm married to a 6 footer, and she's married to a fellow who's 5 feet 4. Our babies were exactly the same length and weight—20 inches, 7 pounds 5½ ounces—at birth. But at 1 year old, her daughter was a short 34 inches, and mine was a tall 37 inches. Now the girls are 8 years old, and you can still see the difference. Lainie is short and broad like her father, and Nancy is tall and lanky like *her* father.

An infant's sex and order of birth also affect weight and maturity at birth. On average, boys are half an ounce heavier, have larger skulls and more muscle, and are longer than girls, whereas girls' skeletal and nervous systems are two weeks more mature than boys'. Firstborns usually weigh less than later-borns and grow faster after birth until they make up the deficit (Tanner, 1974). Most twins and all triplets are born underweight because they are born prematurely.

As the newborn begins to ingest and digest on his or her own, typically about 10 percent of body weight is lost. After about five days and ready to solo, the newborn begins to gain about an ounce a day.

> Sam weighed 7 pounds 5 ounces and was 21 inches long at birth—both 50th percentile. Within two weeks, though, he had begun to grow extremely fast. He's been off the charts ever since. At 1 year, he weighed over 30 pounds. He looked a bit like Winston Churchill. My husband swore that if we were quiet enough, we could *hear* him growing!

GROWTH CHARTS, HEIGHT AND WEIGHT

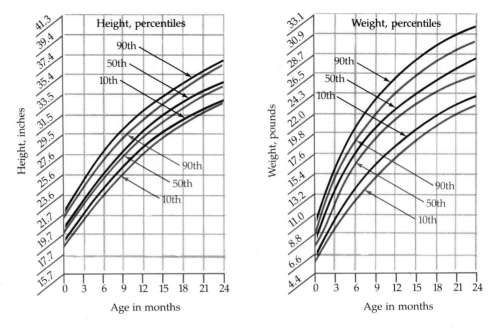

Figure 5.2 These charts show American infants' ranges of heights and weights over the first two years. Fiftieth percentile represents the average; 90th percentile represents infants who are larger or heavier than 90 percent of those their age. Girls (colored lines) average somewhat shorter and lighter than boys (black lines).

On average, babies double their birth weight by 4 months and triple it by 1 year. Smaller than average babies gain even faster. The faster **catch-up growth** of a baby kept small by a small mother's restraining womb takes place largely in the first five months of life. The 4-pound newborn may weigh 8 pounds at 2 or 3 months and 20 pounds at 1 year. Heredity has surprisingly little effect on prenatal size, but it has a sizable effect on catch-up growth (Tanner, 1974).

The quick weight gain of the infant's first year is mainly body fat, which is why many infants look round and dimpled. Although some of this padding is necessary insulation against cold and a food reserve during teething, infants need not be fat. Overfeeding actually may predispose them to weight problems later on (see discussion in Chapter 8).

> Natalie was 7 pounds 10 ounces at birth and 19 inches long. But she's been getting progressively rounder and shorter, roughly the 25th percentile in height and 75th in weight. We're starting to worry that her "baby fat" won't go away.

During their second year, toddlers' bodies lengthen, and they gain less weight. By 24 months, an average child in this country weighs 30 pounds and stands 34½ inches tall (Figure 5.2).

Reflexes of the newborn

The healthy newborn infant shows a remarkable range of **reflexes**, swift and finely coordinated involuntary responses to falling, to being stroked on the cheek or the sole of the foot, suspended by the fingers, or "walked" across a flat surface. More than 20 reflexes in the newborn have been identified (see Table 5.4). In the moments after birth, a doctor usually puts an infant through his or her paces to check these reflexes, for their presence is assurance that the nervous system is well developed. Abnormal or missing reflexes are warning signs of neurological problems.

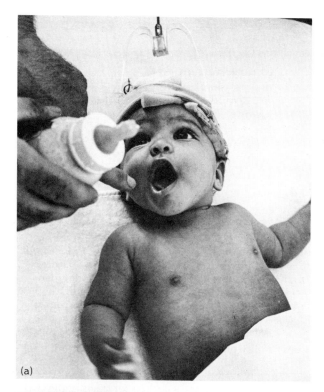

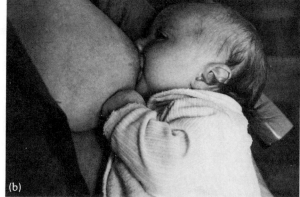

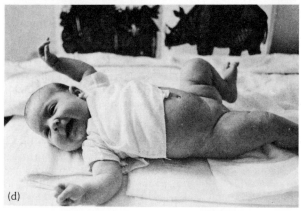

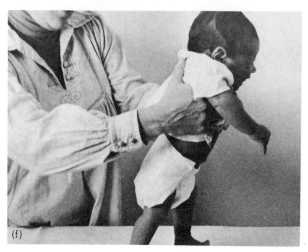

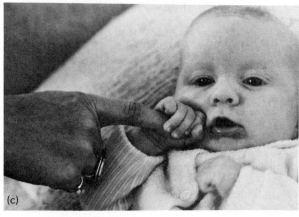

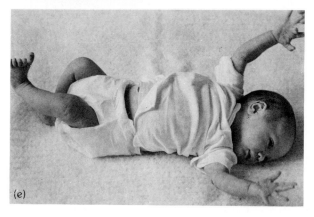

The reflexes of the newborn help ensure the physical survival of the not-so-helpless infant. (a) The rooting, (b) sucking, (c) palmar reflexes, (d) tonic neck, (e) Moro, and (f) stepping.

Table 5.4
Reflexes in the newborn

Name	Testing method	Response	Developmental course	Significance
Blink	Flash a light in infant's eyes	Closes both eyes	Permanent	Protects eyes from strong stimuli
Biceps reflex	Tap on the tendon of the biceps muscle	Contracts the biceps muscle	Brisker in the first few days than later	Absent in depressed infants or those with congenital muscular disease
Knee jerk or patellar tendon reflex	Tap on the tendon below the patella, or kneecap	Quickly extends or kicks the knee	More pronounced in the first two days than later	Absent or difficult to obtain in depressed infants or infants with muscular disease; exaggerated in hyperexcitable infants
Babinski	Gently stroke the side of the infant's foot from heel to toes	Flexes the big toe dorsally; fans out the other toes; twists foot inward	Usually disappears near the end of the first year; replaced by plantar flexion of big toe in the normal adult	Absent in infants with defects of the lower spine; retention important in diagnosing poor myelination of motor tracts of the brain stem in older children and adults
Withdrawal reflex	Prick the sole of the infant's foot with a pin	Flexes leg	Constantly present during the first 10 days; present but less intense later	Absent with sciatic nerve damage
Plantar or toe grasp	Press finger against the ball of the infant's foot	Curls all toes under	Disappears between 8 and 12 months	Absent in infants with defects of the lower spinal cord
Tonic neck reflex	Lay baby down on back	Turns head to one side; baby assumes fencing position, extending arm and leg on this side, bending opposite limbs, and arching body away from direction faced	Found as early as 28th prenatal week; frequently present in first weeks, disappears by 3 or 4 months	Paves way for eye–hand coordination
Palmar or hand grasp	Press rod or finger against the infant's palm	Grasps the object with fingers; can suspend own weight for brief period of time	Increases during the first month and then gradually declines and is gone by 3 or 4 months	Weak or absent in depressed babies
Moro reflex (embracing reflex)	Make a sudden loud sound; let the baby's head drop back a few inches; or suspend baby horizontally, and then lower hands rapidly about 6 inches and stop abruptly	Extends arms and legs and then brings arms toward each other in a convulsive manner; fans hands out at first, then clenches them tightly	Begins to decline in third month, generally gone by fifth month	Absent or constantly weak Moro reflex indicates serious disturbance of central nervous system; may have originated with primate clinging

Table 5.4
Reflexes in the newborn (*continued*)

Name	Testing method	Response	Developmental course	Significance
Stepping or automatic walking reflex	Support baby in upright position with bare feet on flat surface; move the infant forward and tilt the infant slightly from side to side	Makes rhythmic stepping movements	Disappears at 2 to 3 months	Absent in depressed infants
Swimming reflex	Hold baby horizontally on stomach in water	Alternates arm and leg movements, exhaling through the mouth	Disappears at 6 months	Demonstrates coordination of arms and legs
Rooting reflex	Stroke cheek of infant lightly with finger or nipple	Turns head toward finger, opens mouth, and tries to suck finger	Disappears at approximately 3 to 4 months	Absent in depressed infants; appears in adults with severe cerebral palsy
Sucking response	Insert finger about 1 to 1½ inches into the baby's mouth	Sucks rhythmically	Sucking often less intense and less regular during the first 3 to 4 days	Poor sucking (weak, slow, and in short bursts) found in apathetic babies; depressed by maternal medication during childbirth
Babkin, or palmarmental reflex	Apply pressure on both the baby's palms when lying on back	Opens mouth, closes eyes, and turns head to midline	Disappears at 3 to 4 months	Inhibited by general depression of central nervous system

Above and beyond their value as diagnostic tools, reflexes offer infants survival advantages, and investigators continue to turn up intriguing possibilities for the purposes that reflexes serve. Two reflexes that are necessary for survival are the rooting reflex and the sucking reflex. In the **rooting reflex**, the newborn automatically turns his or her mouth toward the nipple that touches cheek or lips. In the **sucking reflex**, the newborn sucks on anything that touches his or her lips. With these two reflexes, the infant may feed—an act critical to survival. Sucking is the first step in a complex pattern of behavior. Infants form a seal around the nipple with their lips and create a vacuum in their mouths by moving their jaws. This vacuum helps to draw milk from the nipple. At the same time, infants use their tongues to draw milk from the nipple and toward the back of their mouths. Infants can suck and inhale simultaneously, swallowing between breaths three times faster than adults can. After a week or two, most infants have mastered the complex pattern of synchronizing sucking, swallowing, and breathing.

The **palmar grasp** is another reflex in the newborn's repertoire. Also called the "automatic hand grasp," this reflex appears when someone's finger or another narrow object touches the newborn's palm. The newborn's fingers then fold so tightly around the finger or other object that they can support the baby's entire weight. The palmar grasp grows stronger for several weeks after birth, then weakens, and finally disappears altogether by the time the infant is 3 or 4 months old. Not until the age of 5 years do children have the same strength of grasp as in the newborn period.

When the newborn is startled or begins to fall, arms and legs fling outward, hands open, and fingers spread in what is called the embracing, or **Moro reflex**. As the Moro reflex continues, the infant draws arms to body, clenches his fists, arches his back, fully stretches out his legs, and opens his eyes wide. Then comes a loud wail. If the Moro reflex does not disappear from the baby's repertoire within a few months, it indicates a problem in the central nervous system. In the ordinary course of development, reflexes that do not disappear may give cause for alarm. In cerebral palsy, for example, a condition that affects motor centers in the brain, early reflexes persist. In normal infants, most reflexes disappear within the first few months after birth. Reflexes are under the control of centers in the newborn's brain stem. As the higher level cortex of the brain develops, it acts on the reflexes, and the infant's voluntary, willed actions come to replace the early reflexes.

Why do newborns possess these fleeting reflexes in the first place? Some help the newborn to feed. As we have seen, the rooting and sucking reflexes allow newborns to drink milk. The palmar grasp probably evolved among primates so that infants could cling to their mothers as they moved about. Several of the newborn's reflexes look much like actions that will appear later after much effort. Walking and swimming, for example, have antecedents in the reflexes of early infancy. Hold an infant under her arms, put her feet on a flat surface, and she "walks." Hold the infant on her stomach in a tub or pool of water, and her arms and legs make swimming motions. Researchers are looking into the possible connections between these early actions and the later skills that they resemble. The **stepping reflex**, for example, in which the infant seems to walk, traditionally has been explained as one of the primitive reflexes that disappear after a few months, when the cerebral cortex is mature enough to inhibit them. But perhaps stepping disappears out of simple disuse. In one study, when a group of parents "walked" their infants every day, not only did the stepping reflex not disappear, but it grew more frequent, and the infants walked on their own a month earlier than infants who had not practiced walking (Zelazo, 1976, 1983; Zelazo, Zelazo, and Kolb, 1972). One intriguing hypothesis is that stepping is not a reflex at all, but part of a more complex innate pattern of movement (Thelen, Fisher, and Ridley-Johnson, 1984). Kicking and stepping are parts of the same pattern. Put an infant on her back, and she kicks. Stand her up, and those kicks turn into steps. But stepping disappears as the infant's legs become too heavy with fat for her slower-growing muscles to raise comfortably against gravity. Kicking, which requires less muscle strength, does not disappear. Despite all we know, we still need further research to complete the story of newborns' reflexes.

Infant states

From the time they are born, infants spend their days in a range of states of consciousness, from deep sleep to frantic squalling. What infants are capable of doing is very much affected by their state at the time. Try to get an infant to look at something—no matter how interesting—when she's sleepy, and you are bound to fail. These states are largely determined by the infant's central nervous system and other physiological systems, rather than by external stimulation. Infants can sleep—or wail—through earthquakes and concerts.

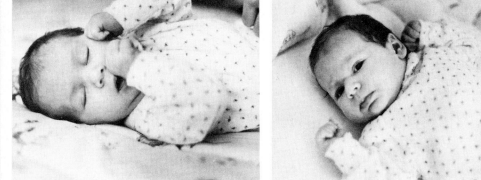

The three common states of sleep–wakefulness are (left to right) quiet, regular and restful sleep; active sleep, during which the baby moves, smiles, grimaces, and has rapid eye movements; and alert inactivity, the best state for learning.

The state of consciousness most common to the young infant is sleep. Newborns sleep nearly 70 percent of the time, in seven or eight segments over the course of 24 hours (Figure 5.3). In fact, most parents, who are eager to play with the infant they have been awaiting for nine months, are surprised to find that all the newborn does is sleep. Gradually, the segments of sleep grow fewer and longer. In a matter of months, most infants need only two or three naps a day, and after they reach the age of about 1 year, their naps are even fewer. When do infants reach that blessed milestone, sleeping through the night? There is no hard and fast rule, although many weary parents find encouragement in looking forward to ''12 weeks or 12 pounds, whichever comes first.''

> Do I remember when Sam first slept through the night? I'll never forget it. I heard him cry and groaned as I hoisted myself out of bed to go and feed him. But I literally did a double take when I saw the clock on my night table. It was 5 AM. He had slept for *seven* hours, right through his 2:30 feeding. Maybe only an exhausted new parent can understand how one could positively *rejoice* at being awakened at 5:00 in the morning. But rejoice I did.

Bottle-fed infants are likely to sleep through the night earlier than breast-fed infants. Observational studies of breast-fed and bottle-fed infants show that the 24-hour sleep patterns of the two groups begin to diverge in their second six months of life (Bernal and Richards, 1969; Elias, 1984). Bottle-fed babies sleep a total of 13 to 14 hours a day from the time they are 6 months old until they are 2 years old. At 2 years, three-quarters of them sleep through the night. But breast-fed babies sleep less overall, wake up more at night, and, on the average, sleep for only five hours at a stretch even at the age of 2 years. Breast-fed infants probably are not as full after a feeding as bottle-fed infants are, and so they wake up hungry. Sleep patterns established in infancy are hard to change later on. Infants whose sleeping and waking patterns are stable from one day to the next are less likely to develop medical or behavioral problems in infancy than those with erratic patterns (Tynan, 1986).

NEWBORN STATES

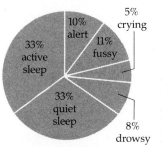

5% crying
10% alert
11% fussy
33% active sleep
33% quiet sleep
8% drowsy

Figure 5.3 This chart pictures the amounts of time that infants spend, on the average, in different physiological states (Berg, Adkinson, and Strock, 1973; Roffwarg, Muzio, and Dement, 1966).

Infants experience two different kinds of sleep: active, irregular sleep, and quiet, regular sleep. In active sleep, the infants' blood pressure, heart rate, and breathing rate are high, brain waves are speeded up, and the level of arousal, indicated by the galvanic skin response, is at the same level as when infants are awake. The infants may smile, grimace, pucker their lips, and move their arms and legs during active sleep. Their eyes, though closed, make rapid movements from side to side and top to bottom. Natalie's mother is describing active sleep when she says,

Natalie is so quiet when she's awake that it always surprises me when I hear her noisy sleeping. She flails her arms, tosses and turns. The covers fly off. Sometimes she whimpers like a kitten, and I wonder if I should waken her from a bad dream.

Newborns spend about half of their sleep time in active sleep, half in quiet sleep. By their first birthday, they spend only one-quarter of their sleeping time in active sleep (see Figure 5.4).

We know that in adults, rapid eye movements (REMs) occur during dreaming. It is possible that newborns spend as much time as they do in active sleep because the higher parts of their brains are working through the stimulation they have received when they are awake. As their brains grow practiced at coordinating and consolidating sensory stimulation, infants come to need less "exercise" time (Roffwarg, Muzio, and Dement, 1966).

If they are not sleeping, infants may be drowsy; awake and active; awake and inactive; or crying. Infants who are crying or actively moving around are less likely to be listening to or looking at what's happening around them.

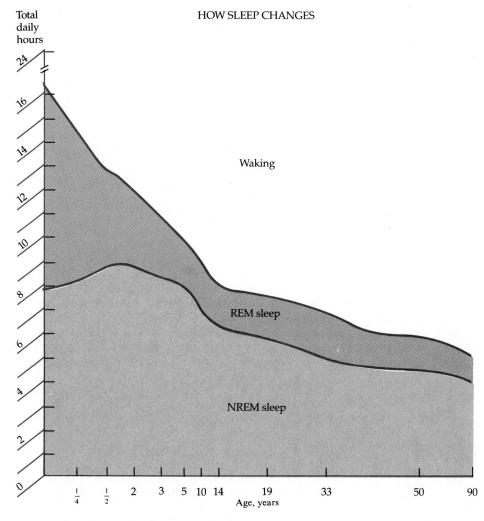

Figure 5.4 The daily amounts of quiet (NREM) and active (REM) sleep change during the life span, but the percentage of REM sleep drops significantly during early childhood. Newborns spend half their time in quiet sleep and half in REM sleep. Two- to 3-year-olds spend only one-quarter of their sleeping time in REM sleep, although they get about the same amount of quiet sleep as younger infants (Roffwarg, Muzio, and Dement, 1966).

HOW SLEEP CHANGES

Total daily hours

Waking

REM sleep

NREM sleep

Age, years

Infants in a state of alert inactivity can focus on and follow things with their eyes, listen, and learn (Korner, 1970, 1972).

focus ___Is my baby all right?___

All new parents want to know right away whether their baby is healthy and sound. The healthy skin tone, the strong muscles, and the curious gaze of their newborn are reassurance indeed. But as we have come to understand more about the rather remarkable range of abilities newborns have, the answer to that question, "Is my baby all right?" has come to require more complex answers. Newborns can be judged by their color and their reflexes, their responses to stress, their control of certain movements, their alertness, even their initiation of social interactions.

The Neonatal Behavior Assessment Scale (NBAS) was devised by Boston pediatrician T. Berry Brazelton to shorten the four-month period that doctors once waited to certify that infants were normal and ready for adoption. With the NBAS, a doctor can tell right away whether the newborn is all right. The test uses props like a pocket flashlight, an orange rubber ball, a paper clip, and some kernels of popcorn to evaluate a newborn infant. As the test begins, the newborn is sleeping, and the tester checks to see how the infant reacts to various stimuli. Twenty minutes into the test, the newborn is alert—and may be protesting noisily. Because all new infants' behavior is strongly influenced by their state of consciousness, and because infants perform best when they are quietly alert, testers must wait for a quiet alert state before they can continue the test. By watching how the infant responds to comforting, the tester also can check the infant's **lability**, or how quickly the infant moves between of states of consciousness. This is an important measure because infants who make swift transitions and become alert quickly can orient themselves to sights and sounds and learn most readily about their world.

Altogether, the NBAS tester assesses newborns' capacities in the following general areas:

1. Attention and social responsiveness. Does the infant look at an object? turn toward a sound or voice? look at the face of someone speaking? Is the infant alert? cuddly? consolable when crying?

2. Motor and muscle tone. Is the infant's muscle tone tense, taut, or flabby? What is the infant's activity level? maturity of movement? Can the infant bring his fist to his mouth? Can the infant flinch, exhibit the Moro reflex, and make other defensive movements? Can the infant be pulled into a sitting position?

3. Control of state of consciousness. How quickly does the infant tire of repeated stimuli—a light, a rattle, a bell, a pin prick? How quickly does the infant work up to a full cry? How excited does the infant get? How irritable is the infant? How quickly can the infant quiet himself after crying?

4. Response to stress. Can the infant contain his startle response? trembling? change in skin color?

As the tester observes the newborn's patterns of actions and reactions, a profile of the newborn's general health and style of activity emerges. If the infant is attentive and responsive, cuddly and consolable, firm and active, quick to tire of a stimulus and quick to quiet, the skilled observer can quite accurately assure the parents that their baby is "all right."

Motor development

Infants acquire motor abilities in the same cephalocaudal–proximodistal—head to toe and center to periphery—direction in which the body grew before birth. First, infants lift their heads and necks. They control their shoulders, then their elbows, then their fingers. They control their knees before their toes. These tendencies traditionally have been ascribed to the direction in which the nervous system matures. Nerves are **myelinated**—insulated with sheaths of a protective substance called **myelin**—in the following order: head, shoulders, arms, upper chest, abdomen, legs, and feet. But this explanation of motor development recently has been challenged. When 4- to 8-month-old infants are allowed to move freely in water, they kick their feet more than they move their arms—an apparent reversal of the arm-before-leg order (Weiss and Zelazo, 1984). It just might be that in the usual course of things—on dry land—infants use their legs after their arms because their legs are heavier and harder to move than their arms are, and not because their nerves are myelinated in that order (Thelen et al., 1984).

Infants also perform gross motor acts before fine motor acts: their whole arm swipes at the toy before their hand can grasp it. They push their big toys across the floor by using their whole upper body, their shoulders, and both arms and only months later become engrossed in trying to pinch a penny from the floor between fingers and thumb.

> Natalie held up her head on her own three weeks to the day after she was born. We instantly snapped a picture of it. The day she first grasped a little toy bird with her fingers we photographed as well. One of the amazing things about parenthood is how engrossed you get in the tiniest developments in your baby.

> Sam seemed to work so long and hard to get his arms and hands to do things. It was very touching to watch him practice over and over again bringing his fist to his mouth. Sometimes he would stare at his fingertips for long periods, moving them gently. There was something almost scientific in his single-minded concentration and perseverance.

Motor milestones

Although, as we shall see, infants vary somewhat in how fast their motor skills develop, the order in which these skills develop (see Figure 1.1) and the age *ranges* when they develop are quite consistent from infant to infant.

Birth to 3 months

From birth, many newborns can turn their heads and lift their chins as they lie on their backs. Put them on their stomachs, and they can lift their heads just enough to turn from side to side. Soon they're raising shoulders and chest, and by 2 months usually they can lift their heads up when they're lying on their backs. Sit these 2-month-olds up though, and their heads soon droop or loll to the side. At 3 months, most babies can keep their heads slightly forward but upright. Put them on their stomachs, and they rest on their knees, abdomen, chest, and cheek. Turn them onto their backs, and the head turns to one side, arm and leg on that side of the body extend forward, arm and leg on the other side are pulled in—a fencing pose, the **tonic neck reflex**. Still too young to try creeping or walking, 3-month-olds nonetheless push their feet against your hand. Newborns have no control over their arms. But within a few weeks, they can use their arm, hand, and fingers together, rather like a flipper. Put a shiny toy in front of him, and the 1-month-old does

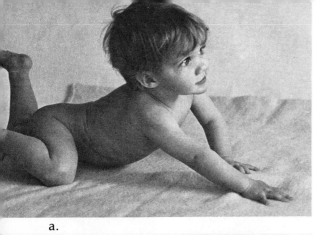

a.

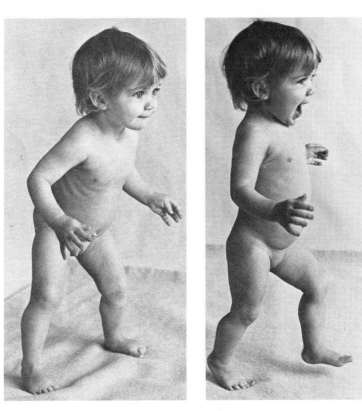

b.   c.   d.

Motor milestones. (a) By 7 or 8 months, most babies can creep forward on their stomachs. (b) By 9 months, they can move on all fours and, soon afterwards, (c) pull themselves up to stand alone. (d) By 12 months of age, most babies can walk alone—unsteadily but with great pride.

not even try to grasp it. The 2-month-old can hold his fingers against his palms and grasp objects handed to him, at least for a short while. The 3-month-old swipes at the shiny toy with his curled fist.

4 to 6 months

At 4 months, most infants can roll onto their sides from their stomachs. By this age, the infant's cortex can direct voluntary movements to the arms. The 4-month-old watches fascinated as his fingers reach. Over and over again, he glances at his hand and then at its target, bringing them into alignment. His concentration is intense. At 5 months, infants can roll onto their backs. They grasp objects by holding them to their palms with their fourth and fifth fingers (see Figure 5.5). At 6 months, they can touch their hands together in front of them and their hands go up and down, side to side at will. They can reliably reach, grasp, and hold things between their palms and fingers. They can coordinate their posture and gaze with the movements of their arms and hands. The tonic neck reflex has disappeared, and most babies can move more freely on their own. Sit them up and their heads stay upright; their trunks have better muscle tone. By the end of the period, they can even sit for a short time without support, and their perspective changes from horizontal to vertical.

7 to 9 months

By 7 to 8 months of age, most infants can roll from their backs to their stomachs, pull themselves up to standing, and stand by holding onto the edge of crib or playpen.

When Erica was 7 1/2 months old, I heard her making noises a few minutes after my husband supposedly had put her down for a nap. Erica

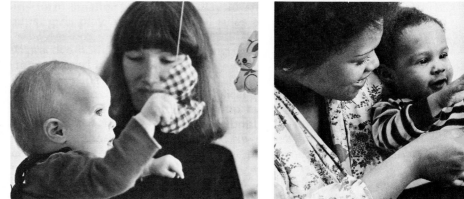

During the first year, infants acquire fine hand skills. They progress from an interest in their own tiny fingers, to grasping a toy, to manipulating and making a toy work.

was standing in her crib, babbling away. I thought my husband had neglected to lay Erica down. I would certainly speak to him about *that*. So I lay her down in the crib, said ''Night night,'' and left the room. Three minutes later I heard more babbling. There was Erica, standing up again in her crib—proud as a peacock at her new trick.

From the moment he was born, Peter was happier in an upright position than lying down. None of those reclining infant seats for him. He struggled to raise himself upright. Even to get him to stop crying, the best thing was to hold him up under his arms and let him swing freely. He finally managed to pull himself up at about 7 months, and the smile on his face went from ear to ear.

Seven-month-olds can get around by wriggling forward on their stomachs with a little help from arms and feet and can hold objects in their hands. They use their opposable thumbs against several fingers; 8-month-olds can shift the toy from one hand to another. These new physical abilities allow babies to play alone for a few minutes for the first time. Because their hands now can grasp a bottle or a crust of bread, some of these independent 8-month-olds may try to feed themselves. By 9 months, most babies can rise up on tiptoes or play with their feet as they lie on their backs. They can sit unsupported for ten minutes or more and right themselves if they begin to fall over. Some even manage to push themselves up into a sitting position from a prone position. Now babies begin to move around on their own. Some crawl, some creep, some scoot, some walk like bears on all fours, some edge sideways like crabs. They are endlessly inventive as they embark on this wonderful new game of getting around. They can also pick up an object between thumb and forefinger, and this gives them an enormous advantage over younger infants. Infants at this age can get about, explore, and do things for themselves. Their combined motor skills let them explore and manipulate objects as they learn about three-dimensional space, actions and reactions, and the connections between events. Now is the time for them to learn about the noise a pot on the stove makes when it hits the kitchen floor, the interesting swinging action of opening and closing a cabinet door, the joy of playing peekaboo with Mommy, and seventeen different things you can do with an egg whisk.

10 to 11 months

Lay a 10-month-old on her back, and she is likely to squawk in protest. She'd much rather be sitting or standing up. She can sit long and comfortably now, pivot from side to side, move from sitting to lying and back. Hold her hands, and she'll walk with you. On her own, she'll walk along by holding the

FINE MOTOR DEVELOPMENT

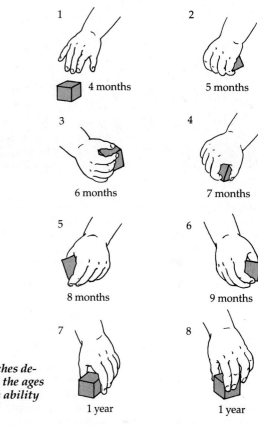

Figure 5.5 These sketches depict changes, between the ages of 4 and 12 months, in ability to grasp an object.

edges of cabinets and furniture. Baby handprints begin appearing along the bottoms of the windows. There is so much to see! By 11 months, she can stand alone. She takes her first step—and quickly plops to the floor.

12 months onward

By 12 months, most babies in this country begin to walk alone, without holding on. They're not too steady at it yet, and they topple often, but they keep at it with enormous pride and excitement.

> Sam began walking at 11½ months. He was so thrilled to be able to walk that he almost never sat down for nearly six months. I even had to put his food at the edge of his table so that he could peck at it in his travels. If we tried to contain him in his high chair, he would stiffen his legs and throw a tantrum. Boy, did he start to shed fat in those months!

Soon babies at this age can walk well enough to try to get themselves to certain places. Whether on their own or in a walker, babies who can walk are likely to approach adults (Gustafson, 1984). They look often at the adults, smile, and vocalize, and the adults respond to them. Walking also helps babies to explore new kinds of things—the cracks between the kitchen floor tiles, the dog's tail, the underside of chairs—and to engage other people in their explorations.

> Natalie was a bit late in walking—nearly 15 months. She always preferred to sit quietly and use her fingers, sometimes to hold a picture book,

sometimes to explore the texture of things like a doll's hair, a piece of fabric, a puddle of milk. But when she did start to walk, it opened up vast vistas for her to explore. She went from one room to another in her very deliberate way.

After 12 months, walking and balance get smoother and smoother. By the end of the second year, the toddling toddler is able to run and climb stairs.

Variations in Development

As Sam's and Natalie's ages of first walking show, infants reach milestones of motor development at somewhat different ages. Knowing the age range within which most children reach certain milestones of motor development—sitting alone, standing, and walking—helps parents and doctors to spot a child who is lagging behind and to inquire into the cause. Some lags in development are normal variations in a healthy child; others signal problems.

> Tim didn't hold up his head on his own until he was 6 months old, and he sat up late as well. But the pediatrician thought, because Tim could bring his hands together at the midline and because his skull was growing, that he was just developing at his own pace. We've had no other problems with Tim since then. He just needed some extra time.

> A woman I know has a 2-year-old who is just beginning to walk. He also shows some repetitive, self-stimulating behaviors. I think he has some problems that a specialist should check out, even though the mother hasn't indicated that *she* thinks there's a problem with her son.

From one generation to another, from one culture to another, the age at which normal infants achieve milestones in motor development varies by as much as three months. In two studies done in the 1930s, for example, babies in a California sample walked on the average at 13 months, and babies in a Minnesota sample walked at 15 months (Bayley, 1971a). In a study done in the 1960s, babies in a sample from Colorado walked on the average at 12 months (Frankenberg and Dodds, 1967).

When we try to figure out the reasons that some infants—whether individual infants like Sam or groups of infants like those in California—develop faster than others, diet, practice, parents' encouragement, and the chance to move freely all suggest themselves. A study of two twin boys conducted half a century ago (McGraw, 1935) offers support for the importance of practice and encouragement. One of the twins, Jimmy, was allowed the usual opportunities to walk, run, and climb and was moderately encouraged in motor skills. But his fraternal twin brother, Johnny, was given more freedom, daily practice in physical skills, and lots of encouragement. Johnny grew into a more athletic and better coordinated child than Jimmy, and the advantage lasted into adulthood. Clearly, practice makes for precocity. In another study, too (mentioned earlier in connection with the stepping reflex), when infants were actively exercised—given three-minute sessions to practice stepping four times a day between the ages of 2 and 8 weeks—they walked earlier than infants who did not get this practice (Zelazo, Zelazo, and Kolb, 1972). But even with exercise, infants achieve motor milestones like walking on a relatively fixed maturational timetable. In the experiment just described, for example, exercise speeded up walking—but by only one month. The size of the reaction range (see Figure 3.2) for basic physical abilities is quite small because these abilities are deeply canalized, that is, under strong genetic control.

Heredity clearly plays a role in an individual infant's rate of motor development. Identical twins reach motor milestones at the same age more often than fraternal twins do (Wilson and Harpring, 1972). American babies of African ancestry, who inherit one body type, are likely to walk a couple of months earlier than American babies of European ancestry, who inherit another body type, even though they are reared similarly (Tanner, 1970). An infant's activity level and adventurousness, also inherited, contribute to the pace at which he or she reaches motor milestones. It comes as no surprise that a slower-moving, more sedentary, and cautious infant will not walk until 15 months while an active, energetic, adventurous one will be walking at 11 months, climbing ladders at 16 months, and jumping off fences at 5 years.

Sensory and perceptual abilities

By watching infants at their daily activities—reaching, walking, climbing—one can easily see the development of their motor abilities. But what about the development of sensory and perceptual abilities? These abilities are much harder to observe. Infants cannot speak, and so everything about their sensory abilities must be inferred indirectly. Researchers face formidable problems in finding out what infants can see, hear, smell, and taste. Not only must they come up with clever tests to probe the infants' sensations, but they also must deal with subjects who don't know the meaning of cooperating with experimenters. Infants make very poor research subjects! Put them on their backs, and they fall asleep; sit them up and they move their arms and heads to keep their balance. Swaddle them, and they doze off; dress them loosely, and they cry. Keep the room warm, and they nap; keep it cool, and they fuss. Turn up the lights, and they squint; turn them down, and back to sleep they go. Six minutes of wakefulness is about all that anyone can count on from a newborn. No response? The infant either can't see it or can't hear it—or couldn't care less.

Researchers persevere even so, devising ingenious procedures to use with their tiny subjects. One procedure they follow is to record infants' eye movements. Like anyone else, infants look longer at some things than others. To monitor an infant's visual responses, researchers film the light reflected from the infant's cornea. This reflection tells them precisely where the infant is looking. In another procedure, researchers give an infant a pacifier wired to record the infant's sucking. By first recording a baseline rate of sucking, the researcher can compare the infant's faster or slower sucking in response to particular sights and sounds. When the sucking rate returns to the baseline, the infant has gotten used to or bored by—**habituated** to—the stimulus. If the researcher then shows the infant another stimulus and the sucking rate stays the same, the researcher can assume that the infant probably does not notice any difference between the two stimuli. If the sucking rate changes, the researcher can assume that the infant does notice the difference between the two stimuli. In a different procedure to assess infants' hearing and vision, pacifiers are wired to devices that let the infant turn on a recorded sound or bring a picture into focus by sucking. In yet another procedure, stabilimeters are used to measure the infants' movements, pneumographs to measure their breathing, or electrocardiographs to measure changes in heart rate when they see or hear a stimulus. Reaching and head turning may be used to indicate that the infant sees or hears as well. By using all these procedures, researchers have learned important things about how infants see, hear, taste, and smell.

Vision

Until about 20 years ago, people did not really know just what or how very young infants could see. Some doctors claimed that infants couldn't really see

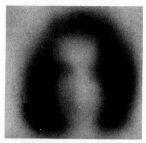 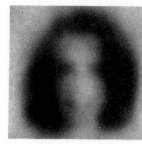 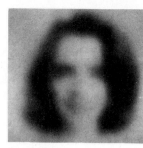 

1 month 2 months 3 months Adult

These photographs simulate what mother looks like to her infant at 1 month, 2 months, and 3 months. By 3 months the child has sufficient spatial resolution and experience to recognize the mother's face.

until they were 3, 4, or 6 weeks old, although they might flinch at a bright light shone in their eyes. Parents, in contrast, argued that their infants were quite obviously gazing at their faces during nursing or other periods of cuddling. In the last 20 years, scientists have learned much about the functioning, the anatomy, and the physiology of infants' vision (See Figure 5.6).

Visual capacities

The infant's retina, the part of the eye that turns light into nerve signals to the brain, has been found to be like an adult's in its components—rods, cones, and synapses—but it has no distinct **fovea**, the area in the adult retina on which central visual images are formed. Without a fovea, the central

Figure 5.6 This diagram compares the eyes of an adult and a newborn infant. It shows some of the ways in which the infant's visual system is limited. The diagram does not show the infant's jerky, inefficient eye movements and the immaturity of nerves in the visual cortex of the brain, which also limit the newborn's vision.

ADULT AND NEWBORN EYES

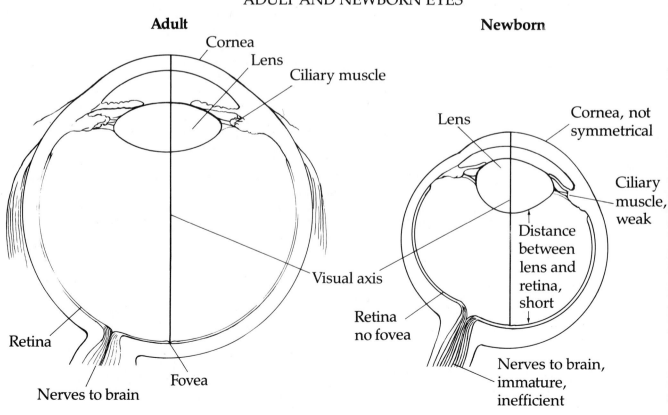

retina's handling of spatial resolution is poor. Therefore, researchers infer, the newborn's sight is not sharp. The retina matures fairly quickly, though, and by 11 months or earlier, its major structures are adult-like. During this period of maturation, the part of the nervous system that relays visual impressions between the retina and the cortex of the brain also gets more efficient until it is like an adult's. In the visual cortex, **dendrites** at the ends of the nerve cells form more branches, and the myelin sheaths that insulate the nerve cells continue to form. At about the age of 2 months, the infant's visual cortex begins to process visual stimuli (Hoffman, 1975).

Eye movements change, too. In young infants, the **saccadic eye movements**, which are the rapid movements between one point of visual fixation and another, are slower and more numerous than those of adults. In an adult, a saccade moves the eye 90 percent of the way to the visual target, but infants need several saccades to reach their visual target. The infant's eyes also do not move as smoothly as an adult's in tracking a moving target. Although they actually seem to prefer to look at moving objects over still ones (Haith, 1966), infants trying to track a moving stimulus refixate their eyes often, first gazing at one spot and then another. This jerkiness may be necessary because convergence, the focusing of both eyes on the same point so that only one stimulus is seen, is difficult for newborns. By 48 hours after birth, most infants can track a slowly moving object (Haith, 1966). But only at 6 weeks of age do infants track a moving object smoothly (Dayton et al., 1964; see Figure 5.7). By 2 to 3 months, infants' perception of movement apparently is as good as adults'.

The shape and structure of the eye also are important in determining how well someone can see. The newborn's eyeball is short and the distance between the retina and lens reduced. Therefore, most infants are quite far-sighted. Many also have an **astigmatism** during their first year, a difficulty in focusing that arises because their cornea is not symmetrical. Because of weak ciliary muscles, moreover, newborns cannot change the shape of the lens of the eye to **accommodate** to the shifting plane of focus for visual targets. Until they are 1 month old, babies can adjust their focus only for targets that are between 5 and 10 inches away. Although it seems logical to expect that infants at this age could see objects more clearly at a distance of 5 to 10 inches, they cannot. Apparently the infant's **depth of focus**, the distance that an object can be moved without a perceptible change in sharpness, is so large because other inadequacies in the visual system keep even substantial focusing errors from causing a noticeable increase in blurring. By 4 months of age, infants can accommodate to shifting planes of focus as well as adults can.

As a result of all these limitations in the visual system, but particularly because of the lack of a fovea and the immaturity of neurons, **visual acuity** is poor early in infancy and improves greatly in the first year. In one investigation of infants' visual acuity (Allen, 1978), infants between 2 weeks and 6 months old were shown two slides at the same time that were equal in size, brightness, and color. One had no pattern on it, and the other had high-

Figure 5.7 Records of eye movements made by infants of two different ages as they tracked a moving target. The motion of the target is represented by the smooth lines; the eye movements are represented by the other lines (Aslin, 1981).

TRACKING A MOVING TARGET

8-week-old   12-week-old

Figure 5.8 Newborn infants prefer to look at a moderately complex stimulus—in this set of stimuli the drawing of a face (Fantz, 1963).

NEWBORN'S VISUAL PREFERENCE

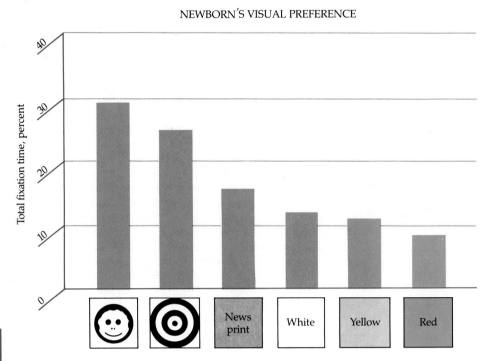

NORMAL AND
SCRAMBLED FACES

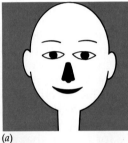

(a)

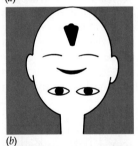

(b)

(c)

Figure 5.9 Newborn infants show no preference for (a) normal versus (b, c) scrambled faces.

contrast stripes. The experimenter progressively increased the width of these stripes from narrow to wide. By recording the point at which infants first discriminated between the unpatterned and the striped slides (by sucking faster on a nipple when they were shown a new slide), the experimenter measured the infants' visual acuity. At 2 weeks, he found, infants could make out stripes that were one-eighth inch wide; at 6 months they could make out stripes one-fortieth of an inch wide. In another study, newborns' visual acuity was shown to range from about 20/150 to 20/800 (Fantz, 1961). (A person with 20/150 visual acuity sees an object 20 feet away as if it were 150 feet away.) By the second half of their first year, infants have 20/20 vision.

But even in the first six months, infants are far from blind. Martin Banks and Philip Salapatek (1981) suggested a useful way of thinking about the visual limitations of infants. They referred to the amount of information in a pattern that an infant can see as his or her visual "window." Early in life, an infant's visual window is quite limited, but the contours of many common objects are well within this "window." Young infants can see the contrast between hair and skin on a parent's face, for example. Although infants cannot see small things on the other side of a room, they can see large objects close up—the distance at which much of the interaction between young infants and their parents takes place.

Visual preferences

Psychologists have been interested not only in finding out how *well* infants can see, but in finding out what they like to look at. Infants show clear preferences for looking at certain *kinds* of objects up close. They look longer at a pattern than at a plain surface (Fantz, 1965). But too much pattern can make them tune out. In the first month, infants look longer at a pattern made up of a four-square checkerboard than at a more complex checkerboard (Brennan, Ames, and Moore; 1965; Hershenson, 1964). Infants also like to look at pictures of faces (Fantz, 1963; see Figure 5.8).

LOOKING AT A
CHECKERBOARD THROUGH
THE EYES OF A NEWBORN

Adult sees:

6 × 6

16 × 16

Infant sees:

6 × 6

16 × 16

Figure 5.10 No wonder 1-month-old infants prefer to look at a 6×6 checkerboard instead of one with 256 squares. In the infant's limited visual system, the complex patterning of a 16×16 checkerboard is lost (Banks and Salapatek, 1983).

Is there something about faces that attracts infants? When researchers showed newborns pictures of faces with normal or scrambled features, they found no difference in how far the infants turned their heads or their eyes to follow the pictures (Maurer and Young, 1983). Other studies support these results and show that infants younger than 2 months do not look at normal looking faces in preference to scrambled faces (Fantz, 1961; Fantz and Nevis, 1967; Maurer and Barrera, 1981; see Figure 5.9). It is now generally thought that faces have no innate attractiveness for babies but instead contain attractive elements—like curved contours, a moderate amount of complexity, and movement (Olson, 1983).

Why *do* young infants like to look at patterns with these characteristics? The most recent suggestion is that infants prefer patterns that are the most salient and visible and have the largest discernible elements that fit their visual ''window'' (Banks and Salapatek, 1983; see Figure 5.10). This appears to be true for infants up to 3 months old (Gayl, Roberts, and Werner, 1983).

Because infants have only a limited ability to perceive complex patterns, they tend to look at the most striking aspect of a pattern, the part that is moving, or largest, or of greatest contrast—the part they can see best. For such young infants, this is usually the outside contour of a figure or face (Figure 5.11). At 2 to 4 months, when infants see a face, they focus on the now visible eyes and mouth as well. Infants focus on contrast, it has been suggested, to keep the neurons of the visual cortex firing at a high level. This firing seems to prod the development of the visual cortex. Looking at contrast also allows infants to get the most information a stimulus affords. Later, at 5 to 7 months, infants also gaze at the nose when they see a face. By then they seem to know something about what faces are and distinguish between scrambled and normal arrangements of features. They are doing more than looking simply at what they see best (Caron, Caron, Caldwell, and Weiss, 1973; Haith, Bergman, and Moore, 1977; Salapatek, 1975).

Seeing colors

From the time they are born, infants can see the difference between brightness and darkness. Whether newborns can also notice the differences among red, blue, yellow, and green is not yet settled, although there is some evidence to suggest that they can (Adams and Maurer, 1983, 1984). The

Figure 5.11 Infrared marker lights placed behind a stimulus reflect off babies' eyes, permitting the photographing of their pupils' movements and the tracking of their visual scanning. One-month-old infants concentrate on areas of greatest contrast in faces, particularly the edges of the face and head. Two-month-old infants scan features, especially the eyes and mouth (Maurer and Salapatek, 1975).

INFANT VISUAL SCANNING

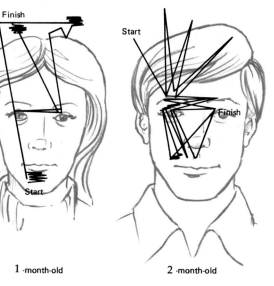

1-month-old   2-month-old

Looking at faces

Can 1-month-old babies recognize their own mother's face? Edward Melhuish (1982), an English psychologist, set out to explore this question. He tested 31 babies between 24 and 35 days old. Each was seated facing a screen in an observation chamber with cloth sides. Through an opening in the screen that was 10 inches in front of the baby, the mother's or a female stranger's face appeared.

When naive observers tried to tell from videotapes of the babies' reactions which faces the babies had seen, they could not guess beyond a chance level. Melhuish concluded that 1-month-olds did not recognize their mothers by sight. But Melhuish had presented his own dark-haired, dark-bearded, pale-skinned face to the babies as a way of checking the observers' accuracy at judging where a baby was looking. As he examined the videotapes of all the trials in the experiment, he noticed that the babies usually had paid more attention to his face than to either of the women's faces. He went back and reclassified his data according to the hair color of the mother and of the female stranger. (All the adults were white-skinned.)

This time, Melhuish found that the infants looked significantly longer at dark-haired adults. He concluded that contrast between light and dark is most important in 1-month-olds' visual attention to faces, not whether the face belongs to their constant companion or a total stranger. Not until a month or two later, research suggests, can infants recognize their parents and some months after that distinguish between familiar and unfamiliar faces (see Chapter 7, "Crying").

capacity to discriminate among colors is clearly present a few months later (Bornstein, 1985). By this age, what is more, the amount of time infants spend gazing at each of the colors corresponds to adults' ratings of each color's pleasantness—high for red and blue, low for yellow and green (Bornstein, 1975).

> Sam always gravitated towards things that are red. First he sucked on a little red plastic dumbbell someone gave him. Then he always chose the red ball over any other color. At a birthday party for another 1-year-old, he stuck his finger right into the red-frosting balloon on the birthday cake.

Perceiving distance

Psychologists long have been interested in whether babies can tell when things are near or far away. Because newborns have had no experience with objects and have lived in the dimly lit uterus, how can they know about visual cues to distance? Some researchers (Bower, Broughton, and Moore, 1970) have suggested that newborns do perceive distance. In their studies, infants were put at the end of a table, and a large box was moved toward them. As the box approached, the infants pulled in their heads, raised their arms protectively, put their hands in front of their faces, and widened their eyes or grew distressed. The researchers inferred that when babies saw the box getting larger, they understood that it was getting closer. This interpretation is speculative, however. Another interpretation is that infants were not reacting to an impending collision but were simply moving their arms or heads to parallel the rising or falling contours of the visual stimulus as it got closer (Yonas and Pettersen, 1979).

This young fellow is clearly aware of depth and does not want to venture from the "safe" runway of the visual cliff.

Other researchers have tested infants' defensive reactions to objects that seem to be coming toward them on a collision course and that then veer away. They use blinking to indicate a defensive reaction to an impending collision. In one study, for example, researchers tested 6-week-old infants for their reactions to a triangle that loomed toward them (Pettersen, Yonas, and Fisch, 1980). The infants blinked on only 16 percent of the approaches. Apparently distance perception is not present at birth.

Another way of testing whether infants can tell that things are near or far away relies on the **visual cliff**. Infants old enough to crawl are put on a slightly raised runway in the center of a large glass table several feet high. On one side of the runway, a checkerboard pattern is fixed to the underside of the glass. On the other side, the checkerboard extends from the runway down and across the floor, creating the illusion of a steep cliff. Infants are beckoned by their mothers to cross the glass over the "cliff." In one of the early studies with the visual cliff, 6- to 14-month-old infants would not cross the cliff, suggesting that they could, indeed, recognize that the deep side was farther away (Gibson and Walk, 1960).

PERCEIVING DISTANCE

*Figure 5.12 Infants reach for the side of a "trapezoidal window" that **appears** closer to them, showing that they can perceive distance.*

But what about younger infants? In a study of 2- to 4-month-olds (Campos, Langer, and Krowitz, 1970), infants were placed on their stomachs on the cliff side. Their heart rates slowed noticeably, they cried less, and they were more attentive to what lay below them—all signs that they may have perceived the drop-off beneath them. Some researchers remain skeptical, however, that these findings prove that infants so young can perceive distance. An alternative explanation for the slowed heart rates and other signs is that the infants were responding to a perceived difference in the patterns' visibility rather than to the distance they were away.

In yet another test of when infants begin to perceive distance, researchers use a different visual illusion: a trapezoidal "window." This is a two-dimensional cutout of a window shaped like a trapezoid (see Figure 5.12). Viewing with one eye, adults think that the longer end of the trapezoidal window is nearer to them than the short end, and so, apparently, do 7-month-olds. But 5-month-olds do not. On the basis of studies designed around this technique and others, researchers have concluded that infants develop sensitivity to distance cues between 5 and 7 months of age. In trying to sum up what psychologists know about distance perception, we can say that it seems unlikely that infants are born with the same appreciation of distance that adults have. More likely, they develop the abilities to perceive distance during

*research
focus*

Familiar size as a cue to distance

When do infants develop distance perception? What do they use to judge how far away an object is? To answer those questions, Albert Yonas and his fellow researchers tested how infants reacted to photographs of familiar and unfamiliar faces (Yonas, Pettersen, and Granrud, 1982). First they asked adults to judge how far away the photographs looked to them. In front of each adult, who had closed his or her eyes, a yardstick was placed across the table for reference. When the adult opened one eye, the photograph was uncovered, and the adult was asked to judge how far away it looked. The photographs were actually all the same size, and all were 12 inches from the viewer.

Adults, on the average, thought that a photograph of a large face was 9 inches away and a photograph of a small face was 20 inches away. Thus they judged the large face to be within an infant's reaching distance and the small face to be out of reach. If the infants saw the photographs as the adults did, they could be expected to reach more to the large than to the small face.

To test this expectation. Yonas presented 78 infants of 7 months with the same pictures as the adults had seen. Only infants whose parents said that they had begun reaching were used as subjects. Each infant was shown a set of pictures portraying a large and a small photograph of the same face.

Infants were seated in a canvas infant seat that was placed on a table. The photographs were presented on the tabletop, and a videotape camera recorded the infants' responses. Infants wore an eye patch over their left eye. Every time the infant looked at the photograph, the experimenter pushed a button. If an infant's attention wandered, the experimenter tried to redirect it by tapping on the back of the photo. Infants who fussed were taken out of the infant seat and soothed. All the infants viewed the large and small photographs alternately until they grew too fussy or bored to go on. Babies were considered to have reached for a picture if, while looking at it, they moved one or both hands forward with a grasping or swiping motion that crossed a line 4 inches in front of them.

Like the adults, 7-month-olds who had viewed the faces with one eye reached significantly more often and longer for the larger face. This response suggests that they perceived the large faces but not the small faces to be within their reach. Younger infants did not differentiate between the large and small photographs. This study joins a number of others in suggesting that infants learn to perceive distance at some time between 5 and 7 months of age.

their first six months of life, as their visual and motor systems mature and as they learn to interpret what they see.

Hearing

Newborns clearly are physiologically equipped to hear. As we saw in Chapter 4, in fact, even fetuses can hear. Newborns' ears have a nearly adult-sized **tympanum** and a well formed **cochlea**, and their auditory system is functioning (Northern and Downs, 1974). But, just as clearly, they do not hear as well as adults do. Although data from various investigations are not completely consistent, it seems that the softest sound that a newborn can hear is 10 to 20 decibels louder than the softest sound an adult can hear. There are several reasons for this deficiency in infants' hearing, which is approximately the amount of hearing an adult loses during a head cold.

At first, the amniotic fluid that remains in the outer ear plus the fluid and residual tissue left in the middle ear may impair the newborn's hearing. In the first few days after birth, the outer ear drains and the middle ear absorbs nearly all the fluid and tissue. At that point, researchers can investigate infants' hearing by recording changes in their heart rates, sucking rates, or brain-wave patterns when a sound is presented. By using these techniques, researchers have found that infants 1 to 2 weeks old can discriminate between loud and soft sounds and high and low ones. They can detect the difference between two notes on a musical scale (Weir, 1979). The softest sounds they respond to are, on the average, about 20 to 30 decibels—the sound of a soft voice—although there are significant differences among individuals, and the exact level of sound responded to depends on the measurement technique used (Acredolo and Hake, 1982). Past the newborn period, hearing gradually improves. But even in their second six months of life, infants are about four times less sensitive to differences in sound frequencies than adults (Aslin and Sinnott, 1984). Hearing improves to adult levels over the first two years of life.

Speech perception

Of special interest to developmental psychologists is infants' ability to hear the sounds of speech. Interestingly, newborns have better hearing for sounds in the range of speech than for higher or lower sounds (Eisenberg, 1965, 1979). Also, although they show large body movements and a faster heartbeat when listening to single tones and noises, when they hear someone talking, newborns show small movements, such as grimaces, crying (or stopping crying), dilation of the pupils, and movement of their eyes toward the source of the sound (Eisenberg, 1976, 1979). By 2 weeks of age, infants notice the difference between a human voice and other sounds, such as the sound of a bell. At 4 weeks, they can discriminate between small differences in spoken sounds. In a study by Peter Eimas and his colleagues (Eimas, Siqueland, Jusczyk, and Vigorito, 1971), babies sucked on a nipple that turned on a recording of /b/ sounds. But after they had heard the sound repeatedly, they grew used to it—they habituated—and sucked less. Gradually the recording changed to a /p/ sound. When the sound was clearly /p/ and not something in between /b/ and /p/, the babies sucked harder again. The study showed that infants perceive speech sounds in the same categories as adults do (such as /b/ and /p/). Infants can discriminate between even subtly different sounds, like the /a/ in "cot" versus the /ɔ/ in "caught" other researchers have shown (Kuhl, 1983). They can discriminate between these sounds despite changes in speaker—man, woman, or child—and, in some cases, despite changes in rising or falling pitch.

The ability to discriminate between sounds like these probably is innate rather than learned, for it precedes infants' exposure to much language. Cross-language studies (for example, Lasky, Syrdal-Lasky, and Klein, 1975; Trehub, 1973) show that infants from many different linguistic backgrounds can discriminate between similar sounds. Young infants can even hear contrasts in a foreign language that adults who do not speak the language cannot hear. Japanese babies, for instance, have no trouble with the /l/–/r/ distinction that their parents find difficult. Adults apparently have had long practice at learning *not* to hear many sounds that are not significant in their own language. This effect sets in early. Even at 1 year of age, infants have more trouble than they did earlier distinguishing sounds that are not used in their own language (Werker and Tees, in Friedrich, 1983).

The reason that infants discriminate between speech sounds seems to be that some acoustical attributes are more striking than others, rather than that humans have some special "speech processor." For one thing, infants discriminate between nonspeech sounds as well as speech sounds (Jusczyk,

Rosner, Cutting, Foard, and Smith, 1977). For another, lower species of animals, like chinchillas, as well as humans, discriminate between speech sounds (Kuhl, 1981). This does not mean that speech is not special to infants though, because it is. Infants pay more attention to a human voice than to a synthesizer making the same sounds, for instance (Trehub and Curran, 1979).

Even though infants *can* discriminate between similar spoken sounds in an experiment, psychologists still do not have the answer to how babies actually *do* segment the speech they hear. Do they segment it into **phonemes**— the smallest units of language, such as /b/ed versus /r/ed—into syllables, into words, into all of these, or into none? Although researchers have shown that infants *can* discriminate between phonemes like /b/ and /p/, syllables like /bah/ and /pah/, and words like *ball* and *Paul*, they have not yet demonstrated that infants *do* divide the speech stream they hear in these ways. At some point, infants must begin to segment speech in some meaningful way, or they would never learn to talk. But they may not begin to do so until they have communication as their goal and have received feedback from adults about the meaning of their utterances. It seems plausible that syllables or single-syllable words are the first divisions that infants make (Bertoncini and Mehler, 1981). Finer distinctions, like categorization into phonemes, may not happen until children are learning to read (Jusczyk, 1977; Liberman, Shankweiler, Fischer, and Carter, 1974).

Baby talk

No matter how they segment sounds, babies often hear speech that is especially adapted to their hearing. Adults the world over talk to babies in a special way—in "baby talk," of course. **Baby talk** is a whole range of changes worked on the usual patterns of adult speech. People speak to babies at a high pitch, exaggerate their tones from bass to squeaks, and swoop exaggeratedly from whispers to shouts. "Hi baby-baby. Izzata baby-baby?" They speak quickly or slowly, repeat words and phrases, and draw out their vowels. They make nonsense sounds and speak in a singsong rhythm. " "Im luva Mommy? *At's* a goo' boy." In languages from Arabic to Latvian, people from grandfathers to older sisters pitch their voices high when they speak to infants (Ferguson, 1964; Ruke-Dravina, 1977; Fernald and Simon, 1984; Fourcin, 1978). Listening to a tape of an adult speaking baby talk, one researcher thought that the adult was a woman—until the adult spoke to the baby's grandmother in *his* normal tone of voice (Tuaycharoen, 1978). This higher

Adults around the world talk to babies in a special way—in baby talk. Infants prefer the high pitch and exaggerated intonations of this special speech.

pitch is not universal. It is not found among Quiche Mayan mothers, for example (Ratner and Pye, 1984), but it is very widespread.

Infants love this baby talk. Infants from 4 to 18 months old who could choose between hearing adult conversation and baby talk chose to listen to—and, presumably, preferred—the baby talk (Fernald, 1981, 1985; Glenn and Cunningham, 1983). What do infants like about baby talk? Judging by their listening choices, they like its rising tones—''This little piggy went to market'' rather than ''No, no, don't touch'' (Sullivan and Horowitz, 1983). They like its expressive and exaggerated intonation—''And *this* little piggy ran *all* the way home'' (Lieberman, 1967; Turnure, 1971; Kearsley, 1973). They particularly like its high pitch (Fernald, 1982). A mother's voice is probably especially appealing to her infant because it has all these qualities. When 4- to 6-week-old infants heard brief speeches by their mothers and by another woman, some of which were highly intonated and some of which were monotonous, they preferred their mothers' voices, but only when they were intonated (Mehler, Bertoncini, Barriere, and Jassik-Gerschenfeld, 1978).

> Even before he could focus his eyes clearly, Sam would stop, listen, and perk up whenever he heard my voice as I entered the room he was in.
>
> After Jason took a bottle, he usually was responsive and not irritable. I'd entertain him with an old high-school cheer that I knew. It was full of nonsense syllables and heavily rhythmical.
>
> *Ah-ba-la-ba, goo-ba-la-ba, goo-ba-la-ba, vee-stay.*
> *Ah-ba-la-ba, goo-ba-la-ba, goo-ba-la-ba, vee-stay.*
> *Oh, no, no, no, no, vee-stay, vee-stay.*
> *Eenie-meanie dixie-deenie ooh-la thumbeleenie,*
> *Aatchie, patchie Liberace, I mean you!*
>
> Jason would stare at me, transfixed, and I had a wonderful time sing-songing to him. Of course, anyone who heard us would have thought that we had lost our minds.

Infants also like to listen to baby talk because baby talk is salient, tuned to infants' sensory capacitites, and infants may be biologically predisposed to hear and pay attention to it (Fernald, 1984; Sachs, 1977). For one thing, the pitch of baby talk makes it subjectively louder than speech at lower pitch, so it stands out against background noise. For another, the contours of baby talk—long, smooth, gradual—are simple, separated by pauses, and easy to track. Baby talk is like a simple melody, and because infants' auditory systems are immature, simple patterns are easier for them to perceive. Infants react physiologically to the pitch contours of baby talk. They are aroused by a high, rising pitch and soothed by a low, falling one—another reason that baby talk stands out for them. Baby talk is tuned not only to babies' hearing but also to their vocal capacities. Baby talk contains many syllables that begin with the very initial-stop consonants—baba, papa, dada—that infants burble themselves (Pierce, 1974). The high pitch, special tones, patterns, and rhythms that characterize baby talk are used in infants' own speech. When infants hear a high-pitched voice, they immediately raise their own pitch, for example (Webster, Steinhardt, and Senter, 1972). Baby talk is clearly an appropriate way to talk to infants.

Looking and listening

In real life, infants see and hear at the same time, integrating the information from the two domains to make sense of their world. One way they do this is by looking to locate the source of a sound. Even newborns do this in a rudimentary way. In one study of 2- to 4-day-old infants (Muir and Field, 1979), a tape-recorded rattle sounded from one of two loudspeakers on either side of the infant. Three-quarters of the time, infants turned toward the sound, although it took them about 2½ seconds to begin responding and nearly 6 seconds to turn their heads all the way. By 4 months of age, infants can look toward the right person when their mother or father talks to them (Spelke and Owsley, 1979). They can demonstrate their coordination of sight and sound in other ways as well. When shown a film of a bouncing toy donkey on one screen and a bouncing toy kangaroo on another, infants preferred to watch the film of the animal that bounced in time to the sound track (Spelke, 1976, 1978, 1979a, 1979b).

Taste and smell

Newborns can tell water, sugar, and salt from milk, and they respond differently to different concentrations of sweet, salty, and bitter solutions (Ganchrow, Steiner, and Daher, 1983; Jensen, 1932). Newborns suck longer and pause for shorter periods when they are given a sweet solution (Lipsitt, Reilly, Butcher, and Greenwood, 1976). They also suck more slowly, as if they are savoring the sweetness. In addition to sucking, newborns smile and lick their upper lip when they taste a sweet solution (Ganchrow et al., 1983).

Newborns also have a good sense of smell, although they cannot discriminate smells as acutely as they will later on. Infants turn away from a strong smell, such as ammonia. They breathe faster and move around more when they smell asatfetida, which smells like garlic (Lipsitt, Engen, and Kaye, 1963). They turn their faces toward a sweet smell, and their heart rates and breathing slow down (Brazelton, 1969). They smile at the smell of vanilla and banana but protest the smell of rotten eggs and shrimp. Within days after birth, breast-fed newborns prefer the odor of their mother's milk to that of another mother (Russell, 1976).

Perceptual processes

So far in this chapter, we have discussed infants' abilities to see, hear, taste, smell, and move. But infants are not just passive receivers of the sights, sounds, tastes, and smells that the environment throws their way. They actively seek some sights—faces—and some sounds—baby talk—rather than others. How and why do they do this, and how do they make sense of what they see and hear? Which processes do they use in actively perceiving not only lines, colors, and sounds but things, places, and events in the world?

The traditional view in philosophy and psychology is that we begin life with minimal perceptual capacities and build them up only with years of experience. We now know that infants have some perceptual capacities even at birth. Much of what we know about infants' perceptual development is the result of the theory and research conducted and inspired by James and Eleanor Gibson (Gibson, 1966, 1969; Gibson and Spelke, 1983). In their view, infants are endowed with powerful perceptual capacities from birth. With experience infants become increasingly aware of information in the world, and their perception becomes more exact and differentiated. They learn to extract more and more of this information from objects and to make more and more subtle distinctions among objects. Unlike Piaget, who held that infants construct their perception of objects by acting on them (see Chapter 6), the Gibsons theorized that the information is in the object and that all infants have to do is seek, and they will find.

Exploring

The first step in this seeking and finding is attending to the environment, exploring its features, and focusing on some action or object out of the vast array available. Even newborns pay attention to the sights and sounds in their world, although often the only sign that they have noticed something is a slowed heartbeat. They notice especially the *onsets* of sights and sounds and, as we have discussed, sights and sounds that are contrasting and relatively intense.

> As I came up to 2-month-old Natalie's stroller and said hello, her eyes flickered. Then she seemed to stare hard at my face for almost a minute. But she looked past my shoulder when a noisy truck passed by.

Very young infants can attend to the environment for only short periods of time, but as they mature, infants' periods of attentiveness lengthen. In these attentive periods, infants actively explore, with eyes and ears, hands and mouths, the sights, sounds, objects, and events that have caught their attention. With age their exploration becomes more swift, efficient, systematic, and focused in direction. But right from the beginning, it is purposeful and directed. Even newborns actively scan visual objects, moving their eyes back and forth systematically when they come across contrast, contours, or corners. At this age, though, they move their eyes back and forth in one place rather than searching whole scenes. As they get older, they look at whole objects. In the early months, infants also explore by putting things into their mouths, and for the first six months or so, they prefer mouthing to exploring with their hands. By 8 or 9 months of age, with improved motor control and coordination they explore more with their hands, bang and squeeze things. They also coordinate their tactile manipulating of objects—fingering, turning, poking—with their visual examination. When given a new object, infants at this age examine by touching and looking (Ruff, 1986). The fact that similar developmental changes occur in scanning by touch as well as in visual scanning suggests that central processes direct exploration in all the senses.

Infants also become increasingly selective about which features of the environment they explore and focus on. As we have already seen, they prefer at first to look at edges and angles, contours and corners. These early visual preferences, we suggested, are determined largely by the infant's cortical and visual capacities rather than by the properties of the stimuli. Beginning at the age of 3 or 4 months and thereafter, however, the properties of the stimuli themselves affect infants' attention and exploration. Some infants attend to color more than size; others attend to shape more than color (Odom, 1978). An infant may attend first to color, then to shape, then to size, and so on. But whatever the differences among individuals, all infants grow increasingly selective and focused as they get older. They learn to tailor their perception to the particular object and situation.

Detecting invariances

According to the Gibsons' theory of perception, infants perceive events, objects, and places by detecting **invariants**—that is, actions or things that look or sound the same every time they appear. The ability to perceive these invariants is based on innate perceptual abilities and, like the ability to explore the environment, they suggest, improves with physical maturation and with experience.

The process by which infants come to know that things are objects typifies the process. To study infants' perception of objects, a researcher might show the infants an object in which part is hidden, then show them the

PERCEIVING A SQUARE

Habituation stimulus

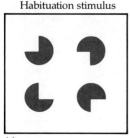

(a)

Novel stimulus

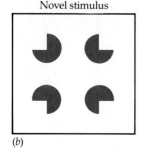

(b)

Novel stimulus

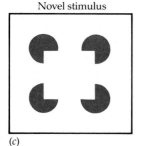

(c)

Figure 5.13 Adults see a square only in stimulus c. Researchers using habituation techniques have found that 3-month-olds respond as though all three arrangements are alike, whereas 7-month-olds pay more attention to stimulus c, suggesting that they perceive a square or part of it (Bertenthal et al., 1980).

complete object, and then see whether they discriminate between the two. Results of experiments like this suggest that, from the beginning, infants know something about the nature of objects. They seem to know that if two points move together or touch each other, they are part of the same object (Spelke, 1982). They perceive an object when they see connected surfaces that remain connected while in motion, and they perceive the difference between object and background as the object moves and the texture of the background is added to and subtracted from along the moving object's edges. By perceiving the connected movements of a caterpillar crawling along a leaf, a ball rolling along a sidewalk, or Dad entering a room, infants come to perceive caterpillar, ball, and Dad as objects. Infants fail to track objects moving in tandem with their backgrounds, perhaps because they perceive object and background as a single unit moving together. Only after experience with many objects do infants learn that objects are separate from their backgrounds.

Part of perceiving invariants is recognizing that an object's size and shape remain constant even if the object is moved closer or farther away or tilted to the left or right. The 7-month-olds in the study of distance perception described in the Research Focus: Familiar Size as a Cue to Distance demonstrated that they knew that faces are always the same size. But what about younger infants? By the time infants are 3 or 4 months old, researchers have found, they have this knowledge (Day and MacKenzie, 1973, 1981). In fact, even at birth infants appear to have **shape constancy** for simple shapes (Slater, 1986). That is, they respond to identical simple shapes in the same way even if the shapes are tilted at different angles. Researchers are still exploring how precise and detailed infants' perception of sizes and shapes is over the first months (Gibson and Spelke, 1983). The perception of more complex shapes seems to take time to develop (see Figure 5.13). Newborn infants do not seem to perceive patterns. By the age of 3 months, infants do perceive simple patterns, and by 8 months, they perceive complex patterns. Experts still disagree to some extent about what is inborn, what matures, and what is learned in the first months of life. But there is agreement that by the end of infancy, the basic perceptual competencies are in place.

Recognizing affordances

In the Gibsons' theory, infants learn not only about invariances but about the properties of objects. They learn what they can *do* with objects and what they can expect from them. Places, objects, and events all offer such **affordances.** Water affords wetness, and floors afford support. Fires afford warming and light to read by. A wall is an obstacle that affords collision, but a doorway in the wall affords passage. Affordances are not determined solely by the properties of objects. They are also related to the observer: a floor affords support to people but not to elephants, and a leaf affords shade to a person but support to a caterpillar. Affordances may derive from an object's texture, shape, or substance and may involve more than one sense. To judge affordances, we use information that we take in with our eyes—a floor must be level, solid, rigid, neither too slippery nor too rough to be walkable upon—plus information from our ears—the creak of the floor—and from touch—the give of the floor under our weight.

When do infants first begin to perceive the properties of objects, properties like flexibility, texture, and shape, from which they can judge the objects' affordances? Even very young infants have rudimentary abilities to perceive the properties of objects. At 1 month, infants can differentiate between rigid and flexible substances in their mouths, like teething rings and nipples. At 3½ months, they can see the difference between rigid and flexible motion—the difference between a ball being rolled and a ball being squeezed, for instance.

Infants explore the features of their surroundings. This 8-month-old looks, touches, and tastes.

They can see the difference between flat and solid objects and between objects of different simple shapes like spheres and cubes. At 6 months, infants can feel the difference between rough and smooth textures. One-year-olds distinguish between rigid and elastic substances by banging the hard objects and squeezing, pressing, and wiping with the spongy ones. They recognize by sight or by touch simple shapes they have manipulated (Gottfried, Rose, and Bridger, 1977). As they get older and develop strategies of exploring and manipulating, infants' perceptions of objects become increasingly differentiated. In addition to perceiving the properties of flexibility, shape, and texture, infants perceive the color, temperature, scent, size, and animacy of the objects around them (Gibson and Spelke, 1983). From their perceptions, they predict objects' affordances.

> Sam never had any trouble knowing which things were good to eat. Later on he got good at knowing just what to do with a new toy—bang with the hard ones and squeeze the soft ones.

> Natalie's babysitter arrived one morning with a cake of soap that looked exactly like a piece of layer cake, complete with ''frosting'' and a ''cherry'' on top. Poor Natalie bit off a big mouthful, then let out a startled wail, and made the most horrible grimace of disgust I have ever seen.

Summary

1. An infant's first month after birth is a risky time, when untested biological systems must function independently in a germ-filled environment. The newborn's immediate tasks include breathing, eating, stabilizing

body temperature, and circulating blood. The Apgar test is used to assess the condition of the newborn immediately after birth.

2. Among the risks to infants' survival in their first year of life are prematurity, low birth weight, disease, malnutrition, sudden infant death syndrome (SIDS), and neglect. An infant's sex and birth order influence weight and maturity at birth.

3. The average newborn weighs 7½ pounds and is 20 inches long. Newborns whose size was restrained by their mother's small uterus go through catch-up growth after birth. Heredity has but a small effect on prenatal size, but it strongly affects catch-up growth.

4. Healthy newborns have more than 20 reflexes. Some reflexes help the newborn to feed, some to maintain contact with the mother, and others anticipate actions—like swimming and walking—that are learned later only by deliberate effort. Tests of reflexes help doctors to detect central nervous system disorders. Most reflexes disappear within a matter of months after birth.

5. Infants go through a range of states of consciousness from deep to active sleep, drowsiness to quiet alertness, calm activity to restlessness, soft crying to loud squalling. Newborns sleep up to 70 percent of the time; half of that sleep time is active sleep, half quiet sleep.

6. Infants acquire motor abilities in the same order that body parts grew before birth. In the first months, infants are able to lift and support their heads. Later, they learn to roll from stomach to side or back and to sit unsupported. At 6 months, they can touch their hands together in front of them and move them up and down and side to side. At 7 months, they may pull themselves into a standing position. Soon comes creeping, crawling, and sometime around the first birthday, the first independent steps. Individual variations in reaching motor milestones are common, and both heredity and environmental conditions affect infants' rates of motor development.

7. The infant's visual system matures gradually over the first two years. In early infancy, the abilities to focus, to track objects, to accommodate to the shifting planes of visual targets, and to discriminate details all are worse than adults'. Infants can see clearly only objects that are large, close to them, and high in contrast—and a parent's face during feeding, for instance, precisely fits this description. Infants also prefer to look at things with high contrast, contours, a moderate degree of complexity, and movement.

8. Researchers have used several different techniques to determine that the perception of distance develops in infants when they are between 5 and 7 months old.

9. Newborns can hear the difference between loud and soft, high and low tones. But their hearing is not as acute as adults' throughout their first year of life. Infants prefer human speech to other sounds. They especially like baby talk, which typically has a high pitch, exaggerated tone, slow and repetitive wording, and drawn-out vowel sounds.

10. Newborns coordinate what they hear with what they see. They can also taste and smell at birth.

11. Newborns pay attention to their environments and notice the onset of sights and sounds. As they mature, they can pay attention for longer periods. They actively explore with their senses and select things to focus on. They detect the invariance of objects in the environment and perceive what they can do with these things.

Key terms

Apgar test
restraining effect
small for gestational age (small for dates)
sudden infant death syndrome (SIDS)
apnea
marasmus
colostrum
placebo
failure to thrive
catch-up growth
reflex
rooting reflex

sucking reflex
palmar grasp
Moro (embracing) reflex
stepping reflex
lability
myelination
tonic neck reflex
habituation
fovea
dendrites
saccadic eye movements
astigmatism

accommodate
depth of focus
visual acuity
visual cliff
tympanum
cochlea
phoneme
baby talk
invariants
shape constancy
affordances

Suggested readings

Bower, T. G. R. *The Perceptual World of the Child.* Cambridge, MA: Harvard University Press, 1977. An easy to read discussion of the perceptual capacities and development of infants and young children.

Gesell, Arnold, Ilg, Frances, and Ames, Louise. *Infant and Child in the Culture of Today.* New York: Harper and Row, 1974. Milestones of motor and perceptual development in infancy and childhood.

Klaus, Marshall and Klaus, Phyllis. *The Amazing Newborn.* Reading, MA: Addison-Wesley, 1985. Discussion of the awareness, sensory capacities, and abilities of the newborn, amply illustrated with photos.

chapter six
Cognitive development

If you have ever seen, or been, an adult in physical therapy, trying to relearn some lost physical skill—walking, grasping, flexing an ankle or knee, forming words—and expending enormous concentration and effort, then perhaps you can imagine life for the infant, for whom everything is new and must be learned through repetition, practice, and perseverence. If you have ever forgotten where you left your keys, if you have ever been stumped in remembering a teacher's name, perhaps you can imagine life for the infant, for whom sustained memory is impossible. If you have ever seen a videotape of Neil Armstrong taking a giant step on the moon, perhaps you can imagine life for the infant, for whom each new achievement is occasion for great excitement. But imaginings aren't really enough for developmental psychologists. Analogies are not necessarily apt. *Is* this what life is like for the infant? What *does* go on inside that fuzzy head with the angelic smile? What do babies remember from yesterday? What do they think about their toys? their parents? their first steps? How do they learn that something delicious is in the bottle? How do they learn to play with spoons, blocks, cars? How do they learn that they are unique and separate beings?

Developmental psychologists have asked these questions—and have found them hard to answer. They cannot just ask 6-month-olds what's on their minds, and so they have designed experiments to try to find the answers. In the last chapter, we discussed how infants take in the sights and sounds and smells around them. In this chapter, we will discuss how infants learn, remember, think, and know about the world.

Learning in infancy

> For his first few months, Sam slept in a bassinet with a string of bright red, yellow, and blue plastic horses draped over one side. The horses rattled when they were moved. One night at about midnight, I was awakened by the sound of the horses rattling. Sam's hand must have brushed against them by accident in the dark. The sound stopped. An hour later, I heard them rattling again: once, twice, three times. The sound stopped. I fell asleep again. Soon the horses were rattling again—and again and again. Sam rattled the horses in bursts all night long. He had learned his first trick. The next night, I made sure that the horses were draped *outside* of the bassinet!

Ingenious experiments have offered developmental psychologists a baby's-eye view of learning. In these experiments researchers have probed the ways in which babies learn. One way infants might learn is by classical conditioning, associating events that repeatedly happen together. Ivan Pavlov, you will recall, demonstrated that animals can learn in this way. In his classic experiment, Pavlov rang a bell (the **conditioned stimulus**—CS) just before food (the **unconditioned stimulus**—the UCS) was put into a dog's mouth. The dog responded to the food by salivating (the **unconditioned response**—UCR). After the food and the bell had been paired repeatedly, the dog began to salivate (the **conditioned response**—CR) as soon as it heard the bell. Later, John Watson demonstrated that infants, too, could learn by classical conditioning (Watson and Rayner, 1920). In his most famous demonstration, Watson chose a 9-month-old named Albert as his subject and set out to make Albert afraid of a white rat. First, he demonstrated that Albert was not afraid of the white rat, a white rabbit, cotton batting, or other white things. He then demonstrated that when Albert heard a steel bar rapped loudly behind his head (UCS), he jumped (UCR). Two months later, Watson began to condition

Albert. Whenever Albert saw the white rat (CS) and reached out to play with it, Watson rapped the steel bar behind the baby's head. After seven repetitions, Albert drew back at the sight of the rat, cried, and tried to crawl away (CR). Five days later and at two other sessions, Albert reacted fearfully to the white rat and to some extent to the other white things, too. He now was conditioned to fear previously positive stimuli, and his fear generalized to other, similar objects. Classical conditioning can take place in everyday situations, too, not just in the laboratory. The infant whose doctor comes to be associated with painful injections or the aunt who comes to be associated with painful, cheek-pinching greetings make the infant recoil in fear, just as Albert recoiled from the white rat. But how old do infants have to be before they begin to associate things in this way? Do even newborn infants learn through classical conditioning?

Psychologists have tried to condition very young infants under controlled conditions to provide answers to these questions—only to be frustrated at the obstacles. One researcher may report that he has demonstrated conditioning, but another researcher will not be able to duplicate his results. Some researchers have worked with groups of infants so small that it is not meaningful to generalize from their results. Others have neglected to take into account the infants' state of wakefulness, and, as we suggested in Chapter 5, it is unlikely that infants learn unless they are actively awake and alert. These obstacles aside, there is little evidence that infants under 2 or 3 months old can be classically conditioned. Most attempts to classically condition very young infants have failed (Sameroff and Cavanaugh, 1979). Psychologists now tend to be skeptical that infants in their first few months learn through classical conditioning.

Another way that infants might learn is through operant, or instrumental conditioning. In this kind of learning, a person or an animal does something, finds the consequences of the action rewarding, and therefore repeats the action. A laboratory pigeon, for example, pecks at a bar on the side of its cage (the operant response). The peck releases a pellet of food (the reinforcer) into the cage. The pigeon pecks again at the bar and receives another pellet of food. The rate at which the pigeon pecks the bar is increased by the presentation of food pellets. As long as food is presented at least some of the time after the bar is pressed, the pigeon will press the bar at a high rate. If reinforcement is discontinued, bar pressing will decline. Pigeons are not the only creatures to learn to do things for rewards. People do, too, of course. But do infants learn through instrumental conditioning?

With young infants, researchers' attempts to demonstrate operant conditioning have been more successful than their attempts to demonstrate classical conditioning. In one study, for example, newborn infants' sucking on a nipple became stronger or faster if only strong or fast sucking was rewarded with milk (Sameroff, 1968). To keep the milk flowing, infants also learned to change the way they sucked. In another successful demonstration of instrumental conditioning, newborn infants learned to turn their heads to the side if the experimenter brushed their cheeks and gave them sweetened water every time they did so (Siqueland and Lipsitt, 1966). These successful demonstrations of instrumental conditioning in young infants, you will notice, relied on the infants' sucking and rooting reflexes. Researchers now suspect that the reflexes of newborns can be conditioned because newborns are already physiologically prepared to take in stimuli and to learn from the environment by using these reflexes (Sameroff and Cavanaugh, 1979). If this is true, the instrumental learning of newborns seen in these experiments may differ in kind from that seen in older infants and adults, reflecting simply a basic adaptation of reflexes rather than the modification of a voluntary or operant action.

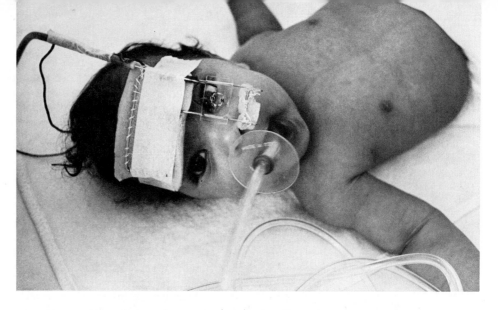

In this classical conditioning experiment, researchers attempted to condition the infant to blink, a reflex (UCR), when a tone (CS) was played. They originally elicited the blink by directing a puff of air (UCS) into the infant's eye as the tone sounded.

Beginning when infants are 3 months old, however, a broader range of behavior—not just reflexes—can be modified through instrumental conditioning. At 3 to 6 months, it has been demonstrated, infants coo, smile, look, reach, press, and touch if they are rewarded for doing so. But even at this age, infants seem to have been prepared either by past experience or by biological predisposition to respond in certain ways. In one experiment, for example, 6-month-olds were seated in front of a clear panel on which they could press (Cavanaugh and Davidson, 1977). Infants in one group were rewarded by seeing lights behind the panel and hearing a bell each time they pressed the panel. Infants in a second group saw lights behind the panel and heard a bell, but the sound of the bell was not timed to their pressing. A third group of infants saw lights go on every 20 seconds, but the lights were not behind the panel. Infants in *each* group pressed the panel more often as time went by—even though only those in the first group were systematically rewarded for doing so. Why? Presumably, the infants had had lots of practice pressing things like buzzers and busy boxes, and so when they saw something to press, they reacted naturally by reaching out and pressing, and the pressing itself was rewarding. Infants in the first group did show some effects of their conditioning, however. During the *extinction* phase of the study, when the infants saw no lights and heard no bell, their rate of pressing fell below what it had been before the experiment began. Infants do learn through instrumental conditioning, but their learning at this age is still closely tied to a limited array of familiar behaviors.

Memory

Parents know from their everyday experiences what conditioning experiments demonstrate—that babies in their first year remember things: the 9-month-old baby smiles when Mother or Father, but not a stranger, appears by the crib; the 8-month-old baby who once tensed up now splashes happily in the familiar bathtub.

> Sam and I had a raucous routine that we both loved. It was a rollicking rhyme that we bounced and swung around in time to. When Sam was looking at me and I knew I had his attention, I'd begin with a loud, "Ah *one*, ah *two*, I'm talking to *you*." After a couple of times, all I had to say was "Ah *one*," and he would chortle with delight.

The problem for developmental psychologists is to demonstrate systematically and scientifically what infants can remember.

194

research focus

Infants learn to chat

Many researchers have investigated instrumental conditioning in infants by contrasting what happens when a behavior is reinforced with what happens when it is no longer reinforced. But this experimental design raises problems. The first problem is that infants tend to cry a lot during the nonreinforcement, or extinction, phase of the experiment. The second is that this experimental design does not separate the effects of *reinforcing* a response from the effects of *eliciting* a response. To reinforce an infant's response, the experimenter might systematically talk, smile, bounce, or cuddle the infant as a rewarding consequence immediately after the infant has vocalized or smiled. But talking, smiling, bouncing, and cuddling are likely to bring out infants' smiling and vocalizing by themselves. When the social stimulation used as a reinforcer is also an inherent elicitor of infants' responses, then, in the extinction phase of the study, the researcher does not know whether lack of stimulation or lack of reinforcement is causing the infant to vocalize less. The researcher does not know whether vocalization has been instrumentally conditioned.

Claire Poulson (1983) wanted to find out whether reinforcement itself would increase how much infants vocalize. She reasoned that she could do this by showing that the rate of vocalization increased when it was reinforced and decreased when silence was reinforced. Her subjects were four infants about 3 months old who came to the laboratory once a day, at least 20 times. The infants sat in a car seat facing a playhouse with a window that opened and closed. Mothers were asked, whenever the window was open, to do what they normally did to get their infant to "talk" to them. Each daily session lasted about 12 minutes, fewer if the infant fussed, cried, or fell asleep.

During each session, the infants were observed under two conditions. During the reinforcement-of-vocalization condition, as soon as the infant vocalized, the window opened and for eight seconds the mother reinforced the infant by making eye contact, talking, touching, or showing toys. In the second, reinforcement-of-silence condition, every two seconds so long as the infant did *not* vocalize the window opened for eight seconds of eye contact, talking, touching, and showing toys by the mother. If the infant vocalized, the window did not open until there had been at least four seconds of silence.

How much did the infants vocalize under these two conditions? All vocalized significantly more during the reinforcement-of-vocalization condition than during the reinforcement-of-silence condition, even though the amount of eye contact, talk, touching, and playing with the mother in the two conditions was the same. This proved that mothers' social interaction with their infants had controlled how much they vocalized through reinforcement rather than through simple stimulation or elicitation. It also suggests that the frequency of infants' vocalization at home can be affected directly by social reinforcement. Infants who learn that vocalizing brings about a big reward—attention from Mom and Dad—are likely to grow more and more chatty.

Methods of studying infants' memory

Researchers can use any of several different methods to find out how much and for how long infants remember. One method they have used is to show infants a pair of patterns. Then the infants are shown one of the patterns they have just seen plus a new one. If the infants look at the new pattern in the pair longer than they look at the familiar one, it can be inferred that they remember the familiar pattern. Infants can be shown pairs of patterns after hours, days, or weeks have elapsed to test the length of their memories. With this method of **paired comparisons**, researchers have found that 1-month-olds remember nursery mobiles for up to one day and 5-month-olds remember simple visual patterns for up to two days and pictures of faces for two weeks (Fagan, 1973; Weizmann, Cohen, and Pratt, 1971). In one study using the paired comparison method, researchers tested 5-month-old infants' memories of a three-dimensional object immediately, after 10 minutes, and again after 24 hours, by comparing it with another figure that differed in shape, color, size, and slant (Strauss and Cohen, 1978). Immediately after seeing the object, all the infants remembered all four of these characteristics. But after 10 minutes, they remembered only the object's color and form. After 24 hours, they remembered only its form. Some features are remembered better than others, even by babies, just as we saw in Chapter 5, some features are noticed more readily than others.

Just like older people, infants eventually tire of looking at the same old patterns and pictures—they *habituate* (see Chapter 5). Researchers capitalize on this human tendency to grow bored with the old in a second method of studying infants' memory. Researchers show infants a pattern and see how quickly they habituate. When they habituate, the assumption is that they remember having seen the pattern. Newborns, even premature ones, this method shows, eventually habituate to simple shapes (Werner and Siqueland, 1978). But as they mature, infants habituate more and more quickly with more and more complex patterns. One reason they do so is that it takes them progressively less time to scan what they see and to **encode** their sensory impressions in their brains. Individual abilities also play a role in how quickly infants habituate. Infants who habituate quickly are likely to have had a high Apgar score at birth and a well-functioning central nervous system and to perform well on tests of learning and intelligence (Lewis, 1971). Yet once infants have absorbed information, they all seem to retain that information for the same length of time (Werner and Perlmutter, 1980). Individual infants vary in their speed and thoroughness at recognizing objects and patterns as familiar but apparently not in retaining their images.

Researchers rely on infants' retention of learned responses as a third measure of their memories. One- and 2-month-olds, so studies using this measure indicate, can retain a learned response from one day to another, and 3-month-olds can retain information even longer (Papousek, 1959, 1961, 1967; Weizmann et al., 1971). In one ingenious study, 3-month-olds were put in their own cribs at home, with a ribbon tying one of their feet to a lever that turned a mobile (Rovee-Collier, Sullivan, Enright, Lucas, and Fagen, 1980). As the infants kicked, the mobile turned, and this interesting motion reinforced their kicking. They had two learning sessions one day apart; during each of them, the infants moved the mobile for about ten minutes. Several weeks later, the infants got a three-minute ''refresher'' session with the mobile. A day after the refresher session, the infants all could turn the mobile like pros. Infants who had not had the learning experience could not. In short, 3-month-old infants retained what they had learned for several weeks, if their memories were jogged by reminders of the learning experience.

A fourth method of studying infants' memories relies on observation of the infants' spontaneous behavior. Common sense tells us that infants do not behave in the same way at home as they do in a laboratory—where much of the research on their memory abilities has taken place. The laboratory is unfamiliar, devoid of informal social stimulation, and as carefully controlled for outside influences as the investigator can arrange. Some researchers therefore have looked for signs of infants' memories at home, in their natural surroundings. Home is rich in stimulation and support, and the kinds of learning and remembering that children show there can be quite different from what they show in more sterile and objective assessments. When the test materials are familiar and meaningful, and when the surroundings are comfortable and relaxed, infants are more likely to show that they retain complex memories. Parents and psychologists therefore sometimes hold quite divergent views of infants' abilities. Psychologists tend to view children as cognitively immature—as *unable* until proved otherwise. But parents, who watch their infants every day, cheering every cognitive advance they make, tend to think that their infants have impressive powers of thought—*able* unless proved otherwise.

When parents were asked to keep systematic records of any behavior their infants made at home that was based on past experience (Ashmead and Perlmutter, 1980), their records were much richer and more complex than those collected by unfamiliar observers. The little girl in the following observation would never have acted as she did in a laboratory. Asked by her father to go get her doll, the 11-month-old left the room she was in, found her doll, returned to the room, and began playing with the doll. To do so, she had had to retrieve from memory the mental image of the doll at her father's mention of the word "doll," plus recall where she had left it and how to get there and back. Another 11-month-old was playing with her bottle in the kitchen of her house, when the bottle rolled part way under the refrigerator. She left the kitchen, played for 20 minutes or so, then returned and retrieved the bottle from beneath the refrigerator and took up playing where she had left off. In their records, parents noted that their 7- to 11-month-old infants could recall games like peekaboo and pattycake, bath and mealtime routines, and where to find familiar toys and objects. These are simple and routine events, of course, but they clearly show that infants can remember past events and experiences.

Social situations especially afford infants with rich memories. In one study, toddlers between 18 and 30 months performed extremely well on a hide-and-seek game at home (DeLoache, 1980; DeLoache and Brown, 1983). Their parents taught them that Big Bird was going to hide and that they should remember where Big Bird was hidden so that they could find him later. They watched their parents hide Big Bird somewhere in the house and then, when a kitchen timer rang in three to five minutes—a long time for such young children—they usually jumped up and found the toy without mistakes. Even when they had to wait for much longer periods, the children were fairly accurate in remembering where Big Bird was hidden, especially when he was hidden in a natural spot such as in the toy chest or on a shelf.

After putting together evidence from all these different methods of research—comparing infants' reactions to pairs of familiar and unfamiliar patterns, seeing whether infants habituate to a pattern, finding out how long infants retain a learned response, and observing what infants spontaneously recall—we begin to get a picture of what infants can and do remember.

Phases and functions of infant memory

Although some kind of memory is possible right from the start, there is a vast difference between the memory of the newborn, who can recognize a simple pattern, and the 1-year-old, whose face lights up as Father's approaching footsteps sound on the stairs and who greets the babysitter by diving into Mother's lap. In the first year of life, memory develops into increasingly elaborate and sophisticated patterns—carrying along the infant from the largely helpless, speechless being of the early weeks to the remembering, speaking, active reasoner of a year later.

In this study, the infant sees a checkerboard pattern on a television-like screen. By sucking on a pacifier connected to the projector, he can keep the pattern in sharp focus. For awhile the infant sucks with great energy and interest, but like most babies, he eventually becomes bored with what he is attending to. This is called habituation. As he slows his sucking, the checkerboard fades. When the screen offers another picture, he will suck energetically again.

The development of memory during this crucial first year can be divided into several phases (Mandler, 1981; Olson and Strauss, 1981; Schacter and Moscovitch, 1981). In the first phase, the infant's memories apparently depend on neurological "wiring." Show the newborn an object—Mother's face, a bright toy, a nipple, a pattern—and neurons fire in the brain's visual cortex. Infants fix their eyes on new and interesting patterns, and their neurons fire. But as the infant continues to stare, the firing decreases, and the infant becomes habituated to the pattern. Once habituated to this particular pattern, the infant may turn away. "Oh, that," the infant may seem to be saying, "I've seen that before. How about something new?" In fact, the infant probably isn't thinking at all, and the seeming recognition of the pattern is simply the effect of tired neurons.

At about 3 months of age, infants begin a second phase in the development of memory. Their memories seem to become cognitive rather than sensory. Now they can both control their attention and actively explore with it. They can learn and take in information readily and rapidly—sometimes after only a few seconds of experience—remember for relatively long periods, and build on what they have learned. Able now to reach, touch, grasp, turn, look, and pull, they actively explore their world. By the end of this phase, 6- to 7-month-old infants recognize not only bold patterns and sharp contrasts but subtleties and details.

Another major change in infants' abilities to remember takes place between the ages of 8 and 10 months. Infants start to organize the vast array of information that they absorb into systematic categories. They can generalize across time and place. Their memories now include general categories like ducks and geese and clowns and puppies, not just specific objects like Daffy Duck, Mother Goose, Bozo, and Fido. In the laboratory, infants' memory for categories can be tested. First they are shown several objects from one category—perhaps women's faces—and then an object from a new category—a man's face. If they look longer at the new object, the infants are assumed to have noticed the abstract properties common to the first category, women's faces. When just such a test was run, 8-month-old infants did remember the women's faces; 4-month-olds did not (Cohen and Strauss, 1979).

By 8 to 10 months, infants have been found to categorize shapes regardless of their size, color, or orientation in space and faces regardless of their

The simplest kind of remembering is recognizing an object or an image as one seen before. Infants do this from an early age.

poses; to differentiate between faces with familiar features and faces with unfamiliar features; to categorize kinds of movement and toys representing men, letters, animals, food, furniture, and moving vehicles (Olson and Strauss, 1981). Their ability to form categories of things that are wet versus things that are dry, things that are good to eat versus things that are bad to eat, things that are rough versus smooth, and so on provides the basis for an organizational framework for memory. It allows infants to represent information in a summary fashion, thereby significantly reducing their memory load.

These changes in classification and memory abilities have important implications for how infants act. Beginning between 8 and 10 months, infants approach familiar people and things but are wary of strangers. They remember previous departures, and so now the sight of their parents leaving is crushing to them. They begin to recall things that are not immediately available to their senses, and so now they can look for their toys in familiar places. Although they are probably still without any conscious notion of the past, they have begun to build on their backlog of remembered experiences. By the end of the first year, the walking, seeing, hearing infant is also a thinking and remembering infant. The memory systems that will last a lifetime are in operation. Although the abilities to recognize, encode, recall, and retrieve information from memory will grow more elaborate, efficient, complex, and better integrated, no new memory systems will appear. The neural equipment that underlies the ability to remember the past is in place.

Sensorimotor intelligence

One person who was especially interested in infants' abilities to think and remember was Jean Piaget. Piaget carefully investigated, charted, and tried to explain the fascinating journey infants take over their first two years, from early reflexive—unthinking—behavior to later—thinking—mental images. Although he was mistaken in some particulars, it is important that we know what Piaget said, because his was the first truly careful, sustained, empirical and theoretical exploration of infant cognitive development.

During the sensorimotor period, the infant's schemes revolve around actions such as grasping, shaking, patting, and looking at objects.

Schemes

Piaget called the period from birth to about 2 years the **sensorimotor period**, because, he claimed, infants' mental activity then depends solely on sensory and motor abilities and experiences. During the sensorimotor period, according to Piaget, babies do not yet reflect on or consciously think about their world. But they do have notions about the world that Piaget called sensorimotor **schemes**. Reflexes like sucking and grasping and simple sensory acts like looking and hearing are basic building blocks for the development of sensorimotor schemes. Schemes are primitive mental structures, the most basic units of knowledge. As babies experience regularities—the constant properties of objects, the consistent reactions of people—they form schemes that incorporate the information they have gleaned. Schemes are generalizations built up from specific, repeated, single events and experiences. They are built out of sensorimotor actions like sucking on a nipple, looking at Mother's face, or nibbling one's toes (a favorite activity of the 6-month-old set).

Schemes are many, complex, and varied. As infants' senses, muscles, and memories mature, their schemes grow and change. Primitive action schemes built upon reflexive sucking and grasping grow into voluntary mouthing, hitting, shaking, waving, banging, sliding, swinging, dropping, and tearing schemes. Give the 7- to 9-month-old a block and a cup, and he hits, pats, and shakes them, puts them in his mouth, bangs them on the table.

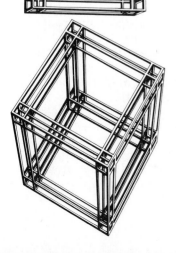

Figure 6.1 In this illustration, each structure is formed from the simpler structures above it. According to Piaget, sensorimotor intelligence develops in this way. Abilities and knowledge from previous stages do not disappear; they are integrated into a new, more complex structure as the infant develops.

Later, as a 10- or 12-month-old, he examines them intently and turns them around and around. He slides them along the highchair tray, rubs them together, and places the block in and out of the cup. He puts the cup on the saucer and the spoon to his lips. Soon he graduates to letting go with his fingers, dropping the block onto the floor. The 14-month-old engages in building schemes—turning over the cup and putting the block on top of it; drinking schemes—putting the cup to his own and to his parents' lips; and grooming schemes—applying the hairbrush (none too expertly) to his hair, as he uses objects for their intended purposes. He seems to know what things are *for*. He looks first. Then he rolls the truck along the tabletop, or, in perfect sequence, puts the cup on the saucer and stirs with the spoon before he "drinks." He can combine actions into longer and more coherent sequences. He stirs the "food" in a pot, then eats it from a plate, and then "washes" the pot with water.

In addition to advances in perceptual, motor, and memory development, in Piaget's theory, there are two mental processes that guide the infant's development of schemes. **Adaptation** is the process by which infants modify their schemes. Adaptation has two complementary aspects: **accommodation** and **assimilation**. To assimilate is to take in. Infants take in new objects to fit their existing schemes. Give the 9-month-old a cup with a spout on it, and he will be sucking on it in a flash, for spouts are not much different from nipples. Nipples are not much different from pacifiers, or drinking straws, or garden hoses, or pipestems, or (to Mother's horror) pens—all the common household objects that infants can and do apply their sucking scheme to. Luckily, there is more to development than assimilation, however, or you might be sucking on the corner of this textbook right now. Infants also accommodate, or modify, their existing schemes when they encounter new objects that do not fit. Breast-fed babies given a bottle for the first time change their sucking scheme slightly, moving their heads a bit, adjusting their mouths to the new nipple, and modifying the movements of their jaws and tongues. The 9-month-old learns that pipes taste yucky and eliminates them from his sucking scheme. The 1-year-old discovers that books are not suitable for sucking but have pages that turn and tear in an especially interesting way. Assimilation and accommodation are complementary processes of adaptation. The other process that guides the infant's development of schemes, according to Piaget, is **organization**. This is the process by which the infant combines and integrates separate schemes. The 3-month-old stares at and then reaches for his rattle, combining the staring scheme with the reaching scheme. The 5-month-old can combine three schemes—mouthing, staring, and reaching—as he puts his rattle to his lips. With these two processes, adaptation and organization, the infant makes rapid progress to higher levels of sensorimotor intelligence.

Stages

The progress that infants make as they organize and adapt their schemes moves them along in their developmental journey in an unvarying sequence of stages, according to Piaget. Each advance emerges from earlier experiences, and each stage incorporates the mental structures that developed in the previous stage (see Figure 6.1). For the sensorimotor period, Piaget outlined six successive stages of development (see Figure 6.2). The age ranges for these stages are approximate. More important is the order in which the stages occur.

Stage 1: practice and repetition of reflexes
(birth to approximately 1 month)
In the first stage, the newborn practices reflexive actions like sucking,

grasping, looking, and listening. A toy touches her lips, and she begins sucking. A nipple is put to her mouth, and she will suck. Her own hand touches her lips, and she sucks. She spends her time fitting the world into her limited range of reflexes.

Stage 2: the first acquired adaptations (approximately 1 month to 4 months)

At about 1 month, the infant begins exercising simple actions for pleasure. Her hand moves, and the movement is pleasant, and so she repeats it. She kicks her legs gleefully over and over again. Piaget called these repetitions of what begin as random or reflexive actions **primary circular reactions**. Circular reactions are the first kind of accommodation, for they are the willful modification of behavior through repetition.

At this stage also, infants begin to develop the notion that objects are separate from themselves. When they drop their rattle, they stare at their fingers, a bit perplexed. But within moments, they have gone on to something else. They do not search for objects they cannot see; out of sight is literally out of mind. They do not realize that objects are permanent, a realization Piaget called **object permanence**.

Stage 3: procedures for making interesting sights last (approximately 4 to 8 months)

At the age of 3 months, Piaget's daughter, Lucienne, noticed that shaking her leg, which she'd been doing just for fun, also made some dolls attached to her bassinet swing back and forth.

> At 0;3 (5) Lucienne shakes her bassinet by moving her legs violently (bending and unbending them, etc.) which makes the cloth dolls swing from the hood. Lucienne looks at them, smiling, and recommences at once. These movements appear simply to be the concomitants of joy. . . . The next day. . .I present the dolls: Lucienne immediately moves, shakes her legs, but this time without smiling. Her interest is intense and sustained. . . .
>
> 0;3 (8). . .a chance movement disturbs the dolls: Lucienne. . .looks at them. . .and shakes herself with regularity. She stares at the dolls, barely smiles and moves her leg vigorously and thoroughly. . . .
>
> At 0;3 (16) as soon as I suspended the dolls she immediately shakes them, without smiling, with precise and rhythmical movements with quite an interval between shakes, as though she were studying the phenomenon. Success gradually causes her to smile (Piaget, 1952, pp. 157–158).

When the baby began repeating her action, shaking her legs to see its effect on the movement of the dolls, she was engaged in what Piaget called a **secondary circular reaction**. Secondary circular reactions extend beyond the baby's own body, to an object or a person who responds to the baby's acts. In this stage, babies try to prolong interesting sights, like dolls bouncing, although it takes them some experimentation to learn which of their actions cause which reactions in the world outside of them. Piaget's son, for example, pulled a rope hanging from the top of his cradle, and the rope made an interesting rattle. But he also pulled the rope in a vain attempt to make his mother stay in the room with him (Piaget, 1952). His mother, of course, was not attached to the rope, a mistake in inferring causality that Piaget called **magico-phenomenistic thinking**. By this term, Piaget referred to the way that infants, with their imperfect understanding of cause and effect, often act as though things happened by magic. To someone so new to this complex world, magic

---

SUBSTAGES IN THE SENSORIMOTOR PERIOD

Stage 1. Use of reflexes and such innate schemes as sucking and grasping

↓

Stage 2. Modification and repetition of schemes to achieve interesting sensations; coordination of different schemes such as looking and grasping

↓

Stage 3. Development of a variety of schemes that produce interesting effects

↓

Stage 4. Coordination of schemes into intentional, "intelligent"-looking means-end sequences, in which one scheme leads to another

↓

Stage 5. Trial-and-error experimentation, often leading to the discovery of new means to achieve goals

↓

Stage 6. Invention of new means through internal mental combinations; first appearance of deferred imitation, symbolic play, and speech

Figure 6.2 In Piaget's theory of the development of sensorimotor intelligence, these are the major substages.

must seem to be everywhere: *presto!* and the room is lit up; *presto!* and Mommy appears by the crib; *presto!* and flames appear under the shiny pots; *presto!* and the telephone bell rings.

At this stage, babies begin to understand something about the permanence of physical objects. If they see their ball on the floor, peeking out from beneath a blanket, they may move the blanket aside. With this action, they show that they can reconstruct the whole object from seeing just part of it, a sign that they have developed a primitive mental image of the ball. But if the ball is invisible beneath the blanket, they will ignore it completely. It will seem like magic when someone pulls the blanket off the hidden ball. The magic with which people and things disappear and reappear makes games like peekaboo and jack-in-the-box lots of fun for babies at this stage.

Stage 4: coordination of means and ends (approximately 8 to 12 months)

The budding scientist of 8 to 12 months old is quickly learning more and more about cause and effect. Play peekaboo with her now, and she'll pull your fingers from your face (a month or so ago, she waited until *you* took your hands down). She's no fool; she knows you're in there! Now she watches as Daddy picks up her ball, tosses it into the toy chest, and closes the cover. She goes to the toy chest, finds the cover too heavy to lift, and bangs on it. Daddy is oblivious. So she goes to Daddy, pulls him to the toy chest, and presses his hand on the cover. The light dawns; Daddy opens the cover; and she reaches in for her ball. Her understanding of cause and effect is much more sophisticated now, although she still apparently believes that it is she who initiates and causes all actions.

She knows lots about the properties of different kinds of objects now, and her schemes are more varied and appropriately used. No longer is every object sucked, shaken, or dropped to the floor. Now her stuffed bear is carried, hugged, and propped on the living room couch. Her toy telephone is babbled into. Pots and pans are nested, drummed upon, and their lids—after Daddy is led by the hand to perform—are spun like tops. Cabinets doors are swung, opened, and closed. She has begun to learn about the positions of objects in three-dimensional space.

When Sam was just over a year old, he loved to put things inside one another. I always found it very funny to discover things like the dog's

As the infant's understanding of cause and effect increases, she is able to use objects as means to an end.

The year-old infant is an enquiring scientist who performs endless experiments—drop the cup, open the door, smear the dirt—just to see what will happen.

brush, a toy xylophone, a plastic ladle, and one mitten inside of the soup kettle, all piled in front of the back door and covered with a towel.

But move her ball from one hiding place to another, and the baby cannot follow your sleight of hand. She may watch your every move as you hide the ball under the pillow, take it out, and then hide it under the blanket. Ask her where it is, and she goes to the pillow. Even so, this mistake shows that she has some grasp of object permanence. For now she searches for the ball even when it is completely hidden; even when she cannot see any part of it, she knows that the object still exists. Until now, she had to be able to see at least some part of the object to credit its existence. Although she now has a mental image of the ball, it is bound up with the *act* of searching for it and with the specific place where she first saw it hidden. According to Piaget, at this stage the infant still does not have a fully mature image of the object as *separate* from all other objects and from her own actions.

Stage 5: experiments in order to see (approximately 12 to 18 months)

At around her first birthday, the baby is a confirmed scientist. Now that walking has freed her hands to explore the world at will, she performs endless experiments in order to see what will happen. She pulls the cabinet doors open, pulls the dog's fur, pulls the highchair across the floor, pulls her own hair, pulls Mommy's and Daddy's hair. Through **tertiary circular reactions**, she repeats her pulling action, modifying it slightly each time to see the effects of the modification. Pull Mommy's hair, she learns, and Mommy squawks; pull the cabinet doors and they swing open; pull her own hair, and she can't see it but it hurts.

When Sam was 12 months old, he deliberately spilled his food, bit by bit, onto the floor. We knew that he was experimenting, and we knew that he wasn't being naughty on purpose. But it was hard to live with the mess our little scientist was creating at every meal.

Babies now can infer the cause from seeing just its effect. Bedroom door opening? Mommy coming in! Kettle whistling? Hot! Stroller rolling? Someone pushing it! Now infants can follow the path of the hidden ball being moved from under the pillow to beneath the blanket and can retrieve it from its hiding

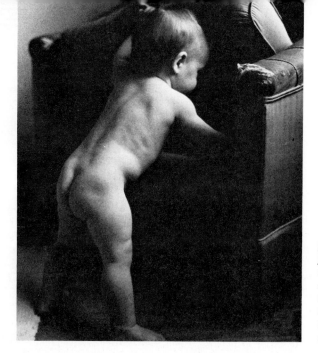

When infants achieve object permanence, they can search for hidden objects even when they have not seen them being hidden. This ability means that the infants have mental representations of objects that transcend their immediate perceptions.

place—as long as they saw it being hidden. Hide things when they are not watching, and they will not be able to find them. Their concept of objects is still tied to their immediate perceptions.

Stage 6: invention of new means through mental combinations: the beginnings of thought (approximately 18 to 24 months)

In the sixth and final stage of the sensorimotor period, children form mental representations of cause and effect independent of their immediate perceptions. A few months ago, they would open a door even though their chair was in the way—and knock over the chair. Now they move the chair out of the way before they open the door, for now they understand how the door will affect the chair. They can perform mental combinations as they invent solutions to their problems. If they want out of the playpen, they may cry, call, or pretend they want a drink. If they want to go outside, they may grab their shoes and coat and present them to the nearest available parent.

The concept of object permanence is mature enough now that toddlers can search for a ball hidden under the couch even when they haven't watched it being hidden there. If the ball rolls under the couch, the child can understand that it may have rolled out the other side. She can walk around the couch, taking a path different from the ball's, and find the ball a few inches behind the couch. Her ability to follow such an invisible path is evidence that her mental representations of objects have transcended her immediate perceptions. Now when her parents forget to take her favorite blanket on a car ride, she protests. When her mother disappears into the bathroom and closes the door, she finds the baby impatiently waiting outside—or pounding on the door to be let in. The ability to create mental representations is the culminating achievement of the sensorimotor period. It ushers in a new world for children and their parents, who will always remember fondly the happy days of distraction when, for their infant, out of sight was out of mind.

Problems in Piaget's theory of sensorimotor development

Piaget's descriptions of changes in babies' behavior during the sensorimotor period are vivid and appealing. But not everyone is persuaded by Piaget's

204

explanations of what is going on in babies' heads. Some developmental psychologists have questioned Piaget's explanation of how infants develop object permanence, for instance. They have questioned both the way Piaget tested object permanence and the inferences he made about his results.

Piaget's test of infants' object permanence gave infants a choice of two locations in which they could search for a hidden object. One location was where the object first was hidden, and the other was where the object was hidden second and remained. In this test, Piaget found that Stage 4 (8- to 12-month-old) infants were likely to continue to search where they had found the object earlier—at point *A*—rather than at the location where the object actually was hidden—at point *B*. Recently researchers have suggested that such *A not B* errors may be artifacts of the particular test, rather than a milestone in cognitive development, as Piaget suggested. In one series of studies, researchers lined up five locations for hiding objects, with the points *A* and *B* at either end (Bjork and Cummings, 1979; Cummings and Bjork, 1981). Infants 9 to 12 months old first had five tries to look for the object when it was hidden at point *A*. Most of them looked at point *A* or very near it. Then, in plain view, the experimenter moved the object and hid it at point *B*. But the infants did not make *A not B* errors, as Piaget would have predicted. Instead, they searched at or near point *B*. The researchers suggested that the reasons infants succeeded on this test and not on Piaget's were that they had more experience with the hiding-and-seeking procedure and that the *A* and *B* locations were clearly separated. They failed on Piaget's test, these researchers suggested, not because they did not realize that the object was permanent, but because they simply had forgotten where they had seen the object last hidden. Evidence from the laboratory supports this idea that babies get confused when they have to remember in which of two locations something disappeared. In another study, for example, 8-month-olds—who clearly knew something about the permanence of Mother—watched their mothers leave a room through door *A*. After the mother had disappeared, the infants looked first at that door—a sign that they had registered the spot where their mothers had disappeared—but then—apparently forgetting—they looked randomly at doors *A* and *B* (Zucker, 1982).

Another source of evidence that throws doubt on Piaget's interpretation of the *A not B* error is research demonstrating that infants tend not to make *A not B* errors if they can begin searching for an object immediately after it has been hidden rather than having to wait for several seconds (Fox et al., 1979; Gratch, Appel, Evans, Le Compte, and Wright, 1974). This evidence suggests that Piaget's infants may have failed his test not because they had no idea of object permanence but because their memory span for where the object was hidden had been exceeded. In support of this suggestion, research also shows that infants do better at finding hidden objects when there is a marker—a reminder—at the place the object is hidden and no marker at the place it is not hidden (Freeman, Lloyd, and Sinha, 1980; Lucas and Uzgiris, 1977).

In other research, psychologists have found that infants make *A not B* errors when the object is not even *hidden* but remains in full view of the infant at all times. In one study, for example, 10-month-old infants searched at a point at which an object had been hidden earlier, even while the object was fully visible somewhere else (Harris, 1974). This suggests that in Piaget's test, infants may have been perseverating because they had succeeded at point *A* before, rather than that they lacked the awareness that a permanent object had been moved. You may do the same thing, in fact, when you "lose" your car in the parking lot if you have parked in an unaccustomed spot. You go first to the accustomed spot, blanch when the car is missing, and then remember to search in the right spot. But the most recent research suggests that infants do not necessarily perseverate at point A, even in a test just like Piaget's. In a study of 9-month-olds, 47 percent did search at *A*, but 53 percent searched at *B*; the probability of searching at each location was chance (Sophian, 1985).

As Paul Harris (1983) points out, finding a hidden object requires two things: (1) mentally representing the hidden object and (2) figuring out where it might be. Piaget did not allow for the possibility that an infant might be capable of the first but not the second, that an infant might know that an object exists without being able to find it. Developmental changes on Piaget's hidden-object test may reveal infants' ever improving search strategies rather than their dawning realization of the permanence of objects.

Evidence that infants have some notion that objects are permanent has been uncovered even before the 8- to 12-month period. In one experiment, 5-month-olds first were shown briefly an attractive object. Then the lights in the room suddenly went off, and the object disappeared completely from their view. Even so, the babies reached right toward the place where they had just seen the object, something that they would not be likely to do if they had no mental image of the vanished object (Bower and Wishart, 1972; Hood and Willatts, 1986). In other experiments, babies as young as 3½ months showed that they had some notion of the permanence of objects because they stared longer at physically impossible actions (like a toy car rolling along a ramp and apparently *through* a solid box) than at physically possible actions (a car rolling *in front of* the box) (Baillargeon, 1984, 1986).

Altogether, then, a substantial amount of evidence makes us cautious about accepting as fact Piaget's interpretation of what infants think and know in the first year of life. Many American researchers today doubt that infant intelligence is limited to sensory and motor procedures and routines, doubt that thought plays so little part in the first two years. Research evidence from the last fifteen years suggests that infants have acquired some semblance of object permanence by 9 months or even earlier and that thereafter their ability consolidates, becomes more widely and consistently applied and becomes better connected to other response systems such as search routines. Despite the disagreement between these researchers and Piaget about the age when infants first can mentally represent objects to themselves, there is no doubt that infants are not born with this ability, that they do develop it sometime during the first two years, and that when this ability *does* develop, a profound change in thinking and understanding has taken place. The infant has moved to a higher level of cognition.

Imitation

Just as infants gradually come to form mental representations of objects, they gradually come to form mental representations of actions. Imitation is part of this process. According to Piaget, imitation, like the other aspects of sensorimotor intelligence, develops in stages. At first, imitation is a way to prolong the pleasures of looking and other sensations. A bit later it is a way to prolong those interesting early circular reactions. The 4-month-old pats her blanket with her hand. Her mother pats the blanket. The 4-month-old pats again, *as though* she were imitating. In this game, the infant must be the initiator, and her partner must play into her circular reactions. At this stage, the infant engages in **pseudoimitation**, for she imitates only those actions she can perform already. True imitation develops only when she can imitate behavior that is brand new to her. It develops in the third stage of sensorimotor development, according to Piaget, when the infant is between 4 and 8 months old, so long as the imitation involves her hands and feet, the parts of her body that she can see. "Bye-bye," Daddy waves. "Bye-bye," the infant imitates. Not until the fourth stage of sensorimotor development, Piaget claimed, when the infant is between 8 and 12 months old, can she imitate

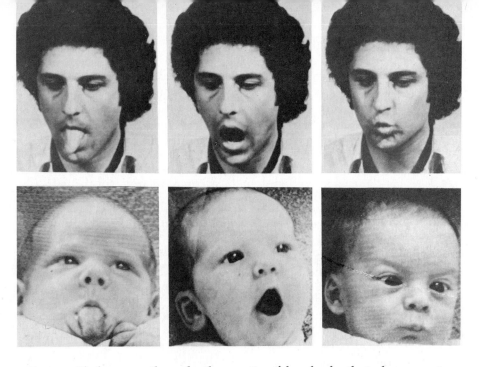

These photographs, well selected by Andrew Meltzoff and Keith Moore, show a 2-week-old imitating an adult experimenter's tongue protrusion, open mouth, and lip protrusion.

actions with her mouth and other parts of her body that she cannot see—blowing out a candle or wrinkling her nose. By the sixth stage of the sensorimotor period, when the infant is 1½ to 2 years old, she can imitate gestures she has seen earlier as well as those she has just watched in so-called **deferred imitation**. Last night at bedtime Mommy started the story with "Once upon a time," and today the infant burbles, "Onceuponatime. . ." in the same tone of voice as soon as the covers are pulled up. Piaget described his daughter's deferred imitation:

> At 1;4, J. had a visit from a little boy of 1;6 whom she used to see from time to time, and who, in the course of the afternoon, got into a terrible temper. He screamed as he tried to get out of his play-pen and pushed it backwards, stamping his feet. J. stood watching him in amazement, never having witnessed such a scene before. The next day, she herself screamed in her play-pen and tried to move it, stamping her foot lightly several times in succession. The imitation of the whole scene was most striking. Had it been immediate, [the imitation] would naturally not have involved representation, but coming as it did after an interval of more than twelve hours, it must have involved some representative or pre-representative element (Piaget, 1962, p. 63).

American psychologists have conducted research to confirm—or disconfirm—Piaget's work on imitation. Their findings are not without surprises and controversy. In 1973, a doctoral student named Olga Maratsos spoke with Piaget.

> "I am sticking out my tongue at the [7-week-old] babies, and do you know what they are doing?"
>
> "You may tell me," Piaget murmured.
>
> "They are sticking out their tongues right back at me! What do you think of that?"
>
> . . ."I think that's very rude," he said (Friedrich, 1983, p. 63).

Were these very young infants performing the kinds of imitation Piaget claimed would not occur until they were 8 to 12 months old? Perhaps so. Andrew Meltzoff and Keith Moore, in a controversial study a few years later, also got infants in their first two weeks of life to imitate various facial expressions modeled by an adult—sticking out tongue and lips, opening the mouth

207

(Meltzoff and Moore, 1977). Meltzoff and Moore argued that this early imitation showed that babies have innate sensorimotor coordination that allows them to match their movements with those of another person and that they have some knowledge of this matching. Not everyone accepted this explanation, however. For instance, Kenneth Kaye and Janet Marcus (1978) argued that the newborns' responses were more like reflexes than imitations. They stated that the photographs Meltzoff and Moore presented did not demonstrate "systematic accommodation" of the baby's mouth to the mouth movements of the model. Only that kind of demonstration, they argued, would prove that the newborn's responses were imitative rather than reflexive.

More recently, a number of other investigators, who have taken more precautions to control the experimental situation, have not been able to replicate Meltzoff and Moore's results (Abravenel and Sigafoos, 1984; Kleiner and Fagan, 1984; Koepke, Hamm, Legerstee, and Russell, 1983; McKenzie and Over, 1983; 1983b). In one study, for example, researchers tested 14 babies between 9 and 30 days old (McKenzie and Over, 1983). They modeled facial and arm gestures, such as mouth opening, tongue protrusion, bringing hand to face, moving hand to and from the midline of the body and videotaped the babies' reactions. When 16 judges tried to identify from the videotape which gestures the model had demonstrated, they found only weak and statistically insignificant relations between the adult's behavior and that of the infants. The researchers concluded that their results were not consistent with claims that newborns can imitate gestures of the face and hands. The question of which gestures newborn infants even can see—given the serious limitations of their visual acuity that we discussed in Chapter 5—does tend to undermine the believability of Meltzoff and Moore's claims of newborn imitation. The debate continues, however, and the question of whether newborns can imitate remains open. An answer would add to our knowledge of innate human abilities, help us to interpret the meaning of imitation for cognitive development, and help us to evaluate Piaget's theory of sensorimotor development.

Researchers studying imitation in older infants also have come up with results that do not entirely agree with Piaget's. They have found that infants can imitate gestures that they cannot see themselves perform at younger ages than Piaget found. For example, in one study, 6-month-olds imitated a burst of five openings and closings of the mouth (Kaye and Marcus, 1978), imitation that Piaget said did not occur until 8 to 12 months. But infants do not so readily imitate *all* gestures that they cannot see themselves perform. In another study, 10-month-olds did not reliably imitate the invisible gestures of looking at the ceiling or patting the tops of their heads (Masur and Ritz, 1984). Perhaps infants are born with the ability to notice similarities between what someone else's mouth and their own mouth is doing (Kaye and Marcus, 1978)—a possibility that might also account for Meltzoff and Moore's success in getting newborns to imitate sticking out their tongues. In general, infants imitate mouth and other facial gestures before they imitate arm movements, arm movements before finger movements. This progression does not agree with Piaget's claim that the order of imitation is from actions that are visible to those that are invisible to the infant. Rather, the actions infants imitate parallel the order of their developing motor skills. This *does* fit with Piaget's proposal that early imitation relies on the infant's available repertoire of schemes. More evidence of this repertoire effect comes from an investigation in which it was found that infants were likelier to imitate meaningful gestures—shaking their heads, pointing—and familiar actions—raising their arms for "so big"—than unfamiliar gestures—opening their fists (Masur and Ritz, 1984).

Research on deferred imitation also offers limited support for Piaget's claims. One investigation of infants between 1 and 3 years old did show that 24 hours after watching a model do things like slide a block, put on a necklace, and say "bye-bye" into a phone, 1-year-olds showed little evidence of deferred imitation, whereas 2-year-olds did (McCall, Parke, and Kavanaugh, 1977). This finding is consistent with Piaget's finding that deferred imitation first appeared only at about 1½ years. Meltzoff again, however, has come up with evidence of imitation in younger infants (Meltzoff, 1985). In his recent study, 45 percent of the 14-month-olds observed imitated simple motions with an unfamiliar toy after a delay of 24 hours. Similarly, in another study, one-third of the 12-month-olds studied imitated simple actions like taking apart a toy barrel or putting a crown on a doll's head after a ten-minute delay. But they did not imitate more complicated actions like stacking five dolls together (Abravanel and Gingold, 1985).

Clearly, infants' ability to imitate actions right away or after a delay depends on the nature and complexity of the action. The more complex the action, the more information the infant must encode, the more difficult the task, and the less likely the infant is to imitate it. Piaget may have been correct about one function of imitation in infants' cognitive development—accommodating their schemes to a model's. He undoubtedly was correct in suggesting that deferred imitation is more advanced than immediate imitation because it demonstrates that an infant can mentally represent actions. He also was correct that imitation develops and changes over the first two years. But Piaget did not give enough attention to the influence of the complexity of the action on the likelihood that it would be imitated. He also paid little attention to individual differences among infants. Recent studies such as those just described, in which some infants have been found to imitate particular actions at certain ages, also show that just as many infants do *not* imitate the actions. These infants may be unable or unwilling to imitate the action. There is still much to learn about what, how, when, and why infants imitate the actions they see.

Developing a sense of self

It's an ability that adults take thoroughly for granted. Of *course* we know where we end and our surroundings begin. But infants, Piaget suggested, do not know this, and it takes them many months to learn the boundaries of their separate selves. During the sensorimotor period, Piaget claimed, infants cannot tell the difference between events that they cause or control and those that they do not. They cannot tell the difference between a change or a movement in an object and in themselves. To them, when something disappears it's all the same whether it went up in smoke, was hidden under a blanket, or went out of sight because they moved their head. Recent research supports Piaget's notion that infants do not understand the distinction between self and surroundings.

Infants who had just learned to stand up by themselves were tested in a room that had a stable floor but three walls and a ceiling that could be moved (Lee and Aronson, 1974). When the infants saw the end wall moving away from them, apparently they felt as though they were falling backward. In an effort to keep their balance, they toppled forward. Younger infants, who were sitting down, compensated in the same way for the sense of losing their balance (Butterworth and Hicks, 1977). Tests of older infants who had learned to walk showed that with increasing practice, the infants began to understand that the moving walls were incongruous (Butterworth and Cicchetti, 1978). When those who had been walking for a year saw the room "move," they swayed only slightly, laughing as they looked to see what was causing the movement. As they mature, infants gain voluntary control over their bodies, by calibrating their movements against their stable surroundings. Infants gradually learn to coordinate floor, walls, and body as they move through sitting, to standing, to walking. As human beings, we may be born with the potential to distinguish ourselves from our surroundings, but we develop the actual ability only with practice. Only gradually, with experience, does the infant gain voluntary control over himself or herself.

Watching infants as they learn to recognize themselves is another—quite charming—way to see the sense of self unfolding.

> When Sam was about 7 months old, he liked to sit in front of a full-length mirror and kiss the reflection of his lips. At 9 months, he played peek-a-boo with himself. By the time he was 2, he ran to the mirror to admire himself whenever anyone complimented him on his fireman's hat.

Several researchers have studied infants between 5 and 24 months old to see how and when the recognition of self begins (Bertenthal and Fischer, 1978; Fisher, 1980; Lewis and Brooks-Gunn, 1979). They have found that between 5 and 8 months of age, infants smile at their image in a mirror or on videotape, gaze intently at it, touch it, and bounce, wave, or clap. But at this early age, there is no evidence that infants distinguish their own image from that of another person whose action is contingent on theirs.

Between 9 and 12 months, infants in these studies use their mirror image to guide their reaching, as they begin to understand that mirrors show reflections. At this age, for instance, the infants studied reached for a hat hanging over their head after seeing it reflected in a mirror. Between about 15 and 18 months, infants touched their own nose when they noticed in the mirror a spot of rouge that the researcher had surreptitiously put on it, and turned to see a toy behind them after watching it appear first in a mirror. At this age, too, some infants can point to and name pictures of themselves. By 21 to 24 months, most infants can use their own name and personal pronouns for themselves and others. They answer appropriately when their mothers point to the children's mirror image and ask, ''Who's that?'' They can reliably differentiate between themselves and others.

From these observations, a developmental sequence suggests itself (Harter, 1983). In the first stage, infants are interested in their mirror image but give no sign that they perceive themselves as independent, causal agents. In the second stage, infants understand how their actions affect reflected images. In the third stage, they understand the difference between mirror images that reflect their own and other people's actions. In the fourth stage, infants recognize that they are objects and can distinguish between themselves and others. They have an internal image of their own face that they can compare with an external image. Finally, infants understand that they have unique features that can be named and labeled with words. Thus over the first two years of life, infants develop a primitive understanding not only of the external world of objects but also of the internal world of the self.

Infants between 9 and 10 months old smile at and reach for their image in a mirror. They are beginning to understand that mirrors show reflections and to recognize themselves.

Play

Play is the work of infancy, for during play the infant practices many skills and schemes. In playing, the infant combines bits of skills into new wholes and finds out what works and how it works. If infants were always engaged in seeing new sights or hearing new sounds, they might never master the basic skills that they will use for solving problems when they are older. The countless hours they spend repetitively banging spoons on pots and pans, running their hands through water, milk puddles, their own and the dog's hair, scribbling on paper and the forbidden walls, stuffing little things inside of big things, jamming big things inside of little things, emptying drawers and boxes, stacking, carrying, stirring, dragging, and overturning exercise their endlessly resourceful minds and bodies. All work and no play may *indeed* make Jack a dull boy. Only higher animals play, and the higher they are on the evolutionary scale, the more playing they do. It has even been proposed that human beings have a prolonged infancy to allow lots of time for play so they may develop their sophisticated cognitive abilities (Bruner, 1972). It is likely that play fosters lively minds and that lively minds foster curiosity, exploration, and *play*fulness.

Play has no immediate goal except the repetition of actions for the sheer pleasure of it. Piaget thought of play as pure assimilation, the infant's exercise in fitting the world into his own schemes without changing those schemes to fit the world. Give an infant a doll and a blanket, and let him do with them what he will. If he tucks the blanket around the doll, he is playing. If he bounces her happily up and down, he is playing. If he covers the doll with the blanket and sits on her, he is playing. But ask him to bring you the doll, and as he uncovers it from beneath the blanket and carries it to you, he is no longer playing. You have given him a goal to meet.

Through their spontaneous play, infants reveal their constantly maturing cognition. Play changes markedly from month to month during infancy. In the first seven months, infants play with one object at a time—banging, waving, sliding, and so on. Between 7 and 18 months, this simple object play decreases from about 90 percent to less than 20 percent of infants' play (Rubin, Fein, and Vandenberg, 1983). Playful imitation of real-life activities—talking on the phone, drinking from a cup, and the like—appears first around 12 months and increases between 12 and 18 months. This pretend play—for example, playful drinking from a cup, complete with head tilted back and mouth sipping, or playful sleeping with eyes closed, body curled and still—captures many of the actual details of the real-life activity, but it is not performed at the same time as the real activity—mealtime or bedtime. Infants may incorporate toys and miniatures or adult-size objects as props in this play. From 12 to 18 months infants usually play pretend alone. Later, as we shall see in Chapter 9, pretend play is done with dolls and other children. Thus infants' play reveals the same kinds of development that we have discussed already—decreasing simple sensorimotor activity, increasing mental representation, and increasing awareness of self and others.

Testing intelligence

So far in this chapter, we have been describing the development in cognition that *all* infants go through. But all infants do not develop at the same rate. Even children within the same family show wide differences in their rates of cognitive development, some leaping and some just creeping ahead. To chart individual children's rates of mental development, psychologists need tests that reflect the relative abilities of different infants at the same age. By observing how infants at different ages behave when they are presented with particular objects under controlled and standardized conditions, psychologists can measure the infants' development against established norms for all infants of that age. This is the goal of infant intelligence tests.

Arnold Gesell was the pioneer of infant intelligence testing, and his work has influenced the content of all existing infant intelligence tests. Gesell tested infants' hand–eye coordination by giving them objects like a red ring on a string and seeing whether they could grasp them. He tested infants' fine motor skills by giving them objects like red one-inch cubes and seeing whether they could pick them up and build with them. He tested gross motor skills by seeing whether infants could sit up, walk, and climb stairs. He tested language abilities by seeing if infants could label or point to objects, and he tested personal–social behavior by seeing how infants responded to the tester. How a particular infant compared to the norms for these items collected on hundreds of infants of the same age was used as an indication of the child's developmental maturity. Other tests have been devised that follow and expand on Gesell's (for example, see Table 6.1).

These tests have been used not only to evaluate infants' level of development at the time, but to predict their later level of intelligence. Unfortunately, these predictions have not proved especially accurate. Correlations between intelligence test scores in infancy and later are usually not significant for boys and only marginally significant for girls (McCall, Hogarty, and Hurlburt, 1972; Bornstein and Sigman, 1986). When significant correlations between infant and later test scores have been found, it is only because subjects with extremely low scores have been included in the study. People who score at the extreme low end in infancy continue to get low scores, probably because they have a serious and permanent retardation that can be observed even in the infant test. But within the normal range of intelligence, there is little predictability from infant to later tests.

Table 6.1
Some items from the Bayley Scale of Infant Mental Development

Item number	Age, months	Item
1	0.1	Responds to sound of bell
5	0.1	Momentary regard of red ring
10	0.7	Eyes follow moving person
11	0.7	Responds to voice
13	0.9	Vocalizes once or twice
14	1.6	Turns eyes to red ring
24	1.9	Blinks at shadow of hand
28	2.2	Searches with eyes for sound
30	2.3	Vocalizes two different sounds
33	2.6	Manipulates red ring
36	2.8	Simple play with rattle
44	3.8	Carries ring to mouth
47	3.8	Turns head to sound of bell
49	4.1	Reaches for cube
54	4.6	Picks up cube
60	5.0	Reaches persistently
63	5.2	Lifts inverted cup
65	5.4	Smiles at mirror image
69	5.5	Transfers object hand to hand
73	5.8	Lifts cup with handle
76	6.2	Playful response to mirror
78	6.5	Manipulates bell: interest in detail
83	7.8	Rings bell purposively
84	7.9	Listens selectively to familiar words
87	8.9	Fingers holes in pegboard

Table 6.1 (*continued*)
Some items from the Bayley Scale of Infant Mental Development

Item number	Age, months	Item
92	9.7	Stirs with spoon in imitation
95	10.4	Attempts to imitate scribble
99	11.3	Pushes car along
103	12.0	Turns pages of book
107	12.9	Puts beads in box
111	13.8	Builds tower of two cubes
113	14.2	Says two words
118	16.4	Pegs in pegboard placed in 70 seconds
119	16.7	Builds tower of three cubes
123	17.6	Pegs placed in 42 seconds
124	17.8	Names one object _____ Ball _____ Scissors _____ Watch _____ Cup _____ Pencil
130	19.3	Names one picture
132	19.9	Points to three pictures
132	20.6	Utters sentence of two words
138	21.4	Names two objects
143	23.0	Builds tower of six cubes
146	24.0	Names three objects
152	25.6	Discriminates among cup, plate, box
156	26.6	Pegs placed in 22 seconds
158	28.2	Understands two prepositions
161	30 +	Builds tower of eight cubes

SOURCE: The Psychological Corporation, 1969.

When Jason was 1½, we had his intelligence tested. When the psychologist who tested him told me that he had gotten a score of 85, I was scared. But she said not to worry, that some boys are slower to develop and that how they do at 1½ doesn't have much to do with how well they'll do in school.

Why do intelligence test scores from the early years rarely agree with scores later on? For one thing, development in infancy occurs in fits and starts. Sometimes infants develop rapidly, sometimes slowly, and so it can be difficult to get a fix on their abilities. For another thing, performance on infant tests may be affected by individual differences in temperament. Researchers who conducted one study (Brucefors et al., 1974) suggested that less active 3-month-olds responded less to test objects and tasks and therefore scored lower than their more active counterparts but were learning in ways that allowed them to consolidate their gains when they were older. Yet another reason for differences between infant and later test scores is the difficulty of giving tests to infants. Accurate measurement of infants' rapidly developing mental abilities depends not only on the adequacy of the test, but also on the

The Bayley Scale of Infant Mental Development is often used to test infants' power of perception, sensation and cognitive skills. Unfortunately, predictability from scores on this test to later IQ scores is limited.

skill of the tester and, perhaps most important, on the state of the infant. The ideal time to test an infant, of course, is when the infant is quietly alert, interested, and responsive. The ideal time is hard to catch, however, and many a subject dozes off, cries, squirms, protests, or ignores the tester. But perhaps the most powerful explanation for the lack of predictability from infant tests to later IQ scores is that it has been difficult to identify the precursors in infancy of the abilities we consider intelligence later in childhood and adulthood. Infant intelligence tests focus on perceptual and sensorimotor abilities—because that is what infants have. Intelligence tests for older children and adults focus on quite different skills, particularly on verbal and abstract skills—because that is where intelligent adults excel.

Recently, researchers have hypothesized that an infant's quickness to recognize a stimulus as familiar or new reflects the same ability that later intelligence tests tap, because both involve the ability to process and remember information. They have tested this hypothesis with a number of samples of children and found that, indeed, infants' abilities to recognize stimuli are significantly correlated with how they do on later tests of verbal intelligence (Fagan and Singer, 1983; Bornstein, 1984). The relation holds for samples of children with normal intelligence and those with Down's syndrome, and it holds for all socioeconomic groups and for both boys and girls. It has been replicated in other studies (Bornstein and Sigman, 1986). These results suggest that psychologists soon may be able to predict with greater confidence how a child will develop intellectually from the time he or she is an infant.

Language

By the time he was 2½, Jason was still saying only a few words—"baba" for bottle, "guck" for duck, "caw" for car, and some others. He seemed to understand well, but he couldn't express himself. He preferred running around to sitting still for a story, and he couldn't have cared less about looking at books.

Natalie started saying recognizable words when she was 9 or 10 months old. She could use simple sentences by the time she was 1½—"Go bye-bye car," and "She talkin' me."

One of the most impressive developments in infancy and one that clearly reveals individual differences among children is the beginning of language

214

Table 6.2
Milestones in language development

3 months	Smiles when talked to and nodded at; smiles followed by gurgling, squealing, cooing in vowel-like sounds for 15 to 20 seconds; laughs in social interaction.
4 months	Clear responses to human sounds; turns head and looks for speaker with eyes; babbles; chuckles.
5 months	Cooing interspersed with consonant sounds.
6 months	Babbling sounds like single words; sounds like *ma, mu, da, di, mamama,* and *bababa* most common; turns toward speaker; laughs.
8 months	Babbles in reduplicated and repeated sounds; intonation patterns distinct; utterances convey emotions and emphases; occasionally imitates sounds.
12 months	Words (*mama, dada*) begin to emerge; shows signs of understanding of words and simple commands ("Show me your eyes"); intones patterns that sound like sentences.
18 months	Has vocabulary of between 3 and 50 words; babbles in several syllables and complex intonations; doesn't try to communicate information and not frustrated when not understood; may say "thank you" or "come here" but does not join words into two-word sentences; understands simple sentences and lots of words.
24 months	Has vocabulary of over 50 words; joins words to form two-word or slightly longer sentences; shows interest in language and in communicating; understands well.
30 months	Rapidly increases vocabulary; babbling gone; feels frustrated when not understood; utters two-word, three-word, and even longer sentences with typically immature grammar; speech still difficult to understand (though children vary widely in this respect); understands nearly everything that is said.

SOURCE: Lenneberg, 1967, pp. 128–130.

(Table 6.2). How and when infants begin to talk and to understand speech is a story that has fascinated linguists, developmental psychologists, and parents. But it is a story that is still being written, as we shall see later in this chapter and in Chapter 9. Learning language poses awesome challenges for infants. How do infants learn that the sounds of language are different from the surrounding din of humming, coughing, chuckling, and harrumphing? Even more difficult, how do they learn what the language sounds mean? How does infant Sam, for example, learn that "dog," means dog, when he hears the word "dog" applied to a Great Dane, a dachshund, a poodle, and a stuffed toy, and the family pet referred to as "Airedale," "Rosie," "Good girl!" and "Bad dog!"? How does he figure out whether "dog" means this dog only, all dogs, all animals, all four-legged or brown or long-tailed creatures, or this dog's hind leg? The fact is, though, that infants do meet these challenges.

Before words: basic abilities

Sometime around 10 to 13 months, most infants utter their first word. But the infant's first word does not appear out of the blue. To reach this milestone, infants have been practicing sounds for months and listening intently to those around them. Both nature and nurture contribute to the achievement of these first words. From the very beginning, as we discussed in Chapter 5, infants are tuned in to the sounds of speech, and the speech they hear is tuned to their capacities. They are innately prepared to perceive the phonemes in spoken language and to listen to the high pitch of baby talk. They also apparently have innate cognitive abilities to categorize the world and to map ideas onto language. They seem to assume, for example, that each word they hear represents a single concept (Gleitman and Wanner, 1982; Mervis, 1985; Slobin, 1973). Infants' developing knowledge of language parallels and depends on the development of the ability to represent objects and actions that we discussed previously. The understanding that is reflected in object permanence, deferred imitation, and pretend play enables the infant to know that words are symbols and to try to express meaning in words.

Long before they produce intelligible words on their own, many infants give signs that they understand other people's words. As many a parent has remarked, the baby "doesn't talk yet, but she understands everything." "Everything" is probably an exaggeration, but year-old infants do understand lots of things that people say to them, especially when they can rely on other cues. When Daddy says, "Roll the ball to me," the baby does so. She uses the ball itself as the cue, and there's not much else she could do with the ball. Daddy might also say, "Where's the ball?" and look or point at it with large, plain gestures. By removing prompts and cues like these, researchers have shown that infants first understand the meanings of some proper names—*Mommy, Baby,*—and object names—*ball, egg, bottle*—at around 10 months (Huttenlocher, 1974). They recognize words that their caregivers use all the time—"light," "bottle"—as early as 5 to 8 months.

Besides basic abilities for understanding speech, infants also have basic abilities for producing speech. At first, when they are very young, infants coo little relaxed sounds. Then, when they are about 4 months old, they begin to produce more and different sounds, vowels especially. Over the next few months, they discover and invent many sounds, alternating vowels and consonants—the "Mamamamama" and "Babababa" that so delight parents. This **babbling** is the earliest of an infant's speech-like sounds. Repeating syllables gives infants practice in combining sounds that eventually they will use to form meaningful words. Included in the stream of sounds, however, are those that the infant has not heard and will not use later on. The babbling of hearing and deaf infants, the world over, is the same. Only the accident of birth turns an infant into an English-speaking, Swahili-speaking, or Japanese-speaking specialist. At about 9 months, the babbling of English-speakers-in-the-making begins to lose its German gutturals and French nasals. Babbling grows increasingly complex, taking on the intonation and stress patterns of adult speech, and infants seem to speak in long "sentences" that mimic the sounds of the language they are beginning to learn. By listening to these wordless "sentences," adults can identify the language that the infants soon will speak (DeBoysson-Bardies, Sagart, and Durand, 1984).

But the continuity between babbling and talking is not entirely straightforward. Although infants babble many sounds, they do not babble *all* the sounds later used in words. Conversely, they cannot later say in words *all* the sounds they once babbled. The relation between babbling and speech seems to be indirect. To a great extent, babbling is simply exercise for the mouth and vocal tract and practice in producing sequences of sounds and tones (Clark and Clark, 1977).

At around 9 months, infants begin to use sounds like "duh," "da," and "ma." These new sounds soon replace babbling. Although they bear little or no relation to any adult words, they *seem* very much like words. Their combination of short utterance, communicative intention, and appropriateness to context makes them seem as though they should be understood. In this period between babbling and the first real words, infants use these shortened speech sounds repeatedly, on purpose, and in specific contexts (Dore, 1978a). They express emotions: "ooh wow," to convey joy, for example, and "uh-uhuh'' to convey anger. They express desires: short, urgent little cries to get a parent to reach something on a high shelf that the infant wants. They point things out: ''duh'' or ''dah'' plus a pointed finger to catch an adult's attention and to indicate something like ''this'' or ''look'' or ''I'm seeing this.'' They designate similar objects: a single sound applied to any one of a group of objects, for example, ''oo'' referring to boots, shoes, slippers, and socks. These expressions are not words, but unlike babbling, they act like words. These expressions also show that in addition to their basic abilities to hear phonemes and words, to understand meaning, and to produce speech sounds, infants have basic communication skills. As we will discuss further in Chapter 7, through interaction with ready partners like Mom and Dad, infants learn to vocalize when others talk to them, to use vocalization to express feelings and wishes, to refer to interesting objects, and to take turns in ''conversation.''

First words

Finally, infants begin to use real words. These words are accompanied by lots of cues to make the message clear—pointing, reaching, grunting, staring. With the combination of word, gesture, facial expression, and action, the year-old infant requests and demands, labels people and things, describes actions, and expresses joy, displeasure, and surprise. These one-word utterances plus associated gestures, called **holophrases**, can do the work of whole paragraphs.

> Natalie would place herself squarely in front of me, reach her arms over her head, assume a supplicating face, and command, ''Up.'' Once perched in my arms, she showed me by looking and pointing, emitting guiding grunts, and saying something that sounded like ''mih'' what she was after.

Pronunciation
Infants' first words sound imperfect because their speech sounds remain limited. Their first words use relatively easy sounds. They are likely to include the consonants *p, b, t, d, m,* and *n,* which are formed with the tongue at the front of the mouth, and the vowels *a* and *e,* which come from the back of a relaxed mouth. Perhaps because of these limitations in infants' articulation, in most languages, the names for the people dearest to an infant's heart are made of these easy sounds: ''nana,'' ''baba,'' ''mama,'' ''papa.''

This 18-month-old makes her wishes clear as she reaches for her sister's pen and says ''peh.'' This is a typical early use of language.

For ease of pronunciation, infants often drop final consonants—duck is "duh," and bed is "beh," milk is "mih," and ball is "bah," or they drop initial consonants—cup is "up" (de Villiers and de Villiers, 1979). Only later do infants manage to produce whole sound clusters beginning with a vowel— "appuh" for apple, "itty" for kitty. Clusters of consonants are difficult for infants to say and may be simplified—spoon to "poon" and stop to "top" (Greenfield and Smith, 1976; Waterson, 1978). Infants also tend to use voiced consonants (*b, d*) at the beginnings of words and unvoiced (*k, p*) at the ends. Pie becomes "bie," and dog becomes "dok." In trying to say two-syllable words, infants often repeat one of the syllables—"Zeezee" for Rosie and the familiar "baba" for bottle. They can't produce two different syllables in one word, but hearing that the word has two syllables, they do their best. Simplifying the word by using the same vowel or consonant twice is another solution. Thus doggy becomes "goggy" or "doddy." In words with two or more syllables, they may simply drop the unexpressed one and say the stressed syllable: "raff" for giraffe "'mote 'trol" for remote control. Later, they may substitute an "uh" sound (ə)—"tape uhcorder"—for the unstressed syllable.

Content

The particular words that infants first say usually are social or functional expressions like *hi, bye-bye, thanks, yes, ouch, this, up,* and *on;* names for objects that are important, familiar, permanent, and usually movable, like *ball,* "Dada," and "b'anket"; simple adjectives like *hot* and *big;* and action words like *push* and *give.* They do not use less salient, filler words like *and, be,* or *the.* They use words to comment when the object has just changed in some way. Someone or something may just have appeared or disappeared, opened or closed, moved or brightened. Infants chirp "Daddy" as he walks in the door and "ight" as the lamp clicks on. Early vocabularies of object words are quite similar for different children, covering the categories of foods, animals, and toys. In one longitudinal study of language development, for example, the following words were found in the first 50 words of 18 toddlers (Nelson, 1973):

"juice," "milk," "cookie" (foods)

"dog," "cat," "duck" (animals)

"ball," "block" (toys)

"ear," "eye," "nose" (body parts)

"shoe," "hat," "sock" (clothes)

"car," "boat," "truck" (vehicles)

"momma," "dadda" (people)

Infants usually acquire nouns for basic categories—flower or dog—before they acquire more general words—plant or animal—or more specific ones—rose or collie (Brown, 1958; Rosch, Mervis, Gray, Johnson, and Boyes-Braem, 1976).

It is often difficult for others to know what infants understand and mean by certain of the words they use. Does the infant's "goggy" mean dog, animal, furry thing with a tail, or dog's hind leg? The problem for the adult in interpreting the infant's language is the same as for the infant in interpreting the adult's language.

Process

Infants learn the meanings of words by induction. They hear others speak words or react to their own utterances, and they draw inferences about the words' meanings (Carey, 1985; Figure 6.3). Like young interrogators, infants learn word meanings by pointing to possible referents, saying the

Among this infant's first words are basic nouns like "flower." It is unusual for first words to be either more specific—"geranium"—or more general—"plant."

Figure 6.3 What does Mother mean when she says "bowwow!"? This is the challenge that confronts the infant who first hears the sound. He attempts to find out by saying a few "bowwows" himself.

word in question, and observing the reactions of others. Infants formulate hypotheses—*dog* means dog? *dog* means pet? *dog* means hind leg?—that are constrained to converge on the correct meaning relatively quickly, sometimes after just one trial. Constraints on an infant's induction are imposed by the infant's understanding of objects, causes, people, and intentions. Although the infant may make the category of dog slightly too narrow—only this dog is *dog*—or too wide—*dog* refers to all four-legged animals—the infant is extremely unlikely to mistake bone or floor for *dog*, even though he or she often sees them together.

Toddlers often **overextend**, or overgeneralize, their words, using the words they do know to cover extra meanings. These overextensions are based on common properties or functions of objects—shapes, movements, sizes, sounds, textures. "Fly" may mean all small, dark objects, from insects to raisins. "Bowwow" may mean all small and furry animals, "dance" any kind of turning around (Brown, 1958; Clark and Clark, 1977; Rosch, 1975). Toddlers also may **underextend**, or undergeneralize, some words (Anglin, 1975). "Dog" may mean only *their* dog, not any other dogs. Are overextensions the result of problems in making categories or in knowing words? Does the infant use the overextended term to find out what the right word is, if he knows that when he says "dog," his father will say something else, perhaps "cat"? Does he overextend his words because it's the best he can do to communicate?

The main reason for overextensions seems to be that infants have limited vocabularies. Children use overextensions even when they understand more specific terms. In one study, for example, even toddlers who could point correctly to pictures of a dog and cat called them both "dog" (Fremgen and Fay, 1980). In another study, researchers found that like adults, infants categorized objects by applying the same word to all members of the category. But because their vocabularies were so limited, they overextended the name of one of the category members to the other members of the category rather than using the category name (Rescorla, 1981). In the study, six infants were followed from the time they were about 1 year old for at least six months. Their mothers kept diaries of the children's new words, and the researcher visited with the infants at home. When she visited, she brought a variety of small toys, and she recorded the names the children gave the toys and the names they understood, to see how they categorized these objects. All the infants organized vehicles, at first, around the word *car*. For about a month, cars were just cars, but thereafter the children overextended the word *car* to denote trucks, buses, planes, trains, and strollers. After the period of overextension, the children's concepts of car narrowed, and they acquired a new word—*truck*—and a new category—large commercial vehicles. Then they overextended the word *truck* to label buses, trains, bulldozers, cement mixers, and fire engines. They also discovered, before the end of the study, the word *plane* and used it for all aircraft, including helicopters, blimps, rockets, and gliders. When the researcher used the specific vehicle words in talking to the children, however, she found that they could *understand* finer distinctions among vehicle words than they could actually say.

Eve Clark (1983) has described the processes that young children use to increase their vocabularies. When children notice a gap in their ability to talk about something, they actively search for words to fill it. They look for words to label objects that are salient to them. A child interested in cars and trucks will attend more to words in this category than to words for animals, for example. Later, this child may set up several categories for trucks—moving trucks, delivery vans, mail trucks, big trucks, noisy trucks, dump trucks, and so on—and listen for new words to describe them. Hearing new words applied to trucks, he also starts looking for the kinds of trucks they name. In the meantime, he fills gaps in his vocabulary by overextending the words he has, by relying on general-purpose words like "that," and by coining new words whose meanings contrast with those of words he knows already. Children often coin words for actions—"Mommy *nippled* Anna," "I'm going to *gun* you"—and for objects—"chop" for an axe or "knock-thing" for something to knock with. They also coin words for people—"a smile-person" for someone friendly who smiles or a "hitter-man" for someone who hits things.

> Peter's expressions were wonderfully inventive. "It's not pepping," he complained about an empty pepper shaker. "Can I sprink the lawn?" "The fan breezed me." I still call sirens "ers," from Peter's baby word for the sound they make.

What part do parents play in children's acquisition of early words? For one thing, as we discussed in Chapter 5, parents' use of baby talk simplifies the language the baby hears. For another, parents' labeling of objects draws the baby's attention to the connection between words and things. Also, parents usually use nouns from the basic categories when they name things for their toddlers, and these are the words that the toddlers themselves use (Mervis and Mervis, 1982). Asked to label pictures for their 2-year-olds, one group of mothers labeled a Collie a "dog," a sandal a "shoe," a pigeon a "bird," and a dime "money," although they used the words "Collie," "sandal," "pigeon," and "dime" when speaking to another adult (Anglin, 1977). But mothers in this study also labeled some pictures with specific words: "pineapple" and not "fruit," "typewriter" and not "machine," "butterfly" and not "insect." What determines the kind of label that mothers use and children learn? Common sense, perhaps. Mothers use common labels for objects that are similar or that people use or respond to similarly. Thus mothers give both a Collie and a Miniature Poodle the label "dog," because both are pets, both gnaw bones, and both walk on a leash. But mothers call a cockroach an "insect" and butterfly a "butterfly," because cockroaches, like most insects, are disgusting and butterflies, unlike other insects, are beautiful.

Parents' responsiveness to their infants' attempts to talk also affects the infants' language development. Responsive parents accept and reinforce their children's attempts at pronouncing words. They treat their children's speech as meaningful, they echo their words, and they give them examples of more words. Here is a dialogue between a responsive mother and her 14-month-old daughter.

> MOTHER: Is that a car?
>
> JANE: Bah.
>
> MOTHER: Yes, car. Here's another car.
>
> JANE: Gah.
>
> MOTHER: Car, yes.
>
> JANE: Bah. Daddy.
>
> MOTHER: Daddy. Daddy's car is all gone (Nelson, 1973, p. 105).

Unresponsive parents, in contrast, are critical of their children's language, offer no reinforcements or appropriate models, and do not accept their children's language as meaningful. Here is a conversation between Paul, age 17 months, and his mother as they look at a picture book.

> PAUL: Go.
>
> MOTHER: What? Feel.
>
> PAUL: Fe.

MOTHER: What's that? A dog. What does the dog say? One page at a time. Oh, that one over there. What's that one there?

PAUL: Baoh.

MOTHER: What? You know that.

PAUL: Bah.

MOTHER: What?

PAUL: Ah wah.

MOTHER: What?

PAUL: Caw.

MOTHER: Car?

PAUL: Caw, awh.

MOTHER: Little kitty, you know that (Nelson, 1973, pp. 105–106).

Children of unresponsive, critical mothers tend to lag behind in their language development.

Stimulating cognitive development

Developmental psychologists have not been content simply to describe infants' language and cognitive development. They have wanted to learn how factors in the environment stimulate them. What helps and what hinders cognitive development? Given the constraints of an infant's genetic potential, what are the limits on enhancing the rate or level of cognitive development?

Infants in institutions

One thing psychologists have done to answer questions like these is to observe what happens to infants who are deprived of certain kinds of experience. To study the effects of deprivation, researchers have observed infants raised in institutions. In some of these institutions, although the infants were kept clean, dry, and well fed, they received no continuous care from a single caregiver of whom they might grow fond. They received no educational stimulation. Toys were scarce, the infants rarely moved about, and no one played with them or talked to them. They lay in white-sheeted cribs where they saw and heard almost nothing and where the hurried ministrations of an attendant were their only regular contact with adults. Many studies showed that infants in such institutions developed less quickly and less fully than other children (for example, Dennis, 1973; Goldfarb, 1945; Spitz and Wolf, 1946). These infants progressed normally for the first three months of life in the institution as long as their basic physical needs were met. But by 3 to 6 months of age, smiling, vocalizing, and motor development all were delayed. By the time the infants were 1 year old, intellectual development was impaired by as much as 50 IQ points (Clarke-Stewart and Apfel, 1979; Rutter, 1974).

Early investigators saw the pale and retarded children in institutions and asserted that the reason these children were doing so poorly was that they were suffering from a lack of mother love. Soon the investigators realized that the institutionalized children were deprived of other kinds of stimulation as well. Although these investigators did not specify which of the depriving conditions accounted for the observed developmental delays, they did show clearly that extreme environmental deprivation affects children's development.

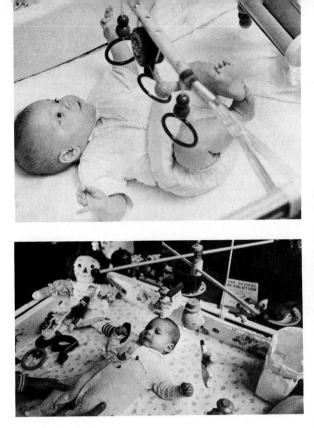

Moderate stimulation is best for infants' cognitive development; it arouses interest. Overstimulation is confusing, and understimulation is boring.

The stimulation of toys

But what of infants brought up in less extreme conditions—at home—as, of course, most are? We can infer from what is known about sensorimotor development that normal cognitive development requires infants to have practice in manipulating different objects. These little scientists undoubtedly need the chance to collect information as they experiment with objects and interpret their growing cache of information according to their ever-changing working knowledge of their surroundings. Be the objects bright or dull, colorful or drab, natural or synthetic, bought or homemade, designed for adults or for children, inanimate objects are likely to stimulate children's vision, exploration, schemes, and play. All the available research evidence suggests that children's early cognitive growth depends to some extent on the availability of a variety of stimulating objects.

In one study, for instance, when 5-month-old black infants from various socioeconomic groups were observed at home, it was found that the variety of objects available to the infants was related to their scores on tests of intelligence, problem solving, object permanence, and exploration (Yarrow, Rubenstein, and Pedersen, 1975). A number of other studies, too, suggest that young children's mental abilities are stimulated when they can play with a variety of interesting things, when they are allowed to explore their surroundings, and when their parents encourage them to do both these things (Wachs and Gruen, 1982). It also may be beneficial if the objects respond to infants' actions—if jack-in-the-boxes pop open, squeeze toys squeak, and bath toys float and bob (McCall, 1977). Of course, it is impossible to say, from correlational studies like these, that toys *alone* influence infants' development. There is likely to be a strong genetic component linking advanced infant development with greater availability of toys. But the results do strongly hint that objects that are varied, interesting, and responsive, objects that force infants to reach a bit but are not overwhelming, are best for fostering infants' cognitive development.

223

Parents at home

For most infants, toys and other play objects are part of the stimulation provided by parents. These objects may be especially important if parents play with them with the infant (Smith, Adamson, and Bakeman, 1986). Many psychologists have studied the relations between infants' cognitive development and parents' stimulating play—with and without toys. In one observational study, 25 pairs of mothers and infants were observed for 3½ hours when the infants were 3 months old (Crockenberg, 1983). What the mothers did with their babies—smiling, making eye contact, responding to the baby's crying, and the like—was recorded. Then, when the babies were 21 months old, they were tested on the Bayley Scale of Infant Mental Development (see Table 6.1). The test results were clear-cut: infants who scored high on the test had mothers who were more educated and more responsive to the infants' needs, who smiled and made more frequent eye contact with the infants, and who spent less of their time with the infant in such routine caretaking as diapering and feeding. In short, there was a clear connection between the quality and quantity of the mothers' stimulation of their infants and the infants' cognitive development.

In another study, 168 pairs of mothers and infants, from working-class to upper-middle-class backgrounds, were observed three times at home (Olson, Bates, and Bayles, 1984). When the infants were 6 months old, inventories of their home environments were taken, and the infants were given the Bayley Scale of Infant Mental Development. Again when the infants were 13 and 24 months old, the mothers and infants were retested. By the time the children were 24 months old, their IQ scores were significantly related to how frequently their mothers talked to them. Mothers who talked to their children and who did relatively little restricting or punishing tended to have the most advanced 2-year-olds. These were the mothers, many from the upper middle class, who earlier had kept in close physical contact with their infants, had offered them stimulating and appropriate objects to play with, had been highly involved with them, and had been both emotionally and verbally responsive.

These studies are fairly typical of the kind of research that has been done in this area in the past 15 years. Many other studies (reviewed by Appleton, Clifton, and Goldberg, 1975; Clarke-Stewart, 1977; Yarrow et al., 1975) have shown that mothers' education, responsiveness, and stimulation of their infants are related to how the infants develop. Mothers with more education talk more to their babies. They respond to their babies' babbling by talking. They provide more interesting toys for them, and they are more effective teachers. (Better educated mothers also are more likely than less educated mothers to have a husband living at home, more money, fewer children, and quieter households—factors that make it easier for them to provide this kind of attention, responsiveness, and stimulation to their infants.) When parents act in these stimulating and responsive ways with their infants, the infants do better on tests of cognitive development. These parents are providing their infants with interesting information about the world and, presumably, teaching them that the world is a place of predictable actions and reactions, a place worth exploring and learning about.

Is this why these children do better on the cognitive tests? When psychologists observe how infants' cognitive development is related to their parents' behavior, they do not really know whether more stimulating and responsive parents are *causing* the infants to develop quickly or more intelligent infants are *eliciting* more stimulation and more appropriate responsiveness from their parents. (This is a problem with correlational research in general, as we discussed in Chapter 2.) To try to separate these two possibilities, researchers

A mother stimulates her 3-month-old baby with a toy. There is a clear connection between the parents' stimulation and their infant's cognitive development. But at this age it is unlikely that the parent is having an immediate or irreversible effect on the baby's development.

at the University of Colorado (Hardy-Brown, Plomin, and DeFries, 1981) studied 50 adopted 1-year-olds and their biological and adopted parents. The *adoptive* parents' socioeconomic status and educational level, cognitive ability and vocabulary level, overall frequency of speaking or reading to their 1-year-olds, they found, were not related to the infants' language development. In contrast, the *biological* mothers' cognitive ability, especially memory ability, was significantly related to their 1-year-olds' language competence. This finding suggested that language development in the first year of life is influenced by genetic factors more than by parents' behavior. This finding is consistent with other studies (some of them discussed in Chapter 3) that suggest that the link between parents' behavior and individual differences in infants' intelligence in the first two years of life is largely genetic. Infants are by no means empty vessels into which parents pour intelligence merely by their stimulation and responsiveness. But parents do encourage their infants' natural intelligence to come out, and their influence increases as infants get older. Moreover, although parents' behavior may not always be correlated with individual differences in infants' intelligence, some stimulation and responsiveness from parents are still necessary for infants' development. It just may be than most parents provide *enough* stimulation and responsiveness to foster their infant's development so that *more* stimulation does not advance development faster.

To add to the complexity of the nature–nurture issue, other innate characteristics, such as the baby's sex and temperament, also are likely to affect both parents' activities with their infants and the consequences of these activities. Apparently not all ''positive'' early experiences enhance development, and not all ''negative'' early experiences interfere with it. In one study to consider this possibility, easygoing infants whose parents allowed them to explore freely, in homes where the toys and decorations were plentiful and where mothers smiled and responded to the infants' vocalizations, did well on tests of cognitive development (Wachs and Gandour, 1983). In contrast, more difficult and irritable infants reacted negatively to interactions with people and were more sensitive than easygoing infants to noise, confusion, and other stressful aspects of their physical environments; they did worse on tests of cognitive development. What is moderate stimulation for one infant may be overwhelming to another infant. Parents must consider the unique qualities of their own baby as they try to offer that baby experiences that will stimulate cognitive development. An infant's innate resilience or vulnerability to assaults from the environment also affects cognitive development. For infants who are relatively invulnerable, cognitive development is likely to proceed well even in a difficult environment. But for those who are vulnerable, cognitive development may proceed well only if the environment is favorable. The process of stimulating infants' cognitive development is clearly a reciprocal one, to which both infants and parents contribute.

Special programs

Not all parents do as much as they can to stimulate their infants' development, however. For these parents and their children, psychologists have designed special enrichment programs. Most of these enrichment programs involve the mothers, for it is they who provide much of the stimulation that infants receive. Many attempts to train, involve, and guide mothers have been made, and many have been quite successful.

One comprehensive enrichment program was the elaborate and extensive New Orleans Parent Child Development Center program (Andrews et al., 1982). This program included a curriculum that provided mothers with information about infant development and child rearing, home management,

focus Superbabies

Ambitious parents are not new under the sun. Mozart's father taught him the harpsichord at 2, and philosopher John Stuart Mill was taught Greek at the age of 3. Modern mothers and fathers, too, want their children to succeed in a competitive world. Some of them take their desire to an extreme. They would do anything to give their "superbabies" a head start on the road to achievement. Getting accepted by the "right" infant program can mean acceptance later at the "right" nursery school and kindergarten.

> There's so much pressure to get into college. You have to start them young and push them toward their goal. They have to be aware of everything—the alphabet, numbers, reading. I want to fill these little sponges as much as possible (a mother quoted in *Newsweek*, March 28, 1983, p. 62).

Compared to the generation of mothers before them, mothers today put greater stock in looking at books, providing their children with playthings, and teaching their children reading and cultural norms (Myers, 1984). Competitive parents want their children to have educational toys, lessons, and developmental preschool. Special programs that foster precocious physical and intellectual abilities have sprouted all over the country, and many infants and their panicky parents must interview for such coveted slots.

Philadelphia's Better Baby Institute trains mothers to teach their infants to swim, read, calculate, speak foreign languages, and play the violin. To instruct their potential prodigies in reading, art history, or zoology, parents should smile as they flash appropriate cards for brief periods three times a day. When they finish the course, the parents get a "professional mothering certificate." The institute's founder, Glenn Doman, who has written best sellers on *How to Teach Your Baby to Read* (1964); *Teach Your Baby Math* (1982); *How to Multiply Your Baby's Intelligence* (1984), contends that anyone has the genetic potential of Leonardo, Shakespeare, Michelangelo, Edison, or Ein-

Many parents deliberately and systematically work with their infants in an attempt to speed up their cognitive development.

nutrition, and health, as well as information about their own personal development and community and government resources. It also provided education for the children and broad support services. Mothers and their 2-month-old infants were assigned randomly either to the program or to a control group. They stayed in the program until the children were 3 years old. First, the researchers assessed whether the mothers' behavior changed as a result of being in the program. Trained observers coded the mothers' behavior with their infants in a waiting room when the children were 2, 12, 24, and 36 months old. The observers coded the mothers' interactions (teaching, showing affection, talking, restricting, punishing, or ignoring the child); their language (elaborating, suggesting, praising, generally conversing, questioning, teasing, warning, or criticizing); and their sensitivity to the child's communications and actions. The infants were tested at regular intervals on the Bayley Scale and scales of sensorimotor development.

After two years in the program, the mothers were more sensitive, accepting, and cooperative than control mothers. But neither their language nor their techniques of interacting with their children were significantly more positive than that of the controls. After three years in the program, mothers were more sensitive and accepting and were using more positive techniques with their children (playing, helping, and showing interest and affection). Their lanstein. In more specialized programs, children at tender ages practice computer programming, play Suzuki violin, and learn to swim, ski, and do gymnastics.

Although superbabies may be able to translate sentences into Japanese, French, and English, play the violin, and name the parts of the brain, the trend toward competitive early enrichment has a number of critics among specialists in child development. Developmental psychologists point out that infants are not born mere passive, empty creatures whom parents must cram full if they are to function intelligently in the world, and many doubt the wisdom of formal schooling before the age of 3 or 4 at the earliest. They point to developmental theories like those of Piaget and Gesell, which stress how important it is for infants to achieve things only when they are developmentally ready. They suggest that learning too early may create problems in development. Concentrating on letters and numbers teaches the child to parrot facts rather than to develop a creative and curious mind, and superbabies may perform by rote without any real understanding, burn out intellectually, or grow grim and striving. Some infants get frightened by the pressure of flash cards and drill. Perhaps the most serious problem that child care specialists warn against is the damage done when emotional and creative growth are sacrificed to academic achievement. Says Lee Salk,

> This pressure for high achievement really sets children up for failure. Love should be unconditional where children are concerned; it should not be based on IQ (*Newsweek*, March 28, 1983, pp. 65–66).

Superbabies' parents confirm the claims of baby trainers that their children devour facts, but some of them, too, are concerned about how valuable that is. Most troubling for all, the long-term effects of superbabyhood have not been evaluated. When they are evaluated, it is likely to turn out that what is most important is the *way* that training is presented to infants. Too much pressure is likely to make the baby anxious and to impede the development of other skills and ultimately may backfire when a child gets old enough to say, "Enough!"

guage now was significantly more positive than that of the control mothers. Program mothers also were significantly more effective than control mothers at teaching their children. As for the program's effects on the children, when the children were 3 years old, the program children scored significantly higher on tests of mental development. The program had intervened successfully in the early development of poor, black, inner-city children. Their intellectual skills and patterns of interaction with their mothers were significantly more positive and promising than they otherwise might have been. But it was not clear in this study, any more than in the correlational research on parent–infant interaction, that this was solely because mothers influenced their children's development. There was also evidence that the infants influenced their mothers. Again we see that the process of stimulating infants' development is reciprocal.

Most special programs for infants and parents are less comprehensive than this one—and so are their results. Modest programs generally have modest effects on parents' behavior and infants' development (Clarke-Stewart and Apfel, 1979). The important ingredients seem to be that the parents and children be truly involved in the program, that the program be right for the particular parent–child pair, and that the messages to the parents be unambiguous and clear.

Summary

1. Investigations of how early and in what ways infants learn show that classical conditioning generally is unsuccessful with infants under 2 or 3 months old. Operant conditioning with very young infants involves only reflexes; after 3 months of age or so, a broader range of behavior is affected by reinforcement.

2. By using various methods—paired comparison, habituation, retention of learned responses, and observing spontaneous behavior—researchers have learned what and for how long infants remember. At first, apparently, memory consists of primitive, sensory, wired-in recognition, without thought. At about 3 months, memory becomes more cognitive, as infants begin to control what they look at, listen to, and pay attention to. By 8 to 10 months, infants form mental categories, which allow them to summarize information, thus reducing their memory load.

3. According to Jean Piaget, the early mental activity of infants, called sensorimotor intelligence, is limited to what can be sensed and acted on. Out of their sensorimotor experiences with objects, infants develop action schemes. They organize—combine and integrate—their schemes and adapt them as their experience increases. Infants assimilate new objects and experiences into their existing schemes; they accommodate, or modify, schemes when they encounter new objects and experiences that do not fit their schemes.

4. According to Piaget, infants progress through an unvarying sequence of developmental stages, each of which incorporates the knowledge gained in the previous stage. During the sensorimotor period, Piaget claimed, infants progress from a stage of practicing and repeating reflexes, to acquiring adaptations, to making interesting sights last. During this stage, they engage in magico-phenomenistic thinking. They also begin to develop object permanence, the knowledge that even when objects are out of sight they continue to exist. Later stages bring fuller understanding of object permanence, cause and effect, the physical properties of objects, and of the self as a separate being.

5. Other developmental psychologists have found problems in Piaget's theory of sensorimotor development and his suggestion that infants do not begin to form mental representations of objects until the middle of their second year. They have found evidence that infants form mental representations of objects in the first year and suggest that Piaget's hidden object task is difficult for infants not because they don't realize that objects are permanent but because they are not good at searching for objects or remembering where they are hidden.

6. Infants act out their mental representations of actions through successively more advanced stages of imitation. They go from pseudoimitations—imitations of acts they can perform already—to true imitations of unfamiliar actions to deferred imitations, imitations that occur sometime after the infant has seen the original act. Infants seem to be tuned in to imitating others' mouth movements particularly early.

7. The sense of self develops in stages, too. Infants at first are interested in their mirror images but do not realize that they are seeing their own image. Later, they distinguish between their own and others' reflected images. Still later they understand that they have unique features that can be named and labeled with words.

8. Play is the work of infancy, the repetition of actions for sheer enjoyment. A major developmental change in play occurs when pretend play begins at the age of about 1 year.

9. Not all infants develop cognitively at the same rate. Psychologists test individuals' cognitive levels with infant intelligence tests. These tests are useful for assessing whether infants are progressing normally, but they generally do not predict individuals' later IQ scores. One reason is that intelligence tests in infancy center on perceptual and sensorimotor abilities, whereas later intelligence tests center on verbal and abstract abilities. Infants' recognition of new and familiar stimuli is more predictive of later IQ scores than these infant IQ tests.

10. Language develops in infancy, too, out of basic capacities like speech perception and categorization, understanding of the meaning of words, the articulation aspects of babbling, and a conducive learning environment. At first, because of their limited vocabularies infants may overextend words (using ''dog'' for cats, dogs, and rabbits) or underextend them (using ''dog'' just for Spot).

11. Unresponsive and unstimulating care in infancy retards cognitive development. Although parents cannot create intelligence in their children, they can foster its development. Special programs to train and support parents to become more stimulating have been successful.

Key terms

conditional stimulus
unconditioned stimulus
unconditioned response
conditioned response
paired comparisons
encoding
sensorimotor period
schemes

adaptation
accommodation
assimilation
organization
circular reactions (primary, secondary, and tertiary)
object permanence
magico-phenomenistic thinking

A not B phenomenon
pseudoimitation
deferred imitation
babbling
holophrase
overextend
underextend

Suggested readings

CLARKE, ANN M., and CLARKE, A. D. B. (EDS.) *Early Experience: Myth and Evidence.* New York: The Free Press, 1976. A collection of articles demonstrating the remarkable ability of children to recover from extremely depriving and depressing early experiences. This book takes the position that early childhood is not the only important period for intellectual and social development.

McCALL, ROBERT C. *Infants.* Cambridge, Mass.: Harvard University Press, 1979. Developmental milestones of the infant's cognitive and social progress, clearly explained for parents.

PIAGET, JEAN. *The Origins of Intelligence in Children.* New York: International University Press, 1966. Piaget's own account of the evidence for and theory behind sensorimotor development in infancy.

WEIR, RUTH H. *Language in the Crib.* The Hague: Mouton, 1970. An in-depth analysis of a child's very early speech.

chapter seven

Social and emotional development

A new baby seems helpless, incapable of turning over, lifting her head, or moving around without someone's help. But look more closely, and you will see this same baby's formidable capacity to attract people to herself. The baby cries for food—and her parents come, meal at the ready. She whimpers for comfort—and arms scoop her into an embrace. She opens her eyes—and her parents fix their gaze on her tiny face, waiting for eye contact. She hiccoughs after her milk—and someone props her up, taps her back, and waits for the air bubbles to come up. She fusses—and hands come to check the sogginess of her diaper. Over and over again, hundreds of times a day, the new baby draws people to herself with gazes, cries, snuggles, and sniffles. She participates actively in a world prepared to support and encourage her social inclinations. This tiny creature has begun in her own way to build the social ties that will shape her lifelong experience. In this chapter, we will follow the infant's progress in the social world from the first moments after her birth to her first love affair.

The first meeting

> Look at his little face. His little nails. Oh. His little squashed up nose like your nose. He has red hair.
>
> Little baby got big feet—he has got big feet, hasn't he?
>
> He's blowing bubbles. His little hands are all wrinkled—looks like he's done the washing up, doesn't he?
>
> Yes (laughs). Oh dear!
>
> Oh, he's opened his eyes, there—look.
>
> Hello (as baby opens his eyes for the first time)! (Macfarlane, 1977, pp. 91, 94, 95).

When mother and infant first look at each other, they are not really strangers. They have been intimately connected for the infant's entire existence in the womb. Now, when they meet face to face, the mother gets to know this new arrival by looking, touching, and talking (Klaus, Kennell, Plumb, and Zuehlke, 1970). Most mothers follow a similar pattern in getting to know their infants in these first minutes after birth. They reach out and tentatively touch the infant's fingertips, then the arms and legs. Within a few minutes, they place their palms on the infant's trunk and massage and stroke the tiny body. They look, the infant looks, and their eyes meet. Even right after birth, infants will follow the mother's face. Mothers of blind infants say that they feel ''lost,'' because their infants cannot return their gaze (Fraiberg, 1974). For as long as an hour after birth (unless the mother has been heavily sedated during the delivery), the infant is quiet, alert, and open-eyed.

> Right after she was born, Natalie was wide awake and nursed hungrily at my breast. I kept gazing at those beautiful blue eyes and stroking her all over. It was hard to believe that we had created anything so wonderful as that baby in my arms.

The first hour after birth can be an important time, because the infant is alert and gazing, and the mother's receptivity is intensified by high hormone levels. The two ''converse'': Mother talks to the infant, and, some observers have suggested, the infant moves in time to her words (Condon and Sander, 1974). Seeing her infant move and look into her face encourages the mother to keep on speaking, touching, and looking. It pleases her deeply to hold the

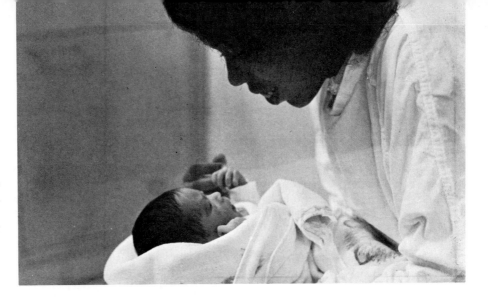

The mother–infant bond has its earliest expression in mutual gazing, which begins in the first hour after birth as the mother holds, touches, and studies her newborn.

infant. When the infant is attentive and the mother welcoming their relationship is off to a good start.

The bond between mother and infant

The special feeling that mothers have for their new infants even in the first moments after birth usually deepens over the first few months into a strong emotional bond. Most mothers feel nurturant and caring toward their infants. They are disturbed by separation or the thought of separation, and they are willing to make the sacrifices necessary for their infant's survival—like getting up several times every night to feed and comfort the infant. But this bond does not always form. In the 1970s, Marshall Klaus and John Kennell (1976), two pediatricians, observed that mothers who were separated from their newborns immediately after the birth treated their infants differently from mothers who remained in contact with their newborns. Mothers who were separated from their infants, usually either because mother or infant was ill or because the infant was premature, were more likely to neglect or abuse their infant. According to Klaus and Kennell, these mothers seemed to have missed an early chance to form deep emotional bonds with their infants. When they handled them, the mothers seemed fearful and unsure. Some felt uncertain that the infants really were theirs. ''Are you mine? Are you really mine? Are you alive? Are you really alive?'' asked one mother reunited with her baby (Klaus and Kennell, 1976, p. 10). Perhaps the moments immediately after birth, Klaus and Kennell suggested, are a **sensitive period** when mothers easily form emotional bonds with their infants. Preventing the pair from **bonding** in these early moments, they argued, hampers the development of this important tie.

Researchers began to test this suggestion. At the time the researchers began their investigations, newborns in American hospitals were routinely removed from their mothers immediately after birth and kept in infant nurseries, except for feeding visits to their mothers. By increasing the contact between mothers and infants beyond this usual level, investigators could gauge how early contact affected the bond between mother and infant. Researchers compared mothers whose infants went to the newborn nursery with those who kept their infants with them, a procedure called **rooming in**. They experimented with keeping infants and mothers together for several hours right after birth and with keeping infants and mothers together for extra hours every day. Several of the studies showed that mothers who had more early

233

contact with their infants reported feeling more competent than mothers who were separated from their infants by ordinary hospital routine. They were less willing to turn their infants over to anyone else. They kept their infants closer to them, touched and soothed, kissed and caressed them more often—not only when their infants were newborns but a year later as well (Greenberg, Rosenberg, and Lind, 1973; Hales, Lozoff, Sosa, and Kennell, 1977; Kennell et al., 1974).

These effects of early contact were not apparent in all studies, however. Middle-class mothers in particular did not always benefit so clearly from extra early contact with their infants. In one investigation of the short-term effects of early contact, for example, 30 middle-class parents were randomly assigned to one of two groups when their first baby was born (Svejda, Pannabecker, and Emde, 1982). In the early-contact group, mothers were given 15 minutes of skin-to-skin contact with their newborn in the delivery room, 45 minutes with the baby in the recovery room, and 1½ hour at each of the next seven feedings. Mothers in the routine-contact group had five minutes together with their baby as they were wheeled to the recovery room, where there was no further contact, and then 20 to 30 minutes of contact at each feeding. The investigators found no differences between the two groups in the bond that mothers felt toward their babies.

Effects of early contact that last beyond the period of infancy have been especially difficult to demonstrate (Whiten, 1977; Taylor, Taylor, Campbell, Maloni, and Dickey, 1979). In one carefully done study in Germany, for example, investigators found some weak effects of early contact, but these effects diminished over time (Grossmann, Thane, and Grossmann, 1981). On the second and third days after the birth, mothers in the early-contact group touched their babies more tenderly and cuddled them more during feedings than the mothers in the routine contact group. But by the next day, the effects had disappeared. Weak effects also were found in a study of 200 mothers, most of whom were black and single (Siegel, Bauman, Schaefer, Saunders, and Ingram, 1980). When the mothers were interviewed and observed with their infants at 4 and 12 months after the birth, differences in early contact accounted for only about 3 percent of the differences in mothers' acceptance and consoling of their infants. In yet another study, mothers who had had early contact with their infants and were not separated from them in the hospital felt more confident and less anxious in the first weeks after the baby was born. But by 4 to 6 weeks after their infants' births, mothers who had had early contact did not differ discernibly in either anxiety or self-confidence from mothers who had been separated from their infants after birth (Sostek, Scanlon, and Abramson, 1982).

Early contact, then, *sometimes* affects mothers' feelings toward their infants. These effects are not universal. Human mothers differ from mothers of many other animal species in that they form bonds with their infants even if the early sensitive period is missed or disrupted. Many human mothers miss the early moments after an infant's birth because they have been under anesthesia for a cesarean section or other obstetrical procedure or because the infant is whisked away to an incubator or intensive care. Most of these mothers do form strong and abiding emotional bonds to their infants. So, too, adoptive parents, fathers who missed their infant's birth, and many other people form emotional bonds with the infant. Early contact may start the bonds forming earlier, but later contact is likely to lead to an attachment that is just as deep and enduring.

The main value in Klaus and Kennell's original ideas about the danger of separating mothers and babies immediately after birth may turn out to have been practical: the humanizing of hospital procedure.

Postpartum blues

No matter whether they have been separated from their infants in the hospital or not, mothers face a difficult transition when they arrive home and take on the enormous task of caring for a newborn infant. Most new mothers find their moods swinging and swaying. From half to three-quarters of new mothers have crying jags during the first ten days after delivery (Davidson, 1972; Pitt, 1973; Yalom, Lunde, Moos, and Hamburg, 1968).

> I was so happy after Sam was born that I found it amazing when I started to cry at the oddest things. When we brought him home from the hospital, I cried. I chalked that up to joy. A few days later, I cried miserably because I'd gotten a drop of ketchup on my bathrobe.

New mothers feel vulnerable and sensitive, a consequence of both physical and psychological changes following childbirth. They are tired from the hard work of labor and delivery and from meeting the round-the-clock demands of their newborn infant. In the days and weeks following childbirth, mothers need time to rest. They also need the support of family and friends. In one study it was found that new mothers who lacked emotional and practical support from relatives and friends were more likely to need psychiatric care (Gordon and Gordon, 1960). Expectant mothers who had been told to set up a support network—of husband, grandparents or other relatives, friends, and babysitters—and who had been taught how to minimize stress while they were pregnant suffered fewer emotional problems in the adjustment period after childbirth than mothers who did not (Gordon, Kapostins, and Gordon, 1965).

> Our Lamaze teacher told our class of expectant parents that the best gifts for new mothers were phone calls that said, ''I'm going grocery shopping now. Tell me what you need,'' or, ''I'll be at your house at 4 o'clock to do your laundry and make supper. You rest.''

Not only social support, but the mother's personality and expectations also affect her adjustment to the new baby. Mothers adapt most readily if they are nurturant, self-confident, interested in child rearing, see themselves as mothers, and remember their own mothers as close, warm, and happy (Shereshefsy and Yarrow, 1973). They also adapt well if they really wanted the baby (Field, Sandberg, Vega-Lahr, Goldstein, and Guy, 1985).

How the infant acts also has a lot to do with the new mother's postpartum adjustment. One pair of investigators found that three-quarters of the mothers who reported strong positive feelings for their infants in the first three months explained that the reason was their infant's responsiveness (Robson and Moss, 1970). Mothers want healthy infants—infants who nurse well and gain weight, infants who sleep well and are quiet. But they also want infants who are responsive and communicative—smiling, laughing, making eye contact. A responsive, communicative infant makes the postpartum adjustment easier and deepens the mother's bond to her infant.

Infant communication

Infants communicate in a number of ways, active and passive, noisy and quiet, by vocalization, facial expression, and gesture.

"Babyness"

Parents and grandparents, brothers and sisters, even strangers who peek into the baby carriage nearly all smile and coo, open their eyes wide, exaggerate the expressions on their faces, and talk baby talk in high voices. Why do otherwise sober people act so dotty? The cute "babyness" of that tiny infant does it, with a big round head on a little body, a rounded forehead, big eyes, plump cheeks, small face and mouth. The baby's helplessness is touching, her grins and bright eyes are charming, her sweet pink mouth is alluring, and her squeaks and gurgles are endearing. Human babies, like puppies, kittens, calves, and colts, have a special appeal.

This cute "babyness" equips infants with a powerful means of attracting the nurturance they need. Ethologists maintain that "babyness" helps to ensure the infant's survival (Bowlby, 1969; Lorenz, 1971). It keeps adults nearby and interested in feeding, sheltering, and stimulating their offspring. Actively caring for and touching the infant seems to intensify the attraction. Nurses feel more strongly attracted to newborn infants after caring for them, and doctors feel more strongly attracted after examining them (Corter et al., 1978; Klaus and Kennell, 1976).

At the same time as infants are attractive to adults, adults are extremely attractive to babies. The baby talk and exaggerated facial expressions that parents direct toward their infants seem especially well suited to the infant's limited sensory abilities. Mouths that move and eyes that widen suit the infant's visual attraction to movement and to contrasts between bright and dark. People around the world, parents and nonparents, of both sexes and all ages, respond in these ways to human and animal infants (Stern, 1977). Parents greet their new babies like this even if they think the babies cannot see (Papousek and Papousek, 1978). The mutual attraction of infant and parent is powerful and, at least in part, biologically determined.

Gazing

Babies also communicate with the people around them by gazing. As we described in Chapter 5, from the time they are born infants can see things that are large and close up. When infants are held close, they can see their parent's face and hair or a proffered hand or toy. During feeding and play, parents hold their infants at a distance that is well within the infant's visual "window." That interesting face, as Mom or Dad talks to and looks at the infant, turns feeding and playtime into excellent opportunities for forming social and emotional ties.

The enrapt mother and her infant are clearly communicating, but without a single syllable being exchanged. Their mutual gazing tells it all.

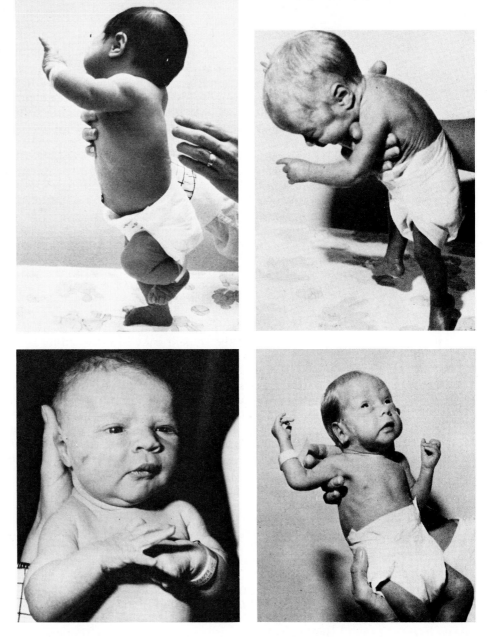

(Left) The automatic walking reflex of the full-term baby—her strong back, firmly planted foot, arm and head in upright balance—spells competence to her parents. (Right) The overextended limbs and weak and curved back of the premature baby project a sense of fragility and incompetence to her parents. As her mother said, "Oh, don't do that with her. It looks grotesque."

(Left) In **en face** interaction, the full-term baby, only 24 hours old, looks steadily and calmly at his mother. (Right) When parents attempt the same intimate contact with the premature infant, she startles, trembles, and breaks away, eliciting from her mother a worried, "She doesn't seem to **want** to look at me."

When infants are about 6 weeks old, their visual and motor systems have matured enough so that they can focus on their mother's eyes, with their own bright eyes wide open (Wolff, 1963). For the first time, the mother feels that the baby is looking *at her*. Even mothers who are not consciously aware of this wonderful new development step up the pace of their interactions noticeably—doing more playing, talking, and bouncing.

> Jason was such a handful in the first month and a half. He cried and cried; we paced the floors with him for hours on end. He stopped crying only long enough to take a bottle. Then he'd spit it all up. But one day, as I was changing his diaper, my hand on his stomach, Jason stopped squirming, opened his eyes wide, and looked *at me*. I was so thrilled! It had been weeks of torture, but now it was okay. There was someone inside that baby head.

When they are about 3 months old, infants become able to maintain eye contact with their mothers, to gaze into their eyes for several seconds, and the mother's feelings of attachment to the infant deepen. Now mothers are likely to feel so strongly attached that being away from their infant feels uncomfortable, and imagining its loss is unbearable (Robson and Moss, 1970). Mothers of blind infants, who do not maintain eye contact, have difficulty forming an attachment (Fraiberg, 1974). They find their infants perplexing and unresponsive.

The infant's intent gaze not only affects how the mother feels, but it also communicates a useful message about how the infant is feeling. Videotapes of typical middle-class mothers show that on the average these mothers spend three-quarters of the time that they are feeding or playing with their infants gazing at the infant's face, and the infant's gaze signals the mother about how to proceed (Peery and Stern, 1976; Schaffer, Collis, and Parsons, 1977). So long as the infant is looking at her, the mother continues to play. But when the infant turns away, the mother stops playing. Mothers interpret the turning away as a signal that the infant wants a change. Thus, gazing is an effective means by which the infant communicates with parents.

Vocalizing

Vocalizing is another means by which the infant communicates. For the first few months, the infant's vocal sounds are coos and gurgles, uttered after meals and naps, when the infant is relaxed and being held. By about 4 months, infants utter relaxed consonant and vowel sounds when they hear their parents' voices or see their faces approaching. They string these sounds together—"babababababa," "dahdahdah"—in sentence-like patterns. This babbling is vocal play, not a deliberate attempt to say something. Infants vocalize in this way even when there is no one around to listen. But although infants do not intend these sounds to convey meaning, parents react to them—as they do to yawns, burps, smiles, and hand movements—as though they were *full* of meaning. While the infant is vocalizing or right after, the mother is likely to speak (Jones and Moss, 1971; Lewis and Freedle, 1973). "Oh, is dat so," she may say, "Is oo trying to tell me somethin'?"

Soon, infants are imitating the sounds they hear, and synchronizing their babbling with their parents' speech. They grow quiet when someone nearby speaks, then babble excitedly, and then listen again. Parents treat this "conversational" babbling, too, as though it were meaningful and respond with talk, delight, and affection. Although vocalization at this age is not language, it can communicate an infant's intention. One 6-month-old vocalized when he was playing with objects in a higher pitch than he used when he wanted his mother. When his pitch dropped, his mother checked to see what he wanted. Another baby's vocalizations grew sharper when he wanted something beyond his reach, and his mother responded to this change in sound by fetching the thing he wanted (Bruner, 1978). The infant's vocalization is a means of communicating with parents who are willing to listen.

Smiling and laughing

Smiles and laughter are arguably the infant's most irresistable means of communicating. During the first two weeks of life, infants ordinarily smile when they are drowsy or sleeping lightly rather than when they are awake. These smiles are not triggered by social stimulation. Instead, they come from completely internal events within the brain: the infant's rising and falling levels of arousal. They are, therefore, called **endogenous smiles**. As infants relax after being aroused, their muscles relax, and a smile appears on their face (Figure 7.1). As infants sleep lightly, their level of physiological arousal stays near this "smile threshold," and little endogenous smiles play across their faces. Startle them with a loud noise, and they grow too highly aroused

Spontaneous smiles suffuse the infant's face in sleep.

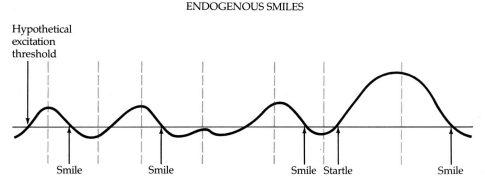

ENDOGENOUS SMILES

Figure 7.1 **This schematic drawing of excitation and arousal shows an infant's behavior in relation to a hypothetical threshold of arousal. When infants are aroused and then relax just below the threshold, they give a tiny spontaneous (endogenous) smile (Sroufe, 1979).**

to smile. But touch them softly or whisper, and in six to eight seconds an endogenous smile may appear.

In the second two weeks of life, smiles can be coaxed from infants by gentle stimulation while they are awake. At the end of the first month, bouncing and other forms of moderate stimulation coax those smiles from the infant. In each case, the infant is stimulated to a point above threshold, and then, six to eight seconds after the stimulation ends, a smile appears. Although parents get great pleasure from seeing these endogenous smiles, they do not really signify pleasure or sociability in the infant. These early smiles *look* like later smiles, and like later smiles they arise from arousal and relaxation. But it will be another few weeks until the infant is smiling with real pleasure.

When infants are about 1 month old, they begin to smile **exogenous smiles** that are responses to events in the outside world. They smile when heads nod at them silently or speak in a high voice, when lights blink, and when they perceive rhythm or repetition (Sroufe, 1979). By 3 months infants smile when they see a human face, a doll, or other familiar object. Now their smiles are truly social. Three-month-olds smile when they see Mom or Dad. Their smiles may reflect pleasure, or they may signal that the infants have recognized someone or something (Kagan, 1971). When babies are 4 months old, the motionless face that just a few weeks ago made them smile now does not, perhaps because it's too easy to recognize. But a moving face is more grist for their mill, and so they smile. The 5-month-old smiles after he has done something like move a ball or a mobile and then shown his mastery by moving it again. His smiles show that in his earliest months of life, he already takes pleasure from learning and doing.

Whatever their cause, young infants' smiles draw others to them because they are so rewarding. The more infants smile, the more their parents are "hooked," eager to watch and interact, and the more they smile back. The upward spiral is quite lovely: the more the infant smiles, the more his parents smile back, and so the more he smiles, and so the more they smile. . . .

> Sam grinned when I came into his room to pick him up after his nap, and he grinned when he first saw me in the morning. He grinned when he saw his father, or his rice cereal, or the brightly colored horses on the side of his bassinet. He grinned when he was changed, and he grinned when he was sung to. We were so in love with those grins of his that his father at one point said, "That kid's got us trained like seals."

Laughter is another sign of joy. Laughter is also a reaction to arousal and a fine means of communication, like smiling. Infants begin laughing when they are 3 or 4 months old (Berlyne, 1969). Arousal that at an earlier age would have overwhelmed them and sent them into tears now brings them to laughter. Bouncing, tickling, clapping, and singing all may arouse infants at this age enough to make them laugh. To keep them laughing, the sounds and movements must change or intensify. Parents may find themselves working harder and harder to keep the baby laughing. They do it because the laughter is immensely rewarding.

Five-month-olds laugh when they are jiggled and tickled under the chin but also when Mom or Dad plays peekaboo. In the laboratory, 7- and 8-month-olds laugh when Mom, that great entertainer, acts silly and shakes her hair, or, at the request of an experimenter, puts a cloth in her mouth, says "coochy coo," or neighs like a horse (Sroufe and Wunsch, 1972). Twelve-month-olds laugh when Mom acts incongruously, walking like a penguin, sticking out her tongue, or sucking on the baby's bottle. They also laugh when they know some fun is about to happen—when Mom is about to nibble their tummy—or when they can do something funny themselves, like grabbing the cloth that covered up Mom's face or sticking it in her mouth. Laughing, like smiling, happens first in direct response to an event and later in response to the infant's interpreting, expecting, or participating in the event (Sroufe, 1979).

Crying

Laughter is the sound that parents most love to hear from their infants. Not so beloved is crying, another powerful means of communication. The sound or sight of an infant crying galvanizes most people into action. A nursing mother has only to hear her own or another infant cry, and her breasts fill with milk. A mother has only to watch a *silent* videotape of an infant the same age as her own crying, and her heart races (Donovan, Leavitt, and Balling, 1978). If she watches a videotape of her own infant crying, or if a soundtrack is added to the tape, her heart races faster still (Wiesenfeld and Klorman, 1978). Not only does crying arouse people, but it also irritates and angers them (Frodi, Lamb, Leavitt, and Donovan, 1978; Freudenberg, Driscoll, and Stern, 1978). Even infants a few months old start to wail when they hear recordings of newborns' cries (Simner, 1971).

Once infants start crying, it is not always so easy for people to quiet them. They may not know precisely what the baby is crying about—pain? hunger? sleepiness? illness?

When Mikey was an infant, I read books that said "experienced mothers" could distinguish their babies' hunger, pain, and tiredness cries. Much as I wanted to know how to get him to stop crying some-

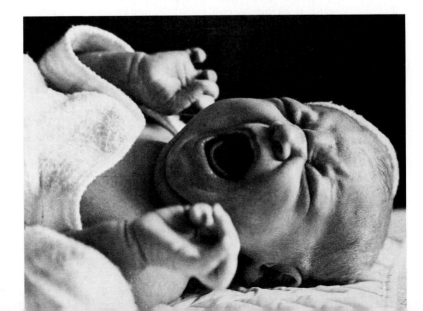

The infant's cry: a frowning, screwed-up face; eyes closed and mouth open; a lusty wail.

times, *I* couldn't tell his cries apart very well. His pain cry did sound different. But with the other cries, I just groped my way along. If he was crying at mealtime, I figured he was hungry.

Although some people who have been around lots of infants—midwives, children's doctors and nurses, and some parents—can tell various cries apart, and although sound wave recordings of birth cries, pain, hunger, and angry cries do look different, most people cannot tell them apart in everyday practice (Mueller, Hollien, and Murry, 1974; Wasz-Hoeckert, Lind, Vuorenkoski, Partanen, and Valanne, 1968; Wolff, 1969). If an infant cries for long enough, for whatever reason, the crying eventually takes on the same rhythmic pattern as the hunger cry (Wolff, 1969). Sometimes, too, infants cry for more than a single reason.

> There were days when Sam was a few months old when the crying just seemed to go on and on. Those were days that he had a cold, was teething, and hadn't slept well.

Why infants cry

To learn about the causes of infants' crying, Peter Wolff (1969) observed infants for 15 to 30 hours a week in their homes for their first six months. He also observed a group of hospitalized infants. New babies, he found, cried when they were hungry. Both hospitalized infants being fed through stomach tubes and healthy infants who sucked under their own power cried less when their stomachs were full. Infants whose rooms were heated to a toasty 88 degrees Fahrenheit cried less—and slept more soundly—than those in rooms of a merely tropical 78 degrees. Warmth and sleep both may insulate infants from crying. No matter how warm their room, infants fussed when they were undressed. Quick, sharp noises or movements that startled the infants often made them cry as well. Other researchers later found that babies also cry if they are overstimulated. Even gazing too long at a bright toy or mobile may overstimulate them, and they cry to break away from it (Sroufe, 1979; Tennes, Kisley, and Metcalf, 1972).

Babies 2 to 3 months old cry for different reasons—if someone interrupts their feeding, takes something out of their hand, approaches suddenly, makes a loud noise, or stares at them unresponsively (Bernal, 1972; Wolff, 1969). When one investigator asked a group of mothers to stare unresponsively at their babies, for instance, the babies' expressions became serious, they tried to catch their mother's attention, then turned away, grew fussy, and either cried or avoided looking at the mothers (Stern, 1974). Babies at this age also sometimes cry for a moment when their mother or another person leaves them.

By 4 to 6 months, infants develop intentions, the motivation to complete an action, and cry if they are frustrated. Infants begin to distinguish between familiar and unfamiliar people. When an unfamiliar person appears, the baby studies the person's face intently, frowns, takes a deep breath, and usually looks or turns away; he then may cry (Bronson, 1972). This *wariness* of strangers is an important new development that demonstrates the infant's growing awareness of the social environment. The infant's interest is caught by the interesting human face of the stranger. His mind engaged and his body aroused, the infant works at recognizing, or assimilating, the stranger's face. If he cannot assimilate the person, he acts wary. Over the period from 6 to 12 months, as cognitive awareness increases, the likelihood that the infant will be wary increases (see Figure 7.2). The baby also acts wary if someone familiar acts strangely or looks different—perhaps wearing new glasses or a mask (Brazelton, Tronick, Adamson, Als, and Wise, 1975). The process is the same

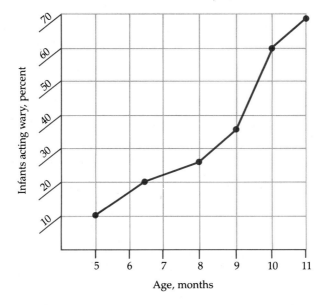

WARINESS OF STRANGERS

Figure 7.2 The likelihood that an infant will act wary of a stranger increases noticeably from 5 to 11 months of age (Decarie, 1974; Skarin, 1977; Waters, Matas, and Sroufe, 1975).

when a familiar face looks strange as when an unfamiliar face appears. The *incongruity* confuses and upsets the infant (Bronson, 1972).

Sometime during this period infants act not only wary but actually fearful. They cling to their parent, burst into tears, scream, or scoot away. This fear may be the infant's first true negative emotion. Earlier, crying is brought about by physical conditions like hunger or cold, or it is an immediate reaction to an event like a face not responding. But this **stranger anxiety** or **fear of strangers** involves cognitive processing, and this, psychologists think, makes the crying qualitatively different from the crying caused by pain or over-stimulation. Developmental psychologists now think that infants' fearful reaction to strangers depend on their interpretation of the stranger and the situation—who else is there, how the stranger acts, and so on. Safe in his mother's arms when a stranger appears, an infant acts wary (frowns, looks away, has a racing heart) but usually does not react fearfully (tearfully) to the

This baby is showing her "stranger anxiety" as she turns away from the unfamiliar woman to the comforting arms of her mother.

stranger. But if the infant is alone, upset, or in an unfamiliar place, or if the stranger comes too close, too quickly, looks too serious or scary, or does not back off when the infant looks away, the infant is likely to react fearfully (Bronson, 1978; Brooks and Lewis, 1976; Emde, Gaensbauer, and Harmon, 1976; Skarin, 1977; Sroufe, 1977).

If the stranger reminds the infant of some past experience with a stranger, the infant also may act fearful. Beginning at 8 to 10 months, as we discussed in Chapter 6, infants can form rudimentary categories—like "scary stranger," or "noisy new person," or "nice new playmate." They can make guesses about the new stranger based on their past experiences. Frightened by one stranger, they are more likely to be frightened by a second. Once frightened by a nurse in white uniform who gave her a painful injection, for example, the infant is likely to cry in fear when anyone else in white uniform appears.

> When Sam was 9 months old, he stayed with his grandparents one afternoon. They couldn't understand why he cried so hard when the teenaged girl from next door stopped by for a few minutes. He probably thought she was a babysitter, and he got scared that his grandparents were going to leave him alone with her. After all, most of the other teenaged girls he'd seen *had* been babysitters.

Not all infants show fear of strangers, and not all strangers are feared. But most infants can be intimidated by an insensitive newcomer. It takes a certain sensitivity to make friends with a baby.

All these factors—pain, hunger, cold, fatigue, frustration, overstimulation, incongruity, and fear—contribute to the likelihood than an infant will cry.

Parents' response to crying

> My mother was from the school of child rearing that believed in letting babies "cry it out." But I don't think it's good for them to cry it out. So pretty much every time Natalie or the other kids cried, I tried to comfort them.

Crying quite simply is not good for babies. It saps their energy, increases the pressure on their brains, removes oxygen and adds white cells to their blood. In newborns, crying may even revert blood circulation to its fetal direction (Anderson, 1984). Even so, the question of whether it is best to respond every time a baby cries remains controversial. Parents turn to experts in child care, only to get conflicting advice. Most of the experts agree that cries of pain and hunger should be met promptly. But what about all those other cries, even assuming that parents could identify them precisely—which they cannot? Under controlled circumstances in the short run, babies can be conditioned to cry less and smile more if their crying is ignored and their smiling is rewarded or, conversely, to cry more if their crying is rewarded (Etzel and Gewirtz, 1967; Gewirtz, in press). But at home, in the long run, if the infant is ignored, crying spells gradually grow longer and more frequent (Bell and Ainsworth, 1972; Clarke-Stewart, 1973; Belsky, Rovine, and Taylor, 1984). Perhaps if the parents respond right away, they reinforce a short cry, and so the infant's crying spells over time grow shorter. It has been observed that infants develop a "request cry," a signal that begins with a short cry and a pause for the parent's response (Bruner, 1978). If the parent responds to the request cry, the crying ends. If the parent does not, the infant moves into a longer, full-blown "demand cry." In fact, a very alert parent may nip a crying spell in the bud by responding to the infant's intensifying signs of distress *before* he begins to cry. During the half hour before he starts crying, the baby may put his hand to his mouth, suck on his hand, stick his tongue in and out,

focus *Making friends with baby*

Natalie has always been shy with most people outside the family. But one of our friends won her over the first time they met. She said hello and smiled at Natalie when she came in, and she made it clear by her body language that she was interested in her. But she never pushed. When Natalie went near her, she told her softly how pretty she looked and offered her a toy to hold. In 10 or 15 minutes, Natalie was hanging on the side of her chair and trying to climb into her lap. When our friend saw that, she turned her full attention to Natalie and played wonderful games with her—making animals with her fingers, making faces, and telling silly rhymes. By the time Natalie was 2, our friend was her ''best friend.''

Many adults are afraid of 9-month-old babies, scared off by the screams of one baby's ''stranger anxiety.'' But it *is* possible to make friends with these creatures, even during this wary period. Strangers can melt an infant's reserve by treading lightly, letting the infant warm up slowly, and not overwhelming the infant with too much too soon. If the adult just sits quietly but smiles responsively, the infant is likely to smile and stare (Eckerman and Whatley, 1975; Rheingold and Eckerman, 1973). Babies first size up a stranger. They check to see whether the stranger is a child or an adult, male or female, tall or short. When the stranger beckons to the baby, the baby approaches or backs away according to whether she has judged the stranger's looks as reassuring or scary. If the stranger touches the baby, the baby's tendency to approach or back away intensifies.

The success of the ''play it cool'' approach for strangers was supported in an experiment with 3-month-old babies in which one stranger rocked and touched the babies, one stranger did not respond at all, and one stranger smiled, talked, played, and stayed nearby but did not touch (Roedell and Slaby, 1977). After three weeks, the babies spent the most time with the stranger who smiled but did not touch. They preferred that person to the neutral stranger and the neutral stranger to the ''toucher.'' The toucher proba-

or whimper quietly (Gill, White, and Anderson, 1984). A parent who responds consistently and promptly to these early warning signals teaches the infant that he does not have to cry to get what he wants.

How then to stop infants' crying? During the first two weeks, a baby may be comforted by rhythmic motion—rocking or gentle patting (Ambrose, 1961; Korner and Thoman, 1972). Swaddling the new baby in a blanket also stops crying, by preventing overstimulation from kicking and arm waving. Picking up a swaddled baby and carrying it upright often can stop crying (Korner and Thoman, 1972). So can white noise, recordings of sounds heard in the womb, the noise of an air conditioner, vacuum cleaner, or blender, or Beethoven played loudly (Brackbill, 1958; Rosner and Doherty, 1979).

One night Sam was really tough to soothe. His father put earphones on him and played a recording of Mozart. No go. But when the music was changed to the Rolling Stones, Sam calmed down right away.

Some babies quiet if they can suck on a pacifier. The rhythm of their sucking seems to soothe them. Nursing also soothes because it has the qualities of sucking and movement, provides food, warmth, faces, and voices. It is a biological pattern well adapted to soothing the crying infant.

bly came on too strong for the babies' comfort. Vigorous, gruff male strangers scare most babies (Clarke-Stewart, 1978b; Lemly and Schwarz, 1979).

> Poor Jason! I took him to sit on Santa Claus's lap when he was 9 months old. I put him on Santa's red flannel knee, and when Jason turned to look at that long white beard and bushy eyebrows, he froze in shock. When Santa went "Ho! Ho! Ho!" Jason's shock turned to terror, and he let out a piercing scream that must have carried for blocks.

Young babies like strangers who are calm and cuddly rather than boisterous and bouncy; older babies like tickling (Weisberg, 1975).

The context also makes a difference. Babies can deal with strangers best when they are in a familiar setting and when their parent is at their side (Campos, Emde, Gaensbauer, and Sorce, 1973; Feinman and Lewis, 1983). With Mom or Dad around to make a baby feel safe, the baby may enjoy vocalizing, laughing, and playing with a stranger who sits down and offers toys (Bretherton, 1978; Ross and Goldman, 1977b). If the stranger is paying attention to the baby and not talking to the mother, the baby is even more likely to want to play.

Individual babies vary in their friendliness, in part because their mothers vary in *their* friendliness to strangers (Babad, Alexander, and Babad, 1983; Feiring, Lewis, and Starr, 1984). If mothers are warm and friendly to strangers, then infants tend to be the same. In one study, for example, researchers asked mothers of 8½-month-olds to greet a stranger either by uttering an abrupt, unfriendly hello and frowning or by smiling at the baby and stranger and saying hello cheerfully. When the mother acted unfriendly, the infants' heart rates sped up, they smiled less, and they showed more distress. When the mother greeted the stranger cheerfully, the heart rates of the infants slowed down (Boccia and Campos, 1983). It sometimes overcomes a 1-year-old's shyness if a stranger copies some game or other activity that the mother plays with the baby (Rafman, 1974).

After several hours of feeding, playing with, and talking to a baby, a stranger usually can get the baby to approach and even to cry when he or she leaves (Fleener, 1973). Strangers who are friendly and responsive have a good chance at getting the baby to act friendly in return (Connolly and Smith, 1972).

Making faces and gestures

Another means by which infants communicate with others is by the gestures of their arms and legs and the expressions on their faces—their frowns and furrows, glares and grimaces. Even young infants' faces show expressions that in adults indicate pleasure and displeasure, anger and fear, joy, surprise, sorrow, and disgust (Charlesworth and Kreutzer, 1973). Take teething biscuits away from infants, restrain their arms, or give them a painful injection, and their faces register anger—frowns, hard stares, lips pulled back to reveal clenched gums, and red flushed skin (Izard, Hembree, Dougherty, Spizzirri, 1983; Stenberg, 1982; Stenberg, Campos, and Emde, 1983). Give infants something unpleasant to taste, and they react with frowns of displeasure (Rosenstein and Oster, 1981).

Robert Emde (1980) took photographs of infants playing with their mothers, meeting a stranger, and looking at a pattern. He then asked adults to give a single word or phrase for "the strongest and clearest feeling that the baby is expressing." The adults categorized over 99 percent of the photos as belonging to one of the basic emotional expressions that have been identified in adults, plus the category ''bored-sleepy.'' Interest, joy, and distress were the most common expressions seen in 3½-month-olds. Fear, surprise, and anger were common in the second half of the infants' first year. These latter emotions, as we have suggested about fear, require more experience and more cognitive awareness.

Parents interpret babies' facial expressions and gestures as communication. One infant, Sarah, videotaped by researchers, for example, shakes her head, and her mother says, ''You're looking very pensive, aren't you? You don't want to smile'' (Sylvester-Bradley and Trevarthen, 1978). Mothers hardly ever refer to themselves when they are interacting with their infants. Fewer than 10 percent of Sarah's mother's sentences were about herself; 77 percent were about Sarah. The mother talked mostly about Sarah's psychological state and continually interpreted Sarah's moods from the baby's facial expressions and gestures. In interactions like these, infants learn that others will react in particular ways to their expressions and gestures. Parents also learn to interpret the infant's signals accurately.

Developing emotions

Infants, as we have just seen, express their emotions in smiles, cries, frowns, and grimaces from the very beginning of life. These facial expressions are part of the infant's inborn repertoire. Even blind infants have these facial expressions (Eibl-Eibesfeldt, 1973). But the emotions of infants differ from those of adults. They are elicited by different events, experienced in different feelings, and expressed in different ways. Adults, for example, usually do not cry when they are angry; infants do. Adults usually mask their smiles of delight when a competitor stumbles; youngsters do not. Over the course of childhood, the rules for expressing and responding to emotions must be learned. This learning begins in infancy.

Rules of expression

Children must learn how to modulate and control their expressions of emotions. They must learn when to express, to exaggerate, to mask, to pretend, and to neutralize emotions, consistent with the rules of their culture. Learning about emotions begins as infants interact with adults (Lewis and Michalson, 1982).

> At her second birthday party, Erica noticed one of the adult guests laughing loudly. She asked her, ''Anne happy? Erica happy too.''

> One morning when Sam and Natalie had been playing together, Natalie's mother said that it was time for Natalie to think about getting her coat on to go home. ''I don't want to,'' Natalie complained.

> ''You go home *now*,'' Sam said, tired of sharing his toys.

> ''Sam, we don't say things like that to people,'' his mother interjected. ''It hurts their feelings.''

Children learn when and where they may express feelings. Learning these display rules, it seems, is a slow and gradual process. The first rule about feelings that infants learn is to smile often (Demos, 1982). Later, they learn to modify or suppress socially unacceptable feelings like displays of temper, dislike, and distress. Even infants just under 1 year old may do some of this when they interact with people they know well (Feinman and Lewis, 1981). In their second year, they try to control expressions of distress by pressing, sucking, or funneling their lips (Demos, 1982). As they learn language, infants learn the labels for emotions.

Children probably learn most about feelings from their parents. Parents are the ones who model expressions of emotion. It has been estimated that infants between the ages of 3 and 6 months are exposed to 32,000 facial expressions of emotion (Malatesta and Haviland, 1982)—not a trivial learning experience. Parents also talk about emotions to their infants, saying things like ''Don't be afraid, baby,'' ''I know you love Mommy,'' and ''Oh, you're embarrassed'' (Pannabecker, Emde, Johnson, Stenberg, and Davis, 1980). A parent can turn any emotional incident into a learning experience. For example, a 1-year-old starts to cry after a tower of blocks she has built falls down on her leg. Her mother may say, ''You're frustrated'' and help to rebuild the tower. The mother has labeled the feeling of frustration. Instead, the mother may bark, ''Stop crying! If you can't build it that high, don't try. You're driving me crazy.'' The mother has labeled her own emotions. Maybe the mother says, ''Oh, you hurt yourself'' and cuddles the baby. She has labeled the baby's response to pain. Three quite different learning experiences have followed from the infant's crying, a single emotional expression.

Parents' labeling of infants' emotions is, of course, related to the infants' expression of emotion. In one study, for example, mothers who had been separated from their infants until the infants started crying said to them, ''Oh, you're mad'' if the infants had thrown toys around and ''Oh, you're tired'' (or sad) if the infants were crying quietly (Lewis and Michalson, 1981). Other factors, such as the infant's sex, also come into play. When undergraduates were shown a film of a 9-month-old infant playing with four unfamiliar toys, and half the undergraduates were told that they were observing David and the other half that they were observing a girl named Dana, the infant in the film was considered to have different emotions and levels of emotional intensity, depending on the sex of the observer and the supposed sex of the infant. David was observed to express considerable pleasure and little fear as he played. Dana was observed to express less pleasure and more fear. When the infant in the film reacted negatively to a jack-in-the-box, David was presumed to be angry, and Dana was presumed to be afraid. Male undergraduates distinguished especially sharply in describing the emotions of David and Dana (Condry and Condry, 1976).

Responding to emotions

Just as we feel and express emotions, we also respond to them in other people. How does the infant's ability to respond to others' expressions of emotions develop? How early does the ability develop?

From an early age, infants respond to differences in other people's emotional expressions if these are reflected in direct interaction with the infant. In one study, for example, researchers tested the responses of 3-month-old babies to the emotional expressions of their mothers while interacting with the infants (Cohn and Tronick, 1983). Some mothers were asked to act as they normally would, some to act depressed—to slow their speech, keep their face still, and minimize touching their infant or moving their own body. The babies responded quite differently to normal and ''depressed'' mothers. Babies of ''depressed'' mothers spent half the time protesting, reacting warily, or giving but fleeting smiles. Babies of normal acting mothers showed much more variety in their play, protested or acted wary only rarely, and when they smiled, did so for significant periods of time.

Young infants also respond to others' emotional expressions if the expressions are clear and salient—like crying. Investigators have observed, for example, that 6-month-olds are responsive to the distress of other babies (Hay,

Nash, and Pedersen, 1981). When infants were placed in a room with another infant who began to cry, nearly all of them (84 percent) looked at the distressed infant for nearly the whole time he or she cried. Some infants also leaned, gestured, or touched the crying baby. Moreover, if there were no toys present and the infant went on crying, the other infant was likely to grow distressed too. Clearly, infants respond to crying. But what about more subtle emotional expressions, such as smiles and frowns?

Some researchers have reported that 3-month-olds who saw a frowning face cried more than infants who saw a smiling face (Barrera and Maurer, 1979). But were the infants crying because, as the investigators suggested, they recognized that a frown meant sadness or because they found the frowning face uninteresting? Do infants look longer at a face with a toothy grin because they read the pattern as a smile or because the teeth make the face more salient and, therefore, more pleasant? In an experiment with 4-month-olds, Harriet Oster (Oster and Ewy, 1980) showed infants in one group pictures of a sad face and a face with a closed-mouth smile and infants in another group a sad face and a face with a toothy open-mouthed smile. A third group of infants saw the sad face and a face with a toothy grin upside down. The investigators found that the infants looked longer at the face with the right-side-up toothy grin than at the sad face but did not look longer at the face with the upside-down toothy grin. They suggested that infants respond to differences in facial patterns rather than simply to differences in contrast, contour, or the like. But because the infants did not look longer at the face with the closed-mouth smile than at the sad face, it is possible that 4-month-olds cannot yet read smiles from the position of the mouth alone without seeing teeth.

Other researchers looked into the abilities of 4- to 9-month old babies to read emotional expressions, some of which showed teeth and some of which did not (Caron and Myers, 1984; Caron, Caron, and Myers, 1985). The researchers used a habituation design in which the infants were first habituated to a picture of a woman posing one facial expression and then shown a picture of another woman posing either the familiar expression or a new one. At all ages, the babies could distinguish faces with toothy smiles from those with closed mouths (either angry or smiling). But they could not distinguish toothy smiles from toothy angry expressions. Clearly, young infants pick up some information about other people's emotions from what they see on their faces, but that information is incomplete. To know whether Mother is happy or angry, the infant must depend on movement and sound. Tone of voice is an emotional expression that infants also respond to. When researchers looked angry and uttered a nonsense word in an angry tone of voice, 10-month-old infants inhibited their touching of an attractive object. Infants who heard the same word uttered without emotion did not inhibit their touching (Bradshaw, Campos, and Klinnert, 1986).

A mother's laughter can assuage an infant's fear. A mother's fear can turn her infant's worry into panic. In an unfamiliar situation, infants tend to orient themselves so that they can see their mother's face (Carr, Dabbs, and Carr, 1975). Perhaps they do so because they can get important cues about how to act in the unfamiliar situation from their mother's face and gestures. If the mother is out of sight, infants will rely on cues from her voice (Campos and Stenberg, 1981). In one study of this **social referencing** (Sorce, Emde, Campos, and Klinnert, 1981, 1985), one group of infants, who had to cross a visual cliff with an apparent drop-off of four feet, refused to cross the glass. A second group, who faced no apparent drop-off, crossed immediately without checking their mothers' faces. But a third group, confronting a drop-off of two feet—an ambiguous situation—looked at their mothers for cues before they did anything. When the mother looked afraid, not a single infant crossed the glass. When she looked happy, 80 percent of the infants crossed, but when she looked angry, only 10 percent crossed. When mothers looked sad—an inappropriate response—one third of the infants crossed but vacillated before doing so. In short, it was shown that infants not only referred to their mothers' expressions for cues in an unfamiliar situation, but also behaved differently depending on the sort of emotional messages they got from their mothers' faces. As they continue to develop cognitively and socially, children come to depend less on social referencing and more on their own, internal strategies for evaluating events. But it is likely that people never completely outgrow referring to others when they need to evaluate ambiguous situations.

A social partner

It is clear that infants communicate with the people around them. They gaze and babble, smile and cry, frown and reach. They react to the behavior of others. But when do infants first turn into real social "partners"? When do they first hold up their end of a dialogue or a game? When do they first become part of a true "system" of interaction?

The parent–infant "system"

From birth, as we mentioned in Chapter 5, the infant's physiological systems are "prewired" in such a way that the infant pays attention to the kinds of stimulation that parents' faces usually provide. The infant's eyes rest on the contrasts at the edges of the face, on the moving, blinking eyes, on the animated red mouth. But the infant is still too young to be a true social partner. In the early months, parents work at enfolding the infant within an interactive system. They project their own feelings and intentions onto the infant's built-in rhythms and actions, and in doing so, they begin to create a repertoire of shared routines with their infant (Kaye, 1982).

Even during pregnancy, parents speak for their infant and draw the still unborn participant into the family. As they feel the fetus moving,

"He says," explains the mother-to-be, " 'No more beans, please!' "

"She says, 'It's getting crowded in here!' "

Once the infant is born, the parents continue to speak for it:

"She says, 'I'm hungry, Mom.' "

"He says, 'I'm sleepy, Daddy; don't bounce me so much.' "

They interpret the baby's cries from hunger and pain or motions of restless sleepiness as though the infant were trying to scare up a meal or find a resting place. As infants begin to show their intentions—by reaching for the toy that Daddy holds up, reaching for Mommy's mouth as she talks, or turning their head to search for a voice, parents continue talking for them.

"He says, 'Give it to me, Dad. I want to put that in my mouth.' "

"She says, " 'Where'd it go?' "

Parents interpret their infant's expressions and behavior as meaningful and communicative. They act *as though* their infant were a little person and an intelligent partner. As they treat the infant as a contributing member of the family, they gradually draw the infant into the family system.

Taking turns

The evolving social system of parents and infant shows itself in the way parent and infant take turns. Only recently, since investigators have been able to use stop-frame and slow-motion **microanalysis** of films and videotapes, have they been able to pick out the fine details of these turns. They have shown that mothers and infants begin the interactive turns from the moment the infant is born. From birth, for example, babies suck in a regular pattern of bursts—suck, suck, suck—and pauses. Mothers pick up on this pattern and act in time to it. When the baby sucks, Mother is quiet. When the baby pauses, Mother bounces, touches, and talks. The baby will suck and pause whether the mother responds or not, but her behavior serves to make feeding time a turn-taking *interaction*. She treats the baby's bursts of sucking as a turn, and she treats the baby's pause as though he were saying, "There, my turn is over. It's your turn, Mom." During her turn, she bounces the baby and says, "Hi there, cutie" (Kaye, 1977).

In the early months, too, the mother may act as if the baby were taking turns in "conversations." To give their babies turns, mothers generally wait the length of a pause in adult conversation and listen for an imagined response. They then wait the length of another pause in adult conversation before they talk. Mothers have been observed in these "conversations" with babies as young as 3 months (Stern, 1977).

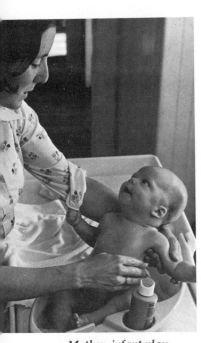

Mother–infant play makes an enjoyable break from the bath for the young infant. The behavior of mother and baby is finely meshed and in tune.

MOTHER: "Aren't you my cutie?"

   Pause: (0.60 second)

Imagined response from baby:
       "Yes"

   Pause: (0.60 second)

MOTHER: "You sure are!"

These "conversations" are even more clearly etched once the baby is old enough to babble (Trevarthan, 1977).

MOTHER: "Are you talking to me?"

   BABY: (Babbles)

MOTHER: "Are you telling me a story?"

   BABY: (Babbles)

MOTHER: "Are you telling me a story?"

   BABY: (Babbles)

When mothers do respond to their infants' babbling with this turn taking, the infants' babbling increases (Bloom, Russell, and Davis, 1986). Turn taking in these first **pseudodialogues**, of course, is up to the parent. Infants' rhythmic behavior—suck, suck, suck, pause, suck, suck, suck; babble, pause, babble, pause—allow the appearance of turn taking. But parents still have to speak babies' parts for them—to fill in the blanks.

By the time they are about a year old, babies can speak their own parts. They can vocalize when their parents pause expectantly. Pseudodialogues have become true dialogues and infants, true social partners (Table 7.1; Newson, 1977).

   BABY: (Looks at a toy top.)

MOTHER: "Do you like that?"

   BABY: "Da!"

MOTHER: "Yes, it's a nice toy, isn't it?"

   BABY: "Da! Da!"

Table 7.1
Social milestones

Birth to 3 months: the Dance Begins

- Fixes eyes on parent's eyes and holds gaze.
- Smiles at a nodding head or high voice.
- Smiles at parent's face (the first *social* smile).
- Cries when parent does not interact as usual.
- Discriminates between sight of parent and others.

---

3 to 6 months: Emotions Appear

- Laughs.
- May act wary with strangers.
- Acts differently toward parents and other people.

---

6 to 12 months: Focused Relationships Develop

- Laughs at incongruity.
- Acts fearful with strangers in threatening situations.
- Acts as a real partner in social interactions.
- Deliberately seeks out and stays near parents.

Individual differences

Most infants are born with regular cycles of behavior that offer their parents these "handles" for social interaction. Infants who feed and behave predictably are easier for parents to engage in social exchanges than those whose inborn cycles of behavior are disorganized and hard to predict. In the developing social system of infant and parent, it takes two to tango, and not all parents and infants dance together smoothly. Sometimes it is the infant who is clumsy, sometimes the parent.

Skilled and unskilled mothers

A mother may be depressed and understimulating; she may be hyperactive and overstimulating; or she just may not know how to play with her baby. She may not be able to muster the energy for play because she is so preoccupied with her other responsibilities at work and at home. She may be under psychological strain, or she may be inhibited or fearful around the baby. She may resent the baby and all the care required. She may be personally insecure and interpret the baby's cries or averted eyes as a personal rejection. There are many reasons that a mother may be a less than perfect partner to her baby.

The mother of one pair of twins, Fred and Mark, for example, felt differently toward each of them even during her pregnancy (Stern, 1971). One baby, she could tell, kicked more, and because the mother thought of herself as lively and energetic, she identified with this more active presence. Once the twins were born, the mother assumed that the more active twin, Mark, had been the one who had kicked more in her womb. She felt more negative toward Fred, the quieter twin, who was "more like his father." When the twins were 3 months old, they were filmed as they played with their mother. Mark and his mother were in step with each other: he moved in time with her voice and actions when they were looking at each other face to face, and he did not pay attention to her when they were not. But Fred and his mother were out of step with each other. When she approached him, he turned away; when he approached her, she turned away. Never entirely in step, the two never quite got their dance going.

In the dance between parent and infant, some parents continually misread the cues that their infants send out. If during spirited play, the infant frowns or looks away, parents should read those reactions as cues for them to back off and ease the stimulation. But an intrusive parent instead acts *more* intensely, and the infant has lost a chance to regulate his environment, to learn that his wishes matter and that he can exert control over what happens to him. After enough such frustrating social exchanges, the infant may stop trying. Parents who are insensitive to their infants' signals may end up teaching the infants that the world is totally beyond their control. The smoothness of the exchanges between parents and infants depends on parents' abilities to interpret their infants' signals and intentions, complete their actions, and anticipate their reactions.

Mothers who, because they are young, poor, and have problems feeding their infant, are classified as "at risk" for neglecting or abusing their infants. These mothers are not as good at interpreting infants' emotional expression as mothers who are not classified as at risk. At-risk mothers, in one recent study, were more likely to see their infants as expressing sadness, anger, shame, and joy and less likely to see them as expressing fear and interest (Butterfield, 1986).

In some cases, mothers who have trouble interpreting their infants' signals can be helped by training or therapy. All parents need support and encouragement in their attempts to care for their infants, but programs specifically for troubled mothers are particularly important. Professionals can teach these mothers how to stimulate difficult or listless infants and how to read the signals of quiet infants. Troubled, disturbed mothers may not know how to nurture their infants because they themselves were nurtured poorly. They may misunderstand things that their infants do because they do not know how normal infants develop. For example, one mother of a 4-month-old interpreted his arching his back when she tried to hold him as rejection (Peterson, 1982). In fact, the infant's muscles simply were too immature for him to support his back. He wasn't rejecting his mother at all.

In one study, a simple attempt was made to help high-risk mothers appreciate their infants' abilities. Teenaged mothers watched while their prematurely born infants were tested on the Brazelton scale (discussed in Chapter 5) and then each week filled out rating scales modeled on this test (Widmayer and Field, 1980). The mothers saw how their infants could track objects like a red ball with their eyes, quiet themselves, orient to stimulation, and generally engage the intense interest of another adult for half an hour. Many of the mothers said later that they had really enjoyed watching the examination. The effects of this program showed in more close, face-to-face play and smoother feedings between mothers and infants than between mothers who had not seen their newborns examined.

Easy and difficult infants

All problems in the social interactions of mothers and infants cannot be laid at the mothers' feet, of course. Some infants are more difficult than others. Even the most responsive and sensitive of parents may have a hard time getting along with these infants.

> Jason was brought from the hospital nursery into my room. As he lay in his crib, he seemed fussy and fretful. His mouth grimaced, his face and scalp went red, and he grumbled as his eyes flickered open. We thought

that he might be hungry. Charlie picked him up tenderly, and I started to arrange myself to try and nurse him. Within a few seconds, Jason was flailing his arms, kicking his legs, and screaming so hard that we both got scared. His little body was rigid with tension, his eyes were clenched shut, and I had no idea how to get him to suck. I called for a nurse, and she showed us how to quiet him by swaddling him and propping him on her shoulder. She helped me put Jason to my breast. But he spluttered and started to cry again—fiercely. The nurse said she'd take him back to the nursery and we could try again later. I looked at Charlie and burst into tears.

Alexander Thomas and Stella Chess (whose study we mentioned in Chapter 3) were among the first researchers to study individual differences in infants' behavior during the first weeks of their lives. They knew about the prevailing inclination to blame mothers for children's psychological problems. But how, they asked, could behavior that appeared so early be attributed to mothers? To explore this issue and to trace the development of temperament from infancy onward, they began the New York Longitudinal Study. Parents in the study were interviewed when the infants were 2 months, 6 months, and 1 year old. The questions were specific. For instance, in the past several weeks, how had the infant acted in the bath, when a diaper was wet, when tasting a new food? The researchers asked for descriptions of infants' behavior in specific situations in an attempt to steer as clear of parents' biases as possible. When the children were older, the researchers observed them directly and questioned their teachers. When the children were 16 years old, they and their parents were interviewed separately. The data collected from all these sources strongly suggested that individual differences in temperament were apparent in infancy and left a trail right through childhood and adolescence (Thomas and Chess, 1981).

The infants' behavior varied along nine dimensions.

1. Activity level. Some infants brim with energy. They rove around the crib in their sleep; they kick and roll when they are being dressed. Other infants are more still and quiet.

2. Physical rhythms. Some infants feel hungry, sleepy, and move their bowels at regular intervals. Others eat, sleep, and move their bowels irregularly and at unpredictable intervals.

3. Approach and avoidance. Some infants go right after new objects and people. They clap delightedly at a new toy and smile openly at a new face. Others turn their heads away from a new food and cry at new faces.

4. Adaptability. Some infants fall asleep right away in new places and greet most new experiences with gusto. Others cringe at every change in routine and take a long time to adapt to new experiences.

5. Threshold of reaction. Some infants are alert to every sight and sound in their environment. Others march to the sound of a different drummer and barely notice loud thunderclaps or soaking diapers.

6. Intensity of reaction. Some infants howl when their diapers are changed and scream themselves blue in the face when their fingernails are clipped. Others hardly cry when they crunch their heads on swinging doors or get a painful injection from the doctor.

7. Usual mood. Some infants are happy most of the time. Others are constantly dissatisfied, even when their mothers are holding them tenderly and rocking them gently.

8. Distractibility. Some infants are easily distracted by new objects and events. Others will not be swayed. Infants in the first group will stop

Table 7.2
Infant temperament

Trait	Easy temperament	Difficult temperament	Slow-to-warm-up temperament
Activity level:	Variable	Variable	Low to moderate
Rhythms:	Regular	Irregular	Variable
Approach or avoidance:	Approaches	Withdraws	Withdraws at first
Adaptability:	Adapts readily	Adapts slowly	Adapts slowly
Usual mood:	Positive	Negative	Mildly negative

crying if you hand them a rattle. Infants in the second will cry until they get what they want.

9. Attention span and persistence. Some infants play with Mom or Dad or the kitchen pots for many minutes. Others move restlessly from one thing to another.

These dimensions, Thomas and Chess found, came together into three broad patterns of temperament (see Table 7.2).

1. *Easy babies* are usually happy and receive people and things enthusiastically. They do not react to small discomforts or frustrations. They get hungry and sleepy at pretty much the same times every day. About 40 percent of the babies in the New York study were easy.

2. *Difficult babies* take most things hard. They cry often, run on irregular schedules, and adapt to new people and places with difficulty. Their mood tends to be down. About 10 percent of the babies in the study were difficult.

3. *Slow-to-warm-up babies* take a while to adjust to new people, places, and events. They react mildly to things and run on moderately irregular schedules. But once they get used to something or someone, they like and enjoy them. About 15 percent of the babies in the study were slow to warm up.

Babies with these three types of temperament were found in all kinds of families, regardless of social class or child-rearing style and regardless of the babies' sex.

Evidence from other studies, in which unbiased observers (and not parents) watched infants, supports these findings (for example, Korner, 1973; Schaffer and Emerson, 1964b). From the first week of life, babies show individual styles of responding. Some babies, for example, are more cuddly than others. Cuddly babies are more placid and sleep longer and are more likely than other babies to take comfort from people, thumb sucking, or a soft blanket.

> The lights went on at 2 A.M., and I opened my eyes to see a nurse taking Natalie out of her crib. It was time to nurse her. We were up to three minutes at each breast. I took Natalie in my arms. She felt like a warm little ball. She opened her eyes long enough to see my breast, and I touched her lips with my nipple. She caught it after a couple of tries, closed her eyes, and sucked away. I felt a little sore, but I also felt incredible pleasure that I could nourish my baby with my body.

In contrast, uncuddly babies are restless and active. They are quickly aroused and dislike physical restraints—and to a restless ''noncuddler,'' even a

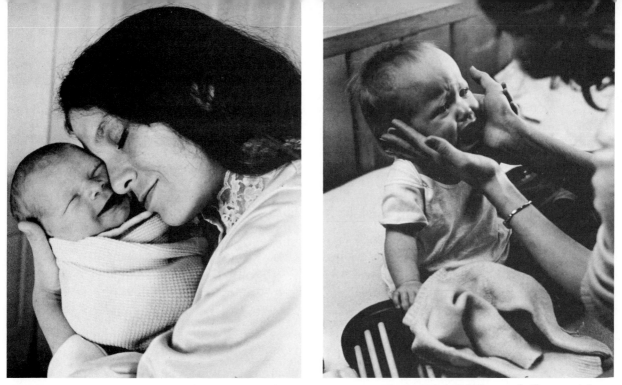

The infant's easy or difficult temperament makes a profound difference in the parents' "quality of life."

mother's hug may feel like a restraint. When it comes to soothing, some babies can soothe themselves by sucking their thumb or fingers. But others need to be soothed by someone else. Some babies can be calmed easily and for long periods; others are difficult to calm. More active babies express their feelings in cries, grimaces, and noises. They like new things and strong excitement. Quiet babies spend more time looking around and making small movements. They need gentler stimulation that they can sift through, reduce, or turn away from.

Despite this seemingly unbiased evidence for individual differences in infants' behavior, some psychologists have suggested that temperament is not really a characteristic of infants. Instead, they say, temperament is something that parents project onto their infants. Some researchers have found little agreement between parents' ratings and objective observers' ratings of the children's temperaments or behavior (for example, Bates, 1980; Isabella, Ward, and Belsky, 1985). Others have found some agreement. In one study, for example (Dunn and Kendrick, 1980), mothers' descriptions of their 1- to 3-year-olds' behavior agreed strongly with the records of behavior collected by familiar observers who watched the children in their homes. When parents and children feel at ease and when the observations are carried out in a familiar setting and for relatively long periods of time, the slice of life that observers see may be more like the one that parents report.

But most parents probably do project ideas about temperament onto their infants. Parents are not unbiased observers trained to collect objective data about infants' behavior. Their ratings of their infant's temperament are related to their own characteristics, social class, race, and attitudes (Bates, Freeland, and Lounsbury, 1979; Crockenberg and Acredolo, 1983; Sameroff, Seifer, and Elias, 1982). In one study, for example, mothers who were more upset when they heard an unfamiliar infant crying and whose child-rearing attitudes were more punitive—even *before* their own infants were born—later were more likely to claim that their own infants were "difficult" (Frodi, Bridges, Shonk, and Greene, 1986). In another study, mothers' ratings of their infants' temperaments were found in one study to be more closely related to the mothers' behavior than to the infants' (Gordon, 1983). Parents' ratings of their infants' temperaments do clearly reflect something about the parents.

Parents' ratings of their infants also, however, reveal something about the infants. Although parents' ratings of their infants' temperaments may be biased, infants do exhibit different temperamental characteristics and these characteristics are relatively enduring and stable over time. The evaluations of parents as well as objective observers reveal this stability over time. One-year-olds, for example, who approach new situations cautiously also tend to act that way as 3-year-olds (Gibbons, Johnson, McDonough, and Reznick, 1986). Difficult babies continue to protest, fuss, and cry as toddlers (Worobey, 1984; Riese, 1986). Boys who are difficult as infants are usually still difficult at 3 years (Bates and Bayles, 1984), have more behavior problems at 4 (Guerin and Gottfried, 1986), and often still are difficult as young adults (Korn, 1984).

> Jason was a fussy and stubborn infant, and he turned into a fussy and stubborn toddler. He hit and fought with the other kids so often that even his nursery school teachers, who were extra patient, agreed that he was "high strung." He's always been alert, but he's touchy and aggressive, and so he gets into lots of fights.

But temperamental traits are not cast in stone. The way temperament is expressed changes as children get older, and parents' feelings about it may change as well. The extent to which a temperamental trait is transformed into either problem or productive behavior is likely to depend on how it fits with the parents' goals, values, expectations, and styles of behaving. Infants' traits may mesh well or poorly with their surroundings. If the fit is good between the behavior of infants and their parents' expectations and behavior, the infants are likely to develop well. If the fit is poor, development may be compromised (Thomas and Chess, 1977; Lerner, 1984). It makes sense that easy babies would mesh better with some mothers, difficult babies with others. An easy baby might reassure a mother who lacks confidence that she is doing a good job.

> Sam was so healthy and sturdy and good natured in his first months that he kept me from worrying about whether he was getting enough to eat or whether I was letting too many people handle him or any of the scary things I imagined as a brand new mother.

A difficult baby might fit better with a mother who needs an assertive infant to reassure her that her child will not be victimized easily. But a difficult baby might have trouble with a mother who detests noise and nuisance. A slow-to-warm-up baby might be resented by some mothers. An impatient or tense mother could pressure and push this reluctant baby so hard that things would get even more difficult, rather than patiently exposing him to new things that he might eventually learn to enjoy.

> When Natalie was just a few months old, it became clear to me that it took her a long time to get used to things, and that was something we were just going to have to learn to live with. I try to give her lots of time to get her feet wet. I introduce new babysitters, new foods, new places very slowly. When she was 3½ and started nursery school, she needed her pacifier and blanket for the first few weeks. I car-pooled with Sam's mother, and even though Natalie has known her forever, I waited a whole month before Natalie went in their car without me. If I pushed Natalie too fast too soon, she just couldn't handle it.

A noncuddler could put off a mother who craved physical closeness. In one study, noncuddlers and infants who were not soothed easily made mothers, especially new mothers, feel less competent (Korner, 1973). Cuddlers need lots of physical contact and comfort to develop well, and mothers who aren't cuddlers themselves could do better with a baby with the same inclination.

> I've never been long on cuddling. I'm just too restless for that. My style is to do more bouncing, jiggling, clapping, and pacing when I hold my kids. Looking back on it, Tim could have used more cuddling. He's always been kind of sensitive and soulful. But Willy just ate up my bouncing him around. He's more physical.

We need more research on goodness of fit to confirm or disconfirm its importance for infants' development (Windle and Lerner, 1986). We also need more research to find out exactly how infants' temperaments affect the behavior and attitudes of those around them (Crockenberg, 1986). In one study, new parents who perceived their infant as difficult felt less in control than they had before the infant was born (Sirignano and Lachman, 1985). In another study, simply being told beforehand that an infant was difficult made women less effective at stopping the infant's crying (Donovan and Leavitt, 1984). The belief that they would be unable to soothe the infant apparently made these women feel helpless, and their feeling of helplessness in turn made them less likely to console the infant. In yet another study, the effort that mothers put into teaching their children varied according to how easy or difficult the children had been as infants (Maccoby, Snow, and Jacklin, 1984). Mothers of boys who had been difficult infants later put less effort into teaching their sons. Thus temperament—real or imagined—may feed into a vicious circle. Either a difficult infant or an unskilled parent may start things off on the wrong foot, and the interactions between infant and parent that follow are likely to be bumpy. It undoubtedly takes especially sensitive, patient parents to avoid falling into difficult interactions with difficult infants, and especially easy, responsive infants to smooth the interactions with troubled parents.

Becoming attached

Out of these bumpy or smooth interactions between infants and their parents develop relationships. In the first year of life, infants form their first relationships—lasting, loving ties, or **attachments**, to the most important people in their world. These attachments are the infant's first love affairs, and like any love affairs they have their pleasures and heartbreaks—the delight of being together, the pain of being apart. Love this deep does not blossom overnight. It develops gradually (Ainsworth, 1973; Bowlby, 1969):

1. During the *preattachment* phase, new babies look and smile at and can be comforted by everyone. This phase ends when babies can tell people apart and recognize the difference between familiar folks and strangers. Although babies can tell the difference between familiar and new people by smell, touch, and hearing even earlier, the preattachment phase is generally considered to be over when the 2- or 3-month-old baby consistently responds differently when he or she *sees* Mom and Dad or a stranger.

2. The second phase of a baby's developing social attachment, when the baby responds differently to familiar and unfamiliar people, is called the *attachment-in-the-making* phase. The baby smiles and ''talks'' more to the familiar people and later greets them and cries when they walk away. Familiar people can console the baby better than unfamiliar ones can.

When the baby is 6 or 7 months old, he or she begins to stay close to one of these familiar people, and an attachment is said to be formed.

3. During the third, *clear-cut attachment* phase, the baby is truly attached to that specific person. She tries to stay near the person by crawling, calling, pulling, and hugging. She protests when the person leaves. In families in which the mother is the infant's primary caregiver, this person is usually the mother (Cohen and Campos, 1974; Kotelchuck, 1976; Lamb, 1976a, b). But although most babies grow attached to their mothers first, soon they also are likely to grow attached to their fathers, grandparents, older brothers and sisters, or even a neighbor or other relative they see often. By the time they are a year old, babies usually have grown attached to one, two, or possibly three people. The phase of clear-cut attachment lasts until the baby is 2 to 3 years old.

Theories of attachment

Many developmental theorists have noted the importance of the infant's attachment to the mother. Freud called it "unique, without parallel, established unalterably for a whole lifetime as the first and strongest love object" (1938, p. 85) and proposed that it develops out of the infant's oral pleasure at the mother's breast. Erikson (1968) made attachment the cornerstone of his theory of psychosocial development when he claimed that the first and most basic human crisis is the development of a sense of trust or mistrust, based on the infant's expectation that the mother will or will not meet his or her needs. For social learning theorists, the infant's attachment to the mother was important because it illustrated learning principles. They explained the infant's desire to be close to the mother as a secondary drive, learned through association of the mother with satisfaction of hunger, a primary drive. Each of these theories, however, has been found wanting in some way or another. The theories have been criticized on the grounds that the details of how the attachment develops are sketched incompletely and on the grounds that the proposed course of development does not fit with the facts (for example, that sucking and feeding do not form the bases for attachment).

The most complete and persuasive description of the development of attachment comes from John Bowlby (1969). His account draws from the fields of ethology, psychoanalysis, control systems, and cognitive development. Bowlby suggests that attachment has its origins in inherited behavior that is characteristic of the human species. Through crying, sucking, clinging, smiling, vocalizing, and following, infants draw their mother or other caretaker to them and keep the adult nearby. Nearness to a caring adult is essential to an infant's survival. Although all human infants inherit the tendency to seek this kind of physical closeness, though, how much closeness they need depends on their experiences and their circumstances. Through repeated interactions with the attachment figure, infants construct mental models of the adult and of themselves. These models help infants to appraise new situations and guide their behavior. If their experiences have led them to construct a model of the attachment figure as someone who gives necessary support, infants do not have to stay nearby constantly to monitor the person's whereabouts. But if infants cannot count on this responsiveness, they may seek more closeness. The need for closeness, Bowlby suggested, is a **set goal** that each infant strives for. If the amount of closeness infants get falls below their set goal, they strive for more. Infants whose parents have been away may seek more closeness when they return than infants whose parents have been available. Infants who are sick or tired may seek more closeness with their attachment figure than when they are well and bursting with energy. Infants who feel threatened by, say, the appearance of a stranger or sudden darkness also seek closeness. Infants may crawl or call to their parents when the parents move away from the infants or even when they make the first signs of moving away—for example, putting on their coat or taking keys in hand. If crawling, calling, and clinging do not bring the parents close enough to reassure them— and meet their set goals—infants may start to cry.

Others have added to Bowlby's theory of attachment. Mary Ainsworth (1973) suggested that the infant's set goal of seeking closeness to the mother must be balanced against a second set goal, the infant's wish to explore the surroundings. Alan Sroufe (Sroufe and Waters, 1977) suggested that the infant's set goal is not simply physical closeness, but the feeling of security that closeness brings.

Assessing attachment

Babies *feel* attached to their mothers. But how can psychologists measure these feelings? They cannot directly photograph or weigh attachment. They have to draw conclusions about attachment by watching how babies act. For one thing, they observe how babies act when their mothers leave them. For another, they count up the number of times a baby crawls after or looks toward the mother. But the baby's actions must be taken in context. A baby may turn her face away when her mother picks her up, and she may turn away when her mother offers her a new food. The meaning of the behavior depends on the situation. In one study, for example, babies went up to either their mother or a stranger when they wanted to play. But when they wanted to be picked up, they went only to their mother (Tracy, Lamb, and Ainsworth, 1976). If the researchers had paid attention only to the infants' behavior of approaching and not to the context, they might have misinterpreted the behavior.

One procedure has become the accepted standard for assessing the feelings of attachment in 1- to 1½-year-old babies. In the so-called **strange situation,** the baby is brought by the mother into an unfamiliar but un-threatening playroom with a one-way window in it. The mother has been coached ahead of time about how she is to act. She puts the baby down a little way from some toys and sits in a chair. A stranger comes into the room, remains quiet for a while, then talks with the mother, and eventually tries to play with the baby. The mother hears a tap on the one-way window, her signal to leave the room for three minutes. Then she goes back into the room, the stranger leaves, and the mother stays with her baby until she hears another tap on the window. The mother then leaves the room for a second time, and the baby is alone. Next, the stranger goes back into the room and tries again to play with or console the baby. Finally, the mother goes back in, speaks with, and picks up the baby.

Most babies studied in this country (for example, Ainsworth, Blehar, Waters, and Wall, 1978) do not protest when their mothers put them on the floor, and over three-quarters make for the toys in less than a minute. Few babies are distressed at this point. Most begin exploring their surroundings, keeping their mother in sight, smiling and calling to her, and showing her the toys. But when the mothers leave the room for the first time, about one-fifth of the babies start crying, and about half cry at some time during the separation. Some babies try to find the mother at the door, some at the chair she was sitting in. When the mothers return, over three-quarters of the babies smile, go toward, reach for, touch, or talk to them. One-third of the babies cry.

The second time the mother leaves the room, babies are more likely to get upset. Over three-quarters cry; half cry so hard that their mother has to return before the allotted three minutes are up. Almost none of the babies pays attention to the toys, and the stranger can stop only about one-quarter of the

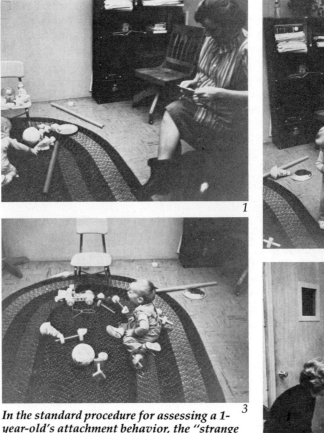

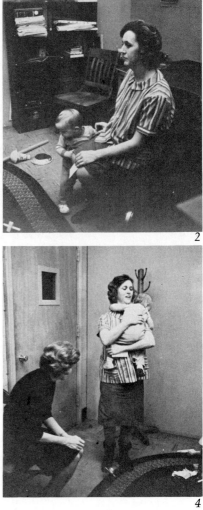

In the standard procedure for assessing a 1-year-old's attachment behavior, the "strange situation," 1 the infant first is allowed to explore the unfamiliar room while his mother is present. 2 He briefly approaches her. 3 Next, left alone in the room, he cries and rocks himself. 4 When the mother returns to the room after a brief absence, this securely attached infant hugs her.

babies from crying. When the mothers come back a second time, half of the babies cry, and three-quarters hold onto her tightly (compared to one-third who held on tightly after the first separation).

This assessment procedure has been used in many studies of attachment here and abroad. In other countries, such as Israel, Japan, and Germany, infants sometimes act differently from American infants to the strange situation. It is an open question whether this is because their attachments to their mother are different from those of American infants or because they interpret the strange situation differently. By using other assessment procedures, researchers are trying to answer these questions.

Patterns of attachment

The reactions of the 1-year-olds in this country to the strange situation have been grouped into three patterns of attachment (Ainsworth et al., 1978). Babies with a **secure attachment** try to stay near their mother and pay more attention to her than to the stranger. The mother's presence in the room offers them a secure base from which to explore the room and the toys. When their mother returns to the room after the brief separation, the babies act happy, greet her, and play nearby. Most babies in this country have secure attachments to their parents (two-thirds of the infants in the Ainsworth study, for example).

Babies with an **insecure-avoidant attachment** ignore and turn or look away from their mother when she returns to the room after the separation. These babies, about one-fifth of Ainsworth's sample, do not try to stay near their mother, cry little or not at all when their mother leaves, and can be comforted by the stranger.

The babies with an **insecure-ambivalent attachment** are quite distressed when their mother leaves the room. When the mother returns, some of the babies approach her. But they are not comforted when she picks them up, and they soon wriggle to be put down. These ambivalently or resistantly attached babies made up just over one-tenth of Ainsworth's sample.

Forming a secure attachment

All infants form some kind of attachment to the primary person in their lives. But what qualities in that person are most likely to foster a *secure* attachment? What kind and how much contact work best? Bowlby (1951) suggested that to develop a secure attachment, an infant needs a loving relationship with the same person, which continues unbroken from birth, through infancy, and childhood. What is the evidence for this claim?

Rx: loving care

Secure attachments do not grow automatically within infants with ever-present caregivers who provide adequate food and physical care (Ainsworth, 1973; Rutter, 1974). It is the *quality* of the interactions with the caregiver that seems to be crucial. Infants with secure attachments are more likely to have caregivers who treat them warmly and affectionately, smile at them and play happily with them, hold and cuddle them often and tenderly, and enjoy the everyday details of taking care of the infant. Mothers of securely attached infants give their infants orders more pleasantly and are more supportive, helpful, affectionate, and playful with their infants than mothers of insecurely attached infants (Arend, Gove, and Sroufe, 1979; Clarke-Stewart, 1973; Pastor, 1981).

Loving caregivers are not always Pollyannas, however. Love intensifies *all* emotions, both the pleasant ones and the unpleasant ones (Schaffer and Crook, 1978). The most loving of mothers can and does lose her temper. Anger and upset also reflect a mother's emotional involvement with her infant. In one study of mothers and nurses in a live-in institution, for example, the mothers were both more loving and more often angry than the nurses (Tizard and Tizard, 1971). For infants, the important thing is the relative proportion of warmth and affection to coolness or anger. Infants whose mothers are *often* angry, critical, rejecting, and interfering are likely to be insecure and avoidant with them (Ainsworth, 1973; Beckwith, 1972; Egeland and Farber, 1984; Radke-Yarrow, Cummings, Kuczyncki, and Chapman, 1985). Infants whose mothers are actually abusive or neglectful are especially likely to be insecure and anxious (Egeland and Sroufe, 1981; Schneider-Rosen, and Cicchetti, 1984). The loving care that babies need to form secure relationships is likelier to flourish in a family setting than in an institution. It is the *love* that is important, though, not where or by whom it is offered. Babies thrive on love from adoptive parents just as well as on love from biological parents and are just as likely to form secure attachments to them (Singer, Brodzinsky, Ramsay, Steir, and Walters, 1985; Tizard and Rees, 1974).

Not only affection but also empathy is important in the loving relationship of mother and infant. The empathic mother sees things through the

A loving relationship with mother, or another caregiver, is essential for the baby's social and emotional development.

infant's eyes, picks up and understands the infant's cues, and responds quickly, reliably, and appropriately. Sensitive, empathic mothers are likely to have children who are securely attached, happy, and sociable (Ainsworth, 1973; Clarke-Stewart, 1973; Egeland and Farber, 1984; Schaffer and Emerson, 1964a). Mothers of securely attached infants also are moderately stimulating and playful with their babies (Belsky, Rovine, and Taylor, 1984). They are not too stimulating—overstimulation makes infants avoid their mothers—nor are they understimulating—understimulation makes babies angry. It is not a simple matter of ''more is better,'' but a matter of a happy medium. As we have pointed out with respect to cognitive development, stimulation has to be geared sensitively to the infant's needs.

Mothers who are psychologically healthier—strong, self-confident, affectionate—in situations not involving their infants may also behave more sensitively with their infants and have securely attached infants (Belsky and Isabella, in press; Benn, 1985). In contrast, mothers of avoidant infants have reported themselves to be relatively intense, and mothers of resistant infants have reported themselves to be less adaptable to new situations (Weber, Levitt, and Clark, 1986). Mothers who recall their childhoods as painful also may be rejecting and have avoidant infants. Mothers in one study who reported being rejected by their own mothers, who could not remember their own childhoods, or who idealized their own rejecting mothers were more likely to reject their own infants. Mothers who did not feel rejected by their own mothers or who could express their anger and resentment toward their mothers were less likely to reject their own infants (Main and Goldwyn, 1984).

These studies provide suggestions about how parents' personalities and experiences affect infants' attachments. But we still do not understand the whole picture. For example, we still do not know whether sensitive parents foster secure attachments by reinforcing their infants' social skills, by creating positive expectations, by encouraging a sense of personal efficacy, by all (or none) of these (Lamb, Thompson, Gardner, and Charnov, 1985).

262

Continuous care

Babies who have grown attached to their caregivers are distressed when they are separated for long. They react to separation from their mothers during a hospital stay, for example, by first crying and rejecting other people's attempts to comfort them. After a few days of noisy protest, they grow quietly hopeless and despondent. They seem to be in mourning. If the separation continues, the babies *seem* to adjust to it and to lose interest in their mothers. When the mother returns at this point, the baby is likely to avoid and ignore her (Robertson and Robertson, 1971).

> When Tim was about 1½, his grandparents offered to take care of him while my husband and I took a vacation. I agonized about whether to leave him, and we finally decided that the vacation would do us good. We were gone for a week. When we got home, I ran into the house to see Tim. But he took one look at me and turned his back. I was crushed. I burst into tears. It took him several weeks to accept me again. That really was hard.

Parents cannot always protect their babies from the emotional loss of separations. But they can take steps to make the separations less painful. If the baby is in the hospital, a parent can visit often or stay with the baby as much of the time as hospital routine permits. Someone whom the baby knows well can stand in for the parents if they have to be away. When they return, they can make a special effort to comfort and care for the child.

> Megan had to have surgery on her eye when she was a year old. The hospital was very sensitive to babies' needs. There was a bed for me near her so that we didn't have to be separated overnight, and I stayed with her nearly all the time except when she was in the operating and recovery rooms. I wouldn't say that the experience was *fun* for anyone, but at least it wasn't the horror show it might have been.

An easy baby

One factor that Bowlby did not consider in predicting the quality of infants' attachments was the baby's own temperament. We now have evidence that infants' attachments to their caretakers depend on the infants' characteristics as well as on their caretakers'. In one study, for example, children's attachment to their mother was related to how difficult they were as newborns (Holmes, Ruble, Kowalski, and Lauesen, 1984). Securely attached 1-year-olds as newborns cried relatively little; insecurely attached 1-year-olds were more likely to have been difficult newborns. Other researchers, similarly, have reported finding a link between infants' difficult temperament at 6 months and insecure attachment at 1 year (Egeland and Farber, 1984; Maslin and Bates, 1983).

In a recent review of all the studies in which researchers have looked for links between temperament and attachment (Goldsmith, Bradshaw, and Riesser-Danner, 1986), it was concluded that, although the link is not strong, infants who are temperamentally prone to distress are more likely to develop resistant, ambivalent attachments, and infants who are temperamentally more interested, persistent, and happy are more likely to develop avoidant attachments. But only further research will explain how temperament influences the development of attachment. For example, we do not know whether temperament affects infants' reactions to the strange situation, their reactions to their caretakers, or their caretakers' reactions to them. In one study, it has even been shown that after infants developed secure attachments, their mothers regarded them as having become less difficult, whereas if infants developed insecure attachments, their mothers regarded them as more diffi-

focus *Attachment and the working mother*

Mothers who work full-time and put their infants in some kind of day care test some of the assumptions about the formation of attachments. After reviewing the available studies of infants in day care, Alison Clarke-Stewart and Greta Fein (1983) drew several conclusions about the effects of these programs. First, infants in day care, like those reared exclusively at home, do become attached to their mothers. Their relationships with the caregivers in day care do not replace their attachments to their mothers. But are children in day care as *securely* attached as children cared for at home? Some studies show that day care causes no ill effects on the security of infants' attachment. For example, in one study researchers inquired into how mothers' working affected the attachment of firstborn children in intact, middle-class families (Chase-Lansdale, 1981). In all these families, the mothers had returned to work before their infant was 3 months old—therefore, before a true attachment had formed. No relation between the mother's working and the security of her child's attachment was found. But some studies have shown that infants, boys especially, in full-time day care keep more distance between themselves and their mothers in the strange situation than home-reared infants do. They are more likely to show an avoidant attachment pattern with their mothers than home-reared children (Barglow, Vaughn and Molitor, in press; Schwartz, 1983; Vaughn, Joffe, Egeland, Dienard, and Waters, 1979). This effect is especially likely if day care begins in the first half of the first year, before a strong and stable attachment to the mother has formed. Day-care infants are not more likely than home-care infants to be anxious or angry or to protest their mother's leaving, however.

What can explain the observed tendency for day-care infants to distance themselves more from their mothers? Is it because their mothers spend less time with them than home-care mothers? This explanation is unlikely. Working mothers may have less time at home, but they spend just about as much time as homebound mothers do in actual interaction with their children. A likelier explanation is that working mothers are less emotionally and psychologically accessible to their children than home-care mothers are. Working mothers tend to feel overworked and overtired. Although working often improves their self-image and even their health, they may feel guilty about taking time from their children and feel that their mothering is rushed and harried. Could this account for the physical distance between day-care children and their mothers? *Home-reared* children who avoid their mothers, we have seen, have mothers who are rejecting and angry or who do not reciprocate their children's initiation of physical contact. Yet the few studies that bear on this issue suggest that day-care mothers do not, as a group, differ from home-care mothers on measures of rejection or reciprocity with their children. It has been suggested by some that infants in day care interpret their daily separations from their mothers as rejections. But it is unlikely that young infants, with their limited understanding, can draw this kind of inference. Is it then simply that day-care children get used to being with many different people outside of their families and become more independent of their mothers? Does their greater distance from their mother reflect generally advanced development? There is some evidence to support these explanations. It does seem that for *most* children, the pattern of greater distance from their mother probably reflects an adaptive reaction to a realistic appraisal of the situation rather than an emotional disturbance. Even so, because most available studies have been focused on high-quality day care, and the measures of attachment they have included are not necessarily the most sensitive, the question merits further investigation. As more and more working mothers rely on day care for their infants, effects on attachment should be monitored closely.

cult (Belsky and Isabella, in press). What we do know is that the links between attachment and temperament are many and complex.

An easy life

Another potentially important influence on infants' development of attachments is the circumstances surrounding the caretaker–infant pair. It seems that it takes more than two for this tango. When families are poor, when mothers are chronically stressed, when they are without social support, when neighbors are felt to be unsupportive, when a marriage is unsatisfying, or when the quality of a marriage declines after an infant is born, the chances increase that infants will develop insecure attachments (Crockenberg, 1981; Goldberg and Easterbrooks, 1984; Belsky and Isabella, in press). Conversely, when circumstances are more favorable, infants and caretakers have better chances of developing secure relationships. In general, good marriages and sensitive parents produce healthy, secure infants, and poor marriages are associated with insensitive parents and insecure infants. In sum, when all three systems—parents' personalities, infant's temperament, and surrounding circumstances—are positive, most infants develop secure attachments. When all three systems are negative, infants are likely to develop insecure attachments.

Significance of a secure attachment

For parents, the security of an infant's attachment is of central importance. But do secure attachments have more far-reaching consequences? Possibly so. In a number of studies, it has been found that infants who are securely attached to their mothers generally are more socially and emotionally competent than infants who are insecurely attached, and these advantages persist well into childhood (Cassidy and Main, 1984; Schneider-Rosen and Cicchetti, 1984; Waters, Wippman, and Sroufe, 1979). Securely attached toddlers have been observed to be more sociable than insecure ones when playing with others their age (Pastor, 1981) or with adult strangers (Main and Weston, 1981; Thompson and Lamb, 1983). They are more cooperative, enthusiastic, persistent, and competent at solving problems than insecurely attached toddlers, more compliant and likelier to have internalized controls—they obey past commands even when no one is watching (Frankel, 1984; Londerville and Main, 1981; Matas, Arend, and Sroufe, 1978). At age 3, children who were securely attached to their mothers as toddlers have been found to attract more positive responses from unfamiliar peers, children with avoidant attachments to elicit less positive responses, and children with ambivalent attachments to provoke more antagonistic and resistant responses (Jacobson and Wille, 1986). In preschool, children who were ambivalent and resistant as infants have been described by their teachers as impulsive and tense or as helpless and fearful, whereas those who were avoidant have been described as either hostile or restrained and socially isolated from other children (Arend et al., 1979; Sroufe, 1983). In kindergarten and first grade, children who were securely attached to both parents are more trusting and open with an unfamiliar woman (Weston and Richardson, 1985) and have fewer psychological problems (Lewis, Feiring, McGuffog, and Jaskir, 1984).

But attachment is just one of a number of factors—including stressful events and family characteristics—that affect the course of children's social and psychological development (Lewis et al., 1984). The link between attachment and later competence probably appears consistently not only because secure attachment gives a good emotional start to infants' development but also because it reflects infants' competence and because the infants observed in most studies were growing up in relatively stable circumstances, which foster the development of secure attachments and other forms of competence as well (Lamb et al., 1985). A secure attachment to one's parents does not guarantee later social success in the world; an insecure attachment does not condemn the child to later psychopathology. Attachment is a significant part of a whole constellation of social competencies, which can be modified over time.

Fathers are special, too

Once upon a time, developmental psychologists focused exclusively on infants' relationships with their mothers. Mothers were central in the theories of development and responsible for virtually all the daily infant care. But recently researchers have trained their focus on fathers, too. Their work tells something about how fathers take care of, enjoy, and think about their infants, and it suggests that a father plays a special role in his infant's development. Mothers and fathers, it seems, typically offer their children somewhat different kinds of experiences.

Fathers' behavior

In our family, when Ron comes home from work, the kids squeal with delight. He gets down on the floor with them and roughhouses; he tosses the baby in the air; he gives them horsey rides on his back. Then he says, "Okay, kids, that's it," and he hands the baby back to me and shoos Natalie and her sister off to their toys. When *I* come home from work, the kids say "feed me, feed me."

In our family, Daddy's always been the one who did special things for us kids—played piggyback or bought us cute T-shirts, took us out for ice cream or to the movies. But he's also the one with the short fuse. He can be with us kids in short, intense bursts, but it's Mommy who has had to stay in for the long haul.

Most new fathers are thrilled, absorbed, and preoccupied with their new babies (Greenberg and Morris, 1974). In their fond eyes, their baby is beautiful and special. They like to hold and touch, gaze and smile, talk and stroke their new baby just as much as new mothers do (Parke and O'Leary, 1976). Fathers are no less sensitive to their baby's cries, sneezes, and coughs than mothers are; they may stop a feeding to soothe, and they are likely to feed a baby just as much milk as new mothers do (Frodi, Lamb, Leavitt, and Donovan, 1978a; Parke and Sawin, 1975). But on the average, fathers do not spend as much time actively "on duty" with their infants as mothers do. American mothers are still the ones who spend the most time and do the lion(ess)'s share of the feeding, bathing, and dressing. Among one group of middle-class Boston families, for example, three-quarters of the fathers did not regularly take part in the physical care of their infants (Kotelchuck, 1976). Nearly half had never changed diapers. In the time they did spend with their babies, the fathers spent some 38 percent in play, compared to the mothers' 26 percent. This pattern appeared in other studies of families with fathers who worked and mothers who stayed at home, too (Clarke-Stewart, 1978a, 1980; Lamb, 1977). Observations of both parents at home with their infants have shown that fathers are more likely to watch television and read, while mothers are actively engaged with their infants (Belsky, Gilstrap, and Rovine, 1984). Over the first

Fathers are more likely than mothers to engage in rough-and-tumble play with their infants and young children.

year, these differences decrease somewhat. Fathers grow more comfortable with their infants and give them, especially firstborns, more stimulation, and mothers grow less involved in breast feeding and other aspects of physical caretaking.

When fathers play with their infants, they play more roughly and physically, doing more tapping and poking, bouncing and tossing, than mothers (Clarke-Stewart, 1978a, 1980; Kotelchuck, 1976; Lamb, 1977; Parke and Sawin, 1975; Yogman, 1977). Mothers are more likely than fathers to use a soft, repetitive kind of talking in their play with the baby. Mothers sing and rhyme; fathers hoist and toss. Few differences have been found in the length of time mothers and fathers play with their infants when the infants are playing happily with their toys. But when the baby's attention and interest wane, researchers have observed, mothers and fathers react differently (Power and Parke, 1983). Mothers tend to take cues from the baby, following the baby's gaze at a particular toy and then playing with that toy. They spend more time watching or holding toys when the baby's interest flags. Fathers do not so consistently follow the baby's gaze, and they often try unsuccessfully to get the baby to play with a toy in which the baby is not interested. When the baby's interest in toys flags, fathers do what comes naturally. They begin to play physically with the baby. Not surprisingly, babies react to their mothers and fathers somewhat differently—frowning or giggling at fathers' poking and tossing, gazing and smiling at mothers' soft sounds (Clarke-Stewart, 1978a; Lamb, 1977; Yogman, 1977).

Are the differences between mothers' and fathers' behavior with their babies and the parallel differences in the babies' behavior the results of learning or biology? To examine this question, one researcher (Field, 1978) compared the behavior of fathers who were the primary caretakers for their babies with the behavior of fathers who were secondary caretakers. Primary caretakers presumably would have had more chances to learn how to interact with their infants. No matter which their role, fathers poked and played physically more often than mothers. Fathers probably are *both* biologically and culturally primed to play physically with their babies. Not only human fathers, but monkey fathers, too, like to roughhouse with their offspring (Suomi, 1977). In Sweden, where it is more common for fathers to be primary caretakers for their babies than it is here, researchers have observed that mothers and fathers play similarly with their babies, but the mothers hold, pick up, and tend to the babies' needs more than the fathers do, no matter

267

research focus

child care in nontraditional families

Michael Lamb and his associates (Lamb et al., 1982) wondered whether mothers and fathers who assumed nontraditional caretaking roles act differently with their infants from those who assume traditional caretaking roles. To find out, they first located Swedish families in which the fathers had been serving as primary caretakers of their firstborn 8-month-old infants while the mothers went to work. Swedish national policy allows every parent nine months paid leave following the birth of a child. Couples are free to divide the nine months between them, and about 10 percent of Swedish fathers take some paid leave. The researchers' major question was whether these caretaking fathers would act more like traditional fathers or like traditional mothers. In observations lasting over an hour of parents acting "as naturally as possible" at home with their infants, the research team noted when either parent picked up or held the infant in the course of disciplining, playing, kissing, soothing, or responding to the infant's request to be picked up. They also noted when the parents acted affectionately, smiled, vocalized, or actively tended to the infant's needs. Different styles of play—reciprocal, parallel, gently stimulating, vigorously physical, conventional, or idiosyncratic—were recorded as well.

The researchers admitted to being surprised by their results. The nontraditional Swedish parents acted much like their traditional American counterparts. In every case, mothers did more disciplining, kissing, soothing, vocalizing, holding, and tending to the infant's needs than fathers did, regardless of their caretaking role. There was no difference in the parents' styles of play with the infants. Thus, contrary to their expectations, the researchers found that sex had a stronger effect on parents' behavior than did caretaking role. This finding suggests that differences in parents' behavior are not simply artifacts of their current roles. Such differences may be deeply rooted in individuals' childhood socialization, or they may have biological roots. Only further research will tell.

whether the fathers are primary caregivers or not (Lamb, Frodi, Hwang, Frodi, and Steinberg, 1982).

Today, in our society, the range of fathers' behavior toward their infants is wide. Fathers can be caretakers or teachers, playmates or strangers. Attitudes toward fatherhood are changing, as the shape of the traditional family—working father, housewife, and their children—changes to encompass working mothers and single fathers. These changes have given some fathers an added incentive to be involved with their children. But fathers lack a single clear model of how they are to act and have no set biological programs to guide them in their caretaking activities. What is more, fathers have not been uniformly socialized, as most mothers have been since they were young, to play with dolls and look after babies. As a consequence, fathers vary widely in the extent and content of their activities with their infants. Although, on the average, mothers are more involved in caring for their infants than fathers are, many fathers today are deeply involved in infant care.

This kind of involved fathering, not surprisingly, improves the family relationships. The more the father is involved with the infant, and the more sensitive he is to the infant's needs, the more likely the relationship between father and child is to be joyful and secure, and, it has been found, the more likely the *mother* is to talk and play with the infant (Clarke-Stewart, 1980;

Easterbrooks and Goldberg, 1984). In one recent study, 75 firstborn 20-month-olds and their parents were observed in the strange situation and, later, doing a jigsaw puzzle with each parent (Easterbrooks and Goldberg, 1984). Fathers' involvement with their infants was measured by how much time fathers spent alone each day with their children and how much time they spent playing with them at home. Uninvolved fathers spent less than an hour a day alone with their infants; moderately involved fathers spent about one and a half hours; highly involved fathers spent over three hours alone every day with their infants. The researchers found that the infants, sons especially, who were developing well—securely attached, happy, and attentive to tasks—had fathers who were highly involved in their care, who were sensitive in doing the jigsaw puzzle with their child, who encouraged the child's autonomy, and who expressed little annoyance toward the child. The amount of routine caretaking that fathers did—diapering, arranging for babysitters, feeding and so on—was not related to the infants' development.

Fathers' close involvement with their infant sons thus predicts good social and emotional development in infancy and early childhood. Fathers' involvement with their infant daughters may have consequences that do not show up until later. One study of fathers and stepfathers who had sexually abused their daughters showed that these men had had little physical and social contact with their daughters as infants (Parker and Parker, 1985). They had not spent much time at home in their daughters' first three years of life and had provided scarcely any nurturing or care. Early father–daughter contact may help prevent later abuse. This possibility requires further research.

The significance of fathers' involvement in infant care is just now beginning to receive more attention by developmental psychologists. Now that the blinders are off, we all are likely to learn more about parents' and infants' interactions and about how mothers, fathers, and infants become families. Father and infant do not, of course, operate in a vacuum any more than mother and infant do. They influence and are influenced in turn by other family members. And this brings us to our next topic: the development of relationships and mutual influences in the family as a whole.

Family development

Just as each child grows from one tiny cell into a complex being, the family itself grows in complexity and richness as, over time, individual members join it and leave it. When an infant is born, or an adolescent leaves the nest, or the mother gets a job, or the couple gets divorced, or the father remarries, or the grandparents move in, or a grown child returns—the family now shrinks and now expands. In families, the behavior of each member ripples through the entire structure. The actions of one member are felt by all the others. Few events make such oceanic waves in a family as the arrival of a new baby. Somehow all routines stop, and all relationships change in the wake of this powerful new creature.

> Our marriage was very strong before we had Sam. It's different now, because we're different people. When Sam is going through a difficult phase, we all suffer. We bicker and slam doors. But when he's peaceful, we're a pretty happy group.

> Looking back on it, Jason's birth put strains on what was already a crumbling marriage. I didn't want to think that it was crumbling, so I ignored the signs for a long time. But when Jason was just a tiny baby—and difficult—Charlie began working longer and longer hours. He began missing not just week-night suppers, but important family times—weddings, holidays, birthday parties. He was never there to walk the

floor to get Jason to sleep, or to watch him doing the nice, normal kid things like learning to walk and talk, or, later, to talk to the teachers about things that came up at school. I ended up taking care of everything to do with Jason, and finally it was just as easy to ignore Charlie altogether.

For the first six months after a baby is born, a family undergoes many changes—some for better and some for worse (Collins, 1985). In most cases, the husband and wife act less affectionately toward each other and have less free time together; they lose some of the romance from their marriage. Yet despite the waning of romance, they feel a greater sense of partnership and shared caretaking. Couples suffer most in making the transition to parenthood if their expectations of parenthood are unrealistic, if one spouse has job-related problems, or if the division of household chores falls much more heavily on the wife. When husband and wife feel supported and encouraged by their coworkers who are parents, positive feelings about parenthood and marriage increase. Although the new parents go through a sea change after the baby arrives, there are important continuities in the quality of a marriage. ''The best marriages seem to stay the best after the arrival of the baby, and the worst marriages stay the worst,'' (Belsky, in Collins, 1985, p. 44)

The families who seem to adjust best to the birth of an infant are those in which the quality of the marriage stays high before and after the birth and in which the father actively participates in daily care of the infant (Grossman Eichler, and Winikoff, 1980; Goldberg, Michaels, and Lamb, 1985; Heinicke, Diskin, Ramsey-Klee, and Oates, 1983).

Relationships with other caregivers

Families do not exist in isolation, of course. Family members—children and parents alike—form relationships with many other people. Infants meet, approach, withdraw from, like, love, and loathe neighbors and strangers, aunts, uncles, and babysitters.

One person outside the family circle with whom a baby is likely to form a close relationship is a caregiver in day care. In one study, 7-month-old babies who had spent half-days for several months in day care reacted to a brief separation from their caregiver much as they reacted when their mothers left them (Ricciuti, 1974). The babies apparently had formed a relationship with their caregiver. Clearly, these caregivers were psychologically important and meaningful to the children. Caregivers may be less important than parents, but they are important nevertheless. Children do not see them as mere hired hands.

A recent study of infants in full-time day care was focused on the nature of their attachments to their caregivers (Ainslie and Anderson, 1984). In this study, researchers measured the infants' responses both to their mother and to their primary caregiver from the day-care center in two separate sessions of the strange situation. In certain respects—crying, looking around, vocalizing, and keeping the adult in sight—the infants did not react differently to mother and caregiver. But the infants used their mother more than the caregiver as a secure base for exploration, and they interacted more sociably when alone with her. When alone with the caregiver, infants were likelier to play with objects. The differences in the infants' behavior toward their mothers and their caregivers were substantial enough to make the researchers suggest that although the infants had developed familiar relationships with their caregivers, they were probably not equivalent to the attachment relationships that they had with their parents.

A second group of psychologists observed infants interacting with their regular caregivers in the day-care center (Farran, Burchinal, Hutaff, and Ramey, 1984). The infants clearly focused on the regular caregivers in preference to other adults or children present in the room. They vocalized, touched, approached, and played more with the regular caregivers. In fact, nearly half of each infant's actions were directed toward a single preferred caregiver. The infant vocalized, played with, and touched this caregiver more than any other person. Clearly, the infants were differentiating among the staff members. Did the caregivers reciprocate? In most cases, they did. Just as infants directed their attentions to a favorite caregiver, caregivers directed their attentions to particular infants. Even when the infants were only 6 months old, the beginnings of reciprocal relationships were in evidence. By the time the infants were 12 months old, the reciprocity was strong. The infants were quite democratic in their preferences. All the caregivers were favored by different infants. Unlike the true attachment of infants and mothers, however, the reciprocal relationships between infants and preferred caregivers did not last long. The observers saw almost no stability in the relationships from 6 to 9 to 12 months.

Presumably these observations, in part, reflected the shifting staffing patterns common to day-care centers. Day-care centers are in a constant state of flux. Infants come and go; caregivers are sick; substitutes appear; caregivers leave; shifts of caregivers move in and out. For infants who come from chaotic or unstable families, where it may be hard for them to develop secure attachments, day care is unlikely to provide the secure base that they need. Day care often is less stable than the family environment, and the relationships between infants and their caregivers are neither as deep nor as enduring as the attachment of children and their parents. Day care may not interfere with infants' relationships with their parents, but it clearly is no substitute for them.

Summary

1. In the first hour after birth, when an infant is alert and gazing and the mother's receptivity is heightened by high hormone levels, the mother begins to form emotional ties to the infant. Mothers who miss this sensitive period for bonding have many opportunities later on to grow emotionally attached to their infants.

2. Infants communicate with those around them with their appealing babyness, gazes, vocalizations, smiles, laughter, and cries. They communicate by facial expressions and bodily gestures. Mothers interpret babies' expressions and gestures as communication, even when the baby is not intentionally sending messages. Eventually, the infant does learn to communicate and becomes a truly interactive partner in these social exchanges. Mothers and infants take turns and play "duets" in feeding, vocalizing, and playing games.

3. In their interactions with adults, infants begin to learn their culture's rules about when and where they may display emotions. They learn to smile often and to control expressions of distress. Infants also respond to other people's expressions of emotions and use them to guide their own behavior.

4. The newborn is physiologically primed to pay attention to the kinds of stimulation provided by parents' faces—the contrasts between skin and hair, the moving eyes and red mouth. In turn, parents project their own feelings and rhythms onto the infant and act *as though* those actions were social. So begins the interactive "system" of parents and child.

5. Some mothers and infants mesh well, others not so well. Mothers may be overstimulating, anxious, insecure, depressed, even mentally ill. Some babies are temperamentally unresponsive, difficult, irritable, and rejecting of mothers' attempts at social communication.

6. Temperament is generally stable over time, although the course of any infant's development depends to some extent on the fit of his or her temperament with parents' expectations and behavior.

7. The most important social and emotional development of an infant's first year is the formation of a lasting, loving tie with the person he or she interacts with the most. This attachment develops in the second six months of life. By observing infants and mothers in the "strange situation," psychologists have found that infants are either securely or insecurely attached to their mothers. Insecure infants avoid contact with their mothers or act ambivalently toward them. Mothers who are loving, responsive, and sensitive are likely to offer the infant appropriate levels of stimulation and to foster secure attachments in their infants. Mothers who are tense and angry are likely to foster avoidance in their infants.

8. Secure attachments are likely to flourish when a baby has one regular caretaker who gives loving and sensitive attention and who keeps long separations to a minimum.

9. Securely attached infants typically become children who are more socially and emotionally competent than those who are insecurely attached.

10. Mothers do most of the physical care of infants. Fathers are more likely to play and roughhouse. There are, of course, marked individual differences in how fathers behave with their infants.

11. In families, the behavior of each member is felt by all the others. The arrival of a new baby is a momentous event within any family and causes substantial changes in family relationships.

12. Infants form relationships outside their families, with caregivers in day care, but these do not substitute for their attachments to their parents.

Key terms

sensitive period	stranger anxiety (fear of strangers)	set goal
bonding	social referencing	strange situation
rooming in	microanalysis	secure attachment
endogenous smiles	pseudodialogues	insecure-avoidant attachment
exogenous smiles	attachment	insecure-ambivalent attachment

Suggested readings

AINSWORTH, MARY D. S., BLEHAR, MARY C., WATERS, EVERETT, and WALL, SALLY. *Patterns of Attachment: a Psychological Study of the Strange Situation*. Hillsdale, N.J.: Lawrence Erlbaum Associates, 1978. Details Ainsworth's procedure for studying qualitative differences in infant–mother attachment and reviews the results of research using the strange situation assessment procedure.

BOWLBY, JOHN. *Attachment and Loss*, Vol. 1, *Attachment*. New York: Basic Books, 1969. The first of Bowlby's influential trilogy on the theory of attachment; a seminal book that inspired a whole line of research on children's early social relations with their mothers.

CHESS, STELLA, and THOMAS, ALEXANDER. *Your Child Is a Person*. New York: Viking Press, 1965. An excellent book integrating the notion of temperamental differences in children with practical advice on child rearing.

KAYE, KENNETH. *The Mental and Social Life of Babies: How Parents Create Persons.* Chicago: University of Chicago Press, 1982. An original theory of the roles of mothers and infants in their early face-to-face interactions.

KLAUS, MARSHALL H., and KENNELL, JOHN H. *Parent-Infant Bonding.* St. Louis: C. V. Mosby, 1982. Support for the critical period explanation of maternal bonding, gathered by its chief proponents from animal and human studies.

LAMB, MICHAEL, THOMPSON, ROSS, GARDNER, WILLIAM, and CHARNOV, ERIC. *Infant-Mother Attachment.* Hillsdale, N.J.: Lawrence Erlbaum Associates, 1985. A comprehensive review of the research on the development of infants' relationships with their mothers.

PARKE, ROSS D. *Fathers.* Cambridge, Mass.: Harvard University Press, 1977. A comprehensive, readable presentation that reviews the research on the roles of the father, how they differ from those of the mother, and what effects they have on children's development.

SCHAFFER, H. RUDOLPH. *Mothering.* Cambridge, Mass.: Harvard University Press, 1977. A lucid review of psychological research on the different roles that an infant's mother fills and how they relate to the infant's development.

SLUCKIN, WLADYSLAW, HERBERT, MARTIN, and SLUCKIN, ALICE. *Maternal Bonding.* Oxford: Basil Blackwell, 1983. A brief but balanced discussion of the issues and research on the formation of emotional bonds between mothers and their infants.

Early Childhood

chapter eight
Physical development

Physical growth

In Chapter 5, we saw the marvelous changes in size and motor abilities that take place during infancy. At the end of that discussion, we left the infant of about 2 toddling around, getting into things, having stretched to some 34 inches and 27 pounds, and sleeping about 12 hours a day. In this chapter, we look at the physical growth and development that take place in early childhood, the ages from 2 to 6 years.

It is with mixed feelings that parents watch their infants and children put on inches and pounds. Parents take pride in these outward signs of their children's robust good health. They take satisfaction in knowing that all those proddings—"Finish your milk before you go out to play, dear," "But broccoli's *good* for you," "I don't *care* if George can have cookies for breakfast. In this house . . ."—have paid off. But parents also sigh as they set off once again to buy shoes for toes that seem always to be poking through the front of the sneakers and jeans to cover ankles that seem always to be showing. And they sigh again when their armful of an infant has so quickly grown into more than a comfortable lapful of young girl or boy. Between the ages of 2 and 6, the average American child grows 3 inches and gains 4½ pounds a year. The average 5-year-old weighs 40 pounds and stands 43 inches tall. That's a long way from the newborn of 7 pounds and 20 inches. But the visible does-a-parent's-heart-good growth of a child in inches and pounds masks complex and varied patterns of cell and tissue growth.

Growth patterns

Within the child's body, growth creates a state of constant change. Nutrients are continually ingested, broken down into their components, and used for fuel. Some cells divide, others stop dividing and change in size, and still others stay relatively stable. At any time during infancy and early childhood, one part or organ of the body is likely to be growing faster than another. This **asynchrony** is typical of how human beings grow both before and after birth (see Figure 8.1). Vital organs grow at different rates because their cells divide and grow at different rates. The physical growth that we notice—the longer arms sticking out of the sleeves that were just the right length a few months ago, the broader rib cage stretching taut the sweater that was loose just last season—is the result of microscopically small changes in body cells.

Cells grow in one of three ways. Some cells, such as those that line the gut and make up skin and blood, continuously die and are replaced. Other cells, such as those in glands and parts of the liver and kidneys, live for long periods. The third kind of cells, such as those in nerves, muscles, and fat, form only during certain periods of growth. Most of the nerve cells in the central nervous system have formed by the 18th week of prenatal life. The newborn has all of the muscle cells it will ever have. Fat cells generally multiply only in the weeks before birth, during the first two years of life, and in early adolescence (Hirsch, 1975).

All this activity, with cells asynchronously dividing and multiplying, goes on *inside*. Outside, to the pediatrician who weighs and measures infant and child, the process of growth proceeds gradually and, for the most part, regularly. A **growth curve** is a record of a child's pattern of physical change over time. If the curve of a child's growth from birth to maturity is drawn on a graph, it shows how far and fast the child has grown. The two curves in Figure 8.2 are the earliest-known growth curves recorded. They plot the growth in height of an 18th-century French nobleman's son from the time he was 6 months old until he was 18. The upper curve, which shows his *height* at different ages, rises gradually, as de Montbeillard's son grew taller. The lower

GROWTH PATTERNS

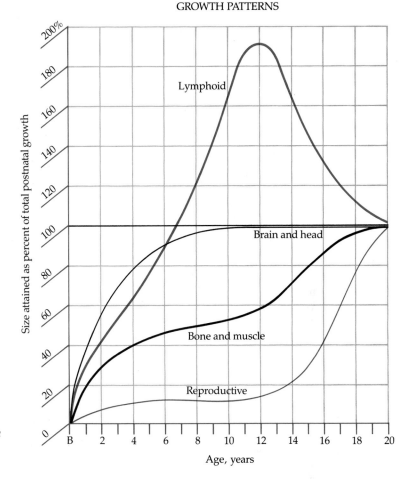

Figure 8.1 **These growth curves for parts and tissues of the body show the asynchrony of human growth after birth (Harrison, Weiner, Tanner, and Barnicot, 1964).**

curve, which shows *changes* in height from one age to the next, declines over time, as the boy's *rate* of growth slowed down after infancy. Then it rises sharply, as the boy reached the growth spurt of early adolescence. Had the boy's rate of growth been plotted from conception, the slowdown would have begun in the fourth month of prenatal development (Tanner, 1978).

Growth curves can be plotted for groups of children as well as for individuals like de Montbeillard's son. Although individual children grow taller or heavier at slightly different rates, plotting these average curves for large groups of children can help in identifying children whose growth is markedly abnormal (Figure 8.3). It is not uncommon for parents to talk about their children in terms of their places on growth curves for height and weight.

"Tim is 25th percentile in weight and 90th in height—tall and skinny like his father."

"Denny is a pip-squeak—10th percentile height and weight."

A child whose growth departs radically from these growth norms may have a genetic problem or may be getting poor care. A child who is below the third percentile in height, for example, is so small that his or her condition needs investigating. Of course, if the assessment of abnormality is to be meaningful, the norms themselves must be based on a broad and up-to-date cross section of the population. In countries like the United States, which are

THE FIRST GROWTH CURVE

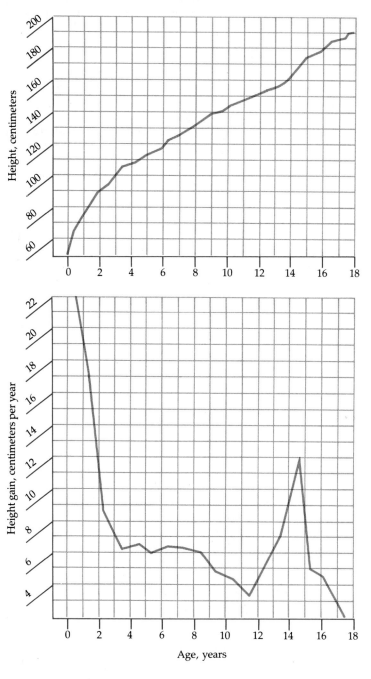

*Figure 8.2 **The growth curve at the top traces the increasing height of de Montbeillard's son, who grew to be 18 back in the years 1759 to 1777. The bottom growth curve shows that his rate of growth decreased, except for a spurt in adolescence (Tanner, 1978). (10 centimeters = 3.9 inches.)***

made up of many different ethnic and racial groups, separate growth norms for various groups are needed.

In our Midwestern town, there are lots of children of Scandinavian descent and lots of children whose parents recently emigrated from Southeast Asia. In the nursery and grade school classes where they mix together, the impression one gets is of one clump of big, tall, rangy, fair-haired kids and another clump of small, short, neat, dark-haired kids.

GROWTH NORMS

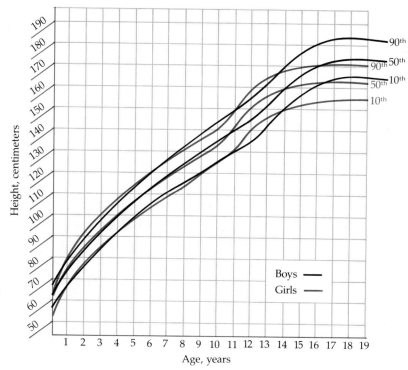

Figure 8.3 **The darker lines trace the norms of height from birth to 19 years of age for tall American boys, those in the 90th percentile (taller than 90 percent of their contemporaries); average American boys (50th percentile); and short American boys (10th percentile). The lighter lines show the norms of height for tall, average, and short American girls from birth to 19 years of age. (10 centimeters = 3.9 inches.)**

If children from genetically small populations—such as the Vietnamese and Cambodian—are measured against norms set for children from genetically large populations—such as Scandinavian and Afro-American—they may be singled out as abnormally short when they are actually growing normally. Similarly, if children from groups of large people are measured against norms set for children from groups of small people, they may be judged normal when they are actually growing abnormally slowly because of illness or malnutrition. It is also possible that a whole subgroup of the population is not growing at a normal rate because of a dietary deficiency. Only if the growth of this whole subgroup is measured against a national or international sample will the growth problem of an entire subgroup show up (Figure 8.4).

Measures of maturity

The visible signs—the inches and pounds added—tell us that children are growing, but they are not really the most precise indicators of children's physical maturity. For that, the best indicators are the length, thickness, and hardness of the bones. The maturity of a child's skeleton can be read from X rays. X rays of the hand, for example, show how fully the immature, central cartilage cells have broken down and hardened into bone. By the time most children are 1 year old, three of the twenty-eight bones in the hand and wrist have ossified. By the time they are 2, the skull has completely ossified. By then, the six **fontanels**, the soft spots in the skull that allow it to mold during childbirth, have hardened. Only after the growth spurt of puberty does the growth of the limbs stop. By the end of puberty, people have reached their full height.

The appearance of the first baby tooth is another milestone of physical maturity. In most babies, the first tooth appears at the front of the lower jaw

HEIGHT AROUND THE WORLD

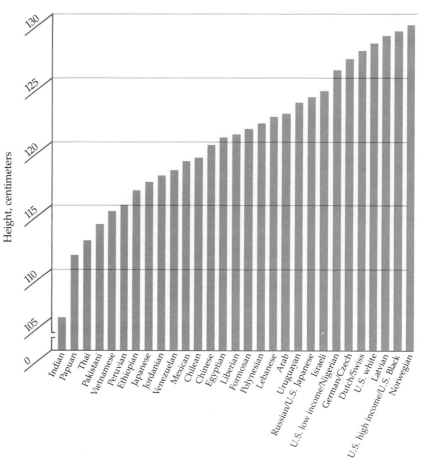

*Figure 8.4 **The heights of 8-year-old boys from around the world are compared to those of 8-year-old boys from white and black, high- and low-income families in the United States (Meredith, 1978). (10 centimeters = 3.9 inches.)***

when the baby is 6 to 9 months old. The other baby teeth fill in by about the second birthday, at a rate usually governed by heredity.

Changing size and proportions

Children grow faster during their first few years than they will at any other time in their lives, except during the growth spurt of adolescence (see Table 8.1). They gain 15 pounds and 10 inches in the first year, 5 pounds and 5 inches in the second year, and 4½ pounds and 4 inches in the third year. They grow faster both in absolute terms—inches—and in relative terms—proportion of baby height.

> Sam grew so fast in his first few years that I used to joke that I had to keep the car running so that I could dash out fast enough to buy him bigger clothes.

The 3-year-old, who grows 3 inches, is gaining a greater proportion—one-twelfth compared to one-nineteenth—of her height than the 10-year-old who grows 3 inches. But her growth is slowing down. If it continued at the same rate as in the first year, the toddling 2-year-old would be a mammoth 63 pounds—much too heavy for mother to lift into the shopping cart.

Because growth of different body parts is uneven, as children grow they change in physical proportions as well as size. The newborn's head is fully

Table 8.1
Expected increase in height per year

Age, years	Growth, inches	
0–1	9.8	
1–2	4.8	
2–3	3.1	
3–4	2.9	
4–5	2.7	
5–6	2.7	
6–7	2.4	
7–8	2.2	
8–9	2.2	
9–10	2.0	
10–11	1.9 (boys)	2.3 (girls)
11–12	1.9 (boys)	2.5 (girls)
12–13	2.2 (boys)	2.6 (girls)
13–14	2.8 (boys)	1.9 (girls)

SOURCE: Lowrey, 1978.

one-fourth of its body size, but its legs are short—just a bit longer than that big head—and its feet are proportionally the tiniest part of its body. After birth, the baby's head continues to grow most rapidly. Toward the end of the first year, muscle and bone growth quickens, and the baby's trunk grows fastest of all. After the first year, the baby's arms and legs grow more quickly than the body. With their longer limbs and increased mobility, most 2- and 3-year-olds lose much of their baby fat (and pot bellies). The chubby infant usually thins down to the slimmer, more active toddler, who may have a much smaller appetite and very definite ideas about what is good to eat. By age 2, a boy is

The photographs of this boy, taken at successive ages, show the typical changes in proportions from infancy to maturity. His head, which was half his body at 2 months after conception, makes up less and less of his body size. The ages, left to right, are 15 months, 30 months and 6, 7, 11, 14, and 18 years.

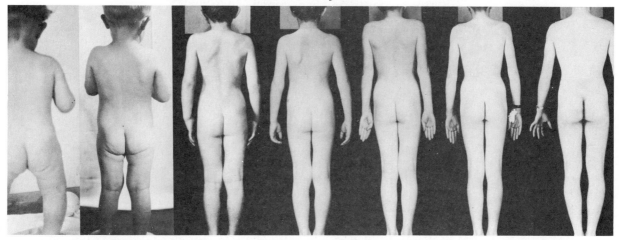

about half his adult height, a girl slightly more than half her adult height (Lowrey, 1973). By age 6, children are about 70 percent of their adult height.

Many children, especially those whose parents are very different in size, do not fall neatly into predictable slots, however. There are marked individual differences in growth patterns, height, and weight.

> Sam was so regularly off the growth charts that we worried he'd grow up gigantic. But then he slowed down, thank goodness. Now the doctor tells us that he'll probably top out at about 6 feet 3 inches.

> Erica has stayed proportionally pretty much the same since she was a few months old—30th percentile for height and 80th percentile for weight. We figure she'll keep on being short and solid.

Factors affecting growth

Genetic and inborn factors

Normal physical growth, as we mentioned in Chapter 5, is largely under genetic control. The brain's pituitary gland follows genetic instructions that cause it to produce growth hormone and other hormones that affect growth. We know from longitudinal studies like the Berkeley Growth Study that parents and their children are likely to follow similar patterns in their rates of growth, although they may differ slightly in their final sizes (Tanner, 1970).

In rare cases—about 1 child in 1000—the instructions that control growth go awry, and the children grow extremely short or extremely tall. **Dwarfism** and **giantism** may be genetic in origin or the result of abnormalities in prenatal development. When children are abnormally short or, more rarely, abnormally tall for their age, tests of bone age are done. If their bone age differs significantly from their chronological age, children may be given growth hormones or other treatment to bring their height more into line with the norm for their age. Abnormal growth in height sometimes is just one piece in a complex problem requiring careful physical and psychological treatment.

> A first-grade classmate of Kristy began to develop breasts and show signs of entering puberty at the age of 6. Her parents had to find help in dealing with her disorder and with the other children's reactions to the changes in her appearance. She was treated by a team of pediatricians, psychologists, and endocrinologists.

Even when extremes in growth are not associated with more serious underlying conditions, exceptionally tall children may look so much older than their age that people may expect too much from them, and very small children may be babied (Scharf, 1986).

> Sam was so large as an infant and toddler that his pediatrician warned us not to be fooled by his appearance into being too hard on him. Good as it was, that wasn't always easy advice to follow. Once when we were at the supermarket when Sam was about 1½—but looked at least 3½—he was talking baby talk. A few people stared hard at him, clearly assuming he was retarded. I bit my tongue and decided then and there that I was not going to apologize for my son.

Sex differences

A particular kind of genetic influence over growth shows up in the differences between males and females. From early on in prenatal development, there are physical differences between boys and girls. Newborn girls' skeletal systems are several weeks more mature than newborn boys'. Their permanent teeth come in sooner than boys' do. By adolescence, girls' skeletal systems are, on average, three years more mature than boys'.

As a result of this difference, girls tend to excel at different sorts of motor activities from boys. Girls are likely to do better at fine motor skills like writing, drawing, and buttoning, and they do better than boys when the fine motor tasks require quickness.

> Natalie is very dextrous. At 2, she could button her sweater and buckle her belt. At 3, she could tie her shoelaces, comb her hair, and zip her jacket. She's always liked toys with little pieces and parts—toy phones with little holes in the dial, spelling games with lots of keys to press, beads and buttons to string for necklaces.

At age 4 or 5, girls may also skip and run with greater coordination than boys. But not all differences favor girls. For their first seven years, boys are slightly taller and more muscular than girls. Their baby fat disappears sooner than girls', and they are a bit leaner throughout childhood. Boys throw, bat, and hit better than girls. Some boys do better at gross motor skills, especially those that use the muscles of the upper body. In the schoolyard, while the girls are jumping rope and playing kickball, the boys are playing hockey and baseball.

> Sam spent lots of time at nursery school building towers and castles with sturdy wooden blocks, clambering around a jungle gym, running toy ''hepticopters'' and ''hairplanes''—and asking when he'd be old enough to ice skate, play hockey, and be as strong as He-Man.

Whatever the inborn differences between them, boys and girls differ in the amounts of experience they have with particular physical activities. These experiences may enhance inborn differences—with boys climbing, pedaling toy cars and tricycles, throwing and batting balls; and girls turning the pages of books, writing, and painting—but not always. Differences in group averages do not tell about the skills of individual girls and individual boys. Many boys excel at painting and writing, and many girls are very adept at pitching balls and riding bicycles. Even the group differences in abilities between boys and girls tend to be quite small. In a study comparing kindergarten boys and girls in running and jumping, for example, 50 percent of the boys and 45 percent of the girls could do a standing jump of 35 inches and dash 400 feet in 50 seconds (Milne, Seefeldt, and Reuschlein, 1976). Although the averages for the boys were slightly ahead of those for the girls, in each class there were some girls who could run faster and jump farther than most of the boys in the class.

Nutrition

Without nutrients, children's bodies cannot grow. The earlier and the more severe their malnutrition, the worse the prospects for their normal development. One kind of severe malnutrition that children between 2 and 4 years may suffer from is a protein deficiency called **kwashiorkor**. With bloated bellies, thin and colorless hair, skin lesions, these children are apathetic, withdrawn, and irritable. Their motor skills are poor, and their intellects are impaired (Thomson and Pollitt, 1977). Malnutrition also lowers children's resistance to disease. They are less able to resist viruses, bacteria, and fungi than other children (Edelman, 1977; Edelman, Suskind, Sirisinha, and Olson, 1973). Because they are susceptible to diarrhea, malnourished children may not be able to use what little food they take in. The poor sanitation of a

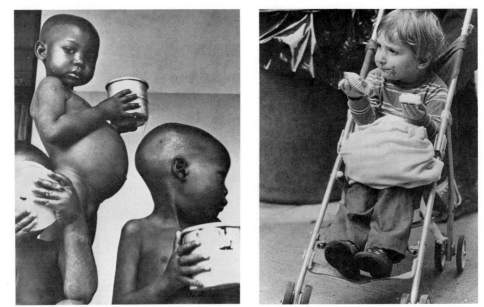

Malnutrition is a world-wide problem. In Africa, many children live on too few calories and too little protein. In the United States, many children live on junk food and "empty" calories.

poverty-stricken environment means that poorly nourished children are exposed to many infectious diseases.

Evidence from around the world attests to the toll malnutrition takes on children's intellectual abilities. In Indonesia, the IQ scores of children classified as "poorly" or "fairly" nourished were significantly lower than those of a group classified "acceptably" nourished (Soewondo, Abednedo, Pekerti, and Karjadi, 1971). In India, children's IQ scores decreased in direct proportion to how underweight they were (Gupta, Dhingra, Singh, and Anand, 1975). In Barbados, children who had suffered moderate to severe protein and calorie malnutrition in their first year of life did worse in school subjects ranging from reading, math, and social science, to health, religion, and art than children who had been adequately nourished (Galler, Ramsey, and Solimano, 1984). Even when IQ was held constant, the malnourished children's classroom performance was poorer than the other children's. Other studies confirm the finding that children who suffer severe malnutrition early in life are likely to do poorly in school even when their diets later have improved so that they have caught up in height and weight to others their age (Brozek, 1978).

Food supplements given early do help. In Guatemala, a longitudinal study showed that children given high-calorie supplements in infancy turned out to be more socially involved, more capable of strong feelings of both happiness and anger, and more physically active when they were 6 to 8 years old than children who did not get the food supplements (Barrett, Radke-Yarrow, and Klein, 1982).

But malnutrition is an ecological problem. It does not occur in isolation. Its consorts are poverty, chaotic family structure, poor housing, ignorance, and despair. Chaotic families mean more children who are neglected, more children with blighted chances for optimal development. Although the need for dietary supplements is critical, the problem of malnutrition is larger than diet alone. Malnutrition is so often found enmeshed in the circumstances of poverty that it is impossible to eradicate without major economic and social reform. Mothers of malnourished children, for instance, tend to be less educated, in poorer health, and less responsive to their children than mothers of well-nourished children (Thomson and Pollitt, 1977).

focus *Feeding fussy eaters*

"This child eats half an egg for breakfast and 2 bites of cheese for lunch. She's going to waste away," one mother moans.

"My son refuses everything but peanut butter and tomato soup," says another mother. "He's going to shrivel up from malnutrition."

Many parents see the food their children leave untouched on their plates, see their children's pickiness, dawdling, and mealtime battles and worry that their children are eating too little to survive on. For these parents, pediatricians offer some tips:

- Most toddlers *are* fussy. So long as they get 16 ounces of milk a day, a few ounces of orange juice, and perhaps some multivitamin drops, they are doing just fine.

- Put the food in front of the child *without comment*. No bribes ("If you eat your spinach, you can watch TV."), no threats ("You are going to sit there until every pea is gone."), and no ultimatums ("No potato chips in this house again *ever*!").

- It's the child's business to eat as much or as little as he or she wishes. At the end of the meal, take away the full or empty plate *without comment*. Food is for satisfying hunger, not for reward or punishment.

- Serve small portions, perhaps two or three spoonfuls. Give a child the chance to finish. Kids are not bashful about asking for more when they're hungry.

- Serve food from the basic four food groups each day. (But don't be rigid about it. Children balance their diets over weeks or months, not on single days.) A well balanced diet includes on the average: two small servings of protein (meat, fish, eggs, peanut butter, lentils, or cheese); four servings of vegetables and fruit; two or three 8-ounce glasses of milk (or the equivalent in yogurt or cheese); and four servings of bread or cereal foods each day.

- If you're really worried about a child's diet, write down everything the child eats and drinks for one or two weeks. Then show the list to the child's pediatrician for his or her advice.

- Variety is not necessary to sustain life. Perfectly healthy children go for months on nothing but milk and hamburger, or chicken and green grapes. Offer new foods once in a while, but do not insist.

- Keep between-meal eating to a minimum so that the child is really hungry at mealtime. If the child really needs a midmorning or midafternoon snack, serve some fresh fruit, real juice (not a "juice drink"), or milk.

- Serve meals at regular times, and serve them when a child is hungry. If the child is hungry for supper at four in the afternoon, forget social custom, and serve supper then.

- Don't turn your child into a dessert addict. If you serve desserts, serve fruit.

The dramatic pictures of entire peoples starving in North Africa are among the most gruesome signs of malnutrition. Much of the world's population—in North America as well as North Africa—lives on too few calories and far too little protein. A survey of Asian, African, and South American children found 80 percent of them to be suffering from moderate to severe malnutrition. Estimates are that one hundred million children under 5 years of age suffer from malnutrition (Suskind, 1977). In the United States, surveys have found chronically poor nutrition in 20 percent of the children under 6 years and in 30 percent of the children from poor families. Many preschool-aged children do not get enough iron, and nearly half of them get less vitamin A and vitamin C than is recommended (National Center for Health Statistics, 1975). In the United States, a study of children between 6 and 11 showed that children from wealthy families were 1.2 inches taller than children from poor families (Goldstein, 1971). In contrast, a study of children in Swedish cities showed no connection between children's height and family income, presumably because in Sweden poor and rich alike have access to food and social services, and the link between poverty and malnutrition is broken (Lindgren, 1976).

In this country, where shelves are stocked with prepared and packaged foods, even parents who have money to buy their children enough food face the problem of checking food additives. Too much sugar, salt, or chemical preservatives? Too few minerals and vitamins in processed foods? Too many junk foods—lurid orange puffed cheese, greasy chips, sugary soda and cookies—competing for the preschool-aged child's already limited appetite? As we've seen, once they are past the extremely rapid growth of infancy, children need fewer calories per pound, and so their appetites decrease. Feeding preschoolers can be a problem even for affluent parents.

Climate and altitude

Unless the physical climate, hot or cold, is linked to a difference in nutrition, temperature seems to have little effect on children's physical growth. Contrary to some popular beliefs, children living in hotter climates do not mature earlier than those living in more temperate zones (Tanner, 1970). Altitude appears to slow up growth, but people in mountainous areas also tend to be undernourished. High altitude does induce larger chest circumference and bigger lungs, as proved by a study comparing coastal and mountain children in Peru (Tanner, 1978). Similar adaptations eons ago are probably responsible for the different body types of Africans, Asians, and Caucasians.

Disease

Children born with defects of the heart, lungs, kidneys, or any of the endocrine glands may not grow normally in height and weight. Children with heart defects, for example, may lag two years behind in growth. After they have corrective surgery, they often catch up to others their age. One child added four years of bone age in six months. Major diseases and chronic conditions like untreated diabetes, hookworm, and dysentery stunt children's growth (Lowrey, 1978)). But minor diseases caused by viruses and bacteria—measles, flu, even pneumonia—usually have little if any effect on growth (Lowrey, 1973). In nearly all children whose growth has been slowed by illness, catch-up growth begins when they recover (*How Children Grow*, 1972). Children's bodies have almost miraculous abilities to compensate for lost growth.

Neglect

Severe emotional stress is another factor than affects children's growth. Unloving care or extreme neglect can cause a child to stop growing, even if the child is fed adequately. The child's pituitary gland stops producing enough growth hormone for normal physical development. The children in these cases are short and immature in bone development. A child of 6 might have the bone age of a 3½-year-old, for example. These children come from strife-torn families where they are neglected by their parents. In one such family, the mother of infant twins unhappily found herself pregnant again when the twins were 4 months old (Gardner, 1972). Their father first lost his job, fought with the mother, and finally left the family. The mother took out her rage on one of the twins—the boy. Although his twin sister continued to grow normally, the boy did not. When he was examined at 13 months, he was the size of an infant six months younger. He was placed in the hospital for treatment and began to grow normally. After his father returned to the family, he was discharged from the hospital, and when the twins were examined 2½ years later, both were of nearly normal height. Children in such dire circumstances are often treated by being placed in foster care. Deciding to remove a young child from the family is difficult because of the child's attachment to the parents (see Chapter 7). But sometimes the situation requires it. In their new surroundings, without any hormone therapy, and eating an ordinary diet, the children usually begin to develop and grow more lively and sociable. Children who have been growing only about 1½ inches a year suddenly gain, on the average, 6.3 inches a year (*How Children Grow*, 1972; Powell, Brasel, Raiti, and Blizzard, 1967).

Obesity

Not so long ago, parents were congratulated for their healthy, chubby babies. Double chins and rippling thighs were considered signs of robust good health. No more. (See Figure 8.5.)

> Since I'm overweight, I was extremely careful when my two kids were little not to let them get fat. I've heard that the first two years are when kids develop their lifetime supply of fat cells, and I didn't want to take any chances with them. They're 5 and 8 now and still thin. I hope they're out of the woods.

> Natalie was plump as a young child, and we were kind of worried that she'd turn into a fat child. It was really awful to wrangle with her about everything she ate, though.

Chunky toddlers may well turn into fat children and, later, adults, and fatness can cause psychological as well as physical ills. Five percent of American schoolchildren are obese, weighing more than 85 pounds at age 9, compared to the norm of 66 pounds. The prevalence of obesity has increased by more than 50 percent in the past 15 to 20 years and even more so for black children (Dietz, 1986). Forty percent of the children who are obese at age 7 become obese adults (Epstein, 1986).

Why are there so many fat children? There are many reasons (see Table 8.2). For one thing, there are a lot of fat children because there are a lot of fat parents—who pass on both their body type and their eating habits to their children (Stunkard, 1986). They begin to do this in infancy by overfeeding the baby. By the time a child is 6 years old, overeating has become a habit that is hard to break. A child need eat only an extra 100 calories a day—a cookie or

Table 8.2
Causes of overweight

- *Body build.* Children inherit a body build that is lean or heavy.
- *Activity level.* They also inherit a characteristic level of activity that burns off more or fewer calories.
- *Taste preference.* Infants are born with taste preferences. Some have a ''sweet tooth'' before they even have teeth. They prefer to drink sugary water more than other infants do.
- *Basal metabolism.* Even at rest, people's rates of using the calories they take in varies by as much as 400 to 500 calories a day.
- *Endorphins.* Overweight people may produce too many endorphins, with the effect that they crave food all the time.
- *Food consumed.* Parents often urge their children to ''clean their plates'' and thereby overeat.
- *Sugar and fat.* People may know that candy and cookies are sugary and fattening, but they may not know about the sugar hidden in processed foods like peanut butter, ketchup, and cold cereals. Foods low in sugar and fats—fresh vegetables, fish, poultry, and lean meats, and, for infants, breast milk—rarely cause obesity.
- *Stress and anxiety.* Anxiety, loneliness, boredom, and stress can all cause people to overeat.

CAMPBELL SOUP KIDS
THEN AND NOW

Figure 8.5 Recognizing that today's public no longer believes that ''a fat baby is a healthy baby,'' the Campbell Soup Company has slimmed down the Campbell soup kids. New advertising features the formerly chubby pair engaging in sports and exercise, to promote the idea of eating right and staying fit.

two, a bag of potato chips, a glass of cola—to gain 3000 calories in a month. Only 3500 extra calories add up to a weight gain of 1 pound.

According to one hypothesis, the first year or two of life is a critical period during which the infant's diet affects how many fat cells form. Malnourished infants develop few fat cells; overfed infants, many (Winick, 1975). Overfed infants then are permanently predisposed to obesity, turning into children and adults who crave more food and gain weight more easily than those with fewer fat cells (Harding, 1971). But some evidence suggests that fat babies are not necessarily doomed to be fat adults. One researcher (Roche, 1981) has challenged this hypothesis with data from animal experiments, which suggest that the number of fat cells is *not* fixed in the early years. Furthermore, in humans, he points out, measures of obesity in infancy are not significantly correlated with measures of obesity in adulthood. In addition, factors besides the number of fat cells have been shown to influence one's weight. The *size* of fat cells, for example, also influences how much a person weighs (Brownell, in Turkington, 1984).

Another factor that contributes to leanness or obesity is a person's general body **metabolism**, the rate at which calories are burned. How efficiently people burn calories is more important in determining obesity than simply the number of calories they take in. Lean people burn the extra calories they take in without turning them into deposits of fat. Some governing mechanism in their brain makes their body ''waste'' extra calories. But the metabolism of obese people makes their bodies thrifty about burning extra calories; they store those calories as fat (Bennett and Gurin, 1982). Related to this, perhaps, is another factor: activity level. Quiet, placid babies who eat only moderately are fatter than thin, tense babies who cry often and eat a lot (Mayer, 1975). Later, sitting passively while watching television and munching aggravates the tendency to obesity (Dietz, 1986). Taste preferences also may contribute to obesity. From the very beginning, it has been found, some infants prefer sweet flavors more than other infants do (Milstein, 1978). These infants are thought to be likely candidates for later overweight.

Obesity affects more than an individual's appearance. In adulthood, obesity poses health risks like diabetes and high blood pressure. But in childhood, the risks are mainly to mental health. Overweight children often

Heredity, metabolism, activity level, taste preferences, and other social and psychological factors all contribute to obesity in early childhood.

feel rejected by others. When one researcher (Mayer, 1975) showed girls a picture of a girl a short distance away from a group of other girls, thin girls usually interpreted the picture to mean that the girl was walking *toward* the group; fat girls interpreted the picture to mean that the girl had been *left out* of the group. In fact, overweight children, especially girls, may be left out of social activities. One study of college admissions showed that, if applicants were interviewed in person, obese girls had only one-third the chance of acceptance at their chosen college as thin girls (Canning and Mayer, 1966). Many other studies support the suggestion that both children and adults hold negative stereotypes about, keep farther away from, and discriminate against obese people (Jarvie, Lahey, Graziano, and Framer, 1983). In middle childhood and adolescence, fat children are more likely to have low self-esteem (Mendelson and White, 1985).

Brain growth

For psychologists, perhaps the most important aspect of physical growth is the growth of the brain. Recent technical improvements in recording the activity and mapping the structure of the brain have made it possible for the first time to peek at how this most important organ develops. Brain development and function depend on several different properties and processes:

- The number, size, and structure of neurons, or nerve cells, in the brain.
- The branching dendrites at the ends of the nerve cells.
- The arcs and connections among the nerve cells.
- The covering of myelin on the nerve cells.
- The location and arrangement of the nerve cells.

Each is important to the development of the brain and behavior.

Brain structure and organization

Neurons first appear in the brain during the second prenatal month and, in the eighth prenatal month, develop branching dendrites, effective **neurotransmitters**, and the ability to metabolize glucose. Neurons continue to develop, grow, and change in all these ways from that point into childhood. First, dendrites increase in length and number of branches. There are individual variations in the rate at which this occurs, and some evidence suggests that stimulation from the environment can increase the growth of dendrites. In one study, for example, kittens were trained to pull back one of their front paws to avoid a mild electric shock (Spinelli, Jensen, and Viana Di Prisco, 1980). Examination under the microscope showed that in the corresponding area of the brain, the dendrites had developed more branches. This kind of branching of dendrites is the most important clue to the functional capacity of the brain. The more branches, the wider the range of behavior possible (Tanner, 1978). Second, during the course of development, the types and strengths of the chemical transmitters between neurons at various sites in the brain change (Axelrod, 1974; Iverson, 1979). These changes make the brain more efficient. Third, glucose metabolism increases until children are 11 years old, which indicates an increase in the brain's functioning (Farkas-Bargeton and Diebler, 1978).

Neurons also grow in physical size. At birth, the infant's brain contains all the neurons it will ever have, but it weighs only about one-fourth of its adult weight. The infant's brain must be small to allow the head to pass through the birth canal. After birth, nerve cells increase in size, and other, supporting cells called **neuroglia** continue to multiply until one or two years after birth (Tanner, 1978). The brain doubles in volume during the first year and reaches about 90 percent of its adult size by age 3 (Trevarthan, 1983). During childhood and into adulthood, myelin, the white fatty substance that improves the transmission of signals along the neurons, is deposited around the axons of these cells. Myelination also contributes to the increased size and weight of the brain and to changes in its appearance. In the first six years, the brain's surface area increases, and **fissures** develop as the neurons enlarge and are myelinated. The substances and structures *within* the neurons also develop gradually during childhood. Neurons include a cell nucleus and, surrounding the nucleus, **Nissl substance**. This substance often appears at the same time as a new behavioral function appears. Finally, neurons in the brain congregate into functional groups.

In sum, brain maturation is a system of closely coordinated developments at many different levels: the growth and formation of brain cells, myelination, complexity of branching dendrites, and the connections between cells. But brain development is not all growth. Brain regions originally develop an excess of cells. In the course of normal development, the extra cells die off and the extra connections between cells are reduced. After the first two years of life, unnecessary branches are discarded and replaced by more efficient ones (Huttenlocher, 1979; Mark, 1974). Thus, brain development also includes the elimination of redundant or inefficient pathways.

Brain and behavior

Increases in brain size, complexity, and myelination are related to advances in children's thinking and talking. As myelin forms in the brainstem before and soon after birth, the infant develops the ability to babble (Lecours, 1975; Figure 8.6). During a second cycle of myelination, which lasts from soon after birth until a child is between 3½ and 4½, the child's earliest actual speech develops. The muscles for producing speech are primarily controlled by **Broca's area** in the motor cortex. Neurons connect Broca's area to **Wernicke's area**, which is involved in hearing and understanding speech. As these areas of the cortex mature and are myelinated, children begin to speak and to understand language. And from infancy until the age of 15 or so there is a third cycle of myelination, in the association areas of the cortex. Cognitive

BRAIN AND BEHAVIOR

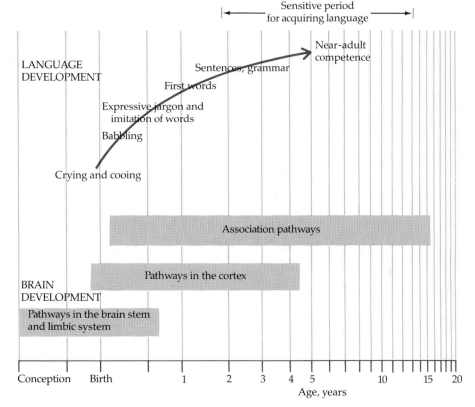

*Figure 8.6 **Cycles of my-elination in the brain and the development of language. Babbling develops during the first cycle, when the brain stem and limbic system are myelinated. The second cycle, when parts of the cortex are myelinated, accompanies the development of early speech. The third cycle, when association areas are myelinated, accompanies the sensitive period for the development of language. This cycle of myelination begins at birth and continues gradually to encase axons until the individual reaches full maturity.***

functions develop during this cycle (Bay, 1975; Yacovlev and Lecours, 1967). Unfortunately, although it has been suggested—and seems sensible—that these changes in brain maturation are *causing* the advances in language and cognitive development that occur at the same time, it has not been proved. Research shows only that the changes in the brain's structure and the development of abilities occur at the same time (Pappas, 1983). It may be that the behavioral changes are causing changes in the brain. We have not yet been able to trace the links from physiology to psychology, from brain to behavior, from nerve cells to thoughts.

One possibility for tracing these connections is to study children who are brain-damaged. If damage occurs to the areas of the brain that govern speech—and the association areas especially—children may not speak normally and the extent of damage will depend in part on the age of the child at the time of the injury. Because most of the child's brain growth takes place before the age of 5 and then slows down, it seems likely that preschool children whose brains are damaged will lose only part of their ability to speak, whereas adolescents and adults are more likely to lose the ability completely. More longitudinal research is needed for tracking the extent of brain injuries and the recovery of function in infants and children.

Brain lateralization

The cortex is divided into two halves, or hemispheres, connected by a tough band of myelinated tissue called the **corpus callosum**. Each hemisphere has its own specialized functions, a characteristic called **lateralization**. For example, muscles on one side of the body are controlled by areas of the brain in the opposite hemisphere. Although the hemispheres seem physically symmetrical, closer analysis shows that they are not completely so. The area governing language is larger in one hemisphere than in the other, for example. In most people, electrical activity is greater in the left than the right hemisphere when they listen to spoken sounds, and it is greater in the right cortex when they listen to music. This division is related to processing and producing language and music. In right-handed people, language is usually governed by the left hemisphere, and music and nonspeech sounds, emotions, and spatial abilities like map reading and figure drawing by the right hemisphere (Figure 8.7). Studies have shown, for example, that people whose right hemisphere has been damaged show inappropriate emotional responses, misperceive other people's emotions, and cannot draw or build a model from a plan (Geschwind, 1979; Kimura, 1975). In most adults, the left hemisphere is more efficient at logic, sequential tasks, and the processing of rapidly changing stimuli, and the right is more efficient at spatial processing, emotion, and intuition (Ornstein, 1978).

It is worth noting that in most daily activities, both hemispheres are involved. As you read this text, for instance, the right hemisphere may play a special role in decoding visual information, maintaining an integrated story, and appreciating humor, emotion, and metaphor. Meanwhile, the left hemisphere plays a special role in understanding sentence structure and word meanings. No activity and no person is entirely "right-brained" or "left-brained," as the popular press might like us to think. The two hemispheres in each of us are specialized but integrated.

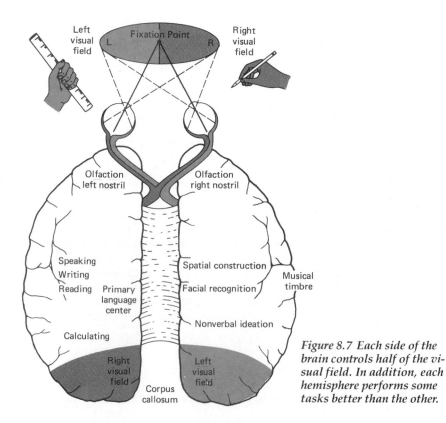

Figure 8.7 Each side of the brain controls half of the visual field. In addition, each hemisphere performs some tasks better than the other.

But what about children? In one study, researchers simultaneously played different sentences into children's two ears to see which ear they favored for processing sentences with emotional content and sentences with just verbal content (Saxby and Bryden, 1984). Even 5-year-old children favored the right hemisphere for processing emotional material and the left hemisphere for processing verbal material. In another study, researchers found that infants showed greater electrical activity in the left hemisphere when they heard words that they knew (Molfese and Molfese, 1985). Some scientists now suggest that lateralization develops before birth (Levine, 1983). However, research on children who suffer brain injuries in the first two years of life suggests that there is considerable plasticity in the development of lateralization over this period.

Physical abilities

Between the ages of 2 and 6 years, children shed much of their babyishness and grow more competent in a whole range of ways. The overall result is the emergence of physically skilled and coordinated children—good jumpers, runners, pitchers, catchers. Preschoolers spend many of their waking hours on the go. Curious, energetic, resourceful, and eager, they dance, prance, climb, run, push, dart, throw, stack, and fall down in a heap—only to be back up within seconds dancing and prancing. All this play exercises and develops muscles, senses, and coordination. Large motor skills refine noticeably in the preschool years. In general, the 2-year-old who falls and bumps and tips things over emerges as the 6-year-old who can carry dish and cup without mishap. The 6-year-old is thinner, stronger, taller, and better coordinated than the 2-year-old. The 6-year-old not only may be able to pedal a tricycle, catch a ball, and climb a ladder, but may do so gracefully. These skills develop according to a maturational timetable, helped along by experience. The balance of the 6-year-old allows for riding bicycles, skiing, skating, and skateboarding.

Preschoolers' play and excercise develop their muscles, senses, and co-ordination. Both large and fine motor skills refine noticeably over the years of early child-hood.

Preschoolers also develop their fine motor and perceptual skills. The average 5- or 6-year-old can both hold a pencil and focus on a line of print.

(Before this age, children tend to focus more easily on objects at a distance than up close.) To most children, the worlds of reading and writing now open for the first time. Of course, children vary widely in their fine motor skills. One 4-year-old can tie her shoelaces and cut her food with the side of her fork, but another cannot even manipulate the large pieces of a puzzle or string chunky beads. In general, preschool children—with their chubby fingers and farsighted eyes—are more adept at large than fine motor skills. Much of their play—stacking blocks, holding pencil and paintbrush, playing with the dials on telephone, television, radio, and stove—is an exercise in developing these important fine motor skills.

> Sam loved to play with the things on my desk when he was 3 or 4. I remember the delight he took in stapling together endless pieces of paper, punching holes with a metal punch, trying to manipulate paper clips, bundling things with elastic bands, and, joy of joys, getting to press the keys on the word processor. Pens, pencils, tape dispensers, erasers simply fascinated him. But he was more interested in building with them than writing.

Health and well-being

Physiological changes

After the age of 2, children's heart and breathing rates slow. Average body temperature falls, and even fevers get lower. The average body temperature of the 1-year-old is 99.7 degrees Fahrenheit. That of the average 5-year-old is, like adults', 98.6 (Lowrey, 1978). Kindergartners play for longer periods in one spot, sit still longer without fidgeting, need if any, fewer, shorter naps, and even sleep less restlessly (Routh, Schroeder, and O'Tuama, 1974). Their physical systems "tune up" and function more smoothly and efficiently. A number of the small physical nuisances of the early years begin to disappear. Most children who wet the bed at 2, 3, and 4 years are dry at 5 or 6, their bladder capacity having enlarged or their sleep patterns now allowing them to awaken in response to a full bladder. During the day, too, the children need to make fewer trips to the bathroom, and there are fewer "accidents." Sensitivities to foods, dust, and other allergens seem to die down in many children. As middle and inner ears grow larger, ear infections wane. As windpipes grow larger, too, upper respiratory illnesses are less frequent. Children who as toddlers always seemed to have flu, colds, throat and ear infections as preschoolers stay healthy for longer spells. Those who as infants were colicky or subject to stomachaches now digest more smoothly.

> One winter, Kristy stayed home from nursery school every day except three between February 3 and March 22 because she had ear or strep infections. But in kindergarten, she missed only six days all winter. What a *relief*.

> Sam used to be extremely sensitive to red dyes when he was an infant. Even the red coloring in baby aspirin would send him off the wall. But after he turned 3, he seemed lots less sensitive. Now all he gets from a bright red lollipop is sticky fingers.

Illness

Nevertheless, children still face the classic childhood illnesses. Children are born with immunity to only a few diseases, and because they lack immunity, they contract more of these diseases than older people do. "Childhood"

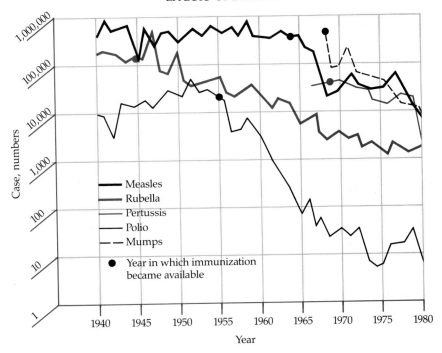

EFFECTS OF IMMUNIZATION

Figure 8.8 Reported cases of certain diseases before and after the availability of immunization in the United States (Centers for Disease Control).

diseases can strike vulnerable people of any age. Measles and mumps, for example, strike adults and old people, but most people get them in childhood, acquire immunity to them, and do not come down with them again.

Immunization has wiped out or dramatically reduced the incidence of many previously common childhood diseases—measles, rubella (German measles), pertussis (whooping cough), and mumps (Figure 8.8). In the United States, polio vaccine reduced the number of cases from 29,000 in 1955 to 8 in 1975, for example. Smallpox has been virtually eliminated throughout the world. Chicken pox is still common, however, and epidemiologists are concerned because the number of children being immunized against measles, rubella, DPT (diphtheria, pertussis, and tetanus), and polio has declined since 1975. Currently 37 percent of American children are not immunized for mumps, 45 percent for polio, and 40 percent for DPT (Miller, 1986). In consequence, these illnesses are becoming more common again.

Among preschoolers the most common health problems are acute infectious diseases, of which 80 percent are respiratory infections. Of these, the common cold is the most frequent. Children between 1 and 2 average eight or nine colds a year, and until age 15, children average four colds a year (Ray, 1977). Although most are self-limiting, colds may produce complications, such as ear infections. As with other viral infections, antibiotics are useless, and treatment—bed rest, increased fluids, medication to reduce fever and congestion—is directed at the symptoms. Middle-ear infections, **otitis media**, strike one-half to two-thirds of all children by the time they are 2 (Krugman, Ward, and Katz, 1977). Viral throat infections are more common among 4- to 7-year-olds.

Accidents and poisons

In the United States every year, accidents kill more children than any other cause. Accidents kill 16,000 and permanently injure 40,000 to 50,000 children every year (U.S. Department of Health and Human Services, 1982). The types

Young children are injured accidentally when they play with dangerous objects or in dangerous places and when they are active, daring, irresponsible, or in poor neurological control of their movements.

Figure 8.9 Deaths from accidents among children aged 1 to 14 years (1982).

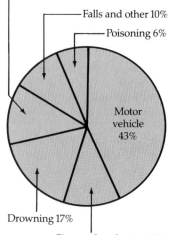

Inhalation and ingestion 12%

Falls and other 10%

Poisoning 6%

Motor vehicle 43%

Drowning 17%

Fires and explosions 12%

of accidents that befall young children include poisoning, drowning, falls, fires and explosions, and inhaling and ingesting substances. Deaths from accidental poisonings have declined markedly in the past few decades. It has been estimated that of the half million children who ingest poison every year, only 2000 die. A large study of children admitted to a city hospital for treatment of poisoning showed that aspirin was the major culprit (35 percent of the cases) (Deeths and Breeden, 1971). Most of the accidental deaths among children result from car accidents (Figure 8.9). Children are killed when they ride as passengers in cars, when they fall from cars, and when the passenger compartment overheats (King, Negus, and Vance, 1981).

When data from hospital emergency room records of 197,000 cases of injury to children between birth and 19 years were analyzed, it was found that children 1 and 2 years old are most likely to have accidents, but at every age boys have more accidents than girls do (Rivara, 1982). Most injuries take place in the home: children fall downstairs; they are cut by broken windows; they hurt themselves on the sharp corners of tables; they fall in the bathtub (NEISS, 1980). Drowning is also common; one-half of all drowning victims in the United States are children under 10 (Iskrant and Joliet, 1968).

Because accidents injure and kill so many children, many researchers have investigated environmental and social factors leading to accidents. They have found that fatigue, hunger, illness, death in a family, or the presence of a new caretaker are all factors associated with the occurrence of accidents to children (Mofenson and Greensher, 1978). As for the personal characteristics of young accident victims, it has been found that about 30 percent have had accidents before, leading some investigators to hypothesize an "accident-prone syndrome." Accident-prone children tend to be physically active but immature in their neurological control of movement. They may also have trouble anticipating, judging, and accommodating to the consequences of their behavior (Wright, Schaefer, and Solomons, 1979). Some children are more cautious than others. Older children are generally more cautious and exercise better judgment than younger children do, but because older children are more capable and independent, they get more latitude than younger children. As a result, they, too, may be injured.

Injuries result when children are not supervised by responsible adults, when they play with dangerous objects or in dangerous places, and when they are very active, daring, or irresponsible. Both laws and education have been helpful in preventing childhood injuries. To prevent injuries in cars, there are seat restraints and specially padded and constructed car seats. Deaths from poisonings have declined in response to an increase in the number of poison control centers, better treatments, protective packaging of medicine and dangerous household products, and health education. Falls from high windows have been prevented by such laws as that passed by the New York City Board of Health requiring apartment landlords to install window guards in apartments where there are children under age 10. As a society, we have become more concerned about the health and safety of our children, and the future should see further advances in promoting health and preventing injury to young Americans.

Yet sometimes what makes a place dangerous is not immediately obvious. Lead and other substances in the environment can be hazards to children's health and development. In one study of the effects of chemical toxins on development, researchers found that many of the prenatal and postnatal exposures had caused no gross abnormalities (Fein, Schwartz, Jacobson, and Jacobson, 1983). But low levels of exposure may produce subtle effects: slightly lower than normal size at birth, slightly increased susceptibility to infections, slight behavioral changes. Different people react differently to any given dose of toxin, and the effects of toxic substances vary

focus Lead poisoning

Death and the injuries that result from accidents are disturbingly obvious, but there also are more subtle health hazards in the environment, in the water we drink, the air we breathe, the places where we live. Because mercury, lead, the PCBs, and many other toxins have no taste, color, or odor, parents and children may not realize when they are being exposed to them. Lead, for example, may be present in food, car exhaust, old paint chips or dust, plumbing lines and fixtures, soil, air, and water. People who live in cities have higher blood levels of lead than people who live in rural areas. In a study of children living in Omaha, Nebraska, the highest levels of lead were found in those who lived in a commercial area of the city near a small factory that produced batteries; the next highest levels were in those who lived in a residential area of the city; the lowest levels were in suburban children (Angle and McIntire, 1979; McIntire and Angle, 1973). Children who lived within 500 feet of a major road had higher lead levels than children who lived farther away (Angle, McIntire, and Vest, 1975). A study of preschool children in 14 Illinois cities revealed that nearly 20 percent had elevated levels of lead in their blood (Fine, Thomas, Subs, Cohnberg, and Flashner, 1972; Fine and Dobin, 1974). Extremely large doses of lead—lead poisoning—damage children's brains.

But do lower levels of lead have any effects? Consistent links between higher than normal levels of lead and lower than normal levels of intelligence have been demonstrated in research. These links are most often observed in poor children, who live in old houses with peeling paint, dirt, and dust (Smith, Delves, Lansdown, Clayton, and Graham, 1983). Because it is often difficult to separate the effects of lead from those of stress, poverty, and other pollutants with which they are associated, however, there is some debate about whether exposure to lead directly *causes* children intellectual and behavioral problems. In one study of 6- and 7-year-old children in London (Smith et al., 1983), those who had higher lead levels, measured by the lead content in the baby teeth they had just lost, scored lower on intelligence tests. When social factors like the parents' level of education and social status were statistically controlled, however, the differences in intelligence of children with high levels of lead and of those with low levels of lead were reduced below the point of statistical significance. It does seem likely that for poor, inner-city children intellectual development is hindered not just by lead levels but by a combination of other factors.

Does this mean that we should not try to remove lead from the environments of poor children? Absolutely not. Statistical analyses cannot provide a reliable estimate of the effects of any one variable, such as lead, as it would behave in isolation from the others it is associated with. In an attempt to study the effects of lead alone, another team of researchers studied children from white, working-class families who did not have the other confounding factors of poverty and stress (Needleman et al., 1979). The children with higher lead levels were more likely to have IQs below 80 and less likely to have IQs above 125. Even when family factors like socioeconomic status were statistically controlled, IQ was significantly—and negatively—correlated with lead level (Needleman, Geiger, and Frank, 1985). Reducing lead exposure should be a priority for children at all social levels.

according to genetic vulnerability, time of exposure during development, type of toxin, and length of exposure. Although high levels of exposure are likely to have recognizable clinical effects, low levels of exposure may produce symptoms like fatigue, distractibility, and tremors. It may be only in subtle changes in behavior and in emotional or sensorimotor problems that symptoms of exposure show themselves.

Child abuse

Unfortunately, sometimes the physical well-being of children is directly threatened by their parents. Each day in this country abusive parents are responsible for the deaths of one or two children. The number of children under 5 killed each year by their own parents may be greater than the number of those who die from disease (Kempe and Helfer, 1972). An estimated 500,000 children are beaten, burned, thrown, kicked, and battered without losing their lives. Exact figures are not known. Since 1967 all 50 states have had laws requiring that suspected cases of **child abuse** be reported; most require doctors, clinic and hospital personnel, teachers, social workers, psychologists, lawyers, police officers, and coroners to do so. In 1974, the U.S. Congress passed the Child Abuse Prevention and Treatment Act. The numbers of cases reported jumped by tens of thousands after these laws were enacted.

Most abusive parents say that they love their children. Few have any specific psychiatric illness. Nevertheless, research suggests that abusive parents share certain characteristics (Bee, Disbrow, Johnson-Crowley, and Barnard, 1981; deLissovoy, 1973; Dibble and Straus, 1980; Kempe and Helfer, 1972; Steele, 1975; Terr, 1970).

ABUSIVE PARENTS

- Report that they were harshly treated and abused by their own parents.
- Are impatient.
- Feel personally inadequate, have little self-esteem, worry that they have failed in one undertaking after another.
- Are immature.
- Know little about child development.

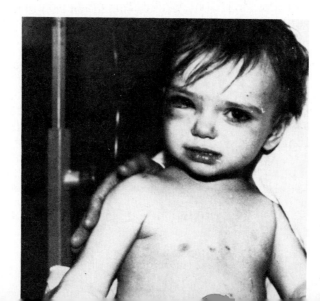

This 15-month-old child is one of 500,000 who are abused by their own parents every year in the United States.

- Hold unrealistic expectations of what infants and children can do—expecting, for example, that an infant will not cry, that a toddler will hold a glass or manage a spoon without spilling, that an energetic child will sit still through a long conversation between adults.
- Interpret children's normal behavior as intentional wrongdoing; interpret failure to follow instructions as willful disobedience, malice, or stubbornness.
- Believe that children ought to act in ways that please their parents.
- Expect their children to understand their problems—but ignore their children's problems.
- Depend on their children for emotional support and expect their children's love to compensate for their own feelings of emptiness or despair, then feel disappointed when their children do not meet their (misguided) expectations.
- Are less sensitive to their children's cues and generally less competent at fostering their children's cognitive, social, and emotional growth than other parents.
- Fear their children, especially when their children act helpless or sexual.
- Consider severe physical punishment necessary to ensure that their children behave "properly."
- Respond angrily to infants' crying.
- Are violent toward their spouse as well as toward their children.
- Are unstable and may be dismissed from jobs often and move from one community to another.
- Have no ties to community, neighbors, or extended family members, no relatives, close friends, or neighbors to call on in times of stress or need. They isolate their children, forbidding them to play with other children or to attend children's gatherings like birthday parties.
- Are too poor to pay babysitters for relief from the 24-hour-a-day responsibilities of parenthood.

The picture that emerges is one of parents who are violent, immature, unrealistic, impatient and weak, isolated, and rootless. These parents are plagued with stress yet without the psychological or social resources for dealing effectively with that stress.

In an estimated one-quarter of the cases of child abuse, qualities in the child trigger the abuse (Gil, 1971). All children put stress on their parents, but overburdened parents are more likely to abuse a particularly troublesome child. We can also compile a profile of the abused child (deLissovoy, 1973; Elmer and Gregg, 1967; Hoffman-Plotkin and Twentyman, 1984; Main and George, 1985; McCabe, 1984; Morse, Sahler, and Friedman, 1970; Gil, 1971; Ounsted, Oppenheimer, and Lindsay, 1974; Spinetta and Rigler, 1972).

ABUSED CHILDREN

- Were underweight at birth and therefore as infants cry often, mature slowly, need special feeding and care, and look thin and pinched.
- Are aggressive, annoying, hyperactive, mentally retarded, or learning-disabled.
- Are clingy, irritable, restless, sleep poorly, cry excessively, and vomit frequently.
- Are unresponsive, difficult to manage, give unclear social cues, and react poorly to discipline.

focus *Child abuse—a vicious cycle*

As a child, I never knew what to expect from my mother. There didn't seem to be any relationship between what I did and the result it achieved. Of course, my mother blamed my "bad behavior" for the unending *years* of punishment she doled out, but I learned as an adult that the chaos in our home was not so much the outcome of what I did as it was how she felt about herself and her own life problems. I was just the available scapegoat, the place to vent her rage, frustration, and impatience with the outside world. It was not unlike the way she'd been treated when she was a little girl, so she didn't see anything wrong with her behavior.

There were times when I thought the things she did were wrong. Even if I didn't say anything, she knew and it made her crazy. Then she'd fly into one of her fits of temper and accuse me of doing things I'd never done. . .punish me for the story *she'd* made up! If I denied it. . .she called me a liar. No one believed me. I was living with a lunatic. It was a living nightmare (Crawford, 1985, p. 36).

These angry words, from the abused daughter of actress Joan Crawford, give us a glimpse of the vicious cycle that enmeshes child abusers. Abusive parents describe their own childhoods as filled with physical punishment and abuse. In a cycle that repeats itself in one generation after another, the abused children often grow up and abuse in turn.

In order to understand and, they hope, ultimately to break the vicious cycle, psychologists have tried to uncover the origin of child abuse. In one recent study, Mary Main and Carol George (George and Main, 1979; Main and Goldwyn, 1984) compared a group of abused children and their mothers with a matched group of nonabused children and their mothers. The abused children, only 1 and 2 years old, already had begun to imitate the destructive

– Are unattractive or unappealing.
– Have "old-looking" faces, leading parents to expect mature behavior from them.

Infants and children who demand lots of attention and unusual sensitivity from parents may be abused by parents who lack even the ordinary social and psychological resources. The important question, though, is whether the abused children's physical, psychological, and social shortcomings *result* from the abuse they receive or whether they *invite* that abuse. As with so many of the problems that children have, separating cause from effect is difficult. The answer, however, is probably that these shortcomings are both causes *and* effects of the abuse that children receive. Abuse is part of a vicious cycle set in motion by problems in both parents and children, a vicious cycle that is perpetuated across generations.

To break the vicious cycle of abusive parents raising children who later abuse their own children, parents must receive therapy to raise their low self-esteem and to learn—for the first time—how to take competent care of children. With training, most parents can learn gentler means of discipline and can break out of their self-imposed isolation from family and friends. Parents Anonymous, a self-help organization with chapters in major cities, allows ways of their parents. They more often hit, slapped, kicked, and assaulted their playmates than nonabused children. They also assaulted and threatened their caregivers more often than the other children did. They seemed to *harass* their caregivers, to act aggressive without provocation, apparently just to hurt the other person. An abused toddler might suddenly spit at a caregiver, threaten another child with a shovel, or slap another child after having been scolded. Seven out of ten abused children harassed their caregivers, compared to two of the ten nonabused children. The abused children also avoided other people's friendly overtures, by moving away or turning away as another child or a caregiver approached them, or ambivalently approached others—crawling toward someone with head averted and then suddenly turning away. None of the children in the comparison group of nonabused children showed this ambivalent behavior.

Although several of the nonabused toddlers responded to another child's distress with sadness, concern, or empathy, none of the abused toddlers did so. What is more, all but one of the abused toddlers responded more than half of the time to another child's crying with fear, anger, or physical abuse—slapping, hitting, or kicking.

> Martin, a 2-year-old boy who'd been abused, slapped a crying child on the arm. Then he turned away from her, looked at the ground, and said, ''Cut it out! Cut it out!'' with more and more agitation and vehemence. He then patted the girl on the back, but she didn't like that, and so he backed away, hissing and baring his teeth. He patted her back again, but the patting turned into beating, and he beat the little girl as she screamed (Main and Goldwyn, 1984, p. 207).

What can we learn from these observations of abusive toddlers? We learn that hostility and abuse are passed from one generation to the next, beginning with the aggression evident in early childhood and continuing as the abused toddlers grow up and abuse their own children.

child abusers to admit what they have done, to experience social support, and to learn from other abusive parents how they can stop the cycle of abuse. Luckily, most parents *can* handle the demands of their children, especially when they have the support of caring family and community members. When they themselves have the necessary physical, psychological, and social resources, parents can raise healthy, thriving children.

Summary

1. Growth creates a state of constant, asynchronous change in children's bodies. Cells die and are replaced, live for long periods, or form only during certain periods of growth.

2. Growth curves chart the changes in children's height, weight, and other physical signs of maturity. Growth curves plotted for subgroups in the population help in identifying children whose growth is abnormal.

3. The most precise indicators of children's growth are the length, thickness, and hardness of the bones.

4. Children grow faster in the first three years than at any other time until the adolescent growth spurt. As they change in size, they change in physical proportions, too—from the infant with large head and tiny feet to the 5-year-old with long legs and arms.

5. Normal physical growth is largely under genetic control. Abnormalities in growth, such as dwarfism and giantism, usually are genetic in origin or result from abnormalities in prenatal development. Occasionally, children do not grow because they are severely neglected by their parents. Inborn sex differences account for some differences in physical growth, and these differences are enhanced by differences in boys' and girls' experiences.

6. Nutrients are necessary for children's physical growth. The earlier and more severe a child's malnutrition, the worse the prospects for normal physical growth or full development of intellectual abilities.

7. Children's physical growth is also affected by chronic, serious diseases—heart defects, lung and kidney diseases, untreated diabetes, dysentery, hookworm. Minor ailments usually do not interfere with children's physical growth.

8. Obesity is unhealthy at any age, and overweight children are at risk for lifelong obesity. The causes of obesity are many: inherited body type, low activity level, preferences for sweet taste, and poor eating habits. Prevention of obesity requires a controlled diet from infancy onward.

9. Brain development and function depend on the number, size, structure, location, covering, arrangement, and branching of nerve cells and the connections among nerve cells.

10. As various areas of the child's brain develop, behavior changes. Although it seems sensible that brain maturation *causes* these concurrent changes—for example, advances in language and cognition—it has not yet been proved.

11. Each half, or hemisphere, of the brain has its own specialized functions, which appear from infancy onward.

12. During early childhood, children grow more competent in a wide range of physical skills, and many of their earlier physical sensitivities and physiological vulnerabilities diminish.

13. Children suffer their share of illnesses, although they can be immunized against some of the most serious—polio, diphtheria, whooping cough, tetanus, and others. Preschoolers get many colds and ear and upper respiratory infections. Many also are hurt in accidents or by poisoning.

14. Child abuse threatens the physical well-being of many children. Child abuse is part of a vicious cycle set in motion by both child problems (irritability, unattractiveness, aggressiveness) and parent problems (ignorance, impatience, inadequacy). It passes from one generation to the next.

Key terms

asynchrony	kwashiorkor	fissures	corpus callosum
growth curve	metabolism	Nissl substance	lateralization
fontanels	neurotransmitters	Broca's area	otitis media
dwarfism	neuroglia	Wernicke's area	child abuse
giantism			

Suggested readings

FEATHERSTONE, HELEN. *A Difference in the Family: Living with a Disabled Child.* New York: Penguin, 1981. A discussion of the difficulties confronted by the rest of family when there is a handicapped child.

KEMPE, RUTH, and KEMPE, C. HENRY. *The Common Secret: Sexual Abuse of Children and Adolescents.* New York: W. H. Freeman, 1984. A book that helps explain the increase in sexual abuse in this society and sheds new light on the family's role. It is vividly illustrated by case studies.

KEMPE, RUTH, and KEMPE, C. HENRY. *Child Abuse.* Cambridge, Mass.: Harvard University Press, 1985. A discussion of the reasons for all kinds of child abuse and neglect and suggestions for their prevention and treatment.

chapter nine
Cognitive development

Two-year-olds are on the threshold of a whole new phase of thinking and knowing. Soon they will be able to count, to make believe, and to imagine things in ways that take them far beyond the here-and-nowness of infancy. No longer will their imaginations be bound by their immediate perceptions of people and things. Soon they will be talking about dreams, playing super-heroes, and pretending that dolls are real. In this chapter, we will look at the cognitive development of young children: at the symbolic thought they show in fantasy play, drawings, and words; at the intuitive thought they show in dreams and animistic beliefs. We will discuss the stages of cognitive development and language development that young children go through and describe their attention and memory capacities. Finally, we will discuss the context within which cognitive development unfolds—the contexts of toys and television, parents and peers.

Symbolic thought

During infancy, as we saw in Chapter 6, children develop the ability to mentally represent objects and actions. In early childhood, they begin to use **symbols** to represent them. This ability to symbolize opens up new worlds for children. They begin to draw, to pretend, and most important, to use language meaningfully. They use symbols to remember things that have happened and to imagine those that never will.

According to Piaget (Piaget and Inhelder, 1969), symbolic thought is the major new cognitive activity in the years from 1 to 4. A symbolic representation may be verbal—a word, a made-up name—or it may be physical—a drawing, a doll, a stick used as a gun, a plastic letter stuck to the refrigerator door. At age 1 year, 3 months, Piaget's daughter, Jacqueline, used her own finger as a symbol:

> J. was playing with a clown with long feet and happened to catch the feet in the low neck of her dress. She had difficulty in getting them out, but as soon as she had done so, she tried to put them back in the same position. There can be no doubt that this was an effort to understand what had happened: otherwise the child's behavior would be pointless. As she did not succeed, she put out her hand in front of her, bent her fore-finger at a right angle to reproduce the shape of the clown's feet, de-scribed exactly the same trajectory as the clown and thus succeeded in putting her finger into the neck of her dress. She looked at the motion-less finger for a moment, then pulled at her dress, without of course being able to see what she was doing. Then, satisfied, she removed her finger and went on to something else (Piaget, 1962, p. 65).

Piaget divided symbols into two categories, those that are personal and those that are shared and conventional. He called the first *symbols* and the second *signs*. The most important signs are words. Words are used and understood by whole groups of people to represent the same specific things, actions, and events. Piaget suggested that children think first in symbols and that these prepare them for using signs.

Fantasy play

Kristy at 2½ was always underfoot and as bossy as could be—a difficult combination to take sometimes. When I needed a few minutes respite, I wheeled her miniature plastic shopping cart over to her and com-manded, "Okay, Kristy. Go shopping." She usually responded by tak-ing the cart all over the kitchen and living room, tossing things in, and naming all her groceries.

In their symbolic play—here, games of "office" and "school"—young children show their understanding of objects and roles.

Toddlers' pretend play is the earliest evidence of symbolic thinking. Pretending to be a bird, or pretending that a postcard is a car or that a piece of cloth is a pillow are examples of the simplest kind of fantasy play, **symbolic play**. A 2½-year-old is looking at a book showing a picture of a child licking an ice cream cone. She puts her lips to the picture of the ice-cream and says, "Yummy." Young children pretend that they are Mommy or Daddy or Big Bird. They may have an imaginary playmate or make up a new brother or sister.

Pretending, at this age, can be serious business. Children often cannot separate fantasy from reality. Piaget's daughter stood beside him making the sound of bells at the top of her lungs. When asked to move and be quiet, she refused angrily and stated, "Don't. I'm a church." And woe be to anyone who tries to sit where an imaginary playmate has already settled himself.

> Three-and-a-half-year-old Sam told his mother about his doll, Betsy, "She was just talkin' to me." "She was? That's nice. When I was a little girl, sometimes I had trouble knowing whether my dolls could talk and whether they really couldn't. Do you have that trouble?" "No," Sam announced firmly, "Betsy can talk."

According to Erik Erikson (1968), children use their symbolic play to work through fears and frustrations, relive unpleasant events, or carry out in play acts forbidden in reality. One child pretends to cook at a make-believe stove after being scolded for going near the real stove. Another "shaves" with an empty—and harmless—razor. Another guides her doll through a reenactment of a scene from the previous day when she had cut her lip, telling the doll not to be upset, because her lip would be all right.

> When Natalie was 3 years old, every night before bed she had to stand at each window in her bedroom and swing her arms, saying "Good-bye, school buses. Good-bye, trucks. Good-bye, cars." She often dreamed of being overrun by these things, and so she needed to throw them out the window before she could let herself sleep.

> Every night before Sam fell asleep, we had to pile his half-dozen or more stuffed animals and dolls against the wall at the head of the bed. He was very insistent on this procedure, but it was only by chance that he let on why. "Lambie" had slipped off the pile, its body wedged in the space between headboard and wall. "Move him," Sam's voice quivered, "or else The Scareds will get him." The Scareds were the monsters under the bed.

Fantasy play lets children feel in control of situations that threaten to overwhelm them. In play they can push the mother down the stairs, drown the baby in the bathtub, and make the bedroom unsafe for monsters.

Between the ages of 1 and 4, the nature of children's fantasy play changes. They progress from symbolic play with objects, to pretend play in which they act like a grown-up, and finally to dramatic play with roles announced ahead of time—"Let's play. . ." (Field, DeStefano, and Koewler, 1982). The 2½-year-old sticks a miniature plastic man in the driver's seat and loads the truck with miniature pieces of furniture. The 3½-year-old puts on a hat that turns him into a "moving man" who uses his toy hammer and screwdriver to move the "family" into their cardboard box "new house." The 4½-year-old says, "Let's play 'moving man.' I'm the driver. Peter, you're my helper. Sarah, you're the mother. George, you're the baby. This box is the suitcase we have to move into the new house. This cup is your baby bottle, George. . . ."

Over this period, too, children's fantasy play becomes more elaborate and intricately detailed. "Let's pretend," by 4 or 5, often turns to doctor and nurse, fire fighters, school, baby, Superman and Wonder Woman, He-Man and Skeletor. Many dramatic themes come from television programs and products advertised to children. Playing superheroes and adult roles invests children with feelings of power. In their dramatic roles, children don costumes—the same tablecloth that makes Natalie She-Ra, Princess of Power, later makes Sam's Superman cape—and they assume the voices, postures, and actions of the characters they enact. Preschoolers enact fairly limited improvised dramas, for they cannot yet imagine entire plots. But in their play, as preschoolers recall and organize ideas and give new meanings to words and objects, they lay the groundwork for creativity and storytelling.

How does fantasy play affect children's development? In one piece of research to address these questions, 3- to 5-year-olds were randomly assigned to one of four groups (Saltz, Dixon, and Johnson, 1977). Those in the pretend play group acted out everyday experiences like trips to the grocery store or the zoo. Those in the dramatic play group acted out popular fairy tales like "Little Red Riding Hood." Those in the discussion group heard and discussed the same fairy tales. Children in the control group just went about their usual activities. After seven months, all the children were tested. The children in the two fantasy play groups, especially those in the dramatic play group, had higher IQ scores and did better on tests of taking the perspective of another person, telling a story, and distinguishing reality from fantasy. Acting in play seemed to help the children to understand how others feel, to learn new words, to communicate new thoughts, and to separate real from unreal. Because dramatic play has a story plot (unlike simple pretend play), it may also help children to organize and order events in time and to understand cause and effect. Preschool children's fantasy play apparently both reflects and promotes development.

Drawing

Children's drawings, which festoon the walls of nursery schools, bedrooms, and kitchens, also reflect the development of symbolic thought. The earliest drawings are scribblings that reveal children's pleasure in putting crayon to paper and watching marks appear. Scribblers cover the paper with marks that are random and repetitive, first with straight lines, then curves and spirals (Kellogg, 1970). But soon young children are explaining what their pictures show. "This is a house and a mommy and a daddy going for a walk," said one 3-year-old of his page of large and small lines.

Three-year-olds have obvious artistic limitations. A circle can be a person or a tree; a line is a bicycle or a chimney. In Western societies, researchers have observed that children's drawing progresses through three stages toward increasingly realistic representation (Lark-Horovitz, Lewis, and Luca, 1973). First, when they are between 1½ and 3, children simply scribble. Next, when they are 3 or 4 years old, children begin to represent things in their drawings. After hearing parents and teachers ask for drawings of a house, a man, a car, they draw outlines of shapes that partly resemble real objects. The drawings are general—any man and any house, not ''Mr. Jones'' or ''our house''—and usually represent only part of the object. In the third stage, usually by school age, children draw realistically. They incorporate perspective, color, proportion, and relations between objects.

Are these stages automatic and inevitable in normal children's development? Cross-cultural work suggests that they are not. One researcher (Alland, 1983) collected drawings from preschool children in cultures around the world, from the United States to Ponape, one of the Caroline Islands in the South Pacific. He found that drawing does not necessarily grow more representational as children get older. Children from Ponape, when asked to draw something, tended to draw connected abstract designs. They did not include representational or symbolic objects in their drawings. Balinese children used lots of colors and filled the page with a dense pattern of small, separated marks or simple ovals and circles; they also did not draw real objects. Taiwanese children filled the page with small units, but the units were not representational. Children from the United States and Japan, in contrast, drew houses and trees, cars and boats. Why do children in some cultures but not others draw representationally? This researcher suggested that it is because adults and other children teach them, both intentionally and unintentionally, to do so. Children everywhere begin as scribblers, but after the scribbling stage, the pattern of picture making is shaped by adult expectations, lessons, and conventions for how drawings should represent reality. Children in our culture hear the demand to draw objects, ''Draw me a house. Now draw me a man going up the stairs. Now put an airplane in the sky over the house. And don't forget the smoke coming out of the chimney . . .'' and become increasingly skilled at doing it.

Children's drawings of figures, at first, leave out parts of the body—the torso, for instance—but include others—head, eyes, legs, arms, hair, and hands. The ''tadpole'' drawing (see Figure 9.1) is an example. It shows how a 4-year-old commonly draws a person: a round body—which looks like a big face—out of which stick two vertical lines for legs and two horizontal lines for arms. According to Piaget, these incomplete drawings reflect young children's incomplete and global mental images. Other developmental psychologists have suggested that children omit details because their memories or their physical abilities are limited or because they have trouble turning what they

Children's first drawings and paintings are scribblings that please their creators with their shapes and colors. Soon after, children in this society learn to make representations of real objects.

Figure 9.1 Four-year-old children's drawings of people usually consist of a large head or face, to which they attach sticks or other thin lines for arms or legs (Golomb, 1974). The question is: Why do they leave out the body?

"TADPOLE" DRAWINGS

imagine into a drawing (Freeman, 1980; Golomb, 1974; Goodnow, 1977). Perhaps children have accurate mental images of what to draw but inadequate strategies for drawing them. In support of this view, researchers have shown that children can be taught to draw complete figures. In one study (Brown, 1981), kindergartners first were asked what they would include in drawings of themselves to grace their work folders, and they and their teacher went through the details of the body to be represented. With questions and answers, beginning with top of the head and moving to hair, eyebrows, eyes, ears, neck, and so forth, the children suggested details. They clearly knew parts of the body and what people look like. Then they drew pictures of themselves—with a wealth of detail. Their teacher was astonished; all the children's earlier drawings of people had been global and barren.

Words

The most important form of symbolic representation is language—using words to stand for things and actions.

It is impossible for any of us to remember uttering our first word, but the significance of this achievement was vividly recalled by Helen Keller, who lost her sight and hearing after she was stricken with an infectious disease at the age of 1½. Just before her seventh birthday, Keller's teacher, Anne Sullivan, arrived.

> We walked down the path to the well-house. . . .Someone was drawing water and my teacher placed my hand under the spout. As the cool stream gushed over one hand she spelled into the other the word *water*, first slowly, then rapidly. I stood still, my whole attention fixed upon the motions of her fingers. Suddenly I felt a misty consciousness as of something forgotten—a thrill of returning thought; and somehow the mystery of language was revealed to me. I knew then that ''w-a-t-e-r'' meant the wonderful cool something that was flowing over my hand. That living word awakened my soul, gave it light, hope, joy, set it free! . . .
>
> Everything had a name, and each name gave birth to a new thought (Keller, 1905, p. 37).

As we described in Chapter 6, children usually have acquired their first recognizable words by their first birthday. By the time they are 1½ to 2, they are adding an average of five to seven new words each day (Carey, 1982). Increasingly, their words are restricted to conventional signs and accurately match accepted meanings. By the time they are 5, children have vocabularies of 5000 to 10,000 words. The words that children utter and understand clearly reflect their symbolic thought. Only when they understand the connection between language and the objects, events, and relationships it represents can they use words appropriately.

It is not always easy for adults to find out whether the preschool child's concepts of word meanings match those of adults, though.

> INTERVIEWER: Can you tell me what a car is, Peter?
>
> PETER (AGE 2 YEARS, 8 MONTHS):
> Okay, A car is a truck and a car is a truck (*laughs*).
>
> INTERVIEWER: What does a car look like?
>
> PETER: A truck.
>
> INTERVIEWER: A truck? What does a car do?
>
> *Peter crawls on hands and knees away from table, demonstrating what a car does* (Anglin, 1977, p. 193).

focus *When children talk to themselves*

The other night I was making supper while Sam played nearby. Suddenly he lunged through the doorway, yelling "Ka-powie!" and charging at some imaginary demon with He-Man in his fist. Then last night, we heard him in bed alone talking—"Steg-o-saurus, steg-a-saurus, steg-ee-saurus"—and giggling and, finally, laughing so uproariously that I had to tell him to quiet down and go to sleep.

Many young children whisper, sing, rhyme, converse, count, and plan to themselves aloud when they play and solve problems. Several psychologists have offered theories about the functions of this often charming **private speech**. The behaviorist John Watson considered private speech inappropriate muttering that parents and teachers ultimately persuade young children to stop using. Piaget considered private speech egocentric and without social purpose. He theorized that the cognitively maturing child drops private speech in favor of social speech. In contrast, the Russian psychologist, Lev Semenovich Vygotsky, thought that private speech served a positive function in children's development. He theorized that private speech helps children to coordinate their speech with their actions and is a kind of communication with the self. Vygotsky suggested that private speech increases during early childhood—as children try to master their behavior—and decreases during middle childhood—as they do master their behavior.

Vygotsky's suggestion was confirmed by observations of 4- to 10-year-old children (Kohlberg, Yaeger, and Hjertholm, 1968). All the children observed spoke to themselves as they played and made designs with stickers. The youngest children simply and playfully repeated words and noises, the older children talked about what they were doing, and the oldest children talked to themselves briefly and almost inaudibly. The frequency of using private speech peaked among the children of above-average intelligence at age 4 and among those of average intelligence at age 5 to 7. Nearly all of the children had stopped using private speech by the age of 9. Vygotsky also suggested that young children's social experiences stimulate their private speech, and this, too, was supported by the finding that the most outgoing children observed used private speech most often.

In observations of children in class, in school corridors and cafeterias, and at play, researchers have found that the egocentric speech Piaget described is nearly nonexistent. In one series of studies, only 1 percent of school-age children's speech was egocentric, and even among 3- to 5-year-olds in nursery school and day-care centers, egocentric speech was virtually nonexistent (Berk and Garvin, 1984; Berk, 1986). School-age children who intended to communicate with others, the researchers found, spoke intelligibly. But when the children had to solve tough problems, their use of private speech increased noticeably. First and third graders working at their desks on arithmetic problems spoke to themselves 60 percent of the time. The first-grade children spoke aloud; the third-grade children and the brighter first graders spoke more softly and infrequently.

Should parents and teachers discourage children from private speech? Probably not. Private speech seems important in helping children learn how to organize, comprehend, and master their behavior.

Showing children pictures and asking them questions—''What is this?'' ''Is this an animal?''—can be more successful than asking ''What is a car?'' when it comes to unlocking the mysteries of their comprehension. Using both these techniques, researchers (for example, Anglin, 1977; Rosch, Mervis, Gray, Johnson, and Boyes-Braem, 1976) have explored what young children understand about the names of things. Preschool children, they have found, understand the meanings of the most common, basic labels for things first—tree, car, dog. (Recall from Chapter 6 that this is the level of word infants are likely to say first.) Only later do they understand superordinate category names like ''plant,'' ''vehicle,'' or ''animal'' or subordinate category names like ''collie'' or ''boxer.'' Shown a picture of a tree and asked, ''Is this a plant?'' most preschool children say, ''No, that's a tree.'' Shown a picture of a caterpillar and a praying mantis, few preschoolers agree that they are ''animals.'' None agrees to label a picture of a woman as an ''animal.'' Throughout the preschool years, children's abilities to define, understand, and use words continue to build. By age 5, children can say that a dog is ''a kind of animal'' and food is ''something we eat.''

Intuitive thought

The thought of 4-, 5-, and 6-year-old children, according to Piaget (1970) is dominated not by fantasy but by **intuition**—by guesses about reality rather than rational inferences. Preschool children know many things about people, animals, toys, and food. They work at tasks and at increasingly complex forms of reasoning. But the solutions they propose often are wrong when judged by adult standards. Although recent research suggests that Piaget underestimated the knowledge and reasoning abilities of preschoolers, it still is true that preschoolers do not think like older children.

Dreams

The intuitive way that young children think shows in the way they describe their dreams. Piaget found three developmental stages in children's understanding of dreams. First, at around 4, young children think that dreams are real events that happen outside of themselves.

> When Natalie was 4, she told us with complete conviction that she had driven the car to her cousin Jerry's house. She described the trip and the route she had taken in perfect detail, right down to having put on the parking brake at Cousin Jerry's house. When we told her that she had dreamed it, she did not believe us.

They sometimes wake up frightened because their dreams are so real to them.

> At 3;7, when [the child] was trying to overcome a tendency to bite her nails, she said when she woke, but was still half asleep: ''When I was little, a dog bit my fingers,'' and showed the finger she most often put in her mouth, as she had probably been doing in her sleep (Piaget, 1962, p. 178).

One characteristic of intuitive thought is this blending of the real and the imagined. Young children cannot separate dreamed from real events: ''We had a circus in my room last night,'' ''I get pictures on my windows at night when it's dark.'' When Piaget asked 4-year-olds about their dreams, these were typical replies:

> When do you dream? *At night*. Where is the dream when you are dreaming? *In the sky*. Can you touch the dream? *No, you can't see and besides*

you're asleep. When you are asleep, could another person see your dream? *No, because you're asleep.* Why can't one see it? *Because it is night.* Where do dreams come from? *From the sky* (Piaget, 1975, pp. 93–94).

In the second stage of understanding dreams, 5- and 6-year-olds understand that dreams come from inside a person's head but, even so, think that they happen outside of it:

What is a dream? *You dream at night. You are thinking of something.* Where does it come from? *I don't know.* What do you think? *That we make them ourselves.* Where is the dream while you are dreaming? *Outside.* Where? *There (pointing to the street, through the window)* (Piaget, 1975, p. 107).

Only when they are about 7 years old do children clearly understand that dreams are thoughts and imaginings that come from within a person.

Animism

Another characteristic of intuitive thought, according to Piaget, is that children think that inanimate things are living and have feelings, intentions, and thoughts just as they do. Piaget called this belief **animism**. Balls roll and waves break because they want to. Snow-covered trees feel cold, and empty cars feel lonely.

The moon moves; it moves because it's alive.

The clouds go very slowly because they haven't any paws or legs; they stretch out like worms and caterpillars; that's why they go slowly.

The moon's hiding in the clouds again. It's cold (Piaget, 1962, p. 251).

Because an object is alive, its motions are intended. The sun sets to go to sleep; the rain falls to bring us flowers; the highway stretches to reach Grandma's house; and the oven makes our supper. Someone—divine or human—has created all things in the universe. Thus, stones were planted and grew into mountains. People built cities, then scooped out lake beds and filled them with water so that the people in the cities could go swimming and have pretty lakes to look at.

When children do not have factual information about things and the way they work, they use their intuition to come up with explanations like these. But when children do have information, researchers have found, they do not appear so naive. Preschool children may well say that inanimate objects they know little about or that they have heard about in fairy tales—clouds, wind, moon—are alive. But apparently they do not think that *all* inanimate objects are alive. Even in this early period, children's intuitions are readily modified by observable, concrete facts. When researchers have interviewed preschool children about familiar objects—not remote things like clouds and wind—they have found that the children's responses do not show the same belief in animism. In one study, researchers asked preschoolers about the differences between a person, a doll, and a rock (Gelman, Spelke, and Meck, in Pines, 1983).

Can a person make a wish? *Yes.* Can a rock make a wish? *No.* How is it that a person can, but a doll and a rock can't? *A rock is just chemicals, made of little stones. Dolls are made out of plastic sometimes.* What about a person? *A person is made out of a seed* (Pines, 1983, p. 50).

Children answered in ways that showed that they believed that objects made to move from outside are inanimate and objects that can move from within are animate. None of the children questioned said that rocks had thoughts or feelings, although some said, perhaps in make-believe, that dolls had feelings.

In another recent study, 3- to 5-year-olds were shown videotapes of moving objects—animate objects—a girl, a rabbit—and inanimate objects—blocks, a windup worm—and were asked questions about what was happening (Bullock, 1985). The questions were designed to elicit the children's understanding of animacy. They were asked whether the objects had a brain, could grow, would get hungry, and were alive, whether they could be fixed with glue, thrown, or bought in another color. The findings suggested that preschoolers do not have an animistic view of all objects. They were just as likely to say that animate objects had inanimate properties as the reverse. Their problem seemed to be a lack of knowledge about the properties of many objects, especially those they had not had the chance to explore. Another study contributed evidence that children have a better grasp of animacy than Piaget thought (Richards and Siegler, 1984). Most 4- and 5-year-olds in the study believed that people and animals were alive; some believed that trees and plants were alive; but none believed that vehicles or objects were alive. When asked to name "living things," they did not mention sun or moon.

There are, however, gaps in preschoolers' information about the biology of digestion and reproduction and the meaning of alive and dead (Carey, 1985). One area in which animistic explanations predominate is children's understanding of where babies come from. No matter how carefully their parents spell out the details of conception and birth, preschool children's understanding of these remote and complex events is limited. Psychologists have interviewed children between 3 and 15 years old in Australia, England, Sweden, the United States, and Canada on this subject (Bernstein and Cowan, 1975; Goldman and Goldman, 1982). When asked, "How are babies made?" preschool children answered:

I don't know. I never saw. Jesus makes them in a factory.

The father does it. He buys the seed from the seed shop and puts it into the mummy.

By eating good food. She swallows it and it grows into a baby, if it's good food.

God makes mommies and daddies with a little seed. He puts it down on the table. The people grow together. He makes them eat the seed and

Even when their parents take pains to explain the details of conception, prenatal development, and birth, young children's understanding of these remote and complex events is sketchy.

then they grow to be people from skel'tons at God's place. They then stand up and go someplace else where they could live (Goldman and Goldman, 1982, p. 494).

Some children whose parents had obviously given them specific information thought that a tiny baby lives within either sperm or egg.

Sperm hits the egg and sets it off. The baby's in the egg (Goldman and Goldman, 1982, p. 495).

With their wonderfully vivid imaginations and an unrepressed sense of their own understanding, preschool children are not troubled by mere lack of knowledge. Intuitive thought is quite enough for filling in the gaps between their constant "whys?"

Perspective taking

Another characteristic of intuitive thought, according to Piaget, is its **egocentrism**. Preschool-age children rarely stop to think that others do not see things through their eyes. "What dis?" the 3-year-old asks from two rooms away, as if her mother can see through walls. She holds a picture book to face herself and asks her mother across the room, "Why is dis doggy running?"

Piaget called this apparent inability to take the perspective of another person *egocentric* and documented young children's egocentric thought with his "three mountains" test. In this test, a three-dimensional model of three mountains of different heights is set on a table that is surrounded by four chairs (Figure 9.2). A child looks at the mountains from all sides and then sits in one chair, and a wooden doll is placed on another chair. The child then looks at ten photographs to find the one that shows the mountains as the doll would see them. Four-year-olds, Piaget found, chose any picture at random. Five-year-olds chose the picture that showed their own view. Six- and 7-year-olds understood that point of view affects what one sees, but they could not always choose the picture showing the doll's point of view. They guessed, changed their minds, tried another picture, and then went back to their first choice. Only after age 7 or 8 did children reliably choose the right picture. Others have shown, similarly, that preschoolers have only a limited appreciation of another person's point of view in this kind of task (Flavell, Botkin, Fry, Wright, and Jarvis, 1968; Flavell, Everett, Croft, and Flavell, 1981; Flavell, Shipstead, and Croft, 1978).

Figure 9.2 In Piaget's three-mountain task, the child is asked how the scene appears to the doll, which the experimenter seats in different positions (B, C, D) around the table. The experimenter may ask the child to describe the scene that the doll sees, to construct it from cardboard models, or to pick the correct picture from a collection of ten (Piaget and Inhelder, 1967).

PERSPECTIVE TAKING

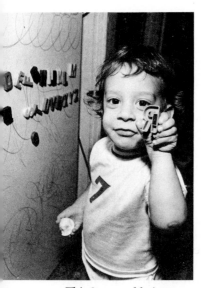

This 2-year-old gives away his egocentric thinking by showing the photographer his "R."

But young children are not always egocentric. When the task is simple, preschool children show that they realize that other people have different points of view from theirs. In one study, when 1- to 3-year-olds were given a cube with a picture pasted to the bottom and asked to show it to a person across the room, for example, all the children over 2 could do it (Lempers, Flavell, and Flavell, 1977). In another study, many 2- and 3-year-olds could hide an object from someone else behind a screen, even though they themselves could still see it (Flavell et al., 1978).

The understanding of *how* things look to another person develops later than the realization that they *do* look different (Flavell et al., 1981). The age at which children can figure out how things look to another person largely depends on the difficulty of the task and the kind of response the children must give. For example, in one study (Borke, 1975), when the display that the child was shown contained familiar objects, such as a toy sailboat on a lake, children as young as 3 said correctly what the doll could see. In other studies, too, it has been shown that preschool children can take another's perspective if they can actually turn the display instead of picking a picture or if they can say what the other's point of view is without having to look at the display at the same time (Hardwick, McIntye, and Pick, 1976; Huttenlocher and Presson, 1973). Children often do *act* egocentric—in real life as well as in experiments. But the findings from all these studies suggest that young children are limited by their ability to perform mental operations (like rotating a scene in their minds) rather than that they simply do not realize that other people have perspectives that are different from their own.

Preoperational logic

Unlike older children, young children do not rely on logical rules. Young children show in numberless ways that they have yet to develop mature abilities to reason logically. While they are in this period of early childhood, they cannot perform logical **operations**, like addition, multiplication, subtraction, which transform information and form an organized network of knowledge. For this reason, Piaget called the logic of 2- to 6-year-old children *preoperational* and the developmental stage they are in the **preoperational period**. Although Piaget to some extent underestimated young children's knowledge and capacities in this area (as in some others we have discussed) his influence on thinking about child development has been so strong that it is useful to present his views and the evidence on which they are based. According to Piaget, preoperational logic shows clearly in children's abilities to classify, reason, and understand numbers.

Classification

To be able to **classify** objects, children must notice that certain objects are alike in one way, others in a second way, and then separate them into groups depending on these similarities. Piaget demonstrated preschool children's limited ability to classify objects by using cutouts of rectangles, triangles, and arcs that were red, blue, and yellow. He found that 2- and 3-year-old children arranged the cutouts in a line or big circle, or they made a house or a wagon with them. But they paid no attention at all to the shapes or colors of the cutouts. Four- to 6-year-olds began to pair the cutouts, sometimes by shape and sometimes by color. But as they arranged the cutouts in, say, a line, they were distracted from one property to another and set down a few blue rectangles, then a yellow one, then two yellow arcs, and finally a red and a blue arc. They had begun to sort the cutouts but were still easily distracted.

Only at about age 7, Piaget found, could the children carry out their plan to arrange all the cutouts by shape, by color, or by both.

Today in the United States, where many youngsters watch "Sesame Street" and go to nursery school, preschool children are more likely to know something about classification. In one study (Denney, 1972), for example, about half of the 2-year-olds could sort cardboard cutouts of four different shapes, two sizes, and four colors. Two-thirds of the 4-year-olds sorted the cutouts correctly or nearly so, according to two of the three properties. In another study (Rosch et al., 1976), children were asked to sort pictures of familiar pieces of clothing, furniture, vehicles, and people's faces into categories. One kind of category was described in terms of the basic, functional properties of the items, such as "things people put on their bodies." The other kind of category was described in more abstract, general terms, such as "clothing." Preschool children were able to sort the objects into the basic, functional categories. But only half of the kindergartners could sort the objects into general categories. Even preschoolers, it appears, can classify objects—but only if they are familiar enough and are described in simple, specific enough terms.

One particular classification skill that Piaget found that preschool children had trouble with was **class inclusion**, the understanding that a general class of items can be divided into subclasses. When he showed preschool children a picture of nine tulips and five daisies, for example and asked them to point to the "flowers," they pointed to both the daisies and the tulips. When he asked them to point to the tulips, they pointed to the tulips. But when he then asked them, "Are there more tulips or more flowers?" they answered, "more tulips." Their ability to integrate the general class, "flowers," with the subclass, "tulips," apparently was limited.

According to Piaget, children failed to solve these problems because they could not perform the necessary mental operations. They did not understand that although there may be *more* tulips than daisies, there are *fewer* tulips than flowers. In more recent research, when children have been encouraged to focus on the general class rather than on the subclass, researchers have found that even preschool children can solve class inclusion problems. When 3- and 4-year-olds, for example, were asked, "Are there more Smarties [Canadian M&Ms] or more of *all* the candies?" they answered correctly (Siegel, McCabe, Brand, and Matthews, 1978). When 7-year-olds who had failed Piaget's class inclusion problem were shown a picture of two big dogs and four small dogs and asked, "Who would have more pets, someone who owned the baby dogs or someone who owned the *family* [of dogs]?" more than half answered correctly (Markman, 1973). When questions are phrased so that children hear collective terms like "family," "group," and "pile," they are more successful at solving class inclusion problems. Class inclusion clearly depends on language abilities as well as logical abilities.

Reasoning

Even without giving children particular problems to solve, researchers can gather evidence of their preoperational logic. As Piaget listened to children's attempts to reason things out, one kind of preoperational reasoning he heard was **transductive reasoning**—reasoning from one particular to another rather than from the general to the particular.

> J. had a temperature and wanted oranges. It was too early in the season for oranges to be in the shops, and we tried to explain to her that they were not yet ripe. "They're still green. We can't eat them. They haven't yet got their lovely yellow color." J. seemed to accept this, but a moment later, as she was drinking her camomile tea, she said, "Camomile isn't

green; it's yellow already. Give me some oranges'' (Piaget, 1962, p. 23).

Confusing oranges, which ripen as they turn yellow, with tea leaves, which turn the tea water yellow, Jacqueline failed to understand that not all things turn from green to yellow for the same reasons. Children are trying hard to put things together, and so they often string together thoughts that apparently have no logical relation.

The sun does not fall down. *Why*? Because it is hot. The sun stops there. *How*? Because it is yellow. *And the moon, how does it stop there*? The same as the sun, because it is lying down on the sky. Because it is very high up, because there is [no more] sun, because it is very high up (Piaget, 1962, p. 229).

From Piaget's observations, one gets the impression that preschoolers' reasoning is a muddle of illogic. More recent research, however, demonstrates that children as young as 4 sometimes can reason correctly and deductively. In the exchange that follows, a 5-year-old girl correctly deduces that there must be two Mr. Campbells. She has heard of Donald Campbell, who had died not long before in an attempt to break the world's water speed record. She also has heard of another "Mr. Campbell," a research worker named Robin Campbell, who had come to her school.

CHILD: Is that Mr. Campbell who came here. . .*dead*? (Dramatic stress on the word "dead.")

ADULT (SURPRISED):
No, I'm quite sure he isn't dead.

CHILD: Well, there must be two Mr. Campbells then, because Mr. Campbell's dead, under the water (Donaldson, 1983, p. 233).

When children listen to stories or look at picture books, their comments reveal a rich store of valid deductions:

But how can it be [that they are getting married]? You have to have a man too.'' (The book contains an illustration of a wedding in which the man looks rather like a woman. The child thinks it is a picture of two women.)
First premise: You need a man for a wedding.
Second premise: There is no man in the picture.
Conclusion: It can't be a wedding (Donaldson, 1983, p. 234).

In fact, children even younger than 4 have been heard to reason deductively— especially when it's in their best interests. A 3-year-old child tries to keep her younger sibling from jumping on and off the couch with her. First she tried physical means, but then she gets out the big guns:

People with shoes on can't jump. I haven't got them on, so I can jump. but you can't; you've got on shoes. So there (Mills and Funnell, 1983, p. 167).

From exchanges like these, we can deduce that young children can reason deductively, even though they may not be able to do so when asked about things they know nothing about—like sun and moon or tea and oranges.

Even in the laboratory, they can reason. In a recent study of 4-year-olds' ability to reason, children were presented with different kinds of logical problems (Hawkins, Pea, Glick, and Scribner, 1984). They could reason correctly when the problem was purely fictional.

Merds laugh when they're happy.
All animals that laugh like mushrooms.
Do merds like mushrooms? [Yes.]

They also could reason correctly when their real-life knowledge did not conflict with the right answer. But they could not correctly solve problems like the following:

> Glasses bounce when they fall.
> Everything that bounces is made of rubber.
> Are glasses made of rubber? [Yes.]

Preschool children have trouble ignoring the evidence that they see in front of them or facts that they know to be true; they have trouble concentrating on just the logic of a proposition.

Piaget also claimed that young children's thinking was illogical because they did not understand the difference between cause and effect. Children, he reported, sometimes think that the cause is the effect.

> The man fell from his bicycle because he broke his arm.
>
> I had a bath because afterwards I was clean.
>
> I've lost my pen because I'm not writing (Piaget, 1926, pp. 17–18).

The boy who said these things clearly sensed that the events were connected, but he either did not understand or could not express their causal relation.

Researchers since Piaget have investigated children's understanding of cause and effect by means other than interviews. In one study by Rochel Gelman, for example, 3- and 4-year-olds were shown how to tell a story from a series of three picture cards from left to right (Gelman et al., 1980). Then they were shown two picture cards—perhaps one of a dog and one of water pouring from a pail—and were asked to pick a third card that would complete the story about the first two cards. (The choices might be pictures of a cat, a wet apple, and a wet dog.) The children were very good at choosing a third card that told a logical story—in this case, the picture of the wet dog. "First you have a dry doggie, and then the water puts water on that doggie, and you end up with a wet doggie," said a 3-year-old to explain her quite logical choice. As children got older, they made fewer mistakes and gave fuller explanations, but even the youngest children could infer cause and effect in these stories.

Preschoolers can also understand quite a lot about causal relations between objects and events. In another experiment (Gelman and Bullock, in Pines, 1983), children saw a contraption that looked as though two runways led inside a box where there was a pop-up Snoopy. Actually, the runways came to dead ends, and the Snoopy appeared when the researcher touched a hidden lever. First the researchers inserted a ball into a hole at the top of one runway that led to Snoopy's box, then they made Snoopy appear, and then they dropped a second ball into a hole at the top of the second runway. When they asked the children, "Which ball made Snoopy come up," 75 percent of the 3-year-olds, 87 percent of the 4-year-olds, and 100 percent of the 5-year-olds said that the first ball had made Snoopy come up. They understood that a physical cause precedes its effect. Next, the researchers removed the runway that led to Snoopy's box and then inserted a ball into a hole at the top of the unconnected runway. When the children saw Snoopy pop up, they were amazed. Apparently they also understood that physical causes do not act at a distance. When the researchers dropped a second ball into the hole at the top of Snoopy's runway, though, the children insisted that the first ball had made Snoopy come up (even though the first ball had rolled down the unconnected runway). What the children did not understand was that for something to be the cause of an event, it must *always* be followed by the event. When the runways were connected to Snoopy's box again, the ball dropped down the first hole, and Snoopy popped up, the children once again claimed that the ball down the hole caused Snoopy to pop up—even though they had seen Snoopy pop up when no ball was put down the hole. Preschool children know more than Piaget gave them credit for, but they do not completely understand cause and effect.

Concepts of number and age

Preschoolers generally understand concepts of concrete objects—bed, house, car, tree—fairly early. Understanding of more abstract concepts, such as number and age, comes later. Many 2- to 3-year-olds can count from 1 to 2. The number 3, if they know it at all, is likely to refer to anything above 2. Natalie at 2½ counted, "1, 2, 3, 8, tree!" A 4-year-old might count accurately from 1 to 39. But even if she has memorized this counting string, and even if she knows the principle of counting—that one number is assigned to each object (Gelman, Merk, and Merkin, 1986)—she has not yet acquired an understanding of the *concept* of number. She does not understand that 3 is a number, that the number is intermediate between 2 and 4, and that the interval between 3 and 5 is the same as that between 1 and 3.

In a series of studies to probe children's developing concepts of number, Piaget showed that the concept of number is still shaky for 4- and 5-year-olds. If children are presented with two rows of objects that differ in number—say, one row with six bottles and one with twelve glasses—and are asked to make the numbers of bottles and glasses the same, 4- and 5-year-olds cannot do it. Instead, they spread out the bottles so that the two lines are the same length (Figure 9.3). If the row of six bottles is already longer than the row of twelve glasses—because the bottles are farther apart than the glasses—children say that there are more bottles than glasses. Only when they are 6 or 7 can children consistently match glasses to bottles without getting thrown off the track by the length of the rows.

In a more recent study of children's concepts of number (Gelman, 1972), 3- to 5-year-olds were shown sets of cards that had different numbers of dots spaced closer together or farther apart (Figure 9.4). So long as they could count the dots, the children could answer correctly which cards had the same

The counting ability of a preschooler typically depends on her memory and confidence. But even though she can count, a preschooler is unlikely to have a concept of number.

Figure 9.3 The preschool child will agree that bottles and glasses lined up on a one-to-one correspondence are the same in number. When the glasses are put close together and the bottles are spread out, the child often thinks that there are more bottles than glasses.

numbers of dots. But when there were more dots than they could count, the children went by the length of the row of dots. The results gave some support to Piaget's findings. Preschool children clearly have a limited understanding of number.

Just as they confuse number with length, preschool children often confuse age with size.

Natalie at age 4½ to her mother: "See? These two books are the same age."

Rom, 4;6, has a small sister called Erica: How old is she? *Don't know.* Is she a baby? *No, she can walk.* Who is the older of you two? *Me.* Why? *Because I'm the bigger one* (Piaget, 1969, p. 203).

CONCEPT OF NUMBER

Figure 9.4 Gelman (1972) gave children sets of three cards and asked them which two cards had the same number of dots. (1) When the number of dots was small enough so that the children could count them, they answered correctly a and b. (2) When there were more dots than the children could count, they went by the length of the line formed by the dots, choosing a and c.

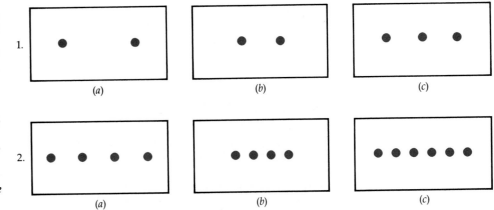

Preschool children may also believe that people can get older *or* younger over time. They talk about "growing up" and "growing down" as well.

> Mikey to his father: "When I grow up and you grow down, I will be your daddy and make *you* go to bed early."

They do not understand that age is related to when one is born.

> Sam at 3½ was invited to his friend Jennifer's fourth birthday party. "You'll have a fourth birthday party in half a year, Sam, and you'll be as old as Jennifer is now," I explained.
>
> "And Jennifer will be the same as me then?"
>
> "No, Jennifer will always be older than you."
>
> "Uh uh," he said, frowning, "no she won't."

Preschool children may be able to tell a researcher how old they are, but when asked how many years it has been since they were born, they say things like, "Oh, about a hundred" (Mebert and Sandoval, 1985). Even in the early school years, children may have difficulty understanding the concept of age:

> *I have a little sister, Liliane, and a nine-month-old brother, Florian.* Are you the same age? *No. First of all there's my brother, then my sister, then me, then Mama and then Papa.* Who was born first? *Me, then my sister and then my brother.* When you are old, will Florian still be younger than you? *No, not always.* Does your father grow older every year? *No, he remains the same.* And you? *Me, I keep growing bigger* (Piaget, 1969, p. 207).

> How old are you? *Seven and a half.* Have you any brothers or sisters? *No.* Any friends? *Yes, Gerald.* Is he older or younger than you? *A little older; he's twelve years old.* How much older is he than you? *Five years.* Was he born before or after you? *I don't know.* But think about it. Haven't you just told me his age? Was he born before or after you? *He didn't tell me.* But is there no way of finding out whether he was born before or after you? *I could ask him.* But couldn't you tell without asking? *No* (Piaget, 1969, p. 209).

Conservation

Conservation is the name given to the understanding that even though an object's outward appearance may change, its length, quantity, mass, area, weight, and volume do not change as well. When children know that milk in a tall, narrow glass is the same amount as milk in a short, wide glass, they understand conservation of liquid quantity. When they know that four cookies are four cookies, no matter whether they are spread out or squeezed together on a plate, they understand conservation of number.

Piaget's experiments on conservation suggest that there are three stages in the development of children's understanding of conservation (Piaget and Inhelder, 1969). In his classic experiment on conservation of the amount of substance, Piaget showed children two balls of clay and asked them to add more clay to the balls until both were the same. Once the children said that the balls had the same amount of clay, Piaget rolled one of the balls into a long snake and asked the children, "Now, do both these pieces have the same amount of clay?"

Four- and 5-year-old children, in the first stage, thought that the long snake had more clay and could not be convinced otherwise. They could only focus, or *center*, on the one dimension—the salient dimension of length; they could not take thinness into account at the same time. They did not appreciate that the act of making the snake could be reversed and the clay turned back

A psychologist tests a boy's understanding of the conservation of liquid quantity. When the liquid is poured into the tall, thin beaker, it looks to the boy as though it is more than the liquid in the short jar. The psychologist then encourages the boy to pour the liquid into the other jar. But until he understands conservation, the boy continues to think that the liquid has changed in amounts.

into a ball. Five- and 6-year olds, in the second, transition stage, could not decide whether the snake or the ball had more clay. They might say that the amounts were the same when the snake was short, but when the snake was long, they would say that the snake had more clay. They might guess correctly before Piaget rolled out the clay, but when they saw the snake, they would say that it had more clay. They were still strongly influenced by the way things *look*. Six- and 7-year-olds, in the third stage, realized that the ball and the snake had equal amounts of clay, no matter how long the snake looked. They understood that the process of rolling the clay was reversible and the snake could be rolled back into a ball. They also understood that the dimensions of length and thickness were reciprocal—that the snake was long—but also skinny. They could explain why the amounts of clay were the same. They understood conservation of substance.

In similar experiments on conservation of number, length, weight, and so on (Figure 9.5), Piaget found that children went through the same stages of mastering conservation for all these quantities. He described children's thinking in the preconserving stage as preoperational because children at this stage could not perform mental operations like **reversibility**, understanding that some transformations are reversible, and **reciprocity**, understanding that dimensions like height and width or length and thickness are reciprocal or complementary.

Since Piaget carried out his experiments on conservation, many researchers in this country have tried to duplicate, understand, and explain his results. In one study (O'Bryan and Boersma, 1971), for example, researchers recorded the eye movements of children who were taking part in experiments like Piaget's on conservation of length, area, and liquid quantity. Nonconservers, they found, spent most of their viewing time looking at only one dimension, the "dominant" one. Children in the second, transitional stage shifted focus from one dimension to another now and then. But conservers shifted their focus often and quickly, supporting Piaget's claim that **decentration**—being able to focus on more than one dimension at a time—is necessary if children are to conserve quantity.

Other investigators have been more critical of Piaget's work (see for example, Scholnick, 1983). They have suggested that sometimes the wording of Piaget's questions actually hid children's conservation abilities rather than revealing them. For example, when children see two plates, each of which has the same number of cookies, they may say "yes" to the question, "Does one have more?" To the young child, "more" may describe the amount of space

*Figure 9.5 **These procedures are traditional methods of testing children's abilities to conserve length, liquid quantity, substance amount, area, and volume.***

Type of Conservation	Child sees	Experimenter then transforms display	Child is asked conservation question
Length	Two sticks of equal length and agrees that they are of equal length	Moves stick over.	*Which stick is longer?* *Preconserving* child will say that one of the sticks is longer. *Conserving* child will say that they are both the same length.
Liquid quantity	Two beakers filled with water and says that they both contain the same amount of water.	Pours water from *B* into a tall, thin beaker *C*, so that water level in *C* is higher than in *A*.	*Which beaker has more water?* *Preconserving* child will say that *C* has more water: "See, it's higher" *Conserving* child will say that they have the same amount of water: "You only poured it!"
Substance amount	Two identical clay balls and acknowledges that the two have equal amounts of clay.	Rolls out one of the balls.	*Do the two pieces have the same amount of clay?* *Preconserving* child will say that the long piece has more clay. *Conserving* child will say that the two pieces have the same amount of clay.
Area	Two identical sheets of cardboard with wooden blocks placed on them in identical positions. The child acknowledges that the same amount of space is left open on each piece of cardboard.	Scatters the blocks on one piece of cardboard.	*Do the two pieces of cardboard have the same amount of open space?* *Preconserving* child will say that the cardboard with scattered blocks has less open space. *Conserving* child will say that both pieces have the same amount of open space.
Volume	Two balls of clay in two identical glasses with an equal amount of water. The child acknowledges that they displace equal amounts of water.	Changes the shape of one of the balls.	*Do the two pieces of clay displace the same amount of water?* *Preconserving* child will say that the longer piece displaces more water. *Conserving* child will say that both pieces displace the same amount of water.

the cookies take up, not the number of cookies. ''Bigger'' may mean ''longer'' or ''taller'' to young children, not having greater mass or quantity. In one study of third graders' conservation abilities, researchers first asked Piaget's standard questions and then tried to reword them to make sure that the wording was not obscuring the children's conservation abilities (Pennington, Wallach, and Wallach, 1980). When the children were asked, ''Are there still 13 objects?'' and not ''Are there the same as before?'' the number of children who answered correctly increased. Even questioning a child right before and right after the experimenter transforms the objects may suggest to the child that the first answer was wrong. Children more often answer questions about conservation correctly when they are asked only once how many objects there are (Rose and Blank, 1969; Samuel and Bryant, 1984).

Piaget's standard tasks for assessing conservation abilities may also make children seem less cognitively advanced than they, in fact, are because they distract the children unnecessarily. When a screen was put in front of the containers in a conservation of liquid task so that the children would not be distracted by seeing the different liquid levels, half of the 4-year-olds, 90 percent of the 5-year-olds, and all the 6- and 7-year-olds who had previously failed on the task answered correctly, saying something like ''It's still the same water'' or ''The water was only poured'' (Bruner, 1964). When the screen was taken away, and the children were asked again which container had more water, the 4-year-olds said that the tall container had more, but most of the older children stuck by their correct answers.

To some extent, children can be tricked into answering as though they can or cannot conserve by the way an experimenter presents a task, asks questions, and encourages a child to agree. Therefore it is difficult to say just when children develop the ability to conserve or exactly what conservation means. Piaget's age ranges are no longer accepted as invariable. But it does seem that in the preschool years, most children do *not* figure out the implica-

research focus *Conservation of length*

Are there more accurate tests of children's conservation abilities than Piaget's? William Schiff (1983) is one researcher who has looked for them. Schiff tested 3½- to 5½-year-old children's understanding of conservation of length. Using Piaget's traditional method, he first asked children whether in each pair of two identical sticks, with their ends either aligned or not, the sticks were ''the same length'' or ''one is longer than the other.'' The children said that the stick that stuck out farther was longer. Their answers suggested that they could not conserve length. Then Schiff showed the children two identical sticks with their ends aligned or not and also showed them a selection of wooden boxes of different lengths. The children were asked to put each stick into the box where ''it fits just right.'' Finally, two sticks of unequal length were placed on the table and the question was repeated.

On Schiff's tasks, children were able to conserve length. The same children who had said that the identical sticks were not the same length when they had had to solve Piaget's problem realized that the sticks would both ''fit just right'' into the same box (and that sticks of different lengths would fit into different boxes). It is very likely, Schiff concluded, that immature language, not immature perception, interferes with children's performance on Piaget's conservation tasks.

tions of reciprocity and reversibility and number and size, use mental operations consistently, or understand conservation problems so that they can answer correctly, regardless of the wording of the questions or the appearance of the objects, backing up their judgments with sound, logical reasoning.

Seriation

Seriation is the process of arranging similar objects in a systematic series—for example, arranging sticks from longest to shortest.

> When Sam was little, he responded to my asking him to put his toys away by plopping everything on his shelves in a complete jumble. Now he likes to line up all his robots in order from big to little, then his dinosaurs, then his trucks and cars from Matchbox size to mammoth.

Children also go through three stages in mastering seriation, according to Piaget. In the first stage, before they can perform mental operations, 4- and 5-year-olds separate the sticks into two or three bunches, short, medium, and long, and then seriate the sticks within each of the three bunches. They cannot seriate the three bunches into one coordinated series. In the second stage, 5- and 6-year-olds can seriate all the sticks, but it takes them many back and forth looks and tries to get it right. In the third stage, 6- and 7-year-olds can seriate the sticks easily. They look for the longest or shortest sticks and work their way through the pile systematically and surely (Piaget and Inhelder, 1969).

Beyond seriating sticks, children may go on to seriating cookies and kids, robots and Gobots, dolls and trucks. Seven-year-old Sam has a Matchbox Volkswagen and a much larger dune buggy. His friend Robbie says that he has a pickup truck even bigger than Sam's dune buggy. Crushed, Sam doesn't have to see the pickup truck to know that it's bigger than the Matchbox Volkswagen as well. This kind of seriation is called a **transitive inference**. According to Piaget, children can make transitive inferences—if A is bigger than B, and B is bigger than C, then A is bigger than C—only when they can hold in mind the logical relationship of seriation: $A > B > C$.

As with conservation, questions have been raised about the age at which children first can understand transitivity. In Piaget's tests of transitive inference, children were asked questions like: Mary is taller than Jane. Jane is taller than Susan. Who is taller, Mary or Susan? On such tests, children younger than 6 did not succeed. It is likely that preschool children can understand what ''small'' and ''big'' mean and can judge the relative *size* of things, but not relative *terms* such as ''smaller'' and ''bigger.'' In experiments in which the problem is presented to children nonverbally, however, younger children have been found to make transitive inferences. In one experiment, 4-year-olds saw two strips of colored paper only one-quarter inch different in length (Harris et al., in Donaldson, 1983). The strips were on the floor, about three feet apart—too far for the difference in length to be noticeable. Then another strip of paper, the same length as one of the other two, was briefly put next to each of them. The children could see the difference in length, and when they were asked which strip was longer, they answered correctly. These children had inferred that if A equals B and B is longer than C, then A must be longer than C.

Stages of cognitive development

According to Piaget, the developmental stages observed for conservation and seriation—preoperational, transitional, and operational—occur across all domains. They appear in a fixed and irreversible sequence, such that no child who achieves the stage of operational thought ever backslides to preoperational thought. They are discontinuous; that is, the shift from one stage to the next is relatively sudden. And they are universal; all children everywhere go through these stages.

Researchers have tested the accuracy of these claims that cognitive development occurs in stages. One thing they have tested is whether children reach the same stage in different areas at the same time. For example, does a child acquire conservation of weight, length, and volume, seriation, and transitive inference at the same time? Most of the researchers who have looked for consistency in stage level across areas have found inconsistencies (Gelman and Baillargeon, 1983). Children develop particular concrete operations at different times, they have found, and not necessarily even in the order that Piaget proposed. Piaget himself observed that children acquire conservation of different quantities at different ages. Piaget named this phenomenon **horizontal décalage**—after the French *décaler*, meaning to unwedge or displace—to suggest that children learn conservation of different quantities at different times. But giving it a name does not reconcile this phenomenon with a theory of general, cross-domain cognitive stages.

Another claim about stages that researchers have tested is whether children in Europe, Africa, China, and Australia all go through the same developmental stages in the same order. In general, these tests have been positive. Cross-cultural studies show that although environment affects the *rate* at which children develop, it rarely and minimally affects the *sequence* of stages. Children everywhere develop the same mental operations, although children may grow more skillful in using the operations that are valued and practical in their particular culture (Cole, Gay, Glick, and Sharp, 1971; Dasen, 1977).

A third test of Piaget's theory of stages has been to see whether children can be taught the operations from a cognitive stage more advanced than their own. According to Piaget, children must work out these operations at their own pace and within the context of their own everyday activities. Deliberate training as a way to speed children's development is not necessary or helpful. Piaget did allow that the child in the transitional stage of mastering an operation might find training useful but only if the training were geared to the child's present level of understanding and if it offered the child information about concepts at the next stage of development. Short-term training, according to Piaget, could not create new cognitive abilities or structures.

American researchers have conducted many studies to test this aspect of Piaget's theory. In one study (Gelman, 1969), the researcher tried to train 5-year-olds to conserve number and length. She showed children rows of chips or sticks with different numbers and spacing (Figure 9.6). The children were asked to point to the rows that had either the same or different numbers of chips or sticks. When children in one group got it right, they got a prize. Children in another group were not rewarded or told when their answers were correct. The children whose right answers were rewarded quickly learned to tell the difference between number and length; those who were not rewarded learned little. When the children were tested the next day and again two to three weeks later, those who had been rewarded could conserve number and length 95 percent of the time and mass and liquid two-thirds of the time. Their reasoning showed clearly that they understood conservation. The children who had not been given feedback did not acquire these abilities. Training apparently did help preoperational children to learn conservation. Mere exposure to the materials on number and length did not allow the children to discover conservation on their own.

In another training study, third graders who understood conservation were paired with third graders who did not (Silverman and Stone, 1972).

TRAINING IN CONSERVATION

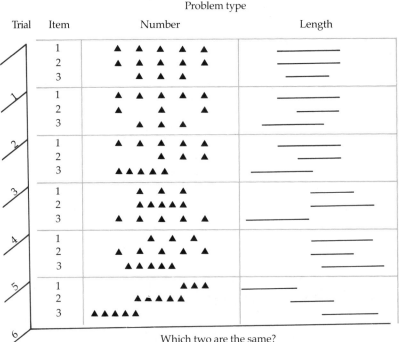

Figure 9.6 These sets of chips and sticks are examples of the groups of items that Gelman (1969) used in training children to discriminate number and length.

After the pairs had talked about conservation of area, 11 of the 14 original nonconservers could understand conservation of area. Retested a month later, the children still understood the concept.

Children also have been trained to make transitive inferences about relative length and height. Once they are taught that $A > B$ and so forth, they can infer that $A > D$. Children as young as 4 or 5, well below Piaget's age for concrete operations, can be trained to make transitive inferences (Harris and Bassett, 1975; Stetson, 1974).

Researchers have tested whether children can be trained in virtually every ability that Piaget described as developing in stages: perspective taking, class inclusion, conservation, seriation, transitivity, and so on (Brainerd, 1983). Although children in middle childhood are easier to train than preschoolers, even the younger children can be trained to apply rules and strategies that help them to acquire these abilities. In general, training studies have not supported Piaget's proposal that only children in transition between stages can be trained. Children at lower stages have benefited from training just as much as those in transitional stages (Brainerd, 1978). Although most normal children, who do not have the advantages of training by a researcher, likely do proceed through the cognitive stages as Piaget proposed, training studies demonstrate that cognition can be affected by many factors besides a child's everyday interactions with the physical world. In fact, for teaching concrete operations, training seems to be a more effective teacher than a child's own discoveries.

Piaget provided a useful framework for thinking about children's cognitive development. But it now seems clear that the ages at which children can succeed at particular tasks can be modified when the tasks are presented in a simpler way or when children are given training. Of course age was never the important thing to Piaget. The fact remains that younger children do not spontaneously succeed on Piaget's tests, whereas older children do, and this fact reflects real differences in the thinking of younger and older children.

Much of the difference between the thinking of children in early and middle childhood is a result of increased knowledge. But three qualitative changes seen on Piaget's tasks do seem to differentiate the thinking of preschoolers and school-age children.

1. Preschool children depend on the appearance of things rather than inferred reality. School-age children are more sensitive to distinctions between what *seems* to be and what really *is*.

2. Preschool children tend to concentrate their attention on one particularly interesting or salient feature and neglect others. School-age children pay attention to more features.

3. Preschool children do not understand reversibility; older children do.

Most developmental psychologists today do not subscribe to a strong, monolithic stage theory as was laid out by Piaget. But because of developmental differences such as these three, many psychologists still are convinced that there are stages in cognitive development (for example, Fischer, 1980; Case, 1985). Whether children can perform at their highest stage, these psychologists suggest, depends on the difficulty or complexity of tasks and the amount of help the children get in solving them (Fischer and Canfield, 1986). In most situations, children do not function at their highest level. When children are given help, and when the task is simple, development does appear to take place in discrete stages, as Piaget suggested. Neo-Piagetian psychologists support a more liberal view of stages in which children's progress in different domains is somewhat independent but constrained by certain age-related factors (Case, 1985).

One such constraint is working memory. One explanation of why training succeeds is that it acts to improve children's working memory (Brainerd, 1983). Children need to encode and remember the facts of the situation—like the height and width of two glasses—while they figure out the problem. Training that improves children's abilities to encode or to remember facts thus may help them to solve problems in cognition. The issue of what preschool children can encode and remember is taken up in the next section.

Information processing

Piaget has provided one framework for describing preschool children's thinking. Another framework is provided by the information-processing approach (see Chapter 1). This approach emphasizes quantitative changes in children's abilities, not stages. The preschool child's thought is not seen as qualitatively different from the school-age child's but as constrained by context, complexity, the verbal demands of tasks, by general abilities such as memory, and by specific limits like lack of knowledge. According to the information-processing approach, as children get older, their skills and their ability to apply them to more tasks increase. Researchers who have followed this approach have focused on how children attend to information in the environment and store that information in memory. They have studied the amount of information children can take in, how quickly they process it, and how well they remember it. In this section, we discuss the results of research on children's processing of information.

Attention

Preschool children attend to sights and sounds by extensively scanning the environment, but their exploration is not systematic.

For a long time, I was worried at how poor Jason was at finding things. He would open the toy cabinet but consistently miss the toy he was after. He would rummage through the paper on the top of his father's desk but miss the toy car. I thought there might be something wrong with his eyesight. But as he got older, he got much better at finding things. The other day he even found a ring I had lost.

In one study, 4- to 8-year-olds were shown pictures of houses in pairs (Vurpillot, 1968; Figure 9.7). They were asked whether the houses were the same or different. The most efficient way to decide this is to compare the houses systematically, looking from one house to the other and back, window by window, row by row. The 8-year-olds did follow this strategy, and when they had found a difference between two windows, they efficiently stopped searching and said that the houses were different. The 5-year-olds, however, did not scan systematically. They did not compare the two houses window by window; they did not start at one corner and work toward another. They did not even look at every window. In another study (Elkind, 1977), children were asked to name the pictures that they saw pasted onto a card—hat, parrot, chair, and so on. Eight-year-olds named all the pictures systematically from left to right and top to bottom. Five-year-olds left out some pictures and named others twice because they jumped from one picture to another. Only

SYSTEMATIC SCANNING

Figure 9.7 A pair of different houses (top) and a pair of identical houses (bottom) (Vurpillot, 1968). When children are asked to say which pair of houses is the same, preschool children do not scan as systematically as older children.

when a system was imposed on the pictures by the researcher and they were pasted in a triangular shape did the 5-year-olds, like the 8-year-olds, name the pictures in order.

Clearly, preschool children are not as systematic as older children in paying attention to the environment. They are also not as selective as older children in what they pay attention to. In studies of children watching television, for example, 2-year-olds have been found to be more easily distracted, to talk more to other people, to play more with toys, and to look around the room more than 4-year-olds (Anderson and Levin, 1976). As they get older, children get better at picking out one object or picture from a clutter and listening to one voice while ignoring another (Geffen and Sexton, 1978; Sexton and Geffen, 1979). They become increasingly skilled at selecting stimuli to attend to and focusing their attention at will. In one study, children were shown a row of cards, each containing a picture of a common household object and a picture of an animal (Hagen and Hale, 1973). Then the cards were turned face down, and the children were asked to locate the animals. Later, after the game was over, the children were asked which objects had been on the same cards as the animals. Younger children did better than older ones on this task, because the task-oriented older children had focused their attention only on the animals.

Why are preschoolers less selective about the information they attend to than older children? For one thing, young children may be less *efficient* at processing information and so, because they use more of their limited ability to process irrelevant stimuli, they cannot pay as much attention to important stimuli. In support of this explanation is the finding that young children are more easily distracted by irrelevant stimuli (Smith, Kemler, and Aronfreed, 1975). For another thing, perhaps young children do not understand what experimenters want from them. Perhaps they do not select as important the elements that an experimenter intends as important and instead focus on the elements that are more salient for them. Research has shown that if the stimuli the experimenter intends to be important are also salient to the child, young children do not differ from older children in what they pay attention to or remember (Odom, 1982). Finally, perhaps young children do not have the *strategy* of consciously controlling or directing their attention so that they focus only on relevant aspects of tasks. Older children know that they should be selective and have conscious strategies for paying attention.

In brief, 5-year-olds are explorers. They approach the environment curiously and playfully, move quickly from one thing to another, are easily distracted, and respond to whatever attracts them. Six-year-olds are searchers. They investigate the environment systematically, with plan and purpose.

Memory

After children have attended to information and taken it into their information-processing system, they must remember it. Attention determines which information enters the ''computer,'' and memory determines which information stays in it and how it is filed.

Recognition of an object or image one has seen before is the simplest kind of remembering. Even preschoolers are quite good at this kind of remembering—if what they are asked to remember is simple and familiar. In one study, researchers showed 2- and 4-year-olds 18 small, familiar, attractive objects (Myers and Perlmutter, 1978). Later, they showed them 36 objects, the original 18 plus another 18. The 2-year-olds recognized over 80 percent of the original objects; the 4-year-olds recognized over 90 percent. Both groups were extremely accurate at realizing which objects they had never seen. Preschoolers are less accurate at recognizing complex, abstract forms, however (Nelson and Kosslyn, 1976). Presumably, this is because they are not as good at encoding information into their information-processing system as older children. It is clearly not that they cannot retain information in memory once it is there.

Recall is a more difficult process than recognition, because information must be retrieved from memory with no prompts from the environment. No person or object is present to trigger memory, as in recognition.

> Whenever I asked Peter about something he couldn't remember—"What was the name of the boy you were playing with when I picked you up?" "What was that snack you wanted me to buy for you?" "Where does Sam live?"—he'd answer, "Do you know? Tell me all the names [or snacks or streets] you know." Then, when I hit the missing word, his face lit up, and he crowed, "You got it!"

How well people recall information depends, for one thing, on how much practice they have had in recalling. Unlike recognition memory, which is similar in all cultures (Cole and Scribner, 1977), recall varies widely from one culture to another. In our society, we rely heavily on written material to help us remember: students take notes in class and read textbooks; actors use cue cards; and children are not expected to memorize much more than their ABCs. But in some societies, people develop their powers of recall to great heights. The poet Homer, for example, sang the entire *Iliad* and *Odyssey* from memory—a staggering feat of recall.

How much can preschoolers in this society recall in tests of memory? In one study, researchers showed preschool children nine small objects one at a time from nine different conceptual categories, such as animals, utensils, vehicles, and the like, labeled them, and put them in a box (Perlmutter and Myers, 1979). Even though they were told that they could keep the objects they could name, the 3-year-olds recalled only two of the objects, the 4-year-olds three or four objects. Most of the children recalled the last object they had seen. When the nine objects were from just three categories, the children remembered more of them, perhaps because by this age, children's recall is organized into conceptual categories. When the experimenter prompted the children with a clue—"Do you remember any other animals?"—they recalled even more. Marion Perlmutter (1980) suggests that preschoolers recall poorly because they lack language for encoding information and strategies for memorizing and retrieving it. Preschool children lack the organization of memory that older children have. They do not yet have a filing system, so their memories may be jumbled and inaccurate. Preschoolers also have a more limited memory capacity (Brown, Bransford, Ferrera, and Campione, 1983; Case, 1985). They can remember fewer units or bits of information than older children, and they use up more of their mental "space" encoding information, so less is left over for actually storing information.

Out of the laboratory and in familiar surroundings, preschoolers can recall better. They recall social interactions and cartoon characters (though only rarely objects—the usual target of laboratory research), and their recall extends back for several months (Todd and Perlmutter, 1980). They also recall "scripts" for familiar events and routines like going shopping, taking a bath, going to school, or having a party. Katherine Nelson and Janice Gruendel (1979) interviewed children between 3 and 8 years old about "what happens" when you have a birthday party, plant a garden, and other familiar situations. The youngest children's scripts were sketchy and general—"You cook a cake and eat it." The older children included social aspects in their scripts, such as children arriving at a birthday party and playing games, and they described them with more complex details. Scripts are representations of what *usually* happens rather than descriptions of what happened last week.

Preschoolers can tell you about having dinner at a restaurant or having birthday parties, but they may be incapable of describing last night's dinner or cousin Lainie's third birthday party. In a study of one group of 5-year-olds' school scripts (Fivush, 1984), the children had lots to say about what happens at school but little to say about what happened "yesterday" at school.

> Why was it that every time I asked Kristy what she'd done at nursery school today, she answered with utter silence or, at most, "Nuffin'"? But if I asked her, "What do kids do at school?" she could tell me they line up and go inside, play, eat snacks, and go back outside to the swings.

These "scripts" are one way that preschoolers have for remembering things. They offer them some organization, as one study in which 3- and 4-year-olds were asked to recall lists of words showed (Lucariello and Nelson, 1985). Children recalled more words when the lists had been made up from children's scripts (for getting dressed in the morning, having lunch, going to the zoo) rather than from the adult categories of clothes, food, and animals. They remembered the most words when they were given the script list and were prompted with questions such as, "Tell me which of those things you could put on in the morning (eat for lunch, see at the zoo)." Thus, although, as Perlmutter showed, preschool children find adult category organization helpful, because script organization is *more* helpful, children's knowledge of general events may be more accessible than their knowledge of categories.[1]

Factors that influence memory

Why are some things remembered better than others? For one thing, the mode in which information is presented—written words, spoken words, or pictures—affects how well it is remembered. The old saying, "A picture is worth a thousand words" is supported by research. In one study, for example, children recalled pictures better than spoken words and spoken words better than printed words (Dempster and Rohwer, 1983). In another study, 3- to 5-year-olds recognized advertised products better when they had seen or had seen and heard advertisements rather than when they had just heard the advertisements (Stoneman and Brody, 1983). A study of 5-year-olds' memory of the images and sound from a "Sesame Street" episode also suggested that visual images are more salient and memorable than sounds (Pezdek and Stevens, 1984).

A person's interests, motives, and feelings also affect what he or she remembers. In one recent study, 3-year-olds' interests were identified by researchers who watched what the children played with most often in their nursery school classroom—blocks, cars, dolls, and so forth (Renninger and Wozniak, 1985). They then asked the children to remember pictures of "birthday presents" or to recall which toys had been hidden in a box. Individual children's abilities to recognize and to recall particular pictures and objects were found to be strongly related to their interests.

In a study of how motives affect memory, researchers first asked teachers to rate children on dominance, affiliation, hostility to their peers, and academic mastery (Moore, Kagan, and Haith, 1978). The children who were rated highest and lowest acted as subjects. They were asked to listen to 20 sentences

---

[1]See Chapter 12 for a discussion of the finding that preschool children's first choice for sorting things is to put together things that are used together rather than things that are in the same category.

focus   *Children as witnesses*

With the recent rash of court cases concerning both the rights and the abuse of children, many children have taken the stand and told their tales to judge and jury. Just how accurate are children as witnesses? Should their testimony be allowed? What about 3-year-old Lori?

> One summer day a man in an orange Datsun pulled up in front of the neighbor's yard where Lori was playing and told her to get in. She did. Three days later the police found Lori, crying and bruised, in the pit of a deserted outhouse. Lori told the police that the ''bad man'' had hit her and left her there. The next day, when the police showed her a set of twelve photographs, she gasped and identified one man as her abductor. The man Lori identified was arrested, and a week before the case was scheduled to come to trial, he confessed (Goleman, 1984, p. 19).

But when a case of sexual abuse of children in Minnesota was dropped because of insufficient evidence, people began to ask whether the complaining children had lied.

> A tense and deeply embarrassed 11-year-old boy, the first of six children scheduled to take the stand, testified that the Bentzes had sexually abused him over the previous two summers. But the next day, the youth recanted part of his testimony, saying he had lied the day before when he described the sex acts with Robert Benz. When defense attorney Earl Gray asked, ''Was that a big lie or a little lie?'' the child answered, ''A big one.'' But then the boy insisted other stories he had told about sexual acts with Lois Bentz and other adults were true (Siegel, 1984, p. 28).

Lawyers on one side held that adults had threatened the children, put words into their mouths, and educated them about sex by using anatomically correct dolls as models. The other side countered that no one could have coached the children to make up such sexually explicit stories.

and, on the next day, to choose from pairs of sentences those that they had heard the day before. Unbeknownst to the children, none of the sentence pairs had actually appeared the day before but had been constructed to reflect the motives on which the students originally had been rated. For example, hostility to peers was reflected in the sentence, ''The child was mad at his friend for not sharing his Coca-Cola,'' and dominance was reflected in, ''The child could drink Coca-Cola faster than anyone.'' Asked whether they had seen either of these sentences, in 70 percent of the cases the children claimed to remember those that reflected their own strong motives, a finding that suggests that motives do affect memory.

The meaningfulness of information also affects people's ability to remember it. Some psychologists (Craik and Lockhart, 1972) have suggested that information processing occurs at different levels, from a shallow perceptual level, to deeper and more meaningful levels. Information that receives scant and superficial analysis is soon forgotten; information processed at deeper levels is remembered better and longer. Development seems to improve children's abilities to process information at the deepest levels (Naus, Ornstein, and Hoving, 1978). In one recent study to explore how this aspect of

What does research suggest about children's capabilities as witnesses? In some ways, children make better witnesses than adults. Because young children do not attend to information as selectively as older children or adults, they may notice and recall details that older people ignore. For example, in one study, when children and adults watched a basketball game on videotape, 75 percent of the first graders, 22 percent of the fourth graders, and no adults recalled seeing a woman with an umbrella walk through the gym (Neisser, 1979). Although their stories tend to come out in bits and pieces, children's recall of simple events may be no less accurate than adults'. Children are also good at recognizing faces. Children under 12 do, however, remember fewer details than adults, especially those they do not understand or follow well (Goleman, 1984). They also sometimes mix reality and imagination. In one study, children 6 years old distinguished an imaginary from a real, remembered event as well as adults, but they confused what they had really done in the situation with what they had only thought about doing (Foley and Johnson, 1985). They also may mix a memory of a single event with their general knowledge of what usually happens (their "script"). Children's recall of what happened to them in preschool is influenced by their general knowledge of what happens in school, for example (Myles-Worsley, Cromer, and Dodd, 1986).

Four-year-olds may not know how to count or name the days of the week. They may give literal answers that sound contradictory. Asked if he had gone to the defendant's *house*, one child witness said "no." It turned out that he had gone to the defendant's *apartment*. Judges need to be alert to lawyers' questions that exceed children's cognitive capacities. Psychologists suggest that children facing court testimony first be reassured by visiting the courtroom where they will be testifying, or by testifying over closed-circuit television, while sitting in a trusted adult's lap, or in private with a psychiatrist, and by meeting first with the judge, who should intervene to protect them, to remind them that they are not on trial, and to reassure then that nothing bad will happen to them. Then, as long as they are asked simple, straightforward, nonsuggestive, and unthreatening questions, children can make reliable and useful witnesses.

children's memories develops, researchers tested children's recall of words under two conditions (Ghatala, 1984). In one condition, children were asked to give rhymes for the words; in the other condition, they were asked to define the words. The words they were given were either very meaningful or not very meaningful (judging by how many associated words children of the same age could generate). Recall was greatest for meaningful words that the children defined. Older children did better than younger, because more words were meaningful for them.

Finally, how information is remembered depends on the contexts in which it is encoded and recalled. When young children are in familiar surroundings, they are likelier to remember where they left a toy or to do something they have been told than when they are in unfamiliar surroundings (Ashmead and Perlmutter, 1980; Ceci and Bronfenbrenner, 1985; DeLoache and Brown, 1983). How well children remember things depends on where they are, what else they are thinking and doing, and what they are trying to remember. Context, like mode, motive, and meaning, affects children's memory.

Language

We have already described something of children's acquisition of words. But language, of course, is more than a grab bag of words. The remarkable speed with which preschoolers learn words partly depends on their having a framework on which to hang those words. **Syntax** is the name for this framework. Syntax is how words are combined into sentences to express who did what to whom.

Before children can manage complex sentences with subjects, predicates, and objects, though, they use strings of related one-word utterances (Scollon, 1976), or they say two words and then pause (Branigan, 1979). They do not take a flying leap from uttering their first words to putting them together into many-word utterances. They do not develop an entire system of syntax in one swoop. Instead, they make their way slowly and in small steps along a winding path, combining words in ever longer and more complex sentences. In this section, we will first describe the child's progress toward complex sentences and then discuss the processes underlying the child's acquisition of syntax.

Two- and three-word sentences

Children's first "sentences" are two words long and very basic. They include only the most important words in the sentence—like a telegram sent by a miser or a newspaper headline: "Doggy bark," "More car." If she wants her mother to give her a picture book, the child may say, "Give book" or, "Mommy give" or even, "Mommy book," but she does not say, "Mommy, please give me the book that is on the shelf." She is limited to her two word **telegraphic sentence** because of her limited memory and information-processing skills. She expresses the core of the sentence and omits "frills" like the copula verb *(is)*, the article *(the)*, the preposition *(on)*, and the conjunction *(that)*. Why are all these frills omitted? For one thing, they are difficult to learn because there is no one-to-one correspondence between them and their meanings. For another, they are omitted because they are unstressed sounds, and children at this stage often omit unstressed syllables—"e-phant" for elephant, "'mato" for tomato, and "'puter" for computer (Gleitman and Wanner, 1982).

With their two-word sentences, children comment on actions and objects, possession and location. "Milk fell," "Go car," "Molly room," "Daddy home," "Cookie gone." What was once expressed with one word and a gesture is now handily expressed in two little words, "See doggy." "Bottle here." With rare exceptions, the word order in these two-word sentences is the same as that an adult would use in a longer sentence: "Doggy bark" and not "Bark doggy" (de Villiers and de Villiers, 1973). The child apparently knows something about syntax as well as meaning even at this early age. She knows that in English sentences, "doers" come before actions; that actions come before objects. She shows this in the word order of her two-word sentences. (In fact, even in the one-word stage children apparently understand this. In an ingenious study of 16- to 19-month-olds who could say only two or three words themselves, researchers found that when children heard "Cookie Monster is tickling Big Bird. Where is Cookie Monster tickling Big Bird?" they looked more at a videotape of Cookie Monster tickling Big Bird than at a videotape of Big Bird tickling Cookie Monster shown at the same time (Hirsh-Pasek, Golinkoff, Fletcher, Beaubien, and Cawley, 1985). If they had understood only the meaning of "Cookie Monster" and "Big Bird" and had not been sensitive to the significance of word order, they would not have shown a preference). Two-word speakers appreciate well-formed, complete sentences—with all the frills—even though they cannot yet speak them. In another study, two-word speakers were found to obey more often if their mother said, "Throw me the ball" than if she said, "Throw ball" (Shipley, Smith, and Gleitman, 1969). In yet another study, some 18-month-olds were told that a doll was "Zup," and others were told that the doll was "a zup" (Katz, Baker, and MacNamara, 1974). The children who had been told that the doll was "a zup"—the article suggesting that other zups existed—labeled other dolls they were shown as "zups." But the children who had been told that the doll was "Zup" did not label any other dolls "Zup." Children clearly are aware of syntax even at this early stage of language development.

Children's three-word sentences are still telegraphic and still leave out the nonessential words. But as before, they follow conventional English subject–verb–object form. The child now asks for her picture book, "Mommy give book."

Complex sentences

As sentences become more complex, syntactic "frills" begin to be added, generally in this order (Brown, 1973; de Villiers and de Villiers, 1973):

ing ("Cat drink*ing*.")

in, *on* ("Cat *in* basket.")

s ("Cat*s* playing.")

's ("Cat*'s* milk in bowl.")

is ("Cat *is* fat.")

a, the ("*The* cat is drinking.")

ed ("The cat play*ed*.")

Thus in trying to communicate, "The cat is drinking," the child who once said, "Cat drink," is now more likely to say, "Cat drinking," than to say "Cat is drink" or "The cat drink."

Why are elements added in this order? According to one careful analysis (Moerk, 1983), it is not semantic complexity but the frequency with which the child hears these elements in the parents' speech and their acoustical distinctiveness that affect the order of acquisition. The child's own need for language may also contribute. Thus the child may learn to say "my" before "his," because the child needs to talk about herself before she talks about someone else.

At first, in their early complex sentences, although children know how to make a sentence, they do not always do so. They may know how to say "Daddy drive car," a complete sentence, but still use a sentence fragment like "Daddy car." They also may know how to add *-ed* or *-ing*, for example, but not do so. Michael Maratsos (1983) has suggested that at first children may not assume that a grammatical form that is expressed *sometimes* has to be expressed *every* time.

By the time they are correctly using the *-ed* ending to indicate the past tense about half of the time, though, young children do figure this out. They begin to **overregularize** their verbs and tack *-ed* onto irregular verbs that they once said correctly—"I break*ed* my crayon," "We go*ed* to the store," "He make*d* a drawing," and "She bring*ed* her shoes." Similarly, they overregularize words with irregular plural endings—"My foot*s* hurted," "How many goos*es* in there?" and "Daddy and me are man*s*." The child now seems to be searching for general rules of language that operate consistently and, having found one, sticks to it most determinedly.

CHILD: My teacher *holded* the baby rabbits and we *patted* them.

ADULT: Did you say your teacher *held* the baby rabbits?

CHILD: Yes.

ADULT: What did you say she did?

CHILD: She *holded* the baby rabbits and we *patted* them.

ADULT: Did you say she *held* them tightly?

CHILD: No, she *holded them loosely* (Gleason, 1967).

Most children relearn irregular past tenses and plurals by the time they start school—through tedious memorization. But even then for unfamiliar words, they are likely first to try out regular rules (''wring, wringed'' ''bleed, bleeded'').

Along with pronouns and suffixes, children add adjectives and adverbs to their sentences. They learn the most general ones first: *big, nice, little,* before *tall, naughty, short.* The former are the adjectives the child probably hears most often, and they are useful in a variety of situations and sentences.

Children also learn to ask questions. In their two-word sentences, children signal questions simply with a rising intonation: ''Me go?'' ''Doggy eat?'' When they begin to use auxiliary verbs, they first say: ''Doggy can eat?'' ''Where I am going?'' They keep the verb and the auxiliary verb together. Only later do they learn to reverse the order of auxiliary and subject: ''Can doggy eat?'' ''Where am I going?'' This is a syntactically more complex form. Children also ask the simpler ''wh-'' questions: ''where,'' ''what,'' ''who,'' and ''whose'' first. Locations (where), objects (what), and agents (who), you will recall, were the first concepts that children put into their two-word sentences. Causation (why), manner (how), and time (when) are more difficult concepts and so are learned later and appear in sentences later (de Villiers and de Villiers, 1979; Ervin-Tripp, 1970). Children continue to think that ''when'' means ''where'' as late as 3 years of age:

MOTHER: When are you having lunch?

CHILD: In the kitchen.

It takes several more years of listening to and using language before children have figured out how to ask indirect questions. When preschool children in one study were asked to relay a question to a third party, for example, the children were likely to make mistakes (Tanz, 1980). When the experimenter said, ''Ask Tom where I should put this,'' the children were likely to say, ''Where should you put this?'' or ''Where should I put this?'' rather than ''Where should she put this?'' They did much better with, ''Tell Tom where I should put this'' (C. Chomsky, 1969).

As their language increases in complexity, children learn how to put more than one idea in a single sentence. They join ideas with *and, but,* and *or.* These conjunctions can make a sentence go on forever. ''Daddy took me to the grocery store, *and* we bought carrots, *and* then we bought peanut butter, *and* Daddy said, 'Where's the bread?' *and* we found the bread, *and* we put it in our cart, *and*. . . .'' Three-year-olds also use the conjunctions *if, when,* and *because:* ''If I brush my teeth, can I have two stories?'' ''When it gets dark, I go to sleep.'' ''I like you because you are my friend.'' They use *before, after,* and *until* less often, because these words express temporal relations that are quite sophisticated.

Until they are about 5 years old, children describe events in their actual order of occurrence: ''I brushed my teeth, and then I got in bed.'' ''The mailman rang the bell, and I got a letter.'' Not until later will they say, ''I got in bed after I brushed my teeth'' or ''Before I got a letter, the mailman rang the bell.'' Of practical importance, children *understand* compound sentences more easily if they mirror the real order of events and if the order is logical or irreversible. It is easier for them to understand—''Feed the baby before you put her to bed'' than ''Feed the baby before you pick up the phone'' (E. Clark, 1971; Kavanaugh, 1979). Knowing this can help adults when they give children instructions. Giving directions in the actual order they want them followed—''Wash your hands, and then come to the table''—is likely to be more effective than saying, ''Before you come to the table, wash your hands.'' During the preschool period, children gradually learn to use even more complex sentence structures like relative clauses—''Here's the doll that I need''—and embedded relative clauses—''The doll that I need is up there.''

By the time they reach first grade, most children have at their disposal all the basic sentence forms in their native language.

How do children acquire syntax?

In just a few short years, most children have become fluent sentence makers. They learn language with an ease and eagerness that older people, struggling over their foreign-language texts, can only envy. Just how *do* young children acquire syntax? On one level it is obvious that both innate abilities and environmental input are involved in the acquisition of language. Innate abilities clearly are involved because only children, not their pets, learn to speak in sentences, despite the fact that they both hear sentences. Environmental input clearly is involved because American children learn to speak English whereas Mexican children learn to speak Spanish, despite the fact that they both have the same innate language abilities. The *emphasis* given to innate versus environmental factors in explaining how children acquire language, however, has been a matter of some debate.

Behaviorist B.F. Skinner (1957) suggested that children learn language as adults systematically reinforce their efforts. When parents hear their baby babble ''nananana,'' Skinner proposed, they smile with delight and talk back to the baby. Pleased, the baby babbles again. Mothers give big hugs and lots of praise when babies first say ''Mama.'' They fill the bottle with milk when babies say ''baba,'' and later, as their children are learning to put words together, parents are responding, mirroring, modeling, and correcting. Their children then imitate the correct forms they hear from their parents.

Noam Chomsky (1957, 1965, 1968), a linguist, had a different explanation of how children learn language. He admitted that reinforcement and imitation were important but claimed that they were not sufficient to account for children's acquisition of language. Children, he pointed out, utter sentences for which they have never been reinforced. In fact, they constantly utter expressions they have never even heard before—original creations, ''We go store now buy present Jerry baby,'' and mistaken constructions found nowhere in adult speech—''foots,'' ''runned,'' ''breaked,'' and ''Allgone wet.'' Children also vary considerably in the degree to which they imitate the speech they hear from others. Some children imitate hardly at all. Others, much to an embarrassed parent's dismay, are amazing in their ability to echo something someone has said, even days later. Chomsky called attention to the remarkable capacity of the child to understand and create sentences, to generalize, and to process language in a variety of very special and complex ways that must be largely innate.

Imitation may be how children say words for the first time. But they then apply these words to new objects and use them in new sentences. In learning syntax, children first must understand the form of the sentences they hear; then they may imitate the form; finally, they use the form in their own sentences (Whitehurst and Vasta, 1975). Children seldom imitate entire sentences verbatim. Hearing ''I love you, Peter,'' the child does not say, ''I love you, Peter.'' If he imitates it at all, he is more likely to say, ''I love you, Mommy,'' imitating the *form* of the sentence. Even with encouragement, though, children do not imitate syntactic forms that they do not use spontaneously.

ADULT: Adam, say what I say: ''Where can I put them?''

ADAM: ''Where I can put them?'' (Slobin, 1971, p. 52)

ADULT: This one is the giant, but this one is little.

CHILD: Dis one little, annat one big (Slobin and Welsh, 1973, p. 490).

Children seem to imitate constructions that are just entering their repertoire, not those that are totally new (Bloom, Hood, and Lightbown, 1974).

Just as children seldom imitate their parents' sentences, their parents seldom correct their children's sentences—at least not their syntax. If they try, usually they are unsuccessful.

CHILD: Nobody don't like me.

MOTHER: No, say ''Nobody likes me.''

CHILD: Nobody don't like me.

MOTHER: No, say ''Nobody likes me.''

CHILD: Nobody don't like me.

MOTHER: No, now listen carefully: ''Nobody likes me.''

CHILD: Oh! Nobody don't likes me (McNeill, 1966, p. 69).

Inspired by Chomsky, developmental psychologists now ask *how* the child's innate language abilities interact with environmental factors to create a speaking, comprehending child.

How parents talk to children

Day in and day out, as parents and children do things together, parents talk. They talk about people, about things, and about events. Parents comment on what is obvious and salient to their children. We have already discussed (in Chapter 6) the process of early *word* learning. Here we are

Motherese is an attempt to talk so that the young child can understand. Sentences are short, simplified, and repetitive.

concerned with how children learn *syntax* from their parents' speech. As parents talk to their youngsters, the children may learn something about the order of words. Parents format conversations with their young children: "What's that? You know. A kitty." They also mend their children's failed messages: "What's 'itty'? Do you mean 'kitty'? No? Oh, you mean, 'Sit here'" (Bruner, 1983).

But parents do not usually give specific lessons in syntax to their children. They do not usually correct their children's grammatical mistakes. Instead, parents attend to the messages their children are trying to convey (Brown and Hanlon, 1970; Hirsh-Pasek, Treiman, and Schneiderman, 1984; Slobin, 1975). As in adult conversation, the goal is communication, not instruction. When a girl with sopping overalls says, "I not wet my pants," her mother is more likely to respond, "Yes, you did," than to ask the child to say, "I did not wet my pants." Parents may correct a child's incorrect sentence *indirectly* by saying it in correct form, but they do not scold the child for making a mistake in syntax (Hirsh-Pasek et al., 1984).

Adults typically speak to young children in a special, simplified way called **motherese** (Newport, 1976). Motherese consists of short, simple sentences that may be repeated in different forms for emphasis—"Don't fall, Mikey. Don't fall. Watch out. You'll fall." "Megan, come here. Put the ball down. Good girl." In contrast to speech to adults, motherese has shorter sentences separated by longer pauses, more commands and questions, more present tenses and references to the here and now, fewer pronouns, modifiers, and conjunctions. Mothers use the simple, basic words that their children understand, overextending terms just as their children do. To a child who has just learned the word "car," a mother calls trucks, vans, ambulances, and mobile homes "car" (Blewitt, 1983; Mervis and Mervis, 1982). Pronouns, which are difficult for young children, may be dropped in favor of names:

Did *Natalie* make that?

Tell *Mommy* a story.

As children learn more language, their parents' speech to them changes (Kavanaugh and Jirkovsky, 1982; Slobin, 1975). The parents' sentences get longer; declarative forms replace questions and commands (Maratsos, 1983; Newport, 1976). But there is no *simple* relation between parents' and children's syntax (Chesnick, Menyuk, Liebergott, Ferrier, and Strand, 1983; Kavanaugh and Jirkovsky, 1982; Nelson, Denninger, Bonvillian, Kaplan, and Baker, 1983). Motherese is not a deliberate attempt by adults to teach children language. In fact, adults talk to their dogs with the same kind of language as motherese, and clearly they are not trying to teach their dogs syntax (Hirsh-Pasek and Trieman, 1982). Motherese is mainly an adult's attempt to speak so that a child can *understand*. In one study, for example, adult subjects told stories to a 2-year-old boy. Whenever the boy said "What?" or "Huh?" to indicate he hadn't understood, the adults shortened their next sentence—in good motherese fashion (Bohannon and Marquis, 1977). Shorter utterances very likely ease children's comprehension, because young children's memories are limited. Pauses between sentences likely help children to pick out syntactic units (Hirsh-Pasek, Nelson, Jusczyk, and Wright, 1986). Utterances repeated in slightly different forms illustrate different syntactic arrangements and are related to increases in children's use of longer and more complex sentences (Hoff-Ginsberg, 1986). Simpler sentences probably help children to pick out important words and sentence forms. But although some simplification probably does help children to learn language, it does not follow that the simpler the language spoken to children, the better. Children are not encouraged to advance linguistically if the language they hear is reduced to their level; it should be somewhat more complex (Clarke-Stewart, VanderStoep, and Killian, 1979; Gleitman, Newport, and Gleitman, 1984).

In helping children to learn language, extending or expanding their speech is more effective than speaking simply, it seems.

CHILD: Doggy out?
MOTHER: Doggy wants to go out?

CHILD: Get bear.
MOTHER: Will Mommy get the teddy bear?

Expanding children's utterances does seem to be related to their language competence—as long as the expansions are simple and to the point. Keith Nelson and his colleagues (Nelson, 1980; Nelson, Denninger, Bonvillian, Kaplan, and Baker, 1983) found that some mothers of 2-year-olds expanded just one part of the children's utterances:

CHILD: Broke.
MOTHER: The truck broke.

CHILD: Baby sleep.
MOTHER: Baby is sleeping.

Other mothers expanded on two or three parts of the children's utterances:

CHILD: Broke.
MOTHER: The big truck broke its wheel.

CHILD: Baby sleep.
MOTHER: The baby is sleeping in the crib.

Two-year-olds whose mothers made simple expansions of what they said spoke in longer sentences and used more auxiliary verbs at younger ages. The 2-year-olds who heard complex expansions progressed more slowly. Simple expansions help children to notice and analyze a new syntactical structure. When mothers expand on their children's speech simply and reasonably, they hold the children's attention and apparently help them to acquire language.

But does parents' speech actually *cause* their child's language to improve? In a study designed to answer this question, Nelson (1981) had adults deliberately expand children's sentences, either by fixing the verb:

CHILD: It go here?
ADULT: Yes, it goes here.

or by restating the statement as a question:

CHILD: Fox run.
ADULT: Did the fox run?

After five one-hour sessions with the experimenter, children's language was assessed. Children who had heard expanded verbs advanced in their use of verbs, but not of questions; children who heard restated questions advanced in their use of questions but not of verbs. It seems that children do notice extensions of their language and learn from them.

Other deliberate attempts to accelerate children's language development also have succeeded. One researcher (Roth, 1984), for example, worked on syntax with a group of children between 3½ and 4½ years old. She found that after they heard sentences like ''The dog chases the pig that sits on the duck,'' watched them enacted, and then enacted them themselves, the children could learn several kinds of relative clauses that at first were beyond their grasp. These and other studies suggest that the kind of language teaching that is most successful is reciprocal and engaging—not a one-way drill to correct children's mistakes; it extends children's sentences, asks them questions, gets them involved, and is responsive to what they say. Parents' speech to children provides the children with information about language and prods them to analyze it. Parents' complex utterances illustrate regularities in language, and parents' questions to their children prod the children to produce new utterances. In a recent study, it was found that when mothers' language to their children contained more complex utterances, more repetitions, and more questions that required more than yes/no answers, children's language developed more quickly (Hoff-Ginsburg, 1986).

Although parents' expansions, questions, and repetitions speed up their children's early language growth, it is worth noting that even the children of parents who do not expand their children's sentences turn into fluent speakers by 4½ or 5 years. What is more, in some other cultures, parents do not modify their speech in the ways that American parents do. Among the Pacific Kaluli tribe, for example, there is no motherese (Schieffelin and Ochs, 1983), because parents there believe that if adults spoke baby talk, children would sound babyish—not a desirable state of affairs to the Kaluli. But Kaluli children still learn to talk. Given the wide variety of conditions under which children learn to speak, from occasional comments to endless expansions, from casual conversations to deliberate instruction, it is clear that children have many chances to learn this crucial skill.

Innate abilities and constraints

Ultimately the task of learning language is up to the child. No matter how much or how little adult speech is directed to children's ears, no matter how much or how little it is modified, children must still make sense of the underlying patterns within the surrounding babble. How much of language learning is the result of children's innate language abilities? Cases in which children have never been exposed to language tell us something about innate predispositions to learn language.

Deaf children, for example, do not hear language. Yet when the spontaneous gestures of deaf children who have not been taught sign language are analyzed, they are found to have a number of properties of spoken language (Goldin-Meadow and Feldman, 1977; Goldin-Meadow and Mylander, 1985). Like hearing children, those who are deaf begin with single gestures and use them to point to familiar objects. Deaf children acquire a vocabulary of gestures that, like hearing children's words, refer to actions, objects, and people and are used in a consistent order. The abilities to use and order signs may be innate. Unlike hearing children, though, deaf children never acquire ''frills,'' like articles. These aspects of language depend more on environmental input.

Occasionally, even hearing children are deprived of normal language. One child, Genie, for example, was discovered and rescued at the age of 13, unable to speak or understand language, unable even to stand up (Curtiss, 1977). Genie had been isolated, abused, and neglected. Her father had strapped her to a potty seat and confined her to a small bedroom all day. At night, he had either ignored her altogether or tied her inside a sleeping bag, put it in a crib, and covered the crib tops and sides with wire mesh. If she made noise, she was beaten. After she was discovered, Genie was given intensive therapy and language lessons. By the age of 19, she spoke in sentences and expressed normal feelings. But she had not mastered all aspects of language. She could not use words like *what*, *that*, and *which*. She could not use the passive voice (''The child was found'') or questions with an inverted auxiliary verb (''Is she talking?''). She used few auxiliary verbs at all and said, ''She gone home'' rather than ''She *has* gone home.'' She could not put more than one simple idea into a sentence. Despite the great progress that Genie had made in language and in social behavior, she had the telegraphic speech of a typical 2- or 3-year-old.

It has been suggested that children must learn language during a critical period between infancy and puberty, if they are to speak normally. The preschool years may well be a period when children are especially primed to acquire language (Lenneberg, 1967). Once beyond this critical period, the very physiology of the brain may prevent full and easy language acquisition. Genie did learn to speak after she was 13. But she did not master an adult's level of complexity in her language.

Research on both deaf children and deprived children thus suggests that children have innate abilities to make up sentences from the syntactic units of subject, action, and object. More complex sentence forms, however, such as those with auxiliary verbs and relative clauses, are apparently more fragile. They appear later or not at all in a child's speech if the environment does not provide models as the child is learning to put sentences together. Other abilities that seem to be innate and that affect children's acquisition of language are children's predisposition to look for regularities in language, to generalize about syntax from the sentences they hear, and to hypothesize about the rules of language—''-*ed* means it happened in the past.'' According to Chomsky, innate constraints limit these hypotheses. Young children's limited memory capacity also innately constrains the length of the sentences that they can utter. In their short sentences, children therefore say the words that they hear best—those that are stressed in adults' speech—and those that are the most informative and communicative. Mature, complex speech clearly requires both innate abilities and environmental input.

Hearing two languages

In nations like the United States and Canada, many children grow up hearing two or more languages—English, Vietnamese, Spanish, French, Polish, Navajo. Are these children delayed in learning language because they must learn two languages rather than just one? The question of whether children who hear two languages learn to speak, think, and understand better or worse than other children is controversial.

Children who hear two languages face the challenge of making sense out of two sets of words and two systems of syntactic rules instead of one. Despite this challenge, by age 3 most children who hear two languages spoken at home can speak and understand both. They may be slower in building their early vocabularies, and they do sometimes get mixed up. One of their most common mix-ups is ''lexical borrowing,'' using a word from one language when they do not know the word in the other language (Ben-Zeev, 1977; Lindholm and Padilla, 1978). Bilingual children seem to move through three stages before they speak their two languages fluently by about 4 years old (Volterra and Taeschner, 1978). First, they learn a word in one language, not both. Second, they apply one set of syntactic rules to both sets of words. Third, they strongly associate each language with the people and places in which they hear it. If they hear Mama, who has always spoken French, begin to speak in German, young children may grow quite upset. Some people have suggested that children learn two languages best if they learn them in two separate contexts—one in school and one at home, one from mother and one from father—but the research generally does not support this idea (Doyle, Champagne, and Segalowitz, 1978).

What are the effects of bilingualism on children's cognitive development? Research suggests that they are generally positive. Bilingual children

Bilingual children usually do as well as or better than monolingual children both verbally and nonverbally.

do as well as monolingual children on tests of both verbal and nonverbal abilities (Bain, 1976; Lambert, 1972). In tests of storytelling, they tend to express more ideas than monolingual children (Doyle, Champagne, and Segalowitz, 1978). Children who speak two languages, it seems, not only have adequate intellectual and verbal skills but may have some advantages over children who speak only one language. They see the world from two different perspectives, can try out two different approaches to situations, and learn firsthand that language is arbitrary (Diaz, 1985a, b). Bilingualism may make children more cognitively flexible. Bilingual preschoolers in one study were better than monolingual children at understanding that names are merely labels for things and that changing a label does not change the properties of an object (Oren, 1981). Bilingual children seem to understand better the difference between symbols and objects and to understand the functions of language. (Children who enter schools in the United States without knowing English face a different problem. We discuss this problem in Chapter 12.)

The context of cognitive development

Just as language development depends on innate abilities and environmental input, so does cognitive development in general. Even children who inherit genes for brilliance will stagnate mentally if they have no chances to learn first-hand about people and things. In this section, we discuss how several factors in the environment affect children's cognitive development in the preschool years.

Toys

Sam stayed in bed unusually late one morning. When I peeked in, he was sitting up in bed "reading" a story to his animals and dolls, fireman's helmet on his head, slippers on his feet, and a necklace made of dry noodles around his neck.

Natalie took a coffee tin from the kitchen counter and banged on the lid with two spoons. "This is the drum," she told her younger sister. "You follow me and be a horn."

The best toy Erica ever got was the crate from a washing machine. She turned it into a house, a fort, a hospital, a school—an endless array of spaces for playing in.

Toys need not be elaborate, complex, and expensive to satisfy children's needs to explore, experiment, and learn. Two- and 3-year-olds rifle through drawers and boxes, pull books off shelves, push brooms and vacuum cleaners, crawl into closets and under beds, scribble with crayons, and dress dolls. They try to ride the family dog, wear Daddy's glasses to "read" the *TV Guide*, swathe themselves in Mommy's scarves and high heels, and bathe their dolls in the sink. They slide down sliding boards, climb jungle gyms, pump swings, tunnel through sand, and run after ants and butterflies. As they do, they satisfy their curiosity, add to their knowledge about the world, and adapt to it.

Not surprisingly, children's preferences in toys change with age and cognitive ability. Among nursery schoolers in one study, for example, 2-year-olds liked best to play with sand and ride kiddie cars—objects that allow simple manipulation and motor activity; 3-year-olds liked best to play house—with toys that allow for pretending; and 4-year-olds liked best construction materials like clay, paint, and blocks—objects that allow more advanced symbolic activities (Parten, 1933). In another study, 2-year-olds preferred realistic toys that they could use for their intended functions—"vrooming" a truck, "drinking" from a cup, "feeding" a doll—whereas older children preferred nonrealistic toys—boxes, paper tubes—around which they could embroider fantasies (Fein and Robertson, 1975).

> One day when he was 2½, Sam lay on the floor playing with a toy ambulance. I reached into the toy cabinet and took out a small figure of a nurse and a doctor, put them on the floor about a foot from the ambulance. Sam immediately incorporated them into his play, which then grew much more elaborate. When he was 3½, his favorite toy was a key on a chain, which he used as a car, a "poker," and, of course, a "shooter."

Curiosity bubbles from most children like water from a garden hose, especially when they are exposed to stimulating surroundings and intriguing new objects (Berlyne, 1950; Sussman, 1979; Switsky, Haywood, and Isett, 1974). New objects should be complex enough to catch and keep children's interest but not so complex as to be overwhelming. The 3-year-old faced with a 10-piece mouse puzzle is likely to be fascinated but faced with a 50-piece abstract puzzle is likely to be overwhelmed and frustrated. When their toys and play spaces are stimulating and right for their age, they help children in both their make-believe and exploratory play (Bradley, Caldwell, and Elardo, 1977).

Toys also can teach children about colors, shapes, sizes, numbers, and words. Puzzles teach that things can be broken down into pieces—and rebuilt. Crayons, paint, and clay allow children to create symbols. Researchers who have observed children's play with different kinds of toys have found that building materials like blocks and boards, pretend materials like dolls and dress-up clothes, and academic materials like books and puzzles are most likely to promote rich and complex play in preschoolers (Sylva, Roy, and Painter, 1980, and other studies reviewed in Clarke-Stewart, 1982; Minuchin and Shapiro, 1983). Sand, clay, buttons, and other materials for "messing around" encourage creative, experimental, but somewhat less complex play. Small toys like guns or checkers, microscopes or gyroscopes, encourage still less complex play, for children simply do what the materials suggest. When materials are scarce or inflexible, children do less playing, and their play is neither complex nor intellectually challenging.

In their play with toys, young children learn about the way things work, and they grow ever more skillful and adept. Children may first explore the properties of unfamiliar objects—looking, touching, moving, opening,

Stimulating toys satisfy children's needs to explore, experiment, and learn. Two-year-olds may favor playthings that allow simple manipulation and movement. Four-year-olds favor objects that allow for more advanced symbolic play.

closing—and wondering, "Hmm, what does this thing *do*?" Later, as the object becomes familiar, they engage in play that answers, "Now what can *I* do with this?" Exploration and play with objects also can help children to solve simple problems. In one study, for example, 3- to 5-year-olds were asked to remove a piece of chalk from a box they could not reach (Sylva, Bruner, and Genova, 1976). To get the chalk, the children had to clamp together two sticks and extend them toward the box. Children who had been allowed to play with the sticks first were as successful in reaching the box with the sticks as were children who first saw an adult demonstrate how to solve the problem. By exploring and playing at home, children learn how to get the mail, reach cookies on top of the refrigerator, open doors, turn on the oven, stack pots, nest spoons, and dial the telephone.

Television

Mikey used to go to a babysitter who *seemed* to take excellent care of him. But I found out that she parked him in front of the television for most of every afternoon, especially on days when they couldn't go outside, and so I found other day care for him. We just felt that watching television wouldn't stimulate him the way we thought he needed.

In many households, the television plays as long as anyone is at home, and it is often a child who perches intently before the screen, waiting for the next scene. Nearly every household in the United States—97 percent—contains a television set. No wonder that many children watch television more than they do anything else except sleep (Keye, 1974). Although children average close to four hours a day in front of the television, they get little intellectual stimulation from the programs they watch most often (Liebert and Poulos, 1975). The young children who spend the most time watching television, in fact, develop intellectually more slowly than other children (Carew, 1980; Nelson, 1973). In one study, a group of children randomly assigned to restricted television viewing were found to spend more time reading, to be more careful and reflective on tests, and to improve in their performance scores on IQ tests (Gadberry, 1980).

Spending time watching television generally does not speed children's language development. Children of deaf parents, for example, do not learn language if all they have to listen to is television (Sachs and Johnson, 1976), and probably for many of the same reasons, children do not learn to speak a foreign language simply by watching foreign television programs (Friedlander, Jacobs, David, and Wetstone, 1972). But although television *in general* does not teach children cognitive or language skills, certain children's television programs actually may (Rice, 1983). Some educational shows ("Mr. Rogers' Neighborhood," "Sesame Street," "Electric Company") highlight words and phrases, repeat, and refer to things that are present, concrete, and explicitly clear. Children who watch "Sesame Street" learn the alphabet, parts of the body, and properties of objects such as size, amount, and position earlier than children who do not. After a year of watching "Sesame Street," they do better on alphabet and vocabulary tests than other children (Bogatz and Ball, 1971; Minton, 1972). Television may be good or bad for children's intellectual development. It all depends on what the children watch.

Parents

It is, of course, parents who buy the toys and turn on (and off) the television set. They are their children's first teachers, and so they have the enormous responsibility for making their home stimulating enough to keep their preschool children's minds alert and active. It must be safe yet challenging, organized but not too restrictive, intriguing but not overwhelming. Parents also have the responsibility for offering their children the activities that foster exploration and learning, and they are children's first models for intellectual interests. Several researchers have shown that parents who provide appropriate and varied play materials, who are responsive, who participate in their children's games and activities, and who help them with exploratory play encourage their children's development (for example, Bradley, Caldwell, and Elardo, 1977; Bradley and Caldwell, 1984)

Parents can deliberately guide and educate older preschool children as well as provide them with a stimulating environment. Parents who show their children how to complete puzzles, to give the doll a ride in the carriage, to build a skyscraper out of blocks, and who read stories to their children are helping them develop intellectually. Mothers who rehearse specific content with their children, as opposed to just chatting or playing with them, foster their children's learning of specific content—for example, knowledge of letters and numbers—research with 4-year-olds shows (Price, Hess, and Dickson, 1981). When mothers ask their preschoolers to remember things and help them to do so, the children remember better. In one study of 3-year-olds, for example, the children whose mothers asked questions that made demands on their memories remembered better than other children (Ratner, 1984). When parents link their children's current experiences to a broader family and social context, children are more likely to reason deductively. When a child points to a picture and says, "That a cow," all mothers are likely to respond by saying, "Yes, and it says 'moo' " or "Yes, and there are two of them. Can you see the other cow?" But only some mothers create "world links" and say, "Yes, and do you remember when we all went on a picnic and the cow nibbled your hat?" or "Yes, and it's the same color as the cow who jumped over the moon. You used to love that rhyme when you were a baby." In one study, only mothers who made these world links were found to have preschoolers who reasoned deductively (Mills and Funnell, 1983).

In infancy, you will recall from Chapter 6, it was not so clear that the environment had an effect on children's cognitive development. The primary link between infants' and parents' intelligence seemed to be genetic (for example, Yeates et al., 1983). In the preschool years, the effect of home environment and parents' behavior is more marked. In fact it is in this age period that parents may have their greatest effect on their children's cognitive development. In middle childhood, instruction and experiences at school are likely to contribute more than parents to children's intellectual progress.

Parents foster the cognitive development of children by providing a stimulating environment, by being responsive, and by deliberately guiding and educating them. Studies of transracial adoptions can help tease apart the relative influences of heredity and environment on intelligence.

Programs

In the past 20 years, many attempts have been made to improve the learning opportunities of children from disadvantaged families. These attempts have been focused on changing the children's home environments or on enriching their education. One such program designed to enrich preschool children's education was the Abcedarian Project carried out at the Frank Parker Graham Center in Chapel Hill, North Carolina. This program provided full-time day care in a high quality center for children from poor black families. Children were assigned at random to attend the program or to remain at home with their mothers from infancy to school age. The program was a significant success. Children who attended the program scored higher than the control group on IQ tests at ages 2 and 3 (by 10 and 15 points) (Ramey and Campbell, 1979). When they were 4 and 5 years old, children in the program still scored higher than the control children (by 12 and 7 IQ points) (Ramey and Haskins, 1981).

The **Head Start** program is perhaps the best known and certainly the most comprehensive enrichment program for preschoolers. It began in the 1960s as an eight-week summer program for children who were about to enter school but soon turned into a year-round, center-based program for disadvantaged preschool children. Currently, about 450,000 poor and minority children attend Head Start every year. Head Start programs provide medical and dental examinations and immunizations for children, a hot meal and a snack, as well as educational activities for the children and classes for parents in home economics, buying and preparing food, and child care. The educational activities for children, in some Head Start programs, consist of traditional middle-class nursery school routines such as coloring and dress-up, being read to, learning rhymes, drawing, coloring, cutting, playing with blocks and puzzles, riding tricycles, and learning about animals. In other programs, children's education comes from a strictly scheduled and highly structured academic curriculum. Still other Head Start programs have adopted a low-key ''discovery'' approach to education. Children are free to explore and learn from a smorgasbord of materials—wooden blocks, sand, water, weights, sci-

A model preschool program can successfully intervene to modify preschoolers' intelligence. Many investigators have reported IQ increases of from 5 to 15 points in children who attended educational programs.

ence materials, geometric forms, books—laid out for them by the teacher. The teacher responds with a "mini-lesson" only when specifically asked by a child. There also are programs that stress language and communication skills, others that emphasize emotional expressiveness and creativity, and still others that focus on social interaction and adjustment.

A number of evaluative studies have been conducted to measure the effect of Head Start on preschool children. One of the first, the Westinghouse Learning Corporation and Ohio University study (1973), indicated that Head Start had a significant effect on children's IQ scores, raising them 10 points, but that the gains made did not last once the children entered school. Other studies revealed that Head Start children, compared to other disadvantaged children not in the program, were more attentive and less impulsive, were more receptive to language, and had greater curiosity and motivation (Brink, Ellis, and Sarason, 1968; Lesser and Fox, 1968).

Many other smaller and more carefully controlled programs have also produced IQ gains of 5 to 15 points for the children attending them. These IQ gains last a year or two and then begin to diminish. If no further intervention occurs, the gains have disappeared by the time children are 10 to 17 years old (Gray, Ramsey, and Klaus, 1982; Lazar, Darlington, Murray, Royce, and Snipper, 1982; see Figure 9.8). Indirect benefits like improved self-esteem and more positive feelings about school are likely to endure, however. Disadvantaged children who attended preschool enrichment programs are less likely to stay back a grade in school or to need special education than those who did not (Lazar et al., 1982). Even their brothers and sisters benefit indirectly from the effects of their participation in an early intervention program (Klaus and Gray, 1968). Later, Head Start children are more likely to graduate from high school and get full-time jobs than disadvantaged students who did not attend Head Start (Deutsch, 1985).

Not all preschool interventions have been aimed directly at the child; some have approached the child indirectly through the mother. In one study of Chicago mothers and children from low-income housing (Slaughter, 1983), researchers compared mothers who had participated in one of two parent education programs with those who had not, over the period when their children were 2 to 4 years old. Mothers who had participated in discussion groups where they shared their experiences of child rearing and social life

352

PROGRAM EFFECT FADE-OUT

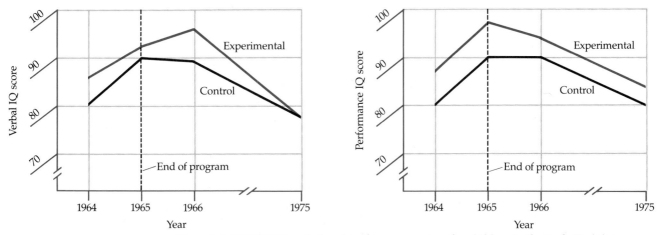

Figure 9.8 IQ (WISC) verbal and performance scores for children in the Early Training Project, taken during and after the program ended and showing that the program effects faded out with time (Gray, Ramsey, and Klaus, 1982).

interacted more and played more elaborately with their children. Their children in turn tested higher on IQ tests and talked more than children in the control group. This study is one of many to demonstrate that involving mothers in their children's education can benefit the children. Parent training is not a panacea for problems or a guarantee of high intelligence in children. But if parents are motivated, children are interested, and training is thorough, it can improve the quality of parents' teaching and interacting with their young children.

Middle-class children as well as poor children can benefit from educational enrichment. By the time they are 4 years old, most children in the United States are attending some form of **nursery school** or day-care program, and with each passing year, so are more and more 3-, 2-, and even 1-year-olds. Nursery schools traditionally have prepared children for kindergarten and first grade. Over the years, many evaluations have shown that when children start school, those whose parents have sent them to nursery school are advanced over children without this experience (Clarke-Stewart and Fein, 1983). Day-care programs with an educational component, research shows, also temporarily accelerate children's intellectual development. Day-care-center children are more advanced than home-care children on both verbal and nonverbal skills: language comprehension and fluency, eye–hand coordination, and drawing. In the Chicago Study of Child Care and Development (Clarke-Stewart, 1984), for example, 2- to 4-year-old children in nursery school or day-care-center programs were 6 to 9 months ahead of home-care children on tests of intellectual development. This intellectual advancement may stem from the stimulation offered in these programs, the availability of a variety of materials and equipment, and the more systematically educational environment of the early childhood program compared to a home. Like the advantages that children get from Head Start and other intervention programs, however, the intellectual acceleration of children who were in day care relative to that of children who stayed at home diminishes by the time first grade rolls around.[2]

---

[2]In Chapter 10, we discuss how day care and nursery school may affect children's social development.

Peers

Another reason that children in preschool programs are intellectually advanced may be that they interact more with peers. Children can stimulate and enrich each others' development, especially if they are together in a preschool program of some kind. In the Chicago study (Clarke-Stewart, 1984), for example, the children who gained the most intellectually were in programs where there were older, more advanced, and more responsive children to watch and do things with. A study of how preschoolers learn by imitating their peers supports this suggestion (Morrison and Kuhn, 1983). In the study, 4- and 6-year-olds observed behavior slightly more advanced or complex than their own. First the researchers watched the children playing alone with a construction toy in which pieces could be combined to make a ramp or roadway on which marbles would roll. The children's play, they found, could be coded into seven levels of performance, ranging from no understanding of the toy's possibilities, through simple to complex constructions, and finally to the successful construction of an incline and an angle. Then the researchers observed the children playing with the toy in groups each made up of four children. In each group, the target child could observe play that was on the same level, a level or two above, or a level or two below his or her own previous performance. The children who advanced to higher levels of play with the toy spent more time playing with the toy and more time watching their peers. The children they watched most were those who were one level more advanced than they were. Clearly, preschool children can and do learn from their peers.

Summary

1. Children use symbols that are verbal—a word, a made-up name—and physical—a drawing, a doll, a stick used as a gun. Piaget called personal symbols *symbols*; he called shared symbols *signs*. Toddlers' pretend play is the first evidence of their symbolic thinking. During the preschool period, pretend play changes from symbolic play with objects, to play in which children act out roles, to dramatic play with roles announced ahead of time.

2. In their drawing, children everywhere begin as scribblers, but after this stage, the pattern of their drawing is shaped by cultural convention.

3. Children between 4 and 6 years old think intuitively and therefore sometimes confuse the real with the imagined, the animate with the inanimate, and their own perspective with others'.

4. Young children cannot perform logical operations such as addition, subtraction, or multiplication, and so their thought, according to Piaget, is "preoperational." Their ability to classify objects is limited to basic, functional categories. They sometimes reason transductively—from one particular to another rather than from the general to the particular—although they are capable of simple deductive reasoning. Slowly, they acquire concepts of number and age.

5. Preschool children are neither as systematic nor as selective in paying attention as older children are, perhaps because they are less efficient at encoding information, because they do not understand what others think it is important for them to pay attention to, or because they cannot consciously direct their attention so that they focus only on relevant aspects of tasks. Memory improves with age, as children get better at encoding information.

6. Children begin speaking in one-word and then two-word telegraphic utterances. Overregularization is a common kind of mistake children make as they are learning to speak in sentences and shows that they have learned the rules for making past tenses and plurals. Language is the result of both innate abilities and environmental input.

7. Although adults do not give children deliberate language lessons, they speak to them in motherese, a special and simplified language adapted to young children's limited language abilities, and they expand their simple utterences into more complex sentences.

8. The number and kind of toys they play with, television shows they watch, and the stimulation they receive from their parents and peers all affect the cognitive development of children.

9. Programs to improve the learning environments of young children, whether focused on the children or their parents or both, can improve children's performance on intelligence tests. Young children's cognitive development is also affected by their attendance at nursery school and day-care programs with an educational component.

Key terms

symbol	operations	reciprocity	recall
sign	preoperational period	decentration	syntax
symbolic play	classification	seriation	telegraphic sentence
private speech	class inclusion	transitive inference	overregularize
intuition	transductive reasoning	horizontal décalage	motherese
animism	conservation	encode	Head Start
egocentrism	reversibility	recognition	nursery school

Suggested readings

CLARKE, ANN M., and CLARKE, A. D. B. (Eds.). *Early Experience: Myth and Evidence.* New York: The Free Press, 1976. A collection of chapters demonstrating the remarkable ability of children to recover from extremely depriving and depressing early experiences. This book takes the position that early childhood is not a critical period for intellectual and social development.

DE VILLIERS, PETER A., and DE VILLIERS, JILL G. *Early Language.* Cambridge, Mass.: Harvard University Press, 1979. A concise guide to the major advances between birth and six years of age as children learn language. The book includes recent findings in psycholinguistics and engaging examples of children's speech.

FLAVELL, JOHN. *Cognitive Development* (2nd ed.) Englewood Cliffs, N.J.: Prentice-Hall, 1985. Well written textbook on cognitive development by an eminent researcher in the field, who is sympathetic to Piaget's views but at the same time responsive to the findings of contemporary researchers in cognitive development.

GARDNER, H. *Artful Scribbles: the Significance of Children's Drawings.* New York: Basic Books, 1980. This book takes children's artwork seriously and ties the development of drawing, from scribbles to abstract forms, to other aspects of child development.

GOODNOW, JACQUELINE. *Children's Drawings.* Cambridge, Mass.: Harvard University Press, 1977. This book analyzes children's drawings as a medium of expressing thought and social development and answers probing questions about what children are doing when they draw.

PERLMUTTER, MARION (Ed.). *Children's Memory.* San Francisco: Jossey-Bass, 1980. The studies reported in this volume of the New Directions for Child Development series focus on infants' and young children's cognition and memory as demonstrated in everyday life.

PIAGET, JEAN. *Play, Dreams and Imitation in Childhood.* New York: Norton, 1962. A classic that weaves together Piaget's theory with wonderful examples of children's play, dreams, and imitation.

chapter ten
Social and emotional development

Between their first and sixth birthdays, children emerge bit by bit from the close confines of Mommy's skirts, and the totally dependent infant is transformed into a proudly independent child ready to venture forth and meet the rest of the world. The bravery of the young child who dares, for the first time, to stay alone at nursery school, or at Auntie's house, or in the doctor's examining room is touching evidence of this progress. During the preschool years, young children develop autonomy and extend relationships beyond the family. They learn social skills and social rules, they learn how to interpret social situations, and they learn how to express and control their emotions. They find out how boys play and girls play. And they find out more about themselves, as their self-concept and understanding of gender roles deepen.

Relations with parents

During the preschool years, the close, constant physical contact between parents and infant, so important to the infant's physical and emotional well-being, gradually gives way to a more autonomous relationship. Toward the end of the first year, the infant crawls away from the parents for brief periods of exploration. The toddler ventures out of the parent's sight, to find a toy or to follow someone into another room. The preschool child becomes less distressed by a separation from the mother or father, and the distance that the child can tolerate away from their comforting presence gradually increases.

Between the ages of 2 and 4, children comfortably play and explore farther and farther away from their mothers and need less physical contact than they did in their earliest years.

Developing autonomy

To study the gradual growth of autonomy, researchers have asked mothers to leave their children briefly in a university playroom either with a stranger or alone (Feldman and Ingham, 1975; Maccoby and Feldman, 1972) or have observed naturally occurring separations between parents and children (Clarke-Stewart, 1973; Clarke-Stewart and Hevey, 1981). Children between 1 and 4 years old, they have found, show less and less distress at these brief separations and, between 2 and 4 years, seek less physical contact and closeness to their mother. As long as they can still see and hear their mother, 2-year-olds are willing to leave her side (Carr, Dabbs, and Carr, 1975; Mahler, Pine, and Bergman, 1975). Even the sound of their mother's voice or the televised image of her face helps 3-year-olds to enter and play more comfortably in an unfamiliar playroom than if they are alone. But let a stranger be present or the situation be stressful in some other way, and 3-year-olds tend to be upset at separations from their mothers (Adams and Passman, 1979). One-third of the 3-year-olds in one study (Murphy, 1962) had trouble separating from their mothers to leave home or to go upstairs with an examiner. Only among 4-year-olds is distress at brief separations from their mothers really rare (Marvin, 1977).

> Robbie was 2½ when he started day care in the home of a woman who took care of three other children. For several weeks, he stood at the door, crying ''Mommy, Mommy'' as I left. As he got to know the babysitter and the other children, he stopped crying. But he acted subdued when he was dropped off every day until he was about 4.

When they are playing outdoors—in a park or playground, for example—children establish physical boundaries and stay within them without having to be retrieved. They move around in brief bouts, move, stop, look, and return, as long as their mother is in view and facing them. In these unfamiliar outdoor settings, children venture from their mothers a distance that increases with impressive mathematical regularity: for every month of increasing age,

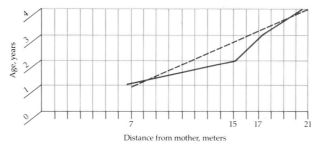

INCREASING INDEPENDENCE

Age, years

Distance from mother, meters

*Figure 10.1 **The distance a child is willing to venture from mother's side increases systematically with age (Rheingold and Eckerman, 1971).***

the children will venture about one foot farther from their mothers in 15 minutes of play (Rheingold and Eckerman, 1971; Figure 10.1).

Although they venture farther away from their parents and tolerate longer separations from them, older children are no less emotionally attached. Physical contact may diminish, but the attachment to parents remains strong. Older children show their attachment in new ways. Now they show their mothers a toy, smile, and talk to her from a distance rather than hanging on to her hand or sitting in her lap (Clarke-Stewart and Hevey, 1981; Maccoby and Feldman, 1972).

As young children are venturing ever farther from their parents, their parents are gradually letting go of the children. In small ways, parents encourage their children to be independent. First they lessen their physical contact with the child, then they relax their constant attention and surveillance, and finally they start fewer interactions (Clarke-Stewart and Hevey, 1981).

During the so-called terrible twos, the young child may occasionally become a tiny tyrant, all in the quest for autonomy.

One evening when Sam was 2½, I realized that for the very first time in his life, 20 waking minutes had passed in which he hadn't needed me or his father. Sam was intent upon sitting under a chair, which he pretended was a hotel. From then on, those brief periods of independence— and relaxation for us—grew more frequent and longer.

The development of autonomy has its rocky moments at first. When 1½- or 2-year-olds get a whiff of independence and strike out farther on their own, they turn their backs on their parents not only literally but figuratively, too. They want to do everything by themselves and for themselves. They want to see, feel, *test* everything for themselves. ''*Me* do it!'' is the rallying cry of the 2-year-old. If they meet resistance, as they often do, they may explode in anger, throw their food on the floor, kick and bite, yell and wail, hold their breath until they turn blue. Tantrums may rain down like hailstones, and the shrieks emanating from the home of a normal 2-year-old may make the neighbors wonder just what is *going on* in that family. These moments—which led some psychologists to refer to this period as the **terrible twos**—reflect the child's bid for autonomy raised to fever pitch. For 2-year-olds, the world is full of temptation and frustration.

When Kristy was 2, in the space of one morning she jammed something in the dishwasher so that it wouldn't work, spilled the contents of the refrigerator into the trash can, peeled all the labels off the cans of food in the pantry, spilled the dog's water on the floor, and threw a tantrum when I wouldn't let her ''skate'' on it. She threw another tantrum when she couldn't mop it up.

Luckily for children and their parents, this phase passes. In secure parent–child relationships, it passes within a year or so, and children move toward a point of balance between their wishes and those of their parents. By the time children are 3, mothers and children are approximately equal partners in the initiation of social exchanges (Clarke-Stewart and Hevey, 1981). Once children can communicate in words, their parents try to mesh their plans with those of their children—''It's going to be bath time in five minutes, Tim,'' or ''Would you like to go in the car with me?'' or ''Please get your sneakers, Robbie. They're in your bedroom.'' The pattern of child as master and parent as slave, which prevails during infancy, gradually breaks down. Young children can wait until their parents finish what they are doing to have their demands satisfied. When Mom says that she has to leave her child alone so that she can go and make a phone call—and the child agrees—then the child is not disturbed at the brief separation (Marvin, 1977).

Continuing patterns of attachment

Not only do young children remain emotionally attached to their parents during the preschool years, but their individual patterns of attachment usually remain stable over time as well. In general, unless there are major changes in the family, children's patterns of attachment—secure, avoidant, ambivalent—remain stable between 1 and 6 years of age (Cassidy and Main, 1984). Infants who were securely attached to their mothers continue to be securely attached as young children, and the same tendency holds true for infants who were ambivalently attached or avoidant.

What is more, as we mentioned in Chapter 7, the pattern of the child's attachment to parents is related to his or her interactions with other people in the preschool period. Securely attached preschoolers, in contrast to those less securely attached, have been observed to enter a relationship with an unfamiliar man more quickly and easily, to be more relaxed and productive in competing with him to build a tower and to be more openly sad when they failed the competition (Lutkenhaus, 1984). They elicit more positive reactions and play in more interesting and innovative ways with an unfamiliar child (Jacobson and Wille, 1984), and they score significantly higher on measures of initiative and skill in getting along with other children at nursery school than insecurely attached children (LaFreniere and Sroufe, 1985; Waters, Wippman, and Sroufe, 1979). There are clear continuities in children's social and emotional behavior—over time and across partners.

Socialization and discipline

In the preschool years, the relationship between parents and children changes in another way: parents begin more actively to socialize and discipline the children, trying to shape and mold them into mature, responsible, productive, functioning members of society. As children near their second birthday, parents tend to perceive them as increasingly competent and assertive. They refuse more of the children's demands and expect from them at least some compliance and cooperation. As children grow more independent and venturesome, parents become less forgiving and more demanding. As children extend the boundaries of their experience, parents begin the process of setting limits and training their children to exercise self-restraint and respect for other people's boundaries. As children become capable of learning the habits, skills, and standards that adults consider important, parents teach them which behavior is acceptable and which unacceptable and impart to them the accumulated knowledge of their culture. There is little correspondence between the controlling behavior parents use with 1- and with 2-year olds (Dunn, Plomin, and Daniels, 1986).

Patterns of authority

How do parents try to influence their preschool children? In extensive research on parents' disciplinary styles by Diana Baumrind (1971, 1979), three distinct patterns of discipline emerged. **Authoritarian parents**, it was found, are firm, punitive, unaffectionate, unsympathetic, detached, and sparing in their praise. They give edicts and expect their children to obey them. Rules are not discussed ahead of time and are not subject to bargaining. The parents try to curb their children's will rather than encouraging their independence. Children who disobey may be punished severely and, in many cases, physically. Children in these families have few rights. Their parents make demands on them but do not reciprocally accept their children's demands. Children are expected to curb their demanding and begging. In extreme cases, children may not speak until spoken to.

> When we were bad as kids, my mother would promise, ''Just wait until your father gets home. He'll give you such a licking.'' She couldn't do anything with us. But my father would walk in, ask how things were, and when he heard that we'd done such and such, he got the strap and walloped our backsides.

Permissive parents do not exert control over their children. The children are given considerable freedom, few responsibilities, and rights similar to adults'. Permissive parents avoid laying down rules, asserting authority, or imposing restrictions. They tolerate and accept their children's impulses,

Authoritative parents set firm limits on their children's behavior but treat the youngsters with respect, explaining carefully and emphatically the reasons for restrictions. Authoritarian parents simply apply force to shape their children's behavior.

including their aggressive and sexual impulses. Children are expected to regulate their own behavior and to make decisions on their own—when and what to eat, what to watch on television, what to read, when to sleep.

> The two girls who live across the street from us are spoiled rotten. Their parents cater to them and give them anything they want. All one of the girls has to do is pout, and the mother caves in. I've heard them yell at their parents, "Get over here right now!"—and the parents do it!

Authoritative parents see the rights and responsibilities of parents and children as complementary. As children mature, they are allowed greater responsibility for their own actions. Authoritative parents reason with their children, encourage give and take, and listen to objections. They keep the level of conflict with their children low. They are firm, loving, and understanding. They try to make their demands reasonable, rational, and consistent. They set limits, but they also encourage independence. They let their children know that they are loved, and they give them a clear idea of what is expected of them.

> If I told my parents that I *really* objected to some law they'd laid down, they always listened to my side of things. Sometimes they would even change their minds, but not often.

For their part, children actually *prefer* parents who explain, reason, and occasionally back up their reasons with physical punishment. When researchers have read children little stories about how parents might discipline their children, the children generally have said that they do not like permissive discipline and that they want parents to set limits (Siegal and Cowen, 1984; Siegal and Barclay, 1985). Children themselves, in other words, favor an authoritative style of disciplining, based on parents' sensitivity *and* firmness.

In the real world of parents and children, the distinctions in disciplinary patterns blur. Although it is true that some parents never hit and some hit a lot, that some parents often reason and some never do, even the most dogmatic parent can be lenient at times, and even the most permissive one can occasionally clamp down. In moments of calm reflection—reading a textbook or talking with another adult about how parents *ought to* enforce discipline—most people favor the path of setting firm limits for children and reasoning with them. But in moments of heat and passion, of which there are *many* in the life of even the best adjusted, most secure and loving, perfectly normal children, reasoning may fly out the window, limits may crumble, and usually measured voices may cause the dishes to rattle.

> Natalie had refused to nap, refused to get dressed, refused her lunch, sulked, hit the baby when I wasn't looking, and was generally a pain all day. When she took a big kettle and spilled water all over the kitchen floor, I slapped her bottom so hard that she was stunned. I stunned myself, too.

Despite these occasional lapses, parents hold strong—and divergent—views on whether children should be physically punished. In a recent survey of 500 readers of *Psychology Today* (Stark, 1985), 49 percent thought that children should never be physically punished, and 51 percent thought that they should be, although most were against anything more than a simple spanking on the behind. The respondents argued against physical punishment for children on the grounds that "violence begets violence" and that it gives children the message that bigger, more powerful people can act abusively. Many said that physical punishment should be reserved for occasions when children run into the street, play with matches, or reach on top of a lighted stove. Others said that spankings are warranted when children talk back, throw tantrums, bite, or lie.

My parents spanked me twice, both times for lying. My mother always said she thought it was terrible to punish children physically. She especially hated punishments like washing a child's mouth out with soap because he'd said something dirty. She used banishment—"Go to your room until you can behave," "Sit on the stairs until you're ready to apologize"—and the silent treatment.

Social and emotional consequences

Although in real families disciplinary styles are not always crisply defined, the three general styles Baumrind found—authoritarian, permissive, and authoritative—have been found to be related to consistent patterns in preschool children's behavior at home, in nursery school, and in the laboratory (Baumrind, 1971, 1979; Becker, 1964; Hoffman, 1970; Maccoby and Martin, 1983). Children reared by authoritarian parents tend to be suspicious and withdrawn, unfriendly and discontented. Although they may be well controlled, they are also likely to be fearful, dependent, and submissive, slow to explore and less likely to strive intellectually. Authoritarian discipline, with its threat of severe punishment, may arouse so much emotion in children that they cannot concentrate on moral reasoning, such as how wrongdoing affects other people. For this reason, these children are more likely to cheat and less likely than other children to feel guilt or to accept blame. Children heavily disciplined in their first two or three years are likely to be conforming, dependent, and inhibited; children given heavy discipline later are likely to be hostile and aggressive.

Like the children with authoritarian parents, children with permissive parents tend to be dependent and unhappy. They are more likely than children with authoritarian parents to be outgoing and sociable and to strive intellectually, but like these children they tend to be immature and aggressive and to lack persistence and self-reliance.

Children whose parents are authoritative are most likely to be friendly, cooperative, competent, intellectually assertive, self-reliant, independent, happy, and socially responsible—an ideal combination of qualities. The best discipline for parents who wish to foster their children's social, cognitive, and moral development seems to be to create an atmosphere of warm approval, praise, and acceptance, and then to explain why the child *should* act in particular ways and to intervene actively when the child acts otherwise. Children are most likely to behave as their parents wish if the parents point out how the child's misbehavior will affect other people—"If you throw snow on their walk, they will have to clean it up again"; if they stop the child from continuing the misbehavior—"Stop throwing that snow!"; and if they enlist the child's help in repairing the damage—"Now help me shovel the snow off again." It also helps if parents explain other people's motives or needs to the child—"Don't hit him. He didn't mean to push you. He tripped." "She's afraid of dogs, so don't let Rusty jump on her." "No loud playing while Daddy is sleeping. He needs his sleep." This kind of discipline appeals to children's pride, competence, and concern for others. It shows them how their own behavior affects other people, and it helps them to integrate this knowledge with their capacity for empathy.

Within these associations between parents' disciplinary styles and children's behavior, though, what is cause and what is effect? It has long been assumed that discipline causes the differences observed in children's behavior. But it is entirely possible that parents of more mature and competent children follow their regimen of moderate, authoritative discipline *because* their children act compliantly and cooperatively, rather than the reverse (Lewis, 1981). Discipline is undoubtedly a two-way street. On one side, it is affected by parents' attitudes, values, and circumstances and, on the other side, it is affected by characteristics of the child like temperament and sex. Researchers have found, for example, that authoritarian discipline is related to aggressiveness and social incompetence in boys but not in girls (Baumrind, 1979; Maccoby, Snow, and Jacklin, 1984; Martin, 1975). Girls are more likely to lack social competence if their parents are permissive and do not challenge them or make demands on them to act maturely. Many gaps remain in psychologists' attempts to chart the course of disciplinary styles and their long-term social consequences, but there are clear suggestions that the effects of parents' discipline are neither simple nor one-sided.

Control and compliance

What about the immediate effects of parents' attempts to control their children's behavior? Are these more straighforward? Can we say what kinds of requests, commands, incentives, and rewards are most effective in getting children to comply right away? Some of the most detailed descriptions of control and compliance come from naturalistic observations of parents actually trying to control the behavior of their young children at home. Here, for example, a mother tries to teach her 2-year-old son table manners (Lytton, 1976, p. 301).

C: My nose is dirty.

M: What do you say?

C: My dirty nose.

M: What do you say?

C: Clean it off.

M: Say "please."

C: Clean it off.

M: What do you say?

C: (Demands again.)

M: Is that how you ask nice?

C: (Demands again, then whines, then demands again with a yell.)

M: Where's "please"?

C: (Demands again.)

M: Where's "please"?

C: (Demands again.)

M: Say "please."

C: (Still does not comply. M feeds him.)

M: Don't spill this milk.

C: My nose is dirty.

M: What do you say?

C: Please.

M: (Shows her approval and cleans his nose.) You can say "sorry."

C: Sorry.

M: Just bad boys say bad words. Don't say bad words.

C: (Says something in compliance with M's wishes, and M shows her approval.)

These naturalistic observations of 2-year-olds suggest that the most common method of attempting to control children of this age is to use commands and prohibitions. Adding physical control to a simple command, surprisingly, *detracts* from its effectiveness. But hugging the child as a parent asks him to do something increases the likelihood of compliance, and making a suggestion is more effective than giving a command. Parents tend to be somewhat erratic, however, in trying to control their children. Regardless of whether the child complied with a request or not, the parents observed in these studies usually ignored the child's behavior. The occasions when parents praised children for complying or spanked them for not complying were rare indeed. Children who complied were more likely to be faced with another request or suggestion than with a respite or a word of praise.

For 3- and 4-year-olds, temporarily withdrawing affection and attention can be a powerful way for parents to gain their children's compliance. Most parents combine this tactic with other disciplinary techniques like physical coercion, warnings and prohibitions, explanations and teaching. But for young children, withdrawal of affection is perhaps the most effective single weapon in a parent's arsenal for gaining compliance (Chapman and Zahn-Waxler, 1982). The parent's tone of voice also is important for controlling the child. A neutral tone has little effect—"Timmy is crying because you took his tricycle." "Ho hum," the child thinks. A tone of conviction, even passion, does have effect—"Kristy, don't let me see you taking Timmy's tricycle *ever again*!" (Zahn-Waxler, Radke-Yarrow, and King, 1979). Control is also more effective when parents make their demands clear and explicit. First, they need to capture the child's attention—"Hey, Mikey" or "Kristy, I want to talk to you for a minute." And then they need to narrow their demands to the task at hand—"I want you to give Timmy a turn on the tricycle now." Parents who monitor their young children's attention and adapt their demands to it gain more compliance than parents who pay less attention (Schaffer and Crook, 1980).

Naturalistic observations and experiments done in the laboratory suggest that effective control has the following characteristics (Parke, 1977). First, it is prompt. The less time that elapses between a child's misbehavior and an adult's discipline, the more effective the discipline is likely to be. Best of all is to stop the child in the act of misbehaving. Second, punishment must be neither too severe—for a child may become anxious and withdrawn—nor too lenient. Moderate punishment is best. Third, discipline from a person who is on good terms with the child is effective, because the child loses more if a scolding comes from someone who is usually warm and affectionate. Fourth, an explanation should accompany the discipline. This criterion may be the most important of all. Children are likely to ignore their parents when they do not explain why they are forbidding a certain activity. The explanation must be right for the child's level of understanding, though. "You don't hit other children" may be enough explanation for a young child. Anything more elaborate would be confusing. Finally, effective discipline is consistent. The best rule is for parents to discipline on the few issues that matter most.

Control is not simply a matter of applying tried-and-true techniques, though. Even immediate control and compliance occur within the context of the history of disciplinary interactions between parents and children, as a researcher in one longitudinal study discovered. By observing the earlier interactions between mothers and children, John Martin (1981) found that children's compliance in specific situations was associated more with the history of their interactions with their mothers than with the mothers' controlling behavior alone. In another study, researchers observed 3½-year-old children's compliance with their mothers' requests to put away toys, after they had gone through one of three kinds of interaction in the laboratory (Parpal and Maccoby, 1985). Some of the children and mothers had played freely for 15 minutes, as they would at home; some of the children had played with their mothers while they acted responsively, letting the child initiate all the play with toys and going along with the child's ideas; and some of the children had played alone while their mothers filled out a questionnaire. Children were more likely to comply after the noninteractive session—presumably in response to the withdrawal of the mother's attention—and after responsive play—presumably because they were very pleased with the interaction they had gone through.

Interactive chains

The control techniques that parents use and their immediate effectiveness, like the long-term consequences of different disciplinary styles, are affected both by parents' own characteristics and perceptions and by characteristics of their children.

Parents' characteristics

In attempts to control children's behavior, parents do not react objectively to the children's actions. They react according to their *interpretation* of the actions. One variable that affects parents' perceptions of their children's actions is the extent to which parents feel that they are in control of the situation. In one series of investigations, experimental confederates, who were children aged 7 to 9, were asked to act uncooperatively, unresponsively, or shyly with an unfamiliar woman while the two were building something together in the laboratory (Bugental, Caporael, and Shennum, 1980; Bugental and Shennum, 1981, 1984). Women who felt in control of their lives and the situation responded to the uncooperative boys with negative comments and a more assertive tone of voice; women who did not feel in control did not grow more assertive and let the boys go on acting unruly. Women who considered themselves *and* the children to be in control were not reduced to helplessness when the boys were unresponsive or shy; they adapted their own behavior to fit the boys' competence and offered reassurance and stimulation.

Characteristics of children

Control rests not just in parents' hands, of course. Some control also rests in children's hands. Children's individual characteristics affect the ways that parents attempt to control them and how effective their efforts are. Even in the same family, parents differ markedly in the controlling behavior they direct to their children. In one study, for example, mothers were observed with their two children when the children were each 2 years old (Dunn, Plomin, and Daniels, 1986). There was no significant correlation between the mothers' discipline with the two children.

This lack of a relation is most likely the result of differences in the children's temperaments. Some children are imps, constantly testing their parents' limits—and tempers. Others are perfect angels.

> With Mikey, one unkind word, and he would absolutely crumple. We have never spanked him; he couldn't take it—and he's never needed it. But Erica is a different story. We could spank her until we were exhausted, and she wouldn't obey. No, with Erica, either we enlist her cooperation or forget it.

Mothers of children with difficult temperaments, it has been observed, do more controlling, warning, forbidding, taking away objects, and asserting their power than do mothers of children with easy temperaments (Bates, 1980). Their difficult children, in turn, keep on disobeying and testing limits longer than other children, and they ignore, protest, and talk back to their parents—"I didn't do it. She did it." Mothers of difficult 3- and 4-year-olds report that they are likely to discipline the children by ignoring them or giving in, rather than by asserting power over them, more than do mothers of easy children (Gordon, 1983). Parents of especially active children also get into power struggles with their children and have trouble controlling them (Buss, 1981).

Handicapped children, too, present their parents with management problems. In one group of toddlers with physical handicaps, for example, the children were observed to initiate fewer social interactions, to engage in focused play less often, to speak less clearly, and to be more easily distracted, clingy, and disobedient than nonhandicapped young children (Wasserman, Allen, and Solomon, 1985). Their mothers needed to work harder to interact with and control them than mothers of nonhandicapped children. Blind and deaf children behave less predictably in interactions with their parents than nonhandicapped children (Walker and Kershman, 1981). They are prevented from returning their parents' loving gazes, from hearing the sounds of language, from learning through observation of a thousand daily actions, and from developing the usual physical independence—and the consequences are profound; these children are likely to develop severe social problems, and their parents may feel unsure and anxious about how to act with them (Fraiberg, 1974, 1975, 1977). Children who have serious physical or behavior problems constantly confront family members with frustrating, painful episodes of interaction. Even experienced, skillful parents have trouble avoiding aversive episodes when they must cope with a chronically ill, handicapped, or difficult child. Not surprisingly, questionnaires and self-reports show that parents of handicapped children are more psychologically troubled than the parents of normal children (Tavormina, Boll, Dunn, Luscomb, and Taylor, 1975).

Strings of interaction

In each family, parents' characteristics and children's combine into strings of interactions, which may be either harmonious or destructive. Too often, exhausted parents must deal with and discipline tired, cranky children. At a time when everyone needs a breather, it's often the case that none is available. Mothers (or fathers) may be cooped up in a few rooms all day with a child who, for any one of a number of reasons—a terrible cold, a terrible handicap, a terrible disposition—test their patience and coping abilities. After a few hours with any such child, parents need a break.

> After our third baby was born, we decided to hire a babysitter to come in between 4 and 8 every day. That was always the time when we all hit bottom.

In the days of the pony express, when the mail had to get through, riders changed horses to keep up the grueling pace. What made sense then for horses would make sense now for parents, if only some version of a parent express could be arranged. The need for ''fresh horses'' is all too clear when children are difficult or balky. When children comply with mild pressure from their mothers—''Turn down the television, Tim.'' ''Okay, Mom,''—the string of potentially unpleasant interactions ends there. But when children do not comply, mothers redouble their efforts at control—''Tim, I said turn down that television. Turn it down *now*, or I'll send you to your room.'' ''Okay, Tim, you're going to your room. Don't you talk back to me.'' For families to avoid intense conflict, children must learn to comply with parents' mild pressure. When children do not comply, actions cause reactions, and when these are hostile, tense, or defeating, they build into seemingly endless vicious circles. The end result in the family is disruption, despair, and low self-esteem (Patterson, 1980).

In most families, mother and father together manage the routine problems that crop up in the course of child rearing. But in families with problem children, the mother usually becomes the lone crisis manager (Patterson, 1980). She often engages in long coercive exchanges with the problem child, in which the child attacks her and quickly escalates the battle, even though the mother did nothing to provoke the attack, and even though she escalates only slightly and tries to withdraw as quickly as possible. Fathers seem to have less trouble than mothers in dealing with active sons, because fathers can defuse the situation with jokes about the boys' pranks or dramatizations, whereas mothers are more likely to become hostile.

In families with extremely difficult and aggressive children, one person's aversive behavior seems to set off long strings of coercion and unpleasant behavior. Brothers and sisters, too, get into the act. They behave coercively, using punishment and negative reinforcement to control others' behavior

(Patterson, 1982). When there is no problem with parents' skills or children's temperaments, parents are more likely to ignore their child's aversive behavior, but once they do notice it, they step in firmly and stop it at once. Their discipline effectively ends the coercion before it can develop into a long and painful chain of actions and reactions; their children stop doing what they had been punished for. But in problem families, the children keep on misbehaving, despite their parents' punishment, and the parents keep on punishing, despite the children's behavior. Neither side is sensitive to the needs or signals of the other.

Looking and learning

In attempting to socialize their children, parents often use less direct methods than telling children what to do and punishing them if they disobey. One way in which children learn appropriate social behavior is through being rewarded for social acts. The power of instrumental conditioning has been amply demonstrated in laboratory experiments. Parents as well as experimeters often use tangible rewards to shape their children's behavior: ''Behave in the store, and I'll buy you a balloon.'' ''Good girl; here's a piece of gum.'' But parents have to be careful about how they dole out the rewards, for the effect is not always to increase the frequency of the rewarded behavior. Children come to dislike foods and activities they once liked, researchers have shown, if they are rewarded for them (Birch, Marlin, and Rotter, 1984; Lepper and Greene, 1975, 1978). It's as though the child thinks, ''If she has to give me something for eating this stuff, I must not like it,'' or ''If I'm going to get a prize for doing this, it must be work.'' In contrast, children who are praised are likely to keep doing the things they are praised for. Whenever possible, parents should stick to compliments—''What a helpful boy you are,'' ''That's a grown-up thing to do''—rather than chocolate chip cookies or quarters for walking the dog or playing quietly.

Children also learn vast quantities of information incidentally, casually, as they observe everyday events, with no cookies, quarters, or compliments to motivate them. Children learn many things simply from watching their par-

Children learn many things just by watching their parents and other people. They do not need any kind of tangible reward for imitating what they see.

ents. In one controlled experiment, over 90 percent of the 4-year-olds studied imitated the adult experimenter knocking over a doll, and 45 percent marched around the room in the same unusual way as the adult had (Bandura and Huston, 1961).

> When Jason was 2½, he turned around to watch me just as I was popping an aspirin into my mouth and started to drink some water. All he saw was my hand cover my mouth; he didn't see the aspirin. For the rest of the day, he drank by first tapping his mouth and then drinking.

In one study of observational learning in the real world, researchers watched mothers with their children during half an hour of free play with a set of toys (Waxler and Radke-Yarrow, 1975). *All* children imitated the way their mother played with the toys at least once. They were especially likely to imitate her if she was enthusiastic and demonstrated only a few ways of playing with the toys and if the child had a good relationship with her. Children do not automatically copy their parents' behavior. As children observe other people's actions, they encode their observations in words or images; they form mental representations of what they see. Then, in *some* instances, depending on how they interpret what is wanted or needed or will be rewarded, and depending on their relationship with the person, children imitate what they have observed (Bandura, 1977).

Family stressors

When we imagine "the typical American family," most of us probably conjure up an image of a father who kisses his wife and two children—Sis and Junior—goodbye every morning before he drives to work. Mom, still in her bathrobe, clears the breakfast dishes and then gets Junior and Sis ready for school. The problem with this image is that it no longer represents the typical family. Today fewer than one in five American families fit this image. The rest of us live in families where Dad may well go off to work—but Mom does too. The children—or *child*, for many families stop at one child—goes to day care or to preschool, and preschool may well have a special group for children of divorced parents. After their parents divorce, children may live with one parent and visit the other. They also may have to cope with stepparents, stepsiblings, and stepgrandparents. Divorce and full-time jobs for both parents are stressful circumstances for adults and children. They affect parents' well-being, children's development, and family dynamics.

Divorce

> When the kids' father and I got divorced, Kristy and Jason had a few rocky years. But I knew that Kristy at least had turned the corner when she saw a *Newsweek* cover story on "children of divorce" and joked, "Well, we may be miserable, but at least we're typical." It's been harder for Jason not to have his father around. I'm still not sure how it's all going to turn out for him.

> As I pushed Sam and some of the other 4-year-olds on the swings, I heard one kid ask, "How many dads do you have?"

> Every time there's any problem with Megan at school, it's always chalked up to the fact that her mother and I are separated.

Over one million couples in this country divorce every year, and 70 percent of them have children. Among parents of preschoolers, the divorce rate climbed from 8 percent in 1950 to 20 percent in 1980. At the present divorce rate, half of the children born in this decade will live at least temporarily with one parent, typically their mother. Not only do children suffer when they are separated from a parent, but the parent does too. Even the parent with custody of the children usually suffers, by losing the economic, emotional, and practical support of the other parent.

In one of the most comprehensive studies yet done of the psychological effects of divorce on children and parents, researchers collected data on 96 families with 4-year-old children through interviews, personal records, psychological tests, and observations at 2 months, 1 year, and 2 years after the divorce (Hetherington, Cox, and Cox, 1976, 1978, 1982). In all families, the mother retained custody of the child or children. In the year after the divorce, it was found, mothers became more authoritarian and less affectionate with their youngsters. Family routine became more chaotic. Children became more unruly. Boys especially were aggressive and ornery at home and in nursery school. For fathers, the first year after the divorce marked the beginning of decreasing emotional attachment to their children; the emotional bond deteriorated and the number of contacts diminished. Two years after the divorce, mothers were more patient than they had been the year before, children were more cooperative, and family routines were more stable. But there were still problems. Fewer than one-half of the fathers saw their children as often as once a week—although all lived nearby—and the boys were suffering. Most of them were more feminine and less mature than boys whose parents were not divorced. Their aggressiveness, which had been physical the first year, had been transformed into a more feminine form, verbal aggression. Many preschool sons had become ''sissies.'' Only the boys who continued to see their fathers were unlikely to have developed this problem.

One reason that preschool children may find their parents' divorce so difficult is that they lack a firm sense of the continuity of family relationships. They tend to think that a family consists of people living in the same house. If the father moves out, it seems to the child that he is no longer part of the family. Preschool children also may blame themselves for the divorce. In another study, researchers interviewed children in 60 middle-class families at the time of the divorce and one year later (Wallerstein and Kelly, 1980). Between ages 3½ and 6, children's main feeling about the divorce was self-blame. They saw the difficulty in their parents' marriage not as an issue between mother and father but as something that had gone wrong between themselves and their parents.

After a marriage breaks up, parents often become absorbed in their own difficulties, and the quality of the attention and care they offer their children deteriorates, which is another reason that children suffer from their parents' divorce. Divorce itself creates stress, and stress preoccupies parents. Parents who are preoccupied play less with their children and stimulate, support, and help them less. Their interactions are more curt, critical, and interfering (Zussman, 1980). Stress causes parents to withdraw from interaction or to act irritably and aversively with their children (Forgatch and Wieder, cited in Patterson, 1982). Continued conflict between divorced parents is still another reason that children suffer. When parents do not get along, when they fight in front of their children, no matter whether they are divorced or married, their children suffer and are likely to act out and act up. They are more likely to develop behavior problems (Richman, Stevenson, and Graham, 1983), and they act more disruptively, if their parents fight openly (Hetherington, Cox, and Cox, 1982). Exactly what makes children act up is not clear. Perhaps they imitate their parents' aggressive actions toward each other. Perhaps they absorb and reflect their parents' anger. The finding that children who lose a parent to death do not usually act disruptively points to discord between the

For both parent and child, life in a single-parent family can bring special stresses and pain.

parents as the decisive factor. Whether children develop long-term problems depends in large part on how their parents handle the divorce—whether they part amicably or bitterly, whether they fight openly or not—and on the relationships that they maintain with their children (Wallerstein and Kelly, 1980).

When parents remarry, the children may find themselves experiencing more problems—plunked into a stepfamily where relationships are unfamiliar and difficult. Now there may be six sets of grandparents, a stepmother or stepfather, and an assortment of brothers and sisters, each of whom has definite ideas about the best way to stuff the Thanksgiving turkey and every other aspect of family life. The more complex the stepfamily, the more stressful life within it can be. Who should discipline the children? Whose way of doing things should prevail? Who should share a room with whom? The child may feel that the stepparent is an intruder who is taking away the "real" parent. The child may be confused by inconsistent discipline. The stepparent may not have the same commitment to the child as the biological parent. Sexual abuse is more common in stepfamilies, for example. (In one San Francisco sample, 17 percent of the women with stepfathers had as children been sexually abused by them; the comparable figure for biological fathers was 2 percent [Russell, 1984].) Divorce and remarriage clearly can put stress on preschool children's social development.

Mother's work

Mother's work, too, can be a source of stress for the child and for the family. We all cherish the image of a mother who greets her child's return from nursery school with an enveloping hug and a batch of warm cookies. But nowadays, about half of the mothers of preschool children work away from home. Working mothers spend less time taking care of their children than do mothers who are housewives (Hill and Stafford, 1978), and they spend less time within calling distance or in the same room but doing something without their children, like ironing, cooking, reading, or watching television (Goldberg, 1977). But there is generally no difference in the amount of time working

Stress and the single parent

Marsha Weinraub and Barbara Wolf (1983), of Temple University, wanted to know what it is like for children to grow up in a family with only one parent, their mother. They wondered whether single mothers face more life changes and stresses and fewer social supports or community ties than married mothers. They wondered whether single mothers have more difficulty coping with their stresses and responsibilities than married mothers. They wondered also whether interaction between parents and children is influenced by social supports and whether the relationship among stresses, support, and mother–child interactions differs in single- and two-parent families. Their subjects were 14 single mothers and their children and 14 married mothers and their children, matched for the child's age (2 to 4½ years) and the mother's education and income. Half of the single women were divorced; half had chosen to raise a child alone from the beginning. Only women who had raised their child alone from birth or shortly thereafter were included. The women were interviewed in depth and observed with their children.

Single mothers, the researchers found, worked substantially more hours a week than the married mothers. They had experienced significantly more stressful life changes in the previous year than the married mothers had, and the nature of the changes differed as well. Single women faced changes in jobs, living arrangements, and personal goals; married women faced pregnancy, birth, and home mortgages. Single mothers had fewer social contacts and were less likely to confide in people they saw often than married mothers were. Single mothers also considered their friends, relatives, and people in social or church groups less supportive than married mothers did and were less satisfied with the support that they received. Their social networks changed more often than those of the married mothers. Single mothers used twice the amount of day care that married mothers did. Although single mothers had to cope on their own with finances, child care, and household responsibilities, they reported no more difficulty coping than married mothers. Only in the area of household responsibilities did single mothers have more trouble.

Still, despite these differences in stressful circumstances, the *relations* between mothers and children did not differ appreciably in the one- and two-parent families. Single mothers did no better or worse at controlling, nurturing, or communicating with their children, and the children seemed equally compliant and mature. In both kinds of families, mothers who were more stressed were less nurturant. Unexpectedly, Weinraub and Wolf found that single mothers who had the most social contacts tended to be less nurturant and to have less control over their children. These single mothers generally were of two types: young divorced women who had moved in with their parents and whose social contacts included critical relatives, and mothers who lived alone with their children and who sought social contacts through work or dating. The former were placed in a position of immaturity themselves. The latter faced the dilemma of having to choose between spending time with their children and satisfying their own needs for intimacy and support. Social contacts do not assure social support.

In short, Weinraub and Wolf found substantial differences in the lives of single and married mothers. Single mothers are under more stress from life changes and from the longer hours they work. Their social networks offer them less support for their role as parent. Married mothers can more easily integrate their roles as mother, worker, and adult woman. Despite the increased pressures they operate under, however, single mothers are much like married mothers in their ability to handle their children.

mothers and housewives spend *alone* with their children (Goldberg, 1977). Several investigators have suggested that the time working mothers spend playing and talking with their children is especially intense and that they set aside uninterrupted chunks of time to spend with their children (Hoffman, 1980; Pedersen, Cain, Zaslow, and Anderson, 1983). Others have found that when differences in the nature of mother–child interaction are observed, working mothers do pay more attention and talk more to their young children (Hoffman, 1984).

But work is not the same for all women. Some researchers have hypothesized that a job that improves a mother's morale will improve her relationship with her child and that a job that strains her will cut into her relationship with her child, and the data bear out this hypothesis (Hock, 1980; Schubert, Bradley-Johnson, and Nuttal, 1980; Stuckey, McGhee, and Bell, 1982). The cause, however, is not yet clear. It may be that happy work makes happy mothers, or it just may be that some women are more competent and happier wherever they are, at home or at work.

What are the effects on their young children of mothers' working? For one thing a mother's work is likely to enlarge the opportunities that her children can imagine for themselves. Children of working mothers, for example, can think of more possibilities in answer to questions like "What would you like to be when you grow up?" than children of housewives (Zuckerman, 1985).

> I'm an eye doctor, and Natalie's father is a surgeon, so our kids just take it for granted that both parents work. It *is* hard on them sometimes, like when we have a new babysitter or when I have to miss some event at school that's important to them. But the kids know that mommies and daddies go to work, and they've never questioned it. I'm sure Natalie will have a career when she grows up.

For another thing, many daughters of working mothers are more independent and outgoing; they are socially and personally better adjusted; they achieve more; and they admire their mothers and women in general more than do daughters of housewives. Sons of working mothers, however, do not fare so well. They tend to be less well adjusted socially and to achieve less in school (Hoffman, 1984).

Is the increased training in independence that working mothers give their children too much or too soon for sons but not for daughters? Some psychologists (for example, Chase-Lansdale, 1981) have suggested this, but they have not yet tested the hypothesis empirically. Might working mothers favor their daughters? There is some support for this suggestion, too. In one study of 2- to 6-year-olds, it was found that in families in which mothers worked, daughters got more attention than sons. But in families in which mothers did not work, the sons got more attention (Stuckey, McGhee, and Bell, 1982). Similarly, in a study of 3-year-olds and their parents, fathers and mothers who worked full time described their daughters in more positive terms and their sons in less positive terms than parents who did not both work (Bronfenbrenner, Alvarez, and Henderson, 1983; Bronfenbrenner and Crouter, 1982).

Said one mother who taught full time at a university about her daughter:

> Great, incredibly lovable, bright creative. At times she can be a pain in the neck with her strong will. But that can carry into positive as well as negative. She's very opinionated—about books, clothes, where she wants to go and when. But I think it's good that she has confidence and can assert herself (Bronfenbrenner et al., 1983, p. 9).

But another mother who worked full time said this about her son:

> He really is an ornery child. He's very difficult to manage. He fights us on just about everything. I think that's our biggest problem right now, trying to have him control his actions (Bronfenbrenner et al., 1983, p. 10).

Why would parents describe their sons and daughters so differently? Perhaps families in which the wife has a more egalitarian role simply do not subscribe to the traditional pattern of favoring sons and paying more attention to them than to daughters (Hoffman, 1979). Perhaps preschool boys actually are more ornery and difficult than girls and present more of a strain to their working, overburdened mothers. There is some evidence to support this (Bates, 1980b). Perhaps boys are affected more negatively than girls when their mothers work because, as we described earlier, they are more vulnerable to environmental stresses. Perhaps girls benefit more from stress because it makes their parents tougher on them, and as we have already mentioned, that toughness fosters social competence. There are many possibilities. Only further research will sort out the reasons that daughters more often flourish and sons flounder in families with working mothers.

Relationships with brothers and sisters

Most American families have two children, and many of them are preschool-aged at the same time. An important part of many young children's social development, therefore, is learning to get along with another young child. When they are as young as 6 months old, babies begin to interact with their older brothers and sisters (Abramovitch, Pepler, and Corter, 1982; Dale, 1983; Dunn and Kendrick, 1982a). By the time they are 2 years old, they are spending lots of time with their siblings. Four- to 6-year-old siblings have been observed to spend twice as much time alone together as they spend with their parents (Bank and Kahn, 1975).

Siblings show their interest in each other and learn from each other in many ways. One way is by imitating each other. In one study, nearly one-third of the interactions between 2-year-olds and their older siblings consisted of imitation (Pepler, Corter, and Abramovitch, 1982). Younger children imitated their older siblings far more than the reverse, but older siblings imitated their younger siblings as well. Siblings also show their interest in each other by doing things together. They do things in tandem with great excitement and pleasure (Buhler, 1939; Dunn and Kendrick, 1982a; Greenwood, 1983). Interactions of brothers and sisters are marked by strongly positive feelings.

> He loves being with her and her friends—he's very fond of one of her friends. He trails after Laura. . . . They play in the sand a lot . . . making pies. She organizes it, and swipes away things that are dangerous and gives him something else. They go upstairs and bounce on the bed. Then he'll lie there while she sings to him, and reads books to him. And he'll go off in a trance with his hanky [comfort object]. The important thing is there are becoming games that they'll play together. He'll start something by laughing and running towards some toy, turning round to see if she's following. He'll go upstairs and race into one bedroom and shriek, and she joins him (Dunn and Kendrick, 1982a, p. 39).

By the time the younger sibling is 3 years old, siblings often cooperate in games and play, show physical affection and concern, and try actively to help and comfort each other (Dunn, 1983; Dunn and Kendrick, 1982a).

Most siblings are friendly and comforting with each other, but is their relationship like the attachment between children and their parents? Two early studies (Ainsworth, 1967; Schaffer and Emerson, 1964a) showed that many babies acted distressed in the absence of their older siblings and greeted them joyfully on their return at the same age as they showed this sort of attachment behavior to their mother. Similarly, half of the 14-month-olds in another sample missed an absent older sibling, and one-third went to the older sibling when they felt unhappy (Dunn and Kendrick, 1982b). In a strange situation or outdoors, older siblings can comfort younger ones and serve as a secure base when a stranger approaches or when the mother is out of reach (Clark and Krige, 1979; Samuels, 1980). When sibling pairs found themselves in an unfamiliar laboratory setting, in one study, for example, more than half of the 4-year-olds promptly and effectively comforted and reassured their younger siblings who were distressed at their mother's absence (Stewart, 1983). Children admitted to a live-in nursery were far less distressed if an older sibling was with them (Heinicke and Westheimer, 1966). Thus, for the younger child at least, the relationship with an older sibling may be characterized as an attachment.

Not only do older siblings act like parents in providing security to younger ones, but they also speak in the same ways as parents do to young children. Speaking motherese, older siblings repeat, explain, and help a younger child to practice speech. Here a 31-month-old tries to dissuade his younger brother from eating a piece of candy that fell on the floor. Telling him that the family dog, Scottie, will eat it, he urges the baby into the kitchen with ever shorter sentences:

> No don't you eat it. Scottie will eat it. No not you. Scottie will eat it. Not you. Scottie. Not you. Shall we go in door? Right. Come on. Come on. In door Robin. In door (Dunn and Kendrick, 1982a, p. 50).

It has been suggested that the ability to take the sibling's perspective, which these children's actions imply, comes from the children's familiarity with each other and from their reciprocal relationship. Because siblings share so much and understand each other so well, they are well placed to understand each other. Older children often interpret their younger siblings' wishes or feelings; ''Kenny wants cakey, Mom'' or ''Jo-Jo likes monkeys.'' They clearly understand the younger child's point of view. As one older brother said as he watched his younger brother playing with a balloon, ''He going pop in a minute. And he going cry. And he going be frightened of me too. I *like* the pop'' (Dunn and Kendrick, 1982a, p. 46).

Older siblings in many cultures around the world are expected to take care of their younger brothers and sisters. In a review of ethnographic reports on 186 societies, researchers found that more than 80 percent of younger children were cared for by older siblings (Barry and Paxton, 1971). Most older siblings in the United States and Great Britain also show interest in younger

When a new brother or sister is born, the older sibling gains a new playmate and new responsibilities but to some extent also loses a parent.

brothers and sisters, worry when they cry, and try to entertain and take care of them (Brody et al., 1985; Dunn, Kendrick, and MacNamee, 1981; Legg, Sherick, and Wadland, 1974; Trause et al., 1981). Nevertheless, siblings' relationships are very different from parent–child relationships. No matter how positive sibling interactions are, it is unlikely that they are as positive as interactions with parents. Researchers have shown that children interact more often and more positively with parents than with siblings (Baskett and Johnson, 1982). They also have more negative encounters with siblings.

Brothers and sisters understand not only how to comfort their distressed siblings but also how to provoke them, and their interactions are characterized by strongly negative feelings as well as positive ones.

> It's worse now he's on the go. He annoys her. They fight a lot—more than four or five big fights a day, and every day. They're very bad tempered with each other. He makes her cry such a lot (Dunn and Kendrick, 1982a, p. 39).

In a study of three African societies, it was found that older siblings helped, fed, and supervised their younger siblings as much as adults would, but they also played with and acted aggressively toward them more than adults would (Whiting and Pope-Edwards, 1977). Siblings can annoy, tease, and compete with devastating accuracy.

> When our family went on car trips, I sat in the back seat next to my younger sister. Under my breath and too quietly for my parents to hear, I would make a buzzing sound to pester her. It drove my sister crazy. She'd yell to our parents, "She's *bothering* me!" But they would say, "Cut it out now, Lynn. She isn't doing anything at all."

Nearly one-third of the interactions between siblings have been observed to be antagonistic, with older siblings more likely to antagonize younger (Dale, 1983; Dunn and Kendrick, 1982a; Pepler, Corter, and Abramovitch, 1982). With age, younger siblings themselves increase not only their positive actions toward their siblings, but their antagonistic and aggressive actions as well. By the time they are 2 years old, younger siblings can tease their older siblings quite cleverly.

Older siblings also may act as teachers to their younger siblings. Children of 6 and 7 have shown that they can teach younger siblings—more effectively, in fact, than unrelated teachers (Cicirelli, 1972, 1977, 1978). Even preschool children can teach their younger siblings quite well, teaching them physical skills, games, and how to use toys, labels, words, and numbers. They draw the younger siblings' attention and adapt their instructions to the younger ones' actions—at least when their mothers are supervising the proceedings (Pepler, 1981; Stewart, 1983). Older sisters are especially good teachers (Dunn and Kendrick, 1982b; Minnett, Vandell, and Santrock, 1983).

In sum, sibling relationships are both *reciprocal*—full of mutual imitation, play, talk, comforting, and fighting—and *complementary*—as older siblings take care of, help, teach, and manage their younger brothers and sisters. They are both like relations with peers (reciprocal) and like relations with parents (complementary). They are both positive and negative. Siblings cooperate and compete. They help each other and hit each other. They share their treasures, but they also fight over toys. The relationships between siblings may be described as ambivalent, but they are seldom lukewarm (Dunn, 1983).

Sibling relationships are also part of a broader network of family relationships. When a new brother or sister is born, the older sibling doesn't just gain a playmate; he or she loses, to some extent, a parent.

Natalie was the apple of my eye for two years. But when her younger sister was born, something seemed to change. When Natalie acted babyish, I didn't have the patience with her that I used to have. Now I had a real baby to care for, and I got firmer with Natalie. That was hard on her for a while, I know.

After my baby sister was born, suddenly my parents began to tell me all the time that I was "supposed to know better" because I was the older one.

Researchers have observed the changes in parent–child relationships after the birth of another child (Baskett, 1984; Dunn and Kendrick, 1982a; Kendrick and Dunn, 1980, 1983). When the mother and older child have shared an intense, playful relationship before the birth of the second child, the older sibling is likely to greet the baby with hostility. When the mother feeds or tends the baby, confrontations increase. If the mother then shifts her allegiance to the younger child and is more warm and playful with the baby, both siblings are likely to become hostile to each other. Then siblings' quarrels are likely to draw in the mother, and if she responds negatively, hostility between the siblings continues. Another vicious cycle has started rolling. When the interactions between mother and the older child continue to be positive, there is less squabbling between the siblings (Stevenson-Hinde, Hinde, and Simpson, 1986).

Interactions with other children

Brothers and sisters are not the only playmates that preschool children have. Most preschoolers have chances to play with other boys and girls their own age—cousins and neighbors, nursery school classmates, and family friends. Together, they do many of the same things that siblings do: play, teach, cooperate, and help; punch, kick, hit, and wrangle over toys and turns. To find out whether children's interactions with peers are directly affected by their interactions with siblings, researchers have observed preschool children playing at home with their siblings and also at home or nursery school with their peers. In one of these studies, few significant correlations between children's behavior in the two situations were found (Abramovitch, Corter, Pepler, and Stanhope, 1986).Children apparently do not simply generalize from their experiences with their siblings to their encounters with peers. They tended to interact more positively and playfully with their peers than with their siblings. The correlations were higher, however, when the siblings were close in age—and thus more peerlike. In another study (Berndt and Bullitt, 1985), children who were aggressive toward their siblings and children who often ignored their siblings and played alone acted in these same ways with their peers. Aggression and social withdrawal are apparently strong personal characteristics that show up in many different kinds of social interaction. Children also apparently learn something about social interactions just by *having* a sibling. Girls without brothers, in this study, were observed to spend more time at school unoccupied or just watching the other children play.

Children also are likely to learn different patterns of interaction depending on whether they are older or younger siblings. Older siblings are more dominant toward their younger siblings, for example, and this may show up in interactions with other children. In a study of nearly 400 5- to 6-year-olds, each with one older or one younger sibling (Koch, 1955, 1956), boys with younger brothers tended to be rated higher by their teachers on leadership and responsibility and to be less aggressive than boys with younger sisters. Boys with younger sisters were likely to get along with girls their age and to be friendlier to adults. Girls with older brothers tended to be nonconformists, often tomboys. Girls with older sisters tended to be traditionally feminine: sociable, conforming, and dependent. Having a sibling does not by itself determine how a child will interact with other children, but it is one factor that contributes.

Patterns of peer play

Toddler play

With or without siblings, from the time they are infants, children are interested in others their own age. Their small size and interesting antics make them attractive to each other (Lewis and Brooks, 1974). Although infants less than 1 year old smile and laugh at each other, in most of their play they are emotionally neutral, and their interactions are exploratory at most (Ross and Goldman, 1977a). During their second year, toddlers begin to act less neutral. Their expressions of positive and negative feelings increase. In one study of peer play, the meetings of unacquainted 1- and 2-year-olds were videotaped (Ross and Goldman, 1977a; Goldman and Ross, 1978). Even though the children had not played together before, in just 13 hours of tape, researchers identified over 2000 clearly positive social overtures—positive vocalizations, giving toys, and so on. Even at this early age, the children started games of tickling, touching, give and take, and laughing at antics. The play of the 2-year-olds was more intentional, lasted longer, and was more varied, intense, coordinated, and complex than the 1-year-olds'. Their play also consisted of more games with a greater number of turns. Positive overtures appeared more often in the interactions of these 1- and 2-year-olds than withdrawing, hitting, fighting, crying, or swiping. But conflicts do occur. In another study psychologists observed pairs of unacquainted toddlers playing together for the first time and found that nearly half of their interchanges involved conflicts (Hay and Ross, 1982). Although the conflicts were short-lived, nearly 90 percent of the children engaged in at least one of them. Most were struggles for possession of a toy. But even these conflicts had a social flavor. Even when identical toys were available, children still quarreled over a single object; one child's possession seemed to whet the other child's appetite.

In these studies, researchers examined the play of children who were strangers. In another study, researchers followed the play of five boys who met two mornings a week for 3 months, starting when they were 13 to 18 months old (Mueller and Lucas, 1975). They identified three stages of peer contact as the boys became older and better acquainted. In the first stage, one child's curious examination of an object attracted the attention of the other boys, but there was no interaction. If one child acted, the others watched; if one boy gestured or vocalized to another, he was ignored. In the second stage, these social bids were responded to. Often, in the beginning, a second boy imitated the first; later there were longer and longer interaction chains. In the third stage, the boys tried to elicit not imitation but the appropriate complementary response—a take to a give, a catch to a throw, a run to a chase (Table 10.1).

Some social interactions, like give and take, catch and throw, require the presence of an object. But even beyond this, toys were important for these toddlers. The boys spent most of their time playing with toys, and 90 percent of their activities involved toys. Toys are the main avenue for toddlers' social exchanges, and they allow them to show, give, fetch, and grab. At first, the toy itself is the focus of the interaction. The toy acts either as a carrot, attracting a peer, or a stick, forcing a child to notice the child who takes away his toy (Mueller and Vandell, 1979). Later, the toy is used to mediate social interaction, and the peer becomes the focus. All the while, though, the toy is a necessary prop.

Table 10.1
Three stages of early peer play

Stage 1: **Object-Centered Contacts**

Time, seconds	Noah, 14½ months	Larry, 16 months
0	At engine alone, toots horn once.[a] Toots horn once.	Approaches. Hits engine with toy. Grasps steering handle. Looks at Jacob's face. Steps backward.
17	Toots horn, four times. Grasps steering handle.	Grasps steering handle. Steps back again. Grasps steering handle.
34	Reaches for horn, withdraws Bernie's hand.	VOCALIZES AT NOAH'S FACE.
66	Looks at Bernie's face.	Departs.
84	Toots horn, 12 times, then departs.	

Stage 2: **Contingent Interactions**

Time, seconds	Bernie, 13 months	Larry, 15 months
34	VOCALIZES "DA," LOOKING AT LARRY.	LAUGHS, LOOKING AT BERNIE.
40	VOCALIZES "DA," LOOKING AT LARRY.	LAUGHS, LOOKING AT BERNIE.
	Sequence repeated seven more times.	
69	Turns and walks away.	LAUGHS (IN FORCED WAY), LOOKING AT BERNIE, AND WATCHES HIM LEAVE ROOM.

Stage 3: **Complementary Exchanges**

Time, seconds	Bernie, 16 months	Larry, 18 months
32	LOOKS AT LARRY AND PICKS UP PAPER. Puts paper to wall. Releases paper. Picks up paper from floor. OFFERS PAPER AND VOCALIZES TO LARRY.	
51		RECEIVES PAPER FROM BERNIE. Puts paper to wall. Releases paper. BACKS AWAY AND LOOKS AT BERNIE.
65	POINTS AT PAPER AND LOOKS AT LARRY.	
		LOOKS AT BERNIE AND PICKS UP PAPER. Puts paper to wall. Releases paper. BACKS AWAY AND LOOKS AT BERNIE.
72	Departs.	
81		LOOKS AT BERNIE AND PICKS UP PAPER. Puts paper to wall. Releases paper and departs, following Bernie.

[a]Simultaneous events appear on the same line; socially directed behavior is in capital letters.
SOURCE: Adapted from Mueller and Lucas, 1975, pp. 232–231, 243, 250–251.

Toys are central in the play of preschool children. A jack-in-the-box brings two little girls together, in admiration and in a struggle for possession.

Preschool play

In the preschool period, children's social contacts grow more frequent, and their social skills grow more sophisticated. Observations of groups of children between 2 and 5 years show that as children get older, they do less staring, crying, pointing, sucking, fleeing, and playing alone and more talking, smiling, laughing, and playing together (Mueller, 1972; Blurton Jones, 1972; Smith and Connolly, 1972; Parten, 1932). They make more eye contact and talk more, and their communication becomes more effective (Savitsky and Watson, 1975). They can collaborate more and play together with others more successfully and cooperatively—dividing roles and sharing goals—than they could when they were younger (Cooper, 1977; Parten, 1932; Tieszen, 1979).

> In nursery school, Sam and Natalie played beautifully together. One morning, Sam helped to trace Natalie's outline on a long piece of brown paper. Then she got up and helped to trace Sam's outline. Then the two of them drew in their own eyes and mouths.

Over the preschool period, children's play becomes progressively more positive than negative. One group of researchers found the ratio of positive to negative interchanges among preschoolers to be 8:1 (Walters, Pearce, and Dahms, 1957). Although toys are still often used to mediate social interaction, over the preschool period children become increasingly likely to interact without toys. One kind of purely social play that 3- and 4-year-olds engage in is **ritual play**—repetitive, rhythmic exchanges or turns, with exaggerated intonations, distorted rhythms, and broad gestures. ''I can see Amy.'' ''I can't see Ben.'' ''I can see Amy.'' ''I can't see Ben.'' ''I can see Amy . . .'' Five-year-olds also engage in ritual play, but their rituals are shorter than the younger children's. Older preschoolers are more likely than younger preschoolers to engage in **language play**—rhyming, saying nonsense words, and playing with words. ''Mother dear mother near mother tear mother hear,'' they singsong. They also play out complex roles together in pretend fantasies—house, school, doctor, and other play dramas (Garvey, 1984). Of course much of preschoolers' play does still include toys. **Parallel play**, in which children play independently with toys that are like the toys of a nearby child but in which they do not actually play together, predominates with 2-

and younger 3-year-olds, but older 3- and 4-year-olds still play this way occasionally (Parten, 1932, 1933; Rubin, Watson, and Jambor, 1978; Smith, 1978).

focus *Children in day care*

When they are first introduced to new children, preschoolers may be shy, cling to their mother, ignore or even avoid the other children. But as they spend time together, they touch more often, go closer, and stay near one another (Roopnarine and Field, 1983). After a few play sessions together, most children have overcome their shyness and get along skillfully, playfully, and vigorously. Within a few months, they are full members of the group (McGrew, 1972; Mueller and Brenner, 1977; Smith and Connolly, 1972). Children with experience playing with other children, researchers have found, are more cooperative and competent when they first play with a new child (Lewis, Young, Brooks, and Michalson, 1975; Lieberman, 1977). Going to nursery school or day care offers children many opportunities to interact with other children. Does the experience of being in a preschool program enhance children's social development? Evidence from several studies suggests that it does.

Preschool children who attend day-care centers or nursery schools have been found to be, on the average, more self-confident, more outgoing, more socially competent with both peers and adults, and less timid than home-care children (Clarke-Stewart and Fein, 1983; Clarke-Stewart, 1986). Day-care children know more about the social world—gender roles, perspective taking, labels for feelings, how to solve social problems—are less stereotyped and more sophisticated in their play, and are more realistic about their achievements. The advanced social competence of day-care children cuts two ways, however. Not only are day-care children more self-confident, but they are also on occasion likely to be less polite, agreeable, and obedient, more aggressive, bossy, and rebellious than home-care children.

When psychologists sift the evidence to find out why children in day care differ in these ways from their home-reared counterparts, they must answer the question indirectly. It is unlikely, first of all, that these independent, assertive, rebellious day-care children simply reject adults' standards of conduct, for they remain quite responsive to adults' needs and are sympathetic and cooperative under appropriate circumstances. Day-care children's willingness and ability to interact with other people probably is accelerated by their experiences in day care and by their exposure there to social rules, norms, knowledge, and conflicts. Day-care children may practice and learn social skills as they interact with other children and with adults who encourage independence and self-direction. They also may pick up from their peers aggressive or rude behavior. These qualities—good and bad—may, at the same time, be encouraged and reinforced at home by the parents who send their children to early childhood programs.

Children who develop the best social skills, it has been observed, attend smaller classes in the nursery school or day-care center. They play with fewer children there, and those they play with are more mature, more responsive, less aggressive, and older (Clarke-Stewart, in press). The children with advanced social skills also do not spend *all* their time at day care playing with other children; they spend time listening to the teacher and working on their own. Experience playing with other children can promote children's social development, but how much, where, what, and with whom all make a difference.

Moving a log takes the combined and cooperative efforts of several preschoolers. Such cooperation becomes possible only in the later preschool years.

Sharing and caring

Young children love to share things that they find interesting. As they wander through an unfamiliar playroom, for example, toddlers will leave their mother's side to explore and to show or give her the interesting toys they discover. In one series of studies (Rheingold, Hay, and West, 1976), this early form of sharing cropped up in every single 1- and 2-year-old observed. The children showed and gave food and toys to parents and peers, whether they were asked to or not, and whether the other person responded positively or not.

> I took a sip of water from Kristy's glass once when she was about 2. She looked at me, and I expected a scolding. But instead she smiled broadly and said, "We sharing," and offered me some more.

The development of children's caring actions is more gradual. Only slowly do children develop social skills for responding to other people's needs. In the second year of life, researchers have found, many children begin to perform caring acts (Hay and Rheingold, 1983; Rheingold and Emery, 1986). Dolls are bathed and tucked in bed, stuffed animals are dressed and read stories, playmates are given "tea" and cookies. Mothers who cry "ouch" may be patted on the back solicitously and handed one of the child's favorite toys. Mothers who are cold may be covered with a blanket, and hungry dogs may be given teething biscuits. In one laboratory study designed to bring out children's caring acts (Rheingold and Emery, 1986), all the 1½- and 2½-year-old boys and girls acted caring, and most of them acted out a wide range of caring acts—putting a doll to bed, feeding, disciplining, grooming, carrying, giving affection. As they wheeled their dolls in carriages, brushed their hair, diapered, bathed, and carefully seated the toy animals and dolls, the children were affectionate and loving, spoke appropriately—"Night-night, bear." "Oh, poor baby. Too cold. Too cold. I'll wrap you around."

Few children under 1½ respond to another person's distress, though, and some actually taunt or hit a crying playmate. By the age of 2, most children do respond empathically at least part of the time (Zahn-Waxler, Radke-Yarrow, and King, 1983). **Empathy** is a vicarious emotional response in which the emotions of the person observing, to some extent, match those of the person being observed. An empathic response is one in which a person responds *as though* he or she were feeling what another person is feeling, like feeling sad when someone else is crying. Researchers Carolyn Zahn-Waxler and Marian Radke-Yarrow (1979; Zahn-Waxler, Radke-Yarrow, and Brady-Smith, 1977) have found that the earliest emotional reaction most children

382

show to others' distress is empathic—crying or sadness. These researchers had mothers keep diaries in which they recorded their children's responses to others' distress, and they also tested children with simulated incidents in the laboratory that might elicit empathic responses—such as spilling papers or having a mother "accidentally" bump her elbow. They found that at both 2 and 7 years of age, children had about the same intensity of response to distress. But individual children behaved differently. One child at 2 blocked her ears and ran away when she heard crying or saw someone angry. At 7, the same girl complained, "I can't take much more of this crying." A more compassionate child at 2 ran to her mother and buried her head in her lap when her friend got hurt. Later she comforted a crying baby, her own lips quivering. Still later, she gave her sandals to her younger friend to keep her friend's feet from burning as they walked on hot pavement. A third child was detached and rational. At 2 she remarked as she looked at a friend's face and wiped away her tears, "Annie's crying. She's sad. See her tears." At 7, she asked, "Where does it hurt? How much does it hurt? Why does it hurt?"

What distinguished the 2-year-olds from the 7-year-olds was how they expressed their concern in **prosocial** actions. Although empathic, 2-year-olds lack the skills to be really helpful. They may try to offer comfort to people who are crying or hurt by snuggling, patting, hugging, or offering to feed them. But they offer what they themselves find comforting—a bottle, a doll, a cracker, their own mother's hand. Clearly sympathetic and wishing to be helpful, these very young children do not yet know the practical steps that people take to help others. Later, children's offers of comfort grow more elaborate and appropriate. They help directly, offer suggestions, attempt rescues, say sympathetic things, referee fights, and protect victims (Zahn-Waxler and Radke-Yarrow, 1979; Zahn-Waxler, Radke-Yarrow, and Brady Smith, 1977). In one study of 4½- to 5½-year olds in a day-care center, for example, children responded to their peers' sadness by offering to share toys, or coming close and hugging, or by saying comforting things like "That's a nice hat you've got" (Strayer, 1980).

Preschool children are especially likely to act caring toward other children and infants. In one laboratory study, for example, 4- and 5-year-olds were shown an adult who hurt her back while demonstrating a physical exercise, a baby crying from hunger, and a peer who had been hurt on a ladder (Zahn-Waxler, Iannotti, and Chapman, 1982). The investigators noted

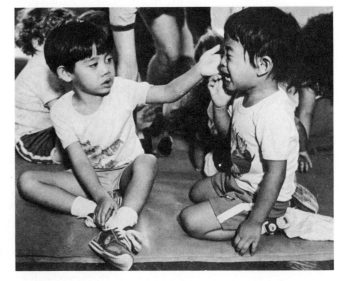

Even preschool children express sympathy and try to comfort someone who is hurt. This young boy tries to pat away the pain felt by his twin brother.

the children's expressions of sympathy, indirect efforts to help (telling some- one else to help), and direct offers of help. The children were much more likely to help the infant than to help the adult. In another study, 3- and 5-year- olds were observed in nursery school (Eisenberg, Lundy, Shell, and Roth, 1985). Every time the children complied with a request from the teacher or another child, an observer asked them why they had done so. Although the children complied with more of the teachers' requests, they gave more proso- cial reasons, like friendship or need, for complying with their peers' requests. Preschool children clearly demonstrate a sensitivity to the needs and feelings of their peers. Although this capacity is not always tapped by traditional measures of perspective taking (discussed in Chapter 9), it may mediate their prosocial behavior in the real world of nursery school (Iannotti, 1985).

At the same time as they are learning to give care and comfort, children are learning to help. Preschool children like to hold the dustpan while some- one else is sweeping, although moving the big broom is much more fun. They like to help fold laundry, pick up and stack magazines, put little things back into their boxes. They say quite explicitly that they are "helping," and they know when a task is done: "All picked up." "Nice and clean now." "I helped Mommy change the sheets." The findings on children's helping are remarka- bly consistent. Over the last 200 years, many incidents of young children's helping, at home and outside, in rich families and poor, with parents and other children have been recorded (Hay and Rheingold, 1983). Nor do these young children simply imitate the prosocial acts of others. They add their own touches; they do not just mimic what the adult is doing. They help, sympath- ize, and offer comfort creatively, genuinely, and in original ways. Thus Sam not only smoothes the quilt with his hands as he helps his mother make his bed but also carefully arranges his dolls and animals on the pillow. Parents, it has been suggested, do not have to teach their children to be helpful (Krebs, 1983). Children have a natural tendency to be caring, empathic, and con- cerned about other people. What parents do have to do is to teach their children to express their naturally prosocial tendencies. Out of their strong need to learn, to be competent, and to be helpful, children will perform positive social acts.

Promoting prosocial behavior

What are the best ways for parents to promote helping, caring, and cooperat- ing in children? To answer this question, one team of researchers interviewed preschool children and their mothers about prosocial issues and child-rearing attitudes (Eisenberg, Lennon, and Roth, 1983). Children who gave more helpful and caring answers, they found, had mothers who claimed that they stepped in forcefully on issues they considered important for the child— getting along with others or getting into danger—but otherwise encouraged the children's independence. In other studies, too, researchers have found that if parents are warm and loving, if they reason with their children rather than punishing or threatening them, and if they act prosocially themselves, they are likely to have children who act helpful and caring (Crockenberg, 1984; Mussen and Eisenberg-Berg, 1977).

Preaching at a child works, at least for a while, especially if the preaching is consistent with how the parent behaves. Researchers have tried to promote children's prosocial behavior in the most direct way: telling them what to do. In one such study (Smith et al., 1983), when adults explicitly told 4- and 5-year-olds such things as "When I play with you, I want you to help," or "Kristy doesn't have any candy kisses. If you share your candy kisses, then she'll have some too," the frequency of the children's prosocial acts dramat- ically increased. The effects seemed to extend beyond the immediate situation and beyond the specific forms of behavior evoked, a sign that might hearten parents. Teaching children and explicitly conveying expectations of prosocial actions may cause them to behave prosocially in other situations, with other people, and in other ways, too (Krebs, 1983). But we know that the ''Do as I say, not as I do'' school of discipline does not work. Children's behavior is more strongly influenced by their parents' *behavior* than by their parents' *words* alone (Bryan, 1975).

The influence of adults' behavior on children's prosocial behavior also has been shown by exposing children to an adult in the laboratory who acts either prosocially or not and then observing the children's behavior in a similar situation. In a typical experiment, the adult seen by some children is selfish; she does not donate her pennies, candy, or toys to (unseen) children who are ''in need''; the adult seen by other children generously donates her winnings. It has been shown consistently in such experiments that watching an adult demonstrate generosity increases the willingness of many children to help and share—especially if the model combines prosocial behavior with warmth, interest, and the exercise of power—as parents do at home (Mussen and Eisenberg-Berg, 1977). Do these effects last? Children in one study watched an adult donate generously and then were given the chance to donate themselves. A week later the children were more likely to donate, and three weeks later they behaved generously in a different situation. Even two to four months later, the effects of watching the model were still evident (Rushton, 1975).

Hitting and hurting

> I worry about Natalie. If someone takes a toy away from her, she just looks lost and never even tries to get it back. Maybe nursery school will toughen her up.

> I wish some of Natalie would rub off on Sam. When he wants something, he bulldozes it away from whoever is holding it.

At one time or another, virtually every parent worries about a child's aggressive behavior—or lack of it. Where do children's antisocial actions come from, when are they expressed, and how do they change over time?

Between the ages of 2 and 4, children become first more and then less aggressive (Hartup, 1974; Blurton Jones, 1972; Walters, Pearce, and Dahms, 1957). After the third year, physical actions like hitting and stamping decrease, and verbal insults and attacks increase (Goodenough, 1931; Jersild and Markey, 1935). Most quarrels are over playthings and possessions that have to be shared with others. Frustration long has been regarded as a major cause of aggression (Dollard, Doob, Miller, Mowrer, and Sears, 1939), and preschoolers are likely to feel frustrated and aggressive when they are left out of a game at nursery school or on the playground or when they cannot play right away with the toys they want because someone else already has them. Preschoolers also are sensitive to anger in others around them. In one recent laboratory study (Cummings, Iannotti, and Zahn-Waxler, 1985), actors simulated an angry interaction while pairs of 2-year-old children played with toys nearby. During the angry exchange the children were clearly distressed; immediately afterward they were more likely to hit, kick, push, or physically attempt to take things from each other. One month later, after witnessing another heated argument, the children were even more upset and aggressive. Anger itself may be contagious, and its effects may be cumulative.

Children learn aggressive acts by directly imitating adults, other children, and even television characters who act aggressively. In studies of observational learning in the laboratory, preschool children have watched an adult punch, throw, kick, and sit on a three-foot inflated rubber Bobo doll, either before their eyes or on film (Bandura, Ross, and Ross, 1961, 1963). Then, later, when they have had a chance to play with the Bobo doll, the children who have watched the Bobo attacked usually copy the attack, blow for blow (see photos in Chapter 1). At home, children may pick up aggressive habits by watching their parents. They may learn to act aggressively through being selectively reinforced for doing so. Parents may pay attention only to the child's naughtiness, for example, and in this way selectively reinforce the aggressive behavior. Naturalistic observations of parents and preschoolers reveal that parents of nonaggressive children communicate often with them— ''What do you want to do?'' ''Do you want a piggyback ride?'' ''Do you want to play with the dolls?'' They listen to what the children answer and pay attention to how they behave (Montagner, in Pines, 1984). They are not aggressive themselves, nor are they overprotective, and they threaten the child only in possibly dangerous situations. Their interactions with children are sensitive, friendly, accepting, and happy (Stevenson-Hinde et al., 1986). Parents of aggressive children, in contrast, are likely to be either aggressive and punitive themselves or overly permissive. A mother may call for her child at day care but turn away to ask the teacher, as the child approaches, ''Was he naughty today? He's always hitting people at home.'' As the child veers away, the mother calls again. She calls, yells, and finally chases him down, grabbing him roughly, and hauling him from the room. Parents who punish their children physically stimulate the children's anger and provide them with a model of aggressive behavior. The long-term effect on children is likely to be increased aggressiveness. Parents who do not attempt to control their children's aggression, also encourage children to have aggressive outbursts. Families with one permissive parent and one punitive parent are especially likely to have children who act aggressively. Children are most likely to learn to control anger and aggression when discipline is consistent and mixed with love and reasoning and when parents are not often angry with them or each other. It is also helpful if parents foster acceptable outlets for the anger children inevitably feel. For example, they might suggest that the children express the anger verbally. Parents of aggressive children often fail to provide positive encouragement for replacing aggression with other behavior, and so their children know what they *cannot* do but not what they *should* do.

Aggression between 2- and 3-year-olds, most often over sharing toys, is direct and physical. Five-year-olds hit and pull less and engage in more verbal attacks and insults.

Not only do family dynamics, child rearing, and discipline contribute to children's aggressiveness; so do a child's hormones, temperament, physical appearance, muscularity, and social skills. Hormones play an important role during prenatal and later development and may modify children's behavior. In one study, males and females who had been exposed prenatally to synthetic progestins were found to act more aggressively than their same-sex siblings who had not been exposed to progestin (Reinisch, 1981). In another study, researchers found a positive relation between blood levels of testosterone and males' aggressive and antisocial behavior. (Kreuz and Rose, 1972). As far as physical appearance goes, a kind of self-fulfilling prophecy may work to make unattractive children more aggressive than their attractive peers. Although the aggressiveness of attractive and unattractive 3-year-olds is not different, by the time they are 5 years old unattractive children tend to be more aggressive and boisterous than attractive ones (Langlois and Downs, 1980). As for temperament, children who develop aggressive behavior problems are more likely to have been difficult infants—more active, irregular, sensitive, nonadaptive and intense (Thomas, Chess, and Birch, 1968). The influences on aggressive behavior in young children are many and complex. This discussion is just a beginning (see also the discussions of television violence and sex differences as influences on aggression later in the chapter).

Friendships

After they have played together for a time, preschool-age children begin to form friendships with a few other children. Friends usually are of the same sex, age, energy and activity levels as the children themselves (Gamer, Thomas, and Kendall, 1975). Preschoolers like to spend time with these friends, to be close to them, and may feel sad when they are separated.

> When Sam's best friend, another 3-year-old boy, left the day-care group, Sam was weepy for several days every time he thought about it. He had to be reassured often that he could still play with his friend—"my Robbie"—on weekends.

If they do not have real friends at this age, preschoolers may create imaginary friends (Manosevitz, Prentice, and Wilson, 1973). The imaginary friend is a companion in play and a scapegoat for the child's naughtiness: "No! I not do it! Burdette doed it."

> *Binker—what I call him—is a secret of my own,*
> *And Binker is the reason why I never feel alone.*
> *Playing in the nursery, sitting on the stair,*
> *Whatever I am busy at, Binker will be there. . . .*
>
> *Well, I'm very fond of Daddy, but he hasn't time to play,*
> *and I'm very fond of Mummy, but she sometimes goes away,*
> *and I'm often cross with Nanny when she wants to brush my hair. . . .*
> *But Binker's always Binker, and is certain to be there (Milne, 1927).*

Compared to the ways they act with unfamiliar children, preschoolers engage in more pretend play with their friends, have more connected dialogues, and are more likely to talk about what they have in common than how they are different (Gottman, 1983). With friends, preschoolers are more agreeable and compliant. They offer friends sympathy and help and ask about their feelings. By what social processes do children become friends? In one study, a number of 3- to 6-year-old children were observed at home as they visited several times with another child their age whom they did not know (Gottman, 1983). The children who hit it off and progressed toward friendship could tell each other things, play at the same activities, talk about themselves and how they were alike or different, resolve their few conflicts, joke, gossip, fantasize, and play dramatic games of house, doctor, and superheroes. Children who did not hit it off did not have these kinds of interactions.

During preschool years, though, friendships are fleeting things. Robert Selman (1981; Selman and Selman, 1979) called this the period of *momentary playmateship*. Friends are valued for their material possessions and for living close by. As one little boy said in an interview with Selman, "He's my friend because he has a giant Superman doll and a real swing set." A little girl explained, "She's my friend—she lives on my street." By the end of the preschool period, the child enters a stage Selman called *one-way assistance*. At this point the friendship may be based on more than Superman dolls; children begin to understand that feelings and intentions, not just things, keep friends together. But they take into account only their *own* needs and satisfaction. Said one child: "She's not my friend anymore because she wouldn't go with me when I wanted her to." And another: "You trust a friend if he does what you want." This is the highest level reached in the preschool period; only later do friendships become reciprocal and intimate.

Social understanding

Understanding the people who make up one's social world, interpreting their emotions and intentions, and communicating with them effectively are important aspects of social understanding. During early childhood, children develop skills that help them to accomplish these tasks.

Interpreting social situations

One kind of social skill preschool children begin to develop is the ability to interpret social situations. They begin to learn to read people's emotional expressions and to infer what emotional states are likely to be provoked by particular situations.

> Peter has always been sharp as a tack about figuring out what people are feeling. As a 2-year-old, he read the facial expressions on the characters in his storybooks. If he didn't recognize an expression, he asked about it. The people on cereal boxes, butter and syrup containers, you name it, and Peter had to talk about whether "Him happy" or "Dem scared" or "Her laughing." Even now, if the slightest frown crosses my face, he asks anxiously, "You mad, Mommy?"

By the time they are 3, children can recognize and label facial expressions that signal happiness, sadness, anger, and fear (Camras, 1977). They also can give examples of being happy, sad, angry, and scared (Harter, 1979). As they get older, they can name and recognize a wider range of emotions and can predict how a person will feel in emotional situations. In one study, children between 3 and 8 years old were read short stories about a child who ate a favorite snack, lost a toy, got lost in the woods, and was made to go to bed (Borke, 1971). Then the children were asked to choose the picture of a face that best expressed how the child in each story felt—happy, sad, afraid, or angry. The older the children, the more accurately they identified the character's feelings. The 3-year-olds could identify happy emotions. Of the 4-year-olds, 60 percent recognized stories about fear, as did all the 6-year-olds. At 5½ children were substantially correct about the sad stories, but only later did children correctly identify the emotion in stories about anger.

In another study, children were interviewed about emotions and emotional situations (Harter, 1979). Preschoolers could not imagine how someone

Gradually children learn to modulate and control their expressions of emotion. They hold back the tears, even though the pain is great.

might feel *two* emotions at the same time or in close succession. "Can you feel good about going to visit grandma but grouchy about having to pack?" They answered, "No way!" or "It's hard to think of this feeling and that feeling because you have one mind," or "I've never done that, you know; I've only lived six years." Similarly, when they were shown conflicting cues, like a smiling face on a child at the dentist's office, preschoolers had only one interpretation. They took things at face value, and their interpretations were consistent with the facial expression rather than the situation. They had trouble reconciling conflicting cues (Gnepp, 1983). As we saw in Chapter 9, preschool children usually do not concentrate on more than one cue or dimension at a time. By preschool age, children clearly are more skillful than toddlers at interpreting emotional expressions and social situations. But their interpretations are still relatively unsophisticated, superficial, and unsubtle.

Expressing and controlling emotions

Over the preschool period, the fears prevalent in infancy, fears of the uncontrollable, the unfamiliar, the unassimilable—loud noises, sudden movements, shadows, flashes of light, strangers—decrease, but fears of animals and imaginary creatures, of the dark and of being left alone, and of bodily injury increase (Jersild and Holmes, 1935). Children increasingly fear death, robbers, imaginary creatures, and being alone (Macfarlane, Allen, and Honzik, 1954). Children who are being toilet trained may fear the toilet. Three-year-olds may fear dogs, and 4-year-olds may fear the dark (Miller, 1983). Interviewing 4- and 5-year-old children about their fears, one researcher (Bauer, 1976) found that half of them were afraid of animals, three-quarters of frightening dreams, ghosts, and monsters. This is the age when monsters appear in the closet and "the scareds" hide under Sam's bed. This is the age when Natalie has bad dreams about getting run over by a big, noisy machine and when Erica cannot sleep without a night-light to chase away the dark.

> Sam was so terrified by the "scary man"—Vincent Price—who cackles ominously on one Michael Jackson song that he sometimes was afraid to listen to *any* music. I reassured him that the scary man wouldn't come on, but he was too frightened to believe me.

Ninety percent of the children interviewed in one study feared some specific thing (Macfarlane et al., 1954), but only about 5 percent have extreme fears or phobias (Miller, 1983). In a controlled study, researchers experimentally assessed fear in 3- to 5-year-olds (Schwarz, 1979). The children, sitting in an unfamiliar room, were suddenly confronted by a toy gorilla, which walked out of a box, stopped, and pounded its chest. Only those children who had a realistic knowledge of toy gorillas or who were allowed by the experimenter to control the toy were not afraid of it.

Fear is only one of the emotions preschool children feel, of course. Preschool children also feel sad, when they are isolated, left out, or rejected. They feel joy, at gifts and parties, friends and family.

> Mikey took a first bite of birthday cake and crowed, "Oh! Oh! I can *taste* it."

They feel anger at obstacles and irritations, at not getting their way, at being punished. They express their fear and sadness openly by crying, clinging, and looking sad; their anger, by hitting and throwing things; their joy, by grins and giggles. But part of growing up (as we mentioned in Chapter 7), part of learning to function in a social world, is learning to control emotions and their expression. Children must learn to shorten and mute their crying and to shift their facial expressions quickly.

> Just before her fourth birthday party, I coached Natalie about how to act when she opened her presents from the other children. "You have to smile and say 'thank you' for every present, even if you don't like it," I told her, feeling somewhat guilty to be teaching her about white lies, "Otherwise you might hurt someone's feelings."

Parents may teach children to modify their expressions of sadness: by punishing them for crying, rewarding them for not crying, or by comforting them and showing them how to cope effectively with the source of distress. Parents may help their children control their fears by minimizing the children's fears and their own and by teaching them to tolerate fear (Izard, 1977). Parents may teach their children to control or conceal angry expressions by expressing anger in words rather than in physical attacks (Bridges, 1931; Goodenough, 1931; Green, 1933; Jersild and Markey, 1935; Muste and Sharpe, 1947; Walters, Pearce, and Dahms, 1957). Children's angry outbursts, especially undirected temper tantrums, have been found to peak at age 2. From then on, most children gradually find socially acceptable ways to express anger. By the end of the preschool period, no matter whether children can or cannot always control their anger and fear, they understand that masking feelings is important, and they begin this masking to avoid embarrassing themselves (Saarni, 1979).

Using language

One of the most important forms of social understanding that preschool children gain is the understanding of language. They learn to use language for conversation, control, and communication.

Conversation

Even before they use real words, as we saw in Chapter 7, infants learn one basic rule of conversation: listen while someone speaks, and then take a turn speaking yourself. Young children, who are learning language, follow this rule. But their vocabularies are still limited. They keep the conversation going by imitating and repeating the other speaker's words.

MOTHER: It fits in the puzzle somewhere.

ADAM: Puzzle? Puzzle someplace?

MOTHER: Turn it around.

ADAM: Turn it around?

MOTHER: No, the other way.

ADAM: Other way?

MOTHER: I guess you have to turn it around.

ADAM: Guess turn it around. Turn round (Slobin, 1968, p. 441).

By imitating, they acknowledge the adults' words, agree, question, or ask for more information. They indicate the function of the imitated utterances with their intonations (Keenan, 1977):

ADULT: We are going out.

CHILD: Out?

The child uses imitation here to express a question. In the following, the child uses imitation to acknowledge the adult's comment:

ADULT: And this is a big man.

CHILD: Big man.

The young child tends to respond in some way, whether with speech or action, every time the adult speaks. When the adult makes a request, the child carries out the act requested. When the adult asks a question, the child answers, and when the adult makes a statement, the child responds by imitating the utterance (Folger and Chapman, 1978).

Later, children elaborate on the adult's words in order to take turns in a conversation. Sometime during the third year, most children become able to converse with an adult about a common topic for at least one turn:

ADULT: Let's get ready for the park.

CHILD: The park has the big slide. I'm going on the big slide.

What about conversations between two children? In an early work, Jean Piaget (1926) suggested that "dialogues" of preschoolers with their peers, as opposed to their talks with adults, were more accurately termed **collective monologues**, because neither child really listens to or responds to the words of the other. It is clear, however, that Piaget underestimated the communication ability of young children. As we have seen in Chapter 9, young children do talk to themselves aloud about what they are doing, repeat themselves, and play with words to a greater extent than older children and adults. But recent research suggests that conversations of preschoolers, even with their peers, are focused more than half the time and that preschool children do respond appropriately to each other's questions and replies (Garvey and Hogan, 1973;) Spilton and Lee, 1977; Wellman and Lempers, 1977).

Children's tendency to converse responsively with each other increases with age. In one play group observed by researchers, the average number of times that a child spoke in response to something one of the other children had said increased from 27 to 64 percent between 2 and 2½ years (Mueller, Bleier, Krakow, Hagedus, and Cournoyer, 1977).

Three-year-olds often converse reciprocally. Here are Tom, 33 months and Judy, 32 months (Garvey, 1984, p. 158):

TOM	JUDY
(*Sits on the wooden car.*) I'm the driver.	(*Stands beside the car.*)
	I'm tired.
Why? Would you like a square dice? (*referring to a plastic block*).	No, thank you. I'm not sick.
They make you better. Do you want one? They make you better. (*Holds it out to her.*)	No, I don't want any.

Most conversations between preschoolers are focused, and the children usually respond appropriately to each other's questions and answers.

All right.	I'm not sick anymore.
Are you sick?	No.
I'm not either. I'm not sick either.	

(*Judy abandons the topic and tells Tom to turn off the car.*)

Five-year-olds converse even more smoothly with their friends (Garvey, 1984, p. 159).

BOY	GIRL
	I think we're gonna be picked up soon, don't you?
Hey, I think they're gonna come over now. (*Turns head to listen.*) I hear someone walking. (*He is hearing steps in the hall.*)	
	(*Goes to door, looks out, then back to partner.*) I think I hear them, don't you?
I don't think it's for us (*as sound of steps passes*).	We just came in here, right?
Yeah.	I think it's juice and cookies time, don't you?
No, it wouldn't be.	

Over the preschool period, children also gradually learn the art of the telephone conversation, an informal but highly structured form of speaking. Although at first they hear only one end of any conversation, children easily learn that phone calls are delimited events, and their first phone calls—real or pretend—are likely to consist of the boundary markers: "Hello. Good-bye." Greetings come next: "Hello. How are you? Fine. Good-bye." Then they introduce a bit of information: "Hello. How are you? I'm fine. I'm ironing. Good-bye." Now, in their phone play, children leave pauses for the replies of the imaginary person at the other end, and they imitate the telephone speaker's typical gaze into middle distance. The sophisticated 4-year-old can actually talk on the phone fairly well, exchange information, and listen for replies. But it is not until they are fluent speakers that children seem to realize that others need feedback, and so the "um-huhs," and "hmms" that adults exchange every five seconds or so during long turns of speaking are relatively late additions to the child's telephone repertoire (Garvey, 1984).

Control

Preschoolers also learn to use and to understand language as a way of controlling how other people act. The Russian linguist Alexander Luria (1961, 1969) described children's growing responsiveness to the control function of language. When they are about 2, he found, children may obey a simple command from another person—or they may not. At this age a child may obey her mother's "No!" and stop hitting her playmate. But she just as well may not obey. A command called to a child in mid-action—"Don't spill that juice!"—may actually provoke the child into continuing even more vigorously than before. Luria found that only when they are about 5 years old could children regularly stop or inhibit their response when they were asked to do so.

Luria's findings have since been confirmed by research done in the United States. In one study, researchers observed how middle-class, Midwestern preschoolers responded to commands (Saltz, Campbell, and Skotko, 1983). After telling the children that they would be playing a game to see how well they could follow instructions, an experimenter played for each child a tape recording of 30 different commands. Half were positive—''Clap your hands''—and half were negative—''Don't touch your toes.'' The experimenter modeled each behavior, even those he was telling the child not to do. The loudness of the commands was varied from soft to a loud shout. The researchers found that most of the children's errors were commissions of forbidden actions rather than omissions of requested actions. That is, the children were likely to touch their toes when told, ''Don't touch your toes.'' They did not fail to clap their hands when told, ''Clap your hands.'' Three- and 4-year olds made more errors than 5- and 6-year-olds. When a command was spoken softly, however, the younger children could respond appropriately. It was when a command was spoken loudly that they were not likely to obey it. The researchers concluded that Luria was right to suggest that children younger than 5 often respond to the physical energy of an instruction—the loudness of a command or the salience of a modeled behavior—even when the instruction is to inhibit their behavior. In other words, shouting ''Don't do that!'' is likely to cause the 2- or 3-year-old to do just the opposite.

Communication

Another function of language is sending and receiving messages. Language communicates information, and to communicate effectively, children must learn how to evaluate the quality of messages, how to identify and label what is important, how to order the elements in the message, and how to change the message when they discover they are not being understood. Researchers have studied how children's ability to communicate effectively develops during the preschool period.

In one study of 4- and 5-year-olds, researchers found that nearly 90 percent of the children interviewed understood that a listener did not know in advance what they were going to tell him and that the purpose of a message was to inform him (Roberts and Patterson, 1983). They knew the basic rationale for communication. Nevertheless, 4- or 5-year-old children often make mistakes; they often give inadequate information (Glucksberg, Krauss, and Higgins, 1975). In part, this is because they do not seem to realize that the listener does not know what they do. Preschoolers have trouble putting themselves in someone else's place, as we saw in Chapter 9. In part it is because they fail to single out what is important to tell the listener. Finally, it is because even when they do know what is important to tell the listener, preschool children often forget to mention it. If 4- and 5-year-olds are asked for more information, they can give it (Cosgrove and Patterson, 1979). But listeners do not often ask. Young children rarely get feedback on the adequacy of their communications. When children do get explicit feedback about their mistakes in communication, their communication becomes clearer (Patterson and Massad, 1980; Sonnenschein and Whitehurst, 1983).

Over the preschool period, children progress to higher levels of social understanding. The differences between 2-year-olds and 5-year-olds in interpreting and expressing emotions and in using language to communicate and control are marked indeed. But there are still serious limits to what 5-year-olds know about other people—and to what they know about themselves.

Self-concept

By the age of 2, as we discussed in Chapter 6, children realize that they are distinct from other people. A little boy now may grab a toy and insist, ''Mine!'' He may see his photograph and pipe, ''Me!'' He begins to tell people, "I a boy," or "I a baby," or "I Mikey." Very young children usually know themselves by their informal "everyday" names—"Mikey," "Kristy," "Sam"—and later learn the difference between given names, nicknames, and polite forms of address such as "Mr." "Miss," "Aunt," or "Uncle" (Garvey, 1984). Older preschool children avidly learn their full names and recite them with pleasure.

> "What's a nickname?" Sam asked when he was 3.
> "It's usually a short form of someone's name." 'Sam' is the nickname for 'Samuel.' 'Tim' is the nickname for 'Timothy.' 'Beth' is your babysitter's nickname.
> "Oh," Sam replied, light dawning in his eyes, "so Beff's real name is Beffnick."

Not only do children learn their names, but they begin to learn their place in the social universe. Preschool children know family members in terms of their relationships to themselves. They call them "Mommy" and "Daddy," not "husband" or "wife," Mary or Jim (Garvey, 1984). Children ask lots of questions about family relationships. Over the course of several months when he was 3, Sam asked his mother, "Who's your mommy?" ("Grandma.") "Who's Grandma's mommy?" ("Grandma's mommy was my 'Nana,' but she died.) "Who's my sister?" ("You don't have a sister.") "Who's your sister?" ("Aunt Laura.") "My aunt's your sister?" ("That's right.")

Although preschoolers know their names and nicknames, they still do not see themselves as others see them. Their **self-concept** is based on fleeting, sometimes faulty, ideas. When asked to describe themselves, preschoolers usually mention something they like to do: "is a helper who does the dishes," "can work hard," and "sits and reads stories." They do not mention more enduring characteristics like "friendly" or "bright." In a study of 3- to 5-year-olds, for example, researchers found that the children thought of themselves in terms of things they did (Keller, Ford, and Meacham, 1978). Asked to tell the researcher about themselves and to complete the sentences, "I am a _____" and "I am a boy/girl who _____," more than half of the children's responses described actions such as "I play ball" and "I walk to school." They mentioned their likes and dislikes only 5 percent of the time. Preschool children define themselves in terms of physical actions and possessions rather than psychological attributes.

Sex differences and gender roles

One important aspect of the preschool child's self-concept is his or her gender. Researchers have long been interested in how children develop concepts of themselves as boys or girls. They have studied children's actions and activities, words and deeds in interviews, experiments, and observations, looking for differences between boys and girls. They have probed the roots of those differences trying to figure out how much is biological, how much learned. From their research, we have learned quite a bit about the development of sex differences and gender roles in the preschool period.

Play styles

At 2, boys and girls look much the same, play much the same, and are interested in many of the same things. But by the time they are 3, boys and girls often act differently, and these differences grow more marked during the preschool period (Pitcher and Schultz, 1984). In nursery school, most girls like to paint, draw, help the teacher, play with dolls, dress up, look at books, and

Differences between boys' and girls' play styles become increasingly noticeable during the preschool period. Girls like to paint, draw, play with dolls, dress up, and hear stories. Boys like to hammer, ride vehicles, stack blocks, and play tough guy.

listen to stories. Most boys like to hammer, ride tricycles, and play with cars and trucks. Most girls like stuffed animals, dolls, cooking utensils, and boys like puzzles, blocks, and tools (Fagot and Leinbech, 1983; Sprafkin et al., 1983). Both boys and girls engage in fantasy play, but girls play house, and boys play superheroes. Girls' fantasies often are tied to everyday, domestic realities. Boys' fantasies often are magical, bizarre, supernatural. A banana becomes a little girl's ''telephone'' and a little boy's ''magic wand'' (Haney, 1984).

In their play, boys act out masculine roles—warriors, mailmen, fire chiefs, plumbers, and fathers—and they love grandiose themes. They are Masters of the Universe, GI Joe, Superman, monsters, and dinosaurs. The few realistic masculine roles that appear in preschool children's play are global and imprecise. Fathers are always off at some vague ''work'' or at home eating, reading the paper, watching television, or sick in bed, tended by mothers. So boys make up their own, more exciting masculine world. They do not give in to girls' romantic overtures. They back away from playing marriage and curl their lips—''Yuck!''—at the thought of a kiss. Boys explore friendship by being ''brothers'' and ''blood brothers,'' by exchanging roles—bad guys and good guys, Batman and Robin, father and little boy—and by protecting one another from danger, fighting wars together, conquering death and destruction on the same side. In their play, preschool girls are more likely to act out masculine roles than boys are to act out feminine ones, but most girls express only a brief interest in the power fantasies that fascinate boys. Most girls like to play at domestic routines, getting married, cooking meals, shopping. Girls do not like to play killers and destroyers, just as boys cannot long tolerate their roles in girls' domestic fantasies. Boy ''babies'' cannot act babyish for long, and a boy who ''irons'' soon is chasing robbers from the house (Pitcher and Schultz, 1984).

> At nursery school, Sam told me, first he saved T.J. from the robbers. Then he and T.J. switched on their giant electric spider webs, and when the robbers attacked, they zapped themselves to death.

In the dialogue that follows, two 5-year-old boys fantasize about building marvelous things—a ''supercave,'' a house, a gas station—and their ideas are imaginative, expansive, full of vitality.

> JOHN: ''I have a space monster in the house, and the rocket comes out of the door and flies up in the air.''
>
> ADAM: ''This is going down in the ocean because he's bad.'' (He has a rubber gorilla wrapped in a flag.)

> JOHN: ''I'm gonna make a supercave.'' . . .
>
> ADAM: We can kill the joker. We can use our sneezer gun to kill the bad guys. We're the good guys.'' . . .
>
> JOHN: ''My gun can break up the whole sun storm.'' (He sneezes.)
>
> ADAM: ''Don't sneeze the sun storm away.'' (John continues to sneeze. Adam ignores it and keeps on blasting. Puts toy gorilla wrapped in flag on rocket.) ''Now I'm gonna do wrecking.'' (Knocks his structure down.)
>
> JOHN: ''Now don't knock mine down. Next time try to be careful.''
>
> ADAM: ''O.K., I'm gonna blast it—now here goes'' (Pitcher and Schultz, 1984, pp. 6–7).

Compare these boys' play to that of two girls, also 5, who have arranged a ''house'' in the block-playing area, near where two other girls are coloring. Their play is subdued, tied to everyday reality, focused on personal relationships.

> WANDA to the other girl (who assumes the role of ''Mom''): ''Mom, I'm going shopping.''
>
> MOM: ''O.K.''
>
> WANDA walks out of room. Returns. Says, ''Ma, I got some new paper and magic markers.''
>
> ''MA'' kisses her and says, ''O.K., put them over there.''
>
> WANDA goes to other side of house. Mom says as she puts papers in slot, ''They're very expensive, so don't waste them.'' . . .
>
> A boy comes up and says, ''Can I play?''
>
> WANDA: ''No, there's already too many people here.''
>
> A girl comes and asks, ''Can I play?''
>
> WANDA: ''Yeah, you can be the dog'' (Pitcher and Schultz, 1984, p. 7).

Boys engage in more rough-and-tumble play than girls do. Teasing, rough-and-tumble play peaks in 5-year-old boys, but few girls play roughly together. Boys tease and say silly words, wrestle, bump into and fall on top of each other, push and pull, shout, make noises like machine guns, chase each other with space guns, fall down laughing at themselves when they make toy horses ''sneeze,'' smear clay in one another's hair, tickle, fall dead, slide from piles of blocks, fall over chairs, and eat fire. Boys talk dirty and love it:

> ''See that spot right there?''
>
> ''It's piss.''
>
> ''Eat this piss.''
>
> ''Eat this ka-ka'' (Pitcher and Schultz, 1984, p. 60).

Girls enjoy telling boys the ''rules,'' and loudly announcing when a boy has broken a rule: ''You marked on the table!'' ''Sit up straight in your chair when you're coloring.'' ''Well, a man's gotta marry a woman and a woman's gotta marry a man.'' Boys' disagreements and reprimands center on intrusion, territorial and property rights, and details of work procedures: ''You stepped on my car!'' ''Hey, you're wrecking my house.'' ''You're stacking those chairs the wrong way.'' When they disagree with girls, they forthrightly refuse—''Nope, I won't''—or make a general judgment—''You're not right.''

Of course not all girls play girl games all the time, nor boys boys' games.

Mikey and Erica, at least so far, have defied most of our expectations about boy kinds of kids and girl kinds of kids. Mikey is sensitive, quiet, obedient—one cross word, and he instantly obeys—has tons of friends whom he loves and is really very kind to. But Erica is the rowdiest, naughtiest child in the world. She runs, bangs, pounds, yells, never obeys, and does exactly what she pleases. Mikey's favorite things at nursery school were the water table, fingerpainting, and having long "telephone" conversations with one friend. But Erica's favorite things were swings, slides, climbing and then jumping from high places, banging on drums, and throwing a ball.

Nevertheless, there are clear and pervasive differences in the ways boys and girls play. There are also, as we shall see, other differences in their behavior.

Nurturant girls

Put a baby in a room with a group of 3- and 4-year-olds, and both girls and boys will pay attention to the baby. But put the baby in a room with 5- and 6-year-olds, and the girls pay much more attention to the baby than the boys do (Berman and Goodman, 1984). Over the preschool period, girls become increasingly nurturant toward other children. Boys become less so. And so begins a major difference between males and females that will last throughout their lives.

From the first months of life, girls have certain sensitivities that may turn them toward social cues and, ultimately, make them more nurturant than boys (see Lever, 1976; Maccoby and Jacklin, 1980). On the average compared to infant boys, girls' skin is more sensitive, and they pay more attention to faces, patterns of speech, and subtle changes of voice. They are more likely to cry when they hear a baby cry. They can recognize their mother's face earlier. They speak earlier, more often, and more fluently and so are likely to be more sociable and readier to start, join, and respond to social exchanges.

By the end of the preschool period, girls play in small groups and emphasize intimacy, mutual support, and sharing secrets, whereas boys in their peer groups tend to emphasize solidarity, loyalty, and doing things together. Girls stay physically closer and make more eye contact with each other than boys do (Hoffman, 1977; Restak, 1979). Both boys and girls are equally able to understand the emotional reactions of others. When assessing an emotional situation, such as seeing pictures of a child who has lost a pet dog, boys and girls are equally adept at inferring how the child feels. But girls are more likely to respond empathically. Their faces, posture, and words of sympathy are more likely to reflect the distress of the person they watch (Cummings et al., 1985; Hoffman, 1977). Boys may try to solve another person's problem when they see that person in a difficult situation, but girls tend to imagine themselves in the other's place.

Girls' nurturance shows up in nursery school play, too. Although both boys and girls play at cooking food, it is mainly the girls who play at serving it. Boys are more taken by the stirring and the mechanics of preparing food. Girls also protect, bathe, diaper, and doctor their dolls and each other. When one girl is the "baby," another girl is likely to kiss, hug, pat, stroke, and speak to her endearingly—"Come, honey, let's go to the house to eat your cake," or "How are you doing, sister?" (Pitcher and Schultz, 1984, p. 63). They help boys put on painters' smocks, comb their hair, hang up their coats and put their pictures in a safe place so they "won't get lost." Girls adjust each other's aprons, veils, hats, and dresses. They wrap bandages, give "medicine," and tend "the wounded" (Pitcher and Schultz, 1984).

Aggressive boys

In all cultures, boys are, on the average, more aggressive toward their peers than girls are. They are more likely to intentionally hurt or harm each other. As we have described, they also are more likely to play rough, mock-fight, and have aggressive fantasies than girls. These differences appear as early as age 2, when boys are likelier to get angry and strike an obstacle or another child to get what they want. In a review of 32 observational studies of preschool children, Eleanor Maccoby and Carol Jacklin (1980) found that in 24 of the studies boys were more aggressive, and in 8 studies neither sex was more aggressive. But in no study were girls more aggressive than boys. Although these findings on aggression are reliable, the average differences are small and getting smaller over time as society places more emphasis on gender equality (Hyde, 1984). Not every boy is more aggressive than every girl, and not every girl is more nurturant than every boy. The differences apply to averages only. The sex differences also are not in *feelings*, research suggests, but in aggressive actions. Girls have just as many hostile feelings as boys do, but they are more likely to express them in words or indirect actions than with physical force (Mallick and McCandless, 1966).

The bases of gender roles

Why do boys and girls differ in playing with dolls and guns, in nurturance and aggression? Are the differences biological or learned? The answer to this question is: probably both.

> When Natalie's mother learned that her third child was going to be a boy—her first—she asked Sam's mother how she had learned about cars and trucks. "Sam taught me, and your boy will teach you, too. Before Sam was born, I really believed that the differences between boys and girls were almost totally socially determined. But now I *know* that they aren't. Sam loves his dolls and stuffed animals, and he plays at cooking the supper—'Me the cooker tonight.' But from the start, he's been fascinated with things that move and roll. He likes to put his face close to the wheels of his toy cars and watch them turn. My husband jokes that there's a 'truck gene' on the Y chromosome. You'll see."

There are certainly biological differences between males and females in muscle structure, build, hormones, and abilities. But contrary to what one might expect were biology the full answer, in the animal kingdom, female lions hunt and kill, and male marmosets nurture their young, and in some non-western societies, females hunt and are not nurturant, and males garden and are not aggressive. Studies exploring the possibility that hormonal differences underlie sex differences in behavior also are not consistent, and behavioral differences between boys and girls appear earlier than physical differences like muscles and build. These facts suggest that learning is an important part of the distinct patterns of masculine and feminine behavior found in American children and adults.

Gender roles are the ways of behaving that are socially prescribed for males and females in a particular culture. They are encouraged, or socialized, in children by parents, peers, teachers, and the community at large. Prescribed gender roles are so intertwined with possible biological tendencies toward physical aggression in males and nurturance in females that the effects are difficult to unravel. Learning experiences may be mediated from within; boys on their own may seek out chances to sharpen their combative skills and girls ways to practice caretaking skills. But in a culture prepared to offer guns to boys and dolls to girls, even the slightest inherited predisposition could be built into a major psychological difference. How do parents, teachers, and peers socialize gender roles in preschool children?

Parents

From birth, boys and girls are treated differently by their parents. Girls are seen as smaller, weaker, prettier; boys as firmer, better coordinated, stronger, and more alert (Rubin, Provenzano, and Luria, 1974). Parents have these biased perceptions, even though newborn boys and girls are not measurably different. Even neutral physical activity of infant boys tends to be interpreted by their parents as aggression.

Later, parents generally encourage their young sons and daughters to act differently in many areas. Dancing, playing with dolls, and dress-up are for girls; climbing, building, and exploring are right for boys. Parents buy vehicles, educational materials, and military toys for their sons, and they decorate their rooms with pictures of animals. They provide dolls, dollhouses, purses, and housekeeping toys such as rolling pins, dishes, and stoves for their daughters, and they decorate their rooms with lace and flowers. They give sons toys that encourage inventiveness, manipulation, and feedback about the physical world. They give daughters toys that encourage imitation, are used near a caretaker, and give less opportunity for innovation or variation (Fagot, 1978; Fein, Johnson, Kosson, Stork, and Wasserman, 1975; Rheingold and Cook, 1975; Rosenfield, 1975). They expect children to play with toys considered fitting for their gender (O'Brien and Huston, 1985; Schau, Kahn, Diepold, and Cherry, 1980). Children are encouraged to choose gender-typed activities—"Let's arrange piano lessons for you, Natalie," "Let's go get you some soccer shoes, Tim"—and, once engaged in these activities, children's gender-typed behavior increases. The structure of these activities themselves further influences children's development. In highly structured activities—which girls engage in—children interact more with adults, imitate, obey, help, and negotiate with them; in unstructured activities—which boys engage in—children are more likely to initiate the interactions, give orders, and act aggressively (Carpenter, 1983). Over time, then, as girls participate in more structured activities and boys in less structured, children and their caregivers, in effect, create distinctive small environments for boys and girls within which gender-typed behavior flourishes.

Children's gender-typed behavior also is fostered by their parents' child rearing attitudes and practices. Reviewers of research done in the 1950s, 1960s, and 1970s (for example, Block, 1983; Shepherd-Look, 1982) note that in general parents describe themselves as encouraging sons more than daughters to achieve, compete, control their feelings, act independently, and assume personal responsibility. Parents claim to punish sons more often than they punish daughters. Fathers especially are more authoritarian with their sons; they are stricter, firmer, less tolerant of behavior that diverges from the traditional masculine stereotype. Fathers encourage instrumentality, mastery, and orientation to tasks with their sons; with their daughters, they encourage expressiveness and dependence. In raising daughters, parents are less punitive, warmer, physically closer, more confident of the child's trustworthiness and truthfulness, expect more "ladylike" behavior, and expect more reflectiveness than they expect from their sons. Mothers supervise their daughters more strictly than they do their sons. Girls are pressured to be nurturant, obedient, responsible, unselfish, kind, well mannered; boys to be self-reliant and successful, ambitious and strong willed (Hoffman, 1977; Tudiver, 1979).

Boys generally are given more room to explore than girls are (Lewis and Weinraub, 1974). The chores they are assigned more often take them outside the house and away from the direct supervision of a caretaker. Girls often are assigned chores as "helpers" (Duncan, Schuman, and Duncan, 1973; Whiting and Edwards, 1975). Parents respond more often to boys' large movements than to girls'; boys are handled and played with more roughly than girls; and girls are treated as if they were more fragile.

Even the subtle ways that parents communicate with their children can reinforce gender roles. When they read a story together, for instance, parents—fathers particularly—are more likely to interrupt daughters than sons (Greif, 1979). The extent to which fathers act in gender-typed ways at home is correlated with what their children think about gender roles. The behavior of mothers at home, in contrast, does not appear to have the same effect. Only when mothers work outside the home do their children seem more aware of gender labels and gender-role differences (Weinraub et al., 1984).

In the area of aggression, the findings are not entirely consistent, but there is certainly no evidence that the greater aggressiveness that has been observed for boys is the result of parents' deliberate encouragement. Some researchers have found no differences in the socialization of boys and girls as far as displaying or returning aggression or settling fights goes (Newson and Newson, 1968; Sears, Rau, and Alpert, 1965). Other researchers have found that boys are punished more severely than girls for aggression (Serbin, O'Leary, Kent, and Tonick, 1973). Although parents do not want their children to be taken advantage of, they do not consider aggression an acceptable way for girls *or* boys to solve problems (Shepherd-Look, 1982). Although boys apparently receive no more direct encouragement of aggression from their parents than girls do, subtle differences in the treatment of boys and girls may affect their aggressiveness. Researchers have found that boys become markedly aggressive when they begin with aggressive temperaments and are raised by punitive fathers (Eron, Walder, and Lefkowitz, 1971; Olweus, 1980). Boys who are severely punished for aggression are more aggressive, and the more they are punished, the more aggressive they become. Children probably learn gender roles not only through their parents' deliberate efforts, but through their indirect influence as well.

Fundamental changes in values could reduce the divergence in parents' socialization of boys and girls. So far researchers studying children's development in families in which mother and father have nontraditional gender-role values and practices have examined only a few, atypical families. But even in traditional families, parents can socialize their children in less gender-stereotyped ways. In a study by Baumrind (1979), some boys were observed to act in the typically feminine way—to be nurturant and friendly. These boys' mothers were particularly responsive to their needs and wishes. Some girls were observed to act in the typically masculine way—to be independent and assertive. Their parents pushed them by being less warm and nurturing and by making strong demands for independent behavior. A recent study of children in the Stanford, California, area suggests that in the last decade, rigid gender socialization by parents may have diminished. After observing and questioning parents and preschool children at home, at school, and in the laboratory, Jacklin and Maccoby (reported in Turkington, 1984) found that parents did not stereotype their children as much as parents in previous studies were reported to do. They treated their sons and daughters similarly and gave them equal amounts of warmth and nurturance, acceptance and restriction. The one exception was that fathers still tended to play more roughly with their sons than with their daughters.

Parents who do not want their children to develop traditional, stereotyped gender roles will still have to make special efforts in the 1980s. Despite the growing opportunities for women to work at jobs not open to them in the past, traditional gender roles remain firmly entrenched in our society. The forces combining to perpetuate them are formidable: biological predispositions, a society that continues to place most child-rearing responsibility with women, obvious and subtle cultural reinforcements, and the traditional upbringing of most of the people who are rearing children. For all these reasons, the socialization of boys is likely to remain different from that of girls. Even today, mothers in single-parent families, who say that they hold nontraditional attitudes toward gender roles and who hope that their sons will develop into ''thoughtful'' men and their daughters into ''self-confident'' women, give their children gender-typed toys and ask the children to do gender-typed chores (Richmond-Abott, 1984).

Child rearing takes some special effort if parents do not want their children to develop stereotyped gender roles. Providing toys and materials that are not traditionally gender-typed and encouraging their use can help.

Teachers

Not only parents, but other adults—including teachers, caregivers, and even strangers—can reinforce gender roles in young children (Condry and Condry, 1976; Frisch, 1977; Pitcher and Schultz, 1984; Seavey, Katz and Zalk, 1975). How can teachers encourage *non*-gender-typed activities in nursery school? One way they might do so is by reinforcing mixed-sex play in their classrooms. In one study, researchers asked preschool teachers to describe loudly and approvingly what they saw boys and girls doing together (Serbin, Tonick, and Sternglanz, 1977). Before the teachers began commenting, the children spent only 5 percent of their time playing cooperatively with members of the other sex. After the teachers began reinforcing the mixed-sex play, children began to play with the other sex twice as often as they had before. But the frequency of such play dropped back to the original level as soon as the teachers stopped reinforcing it. Consequently, the researchers designed a second study (Serbin, Connor, and Denier, 1978). This time the preschool teachers introduced a new toy each day—some stereotypically masculine, like trucks, blocks, and Lincoln Logs, and some stereotypically feminine, like dolls, clay, and beads for stringing—and called on both boys *and* girls to show how the toys could be used. The teachers again reinforced children's mixed-sex play and praised children for choosing cross-sex toys and playmates. As in the first study, children increased their play with other-sex children and toys. After six weeks, teachers stopped reinforcing the mixed-sex play. Once again, mixed-sex play reverted to its original level. The children whose mixed-sex play had been encouraged for six weeks engaged in more such play at the end of the program than children who had been encouraged for only four weeks, but left to their own devices, the preschoolers soon drifted back to playing with members of their own sex. Teachers can influence children's gender-role behavior, if they make continued efforts to do so. But if they are trying to encourage non gender-typed activities they are fighting an uphill battle against the third source of gender-role socialization in early childhood: other children.

Peers

One reason that boys go on being boyish and girls, girlish is that they are strongly influenced, even at this age, by the opinions and behavior of their peers.

Kissy girls. Yuck! Run!

Let's get away from the stinky boys.

As early as 2 years of age and increasingly thereafter (see Figure 10.2), boys and girls segregate themselves into same-sex groups. During free play in nursery school, an invisible curtain divides the girls in the crafts areas from the boys in the block corner (LaFreniere, Strayer, and Gauthier, 1984). At storytime, boys and girls spontaneously arrange themselves on opposite sides of a circle (Paley, 1984). Girls are the in-group, and boys are the intruders. Girls are intimate confidantes, and to them boys are ''crazy'' and ''mean.'' They ignore boys' aggressive overtures. Meanwhile, boys egg on other boys to be He-Man to their Skeletor, to play good guys and shoot bad guys, to be rowdy and loud. They strongly discourage other boys from playing with girls. By age 4, boys direct their aggression only to other boys and get exciting retaliation in return (Pitcher and Schultz, 1984). They may deliberately break the rules of docile nursery school behavior just to get other boys' approval (Dweck and Bush, 1976).

Preschool children create their own male and female worlds—places where they can unambiguously define their own gender, places where they

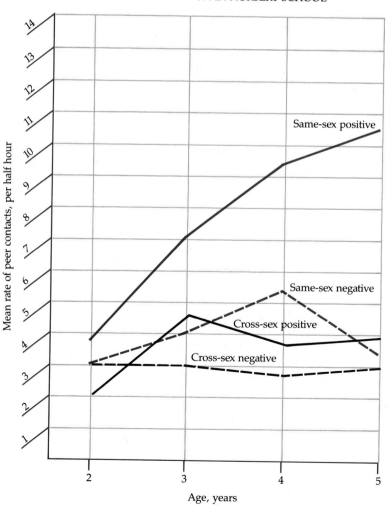

SEX SEGREGATION IN NURSERY SCHOOL

Figure 10.2 As pre-school children get older, they increasingly favor as playmates children of their own sex. By age 5, they are involved in three times as many positive interactions with children of their own sex as with children of the other sex (Pitcher and Schultz, 1984).

can be unforgiving of children who stray from accepted practices, and places where they can almost rigidly pursue gender-typed play. No matter how many times teachers praise them for playing with children of the other sex, no matter how much consciousness raising about gender typing their earnest parents attempt to involve them in, boys still insist on being cowboys and kings of the universe, and girls still insist on dressing their baby dolls and playing at marriage.

Knowledge of sex and gender

In the preschool period, children not only *act* in the gender-stereotyped ways we have described, but they begin to *recognize* and understand the differences between boys and girls, masculine and feminine. Although a boy of 2 or 3 might be able to tell you that he is a boy, he believes that he could be a girl or a mommy if he wanted to be. All he would have to do is play girls' games or wear dresses and grow his hair long. "Boy" may mean no more to him than the name "Tim" or "Jack." Children this young do not understand that sex is anatomical and cannot be changed.

> "When I grow up," Peter told his mother, "I'm going to be a girl." He also expressed an interest in growing up to be a rabbit and a professor.

The development of **sex constancy** has been tested when researchers have asked children to choose pictures, drawings, or dolls of a boy, a girl, a man, a woman (Emmerich, Goldman, Kirsh, and Sharabany, 1977; Thompson, 1975; Thompson and Bentler, 1971). In these studies, researchers have found that 2-year-olds can select which of the pictures is the same sex as they are, but they are not sure whether it is a boy or a girl. Three-year-olds usually select correctly and know that the picture is of a boy or a girl. Children between 4 and 6 can choose appropriate clothes for a man and a woman, but they make their choice according to hair length, not body build or genitals. Few children think that a girl remains a girl if she changes her haircut, clothing, and activities. The immutability of sex is not an easy notion for preschool children to grasp, for it must be distinguished from other personal attributes that *do* change, such as age and size. Children may see themselves as having more in common with a cross-sex age-mate than with a same-sex adult, if they do not yet understand the significance of sex. Learning this takes considerable experience and a degree of cognitive maturity not achieved by most children until age 6 or even older.

Even at age 2 or 3, however, although children do not know that sex is constant, they do have some sense of **gender identity**. In the ways that people talk to young children—"Aren't you a lovely girl!" "What a big boy you are!"—children constantly hear gender labels and soon can label their own gender accurately (Kuhn, Nash, and Brucken, 1978). They are likely to get upset if someone mistakes whether they are a boy or a girl. Research with very young children whose genitals have both male and female characteristics (and for whom corrective surgery often is considered) suggests that by the age of 3, a child has a sense of gender identity that is difficult to alter later (Money, Hampson, and Hampson, 1957).

Young children also have some rudimentary knowledge of gender roles, of what is appropriate behavior for boys and girls, men and women. When 3- and 4-year-olds in one study were questioned about which toys they thought they themselves, another boy, or another girl would like to play with and why, they often justified their choices on the basis of gender roles and stereotypes (although when it came to choosing toys for real play, they rarely resorted to such justifications) (Eisenberg, Murray, and Hite, 1982). Preschoolers in an-

focus *Gender identity*

Identical twin boys were born in 1963. When they were 7 months old, the boys were circumcised. But when the doctor was operating on one boy, he cut an artery, and part of the penis was lost. When the twins were 17 months old, on the advice of doctors, the parents decided to reassign the twin as a girl. They changed the child's name, clothing, and hairstyle, and the first surgery to make the child's genitals look female was done. Psychologists offered the parents guidance, and it was decided not to tell the twins what had happened. If the affected twin knew of the gender reassignment, it was reasoned, her gender identity would be in danger (Money, 1975; Money and Ehrhardt, 1972).

When she was 4, the little girl preferred dresses to jeans and loved her long hair. Her mother reported that she was very feminine—neat and tidy, proud of herself in a new dress, happy to have her mother set her hair. The parents' teachings were taking hold, for the girl was being raised in a traditional gender-typed fashion. Her mother was stricter about sexual modesty in the girl than the boy. When the girl took off her panties in the front yard, her mother spanked her and told her that "nice little girls didn't do that." The mother discouraged the girl's tomboyishness and "bossyness." Her brother became protective of his sister. The mother also encouraged her daughter, but not her son, to help her, gave the girl dolls and feminine toys and the boy, cars, tools, and garages.

Until a few years ago, psychologists had concluded these two boys, perfectly matched genetically and hormonally during their first 1½ years, had been shaped into one child with a thoroughly masculine gender identity and one with a thoroughly feminine gender identity. But then new news appeared. At age 13 and the onset of puberty, the girl was in psychological trouble. She walked and looked masculine. At school she was taunted as "Cavewoman." She had few friends and said that boys have a better life than girls. She planned to become a mechanic. The shaping had not been so successful as people once had hoped.

Because this true story of the identical twins is still unfolding, no one yet knows how it will turn out. This tantalizing case shows how complex is the question of gender identity in childhood and beyond, and it shows once again how development is a matter of both nature and nurture.

other study believed that girls are more likely to play with dolls, help their mothers, be talkative, "never hit," ask for help, clean house, and grow up to be nurses, whereas boys are more likely to help their fathers, hit, mow the lawn, and grow up to be bosses, doctors, and governors. According to the boys, girls cry, cook dinner, and act slowly, whereas boys act naughty and make noise. According to the girls, girls kiss, care for babies, look pretty, and say, "I can do it best"; boys are mean and fight (Kuhn, Nash, and Brucken, 1978). Preschoolers know that men wear suits and shave and that women wear dresses, carry purses, and wear makeup; that men drive trucks, fix cars, and put out fires, and women cook, wash, iron, and clean. Not surprisingly, for preschoolers whose lives are dominated by women—mother, babysitters, nursery school teachers—the masculine gender role stands out. Preschool children's knowledge of male stereotypes develops earlier, and they know more masculine than feminine traits (Best et al., 1977). Boys are more aware of gender roles than girls are (O'Keefe and Hyde, 1983; Weinraub et al., 1984).

Tim made the mistake of telling his pal, Donny, that he wanted to be an artist when he grows up. Donny ridiculed him, "An *artist*! Only sissies are artists."

After they have gleaned this knowledge about gender roles, children at first are likely to subscribe to gender stereotypes with considerable rigidity and oversimplification. For example, 5-year-old Andy may think that only men can be doctors, only women can cook, and only boys can play ball, despite the fact that his mother is a surgeon, his father is a chef, and his sister is captain of the softball team. Gradually, as experience in the school years modifies their views, children allow for more variations. It may be that during this modifying phase parents, siblings, peers, teachers, television, and textbooks can reduce stereotypes significantly. Researchers who have examined the effects of mothers' work on their children's gender-role stereotyping have found stereotypes to be most rigid at 5 to 6 years; influenced most by the mother's work at 7 to 8; and the least stereotyped, regardless of the mother's kind of work, at 9 to 11 (Marantz and Mansfield, 1977). Apparently, 5-year-olds feel that they must conform to gender-role expectations to maintain their gender identity (Ullian, 1976). Only later, with sex constancy firmly established, do children understand that playing a boyish game will not change a girl, that putting on an apron will not change a boy.

The effects of television

The effects of parents, teachers, and other children on preschoolers' development are well established. The effects of television on children are just beginning to be appreciated. For many preschoolers, television is an electronic babysitter, a way for parents to keep children out of trouble—and out of their hair. Few parents restrict their children's television viewing until middle childhood or adolescence, even though the children may have been watching lots of television for years. When parents provide little guidance, children get much of their socialization from television. In one national survey in which children were asked to name a famous person they wanted to be like, most named entertainers and athletes whom they had seen on television (Foundation for Child Development, 1976). Hardly any named politicians, artists, or scientists. Most of the children surveyed said that their television viewing was not limited in length or content.

For many children, television is the primary source of information about other people—about other races and ethnic groups, other social classes, the outside world, our culture. Children probably also learn more about occupational groups from television than from personal contact or from the community. In this sense, "All television is educational television," as former Federal Communications Commissioner Nicholas Johnson has stated (Liebert and Poulos, 1975).

What are children likely to see on television? The content of television programs reflects—and probably magnifies—current social trends. Families on television today have problems—divorce, adolescent upheavals, brushes with drugs and alcohol. There are blacks on television and at least a few representatives of the working class. Women are seen at work as well as at home. Nevertheless, elderly people, who are becoming a larger proportion of the population, and Asians, Hispanics, and native Americans are still rarely seen on television. Of even greater concern, the proportions of violence and stereotyped gender roles in television programs remain high.

In the 1980s, the "dumb blond" is more popular than ever, and the typical victim of violence is a weak woman. Moreover, even though new

Television is one of the most influential socializers for today's preschool children. It conveys values about sex, gender roles, violence, power, and what is right and wrong—values which parents may not share.

programs reflect recent shifts in attitudes, reruns are common in the afternoon; the stereotyped characters in these programs are popular with children long after they have disappeared from prime time. Television constantly bombards children with images of people in traditional gender roles. This is even the case occasionally on educational programs, like "Sesame Street," where Big Bird is told he is "a boy bird and will have to help with men's work, important work, heavy work," and he "should get a girl bird to help Susan with her work of flower arranging" (Gardner, 1970). In one analysis of popular children's programs (Sternglanz and Serbin, 1974), men and boys were found to outnumber women and girls two to one. Males were aggressive, constructive, and rewarded for action; females, passive, deferential, and rewarded for reaction.

What are the effects of watching this television fare? For one thing, children who watch a lot of television, especially gender-stereotyped programs, have more traditional ideas about gender roles than children who do not (Davidson, Yasuna, and Tomer, 1979; Freuh and McGhee, 1975). For another thing, children who watch more television, especially violent shows, are more likely to be aggressive. The effect of television violence has been a special concern in recent years. In research done in the 1970s (Gerbner, 1970; Gerbner et al., 1977), it was found that nearly one-third of the prime-time and Saturday programs were saturated with violence, and nearly two-thirds featured a good deal of violence, with violence defined as an actual act of physical force or one causing pain. On these programs, socially disapproved means, such as force and illegal escape, succeeded more frequently than legal and socially approved means. This was especially true of children's programs. Foreigners were more likely to be involved in causing violence and more likely to pay a price for it. Despite efforts by the PTA and other groups, children's programs in the 1980s continue to portray a great deal of violence. For every hour of "Sesame Street," there are many hours of violent cartoons in which good guys vanquish bad. It is estimated that by graduation from high school the average American child has seen 18,000 televised murders (Brody, 1975).

Does all this watching of televised violence make children more violent themselves?

> I was amazed the first time Peter, age 3, saw an episode of "Spiderman" on TV. When the bad guys started beating up Spiderman, Peter walked right over to the set and began hitting it.

It has been demonstrated that exposure to television violence increases children's subsequent aggression in the laboratory. But it is difficult to generalize from the laboratory situation to real life; children in these studies may just have been trying to do what they thought was expected of them. In a more naturalistic study (which we described in Chapter 2; Friedrich and Stein, 1973), groups of preschoolers watched one of three types of television program daily for four weeks at their own nursery school: violent cartoons "Batman" and "Superman"; episodes of the prosocial "Mr. Rogers' Neighborhood"; or neutral programs, such as children visiting a farm. Two weeks after their television treatment, children in the first group were less willing to exert self-control, less able to tolerate delays in obtaining their desires, and less likely to obey the rules of the nursery school. If they had been aggressive before the four weeks of television viewing, they were more so afterward; but children who were not aggressive did not become so. The differences were not very large, and we do not know how long they lasted beyond the two weeks. Given the extensiveness of most children's television viewing, however, we should not dismiss the possibility that the effects of actual television viewing are profound and persistent.

In another naturalistic study (Singer, Singer, and Sherrod, 1979), 3- and 4-year-old children were observed repeatedly in nursery school. Their behavior during free play—their imaginativeness, emotionality, aggression, cooperation, interaction, and mood—was then related to their parents' reports of the children's television viewing. A strong relation was found between frequent physical aggression in nursery school and frequent viewing of all but educational children's programs. Frequent viewing of educational programs, on the other hand, was related to prosocial behavior and mature language in nursery school. These relations remained strong even when the education of the parents and the child's IQ were controlled for statistically. The study did not, however, establish the basis of the link: whether aggressive children choose to watch a great deal of violent television or whether watching violent televison makes children more aggressive. Probably both forge the link. Whatever the causal direction, this study joins a substantial number of others in suggesting that there is a definite connection between frequent viewing of violent television and aggression in children.

Because the social portrayals that children see on television are complex, young viewers are likely to misinterpret them (Collins, 1983). Young children may not understand crafty characters—"sneaks," "double dealers"—who seem good but actually are not. They understand less about both explicit and implicit content of what they see. What children do understand and remember about television characters and events depends heavily on what they already know about people and sequences of events—even before they turn on the set. One researcher (Dorr, 1979) obtained the self-reports of children, from kindergarten through fifth grade, before and after they viewed television programs. These reports revealed that children remember facts and events seen on television. But younger children were more likely to remember violent episodes and characters. The positive social and moral content of programs became more salient as the children grew older.

Summary

1. As they get older, children become more autonomous, get less upset at brief separations from their parents and seek less physical contact with them. Yet young children remain strongly emotionally attached to their parents. Patterns of attachment—secure, avoidant, and ambivalent— usually remain stable over time.

2. In the preschool period, parents begin to exert more control and discipline over their children. Parents with an authoritarian style of discipline are firm, punitive, unsympathetic, and do not value independence in their children. Their children tend to be suspicious, withdrawn, unfriendly, and unhappy. Permissive parents do not lay down rules or assert their authority over their children. Their children tend to be immature, dependent, and unhappy. Authoritative parents reason with their children, set few but firm limits, and keep conflict to a minimum. Their children are most likely to be friendly, competent, socially responsible, and happy.

3. Parents' interpretations of their children's behavior and children's characteristics affect the parents' disciplinary style and effectiveness. Mothers of difficult young children do more controlling, warning, and forbidding than mothers of easy children, and difficult children ignore, protest, and talk back more to their mothers than other children.

4. Families with handicapped or difficult children may get caught up in seemingly endless vicious cycles of hostile, defeating actions and reactions.

5. Many families in this country experience the stress of divorce. Whether children have long-term problems as a result of divorce depends in large part on whether their parents part amicably or fight openly and on the relationships they maintain with the children.

6. Mothers' work also is a source of stress—and strength—to their children's development. Daughters are more likely than sons to benefit from their mother's working.

7. In families with more than one child, siblings interact from infancy onwards. They imitate each other, compete for toys and their parents' attention and affection, and have many positive interchanges. Older siblings may act like parents to their younger siblings by providing them with security and even speaking motherese to them. Sibling interactions are both reciprocal and complementary.

8. Over the preschool period, children have more chances to play with other children. As 2- and 3-year-olds, their play is mainly parallel and ritualistic—repetitive, rhythmic exchanges or turns. Older preschoolers are more likely to engage in language play and pretend play, to play interactively and cooperatively.

9. Preschool children act in both prosocial and antisocial ways. They help, hit, hurt, disrupt, and fight with other children. Determinants of young children's aggressive behavior are many and complex. They include frustration; selective reinforcement; imitation of aggressive parents, teachers, other children, and television characters; certain hormones; and physical unattractiveness.

10. Preschoolers make friends with children of the same sex, age, energy and activity levels as they, and with their friends they talk, agree and comply, offer sympathy and help, and inquire about one another's feelings.

11. As young children's social understanding improves, they better understand other people's emotions, modulate their own emotional expressions, communicate more effectively, and have smoother conversations.

12. The young child's self-concept is based on fleeting, sometimes inaccurate, perceptions. Young children usually define themselves in terms of physical actions, not psychological traits.

13. By the time they are 3 years old, boys and girls begin to act in different ways. Girls play house, pay attention to people's feelings and relation-

ships; boys have grandiose power fantasies and games. Girls are more likely to be nurturant; boys are more likely to be aggressive. These differences stem, in part, from parents', teachers', and other children's implicit and explicit teachings about gender roles. Children also acquire knowledge about sex constancy and gender roles and develop their gender identity.

14. Television is one way that young children get information about gender roles. They also learn from watching television what kinds of behavior are acceptable. If they watch violent programs, they are more likely to be aggressive. If they watch prosocial programs, they are more likely to be helpful and cooperative.

Key terms

terrible twos	ritual play	prosocial	sex constancy
authoritarian parents	language play	collective monologue	gender identity
permissive parents	parallel play	self-concept	
authoritative parents	empathy	gender roles	

Suggested readings

CLARKE-STEWART, ALISON. *Daycare*. Cambridge, Mass.: Harvard University Press, 1982. All about day care—its history, politics, ecology, effects—with some practical suggestions for parents on how to find and select a good day-care arrangement.

DUNN, JUDY. *Sisters and Brothers*. Cambridge, Mass.: Harvard University Press, 1985. A fresh new discussion of how siblings influence one another's personalities, ways of thinking and talking, and perceptions of themselves, their families, and their friends.

GARVEY, CATHERINE. *Children's Talk*. Cambridge, Mass.: Harvard University Press, 1984. Young children's many uses of spoken language are discussed in this readable book. Liberally illustrated by examples.

GARVEY, CATHERINE. *Play*. Cambridge, Mass.: Harvard University Press, 1977. An excellent discussion of the many forms of children's play. Quotations from children illustrate why children play, what play is, and how it fosters learning and social development.

MURRAY, JOHN. *Television and Youth: 25 Years of Research and Controversy*. Boys Town, Nebr.: Boys Town Center for the Study of Youth Development, 1980. A compilation of the results of thousands of studies done over the past 25 years on the controversial subject of the effects of television on children.

MUSSEN, PAUL H., and EISENBERG-BERG, NANCY. *Roots of Caring, Sharing, and Helping*. San Francisco: W. H. Freeman, 1977. An excellent review of research on prosocial behavior in young children. Suggests how children's generosity, cooperation, and altruism are encouraged by factors in the family, the media, the immediate situation, and the child's own nature.

RUBIN, ZICK. *Children's Friendships*. Cambridge, Mass.: Harvard University Press, 1980. A lucid and lively description of friendships between children in the preschool and early school years. Suggests how their friendship patterns are affected by children's educational and social programs.

TAVRIS, CAROL, and WADE, CAROLE. *The Longest War: Sex Differences in Perspective*. (2nd ed.). San Diego, Calif.: Harcourt Brace Jovanovich, 1984. A witty but serious scientific review of the battle of the sexes and the nature and nurture of sex differences in behavior.

WALLERSTEIN, JUDITH S., and KELLY, JOAN B. *Surviving the Breakup: How Children and Parents Cope with Divorce*. New York: Basic Books, 1980. A detailed account of the results of the California Children of Divorce Project, which shows how children of different ages cope with this stressful event.

Middle Childhood

chapter eleven

Physical development

Physical growth and skills

One day Natalie was a short, chunky preschooler and the next day, it seemed, she had turned into a lovely, well coordinated child who loved to pedal her bike around the neighborhood, jump rope, and draw with chalk on the sidewalks.

As they enter middle childhood, boys and girls begin to grow more slowly than they did as younger children. Each year, they grow an average of 2½ inches and gain about 5 pounds. The typical 10-year-old weighs 70 pounds and stands 4½ feet tall. From 7 to 10 years, girls are taller than boys, but by age 10, boys have caught up and become taller than girls, and this difference in height continues into adulthood. Boys and girls do not differ much in their physical shape and abilities during middle childhood, although boys' forearms are stronger and girls' bodies are more flexible (Tanner, 1970)—an edge to boys on the pitcher's mound and girls on the balance beam. School-age children are less clumsy and more physically coordinated than younger children. They can throw a ball twice as far as a preschooler, manage a screwdriver, hammer, and saw, knit, sew, and crochet, draw, write, and print legibly, cut their own nails—no more fights with Mom, thank heavens—button buttons, zip zippers, and tie laces, ride a bicycle, climb ladders and trees, swim and dive, roller-skate, ice-skate, and skateboard, jump rope, play hopscotch, baseball, football, board games, cards, and jacks.

All this physical activity helps children to develop. As physically active children master skills, they raise their self-esteem and increase their competence in the eyes of others. Children who can run fast, pitch well, do handstands, or jump rope without being ''out'' are popular with other children, and they like themselves. Physically active children do their bodies a favor by developing muscle, keeping weight down, and preventing the chronic diseases of adulthood, such as heart disease, obesity, and high blood pressure, from gaining an early hold.

Physically active children also do something for their minds. More than 30 years ago, French doctors and educators became concerned that children's health was being harmed by too much schoolwork and too little physical exercise and recreation. Schoolchildren between 6 and 11 years old were divided into two groups (Bailey, 1973). The experimental group got schoolwork all morning, and physical exercise, recreation, art, and music all afternoon. They were not assigned written homework overnight. The control group did schoolwork all day and homework at night. The children were given achievement tests and physical examinations; their absence rates from school were recorded; and their teachers' rated the children's behavior problems and observed the children's interactions with other children and with adults. Even though the children in the experimental group had four fewer hours of schoolwork every day, these tests showed, their academic progress surpassed that of the children in the control group. Their health, fitness, behavior, and enthusiasm were also superior. Clearly, physical activity is important for development in middle childhood.

Physical health and handicaps

Not all children develop through middle childhood with physical grace and ease. Some are afflicted with disease, disorders, or disabling conditions that affect both their physical and psychological development.

Of the children in this country, 10 to 20 percent have physical handicaps. Adjusting to these handicaps requires accommodations on the parts of the children themselves, their parents, and their peers.

Handicapping conditions

Diseases that strike adults often begin in childhood. Risk factors for cardiovascular disease, cancer, and stroke—the cause of two-thirds of deaths among adults in the United States—are common in children. These risk factors include overweight, high levels of cholesterol in the blood, high blood pressure, poor physical fitness, and diabetes. In one sample of elementary schoolboys from California, for example, nearly half had one risk factor associated with heart disease, and over 10 percent had two (Wilmore and McNamara, 1974). In a New York sample, 43 percent of the schoolchildren surveyed had abnormally high cholesterol levels; 10 percent smoked cigarettes; 15 percent were overweight; and 2 percent had high blood pressure. (Williams, Arnold, and Wynder, 1977).

Many researchers believe that prevention of heart disease, cancer, and stroke should begin in childhood. One preventive screening and education program, the "Know Your Body" program, has been instituted in New York to determine whether certain risk factors for chronic disease can be reduced in schoolchildren (Williams et al., 1977). Results over the long term will tell the research team whether the program has motivated the students to change their behavior enough to reduce their risk and, ultimately, their incidence of fatal disease.

In addition to these risks of later health problems, schoolchildren may suffer from handicaps during childhood. At any given time, 10 to 20 percent of the children in this country have a physical handicap (Pless and Satterwhite, 1975). If sensory impairment, mental retardation, and behavior disorders are included, then 30 to 40 percent of children suffer from one or more chronic disorders. The most common of these are asthma, heart problems, cerebral palsy, orthopedic problems, and diabetes (Mattson, 1972). About 25 percent of elementary school children have vision problems, 10 to 20 percent have reading problems, 3 percent have hearing problems, 3 percent are mentally retarded, 1 percent have epilepsy, and 1 percent have a major speech disorder. One common and preventable problem in school-age children is

415

tooth decay. By the age of 12, 90 percent of children have at least one cavity (Nizel, 1977). Scoliosis (lateral curvature of the spine), juvenile rheumatoid arthritis, malnutrition, obesity, poor posture, and sexual abnormalities are less common but still serious problems among children in elementary school.

Cerebral palsy, from the words for "brain"—*cerebral*—and "paralysis"—*palsy*—is a disorder of movement or posture that is caused by a malfunction or damage to the brain and shows up in childhood. It usually results from a disease or disturbance during prenatal development or birth—prematurity, Rh disease, rubella (German measles), viral infections, or anoxia. About 15 percent of cases of cerebral palsy are acquired later in childhood, the results of falls and other injuries to the brain. Cerebral palsy does not get progressively worse, but its severity varies from child to child. Of the 7 in 100,000 children born with cerebral palsy each year, one dies in the first year, two are so severely affected as to need institutional care, three need outpatient care, and one needs no special treatment (Bleck, 1982). Cerebral palsy may extend beyond the motor areas of the brain to cause drooling, tooth grinding, and problems in swallowing, and problems in speech and language. Three-fourths of children with cerebral palsy have impaired intelligence.

Schoolchildren may also suffer from a variety of acute illnesses. But fortunately, for most children, the elementary school years are the healthiest of their lives. Elementary schoolers' incidence of infectious diseases is lower than preschoolers'. Boys are more vulnerable to childhood diseases and disorders than girls are, just as they are more vulnerable to all environmental assaults. More boys than girls contract pneumonia and die from it. More boys suffer from speech, learning, and behavior problems such as stuttering and reading problems. More boys than girls suffer from mental retardation, emotional problems, and sleep disorders (Knopf, 1979). Boys also have far more accidents and need more emergency medical care than girls do (Manheimer, Dewey, Mellinger, and Corsa, 1966; Manheimer and Mellinger, 1967).

Living with a handicap

In addition to their physical disadvantages, children with physical handicaps are also more likely than other children to suffer problems of social or psychological adjustment. Such problems afflict 30 percent of handicapped children (Pless and Roghmann, 1971). "Some teachers," says one handicapped child, "make me feel incapable. What they don't seem to realize is that just because I am physically handicapped doesn't necessarily mean that I am mentally handicapped as well" (MacElman and Burden, 1979, p. 214). But it would be wrong to think that the most severely physically handicapped children are the most psychologically and socially troubled. In fact, the most severely handicapped children often are better adjusted than moderately handicapped children, perhaps because the most severe handicaps limit children's own and others' expectations of what they can or should do (Richman and Harper, 1978).

As they get older, children's perceptions of their handicaps change. Handicapped toddlers may begin to say "I can't" when they face a difficult task and to feel sad and angry when their bodies fail to execute their wishes—turning pages, putting on a jacket, moving over to a favorite toy. Handicapped preschoolers first notice that they are different, but they accept "easy answers" for why they are different: "I can't walk because my muscles aren't strong." They rarely complain if they are clumsy, speak fuzzily, need a walker or help getting dressed. Other, nonhandicapped preschoolers may ask questions, but they are likely to accept handicapped children as playmates.

Megan started wearing leg braces to nursery school when she was 3. The teachers explained to the group that the braces were "to help Megan walk." When I asked Sam why Megan needed the braces, he simply said "to keep her shoes on."

In the school years, handicapped children suddenly want to know where they fit in. They ask "Who do I look like?" "Am I handicapped?" or "Why did you make me this way?" They grow sensitive to how others perceive their differentness, and they may begin to have problems with their image of themselves. Children who cannot walk and climb, children who "look funny" when they run, children who cannot play like the other kids all may feel woebegone and miserable. Said one 6-year-old with cerebral palsy, when asked what her response was to being teased by her classmates because she could not walk, "I want to tell them I hate their guts, but then the teacher would bench me" (Howard, 1982, p. 190). A handicapped 7-year-old boy who was the youngest—and smartest—in a summer school rocket-making class said, "For the first time the kids really like me" (Howard, 1982, p. 190). Friendship and others' respect are especially important to children at this age. By middle childhood, children who once assumed that their handicap would get better in time now may have to abandon that hope. A study of 41 10-year-olds with cerebral palsy showed that half of them were depressed because they knew that they could not be cured (Minde et al., 1972).

When nonhandicapped children participate in experiments that expose them to the daily frustrations of the handicapped—wheeling down a crowded school corridor to the bathroom, trying to eat a snack or drink from a fountain while blindfolded—they grow more curious, concerned, accepting, and comforting to those with handicaps.

> When Sam was 3, he saw a teenager with no arms. He stared intently and asked loudly, "Where's her arms?" I was embarrassed, but I told him I didn't know and to hush because he would hurt her feelings. She smiled at him and continued on her way. When I later told Sam's father about the incident, his reaction was to say that he didn't think it was good for Sam to see handicapped people because it would only scare him.

> I was never so proud of Sarah as I was when she covered up the *adults'* awkwardness and went right up to a blind girl who was being introduced, took her hand to shake it, and said, "Hi, I'm Sarah, and this is my mother."

Treatment at home and at school

Treatment for handicapped children varies widely, depending on the type and severity of the handicap and the wishes of doctors and parents. Therapy with cerebral palsy victims is designed to reduce the effects of the handicap to a minimum, to promote the child's assets, to prevent the handicap from dominating the child's life, and to avoid forms of treatment that further burden the child's family. Generally, if children with cerebral palsy are going to be able to walk, they will have learned to do so by the age of 7. Beyond this age, there is rarely much change. For the children who are up and walking, routine playing on the playground and walking from place to place is all the therapy they need. For more severely handicapped children, one popular form of therapy is the Fay–Doman method. In this kind of therapy, children are taught a progression of movements, starting with those of lower animals—the swimming of amphibians—and working up to those of higher animals—the creeping of human infants—in the belief that the human brain is made up of evolutionary layers, so that the brains of children with cerebral palsy will respond to training in movement that progresses up the evolutionary ladder. One study of 45 severely retarded children, however, showed no more improvement with the Fay–Doman method than with loving care and concern (Sparrow and Zigler, 1978).

At most schools for handicapped children, the method of therapy is eclectic: therapists choose what seems to work best for each child's particular problems and level of development. Handicapped children achieve most when their therapy helps them to function in the outside world as fully as possible. For example, children whose problems of coordination make handwriting a grueling task may do better if they are trained to use an electric typewriter. Electronic and computerized devices that help children to communicate, motorized devices that help them get around, and other therapeutic devices that improve functioning and bolster independence can all help handicapped children to leave segregated, restricted environments and enter the everyday world.

Deaf children may be taught to communicate in sign language. So may children who are not deaf but who are mute—autistic children, for example. Sign language is the most widely used means of communication for these mute children. It is convenient, requires no special apparatus, and is based on the existing language of the deaf. In other cases, children may be taught to use colored symbols—red plastic triangles, yellow squares—to represent words, sentence forms, and complete thoughts. Children with motor handicaps can communicate through boards on which symbols can be arranged or pointed to sequentially. Some parents of mute children worry that if their children depend on sign language or symbolic tokens to communicate, they will never make any progress in speaking. In fact, the opposite is true. Once these children learn to communicate in any form, their frustrations lessen and they may begin to speak more and listen more receptively to spoken language as well (Bonvillian and Nelson, 1982). Handicapped children taught signing master it at about the same rate as nonhandicapped children master spoken language—or earlier. One deaf child had a vocabulary of more than 85 signs and was combining them into sentences—*Mommy shoe; More food*—at 13 months, an age at which most speaking children are just uttering their first word or two (McIntire, 1977). Hearing children who are exposed to signs may also use them before they begin to speak in words. One boy, for example, learned signs because his deaf grandmother lived with the family. At the extraordinary age of 5½ months, he correctly signed for milk (Schlesinger and Meadow, 1972).

Handicapped children who live at home typically need special help from both family members and professionals—teachers, therapists, physicians, and others with special training.

> We adopted Denny when he was 2 days old, with the understanding that the agency would take him back if he wasn't healthy. But he was 9 months old before we acted on our suspicions that he wasn't responding to our voices or to sounds, and by then we were so attached to him that we'd never have given him up. An audiologist at a nearby teaching hospital tested him and told us—brusquely—that Denny is "profoundly deaf." It was horrible news, even though we already suspected it. Our lives since then really have centered on Denny's deafness—how to treat it, how to overcome it, where to find teachers, babysitters, time off for ourselves.

Denny's parents were lucky enough to live near a prestigious school for deaf children, founded by Alexander Graham Bell, where Denny learned both lip reading and signing. Denny's parents were also taught ways to help Denny communicate and put in touch with community resources for families with handicapped children. They installed a special telephone—with a blinking

Parents of physically handicapped children can learn the best ways of helping them to develop as normally, independently, and healthily as possible. Here a father teaches his 2-year-old deaf son sign language.

focus **Living with a handicapped child—
one mother's view**

A special mother with a special child describes the unique feelings and responsibilities that having a child with severe neurological and physical handicaps brings to a family. Robyn was born with Cornelia de Lange syndrome. She has only one finger on each wrist, a cleft palate, mental retardation, deafness, and downturned eyes and mouth.

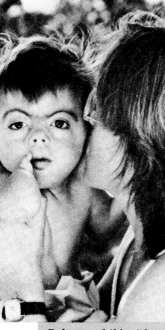

Robyn, a child with the severe physical and neurological handicaps of Cornelia de Lange syndrome, demands extra love and patience.

There were many tears during our life together. Most of them were from me as I tried to keep myself together, emotionally. I didn't know what to expect from all of this. . . . I had plenty of "professionals" giving me advice, but I found that the only way I was going to make it was to live from day to day, using the information and experience that came to me from Robyn herself.

I have a tremendous honor and respect for Robyn. No one can accurately call her life an accident or tragedy. To automatically hold the opinion that a person with a weird body is a less valuable creation is to greatly limit the nature of the universe.

A typical child will cry when hungry, for example, and smile when joyful. Often a child who is handicapped will not initiate this type of interaction. She may not cry to let you know she's hungry. When played with, she may show no obvious signs of pleasure. Depending on the nature and degree of the disability, the appearance of characteristic responses may be extremely delayed, or may not appear at all. Robyn has a downturned mouth, which is typical of the de Lange syndrome. When she smiles, her mouth does not turn up at the corners. Her eyes sparkle, she gets dimples in her cheeks, and she chuckles, but this is not an easily recognizable expression to those who are unfamiliar with her body language. . . .

It is really important for parents to know that the child is expressing love, or discomfort, and that he does recognize his parents. Parents who think their child is rejecting them or doesn't know them can become deeply discouraged and are not easily consoled.

It is very important that you be persistent and consistently provide eye contact in every way available. Make it worthwhile for your child to look at you. First by using your eyes as channels of love—just like faucets—turn on the love and know your child is getting it. This means you have to aim. It takes a while to get the flow right, but your heart knows how and it will do all the work. Talking in a low, soothing voice with much intonation right near the ear will provide excellent audio nourishment. It actually causes the bones in the inner ear to vibrate and stimulate the auditory nerve, even if the child cannot distinguish what he is hearing. Tell your child how you feel about him. Whisper endearments. Tell your child what you love about life.

All in all, what I see to be a wholistic approach to raising a severely handicapped child is just being there, being near, and having it be okay for you and your child to be together. It's opening up new possibilities for loving and caring. It's exploring the deepest parts of yourself with compassion. It's looking deep inside one another—touching and being touched, listening, being led, being taught—being one for the sustenance of two (Craven, 1978, pp. 202 ff).

light to signal a call—and bought a big, gentle dog to sleep in Denny's room at night. All alone in the dark, Denny often has nightmares, and the big, warm dog reassures him.

Parents of children with other kinds of handicaps can learn the best ways of helping them to develop as normally, independently, and healthily as possible. Children with motor handicaps can be exercised, rolled on pillows, clapped and sung with, helped to eat or feed themselves. Parents of handicapped children often have to overcome the urge to do everything for their children. After all, it's so much easier if Mom's normal fingers button those buttons and lift that spoon. But they must learn to stand back and let the children develop their own skills.

Parents of handicapped children face a special set of problems. Not only must they take the practical steps necessary to deal with their child's handicap, but they must also deal with their anguish and sense of loss from not having a normal child. Even as they feel love and tenderness for their handicapped child, parents may also feel anger, despair, worthlessness, and frustration. It not infrequently happens that a child's handicap is difficult to diagnose, to assess and to explain—much less to treat—which leaves anxious parents feeling that their child is ''not a person but a question mark'' (Freeman and Pearson, 1978, p. 36). Adjusting to the news that their child is handicapped, worrying about how they will carry on, feeling burdened by the cost of treatment and exhausted by the effort, suffering, and isolation from friends whose children are not handicapped are just some of the stresses that parents of handicapped children must face.

Even the most experienced parents doubt their abilities to meet the special needs of handicapped children, especially when the children are so seriously disabled that they cannot give their parents much rewarding feedback for their seemingly endless efforts. Asked by professionals to be ''realistic'' about their handicapped child's needs, parents are pressed to superhuman ''objectivity'' in areas of painful emotional sensitivity. Parents must deal with the confusions and intrusions of doctors, therapists, social workers, educators. Support groups can bring parents of handicapped children the sincere joy of meeting people with whom they can share a painful burden, whose families they can see functioning, and from whom they can get help in answering questions from brothers and sisters like ''Why did this happen to my little sister?'' ''Will it happen to my children?''

Since 1975, the law has required that schools provide handicapped children with an appropriate education. Schools must modify existing programs or create new ones to meet the needs of handicapped children, and they must educate handicapped children alongside nonhandicapped children—as fully as possible. **Mainstreaming** integrates handicapped children into the social and academic worlds of their peers and helps them to escape isolation and stigma, which can be more severely disabling than the original handicap. Some children stay in regular classes all day; others take special reading and arithmetic courses or instruction and therapy in special subjects. Teachers of handicapped students must adjust their strategies to the students' abilities. Deaf children, for example, may need classes with lots of visual material—posters, blackboard work, building and drawing projects—rather than lectures. Blind children need Braille books, which they can finger-read, and lots of spoken and tactile material—records, class discussions, music, objects to build and manipulate. Mainstreaming helps educators to correct the tendency to focus on handicapped children's disabilities instead of their abilities and to magnify their weaknesses instead of capitalizing on their strengths. Mainstreaming also can help to draw out the talents of nonhandicapped children to act as tutors and teachers of their handicapped classmates.

Promoting health

Special programs and treatment can help handicapped children, of course. But parents of nonhandicapped children can also take advantage of programs and treatment to keep their children well. Many different forms of injury and illness prevention and treatment have significantly improved the outlook for children today. Not surprisingly, several studies have shown that parents' attitudes toward children's health predict whether they use these programs. One such study of 250 poor mothers showed that those who were interested in preventing illness and who saw their children as basically healthy more commonly used the well-child clinics (Becker, Nathanson, Drachman, and Kirscht, 1977). In another study, children were found to have good health habits, such as exercising or brushing teeth, when their parents encouraged them (Pratt, 1973).

How parents feel about health and illness determines whether and when they seek medical care for their children. Parents with more education are more likely to believe that illness is preventable and to use a physician (Mechanic, 1964). How they feel about the seriousness of their children's illnesses, about the benefits and effectiveness of treatment, about the diagnosis, and about the quality of medical care also influence whether parents comply with physicians' instructions on such issues as giving medicine (Becker, 1974). Two strategies can induce parents to cooperate with medical care: informing them of negative consequences of not complying and making their health care accessible, affordable, responsive, and of good quality (Rosenstock and Kirscht, 1974).

Behavior disorders

Our younger son was a beautiful baby. But by the time he was about a year old, we were worried about the way he wasn't responding to us and wasn't making any progress in talking. By the time he was 2, he not only wasn't talking, but spent hours hitting his head against the side of his crib or rocking back and forth. It was impossible to catch his eye. He seemed to be going backward, into some dark isolated place where we couldn't reach him. We took him to specialists, and the word came back: "autism." He's 8 now and in a residential school for autistic children near our home. We take him home on weekends, and he has made some progress. He can feed himself with a spoon and say a few words. The head banging and rocking are less. But he isn't normal, and God only knows whether he ever will be.

It is not only physical handicaps and illness that present problems for children and parents. Psychological handicaps and behavior disorders can be just as devastating. These behavior disorders range in severity from problems in sleeping and concentrating and outbursts of temper, to extreme hyperactivity and excessive withdrawal or autism.

Sleep disorders

Sleep disorders of various kinds are common in early and middle childhood. The **parasomnias**, which include sleepwalking, sleep terrors, nightmares, head banging, tooth grinding, and bed-wetting, are probably the most common of all. The parasomnias rarely signify more serious underlying problems; at one time or another, they afflict roughly 20 percent of all children, especially boys (Ware and Orr, 1983). Most parasomnias have no clear cause and eventually disappear. Sleepwalking usually occurs in the first third of the night's sleep, during very deep sleep. It can be brought on by a loud noise or by standing a child on his or her feet (Broughton, 1968; Kales, Jacobson Paulson, Kales, and Walter, 1966a, b).

Sleep terrors, like sleepwalking, usually strike during the first two hours of sleep and during very deep sleep. The child sits up in bed, screams loudly, and cries excitedly for several minutes. Typically, the child's pulse rate soars to over 100 beats a minute, but after the episode passes, the child remembers nothing about it. Sleep terrors, like sleepwalking, may set in after a child has had a fever (Kales, Kales, Soldatos, Chamberlin, and Martin, 1979) and seem not to be related to any other forms of pathology. The best treatment for sleep terrors ordinarily is reassurance and education. In some cases, parents have found it effective to wake their child and have him or her urinate just before the parents retire for the night, for a distended bladder has been thought to trigger sleep terrors.

Sleep enuresis (bed-wetting) is found among an estimated 5 to 17 percent of children between the ages of 3 and 15 (Lovibond, 1964). It is more common in boys than in girls (Rutter, Yule, and Graham, 1973). Enuresis may be primary, in children who have never had bladder control during sleep, or secondary, in children who have lost their bladder control. Although secondary enuresis often is ascribed to psychological causes, it may actually have an organic basis (Guilleminault and Anders, 1976). Sleep enuresis is not related to any stage of sleep (Broughton and Gaustaut, 1975), but bed wetters have been found to sleep exceptionally deeply (Hallgren 1957). One treatment for bed-wetting is to use an apparatus that rings a bell and wakes the child as soon as he or she wets the bed. Another kind of treatment is to train a child to increase his or her bladder capacity.

Insomnia is another kind of sleep disorder that afflicts certain children. Insomnia may be a symptom of many different psychological and organic problems. When insomnia is associated with an organic problem, like an ear infection, the cause is usually easy for a physician to detect. But when the insomnia is associated with a psychological problem, the cause may be harder to find. For instance, children who are depressed may also complain of insomnia, and the two may aggravate each other. Treating the depression can often alleviate the insomnia. Other causes of insomnia include neurological problems, food allergies, and nursing on breast milk during infancy (Salzman, 1976; Wright, MacLeod, and Cooper, 1983). Finally, some children sleep badly because they have poor sleep hygiene. Their bedtime routine may interfere with their ability to sleep. Generally, regular bed and awakening times help children to fall asleep promptly and to stay asleep. Light snacks before bedtime can improve sleep, but heavy meals can interfere with it. Milk and cereals promote sleep, but chocolate and caffeinated drinks interfere with it. Regular exercise is likely to improve sleep, but children need a calming transition between periods of exercise and sleep. Environmental disturbances, like noise, lights, temperature, or pets (which often are overlooked) can also interfere with children's sleep (Ware and Orr, 1983).

Hyperactivity

Thomas Edison's teachers complained so about his unrestrained behavior that his mother had to take him out of school and tutor him at home. Winston Churchill's teachers considered his overactivity a problem (Aries, 1962). Today **hyperactivity** is considered a behavior disorder to be treated by psychotherapy, psychoactive drugs, and special education (Ross and Ross, 1982).

Table 11.1
Criteria for hyperactivity

Unusual energy and restlessness.
Short attention span.
Inability to finish work.

plus any six of the following:

Fidgets, rocks	Disobedient
Climbs on roof	Doesn't follow direction
Runs over furniture	Doesn't respond to discipline
Always into things	Defiant
Heedless of danger	Wakes early
Runs away	Hard to get to bed
Constant demands	Wets bed
Easily upset	Many accidents
Impatient	Lies often
Won't accept correction	Takes money
Tantrums	Neighborhood terror
Fights often	Sets fires
Teases	Reckless, daredevil
Destructive	Fears nothing

SOURCE: Stewart et al., 1970. Copyright © 1970, Physicians Post-graduate Press. Reprinted by permission.

At what point does a child's level of activity deserve the label "hyperactive"? (See Table 11.1.) Hyperactive children are restless and have difficulty concentrating. They cannot quiet themselves when someone asks them to. They are distractible, impulsive, easily angered and frustrated, often destructive and aggressive. Unpredictable and disruptive, hyperactive children often are referred by a teacher to a physician for diagnosis and treatment. In the United States, hyperactivity is the most common behavior disorder that child psychiatrists see, affecting some 1 to 6 percent of all schoolchildren (Ross and Ross, 1982). It is a syndrome that has attracted the attention of many researchers) (Abikoff, Gittelman-Klein, and Klein, 1980; Campbell and Paulaukas, 1979; Ceci and Tishman, 1984; Douglas, 1980; Kinsbourne, 1973;

Hyperactive children are distractible and restless; they are often aggressive, destructive, and intolerant of frustration.

Loney, Langhorne, and Paternite, 1978; Routh, Schroeder, and O'Tuama, 1974; Whalen and Henker, 1984).

Specific situations seem to affect hyperactive children in different ways. Some children are hyperactive when they are in groups but not when they are with just one other person. For others, the opposite is true. Some children are hyperactive only in unfamiliar situations; others, only in familiar ones. But almost all hyperactive children have trouble at school. When they can set their own pace, hyperactive children often seem quite competent, but when they must follow someone else's pace—as often happens at school—they seem out of step. In the classroom, hyperactive children are more physically active than other children, acting up at inappropriate times. Compared to normal children, hyperactive children make more mistakes on work that requires focused attention, and they do not control their impulses well. As hyperactive children try to learn their attention is scattered and focused on peripheral attributes—a condition called **attention deficit disorder**. Some hyperactive children also show poor judgment.

Many of the symptoms seen in hyperactive children are associated with delays in maturation. The behavior of hyperactive children is normal for children three to four years younger. As a result of their impulsiveness, poor judgment, and scattered attention, hyperactive children often are in conflict with others, and so many hyperactive children develop a poor self-image and think of themselves as ''bad.'' They have few friends, and others tend to think badly of them. When hyperactive children are also aggressive and hostile, they tend to develop more and more problems as they get older. Hyperactive children often become poorly adjusted adults—regularly changing jobs, homes, and relationships.

What causes hyperactivity? It is possible that hyperactivity stems at least in part from genetic factors. Parents of hyperactive children tend to have more psychiatric problems, including hyperactivity as children, than parents of normal children (Morrison and Stewart, 1971, 1973). Hyperactivity also occurs almost exclusively in boys. For these reasons, and because hyperactivity is strongly related to a deficit in the ability to attend to stimuli, researchers now believe that hyperactivity has a physiological basis. But environmental variables also may contribute. Some people have suggested that hyperactivity is associated with a child's blood sugar level. They recommend eliminating refined sugars from the hyperactive child's diet. This suggestion is based on personal testimony rather than objective data, however. Another school of thought is that food additives set off hyperactivity (Feingold, 1975). Many investigators have not found evidence to support this hypothesis (for example, Conners, 1980). But others have found that food dyes and preservatives have an effect on *some* hyperactive children (Swanson and Kinsbourne, 1980). Still other researchers have suggested that food allergies relate to hyperactivity. The consensus among researchers at present seems to be that dietary factors are likely to be the cause of hyperactivity in at most only a small fraction of children (Henker and Whalen, 1980; Kerasotes and Walker, 1983). Other environmental factors that have been blamed for hyperactivity include exposure to radiation, heavy drinking by the mother during pregnancy, stressful child rearing, stressful experiences in school, chronic low levels of lead in the body, and fluorescent lighting (Henker and Whalen, 1980; Ross and Ross, 1982). Research to establish these links is still continuing. But like so many other kinds of behavior, hyperactivity is doubtless a result of both biological and environmental factors.

What can be done to control hyperactivity? Stimulants like **Ritalin** calm hyperactive children and help them to focus their attention. But the side effects of the stimulants—at first they interfere with sleep and appetite, and for a while, they may stop a child from growing—have led people to question

research
focus

A teacher responds to hyperactive boys

Many children diagnosed as hyperactive are treated successfully with medication. In most cases, drugs, such as Ritalin, have been found to improve hyperactive children's ability to concentrate and to pay attention. Carol Whalen, Barbara Henker, and Sharon Dotemoto (1981) wanted to find out whether Ritalin also affects hyperactive children's interactions with their teachers. They assumed that children whose behavior improves so dramatically would also generate changes in their teachers, and they decided to test this assumption with a group of 22 hyperactive boys who were enrolled in a summer school program. Half of the hyperactive boys were randomly assigned to take a placebo and half to take Ritalin for four days. Then four days were allowed for the effects of the drugs to wash out. Finally, the two conditions were reversed, and the first group of boys got Ritalin and the second the placebo for four more days. Thirty-nine normal boys were chosen as a comparison group. An elementary school teacher taught classes that contained a mixture of normal boys and medicated and unmedicated hyperactive boys. The teacher was not told that any of the boys were considered hyperactive or were medicated. The project was explained to her as one that would assess ''social and academic behaviors under various environmental conditions.''

Four raters who did not know the purpose of the study observed and coded the frequency and kind of contact—primarily attempts at control versus ordinary small talk and information giving—between teacher and each student. They also coded the intensity of contacts, whether they were spoken or physical, whether they were initiated by the student or the teacher, and whether they explicitly included calling the boy's name.

The teacher did more intense controlling, guiding, and disciplining of the hyperactive boys who were on the placebo than of the other boys. She also spoke more often to these boys and called them by name in her attempts to control them. They, in turn, were less attentive to class tasks and showed more bursts of energy, movement, talking, and disruptiveness. They initiated more contacts with the teacher. There were no differences between the hyperactive boys on medication and the normal boys. Both the teacher's beneficial behavior and the students' reflected the effect of medication.

their value as a treatment. Because of this concern about treating children with psychoactive drugs, psychologists have tried to find alternative treatments for hyperactivity. To date, their research suggests that psychoactive drugs are most effective in diminishing the intensity of children's hyperactive behavior, but cognitive and behavioral therapies are effective in improving social behavior and in helping children to manage their anger. In therapeutic programs, children are taught specific strategies for solving problems and for keeping their actions under control when they meet a new child or play a competitive game (Hinshaw, Henker, and Whalen, 1984). They are trained to recognize the external triggers that anger them and to identify the thoughts and feelings that signal their building anger. They learn how to handle teasing and provocation by ignoring it, staring out the window, or talking calmly. The best treatment for hyperactive children at present combines educating children and their parents about the disorder, structuring the children's environments at home and at school—setting firm limits, rules, and providing supervision—and giving the children drug therapy.

Type A behavior

We all recognize them. They are the people who read while they are driving, who chomp their food so quickly they seem to inhale it, who fly off the handle, who rush through the day. They are **Type A** people. Compared to their slower-paced **Type B** fellows, Type A people act, think, and feel more quickly and intensely. Compared to a Type B person with the same intelligence score, a Type A person gets higher grades and undertakes more activities. Type A behavior seems to enhance professional achievement and productivity—a great advantage in a competitive, industrialized society like our own. But Type A behavior has its dangers as well. Type A people often feel hostile, angry, urgently rushed, and anxious (Brody, 1984). These qualities, uncomfortable enough in their own right, have been linked to heart disease in adult men. In fact, it was two San Francisco cardiologists who first described Type A behavior (Friedman and Rosenman, 1974). Although Type A and Type B adults differ on certain neurological, hormonal, and physiological measures, the specific mechanisms by which Type A behavior is translated into heart disease have not yet been uncovered. The connection between Type A behavior and factors associated with heart disease has shown up in studies of young people as well as of adults, however. In an investigation of children between 10 and 17 years old, it was found that the Type A personality traits of eagerness and energy were correlated with blood levels of cholesterol and triglycerides (Hunter, Wolf, Sklov, Webber, and Berenson, 1981).

To explore the differences between Type A and Type B children, researchers have investigated how elementary school children react to a variety of tasks. In one study, for example, the researchers hypothesized that Type A children would perform tasks more hurriedly and intensely than Type B children and that Type B children would perform hurriedly and intensely only if they were so instructed (Wolf, Sklov, Wenz, Hunter, and Berenson, 1982). First, researchers asked the children to rate themselves on scales describing their own behavior. From the children's ratings on scales like ''I am easygoing—I am hard driving,'' ''It does matter if I am late—It doesn't matter if I am late,'' ''I walk fast—I walk slowly,'' the investigators classified them as Type A or Type B. Then, the children were given a number of tasks, which included reading an emotionally charged passage, eating two graham crackers, delivering an envelope to a box, playing marbles, estimating when one minute had passed, and crossing out numbers on a page. The Type A children read more loudly than Type B children, ate their graham crackers and delivered the envelope faster, were more competitive in playing marbles, crossed out more numbers, and estimated that one minute had passed more quickly than Type B children did. All the findings supported the hypothesis that Type A children would act more hurriedly, intensely, aggressively, and competitively than Type B children. The research team concluded that Type A people try harder to exert and maintain control over environmental demands and challenges.

Because it is widely accepted that Type A behavior can contribute to the development of heart disease, researchers have tried to uncover the psychological and social factors that foster Type A behavior. Some have observed how parents encourage their children's competitiveness, aggression, and impatience. For example, one mother encouraged her blindfolded son as he tried to pick up a pile of blocks. When time was up, she said, ''Next time try for six blocks.'' Said another mother to her son, after the same task, ''Next time go a little faster.'' Both sons had been classified as Type A (Brody, 1984).

Other researchers have investigated the contribution of constitutional factors. In one study using subjects from the New York Longitudinal Study (see Chapters 3 and 7), it was shown that Type A behavior in young adult subjects had links to assessments of temperament made when they were children (Steinberg, 1985). Young adults who showed the striving for achievement typical of Type As had been adaptable but irritable and negative in mood as young children. Young adults who were impatient and angry, another characteristic of Type As, were unadaptable, sensitive to stimulation (had low sensory thresholds), and not persistent as young children. It is likely that Type A behavior, like many other behavior patterns that we have discussed, has roots in both nature and nurture.

Signs of the influence of both nature and nurture on Type A behavior emerged clearly in another study of children, some of whom were rated high in Type A characteristics and others, low in Type A characteristics (Thoresen, Eagleston, Kirmil-Gray, and Bracke, 1985). Many of the high Type A children had parents who also were high in Type A behavior. These Type A children reported often feeling stressed and tense and suffering from symptoms of stress such as cardiovascular and sleep problems. They also were more often angry and hostile than the low Type A children. When the children attempted to build a tower of blocks, parents of both high Type As and low Type As praised their children. (Praise for success, research has shown, is likely to instill in children a need to strive for achievement.) But the parents of the high Type A children also criticized their children's failures, gave them more instructions, and made more decisions for them on a ring toss problem. Chronic interference and criticism for failure are likely to impair children's self-confidence.

Autism

One rare but devastating childhood disorder is **autism**. Autism is a form of psychosis that strikes 4 or 5 out of every 10,000 children, usually before they are 2½ (Brask, 1967; Rutter, 1978). In about 70 percent of cases, the autistic child is also seriously mentally retarded (DeMyer, et al., 1974). Although the diagnostic criteria have been debated, generally autism is characterized by a child's profound aloneness and inability to communicate or to form social relationships. Unlike normal children their age, autistic children do not imitate others' social behavior, use objects appropriately, or play simple games. They do not form emotional attachments to their parents or other people, express empathy, or exhibit cooperation. They do not make friends, and they tend to stare at other people's eyes with an unusual gaze. Their behavior is rigid, ritualistic, and compulsive (Rutter, 1978).

Parents of autistic children long were thought to be cold and obsessive (Eisenberg, 1957; Kanner, 1949), but most psychologists now reject this explanation of autism's cause. Instead they look for an organic explanation for autism. The role of several neurotransmitters, particularly serotonin, has been investigated, as has the role of zinc deficiency (Coleman, 1978). But to date autism has not been related conclusively to any one biochemical agent. In one study of 21 same-sex pairs of twins, in which at least one twin was autistic, researchers found that in 4 of 11 monozygotic pairs but none of the 10 dizygotic pairs were both twins autistic (Folstein and Rutter, 1977). In 12 of 17 pairs of twins in which only one twin was autistic, the autistic twin had had a brain injury. But among the twins concordant for autism, there were no histories of brain injury. The researchers concluded that autism probably derives from several causes, including both brain damage and a genetic abnormality. Several investigators have pointed out that the language and cognitive problems typical of autism are problems in left hemisphere functions. Many autistic children show signs of early damage to the left hemisphere (Dawson, 1982). The right hemisphere functions—such as musical, visual, and spatial skills—of many autistic children are normal or even superior (Blackstock, 1978; Lockyer and Rutter, 1970).

Autistic children avoid social interaction and eye contact. They may also have other sensory handicaps, as this child does.

Learning disabilities

In practice, people use the term **learning disabilities** as a catchall to take in everything from hyperactivity to reading disorders (Farnham-Diggory, 1978; see Table 11.2). Because it sounds better to say that Jason has ''a learning disability'' than to say that he is ''slow'' or ''brain-damaged'' or ''retarded'' or ''emotionally disturbed,'' more and more problems have been included under the umbrella ''learning disability.'' But properly speaking, ''learning disabilities'' is a label for the problems that some children have in one or more of the basic processes necessary for using and understanding language and numbers. These children can process some information perfectly well. They have normal eyesight, hearing, intelligence, and physical coordination. But on certain tasks, they cannot function. Children may have problems in reading or spelling, **dyslexia**; in arithmetic, **dyscalcula**; or in writing, **dysgraphia**.

In one survey conducted in the Palo Alto, California, public schools to determine the characteristics of ''learning-disabled'' children, it was found that two-thirds of the children so labeled were between 8 and 11 years old (Owen, 1971). (With younger children, teachers found it difficult to distinguish learning-disabled children from slow learners; older learning-disabled children had entered special-education courses and were not included in the survey.) Four-fifths of the children with learning disabilities were boys—a typical distribution, which reflects the greater vulnerability of males to physical assaults and their slower developmental progress. The learning-disabled children did better on the performance subscales of IQ tests than on the verbal subscales. It was this kind of unevenness, in fact, that alerted teachers to the possibility of the children's learning disabilities.

> When Mikey came home from first grade with a note asking that I call his teacher for an appointment as soon as possible, my heart sank. She had noticed a big disparity between his scores on several of the IQ subtests, and she wanted to tell me that he might have a learning disability.

Table 11.2
A do-it-yourself learning disability terminology generator

DIRECTIONS: Select any word from column 1. Add any word from column 2. Then add any word from column 3. If you don't like the result, try again. They all mean about the same thing. This terminology generator will yield 1000 terms.

1 Qualifier	2 Area of involvement	3 Problem
Minimal	Brain	Dysfunction
Mild	Cerebral	Damage
Minor	Neurological	Disorder
Chronic	Neurologic	Dissynchronization
Diffuse	Central Nervous System	Handicap
Specific	Language	Disability
Primary	Reading	Retardation
Disorganized	Perceptual	Impairment
Organic	Impulse	Pathology
Clumsy	Behavior	Syndrome

SOURCE: Frye, 1968. Copyright © 1968 International Reading Association. Reprinted by permission.

A DYSLEXIC CHILD'S STORY

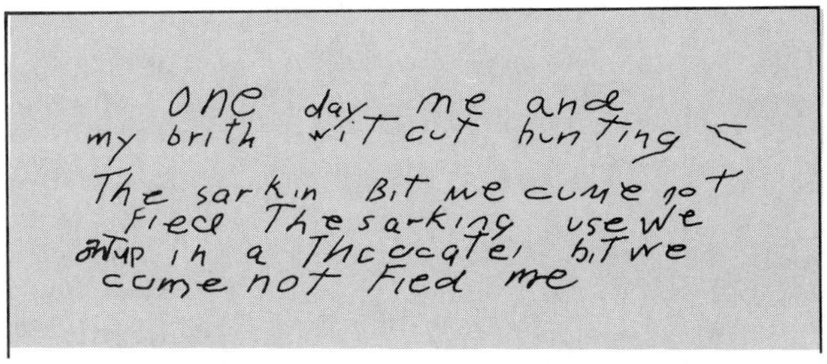

Figure 11.1 This story was written by a dyslexic child. It is meant to say, "One day me and my brother went out hunting the sark. But we could not find the sark. So we went up in a helicopter, but we could not find him" (Farnham-Diggory, 1978, p. 61).

One day me and my brother went out hunting the sark. But we could not find the sark. So we went up in a helicopter but we could not find him.

Compared to other children of their overall IQ and age, children with learning disabilities lag behind by several grades in reading and spelling (Farnham-Diggory, 1978). To a child with dyslexia, letters on a page may seem backward. One dyslexic boy named Fred called himself "Derf" because of the way his name looked to him. Dyslexic children can remember sounds, but they cannot remember images of words. One child, for example, spells "brother" as "birth" and "helicopter" as "thracatei" (Figure 11.1).

What is behind these surprising mistakes? Dyslexic children process visual information unusually slowly. In one study, children first were shown a compound figure—a cross inside a square—and then were shown the two parts separately. For normal children to see the two parts separately, the interval between the two images had to be at least 100 microseconds (Stanley and Hall, 1973). For the dyslexic children to see them separately, the interval had to be at least 140 microseconds. When they were asked to draw the two parts of the picture, the normal children needed 180 microseconds to identify the separate parts, but the dyslexic children needed 230 microseconds. In other words, the image "stayed on" in the minds of the dyslexic children longer.

Another problem for dyslexic children as they read is **masking** (Figure 11.2). Masking happens when the contours of letters are similar, the letters overlap in the visual field, and the time between the visual pickup of the first letter overlaps with the pickup of the second letter. It stands to reason that if dyslexic children process letters slowly, then when they read, masking may make them see a kind of visual jumble.

But dyslexia involves other problems as well. Dyslexic children may perseverate: a letter that they have read may echo in their mind's eye even when they are reading another letter. When 10-year-old Laura, for example, tried to read the word "reverence," she still had not got it right after 51 seconds of trying to sound it out. First she said "rever," but then she said "renay," and then "never." The n apparently was perseverating in her visual memory (Farnham-Diggory, 1984). Many dyslexics have poor visual memories. Compared to normal schoolchildren, for example, dyslexic children were slower to name pictures of common objects (duck, leaf, cat, etc.), colors, and numbers (Spring and Capps, 1974). Dyslexic children also show signs of memory fatigue sooner than other children and do not recover from it when they switch from one kind of mental task to another—from visual to auditory memory, for example—as other children do.

Learning disabilities like dyslexia probably arise from minimal brain dysfunction. In some cases, the connection between the two hemispheres of the brain may be awry, and in other cases, areas controlling vision, hearing, or other senses are defective. Injuries to the brain that prevent a person from

PERCEPTUAL MASKING IN READING

```
     t         o         s
   nte         o         hsx

               o
              bom
             sbomk
            asbomku
           easbomkut
          geasbomkutc
         wgeasbomkutcz
        dwgeasbomkutczh
       idwgeasbomkutczhv
      xidwgeasbomkutczhvp
     fxidwgeasbomkutczhvpn
    rfxidwgeasbomkutczhvpnj
   yrfxidwgeasbomkutczhvpnjl
```

Figure 11.2 In this display, if you look at the o in the top row, you can see it and the letters s and t clearly. But in the second row, s and t are masked by the letters next to them. As you continue down the pyramid of letters, looking at the central o, the end letters continue to be recognizable, but the letters in between are masked.

connecting the words seen via the right hemisphere with the association area in the left hemisphere may produce a reading disability. If the association area is also damaged, a writing disability may occur as well. When children have trouble putting words or letters in a temporal sequence, the problem may arise because the left hemisphere, which controls order and sequence, is inadequate in overall control (Farnham-Diggory, 1978). Some learning disabilities result from brain injuries, but most are inherited (Decker and DeFries, 1981).

Parents do not produce learning disabilities in their children, but their reactions to a child who has them can make things worse. The Palo Alto survey (Owen, 1971) showed that parents thought that their learning-disabled children had problems sticking with things both in school and out, considered them poor readers and spellers, anxious, clumsy, impulsive, in poor control over their surroundings. Mothers were less affectionate if their children—most of them sons—were disorganized and irresponsible, and fathers were less affectionate if their children were apathetic, worried, poor at concentrating, and impulsive. Like all handicaps, learning disabilities can disorganize, upset, and unsettle family members.

Summary

1. Middle childhood is a period of slower growth and greater physical skills. It is also a period when skills in different areas are consolidated. Physical activity sharpens children's minds and helps keep obesity and other problems from developing.

2. Chronic physical disorders, such as cerebral palsy, asthma, orthopedic problems, and diabetes, handicap 10 to 20 percent of all children under 18. Another 10 to 20 percent suffer from sensory impairments, mental retardation, and behavior problems. Boys are more vulnerable than girls to these developmental disorders.

3. By middle childhood, children may feel psychological effects from their physical disorders. In general, children with physical disorders need to be allowed as much independence as possible and to be treated as ordinary people.

4. Therapy for handicapped children is most useful when it focuses on what the child *can* do, encourages the child's independence, and breaks through the isolation and segregation that hamper the development of many handicapped children. Therapy for handicapped children often involves their parents in a network of health professionals, educators, and support services that may be confusing, overwhelming, and insensitive just as well as it may be helpful, supportive, and of real benefit to the whole family.

5. Sleep disorders—sleepwalking, terrors, nightmares, head banging, tooth grinding, and bed-wetting—are common among children and often do not signal any underlying pathology. Some children also suffer from insomnia, the causes of which include organic problems like ear infections, psychological problems like depression, neurological problems, allergies, and poor sleep habits.

6. Hyperactivity is a behavior disorder of children who are so active, distractible, and excitable that they cannot attend to schoolwork or other tasks that other children their age can manage. Hyperactive children's attention seems scattered and peripherally focused. Hyperactivity is sometimes managed successfully with psychoactive drugs, sometimes with cognitive strategies that teach a child to manage actions and outbursts, and sometimes with interventions to structure the child's behavior.

7. Children with learning disabilities may have perceptual problems that interfere with their perception and processing of information. Learning-disabled children have trouble reading, writing, spelling, speaking, or calculating, even though their motor abilities, eyesight, hearing, memory capacity, motivation, and intelligence are normal. Learning disabilities may be the product of brain injury or dysfunction. They seem to run in some families and, like many childhood disorders, afflict more boys than girls.

Key terms

cerebral palsy	sleep enuresis	Type A	dyslexia
mainstreaming	hyperactivity	Type B	dyscalcula
parasomnias	attention deficit disorder	autism	dysgraphia
sleep terrors	Ritalin	learning disability	masking

Suggested readings

FARNHAM-DIGGORY, SYLVIA. *Learning Disabilities*. Cambridge, Mass.: Harvard University Press, 1978. An intriguing discussion of learning disabilities, particularly dyslexia. The discussion of the definitions, causes, and treatments of learning disabilities makes clear how much we have yet to learn about them.

FEATHERSTONE, HELEN. *A Difference in the Family: Living with a Disabled Child*. New York: Penguin, 1981. Writing from her own experience and that of other parents, Featherstone honestly describes the emotional and practical strains of having a seriously disabled child.

ROSS, DOROTHEA M., and ROSS, SHEILA A. *Hyperactivity: Current Issues, Research, and Theory* (2nd ed.).

New York: Wiley, 1982. A description of the course of hyperactivity from infancy through early adulthood and of the drug therapies and special school programs by which it is treated. The hyperactive child's view and those of his or her associates are given.

WHALEN, CAROL K., and HENKER, BARBARA (Eds.). *Hyperactive Children: the Social Ecology of Identification and Treatment*. New York: Academic Press, 1980. A collection of theoretical and empirical articles on hyperactivity, including an examination of factors likely to influence the diagnosis and treatment of hyperactive children.

chapter twelve

Cognitive development

Just as middle childhood is a time when children grow more physically coordinated and skillful, it is a time when children mature cognitively. Children who begin school have shed their intuitive beliefs that balls roll because they want to, that mothers can see through walls, that dreams really happen. They can fathom cause and effect and are beginning to understand the working of numbers. During the elementary school years, children will learn to plan and memorize, to read and calculate. By the end of first grade, they will know how to read simple words and to add pairs of numbers. By the end of sixth grade, they will know rules of spelling, multiplication tables and fractions, and will be able to read and understand complex stories and take tests. In this chapter, we discuss children's progress during the elementary school years and some of the factors that influence how fast and how far individual children go.

Concrete operational thought

The thinking typical of early childhood, as we saw in Chapter 9, is a charming blend of impressions, intuitions, and partial logic. But as children enter school and middle childhood, the flavor of their thinking changes. Armed now with greater understanding of people and things—after all, haven't they dropped things, built towers, aligned sticks, and asked ''why'' at least a million times?—children begin to grasp the logical relations of things, the orderly rules and constant properties that govern the ways in which things happen. Whereas in early childhood, thought was based on the child's immediate perceptions, now thought becomes more integrated and bound by rules of logic.

> When I was 5 years old, my 8-year-old cousin asked me this riddle: ''Which is heavier, a ton of feathers or a ton of bricks?'' I answered ''a ton of bricks.'' She burst into guffaws, and I was mortified.

Reasoning logically about objects was called by Piaget **concrete operational thought**: it is ''concrete'' because children can reason only about concrete, tangible things like milk and cookies, sticks and stones, bricks and feathers. It is ''operational'' because children can perform mental manipulations, or *operations*, on the things in an organized and systematic way.

Children who can use concrete operations know that multiplication is related to division, that subtraction is the opposite of addition, and that ''equals,'' ''greater than,'' and ''less than'' are all interrelated.

> When Erica was 6 we were on a long highway drive, and Erica was getting impatient. As we stopped to pay a toll, she asked, ''Are we off the highway yet?'' ''No,'' her father replied, ''we have four more tolls to pay before we get off the highway.'' At the next tollbooth, Erica said, ''Now we have three more tolls?'' Somewhere along the way she had figured out how to subtract.

They realize that certain transformations of objects are *reversible*—that milk can be poured from one glass to another and then back again, for example. They **decenter**, that is, focus on and coordinate more than a single dimension—height *and* width, for example—at the same time. (In early childhood, you recall, children focused, or centered, on just one dimension at a time.) They also recognize that one dimension may make up for another dimension; that two dimensions may be *reciprocal*, or complementary. The short, wide glass may hold just as much milk as the tall, narrow glass.

For most children, concrete operational thinking first appears between the ages of 5 and 7. It continues to develop during middle childhood, as children apply the operations of addition and subtraction, multiplication and division, reversibility and reciprocity to objects. Concrete operational thinking allows children to solve many problems that elude preschoolers. They can solve problems in conservation, seriation, and velocity. Concrete operational thinking also allows children to appreciate jokes and to understand concepts that they could not earlier.

Conservation

With the ability to perform concrete operations, children realize that the milk poured from a tall, thin glass into a short, fat glass *looks* different but remains the same in quantity. This understanding (discussed in Chapter 9) was called by Piaget *conservation*. During the school years, children master conservation of different quantities in the following order: number, length, liquid quantity, mass, weight, and volume. The 7-year-old knows that a ball of clay rolled out to make a snake retains the same amount of substance, but he may not understand that they weigh the same. The 9-year-old understands that they weigh the same but perhaps not that their volume is the same. Only at age 11 or 12 do most children master conservation of volume. Children seem to learn about conservation first with the simplest tasks, those with the most salient and visible qualities. Only later do they move on to those that are not readily apparent to the eye. Although, as we discussed in Chapter 9, preschool children can be trained to solve simple conservation problems, middle childhood is when most children figure out for themselves the implications of reciprocity and reversibility, number and size, so that they can understand conservation problems regardless of how questions are worded or how objects appear, and can back up their judgments with sound, logical reasoning.

Seriation

During middle childhood, children also come to better understand seriation and transitive relations. At first children's reasoning about transitivity is firmly embedded in its context—in what they already know about the people or things involved. Eight-year-olds, for example, do better at understanding transitivity in relation to *themselves*—''I am taller than Willy. I am shorter than Tim''—than relationships among others—''Mike is taller than Willy. Mike is shorter than Tim'' (Mills and Funnell, 1983). During middle childhood, children's reasoning becomes less tied to direct knowledge about objects.

Velocity

During middle childhood, another kind of problem that children learn to solve involves the speed of moving objects. The first research in this area was done by Piaget. To study children's understanding of time and speed, Piaget set up toy train tracks and asked children to watch two trains move and then to say which train went faster. Four- and 5-year-olds insisted that the train that ended up ahead had traveled faster and gone farther; they completely ignored the trains' starting points. Only when one train came from behind and passed the other train before the children's eyes would they correctly answer that it was traveling faster. Not until children had acquired concrete operations, Piaget found, could they understand the relations among time, distance, and speed. To solve such problems, children had to decenter and concentrate on more than one aspect of the situation at a time—starting point *and* finishing point—and they had to be able to perform the operations of multiplication and division.

In a more recent study of children's abilities to solve problems of time, distance, and speed, children were shown a display of a dog sitting near its house and a bridge that led from the doghouse across a lake (Wilkening,

1981). When the dog barked, a cat got frightened and ran from the dog. The children were to listen to the dog barking for two, five, or eight seconds and then to point to the spot on the bridge reached by the cat. Both 5- and 10-year-olds followed the imaginary path with their eyes and then pointed to the correct spot on the bridge where the cat would have stopped. Even the 5-year-olds could, apparently, multiply speed by time to estimate distance. What they could not do was to divide speed by distance to estimate time. Division is a more complex operation than multiplication, and the relation between speed and time therefore is more difficult to figure out (Acredolo, Adams, and Schmid, 1984).

Humor

Children's understanding of concrete operations shows up outside the laboratory as well as in researchers' tests. Children with concrete operational thought laugh at jokes that earlier would have gone over their heads (and later will be greeted with groans). Preschoolers think that riddles are questions with arbitrary answers—''What has four wheels and flies?'' ''A horse!''—or even factual answers—''Why did the boy tiptoe by the medicine cabinet?'' ''Because everyone was asleep!''

> When he was 4, Peter was always asking, ''Is that funny?'' before he would commit himself to a forced laugh. When he was 5, he thought that a joke was, ''Why did the chicken cross the road?'' ''To eat snakes,'' or ''Knock, knock.'' ''Who's there?'' ''Mickey Mouse's underwear.''

But during middle childhood, with their greater cognitive maturity, children realize that words—like glasses of water—are not always as they appear. They love puns:

> Hey, call me a taxi.

> Okay, you're a taxi.

> I saw a man-eating shark in the aquarium.

> So what? I saw a man eating tuna in the restaurant.

With their developing understanding of conservation, children giggle at a joke like this one:

> WAITER: Do you want me to cut the pizza into eight pieces for you?

> FAT WOMAN: No, no. Cut it into six pieces. I could never eat eight pieces.

The funniest jokes, researchers have found, pose a moderate challenge to a person's cognitive abilities and are understandable but surprising—they violate the person's expectations (Prentice and Fathman, 1975; Zigler, Levine, and Gould, 1967). School-age children who are just working through the nuances of the logical relations involved in reciprocity, reversibility, classification, and transitivity find jokes funny that depend on these operations.

Religion

Children's understanding of concrete operations shows up in more serious discussions, too. On the subject of religion, for example, preschool children have vague and intuitive notions. Three-year-old Sam mentioned that great religious figure, Jesus Rice, to his parents one day. Five-year-old Megan, whose mother is Jewish and whose father is Catholic, announced triumphantly, ''Only Daddy and I are going to heaven, not you Mommy.'' Peter, at 5, was concerned about whether he would see God, angels, or fairies in the clouds on his next airplane trip.

When one researcher (Elkind, 1979) interviewed 800 children between 5 and 14 years old about religion, he found that the youngest children were uncertain about even the terms:

What is a Catholic? "A person."

How is he different from a Protestant? "I don't know."

How do you become Jewish? "God makes you Jewish."

Not understanding the terms, children could not put them into categories:

"Can you be a Protestant and an American at the same time?"

"No way!"

In middle childhood, children were familiar with the labels and understood that one's religious identity fits into a more complex set of characteristics.

Can you be a Protestant and an American at the same time? "Yes."

How is that possible? "Because I live in America and was baptized."

But their ideas about religion were concrete. They defined religion as the things that people *do* to enact their religious identities.

How can you tell people are Catholic? "If you see them go into a Catholic church."

What is a Jew? "A person who goes to temple and to Hebrew school."

More abstract ideas about religion must wait for the cognitive advances of adolescence (discussed in Chapter 15).

Moral reasoning

In middle childhood, children's ideas about right and wrong are also concrete. Piaget was the first researcher to study children's moral reasoning. He developed his theory of children's moral reasoning by watching and questioning children as they played marbles, a game that required children to deal with issues of justice, fairness, and turn taking. He saw that children's rules for playing marbles and their respect for these rules grew more sophisticated as they grew older. At the beginning of middle childhood, children first began to play by strict rules and to play to win. They wanted to settle which players controlled the game, and they wanted all the players to play by the same rules. These children, Piaget suggested, played marbles according to an **external**

Piaget used children's understanding of the rules of games as an index of their level of moral development. Between the ages of 5 and 10, children regard rules as sacrosanct and unalterable.

morality in which rules are seen as cast in stone, handed down by authority figures. Asked who makes up the rules to a game of marbles, children at this age were likely to answer ''God'' or ''Daddy.'' Although the children sometimes bent the rules as they played, they denied that rules can be changed. Here Ben discusses rule making with Piaget:

> Invent a rule. *I couldn't invent one straight away like that.* Yes you could. I can see that you are cleverer than you make yourself out to be. *Well, let's say that you're not caught when you are in the square.* Good. Would that come off with the others? *Oh, yes, they'd like to do that.* Then people could play that way? *Oh, no, because it would be cheating.* But all your pals would like to, wouldn't they? *Yes, they all would.* Then why would it be cheating? *Because I invented it: it isn't a rule! It's a wrong rule because it's outside of the rules. A fair rule is one that is in the game* (Piaget, 1932, pp. 54–55).

Another child told Piaget that if he changed the rules, God would punish him by making him miss during his turn at marbles. Children at this age believed that obeying rules is good and disobeying rules is bad. Their very definition of goodness, in fact, was obedience and conformity to rules.

Children's respect for rules remained rigid, Piaget found, until they reached a level of **internal morality**, in which they understood that people may agree to reason out, discuss, change, and remake rules. They did not reach this level until about age 11, at the end of middle childhood.

Piaget elaborated his theory of moral development by listening to children's reasoning when he asked them moral questions in little stories.

> A little boy who is called John is in his room. He is called to dinner. He goes into the dining room. But behind the door there is a chair, and on the chair there is a tray with fifteen cups on it. John couldn't have known that there was all this behind the door. He goes in, the door knocks against the tray, bang go the fifteen cups and they all get broken!

> Once there was a little boy whose name was Henry. One day when his mother was out he tried to get some jam out of the cupboard. He climbed up on to a chair and stretched out his arm. But the jam was too high up and he couldn't reach it and have any. But while he was trying to get it he knocked over a cup. The cup fell down and broke.

After telling children stories like these, Piaget asked them whether John or Henry was naughtier and who should be punished more severely. Children in middle childhood told Piaget that John was naughtier, because he broke more cups. They were basing their judgment on the severity of the external consequences of the act—15 cups versus one. Eleven- and 12-year-olds, like adults, told Piaget that Henry was naughtier, because he was trying to sneak some jam. They based their judgment on the internal intentions behind the act—innocent versus sneaky.

Stages of moral development

By starting from the external and internal moral reasoning described by Piaget, Lawrence Kohlberg (1969) developed a more complete theory of stages in moral development (Table 12.1). As Piaget had done, Kohlberg based his descriptions on children's responses to hypothetical moral dilemmas such as this one:

> In Europe, a woman was near death from a special kind of cancer. There was one drug that the doctors thought might save her. It was a form of radium that a druggist in the same town had recently discovered. The drug was expensive to make, but the druggist was charging ten times

what the drug cost him to make. He paid $200 for the radium and charged $2000 for a small dose of the drug. The sick woman's husband, Heinz, went to everyone he knew to borrow the money, but could only get together about $1000, which was half of what it cost. He told the druggist that his wife was dying and asked him to sell it cheaper or let him pay later. But the druggist said, "No, I discovered the drug and I'm going to make money from it." So Heinz got desperate and considered breaking into the man's store to steal the drug for his wife. Should Heinz steal the radium? (Kohlberg and Gilligan, 1971, pp. 1072–1073)

Early in middle childhood, Kohlberg found, 6- to 9-year-old children are concerned with getting rewards and avoiding punishments. What they consider moral is determined by authority figures. Children at the first stage of moral development argue on the principle of "might makes right." Heinz should not steal the drug, they might argue, because he will go to jail for it. Or, they might argue, Heinz should steal the drug because he loves his wife very much. Kohlberg was interested in the *reasons* children gave for their moral judgments, not whether they said that Heinz should or should not steal.

In the second stage of moral reasoning, beginning at around 10 years of age, children think that moral action is making fair deals and trades. A child at this second stage might reason that Heinz should not steal because it would not be worth having to go to jail for, or the child might reason that Heinz should steal the drug because that way he would still have his wife. At both these stages, children are basically concerned with looking out for themselves and protecting their own interests. Kohlberg called this **preconventional moral reasoning**, because it was determined by personal interests, not social conventions.

By late middle childhood, around age 11, some children reach a level of **conventional moral reasoning**. They think that moral behavior is following social rules and conventions, and they focus on conforming to social order, family obligations, and caring for other people. In Kohlberg's Stage 3, the first stage of conventional moral reasoning, children do good things so that others will approve of them. This stage has been called the "good boy–nice girl" stage, for it is the stage when children can be motivated by the promise that the teacher will hang their work on the bulletin board or that Mom and Dad will be proud of them. Children at this stage may reason that Heinz should steal the drug because he loves his wife and she will approve of him for stealing it for her. Family is more important to children at this stage than social institutions or outside individuals.

Transitions in moral reasoning

What makes children advance from one stage or level of moral judgment to the next? It has been suggested by some, including Kohlberg, that when children meet with reasoning that is one stage higher than their own, they try to resolve the conflict between what they believe and what they are hearing by reasoning at the higher level. In one study to test this suggestion, researchers measured children's reactions to moral reasoning a stage or two below or a stage above their own (Rest, Turiel, and Kohlberg, 1969). First the children read several moral dilemmas and wrote down their responses to the dilemmas. Then they read other children's advice about what the character in the dilemma ought to do. Finally, the children were asked to decide which advice was the best, the worst, the smartest, and the most reasonable and to put the advice into their own words. The children were considered to understand the advice if their restatement of it was at an equal level of moral reasoning. The researchers found that children were most likely to under-

Table 12.1
Kohlberg's stages of moral development

Moral reasoning	What is right?	How People Answer the Heinz Dilemma	
		Pro	Con
Preconventional Level			
Stage 1: Punishment–obedience orientation	To obey the rules of others in order to avoid punishment. Obedience for its own sake, and avoiding physical damage to persons and property.	He should steal the drug. It is not really bad to take it. It is not like he did not ask to pay for it first. The drug he would take is only worth $200; he is not really taking a $2000 drug.	Heinz shouldn't steal; he should buy the drug. If he steals the drug, he might get put in jail and have to put the drug back anyway.
Stage 2: Instrumental-exchange orientation	Following rules only when it is to your advantage; acting to meet your own interests and needs and letting others do the same. Right is also what is fair, what is an equal exchange, a deal, an agreement.	Heinz should steal the drug to save his wife's life. He might get sent to jail, but he'd still have his wife.	He should not steal it. The druggist is not wrong or bad; he just wants to make a profit. That is what you are in business for, to make money.
Conventional Level			
Stage 3: Good-boy-nice-girl orientation	Living up to what is expected by people close to you or what people generally expect of people in your role as son, brother, friend, and so on. Being "good" is important and means having good motives, showing concern for others. It also means having mutual relationships based on trust, loyalty, respect, and gratitude.	If I were Heinz, I would have stolen the drug for my wife. You can't put a price on love; no amount of gifts makes love. You can't put a price on life either.	He should not steal. If his wife dies, he cannot be blamed. It is not because he is heartless or that he does not love her enough to do everything that he legally can. The druggist is the selfish or heartless one.
Stage 4: System-maintaining orientation	Carrying out the duties that are your obligation. Laws are to be upheld except in the extreme case when they conflict with other fixed social duties. Right is also contributing to society, the group, or institution.	When you get married, you take a vow to love and cherish your wife. Marriage is not only love; it's an obligation like a legal contract.	It is a natural thing for Heinz to want to save his wife, but it is still always wrong to steal. He still knows he is stealing and taking a valuable drug from the man who made it.

Table 12.1 (*continued*)
Kohlberg's stages of moral development

Moral reasoning	What is right?	How People Answer the Heinz Dilemma	
		Pro	Con
Postconventional Level Stage 5: Social-contract orientation	Being aware that people hold a variety of values and opinions, that most values and rules are relative to the group. These relative rules should usually be upheld, however, in the interest of impartiality and because they are a social contract. Some values and rights, such as life and liberty, however, must be upheld in any society, regardless of majority opinion.	The law was not set up for these circumstances. Taking the drug in this situation is not really right, but it is justified to do it.	You cannot completely blame someone for stealing, but extreme circumstances do not really justify taking the law in your own hands. You cannot have people stealing whenever they get desperate. The end may be good, but the ends do not justify the means.
Stage 6: Universal-ethical-principles orientation	Following self-chosen ethical principles. Particular laws or social agreements are usually valid because they rest on such principles. When laws violate these principles, you must act in accordance with the principles, which are universal: giving equal rights to all and respecting the dignity of human beings as individuals.	This is a situation which forces him to choose between stealing and letting his wife die. In a situation where the choice must be made, it is morally right to steal. He has to act in terms of the principle of preserving and respecting life.	Heinz is faced with the decision of whether to consider the other people who need the drug just as badly as his wife. Heinz ought to act not according to his particular feelings toward his wife but considering the value of all the lives involved.

SOURCE: Kohlberg, 1969, pp. 379–380.

stand reasoning one stage below their own, although they considered it the "worst" advice. The children had more trouble understanding reasoning a level or two above their own, but they preferred this more advanced reasoning.

Does this preference for reasoning one stage higher advance children's later moral reasoning? In a study to test this possibility, children were briefly trained in reasoning one stage below, one stage above, or two stages above their own (Turiel, 1966). The children who were most likely to advance were those exposed to reasoning one stage above their own. The evidence supported the hypothesis.

In yet another study, children in fifth through seventh grades heard a man and a woman reasoning about six moral dilemmas at a level that was the same as their own, one stage below it, one stage above it, or two stages above it (Walker, 1982). When the children were tested one week later, the children who had heard reasoning one or two levels above their own had advanced one stage in moral reasoning. They were still reasoning about one-half a stage above their original levels on a follow-up test seven weeks later. Children who were exposed to reasoning at their own or a lower level or to no reasoning at all did not advance. Transitions in moral reasoning, these studies suggest, can be encouraged by exposing children to higher reasoning.

Another approach to training in moral reasoning is to have children discuss moral issues with other children. Piaget himself believed that this kind of discussion contributes importantly to moral development. In one study (Damon and Killen, 1982), children between 5 and 9 years old, in discussion groups of three, talked about moral problems. Their debates, even those that were brief, did modestly—but significantly—advance some of the children's moral reasoning. The children who gained, though, were not those who disagreed, argued, contradicted, or offered contrary solutions; the children who advanced tended to agree with other children's statements and to accept, extend, and clarify them, to work with others, to reciprocate, and, if necessary, to compromise. Overt conflict or arguments apparently were not necessary for advances in moral reasoning.

Yet another approach to moral training is to capitalize on real moral problems that confront children—like fighting in class, taking someone's lunch money, or making someone feel bad. While children are reflecting on these problems, the experimenter suggests to them higher-level solutions and encourages them to try out these solutions in real situations. This approach, too, has been used successfully with school-age children to advance both social and moral reasoning (Enright, Lapsley, and Levy, 1983).

There is still some debate among researchers about the *best* way to advance children's moral reasoning, however. Is it better to present them with a cognitive conflict in which they hear a view different from their own in a hypothetical moral dilemma, or is it better to involve them in a social conflict in which they have to discuss their views with others? These two methods were compared in a recent study (Haan, 1985). In the cognitive-conflict condition, groups of friends discussed hypothetical moral dilemmas for five sessions. In the social-conflict condition, groups of friends met for five sessions and played "games" designed to simulate actual moral problems—for example, the friends were representatives from three nations that were in competition for food to feed their citizens. All the students were interviewed on moral issues before and after the experiment. The students who played the social-conflict games were significantly more likely to gain in moral reasoning (60 percent gained) than the students who discussed the hypothetical dilemmas (30 percent gained). Personal confrontation with moral problems may be more effective in advancing moral reasoning than mere exposure to cognitive conflict. But some researchers have questioned the value of any brief training

(Rest, 1983). They have argued that training may be too short or too narrowly focused, that assessments of children's stages of moral reasoning are crude, and that real moral growth takes time. Longitudinal studies of normal children show that moving through a full stage of moral development typically takes at least four years.

Memory

Another aspect of cognitive development in middle childhood is the growth of memory. School-age children can remember lots of new information and integrate it with what they already know. They can remember more than preschoolers for several reasons, which we discuss in this section.

Strategies

One reason that school-age children remember more than preschoolers is that they use deliberate strategies for remembering. What are the strategies school-age children use?

Rehearsal

One simple strategy for remembering information is **rehearsal**, the process of repeating something until it is memorized. Actors rehearse their lines, young children rehearse their names and addresses, and college students rehearse their class notes before exams. Strictly speaking, preschool children do not use this strategy for memorizing information (Perlmutter and Myers, 1979), although even they use rudimentary rehearsal strategies—talking about a hidden toy or its hiding place, staring or pointing at the hiding place, resting their hand on it and nodding yes (DeLoache, Cassidy, and Brown, 1985; Wellman, Ritter, and Flavell, 1975).

A Soviet psychologist, Z. M. Istomina (1975), found that when children were asked to remember a short shopping list, even preschoolers made attempts at rehearsal, but the attempts children made grew more deliberate and effective with age.

Alik (4 years, 3 months) listened to the instructions to the end, nodding his head after each word, and saying, "Uhuh." He recalled correctly two

School-age children can remember more than preschoolers because they use deliberate strategies like rehearsal for memorizing words and actions. These children have memorized a dance routine about Andrew Jackson.

items on the list and when asked, ''What else do you have to buy?'' he answered calmly: ''Nothing else; we have everything.''

Serezha (5 years, 4 months) listened attentively to the list and repeated each of the experimenter's words in a whisper. He recalled four items, but could not recall the fifth. He looked confusedly at the experimenter and repeated the same words one more time. ''There's something else I have to buy, but I've forgotten it.''

Dima (6 years, 6 months) listened to the list, muttering silently, and then repeated it almost as if to himself. He quickly recalled three items, then paused, screwed up his eyes, and said, with concern: ''Oh! What else was there? Nope, I can't remember what else I have to buy'' (Istomina, 1975, pp. 24–26).

Although 5-year-olds rarely rehearse spontaneously, they can be trained to rehearse, and rehearsal improves their recall. In one series of studies (Flavell, Beach, and Chinsky, 1966; Keeney, Canizzo, and Flavell, 1967), 5- and 10-year-olds were asked to memorize the order in which an experimenter pointed to pictures of objects. After they were shown the pictures, the children had to wait 15 seconds. During this interval, few of the 5-year-olds rehearsed the names of the objects—assessed by reading their lip movements while their eyes were hidden by a space helmet! Nearly all the 10-year-olds did. When the 5-year-olds were instructed by the experimenter to whisper the names of the objects while they were waiting, their recall improved. But when the children were later given another memorization task, the 5-year-olds again did not rehearse the items, and their recall declined. Training can make young children perform as well as older children and, conversely, if older children are prevented from rehearsing, their memories are as spotty as those of young nonrehearsers. But these effects of training are not permanent. Rehearsal is clearly one aspect of cognitive processing that needs time, and rehearsal, to develop.

By the time they are 8 years old, children asked to memorize a list of words do rehearse—but not very effectively. They repeat each word by itself (Ornstein, Naus, and Liberty, 1975):

ADULT: yard.

CHILD: yard, yard, yard, yard

ADULT: cat.

CHILD: cat, cat, yard

ADULT: man.

CHILD: man, man, man.

ADULT: desk.

CHILD: desk, desk, desk, desk.

If 8-year-old children are given more time on each word and a chance to look at the words already presented, they are more likely to rehearse appropriately and to recall more words (Ornstein, Medlin, Stone, and Naus, 1985). It seems that they are aware of the importance of rehearsal but are less skilled than older children at retrieving the words to be rehearsed together. By age 12, children can retrieve words and rehearse the whole list cumulatively.

ADULT: yard.

CHILD: yard, yard, yard.

ADULT: cat.

CHILD: cat, yard, yard, cat.

ADULT: man.

CHILD: man, cat, yard, man, yard, cat.

ADULT: desk.

CHILD: desk, man, cat, man, desk, cat, yard.

Organization

Another strategy that children can use to increase their recall is grouping items into meaningful clusters or chunks. Most people can remember only about seven separate chunks of information. But by including several related items in each chunk, they can remember substantial amounts of information.

Even 2-years-old remember related items better than those that are unrelated. "Big and tall" is easier for them to remember than "big and sad," for example (Goldberg, Perlmutter, and Myers, 1974). But they do not form chunks or categories the way school-age children do. Preschool children may organize words by rhyming or by similar sounds—"big" and "pig," "bat" and "pat"—but school-age children are more likely to organize words by their meanings (Bach and Underwood, 1970; Hasher and Clifton, 1974). Preschool children also organize more according to function—things that go together (bat and ball); school-age children organize more according to taxonomy— things that belong to the same category or class (bat and racquet) (Flavell, 1970). It is difficult, though, to tell whether preschool children *cannot* form taxonomic categories, or just *do not*. In one study (Smiley and Brown, 1979), researchers asked kindergartners, grade school children, and adults to say which two pictures out of three were alike. Subjects could pair the pictures either functionally (horse with saddle or needle with thread) or taxonomically (horse with cow or needle with pin). Kindergartners paired the pictures functionally, older children and adults taxonomically. But when the kindergartners were asked for an alternative choice, and to justify it, they provided and justified it easily. They had chosen according to personal preference, not ability, a preference that affected both their learning and their recall (Overcast, Murphy, Smiley, and Brown, 1975; Smiley and Brown, 1979). Whether taxonomic classification is more accessible or simply preferred, it helps older children remember more items.

Social and spatial information also seems to help children organize their memories. Children may remember things like their classmates' names according to seating plans and reading groups, groups of friends and cliques (Bjørkland and Zeman, 1982; Chi, 1981).

> Natalie reeled off the names of the kids at school each day by thinking of who sat around the table at snack time.

> Sam remembers people by the kinds of cars they drive. People with trucks or motorcycles will live in his memory forever.

Another kind of organization that can improve memory is a story line. Children remember things better when they are organized into meaningful, logical, and coherent scripts, or stories. Children remember the locations of things better, for example, if they have a story around which to organize their memories of the locations (Herman and Roth, 1984). In one study (Buss, Yussen, Mathews, Miller, and Rembold, 1983), children from second and sixth grades heard a tape of a story about a fish named Albert. Some got a straightforward version of the story, and others got a version in which the sentence order was scrambled. Children recalled less of the scrambled stories than of the straightforward ones. Then the researchers gave children training in how to order sentences into a proper story sequence—first the name of the character, then what made the story begin, then what the character did, and then how the story ended—and asked them to retell the stories in the right order. The instruction proved effective, for the children could accurately retrieve and reorder information according to a typical story form.

Preschool children can be trained to use organizational strategies, as they can be trained to rehearse, but the effects are weaker and less durable than the effects of training school-age children (Moely, Olson, Halwes, and Flavell, 1969; Williams and Goulet, 1975). The ability to organize items into meaningful chunks continues to improve over the course of middle childhood and adolescence. In one study of 8- to 21-year-olds, for example, the older subjects remembered the same numbers of chunks as the younger subjects, judging by the bursts and pauses in their recital of the names of animals and furniture. More information was included in each chunk, however, and the older subjects' total memory scores were significantly higher (Kail and Nippold, 1984). Organizing strategies for *retrieving* items from memory also improve over the years of childhood (Morrison and Lord, 1982).

Imagery

Using imagery is the strategy of imagining pictures of items to be remembered. Imagery can help people to remember names (for example, a sand-covered cat for "Sandra Katz"). Children who do not discover this mnemonic technique on their own can be trained to use it. One researcher (Levin, 1980) used imagery to help fourth and fifth graders learn the 50 capital cities of the United States. After providing the students with concrete "keywords" for each place name—"apple" for "Annapolis," "marry" for "Maryland," and showing them illustrations in which the keywords for each state and its capital were combined pictorially—for example, a judge "marrying" two apples—the experimenter found that the children could recall the names of the states and capitals better than a group of children who had been allowed to study the names on their own.

Why does imagery strengthen recall? Perhaps it underscores associations between items to be remembered. Perhaps it provides two forms—words and pictures—in which information can be recalled. Perhaps it makes learning pleasant, personal, and vivid. Perhaps it subjects the information to deeper and thus better remembered levels of cognitive processing. Perhaps it does all these things.

Elaboration

When people link together two or more unrelated items in order to remember them, they are using another memory strategy called elaboration. Elaboration is at work in the mnemonic, "In fourteen hundred ninety-two, Columbus sailed the ocean blue." Children recall better when their elaborations are active—"The lady flew on a broom"—rather than static—"The lady had a broom" (Buckhalt, Mahoney, and Paris, 1976). Again, older children use this strategy for remembering more than younger children do (Paris and Lindauer, 1976). They also use more active elaborations than younger children do (Reese, 1977). Older children remember better when they generate the elaborations themselves than when an experimenter does; younger children benefit more from an experimenter's elaborations, perhaps because the adult's are of better quality (Turnure, Buium, and Thurlow, 1976).

Studying

As they get older, children spend more time studying, and this, too, improves their recall. They also learn strategies for studying. They learn notetaking, underlining, outlining, and how to use study aids (Brown, Bransford, Ferrara, and Campione, 1983). Study strategies, like other cognitive strategies, change quantitatively and qualitatively during the school years. Young schoolchildren spend less time focusing on items they have forgotten on a test; older children study items they have missed (Masur, McIntyre, and Flavell, 1973). Older children use different memory strategies when they think they will be asked to recall rather than recognize objects (Horowitz and Horowitz, 1975). Older children can better predict and identify what is important to remember in a lesson or for a test; they delete trivia and repetition, substitute superordinate terms for subordinate examples or episodes, and focus on topic sentences (Brown and Smiley, 1977; Brown and Day, 1983).

External cues

Finally, using external cues can improve recall. Thus, seeing the string tied around your finger can remind you to return the library book, call home, or turn off the lights. Young children cannot use external cues very well in remembering. In one study, 25 percent of the 3-year-old children and 75 percent of the 5-year-olds spontaneously turned over pictures lying face down on the floor to remind themselves of toys earlier paired with the pictures (Ritter, Kaprove, Fitch, and Flavell, 1973). But even with coaching, 30 percent of the 3-year-olds could not use the pictures to retrieve information. Using external cues is difficult even for 6-year-olds. When 6-year-olds were allowed to use cue cards to help them recall pictures on cards they had seen earlier, only one-third of the children did so, and inefficiently at that, using the cue card to remember only one out of three possible pictures before taking the next cue card. Eleven-year-olds, in contrast, used the cue cards to remember as many pictures as they could (Kobasigawa, 1974).

Metamemory

Metamemory is what people understand and know of their own memory processes. One reason young children do not use the memorization strategies we have just discussed may be that they lack this kind of awareness. Metamemory includes knowing which situations call for conscious efforts at memorization and which factors affect memory. It includes, for example, knowing that faces are easier to remember than names, that everybody forgets things sometimes, that poorly organized material is difficult to recall, and that repeating a fact will help in memorizing it. A number of studies have been done to find out what children understand of their own memories' limitations. Asked, "Do you forget?" school-age children said that they forgot at times; preschool children denied ever forgetting (Kreutzer, Leonard, and Flavell, 1975). Asked how many of ten pictures they thought they could remember, school-age children realized that they would not be able to remember all of them, but preschoolers said that they could perform this feat (Flavell, Friedrichs, and Hoyt, 1970). Preschoolers do understand some things about memory. They know that some things about people—their clothing, their physical build—do not affect memory. They know that noise interferes with memory; and they know that it is harder to remember many items than a few (Wellman, 1977b). They know what remembering, forgetting, and learning are. They know that it is hard to remember long-ago events and easier to relearn information than to learn it fresh. They also know that studying for some time makes it easier to remember information (Kreutzer et al., 1975). But beyond knowing these things, preschool children are limited in their metamemories.

Schoolchildren know that time affects memory, that pairs of antonyms are easier to remember than unrelated words, and that they would be likelier to remember a short list studied for a short time than a long list studied for a long time. They also know about ways to improve memory—tying strings around fingers, reading notes, listening to tape recordings, and asking for information from other people (Kreutzer et al., 1975). When researchers in one study (Kreutzer et al., 1975) asked children how they might remember a telephone number, nearly all third and fifth graders, but only 40 percent of the kindergartners, said that they should phone right away. Most of the older children, but only 60 percent of the kindergartners, said that they would write down the number and rehearse it or use some other mnemonic strategy. In another study (Yussen and Levy, 1977), when children between third and ninth grades were quizzed about how they might try to recall a forgotten idea or a lost item, the youngest children gave one or two suggestions and then stopped. But older children offered many plausible suggestions. In yet another study, researchers found that second graders knew that rehearsal and categorization are useful strategies for memorizing, but only sixth graders consistently realized that categorization is more effective than rehearsal, and used it (Justice, 1985).

Just knowing about memory is not the same thing as remembering, however. Metamemory does not directly predict a person's performance on a memory task (Siegler, 1983). The accuracy of children's reports about how memory works and their actual memorization abilities often bear only a moderate relation (Brown et al., 1983). Children sometimes know *how to* remember something but still are not able to remember it (Chi, 1985). Such vagaries of children's behavior make psychologists realize that they have a way to go before they understand metamemory and its relation to memory. Some psychologists (for example, Cavanaugh and Perlmutter, 1982) have commented that the concept of metamemory has not yet contributed much to the understanding of how memory works. Others have questioned how accurately children can report on their own thinking. Further research is necessary to specify how thinking about memory affects memory itself.

Knowledge

Another way in which school-age children differ from younger ones is in the amount of knowledge they have accumulated. One kind of knowledge that children have, as we mentioned in Chapter 9, is of familiar routines or scripts—eating in a restaurant, having birthday parties, and so on (Hudson and Nelson, 1983). Another kind of knowledge is conceptual. A third kind is factual. School-age children have more of all these kinds of knowledge than younger children do, and this knowledge also increases their ability to remember things.

A study by Michelene Chi of a 4½-year-old expert on dinosaurs illuminates the importance of knowledge for remembering (Chi and Koeske, 1983). First, the boy was asked to name all the dinosaurs he knew. In seven sessions, he named 46 different kinds of dinosaur, of which the investigators chose 20 as better known (the boy had mentioned them each an average of 4.5 times) and another 20 as less well known (each mentioned only once). The investigators also identified the properties of dinosaurs that the boy could recognize and generate—habitat, locomotion, appearance, size, diet, and so on. Later, the investigators read the two lists of dinosaur names to the boy and asked him to recall the names that were on the lists. He recalled ten from the list of well-known dinosaurs and only five from the less known list, showing that knowledge significantly affects memory.

The powerful effect of knowledge on memory was further demonstrated in a study of children who were experts and adults who were novices at chess (Chi, 1978). For ten seconds, the subjects were shown a chessboard with pieces set up on it; then the board was covered and they were asked to reproduce the arrangement of chess pieces they had seen. The young experts reproduced the arrangement much more accurately than the adult novices, a finding that could not be ascribed to their superior intelligence or memory

School-age children have more knowledge than younger children, which helps them remember more. Children who are experts at chess, researchers have found, are better at remembering the arrangement of chess pieces than adults who are novice players. This difference can only be ascribed to the children's superior knowledge of chess.

abilities, but only to their superior knowledge of chess. When children know as much about a subject as adults do, the usual advantage that adults have all but disappears (Roth, 1983).

How is it that knowing more about a subject helps one remember more new information? For one thing, being familiar with the terms used simplifies and speeds up the encoding of the new information. For another, more knowledge allows a person to draw more inferences and to integrate incoming information into a more complete network of facts. Asked whether they have ever heard certain sentences before, adults often cannot distinguish between those they have heard before and those they have inferred, if the subject matter is familiar (Bransford and McCarrell, 1974). Children are the same way. One researcher (Landis, 1982) tested school-age children on their recognition of a sentence from a story read to them a week earlier. This story was about either a famous person or a fictitious character. Children who had heard the famous-person story thought that well known facts about the character, which had *not* been included in the story they were read, were in fact in it. Because they were familiar with the subject, they had integrated the new information into their existing network of knowledge. Later on they could not tell what they had heard in the story and what they already had known about the person.

Knowledge of stereotypes—preconceived notions about certain people—act on memory in a similar fashion. They may prevent people from remembering new facts if they contradict the stereotype (List and Collins, 1983). Children who have rigid gender-role stereotypes, for example, have been found to be less likely to remember that a woman in a story was a doctor or an army officer than children with less rigid gender stereotypes. Remembering is not just a parroting back of random facts; it is a process of constructing, of adding within an existing framework, of checking for plausibility against existing knowledge, and of making inferences about new information (Siegler, 1983). Clearly, knowledge is an essential part of the complex process of remembering.

Basic processes

Finally, some evidence shows that the capacity of **short-term memory**—what children remember for a few seconds to a minute—increases with age. Up to a

449

point, older children can hold more chunks of information in short-term memory than younger children. In one study, for example, 3-year-olds could recall only three things, 5-year-olds four, and 7-year-olds five (Morrison, Holmes, and Haith, 1974). Not all researchers agree that children's short-term memory capacity increases with age, however (Siegler, 1986). Some psychologists believe that more important in explaining why older children remember more is the fact that children's ability to encode information and get it into short-term memory improves with age. In one recent study that supports this idea (Howard and Polich, 1985), researchers found that 5- to 14-year-olds who could remember more items on a test of memory also encoded new information (tones) faster, as indicated by their brain waves. As processing grows speedier and more efficient, then, operating space in memory, once needed for encoding, is freed for remembering (Case, Kurland, and Goldberg, 1982).

In sum, then, there are many reasons that children in middle childhood remember more and better than younger children, and that memory continues to improve with age. Older children know numerous and more sophisticated memorization and retrieval strategies, use them in more diverse situations, and are more flexible in tailoring strategies to situations. They use memory strategies that are more appropriate to the task, pay more attention to detail, and care more about remembering. They know more about the subject matter and more about how to remember. They have a larger and more efficient memory storage system.

Learning to read

One of the practical implications of children's increased ability to remember is that they learn to read. Most of us breeze through magazines as we wait at the grocery checkout counter, absorb road signs and television commercials without a thought, and gobble our favorite kinds of information—be it the encyclopedia, *True Romances*, *Sports Illustrated*, or the menu at McDonald's—like peanuts. But we take for granted the remarkable skills that we have mastered—and that we expect school-age children to acquire.

To begin with, reading requires some understanding of what letters and words *are*. By asking 5-year-old children questions about reading, Jessie Reid (1983) turned up some amazing information—or *mis*information—on this score. One girl said that she was "past reading. We finished it yesterday. . . . Yes, we read all the pages." Other children had not the foggiest idea that people could read street names on buses and addresses on letters. Some did not know what letters are, calling them "numbers" or "words," calling words "names" or "the writing," and calling sentences "stories." "Big letters"—capitals—were "for big animals" or "made a different sort of word." Children said things like "I'll write a house," "I'll draw my name" (Reid, 1983, pp. 153–154). The best predictor of whether children would be reading at age 7, in one study, in fact, was how well they understood what printed and written language was when they first started school (Wells and Raban, 1978).

After children learn what letters are—that they are not numbers, or pictures, or scribbles, they must learn to recognize the particular letters of the alphabet by sight. Our alphabet offers many chances for confusion: *d* for *b*, *m* for *n*, or *u* for *n*. Children must then master the correspondence between letters and sounds: *b* sounds like the "buh" in *boy*, and *o* sounds like "ah" in *hot*. English rules of sound-to-letter correspondence are much more difficult than those in languages like Spanish or Japanese, where what you see is what you say. English-speaking children must learn not only the regular sound-to-

Perhaps the most salient cognitive achievement of the early school years is learning to read. This achievement opens the doors to further cognitive advances.

letter rules but exceptions and variations: *s* sounds like the "ss" in *sweet* or like the "sh" in *sure*; *c* sounds different in *cat* and *circle*. They must learn to break down the words they see into the sounds that make them up: *see* equals "s" plus "ee." They must process and understand what they have decoded (Morrison, 1984). As children read, they use two processes to identify strings of letters. They sound out the letters as they look at them, then blend the sounds and say the whole sounded-out word—l-e-p-i-d-o-p-t-e-r-a—a *phonic* process. They also compare the *meaning* of the word to the words they know— "leopard," "opera"—a *lexical* process. Finally, not only must they learn to read single words, but they must also learn to understand sentences. Simply recognizing letters is not enough for understanding words, and simply recognizing words is not enough for understanding sentences. Who ever said that reading was easy?

In one study of how people read, researchers photographed people's eye movements as they read (Just and Carpenter, 1980). They found that the eye remains on connectives like *and* or *but* only one-sixth as long as it remains on more important words, especially those that are unfamiliar. Apparently, these words take longer to process. A person looks at the word *automobile* for less time than the word *Ferrari*. Words that occur in central clauses are looked at longer than words in peripheral clauses, which expand or embellish the main point. People also fix their eyes longer at the ends of sentences, as they integrate information and make sense out of the sentence they have just read. Reading is not a smooth glide, but a series of stops and starts for clarification and interpretation.

Why are some children good readers whereas others stumble and stammer or miss the point as they read? This question has concerned parents and teachers for generations. Now researchers are coming up with some possible explanations. Poor readers, they have found, are less skillful than good readers at encoding words into short-term memory. When second graders were shown nameless doodles and drawings of objects with familiar names like *horse* and *tree*, the good and poor readers did equally poorly at remembering the doodles, but the good readers were far better at remembering the objects (Katz, Shankweiler, and Liberman, 1981). The good readers, suggested the researchers, probably had said to themselves, "horse, tree, fish, kite," encoding the words in their memories as they were shown the pictures. But the poor readers had not said these words to themselves. Another possible explanation for differences in reading ability is that poor readers just say words to themselves more slowly than good readers do, with the effect that they have forgotten the beginning of a sentence as they approach the end (Manis and Morrison, 1982). According to one researcher, the main problem with most poor readers is that they are innately less sensitive to the sounds that make up words—rhymes, alliteration, syllables (Bryant and Bradley, 1985). Training these children to listen to word sounds before they even begin learning to read can ease their transition to reading.

Teaching reading

Although poor readers may come to the task of reading with disadvantages, these disadvantages can be minimized or maximized by how they are taught. A number of different methods of teaching reading are in use today. In the whole-word, look-say, or **sight-word method** of teaching reading, children are taught to recognize entire words rather than to sound out the letters and then blend them together. These children learn, for instance, to recognize *pit*, *sit*, and *kite* as whole words. In the **phonic method**, children are taught to sound out the words letter by letter. In English, the 26 letters of the alphabet represent about 44 different sounds. In phonics instruction, children learn the rules and exceptions for the correspondences between letters and these sounds. They learn that letters sometimes function alone—as *t* and as *h*—and sometimes function in groups—as *th*—and that single letters and groups of letters both can have more than one sound—*was*, *cat*, and *make*. If they do not learn these facts, children may get bogged down by assuming that one letter equals one sound, when in fact there are a great many words that are, in the words of a 5-year-old,"funny—not the same letters as you say them in" (Reid, 1983, p. 163).

In the "breakthrough to literacy" method of teaching reading, the teacher writes down words that the child knows already, and these make up the child's word bank. Children copy the written words, make sentences with them, and draw pictures about their sentences. In one comparison of the reading skills of 6- and 7-year-old children taught by the breakthrough to literacy method or the phonics method, the two groups were equally good at pronouncing common words. But with unfamiliar words, children taught by the breakthrough to literacy method relied on the first parts of words, whereas the phonics children sounded out the whole word (Rao, 1982). When children from the breakthrough group saw nonsense words that looked like real words, they substituted real words nearly half the time; those from the phonics group did not.

In a similar study (Evans, 1985), researchers compared first graders in a "language" curriculum, which focused on integrating reading with learning about the wider world, with first graders in a "skills" curriculum, which focused on letter and word recognition and phonic decoding. The children in the skills curriculum, as a group, they found, were better basic readers. They could all read a simple book, whereas many of the children in the language curriculum could not. When only the best readers of the two groups were compared, however, the differences between them were not significant. The practical lesson to be drawn from this study may be that for good readers, a variety of methods of teaching reading will do. In fact, many children who are good readers seem to pick up reading without *any* formal instruction (Durkin, 1966). But for children who need more help, a skills-based phonics approach, with lots of sounding out, copying, and exercises in the correspondence of print to sound, may be more effective.

One last method of teaching reading might be called the picture method. In one variety of the picture method, children see a picture of the object for which they are to learn the name—a boy for a *boy*, a coffee cup for *cup*, and the like. In another variety of the picture method, children see a picture that illustrates the sound of the letter they are to learn—a pumpkin or a boy puffing out a candle for the letter *p*. In a third variety of this method, the child sees a picture of a letter that actually looks like the word it is being associated with—a mountainous *M* for "mountain," a serpentine *S* for "snake." Researchers have found that only the third variety of the picture method helps children to read (Levin, 1983). When the pictures on the page do not relate to the word or sound being presented, children actually read more slowly than they do without pictures. Even when pictures and words are related—when a picture of a coat appears above the word *coat*—children are slower at reading easy words and are helped to read only difficult words. Children are easily distracted by pictures, it seems, and as with other methods of teaching reading, it is poor readers who suffer most (Levin, 1983).

Whichever teaching method they use, teachers can better help young children to read by communicating real messages—writing notes and notices, captioning children's drawings, showing them street signs, advertisements, newspapers, and other readable items from the everyday world. Children who dictate sentences for their teachers to write down get practice not just in vocabulary but in sentence form. They also overcome one of the problems of many reading texts—stilted language. When language is stilted, children may not be able to recognize words that they easily recognize and understand in other contexts. Children faced with sentences like "Darkness was upon the face of the deep" said that they could not understand "hard words" like *face*, and *darkness* when they had just read them in easier sentences like "I can see his face in the darkness." (Reid, 1958). Not only can starchy syntax throw children, but starchy exhortations may throw them as well. Often children do not know who is giving the exhortations to "look," "see," "come" and just what they mean. They cannot always tell whether the words they read belong to the characters or to an unnamed narrator. When teachers realize that in learning to read, children deal not just with words but with sentence forms and conventions of narration, they can teach much more effectively (Reid, 1983).

The easiest way for beginning readers to bridge the gap between the spoken and written word is to read things that are richly meaningful—not the stilted, bare prose of "Run, Spot, run" or "Look, John, look." Stories about what they have seen and done, notes to people they know, recipes for peanut butter sandwiches, lyrics to songs they sing, captions for pictures they have drawn, baseball facts, and jump-rope jingles all help children to understand the function of reading and writing in the real world.

Reading readiness

When are children ready to read? at 5? 6? 10? The answer seems to be that it all depends on the child. Some children are ready to read at age 3. They absorb the skills basic to reading as though by osmosis. Their eyes scan the words on the page systematically, they see letters and remember them, they are forever asking, "What's this say?" and "What's that word?" and they are fascinated with books. They guess at words by relying on clues in sentence structure and filling in the blanks, or they fall silent when they do not know a word and try to puzzle it out by using their own knowledge of phonics. These children are making excellent progress in learning to read. Other children are not ready to read when their first-grade teachers are ready to teach them. They are not inclined toward books, words, or letters. They mix up their *p*'s and *q*'s and would probably rather be outside playing Star Wars.

Are there dangers in pushing a child to read too soon or in missing a magic moment by waiting too long to begin teaching reading? A real controversy exists between those who think that children who are not ready to read should stay out of school, at the bottom of the class, or in a separate group until they are ready and those who think that schools should make them ready. At one extreme are those who advocate teaching 2-year-olds to read, saying that waiting until they are in first grade represents a "paralyzing prejudice" (Emery, 1975). At the other extreme are those who advocate keeping children, many of them boys, from formal instruction in reading until they are mature enough—at 8 or 10—to perceive and interpret written words (Moore and Moore, 1975). The traditional, middle-of-the-road position is that children should begin formal instruction in reading in first grade, at 6 or 7, and those few younger children who want to read—and are not being pressured to do so by adults—can be given their head to page through story books, look at written words, scribble, and play word games (Elkind, 1981).

Reading comprehension

After they have mastered the basics of reading, children begin to read for comprehension. In the primary grades, it has been said, children learn to read, but in the higher grades they read to learn. Comprehension of written material involves identifying words, understanding the connections of words, combining sentences into larger units of meaning, making inferences, and relating what is being read to what is known (Perfetti, 1984). As elementary school children become better at these processes, their reading comprehension improves, and they can understand more difficult material. Word identification becomes more automatic and eventually requires little attention or memory capacity. As children's memories increase with age, they can remember longer phrases and integrate what they are reading with what they have read (Daneman, 1981). Children's increasing knowledge improves comprehension by giving them a frame of reference for checking plausibility and making inferences (Beck, Perfetti, and McKeown, 1982). Flexibility in adapting reading strategies to the material—*studying* a text, *reading* a novel, *skimming* a newspaper—is another facet of reading that increases with age (Kobasigawa, Ransom, and Holland, 1980). Sixth-grade readers know more different strategies and when to apply them than third graders (Forrest-Pressley and Waller, 1984). For example, sixth graders are likely to know that they should take notes, memorize main points, and test themselves if they are reading for a test, that they should skim if they are searching for a name in a story, and that they should try to remember important points if they are reading in order to retell a story to a friend. Finally, children's ability to monitor their comprehension increases with age.

All these developmental trends in reading comprehension have implications for reading instruction in elementary school. In one study (Palincsar and Brown, 1984), seventh graders who were behind in reading comprehension were taught four skills: to summarize, clarify, anticipate future questions, and predict the content of the next paragraph. Before this instruction, the students answered about 20 percent of comprehension questions correctly after reading a paragraph. Afterward, they answered about 80 percent correctly, and the improvement was still evident six months later. In another study (Paris and Oka, 1986), 1000 third- and fifth-grade children were informed, coached, and participated in class discussion about when and why to use cognitive strategies while reading. The strategies included thinking about the title and topic before reading, declaring reading goals, stopping to paraphrase, slowing down on difficult passages, checking to see whether information made sense, skimming or rereading to review, and summarizing the text. Compared to 600 children who did not receive this instruction, at the end of the school year, the children in the program scored higher on an index of reading awareness, used more comprehension strategies, and understood more of what they read.

As research in this area advances, we will see more programs like these and perhaps more efforts to sort out which components of comprehension are the most important for teaching children to understand what they read (Pressley, Forrest-Pressley, Elliot-Faust, and Miller, 1985).

Individual differences in cognition

Individual children differ in many different cognitive abilities.

Natalie can think quickly and accurately. When they have spelling or arithmetic speed drills in school, she almost always gets a 100. She reads all the time, and she seems to inhale what she calls "fact books"—almanacs, the encyclopedia, books about real people and things. She's imaginative—she writes poems and is going to collaborate with her best friend on the class play. After I had a conference with her fourth grade teacher, I said, "Nat, this is pretty terrific. Every teacher you have tells me the same thing—what a wonderful, bright student you are and what a pleasure you are to have in class."

Intelligence

Not all children develop cognitive skills at the same age or rate or reach the same ultimate levels of ability. Some children are clearly more advanced at any given age than others. They talk and read earlier and better, understand mathematical and logical operations more quickly, and remember more things more clearly. This advanced rate of cognitive development in childhood and the ultimate differences in cognitive levels in adulthood are important ingredients in what we call intelligence.

> Bobby and Gary are brothers. Bobby is bright, but Gary is super bright. When he was 28 months old, his grandmother asked him to count out loud for her. When he was still going strong at 129, she decided to have his IQ tested.

> Sarah is one of several gifted children in her class at school. She talked early; at 16 months her mother remembers her saying, "Daddy go bye-bye car." She had taught herself to read by the time she was 3, and her vocabulary was larger than most adults' by the time she was 8.

Defining and measuring intelligence have posed problems for psychologists. Although people have a general idea of what they mean by saying that someone is "intelligent," reducing that idea to something measurable and getting agreement among various people's general ideas is no easy task. The question of what intelligence is has intrigued philosophers, scientists, and theologians for 3000 years. In attempts to define it, they have suggested that intelligence is "moral uprightness," "the ability to reason well," "learning thoroughly and quickly," "perseverance," "creative imagination," and "the ability to make fine sensory or esthetic discriminations."

Because the definitions of intelligence are so varied, many people have thrown up their hands and decided that intelligence is whatever intelligence tests measure. **Psychometrics** is the field of standardized testing of intelligence and achievement. Psychometricians define intelligence as the ability to respond correctly to questions on intelligence tests. They search for patterns of individual differences across tests and presume that they derive from individual mental abilities. Psychometrics probably has been the most influential approach to defining intelligence in this century.

Testing IQ

In 1905, Alfred Binet and Théophile Simon published the first psychometric test of children's intelligence, a test of "good sense" and knowledge. (Recall the discussion in Chapter 1 of the significance of this event in the history of developmental psychology.) By testing many children, Binet and Simon found the normative age at which most could answer each question correctly. Children's mental ages (MA) were determined through comparisons of their answers to these norms. In 1912, William Stern hit upon the concept of the **intelligence quotient (IQ)**. To find someone's IQ, he divided their mental age by their chronological age and multiplied by 100. "Normal" children thus had an IQ of 100. Today, IQs are computed so that the mean IQ score for children at each age is adjusted to 100 with a **standard deviation** of 15 points. Thus two-thirds of all people come within the "normal" IQ range between 85 and 115 points, and 95 percent fall within the IQ range of 70 and 130 (Figure 12.1).

In 1916, more items were added to the Binet-Simon test to reflect children's ability to think abstractly and to use verbal symbols. Today, the Stanford-Binet scale can be used to test the intelligence of children as young as 2. It extends through middle childhood and taps children's abilities to define words, recognize verbal absurdities, identify similarities and differences between objects, propose solutions to everyday problems, and name the days of

When conditions for testing are relaxed, black children do as well or better with white testers as with black testers. But when conditions are stressful, black children do better with black testers.

NORMAL DISTRIBUTION OF IQ SCORES

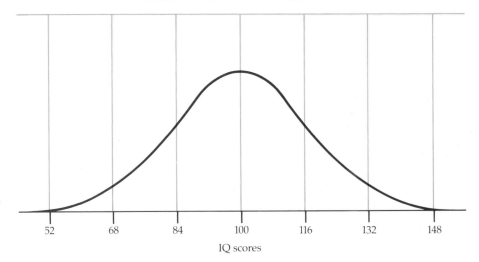

Figure 12.1 The distribution of IQ scores of the general population follows the normal curve.

IQ scores

the week. Since 1938, another intelligence test has been in use, devised by David Wechsler. Wechsler considered intelligence ''the overall capacity of an individual to cope with the world'' (1974, p. 5). His test, the Wechsler Intelligence Scale for Children (WISC), is divided into *verbal* and *performance* subtests. The former taps the child's knowledge and information, vocabulary, comprehension of everyday skills, mathematical ability, recall, and interpretation. The latter taps intelligence through a child's abilities to code numbers into symbols, copy designs made with blocks, put pictures into logical order, complete a picture, and assemble a cut-up picture of an object (see Figure 12.2). The tester begins with problems the child can answer easily and ends with those the child consistently fails.

Although psychologists usually avoid using the subtests in isolation, the vocabulary subtests of the Wechsler and Stanford-Binet scales are a better predictor of children's general intelligence than the performance subtests (Saddler, 1974). Tests that measure only verbal abilities have, therefore, been devised and have proved quite useful. One of the best known of these, the Peabody Picture Vocabulary Test (PPVT), measures intelligence by having a child point to the picture named by the tester. Because this test does not rely on a child's spoken responses, it was once thought to be a fairer test of the abilities of children from minority groups than other IQ tests, which require children to speak standard English. However, research showed that the scores of minority-group children on the PPVT were actually lower than on other IQ tests (Cundick, 1970), and so it was no solution after all. Although it measures the size of a child's vocabulary, the PPVT does not assess how children use or remember language. But the PPVT has its advantages: the main one is that it takes only 15 minutes to administer.

Both the Wechsler and the Stanford-Binet tests are administered by an experienced tester to an individual child. The tester has to be trained to administer, score, and interpret the results of the test and to issue instructions neutrally and in a form that does not vary from one child to the next. A tester also must be able to establish rapport with the child and to detect when the child is confused, sick, or overly nervous.

For children in middle childhood, intelligence testing may be conducted individually, with the Stanford-Binet or WISC. More often, however, children's intelligence in the school years is assessed by tests administered to a whole class. These group tests do not allow examiners to identify children who are ill or nervous, nor to account for any child's especially good or poor performance. They make no allowances for mood or temperament, headaches

STANDARD IQ TEST ITEMS

Verbal Subtests

1. *Information and Knowledge*
   How many wings does a bird have?
   Who wrote *Tom Sawyer*?
   What is steam made of?

2. *Comprehension*
   What should you do if you see someone forget his book when he leaves a restaurant?
   What is the advantage of keeping money in a bank?

3. *Arithmetic and Numerical Reasoning*
   Sam had three pieces of candy and Joe gave him four more. How many pieces of candy did Sam have altogether?

4. *Verbal Similarities*
   In what way are a lion and a tiger alike?
   In what way are an hour and a week alike?

5. *Digit Span and Memory*
   Repeat these numbers: 9 3 4 8 7 1

6. *Vocabulary*
   What does _____ mean or what is a _____ ?
   (The words given cover a wide range of familiarity and difficulty.)

Performance Subtests

1. *Digit Symbol*

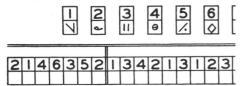

2. *Block Design*

3. *Picture Arrangement*

4. *Picture Completion*

Figure 12.2 These items are like those on the WISC.

5. *Object Assembly*

or anxiety, boredom or sleepiness. The tests also generally penalize children's creativity, originality, or even their perception of two right answers to a single question. In their favor, these tests require little special training of the tester, can be given economically to many children at once, produce objective scores, and have been standardized on large samples.

Whether the test is administered to one child or a class, who the tester is makes a difference. Many testers are white, and black children may feel too suspicious of them to perform well (Edwards, 1979). Black children also may feel suspicious of black testers if they are men (Wubberhorst, Gradford, and Willis, 1971). Trusting and helping an unfamiliar black man runs contrary to children's survival training in communities where most criminals are black and male. Under stressful conditions, when poor black children are anxious about their performance—and in danger of ''choking''—they do better with black testers (Katz, Roberts, and Robinson, 1965). When a test is given under relaxed conditions, however, black children sometimes perform better with white than black testers (Bucky and Banta, 1972). In general, all children do best when they have a chance to grow familiar with the tester and the testing situation and when the atmosphere is friendly and relaxed.

IQ tests: how fair? how useful?

Intelligence tests are relative. They give one child's score in relation to the scores of others who have taken the test. The norms to which a child's scores are compared are based on his or her age. But age does not guarantee that children have had the same experiences. Many intelligence tests are biased towards knowledge that reflects white, middle-class culture. In one extensive sampling of the ways that children speak naturally at home, middle-class children were found to use the language contained in the PPVT and WISC significantly more than children from working-class families (Hall, Nagy, and Linn, 1984). IQ tests also contain questions about such esoteric things as xylophones, tubas, and marimbas, which penalize children who have never seen a band. On the Binet test, children are asked questions like, ''What is the thing for you to do if another boy hits you without meaning to do it?'' The correct answer is to assume that it was an accident and to walk away—a suicidal answer in some black communities (Williams, 1970).

To avoid the bias against children from lower-class families, some researchers have designed intelligence tests around spatial perception and reasoning. One such test is the Raven Progressive Matrices Test. The Raven test relies on 60 different designs, each with a missing piece (see Figure 12.3). The child tries to supply the missing piece from several possible choices. Other ''culture-fair'' tests have been designed to tap only a carefully limited vocabulary and set of ideas. Unfortunately, even these tests usually reveal differences in IQ scores for children from different cultural and economic backgrounds. What is more, they are less predictive than traditional IQ tests of how well children will do in school. For better or worse, traditional IQ scores are highly predictive of school grades (the correlation is approximately .70 in most studies [McClelland, 1973]). They are also predictive of economic success in adulthood (at about the same level [Jencks et al., 1972]). Although intelligence tests may be culturally biased, they do reflect certain realities of life today in the United States. In our society, success on intelligence tests, in schools, and, to some extent, in life is related to middle-class knowledge, values, and norms.

Middle-class norms apply to the way that IQ tests are presented as well as to their content. Intelligence tests, it should be remembered, are not perfect measures of children's basic *competence* to think, to understand, and to draw logical conclusions. They are measures of children's *performance* in one particular situation—the IQ test. They are influenced by children's skills in test

CULTURE-FAIR IQ TEST ITEMS

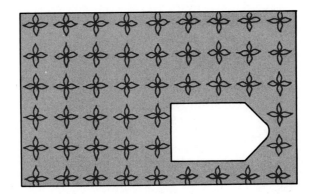

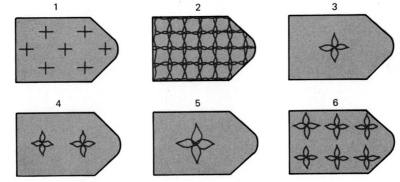

Figure 12.3 Sample item from the Raven Progressive Matrices Test. The child must pick out the piece below that is missing from the matrix above.

taking and working fast under pressure and in their motivation and desire to cooperate and apply themselves to the test. When special efforts are made to motivate children, their scores go up. In one experiment, for example, inner-city children were given tokens for each right answer on an intelligence test. The tokens could be exchanged later for toys. Children who had gotten tokens scored 13 points higher than children in a control group who had gotten no tokens (Bradley-Johnson et al., 1984).

Dissatisfied with traditional IQ tests, some psychologists have proposed alternative methods of evaluating children's intelligence. One such alternative they have suggested is to use individual differences in information-processing speed, choice of memory strategies, and in content of long-term memory as measures of intelligence (Keating and Bobbitt, 1978). This approach to measuring intelligence will no doubt continue to be explored and refined in the 1980s. Another approach that will be explored is a search for different *kinds* of intelligence. Howard Gardner (1983) has proposed that in their richly various thoughts and deeds, people display many kinds of intelligence—linguistic, musical, logical–mathematical, spatial, bodily, personal.

One characteristic not tapped by standard intelligence tests is creativity. Creative children make up new theories, use new ways of seeing, and produce new creations. Their thoughts lead them in fresh directions and into uncharted territory.

When he was 6, Sam put pieces of shrimp shells over his thumbs and called them his Band-aids. When he was 9, he wrote a story that began, "Once upon a time, there was a boy who lived inside a light bulb."

focus *Talent will out?*

Does the child with a particular kind of intelligence, a particular gift, bob to the top automatically, as if talent were a life jacket that always rose safely to the surface? In a word, no. Talent must be tended at home, developed by teachers, and practiced endlessly, or it may sink to the bottom without a trace. Many children who show promise in some area—the musical child with perfect pitch, the gifted early reader and writer, the mathematical whiz—are not given the special training and attention that they need if their promise is to develop into a true and practiced skill.

When a research team from the University of Chicago, led by Benjamin Bloom (1985), interviewed 120 talented concert pianists, sculptors, theoretical mathematicians, research neurologists, and Olympic athletes, they found that all of them had needed help, encouragement, and others' dedication. At every step of the way, parents and teachers had been critical to the talented children's success. Although very few of the children were originally thought of as prodigies, all of them had benefited from their parents' unflagging interest and pride in their accomplishments. The children had been encouraged to work hard, to discipline themselves, and to feel proud of what they accomplished. Parents tried to smooth the way and remove obstacles to their children's progress. If they disliked what they saw of a child's first few lessons in some area, they found another teacher and a new approach. Although they devoted themselves to their special talents, most of the children, like other kids, went to summer camp, joined the Boy Scouts or Girl Scouts, acted in school plays, took dancing lessons, and played baseball.

Beyond the dedication of their parents, the children had had inspiring teachers. Pedantic, demanding teachers, who could kill a child's budding interest, were deliberately avoided. Their first teachers conveyed a deep pleasure—even a playfulness and delight—in learning. Their second teachers stressed accuracy, precision, and hard work. Their third teachers were the ones with high achievements who drew the child toward excellence. And then came practice—the child's investment of hours and hours of time. None of the talented people reached the pinnacle of excellence automatically, none bobbed effortlessly to the top of his or her field. They were lucky enough to have parents who nurtured their talents, teachers who inspired and challenged them, and the persistence to make something of the advantage with which nature had endowed them.

IQ tests measure what children know of the usual and expected right answers—so-called **convergent thinking**. Creative thinking is based on the unusual and unexpected—so-called **divergent thinking**. It is better measured when the creativity of children's drawing and writing and the diversity of their answers to questions are taken into account (see Figure 12.4). A question like, "Tell me all the things that you can do with a brick," might elicit from creative children answers as diverse as "you can build with it, throw it, use it for an anchor, grind it for paint, use it as a step for young children by a water fountain." A theory of intelligence that incorporates creativity as well as more standard aspects of intelligence has recently been proposed by Robert Sternberg (1985). In his book *Beyond IQ*, Sternberg suggests that intelligence includes not only the abilities usually measured on IQ tests but, in addition, the abilities to allocate time, to plan, monitor, and evaluate one's activities, to have insights through selective encoding, combining, and comparing, and to adapt to the real world.

The idea of a single IQ score that sums up a child's intelligence may eventually be a thing of the past. Meanwhile, even with its problems, the IQ score has some usefulness for telling how adequately a child is developing and for predicting how well he or she is likely to do in school and later in life. Scores at the extremes of the IQ continuum are the most useful for predicting success or failure. For scores closer to 100, it is more difficult to predict future learning or performance.

Race and IQ

One major controversy that swirls around IQ tests is whether they show that blacks and whites have different levels of intelligence. The finding that, on the average, whites outperform blacks by about 15 points on IQ tests is not the target of dispute (Brody and Brody, 1976; Jencks et al., 1972; Jensen, 1980). But there is great dispute over how to interpret this finding. At one extreme are those who maintain that the difference in IQ scores is invalid because of defects in the tests or because it reflects the many social, economic, and cultural differences between the two groups. At the other extreme are those who maintain that the difference in IQ reflects differences in innate abilities. As Arthur Jensen (1980) has pointed out, even when blacks and whites of equivalent social and economic status are compared, whites still outperform blacks by 12 points. This difference, maintains Jensen, is too large to be explained by environmental factors alone. What is more, maintains Jensen, blacks do even less well than whites on so-called culture-reduced test items (for example, nonverbal analogies) than they do on so-called culture-loaded items (for example, verbal analogies).

Jensen distinguishes between lower-level intelligence, or *associative intelligence*, and higher-level intelligence, or *conceptual intelligence* (see Figure 12.5). Reviewing the test results of over 9000 children, Jensen (1969, 1973) found that blacks and whites are equal only at the level of associative thinking and memory and that blacks score lower on IQ tests because they cannot learn as well as whites at the higher level of conceptual thinking.

A thorough understanding of the issues involved in this controversy requires an appreciation of heredity and statistics beyond the scope of this book. We will say here that the evidence that racial differences in IQ are genetic is far from clear. For one thing, there is evidence that environment contributes to these differences. Studies of black children reared in white families (Scarr and Weinberg, 1981, 1983), for example, indicate that IQ scores of black children can be increased by 10 to 20 points by adoption into white families, and the earlier the adoption the greater the increase is likely to be. Evidence for the effects of environment also comes from data showing that young black children have higher IQs than their older siblings did at the same age, a difference that has been attributed to improved schooling and other social advantages of the younger children (Kamin, 1978). What is more, studies of children of mixed black and white ancestry do not demonstrate a strict genetic connection between race and IQ scores (Scarr, Pakstis, Katz, and Barker, 1977).

Often forgotten in the emotion of the IQ debate is the fact that the outcome has little practical importance. First, if we ask only whether intelligence is either genetic *or* environmental, we will not find out which environmental conditions are at work or whether they can be overcome. Second, the variation in IQ scores within a single race is three times larger than the difference between blacks and whites. Knowing a person's race is therefore virtually useless as a predictor of that person's intelligence. Finally, if a person's IQ score is within the normal range, it does not by itself indicate how well the person will do in everyday matters. If the goal is to eliminate social and economic injustice, many more practical steps can be taken than to debate endlessly the validity or bias of intelligence tests.

CREATIVE DRAWINGS

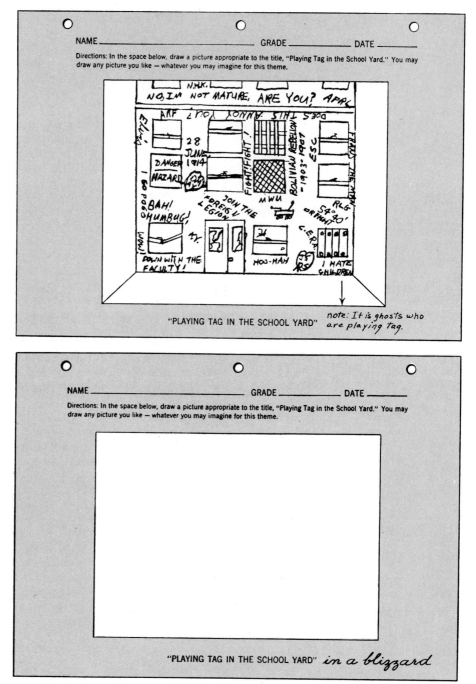

Figure 12.4 Creative children, when asked to draw a picture of an incident, are not literal about it. They may mock convention, depict violence, fashion new creatures, and often use humor (Getzels and Jackson, 1962).

Stability and change in IQ scores

When we look at what happens to a child's knowledge and skills, as measured by intelligence tests, over time, we see a general onward and upward trend. When the *raw scores* on intelligence tests of subjects in the longitudinal Berkeley Growth Study were plotted, they were found to increase rapidly until early adolescence, increase more slowly until midadolescence, and then taper off by late adolescence (Bayley, 1966, 1968). But do

CREATIVE DRAWINGS (*continued*)

NAME _____ GRADE _____ DATE _____

Directions: In the space below, draw a picture appropriate to the title, "Playing Tag in the School Yard." You may draw any picture you like — whatever you may imagine for this theme.

"PLAYING TAG IN THE SCHOOL YARD"

NAME _____ GRADE _____ DATE _____

Directions: In the space below, draw a picture appropriate to the title, "Playing Tag in the School Yard." You may draw any picture you like — whatever you may imagine for this theme.

"PLAYING TAG IN THE SCHOOL YARD"

individual children retain the same *IQ scores* throughout these years? Not often. IQ scores, which reflect the child's position relative to other children of the same age, vary considerably over time. Only one-fifth of the children from the Berkeley Growth Study retained the same IQ scores over their first nine years. For some children, IQ scores shifted enormously. One girl's went from 133 to 77; one boy's went from the middle 90s to 160, then to 135. Over time, thirteen children varied by 30 or more points, one-third of the group varied by

ASSOCIATIVE AND CONCEPTUAL INTELLIGENCE

Level I Associative: Memory and Knowledge
When did Columbus discover America?
Pick out the word that does not belong:
  door kitchen painted garage porch
Underline the word that goes with the set:
  arm, hand, foot, neck: body/man/knee/take

Level II Conceptual: Abstraction and Analogy
What does this mean: ''Fight fire with fire.''
Cat is to *kitten* as *dog* is to _____.
Before is to *behind* as *future* is to _____.

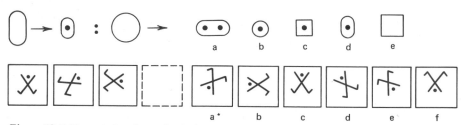

Figure 12.5 Items taken from the Culture Fair Intelligence Test illustrate Jensen's ideas about levels of intelligence.

20 points, and nearly two-thirds varied by 15 or more points. Some of these changes might have resulted from temporary fluctuations in children's moods, health, feelings of stress, and so forth. Some might have resulted from changes in the content of the tests at different ages. Yet others are likely to have reflected changing circumstances in the children's families and schools. In less stable families than the white, middle-class ones in the Berkeley study, the shifts in children's IQ scores could be even greater. IQ scores tend to be more stable the shorter the intervals between tests and the older the child taking them. By age 12, IQ test scores are relatively stable and useful for predicting current and future success.

Mental retardation

Three in every hundred children in this country are ''mentally retarded.'' This label is attached a range of conditions, but in general, individuals who have an IQ score below 70 and are unable to function competently and independently in society are labeled mentally retarded (Edgerton, 1979). *Mildly retarded* children have IQs in the 55 to 69 range. Nearly all of them live at home. They may seem quite normal except in areas like reading or math. *Moderately retarded* children, with IQs from 40 to 55, may have physical as well as mental disabilities. *Severely retarded* children have IQs in the 25 to 39 range. They cannot function independently and need constant supervision and long training to master walking, feeding, and toileting themselves. *Profoundly retarded* children may not be able to speak and may live a vegetative existence under constant medical care. Many are bedridden. They are likely to have short lives.

Many conditions cause mental retardation. Perhaps the best known of these is the chromosomal abnormality of Down's syndrome (discussed in Chapter 3). A child exposed prenatally to rubella, syphilis, alcohol, viral infections, or lead poisoning (as we discussed in Chapter 4) also may be retarded. Severe malnutrition during infancy and childhood can cause mental retardation. Mental retardation that results from any of these biochemical processes is called *clinical retardation*. Clinical retardation accounts for about one quarter of all cases of mental retardation. Educational, economic, and social deprivation accounts for the rest. Growing up in an inner-city ghetto or a poor country hollow is fifteen times more likely to result in *sociocultural retardation* than is growing up in the suburbs. In an Appalachian hollow named Duddie's Branch, for example:

> Not one child has ever seen a sandbox. None has played with finger paints, puzzles, or blocks. Their "toys" consist of broken bottles, sharp metal, discarded tin cans. Ask them about Goldilocks, and they will look at you in bewilderment—they have never heard of a fairy tale. I made a bean bag from an old rag and asked some of the older boys to catch it. They had difficulty. With an old string ball and a heavy stick, I tried to involve them in batting practice. I was unsuccessful. Not only do games fail to interest them, they are almost completely unable to participate in most activities. They could not be taught to whistle, sing, or even hum a simple tune. I wrote 1111, 2222, 3---, --4-, -55- on a sheet of paper and asked a number of 8-year-olds to fill in the missing numbers. They could not. Nor were they able to draw a circle, a square, raise their right arms, raise their left arms, extend their fingers, or spell their names (Gazaway, 1969, in Edgerton, 1979, pp. 54–55).

Most children with sociocultural retardation are only mildly retarded. Brought into stimulating environments and given education that meets their needs, these children can learn and grow into productive members of society. Whether the cause of retardation is biological or environmental, mildly retarded children can learn to read, write, make simple calculations, and perform many everyday tasks. One researcher (Mercer, 1971) who studied the relation between children's scores on standard intelligence tests and their successfully adaptive everyday behavior—whether they could dress and feed themselves, walk alone, remember the names of their classmates, and so on—found that 90 percent of the black children who scored under 70 on the IQ test passed the test of adaptive behavior. Even moderately retarded children, under conditions that are stimulating and challenging, can learn to talk, though few can learn to read or write.

Cognitive style

Not only do children differ in their IQ test scores, but they also differ in their styles of taking in and responding to information. They may take in new subject matter quickly or slowly, be distracted or focused, act with confidence or with uncertainty. These differences reflect children's **cognitive styles**.

Children may attack cognitive problems **reflectively** or **impulsively**. The Matching Familiar Figures Test is one way of assessing the reflectiveness or impulsiveness of a child's cognitive style (Kagan, 1965). On this test, the child is shown seven drawings of a familiar object (Figure 12.6); two of the drawings are identical, and the other five each differ in one tiny detail that is not easily noticed. The child is asked to find the identical pictures. A child who answers quickly, barely scans the pictures and makes many errors has an impulsive style. Impulsive children blurt the first answer they think of and do not stop to consider other possibilities. When they are asked to read out loud, they mispronounce words, substitute the wrong words, leave out some words and add others, and sometimes skip whole lines in their hurry through the passage. They focus on the total stimulus and the total problem rather than on separate components (Zelniker and Jeffrey, 1976; Figure 12.7). Impulsive children can become more deliberate when they are trained to look at all the alternatives and each of their components carefully (Egeland, 1974; Heider, 1971b).

MATCHING FAMILIAR FIGURES TEST

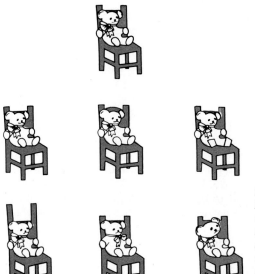

Figure 12.6 In the Matching Familiar Figures Test, the child must pay close attention to details, a challenge that separates reflective from impulsive children. The impulsive child sees that all these bears are similar and, without close scrutiny, chooses any one of them (Kagan, 1965).

The child with a reflective style responds slowly, comparing specific parts of the figures, and makes fewer errors. Reflective children spend more time weighing their hunches, gather more information on which to base their decisions, and gather it more methodically than impulsive children do (Messer, 1976). Reflective children devise better strategies for solving problems and follow them more consistently than impulsive children (Cameron, 1984). On the Raven Progressive Matrices Test both reflective and impulsive children answer the easy questions quickly, but reflective children slow down more and answer more accurately than impulsive children on the hard problems. The impulsive children hurry through the difficult problems, perhaps relying on guesses (Lawry, Welsh, and Jeffrey, 1983). Worry about making mistakes leads reflective children to be more cautious, and they seem very concerned about getting things right on tests of intellectual ability (Messer, 1970).

Another aspect of children's cognitive style is **field independence**—the ability to ignore distractions in the field surrounding a stimulus. One test to measure this ability is the rod and frame test. The child sits in a tilted seat in a dark room and looks at a luminous rod surrounded by a luminous frame. The experimenter turns the rod and frame while the child gives directions on how to turn the rod so that it is vertical. The frame is always tilted; when the rod looks vertical with respect to floor and ceiling, it is not vertical within the frame. Children who are field-independent rely on internal cues to orient the rod in space; they ignore the misleading cues from the frame. But children who are **field-dependent** rely on the frame for spatial orientation. In another test of field independence, children look for a geometrical figure embedded within a larger pattern that makes it difficult to see (Figure 12.8). Children who are field-independent find the hidden figure more easily than those who are field-dependent (Witkin, Dyk, Paterson, Goodenough, and Karp, 1962).

The questions of where differences in cognitive style come from and what they mean have not been answered fully. It once was thought that cognitive style represented broader personality traits. But this link has not been supported consistently by research. Impulsiveness seems to involve making errors rather than just acting quickly, as highly active children do, for instance. There also has been controversy about whether cognitive style is

TEST OF IMPULSIVE OR REFLECTIVE RECALL

Figure 12.7 *When asked to study and then immediately recall this picture, a reflective boy gave this account: "Flowers, trees, a girl, a baby carriage, grass, a frog, two birds, trees, leaves, a baby carriage, a rose leaf, on the water, the frog is on top of the leaf, sky, some earth, and that's it." He scored themes, 0; details, 12. An impulsive boy said, "A girl sailed a doll on the water and the doll ran away and she told the dog to go and save her doll. The dog took hold of the boat and brought it to the bank. There was also a grove and two birds." He scored themes, 5; details, 9 (Zelniker and Jeffrey, 1976).*

EMBEDDED FIGURES

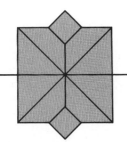

Can you locate the V-shaped figures in the colored design?

Figure 12.8 *Children who are field-dependent have difficulty finding the hidden figures in items on the Embedded Figures Test.*

really separate from cognitive ability. Cognitive style is related to how children do on intelligence tests—those who are field-independent score higher—and to changes as children get older and become more reflective and field-independent. But cognitive style and cognitive ability are not synonymous. Impulsive children are as good at solving cognitive problems as reflective children are, if global processing is possible (Zeniker and Jeffrey, 1976), and field-dependent children perform as well as those who are field-independent if they are trained to look for hidden cues (Globerson, Weinstein, and Sharabany, 1985).

What causes differences in cognitive style? No consistent link to environmental factors such as parents' behavior has been found (Moskowitz, Dreyer, and Kronsberg, 1981). There is some evidence that cognitive style is related to biological factors. Field independence, for example, is associated with a high degree of brain lateralization (Jeffrey, 1980). This may explain why boys, who, we will discuss shortly, have a high degree of brain lateralization, are consistently more field-independent than girls (Linn and Peterson, 1985). But brain lateralization is less plausible as an explanation for differences between ethnic groups—for example, the finding that Mexican-American children are more field dependent than Anglo-American children (Cordes, 1984). There are still many unanswered questions about cognitive styles.

Sex differences

Erica is beginning to clutch in math class. She's not really sure of herself when it comes to things like working with fractions, even though she's doing great in English. I don't really understand what makes girls fall behind boys in math. If it's something biological, then why are there women who make it as stockbrokers, engineers, and physicists, and why are there men who make it as historians, actors, and writers?

In earlier chapters, we have discussed differences between boys and girls in physical size, strength, and vulnerability, in play styles and preferences, in nurturance and aggression. There also may be differences in cognitive abilities, although these are more difficult to pin down. Eleanor Maccoby and Carol Jacklin (1974) combed through 1400 studies to try to find these differences. Unfortunately, many of these studies contained subjective self-reports and potentially biased reports by parents and teachers. Some had not controlled for the sex of the researchers or testers. Some did not take into account children's ages.

In all this research, however, girls quite consistently were found to have greater verbal abilities than boys. In infancy and early childhood, girls, on average, are more responsive to tones, patterns of speech, and subtle changes of voice; they usually begin to speak and sing in tune earlier; and they are more readily startled by loud noises (see also Friedman and Jacobs, 1981; Gunnar and Donahue, 1980). Later, girls learn to read sooner. By the end of middle childhood and thereafter, girls understand and use language more fluently than boys.

In contrast, boys quite consistently were shown in the research to have greater spatial abilities than girls. Boy babies, on average, are more likely to ignore their mother and pay attention to a blinking light or a geometric form than girl babies are. They like to manipulate objects with their hands, pushing, pulling, taking apart, and putting them back together. Preschool-age boys show their greater spatial abilities in the way they fold paper and twist and turn things. By school age, boys can make these spatial twists and turns in their heads (see Figure 12.9), and they do well on tests of finding embedded geometric figures. They can remember three-dimensional objects and imagine rotating them, abilities useful in mathematics. By age 12, boys do better than girls on mathematical problems, although their advantage is not so great as in spatial reasoning. When problems can be solved equally well by verbal or spatial reasoning, boys and girls do equally well. But when problems require verbal solutions, boys are at a disadvantage; when problems require spatial solutions, girls are at a disadvantage.

These differences in boys' and girls' verbal and visual skills (also documented in more recent research reviewed by Linn and Peterson, 1985), though

In general, boys excel in visual and spatial skills; girls excel in verbal skills.

VISUAL-SPATIAL TESTS

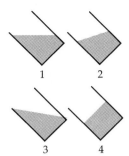

Water level: In which glass is the water horizontal?

Standard

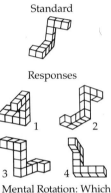

Responses

Mental Rotation: Which response shows the standard form in a different orientation?

Figure 12.9 Boys do better than girls on tests of spatial perception (top) and mental rotation (bottom).

consistent, should not be overestimated. Such differences are statistically significant, but they apply on the average, not to *every* individual, and they may be small in real terms. Among spatial abilities, for example, mental rotation is most strongly linked to sex; for other spatial abilities, sex accounts for not more than 5 percent of the variation in individuals. In addition, boys and girls do equally well when it comes to learning by rote, learning to discriminate between stimuli, shifting to a new solution to a problem, determining probabilities, and analyzing the elements they will need to perform a task.

The origins of sex differences

What are the origins of sex differences in verbal and visual abilities? Scientists have argued that question back and forth for some time. Some have suggested that the differences originate in the X chromosome. They have speculated that spatial ability, like baldness and hemophilia, is sex-linked, or X-linked. Boys, you remember, inherit only one X chromosome along with their one Y chromosome; girls inherit two X chromosomes. If visual–spatial ability came from recessive genes on the X chromosome, it would show up in boys more often than girls because girls would need to inherit the ability from both parents, boys from only one. But the results of studies of verbal and spatial abilities in girls with chromosome abnormalities (such as having only one X chromosome or having three X chromosomes) have not been consistent with the sex-linked hypothesis (Polani, Lessof, and Bishop, 1956; Rovet and Netley, 1983; Vandenberg and Kuse, 1979).

Other scientists have suggested that sex differences in verbal and visual abilities are related to brain structure. As we discussed in Chapter 8, the two hemispheres of the brain are not completely alike in their functions. The left hemisphere apparently controls verbal skills. The right hemisphere processes global configurations. The superiority of girls in verbal tasks and boys in visual and spatial tasks has led some researchers to investigate possible sex differences in brain lateralization. They have found that males generally have a sharper division of function in brain hemispheres. By age 6, a boy's right hemisphere dominates in processing visual and spatial information (Witelson, 1976). When boys work on a spatial task, such as trying to imagine which of three folded shapes can be made from a flat, irregularly shaped piece of paper, their right hemispheres are active. When girls work on a spatial task, both of their hemispheres are active (Restak, 1979). Processing with both hemispheres, as girls do, may be less efficient for solving spatial problems (Levy, 1969), but it also may be one reason that girls suffer less than boys from language disorders.

But the findings on brain lateralization are puzzling. It has been suggested that the timing of maturation, and not sex, determines brain lateralization. Because girls mature earlier than boys, their brains may be less lateralized and their verbal abilities relatively more developed. Early-maturing adolescents of *both* sexes have been found to do better on tests of verbal ability, and late-maturing adolescents of *both* sexes do better on tests of spatial ability (Diamond, Carey, and Back, 1983; Newcombe and Bandura, 1983; Sanders and Soares, 1986; Waber, 1976). But evidence to the contrary also exists. These differences do not show up in all samples or on all measures (Rovet, 1983; Waber et al., 1985; Sanders and Soares, 1986). Maturation, then, is not the whole explanation for sex differences in visual and spatial abilities.

A third possibility is that hormones, those powerful chemicals secreted by the ductless glands of the endocrine system, cause sex differences in visual and spatial abilities. Females with Turner's syndrome and males with androgen insensitivity syndrome do not produce normal levels of sex hormones and are poor at tasks requiring spatial ability (Khan and Cataio, 1984). But there are inconsistencies. In one recent study (Hines and Shipley, 1984), researchers investigated the effects of prenatal exposure to hormones on children's cognitive abilities. They compared girls whose mothers had taken a synthetic estrogen during pregnancy with their sisters who had not been exposed to the estrogen. They found that the girls exposed to estrogen had a more masculine pattern of brain lateralization, but they found no differences between the two groups in verbal or spatial abilities. In another study, researchers investigated the relation between intellectual abilities and body type, which would reflect hormonal influence (Berenbaum and Resnick, 1982). They found no significant relation.

In brief, evidence that sex differences in visual and spatial abilities are biological (based on the X chromosome, brain lateralization, rate of maturation, or hormones) is not especially convincing. Nevertheless, the fact that identical twins are quite similar in verbal IQ and spatial and mathematical abilities suggests that these abilities do have some still unidentified genetic component. There may be a biological foundation for visual and verbal differences, but so far we do not completely understand what it is.

What about the influence of social and psychological factors? If boys are endowed with a slight edge in spatial and mathematical skills, it may be reinforced by the kinds of play they engage in and by the courses they take in school. Boys like to build with blocks, put models together, and practice aiming and throwing things. This kind of play is likely to sharpen boys' spatial and visual perception and coordination. In fact, researchers have found that the more both boys and girls play with "masculine" toys like blocks, tricycles, jungle gyms, Lincoln Logs, Tinkertoys, and ring toss in preschool, the better are their visual and spatial abilities in grade school (Fagot and Littman, 1976; Serbin and Connor, 1979). In an experiment to show the influence of toys on children's spatial abilities (Denier and Serbin, 1978), children were assigned to a group that met with a teacher who showed them masculine toys, suggested interesting ways in which they could play with them, and encouraged and supported their efforts. Before the experiment, the boys had outscored the girls on a test of spatial ability (geometry). After the experiment, both boys and girls who had been trained to use the masculine toys outscored children who had not been trained to use them. Play with "feminine" toys like dolls and doll furniture, crayons and paints, felt boards and kitchen toys does not seem related to children's spatial abilities, but is related to higher verbal abilities (Fagot and Littman, 1976; Serbin and Connor, 1979). Once they are in school, boys take many more courses that rely on spatial skills—math, science, computers—than girls do. Evidence from a number of different sources shows that spatial skills—in both boys and girls—can be sharpened with training in just such subjects (Sprafkin et al., 1983).

The expression of verbal and visual abilities also is likely to depend on parents' and children's expectations and attitudes. Parents usually think that math is more important for sons than for daughters, and this affects children's attitudes more than their own past performance in math class (Parsons, Adler, and Kaczala, 1982). It doesn't seem to make any difference that Mom is a mathematical wizard and Dad a poet. The web of family expectations and attitudes—"He's always been good at math." "Her? She couldn't count her way out of a paper bag"—is what counts in children's approach to math.

At school, too, teachers may reinforce sex differences. Evidence from a number of studies suggests that teachers pay more attention to boys than to girls and respond to them with more ideas about solving problems and with more specific information, which could help them in science and math (Meyer and Thompson, 1956; Sadker and Sadker, 1985; Serbin, O'Leary, Kent, and Tonick, 1973). But girls tend to live up to teachers' expectations that they will be good readers. In one study, first-grade boys whose teachers believed that boys do not learn to read as well as girls, in fact, read less well than first-grade boys whose teachers did not hold those beliefs (Palardy, 1969). When teachers are evenhanded about praising and criticizing boys and girls, both sexes have the same expectations in elementary school about how well they will do (Parson, Kaczala, and Meece, 1982).

Textbooks and tests reinforce teachers' biases and contribute to the differences between boys and girls. Many show boys and men doing math and science as more important doctors, scientists, and professors, whereas girls and women are less important school teachers and mothers (Saario, Jacklin, and Tittle, 1973; Taylor, 1973). But although texts may more often be about men and boys, they do not encourage boys to read because they are not about subjects that boys find more interesting. When boys and girls are asked to read material that *both* consider interesting, boys read as well as girls (Asher, 1980)

The context of cognitive development

Teachers and texts not only magnify or minimize the differences between boys and girls in verbal and spatial abilities, they also affect children's cognitive development more generally. In this section, we discuss some of the important environmental factors that influence children's cognitive development in middle childhood. In the preschool years, as we saw in Chapter 9, the primary context of children's cognitive development is home. Much of children's cognitive development during their school years takes place, not surprisingly, in school, where children are helped or hindered by teachers' expectations, instructional methods, classroom arrangements, courses, and curricula.

Teachers' expectations

Teachers' beliefs and expectations about their students' abilities contribute directly to children's academic self-concepts. These images influence how hard children work and their feelings about school and learning in general.

> When we got the note from Mikey's first-grade teacher that she wanted to talk about the possibility that Mikey might be having trouble with reading, I was really upset. First grade is when kids start forming ideas about how smart they are. They start getting pegged—the fast-reading group and the slow-reading group, the smart ones in arithmetic and the dumb ones, the good spellers and the poor spellers—and if you're pegged as slow in first grade, you may never get over it.

> On the first day of fourth grade, the teacher called the roll. When she got to me, she said, "Oh, I see we have another Dutton with us this year. I hope you do better than your brothers did."

What happens to children tagged by their teachers as "slow learner," "class clown," "a brain," or "another Dutton"? Robert Rosenthal and Lenore Jacobson (1966, 1968) conducted a landmark study of the effects of teacher expectations on children's achievement. Intelligence tests were administered to students in the first to the sixth grades of a school in California. The names of 20 percent of the students were then randomly chosen, and teachers of these students were told that the tests had identified them as "bloomers" who could be expected to show unusual intellectual gains in the coming year. The IQ test was given again eight months later. The randomly selected "bloomers," particularly those in the first and second grades, had made unusual gains—the so-called Pygmalion effect. The younger children improved more than the older children for several possible reasons. First, having sketchier academic self-images, the younger children may have been more susceptible to differential treatment from the teachers. Second, less background information had accumulated about them, and their teachers may have found their promised blooming more credible. The Rosenthal and Jacobson study subsequently was criticized on several grounds. Nevertheless, after a rigorous and comprehensive reanalysis by other researchers, it was concluded that teachers' expectations had probably affected at least the first- and second-grade ''bloomers'' (Elashoff and Snow, 1970).

A number of related studies since have indicated the wide-ranging influence of teachers' expectations. Students with little ability who were taught French by teachers with a positive attitude toward them learned more of the language than did poor students whose teachers had a negative attitude (Durstall, 1975). The reading achievement of students whose teachers overestimated their IQ scores was significantly higher than that of students whose teachers underestimated their IQ scores (Doyle, Hancock, and Kifer, 1971). Even students' physical performance in gym class was influenced by their teachers' expectations (Rosenthal, 1984). Teachers' expectations clearly make a difference in how much children learn in school.

When teachers have high expectations of students, the environment they create is warmer and happier. The teachers smile often, act friendly, nod their head, and look the students in the eye. They talk more, teach more, and teach more challenging material. They give more clues, repeat and rephrase questions more, pay closer attention, and wait longer for students to answer. They praise the students more. Thus on several different levels at once—emotional, body language, spoken language, teaching materials, praise and criticism—teachers express their expectations (Rosenthal, Baratz, and Hall, 1974).

Teachers' expectations and their interactions with students are influenced by many factors: the teacher's own attitudes; the children's appearance, race, social class, abilities, and interest; and teachers' and children's personal, academic, and family histories (Brophy and Good, 1984). The degree of control they have over the students also influences teachers' expectations. Students who respond more predictably, answer teachers' questions, hand in their papers, take their tests, and read their assignments make a good impression and raise teachers' expectations. Students who threaten teachers' sense of control are ignored and criticized.

Ethnic patterns

One problem in elementary schools today arises when teachers' expectations clash with those of pupils from a different ethnic group. The problem is most acute when children arrive at school and do not speak the same language as their teachers. About 3.6 million school-age children in the United States speak a language other than English at home and may have trouble communicating with their English-speaking teachers. What to do about the problem is controversial—a political hot potato—although the goal for most educators and politicians eventually is to get children fluent in English. Some educators advocate teaching children in their native tongue and teaching English as a second language. Some advocate bilingualism in all classes. Others advocate that some classes be taught in English and others in the native language. Still others advocate plunging children into an English-only environment. The effects of these different approaches are not clear, and there have been few adequate evaluations of their effectiveness. Furthermore, what works in one school district may not work in another.

It has been argued that when the two languages develop and function in parallel, bilingualism increases children's cognitive functioning (Diaz, 1985).

As we saw in Chapter 9, children in bilingual families tend to be more cognitively flexible. But when one language is mastered at the expense of the other—which happens when a Spanish-speaking first grader is plunged into an English-only class, for example—bilingualism is a hindrance, and the result is not a bilingual child but a "semilingual" child, who functions inadequately in two languages. For children to have the advantages of bilingualism, it appears, they must continue to learn in their native language as well as in English. Some developmental psychologists who have studied bilingualism favor programs in which children who speak English and those who speak a foreign language take classes in both languages (for example, Hakuta, 1985; Lambert and Taylor, 1985). This kind of program eliminates the problem of poor self-esteem for children whose second language is English and who might otherwise be segregated in special classes and feel that their language and culture are being demeaned. Children generally can learn successfully in a second language if the program has the following features: it is specifically designed for language learning, the children already have mastered their native language, their parents support the program, and the language to be learned and the native language both hold relatively high status in the community (Rotberg, 1982).

More subtle than the clash in languages is the clash in values and learning styles that sometimes reverberates when children from a different culture enter a white, middle-class, American school. Whereas school-age Anglo-Americans are more likely to have a cognitive style that is field-independent than field-dependent, for example, Hispanics, blacks, and native Americans have been found to be more likely to be field-dependent (Cordes, 1984). Whereas most Anglo-American children show high levels of achievement motivation, Mexican-American, native American, and Hawaiian children have lower levels (Adkins, Payne, and Ballif, 1972). Most Anglo-American children feel that they are in control of what happens to them in school, but Mexican-American children often feel that the school controls them, and they have less confidence in their ability to succeed (Anderson and Johnson, 1971; Holtzman, Diaz-Guerrero, and Swartz, 1975). Anglo-American elementary school children tend to be verbal, assertive, competitive; Mexican-American children tend to be quiet, passive, and cooperative with their classmates (Holtzman et al., 1975; Kagan and Madsen, 1971).

If teachers are to promote the learning of children from all ethnic groups, they must be sensitive to the children's family and cultural backgrounds and styles. One successful reading project for native Hawaiian children, for example, was designed around learning in small groups, in which children were given lots of responsibility and helped one another—three elements that meshed with the social organization of the Hawaiian culture (Cordes, 1984). Similarly, native American children have been observed to learn best in cooperative rather than competitive settings, which mesh with codes of sharing and cooperation in their cultural backgrounds. Something as simple as moving desks and chairs out of straight rows and into small clusters can foster cohesiveness and cooperativeness rather than competitiveness.

As the United States becomes increasingly culturally diverse, it will become increasingly important for researchers to study how children in different cultural groups learn best in school and to find modifications of mainstream teaching methods and curricula that best meet the children's needs and mesh with their learning styles most effectively.

Open and structured classes, open and closed classrooms

One possible modification of traditional teaching methods is to reduce the structure in elementary school classes and classrooms.

Tim's in a mixed grade class for first, second, and third graders. The room has lots of activity centers where kids can do different kinds of things like reading, or science projects, or computers, or writing. The classes also do things in large groups. Recently, they all worked on building a model town from the early 1900s. Tim apparently went off to a table and worked by himself all day. When he came back, he had made telephone poles for the whole town. He's really thriving in the open setting. Willy isn't old enough yet, but he's very distractible, very active, and kind of immature. I think he needs a structured environment. Otherwise, he's going to fool around and be the class troublemaker. We're going to have to find a class with walls and desks for Willy.

In the last two decades, many school classrooms have become more open in their physical arrangements—open rooms, movable furniture, room dividers, and activity stations instead of traditional rows of desks. Many school classes have become more open in their routines and curricula—students work at their own pace, on their own projects, instead of listening to the teacher lecture.

Do **open classrooms** help or hinder children's learning? In one study, researchers compared third graders in open and self-contained **closed class-rooms** on tests of vocabulary, reading comprehension, mathematical concepts, and problem solving (Lukasevich and Gray, 1978). The students had been in either open or closed classrooms for three years. Children in the closed classrooms did better on tests of mathematical concepts. Several investigators have reported problems with open classrooms, including noisiness, over-stimulation, and lack of privacy. In some open classrooms, students tend to cluster around the teacher, and this tendency may contribute to students and teachers feeling crowded (Rivlin and Rothenberg, 1976). One experimental study in which children were randomly assigned to crowded or open environments showed that students in crowded spaces felt more tense, annoyed, uncomfortable, and competitive (Aiello, Nicosia, and Thompson, 1979). When classrooms have open spaces around their edges and when ceilings are high, teachers say they feel less crowded (Ahrentzen, 1981). Yet even these classrooms may be so noisy that teachers can be heard no more than 7 feet away. This noisiness is unlikely to benefit children. Children in noisy elementary schools, in the flight paths of the Los Angeles Airport, where planes flew overhead every few minutes, for instance, were found to do more poorly on tests of cognitive ability than children attending quieter schools (Cohen, Evans, Krantz, and Stokols, 1980). Their blood pressure was higher, they were more easily distracted, they felt more helpless, and they were more likely to give up trying to solve a problem before time was up. Living in a quiet home seemed to make no difference in the performance of the children from noisy

Elementary schools and classrooms may be "open" or "closed." Each arrangement has its pros and cons.

schools, and even when noise at school diminished, the children did not score much better than before. Various studies show that the effects of noise on performance are usually cumulative and long lasting (Cohen and Weinstein, 1982).

Because there are few barriers to sight or sound in open classrooms, distraction poses another problem for some students. Teachers must tailor class activities to avoid distracting students who are working on other activities: no movies, slide shows, musical instruments, outside speakers, or cooking demonstrations unless everyone can participate. It takes time for new activities to be set up in open classrooms, interruptions are frequent, and children may spend lots of time looking around doing nothing. Some students, of course, would thrive in any classroom, and some students thrive on the way that open classrooms invite them to respond actively—to move around, to manipulate things, to communicate actively (Gump, in press). But open classrooms are worse for distractible, immature, and disadvantaged students than traditional classrooms are.

In the **open class**, scheduling is flexible, and a changing buffet of materials is available for children to explore and manipulate, at their own pace. Class visitors are likely to see children, often of different ages, scattered around the room and working either individually or in small groups. Older children may help to teach the younger ones, and the teacher studies with the children, discussing subject matter rather than lecturing. The friendly atmosphere and the wealth of educational materials are meant to make learning exciting. Children are more likely to be judged by what they make and by their individual progress than by group tests. In a **structured class**, children spend most of their time on lessons, usually on the three R's. The teacher gives facts and keeps order; subject matter and tests are taken from a curriculum drawn up for the class as a whole. Promotion depends on the children's grades.

What difference does it make if children are in open or structured classes? In a comparison of 100 6-year-olds whose first-grade classes differed in the openness of their curricula, no significant differences in the children's year-end achievement were found to be related to the openness of the class (Day and Brice, 1977). In studies of children who have been in structured or open classes for a longer time, however, more direct, structured teaching is associated with greater student learning and achievement in math and reading (Brophy and Evertson, 1974; Lukasevich and Gray, 1978). In a major study of 871 primary schools in England (Bennett, 1976), researchers found that the more structured style was superior for teaching math, reading, and English, especially to anxious children who need to know what is expected of them. Children in open classes accomplished less academic work than children in more structured classes, but their creative activity was more advanced. Even for creative work, though, a happy medium of moderate structure seemed the most beneficial in this and other studies (Soar and Soar, 1976). An upper limit to the amount of freedom allowed children is apparently better for all kinds of achievement and development. Leaving students entirely on their own is likely to hinder their creativity as well as their academic achievement.

Time in school

Open class or structured, open classroom or closed, high teacher expectations or low, English speaking or Spanish, the more time that children spend on their schoolwork—studying, reading, concentrating, and being taught—the more they learn and the further they progress in school. It seems almost *too* obvious, but the fact remains: the more they work, the more they learn.

Japanese students, for example, spend more time on schoolwork than American students do, and their achievement scores are dramatically higher. Harold Stevenson (1983; Stevenson, Lee, and Stigler, 1986) studied the reading and mathematical abilities of 1440 first and fifth graders in Minneapolis, Minnesota, Taipei, Taiwan, and Sendai, Japan. He found that although the American children were included among the very best and the very worst readers, disproportionately more of them did poorly. Results of the mathematics test were even less favorable for American children. Among the 100 students from the three cities who received the lowest scores in each grade, there were 58 American first-grade children and 67 fifth-grade children. (By chance, there should have been 33 in each grade.) Among the 100 top first-graders in mathematics, there were only 15 American children. Only one American child appeared among the top 100 fifth graders. In not one of the 20 American fifth-grade classrooms was the average score on the mathematics test equivalent to that of children in the worst performing Japanese classroom.

Testing of children's cognitive abilities and interviews with their mothers and teachers helped explain why American children did so poorly. The reason apparently was not the children's level of intelligence—they did just as well on intelligence tests—not the parents' educational status, and not the level of training of the children's teachers. But compared to the Chinese and Japanese children, the American children spent 1000 fewer hours every year in school, received less instruction in mathematics, and spent more class time engaged in inappropriate activities like talking to friends or staring into space. American children also did less homework and spent more time playing, sleeping, and doing household chores.

Research on how well first graders can read points to the importance of the same principle. The longer the school day and the more reading material children cover in class, the better they can read (Barr and Dreeben, 1983). No other condition of instruction seems to affect so strongly how much students learn—not the size of the learning group, the difficulty of the material, the time teachers spend supervising, or the like. More hours of reading are of special benefit to children with low aptitudes for reading.

Learning from computers

A revolution is sweeping this country. By the end of this century, most children will be educated by computers (Kleiman, 1984). A computer that 30 years ago cost $10,000,000 and filled a room today costs less than $1000 and fits in a briefcase. If the automobile industry had made the same strides in price and efficiency as the computer industry has done, we could all buy a Rolls-Royce for $2.75, and it would get 3,000,000 miles to the gallon (Lepper, 1985). As computers continue to grow more affordable, more versatile, and more powerful, parents and educators will use them more to teach children many of the skills once taught only in books, lectures, and written drills.

Children are drawn to computers. Computers respond instantly, a boon to impatient children. They are also impersonal and objective. Computers do not blame children for making mistakes. Said one 7-year-old, "The computer doesn't yell" (Greenfield, 1984. p. 131). Computers do not play favorites. Children appreciate qualities like these. One of the biggest contributions that computers may make to education is simply keeping students in class and learning. In one Los Angeles school in the middle of the barrio, in which the overall absentee rate is 20 percent, the absentee rate for computer classes is 5 percent (Greenfield, 1984).

Computers have the potential for being powerful teachers—and for creating powerful problems as well. They may deepen children's understanding and powers of reasoning and introduce them to facts and situations as no

focus Good schools

According to a survey of London schools, here are the things that characterize good schools, schools where children learn most (Rutter, Maughan, Mortimore, and Ouston, 1979).

- *More time on task.* In good schools, children spend the school day on academic subjects, have assigned homework, are encouraged to take challenging courses, and do not spend their time on busywork, play hooky, or drop out of school.
- *Emphasis on core skills.* In good schools, students are taught the basics—English, math, natural and social science, and foreign language—rigorously.
- *Good teachers.* In good schools, teachers stress learning and achieving academic goals. They teach actively, focus on tasks, make sure students do their homework, and care about the subject they are teaching. They expect a lot from their students and help them to meet their high expectations. They begin and end their classes on time. They give students clear, honest, prompt feedback about their work and about what they are expected to achieve. They praise students' achievements, rather than punishing or humiliating students for failures.
- *Prompt discipline.* In good schools, rules are stated clearly, and infractions are dealt with immediately, privately, briefly, and on the spot.
- *High standards and frequent tests.* In good schools, standards are high, exams are tough, tests are challenging, and assignments are substantial.
- *Small class size.* In good schools, no class is larger than 35 students, and smaller classes are used for teaching young children reading and arithmetic, for teaching handicapped and seriously learning disabled children, and for tutoring.
- *Adequate buildings and equipment.* In good schools, buildings are clean, equipment is in working order, there are pleasant decorations, the furniture is in good repair, and educational resources, books, and materials are available.

Children like to learn from computers because computers respond instantly, play no favorites, and strengthen powers of reasoning. As one child said, "A computer doesn't yell."

other learning tools can do—or they may make children passive, reward superficiality and easy answers. Whether computers work for good or for ill rests in how *people* manage them. Computers are touted as being "fun" tools for learning, but how do they affect children's interest in learning? One set of computer games, for instance, gives children the chance to run a bicycle store, manage a lemonade stand, or rule a small kingdom. The objective is to give the children practice in arithmetic and to expose them to simple economic principles such as the law of supply and demand, the value of advertising, profit and loss, and the like. Games like these have advantages, to be sure. They help children to grasp concrete, action-oriented concepts about how economic variables operate. They may lay a foundation which later will help children to understand the concepts at a more abstract level. But the games allow children to earn endless wealth—without thinking or solving problems. Students who figure out just one simple way to earn can mindlessly repeat it as long as their fingers can punch the buttons (Greenfield, 1984). Computers, it seems, are no different from any other learning tool. Designed well, they can inspire children to learn. Designed poorly, they can rob children of the motivation to learn. When the material to be learned relates naturally and not arbitrarily to its context, students are likely to be drawn in and to learn (see Figure 12.10).

Computers are also "interactive" in a way that books and films are not. Just as children like to pat the squirrels and lambs at the zoo more than they like watching caged animals from afar, they like the give and take of computers. Some people maintain therefore that computers offer children the chance to engage in "discovery-based" learning, which may be more valuable than more traditional, didactic instruction. Children can learn about food chains and ecological niches in the lakes of North America from books, teachers, and class discussion. They can also "discover" the same information by interacting with a computer screen that shows a rainbow trout faced with another fish and a set of decisions about whether to flee, chase, or stop for a meal. When children can experiment and explore, they learn actively, they reason inductively, and they discover principles and facts. Whether such discovery-based learning is more effective in the long run than traditional classroom learning remains an open question.

One area of schoolwork in which computers are definitely helpful is composition. With word-processing programs, children write at the computer keyboard. They type their stories, reports, poems, or dialogues, and the work appears on the screen in front of them. They can change and substitute words, move things around, erase, check their spelling right then and there, with no blots or eraser holes on the paper. When they are satisfied with what they have written, they print a copy. Tomorrow, if they want to make any new changes, all they have to do is call their original up on the screen and edit away. When children are eager to revise, their writing improves. One study of the writing skills of classes of third and fourth graders found that those who had been exposed to computerized word processing used 64 percent more words than they had before, and their adherence to topic and organization improved as well (Levin, Boruta, and Vasconcellos, 1983).

Programming the computer offers children other kinds of learning, too. To program, children must learn to plan, to reason logically, to form models, to break problems into smaller, workable chunks, to use flowcharts, and to "debug" or isolate and correct conceptual errors (Lepper, 1985). They must learn the relation between cause and effect, concentrate, and focus their attention. In a study in which 6-year-old children were randomly assigned to a computer programming class for three months and then tested, the children proved to be more reflective and creative, to know more about thinking, and

COMPUTER GAMES

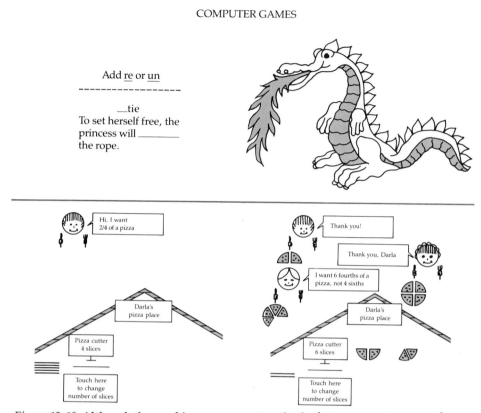

Figure 12.10 *Although the graphics are more attractive in the top computer game, they are not inherently connected to the content. In the bottom game, they are. It might be expected, from what is known about how children learn, that the bottom game would be a better teaching tool.*

to give better directions than children in a control group (Clements and Gullo, 1984).

The power of computers for teaching children school skills and logical ways of thinking, for motivating them to learn and achieve, has just begun to be tapped by researchers and educators. More efforts to study and exploit these modern machines will undoubtedly be made in the future, as the computer revolution continues.

Summary

1. During middle childhood, children begin to grasp the logical relations among things, the orderly rules and constant properties that govern how things happen. Their logical reasoning is concrete—because they can reason only about concrete things—and operational because they can operate mentally on the things in an organized, integrated, and systematic way.

2. With these new abilities children come to understand the conservation of matter: that even though objects' outward appearances may change, their length, quantity, mass, area, weight, and volume do not necessarily change. Children learn to arrange objects in a series and to make transitive inferences. They learn the direct relations between speed and distance and distance and time and then the indirect relation between speed and time.

3. According to Piaget, children between 5 and 10 years old have an external morality, in which rules are seen as inviolable instructions from figures of authority. They do not understand that people may agree to discuss and remake rules. In Kohlberg's stages of moral reasoning, children are first concerned with getting rewards and avoiding punishment. Next they are concerned with making fair deals and trades. At the level of conventional moral reasoning, children think that moral behavior means following social rules and conventions.

4. School-age children remember more than younger children in part because they can use deliberate strategies for remembering, such as imagery, rehearsal, and organizing information into systematic categories, and in part because their broader knowledge of the world gives them organizing frameworks. Short-term memory capacity also increases somewhat with age. School-age children understand their own memory processes better than younger children do, but it is not clear that this understanding helps them to remember.

5. Learning to read requires several skills: attacking and mastering a visual code for spoken sounds; attending to and figuring out the written words on a page; and understanding what words and letters actually are. Poor readers are not as skillful as good readers at encoding words into short-term memory.

6. Individual children develop at different rates and to different levels, and this is reflected in their performance on IQ tests. Children's IQ scores are affected by the cultural content of the test itself and the testing situation as well as by their cognitive competence.

7. Mental retardation ranges from mild to profound. Profound clinical retardation is caused by chromosomal, genetic, and prenatal conditions and by severe malnutrition in infancy and childhood. Sociocultural retardation, which is usually mild, is caused by educational, economic, and social deprivation.

8. Children differ in their cognitive styles of perceiving and responding to the environment, some being reflective and others impulsive, some field-dependent and others field-independent.

9. Girls consistently average higher scores than boys on tests of verbal abilities, and boys, higher scores on tests of spatial abilities. Biological, social, and psychological factors contribute to these observed differences in intellectual abilities.

10. The openness of classes and classrooms, teachers' expectations of students' academic performance, and the amount of time children actually spend on schoolwork all affect how well and how much children learn.

11. Computers have the potential for being powerful teachers and motivators. They are especially valuable in teaching children how to write compositions and how to think logically and systematically as they write computer programs.

Key terms

concrete operational thought
decenter
external morality
internal morality
preconventional moral reasoning

conventional moral reasoning
rehearsal
metamemory
short-term memory
sight–word method
phonic method

psychometrics
intelligence quotient (IQ)
standard deviation
convergent thinking
divergent thinking
cognitive style
reflective

impulsive
field independence
field dependence
open classroom
closed classroom
open class
structured class

Suggested readings

BARTH, ROLAND. *Open Education and the American School*. New York: Agathon Press, 1972. One of many books explaining and criticizing open education. This one was written by an elementary school principal who instituted open instruction in his school.

BRODY, ERNESS BRIGHT, and BRODY, NATHAN (Eds.). *Intelligence: Nature, Determinants, and Consequences*. New York: Academic Press, 1976. Excellent historical background on intelligence testing from the earliest IQ tests to the present, plus a balanced presentation of both sides of the Jensen controversy.

BRYANT, PETER, and BRADLEY, LYNETTE. *Children's Reading Problems*. Oxford: Basil Blackwell, 1985. An intriguing account of why some children have difficulty learning to read and what can be done about it.

DAMON, WILLIAM. (Ed.). *Moral Development*. San Francisco: Jossey-Bass, 1978. A collection of provocative essays on how the culture transmits its standards and values to the young child.

EDGERTON, ROBERT B. *Mental Retardation*. Cambridge, Mass.: Harvard University Press, 1979. An accurate and readable book about the forms, causes, prevention, and treatment of mental retardation, which emphasizes the crucial role of the family in helping a child learn and points out what schools can and cannot be expected to do.

GARDNER, HOWARD. *Frames of Mind*. New York: Basic Books, 1983. A new view of human intelligence in which IQ, or verbal intelligence, is just one of several "intelligences."

GETZELS, JACOB, and CSIKSZENTMIHALYI, MIHALYI. *The Creative Vision: a Longitudinal Study of Problem Finding in Art*. New York: Wiley, 1976. An examination of the personalities, values, and special aptitudes of a group of young artists. They are followed for several years after graduation to determine how the ability to find problems is related to the creative process.

ROSENTHAL, ROBERT, and JACOBSON, LENORE. *Pygmalion in the Classroom: Teacher Expectation and Pupils' Intellectual Development*. New York: Holt, Rinehart and Winston, 1968. The original research that alerted the educational community to the possible effects of teachers' positive and negative expectations about their students' achievement.

chapter thirteen

Social and emotional development

The world of the school-age child is peopled with family members, teachers and classmates, and "the other kids." Although children are still deeply involved in family life in middle childhood, they are independent enough to ride the school bus and play in their neighborhood. After school, they travel on foot or bicycle to local parks, movies, libraries, playing fields, YMCAs and YWCAs, Boys' and Girls' Clubs and Scout troops. Girls may babysit, paint, draw, and do their homework. Boys may make and fix things, skateboard, play team sports, and do their homework. Through all these activities, children's social skills develop. In this chapter, we will discuss changes in children's relationships with parents and peers and improvements in their abilities to cooperate and compete, play and teach, understand rules and other people, as these unfold over the course of middle childhood.

Family relationships

Finding a balance

> Robbie may be independent now and sleep at Sam's house for overnights, ride his bike all over the neighborhood, and be out of the house from 8:00 in the morning till 5:30 in the afternoon, but he still needs to be cuddled and kissed at bedtime. And he still needs a spanking when he's bratty.

When over 2000 school-age children were asked about themselves, their parents, friends, school, and neighbors, 90 percent of them said that they liked their families (Foundation for Child Development, 1976). But 80 percent expressed some worry about their families as well. Many children worried, they said, when they heard their parents argue. Many got angry "when no one pays attention to you at home." Children's feelings and thoughts in middle childhood are still focused largely on their families. Their parents are of central importance, and whether the family is happy or not profoundly influences how children feel about the world and their place within it. True, children of 8 or 10 may be more guarded with their parents than they were as chatty preschoolers who bubbled forth with all the news of the day. Older children may whisper secrets to their friends—"Promise you won't tell anyone *ever*?"—and hide some of their feelings behind an impassive face. But children in middle childhood feel deeply about their families.

> My mamma is the best. I'd like to tell her that, but I never can! All the trying comes to nothing, and then I do something that makes her sad and she knows it. I lie in bed at night and think about it. Suddenly the door opens and my mommy comes in to see if I'm asleep. I quickly close my eyes. She gives me a kiss and then I think that maybe she knows anyway how much I love her (Suzanne, age 6, in Lepman, 1971, p. 6).

At this age, children know that their parents have more and different privileges than they. They may resent the inequity.

> Mothers nibble before meals and tell you not to. That's what a mother is (Mary Claire, age 7, in Lepman, 1971, p. 6).

> A mother doesn't do anything except she wants to. Nobody makes her take baths and naps or takes away her frog (Gary, age 6, in Lepman, 1971, p. 9).

But children also, despite their passing reticence and resentment, love and appreciate their parents, and worry about them. They are more capable of seeing their parents' points of view and care for them with a new tenderness.

Mommy, I see you
With your blue apron
And your pale face
Mommy, I see you,
I always see you.
When you have a minute,
You sit by the fire,
Mending our clothes.
Mommy, I see you
Cooking the steaming soup
For all of us.
Poor Mommy, you work
To help your children.
Mommy, I see you
When you're very tired
You close your blue eyes
(Claude, age 8, in Lepman, 1971, p. 9).

Family rules are important throughout the course of children's development. In the survey of 2000 children, nearly all said that their families imposed rules. Only 3 percent were allowed to swear or curse; only 6 percent had no set bedtime; only 25 percent could snack when and on whatever they wished. But parents adapt rules to their children's changing behavior and needs. The simple, absolute "no crossing the street alone" kind of rule for young children does not work with older children, who have become more independent and who have entered into social relationships with classmates, teammates, teachers, friends, and neighbors. With preschoolers, the basic issues for parents were establishing routines, teaching children to care for themselves, and controlling temper tantrums and sibling fights. But in middle childhood, new issues arise: Which chores should children do? How should parents supervise children's social lives? Should parents help with homework? What should parents do if children have trouble in school (Newson and Newson, 1976)? Ideally, family rules in middle childhood, as earlier, take a middle course between permissiveness and restrictiveness.

School-age children need less monitoring than younger children do, of course, and involved parents have to be sensitive to the changing needs of their growing children. When parents and children trust one another, they constantly telegraph their needs, and the more controlling relationship between involved parents and immature children is gradually reshaped during middle childhood into the less controlling relationship between involved parents and their trustworthy, trusting, mature children. Parents turn over to their children many daily decisions. There is a shift from parents' regulation of the child's activities to *coregulation* by both parent and child. But some rules are still necessary—and children know this. Even when they do not like particular rules and restrictions, children know that some limits are necessary. They think that parents should step in when their children misbehave—for example, when a child hurts a puppy, refuses to return a toy, or acts rude to the grandmother (Appel, 1977; Siegal and Rablin, 1982). When family rules are too restrictive, though, children may have a hard time achieving independence (Trautner, 1972).

Rules are just one path by which parents influence their children. The emotional quality of parents' interaction with their children also continues to be related to children's behavior—with the parents and with other people. When parents are warm and loving, their children tend to be friendly and sociable, too; when parents are cold or hostile, their children are likely to act sulky, withdrawn, or hostile (Armentrout, 1972; Rohner, 1975; Schaefer and

Bayley, 1963). Parents who are loving but set no limits, however, may well turn out children who lack a moral conscience and who are dependent and selfish. As with younger children, parents need to balance love and limits. Research on school-age children (as on preschoolers) supports the value of an authoritative disciplinary style rather than an extremely permissive or excessively authoritarian style (Baumrind, 1985). Authoritative parents accept and support their children's expressions of feeling and opinion but also encourage their autonomy. They care deeply about their children, as their children do about them, and they continue to be involved in their children's lives, as they were in early childhood.

Children with working mothers

One challenge to parents' continued involvement in their children's lives is mothers' full-time employment. Mothers of school-age children who work outside the home now outnumber those who stay at home.

> I went back to work full time when Mikey was 8 years old. Even though I adored what I was doing, and even though we had a good after-school babysitter, I still felt unbelievably guilty. I'd worry that if only I stayed home with him he'd be doing better in school, or be on the debating team, or he wouldn't have caught a cold.

> I worked before Sam was born and went back to work when he was five days old. He's always understood that Mommy has her work, Daddy has his work, and he has his work. First his "work" was staying with his babysitter. Then it was going to nursery school, then grade school. Believe me, I've looked for evidence that my working has scarred Sam in some way, but he seems perfectly fine.

Today the majority of school-age children have mothers who work at jobs outside the home.

Not all children let their mothers go easily off to work, but knowing that their mothers like to work, knowing that most mothers do work, and knowing that they have somewhere to go after school seems to help children cope with the situation (Etaugh, 1974; Hoffman, 1979). School-age children can understand why their mothers want and need to work better than they could when they were younger, and they can feel both pride and worry on the mother's behalf. Some children worry that their mothers have too much to do, and they long for the times—usually on weekends—when they can have some undivided attention.

> My Mom drops me off at school on her way to work every morning at 8:00. After school I go home on the bus and do my homework or watch TV. Mom gets home at 6:00 on nights when she doesn't have a meeting or some dinner to go to. Then she gets home much later. Dad gets home at 7:00 if the train's on time. We have supper together, and I have to go to bed at 8:00. But we spend Saturday mornings "mousing around," just me and Mom doing errands or hanging around the house while Dad sleeps late.—Sarah, age 10

When their mothers work, schoolchildren are more likely to take responsibility for themselves and for doing things around the house. They are also more likely to value women and their abilities. Daughters of working mothers are likely to have higher academic and career goals than other girls (Hoffman, 1979, 1984). When mothers are pleased with their lives—whether they work outside the home or not—their contentment is reflected in their children's contentment and stable adjustment.

Most working mothers feel competent and accomplished, feelings that they radiate to their children, who feel, in turn, pleased and proud of themselves. But things are not always so rosy. In communities where few mothers work, schools are unlikely to cater to the needs of working mothers for supervised before- and after-school activities for their children. As a result, mothers may feel stressed, burdened, and guilty, and their children may sense this. Even in communities where many mothers do work, there may be negative effects on their children's schoolwork (Hoffman, 1984). Although daughters of working mothers generally have been found to be more independent, outgoing, socially and personally adjusted, and to do better in school than daughters of housewives, sons of working mothers often do less well in school and score lower on intelligence tests. Only among boys from poor families do sons of working mothers tend to do better in school. In these families, however, the relationship between father and son may be strained.

One researcher in this area, Lois Hoffman (1979, 1984), suggests that the reason that daughters of working mothers do better than the daughters of nonworking mothers is that they have a female model of social competence and high status and they get more training in independence within their family than daughters of nonworking mothers. Both these factors are likely to benefit girls' development. But the story is different for boys. For the sons of working mothers, a mother's work may carry negative connotations: it can mean that the father has failed to provide financially for the family, or that the mother has failed to conform to the traditional feminine role. It may mean that when mothers work, they do not so intensely socialize their sons to do well in school as stay-at-home mothers do. It may also be that a mother's work creates more stress in families, and boys, being particularly vulnerable to all kinds of environmental stresses, react negatively. The effect of a mother's working is especially damaging to sons if the work itself is stressful. Sons, then, are likely to feel that their mothers are uninvolved or unsupportive to them, and they feel depressed and inadequate (Piotrkowski and Stark, 1985).

It should be remembered that these reported effects of mothers' working on children's development are based on statistical averages from somewhat dated research. A mother's working does not necessarily mean that a son will do poorly in school. It does mean that when a mother works, or when family circumstances make it necessary for a mother to work, there is a somewhat higher risk of this happening, and so special efforts to compensate may be necessary.

Single-parent families

> My mom and dad split up when I was 7 and my sister, Kristy, was 9. It was hard on Mom for a while to take care of us and do her work and everything. We went to a therapist for about a year. One good thing about the divorce is that I get to see my dad more than before. Now he spends every other weekend with us. Before, he was always working.

> I lived with my mother after my parents split up. She cried all the time and never went out except to go to work. We stayed in our old house, so I went to the same school and everything. I visited my dad and his new girlfriend on weekends and vacations. When they moved to New York, I wanted to live with them. I was scared to tell my mother that, but finally I did. I told her it was important for a son to be near his father. So now I live with them in New York and visit my mom on vacations.

Divorce is an unwelcome visitor to school-age children as it is to younger children. It is stressful and painful, and it takes time for children to pick up the pieces and get over the fear, guilt, depression, and loneliness a divorce brings in its wake. It is unusual for children to see divorce as a positive thing for them, even if they realize that it may be best for their parents. Interviews with school-age children whose parents are divorced show that divorce may undermine the children's developing sense of industry and competence (Wallerstein and Kelly, 1980). It may make them turn inward and narrow their intellectual and social horizons, so that it becomes more difficult for them to understand other people's perspectives and get along with others their age. In coping with divorce, school-age children have the advantages of knowing their own feelings and expressing their sense of loss more clearly than younger children can. But they are still afraid of being abandoned—"If my parents can break with each other, what's to prevent them from breaking with me?"—and they express anger that their parents did not stick together. They claim that they feel protective and loyal to their families, but they are also ashamed.

Over the long run, the psychological damage that children sustain as the result of their parents' divorce apparently can be moderated by the parents' actions. When both parents conduct the divorce peaceably and both stay in close touch with their children after the breakup, rather than one parent withdrawing or both parents continuing to battle, the children are less likely to feel stressed, to behave aggressively, to fail in school, or to get along poorly with others (Wallerstein and Kelly, 1980). Other factors also can mediate the effect of the divorce: such as whether the child has another role model or substitute parent to relate to—a stepfather, an uncle, a coach, a friend—or an older brother (Drake and McDougall, 1977); whether the child stays in the same school, neighborhood, and house; whether the financial and social resources of the custodial parent are adequate; and whether the parent himself or herself is coping well with the divorce and single parenthood.

A society of children

As children move through middle childhood, they come increasingly to inhabit two different worlds, the inside world of family and home and the outside world of friends and school. Researchers have studied how children make the transition to the new world of school and peers.

Peer groups

When Ted went to first grade, he didn't have any problems, but *I* did. All of a sudden his friends were much more important to him. He started making his own plans, deciding which kids he wanted to see, hanging around with Robbie and Brandon. They were inseparable.

During middle childhood, groups, clans, and cliques of pals begin to take shape. By the end of middle childhood, children hang out in these groups to go to the movies, play games, go to the beach, or just talk. How do these groups form, and what keeps them together? A series of experiments with boys at a summer camp provides some answers (Sherif and Sherif, 1964; Sherif, Harvey, White, Hood, and Sherif, 1961). Two groups of twelve 11- and 12-year-old boys arrived at camp on separate buses and were kept apart by the camp leaders. The boys within each group were strangers to each other and spent the first few days getting to know each other. Together, group members camped and cooked, took boat trips, and worked on making a swimming hole and a playing field. In just a week, norms, leaders, and followers had emerged in each of the two groups. One group called themselves the Rattlers; the other, the Eagles. When the camp director then set up the two groups to compete against each other in contests and sports, the group members stuck together, competing vigorously against the other group. The rivalry between the groups intensified into scuffles and name calling. Finally, the groups would have nothing to do with each other. Going to movies together and eating together

Schoolgirls have "intensive" relationships with one or two close friends; boys hang out in "extensive" groups or gangs.

in the same dining hall only made matters worse; the boys had more chances to fight. Suddenly (as part of the experimenters' plan) problems at camp developed that threatened everyone's supplies of food and water. To solve the problems, members of the two groups had to cooperate. Gradually, hostility between the two groups diminished. Friendships began to form across group boundaries. One thing that makes children form cohesive groups thus is their desire to achieve a shared goal, whether that goal is beating the other team or beating a problem.

Children also form groups on the basis of sex. The sex segregation that started in the preschool years (see Chapter 10) becomes more marked during the school years (Figure 13.1). The character of girls' groups and boys' groups also differs (Pitcher and Schultz, 1984; Hartup, 1983; Waldrop and Halverson,

Figure 13.1 Children's segregation by sex increases over the years of middle childhood. These observations of over 400 children were made during the summer vacation in a middle-income neighborhood in Salt Lake City (Ellis, Rogoff, and Cromer, 1981).

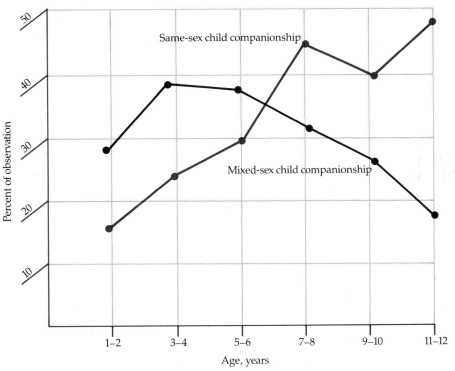

AGE AND SEX SEGREGATION

Same-sex child companionship

Mixed-sex child companionship

Percent of observation

Age, years

1975). Girls form smaller groups and play in smaller spaces than boys. In these groups, girls play at refining social rules and roles. They learn about personal relationships, subtle social cues, and unspoken rules of social contact. They practice noticing and responding to others' needs. Their interactions are intimate and **intensive** as they play with only one or two other girls, express intense feelings about them, and share experiences and fantasies. Boys form larger groups and play more physical games in larger spaces. Their games tend to be competitive and to contain explicit rules for achieving a stated goal. In these activities, boys learn about long-range goals, demand attention and give orders, engage in conflict, rowdiness, and rough play, and experience a feeling of group solidarity. Their peer relations, as they share sports and games with three or more other boys, are **extensive**.

During the elementary school years, boys' and girls' groups generally have nothing to do with one another. Boys' groups devalue girls, and their rough-and-tumble enactment of power relationships excludes girls from the central roles. If the girls find the boys' play exciting and attractive, the boys are likely to insult, humiliate, and reject them. ''Girls have cooties!'' Girls may try to enter boys' groups, but they are usually unsuccessful (Pitcher and Schultz, 1984). During the early school years, the gender-stereotyped roles picked up in the preschool years harden into habits.

Not all children's groups form on the basis of sex, however. The strong segregation of boys' and girls' groups that we see in the United States seems to arise to some extent from cultural demands. The most important factors in finding friends are likely to be compatibility, similarity, and shared goals. In our culture, with its age-segregated elementary school classes, sex is the most likely basis of similarity between children. But in one study, sex was superseded by age as a basis for segregation when children had the chance to form groups from a wider age range (Roopnarine and Johnson, 1984). ''I'm not gonna play with *her*. She's only in second grade.'' More research on children's groups—under naturalistic and under constrained conditions—would show how strong the same-sex ties are. In one study, after a year-long program of mixed-sex work groups in school, children had increased the frequency of cross-sex interactions outside the work groups, but they still *preferred* work and play partners of their own sex (Lockheed, in Maccoby, 1986).

Popularity

> Mikey is very popular with the other kids his age. He's always getting calls from kids who want him to come over and play and invitations to their birthday parties. When he was in first grade, the teachers said that he was so popular that the kids would try to pull him in several different directions at once, and sometimes he ended up doing things he didn't like very much.

> Nancy has one friend in her class who comes to our house to play and sometimes invites Nancy over there. But she really seems to prefer playing by herself, or reading, or just hanging around the house. Sometimes I worry that she isn't more popular.

What makes some children more popular with ''the other kids'' than others? For one thing, good-looking children are likely to be popular (Kleck, Richardson, and Ronald, 1974). Perhaps this is because children think that good looks go along with positive qualities. In one study, for example, when children were shown pictures of attractive and unattractive children, they all said that the attractive children were smarter, friendlier, more generous, more likable, and less mean than the unattractive children (Langlois and Stephan, 1977). In fact, physically attractive children do tend to be more socially

Popular children are likely to have good social skills, to be outgoing, confident, active, and friendly. They adapt to group norms, solve problems constructively, and know how to have fun.

competent (Vaughn and Langlois, 1983). Not just good looks, but a good name increases one's popularity. Researchers have found that children with unattractive names are less popular than those with attractive names (McDavid and Harari, 1966). "Hortense" and "Humbert" are unlikely to be as popular as "Jessica" and "John." Power also makes a difference in children's popularity. Children who are leaders in their own groups are more popular with other children in the class, and so are children who do well at their schoolwork. But being a top student, like being a near flunk-out, wins no popularity contests (Hallinan, 1981; Hartup, 1970).

Even more important in predicting popularity than these qualities are the skills that children bring to social interactions with their peers. When they are with others their age, some children withdraw, mumble, and act shy. Others are disruptive and aggressive. Others are confident and outgoing, active and friendly. They get along with anyone, always know just what to say and when to say it. These are the popular children.

> Sam cannot let pass a chance to greet and chat with a friend or neighbor. His face lights up when he sees someone he knows, and he instantly gives a big cheery "Hi!" Our next door neighbor's daughter, who is in Sam's grade at school, is just the opposite. She walks around glumly, her eyes on the ground, and she never calls out a hello. She doesn't seem to have many friends.

> Erica is one of the most popular kids in her class. I think it's because she's very bright, so she's interesting to talk to, and because she's sunny and outgoing. She really *likes* people, and that comes across and makes people like *her*.

Many studies have been done in the last few years to find out just what sets these children apart (Asher and Renshaw, 1981; Berndt, 1983; Coie and Kupersmidt, 1983; Dodge, 1983; Gottman, Gonso, and Rasmussen, 1975; Putallaz, 1983; Rubin and Daniels-Beirness, 1983; Sroufe, Schork, Motti, Lawroski, and LaFreniere, 1984). Popular children, the researchers have found, know how to act friendly to a newcomer—asking questions, giving information, and inviting the newcomer to visit. With their classmates, popular children are rarely aggressive. They make good suggestions, give praise, and play constructively and cooperatively. They understand and adapt to group norms, use prosocial strategies like taking turns and compromising rather than hitting or yelling for solving problems, act positively, and know how to have fun.

491

Rejected children, these studies show, are likely to be socially inept. They may act inappropriately (like standing on the table in the lunchroom), or they may be distractible, hyperactive, or aggressive. They may have trouble managing conflict. Asked, for example, how they would treat a child who took away their game, they are more likely to say that they would punch or beat him. They may disrupt other children's play, play uncooperatively, and not stick to a task with other children. They may talk a lot but not chat sociably, or they may be withdrawn, working and playing quietly by themselves.

But there is hope even for rejected children. A number of experiments have been designed to change the behavior of unpopular children so that they, too, might win the respect and friendship of their peers. Sherri Oden and Steven Asher (1977) coached socially isolated children in third and fourth grades about how to play with others, pay attention, cooperate, take turns, share, communicate, and give support and encouragement to their peers. Several days after the six coaching sessions had been completed, all third- and fourth-grade children were asked how they enjoyed playing with each of their classmates. The popularity rating for the coached children had increased significantly, and their improvement was still evident one year later. In another successful coaching program (Ladd, 1981), children were taught to use positive and supportive statements, to make useful suggestions to playmates, and also to evaluate their own behavior. Some children do not realize that what they do affects whether classmates like them. Recognizing the effect one has on others is an important step toward peer acceptance, and, possibly, popularity.

Yet another approach has been to pair socially isolated children with a younger playmate for free play (Furman, Rahe, and Hartup, 1979). After ten play sessions, the withdrawn children have been observed to be more sociable when they are back in their classrooms, presumably because they have had the chance to assert themselves and to play dominantly and successfully with the younger children. This is an important area of research and practice, yet it often is overlooked.

Friendship

Even though they win no popularity contests, most children have at least one friend. Friendships are important to children's development for a number of reasons (Hartup and Sancilio, in press). They offer opportunities to learn social skills like communication, cooperation, and self-control; they offer emotional and cognitive resources; they provide a context for developing intimacy; and they serve as precursors of later relationships. Throughout the elementary school years, friends become ever more important to children. Children's joy in learning and doing is heightened when their friends are present.

> Sarah has been my best friend since first grade. Whenever one of our families takes a day trip on the weekend—to an amusement park or the beach or a museum or somewhere like that—we always try to get the other one invited. My parents like Sarah, and her parents like me, so usually they say okay.—Erica, age 10

Interactions with friends are more emotionally expressive and vigorous in exploring materials than interactions with nonfriends (Newcomb and Brady, 1982). With a close or best friend, schoolchildren share, talk, do things together, and form strong bonds. If a close friend moves away, they may mourn. The one-sided quality of preschoolers' friendships, when a friend was ''someone who does what I want when I want it,'' changes into a more cooperative, sympathetic, mutual exchange in middle childhood. Friendships become two-way relationships (Selman, 1981). Friendships last longer in fourth grade than in first (Berndt and Hoyle, 1985). But although friends at this age can give and take somewhat, their friendships are still likely to crumble under the weight of serious conflict.

As children grow older, their understanding of friendship and their depth of feeling increase. Six- and 7-year-olds are likely to say that friendship consists of sharing objects and toys or having fun together (Furman and Bierman, 1984; Selman, 1981; Selman and Selman, 1979; Youniss and Volpe, 1978). Nine- and 10-year-olds say that friendship consists of sharing thoughts and feelings. They understand that friendship is different from mere proximity and that friends feel affection and respect for each other. Friends, they know, can relieve loneliness and unhappiness. When a friend chooses someone else to go somewhere or to do something with, children of this age feel left out and rejected (Selman, 1981; Selman and Selman, 1979). They expect friends to share more and argue less than "kids who simply go to the same school but don't know each other well." But when asked, "How do you know someone is your best friend?" only 2 percent of them mention trust and intimacy as qualities of friendship (Berndt, 1978a).

Eleven- and 12-year-olds think that important qualities in friendship are sharing problems, emotional support, trust, and loyalty (Berndt, 1978a; Selman, 1981). "I tell her everything that happens to me," "I can tell him secrets, and he won't tell anyone else," they say. Friends of this age feel committed to each other; they are loyal to the point of possessiveness. Said one 12-year-old,

> Trust is everything in a friendship. You tell each other things that you don't tell anyone else, how you really feel about personal things. It takes a long time to make a close friend, so you really feel bad if you find out that he is trying to make other close friends, too (Selman and Selman, 1979, p. 74).

Friends at this age have the cognitive capacity to see things from their own *and* a friend's point of view, and they can also appreciate the inherent pleasure and value of friendship. They know their friend's personal characteristics and preferences, what their friend worries about and likes to play (Diaz and Berndt, 1982).

As we have seen already, in middle childhood, boys and girls play in different ways with their friends. They also talk about their friends in different ways. Girls are likely to dwell on how their friends look and on their personalities:

> "I like Hazel because she is a nice girl who always wears a school uniform if possible. She takes great care how she is dressed."

> "My best friend is Vera. She always dresses nicely and walks with her shoulders back. Sometimes she wears brown slip-on shoes, a green cardigan, and a dress. She wears white ankle socks" (Opie and Opie, in Pitcher and Schultz, 1984, p. 126).

But boys talk less about their friends' looks. A friend is a boy who likes playing the same games as you do, who always plays with you on the playground, who calls for you to walk with to school in the morning and walks home with you in the afternoon, who belongs to your "gang," and whom you call your "pal," "partner," or "buddy."

> My best friend is John Corbett, and the reason I like him is that he is so nice to me and we both draw space ships, and what's more he plays with me nearly every time in the playground. Another thing about John is

that he is sensible and nice. Whenever we are playing rocket ships he never starts laughing when we get to an awkward point (Opie and Opie, in Pitcher and Schultz, 1984, p. 127).

Activities with age-mates

What do children do together with their friends? In school, they work together, collaborate on projects, tutor, help, teach one another, and compete as well. Out of school, they also work together, play games and sports, form clubs, go exploring, sit and talk, and share toys, arguments, and fantasies.

Playing games and sports

The play of children in the early years of elementary school often involves sports and games.

> At recess every day in third grade a group of six girls would play "Doggy and Master," in which one partner was the doggy who pranced around and took orders and the other held a leash made of rope and barked the orders.

> When he was 9, Tim played Little League baseball and went to soccer camp for two weeks in the summer. We had taken down the swing set in the backyard, because the kids were too old for it. Tim and his friends liked to play volleyball and softball in our yard or race their bikes around the neighborhood.

With their improved motor skills and their burst of interest in other children, children find games lots of fun. Some games are spontaneous and informal, some elaborate and formal; some require teams, some a partner. Some are ancient, some brand new. Schoolchildren play tag, king of the mountain, Simon says, hopscotch, jump rope, jacks, ring-a-lievo, hide-and-seek, and many other games. Over the last 60 years, children's games have become less formal and, because of increased supervision from adults, less rough (Sutton-Smith and Rosenberg, 1971). More significant, school-age girls now choose to play more active games and sports—more in the style of traditional boys' games and sports—than they did 60 years ago. Girls now swim and play marbles, play on softball and volleyball teams, bounce on trampolines and over sawhorses, and take part in active bouts of fox and hounds. They like to play games that have leaders—statues, Simon says, follow the leader—and still enjoy some traditional girls' games, too, like hopscotch, dress-up, and dolls. Boys meanwhile have taken up even more vigorous games like football, wrestling, soccer, and martial arts, and they enthusiastically play war-like fantasy games. Girls seldom join in these games (Medrich, Roizen, Rubin, and Buckley, 1982).

Games help children make the transition into the larger social world. Games offer practice in following rules, in cooperating and competing. Games offer children challenges to rise to and succeed at. Even kissing games serve a purpose, bridging the gap between boys and girls and setting the stage for the eroticism of adolescence.

Teaching

Although most of their teachers are adults, children can and do teach each other. Some children are trained to teach, and some do it spontaneously. Peer teaching generally has been thought to benefit both the tutor and the child tutored. But evidence for the actual benefits of peer teaching is inconsistent (Hartup, 1983). Tutors are most likely to increase in self-esteem, status, and positive feelings about school if they tutor for an extended period, if they are underachievers who are several years older than the children they teach, if they are carefully trained and supervised, and if they enjoy the tutoring. Children being taught are most likely to improve their knowledge of the subject matter, their reading ability, and their performance on standardized tests if they are tutored for an extended period (Cloward, 1976; Paoni, 1971; Willis, Morris, and Crowder, 1972).

In general, children like to tutor younger children and to be tutored by older children. They like tutors of their own sex, although the sex of the tutor is not related to the success of the tutoring. They are somewhat likelier to make advances in achievement with an older tutor, but tutors of their own age can also be helpful (Guarnaccia, 1983; Hamblin and Hamblin, 1982; Linton, 1972; Thomas, 1970). Children seem to adjust their teaching to meet the abilities of the children they are tutoring. Observations of 9- and 10-year-olds, for example, showed that when they tutored children four years younger than themselves, they did more in the way of focusing the youngster's attention, suggesting strategies for learning, giving redundant information, and praising, helping, and assessing the child's progress than they did when they tutored children only two years younger than they (Ludeke and Hartup, 1978).

Children generally like to teach those who are younger and to learn from those who are older than they. Child tutors like the one pictured here seem able to adjust their teaching to the abilities of their young tutees.

Despite the efforts, popularity, and sometimes effectiveness of child tutors, though, they are no substitute for adult teachers. In one recent study of how children compare to adults as teachers of other children, Shari Ellis and Barbara Rogoff (1982) observed 7-year-olds being taught by either a 9-year-old or an adult. In a room designed to look like a kitchen, the younger children were taught to put groceries on shelves and to sort photographs of common objects into compartments on a tray. Children who had been taught by an adult were better at remembering where to put the groceries and photographs than those who had been taught by an older child. Children taught by the adults correctly placed 68 percent of the items on which they were tested; children taught by older children placed only 45 percent correctly. Why were adult teachers more effective than child teachers? Although the adult and child teachers did not differ in the amounts of nonverbal information they provided—pointing, showing, and so on—adult teachers provided three times as much spoken information as child teachers. The adult teachers also provided more information about *categories* of objects rather than merely about specific objects, and they elicited more participation from the children they were teaching. The child teachers seemed to imitate their own school teachers, using teacherly strategies and language—''That's correct!'' ''Excellent, Katie!''—but without their teachers' effectiveness.

Helping and sharing, cooperating and competing

In the elementary school years, children find new possibilities for cooperation and generosity, for helping, sharing, and caring, for benefiting others. Yet some social values conflict with these prosocial actions. In our society the values of competition, individualism, acquiring property, and winning are also stressed, and these values may interfere with positive social actions.

Perhaps as a result, helping and showing concern in some situations decline toward the end of middle childhood (Staub, 1975). In one experiment, for example, sixth graders alone in a room when they heard a bookcase crash and a child cry for help from another room were less likely than younger

Competition, individualism, and the importance of winning are stressed in our culture and become increasingly salient over the elementary school years.

children to run to the rescue (Staub, 1975). Fourth graders did try to help when they heard these distressing sounds, if they were alone at the time, but not if they were with another child. They may have been inhibited by thinking about how their peers would judge them. (''It's not cool to show concern.'') They may have thought that it was not their responsibility to do anything. (''Why doesn't Sam help?'') By contrast, children in first and second grade were *more* likely to act helpful when they were with another child. For them, it's still a good thing to be helpful, and having another child there makes it easier.

At the same time that prosocial actions decline, competitiveness increases. In school and in play, children learn that it's good to be best. Winning is *fun*. Competitive games, from baseball to badminton, give them arenas in which to assert and confirm their developing sense of self, and getting good marks in school gives them status and approval. But competing is not always adaptive. Even under circumstances in which cooperation would benefit children more, researchers have found, elementary school children may compete. This has been demonstrated in studies using specially designed board games. In one such game, four children sit around a square, paper-covered board (see Figure 13.2). In each corner of the board is an eyelet threaded with a string. The strings are attached to a metal cylinder holding a pen in the center of the board. Each child holds a string and pulls it toward himself, trying to draw a line through the circle on the paper in front of him. But the children have to cooperate to draw the lines; any child can prevent the others from drawing lines through their circles by holding the string tight or pulling it toward himself. When the experimenter gives the instructions, ''When the pen draws a line across one of the circles, only the child whose name is in the circle gets a prize,'' the most effective strategy for getting rewards is for children to take turns letting one another win. Preschool children in the United States cooperate in this way—''Let's help each other. C'mon.'' But 7- to 9-year-old schoolchildren typically choose to compete, trying to get the pen through their circle first, even though it means no one gets a prize (Kagan and Madsen, 1971; Madsen, Kagan and Madsen, 1971). School-age children from cultures in which competition is not stressed as much as it is in this one (like Mexico or the kibbutzim in Israel) are not likely to act competitively.

To some extent, the competitiveness of children playing these board games is a result of the situation itself. When researchers have children do other things that are not so traditionally competitive—building something together, for instance—they find that school-age American children are not

496

THE COOPERATION BOARD

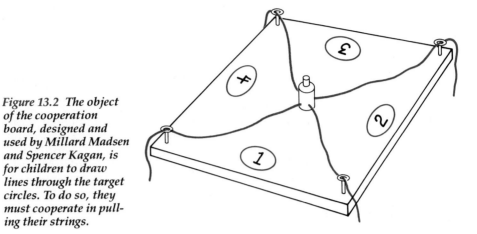

Figure 13.2 The object of the cooperation board, designed and used by Millard Madsen and Spencer Kagan, is for children to draw lines through the target circles. To do so, they must cooperate in pulling their strings.

more likely to compete than to cooperate (Ayman-Nolley, 1985; Brady, Newcomb, and Hartup, 1983). Even so, cultural pressures clearly influence American children to be competitive in many situations.

> A family of Russian emigrants whose son is in Natalie's class have told us that they feel uncomfortable with the stress American schools place on individual excellence at the expense of the group. They ask why it's so important that some kids be in the top reading group, or on the advanced soccer team, or in the accelerated math class. What does this all do to the children in the bottom reading group or the slow math class?

In American society, boys are especially likely to be rewarded for competing and are especially likely to pick up competitive attitudes. Girls are likely to be rewarded for cooperation, and they take a dimmer view of competition (Ahlgren, 1983; Mussen and Eisenberg-Berg, 1977; Stockdale, Galejs, and Wolins, 1983).

The pressure to compete does not, however, seem to destroy either girls' or boys' generosity. Through the school years, both boys and girls increase in generosity and become more likely to share their possessions like pencils, candy, or allowance with other children—at least when an adult demands it (Staub, 1975; Zarbatany, Hartmann, and Gelfand, 1985). More generous children are more self-confident, competent, and self-controlled, more empathic, expressive, active, outgoing, and assertive (Barrett and Radke-Yarrow, 1977; Mussen and Eisenberg-Berg, 1977). The *most* generous children are not always the *best* adjusted psychologically, however. In a study of fourth-grade boys given the opportunity to donate to other children the prizes they had earned, the most generous boys tended to be naive and prone to guilty feelings (Mussen and Eisenberg-Berg, 1977). They were willing to give away everything they had earned. The least generous boys were weak and lacked self-control and perseverence. The best adjusted boys were moderately—perhaps appropriately—generous. They could think of their own interests *and* other children's.

Like competition, though, children's generosity depends not only on these personal qualities but also on the immediate situation—how the child feels at the moment and what he thinks about the other person. Young schoolchildren, in first through fourth grades, researchers have found, are less likely to act generously when they are in bad moods than when they are in neutral or good moods. For example, children who thought that they had performed badly in a game gave less to charity than those who thought they had done well (Isen, Horn, and Rosenhan, 1973). Similarly, children who were asked to think about sad memories gave less to charity than children who were not asked to think sad thoughts (Cialdini and Kendrick, 1976; Moore, Underwood, and Rosenhan, 1973). By the end of middle childhood, however, children are like adults; out of empathy or guilty conscience, they are more inclined to be generous when their mood is negative (Barnett, Howard, Melton, and Dino, 1982; Cialdini and Rosenhan, 1973).

Video games provide a new source of influence on children's generosity. In a recent study (Ascione and Chambers, 1985), researchers had elementary school children play one of two commercial home video games: either an aggressive boxing match or a prosocial adventure in which players try to rescue a fantasy creature from danger. Then the researchers gave each child a dollar in change and told the children they could donate some or all of the money toward a fund for needy local children. Despite the fact that each session lasted only ten minutes, there were clear differences in donations depending on which game the children had played. Those who came to the fantasy character's rescue donated 41 cents, on average; those who punched it donated only an average of 28 cents each. The researchers speculate that the overtly aggressive and competitive nature of the boxing game fostered a self-centered attitude in the children who played it so that they became less inclined to help others when the time came to donate.

Lying and Cheating

> Erica had a rabbit's foot, for good luck I suppose, on top of her bureau when she was in first grade. Mikey really wanted that rabbit's foot. He'd stand around and gaze at it or pat it with his fingertips, and Erica would warn him away. I made it clear to him that it was Erica's and that he was not to touch it without her express permission. Well, one day the rabbit's foot was missing. Erica was frantic. Mikey swore up and down that he hadn't seen it. It turned out that he had taken it and then, afraid to put it back, had sold it to a kid at school for a quarter. Not only had Mikey disobeyed us; he stole, lied, and got rid of the incriminating evidence. We were afraid we were harboring a criminal in the making.

On occasion, almost all children cheat or lie. This is a source of concern to their parents—and it has been to psychologists, too. In a major study of children's dishonesty, done in the 1920s, the researchers tempted some 11,000 children between the ages of 8 and 16 to do something for their own gain that they would not want other people to know about—to copy answers on a test, to cheat on a party game or at a sport, or to lie about doing their chores (Burton, 1963; Hartshorne and May, 1928-1930). Without knowing that they were being observed, the children were tempted at home, at school, at church, on playgrounds, and in clubs. Nearly all the children cheated at least some of the time. But when there was risk of discovery or when cheating took some effort, they were more likely to be cautious—and honest. Resisting temptation depended less on conscience than on circumstance. In some school classes, many children cheated, and in others few did, a finding that the researchers chalked up to differing group pressures to conform. Some children were nearly always honest and some the opposite, but everyone's honesty varied as the circumstances changed (Burton, 1963).

Whether children give in to temptation depends to some extent on what they see other people doing. In one study, fourth-grade boys were asked to sit in a chair and perform a boring job while an exciting movie was shown just out of their sight (Stein, 1967). If they stayed in their chair, they were considered to have resisted temptation. Boys in one group saw a man get out of his chair and peek at the movie. Boys in another group saw a man resist temptation. Boys in the control group saw no model. The boys who saw the man peek at the movie gave in to temptation more readily than the boys in the other two groups. But the boys who saw the unyielding adult were no more resistant to temptation than the boys in the control group. The moral of the story? Honest behavior may not be catching, but dishonest behavior is, if children learn from watching someone else that they are not likely to get caught.

How, then, can one get children to be honest and upright? Simply modeling good behavior apparently is not enough, and neither is simply telling children that cheating is bad (Burton, 1976). Using scare tactics and punishment is not always the most effective strategy either.

> Natalie was half an hour late coming home from school one day in second grade. Why? The teacher discovered that a felt animal was missing from the feltboard, and she kept the entire class after school until she found the culprit. Natalie said that the teacher really scared them. First, the teacher made them sit at their desks, hands folded, and demanded to know who did it. When no one confessed, she made them all close their eyes and put their heads down on their desks. The culprit was supposed to return the animal to the feltboard, and none of the other kids would have to know who did it. That didn't work either. Then the teacher brought in the other second-grade teacher. She lectured them about stealing and lying and shamed them with, "I can't believe that any child in this beautiful new school would stoop so low as to take something that didn't belong to him." Eventually, one of the boys in the class pulled the felt duck out of his desk, and the kids got to go home. I just hope the teachers were as effective in scaring that boy as they were in scaring Natalie.

As we discussed in Chapter 10, punishment tends to be most effective when it follows the wrongdoing right away (Parke, 1977). But this condition gets harder to meet as children grow older and spend more and more time on their own. Parents and teachers are unlikely to find out that the child skipped school, or cheated, or lied until well after the fact, and by then punishment may have lost much of its deterrent effect. If adults can recreate the situation and reconnect the wrongdoing with the punishment, they may be more successful. In one study, children saw themselves misbehaving on a videotape and heard their misbehavior described, or they were told to misbehave again and then were punished (Andres and Walters, 1970). Later on, these children were less likely to misbehave than were children who were simply punished long after the misbehavior.

Sometimes attributing moral qualities to children helps them to resist temptation. In one study, a child was left alone to watch some equipment, while a distraction was staged nearby (Dienstbier, Hillman, Lehnhoff, Hillman, and Valkenaar, 1975). When the child looked away, the equipment was made to malfunction. With some children, the experimenter then returned and said, "You feel bad because I caught you." With others, the experimenter said, "You feel bad because you did something you knew was wrong." It was children from the second group who later resisted temptation more resolutely in later tests.

> One night when Sam was about 9 he was pretending to make trick shots with a cake platter that had been in the family for several generations and acted snippy when I asked him to be careful. The platter smashed on the kitchen floor. For a minute, I was just too angry to speak. Then, instead of snarling at him, I had the presence of mind to say, "I know you didn't mean to break that, Sam. You're too careful a person to have intended that." He really was more careful after that, too.

The issue of how to foster morality in children has been important for many psychologists. According to Freud, morality develops early in childhood out of fear and anxiety at the thought of losing a parent's love and from guilt over incestuous fantasies about the parent of the other sex (Freud, 1940). When the child has developed a sense of guilt, moral sanctions emanate from within. In psychoanalytic theory, the child's ability to identify with the parent is necessary for the formation of conscience. It is *the* essential relationship for fostering moral growth, one that cannot be replaced by other identifications with teachers, peers, or siblings. Taking the role of the parent leads the child to internalize parents' standards wholly and unquestioningly.

Empirical research does not support the contention that conscience is formed only through identification with parents, however. In studies comparing the moral development of kibbutz-reared and family-reared Israeli children (reviewed by Kohlberg, 1964), for example, no differences in the guilt felt by the two groups of children and in their morality have been found, even though kibbutz-reared children received their moral socialization primarily from caregivers and teachers in the Children's House where they lived. Nevertheless, identification with some adult authority and acceptance of that authority's standards probably are necessary for children to feel guilt and behave morally.

How likely children are to behave morally, as we suggested in Chapter 10, may be related to their parents' methods of discipline. When parents simply assert their power with physical punishment, by taking away the child's toys or privileges, by applying force, or by threatening any of these, their children are less likely to behave morally (Hoffman, 1970). They are more likely to cheat, less likely to feel guilt or to accept blame after a moral transgression. The most effective disciplinary method for advancing moral development is to create an atmosphere of warm approval and acceptance for the child, to explain why the child should act in particular ways, and to stress the effects of the child's behaviors.

Acting aggressively

Perhaps the worst thing that children do together is to hurt each other. Preschool children may hit or push other children, but their actions usually are for some instrumental purpose like getting back a toy. In the school years, children begin to direct aggression toward others just to hurt them (Hartup, 1974; Lefkowitz, Eron, Walder, and Huesmann, 1977).

> I'll never forget walking home from school on my eighth birthday, followed by a bunch of girls. As we passed my neighbor on the sidewalk, I taunted her, ''We're going to my birthday party, and you can't come.'' She got even with me later and stole all my Winnie the Pooh books.

> The sixth grader up the street is harassing Sam. Yesterday, when Sam told him he wouldn't carry his books home for him, he ground a baseball bat into Sam's toe with all his might.

This kind of hostile aggression increases steadily during middle childhood (Figure 13.3). Older children hit, punch, kick, make faces, and hurl insults and snide comments if another child gets in their way, takes their things, insults, criticizes, or tattles on them. They break into fights, disrupt class, and occasionally hurt animals or the teacher. Their aggressiveness tends to be expressed openly now, on the playground, in the classroom, on the street, where it is likely to meet with public attention and censure.

What makes schoolchildren act aggressively? Perhaps the most comprehensive attempt to answer this question is a longitudinal study of aggression carried out in New York State's semirural Columbia County (Eron,

Children are likely to respond with aggression to incursions into their space, possessions, or movements. Older children are likelier than younger ones to react aggressively to people who insult, criticize, or tattle on them.

AGE AND AGGRESSION

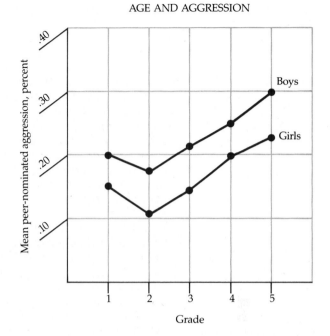

Figure 13.3 Aggressiveness increases for both boys and girls during middle childhood (Eron et al., 1983).

Walder, and Lefkowitz, 1971; Huesmann, Eron, Lefkowitz, and Walder, 1984; Lefkowitz, Eron, Walder, and Huesmann, 1977). After testing all the third graders in the county and interviewing many of their parents, the researchers chose a smaller sample of boys and girls for intensive study. They followed these children from then until they were 30 years old. From their observations, they found that certain qualities of children's experiences at home, and particularly their parents' behavior, were associated with aggressiveness in the children. If parents were rejecting, unloving, and in conflict with each other, their children tended to be aggressive. If parents punished their children for aggression but did not reward them for cooperation or sharing, their children also tended to be aggressive. If children identified strongly with their parents, usually they were too afraid of punishment to act aggressively, but children who did not identify with their parents grew more aggressive the more their parents punished them. Even though they preached nonviolence, parents who were themselves aggressive produced aggressive children. Children clearly learned aggression from their parents. They also learned it from their siblings. It has been suggested that severe aggressive behavior is learned most easily in a family that includes both victims—younger siblings—and models—older siblings (Patterson, 1982).

Family members figure in the socialization of aggression, but so do peers. Peers act to reinforce, model, absorb and provoke hostility. In one experiment (Hall, 1974), for example, pairs of unacquainted 6- and 7-year-old boys played together. One child in each pair had been trained by the researchers to act either aggressively or passively. When that child acted aggressively, the probability of the other child's acting aggressively was .75. Children who were attacked by aggressive peers fought back. In another study (Hicks, 1965), children imitated their peers' aggression—even though it was not directed toward them—when they saw a film of an aggressive child.

Finally, aggression is encouraged by the structure and activities of schoolchildren's play groups. Large groups, playing outdoors unsupervised by adults in rowdy, rough-and-tumble, or competitive games that are concerned with establishing pecking orders, are most likely to bring out aggression.

research focus

Social understanding in aggressive boys

Do aggressive children see the world as a more hostile place, or do they just act more aggressively because they are unable to inhibit their actions? Kenneth Dodge and Cynthia Frame (1982) conducted a study to try to answer this question. Their subjects were elementary schoolboys, chosen on the basis of teachers' and peers' ratings as being aggressive or nonaggressive. Those nominated as aggressive were also observed to start many aggressive acts on the playground. To find out what the boys thought about social situations, the researchers interviewed them privately and confidentially about how they would react to several incidents that might involve them or another child: getting hit in the back with a ball, getting milk spilled on them, losing a pencil and a lunch bag and later seeing another boy with them. In each story, the protagonist was a boy the subject actually knew, and was, according to the teachers' and peers' ratings, aggressive or nonaggressive. Dodge and Frame found that all the subjects attributed more hostility to the aggressive than to the nonaggressive protagonists, especially when the events had negative effects. All subjects were also equally likely to attribute malice to the protagonist when another child was the target. But when they themselves were the victims of aggression, the aggressive subjects said that they would retaliate with aggression to a greater extent than the nonaggressive subjects said that they would.

In a second procedure, aggressive and nonaggressive boys watched short films of a boy actor describing to a woman how he acted with his classmates. They were then asked to recall as much as they could of what the boy had said. Some of his descriptions were of hostile acts, and some were of benevolent or neutral acts. To some of the subjects, the actor was described as a popular boy, to some as aggressive, and to some he was not described at all. When the boy had been labeled as popular, all the subjects recalled more benevolent statements. When the boy had been labeled as aggressive, they recalled more hostile statements. Contrary to the researchers' predictions, the aggressive boys did not recall more hostile statements than the nonaggressive boys. *Both* groups were biased toward recalling more aggressive statements than benevolent.

Thus it appears that aggressive boys are more likely than nonaggressive boys to attribute hostility to ambiguous actions, but only when an action is directed at the aggressive boy himself. Aggressive boys do not indiscriminately misattribute or selectively recall hostility. The investigators suggest that the cause for the heightened aggression in some boys is neither a lack of discrimination nor a lag in cognitive maturity but rather a suspicious interpretation of potentially aggressive actions.

But children's aggressiveness is not simply provoked by aggressiveness in the environment. Children's perceptions and cognition—perhaps built up over repeated encounters in the family or at school—also contribute. Kenneth Dodge (1980) has suggested that children who respond aggressively may be reading the worst into the other person's intentions. This researcher exposed schoolboys, rated by their teachers and classmates as either aggressive or nonaggressive, to frustration meted out by an unfamiliar peer. The boy heard the peer in the next room breaking the puzzle that the first boy had been working on. The peer's intent was hostile ("I don't want him to win." *Crash*.); benign ("I think I'll help him with the puzzle." *Crash*.); or ambiguous ("It looks like he's got a lot done.'' *Crash*.). All boys reacted more aggressively to the peer whose intent was hostile than to the peer whose intent was benign. But when the peer's intent was ambiguous, the aggressive boys reacted as though the peer had acted hostilely, and the nonaggressive boys reacted as though he had acted benignly.

One further cause of aggressiveness in school-age children, as with younger ones, is the violence they see on television. In studies of the relation between watching violence on television and aggressive behavior in inner-city and suburban Chicago children and in children in Finland, researchers have found that television violence has a particularly strong influence on children's aggressiveness beginning when they are about 8 or 9 years old (Eron, Huesmann, Brice, Fischer, and Mermelstein, 1983; Huesmann, Lagerspetz, and Eron, 1984). Beginning at this age, the effects of television seem to intensify. The more often children watch violent shows and the more violent the shows are, the more aggressive are the children. It is likely that children learn to act aggressively from what they observe on television and that televised violence justifies aggression and makes it more palatable to children, repeatedly showing people who solve their problems violently. Not only did watching violence on television beget aggressive behavior but aggressive behavior also tended to increase the amount of violence children watched on television—a two-way street.

Surprisingly, in the Chicago sample, unlike the New York sample studied earlier (Eron et al., 1971; Huesmann et al., 1984) or the Finnish sample, even though girls acted less aggressively than boys and watched less violent television, their behavior grew increasingly aggressive over time, just as the boys' did. In the New York sample, only the girls who liked masculine games had been affected as much as boys were by televised violence. The shift, the researchers suggest, may derive from social changes in this country and on television over the last two decades. Today, girls are allowed to be more active, assertive, and aggressive than they were 20 years ago, and today there are more aggressive female characters on television.

In brief, it appears that children are most likely to act aggressively if they

- Watch a lot of violent television shows.
- Believe that these shows are real, not fiction.
- Identify strongly with the aggressive characters on the shows.
- Have aggressive fantasies.
- Prefer activities that are physically rough and active.
- Have parents, especially mothers, who act aggressively towards them.
- Observe aggression of their parents, friends, and heroes.
- Are reinforced for their own aggressive behavior.
- Are objects of aggression.

Aggression has many sources, and when these sources come together in one child's life, the result inevitably is antisocial behavior.

How can parents or teachers reduce children's aggressiveness? First, they can reduce their own aggressiveness toward the children. Then they can try to change children's perceptions of those who frustrate them. In one study (Mallick and McCandless, 1966), third graders were prevented from finishing a task and winning a cash prize by a frustrator. If the children were told that the frustrator was sleepy or upset, they attacked less, both verbally and physically. Parents and teachers also can encourage children to excuse their classmates' slights or shoves and promote their children's cooperative ventures. In the boys' camp experiment that we discussed earlier (Sherif and

Sherif, 1964; Sherif et al., 1961), shifting to a shared goal changed the way the campers perceived the "others." Instead of frustrators and rivals, they became friends. Much more research needs to be done to find alternatives to aggression and ways to replace it with a healthy assertiveness that helps children to cope in the face of pressure and to persist in the face of frustration.

Life in school

> Finally, I would be able to read, to write my own name, to learn to add and subtract like my brother, to meet and play with lots of other children. It was so great to walk with my mother into the classroom. Then, meeting the teacher and finding a desk of my own assured me that I was off on the thrilling adventure I was so sure school would be. It's hard to describe that feeling of anticipation I felt. I wanted so much to be a participant in life. School I saw as my pathway to "growing up." My waiting had ended (Schultz, Heuchert, and Stampf, 1973, p. 43).

Public or private, rural or city, one-room schoolhouse or classes without walls, school is a nearly universal experience for children over the age of 5 or 6. In middle childhood, children spend almost half their waking hours at school, and it is there that they meet most of their friends. It is there that they are given new academic and social challenges. If the teacher scolds, if they do poorly on a test, if they are laughed at in class, school is a place of acute pain. If the teacher praises them, if they ace a test, if the other kids ask them to be on a team, school is a place of pleasure, pride, and accomplishment. It is not surprising, therefore, that children have mixed feelings about school. In one large survey (Foundation for Child Development, 1976), three-fourths of the children interviewed said that they liked or loved school. But two-thirds also said that they worried about tests and that making mistakes in class made them feel ashamed. In another major survey (Search Institute, 1984), the most common fear reported by children in the fifth through eighth grades concerned their achievement in school. Even students who say that they are satisfied with school admit that often they are bored there (Jackson, 1968).

> I was bored so much of the time in elementary school that I would try to occupy myself by counting all the lights on the ceiling or all the holes in the acoustical ceiling tiles.—Sarah, age 13

The teacher

In school, the intimacy and concern of parents, babysitters, and other familiar adults give way to the demands of less forgiving teachers. Children must adapt to the "spirit of evaluation" of their teachers, who expect them to perform well and who judge them on their performance.

> My first morning [in first grade], our teacher took us through a singing lesson. I loved to sing, so I really opened up. After a minute or two of this, she stopped us, turned to me—right in front of the class—and said, "Stop singing at once! Your notes are all wrong and you are so much louder than the rest of the class." It was just a thoughtless act, but when I went home that afternoon, I cried and told my mother all about it (Schultz, Heuchert, and Stampf, 1973, p. 17).

Schoolchildren must conform to the norms of a classroom and to the special likes and dislikes of teachers. Some teachers do better than others at gaining children's respect and affection. As researchers in one study found, children prefer teachers who explain things so that they can grasp them and convey information that is interesting and clear (Jersild, 1940). They dislike teachers who are unfair, strict, or play favorites. Teachers, too, have favorites among their students. They like students whose demands on their energies are few. They dislike students who are so disruptive and demanding that their needs overwhelm them (Silberman, 1971). Aggressive boys often incur the wrath of their teachers, many of whom are women. Girls are more likely to obey school rules (Meyer and Thompson, 1956). Teachers are therefore more likely to reject boys and to grow attached to girls. Children who are good-looking and who sit near the teacher, who are smart, achievement-oriented, and well adjusted, who are not passive, disruptive, hostile, or heedless of the group attract teachers' praise and attention (Adams and Cohen, 1974; Adams and Biddle, 1967; Delefes and Jackson, 1972; Glidewell, Kantor, Smith, and Stringer, 1965). Many teachers are themselves from middle-class backgrounds and prefer students whose behavior conforms to middle-class norms. Although teachers may pay as much attention to students from poor families as to those from middle-class families, their attention to those from poor families is more likely to consist of attempts to control behavior and correct speech than of attempts to challenge or stimulate (Brophy and Evertson, 1974).

Classroom management

No matter how teachers feel about each student personally, they must manage a whole class full of energetic and not always willing boys and girls, and keep them in line, working productively and pleasantly. How can teachers do this? One technique that has proved successful is systematic reinforcement (Figure 13.4). As a classroom management technique, this involves several steps:

1. Class time is divided into brief intervals.
2. The frequency of children's desired behavior during these periods is recorded.
3. Students are rewarded for desired behavior every time it occurs; undesired behavior is ignored.

Teachers have successfully managed in this way to get their students to quiet down, to pay attention, to raise their hands, to work together. The rewards they have used include privileges like longer periods of free play, gifts, candy, money, and the old standby, gold stars. Tokens, stars, or points then may be exchanged for prizes or privileges. These "token economy"

Teachers almost always have favorite pupils to whom they give more attention and help than others.

BEHAVIOR MODIFICATION IN THE CLASSROOM

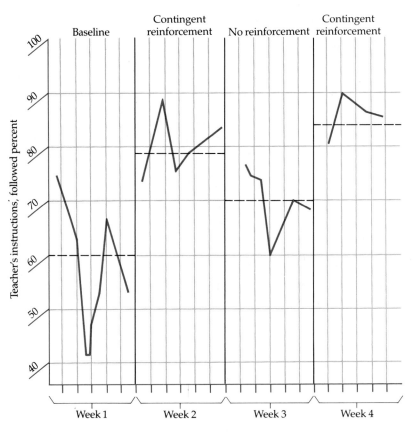

Figure 13.4 Children's behavior improves when the teacher consistently praises the class for following instructions. The broken lines show the mean percentage of good behavior in the classroom for each week.

rewards often prove effective in gaining children's compliance. Many a boy has complied who knew that by sitting still until recess time, or by reading the story in front of him, he would earn enough points to buy a toy or extra time on the baseball field. Using tokens often succeeds where simply praising, setting rules, or ignoring misbehavior has failed. The drawback is that when the tokens stop, so may the desirable behavior. To overcome this drawback, teachers may build intangible reinforcements like verbal praise and approval into their program and get students to work toward long-term rather than immediate rewards (Sherman and Bushnell, 1975). Another drawback is that tangible rewards sometimes backfire. They may actually interfere with how well a child performs the task being rewarded (Lepper, 1983). External rewards can undermine children's **intrinsic motivation**. Children who expect a reward for doing something they like will be less likely to do it once they have been rewarded than children who either are not rewarded at all or are rewarded as a surprise (Lepper, Greene, and Nisbett, 1973).

Not only extrinsic rewards, but also very close supervision, tight deadlines, and forced practice may undermine children's interest in continuing to do something they were originally interested in. Once children feel that their actions are extrinsically controlled, it seems, they lose interest. Because they focus on the reward, the quality of their work may suffer. When sixth grade girls tutored first graders, for example the tutors who expected extrinsic rewards were more critical, impatient, and inefficient than those whose reward was the tutoring itself, and the first graders learned less as a result (Garbarino, 1975). Rewards are useful when they stress the positive and they *focus* *Teacher, spare the rod*

It may be against the law for parents to physically abuse their children, but in many places it is not against the law for children to be slapped, hit, kicked, paddled, or beaten by their teachers or school principals. Some schools keep ''regulation'' instruments of punishment: paddles, leather straps, a ''thin rattan.'' But teachers also resort to using their hands and fists, rulers and yardsticks, belts, bats, planks, pipes, and even cattle prods. Not only are children beaten, choked, and tied to their chairs, but they may have their hair cut off, be thrown into a closet, box, or school vault, be thrown against walls, desks, or concrete pillars, undressed, forced to do push ups, stand on tiptoe, or to eat cigarettes (Hyman and Clarke, 1984). The injuries that children sustain may be severe and permanent, and students with physical and emotional disabilities are not exempt.

Corporal punishment in schools is illegal in seven of the United States, the District of Columbia, Puerto Rico, and in many cities, especially wealthy suburbs in the Northeast, Midwest, and West. But in rural and inner-city schools with little money to spend on education or psychological services, it is quite common. Although firm figures on how often students are hit are difficult to get, estimates run from just under 1 million to 3 million incidents in this country every year (Hyman and Clarke, 1984).

Teachers use corporal punishment because they believe it helps to correct children's misbehavior and make them more obedient and docile. Many say they, would feel helpless to control their students if they could not resort to corporal punishment. Yet research on the effects of corporal punishment on children shows overwhelmingly that it is counterproductive, that it does not increase learning, and that it perpetuates seriously harmful attitudes and behavior. It may stop children's misbehavior for a time, but it does not teach them new or better ways to act. When teachers strike children, they serve as models of aggression both for the children and for their parents. The message they convey is that violence is an acceptable way to solve problems. Corporal punishment therefore tends to increase students' aggression against other people and against school property. It also implicitly condones the abuse of children by parents or other adults.

The most effective way to root out discipline problems is to use not corporal punishment, criticism, ridicule, or sarcasm, but positive methods of discipline—praise, rewarding, and building up children's self-esteem (Brophy, 1981; Peterson and Walberg, 1980; Squires, Huit, and Segars, 1984).

make children feel that their competence has been enhanced. Wise is the teacher who tells a child that doing his math problems will enable him to compute batting averages, rather than telling him that if he doesn't he'll have to stay after school, or that if he finishes his worksheet he'll get a ball and bat.

Praise and attention are powerful rewards that do not have the same tendency to backfire as tangible rewards (Pittman, Boggiano, and Ruble, 1983). They can even undo some of the damage that tangible rewards may have caused (Swann and Pittman, 1977). Praise and encouragement can make children feel competent, successful, and determined. They can leave behind a warm glow that does not make children feel manipulated—only appreciated. When words are used well, they strengthen children's internal motivation. When they are used to reward a job well done, they keep interest high.

Desegregation

Schools reflect the society they serve and the social problems of that society. Attempts in this country to root out racial inequality have deeply affected the schools. Desegregation, ordered by the courts and enacted by individual school systems, has aimed to improve the ratio of minority-group members to whites, to improve the quality of education for those formerly discriminated against, and to improve race relations through contact and interaction. Have schools met these goals? Yes and no. Although busing may integrate a school in theory, in fact, black children bused to a white school may be segregated in their classrooms. When students are actually assigned to work together, however, race relations have been found to improve. In one study of more than 5000 fifth-graders from over 90 schools, researchers showed that when students were assigned projects about racial issues, when they learned about equal racial status in class, and when they worked in class or on sports teams with students of other races and backgrounds, race relations improved (Forehand, Rogosta, and Rock, 1976). When school principals, teachers, or guidance counselors did not encourage integrated work or play, however, desegregation and race relations faltered.

Desegregation tends to improve students' cooperation and relations between races, but, contrary to the hopes and expectations of many people, it does not inevitably enhance the self-esteem of black students (Minuchin and Shapiro, 1983). To the minority-group child, desegregation can offer the first exposure to the values of the dominant white group, an exposure that may prove alienating. Desegregation can intensify hostility and harden differences. It can expose students to racial prejudice, academic competition, and conflicting demands from peers and teachers (Rosenberg and Simmons, 1971). To succeed in a desegregated school, some black students may have to "act white" and court rejection from other blacks. As a simple solution to a complex problem, desegregation clearly fails. To improve race relations and provide psychological and academic support for minority-group children, desegregation may be necessary, but it is clearly not sufficient.

Structure

In Chapter 12, we described the effects of the structure in classrooms and classes on children's academic achievement. But how do open classrooms and classes affect children's social and psychological functioning? Investigators have found that children who are in open classes generally feel more positive about school and themselves than children in traditional classes, although this difference does not always appear (Minuchin and Shapiro, 1983; Giaconia and Hedges, 1982). In open classes, too, children's sense of their individuality is likely to be heightened, and gender roles—girls' especially—are less conventional and stereotyped. Children play in a less gender-typed fashion and tend to play with and make more friends of the other sex (Minuchin, 1965; Minuchin, Biber, Shapiro, and Zimiles, 1969). They are more likely to begin projects on their own and to stick to their own values (Traub, Weiss, and Fisher, 1974). Open classes offer chances for independence and individuality, for a wider variety of interactions, and for greater cooperation on projects, as well as more ways for children to make friends and to be popular. Among children in open classes, dominance and popularity hierarchies are more democratic; there are fewer stars, isolates, and scapegoats. On the negative side, children in open classes—especially boys—feel more anxiety about achievement and are likely to create more disturbances—poking, tormenting, and teasing their classmates—than children in traditional classes (Trickett, 1983).

After school

After school, most children participate in organized activities with their friends. They engage in sports, join clubs and groups, do artwork or play musical instruments, or take lessons.

After school, I walk home with a bunch of other kids from my neighborhood. In the nice weather, we play outside until suppertime. There's a brook at the bottom of our hill where we pitch pebbles and catch polliwogs, or we play in the fields where there aren't any houses yet. One time my friend and me found fool's gold up there. Sometimes I walk home from school with one of my friends and play at his house until my dad picks me up on his way home from work. Sometimes we walk to the store and buy stuff like gum, or wax lips, or comics. Sometimes I have to go straight home and do my homework or something around the house. If we have visitors, I have to go straight home—or else!—Mikey, age 8

I go to church with my mother most nights. I come straight home from school and do my homework until about 5:00. Sometimes I take the bus downtown to do shopping. My mother makes supper, or one of my brothers brings in food from a restaurant, and after we eat, a neighbor takes us to church in her car. We have choir or services—once we were even on TV—and get home about 9:00 or 9:30. I go right to bed then so I won't be tired for school the next morning.—Nadine, age 11

I have lessons—dancing, gymnastics, swimming, and piano—that I have to go to most days after school. My mother drives me, or I'm in a carpool with some other kids. I get home in time for dinner. We wait for everyone to get home so we can all eat together—my mother, my father, my brother, and me. If I don't have a lesson, I might have a friend come over. We go into my room and play with dolls or other stuff. I'm allowed to ride my bike around the neighborhood, but I can't go alone beyond a couple of blocks from my house because you never know what kind of people you might run into in the city.—Alyssa, age 10

What do children do after school? They play, they hang around, they're on teams, they take lessons, they watch television. Much of what they do depends on the kind of neighborhood they live in. One neighborhood offers a ready-made group of playmates, whereas another offers none. One neighborhood offers flat sidewalks for riding bikes and roller skating and empty lots for playing ball, but another has only steep hills with no sidewalks and dangerously busy streets.

In a detailed sociological study of neighborhoods in Oakland, California (Medrich, Roizen, Rubin, and Buckley, 1982), researchers interviewed 764 sixth-grade students about how they spent their time after school. The children's activities and experiences, it turned out, were strongly shaped by the physical and social features of their neighborhoods. In "Mountainside," for example, there were no sidewalks, and the streets were hilly. The houses were set back from the road, there was little public transportation, and it was hard for children to get around the neighborhood. The public spaces—library, shops, park, recreation center—of Mountainside clustered in the center of the "village" and attracted both children and adults. But the children mostly played near their own houses, and they had contact with few adults besides their parents. In "Rosewood," by contrast, the yards of the houses were unbroken by fences, and the sidewalks were generous. Children often rode their bicycles along them and played softball in the streets. The neighborhood centered around the school, and the children could walk there in minutes, sometimes taking shortcuts through a friend's backyard. Because there were so many young families in Rosewood, there were lots of children for games.

The neighborhood of "Bancroft" had no sidewalks or street lights, and most of the houses were hidden from the narrow streets behind huge trees and vegetable gardens. The families, too, seemed insular. Most of the children spent their time with brothers and sisters rather than friends from the neighborhood. The sixth graders of Bancroft usually left their own blocks only to go to school, keep an appointment, or run an errand. Part of this insularity owed to the heavy traffic that ran through the neighborhood. Both the school and the park were near a busy street and right near a freeway exit. The children of Bancroft were frightened by the older people who used the park and the schoolyard. In "Eastside," the streets were stark, the yards were fenced, trees were few, but the neighborhood was alive with people on the streets and sidewalks. The children roamed around in groups, sometimes going to the community center for free meals, sometimes to the corner store. They rambled around, talking, playing basketball. They played a lot of sports, often in vacant lots or dead-end streets.

In sum, where and what the children played revolved around the features of the terrain, their access to various facilities like parks or schools, and the limitations imposed by their need for safety. Although the sixth graders said that they played most often in their own yards or those of friends, they had already begun expanding their ranges. Boys and black children especially said that they often played in public places like schoolyards, recreation areas, streets, and vacant lots and occasionally ventured beyond their own neighborhood. Children from neighborhoods that did not permit easy mobility by bicycle or foot or that did not have public transportation usually had parents with cars, and these somewhat offset the children's limited mobility. Mobility was important to children for keeping a wide circle of friends, for participating in group activities, and for playing team sports. But sometimes, if an adult was not along, children's excursions into the wider world were frightening and dangerous.

In a survey of school children (Foundation for Child Development, 1976), one-fourth of the children interviewed said that they were afraid of getting hurt by someone when they were outside. Asked, "Who is the person you are most afraid of?" most mentioned someone real, and one-third mentioned someone who actually had hurt them. Their fears seemed grounded in the realities of their neighborhoods, for many had had frightening experiences with violence and crime, had been beaten up, hurt by bullies, or menaced by older children.

Children in the Oakland study distinguished clearly between the kinds of places where they went with other children—parks, movies, libraries—and where they went with their parents—churches, cultural and recreational facilities, and restaurants. Aside from the fact that black children were more likely to go to church and white children to restaurants, there were few ethnic differences in what the children did with their families. All the children had jobs around the house, and 40 percent—boys as well as girls—babysat for younger brothers and sisters, especially in families where parents worked. Few of the children held paying jobs. With their parents, children reported watching television, eating dinner, playing games, engaging in hobbies, and getting help with homework. Television was far and away the most common family activity. Nearly all the sixth graders reported watching television some part of every day, and the average child watched an average of 30 hours a week. But few children watched television with their friends. With their friends, the Oakland sixth graders did more physically active things—sports especially. In fact, most of the children participated in some organized after-school activity with their friends: sports—swimming, tennis, skating, martial arts, baseball; art—music, painting, dancing, acting, crafts; clubs—Scouts, YMCA, YWCA, Boys' or Girls' clubs; or other kinds of lessons—cooking, mechanics, ethnic heritage, science. Although the number of hours that children engaged in these organized activities was not great, they were considered important by both the children and their parents.

Playing after school in the neighborhood is when children are most likely to interact with children who are not their age-mates (Ellis, Rogoff, and Cromer, 1981). Interactions between older and younger children are somewhat different from those we have described between peers. Like the asymmetrical interactions between older and younger siblings that we described in Chapter 10, older children interacting with younger children are more likely to act dominant, directive, aggressive, instructive, helpful, and nurturant (French, in press). Having chances to practice these kinds of behaviors is likely to influence children's social styles and skills.

The kind of support available in the neighborhood also may influence children's development of social skills. In a study of 7- and 10-year-olds in rural California neighborhoods (Bryant, 1985), it was found that 10-year-old children were advanced in social understanding and had more prosocial attitudes when they had the following kinds of experiences in their neighborhoods: close contact with a pet ("a boy's best friend"), interaction with a variety of different adults, chances to get off by themselves alone, and informal meeting places. These differences were found in a relatively homogeneous community. There would likely be more significant differences if researchers included a wider range of neighborhoods. As usual, interpreting the results of this study present problems of cause and effect. We don't know whether having a pet led to greater social competence in their owners or whether more socially competent children were able to convince their parents that they were responsible enough to have pets. But the study does demonstrate that in middle childhood children's experiences include more than activities with their parents and classmates. This study, then, underlines the importance of studying children's entire social ecologies, as Urie Bronfenbrenner has urged (see Chapter 1).

Social understanding

Understanding other people

As children get older, they become better at understanding other people's actions and more adept at reading cues about their feelings, intentions, and motives. Preschool children, when asked to comment freely about people's behavior, comment on obvious actions and expressions. But over the school years, children learn to infer more about people's *internal* states and thoughts. In one study of children's social understanding (Flapan, 1968), for example, 6-, 9-, and 12-year-olds were shown a film of a young girl who went through various emotional situations: punishment from her father for not sharing her roller skates; a visit to the circus; a gift of a calf from her father; accidentally killing a squirrel. Children of all these ages could tell when the girl or her father was angry, hurt, or happy. But the 6-year-olds often did not understand the father's intentions. The 9- and 12-year-olds did understand the father's intentions and also understood how the girl deliberately shaped her actions to meet certain goals. The 12-year-olds could deduce what the father thought about the girl's feelings and what the girl thought about the father's.

In another study, Robert Selman (1980) used fictional stories to find out how well children understand how other people think and feel. For example,

> Eight-year-old Tom is trying to decide what to buy his friend, Mike, for a birthday party. By chance, he meets Mike on the street and learns that Mike is extremely upset because his dog, Pepper, has been lost for two

weeks. In fact, Mike is so upset that he tells Tom, ''I miss Pepper so much that I never want to look at another dog again.'' Tom goes off, only to pass a store with a sale on puppies. Only two are left, and these will soon be gone (Selman, 1980, p. 94).

The interviewer then asked the children whether Tom should buy a puppy for Mike's birthday, and why. Children's responses to these dilemmas, Selman found, form three levels of social awareness. At the first level, preschool children do not distinguish between inner, mental events and outer, physical events and observable actions. They typically replied to the dilemmas as though a person's feelings and statements were the same thing. ''If he says that he doesn't want to see a puppy ever again, then he really won't ever want to.'' At the next level of understanding, at around age 6, children distinguished between what people felt and what they said, but they still thought that the two always were in agreement. By age 8, children understood that inner thoughts and outward expressions may be inconsistent or contradictory. In response to the dilemma, they might say that although Mike says he does not want another puppy, inside he really does want one. With the knowledge that people's facades may differ from their inner experiences, children reach a level of reflective, psychological understanding.

Another shift toward greater psychological understanding that occurs during this age period was documented in another study by (Rholes and Ruble, 1984). Children between 5 and 10 years old were read vignettes about children who had either positive or negative characteristics. For example, some children were portrayed as generously sharing a lunch, some as ungenerously refusing to share lunch with a hungry child. The subjects then rated the children in the vignettes as ''nice and kind,'' ''brave,'' ''mean,'' and so on, and were asked how the children might act in other, comparable circumstances. Although children at all these ages rated the story characters as equally generous, stingy, and so on, the 10-year-olds far oftener than the 5-year-olds predicted that the fictional characters would behave consistently from one situation another. They believed, as most adults do, that a person's behavior in different situations can be predicted by an abiding personal disposition.

At around the age of 10, children also made a rapid and pronounced shift from describing other people in terms of their behavior to describing them in terms of these inferred, stable, psychological attributes. In one study, children were asked to describe their classmates (Barenboim, 1981). Children younger than 10 would say something like, ''Billy runs a lot faster than Jason'' or ''Penny draws the best in our whole class.'' But beginning at 10, children would describe a classmate with ''He's really conceited; he thinks he's great'' or ''Linda is real sensitive, a lot more than most people.'' The findings from these studies are consistent with the findings from a sample done in England (Livesley and Bromley, 1983). When researchers in that study recorded how children between 7 and 16 years old described their classmates, they found the same progression from physical and behavioral to psychological descriptions. Younger children described their acquaintances in terms of appearance, name, age, sex, routine habits, possessions, and social roles.

Max sits next to me; his eyes are hazel and he is tall. He hasn't got a very big head; he's got a big pointed nose [age 7 years, 6 months] (Livesley and Bromley, 1973, p. 213).

Older children's descriptions focused on more psychological aspects like personality traits, general habits, motives, values, and attitudes.

Andy is very modest. He is even shyer than I am when near strangers and yet is very talkative with people he knows and likes. He always seems good tempered, and I have never seen him in a bad temper. He tends to degrade other people's achievements and yet never praises his own. He does not seem to voice his opinions to anyone. He easily gets nervous [age 15 years, 8 months] (Livesley and Bromley, 1973, p. 221).

Learning social rules

Another way that children grow in social understanding over the school years is by learning social rules. Part of the task of growing up and getting along with other people involves learning the many rules that govern everyday behavior. There are trivial rules and important rules, implicit rules and explicit rules, rules for school and rules for home. One child came home from her first day in second grade.

CHILD: Mom, guess what. Two and three is five in Mrs. McIntyre's [second-grade teacher] room, too!

MOTHER: What do you mean?

CHILD: It's the *same* as first grade—two and three is five. Is it the same in every room? . . . Everywhere? . . . In China, too?

MOTHER: Yes, it is.

CHILD (musing): It's a rule everywhere. . . . Can't anybody make it be something else?

OLDER SISTER: No, it's a rule. It's always five. And you better not say anything else or Mrs. McIntyre will say you're wrong. You can't fool around with rules about numbers (Shantz, 1982, p. 167).

By school age, children are quite familiar with the culturally defined and arbitrary rules establishing dress codes, forms of address, and table manners—the so-called **social conventions**. Researchers have tried to determine just when children acquire these social rules by interviewing them intensively. In one study the children were told a story about Melissa:

Melissa is a new girl at school. She comes from a country in the Far East. In her country there are different eating habits, and the people there eat many kinds of food with their fingers. One day a teacher saw her eating some spaghetti with her fingers and got upset (Damon, 1977, p. 243).

Preschool children seemed to think that Melissa's behavior was fine. They did not feel bound by the rules of American table etiquette and said that whatever people wanted to do, they could.

INTERVIEWER: Do you think it is okay for Melissa to eat with her fingers?

KAREN (4 YEARS, 2 MONTHS): Yes.

INTERVIEWER: It is? How come that is okay?

KAREN: Because different people eat different ways (Damon, 1977, p. 250).

Kindergarteners no longer confused rules with personal habits, but they thought rules should be respected to avoid the displeasure of authority figures.

INTERVIEWER: Was it wrong for Melissa to eat with her fingers in school?

ANDREA (5 YEARS, 1 MONTH): Yes. . .Because she can't use her fingers.

> INTERVIEWER: Why not?
>
> ANDREA: The mother will hit her (Damon, 1977, p. 255).

At the beginning of middle childhood, children recognized that rules could have exceptions.

> INTERVIEWER: Do you think it was wrong for Melissa to eat with her fingers?
>
> TOM (6 YEARS, 2 MONTHS):
> No, she didn't learn how to eat with other stuff.
>
> INTERVIEWER: Do you think it was wrong?
>
> TOM: No, because she was new to this country anyway.
>
> INTERVIEWER: Why do you think the teacher got really upset when she saw her doing that?
>
> TOM: She may not know that she was new to the country (Damon, 1977, p. 261).

Finally, by the end of middle childhood, children come to respect rules because they understand their social function. They realize that social conventions are necessary for maintaining order.

> INTERVIEWER: What if there was a rule about eating with a fork at Melissa's school?
>
> HEATHER (8 YEARS, 8 MONTHS):
> If there is a rule then she would have to eat that way.
>
> INTERVIEWER: Why is that?
>
> HEATHER: Because then everyone would have to do the same thing no matter how they were taught at home or it wouldn't be fair.
>
> INTERVIEWER: Couldn't Melissa just ignore the rule?
>
> HEATHER: No. Because then everybody would start looking at her and start doing it. . .What a mess! Then if only one person didn't do it they would make fun of him, and they might not think it's fair (Damon, 1977, p. 271).

One kind of social rule that school-age children follow is about gender roles.

> "Why do you think people tell George not to play with dolls?"
>
> "Well, he should only play with things that boys play with. The things that he's playing with now is girls' stuff."
>
> "What makes it girls' stuff?"
>
> "Because it's pictures of girls. But the boys' things are boys'."
>
> "Can George play with Barbie dolls if he wants to?"
>
> "No, sir."
>
> "How come?"
>
> "If he doesn't want to play with dolls, then he's right, but if he does want to play with dolls, he's double wrong."
>
> "Why is he double wrong?"
>
> "All the time he's playing with girls' stuff."
>
> "Do you think people are right when they tell George not to play with girls' dolls?"
>
> "Yes.". . .

''What should George do?''

''He should stop playing with the girls' dolls and start playing with the G.I. Joe'' (Pitcher and Schultz, 1984, p. 114)

In one recent study (Stoddart and Turiel, 1985), school-age children were shown pictures in which children were doing things appropriate for the other gender (a boy wearing a barette or putting on nail polish, a girl with a crew cut or wearing a boy's suit). The 5- and 6-year-olds thought that breaking gender-role rules was worse than the 8- to 10-year-olds did.

Children respond differently to social rules—like playing the right way—and moral rules—like not stealing and lying (Nucci and Nucci, 1982). But in the early school years children do not have quite the same appreciation as in the later elementary school years of the distinction between social conventions, which are arbitrary, and moral rules, which are absolute. In one study, first and second graders were interviewed about rules and heard stories about social transgressions—a boy who gets up in the morning and washes his face but does not comb his hair—and moral transgressions—children refusing to share or hitting (Shantz and Shantz, 1977). The children were then asked to point to the face that best represented what they thought about the naughty child—from a broadly smiling ''very good'' to a frowning ''very bad'' face. Although, on the average, children ranked the moral transgressions as worse than the social transgressions, the children did not rank all moral transgressions as more serious than all social transgressions. They thought that some of the social transgressions, like not combing your hair, were as serious as the moral transgressions, whereas others were not as bad. Development brings with it increasing awareness of subtle distinctions between types of rules and greater flexibility in complying with arbitrary rules.

research focus — *Moral and social rules*

Larry Nucci and Maria Santiago Nucci (1982) decided to investigate how children playing freely and without adult supervision would react to violations of either moral or social rules. Children, they thought, might construe spitting or chewing grass as violations of social rules and throwing sand at a smaller child or taking away a younger child's sled as violations of moral rules—and respond differently to the two kinds of violations. The investigators defined moral rules as those that involved acts having intrinsic effects upon the welfare and rights of individuals or groups and social rules as existing consensual norms. They visited ten suburban Chicago playgrounds and unobtrusively watched children as they played without adult supervision. They focused on play among groups of five or more children who were from 7 to 14 years old. Observers described transgressions against moral and social rules and noted children's responses to these transgressions.

In all, the observers witnessed 900 transgressions. During 80 hours of observation, they found that children responded more often to moral than to social transgressions. In response to moral transgressions, children, and boys especially, retaliated and said things about injury, loss, and unfairness. They focused on features intrinsic to the transgression. In contrast, in response to social transgressions, they focused on the external social organization that had been disrupted—for example, calling two boys riding a sled ''faggots'' or ridiculing two children who were tying their shoes with, ''Bobby and Allison sittin' in a tree, K-I-S-S-I-N-G.''

Development also brings an appreciation for more subtle social rules—like rules of deference and politeness that are implicit in the ways we speak. In many European languages, the pronouns express deference. For example, a French "you" can be expressed by the familiar form, *tu*, or the more formal *vous*. *Tu* not only means "the person to whom I am speaking" but also indicates familiarity and closeness between the speaker and listener. Children, intimates, and people of low status are addressed with *tu*, and *vous* is used to convey respect and formal distance. European children develop an awareness for these social differences in pronouns at about the same age that American children begin to make requests politely—6 years (Hollos, 1977). Children of this age are capable of learning the social conventions of polite speech because they know that other people have perspectives different from their own. They also have had some practice with polite forms. Young children try out the polite phrases that they hear around them. One 4-year-old, on meeting "George" for the first time, said, "My, you look nice today, George." Said 4-year-old Peter to departing guests, as he roused himself from a nap on the living room couch, "Come back again." Three-year-old Sam *acted* polite when he greeted his babysitter with, "You look beau'ful tonight, Beff." But not until the elementary school years are children able to *understand* linguistic rules of politeness and deference.

A speaker may convey a command either directly, "Close the window," or indirectly, "Would you mind closing the window?" or "It's awfully drafty in here." To the ears of English speakers, "Would you mind closing the window," "Could I ask you to close the window," and "I hope you wouldn't mind closing the window," all sound more polite than "Shut the window." Not until they are around 6 years old do children understand that they should make requests politely and indirectly. A 5-year-old will say, "I want the bicycle," or on good days, "I want the bicycle, please." But only after age 6 or so can children use forms like "Can I swing?" or "Please may I swing?" or "Can I have a turn on the swing?" (Bates, 1976; Garvey, 1975).

Even then, children's politeness is spotty. Politeness requires both linguistic and social skills. It requires that children not only know the polite language forms but also understand their listener's signals, status, and other aspects of the social situation. This understanding comes only with advanced cognitive development. In one study, 5- to 10-year-old children were studied as they interacted with adults (Axia and Baroni, 1985). Not until age 9 or so did children master polite requests to overcome difficulties in spontaneous interactions. Five-year-olds did not have the polite forms; 7-year-olds did not discriminate between situations in which politeness was required and those in which it was not.

Solving social problems

Every day children face social problems—acquiring objects, entering interactions, seeking help, initiating friendships. Their ability to suggest solutions to these social problems increases in the school years. In one study (McCoy and Masters, 1985), for example, older elementary school children were able to suggest more useful and helpful strategies to cheer up or calm down fictional children experiencing sadness or anger than younger elementary school children were. In another study (Weiner and Handel, 1985), older elementary school children knew enough to say that they would withhold information that would make another person angry, such as the fact that the reason they hadn't shown up at a friend's house as invited was that they had decided to stay home and watch television (Rubin and Krasnor, 1986). Some psychologists have suggested that solving social problems improves in the school years because children's cognitive understanding increases (Spivack and Shure,

1974). To solve social problems, they have suggested, children need first to recognize the problem, then to generate alternative solutions to solve the problem, then to consider means to accomplish the solution, and finally to figure out consequences of the different alternatives. For this they must be able to take the other person's perspective.

What evidence do we have that this kind of cognitive understanding determines social behavior? Is there a connection between the level of understanding children demonstrate as they reflect about hypothetical situations and their social competence in real-life situations? When researchers in one study (Selman, Schorin, Stone, and Phelps, 1983) interviewed and observed girls in the second, third, fourth, and fifth grades, they found that the answers the girls gave to a dilemma about what a girl should do when her wishes and a friend's conflicted were related to the social interaction strategies they used in real groups. Immature strategies in these groups included grabbing and insulting; commands and tattling were more mature; suggestions and compromises were even more grown-up; and joking and making way for minority rights were the most mature of all. Girls with the lowest levels of reasoning in the social understanding dilemma used the fewest advanced strategies in their groups. Girls who reasoned at a high level of social understanding about hypothetical friendships also used relatively advanced strategies when they were in a group.

Research on socially isolated children, who do not interact with others in the classroom, supports this link between understanding and behavior. The solutions for social problems that these children offer have been found to be less relevant and flexible than those offered by more sociable children, at least in kindergarten (Rubin and Krasnor, 1986). Also, as we have already mentioned, popular children give better answers than rejected children to social problem-solving questions. But is this because advanced reasoning helps children know what to do in social situations, or are both reasoning and social behavior the consequences of children's general level of maturity? One way to find out would be to train children to reason about social problems and then to observe how they act in real problem situations. In one study (Shure and Spivack, 1980), children who were trained to solve hypothetical interpersonal problems were subsequently rated better adjusted by their teachers. But other researchers have not replicated these effects (Rubin and Krasnor, 1986). The strategies children need to solve their social problems are not necessarily the ones that are taught in such programs, and the strategies they are taught are not always used in their daily lives. Some social problems can be solved without thinking, and some cannot be solved even with it. The connection between children's cognitive understanding and their social skills clearly is imperfect. But the usefulness of training children in social problem-solving skills that can be translated into real actions has not yet been adequately explored by researchers. It is an area that is getting—and deserves—more attention.

The self

Middle childhood brings with it rich new developments in children's feelings about themselves. Their self-images grow more complex and sophisticated. Even their fears change.

Fears

Schoolchildren are less likely than younger children to worry about lurking monsters, although many still have bedtime fears and nightmares. But they are more likely to worry about getting hurt by others—"He would have killed me" or "Those guys wanted to cut my head off" (Bauer, 1976). School-age children can better understand why things are dangerous or cause injury. Their understanding of death changes from the imaginary to the more realistic (Grollman, 1967; Childers and Wilmmer, 1971). With this understanding develops a whole new set of anxieties, for if planes and cars crash, children can get hurt or killed. As they progress through elementary school, children begin to fear social disgraces—being sent to the principal's office, getting low marks, failing tests (Scherer and Nakamura, 1968). In a survey of over 8000 fifth through ninth graders, children were most likely to worry about how well they were doing in school, followed by how they looked and how their friends treated them (Search Institute, 1984). School children also worry about nuclear war (Solantaus, Rimpela, and Taipale, 1984).

Identity

In middle childhood, children's views of themselves change dramatically. They begin to recognize that they have unique personal qualities. They begin to feel a strong conscious sense of themselves as male or female and to project ahead to what they will do as grown women and men. To determine how the concept of the self changes in the school years, researchers have asked children to answer the question, "Who am I?" (Montemayor and Eisen, 1977).

> My name is Bruce C. I have brown eyes. I have brown hair. I have brown eyebrows. I'm 9 years old. I LOVE! sports. I have seven people in my family. I have great! eye site. I have lots! of friends. I live on 1923 Pinecrest Dr. I'm going on 10 in September. I'm a boy. I have a uncle that is almost 7 feet tall. My school is Pinecrest. My teacher is Mrs. V. I play Hockey! I'am almost the smartest boy in the class. I LOVE! food. I love freash air. I LOVE School (Montemayor and Eisen, 1977, p. 317).

Most children of 9 or 10 identified themselves as Bruce did, by the concrete facts of their existence. The 9- and 10-year-olds were likely to refer to their sex, age, name, territory, likes, dislikes, and physical self. But by age 11 many children especially girls, began to emphasize their personality and relations with others. A sixth-grade girl of 11½ gave this answer to "Who am I?"

> My name is A. I'm a human being. I'm a girl. I'm a truthful person. I'm not pretty. I do so-so in my studies. I'm a very good cellist. I'm a very good pianist. I'm a little bit tall for my age. I like several boys. I like several girls. I'm old-fashioned. I play tennis. I am a very good swimmer. I try to be helpful. I'm always ready to be friends with anybody. Mostly I'm good, but I lose my temper. I'm not well-liked by some girls. I don't know if I'm liked by boys or not (Montemayor and Eisen, 1977, pp. 317–318).

These developments clearly parallel the changes we discussed in how children describe their classmates.

At the beginning of elementary school, most children do not differentiate their characteristics from those of others. They may love sports, but they do not think of themselves as athletes. They may say, "I ride a bike," but they do not say "I ride a bike better than my brother." Gradually, by selecting and integrating new discoveries about themselves and by using their newly developed cognitive skills, they bring into focus a picture of the self that is sharp and unique. They begin to appreciate their own **identity**.

To learn more about children's ideas of identity, researchers have asked them questions like, "What is the self?" and "What is the mind?" They also have used more indirect means, such as reading children stories like the one about 8-year-old Tom quoted earlier and then asking them questions about the children in the stories (Broughton, 1978; Secord and Peevers, 1974; Selman, 1980). Six-year-olds locate their ''self'' within their body, usually within their head. As one child replied, ''I am the boss of myself. . .[because] my mouth told my arm and my arm does what my mouth tells it to do'' (Selman, 1980, p. 95). At about the age of 8, children begin to understand the difference between self and body. They describe themselves largely in terms of what they do, but they also describe how well they do it compared to other children. In middle childhood comes the understanding that one is unique not solely for physical reasons but also for what one thinks and feels. As one 10-year-old put it:

> I am one of a kind. . . .There could be a person who looks like me, but no one who had every single detail I have. Never a person who thinks exactly like me (Broughton, 1978, p. 86).

Self-esteem

School-age children achieve a deeper and richer understanding not only of who they are but also of their self-worth. **Self-esteem** reflects children's mastery of developmental tasks, their performance on schoolwork, and their success in solving social problems. It also derives in part from other people's reactions to them and their achievements.

> My mother gets mad at me at least every day, and she tells me to get outside and find friends to play with because she doesn't ''need a little friend around the house.'' I asked her once why she gets so mad at me, and she said it's because I need to be taken down a peg. Some days I want to run away, but I don't have anywhere to go.—Nancy, age 9

> Sam painted a wonderful pair of snakes, one lavender and one green, that we liked so much we framed it and hung it on the wall. When he walked into that room and saw his painting, the pride on his face was simply beautiful to see.

Although self-esteem builds over a lifetime, middle childhood is especially important because in this period children first develop more than vague, simple ideas about themselves and their worth.

Self-esteem builds over a lifetime, of course, but the years of middle childhood are critical, for that is when children first go beyond vague, simple ideas of themselves and make more complex evaluations. Once formed, a child's self-esteem is difficult to change. Children with low self-esteem feel inadequate and are afraid of others and their rejection. Extremely low self-esteem is frequently accompanied by serious psychological problems.

Researchers have studied the development of children's self-esteem in middle childhood through extensive interviews with children and their parents. In one of the most detailed of these studies (Coopersmith, 1967), investigators found that boys (all the children in the study were boys) with high self-esteem were more independent and creative than those with lower self-esteem, more readily accepted in social groups as equals and leaders, more assertive, outspoken, and likely to express their opinions, and better at taking criticism. Their parents, in turn, were caring and attentive. They loved and respected their sons, set clear and reasonable limits for them, demonstrated their expectations and communicated the importance of social norms. They did not punish the boys harshly or maintain excessively high standards for their achievement in school. They were themselves self-assured, happily married, and socially active. In sum, children with high self-esteem are likely to have the same kind of warm, supportive, parents who, as we have seen before, are most likely to foster the development of social competence in their children.

As in other studies of parents' discipline and children's behavior, it is impossible to separate cause and effect in these correlations. But it is unlikely that children have high self-esteem simply because they have supportive parents. Children also have high self-esteem because they are successful in school and elsewhere. In one study, researchers traced the connections between boys' self-esteem and their success in school and work (Bachman and O'Malley, 1977). They found that boys with high grades in school later had higher self-esteem. In another study of third through ninth graders, achievement in school was found to influence students' estimations of their competence (Connell, 1981; Harter and Connell, 1982). This estimation of their competence in turn influenced their motivation to achieve. The higher the students' opinion of their academic abilities, the greater was their motivation to do well in school.

Continuity of personality

One of the most intriguing questions about human development concerns the continuity of social and personality traits. Does the irritable infant become a sullen school child? Does the predictable toddler become a predictable preteen? Does the popular preschooler become the college homecoming queen? Does the 4-year-old who never cries, even when her sister hugs her too tightly, later get through painful visits to the dentist without a fuss? Most of us—laypeople and psychologists alike—would be tempted to guess yes. Would we be right? The answer is difficult to come by. Few researchers have followed their subjects from infancy into adulthood, and it is hard to follow the changing and tangled threads of personality across time. The scattered evidence we do have suggests that some aspects of personality are more stable then others. An adult's personality is never a wholesale continuation of the infant's or child's, but parts of early patterns surely do survive.

> Sam got hungry every three hours as an infant, and he got hungry every three hours as a child. He gets hungry every three hours now that he's a teenager, and I expect he's not going to change much later on. You could set a clock by that kid's appetite.

> Natalie was never very intense in her reactions, although she's certainly capable of feeling things strongly. She's always been soft-spoken, slow to get angry or upset. She's like a submarine, I guess, runs silent but deep.

Followed from infancy into early childhood, a few temperamental traits seem to be quite stable. As we saw in Chapter 7, there is some stability in the "difficult" temperament pattern from infancy into adulthood. Data from the New York Longitudinal Study (Thomas and Chess, 1977) suggest that activity level, intensity, adaptability, and rhythmicity are most likely to be the stable traits (Table 13.1; page 522). Infants who moved often in their sleep were likely to be in perpetual motion at age 2. Infants who had regular eating and sleeping schedules as newborns ate and slept predictably at age 3. Infants who cried vigorously at wet diapers were likely to slam doors angrily at age 10. Infants who whimpered quietly when they were hungry later were likely to be stoic in the face of a scolding. Infants who adjusted quickly to new experiences like baths later adjusted easily to new experiences like nursery school. But although these temperamental traits were stable from year to year, they were not stable across the whole period from birth to age 5, and they were not stable enough to provide a basis for solid predictions in individual cases. When another researcher with a different sample (McDevitt, 1976) used the same categories of behavior as were used in the New York Longitudinal Study, he also found some stability between infancy and early childhood in activity level, intensity, adaptability, and, for girls, rhythmicity. But between infancy and middle childhood, the traits were much less stable. Clearly, the longer the interval between the measurements of traits, the less stable they are.

Across childhood and beyond, the greatest degree of stability has been found for two important qualities, aggressiveness and sociability. Aggression toward peers seems to be one of the most stable behavioral characteristics measured by researchers (Huesmann, Eron, Lefkowitz, and Walder, 1984; Olweus, 1979; Kagan and Moss, 1962). Boys, especially, who are aggressive as 5-year-olds turn out to be aggressive as 8-, 18-, and 30-year-olds as well. Children who are inclined to insult or hit other children are, in adulthood, more likely to be guilty of criminal acts, physical abuse of their spouse, speeding, drunk driving, and getting into fights. In the study by Rowell Huesmann and his associates, for example, among 8-year-olds considered by their peers to be *low* in aggression, 10 percent of the males and none of the females were convicted of crimes before age 30. Among 8-year-olds considered *highly* aggressive, 23 percent of the males and 6 percent of the females were guilty of crimes. Aggressiveness is stable, it should be noted, not only because of continuity in constitutional factors—genetic, hormonal, neurological—but because of continuity in environmental factors as well.

Sociability is another quality of personality that seems to be quite stable over time (Beckwith, 1979; Bronson, 1966; Kagan and Moss, 1962; Martin, 1964). Evidence from one longitudinal study (Waldrop and Halverson, 1975), for example, showed that children who at age 2½ were friendly and smiling, involved with and helpful towards other children, and who could cope with aggression from other children, at 7½ were likely to spend their time outside of school with other children, to feel socially at ease, choosing what and with whom they would play. In another longitudinal study (Schaefer and Bayley, 1963), boys who were friendly preschoolers became friendly and cooperative schoolchildren and, later, friendly and outgoing adolescents. The stability of sociability between early and middle childhood was lower for girls than for boys in this and one other study (Kagan and Moss, 1962). But girls who in *late* childhood were friendly, outgoing, and cooperative, tended to stay that way during adolescence.

These personality traits are relatively stable. But it is important to remember that although *some* people change little from year to year, *others* seem in continual process of transformation (Block, 1971). Environmental, physical, and cultural changes influence how stable any individual's personality traits are across the years. People adapt their behavior to the circumstances in which they find themselves and so, in changing circumstances, their behavior changes, often markedly so, as they age.

Summary

1. In middle childhood, the world is made up of family, school, and peers. School-age children feel deeply about their families. They need and want rules and restrictions, but the more controlling relationship between involved parents and younger, immature children gradually changes into a less controlling relationship in which both parents and child are responsible for the child's behavior.

2. Children of mothers who work outside the home are likely to become independent and self-reliant earlier and to value women and their abilities more. Daughters of working mothers tend to be more independent and outgoing and to do better in school than daughters of housewives. But in some middle-class families, sons of working mothers may do less well in school, score lower on intelligence tests, feel that their mothers are uninvolved, and therefore feel depressed and inadequate.

Table 13.1
Expression of temperament

Temperamental quality	At 2 months	At 10 years
1. ACTIVITY LEVEL[a]	Moves often in sleep. Wriggles when diaper is changed.	Plays ball and engages in other sports. Cannot sit still long enough to do homework.
	Does not move when being dressed or during sleep.	Likes chess and reading. Eats very slowly.
2. PHYSICAL RHYTHMS	Has been on four-hour feeding schedule since birth. Regular bowel movement.	Eats only at mealtimes. Sleeps the same amount of time each night.
	Awakes at a different time each morning. Size of feedings varies.	Food intake varies. Falls asleep at different time each night.
3. APPROACH AND AVOIDANCE	Smiles and licks washcloth. Has always liked bottle.	Went to camp happily. Loved to ski the first time.
	Rejected cereal the first time. Cries when stranger appears.	Severely homesick at camp during first days. Does not like new activities.
4. ADAPTABILITY	Was passive during first bath; now enjoys bathing. Smiles at nurse.	Likes camp, although homesick during first days. Learns enthusiastically.
	Still startled by sudden, sharp noise. Resists diapering.	Does not adjust well to new school or new teacher; comes home late for dinner even when punished.
5. INTENSITY OF REACTION	Cries when diapers are wet. Rejects food vigorously when satisfied.	Tears up an entire page of homework if one mistake is made. Slams door of room when teased by younger brother.
	Does not cry when diapers are wet. Whimpers instead of crying when hungry.	When a mistake is made in a model airplane, corrects it quietly. Does not comment when reprimanded.

3. School-age children form friendship cliques, with leaders and followers, in which they do such things together as watch television, go to the movies, play games, go to the beach, and talk. Girls have an intensive style of interacting with each other; they play with one other girl, express intense feelings about her, and share experiences and fantasies with her. Boys have an extensive style of interacting with each other. They play noisily in a group and usually focus on a game like baseball or soccer. In the age-segregated elementary school, boys and girls rarely mix.

4. Popular children are confident, outgoing, active, friendly, and cooperative. They are rarely aggressive, get along with anyone, and know what to say and when to say it. Children who are socially inept, aggressive, disruptive, and act inappropriately are often rejected.

Table 13.1 (*continued*)
Expression of temperament

Temperamental quality	At 2 months	At 10 years
6. THRESHOLD OF RESPONSIVENESS	Stops sucking on bottle when approached.	Rejects fatty foods. Adjusts shower until water is at exactly the right temperature.
	Is not startled by loud noises. Takes bottle and breast equally well.	Never complains when sick. Eats all foods.
7. USUAL MOOD	Smacks lips when first tasting new food. Smiles at parents.	Enjoys new accomplishments. Laughs aloud when reading a funny passage.
	Fusses after nursing. Cries when carriage is rocked.	Cries when he cannot solve a homework problem. Very ''weepy'' if he does not get enough sleep.
8. DISTRACTIBILITY	Will stop crying for food if rocked. Stops fussing if given pacifier when diaper is being changed.	Needs absolute silence for homework. Has a hard time choosing a shirt in a store because they all appeal to him.
	Will not stop crying when diaper is changed. Fusses after eating, even if rocked.	Can read a book while television set is at high volume. Does chores on schedule.
9. ATTENTION SPAN AND PERSISTENCE	If soiled, continues to cry until changed. Repeatedly rejects water if he wants milk.	Reads for two hours before sleeping. Does homework carefully.
	Cries when awakened but stops almost immediately. Objects only mildly if cereal precedes bottle.	Gets up frequently from homework for a snack. Never finishes a book.

[a]High levels and positive behavior appear on white background; low levels and negative behavior on gray background.
SOURCE: Thomas, Chess, and Birch, 1970.

5. Cooperation, helping, and showing concern for others increase during early childhood but decline toward the end of middle childhood. Competitiveness, individualism, and generosity increase over the school years.

6. Almost all schoolchildren sometimes cheat or fib. They also sometimes hurt each other. Children learn aggression from parents who are aggressive, rejecting, and unloving and who punish the children for aggression but do not reward them for sharing or cooperating. Children's peers reinforce, elicit, model, and absorb aggression. When children watch a lot of violent television shows, think that these shows are real, identify with aggressive television characters, are reinforced for their own aggressive behavior, and are objects of aggression, they are likely to act aggressively.

7. Children in open classes generally feel more positive about school and about themselves than children in traditional classes.

8. What children do after school largely depends on the neighborhoods they live in—whether there are parks, stores, community centers, busy streets, fenced yards, sidewalks, streetlights, and other physical features. With their friends, children roam around their neighborhoods on foot, bike, and skateboard, play sports, join clubs and Scout troops, and take lessons.

9. As they get older, children get better at understanding other people's feelings, moods, intentions, and motives. As their social understanding increases, their social competence increases, too.

10. The way that children see themselves changes in middle childhood as they begin to recognize that they have unique qualities. Children's self-esteem derives in part from others' opinions of them and in part from their mastery of developmental tasks, their performance in school, and their ability to deal with social situations.

11. Some temperamental traits—activity level, intensity, adaptability, and rhythmicity—seem somewhat stable from infancy to early childhood. Across childhood and beyond, the most stable qualities are aggressiveness and sociability.

Key terms

intensive peer relations
extensive peer relations

intrinsic motivation
social convention

identity
self-esteem

Suggested readings

ASHER, STEVEN, and GOTTMAN, JOHN (Eds.). *The Development of Children's Friendships.* Cambridge: Cambridge University Press, 1981. A broad sampling of research into peer relations and their effect on children's development. The chapters on children without friends and how training can improve their social standing, and Robert Selman's chapter on children's capacities for friendship are of special interest.

DAMON, WILLIAM. *The Social World of the Child.* San Francisco: Jossey-Bass, 1977. A discussion of how children reorganize their ways of understanding social reality and deal with the principal social relations and regulations of their lives. The book is liberally sprinkled with actual conversations between children and adults.

HIGGINS, E. TORY, RUBLE, DIANE, and HARTUP, WILLARD (Eds.). *Social Cognition and Social Develop-*ment. New York: Cambridge University Press, 1983. An overview of current research and theory concerning social cognition and social behavior in children, with a focus on the developmental roots of social cognitive abilities.

RUBIN, KENNETH, and ROSS, HILDY (Eds.). *Peer Relationships and Social Skills in Childhood.* New York: Springer-Verlag, 1982. A collection of articles examining the development of peer relationships and social skills from infancy through early adolescence, by many of the most eminent researchers in the field.

SILBERMAN, MELVIN L. *The Experience of Schooling.* New York: Holt, Rinehart and Winston, 1971. An interesting, sometimes irreverent, look at school, the bias of teachers, the way certain students affect teachers, and the way school feels to children.

Adolescence

chapter fourteen
Physical development

I look at these kids I've known since they were pip-squeaks, and all of a sudden they're all grown up. Sam and his friends eat *incredible* quantities, their voices crack and embarrass them to death, and they need a bigger shoe size every two weeks. No more Saturday morning cartoons; the kids are *asleep*. The girls are getting curvy and attractive. Natalie comes over to our house now wearing lipstick and perfume, pocketbook over her shoulder. No more dollies. She wants to talk about dates.

Young people go through a series of biological and psychological changes at the end of childhood, as they enter **adolescence**. Their bodies visibly mature, their roles in society change, and the very content and complexity of their thoughts change as well. In this chapter, we begin our discussion of the complexities of development in adolescence by looking at the physical changes adolescence brings and at some of the implications of these changes for the way adolescents think and feel about themselves.

Puberty

The set of biological changes that mark the beginning of adolescence is called **puberty**. Puberty begins as increased levels of hormones enter the bloodstream, in response to signals from the hypothalamus region of the brain

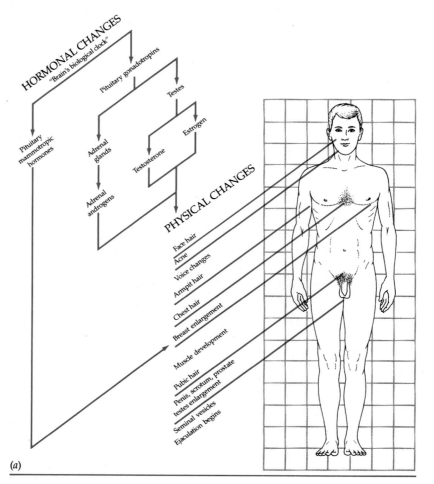

PROCESSES AT PUBERTY

Figure 14.1 Processes of sexual maturation at puberty in males and females.

(a)

(Figure 14.1). Early in prenatal life, sex hormones and other chemicals in the fetus and in the uterine environment program the hypothalamus of a male to develop differently from that of a female. At puberty, signals from these sexually differentiated parts of the hypothalamus communicate to the pituitary gland (also located in the brain) to increase its production of growth hormone and the hormones that stimulate the development of the gonads—ovaries and testes. The gonads then increase their production of sex hormones—estrogens and androgens—that turn the bodies of girls and boys into those of sexually mature young women and men. Throughout childhood, boys' and girls' bodies have produced roughly equal levels of estrogens and androgens. But with puberty, girls' bodies begin producing more estrogens than androgens, and boys' bodies begin producing more androgens than estrogens. As these sex hormones enter the bloodstream, they stimulate the development of particularly sensitive cells elsewhere in the body. In girls, breasts and genitals mature in response to estrogens; in boys, genitals mature in response to androgens.

The growth spurt

> Sam grew five inches in ninth grade. His body changed so fast that for a while he lost his physical coordination. He seemed to be bumping into things all the time and looked really gangly there for a while.

PROCESSES AT PUBERTY

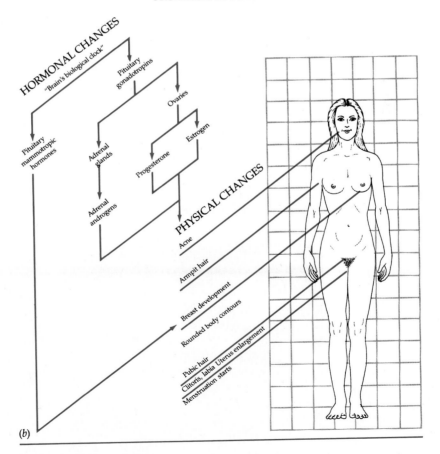

(b)

As the levels of growth hormone rise in the body, the steadily but slowly growing child seems suddenly to spurt up. It is this **growth spurt** that to the outside world visibly signals the beginning of puberty. The rate of growth may double, with young adolescents growing as much as five inches in their peak year. For boys, the growth spurt usually starts at 12 or 13 and peaks at about 14 years, then tapers off after 16, and finally stops at 18 or 19. For girls, the growth spurt starts at 10 or 11, peaks at 12 or 13, and stops at 17 or 18 (Bayer and Bayley, 1976; Faust, 1977; Stolze and Stolze, 1951; Tanner, 1970; see Figure 14.2). But there are wide individual differences in when the growth spurt occurs. One longitudinal study, for example, showed that of 94 girls, one began her growth spurt at the age of 7½, and one began hers at 13 (Faust, 1977).

The growth in height results from the final stages of bone maturation. It is at puberty that the epiphyses—the parts of the long bones made of cartilage—finally turn to bone. The muscles, too, lengthen and strengthen. Internal organs—lungs, heart, stomach, kidneys—grow to adult size and capacity. Boys particularly, in response to androgens, gain muscle mass, strength, and stamina. Their bodies grow more efficient at metabolizing lactic acid, the by-product of strenuous exercise. Girls, in response to estrogen, develop curves as breasts, hips, and buttocks grow larger and padded with fat.

But growth is not smooth and even. It is asynchronous. Legs grow before trunk and shoulders. Forearms grow before upper arms. Whereas growth in infancy and early childhood was from center to periphery—proximodistal—growth at puberty is just the opposite, from periphery to center—distoproximal. Adolescents in the midst of the uneven growth patterns of puberty sometimes look gawky and uncoordinated. Big feet and hands, long legs and arms poke out of pants and shirts. Jaws and ears look too big. At puberty, nose, lips, and ears reach their adult size before the upper part of the head grows. As the eyes grow in size, many adolescents become nearsighted. The sweat and oil glands of their skin make baby-fine complexions coarsen and break out.

Development of sexual characteristics

The most profound transformation of puberty is the development of sexual maturity, the ability to reproduce. The reproductive systems of boys and girls at adolescence enlarge and mature into those of sexually mature men and women. The primary sexual characteristics—genitals and associated structures—have been in existence since birth, but at puberty they become functional. Girls begin to menstruate and then to ovulate, boys to ejaculate semen.

On the average, girls start their growth spurt two years before boys do.

TIMING OF PHYSICAL CHANGES AT PUBERTY

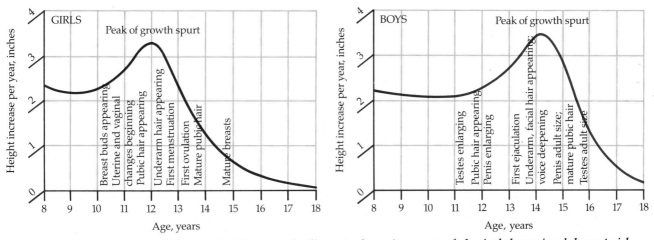

Figure 14.2 These graphs illustrate the main aspects of physical change in adolescent girls and boys at puberty. Curves represent changes in height. Secondary sexual characteristics are shown by typical age of onset. Although individual variations in age are normal, the sequence of onset is essentially as shown (Tanner and Whitehouse, 1976; Tanner, 1978).

At puberty, too, the **secondary sexual characteristics** develop (see Figure 14.2). Before his growth spurt begins, a boy's testes grow larger, downy pubic hair emerges, and the skin of the scrotum turns pinker and coarser. Then, just as growth hormone makes him taller, it makes his penis grow larger. The internal pathways for delivering sperm also develop, and after a year or two, the sperm-producing structures have matured and are producing live sperm. Nocturnal emissions, or wet dreams, may occur. Gradually, the numbers of sperm produced increase to the point that the young man is fertile and biologically capable of fathering a child. Because his hypothalamus signals for the fairly constant production of sex hormones, his production of sperm is also constant—many thousands every day.

It is not only the boy's reproductive system that develops at puberty. Fine hair appears on his upper lip, chin, and cheeks and under his arms. This fine hair then grows coarser and darker. The boy's larynx and vocal cords lengthen, deepening his voice. To his horror, his breasts may enlarge temporarily, a side effect of the high levels of hormones in his body. Eventually though, a boy's body takes on its distinctly masculine outline. The soft contours and plumpness many boys have disappear. Their faces get bonier and more muscular. Androgens make the boy's shoulders widen and his rib cage expand. By the end of puberty, he is likely to have beard and body hair, broad shoulders and chest, narrow hips, and a lean, muscular, angular form.

The parallel transformation for the girl is to take on the curves and padding of fat typical of the feminine outline. First, the girl sees breasts bud and fine pubic hair sprout. Even before she notices these outward signs, her uterus has begun to enlarge and her vaginal lining to thicken. Her hips and thighs grow heavier and wider, and her waist seems narrower. Estrogens cause her pelvis to widen, a development that will make childbearing easier. Her voice loses its girlish reediness. Her breasts continue to grow for several years, the area around the nipple—the areola—darkening and expanding. Her external genitals also enlarge, coarser pubic hair covers her mons and external labia, and underarm hair develops. A year or two after she has reached the peak of her growth spurt, her first menstrual period—**menarche**—appears.

Menstruation usually begins only when a girl weighs over 100 pounds, presumably because at that weight her body has enough fat to store the estrogen needed for menstrual cycles. The first menstrual cycles may be irregular, and the girl's body may not begin to ovulate for a year or so after menstrual cycles have begun. Only when she ovulates does she become fertile, capable of conceiving a child.

By the end of puberty, boys have bigger and stronger muscles than girls, larger hearts and lungs, more blood and more oxygen capacity in their blood, and lower resting heart rates (Faust, 1977; Grinder, 1978; Malina, 1974; Tanner, 1970). With these physical advantages and their greater upper body strength, boys tend to excel in some sports, such as throwing and fielding balls, wrestling, and lifting weights. With their larger reserves of fat and greater flexibility, girls tend to excel at different sports, like gymnastics, distance running, and swimming. Although the *best* male athletes usually can outperform the *best* female athletes in a given sport (in professional basketball or marathon running, for example), the *best* female athletes can outperform the *majority* of males.

Puberty confers on males and females measurable differences in size, shape, and strength. But cultural attitudes intensify the effects of these biological differences. When gender-role expectations are such that females are pressured to be more delicate and weaker than males, adolescent girls actually may perform at reduced levels of strength after puberty. As attitudes toward the participation of women in high school and college athletics have changed, women in many fields have broken records and surpassed traditional expectations. In fact, female athletes have surpassed world records held by males 20 years ago (for example, in swimming). Old-fashioned fears that women should not engage in strenuous activity during their menstrual periods, that the menstrual cycle makes women's performance erratic, and that breasts and uterus make women too delicate to participate safely in sports have all proved unfounded. Surveys conducted at the Olympic Games show that women have set world records at all stages in the menstrual cycle (Grinder, 1978). The uterus is one of the most shock-resistant of all internal organs, and the external genitals of females are less exposed than those of males.

The trend toward earlier maturity

Both the growth spurt and the age of first menstruation have been occurring at younger and younger ages over the past century. This secular trend in maturation has been noted in Canada, the United States, Great Britain, Sweden, Japan, and other places with comprehensive statistics on growth (Moore, 1970). In the United States, for example, girls of a century ago first menstruated at 13 to 15 years; today the age is 11 to 13. Similarly for boys, the growth spurt now, on the average, begins two years earlier than it did at the turn of the century (Blizzard et al., 1974; Bullough, 1981; Hamburg, 1974; Tanner, 1962). Not only does the growth spurt start earlier, but adolescents also grow taller and heavier than they did in the past (see Figure 14.3). Armor worn by medieval knights would fit a 10-year-old today, and the average height of male colonists was five feet. On average, for every ten years between 1910 and 1940, white adolescents grew one-half inch taller; for every ten years between 1940 and 1960, they grew one-quarter inch taller (Espenschade and Meleney, 1961).

Is this trend likely to continue? Are boys and girls going to mature ever earlier and grow ever larger—until they are sexually mature in kindergarten and as tall as giraffes in college? Some researchers have suggested that the timing of sexual development must have a limit (Tanner, 1965), and, in fact, the average age of menarche, 12.6 years, has not altered in the last 30 years (McAnarney and Greydanus, 1979). Puberty probably began earlier primarily

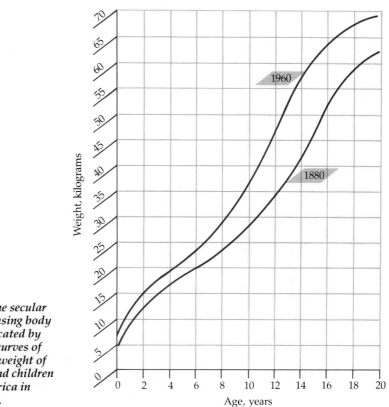

SECULAR TREND IN BODY WEIGHT: 1880 AND 1960

Figure 14.3 The secular trend of increasing body weight is indicated by these growth curves of average body weight of adolescents and children in North America in 1880 and 1960.

because young people were eating better and suffering from fewer diseases than previously (Tanner, 1962). When girls eat well, they reach the critical body weight of 100 pounds earlier and so begin to mature sexually. It is likely that disease and poor nutrition can delay maturation and that good health and nutrition can stimulate it—a kind of biological "greenhouse effect"—but only so much.

Effects of physical change

Do the hormones that trigger the physical changes of puberty also trigger psychological changes? Do the physical changes themselves have psychological ramifications? Yes they do, but the effects are not as simple as one might expect.

Hormones and psychological states

When menarche begins, many adolescent girls undergo profound changes in their self-image (see Figure 14.4), in their attitudes toward others, and even in perceptual abilities. In one investigation (Diamond, Carey, and Back, 1983), for example, girls were found to encode unfamiliar faces less efficiently during puberty than either before or after puberty. What might cause this? It has nothing to do with changing schools, the research showed, and it has nothing to do with any age-related reorganization in knowledge of faces. It is possible

MENARCHE AND SELF-IMAGE

Figure 14.4 The drawing on the left was done by a girl 12 years and 1 month old—before she began menstruating. She saw herself differently six months later, after she had begun to menstruate (Gardner, 1982, from Koff, Rierdan, and Silverstone, 1978).

that the hormones of puberty directly affect the brain's ability to recognize faces. It is also possible that the phenomenon is psychological. Perhaps in adolescence children become interested in different aspects of faces and so, through puberty, go through a period of less efficient encoding. For now the question remains open. Further research is necessary to explore the relations between hormonal and psychological changes during adolescence.

Another study to explore these relations provides evidence that hormonal changes associated with menstruation, especially fluctuations in estrogen, are associated with anxiety and other psychological states in adolescent women (Ivey and Bardwick, 1968). In the study, adolescent women were asked to speak for five minutes on any memorable experience in their lives. On the few days just before menstruation, when their estrogen levels were low, the women's memories contained themes of death, mutilation, helplessness, and loneliness. When their estrogen levels were highest, around the time of ovulation, the themes more often reflected success and coping skills. Said one woman before menstruation,

> They had to teach me how to water ski. I was clumsy. It was really embarrassing 'cause it was kind of like saying to yourself you can't do it, and the people were about to lose patience with me (Bardwick, 1971, p. 31).

But near the time of ovulation, she said:

> So I was elected chairman. I had to establish with them the fact that I knew what I was doing. I remember one particular problematic meeting, and afterwards L. came up to me and said, ''You really handled the meeting well.'' In the end it came out the sort of thing that really bolstered my confidence in myself (Bardwick, 1971, p. 31).

This study was not as carefully controlled as it might have been, and the results have not been replicated. But preliminary findings from a study underway at the National Institute of Mental Health (Nottelmann and Susman, 1985) suggest that a low level of the sex hormone estradiol may be related to psychological adjustment problems in 9- to 14-year-old girls. In boys the link between hormones and behavior is even clearer and stronger. Boys with high adrenal androgen were more likely to have behavior problems—

rebelliousness, talking back, fighting with classmates—or feelings of sadness and confusion. This finding fits with earlier research showing that when adolescents were given androgen, they became more aggressive (Wolstenholme and O'Connor, 1967).

The effect of hormones on adolescents' behavior are complicated by social and psychological factors, however. Cultural and family attitudes make a difference in whether hormones bring about psychological change. Attitudes toward menstruation and toward menarche, for example, affect adolescents' anxiety and physical discomfort around their menstrual periods.

> I have terrible cramps every month. No one can convince me that they're all in my head. It's the "curse."—Megan, age 15

> I almost never have cramps, and I do anything and everything when I have my period. My mother says just to do what I normally do. My friend's mother won't let her swim when she has her period.—Erica, age 15

In the United States, cultural attitudes toward menarche and menstruation are mixed. We have no formal ceremony or other means of recognizing the event, but we may surround the newly menstruating girl in a kind of pall.

> We prescribe no ritual; the girl continues on a round of school or work, but she is constantly confronted by a mysterious apprehensiveness in her parents and guardians. Her society has all the tensity of a room full of people who expect the latest arrival to throw a bomb (Mead, 1971, p. 180).

Although some adolescent girls have been exposed to a bit of education—films on menstruation, talks with their mothers, and the like—in one study of white, middle-class girls, most had little idea about what the inside of the body was like or how it functioned (Whisnant and Zegans, 1975). Although they had been told about showering and changing sanitary pads during their periods, their ideas about the purpose of menstruation were sketchy. Those who had not yet menstruated thought that when their first period came they would proudly announce it to family and friends. But when they did begin to menstruate, most grew secretive and told only their mothers.

> When I first got my period, I knew what it was, and so I wasn't scared. But I was embarrassed and asked my mother not to tell anyone. She was so proud "that her little girl had become a woman" that she crowed about it to everyone. I felt like crawling under the rug.—Sarah, age 15

Some grew closer to their mothers, even those who had not felt close before, and some focused more on their relationships with their fathers. In another study in which 350 adolescent girls were polled, most said that they believed menstruation caused physical pain, emotional upheaval, mood swings, and disruptions in behavior and relationships (Ruble and Brooks, 1977). The girl's age at the time, her knowledge and expectations, her personality, and the support she receives from her family all influence how she interprets menstruation. Girls who are well prepared both physically and psychologically and who begin menstruating at about the same time as most of their friends tend to feel that menstruation is a normal event (Ruble and Brooks-Gunn, 1982).

Body image

> Jason works out with weights, he's a vegetarian, and he runs 50 miles a week. He looks a lot healthier than he did as a young boy, but I worry

sometimes that he's doing all this because underneath he feels that his body doesn't measure up somehow.

Just as menarche changes adolescents' images of themselves, so do other physical changes ushered in by puberty—particularly changes in appearance. Not a few adolescents are unhappy with the way they look; they have a poor **body image**. ''Too fat'' thought nearly half of all 12- to 17-year-olds surveyed in one national poll; ''too short'' thought nearly half the boys (Scanlon, 1975). ''Too pimply'' thought one-third of the girls and one-fifth of the boys at age 12; half the girls and two-thirds of the boys at age 17. **Acne** is only one of the complaints adolescents make about their appearance. Others dislike their posture (Hamburg, 1974). Asynchronous growth makes them feel awkward and ungainly. Many worry that they do not measure up, do not meet a tacit standard among their peers, and differ in some way from what girls or boys ''should'' look like. Boys want to see whether they measure up in height, endurance, muscle strength, and virility. Many worry that their penis is the wrong size, shape, or color; that their chests and chins are not hairy enough; that their voices are not deep enough. Girls, already uncomfortable because from age 11 to 13 they tower over the boys in their class, are concerned about measuring up in prettiness. Many of them worry that their breasts and genitals are the wrong size and shape, that their hair, teeth, hips, legs are not attractive enough. Those with chronic illnesses or handicaps can feel miserably self-conscious and different from ''the other kids'' at a time when being like them is nearly the most important thing in life (Magrab and Calcagno, 1978).

Adolescents who are attractive and who have a favorable body image are likely to have a generally favorable self-image and to be happier, more socially successful, and more pleased with themselves right into their adulthood than unattractive adolescents with poor body images (Berscheid, Walster, and Bohrnstedt, 1973; Jaquish and Savin-Williams, 1981). Adolescents' body images are based not only on what their bodies look like at present but on a lifelong accumulation of perceptions and feelings about their appearance.

> I was a chubby little girl, and so now every time I look in the mirror, I see *fat*. My grandmother tells me to stop dieting, that I look fine. But I don't believe her. Once a tub, always a tub.—Natalie, age 16

Even when their bodies have changed enormously at adolescence—the skinny becoming round, the round becoming skinny, the cute becoming plain, the plain becoming handsome—the things adolescents heard and saw about themselves in childhood do not allow them to perceive themselves objectively.

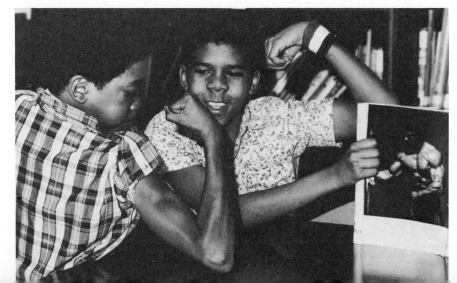

As their body image forms, adolescent boys constantly compare their physical growth and prowess against each other and with those of their ideal.

Adolescents whose self-images in childhood were positive are more likely to approve of their new images than are those whose early self-images were negative and harsh.

How parents, teachers, and peers judge their appearance also contributes to adolescents' body images. During the rapid changes of early adolescence, when many lose the sense of what "normal" looks like for themselves, other people's opinions can be especially important, and those people's judgments usually are based on stereotypes of physical attractiveness. School principals, teachers, and teenagers all tend to think more highly of large, muscular, athletic boys than of smaller, weaker, less athletic boys, for example (Clarke and Clarke, 1961).

Early and late maturation

> Willy worried a lot that he wasn't developing fast enough. He worried because "all the other kids" were starting to shave and talk in deep voices, and he still looked like a child. I told him not to worry, that he was just a late bloomer and that he'd catch up.

Some adolescents, as we have seen, reach puberty earlier and some later than the norm. Some 14-year-olds look and act like sexually mature men and women, but some are still children. Variation in the timing of puberty is normal. Researchers have studied whether this difference in timing has psychological effects.

In one early study, researchers picked out 16 of the earliest maturing and 16 of the latest maturing boys from the Berkeley Growth Study (Jones and Bayley, 1950). They observed the boys on the playing field, in a doctor's waiting room, talking with girls at a dance, and getting along with their classmates, and they talked to the boys' teachers and peers. They found that other adolescents thought that the **late maturers** were restless, immature, and bossy. Adults also considered them restless and immature, as well as tense, eager, energetic, and self-conscious. Many of the late maturers tried to compensate for their physical immaturity with bids for attention and bursts of activity; a few withdrew from others. In contrast, the **early maturers** were self-confident, calm, and considered mature by both adults and other adolescents. They engaged in little compensating or striving for status, though many were leaders in high school. When the boys made up stories about ambiguous pictures in the Thematic Apperception Test (TAT) (Mussen and Jones, 1957), the early maturers' stories were characterized by self-confidence, independence, and social maturity. The late maturers' were characterized by low self-esteem, dependence, rejection, conflict with their parents, and domination by

The early maturing boy has social advantages in high school and is likely to be a leader and greatly admired.

others. The evidence suggests that early maturation confers social advantages, and late maturation, social disadvantages.

In a more recent and comprehensive study, 6000 adolescents were classified into early-, average-, and late-maturing groups (Duke et al., 1982). The adolescents, their parents, and their teachers were asked about the adolescents' school performance, intelligence, and related matters. Again, for late maturing boys, at every age beyond 12 years, disadvantages in development showed up. Compared to mid-maturing boys, late-maturing boys were less likely to intend to finish college and were less likely to be expected by their parents to do so. Their teachers considered late-maturing boys less intelligent and less academically able.

When the adolescents in the Berkeley Growth Study were observed again at the age of 33, the early maturers still bore social advantages, still seemed poised and cooperative, were social leaders and professional successes. But they were also more likely to be rigid and tightly controlled, clinging in later life to the behavior that won them social acceptance in adolescence—and paying a psychological price for it. The late maturers were given to impulses, irritable, rebellious, and less successful and cooperative. Some continued to feel inferior and rejected. But, on the positive side, many had grown to be more flexible, perceptive, assertive, expressive, eager, uninhibited, insightful, and playful than the other men (Jones, 1957; Peskin, 1967). When puberty begins apparently does affect an individual's emotions and social development. But the outcomes are neither all good nor all bad.

These differences have been observed in the United States. In other countries, such as Italy, where physical ability is not so highly prized, self-esteem and social standing are less likely to be affected by the rate of physical maturation (Mussen and Bouterline-Young, 1964).

The effects of the timing of maturation on girls are similar, though more complicated then the effects on boys (Duke et al., 1982). Whereas early-maturing boys are viewed as athletic and as leaders, maturing early can present problems for the adolescent girl because of the ways that parents and peers react to the girl's potential for sexuality. More important than being early or late, for girls, is being "on time." Just as with menarche and physical appearance, it is very important to adolescents how others respond. Reaching puberty when most of their peers do tends to make adjustment easier (Faust, 1960; Greif and Ulman, 1982; Harper and Collins, 1972; Weatherly, 1964; Wilen and Peterson, 1980).

Sexuality

The physical changes of puberty make possible feelings of mature sexuality. Sexuality has been present since infancy, but it has been present in immature form. Infants and young children are no strangers to genital stimulation, exploration, or sexual arousal. In the preschool years, sexual games and fantasies are normal and widespread. In research by Alfred Kinsey and his associates, for example, 56 percent of boys and 30 percent of girls said that they masturbated (Elias and Gebhard, 1969). But mature sexuality is made up of more than genital exploration and stimulation. It is made up of more than the hormones, ova, and sperm that develop at puberty. Mature sexuality is also made up of mature *ideas* about sex. Most adolescents develop a fuller understanding about reproduction than they had as children, new interests in intimate sexual relationships, and new cultural expectations about the who, when, and where of sexual behavior.

Cultural expectations strongly influence sexual behavior during adolescence. As attitudes toward sexual behavior have changed in the last 50 years, so have adolescents' sexual habits (see Figure 14.5). For example, relatively

Cultural expectations strongly influence sexual thoughts and behavior during adolescence.

RATES OF PREMARITAL SEX

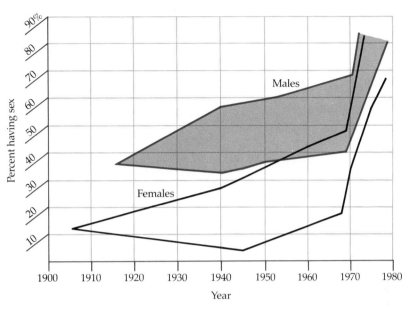

Figure 14.5 Rates of sexual intercourse for never-married male and female college students, based on 35 published studies (Darling, Kallen, and VanDusen, 1984), illustrating both the increase in premarital sex and the decline in the "double standard."

few adolescents in one study reported feeling guilty about masturbating, a change from earlier generations (Sorenson, 1973). Moreover, the number of adolescents having sexual intercourse began to increase in the 1960s and 1970s and continues to increase in the 1980s (Dreyer, 1982). Adolescents today see the world as sexually active, even sexually preoccupied (Miller and Simon, 1980). They feel that social disapproval of sexual activity has weakened and that they must decide as individuals about the degree of sexual intimacy they find comfortable. Most adolescents date for some time without engaging in sexual intercourse, but eventually, after kissing, necking, and petting, most of them do have intercourse with their steady dates. Among 14-year-olds in the recent survey, 20 percent reported having had sexual intercourse (Search Institute, 1984). Among 16-year-olds, in another major survey, 45 percent of the boys and 33 percent of the girls were sexually active. Among 19-year-olds, 80 percent of the boys and 70 percent of the girls were sexually active (Alan Guttmacher Institute, 1981; see Figure 14.6).

The increase in sexual activity over the past two decades may be more a reflection of attempts to achieve personal identity and physical intimacy than a reflection of uncontrolled impulse gratification. For most adolescents, sex is not casual. But neither is sex an obsession. When 600 adolescents were asked to rank the importance of activities in their lives, they ranked sex last, after doing well in school, having friends of their own sex, having friends of the other sex, participating in sports, and being romantically involved (Haas, 1979). The adolescents who have sex differ somewhat from those who do not. They tend to have less conventional attitudes and values, to be less involved in conventional social institutions, to be more likely to use drugs or alcohol, and to have parents who are less controlling (Jessor and Jessor, 1975).

As sexual standards have relaxed, the old double standard—a stricter standard of sexual conduct for women than for men—has relaxed as well (Miller and Simon, 1980). More girls are having sex before marriage. By college, 74 percent of *both* young women and men have had sexual intercourse (Dreyer, 1982). But boys still are likely to have more sexual partners than girls. In one recent study, the majority of the adolescent girls had had sex with only

RATES OF SEXUAL ACTIVITY

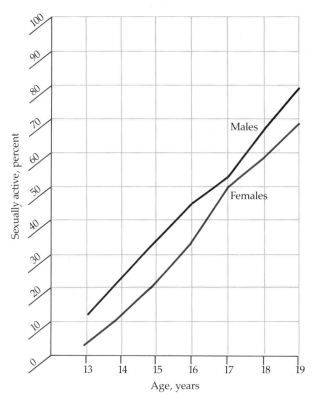

Figure 14.6 Recent statistics show that by age 16, 45 percent of boys and 33 percent of girls in the United States are sexually active. By age 19, the percentages are 79 for boys and 68 for girls (Alan Guttmacher Institute, 1981).

one partner; the majority of boys had had sex with more than two partners (Haas, 1979). Most adolescent girls have sex first with someone they love and hope to marry. Boys are not so likely to have sex with a partner whom they love (Jessor, Costa, Jessor, and Donovan, 1983). The reason for this difference may be biological (boys have spontaneous erections; girls do not) or it may be social (boys brag about their exploits; girls do not). Whichever it is, the **sexual scripts**—norms about how to be sexual, norms about what, when, and with whom one does sexual things, and what they mean—differ for adolescent boys and girls (Gagnon and Simon, 1970). Adolescent boys usually proceed from masturbation to sex with a partner, and they must learn from girls about the interpersonal and the emotional aspects of sex. In contrast, adolescent girls usually begin with sex with a partner and must learn from boys how to focus on the physical aspects of sex. On dates, boys teach girls how to abandon themselves to sensual pleasure and to put aside manners and tidiness. Girls teach boys how to nurture and support. If they learn well, late in adolescence both boys and girls will combine elements of both sexes' scripts into a mature sexuality. In one survey, only 5 percent of the college students questioned said that they were not emotionally involved with their partner, compared with 45 percent of young adolescent boys (Miller and Simon, 1980).

Homosexuality

Most adolescents are sexually attracted to people of the other sex. But some adolescents wish for sexual relationships with members of their own sex. Although few adolescents have committed themselves to homosexuality, a large minority have thought about it. Among adolescents in one study, although they did not identify themselves as homosexual in orientation, 11 percent of the boys and 6 percent of the girls had had some homosexual experience (Sorensen, 1973). In a more recent study, 15 percent of boys and 10 percent of girls reported having had a homosexual experience (Dreyer, 1982). Forty percent of the adolescent boys and girls in the first study agreed that "If two boys and two girls want to have sex together, it's all right so long as they both want to do it." But 75 percent also said, "I'm sure I'd never want to." Typically, boys have their first homosexual experience with an older boy or a man at ages 11 or 12, and with increasing age, they are more likely to have homosexual experiences (Bell, Weinberg, and Hammersmith, 1981). Exclusively homosexual men have homosexual feelings as boys, and their homosexuality usually is well established by their late teens. Bisexual men do not have homosexual feelings as boys, although they do have homosexual experiences; their bisexuality usually emerges after age 19.

> I was *afraid* that I was gay when I was very young. I *knew* it when I was in my teens. But it took me until after college to come out.—Tim, age 25

Girls, in contrast, are most likely to have their first homosexual experience with another girl between the ages of 6 and 10.

In the past, the behavior and feelings of parents and peers were thought to cause a person's homosexuality. But these threads are probably just part of a larger and more complex biological, psychological, and social web. Biological factors probably predispose a person toward homosexuality. These biological factors then make the child act in certain ways that elicit certain reactions from parents and others. A boy who acts girlish, for example, might elicit hostility or rejection from his father and therefore would not want to identify with this masculine figure. Thus, sexual orientation may have its origins in very early hormonal events, and these may shape behavior and elicit reactions to that behavior. In one longitudinal study (Green, in press; Green, Neuberg, Shapiro, and Finch, 1983), young boys referred to a clinic because their parents were worried about their preference for wearing girls' clothes, playing with girls' toys, and doing feminine things, were observed and tested.When dressed to conceal their sex, these boys threw a ball, walked, ran, and told a story in ways that were *neither* markedly feminine nor markedly masculine. In adulthood, 29 out of 43 turned out to be homosexual or bisexual. Only one factor in the boys' environments seemed to correlate with later homosexuality: the absence of the boy's natural father in the family. Why? It may be that although biology disposes a boy toward homosexuality, the presence of a strong father inhibits its expression. The pattern of feelings, attitudes, reactions, and thoughts that makes up any person's sexual orientation takes shape over the course of childhood, is reshaped during adolescence, and typically is confirmed in adulthood. The course of development, in this as in other areas, involves both biology and culture, nature and nurture.

Health problems

Because of the physical changes we have discussed, adolescence ushers in its own special health problems and hazards. Sexual activity brings teenage pregnancies and sexually transmitted diseases. Cigarette smoking, drug use, and drinking alcohol become fairly common. Violence, accidents, self-imposed starvation, and suicide take adolescents' lives (Schroeder, Teplin, and Schroeder, 1982).

Pregnancy, childbirth, and contraception

Mature enough physically to conceive and bear children, few adolescents are socially and emotionally mature enough to take good care of themselves when pregnant, to meet the intense demands of an infant, or to support themselves and their child financially and emotionally. When they do become pregnant, many adolescent girls do not receive adequate prenatal care. Only 40 percent of pregnant 15-year-olds get prenatal care in the first third of their pregnancies, half the number of those over 25 who seek prenatal care (Ventura, 1977). Over and above these problems of psychological maturity, pregnant adolescents face serious physical risks. It is a cruel irony that although adolescent girls can conceive, their bodies are too immature for problem-free pregnancy and delivery. The medical risks for a pregnant teenager are twice those of women who are pregnant in their 20s. Teenagers face the risks of toxemias of pregnancy, long labor, stillbirth, babies of low birth weight, and premature delivery. Recent studies show, however, that many of these complications can be avoided if the pregnant adolescent is identified early and given nutritional, social, prenatal, and perinatal care (Evrard and Gold, 1985).

When teenagers marry because the girl is pregnant, the marriage is likely to break up within six years (Alan Guttmacher Institute, 1976). But more often, the girl chooses to raise the child alone. Few teenagers who are about to become parents have married in the last decade, and out-of-wedlock births have increased (Alan Guttmacher Institute, 1981). Either way, the decision to go ahead and have the baby is often based on storybook notions of becoming a parent and living happily ever after. In the short run, having the baby may satisfy the adolescent's longing for a sense of adult worth. In the long run, when teenagers have babies, both teenage father and mother end up with less education, poorer economic opportunities, and, usually, more children than they want or can afford to support (Card and Wise, 1978). They feel sadder and more tense than those who wait to have their children (Brown, Adams, and Kellam, 1981; Figure 14.7).

Adoption is an alternative that few teenagers choose: 94 percent of the teenagers who give birth keep their babies. The frustration of lives prematurely harnessed to the care and feeding of other utterly dependent human beings soon catches up with these young mothers and their children. Teenage parents have a high incidence of child abuse; their children in turn are more likely to develop behavior problems and to add to the numbers of those who will themselves later have difficulty being self-sufficient people and loving parents.

It is another cruel irony that although the majority of adolescents in this society are sexually active, they are given neither the information nor the support they need to make intelligent choices about their sexual activity. Parents are shy, teachers are distant, peers are uninformed, birth control is forbidden, illegal, or inaccessible, and sex education is scarce. Although

The cruel irony is that although adolescent girls can conceive, their bodies are not mature enough for problem-free pregnancies and childbirth.

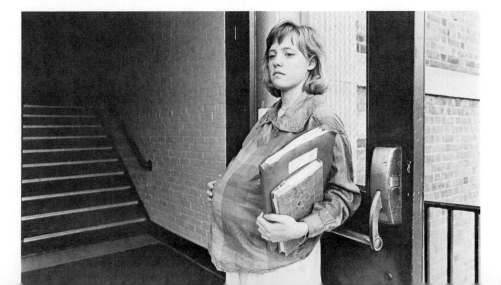

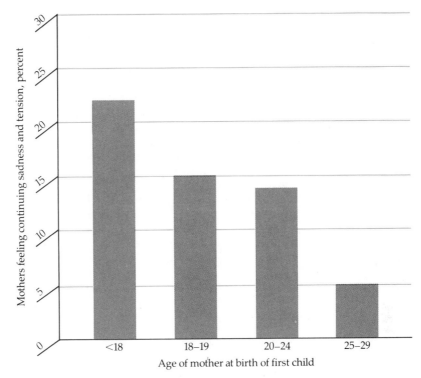

Figure 14.7 The likelihood of a mother's claiming to feel often sad and tense depends on how old she was when she had her first child (Brown, Adams, and Kellam, 1980).

teenagers can make abstract decisions about medical and psychological problems that are not different from adults' (Weithorn and Campbell, 1984), many people contend that adolescents are too immature to make practical decisions about their sexual activity or its consequences. The tug of war on this politically touchy issue is reflected in the contradictory judicial rulings about whether adolescents should have access to contraceptives, whether they are competent to consent to abortions, and whether their parents must give their consent as well. Some argue that requiring parents' consent for contraceptives will prevent many adolescents from using contraception and therefore will increase pregnancy rates. One study of 1200 teenagers showed, in fact, that 23 percent said that they would not use family planning if their parents had to know; 18 percent said that their parents did not know that they were using contraceptives (Torres, Forrest, and Eisman, 1980).

The United States is the only developed country in which teenage pregnancy rates are rising. Compared to 37 other developed nations, including Holland, France, and Canada, the rate of teenage pregnancy, abortion, and childbearing is highest by far in the United States. For every 1000 girls between 15 and 19 in the United States, 96 get pregnant, compared with 43 in France, 35 in Sweden, and 14 in Holland (Mall, 1985). Where attitudes toward sex are more liberal, where sex education is more thorough, and where contraceptives and health services are more readily available, the rates of teenage pregnancies, abortions, and childbirths are lower.

Many adults misguidedly fear that giving teenagers information about sex, contraception, or the right to abortion will increase their rates of sexual activity, pregnancy, abortion, and childbearing. Researchers have shown that sex education plus access to family planning does not prompt adolescents to begin having sex and does not increase pregnancies among sexually experienced adolescents; it does the reverse (Furstenberg, Moore, and Peterson 1985; Zelnick and Kim, 1982). Many high schools in the United States do not offer sex education, and of those that do, the majority do not include discus-

543

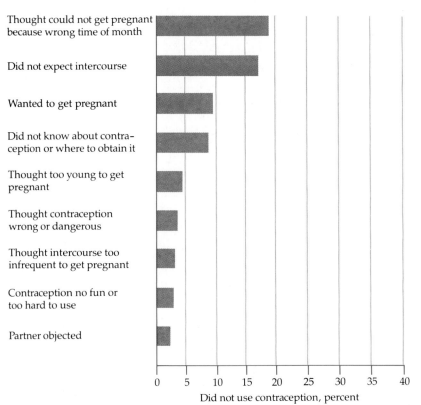

Figure 14.8 **Teenage girls who had had premarital intercourse more than once gave these reasons for not using a contraceptive (Alan Guttmacher Institute, 1981).**

sions of contraception. As a result, although over the past fifteen years increasing numbers of adolescents have used birth control, they still often use the least effective forms such as withdrawal and the rhythm method rather than pills, IUDS, condoms, diaphragms, or vaginal sponges (Mecklenburg and Thompson, 1983; Zelnick and Kantner, 1978).

One reason that adolescents are poor users of contraception is that many have only a vague grasp of the "facts of life." Young adolescents are too cognitively immature to understand the complexities of the unseen processes that make up sexual reproduction. Few know when during their menstrual cycles females are fertile. Some adolescent girls mistakenly believe that they cannot get pregnant, that they are sterile, that they are too young, or that it requires many sexual encounters to conceive. Many are too embarrassed to buy contraceptives or simply cannot find them. Some are too shy to touch their genitals. Some suspect that contraceptives are wrong or interfere with sexual pleasure and spontaneity (Figure 14.8). Of course, pregnancy is not always a result of ignorance or naïveté. Some adolescent girls want to get pregnant to bolster their self-esteem, to prove that they are women, to test their boyfriend's love, get attention or gain independence, or to assuage their loneliness; or they want to because their friends are doing it or they think that their families expect it of them (Chilman, 1979). Nevertheless, at least one study shows that most teenagers do not plan to get pregnant, nor are they happy when they find out that they are. When they are given instruction in contraception, they are less likely to get pregnant (Furstenberg, 1976).

Just where do teenagers get their information about sex? Most teenagers must piece together bits of sexual lore from three principal sources: their parents, their friends, and books. Their peers are teenagers' major source of information about sex. Teenagers talk together about intercourse, contraception, homosexuality, masturbation, prostitution, and ejaculation, and they are

544

virtually the exclusive source of information for one another on petting (Thornberg, 1981). Parents impart their sexual attitudes to their children in more subtle and indirect ways. From the time their children are babies, parents express their attitudes toward sex in the way that they clean their children's genitals, teach them the culture's rules about modesty, and mislabel or ignore their sexual acts. When they are young and inquisitive, children may get special books from their parents about the "birds and the bees," many of which are literally that. But once the children are old enough to be interested in sex, most of the talk stops. Talk about intercourse and contraception is rare.

> The only thing my mother's ever told me about sex is, "You'll just know when it's time." Big help she is.—Megan, age 15

Parents are embarrassed, adolescents sense it, and so both parties withhold information about sex. In one study, many of the teenagers reported that their parents were so "uptight" about sex that they told them only what they thought they could stand hearing. A mere 21 percent asked their parents' advice about sex (Sorenson, 1973). Parents not only find it difficult to talk to their adolescent sons and daughters about sexual matters; they also overestimate what the adolescents know. They rarely go back over the rudimentary information that they gave their young children years before to clarify, explain, or correct the inevitable gaps and misimpressions. It is not surprising then that much of what adolescents know or believe about sex is inaccurate.

Parents are not only silent on the subject of sex; they also disapprove—not always silently—if their adolescent children are sexually active (LoPiccolo, 1973). Even parents who themselves had sexual intercourse before they were married tend to disapprove of it in their adolescent sons and daughters. In one study, although 30 percent of the mothers reported that they had had intercourse before marriage, only 3 percent approved of it in their daughters, and only 9 percent approved of it in their sons. Of the fathers who had had intercourse before marriage, only 10 percent approved of it in their daughters and 20 percent in their sons (Wake, 1969).

> My father is driving me crazy with all his talk about making sure that I keep a "good reputation." I nod and make noises like I agree with him, because I don't want to worry him, but boy is he out of it.—Erica, age 15

The adolescents who listen to their parents are most likely to remain virgins. One study of Canadian university students showed that half of those who were virgins said that their parents were the most important influence on their attitudes. But of those who had had intercourse, only 30 percent ranked their parents that highly. None of the students considered his or her parents major sources of factual information about sex (Barrett, 1980).

In families where parents and children do talk openly and fully about sex, where parents are openly affectionate with each other, and where parents explicitly forbid their daughter to have sex, adolescent daughters are less likely to be sexually active (Darling, 1979; Lenney, 1985; Lewis, 1973; Miller and Simon, 1974). Family discussion of sex is likely to increase the sexual activity of sons, but whether discussions with parents make them more responsible about matters like contraception remains an open question (Darling, 1979). In late adolescence especially, friends' attitudes may be more influential than parents' (Spanier, 1976). Emotionally intimate couples are likely to grow sexually intimate as well, no matter how their parents feel, and the likelihood grows the longer the relationship lasts.

Sexually transmitted diseases

The diseases that are passed from one person to another during sexual encounters are called **sexually transmitted diseases (STDs)**. They include chlamydia, gonorrhea, genital herpes, syphilis, and acquired immune deficiency syndrome (AIDS). Most are caused by microorganisms that thrive in the moist, warm conditions afforded by skin folds, mucous membranes, and genitals covered by pubic hair and underwear. Because so many adolescents are sexually active, have several sexual partners, and do not use birth control methods that create a physical barrier between sexual partners (condoms and spermicide, for example), they are particularly vulnerable to these diseases. In 1980, the federal government estimated that 75 percent of all reported cases of STDs affected people between the ages of 15 and 24 (U.S. Department of Health and Human Services, 1980).

Because most STDs (except herpes and AIDS) can be cured by medical treatment, adolescents who are sexually active can help keep themselves healthy by speaking to a physician about preventive measures; by going for checkups every six months; by using barrier methods of birth control; and by seeing a doctor when symptoms develop.[1]

Alcohol, drugs, and smoking

By the end of tenth grade, 90 percent of all adolescents have drunk alcohol (Figure 14.9). A recent survey showed that 40 percent of the high school juniors in Orange County, California, drank alcohol at least once a week (CBS News, June 1, 1984). In another survey, 41 percent of high school seniors had drunk five or more drinks in a row within the previous two weeks (Johnston, in Mervis, 1985). A sizable number of adolescents—as many as half a million in this country—are problem drinkers (Chafetz, 1974). Most adolescents do their first drinking at home and learn their drinking habits from their parents. Children are likely to drink moderately if their parents do, just as children are likely to drink excessively or to abstain altogether if their parents do (U.S. Public Health Service, 1974).

> I sometimes drink a beer with my dad when I visit him and we're watching a game together or something.—Jason, age 15

> I go drinking with the guys every weekend. We get a keg and party at the beach. My parents stay home and get sloshed on the hard stuff.—Brandon, age 17

[1]The V.D. National Hotline is open from 8:00 A.M. to 8:00 P.M. on weekdays and from 10:00 A.M. to 6:00 P.M. on weekends, and treats all calls confidentially. Its toll free number is 1 (800) 227-8922 or, in California, 1 (800) 982-5883.

Ninety percent of America's high school students drink at least occasionally with their friends or at home.

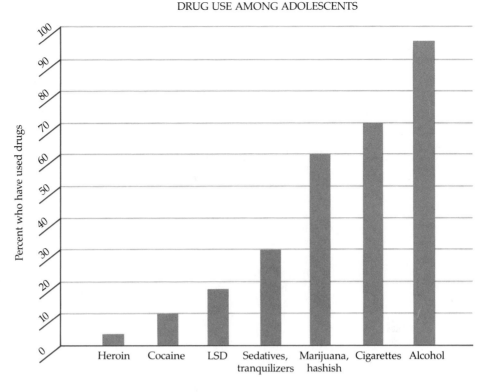

Figure 14.9 These percentages of adolescents graduating from high school have used the drugs indicated, without a doctor's order, at least once (Johnson, in Mervis, 1985; Johnson and Bachman, 1981).

Adolescents who are most likely to drink too much are dependent and rebellious and have poor relations with others (Jones, 1968).

Many adolescents also use marijuana. Young adolescents are especially likely to smoke marijuana if their friends do (Brynner, 1980), and many begin to use drugs when they are most vulnerable to peer pressures—at ages 11 to 13 (see Figure 16.3). Recent surveys show that 40 percent of high school juniors and seniors have tried marijuana, 25 percent use it sometimes, and 5 percent use it every day (CBS News, June 1, 1984; Johnston, O'Malley, and Bachman, 1985). These figures are substantially lower than those of a decade ago, and the number of high school students who disapprove of marijuana smoking—85 percent—is substantially higher.

Although it is not true that marijuana dooms anyone to heroin addiction, it is true that teenagers who use one drug are likely to use several of them and to drink as well. In the last few years, the number of adolescents using marijuana, sedatives, and tranquilizers has decreased, but the number using heroin and other opiates has increased (Johnston, in Mervis, 1985). Twenty percent of adolescents have tried cocaine; 12 percent use it at least once a year; and 6 percent use it every month.

Just which teenagers are prone to using drugs? The profile is: those most likely to smoke marijuana or use other drugs are not interested in school or academic achievement. They strongly value their independence and tolerate deviance. They do not care much for religion. Their parents are distant, unsupportive, uncontrolling, and express little disapproval of drugs. Their fathers are less likely to be well adjusted, to hold traditional values, or to be conventional and religious. Their friends strongly support drug use (Brook, Whiteman, Gordon, and Brook, 1984; Jessor, in Mervis, 1985; Stern, Northman, and Van Slyck, 1984; Tec, 1972).

One study of the factors that predict teenagers' drug use suggests that personality, peers, and family *all* operate (Brook, Whiteman, and Gordon, 1983). Teenagers with personality traits that make them likely drug users may do so even though their families and peers try to persuade them not to.

547

Teenagers with poor family relationships may use drugs, even if their personal values and their peers' opinions are against drugs. Pressures from peers to use drugs can override personal antidrug values and good family relationships. An adolescent under pressure on all three fronts—a vulnerable personality, poor family relationships, and pressure from friends—is a prime candidate for using drugs.

What difference does it make if an adolescent does use drugs? Movies like *Reefer Madness* and antidrug campaigns over the last 20 years have implied that the first puff of marijuana smoke leads inevitably down the path of perdition and straight to heroin addiction. Such exaggerations were designed to scare people away from drugs. But drugs do cause real problems. They can damage the central nervous system and a person's abilities to pay attention and remember. Adolescents who smoke marijuana regularly may grow unresponsive, alienated, and passive. This passivity, in fact, makes marijuana smokers less likely to commit crimes than people who use other kinds of drugs. In this regard, one study has shown that as adolescents smoke more marijuana, the likelihood of their committing crimes drops (Gold and Reimer, 1975). Drugs and alcohol, however, are responsible for an estimated one-half of all the fatal accidents in which teenagers are involved. A recent study by the state of New York (1986) revealed that raising the drinking age from 18 to 19 in 1982 resulted in a 46 percent decrease in driving while intoxicated and a 21 percent decrease in crashes causing deaths and injuries among 18-year-olds.

By seventh grade, one-third of the adolescents in this country have tried smoking cigarettes. About 15 percent of high school seniors are regular smokers (Bachman, 1982).

> On a class trip in eighth grade, I sat in the back of the bus with a friend who had promised to teach me to smoke. The first few cigarettes tasted horrible. But then I got used to them. I liked the way I looked with a cigarette in my hand. I've been smoking ever since.—Sarah, age 16

Cigarettes, too, are harmful to health. Moreover, unlike marijuana, which can create psychological dependency but usually does not create physical addiction, the tobacco in cigarettes is physically addictive. Quitting a cigarette habit is a form of drug withdrawal that is painful and difficult. The best solution to cigarette addiction is never to start smoking in the first place. What then is the best way to keep children from starting to smoke cigarettes? In one recent study, researchers found that the most effective smoking prevention program for seventh graders was one taught by a fellow student and focused on things like appearance, bad breath, and exclusion from public areas (Murray, Johnson, Luepker and Mittelmark, 1984). (It worked only for those students who had not tried cigarettes.) More efforts like this may continue the downward trend in smoking among adolescents (Bachman, 1982).

Acne

> My face started breaking out when I was 11, so my mother took me to a dermatologist. My father and all of my aunts and uncles on his side of the family had acne, and they have the scars to prove it. The medicine helps, but my skin usually is broken out somewhere. I try to tell myself that it's the person underneath who counts, but I really *hate* my skin.—Alyssa, age 16

> Every time exam period rolls around, my face breaks out.—Robbie, age 14

Adolescents are excruciatingly sensitive to how they look. Every mole, freckle, and pimple can seem a horrid disfiguration. At an age when their body images are highly vulnerable, adolescents' complexion troubles can undermine self-esteem. One sympathetic observer has called the adolescent complexion ''a canvas on which the psyche reveals its emotions'' (Zeller, 1970).

Emotional flare-ups are implicated in one-quarter to one-half of all skin problems. The tension brought on by exams, college interviews, proms, breaking up and making up, sports meets, and premenstrual factors can make complexions break out. The androgens secreted by the adrenal glands stimulate glands in the skin to produce oil, and sometimes the ducts to carry this oil away from the skin do not function properly. When the oil in one of these ducts is exposed to the air, it turns into a blackhead. When it is covered by skin, it turns into a whitehead. When it irritates the surrounding tissue, the skin breaks out in acne. Although thorough cleaning, a balanced diet, and general good health can go a long way toward managing oily skin, true acne calls for the help of a dermatologist—a physician who specializes in treating skin disorders. Armed with a combination of topical and oral medications, including antibiotics, vitamin A, and drying agents, and with large amounts of reassurance, dermatologists can bring most cases of acne under control—and most adolescents out of their rooms.

Eating disorders

Anorexia nervosa is a severe eating disorder, a form of self-starvation, which tends to afflict girls who have been good students and compliant daughters.

The same preoccupation with appearance that can make adolescents miserable over a blotchy complexion can make them starve themselves to look ''thin enough.'' When 2000 high school students responded to a questionnaire (Kagan and Squires, 1984), 2 percent showed patterns of seriously disordered eating. Seven percent of the students (11 percent of the girls) were ''emotional eaters''—eating when they were depressed or anxious, for instance. Twenty percent went on binges at least once a week, 5 percent purged themselves afterward by vomiting, and 27 percent felt out of control about eating. In college, these numbers are likely to rise. For example, one-quarter of the women in introductory psychology and sociology courses at one midwestern college binged (Thompson, 1979). During freshman year in college, when students have to cope with separation from their families as well as adjust to a new academic environment, many of them gain weight. Few college men gain weight, because they unwind by exercising. But to cope with the pressures of classes and exams, college women drink, smoke, talk, and eat chocolate, milkshakes, burgers, and pizza (Little and Haar, 1985).

Finding themselves plumper than Brooke Shields, then, some girls may start on a spiral of dieting and gorging themselves. When adolescent girls with shaky self-images look in the mirror, they may see fat where no one else does and embark on a series of diets to control their ''overweight.'' Some diet strenuously and then, feeling starved and deprived, binge on thousands of calories in ''comfort foods'' like cookies, ice cream, cake, and doughnuts until they can stuff themselves no more. Then they make themselves vomit; some purge themselves with laxatives. This pattern of alternate starving, gorging, and purging is called **bulimia**. Bulimia takes both a physical and an emotional toll. The constant vomiting and purging play havoc with the digestive system, and the acidity of vomit corrodes tooth enamel. Many bulimics are secretive, ashamed, and depressed—some of them severely enough to try suicide (Cunningham, 1984).

A less common but more serious eating disorder is **anorexia nervosa**. Many adolescent girls are unhappy about their weight, but one in 300 starves herself and engages in bursts of compulsive exercise until she loses one-quarter or more of her body weight. Most anorexics are girls who are white, middle-class, affluent college students. They are pursuing to an exaggerated degree the thin body idealized in this society. Roughly half of anorexic women alternately binge and starve—the pattern of bulimia. Most are perfectionistic about their appearance, their schoolwork, and their family relationships.

Gymnastics, tennis, basketball, and boxing all demand flexibility, quick reactions, speed, strength, and a slight body and therefore are best done by adolescents.

Laboring hard to be compliant daughters, excellent students, and beautiful girlfriends, and struggling against impending independence from their families all at the same time, they crumble (Bruch, 1969). Many feel out of control, without a sense of mastery over their own behavior, as they labor mightily to please others rather than themselves (Boskind-Lodahl, 1976). Their good grades are for their parents, their good looks for their boyfriends. With no firm sense of self-worth, anorexic women can set no bounds to their dieting. No matter how skinny they are, one look in the mirror convinces them that they are still ''too fat.'' Like many dieters, they grow preoccupied with food, reading recipes, preparing elaborate meals for *others*, counting calories. Without the necessary body weight, many anorexics stop menstruating. Starved and malnourished, some develop symptoms of dehydration, erratic heart rhythms, and other life-threatening conditions. Some anorexics must be hospitalized and force fed. One in five dies (Brody, 1982).

Physical maturity and fitness

Most of the health problems that we have discussed in this chapter affect a minority of adolescents. Most adolescents adjust to their new bodies and new capabilities with good health and good judgment. Some take advantage of their new capabilities to excel in sports and athletics. Gymnastics, tennis, basketball, and boxing, all of which demand flexibility, a slight body, quick reactions, speed, and strength, can be performed best by adolescents. On the average, female swimmers are at their fastest at age 13, male swimmers at about 18 (DeVries, 1980). In general, physical performance improves from early childhood straight through to the late teens, when it is at its height (DeVries, 1966). Then some physical functions—such as maximum oxygen consumption—begin to decline. For most, adolescence is a healthy, exciting time.

Summary

1. Puberty is the set of biological changes that transform children into sexually mature young adults. Puberty marks the beginning of adolescence, the stage of life characterized by social, emotional, and cognitive changes as well.

2. Puberty initiates a rapid growth spurt in height accompanied by the growth of muscles, internal organs, and bones. Secondary sex characteristics develop, primary sex organs and associated structures enlarge and become capable of reproduction, and adolescents' bodies take on the characteristic shapes of men and women.

3. A year or two after an adolescent girl's growth spurt has peaked, and once she has reached a critical body weight of about 100 pounds, her first menstrual period—menarche—begins.

4. The biological changes of puberty make males stronger than females, but cultural attitudes intensify these biological differences. Cultural attitudes also color girls' expectations for and experience of their menstrual cycles.

5. The changes and timing of puberty affect adolescents' behavior and self-image. Those who mature early may differ from those who mature late not only in physical traits but also in social, emotional, perceptual, and behavioral traits.

6. Sexual maturity and sexual activity mean that many teenage girls get pregnant. Most are not equipped physically, emotionally, or financially to meet the needs of an infant. The lack of sex education and the reticence of adults to discuss sex or contraception mean that many teenagers are ignorant of or have no access to effective means of preventing unwanted pregnancies. Many teenagers rely on the less effective methods like withdrawal or rhythm for preventing pregnancy. Many are frightened or shy of taking birth control pills or using other effective forms of contraception.

7. Sexual activity brings sexually transmitted diseases to many adolescents. Among the most common are chlamydia, gonorrhea, genital herpes, and acquired immune deficiency syndrome (AIDS). All can be treated, but not all can be cured.

8. The health problems that afflict many adolescents include use of drugs like nicotine, alcohol, marijuana, and cocaine. Personality factors, peers, and family all influence whether adolescents use drugs.

9. The physical changes of puberty typically usher in a period when adolescents worry about their appearance. Acne can plague them at a time when they are sensitive to every flaw in appearance. Eating disorders such as bulimia—overeating followed by purging—and anorexia nervosa—self-starvation—plague many young women who diet to extreme to meet a cultural ideal of thinness.

Key terms

adolescence
puberty
growth spurt
secondary sexual
  characteristics

menarche
body image
acne
late maturers

early maturers
sexual scripts
withdrawal
rhythm method

sexually transmitted
  diseases (STDs)
bulimia
anorexia nervosa

Suggested readings

ALAN GUTTMACHER INSTITUTE. *Eleven Million Teenagers.* New York: 1976; and *Teenage Pregnancy: the Problem that Hasn't Gone Away.* New York: 1981. Excellent charts, statistics, and studies concerning the ongoing problems of teenage pregnancy, prenatal care, and parenthood.

BELL, ALAN F., WEINBERG, MARTIN S., and HAMMERSMITH, SUE K. *Sexual Preference.* Bloomington: Indiana University Press, 1981. A new perspective that stresses the deep-rooted, multifaceted nature of the choice to be heterosexual or homosexual, in the context of an in-depth survey of San Francisco homosexuals and lesbians.

BROOKS-GUNN, JEANNE, and PETERSEN, ANNE (Eds.). *Girls at Puberty: Biological and Psychological Perspectives.* New York: Plenum, 1982. Recent articles on the biological, social, and psychological components of puberty in young women.

BRUCH, HILDE. *Eating Disorders.* New York: Basic Books, 1973. Anorexia nervosa, obesity, and other eating disorders explained by a woman who has done extensive research in this field. She pays particular attention to their developmental roots.

COLES, ROBERT, and STOKES, GEOFFREY. *Sex and the American Teenager.* New York: Harper and Row, 1985. A thoughtful examination of teenage sexuality, which is not just a survey of sexual behavior but an explanation of how today's teenagers feel about what they do.

COTTLE, THOMAS J. *Time's Children: Impressions of Youth.* Boston: Little, Brown, 1971. A series of impressionistic essays on adolescents' experiences, feelings, and needs, written from a social scientist's frame of reference and with a journalist's flair.

HAAS A. *Teenage Sexuality: A Survey of Teenage Sexual Behavior.* New York: Macmillan, 1979. The detailed report of a survey on adolescents' sexual attitudes and behavior, with quotations and commentary.

KAGAN, JEROME, and COLES, ROBERT (Eds.). *12 to 16: Early Adolescence.* New York: Norton, 1972. A collection of informative essays by experts in the fields of physical growth, sexuality, and cognitive changes. Thomas J. Cottle's "The Connections of Adolescence" and Tina DeVaron's "Growing Up" offer the personal insights of adolescents.

chapter fifteen
Cognitive development

Adolescence is the stage not only for dramatic physical changes but for dramatic cognitive changes as well. It is during adolescence that children become able to think about the possible, not just the actual, to discuss the world as it *might* be, not just as it *is*. It is during adolescence that children become able to reason abstractly and speculatively, to think of hypotheses and imagine their logical consequences, to discuss abstract topics like love, work, politics, religion, and the meaning of life—and to know what they're talking about. Words that were learned in early childhood—*love, country, parent*—take on new, symbolic meanings. Adolescents can construct theories about literature, philosophy, and morality. They can think in general terms and understand how history has affected current events and how current events will affect the future. Understanding this, they are likely to question the validity and goals of social institutions and human actions. They can imagine the world not only as it might be but as it *ought* to be, and many are idealists with strong ideas of how to make the world a better place. Adolescents can grapple with ideological goals—''No more nukes!'' ''Down with abortion!''—favor one political candidate over another, follow a spiritual leader, and think realistically about the work they may do as adults.

In this chapter, we will discuss the kinds of thinking that first become possible during adolescence. We will discuss what they mean, when they occur, and how they develop.

Scientific and logical thought

Although developmental psychologists had recognized for some time that the thinking processes of adolescents were different from those of younger children, these differences were not studied systematically until Piaget began his investigations. Piaget studied the development of adolescents' capacities for logical thought, by focusing primarily on their understanding of physical science.

To do so, Piaget made up many tasks, or problems, that involved scientific principles. Then he asked children of different ages to solve the problems. Children's and adolescents' ways of going about solving the problems revealed differences in their thought processes. In one task, for example, subjects were shown how to make a pendulum from a set of weights and a string. They then were shown how to change the weight, lengthen or shorten the string, adjust the height from which the weight on the pendulum was released, and push firmly or gently on the weight when it was released. Finally they were asked to figure out what made the pendulum swing faster or

Formal operational thinking allows adolescents to form broad concepts and hypotheses, and these skills make for long conversations about themselves, society, love and sex, and the meaning of religion, justice, and life.

FLEXIBLE RODS, TASK

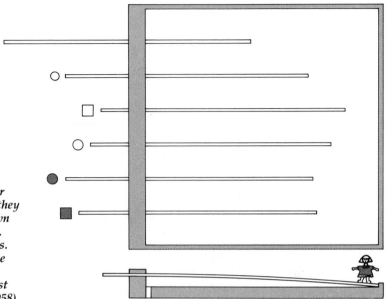

*Figure 15.1 **In the experiment on the flexibility of rods, the rods can be shortened or
lengthened by varying the point at which they
are clamped. Their cross sections are shown
on the left; colored forms show brass rods,
and white forms show rods of other metals.
Dolls of different weights are placed on the
ends of the rods. The task is to figure out
where to clamp each rod so that its end just
touches the water** (Inhelder and Piaget, 1958).*

slower. In another task devised by Piaget, flexible rods could be shortened or
lengthened by varying the point at which they were clamped. Some of the
rods were brass; others were of different metals. Some were round, some
square. When dolls of varying weights were placed on the end of the rods, the
rods bent to a certain degree. The test was for children to make the rods bend
just enough for the doll's end of the rod to touch the water underneath, by
taking into account the material out of which the rod was made, its shape, and
the weight of the doll (see Figure 15.1). In still another task, children were
shown four beakers, each containing a clear, odorless liquid, and a bottle
labeled *g*, also containing a clear, odorless liquid. The child then was shown
that by adding a few drops of *g*, some mixture of the other liquids turns
yellow. The problem was to find out which mixture this was. With tasks such
as these, Piaget probed the thinking of adolescents and compared it with that
of younger children.

Adolescent thought had several distinctive qualities, Piaget discovered
(Inhelder and Piaget, 1958). First of all, adolescents differed from younger
children in their ability to go beyond here-and-now reality to the realm of the
possible. In middle childhood, children approached Piaget's problems as
concrete and practical, and they focused on what was there in front of them.
But adolescents were more likely to examine the problem carefully to try to
determine all the *possible* solutions and only then to try to discover the solution
in that particular instance. An adolescent given the liquids in the beakers, for
example, would realize that there were many possible solutions to the problem: liquid 1 + liquid 2 + *g*; liquid 1 + *g*; liquid 2 + *g*; and so on. A younger child
would not consider all the possibilities. An adolescent asked by Piaget what
people would do if there were no sun would consider the possibilities—that
people would live underground, that they would eat cockroaches, that they
would exploit other forms of energy, and so on. A younger child would flatly
state that there *is* a sun or that it would be dark all the time.

Second, Piaget found that, based on this ability to think about the
possible, adolescents could *hypothesize* and *deduce*. To solve the problems
Piaget had set up, adolescents could apply the scientific method (see Chapter 2). They could:

- Analyze the problem.
- Hypothesize the correct solution.
- Deduce what empirical evidence would be necessary to prove the correctness of the hypothesis.
- Test the hypothesis by collecting the evidence.
- Come up with an alternative hypothesis if the evidence did not support the first hypothesis, and proceed as before.

An adolescent given the string and weights, for example, first might hypothesize that what really determined the speed of the pendulum's swing was its weight. She would test all the different weights and measure the speed of the swing. Finding that the weight did not affect the speed of the swing, she would then hypothesize that the length of the string determined the speed. She would vary the length of the string and measure the speed of swing. Finding that the length of the string did affect the speed, she would feel confident that her hypothesis was correct. But because she knew that she had to consider all the possibilities, she would also try pushing the weight harder or more gently to see whether these actions affected the speed of swing. Similarly, another adolescent given the beakers and liquids would understand that he had to take a systematic approach and test all the possible mixtures of all the liquids: First he would mix g with the contents of each beaker. Then he would systematically mix the contents of beaker 1 with g plus another liquid— liquid $1+g+$liquid 2, liquid $1+g+$liquid 3, liquid $1+g+$liquid 4. Then he would go through the same steps with the liquid in beaker 2, and then in beaker 3, then in beaker 4. Finally, he would systematically try all combinations of three liquids: liquid $1+$liquid $2+$liquid $3+g$, liquid $1+$liquid $2+$liquid $4+g$, liquid $1+$liquid $3+$liquid $4+g$, and liquid $2+$liquid $3+$liquid $4+g$. Many adolescents, Piaget found, were able to think like scientists, separating variables, generating and testing hypotheses, and weighing probabilities.

A third characteristic of adolescents' thinking discovered by Piaget was that, unlike younger children, they could judge the truth of the logical relation between propositions. During the concrete operational period, children could recognize the logic of a single proposition. They could formulate the proposition that there are the same number of cookies in two rows after one row had been spread out, and they could check this single proposition against concrete reality. Adolescents, Piaget found, could infer the logical relations between propositions, regardless of whether they were factually true. Suppose that an 8-year-old and a 16-year-old are told the following:

The development of scientific, logical thought means that adolescents can explore hypotheses and carry out experiments.

All suns are stars.
All stars are black.
Therefore, all suns are black.

The 8-year-old, knowing that the sun he sees is not black, declares the conclusion to be false. The child's reasoning is limited by what he knows to be true from concrete, active experience. He cannot suspend reality and listen to the logic underlying the conclusion. He cannot play with abstract ideas. But the adolescent can logically connect the three statements. *If* all suns are stars, and *if* all stars are black, then—*logically*—all suns must be black. He recognizes the logic of the propositions apart from their content and can combine, negate, and reverse even the most outrageous and blatantly false propositions.

If an experimenter hides a poker chip in his hand and says to a child, "Either this chip is green or it is not green. True or false?" elementary school children are likely to say that they cannot tell because they cannot see the chip. Adolescents can focus on the words and evaluate the truth of the formal proposition (Osherson and Markman, 1975). Similarly, adolescents can figure out the answers to the following logical problems.

1. If this is Belgium, then this is Sunday.
   This is Belgium.
   Is this Sunday? [yes]

2. If this is Belgium, then this is not Sunday.
   This is Belgium.
   Is this Sunday? [no]

3. If this is Belgium, then this is Sunday.
   This is not Belgium.
   Is this Sunday? [can't say]

Children in middle childhood answer the first and second problems correctly but have trouble with the third because they cannot figure out the **inter-propositional logic** (Shapiro and O'Brien, 1970).

Piaget called this kind of scientific and logical thinking, which is first possible in adolescence, **formal operational thinking**. Whereas concrete operational thinking (discussed in Chapter 12) involves real, concrete objects, formal operational thinking involves abstract forms like propositions and hypotheses. A person with formal operational thinking realizes that logical forms and arguments have a life of their own regardless of what the person knows or sees. Because it involves thinking about propositions rather than about objects, formal operational thinking is said to be "second-order" thinking. Thinking about objects is "first-order" thinking.

Apart from Piaget's experiments, what evidence do we have about when and how logical thinking develops? Researchers have used Piaget's tasks and others like them to study the development of logical thinking in children and adolescents. No matter what test they have used, nearly all these researchers have found that between the ages of 11 and 15, children's thinking changes substantially (Neimark, 1975). In one study of several thousand adolescents, for example, researchers found that 14 percent of the 12-year-olds, 18 percent of the 13-year-olds, and 22 percent of the 14-year-olds succeeded on the pendulum task (Shayer, Kucheman, and Wylam, 1976; Shayer and Wylam, 1978). Logical thinking not only increased with age, this study showed, but was tied closely to individual differences in intelligence. Whereas only 22 percent of the 14-year-olds from the general population succeeded on the pendulum test, 85 percent of the 14-year-olds from the top 8 percent in intelligence succeeded. In another study, similarly, only 30 percent of the 14-year-olds from the general population succeeded in the pendulum task; 75 percent of the 14-year-olds who were gifted succeeded (Dulit, 1972).

Levels of formal operational thought

Formal operational thinking does not appear all at once at the beginning of adolescence. According to Piaget, the first level of formal operations is thinking about alternatives, hypotheses, and possibilities. This kind of thinking usually begins in early adolescence (between 11 and 15 years). A second level, thinking *systematically* about possibilities, does not begin until later in adolescence. In the pendulum problem, for example, the early formal operational thinker tries out several possibilities. When he finds one that works, he stops. He does not test every possible variable systematically. The more mature formal operational thinker searches for what is *necessary* as well as what is *sufficient* to change the speed of the pendulum's swing, and therefore he tries out each variable and every combination of variables.

Recent research suggests that there may be even more levels in the development of formal operational abilities than these two. On a variety of Piagetian tasks, researchers have found that adolescents' thinking progresses through four levels (Case, 1985; Furman, 1981; Marini, 1984). One of Piaget's tasks, for example, involves figuring out what will happen when different weights are placed on opposite ends of a balance beam. In solving this problem, the subject must take into account both weight and distance from the fulcrum. Children 7 to 8 years old realize that the beam will balance if it has the same weight on both sides, but they do not realize that distance from the fulcrum is also important. Recognition of this point develops through four substages (see Table 15.1). First, children 9 to 11 years old compare the differences between the two weights with the differences between the two distances and choose the larger as the one that will determine which way the balance beam will tilt. Because they use subtraction, a second-order operation, to solve the problem, the children clearly are a step beyond concrete operational children, who just count the weights. But their strategy is limited.

During the second substage, children 11 to 13 years old formulate a simple ratio to compare the variables of weight and distance. If they are faced with the problem of 2 weights on the left and 1 weight on the right, and 2 units of length on the left and 4 units of length on the right, children see that there are twice the number of weights on the left—the ratio of 2:1—and that there are twice the number of lengths on the right. Therefore they conclude that the two sides will balance. If the ratios are different, they predict that the larger will make the beam tilt. Because they use ratios, a more advanced second-order operation than subtraction, these children are a step ahead of children in the first substage. But they correctly solve only problems in which the weights and lengths can be evenly divided into each other. So their strategy, too, is limited.

In the third substage, 13- to 15-year-olds use division to calculate a ratio even when the units cannot be evenly divided. For example, if there are 2 weights on the right side and 1 on the left, and the distances are 5 units of lengths on the right side and 2 on the left, the subject divides 2 into 5, takes the amount left over—1—and divides it between the 2 lengths on the left—½. She then adds ½ to the lengths on the left—2½—compares this number to the ratio for the weights—2—and picks the larger (2½) as the one that determines the tilt of the beam. In this substage, more elements are represented mentally, and more advanced calculations are made than in the second substage. But the strategy still is not completely effective.

In the fourth substage, 15- to 19-year-olds use division to calculate *two* ratios—one for distance and one for weight—and then compare them. For example, on a balance beam problem in which the sides have, respectively, 7 and 3 weights and lengths of 2 and 5 units, the subject reasons that the weights are in the ratio of 1:2⅓ and the lengths in the ratio of 1:2½, and that

Table 15.1
Percentage of children capable of functioning at each level of second-order thinking

Age range	Level 0: Comparison via addition or subtraction	Level 1: Comparison of unit ratio with simple multiple of it	Level 2: Comparison of unit ratio with nonintegral ratio via two-step reduction	Level 3: Comparison of two nonintegral ratios, with reduction of both
9–11 years	85%	10%	5%	0%
11–13 years	100	80	30	5
13–15½ years	100	95	75	25
15½–18½ years	100	100	95	65

SOURCE: Marini, 1984.

the beam should tip toward the side with the larger ratio—2½. Thinking at this substage is truly abstract because neither of the numbers the subject ends up comparing has any visual counterpart in the physical world. Mature formal operational thinking has been achieved.

Contexts of formal thinking

Logical and scientific thinking is not limited to experiments in physics and chemistry. It also appears in games. The way adolescents play Twenty Questions is different from the way younger children do, for example (Flavell, 1977). Adolescents hypothesize and eliminate broad categories systematically. ''Is it male?'' they ask. ''Living?'' ''Bigger than a breadbox?'' Children, in contrast, guess concretely and specifically. ''Is it George Washington?'' ''Is it a breadbox?'' Logical thinking also appears in the ways children and adolescents reason about stories and events. For example, one researcher told this story to children and adolescents between the ages of 9 and 16 (Peel, 1971):

> Only brave pilots are allowed to fly over high mountains. This summer a fighter pilot flying over the Alps collided with an aerial cable railway and cut a main cable, causing some cars to fall to the glacier below. Several people were killed, and many others had to spend the night suspended above the glacier. Was the pilot a careful airman? Why do you think so?

The 9- to 11-year-olds were likely to answer irrelevantly, some saying, ''Yes, he was brave,'' others saying, ''No, he was a showoff.'' Children 12 to 13 years old reasoned according to the specific information in the story, saying, ''No. If he were careful, he wouldn't have cut the cable.'' Older adolescents knew that they did not have enough information to judge and therefore answered hypothetically and imaginatively: ''*If* the pilot knew the cable was there, then he should have tried to fly above it,'' or ''*If* there was fog, then the pilot might not have been able to keep from flying into the cable.''

The same researcher found similar patterns in the answers of children and adolescents to questions like: ''What causes and prevents soil erosion?'' and ''Were the people of Italy to blame for the water damage to art masterpieces caused by the floods in Florence?'' Children and young adolescents gave simple and sometimes irrelevant answers; older adolescents gave more complex, hypothetical answers and searched actively for new possibilities. This active, imaginative reasoning also occurs in debates. Unlike younger children, adolescents can suspend their own beliefs and take a position for or against a proposition. For example, they can debate either side of the propositions: ''One man, one vote'' or ''All students should be required to learn a foreign language.''

As research in all these domains, from physics to politics, has shown, many older adolescents use formal operational thinking. But not *all* of them do so. Piaget (1972) himself pointed out that although most adolescents have the capacity for formal operational thinking, whether they actually use it depends on their experiences and their education in science and math. Children who had have formal science courses in school usually do better on Piaget's tasks than children who have not had such courses (McClosky, Caramazza, and Green, 1980). In fact, even preadolescent children can succeed on Piaget's tasks if they have been trained in scientific thinking. In one study, for example, 6- and 8-year-olds were tested on the flexible-rods problem (Case, 1974). None of the children could solve the problem. Then the children were trained for four days on how to isolate variables and to test and keep track of possibilities in several problems that were similar to, but not identical with, the flexible-rods problem. When they were tested again on the flexible-rods problem, 75 percent of the 8-year-olds did much better, and many solved it perfectly. Ordinarily, in our society, where the demand for this kind of formal thinking is rare before adolescence, young children do not succeed on tests of formal operations. The fact that they can be trained to do so supports the view that formal operational thinking depends on experience and education.

Formal operational thinking also depends on the situation. Even adolescents who use formal operational thinking sometimes do not use it *all* the time. Whether they use it depends on the demands of the task at hand. They are more likely to use formal operational thinking in more familiar tasks with simpler instructions and concrete objects (Surber and Grzesh, 1984). They are more likely to use it to solve physics problems at school than to solve personal problems at home. In adulthood, an auto mechanic may use formal operational thinking to figure out what is wrong with an engine but not to solve one of Piaget's tasks, whereas a scientist who uses formal operational thinking on a Piagetian task may not do so when his car breaks down.

Nor do *all* adolescents (or adults) use formal operational thinking even to solve Piaget's tasks (Neimark, 1975, 1982). In this sense, formal operational thinking is not universal. In nonliterate, technologically undeveloped cultures where there is little emphasis on science, adults generally do not use formal operational thinking as Piaget defined and measured it (for example, Cole, 1978). But to solve problems of everyday importance within their culture, even people from primitive cultures construct and test hypotheses. Members of the !Kung tribe of the Kalahari Desert, for example, use hypotheses in figuring out the most effective hunting strategies (Tulkin and Konner, 1973).

One researcher (Dulit, 1972) has suggested that even within our own culture, with its emphasis on science, some people use alternative patterns of thought that are also mature and effective for solving everyday problems. Some of them solve problems by applying standard solutions, which they have learned in other situations, rather than reasoning through each new problem systematically and formally. Other, artistic types leap intuitively to solutions, although they cannot explain their reasoning, as formal reasoners can.

Scientific, logical, formal thinking is an important cognitive development that usually occurs for the first time during adolescence. But whether a person uses it in a particular situation depends on the person's level of intelligence, training in scientific reasoning, and experience with similar problems, and on the importance, complexity, and familiarity of the situation itself. Although we often think of adolescent thinking as logical, scientific, and formal operational, clearly this kind of thinking occurs only in some of the people some of the time, not in all of the people all of the time.

Abstract thought

A more common characteristic of adolescents' thinking, perhaps, is making, understanding, and discussing abstract concepts.

> "The principal says the school magazine has to be cleared by him before it can be passed out in school. I say that's censorship, and I believe in freedom of speech."

In making an abstraction, a person must hold in mind a number of facts and recognize the principle or theme that unifies these facts. For example, a person can think about individual laws and abstract a concept of justice. A person can think about the prices in stores and abstract a principle of economics, deriving a notion of supply and demand from watching the price of turkeys at Thanksgiving and Christmas and at other times of the year. This kind of mental work first becomes possible in adolescence. Adolescents can work with abstract equations and formulas in algebra and geometry. They can understand analogies: bird is to flock as fish is to school. They can understand the abstract meanings of proverbs, metaphors, and parables. They can understand how they relate to other people and how other people, in turn, see them. They can, in short, think about intangibles.

Research has shown that these abilities do not appear until early adolescence (Case, 1985; Lunzer, 1965; Sternberg and Nigro, 1980). The majority of 9- to 10-year-olds can solve simple analogies between concrete concepts:

> Black is to white as
> hard is to [steel, solid, soft, blue].
>
> Ink is to pen as
> paint is to [color, spray, brush, paper].

Children at this age may be able to give an accurate, if somewhat concrete, definition of an abstract term like "pity" on the Stanford Binet intelligence test, but they cannot manipulate abstract terms mentally. From age 11 to 13, the majority of children can solve analogies when relations are not obvious and must be abstracted and when alternative answers are not obvious and must be constructed:

> Food is to body as
> water is to [storm, coat, ground, well].
>
> Sheep is to flock as
> [herd, pack, soldier, swarm] is to [cow, ball, regiment, wolf].

The majority of 13- to 15-year-olds can solve analogies that involve abstract associations between entities that are themselves abstract:

> Problem is to solution as
> task is to [completion, work, end, question].

Fifteen- to 18-year-olds can solve even more complex, second-order analogies:

> Bert and Ernie are to friendship as
> Romeo and Juliet are to [relatives, love, make-believe, lovers].

focus *Thinking about democracy*

To investigate the differences between children's and adolescents' thinking about political concepts, Joseph Adelson and his colleagues (Adelson, 1975, 1982; Gallatin, 1980) questioned more than 450 11- to 18-year-olds about a mythical new society founded by 1000 people on a Pacific island. Asked "What is the purpose of government?" some 11- and 12-year-olds couldn't answer at all, and many answered vaguely or simplistically: "To handle the state or whatever it is so it won't get out of hand, because if it gets out of hand you might have to. . .people might get mad or something." Only adolescents over 14 or 15 understood abstract ideas about justice, law, politics, and government. When 18-year-olds were asked about the purpose of laws, for instance, they answered with broad abstractions, "Well, the main purpose would be just to set up a standard of behavior for people, for society living together so they can live peacefully and in harmony with one another."

After interviewing these hundreds of children and adolescents, Adelson realized that junior high school teachers of social and humanistic subjects might profit from his findings. He had come to the conclusion that 11- to 14-year-old children, who reasoned concretely, simply were not grasping the essentials about topics like taxation, human rights, law, freedom, and elections. Junior high school teachers claimed that their students didn't grasp

Cognitive development in adolescence allows children for the first time to begin to understand politics.

Solving this kind of analogy requires two steps:

1. Bert and Ernie are famous *friends*.
   Romeo and Juliet are famous *lovers*.

2. Friends are to friendship as lovers are to love.

Thus, during adolescence, adolescents come to think in more complex ways about more complex concepts.

As a consequence of the ability to think abstractly, adolescents can think reflectively about their own mental processes as another person might do, analyze objectively their thinking and cognitive strategies, and judge whether these concepts because they were bored and, being bored, were not motivated to learn. Taxation might be part of the required civics course in eighth grade, but, their teachers claimed, the students thought taxation had nothing to do with them, and so they put no effort into learning about it. On the basis of his interviews, Adelson thought that it was less a question of motivation than of cognitive readiness. He suggested that the eighth graders were not cognitively mature enough to grasp an abstraction like ''taxation,'' and so they learned little as a result.

Many junior high school students, he had found in his study, often *sound as though* they can reason abstractly. They can mimic what they hear from others. The 13-year-old can talk in class confidently about ''the majority,'' or ''government,'' or ''elections.'' Out come plausible-sounding clichés and pat phrases. But ask that 13-year-old to explain any of these ideas, and the answers are vague, half formed, not quite together. With technical subjects, their ignorance is more obvious. Ask the 13-year-old about the properties of parallelograms, and he is clearly confused. But because the language of social and humanistic subjects overlaps with everyday language and common sense, junior high school students often can carry on seemingly intelligent conversations about these concepts. They do not understand these concepts in the way that older adolescents and adults do, however.

Most junior high schoolers also cannot adopt an ''as though'' attitude. They think that the way things are now is the way they always have been and will always be. Good people are forever good, bad people forever bad. Laws are eternal. Children who cannot reason abstractly have trouble grasping that laws can be amended. They think of laws as the Ten Commandments, chiseled in stone, eternal, and unchanging. Teachers who realize that young adolescents have trouble understanding the principles of change and flux can help them over these rough spots, giving more emphasis to change, possibility, and flexibility in their lessons instead of assuming that their students have the same understanding of these concepts as they do. They can avoid some difficult concepts altogether.

Teachers might be successful in teaching concepts that are just beyond the reach of their students. By teaching about democracy, for example, even if they do not get across the entire abstract concept, they may help their students to form a kernel of understanding of the concept and convey some of the reverence others feel for these things called ''rights'' or ''freedoms.'' Junior high students are likely to have absurd or overblown ideas about what these concepts mean. They may interpret ''freedom of expression'' as a boundless, completely unbridled right to say whatever, whenever, and to whomever. But teachers can plant the beginnings of abstract concepts that in time will mature, find a context, and be qualified. Junior high school civics courses can offer young adolescents their first glimmers of understanding of the social, moral, and political principles that guide this nation and society.

they are appropriate to a particular task.

> When it was time for our final exam in psychology, we pestered the teacher until she told us whether the questions were essay or multiple choice. When she said essay, I knew I had to study harder.—Natalie, age 16

Another consequence of the ability to think abstractly is that adolescents can ponder social and ideological issues, politics, religion, and morality.

> I think that any government that allows apartheid deserves to fall.— Sam, age 16

Information processing

With age and experience, adolescents and adults become increasingly systematic, scientific, logical, and abstract in their thinking. But just what allows them to move to higher levels of thinking? Some psychologists have suggested that improvements in information-processing abilities during adolescence account for these advances. They suggest that the main difference between children's and adolescents' reasoning is the completeness and thoroughness of their information processing. Children stop looking for possible solutions to problems, they suggest, because their memories become overloaded (Sternberg, 1977; Sternberg and Nigro, 1980). Adolescents can keep more information in short-term memory than children can and so are better at solving problems that draw on the ability to move back and forth from information just encoded to information previously stored. Children's memories may not hold enough information to allow them to exhaust the possibilities of a problem. Evidence to support this suggestion comes from a study in which researchers found that children's short-term memory for ratios increased with age (Case, 1985). Children between 9 and 11 years old could remember one ratio (for example, the number of yellow dots per green dot); those between 11 and 13 could remember two ratios (the number of yellow dots per green dot and the number of red dots per blue dot); those between 13 and 15 years, three ratios; and those 15 years and over, four ratios.

As well as having better memories, adolescents also select and plan their information-processing strategies better than children (Brown, 1975). Adolescents who use mnemonics and other cognitive strategies to organize information are likely to remember more than children who do not plan, and adolescents know better than younger children which information-processing strategies are helpful and select among them appropriately. Greater knowledge about the content of scientific and logical problems also enhances adolescents' reasoning and their abilities to solve formal and scientific problems.

Knowledge

Changes in adolescents' knowledge about science, math, and the world thus contribute to improvements in logical and abstract thinking. But how much do adolescents actually know? To find out what American adolescents know, researchers have tested national samples in ten content areas, including math, science, literature, reading, and writing (National Assessment of Educational Progress, 1977). Most 13-year-olds in this country, they have found, can do arithmetic problems on whole numbers but do less well with decimals, fractions, and converting weights and measures (feet into yards or cups into quarts). They know how to make change but not how to calculate a unit price to find out which size package of rice is most economical. Most of them can read phone books and phone bills, and half can understand the membership rules for book clubs and can find the best title for a three-paragraph essay. But only one in three can solve word problems: ''How long will it take a car going 50 miles per hour to travel 225 miles?'' and only one in four can draw inferences from more complex forms of writing. Among 17-year-olds, most can solve one-step word problems and can understand newspaper want ads, the fine print on parking tickets, and book club rules. But many have trouble understanding long, fact-filled written passages. With limited vocabularies, most cannot understand introductory college textbooks or write clear essays on what a musical passage made them think of. Only one-third can convert weights and measures or find the boundaries and internal area of a square. A comparison of adolescents in the United States and in other industrialized countries showed that those from the United States scored last on more than one-third of all the tests given and did not score in the top one or two places on any test (National Commission on Excellence in Education, 1983). Of the adolescents from certain poor city neighborhoods in the United States, nearly half were found to be functionally illiterate.

Tests given to thousands of high school students year after year help us put these findings in a historical framework. Between 1963 and 1980, scores on the best known of these tests, the Scholastic Aptitude Test (SAT), fell sharply. The average score on the math SAT went down 36 points, the verbal, down a whopping 54 points. In 1980, the scores stopped dropping, and since then they seem to have started a slow recovery (see Figure 15.2).

What accounts for the decline in these test scores? Some people blame television. Some blame the deterioration of the nuclear family. Some blame increased use of drugs for slowing cognitive development and the maturation of the brain (Hochhauser, 1978). Others say that schools have been spreading their limited resources too thin in trying to reach more and more students. Others point out that the test-taking population has changed as schools have catered increasingly to large numbers of students who might once have dropped out. Still others point out that as schools have shifted their curricula away from rote learning and toward analysis and interpretation, students test worse on SATs but better on tests that probe these new "process" skills (Bracey, 1979; Jacobson and Doran, 1985). Nobody seems to be pointing a finger at adolescents themselves for watching television and cruising shopping malls instead of doing their homework.

Several reports have appeared recently in response to people's concern about the declining SAT scores (for example, National Commission on Excellence in Education, 1983; Education Commission of the States, Task Force on Education for Economic Growth, 1983). Perhaps the most encouraging finding to come from these reports is that although scores for white students have

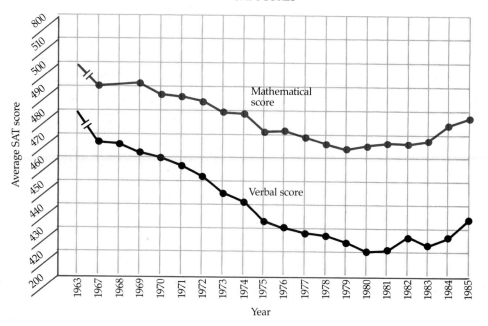

Figure 15.2 As this graph shows, the SAT scores of high school students declined until 1980 and now have started to rise again.

SAT SCORES

dropped, scores for black students have risen (Jones, 1984). For students taking SATs between 1976 and 1983, for example, the average score on the verbal section of the test for whites declined 8 points whereas that for blacks rose 7 points. In quantitative tests, as well as in writing, science, and social studies, the gap between white and black students' scores narrowed appreciably during the 1970s. It is likely that this improvement in black students' scores reflects the social programs designed to increase educational opportunities for minority students, as well as the profound social changes within the black community that have drawn blacks into the academic and professional mainstream and have raised the level of aspirations of many black students. But it is hard to know for sure, and it is hard to know how to improve scores for *both* black and white students. Will plans like the one implemented in California, in which schools that show an improvement in SAT scores from one year to the next receive state money, help to solve the problem? Will revising the SATs to reflect schools' increased emphasis on thinking processes rather than rote memorization improve the picture? Will the SAT scores continue their gradual climb? Only time and continued monitoring will tell.

Writing

Sarah was writing poetry in fourth grade. Erica was putting out a neighborhood newspaper in sixth grade. Together they wrote a play in sixth grade that the class put on. By junior year in high school, they were writing the class play again—this time for a paying audience. They're both very gifted writers.

Ted was in special-education courses but was mainstreamed in high school. When he was a sophomore, he took a creative writing course. His teacher and he worked hard together, and by the second half of the course, Ted was writing in complete sentences. By the time he finished the course, he was using short paragraphs. We were really thrilled by his progress.

Most adolescents speak their native language fluently and clearly. Without much effort, they tell other people their ideas. But when it comes to *writing* those ideas, the rules are more difficult (Bereiter and Scardamalia, 1982; Olson, 1977). Writers must use more formal grammar than speakers do. Spoken communications usually are shorter and less strictly organized than written ones. After a sentence, or two, or three, speakers get feedback— "huh?" "mmhmm," "Say that again?"—that tells them whether they have been understood. Speakers also rely on facial expressions and body language to get their message across. They point with their fingers, punctuate with their hands, smile or frown. But writers have none of these props. To get their message across, they have only the written word.

Writers must think abstractly on several levels. First they must organize their thoughts at the levels of phrases, clauses, and sentences. Then they must organize their sentences into paragraphs and their paragraphs into stories, letters, or essays. They must understand how letters, essays, and stories are shaped, with beginnings, middles, and ends. They must understand the connections between succeeding parts of the composition and the implications of what precedes for what follows. Elementary school children cannot do this. In one interesting study (Wolf, 1985), children and adolescents used microcomputers for writing and editing stories. The 13- to 15-year-olds in the study realized that when they made one change in the story, it called for several types of adjustments to the surrounding text (in tone, tense, co-

From Fall to Spring

In the fall, when the trees grow gold
And the leaves fall side by side.
Then it is that we seem to grow old
And the whole world wide
Is covered, Oh covered with gold.

Then comes spring, glorious spring.
When the buds on the trees break forth.
And the birds begin again to sing.
When they came back up north
And the bluebells start to ring.

LINDA, *age 10*

For a Summer Vacation

The cottage stands facing the lake and from the back road appears lost in the trees. Wild rose bushes surround it, and a slivery, old wooden plank leads from the front door down to the water gently lapping the shore. The screen door at the back is held shut by a piece of wood which when turned proclaims in creaks and groans the length of time it has been there. In the kitchen, the linoleum is worn white by the countless grains of sand ground into it by many swimmers, old and young. In the living-room the antique black loveseat with the claw feet and bright pink roses on it, along with the age-yellowed magazines on Victorian era table, are more evidence of the building's long life span . . .

LINDA, *age 13*

A Real Nightmare

One thought hammered feverishly: ''Why won't they look at me? Why can't they hear? Oh, please, someone help me!'' I struggled to lift my head, but relentless hands held me still; cold fingers stroked my forehead. I looked up into the face above me, but unseeing eyes were dulled with pain. I caught sight of a movement at my side, but felt nothing as the needle emptied its precious cargo into my vein. Once again, desperate now, I attempted to raise myself, but a numbness overtook me. Frantically devoting myself to one last effort, I managed to sit up. I called. But no one heard; and in the silence loneliness, like a pall, descended. I sank back and closed my eyes. Darkness was my world. . . .

LINDA, *age 15*

This Is the Era that Is

In Darien Connecticut the parents sponsor drinking.
Perhaps things would be better if they'd only sponsor thinking.
The child cannot be spanked for fear he'll turn neurotic.
And life among the farmers is ever less bucolic.

But merrily we roll along, money in our clutches.
Trying to put into our lives little human touches.
Education's at its highest peak; Father's working a ten-hour
    [sic!] week.
And happy, Oh, so happy are we,
Around our polyethylene Christmas tree.

SUSAN, *age 16*

herence, and the like). The 11- to 12-year-olds corrected only the pronouns and action sequences that immediately preceded or followed the changes. They changed words but not whole paragraphs or arguments. Only the adolescents realized that composition involves ''the ability to combine what follows with what precedes, all the while keeping in mind what is already written down'' (Tolstoy, quoted in Bertoff, 1978, p. 252).

Few elementary school children know the conventions for writing clear prose. They may not understand which are the most important points, and so they cannot set them out in a logical order. They often cannot organize the sequence of their ideas ahead of time (Brown and Smiley, 1977). Some of them have such a tenuous grasp of written communication that they cannot easily think up things to write about (Siegler, 1983). Only in adolescence do some people become effective writers (see the accompanying box).

The ability to summarize information in written form, a useful skill for studying, also develops during adolescence. In middle childhood, few children have cognitive abilities advanced enough to summarize adequately what they read. Summarizing requires a person to go back through information and condense it into a clear, cogent, brief presentation. It requires the person to separate the important from the trivial and to organize the important points logically. In one study of the development of the ability to summarize written texts, fifth, seventh, and eleventh graders and college students were given two folk stories and told to take them home and learn them perfectly (Brown, Day, and Jones, 1983). One week later, the students were asked to write down all the details they could remember from the stories. Then they were told to pretend that they were newspaper reporters and to write a summary of one of the stories for their paper. College students were most skillful at summarizing. They planned ahead by making a rough draft, appreciated fine differences in importance within the story, expressed more points in fewer words, and ordered points flexibly. Eleventh graders wrote adequate summaries, but they were less succinct than the college students. Seventh graders also could write adequate summaries, if they made a rough draft first. But few of them did so. Fifth graders' summaries were not as concise or as well organized as the older children's.

Adolescents also take better notes when they are studying than younger children (Brown and Smiley, 1978). When fifth and seventh graders decide that they need to learn a particular sentence or paragraph, they copy it word for word, as it appears in the text. Older students paraphrase and condense when they take notes, make outlines, or write reports for school. The same tendencies showed up among the students asked to summarize the folk stories. Fifth and seventh graders summarized in the words of the original stories, but the eleventh graders and college students most often used their own words and did not always follow the order of sentences in the story.

Achievement in school

Our society places heavy emphasis on achievement and success, and therein for many Americans lies the value of abstract thinking, logical analysis, and effective writing. Well before adolescence, children understand the importance of achievement, fear failure, and feel nervous during tests (Feld, 1967). But the issue of achievement in adolescence is especially important because significant—and often irrevocable—educational and career choices are made during adolescence, and adolescents begin to comprehend the implications of these choices and of the possibilities before them. Adolescents have the cognitive capacities to understand and to explore systematically the long-term consequences of their educational and career choices.

> I don't know whether I should go to college right away or take a year off and work. If I work, I may lose some academic momentum, but I'll have a better idea of what I want to do with my life. If I go straight to college, when will I get another chance to take a year off?—Mike, age 17

What determines whether and how much adolescents achieve in school?

School factors

How much adolescents know, how they think, and how well they write is determined to some extent by what they are taught in school, be that mathematics, creative writing, and computer programming, or gym, shop, and home economics.

> At the beginning of high school, we all got our course schedules for the first half-year from our homeroom teachers. We had all heard about "tracking," but those schedules were the first hard evidence of it. I was scheduled for French, algebra, history, and English composition every day, with music and art two or three times a week. But the guy sitting next to me was scheduled for remedial reading, algebra, shop, and study hall every day. Guess which one of us was on the college track.—Sam, age 16

In one study, 5000 adolescents between the ages of 13 and 17 were given 85 mathematics problems to solve (National Assessment of Educational Progress, 1983). How well they did on these problems was then analyzed in relation to a wide range of factors: the students' sex and race, their parents' levels of education and occupations, the amount and kinds of reading material in their homes; the students' year in school and grade point average; the geographic region and type of community where they lived; and the number of courses in high school algebra and geometry they had taken. Among these variables, the best predictor of the students' mathematics test scores was the number of years of high school algebra and geometry they had taken. The more high school courses in mathematics that students had taken, the higher their scores on math achievement tests. This finding is consistent with findings from other tests (Jones, 1984), suggesting—no surprises here—that sheer amount of instruction in a subject is critical to what adolescents know.

So how much instruction are students getting in high school? In one study, in urban Chicago, high school students admitted that they paid attention to class instruction only about 40 percent of the time they were in class (Csikszentmihalyi, Larson, and Prescott, 1977). The rest of the time they daydreamed, whispered, did homework for other classes, and felt bored. Many said that they had trouble concentrating, felt self-conscious, and wanted to be elsewhere. Results from an extensive five-year study of high schools across the United States (Sizer, 1985) painted a similar picture. Interviewing many students and teachers, researchers found that high school students typically spend only five hours a day in classes. Most of that time is spent listening to teachers lecture, memorizing facts for tests (and promptly forgetting them), and earning credit by quietly going along with class routines. Little class time is spent in serious, rigorous, or original thinking. The researchers who conducted the study suggested that to improve the quality and quantity of instruction in high school so that students will achieve more, educators should:

– Insist that students know what of their schoolwork they must master and then clearly master it before they are allowed to graduate.

– Adjust achievement incentives to each individual student.

– Focus on teaching students how to think.

– Make curricula and school structure simpler and more flexible, and less specialized.

Where students are when they are taught also makes a difference in how much they achieve. Students who sit near the front of the class learn more.

> You could always tell the goody-goodies because they took the seats right up in front, near the teacher's desk. The troublemakers always fought for the seats way in back.

When the troublemakers head for the back and the teachers' pets for the front, the groups are self-selected. Do the same effects hold when students are assigned places? In a study conducted years ago, students were assigned seats in a large lecture hall (Griffith, 1921). The students in back got relatively poor grades, and those in the front relatively good ones. Students who sat in the third and fourth rows from the front got the best grades of all. The extreme front, back, and sides of the lecture hall, separated from the main student body by aisles, were seating areas where students did not do as well in their grades. More recent studies have confirmed this finding (Stires, 1980), although a significant relation between grades and seating is not always found (Millard and Simpson, 1980). All other things being equal, there may be an advantage to sitting in class surrounded by other students—being part of the active learning core and not on the distractible fringes—and to being toward the front of the class—seeing and hearing the teacher clearly, but not sitting under the teacher's nose.

Personal factors

Of course things besides the quality and quantity of instruction received in school also affect how much an adolescent achieves. The adolescent's personal characteristics, for example, are an extremely important ingredient in this mix.

> Jason is smart. He remembers batting averages and TV commercials, and he's great at video games. But at the rate he's going, I'm not sure he's ever going to pass ninth grade. The teachers say that he rushes through his work, refuses help, and spends most of his time in class talking to the other kids or looking out the window. Now and then, he completes a project in a way that shows how bright and talented he is. That's what's so frustrating—he's *under*achieving.

Achievement motivation and standards

Underachievers are adolescents whose achievements in school and sometimes in other areas fall short of what could be expected of them, given their high level of abilities. Underachievers are likely to have IQs over 120 but school grades of Cs and below. Although children may not perform up to their potential in elementary school, underachievers usually are first identified in junior high, perhaps because that is when academic demands intensify. Underachievers shirk their homework, do not finish assignments, do not seem to want to do anything academic, and are socially and intellectually immature (McCall, 1986). They have little motivation to strive for success; they have a low **need for achievement**. Need for achievement is the motivation to perform well even in the absence of external rewards (McClelland et al., 1953).

Another aspect of achievement motivation that influences an adolescent's achievement is his or her own personal standards for achievement. For example, two students get a B− on a paper. One feels ashamed of herself for doing so poorly; the other feels proud of herself for doing so well. Their different reactions stem, in part, from their different standards for excellence.

ACHIEVEMENT AND ANXIETY

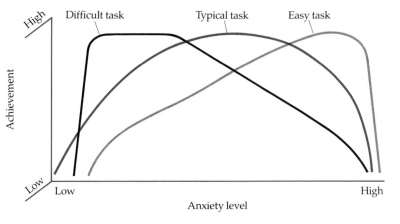

Figure 15.3 Achievement depends on both the difficulty of a task and the person's anxiety. On an easy task, anxiety can enhance achievement. But on a difficult task, it is likely to interfere with achievement. On most tasks, a moderate level of anxiety is best for achievement.

Another aspect of achievement motivation is the adolescent's fear of failing—or succeeding—at tasks. Adolescents who feel anxious about taking tests or going for college interviews, for example, may be afraid of failing. Although some anxiety can help to focus attention and increase motivation and therefore improve performance in a task, too much anxiety is likely to impair performance (Figure 15.3). A high level of anxiety is especially harmful when a person is trying to learn something *new* or solve a *complex* problem (Spielberger, 1966). Consequently, fear of failing often interferes with school performance. In school and on tests, relaxed but alert attentiveness is most conducive to learning and achieving (Hill and Sarason, 1966). Conversely, an adolescent's fear of success also may undermine the need for achievement and lead to ambivalent or negative feelings about doing well in school or on tests.

Locus of control

Not only does an adolescent's motivation to succeed or fail affect his achievement, but so does his explanation of *why* he succeeded or failed. Adolescents may attribute their achievements to their own ability and effort, to luck, or to the difficulty of the task (Dweck and Wortman, 1980). Those who attribute their achievement to their own ability or effort are more likely to feel sure of their ability to achieve, to expect to succeed, and to do so.

I did great on the history test, because I love history, and I really studied.—Nancy, age 15

How much adolescents achieve in school depends on their own personal characteristics—including their abilities, motivation, and work habits—and on the characteristics of their families, such as social class.

Those who attribute their achievement to luck or to the difficulty of the task—factors beyond their personal control—are more likely to feel unsure of their ability to achieve, to expect to fail, and to do so.

> I got lucky last year and got all Bs. But the teacher liked me. I know I'm going to mess up this year.—Ted, age 15

Individuals who aim for a realistically high level of success and who feel personally responsible for their successes and failures are most likely to succeed.

Adolescents who feel that they are in control of their successes and failures are said to have an **internal locus of control**. Those who feel that the events in their lives are beyond their control have an **external locus of control**. To identify children's and adolescents' locus of control, psychologists have used the Intellectual Achievement Responsibility (IAR) questionnaire. The IAR poses questions like ''When you get a high grade on a test, is it (*a*) because you studied hard?''—internal locus of control—or ''*(b)* because the test was easy?''—external locus of control. Several researchers have found that children and adolescents who think that they are personally responsible for their successes, in fact, succeed most often. They do well in reading, math, and language, spend more time on homework, try longer to solve complex logical puzzles, and get higher grades (Crandall, Katkovsky, and Crandall, 1965; Franklin, 1963; McGhee and Crandall, 1968). Students who think that events are beyond their control are likely to get along poorly with their teachers and to attribute more negative qualities to both their teacher and themselves than students who think that they can control the events in their lives (Bryant, 1974).

When adolescents believe that nothing they do makes a difference, that they are not bright enough, that the work is too hard for them or that the teacher dislikes them, they expect to fail. Those who have failed over and over again may begin to believe that failing is inevitable and unavoidable. They sink into **learned helplessness**, an attitude that is likely to fuel the cycle of failures, and stop trying to achieve (Dweck and Licht, 1980). Adolescents who feel helpless are likely to dwell on their failures and the reasons for them. In contrast, those who expect to succeed prefer to move on to something that they can succeed in after they have failed (Diener and Dweck, 1978). In one study of the debilitating effects of learned helplessness, children were asked to do a task that was impossible. In the room with them was a person called a ''failure experimenter.'' Later, the children were asked to perform other tasks with the ''failure experimenter'' present. The children identified as having learned helplessness failed on these tasks when the ''failure experimenter'' was present even though the tasks were well within the children's competence. But when the children with learned helplessness were taught how to take pride in their successes, they succeeded more often. The fact that this feeling of helplessness has been learned implies that it can, with training, be unlearned. When children are trained to connect their own efforts with their successes, they feel—and are—more in control (Dweck, 1976).

Gender

Some differences in achievement in school are related to gender. Boys are likely to achieve more—especially in the physical sciences—and the differences in achievement increase from middle childhood through late adolescence. But just why do these differences exist? In part, they may be the result of biologically based differences in spatial ability (discussed in Chapter 12). In part, the differences may be the result of differences in interests and experience. However, a recent study of the SAT scores of 40,000 high-achieving male and female adolescents showed that males scored higher than females in math, even when the comparison was limited to adolescents who had taken

A child's expectations about his success or failure in solving problems, as well as his teacher's expectations, strongly influence his performance in school.

the same high school math courses and expressed the same degree of interest in math (Benbow and Stanley, 1983).

Socialization by parents, peers, and teachers no doubt contributes to the observed sex differences in achievement. Most adolescent girls get the message that they had better not do *too* well, that competition is aggressive and not feminine, and that achieving can threaten their relationships with boys (Bardwick and Douvan, 1971). What is more, girls are more likely than boys to have been socialized to feel that their failures are attributable to factors beyond their control, such as their lack of ability, and to be victims of learned helplessness (Dweck and Reppucci, 1973; Dweck and Licht, 1980; Nicholls, 1975). Adolescent girls are also more likely than boys to have few expectations of success, low standards of achievement, and considerable anxiety about failing (Stein and Bailey, 1973).

But socialization is unlikely to provide a complete explanation of gender differences in achievement. Among high-achieving adolescents, although girls achieve less than boys in science and math, they achieve more than boys in verbal tasks, especially writing (Benbow and Stanley, 1980; National Center for Educational Statistics, 1985). Is verbal achievement more acceptable for girls than achievement in science and math? Possibly. But other explanations are also possible. For one, the content of the material learned in science and math classes, on the one hand, and that learned in language and literature classes, on the other hand, may help explain the achievement differences between the sexes. In math classes, students are required to master new concepts as they move from arithmetic, to algebra, to geometry, to calculus, whereas in language classes, new concepts build on familiar skills, such as reading, spelling, and vocabulary. Because girls are more likely to fear failure, to feel that they cannot achieve, and to be debilitated by anxiety about their performance, they may be more likely to perform worse than boys in math and science, subjects that regularly call on students to master new concepts (Licht and Dweck, 1984).

Another explanation for boys' higher achievement rests on what happens in the classroom. As one recent study showed, boys dominate class discussion, call out answers more often, and get more of their teachers' attention than girls (Sadker and Sadker, 1985). Girls are encouraged to sit quietly and raise their hands, boys to assert themselves actively. Teachers often did things *for* girls but instructed boys how to do things for themselves. They tended to criticize boys' wrong answers, to help them to find the correct answer, and praise them for answering correctly. But when girls answered incorrectly, teachers tended to move on to another student.

No doubt many factors contribute to observed gender differences in achievement—aptitudes, abilities, interests, experience, socialization, motivation, and attention. These differences remain a focus of investigation—and concern—for researchers and educators. Most upsetting, despite attempts by feminists and equality-minded parents and teachers, the 1985 SAT figures showed girls falling further behind boys—in verbal as well as mathematical and scientific tests.

Family factors

Many of the differences in adolescents' achievement—including the differences related to gender—can be traced to family influences. Family factors are linked to adolescents' opportunities, abilities, and motivation to achieve.

The opportunities for achievement presented to an adolescent depend in part on the family's socioeconomic status and race. Poor and minority students are found in disproportionate numbers in the lower tracks in school (Featherman, 1980). Even the bright students from poor families are likely to achieve less than students from wealthier families if they know that they cannot afford to go to college. Adolescents from middle-class families consistently achieve more in school than those from poorer families (Garbarino and Asp, 1981). Despite attempts to close the gap in educational opportunities between social classes, social class remains a strong determining factor in an adolescent's school achievement (Featherman, 1980).

Adolescents from middle-class families are also likely to achieve more in school than adolescents from poorer families because of differences in their academic abilities. These differences stem from environmental and genetic sources. On the average, middle-class parents have higher IQ scores than parents from lower social classes, and their children are likely to inherit greater intellectual abilities. They also receive the advantages of living in an environment where the importance of learning and achievement is stressed, and good nutrition, health care, and lessons are provided (Featherman, 1980).

Middle-class parents also may instill stronger achievement motivation in their children. Adolescents from families in which parents expect and reward their children's achievement and autonomy have been found to have a higher need for achievement than adolescents whose parents are indifferent to their achievements (Winterbottom, 1958; Rosen and D'Andrade, 1959). In laboratory research, adolescents who have been exposed to a model who rewards himself or herself for excellence are likely to have high standards for achievement (Bandura, 1977).

> My parents have always told me if something is worth doing, it's worth doing well. Of course, I don't always like it when they tell me that. But I think it probably makes me think about trying to do a good job.— Natalie, age 15

Parents of adolescents who are underachievers are likely to be uninterested in education or in their children's school or to be interested but of the opinion that the school, not they, should make their children shape up (McCall, 1986).

Moral reasoning

Moral maturity

Another important change that adolescence brings is the development of greater moral maturity. What *is* moral maturity? Psychologists who subscribe to different theories of development would answer that question in different ways. Those who emphasize cognitive development might say that moral maturity is being able to make moral judgments that are just and fair. Those who accept a psychoanalytic explanation of human development would answer that moral maturity grows out of an internalized sense of guilt, which curbs impulses, lets a person accept blame, and urges the person to make good after doing wrong. Those who subscribe to social learning theory might answer that honest and upright actions characterize mature morality. But followers of each of these theories would agree that adolescence brings with it a higher level of moral maturity. The reasons that adolescents are more morally mature than younger children are many: their cognitive development allows them to think abstractly; their psychological development makes them question rules accepted by their parents and teachers; and their social experience exposes them to a variety of moral positions and moral dilemmas.

In adolescence thinking about moral issues like crime, punishment, and the law undergoes change. A 13-year-old boy might suggest violent, punitive ways to control crime:

> I think that I would . . . well, like if you murder somebody you would punish them with death or something like this. But I don't think that would help because they wouldn't learn their lesson. I think I would give

Many adolescents feel sympathetic distress and social guilt. These feelings compel them to embrace social causes and to worry about the future of humanity.

them some kind of scare or something . . . these people who are in jail for about five years must still own the same grudge, then I would put them in for triple or double the time. I think they would learn their lesson then (Adelson, 1982, p. 8).

But later in adolescence, thinking moves away from this view of law as a way to suppress wayward behavior toward the view that the law protects and helps people. Older adolescents are more likely to believe that laws provide for harmony among people, that they make a nation "a better place to live." Their ideas of justice are more benevolent. They are surer of themselves, more self-controlled, more consistently honest (or dishonest) than younger children. Compared to younger children, adolescents better understand their own reasons for acting as they do, sympathize more with others, and have a more highly developed sense of personal guilt and social injustice.

Adolescents who reach a mature level of moral reasoning make moral judgments based on their own personal values and standards, not on social conventions or the persuasion of authorities. They form their own ideas about moral issues—"Is segregation a moral system?" "Are the immigration laws of the United States fair?"—and reason according to principles of justice and social reciprocity. They acknowledge the rights of individuals to life and liberty as a higher moral good than even such hallowed principles as the interests of the majority.

According to Lawrence Kohlberg (1976), whose theory of moral development was discussed in Chapter 12, mature moral reasoning goes beyond the rules prescribed by social conventions; it is **postconventional**. In the first stage of postconventional reasoning—Stage 5 in Kohlberg's theory—people are oriented toward social contracts. They understand that laws are written by consensus and can be changed by consensus as well. Even though rules may be arbitrary, they guard human rights, and the privilege of living in a society incurs in each individual the obligation to obey its laws and to abide by its social contracts. If laws and rules threaten individual human rights, they can in some instances be superseded, however. As a 24-year-old reasoned when he was asked about the Heinz dilemma,

> It is the husband's duty to save his wife. The fact that her life is in danger transcends every other standard you might use to judge his action. Life is more important than property.
> *Suppose it were a friend, not his wife?*
> I don't think that would be much different from a moral point of view.
> It's still a human being in danger.
> *Suppose it were a stranger?*
> To be consistent, yes, from a moral standpoint.
> *What is this moral standpoint?*
> I think every individual has a right to live, and if there is a way of saving an individual, he should be saved (Kohlberg, 1976, p. 38).

According to this postconventional, Stage 5 argument, the value of human life overrides the value of any convention. A drug to save a life can, therefore, be stolen for a wife, a friend, or a stranger.

In Stage 6, the highest stage of moral reasoning in Kohlberg's theory, people base their judgments on universal principles and unimpeachable ethics. Their ethical values rest on justice, reciprocity, equality, human life, and human rights. Stage 6 reasoners arrive at their moral decisions on their own, sometimes in spite of social conventions. They listen more intently to their conscience than to public opinion or social conventions. The actions of Martin Luther King, Jr., and Mahatma Gandhi exemplify this kind of moral reasoning. These men were guided by strong, individual, ethical principles, and when laws conflicted with their principles, they disobeyed the law:

Martin Luther King went to jail rather than obey the laws that supported segregation, just as Gandhi went to jail rather than capitulate to the inequities of India's system of government. A Stage 6 reasoner might argue that Heinz must steal the drug to preserve life rather than obey a law that would effectively condemn his wife to death.

Kohlberg and his associates now have completed a 20-year longitudinal study of the moral reasoning of a sample of Chicago boys (Colby, Kohlberg, Gibbs, and Lieberman, 1983). Beginning when the boys were 10 years old, the researchers asked them about Kohlberg's moral dilemmas every three to four years, and their responses were recorded. The boys proceeded through the first four of Kohlberg's developmental stages in the order Kohlberg had observed in cross-sectional comparisons of boys of different ages. No subject skipped a stage; only rarely did a subject seem to move back a stage. The subjects' moral reasoning continued to advance for the duration of the study, by the end of which the subjects were men in their 30s (see Figure 15.4).

Even so, in this and other studies, only about one person in five ever reached the postconventional level of reasoning (Stage 5). *No* Stage 6 reasoners were found. Formal operational thought is necessary for postconventional moral reasoning, because postconventional reasoning requires abstract thought and the understanding that social conventions of right and wrong compete with other equally plausible and logical possibilities. But formal operational thinking alone does not guarantee postconventional moral reasoning. Most adults in the United States are at the fourth stage of moral development. At Stage 4, people reason that moral behavior serves the interests of society. People in this "law-and-order" stage believe strongly in rules and social order. Heinz, they may reason, should steal the drug for his wife because he has vowed to protect her until death do them part. His marriage vow and his duty as a husband are of overriding importance. Stage 4 reasoners may argue that Heinz should not steal the drug because stealing is against the law. Most adolescents in this country reason at even lower levels, Kohlberg's levels 2 and 3 (see Table 12.1).

Kohlberg's theory of moral development has come in for its share of criticism. It has been criticized, for example, for being a politically liberal hierarchy in which political conservatism is represented as Stage 4, law-and-order reasoning. It has been criticized for reflecting the values of Western culture and not universal values. To answer this charge, Kohlberg studied boys and adolescents between 10 and 21 years old in cities, tribes, and villages in several different cultures, including Taiwan, Israel, and Mexico's Yucatan Peninsula (Kohlberg, 1969; Edwards, 1981). He found that reasoning corresponding to Stages 1 through 4 unfolded in order as the boys in these cultures grew up. Some adolescents reached Stage 5, although when they did so depended on their intelligence and on their social group; adolescents from poor villages and tribes less often reached Stage 5 reasoning. Some critics claimed that these results did not prove that third-world citizens do not reason at the postconventional level, because Kohlberg's hypothetical moral dilemmas do not represent real-life issues for these people (Simpson, 1974).

In a later study (Nisan and Kohlberg, 1982), Turkish men were presented with six hypothetical moral dilemmas that had been revised for the Turkish culture. For example, the dilemma of Heinz and the drug was changed to the following.

> A man and wife have just migrated from the high mountains. They started to farm, but there was no rain and no crops grew. No one had enough food. The wife became sick from having little food and could only sleep. Finally, she was close to dying from having no food. The husband could not get any work, and the wife could not move to another town. There was only one grocery store in the village, and the store-

STAGES OF MORAL REASONING

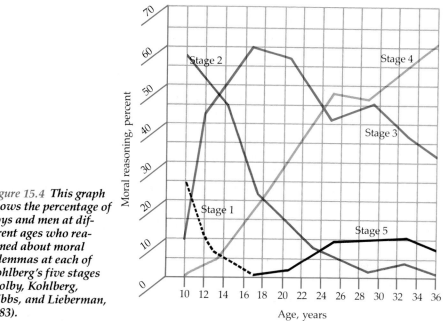

Figure 15.4 **This graph shows the percentage of boys and men at different ages who reasoned about moral dilemmas at each of Kohlberg's five stages (Colby, Kohlberg, Gibbs, and Lieberman, 1983).**

keeper charged a very high price for food because there was no other store and people had no place else to go to buy food. The husband asked the storekeeper for some food for his wife and said he would pay for it later. The storekeeper said, ''No, I won't give you any food unless you pay first.'' The husband went to all the people in the village to ask for food, but no one had food to spare. So he got desperate and broke into the store to steal food for his wife (Nisan and Kohlberg, 1982, p. 868).

Paralleling earlier studies in the third world, only 12 percent of the oldest Turkish subjects used any Stage 4 reasoning, and none of them reached Stage 5. Kohlberg concluded that moral development occurs in the same stages regardless of culture but that people in different cultures are more or less likely to reach the postconventional level. A recent study of adolescents in Israel poses another complication for Kohlberg's scheme, however (Snarey, Reimer, and Kohlberg, 1985). In that study, adolescents who lived on kibbutzim were found to use moral reasoning that is not covered in Kohlberg's scoring manual. In particular, they used moral reasons that emphasized the commune, collective happiness, and the preservation of social solidarity.

Another criticism of Kohlberg's theory has been that it is based on data that may have been affected by particular historical events and conditions (Rest, Davison, and Robbins, 1978). The subjects in Kohlberg's Chicago study had lived through the civil rights struggle, the Vietnam War, Watergate, and the wave of feminism, each of which focused public scrutiny on moral issues, and this may have honed their ideas about fairness. Historical change probably accounts for at least part of the increases in the subjects' scores on tests of moral reasoning.

Most recently, Carol Gilligan (1982) has aroused wide interest with her criticism of Kohlberg's theory as sexist. Gilligan opposes Kohlberg's analysis because it is based on and biased toward male responses. She suggests that women and men differ psychologically in ways that directly affect their moral reasoning. Women are more attuned to the relationships and connections between people; men are more attuned to individual achievement, to the separateness and distinctiveness of each person. Women take much of their personal identities from their personal relationships; men take theirs from their work. Women are likely to be morally concerned with how people are connected, obligated to one another, and generally interdependent. Men are likely to be morally concerned with justice, individual rights and obligations, and equitable solutions to each separate person's conflicting and competing claims. Says Gilligan, women's is a morality of caring, and men's is a morality of justice.

Gilligan contended that women are automatically disadvantaged by Kohlberg's ratings of moral maturity. Kohlberg's moral dilemmas pose conflicts of individual rights and social justice, precisely those areas in which men are trained to reason analytically. These dilemmas draw on men's powers of logical deduction and rational thought. But women, who see the dilemmas more as problems in the web of human relationships, may score lower on Kohlberg's ratings of moral maturity. Gilligan criticized Kohlberg's system for rating all responses centering on caring for others or personal responsibility as Stage 3 reasoning.

Gilligan describes the responses of two 11-year-olds, a boy and a girl, to the Heinz dilemma. Jake feels quite sure that Heinz should steal the drug to save his wife. After analyzing the dilemma as a conflict between life and property, Jake argues logically that life takes priority:

> For one thing, a human life is worth more than money, and if the druggist only makes $1,000, he is still going to live, but if Heinz doesn't steal the drug, his wife is going to die. (*Why is life worth more than money?*) Because the druggist can get $1,000 later from rich people with cancer, but Heinz can't get his wife again. (Gilligan, 1982, p. 26).

Jake sees the dilemma as "sort of like a math problem with humans," a problem in logic, in other words, to be solved rationally.

But Amy responds to the same moral dilemma in quite a different way. Should Heinz steal the drug, Amy is asked.

> Well, I don't think so. I think there might be other ways besides stealing it, like if he could borrow the money or make a loan or something, but he really shouldn't steal the drug—but his wife shouldn't die either (Gilligan, 1982, p. 28).

Why shouldn't Heinz steal the drug, Amy is then asked.

> If he stole the drug, he might save his wife then, but if he did, he might have to go to jail, and then his wife might get sicker again, and he couldn't get more of the drug, and it might not be good. So, they should really just talk it out and find some other way to make the money (Gilligan, 1982, p. 28).

In Amy's eyes, the problem is one of enduring relationships and human needs. The wife's survival is based on the preservation of relationships, and her life is valued in terms of relationships as well: "If she died, it hurts a lot of people and it hurts her." The druggist's failure to respond to another's need thus becomes a central problem. Amy has answered a question the interviewer did not ask. To Amy, the problem is one of impressing the druggist with the dying wife's needs or of appealing to others who might help. The problem is not one of rules that prevail in a world of people standing alone—as it was for Jake and for Kohlberg. Whereas Jake saw the need for agreement mediated through logic and law, Amy sees the need for agreement mediated through the communication among interrelated people. In Kohlberg's analysis, Amy's responses appear a full stage lower in maturity than those of Jake. This impression is misleading, Gilligan contended, because Amy has perceived the central truths in a morality of caring, a central tenet in nonviolent resolutions of conflicts.

Gilligan's criticisms of Kohlberg in turn have been met with criticism. Some argue that Kohlberg's system can be said to discriminate against women only if women actually score lower than men do. But when subjects' educational and work backgrounds are controlled, girls and women do not score lower than boys and men in moral reasoning (Walker, 1984, 1986).

Nevertheless, in one recent study of adolescents between 11 and 21 years old, although no sex differences in stages of moral reasoning were found, girls were twice as likely as boys to justify their Stage 3 moral judgments on the basis of empathically taking another person's position (Gibbs, Arnold, and Burkhart, 1984). Girls were also more likely to justify their moral judgments on the basis of other people's approval and their own conscience. In another study of college students, although again no sex differences in Kohlberg's stages of moral reasoning were found, there were significant differences between students judged masculine and feminine on a scale of traditional gender-role attitudes: masculine students reasoned at higher levels on Kohlberg's dilemmas than feminine students (Lifton, 1985). Gender does seem to be related to moral reasoning in subtle and complex ways, and Kohlberg's stages may not reflect these distinctions.

Moral ideas and moral acts

What is the relation between moral reasoning and moral action? Some people may reason maturely on moral issues but act criminally. Others, whose level of moral judgment is low, never do anything illegal. Moral reasoning is far from an exact predictor of moral action.

In one study, researchers looked at the relation between moral thought and honesty in junior high school students. The students were interviewed about Kohlberg's moral dilemmas and also were tempted to cheat (Krebs and Kohlberg, 1973). Among the preconventional reasoners, three-fourths succumbed to temptation and cheated in at least one of the situations. Among the conventional reasoners, two-thirds cheated. Among the postconventional reasoners, only one-fifth cheated. In this study, the relation between moral reasoning and moral action was clear-cut. But in another study, the relation between more advanced moral reasoning and honest behavior held only when students were interviewed about the moral dilemmas *before* they had a chance to cheat (Krebs, 1967). Interviewed afterward, the more advanced reasoners cheated *more* than less advanced reasoners. Perhaps the interviews put the students on guard not to cheat. Perhaps they made the students think about moral issues and reinforced their tendencies to act honestly. In another study,

Rather than being a definite and fixed personality trait, or a necessary outgrowth of moral understanding, people's honesty seems to depend on the situation, such as the likelihood of being caught in a misdeed.

research focus

Moral reasoning and decision making

It makes sense that people might offer moral reasons for how someone else should act that would differ from those they would offer for their own actions. Richard Weiss (1982) tested whether this is so with a group of 16- to 18-year-old, middle-class, public high school students in California. In their first session with Weiss, half of the students were presented with one of two moral dilemmas. One dilemma was about a teenager who holds a party when her parents are away. The other was about a teenager who leaves the home of vacationing neighbors to join friends, despite the fact that he or she has been given responsibility for the house. Subjects in the "self" perspective were told to imagine themselves in the dilemma. Subjects in the "other" perspective were told to imagine that the dilemma applied to a hypothetical "someone else." All the subjects were asked to decide whether to tell the parents or neighbors what had happened in their absence and to decide, "In this situation, for everybody concerned, what's the best or wisest thing to do, and why?" All the subjects also answered questions designed to probe their moral reasoning. In a second interview about three weeks after the first, Weiss administered the vacation dilemma to the students who previously had evaluated the party dilemma, the party dilemma to those who had responded to the vacation dilemma. In this part of the study, the students who previously had been in the "self" condition were asked to imagine that the dilemma applied to the hypothetical "someone else," and vice versa.

Did the students apply the same moral standards to others as to themselves? Much as Weiss had predicted, the students applied a higher moral standard to others than to themselves. Although the students more often than not decided that the adults in the dilemmas should be told about the unwise acts of the teenagers, they opted for disclosure less often when they imagined themselves in the dilemmas. When they had to imagine themselves in a dilemma, students showed much more concern for getting caught or getting in trouble—what Weiss called "prudential concern"—than they did when they had to imagine someone else in the dilemma. The teenagers tended to separate moral reasoning from decision making and, in dilemmas about others, applied standards that did not apply to themselves. Only when students imagined themselves in the dilemmas did their level of moral reasoning seem integrated with their decisions.

At all levels the teenagers had prudential concerns, but those who were at the highest levels of reasoning were less likely than those at lower levels to make self-serving decisions in either the self or the fictitious-other dilemma.

this one of delinquent and nondelinquent adolescents, it was shown that the moral reasoning of adolescents who had committed antisocial acts was no different from that of those who had not committed antisocial acts (Hains and Ryan, 1983). Yet in another study, eleventh and twelfth graders who reasoned at higher levels on Kohlberg's dilemmas were rated by their teachers as more likely to take morally courageous actions (Gibbs et al., 1986). In sum, although there is a link between moral reasoning and moral behavior, it is tenuous. Moral and immoral actions depend on more than one's abstract judgment.

James Rest (1983) has proposed a model for integrating moral reasoning with moral actions. First, he suggests, people interpret a situation and surmise how their actions might affect others. They also interpret their own feelings in the situation. Once they have thought about alternative possibilities and how these might affect others and themselves, they judge and integrate these alternatives. Then people decide what *ought* to be done in the situation—Kohlberg's moral reasoning. Third, they decide what they actually are *going* to do. Often, values other than moral ones weigh heavily in a person's choice of action. Religious values, ambition, and self-interest are three such possibilities. There is often a gap between what people think they *should* do and what they *will* do. Finally, people carry out a plan of action, a process that involves planning a sequence of actions, surmounting obstacles, fatigue, and disappointment, resisting distractions and other temptations, and keeping the goal in mind. Recent research has shown that the likelihood of a person's acting morally depends on the stress in a particular situation, the cost to the person of acting morally, and the person's ability to assess the situation accurately and choose a practical solution (Haan, Aerts, and Cooper, 1985).

Adolescent egocentrism

Another outcome of the physical, cognitive, social, and psychological changes that take place during adolescence is **adolescent egocentrism** (Elkind, 1967, 1985; Inhelder and Piaget, 1958). Adolescent egocentrism is what makes adolescents think that they are more important and unusual than they really are. In their mind's eye they stand before an audience under a social spotlight. They imagine that the audience can see into their innermost thoughts and is hanging on their every word and deed. After hours fiddling with a hairstyle in front of a mirror, an adolescent girl may expect others to applaud her appearance. A single unsightly pimple can lead a boy to cringe in the certain knowledge that "everybody" will notice. To avoid going to school—and into locker rooms especially—where others might judge how they look, some adolescents develop school phobia (Rutter, 1980).

Whereas younger children can imagine the thoughts of existing people, adolescents can imagine the thoughts of hypothetical people—a second-order symbolic creation (Elkind, 1985). The problem is that at first adolescents fail to distinguish between the concerns of this **imaginary audience** and their own, personal concerns. Results from questionnaires given to hundreds of adolescents show that self-consciousness, which is presumably a reflection of heightened concern with an imaginary audience, is at its peak among 13-year-old girls and 15-year-old boys (Elkind and Bowen, 1979; Gray and Hudson, 1984).

As part of their egocentricism, young adolescents may imagine a **personal fable** for themselves. As if having dressed themselves in the kind of wonderful cape worn by fairy-tale characters, adolescents feel unique and indestructible. They believe that their thoughts and feelings are understood by no one, least of all their parents—"But Daddy, you just don't understand." They feel invincible, immune from death and disaster— "*I* won't get pregnant," "*I* won't crack up the car." They believe that their emotional experiences are new and unique. In failing to differentiate between what is new and thrilling to them and what is new in human experience, adolescents are likely to feel that no one has ever loved or hated as deeply as they—"But Mother, *you've* never been really in love."

What causes adolescent egocentrism? Originally it was suggested that adolescent egocentrism was the result of the onset of formal operational thinking, with its emphasis on speculation and abstraction (Elkind, 1967; Inhelder and Piaget, 1958). This suggestion was supported by studies showing that adolescent egocentrism peaked at the age that formal operational thinking began (Elkind and Bowen, 1979). But this is also the age that dramatic physical changes brought on by puberty and dramatic social changes like heightened conformity to peers and conflict with parents take place.

Figure 15.5 This graph shows the relation between measures of adolescent egocentrism and level of cognitive development. For girls, self-consciousness, which presumably reflects adolescent egocentrism, is most common during the transition between concrete and formal operations. For boys, self-consciousness is most common in the stage of concrete operations (Gray and Hudson, 1984).

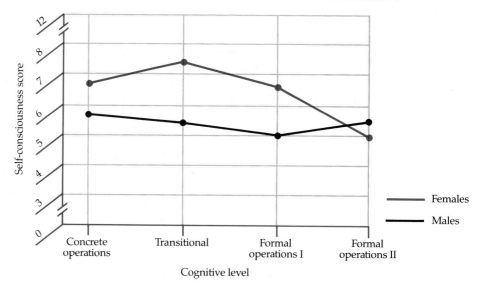

These changes also could lead to increased egocentrism. To test whether adolescent egocentrism is linked to formal operational thinking, researchers in one study gave adolescents tests of formal operational reasoning and logic and assessed their egocentrism (Gray and Hudson, 1984). It was expected that adolescents who were just making the transition from concrete to formal operations would be the most egocentrically self-conscious. The hypothesis was supported for girls but not boys (see Figure 15.5). Apparently, the ability to reason logically and abstractly in the physical domain does not, by itself, account for the increased subjectivity and self-consciousness of adolescence. Advances in social understanding may be even more relevant to the development of adolescent egocentrism (Lapsley and Murphy, 1985). The young adolescent is able for the first time to think about his own perspective, the perspective of another person, and the perspective of a third person observing the first two (Selman, 1980). With this ability, the adolescent can see himself as both actor and object and can imagine his interactions from the perspective of a generalized "average" member of the group observing him.

Fortunately for their *real* audience, adolescent self-consciousness diminishes after early adolescence. It is replaced, as we shall see in the next chapter, by new concerns, about identity and the future.

Summary

1. During adolescence, children can for the first time think abstractly, solve logical problems, and follow the scientific method. Piaget called this level of thinking *formal operational*. Formal operational thinking develops in most, but not all, adolescents by about age 15.

2. Once adolescents can reason abstractly, they understand and can discuss social, political, and moral issues.

3. Many adolescents in this country graduate from high school with a surprising lack of knowledge. People have blamed television, the deterioration of the nuclear family, drug use, poor schooling, and changes in the composition of the test-taking population for declining test scores.

4. Academic achievement is predicted by factors in the school (like the number of courses offered), the family (such as its emphasis on education), and the person (for example, achievement motivation and learned

helplessness).

5. To write clearly, adolescents must think abstractly on several levels. They must organize their thoughts into logical units of grammar and organize the ideas within their messages. With age, adolescents get progressively better at clearly and cogently summarizing what they read.

6. No matter how it is defined, moral maturity does not appear until adolescence. Compared to children, adolescents better understand their reasons for acting as they do, can sympathize more with others, and have a more highly developed sense of personal guilt and social injustice.

7. Adolescents with formal operational thought often reason about moral dilemmas at a postconventional level. They base their moral judgments on their own personal values and standards, not on social conventions or the persuasion of authorities. They acknowledge the rights of individuals to life and liberty as a higher moral good than even such honored principles as the right of the majority. In the first stage of postconventional reasoning, people are oriented toward social contracts. In the second stage, they base their moral judgments on universal principles and unimpeachable ethics.

8. Kohlberg's theory of moral reasoning, in which postconventional reasoning is the morally mature level, has been criticized for being culture-bound and sexist.

9. Moral reasoning is tenuously linked to moral actions; both moral and immoral actions depend on more than a person's awareness and abstract judgment.

10. Adolescents tend to think that they are more important and unusual than they really are and to imagine that they stand before an audience attentive to their every word and action. This is called *adolescent egocentrism*. Adolescent egocentrism may be a result of the increased cognitive and social understanding of adolescents, in which they can think not only about their own perspective but about that of others.

Key terms

interpropositional logic
formal operational thinking
need for achievement
internal locus of control

external locus of control
learned helplessness
postconventional moral reasoning

adolescent egocentrism
imaginary audience
personal fable

Suggested readings

ERIKSON, ERIK. *Gandhi's Truth: On the Origins of Militant Nonviolence.* New York: Norton, 1969. A biography of the man who led India to independence through great leadership and passive resistance, written by one of the outstanding theorists in the field of child development.

GILLIGAN, CAROL. *In a Different Voice: Psychological Theory and Woman's Development.* Cambridge, Mass.: Harvard University Press, 1982. An original theory of moral development in women, one which contrasts their moral and psychological orientations to those of men and is supported by data gathered in extensive interviews with women at various ages.

SIZER, THEODORE R. *Horace's Compromise: the Dilemma of the American High School.* Boston: Houghton Mifflin, 1985. Although Sizer's topic is the American high school, the larger subject of the book is universal—specifically, the ways in which society transmits education and cultural and social values to adolescents.

chapter sixteen
Social and emotional development

The invention of adolescence

In some cultures, there is a clear demarcation between childhood and adulthood. The passage from one to the other, which in our society is long and complex, is quick. The onset of puberty is marked by public events and ''rites of passage.'' Once the physically mature child has completed the rite, be it a circumcision, a ritual offering, a betrothal, or an elaborate ceremony, he or she is considered part of the adult world. In our culture, the gulf between puberty—physical maturity—and an adult social role—social maturity—yawns wider than ever. The period between them is almost as long as that between birth and puberty. Puberty occurs long before marriage, parenthood, or economic independence. For those seeking professional careers, 20 years may elapse between puberty and true economic independence.

Why is adolescence in our society so prolonged? Before the 1880s, the concept of adolescence as we know it did not exist (Demos and Demos, 1969). Although people had become concerned about ''the irreverent and unruly spirit [that] has come to be prevalent, an outrageous evil among the young people of our land'' (Burton, 1863), adolescence was not recognized as a separate period until the end of the 1880s. G. Stanley Hall's two-volume *Adolescence*, published in 1904, brought the subject squarely within the realm of scientific inquiry and into the public consciousness.

By that time, age segregation was beginning to mold the experience and the perception of adolescence. The rise of free, compulsory public education and laws against child labor meant that most adolescents spent most of their days attending school. The idea of adolescence as a separate period then intensified as families migrated from farms to cities, a shift that fractured family life into age-defined units. Whereas rural life had been characterized by a continuum between generations, urban life now gave rise to a view of children and adolescents as special groups, whose behavior, if sometimes unusual, was appropriate to their particular stage in life. During the Roaring Twenties and the Prohibition Era, adolescents became more visible and began to set trends, with their bobbed hair, short skirts, and scandalous dancing. By 1930, adolescents were age-segragated not only at school but in their spare time as well.

In the 1930s and 1940s, adolescents were seasoned by the economic and political stresses of the Depression and World War II. Then in the postwar period, adolescence was lengthened as many returning soldiers went to college on the GI bill. In the 1950s, adolescents of the ''silent generation'' lived in their own separate world of bobby sox and bebop, complacent about their future and the world's. By the 1960s and early 1970s, children born during the postwar baby boom tumultuously entered adolescence. For many, adolescence was strongly marked by political protest—against the war in Vietnam, for civil and women's rights—and rebellious experimentation with drugs and alternative life-styles. The size of this adolescent peer group was the largest ever—adolescents made up more than 10 percent of the population of the United States—and the sheer size of the group created a public image of a youth culture.

In many ways, adolescents, more than younger children and perhaps more than some adults, are affected by the prevailing social and political climate—and affect it. Adolescents are encountering society for the first time. They are discovering what their parents already take for granted. Compared with younger children, they are more willing to express themselves, especially if speaking up makes them more independent. Therefore it is not surprising that many adolescents are interested in social change. Youth movements—for women's rights, civil rights, ecology, or peace—flourish in times of cultural change.

The adolescent experience strongly reflects prevailing historical and cultural trends—in patterns of friendship and family life, opportunities for education, norms for leaving school and getting married, and so on. Because history and culture so thoroughly affect adolescents, it is important to remember that the information in this chapter is specific to contemporary adolescence in the United States. Views of adolescence and perhaps adolescent development itself change right along with adolescents' changing educational, economic, and sexual experiences, expectations, attitudes, fads, values, and norms.

In the 1980s, with the prosperity of the 1950s and the protests of the 1960s long gone, adolescents generally are more concerned with achievement in school and work. When they compare themselves with earlier generations of adolescents (Santrock, 1984), they find themselves to be more money-oriented and more financially dependent on their parents. They claim to be growing up faster and having adult experiences at earlier ages, to be likelier to have jobs, to be more interested in sexual equality, more aware of their own rights, more sexually permissive, more preoccupied with themselves, and more concerned with physical fitness. They also recognize that they are living in more varied family structures. As more mothers of adolescents have entered the paid work force, the age segregation of adolescence has been reinforced in a new way.

Storm and stress

For some, adolescence today is a difficult, stormy time of life. For others, it is a relatively smooth transition between childhood and adulthood. Researchers were once divided into those, like G. Stanley Hall and Anna Freud, who characterized adolescence as a period of **storm and stress**—a stormy decade of emotional turmoil—and those, like Margaret Mead, who did not. One reason for these different views was probably that different observers based their conclusions on different groups of adolescents. Clinicians, seeing patients in psychotherapy, were likely to see adolescents who were experiencing a great deal of stress. Researchers who saw a more representative sample of ''normal'' adolescents would see less stress.

It is probably more accurate to say that some adolescents feel a great deal of stress, some very little, and the others a moderate amount. These differences stem in part from differences in individual temperaments and circumstances and in part from historical and cultural conditions. Although some adolescents experience more stress than others, almost all adolescents are subject to ups and downs in their moods.

> I was feeling on top of the world until I got that note in the cafeteria from my boy friend. He wants to break up, because he says he's feeling ''too penned in.'' I went to the girls' room and cried until I had to be in English class.—Megan, age 15
>
> After school my father drove me to Boston for a college interview. I was really up on the way in, thinking about all the things I was gonna say to the interviewer. But when we got there, it was pouring rain, and I had to run about two blocks from the car to the interview office. I was so rattled that I got bummed out, and the interview was horrible. I *know* I won't get in.—Ted, age 17

One minute a teenager is basking in the glow of a remembered kiss, and the next he is made miserable by a teacher who tells him to stop day dreaming in class. One day, a teenager is feeling warm and friendly toward her family, and the next she is irritated by their demands. As he spends an evening alone, a teenager worries about whether anyone really likes him; the next afternoon, he is buoyed by his friends' infectious high spirits and highjinks.

In one recent study in Chicago (Csikszentmihalyi and Larson, 1984), 75 adolescents, 13 to 18 years old, were paged at random times during the day and night by "beepers" that they carried and were asked what they were doing, whom they were with, and how they were feeling. Within the bland and broad regularity of waking up, going to school, going to work, coming home, doing homework, and going to sleep, there were frequent and rapid changes of mood. From one hour to the next, adolescents went from elation to dejection, from excitement to boredom. For example, one boy in the study, Greg (see Figure 16.1), feels happy as he walks home from school on Tuesday with a girl whom he is beginning to think of as his girlfriend. But he is already "going with" someone else, and as the week goes on this worries him. He wakes up happy on Wednesday, but chemistry class makes him feel down and confused. After class, Greg happily socializes with some friends and admires graffiti he has written: "*Q:* Are we not men? *A:* We are DEVO!" He cheerfully thinks about the song that these lines come from. But 45 minutes later, in typing class, he is emotionally unhinged. By midafternoon, Greg is very happy as he walks by himself to work, because he has just kissed his new girlfriend. Work and the rest of the night are dull. On Thursday, Greg feels guilty and "suicidal" when he thinks about not taking his old girlfriend to the prom. But later that night, he happily plans the costume to wear to the annual Senior Banquet on Saturday. Over the week, Greg alternates between bored unhappiness in class and happy excitement when he is with his friends. Although adults, too, alternate between boredom and excitement in their daily lives, it is the rapidity of the change and their extremes of dejection and exhilaration that mark instability of moods as characteristic of adolescence.

Adolescents in the Chicago study reported far wider variations in moods than adults did in a comparable beeper study (Larson, Csikszentmihalyi, and Graef, 1980). They were more likely than adults to feel euphoric—to see the world as a perfect place—and to be vulnerable to the pain and chaos of unexpected events. Not only were their moods more extreme, but these extreme moods were shorter-lived than adults'. Within 45 minutes of feeling dejection or exhilaration, Greg and the other adolescents studied had usually returned to a neutral mood. But adults were still feeling up or down two hours later. In one respect, the adolescents' moods did resemble the adults'. Their moods were equally predictable from what they were doing at the time. But adolescents move more quickly from one setting to another and get into more emotional situations. They also are more likely to feel overwhelmed—by the demands of a teacher or a parent, and by their own high expectations.

> I thought I would go insane in class today. Who *cares* about memorizing all the losing vice-presidential candidates?—Erica, age 15

> When I heard that we were going to have to do a term paper in English, I panicked. One of the girls burst into tears.—Peter, age 15

Although some individuals have greater difficulty than others, the stresses on most adolescents are real. Some of these stresses are physical—puberty—and others are environmental—rejection by peers, tough exams and bad marks, demands by parents. Even the most competent children may become unpredictable in adolescence. Over the course of adolescence, though, moods become somewhat more stable. In another beeper study which extended for one week during each of several years, adolescents circled words that reflected how they were feeling about themselves when the beeper sounded (Savin-Williams and Demo, 1984). In seventh grade, only 11 percent of the subjects had stable feelings of self-esteem over the week. By tenth

Adolescence is full of ups and downs as situations and moods shift from one hour to the next.

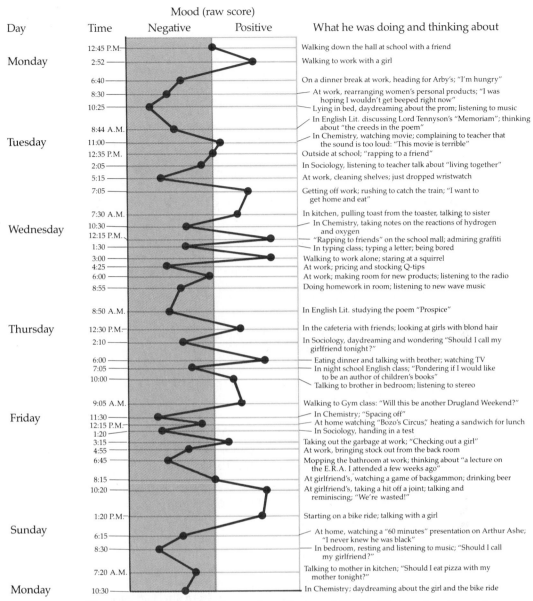

Figure 16.1 *When one adolescent boy, Greg, was "beeped" at random intervals throughout the week and asked to indicate what he was doing and how he was feeling at the time, his ratings showed substantial mood swings (Csikszentmihalyi and Larson, 1984).*

grade, the percentage of adolescents with stable feelings over the week had increased to 41 percent.

Making transitions: early adolescence

The early part of adolescence, from 11 or 12 to 16 or so, is when the storms are stormiest and the stresses most stressful for most adolescents. For this is when the adolescent is making the transition out of childhood.

> I checked on Kristy one night at bedtime when she was 13. She'd fallen asleep with lipstick and heels on, her hair in rollers, and a stuffed animal under her arms. It reminded me of the time when she was 2 and fell asleep with a pacifier in her mouth and sunglasses on her nose. She was straddling two stages of life once again.

In early adolescence, changes occur on all fronts. The child changes physically (as we saw in Chapter 14) and acquires an adult shape and reproductive capacity. These changes and associated side effects (like acne) may create stresses. Worries about physical changes have been found to be most common during early adolescence (Berzonsky, 1982). During early adolescence, children also change cognitively (as we saw in Chapter 15) and begin to acquire adult reasoning abilities. This allows them to worry about social issues, rules, and fairness. It also allows teachers to increase their expectations of what children can achieve and to set more challenging assignments. During this period, adolescents are most likely to mention that one of their greatest worries is nuclear war. Researchers in Finland and Canada, for example, have found that almost twice as many 12-year-olds as 18-year-olds worry most about nuclear war (Goldberg et al., 1985; Solantaus, Rimpela, and Taipale, 1984). During early adolescence, the desire for comformity to peers also is likely to increase, creating in its wake concerns about popularity—"Do people like me?" "Am I too different?" In one study, for example, 11- and 15-year-olds reported that their greatest anxieties were over relationships with members of the other sex and rejection by their peers (Coleman, 1974).

During this period, too, issues of independence may become critical at home. Many young adolescents spend large amounts of time away from home—at school, with friends, or working at a part-time job after school—and resent their parents' requests and questions.

> When I asked Sam where he'd been this afternoon, he snapped, "Here comes the Spanish Inquisition again."

The young adolescent may feel grown up but continue to be treated like a child by parents and older brothers and sisters. It is during early adolescence that family disruptions boil over most often.

> Erica turned impossible on the eve of her thirteenth birthday. We have dinner with my parents—Erica and Mike's grandparents—every Sunday, and we've been doing this for years. All of a sudden, Erica didn't want to go. Why? She had to wash her hair. Couldn't she wash it before or after dinnertime? No. Why? Because she was supposed to wait by the phone for her boyfriend to call her then. I suggested that she call him and change the time of his call to her. Oh no, she couldn't do that. Girls don't call boys, *Mother*. Erica stormed into her bedroom, slammed the door, and put some hideous music on ear splittingly loud. I thought that my blood pressure would blow steam from my ears, I was so frustrated. When I walked by her bedroom door half an hour later, the phone cord was pulled underneath it. She was back "in conference," as my husband puts it. Lord, give us strength to survive the child's adolescence!

In a study of 70 middle-class adolescent boys, family disputes were most common in early adolescence and tended to quiet down after ninth grade (Offer, Ostrov, and Howard, 1981). The 12- and 13-year-olds were the most rebellious, often bickering with their parents.

Self-esteem

Young adolescents are most likely to be plagued with feelings of unhappiness and self-doubt if they are under stress from several sources. In one study of

SELF-ESTEEM AND AGE

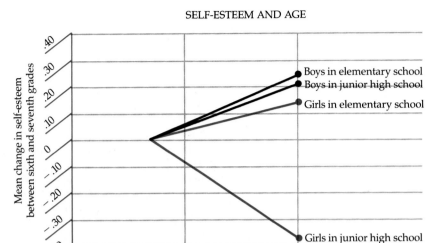

Figure 16.2 **Boys gain some self-esteem between sixth and seventh grade; girls attending seventh grade in an elementary school do, too, although not as much. The self-esteem of girls attending seventh grade in a junior high school plummets (Simmons, Van Cleave, Blyth, and Bush, 1979).**

young adolescents, 12-year-old girls who were going through physical and social changes at the same time—moving to a new school, beginning to date—had the lowest self-confidence and self-esteem (Simmons, Rosenberg, and Rosenberg, 1973; see Figure 16.2). In another study, seventh-grade boys who were going through puberty had lower self-esteem than those who had not yet reached puberty (Jaquish and Savin-Williams, 1981). Many young adolescents just entering junior high school go through a period of questioning their competence (Connell, 1981; Harter and Connell, 1982).

> Our sixth-grade teacher was trying to impress us with what a big change junior high was going to be. She said that she hoped that we would find our way, because it was a much bigger school than the one we were used to. She hoped that we would do well in our courses, because no one would be there to hold our hands the way they'd done up till then. By the end of her talk, I was so terrified of junior high that I nearly passed out.—Natalie, age 13

> I remember sitting in the cafeteria during my first months in junior high and watching the ninth graders. They seemed so nonchalant, so mature, so cool. The boys would casually lean against the wall. The girls would saunter by. And they'd all laugh and joke around. We seventh graders just clumped around our little tables, gawking at them. At the end of seventh grade, I was invited to a party where there were going to be some ninth-grade boys in addition to our regular group. The ninth graders all swooped into the party at once, and the atmosphere turned positively electric. They were *so* sophisticated and cool that when one of them asked me to dance I thought I would levitate through the ceiling.—Sarah, age 17

By later adolescence, the self-doubts of the 13-year-old have eased (McCarthy and Hoge, 1982; O'Malley and Bachman, 1983). Over time, more adolescents answer positively questions like, ''I feel I am a person of worth, on an equal plane with others,'' ''I am able to do things as well as most other people,'' and ''On the whole, I am satisfied with myself'' (O'Malley and Bachman, 1983). Older adolescents are less moody, less irritable, and less self-conscious about their physical changes. Although they are still nestlings, they fly off on forays of their own and begin to set their sights on adulthood. They form plans and engage in reveries about what their lives will be like when they are grown up. They worry about leaving home (Berzonsky, 1982) and conflicts with their parents (Coleman, 1974).

The identity crisis

The most important psychological development in later adolescence—after age 16 or so—is the gradual appearance of a mature identity. A mature identity is both an inner sense of uniqueness and an outward statement of goals, values, and beliefs. Once the rough journey through early adolescence has calmed a bit, the task at hand is to answer the critical question, ''Who am I?'' If adolescents are to move toward an understanding of who they are, in fact and in fantasy, they must navigate new ways of getting along with family members and friends, new ways of feeling and acting sexually—whether in spite of or with the encouragement of peers, parents, and other authority figures—and new ways of conceptualizing themselves and their world.

An important focus of attention in adolescence is the ''identity crisis,'' when young people reflect on their moral and sexual values, religious beliefs, and career options.

> When I grow up I want to be either a poet or a carpenter. I'll *never* be a businessman. My father's a businessman, and I think his values stink.—Tim, age 16

> Who am I? I am a girl, an American, a high school student. I am a Protestant, a Taurus, and a believer in human rights. I want to combine a career with a family life when I get married. I want to travel and see the world. I want to fall in love. I am moody, independent, a good listener, and an idealist.—Megan, age 16

Erik Erikson (1968) theorized that adolescence is a crisis among crises, a period when old issues resurface from childhood and must be resolved once again and put into a new order in a newly emerging sense of self. Issues of sexuality, self-worth or self-doubt, industriousness or passivity, independence or dependence, social recognition or isolation that already have been resolved in infancy and childhood emerge in new forms. If infancy and childhood brought more trust and autonomy, then the adolescent will be more likely to feel autonomous and self-respecting and to believe that others can be loving and trustworthy. But if infancy and childhood brought mistrust, shame, or doubt, then the adolescent may have trouble separating from the family, loving others, trusting to the future, or respecting and believing in himself or herself. If childhood has brought a sense of industry and success in school, then the adolescent is likely to feel that work is rewarded. If it has not, the adolescent is likely to be left feeling inferior, thwarted, and frustrated. All these issues are again scrutinized, sorted, weighed, and tested with the new self-awareness of adolescence, as the adolescent tries to figure out and piece together who he or she is. Graduating from high school, going to college, and forming new relationships challenge adolescents' sense of self and precipitate an **identity crisis** (see the accompanying box). Resolving this identity crisis takes time—time to find and fit together all the pieces, to find the roles, the work, the attitudes, and the social connectedness that will let the adolescent take a place in adult society.

According to Erikson, adolescents enter a period of **psychosocial moratorium** when they have no task more important, no psychological debts more pressing, than those used in the service of finding themselves, as they experiment with roles and look for niches where they might comfortably fit. According to Erikson, adolescents must work out identity issues in four major areas: (1) career, (2) morality and religion, (3) political ideology, and (4) social roles, including gender roles. Adolescents devote attention to each area as they go through an identity crisis. Thus, they contend with questions such as: Should

I go to college? Where? Do I believe in God? Should I have sexual intercourse? With whom? Should I become politically active? Which job should I go after? Whom should I date? Should I take drugs?

> Sometimes I look in the mirror and say to myself, "Okay, who are you *really*, Natalie?" I pull my hair back and put on makeup and look very sophisticated. That's one me. I let my hair fall loosely on my shoulders, put on a Shetland sweater, and that's another me. I write poetry and stay up late to watch the stars and planets through my telescope; that's another me. I get really involved in my chemistry homework and think I'll be a doctor, or I want to be a translator, or I want to be a foreign correspondent. There are almost too many possibilities.—Natalie, age 17

What have researchers found out about the identity "crisis"? Do adolescents experience a crisis? Do their views of themselves change? There is some research support for Erikson's ideas.

When adolescents have been asked to describe themselves, their descriptions show age-related changes in self-perception (Bernstein, 1980; Damon and Hart, 1982). Young adolescents are not troubled by inconsistencies in their self-descriptions. But by mid-adolescence, they recognize these inconsistencies, even though they do not yet integrate them into a consistent whole. At this age, someone might say, "Well, when I'm around my friends, I am really talkative and animated. But just around my family I sort of keep to myself. It's sort of like I'm two different people. I don't know why." By late adolescence, young people reconcile the inconsistencies in their self-descriptions. They begin to think of themselves in terms of stable, abstract, and unifying characteristics.

Some of these older adolescents do consider alternative identities (Waterman, 1982) and try out being rebellious, studious, or detached. Nevertheless, not all adolescents experience a "crisis" or make major shifts in their self-concepts. In one study (Dusek and Flaherty, 1981), researchers repeatedly interviewed a group of adolescents over the period from age 11 to 18. They asked about the beginning of puberty and the intensification of sexual feelings, the changing relations between boys and girls, career choices, the emergence of idealistic thinking, and changes in intellectual performance and self-esteem. For the most part, they found that even important environmental events did not cause major changes in adolescents' identities. Adolescents' self-concepts formed slowly and steadily. The person who entered adolescence was essentially the same person who left it. Their research was supported by data from another longitudinal study (Savin-Williams and Demo, 1984), showing that adolescents' feelings about themselves were basically stable from year to year.

It is worth noting, though, that these data were collected during the middle to late 1970s, a time of relative political and cultural calm. In a more tumultuous era, like the 1960s, there is likely to be more marked change in an individual's identity. For example, during the Vietnam War era, a distinct identity status appeared—**alienated identity achievement** (Marcia, 1980). It appeared among adolescents who concluded that they did not want to pursue the careers offered by "straight" society, participate in a political system that waged an immoral war, or opt for traditional forms of marriage, family, and religion.

As with the experience of storm and stress, there are individual differences in the identity formation process. Although most adolescents have resolved their identity crisis by age 19 or 20, there are wide individual variations in the rate and endpoint of this process (see Table 16.1). Some adolescents emerge with an intact sense of identity, headed for some sort of work,

Table 16.1
Characteristics of different identity statuses

Psychological factor	Identity achievement	Identity foreclosure	Identity diffusion	Identity moratorium
Anxiety	Moderate	Repressed	Moderate	High
Attitude toward parents	Loving and caring	Loving and respectful	Withdrawn	Trying to distance self
Self-esteem	High	Low	Low	High
Ethnic identity	Strong	Strong	Medium	Medium
Prejudice	Low	High	Medium	Medium
Moral stage	Postconventional	Preconventional or conventional	Preconventional or conventional	Postconventional
Dependence on others	Self-directed	Very dependent	Dependent	Self-directed
Cognitive style	Reflective	Impulsive	Impulsive	Reflective
College achievement	High grades	Very satisfied	Variable	Most dissatisfied (likely to change major)
Relations with others	Intimate	Stereotyped	Stereotyped or isolated	Intimate

SOURCE: Adapted from research reviewed by Marcia, 1980.

committed to political views and having examined their religious beliefs. The changes that come with adolescence—changing schools, choosing a major, making job plans, getting along with friends and family—may cause stress, but these adolescents meet the challenges. Out of the many personal, social, cultural, and even historical strands from which they must weave a unified self-image, they emerge as sound, adequate, and successful young men and women. These adolescents have reached a stage of **identity achievement**.

> Junior high was hard for me because most of the other kids—boys, I mean—seemed so *silly*. I felt as though I was wasting a lot of time, and so I concentrated on my schoolwork. I wasn't sure what I wanted to be when I grew up, but I felt more serious somehow than most of the kids in my class. I still hung around with them, went to parties, talked on the phone, all that stuff. When I was in tenth grade, I had an English teacher who really turned me on to poetry and literature. He lent me books of his own and helped me pick out things to read that he thought I'd like. Anyhow, I pretty much decided then that I wanted to be either a writer or a teacher of literature when I grew up. I've had a few other ideas from time to time, but I always come back to that decision. Now I'm majoring in English at a good college, and I've already had a poem published.— Robbie, age 19

Other adolescents remain uncommitted, in a state of **identity diffusion**. They are willing to take the risk of letting go of their secure childhood dependencies and fantasies for an unknown future. They have trouble making decisions and commitments. They lack direction or interest in academic, political, or social questions. According to Erikson, identity diffusion is the major psychological risk of adolescence.

> I might major in history. But if I can get my psych grade up, I might major in psych. You know, I sort of like to read all those case histories.

Changing Thoughts about Identity in Early and Later Adolescence

I have been thinking lately about my future occupation. Planning to take nurses' training, I am undecided as to what branch of nursing I will follow. The starched spotless white uniform of a regular hospital nurse has always fascinated me and the smell of ether "sends" me. But then, since I have travelled so little, I dream of winging my way around the world as an airplane hostess. As a stewardess I might have the luck to see the beautiful northern lights while flying over the North Pole, or watch alligators in the lush equatorial regions. The handsome pilots who are so often heroes in novels are reputed to hold attractions. If there were a war, nurses would be of invaluable service. Florence Nightingale has shown the world how priceless nurses are in war as well as in peacetime. Private nurse, rural nurse, hospital nurse, public health nurse—the opportunities for a qualified nurse are unlimited. This is why I feel nursing has a place for me.

LINDA, *age 14*

It seems hard to realize that already half of my first year at university has passed. I no longer feel lost as I walk from one end of the campus to the other; geographically, I know my way. But often I feel that my mind is full of scorpions. This summer, working in a hospital, I was certain of my ambition; I was sure of my direction. I wanted to be a doctor, and I still do. Now, however, each time I am questioned I become a little less sure, a little more hesitant in answering.

University is a different world, an adult world, and to be successful a student must have a mature outlook. The freshman curriculum requires a comprehensive mind, and the question now confronting me is: am I adult enough?

I have always been a perfectionist; I have always aimed for the top, and usually succeeded in leading my class. I decided before I came to the university that things were going to be different here, and they are. My marks do not seem as important as they once were. One important thing I have learned from this first term. You can honestly learn more when you are not continually striving to be ahead. Perhaps this can be applied the rest of my life; perhaps this will be the key to success and contentment. That is what I want to get out of this confusion: peace, knowledge, happiness, *maturity*.

LINDA, *age 18*

But I don't know what I'd actually do with a psych degree, so I might go into accounting. There's good money in accounting, and you can be your own boss. Well, I don't know.—Jason, age 18

Still other adolescents, actively looking for a way to commit themselves to meaningful work or political views, remain in the state of **identity moratorium** well into adulthood. They may think about religion and politics, they may question their parents' views, but they have not yet found anything with which to replace them. Although they may be preoccupied with questions, their questioning tends to remain unproductive and unresolved.

I've been thinking about working for a political candidate. But I can't decide which one to work for. My father's the head of town Republicans, and I've always been a Republican too. But I might like to give the Democrats a chance. The Republicans haven't done too much for the poor, you know. But I can't see that much difference between the Republicans and the Democrats.—Nancy, age 18

Still other adolescents do not search for identity, never having felt a sense of crisis, and accept the identity that their parents have set for them. They are in a state of **identity foreclosure**. Asked about religious or political questions, they may say something about how ''My family has always been. . . .''

> I'm a member of the Baptist Church. Our whole family goes there. My mother leads the choir, and I teach Sunday school to the little kids. I was baptized when I was 12, and that made my parents very happy. I hope to marry a guy from our youth group so we can get married in our church.—Nadine, age 19

Researchers have found that the proportion of adolescents with identity achievement increases from junior high school to the end of college, while the proportion with identity diffusion and moratorium decreases (Waterman, 1985; see Table 16.2). Achieving gender identity in terms of gender roles may take longer. In one study, the majority (80 percent) of high school students were in a state of identity foreclosure and accepted traditional gender roles. They were naive, especially when it came to understanding how adults might balance the demands of work and family. Only 6 percent of the students were identity achievers and accepted untraditional, egalitarian gender roles.

Family relationships

> My parents don't understand me. They want me to stay home with them all the time and never go anywhere with my friends. I might as well be in prison.—Megan, age 15

> ''Where are you going?'' ''Who else will be there?'' ''Are there going to be any adults there?'' ''How will you get home?'' ''Give me the phone number.'' Every time I set foot out of the house, it's the Spanish Inquisition all over again!—Sam, age 15

One task facing both boys and girls in adolescence is to reshape their relationships with their parents. They must manage a fine balancing act, managing to lean far enough from their families to achieve some autonomy, but not leaning so far as to topple into isolation, rage, depression, or guilt. Most adolescents do manage this balancing act, moving gradually into more autonomous family relationships, but remaining strongly emotionally attached to their parents,

Table 16.2
Developmental change in identity achievement status

	Identity Achievement, percent			Identity Diffusion, percent		
	Career	Religion	Politics	Career	Religion	Politics
Grades 7–8	5	8	2	46	31	88
Grades 9–10	9	9	5	39	57	78
Grades 11–12	21	23	8	29	32	60
College freshman–sophomore	23	20	13	23	16	48
College junior–senior	40	27	19	13	24	52

SOURCE: Waterman, 1985.

brothers, and sisters even so. Among the 17-year-olds interviewed in one study, for example, over 80 percent said that they felt close to their mothers, and over 70 percent, close to their fathers (Greenberger, 1975). In another study, college students, asked to name their top five heroes and heroines, named their mothers and fathers above all others (Farley, in Stark, 1986). Mothers got six times as many first-place votes as anyone else, fathers twice as many. Many studies done in the 1960s and 1970s showed that adolescents, especially girls, generally agreed with their parents about politics, religion, education, and careers (Douvan and Adelson, 1966; Feather, 1980; Lerner et al., 1975; Offer, 1969, 1981).

> When it looked as if I was getting serious with the fellow I was dating, my parents took us out to dinner one night. As we sat around talking, my father asked, ''Well, children, what are your intentions? Jim, what will you do after college? Will you marry, or do you believe in this living together business?'' They were immensely relieved when we described our plans for a conservative life much like their own. Jim wanted to become a stockbroker, and I wanted to teach elementary school when I wasn't at home taking care of babies.—Tim and Willy's mother

Freedom and control

> My father yelled downstairs this morning, ''Who left the cap off the toothpaste *again*?'' I could have killed him, he was so sarcastic. What's the big deal about a stupid tube of toothpaste?—Mike, age 16

> My mother looks so terrible that I told her not to pick me up after school. All the other kids' mothers look natural, but my mother has frosted blonde hair and too much makeup. She makes me sick. You'd think she'd *want* to look decent.—Nancy, age 13

> My parents make me come home by 11 o'clock, so I sleep at my friend's house. Her parents don't care when I come in.—Alyssa, age 14

> Tonight's the night we tell Jason that he can't go to a work camp in Nicaragua this summer. He is going to be so angry that I tense up just thinking about it.

Adolescence is a time when parents' limits are thoroughly tested. Although the issues may vary from day to day and family to family, the underlying battle is to control what the adolescent thinks and does. In one study, college students described the typical relationship between parent and adolescent as like that between guard and prisoner or son-in-law and mother-in-law (Wish, Deutsch, and Kaplan, 1976). When the teenagers in the Chicago beeper study (Csikszentmihalyi and Larson, 1984) were with their families, their negative thoughts outnumbered their positive thoughts ten to one. The kinds of things that they reported included thoughts such as ''How incompetent my mom is,'' ''How pigheaded my mom and dad are,'' ''How much I really don't like my sister's hair,'' and ''Why my mother manipulates the conversation to get me to hate her.'' Here one high school boy describes what he felt as he sat in the car with his parents, as they drove to church on Sunday morning at 10:15:

> I never want to go to church, but I'll go. Finally I get a Sunday off; I don't have to work, so I can sleep a little later. But now I've got to go to church. I've got to wake up earlier than if I'd had to go to work.
>   They always wake you up, and they're always cheerful, and you go, ''Oh, no!'' They act cheerful, but they are really hostile if you don't want to go.

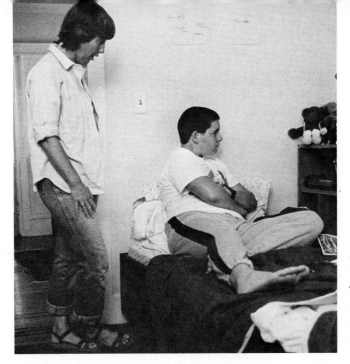

Parents and adolescents are in conflict in all families some of the time and in some families most of the time. For boys, a major source of conflict is keeping their rooms neat.

I'd just asked them to turn the radio channel. They were listening to some opera stuff. They just ignored me; you know, because we were parking and everything. Still, they could have acknowledged me. That's why I was so upset. I went, "Jesus Christ, at least they could answer me" (Csikszentmihalyi and Larson, 1984, p.141).

Adolescents want freedom; parents want control. Whereas from their younger children parents once could demand and expect compliance, now they must explain their reasons and justify their positions. Adolescents are likely to argue, to press for advantage, and to test most of the limits that parents set. It is in early adolescence that children are most sensitive to any hint of parents' control. Irascible and eager to pounce on every perceived flaw in their parents, they are likely to feel their parents' praise or criticism as unbearable intrusions. Wanting autonomy but unskilled at getting it, young adolescents may withdraw into an unsociable, uncommunicative cold war. The more the parents defend their positions, the more the adolescents are likely to defend theirs. Although these arguments with parents may be tiring and unpleasant, they teach adolescents an important social skill. They learn that autonomy can be reached through peaceable compromise.

Dotting the battlefield, of course, are positive feelings and good family times—the night everyone sits around in the Jeep eating chili after they've been sledding all day; the time they sing the songs from *South Pacific* on the ride home from a cousin's wedding; the nights when the whole family watches a special television series together and talks about it afterward. These good, warm feelings are important anchors for adolescents, as they pick their sometimes rocky course through family relationships.

But parents and adolescents are in conflict in "all families some of the time and some families most of the time" (Montemayor, 1983). Because the psychological work of the period is to redefine the childish self into an adult self, conflict with parents is nearly inevitable. Adolescents feel the need to experience life on their *own* terms, not their parents'. Families pay a price for this breaking away. In a study of the problems associated with raising children at different ages, mothers said that there were more problems raising adolescents than any other age-group (Ballenski and Cook, 1982). They reported problems, particularly in disciplining their adolescent children and with the

598

adolescent children's moodiness and desire for independence. Bad as'it seems to the mothers, sometimes adolescents report even more problems than their mothers do (Montemayor, 1983). Why? Imagine a mother telling her daughter to "clean up your room. It looks like a tornado went through there." The daughter complies silently, seething inside. But her mother sees only the clothes hung up and the bed made—and does not register the episode as a conflict.

What kinds of things do families wrangle about? Usually, the sparks fly over the normal, everyday business of life such as schoolwork, social life, friends, chores around the house, disobeying rules, fighting with brothers and sisters, and looking presentable (Montemayor, 1983). One follow-up study of "Middletown," a typical Midwestern town first profiled in a classic sociological study of the 1920s (Lynd and Lynd, 1929), showed that adolescents in the 1980s were disagreeing with their parents about virtually the same matters as adolescents were in the 1920s—"the hours you get in at night" and "home duties" still led the list, half a century later (Caplow, Bahr, Chadwick, Hill, and Williamson, 1982).

> "Take out the garbage, Tim." "Do your homework, Tim." "Have you done your homework yet, Tim?" "No television until your homework's done, Tim." "You can't wear that shirt, Tim." "If you want your allowance, you'll clean up your room, Tim." "No T-shirts at the dinner table, Tim." Get the picture?—Tim, age 16

> Kristy and I had a conversation the other day that I swear I had with my own mother. I said, "I want you home with the car by midnight."
> "Oh, Mom. None of the other kids have to be home that early."
> "I don't care about the other kids. I want you home at midnight."
> "But why?"
> "Because I wait up for you."
> "Then don't wait up. Go to sleep. I'll be quiet when I come in."
> "I'm sorry, Kristy. I can't fall asleep until I know you're home safely, so I want you home at midnight. That's all there is to it."
> "Oh, *Mom*."

Although sex, drugs, religion, and politics are possible sources for rip-snorting arguments, in fact most adolescents and parents do *not* argue about these matters.

By late adolescence, as we have suggested, family conflict usually diminishes. Then, once adolescents reach the age of about 18 and leave home, the amount of stress in most families drops even further. In one study of college boys, researchers found that when the boys moved away from home, their relationships with their families improved (Sullivan and Sullivan, 1980). Their parents became more affectionate, communication improved, and parents and sons alike were happier with their relationships. If boys continued living at home, there was no improvement in family relations. Once the nest empties, and adolescents leave home, mothers report their marriages become happier and their own sense of well-being increases as well (Rubin, 1980).

Sons' and daughters' conflicts

The sometimes choppy path through adolescence differs for girls and boys. In childhood, it is boys who most often have problems. Boys mature more slowly than girls, they inhabit largely female-dominated environments—at home with Mother or in school with a female teacher—and they must conform to stricter gender-role expectations than girls. But come adolescence, it is girls who most often have problems, as they cope with the conflict between their need to remain dependent and their need to strike out on their own—problems that sometimes show up in early pregnancies, unstable marriages, and emotional distress (Werner and Smith, 1982).

In adolescence, boys are likely to begin to separate from their families by relying on their abilities to do things and their knowledge of the outside world. They gradually spend less time with their families and more time at school, at work, or engaged in hobbies and sports. Their identities are based on these activities and abilities (Montemayor, 1982). Girls are more likely to base their emerging identities on their ability to get along with other people, and so they cannot so clearly turn their backs on their families.

Nor can their parents so easily let them go. Parents give daughters less room to maneuver than they give sons. They keep girls in tighter check, worrying about all the things that might happen if they, the parents, were to relax. They worry about whether their daughters are safe on their own, and they worry about their sexual behavior and, worst of all, they worry about the prospect of pregnancy. More tightly confined than boys, girls may have a harder time coming to terms with their independence. They want freedom of thought and expression—but without physically leaving the family (Coleman, 1974). Girls are expected to achieve independence but to maintain close emotional and physical ties with their families at the same time. They often feel ambivalent about asserting independence. If adolescent daughters do not feel close to their mothers, they feel sorry about it (Konopka, 1976), yet adolescent daughters want their parents to acknowledge that they are no longer children. Girls tend to have more conflicts with their parents, especially their mothers, than boys do. They get into more arguments, have more emotional outbursts, and get more threats from their parents. Their conflicts usually are about emotional issues (Kinloch, 1970; Montemayor, 1982).

> I had the chance to go camping with a bunch of kids in my class at school. And I really wanted to go. But my parents said that I couldn't go. "I thought you trusted me," I told them. "We *do* trust you, but it's not the kind of situation you should be in." I got so mad I stayed in my room all weekend.—Erica, age 14

The conflicts that boys have with their parents often involve issues like using the family car, "hanging out with the guys," going to church, having long hair, and doing chores around the house (Offer, Ostrov, and Howard, 1981). Boys also are more likely to feel crowded when they are with their parents and to resent being given orders. They assert themselves unambivalently toward their mothers (Steinberg, 1979), and they behave respectfully—even as they feel rebellious—toward their fathers (Montemayor, 1982).

> *Every* night, my mother makes me wash the dishes after dinner and take out the garbage. When I ask why I have to do it, she says she's "tired after a long day." Well, I have long days, too. How come she gets to sit around with my father and watch TV while I slave in the kitchen?—Ted, age 14

Double trouble: overlapping crises

All families are vulnerable when children are going through adolescence, but they may be especially vulnerable when parents are experiencing a psychological crisis at the same time. Adolescents test their parents as they search for their own emerging identities, and they need parents who can weather the inevitable storms calmly, stably, and good-naturedly. Parents who are coping with the strains of a midlife crisis of their own may feel insecure and prone to depression themselves as they contend with the waning of their physical powers, with the dreams that will never be realized, and with the foreclosing of opportunity. When the psychological turmoil of the parents' mid-life transition gets heaped on top of the surliness, testing, and acting out of the child's adolescence, a family may be in "double trouble."

> I turned 40 less than a week before Sarah turned 15. For the first time ever, I felt miserably depressed by getting a year older. I looked in the mirror the next morning, and I started to cry because there was a middle-aged lady staring back at me. Then at breakfast, Sarah made some crack about "what was the point" of my putting on makeup before work. Some days I pull out of the driveway and swear I'll never come back.

Homemakers, whose children have been their major occupation, and parents who have turned to their children—and away from their spouses—for the satisfaction of emotional needs are most likely to suffer when their children become independent (Birnbaum, 1971; Lidz, 1969). They may feel quite threatened by a teenaged child's normal sexual interests.

> My father put his arm around my shoulders in the car the other day and said, "You'll always be my little princess." But I *won't* always be. That's the problem.—Kristy, age 17

When divorce breaks up the family, the adolescent's identity struggle can be especially severe (Wallerstein and Kelly, 1974, 1980). Some divorced parents act much like their own children both socially and sexually when they primp in front of the mirror on Saturday night, don their designer jeans, and pick up their dates in the family car. Adolescents may feel uncomfortable if they have to listen to parents' harangues about the former spouse's sexual problems or if they run into the parent's date as they stumble into the bathroom the next morning. Said one 15-year-old of her mother,

> I didn't like her going out with other men—I thought she was a tramp. I walked in on her when she had a man in bed—she should go out but not sleep with them (McLoughlin and Whitfield, 1984, p. 166).

In and of itself, divorce need not interfere with normal adolescent development. In fact, if families are riddled with conflict, adolescents may prefer to live with one rather than both parents (McLoughlin and Whitfield, 1984). Most feel that without the constant fighting, shouting, and tears, they can live and work more peacefully and that their schoolwork improves. Some adolescents want nothing more to do with one of their parents after a separation or a divorce.

> My father was running around with every woman in town. That really hurt my mother. It made me and my brother hate him.—Kristy, age 15

But most try to understand both their parents' situations and appreciate them for taking the time to explain their feelings and intentions and for continuing to provide support and security (Wallerstein and Kelly, 1974, 1980).

Parents' continuing influence

The sparks may fly, and the arguments may hurtle around the house. But adolescents continue to feel their parents' influence in this period, as they did earlier. Parents always have influenced their adolescent children and probably always will. When the inventor of the telegraph, Samuel F. B. Morse, attended Yale in 1810, he wrote home to his father that he wanted to be an artist. His horrified father wrote back:

Dear Finley,

I received your letter of the 22nd today by mail.

On the subject of your future pursuits we will converse when I see you and when you get home. It will be best for you to form no plans. Your mama and I have been thinking and planning for you. I shall disclose to you our plan when I see you. Till then suspend your mind.

Your affectionate father,
J. Morse

Parents today may be less directive than the elder Morse, but their adolescent children nevertheless are sensitive to their influence.

Parents' styles of disciplining and communicating with their children tend to be stable as the children develop from childhood into adolescence. In one study, for example, mothers and fathers completed questionnaires about their child-rearing philosophies and methods (Roberts, Block, and Block, 1984). Their answers when their children were 3 years old were consistent with their answers ten years later. The degree of control parents exerted, their investment in their children, and their relative enjoyment of their children all tended to remain stable over time. When parents shifted their child-rearing methods, the shifts were appropriate for the changing needs of their growing children. Thus, all parents were likely to stress achievement more for their 13-year-olds than for their 3-year-olds and to express more affection physically with the 3- than with the 13-year-olds. Younger children were punished more physically; older children were punished by losing privileges. But despite these changes in specific actions, children were exposed to continuous, stable values and attitudes from their parents.

How adolescents think about themselves is related to their parents' attitudes and behavior. As we saw in earlier discussions of discipline (in Chapters 10 and 13), children are most likely to develop competence and confidence if their parents provide a balance of love and limits. Development in adolescence shows the same pattern. In one recent study, adolescents with high self-esteem perceived their parents as accepting and not overly harsh in making or enforcing rules (Litovsky and Dusek, 1985). Adolescents do best when their parents walk a fine line between giving too much support and too much freedom.

In another study, researchers first interviewed adolescents on their thoughts about their identities. Then they asked the adolescents and their

Parents' styles of disciplining and communicating with their children tend to be stable from early childhood into adolescence. Their styles may also have a bearing on the adolescents' exploration of identity issues.

families to make detailed plans for a hypothetical two-week vacation (Cooper, Grotevant, and Condon, 1983). Adolescents who reported that they had thought more about their identities and had explored more different identity possibilities were more likely to come from families in which, when planning their vacation, the father was willing to disagree openly with his wife, the mother was assertive, and both parents were willing to initiate compromises. These were families in which each member was clearly a separate individual with definite opinions and in which all members got along with humor, frankness, support, spontaneity, and vulnerability. As one father in such a family said as the family began planning their vacation (Cooper et al., 1983, pp. 54–55),

> I think probably what we all ought to do is decide the things that we want to do each one of us individually. And then maybe we'll be able to reconcile from that point. . . . Let's go ahead and take a few minutes to decide where we'd like to go and what we would like to do. And maybe we'll be able to work everything everybody wants to do in those fourteen days. Okay?

The mother of this family then said,

> "I think we all have good imaginations," and her husband commented, "I think that's kind of nice. I think we ought to be a rich gang."

In families in which members rarely disagreed or expressed individual opinions, adolescents explored few identity issues. as one such adolescent put it:

> I'm having a hard time deciding what to do. It would be easier if they would tell me what to do, but of course I don't want that.

Here is how her family discussed their vacation plans:

> MOTHER: Where shall we go?
>
> FATHER: Back to Spain.
>
> MOTHER: Back to Spain.
>
> JANET: Back to Spain.
>
> SISTER: Back to Spain.

For supporting the adolescent's quest for identity, the best type of family appears to be one in which members are connected but still individuals, not one in which the members are thoroughly enmeshed with each other, nor one in which they are indifferent or hostile to each other. In another study, adolescents who dealt effectively with identity issues were found to have parents who were curious, task-oriented, and informative with their children rather than being distracted, indifferent, judgmental, or critical (Hauser et al., 1984). Even though their rebelliousness may suggest that they would prefer it to be otherwise, adolescents do best when their parents are supportive, interested, and involved.

Conflict is nearly unavoidable in families with a teenage child, but a *moderate* amount of conflict between adolescents and parents sometimes may be constructive. By creating a certain degree of cognitive disturbance, moderate conflict may help adolescents to develop autonomous and advanced moral thought (Haan, Smith, and Block, 1968; Kohlberg, 1969). *Serious* conflict, a problem for an estimated 15 to 20 percent of all adolescents, does not support psychological growth (Montemayor, 1983). Instead, it is associated with a variety of problems for adolescents, such as leaving home and school, joining a religious cult, getting married or pregnant, becoming a juvenile delinquent, using drugs, or committing suicide. Which comes first, the family conflict or the other problems? It may be either. But whichever is the cause and whichever the effect, the connection between serious family conflict and serious social and psychological problems among adolescents is disturbing and real.

Peers versus parents

The lure of others their own age grows ever stronger throughout childhood, until adolescents are spending hours upon hours with their friends. With friends, adolescents can test their independence and aspects of their developing identities. They can test their sexual attractiveness. They can have a good time with others who like doing what they do (Hunter, 1984).

Time together

Adolescents spend their time in a variety of pursuits. In the Chicago beeper study, adolescents spent slightly less than one-third of their time engaged in productive activities like studying, class work, and holding jobs; slightly less than one-third in ''maintenance'' activities like eating, doing chores and errands, getting places, and personal care; and slightly more than one-third of their time in leisure activities like socializing, sports and games, watching television, listening to music, reading, thinking, resting, and hobbies. Socializing took a full 16 percent of their waking hours, and if the talking that adolescents do as they socialize is added to the talking they do as they eat, watch television, or study, they spend about one-third of their day talking to other people. Adolescents spent half of their waking hours with others their age, both in and out of school, and the time they spent with friends was the most enjoyable part of their lives (see Table 16.3).

> The other night eight of us went to the drive-in. But who could watch the movie? Five of us were in the backseat, and one guy had a leg cast that he slung over everybody's laps. So we left the drive-in and went to the

Table 16.3
Adolescents' most enjoyable activities

Activity	Adolescents reporting as most enjoyable, percent
Social activities with friends	24
Individual sports (tennis, sailing, skiing, etc.)	21
Art activities (singing, dancing, piano, etc.)	17
Team sports (baseball, soccer, etc.)	12
Watching television	7
Productive activities (work, cooking, mowing lawn)	6
Outdoor activities (camping, fishing, etc.)	4
Cars and motorcycles	3
Reading	2
Activities with family	2
Playing cards	1
Being alone	1
Getting high	1

SOURCE: Adapted from Csikszentmihalyi and Larson, 1984.

diner. They're nice there. I had my usual—"Number 5 and a Coke"—and the other kids had whatever they wanted. Then we drove around some more, heard about a party at someone's house. But when we got there, no one was around except the kid's parents. We drove around some more, just hung around at the tennis courts near school, and got home early—about midnight.—Peter, age 16

With friends adolescents talked, joked, and hung out. They were spontaneous, open, and free of adult restraints. They felt excited, friendly, sociable, involved, and motivated. Boys especially felt more open, free, involved, strong, and active when they were with their friends and liked to spend time with them. Often adolescents described having fun with friends as "being rowdy"—getting to say anything, do everything. With friends, adolescents could drive cars from the *back*seat, have fights in school, act silly, and feel uncontrollably gleeful.

The other night we all went "car surfing." You stand on the roof of a car and try to stay on while it goes around corners.—Sam, age 16

Adolescents also sometimes felt self-conscious, impatient, and angry with their friends. Even so, conflict with friends was much rarer than it was with family members.

Although adolescents spend a lot of time being *supervised* by adults—in school, at home, at work—they spend relatively little time actively *involved* with adults. Few adolescents in the beeper study reported spending time alone with adults. On the average, they reported spending only 8 percent of their time with their parents—usually their mother—and another 2 percent with other adults like bosses, teachers, or grandparents. When they did spend time with an adult they usually liked it, though. They loved it when their families played sports or games, and they also liked eating with their families. What they disliked was trying to read or do things privately when other family members were around.

In an interview study of the way that a different group of adolescents—those from Mormon Salt Lake City—spent their time and the amount of conflict they had with their parents, researchers found that these adolescents spent equal amounts of time with parents and friends (Montemayor, 1982). Clearly, there are differences in adolescents' activities depending on their families and their communities. But Mormon adolescents, too, did different kinds of things with their parents—work and chores—and their friends—play and recreation.

Spending time with friends makes adolescents happy and supports their social development. But adolescents in the Chicago study who spent the *most* time with their friends had wider mood swings and more problems in school. Adolescents who spent more time with their families, as boring or as conflict-ridden as that may be sometimes, adapted better to school and to the social system.

Conflict, conformity, and closeness

In the elementary school years, children usually move smoothly between the world of family and the world of friends. But in adolescence, the two worlds often collide. Because adolescence brings increased pressures to look, act, and think like peers, disagreements with parents may multiply. With their peers, adolescents may act outrageously—in their parents' eyes—and their parents may try to stop them.

At the ripe old age of 12, Sarah suddenly began to wear heavy eye makeup and spiky hair, short, tight skirts, and high-top sneakers. We

Most adolescents want to look and act like their friends. Friends' values strongly influence how adolescents act—more, in some cases, than their parents' values.

tried not to criticize, on the grounds that anything we objected to would only incite her further. But when she began criticizing the way I look—''Oh Mom, your hair is so *dowdy*!''—I drew the line.

Not surprisingly, adolescents feel closer to their peers then to their parents. Researchers have studied the development of conformity and closeness to peers and conflict with parents over the course of adolescence. Their findings are as expected: adolescents increasingly say that their friends are more important to them and more intimate than their parents. In a study of fourth, seventh, tenth graders and college graduates (Hunter and Youniss, 1982), for example, fourth graders claimed to be more intimate with their parents than their friends. They claimed that their parents knew how they felt, talked things over with them, did things with them, and were more enjoyable to talk to. Parents were perceived as more nurturant than friends. They helped their childen to solve problems, did things they needed, and the like. But by tenth grade, friends were perceived to be more intimate than parents and just as nurturant.

Conforming to the ways of peers reaches an all-time high at age 13, but adolescents continue to effect uniformity of dress far later than this peak period.

In one crucial way, adolescents' relationships with their friends differ from those with their parents: they want to look and act just like their friends and to belong to the group. They do not want to look and act just like their parents—at least not yet. In adolescence, conformity to one's peer group peaks; it is higher than it was in childhood and higher than it will be in adulthood. When one large sample of adolescents was asked with whom they most strongly identified, the majority—close to 60 percent of both boys and girls—said that they identified with people of their own generation (Sorensen, 1973). Adolescents conform to the values, advice, and judgments of their friends more and follow their parents' advice less than they did when they were younger (Bixenstine, DeCorte, and Bixenstine, 1976; Bowerman and Kinch, 1956; Devereaux, 1970; Utech and Hoving, 1969). In one study, for example, adolescents between 11 and 13 were more likely than younger or older subjects to change their answers to match their peers' (Costanzo and Shaw, 1966). In another study, adolescents were asked whether they would go along with their peers if the peers wanted them to do something prosocial, like helping the peer with schoolwork, or antisocial, like stealing candy (Berndt, 1979). Adolescents were most likely to conform to the prosocial suggestion at 11 to 12 years and the antisocial suggestion at 14 to 15 (see Figure 16.3). When the judgments of classmates and teachers are in conflict, adolescents are inclined to go along with their classmates, even when their suggestions are

CONFORMITY AND AGE

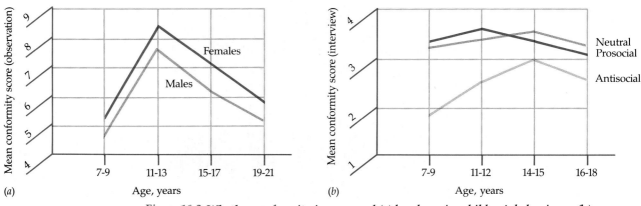

Figure 16.3 **Whether conformity is measured (a) by observing children's behavior or (b) by asking children whether they would go along with a peer's suggestion, it seems to peak in early adolescence: at 11 to 14 for prosocial or neutral suggestions; at 14 to 15 for anti-social suggestions. Girls conform more than boys, and prosocial or neutral suggestions are more readily accepted than antisocial ones (a: Costanzo and Shaw, 1966; b: Berndt, 1979).**

antisocial (Berenda, 1950; Berndt 1978b). Their friends' values strongly influence how adolescents behave (Siman, 1977). When it comes to antisocial behavior like smoking, skipping school, hurting someone, or committing crimes, peer values often override personal or parental values (Condry and Siman, 1974; Krosnick and Judd, 1982).

But adolescents are not mere pawns of their peers. Adolescents turn to peers or to parents for advice on different issues. In one study, perhaps somewhat outdated now, girls were likely to ask their parents about which job to take, whether to enter a beauty contest, and which boy to date (Brittain, 1963, 1966). But they were likely to ask their friends about what to wear to a football game, which subjects to take in school, and which dress to buy. Moreover, although peers' influence increases in adolescence overall, parents are seen by their children as exerting more control over their behavior than friends do—telling them what to do and disagreeing with them—at *all* ages (Hunter and Youniss, 1982). By age 18 or 19, most adolescents have undergone ''a true growth in autonomy'' and make their *own* decisions (Berndt, 1978b).

Peer relations

Cliques and crowds

Adolescents may conform in general to the peer culture, but they share the values of their immediate circle of friends even more. Young adolescents usually hang out in **cliques** of up to half a dozen members of their own sex (Csikszentmihalyi and Larson, 1984; Dunphy, 1963; see Figure 16.4). In these cliques, young adolescents do things together—shop for clothes or records, go to concerts, do school projects, and share good times. Members of a clique usually are of the same age, race, and socioeconomic group. They share attitudes toward school, drugs, music, and clothes, spoken and unspoken norms: a private language, a ''joke of the week,'' an agreement about partying every weekend. They share the attitudes of these friends both because they seek out others who think as they do and because they influence each other (Berndt, 1982; Douvan and Adelson, 1966).

focus *Ultimate conformity*

Some adolescents do not achieve autonomy from their parents smoothly. Without warning, they suddenly abandon their families for the ultimate conformity, to join religious, political, therapeutic, or other ideological communes. Their radical departure may be a necessary rehearsal for separation and practice in growing up.

One afternoon Robbie was helping me with the yardwork, and the next he was missing. When I found out that he'd gone off with a group of Moonies, I didn't know whether to laugh or cry. He's always been so cooperative, so helpful, such a good kid. I've never had any trouble with him at all. But now he's gone and thrown everything away on this crazy cult. He's apparently working at some fried-fish place the Moonies run on Cape Cod. The police told me to sit tight, that there wasn't anything they could do, and that all the kids come home eventually. But I don't understand what would move Robbie to do this. He was an Eagle Scout, an altar boy, on the Honor Roll at school. What could he possibly see in that group of goons?

Most such radical departures are undertaken by apparently well adjusted adolescents and young adults who are between 18 and 26 years old, unmarried, well educated, white, and from intact families. Their flights take family members completely by surprise and frighten, disgust, and enrage them as well. These adolescents move from family to commune in an act of sudden, total transformation. Athletes stop exercising, readers stop reading, musicians stop playing, and sights narrow to an absolute commitment to the new group. Within two years or so, nearly all these adolescents have returned home. One psychologist has suggested that the radical departure may be a desperate attempt to grow up and move away from the family (Levine, 1981). Most of the adolescents who flee their families in this way have been closely tied to their parents until their radical departure. They have not withdrawn gradually from their parents during adolescence and often suffer from low self-esteem. Suddenly, they are offered the chance to move into another all-embracing group, the commune, one that may have values much like those of the family. The radical departure offers adolescents a way to separate quickly from their families with a minimum of suffering. It offers a chance to belong, to abandon at least temporarily the quest for an individual identity, and to merge with a flawless group self. The exaggerated, idealized communal family offers the chance to separate and to join in one and the same act.

Sometimes three or four cliques join into a larger, more loosely organized **crowd** that is organized by activity rather than by close friendship. A big party for the athletic crowd, for example, may include the girls' cheerleading and girls' basketball-playing cliques, which otherwise keep their distance from each other. Crowds serve several functions for adolescents and for adults. School officials, for example, may use crowd leaders to convey and carry out rules and expectations. Crowds therefore can help to maintain order and predictability in schools. Crowds and cliques also contribute to adolescents' sense of identity. Adolescents measure their own abilities against those of other clique members and mold their self-concepts according to the norms and attitudes of the crowd. Crowds and cliques give adolescents a social identity in the eyes of their schoolmates and mark social boundaries.

LATE ADOLESCENCE

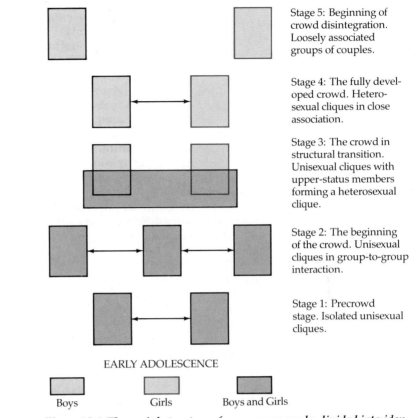

Stage 5: Beginning of crowd disintegration. Loosely associated groups of couples.

Stage 4: The fully developed crowd. Heterosexual cliques in close association.

Stage 3: The crowd in structural transition. Unisexual cliques with upper-status members forming a heterosexual clique.

Stage 2: The beginning of the crowd. Unisexual cliques in group-to-group interaction.

Stage 1: Precrowd stage. Isolated unisexual cliques.

EARLY ADOLESCENCE

Boys   Girls   Boys and Girls

Figure 16.4 **The social structure of peer groups can be divided into iden-tifiable stages during the course of adolescence (Dunphy, 1963).**

The names and nature of the cliques and crowds vary from school to school and community to community—''ropers'' and ''dopers,'' ''kickers'' and ''potheads,'' ''jocks'' and ''freaks,'' ''preppies'' and ''sporties.'' But they have similarities nevertheless. In one widely quoted study of adolescent cliques and crowds in the 1950s, James Coleman (1961) found that regardless of the school, the leading crowds were likely to be male athletes and popular girls—jocks and cheerleaders, not brains. This finding has been confirmed in more recent investigations in the 1970s and 1980s (Eitzen, 1975; Thirer and Wright, 1985). Status within the crowd or clique depends, for boys, on physical maturity, fitness, and athletic ability (Savin-Williams, 1977). For girls, status is most likely to depend on their physical attractiveness (Weisfeld, Bloch, and Ivers, 1984).

Friendship and understanding

Within cliques there may be closer pairs, their friendships based on similarities and shared interests. Friendships are oases where adolescents can learn about themselves and others. In adolescence, friends comfort each other when they are angry, sad, or in trouble (Csikszentmihalyi and Larson, 1984). As in childhood, adolescent girls' friendships are more intimate and more exclusive than boys' friendships. Girls talk about relationships, and boys talk about things to do (Johnson, 1983).

> My best friend and I promised to tell each other everything, including sex.—Sarah, age 14

> When I get together with my friends, we usually listen to records or go to the movies. Sometimes we go shopping for stuff like clothes. Sometimes we shoot baskets or play a little soccer. Lots of times we just hang out.—Sam, age 14

But in adolescence friendship for both boys and girls is likely to be based on empathy, understanding, and self-disclosure (Bigelow, 1977). During adolescence, friendships mature into a fuller appreciation of idiosyncrasies and differences in personality or interests. Friends, adolescents come to realize, may be both dependent and independent at the same time. They trust each other, but they also "give each other a chance to breathe" (Selman and Selman, 1979). Friends are supportive and intimate, but they also act on their own as independent individuals. Adolescents want friends who are loyal and with whom they can identify and share worries. When they just start dating, girls want their girlfriends to remain loyal and supportive. Once they feel more secure about dating, girls' friendships may relax a bit (Douvan and Adelson, 1966).

Interestingly, the quality of adolescents' friendships seems to parallel the quality of their relationships with parents. Among high school girls who were asked to evaluate their relationship with a close girlfriend and with their mother, those who felt close to their mother also felt close to their girlfriend. Girls who had a poor relationship with their mother did not seem able to form a satisfying friendship, which might have compensated for their feelings of being unloved or out of touch with their mother (Gold and Yanof, 1985).

With the increasing intellectual maturity that adolescence brings, young men and women come to appreciate their friends more thoroughly because they understand better what makes them tick. With their abilities to think abstractly and to speculate about possibilities, as we discussed in Chapter 15, adolescents can draw inferences about how others think, feel, and strive, and they can use what they know in interpreting their own experiences. Their increasing powers to understand ambiguity, relative truths, and contradiction deepen adolescents' perceptions of others and themselves. They may understand that someone who *seems* snobbish is really just shy—an understanding of contradictions that younger children lack.

> My boyfriend acts very sophisticated and sarcastic when we're with other people. But when we're alone, he tells me things that he's never told anyone else before. Sometimes he even cries.—Kristy, age 16

They come to understand how one person's behavior changes from one setting to another, and they begin to perceive the unchanging core of the person's personality despite changing setting or circumstance. In so doing, adolescents come to understand what personality means, and they use this understanding in shaping their own emerging identities (Barenboim, 1977; Hill and Palmquist, 1978).

Dating

> My first date was when I was 12. I was fixed up with this really cute 15-year-old guy to go to my cousin's Sweet Sixteen party, a square dance. My mother took me shopping for a dress. It was pink, and I wore white shoes with little heels on them. I was kind of scared, and I worried that my date thought I was a nerd because I was so young. He was polite but didn't spend any time with me. But I had a good time dancing anyway.—Erica, age 16

*By dating, adolescents discover more about their masculinity or femininity, test their popularity, find their social niches, learn how to get along with others, and have **fun**.*

Since the turn of the century, there has been a trend toward dating earlier and marrying later, effectively increasing the span during which adolescents date. The median age at which girls started dating was 16 in the 1920s, 13 in the 1970s, and even younger today (McCabe, 1984). Many girls now begin to date at age 12, boys a year or so later. Whether or not adolescents date, how they feel about dating, and their attitudes toward sex depend on both their physical and their psychological maturity. The adolescent who still has a child's body is likely to feel and act very differently on dates from the adolescent who is sexually mature. Whether, when, and how often adolescents date depend on how they look and think and on the norms prevailing within their family, their peer group, and their community. City adolescents have more sexual experience than country adolescents, for example (McCabe and Collins, 1981), and girls are more likely than boys to be influenced by their parents' wishes and by community standards (McCabe, 1984). Some adolescents do not feel comfortable with members of the other sex until late in adolescence (Douvan and Adelson, 1966). But most adolescents do begin to date at the socially approved age and feel left out if they do not.

Adolescents who begin dating at either extreme of the dating timetable may have problems. Girls who begin dating and then going steady early in adolescence may be hindered because they have not formulated autonomous personal or academic goals, yet girls who do not date by age 16 may have little idea of what boys find attractive (Douvan and Adelson, 1966; Douvan and Gold, 1966). These late daters are likely to be dependent on their families, self-absorbed, and insecure. They usually know that they are different from others their age, and they worry about it.

Dating serves several different functions for adolescents. It is plain fun. It helps adolescents learn to cooperate, consider others' feelings, take responsibility, and get along with others. It even teaches manners. Dating helps adolescents find their social niches, assess their popularity, and develop the social skills that they will need to form a mature, enduring relationship with a mate. It offers companionship and a pathway to achieving intimacy. On dates, adolescents experiment with sex. They reaffirm—or question—their deep personal convictions of their masculinity or femininity that took form during their early childhood. By testing whom they find physically attractive and who finds them attractive in turn, they shape a heterosexual or homosexual identity. Dating gives adolescents a series of temporary relationships within which they can explore their sexual identity. Dating also gives adolescents a chance

611

to test how closely they wish to conform to gender-role stereotypes. Boys experiment with finding a balance between acting macho and being vulnerable, and girls experiment with finding a balance between being emotional and dependent and being strong-willed and self-reliant.

Dates are attracted to each other for their friendliness, popularity, personality, intelligence, shared attitudes, and athletic ability and, perhaps most of all, their looks (Walster, Aronson, Abraham, and Roltman, 1966).

> I met Will at a party in ninth grade, took one look at him, my stomach went *boing*, and I fell in love with him. He's so gorgeous!—Sarah, age 16

> I like girls who are tall, thin, long-legged, smart, funny, and have a good personality.—Sam, age 16

> When someone tries to fix you up with a date, and they say, ''He's got a great personality,'' watch out. That always mean he's ugly.—Natalie, age 16

Adolescent problems

Adolescence can be a difficult time and can bring with it a host of new problems—skipping school, running away from home, stealing, prostitution, and even suicide.

> Four kids in my class died this year. Two who were drunk got killed in a car accident. One overdosed on pills. And one got shot to death by another kid. It was so horrible around school for awhile that they brought in a psychologist to talk to everyone about death.—Peter, age 16

Delinquency

The term **juvenile delinquency** covers a multitude of crimes—murder, assault, theft, prostitution—and a multitude of acts considered wrong because they are committed by a minor—promiscuity, skipping school, running away from home. Most adolescents do things that they know are wrong. In an Illinois survey, for example, of the 3300 14- to 18-year-olds questioned, 73 percent admitted cheating in school, 47 percent admitted skipping school, 46 percent admitted getting drunk, and 23 percent said that they had bought liquor (Puntil, 1972). Fewer adolescents commit serious crimes. The most serious offenses adolescents are charged with usually are robbery, purse

Delinquency has many different causes—neurological and cognitive abnormalities, destructive family relations, and pressure from delinquent peers.

snatching, shoplifting, and pocket picking. Attacks on teachers and fellow students constitute a fairly new kind of serious offense by adolescents. Over 60,000 teachers were attacked by students in 1978 (O'Toole, 1978), and the federal government estimates that up to 280,000 students are attacked every month (U.S. Department of Health, Education, and Welfare and National Institute of Education, 1978). Even so, adolescents generally do not carry guns, injure the victims they rob, or inflict such heavy losses as adult criminals. Although boys are more likely to be delinquent than girls, the rate of delinquency among girls has been rising. For both boys and girls, delinquency peaks at around age 15 (see Figure 16.5).

What are the causes of juvenile delinquency? Neurological and psychological abnormalities are one cause. In a study of Michigan adolescents who had committed a crime, investigators found lower than average scores on tests of rhythm (a test of neurological integration, not musical ability), vision, expressive speech, writing, reading, arithmetic, and general intelligence (Brickman, McManus, Grapentine, and Alessi, 1984). The delinquent adolescents had trouble thinking abstractly, putting things in temporal order, and concentrating. The pattern of abnormalities led the investigators to conclude that these adolescents had not developed the cognitive control to manage their feelings or moods, and this lack of control plus learning problems may have made it difficult for them to deal with their feelings, to pay attention, or to control their actions. In another study (Chandler, 1973), delinquent boys were found to be less able than nondelinquent boys to take the perspective of another person. After being trained in social perspective taking, the boys, according to police records, committed fewer crimes over the next 18 months—or at least did not get caught at them. Interestingly enough, though, delinquents in yet another study were found to be able to reason morally at the same level as others their age (Hains and Ryan, 1983).

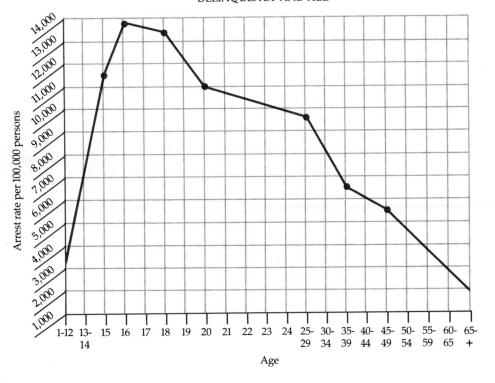

Figure 16.5 Whether one uses official arrest figures, as in this illustration (Sykes, 1980), or people's confidential reports of crimes committed (Gold and Reimer, 1975), the seriousness of delinquent acts appears to peak at about age 15. Boys commit more numerous and more serious delinquent acts than girls.

DELINQUENCY AND AGE

Arrest rate per 100,000 persons

It has long been thought that children who think poorly of themselves misbehave more often. But does low self-esteem cause delinquency? In a recent three-year study (McCarthy and Hoge, 1985), it was shown that students who started out low in self-esteem were no more likely to misbehave or commit crimes than students with high esteem. But delinquent students were more likely to *end up* with low self-esteem. Why? It is possible that breaking rules resulted in condemnation by the people the adolescents cared about, and the condemnation made them think worse of themselves. It is also possible that the adolescents committed delinquent acts to get their friends' approval but reduced their self-esteem in the process. The psychological processes involved in delinquency are not fully understood and no doubt differ from one individual to another.

Destructive family relationships create a backdrop against which adolescents become delinquents.

> Every single kid, I don't care whether their parents are rich or poor, every kid who comes into the program [a residential drug treatment program] has some terrible story to tell. The parents are alcoholics or substance abusers. The kids have been molested, abused, farmed out, neglected. They've been victims of incest, or they've been beaten up. Sometimes the story isn't so blatant, but kids don't get into trouble just out of the blue.—Mike and Erica's father, a drug treatment counselor

In one study of Philadelphia gang members, it was found that the boys tended to be violent at home and had defied, hit, or abused their parents (Friedman, Mann, and Friedman, 1975). In another study of seventh- through tenth-grade boys in Eugene, Oregon, it was shown that delinquency was associated with how closely parents monitored and disciplined the boys' behavior (Patterson and Stouthamer-Loeber, 1984). If the parents supervised their sons and knew where they were, with whom they were spending time, and what they were doing, their sons were less likely to become delinquents. Eighty percent of the delinquent boys were inadequately supervised by their parents; only 10 percent of the nondelinquent boys were inadequately supervised.

Running away from home is a solution that some adolescents use to escape from destructive family relationships. Many runaways have been abused by their parents and have experienced a high level of conflict in their families (D'Angelo, 1974). Runaways are desperate to leave home and desperate once they have left. For adolescents who are legally still minors, running away is itself a delinquent act. Once out in the world, these adolescents may need to commit further delinquent acts to support themselves. Some half a million adolescents in the United States run away from home each year, and to survive most of them turn to acts like prostitution and theft.

Runaways of both sexes may have to turn to delinquency to earn money, but more girls than boys turn to prostitution. According to the results of several studies (Weisberg, 1985), adolescent girls enter prostitution, on the average, at the age of 14, and the great majority are younger than 16. About two-thirds come from divorced families. Some have never had a mother or a father, and about three-fourths relate poorly to one or the other of their parents, describing the situation at home as ''poor'' or ''very bad.'' Some were sexually abused by relatives or others, and the abuse was frequent, began when they were young children, and continued for a long time. About two-thirds were beaten or neglected as children, and nearly that many were beaten as adolescents. The average age at which these adolescent prostitutes first had intercourse was 13 years, substantially earlier than most adolescent girls. Asked how they felt before they became prostitutes, most of the adolescent girls said ''depressed,'' ''unhappy,'' ''lonely,'' ''insecure,'' ''not good,'' or ''ashamed'' (Enablers, 1979, in Weisberg, 1985). A substantial minority—

research focus   *Resilient adolescents*

Why do some adolescents run into social and psychological problems while others, from essentially the same backgrounds, do not? In a 20-year study in which 700 Asian and Polynesian adolescents born in Hawaii in 1955 were followed until early adulthood, researcher Emmy Werner and a team of physicians, nurses, social workers, and psychologists tried to answer this question (Werner and Smith, 1982).

Most of the adolescents in the study came from lower-class backgrounds. Many had been born prematurely or had had difficult births, had been raised in chronic poverty by parents with little education or serious mental health problems, and lived in unstable families. Not surprisingly, about 200 of the children did run into serious problems at some time before they turned 20. About one-third of the children went through an adolescence that was stormy and stressful, and one-fifth had developed serious problems by late adolescence. The boys with problems were aggressive and delinquent. The girls with problems got pregnant or had mental health problems. Many of the troubled adolescents of both sexes felt frustrated and not able to control their own fates.

But most of the adolescents studied—who had been exposed to the same serious stresses—did *not* develop problems. This resilient majority developed into mature, autonomous, and competent young adults who "worked well, played well, loved well, and expected well." Compared to the troubled adolescents, many of the resilient adolescents had been firstborn children and had fewer brothers and sisters. They were described by their mothers as having been physically robust, easy to deal with, active, socially responsive, and good-natured as infants. It is likely that their temperamental characteristics allowed these infants to seek and hold the attention of their parents and other adults—grandparents, friends' parents, babysitters—and that this attention provided the children with important emotional support. Girls who took care of siblings while their mothers had worked outside the home developed reserves of autonomy and feelings of responsibility that further bolstered their development.

Whereas temperament and physical health seemed to have more effect on infants' development, environmental factors like family structure and an individual's own intellectual ability had more effect in early adolescence. By late adolescence, factors like self-esteem and feelings of control or helplessness most heavily affected whether the adolescents ran into trouble. It was this sense of control and faith in the effectiveness of their own actions that seemed most important to a good outcome, according to Werner. By late adolescence, many of the resilient individuals had positive self-concepts, were nurturant, had a sense of coherence to their lives, and were interested in "improving themselves"—that is, continuing to grow psychologically.

some 30 percent—of adolescent prostitutes have mothers who are also prostitutes.

Adolescents from every social class commit delinquent acts. But lower-class adolescents are more likely than middle- or upper-class adolescents to be caught by the police, to be charged with a crime, to be represented by a court-appointed lawyer, to go to prison, and to commit crimes as adults. Adolescents who have served time are likely to be stigmatized as troublemakers by the police as well as by people in the community, and people labeled troublemakers are likely to make a career out of crime (Chambliss, 1977). Thus, although delinquency may have various causes—neurological and cognitive abnormalities, destructive family relations, pressure from delinquent peers— the accident of birth into a lower-class family sometimes closes off an adolescent's avenues of escape from delinquency.

Suicide

Some adolescents look for a way out of their problems that is more final than running away from home or becoming members of a gang. They commit suicide (see Figure 16.6).

> Jennifer was smart and sensitive. From the time she was a child, she took it to heart when she saw people acting cruelly or when someone she knew got hurt. When her father and I argued, the stricken look on her face was pathetic. Jennifer had a few close girlfriends, but she hadn't started dating actively. She spent a lot of time by herself, reading, listening to classical music—''Rock is for street people, not me''—and talked a lot to me or her grandmother. She was devastated when her grandmother died last year of cancer. For a while when she was in junior high, she saw a therapist because she seemed so depressed and lonely. But then she stopped therapy, got more active at school and with other kids her age. She had seemed lonely again lately, and I talked with her about going back into therapy. But she pooh-poohed the idea. I guess you always think back over the things you might have done, and I think that if we had insisted on more therapy, she might still be alive. We found her body on the first anniversary of her grandmother's death.

Figure 16.6 As these figures show, the rate of suicides increases sharply during late adolescence (at 15 to 24 years).

SUICIDE AND AGE

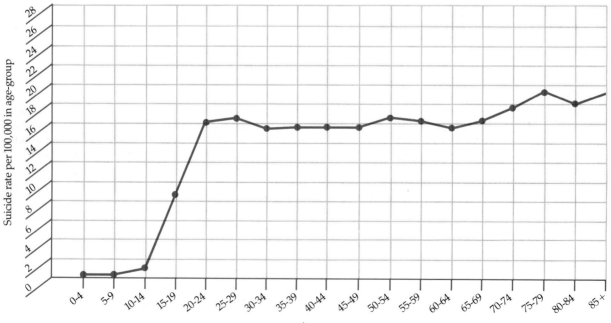

The problems of adolescence can loom so large and insurmountable, the person feels so bleak and despairing, that 14 in every 100,000 people between the ages of 15 and 24 kill themselves every year, and 100 times that many try. Only murder and car accidents kill more people in this age range, and many of these ''accidents'' actually may be suicides (*Monthly Vital Statistics Report*, 1979; Seiden, 1969). The rate of suicide among adolescents has increased 300 percent in the last 30 years (U.S. Department of Commerce, 1981). More girls attempt suicide than boys, but because boys use more violent methods—guns rather than pills—more boys succeed (Cantor, 1985; Petzel and Cline, 1978). Of the adolescents who attempt suicide, 90 percent are firstborn girls who are unusually close to their mothers. Of the adolescents who actually commit suicide, 75 percent are white, middle-class boys. They tend to be later-born children who keep their problems inside themselves and cannot accept help from others. Many feel pressured to achieve but unappreciated and unrecognized by their parents.

Suicide may seem like the only out to adolescents who feel hopeless, powerless, and without options. They have never had experience resolving serious problems. They do not know much about rising above their problems or just waiting them out.

To my family and friends:

I'm sorry it has to be this way. For some reason, I have set unattainable goals for myself. It hurts to live and life is full of so many disappointments and problems. . . . Please don't cry or feel badly. I know what I am doing and why I am doing it. I guess I never really found out what love or responsibility was.

Bill

I might also add that I had had in recent years no great desire to continue living. Saying goodbye to all of you who I was close to would only make things harder for me. Believe me, I tried to cope with my problems, but I couldn't (Jacobs, 1971).

The tendency for adolescents to see things as all black or all white, to narrow their focus into a kind of tunnel vision that shuts out all light, can make bad situations seem utterly hopeless. We do not know which factors make an adolescent turn to suicide, but we do know some of the things that generally can be ruled out: poverty, deprivation, crime, pregnancy, sexually transmitted diseases, and drugs (Wynne, 1978; Yankelovich, 1981). Recently it has been found that adolescents who committed suicide were more likely to have experienced stress before or at birth. In a study comparing suicide victims with a matched comparison group, it was found that 60 percent of the suicide group, compared to 12 percent of the comparison group, had been born of a pregnancy lacking in prenatal care, had experienced respiratory stress at birth, or had a mother who was chronically ill (Lipsitt, 1985). The causal chain between birth stress and adolescent suicide is not yet clear, but this finding does suggest that physical and psychological stresses that begin even before a child is born may culminate in suicide.

Some adolescents are so depressed by the death of a member of their family or a close friend that they try suicide (Tishler, McKenry, and Morgan, 1981). Others try suicide after they have been isolated for a long time, after they have failed repeatedly at things, or when they have been feeling unworthy, desperate, and hopeless. Although many suicides follow depression, hopelessness actually is the key. Some adolescents attempt suicide because they want out of a destructive family; others have problems with members of *focus* *The warning signs of suicide*

The warning signs that an adolescent may be thinking of committing suicide include the following (Cantor, 1985; Lipsitt, 1985):

- Depression.
- A preoccupation with thoughts of death or suicide.
- Earlier attempts at suicide.
- Giving away cherished possessions, writing a will, or making other final arrangements.
- Changes in sleep; sleeping too much or too little.
- Sudden or marked changes in eating patterns, changes in weight.
- Marked changes in behavior or withdrawing from family and friends.
- Changes in behavior at school such as skipping classes, getting worse marks.
- Changes in personality such as nervousness, moodiness, angry outbursts, lack of concern about health or appearance.
- Drug or alcohol abuse.
- Recent suicide of friend or family member.
- Experience of loss or crisis (breakup of a relationship, failure in school, conflict with parents).

the other sex, problems at school, problems with brothers and sisters, or problems with friends (Tishler, McHenry, and Morgan, 1981). Whatever the specific cause—and adolescents themselves may not always know what has driven them to the brink—suicide is one increasingly common reaction to the problems of adolescence.

Work

Part-time jobs

> I have a job at the Boys' Club after school every day watching the 4- and 5-year-olds. It's hard to get my homework done when I've been running around after little kids all afternoon.—Nadine, age 16

Many adolescents hold part-time jobs. In one recent month during a school year, for example, 43 percent of the 16- and 17-year-old boys and 37 percent of the girls in this country held jobs (Greenberger and Steinberg, 1986). Even one-sixth of the 14- and 15-year-olds were working or looking for work in 1983 (Nilsen, 1984). More adolescents hold part-time jobs today than at any other time in the last 40 years. Fully 80 percent of all high school students hold jobs at one time or another. In one short-term, longitudinal study of high school students in Orange County, California, the researchers set out to learn about the costs and benefits of working during adolescence (Greenberger and Steinberg, 1986). Work, they noted, is assumed to benefit adolescents' development and to teach them about taking responsibility, being on time, and being dependable. At work, people are assumed to cooperate and to interact socially. At work, barriers of age and class fall, and tolerance

Many adolescents hold part-time jobs. Although work teaches them to be responsible, punctual, dependable and self-reliant, the jobs also may interfere with their schoolwork and relationships with family and friends.

rises. But are these assumptions valid? Work, the researchers found, apparently did teach adolescents to be responsible, on time, dependable, and self-reliant. But it did not increase their coooperativeness, social interaction, or concern for others. In general, the more time that high school students worked beyond 14 hours a week, the more often they were absent from school, the less time they spent on homework or extracurricular activities, the lower their grades, and the less they enjoyed school. The more time they worked, the less time they spent doing things with their families and the less close they felt to their friends. Students who held jobs had more negative attitudes toward work than students who did not hold jobs, were more tolerant of unethical work practices, and used more drugs, alcohol, and cigarettes. Of course, it is not clear that part-time work itself *causes* these negative outcomes. Adolescents are not randomly assigned to work, and it may be that those adolescents who already smoke and don't care about school choose to or have to work. But it is clear that part-time work does not guarantee benefits to adolescents in psychological, social, or academic development. Moreover, the jobs that adolescents are likely to hold—in food services, manual labor, retail sales, cleaning, office work, and child care—tend to be repetitive, to provide little chance for learning, and to expose the adolescents to environmental, social, and personal stress.

Career development

Whether or not they hold part-time jobs, adolescents are concerned about work, for adolescence is when initial decisions about occupation and careers must be made. Adolescents begin to think about their abilities and interests, to experiment with work roles, and to make vocational plans that are somewhat more realistic than younger children's fantasies about what they will be when they grow up. According to one theory (Super, 1967), from 14 to 18 adolescents first begin to narrow their choices according to their interests and values and seek out information about general categories of occupations and professions—for example, mental health or medicine. From 18 to 21 they specify their vocational interests within one general career category and seek information about specific occupations—for example, social worker, clinical psychologist, psychiatrist. In the real world, not all adolescents are so systematic and rational, however. Many flounder after high school, making repeated job shifts without a clear plan based on adequate information (Super, Kowalski, and Gotkin, 1967). Occupational choices are not based solely on adolescents' interests and values. For one thing, people's interests and values continue to develop past adolescence. For another, there are other factors that affect vocational choices. Another vocational theory (Holland, 1973) suggests that personality is important in the choice of an occupation. ''Realistic'' individuals prefer practical jobs; ''sociable'' individuals are interested in the helping professions; ''enterprising'' individuals look for power and status, and so on. These are the kinds of personality types assessed in inventories of interests that are used in vocational counseling.

Just as important as adolescents' interests and personalities, though, are other people. Parents and peers clearly influence adolescents' career choices. Adolescents from middle-class families with middle-class friends almost always enter middle-class occupations. Why? The reasons include family connections, family pressure, and family expectations. They include educational opportunities, information, and the leisure to explore career options. They also include the more specific example set by parents. In one study (Werts, 1968), for example, it was found that 40 percent of physicians' sons entered the field of medicine. This tendency for sons to take over the family business used to be even more common. Now, adolescents have a wider range of choices and fields than their parents had and are less likely to follow in their father's footsteps. But they still choose occupations of the same socioeconomic level.

Broader conditions in society, like the economy and the job market, also influence adolescents' vocational choices, and so do societal expectations. For example, in our society, expectations for men and women likely are responsible for the fact that adolescent girls' career plans center on a narrower range of occupations than boys' plans do (Marini and Greenberger, 1978). The women's movement has made it more likely for girls to say that they will have jobs when they grow up, but the jobs they aspire to—nurse, teacher, secretary—are as gender-typed as ever (Lueptow, 1984).

One reason for the strong influence of family, friends, and society on adolescents' career choices is the lack of vocational guidance at school. In theory, vocational classes and counseling in high school would seem to be good sources of career guidance, but in fact, they usually do not offer effective guidance (Lueptow, 1984; Sizer, 1985). Most high school guidance counselors have more urgent problems to solve—like getting the students through high school—and most vocational classes are out of date. As a result, adolescents may continue their naive fantasies about their intended occupations. In one study (Sarason, 1980), college seniors who were planning to be doctors or lawyers claimed that they had not considered careers in business because they didn't want to be small cogs in big wheels, to have to struggle to reach the top, or to become morally corrupt in the process. Students who were already in law school or medical school realized that these factors were also part of careers in law and medicine. Career development begins in adolescence, but it certainly doesn't end there.

Psychosocial maturity

Adolescents are faced with the task of learning the patterns of behavior that society requires of its functioning members. At the most basic level, they must learn that there are times for sleeping and eating, working and studying, relaxing and playing. At a higher level, they must learn how to bring pleasure and meaning to the things that they do. They must learn to narrow their sights and concentrate their energies on a limited course of development. One person cannot be a builder, a rock star, a playwright, *and* a dancer. Somehow adolescents must learn to listen to the outer voices— "Read the history chapter," "Let's go bike riding," "Give to the United Way"—and to the inner voices—"I don't care what anyone thinks," "I will never give in," "I love this." They must heed both social and personal values. They must develop constructive attitudes toward working—to know how to perform some kind of work, to persist and to resist distraction, to have standards for and to take pleasure from their work. They also need a clear sense of their own identity—a clear idea of themselves, of their goals and values—and must think well of themselves. They must learn to function independently and to contribute to their society's well-being and survival. All this sounds like a tall order. Can any real-life adolescents fill it?

On a questionnaire designed to test for precisely these aspects of psychological and social maturity, Ellen Greenberger (1974, 1983) found that 1100 sixth, ninth, and twelfth graders advanced significantly over the course of a year in both autonomy and social responsibility. Other studies confirm steady progress toward autonomy among 12- to 17-year-olds and in social responsibility for boys at all ages and for girls until about age 14, when they reach a temporary plateau (Greenberger, 1982). But although girls are more likely

focus *Personhood for adolescents*

> Natalie is 17—going on 70. She's more mature than half the adults I meet.

> Mike got suspended from school for gathering names on a petition against the war in Nicaragua. He's so mad about his right of free speech being violated that he wants to take the school principal to court.

In the eyes of their parents, in the eyes of the state, and in the eyes of the law, adolescents are part children and part adults. They are entitled by law to some rights granted adults but not all. They are entitled to due process of law in delinquency proceedings but not to a jury trial. They have some rights of free speech at school but not the full rights guaranteed adults. They may choose on their own to have an abortion—even against their parents' wishes—but their parents may still "volunteer" them for admission to a mental hospital. Some advocates of minors' rights want to liberate adolescents and increase their powers of self-determination, whereas others want to protect them, and still others see no distinction between the interests of parents and the interests of children. The Supreme Court has ruled as though adolescents do not have the capacity to make mature, independent choices. In the words of Chief Justice Burger:

> Most children, even in adolescence, simply are not able to make sound judgments concerning many decisions, including their need for medical care or treatment. Parents can and must make those judgments (Melton, 1983, p. 100).

But do minors have the ability to make mature choices? In many areas, they do seem able to make mature decisions. For example, adolescents' reasoning is indistinguishable from that of adults when it comes to understanding the concepts of psychotherapy and mental disorders. Adolescents give the same arguments for and against abortion as adults do (Melton, 1983). If adolescents think like adults, perhaps they should be treated like adults. Some psychologists have suggested that the psychological benefits might be substantial (Melton, 1983). If adolescents had more legal rights, they suggest, they would feel more in control of their lives, more competent, less helpless, and would have an easier time developing into independent individuals. Giving children the right balance between freedom and control is essential for the state, just as it is for parents.

It is probable that as the concept of adolescence as a separate stage of development enters its second century, we will see it shifting again in response to social and historical factors. Will the concept of adolescence come full circle, and will adolescents be treated essentially like adults? The weight of the evidence on adolescent development appears to caution society against such a move. For although adolescents seem mature in many ways—with their formal operations and sexual maturity—they still need a protected time in which to form their identities. Without that time, many adolescents are likely to find themselves with identities that are foreclosed rather than integrated and fully resolved.

than boys to say that they should contribute to their communities, at no point in adolescence does a clear majority of either sex endorse this position. Adolescents in this country are clearly more interested in growing independent than in taking social responsibility.

Summary

1. All adolescents go through ups and downs in their moods and feelings about themselves. Some adolescents feel great storm and stress; others find adolescence a fairly smooth transition to adulthood.

2. The early part of adolescence, from age 11 to 16, typically is when physical and psychological pressures are more intense, when family arguments are most heated, and when adolescents' feelings of self-doubt and unhappiness are acute.

3. By later adolescence, moodiness, irritability, and self-consciousness have eased, and the search for a personal identity intensifies, as old issues of personality resurface from childhood and must be put in order in an emerging sense of self. It takes adolescents time to resolve this identity crisis and to find the necessary roles, work, attitudes, and social connectedness.

4. Adolescents face the task of achieving autonomy from their families without removing themselves so far that they feel isolated, enraged, depressed, or guilty. They test their parents' limits and bristle at their parents' attempts to control their behavior. Conflict between adolescent and parents occurs in every family, although it usually diminishes when the adolescent reaches 18 or so.

5. Girls are more likely to have problems coping with the conflict between remaining emotionally close to their parents and breaking away than boys are. Girls argue with their parents most over emotional issues, whereas boys argue over practical issues like using the family car, going to church, or doing chores around the house.

6. Parents continue to influence their children during adolescence. The amount of emotional support they provide influences how successfully adolescent children resolve their identity crises.

7. Adolescents spend many happy, sociable, and exciting hours with their friends. Although they sometimes feel angry and self-conscious with their friends, they are in conflict with them less often and come to feel more intimate with them than with their parents. As they search out their own identities and test their parents' values against their friends', adolescents turn to peers and parents on different issues. By age 19, most adolescents conform less to both peers and parents and are more autonomous.

8. Not only is dating fun, but it helps adolescents learn to cooperate, consider others' feelings, take responsibility, get along with others, test their popularity, develop social skills and manners, and experiment sexually.

9. Few adolescents commit serious crimes. Those who do commit crimes are likely to suffer from neurological and psychological problems. Their family relationships may be destructive and violent, and their parents probably do not supervise them adequately.

10. When adolescents feel that their problems are hopeless, they may attempt suicide. In this country, more girls attempt suicide than boys, but more boys actually kill themselves.

11. Many adolescents hold part-time jobs. Work teaches adolescents to be responsible, dependable, punctual, and self-reliant. But it may interfere with school grades and participation and with an adolescent's family life.

12. The work of adolescence is to develop a coherent sense of personal identity and positive self-esteem, to be autonomous and socially responsible, to enjoy working, and to be capable of making mature decisions.

Key terms

storm and stress	identity achievement	clique
identity crisis	identity moratorium	crowd
psychosocial moratorium	identity diffusion	juvenile delinquency
alienated identity achievement	identity foreclosure	

Suggested readings

COLEMAN, JAMES, and HUSÉN, TORSTEN. *Becoming Adult in a Changing Society.* Paris: Organisation for Economic Co-operation and Development, 1985. An excellent overview of issues and findings concerning changing conceptions of youth and the transition to adulthood.

CSIKSZENTMIHALYI, MIHALY, and LARSON, REED. *Being Adolescent.* New York: Basic Books, 1984. A rich source of information about adolescents' feelings and experiences.

ERIKSON, ERIK. *Identity: Youth and Crisis.* New York: Norton, 1968. Erikson's detailed description of the many paths identity formation can take, with his analysis of literary figures, historical circumstances, and the American scene.

GROTEVANT, HAROLD, and COOPER, CATHERINE (Eds.). *Adolescent Development in the Family.* San Francisco: Jossey-Bass, 1983. Alan Waterman, (Ed.). *Identity in Adolescence: Processes and Contents.* Two collections of brief articles by major researchers in the field of adolescent development (both in the New Direc-tions for Child Development series), which address how identity formation relates to family interaction, religious thinking, political commitment, and vocational development.

LIPSITZ, JOAN. *Growing Up Forgotten.* Lexington, Mass.: D. C. Heath, 1977. A review of research on early adolescence, showing the extent to which we have neglected this age group. Schools, service agencies, and the juvenile justice system are examined and all found wanting.

MEAD, MARGARET. *Coming of Age in Samoa.* NewYork: Morrow, 1971 (originally published in 1928). A readable work that changed the way Americans looked at adolescence because it showed that not *all* adolescents experienced storm and stress.

STEINBERG, L. D. *Understanding Families with Young Adolescents.* Carrboro, N.C.: Center for Early Adolescence, 1980. An easy-to-read overview of the maturation of adolescents and the simultaneous maturation of parents. Ideas for coping with adolescent change in families are included.

Glossary

A not B phenomenon The inability of the child, until 12 months of age, to follow the movements of an object when it is first hidden under cover A, then put, while the child watches, under cover B. The child looks for the object under A.

accommodation In Piaget's theory, the process of adjusting existing ways of thinking, of reworking schemes, to encompass new information, ideas, or objects. In the visual system, the adjustment of the lens of the eye to shifting planes of focus.

acquired immune deficiency syndrome (AIDS) A sexually transmitted disease that impairs the immune system and makes the patient susceptible to opportunistic infections. It may cause dementia and is so far always terminal.

acne An inflammatory disease involving the oil glands and hair follicles of the skin and causing pustular eruptions.

acuity Sharpness of the visual system, which in infancy depends partly on physiological maturity.

adaptation In Piaget's theory, the mental processes by which people extend and modify their thinking. They do so in two ways, by assimilation and by accommodation.

adolescence The biological and psychological changes that individuals go through at the end of childhood.

adolescent egocentrism The tendency of adolescents to think that they are more important and unusual than they actually are.

affordances Properties of objects that afford or allow for certain activities.

afterbirth The placenta and the parts of the fetal membranes that are delivered after the birth of the baby, in the third and final stage of labor.

alienated achievement An identity status of adolescents during the Vietnam War era, in which they rejected certain ''straight'' social conventions.

alternative reproduction Recently developed methods for treating infertility, such as in vitro fertilization, ovum transfer, and surrogate mothering.

alveoli Tiny air sacs of the lungs walled by a very thin epithelial membrane; they are surrounded by capillaries and are the site of respiration.

ambivalent-insecure attachment Relationship of an infant to his or her caregiver in which the child is angry and resistant.

amniocentesis A prenatal medical procedure for diagnosing genetic abnormalities. A small amount of amniotic fluid is withdrawn from the pregnant woman by hollow needle. The chemical contents of the fluid reveal some diseases directly; cells from the fetus are cultured and studied for chromosomal anomalies.

amnion A thin, membranous, fluid-filled sac surrounding the developing embryo and fetus.

anal stage In Freud's theory, the psychosexual stage of toddlerhood, from 12 to 36 months, during which the child receives pleasure through stimulation of the anus and pays much attention to elimination.

anesthesia Loss of sensation and usually consciousness, without loss of vital functions, through administration of an agent that blocks the passage of pain impulses to the brain.

animism The belief that all things are living and endowed with intentions, consciousness, and feelings.

anorexia nervosa A severe disorder in which the person, usually an adolescent girl, eats very little and loses 25 percent or more of original weight. The girl has an intense fear of becoming obese, feeling fat even when emaciated.

Apgar score A rating of the neonate's physical well-being, ranging from 0 to 10, determined by grading the infant's heart rate, breathing effort, muscle tone, reflex irritability, and color at 0, 1, and 2 points—poor, fair, or good.

apnea A transient interruption of breathing.

areola Pigmented ring surrounding the nipple.

artificial insemination A procedure in which either the husband's or a donor's sperm are introduced into the vagina via syringe rather than through sexual intercourse.

assimilation In Piaget's theory, the process of adjusting new information and objects to make them fit existing ways of thinking or scheming.

asynchrony Want of coincidence in time; the condition of two or more events not happening together.

astigmatism A defect of vision owing to corneal irregularity.

attachment An affectionate, close, and enduring relationship between two persons who have shared many experiences; the tie to their parents felt by children 6 months and older.

attention deficit disorder See hyperactivity.

authoritarian parent A parent who rears the child to believe that his or her often arbitrary rules are law, that misconduct by the child will be punished. The authoritarian parent is detached and seldom praises the child.

authoritative parent A parent who sets firm limits and provides direction for the child but at the same time is willing to listen to the child's objections and make compromises.

autism A rare but devastating childhood psychosis characterized by profound aloneness and an indifference to communication and social relationships.

G1

autosome A chromosome other than a sex chromosome. In the human being, any one chromosome of the 22 pairs that carry most of the genetic code for physical size, eye color, hair color, nose structure, chin structure, intelligence, and so on.

avoidant-insecure attachment Relationship of an infant to his or her caregiver in which the infant tends to ignore, turn away from, or avoid the caregiver, even after a brief separation.

axon A long thin fiber that may extend a considerable distance from the nerve cell body and that conducts impulses away from it.

babbling Extending repetitions of consonant–vowel combinations beginning when babies are about 4 months old; vocal play that exercises the speech musculature and gives babies practice in making sounds.

baby talk The special language form used by adults when speaking to infants. The voice is usually high in register but has an exaggerated range of pitch and loudness. The adult chooses simple phrases and nonsense syllables and repeats them in a sing-song fashion.

behaviorism A school of psychology that originated with John Watson and his proposal that only observable behavior should be studied, without reference to consciousness or mental processes.

blastocyst A hollow, fluid-filled sphere whose wall is one cell thick except for the heap of large cells at one side forming the embryonic disk.

blastula A hollow, fluid-filled sphere made up of more than 100 cells; its wall is uniformly one cell thick, but the cells on one side are larger.

bonding The formation of an enduring attachment, such as to one's child, especially in the period immediately following birth.

breech position Position of the fetus during childbirth in which its buttocks or legs come through the birth canal before the head.

Broca's area Part of the brain's motor cortex that primarily controls muscles for speech.

bulimia A disorder in which the individual indulges in secret and episodic eating binges, which often end in self-induced vomiting.

canalized Relatively invulnerable to environmental effects.

case study Research that collects detailed historical or biographical information on a specific individual.

catch-up growth Rapid physical growth during the first 5 months by an infant whose size was restricted by a small womb or by maternal malnutrition; or by a child who has been restored to health after illness or malnutrition.

cephalocaudal (development) A pattern of physical growth and motor development progressing from head to foot; in human beings, followed prenatally and throughout childhood.

cerebellum The region of the brain that coordinates movement and sensory input.

cerebral cortex The outer layer of gray matter covering the brain; responsible for complex information and conscious thoughts.

cerebral palsy A disorder of movement or posture that appears during very early childhood and is caused by a malfunction or direct or indirect damage to the motor centers of the brain, usually before or during birth.

cervix The very small outer or lower opening of the uterus; opens to the vagina.

cesarean section A surgical procedure in which the newborn is delivered through incisions in the abdominal and uterine walls.

child abuse The flagrant mistreatment or neglect of children, which federal and state laws now require doctors, clinic and hospital personnel, teachers, social workers, police officers, coroners, and other professionals to report. Defined by federal law as ''the physical or mental injury, sexual abuse, negligent treatment or maltreatment of a child under the age of 18 by a person who is responsible for the child's welfare.''

childbed fever A disease that results from infection of the placental site following delivery.

chorion The outermost of the membranes surrounding the developing embryo and fetus; villi from the chorion become part of the placenta.

chorionic villi biopsy A test of chromosomes in which a sample of fetal tissue, from the membrane that eventually forms part of the placenta, is taken through the mother's cervix and submitted to analysis.

chromosomes Microscopic threadlike structures, consisting of a linear string of genes; chromosomes are the transmitters of inheritance and are present in the nucleus of every cell.

circular reaction In Piaget's theory, an action that is repeated because it pleases.

classical conditioning A basic form of learning in which a neutral stimulus, through association with a physiologically significant stimulus, eventually comes to evoke the response made spontaneously to the significant stimulus.

classification The process of sorting objects into mutually exclusive groups.

class inclusion In Piaget's theory, the ability to consider an object as belonging simultaneously to a number of categories, each successive one of greater breadth; a concrete operation.

clique A closely knit, small circle of persons who tend to exclude others.

closed classroom A self-contained classroom.

cochlea In the inner ear, a bony, fluid-filled canal, coiled like a snail, containing within it a smaller, membranous, fluid-filled spiral passage wherein lie the nerve endings essential for hearing.

cognitive style The way an individual conceptualizes or approaches tasks; a distinctive way of perceiving, feeling, and solving problems that constitutes part of an individual's personality.

cohort A group of individuals born at the same time or during the same historical period.

cohort–sequential research design A type of research that includes elements of both longitudinal and cross-sectional designs, in which several different-aged samples (cohorts) are studied for a period of time.

collective monologue Piaget's term for the conversation of two preschoolers who talk in turn but are not really listening or responding to each other's words.

colostrum A yellowish protein-rich fluid that is secreted from the mother's breasts a few days before a baby's birth and for two to four days after.

conception The formation of a viable zygote through the union of ovum and sperm, being the first step in the development of a new human being. The act of becoming pregnant.

concordance In genetic studies of twins, their similarity in one or more traits or in a diagnosis.

concrete operational thinking In Piaget's theory, the mental ability of children from ages 7 to 11 by which they can think logically about physical objects and their relations. Concrete operations include conservation, reversibility, seriation, and classification.

conservation In Piaget's theory, the ability to recognize that important properties of a given quantity of matter, such as number, volume, and weight, remain constant despite changes in shape, length, or position.

conventional moral reasoning Kohlberg's intermediate level of moral reasoning, in which conforming to social conventions, or standards, such as pleasing others by being a ''nice guy'' and maintaining ''law and order'' for its own sake, are the primary moral values.

convergent thinking Thinking that has as its goal the selection of a single, acceptable, conventional solution to a problem.

corpus callosum The band of myelinated tissue that connects the two hemispheres of the brain.

correlation The degree and direction of relationship between two variables, which may be positive, with both increasing or decreasing at the same time, or negative, with one increasing and the other decreasing.

couvade A ritual of cultures in many parts of the world in which the father takes to his bed when his child is born and complains that he has suffered the pains of childbirth.

critical period An interval during which certain physical or psychological growth must occur if development is to proceed normally and during which the individual is vulnerable to pertinent harmful events and open to beneficial effects.

cross-over The exchange of portions from strands of homologous chromosomes that have broken at the same level during meiosis.

cross-sectional study A research method in which groups of children of different ages but similar in other important ways—educational level, socioeconomic status, proportion of males to females—are compared at some specific point in time, usually for a specific aspect of behavior. The groups represent different age levels.

crowd A loosely organized group of three or four cliques of adolescents centered on some activity rather than on close friendship.

crowning During childbirth, the first appearance of the newborn's head, usually with the face toward the mother's back.

data Evidence systematically collected during scientific studies.

day-care center An institutional setting in which pre-school children are cared for when their parents are working or otherwise unavailable. Day-care centers usually are open 5 days a week, all day, all year round.

decentration In Piaget's theory, the ability to focus or the process of focusing on more than one dimension, such as length and height, simultaneously; a concrete operation.

deferred imitation The child's ability, beginning between 18 and 24 months of age, to mimic a person's actions witnessed sometime earlier. A term used by Piaget.

dendrites Any of the usually short and branched extensions of a nerve cell that conduct impulses toward the cell body.

deoxyribonucleic acid (DNA) A complex chemical substance whose molecules constitute genes and are able to replicate themselves.

depth of focus The distance that an object can be moved without a viewer perceiving a change in sharpness.

diabetes Illness in which the pancreas does not manufacture sufficient insulin, which is necessary to metabolize sugars and regulate blood sugar.

dialectical view A conception of human development—and especially such processes as communication, language, and problem solving—as a constant process of thesis, antithesis, and synthesis.

diethylstilbestrol (DES) A hormone formerly prescribed to pregnant women to prevent miscarriages. It was found to cause abnormalities and disease in the sex organs of their children when they reached their teens.

divergent thinking Thinking that goes in different directions and searches for new ideas and a number of solutions to a problem.

dizygotic (DZ) twins Birth partners who have developed from two ova fertilized at the same time by two sperm. The genotypes of these twins are as different as those of any siblings.

dominant gene In a pattern of genetic inheritance, the one of a pair of genes that determines the trait and suppresses expression of the other.

double-blind study Research in which neither subjects nor researchers know which subjects are in a treatment group and which are in a control group. Double-blind studies may prevent bias from coloring research results.

Down's syndrome A disorder caused by an extra chromosome 21; the affected child is mentally retarded and has a number of distinctive physical signs.

dwarfism Abnormally short stature and immature physical development found in children under severe emotional stress.

dyscalcula A learning disability that affects calculating skills.

dysgraphia A learning disability that affects writing skills.

dyslexia A pattern of difficulties in reading and spelling that appears in people of normal intelligence. They see letters backward on the page, because they process visual information unusually slowly and because letters echo in their mind's eye.

early maturers Young people who undergo the physical changes of adolescence a year or two before the majority of their age-mates.

ecological approach A view of human behavior that looks at how people are affected throughout their lives by the changing environments within which they live and grow.

ectoderm The outermost of the three primary cell layers of the embryo from which develop the skin, sensory organs, and nervous system.

ego In Freud's theory, the predominantly conscious part of the personality that acts on the reality principle and makes decisions while restraining the id and taking the strictures of the superego into account.

egocentrism One's inability to take another person's point of view; this imbues and colors thinking in early childhood.

Electra conflict The female counterpart of the Oedipal conflict in psychoanalytic theory. In the phallic stage, at about age 4, little girls have an erotic attachment for father and are antagonistic toward mother. These feelings are usually repressed.

embryo In the human being, the developing individual from 2 to 8 weeks following conception, during which time basic body structures and organ systems are forming.

embryonic stage The period extending from the 2nd to the 8th week after conception, during which the organs of the conceptus are differentiated and rudimentary anatomy becomes evident.

empathy The capacity to experience vicariously another person's emotional state.

encoding Putting impressions into short-term memory.

endoderm The innermost of the three primary cell layers of the embryo from which develop the lining of the digestive tract, the salivary glands, pancreas, and liver, and the respiratory system.

endogenous smiles Spontaneous smiles made by the sleeping or drowsy infant during the first 2 weeks

of life; they come when the baby relaxes after an internal neurophysiological arousal.

endometriosis Growth of uterine lining tissue outside the uterus, a common cause of infertility in women.

environment All the conditions, circumstances, and influences that surround an organism.

epidural anesthesia Medication injected under the mother's skin at the bottom of the spine to relieve the pain of childbirth; it numbs the body between chest and knees. Epidural anesthesia may slow the contractions of labor and the newborn's motor abilities.

episiotomy A small incision at the entrance to the vagina to allow an infant's body sufficient clearance for birth.

ethology The observational study of how animals behave in their natural surroundings.

exogenous smiles Smiles made by an infant, beginning at about 1 month of age, stimulated by something in the external world, such as a nodding head speaking with a high voice.

expression In heredity, the display of genetic characteristics in an individual's phenotype.

extensive peer relations The distribution of social interactions and friendships across a number of other children, not just a single, close friend. See intensive peer relations.

external locus of control The belief that success and failure are beyond one's own personal control.

external morality In Piaget's theory, the code of ethics of school-age children that has its origin outside of them. The children obey rules in the belief that the rules have been laid down by authority figures and that they will be punished if they do not obey them.

extrinsic motivation Inducement to do things to get a prize or promised reward.

failure to thrive Want of attaining expected height, weight, and behavior by a baby for no evident organic reason; usually caused by emotional neglect and inattention of parents.

fallopian tubes The pair of tubes that conduct the egg from the ovary to the uterus, having at its upper end a funnel-shaped expansion to capture the egg; fertilization occurs in the fallopian tubes.

fetal alcohol syndrome A congenital condition of infants whose mothers drink excessively during pregnancy. The infants have a small head, widely spaced eyes, a flat nose, and underdeveloped upper jaw, and are retarded in mental and motor development.

fetal stage The period, extending from the 9th week after conception until delivery, during which the conceptus grows large and its organs and muscles begin to function.

fetology A new field of medicine that treats problems of the fetus before birth.

fetus The developing unborn child from approximately 8 weeks after conception until birth.

field dependence A cognitive style in which the individual is unable to ignore misleading perceptual cues when doing certain cognitive tasks and tends to respond to influences in the immediate surroundings.

field independence A cognitive style in which the individual is able to maintain his or her spatial orientation and to ignore misleading perceptual cues.

fissures Folds in the brain that increase its surface area.

fontanel One of the six spaces, covered by membrane, between the bones of the fetal or young skull.

formal operation In Piaget's theory, the mental ability, supposedly attained in adolescence, by which the individual can think logically about abstractions, can speculate, and can consider the future, that is, what might and what ought to be. Formal operations include hypothetico-deductive, inductive, and reflective thinking and interpropositional logic.

fovea The central part of the retina in which focused visual images are formed. In infants the fovea is not distinct.

full-term baby An infant born in the normal range of 259 to 293 days after the first day of mother's last menstrual period.

gender roles The behaviors and attitudes a society considers acceptable for males and females.

gender identity The deeply ingrained sense of being a boy or girl, man or woman. After age 3, gender identity resists change.

gene The basic unit for the transmission of hereditary characteristics; a portion of DNA in a fixed linear position on a chromosome.

genital herpes Sexually transmitted viral infection that causes genital sores.

genital stage In Freud's theory, the last stage of psychosexual development in which the individual has mature sexual relations with the opposite sex.

genotype The individual's genetic makeup, the totality of the genes inherited from the parent cells. The genes are present in each cell of the developing individual, beginning with the fertilized egg.

gentle birth A method of childbirth to give the newborn a welcoming introduction ot the world, advocated by Frederick Leboyer. Lights are dimmed, sounds muffled; the baby is put immediately on the mother's stomach and then into a warm bath.

germinal stage The period from conception until about 14 days later when the many-celled conceptus has become firmly implanted in the wall of the uterus.

giantism Abnormally tall stature.

gonorrhea Sexually transmitted inflammation of the genital mucous membranes caused by the gonococcus; found in both males and females. Sometimes there are no symptoms.

growth curve A graphic representation of the relative growth of an individual or population during successive periods similar in length.

growth spurt In adolescence, the sharp and rapid increase in height and other physical growth that continues for about three years.

guilt A feeling of responsibility or remorse for having violated some ethical, moral, or religious principle.

habituate To become used to, accustomed to something by frequent repetition or prolonged exposure.

Head Start A national preschool program designed to provide children from poor families with the advantages usually afforded middle-class children, including good nutrition, health care, and educational experiences.

holophrase Single-word utterance that 12- to 18-month-old children combine with gesture and intonation to accomplish the work of a whole sentence.

homologous (chromosomes) A pair of chromosomes that are generally similar in size and shape, one having come from the male parent, one from the female parent.

horizontal décalage In Piaget's theory, the notion that the development of similar cognitive abilities is not simultaneous; children do not acquire these abilities all at the same time.

hydrocephaly An abnormal increase in the amount of cerebrospinal fluid within the cranium, especially in infancy, that causes the cerebral ventricles to expand; the skull, in particular the forehead, to enlarge; and the brain to atrophy.

hyperactivity A disorder in which the child cannot remain still or pay attention in situations that demand it. Other symptoms are distractibility, little tolerance for frustration, readily aroused emotions, and problems in learning, listening, and completing tasks. Now more commonly called attention deficit disorder.

hypothesis A guess or prediction about the world that may be tested empirically.

id In Freud's theory, the unconscious aspect of the personality, which is made up of impulses and is governed by the pleasure principle. The id, present at birth, wants whatever satisfies and gratifies and wants it immediately.

identity One's unique psychological picture of oneself.

identity achievement The stage of psychosocial development reached by adolescents who have a sense of identity, have career goals, and are committed to religious and political views.

identity crisis In Erikson's life-cycle theory, the core crisis of adolescence; the urgent need for greater self-understanding and self-definition.

identity diffusion In Erikson's terms, the resolution of the identity crisis of individuals who do not commit themselves to a cause or life course.

identity foreclosure The stage of psychosocial development reached by adolescents who accept the identity set for them by their parents.

imaginary audience Hypothetical people whom adolescents imagine scrutinize them.

implantation The process by which the trophoblast grows into the uterine wall.

imprinting The rapid, innate learning of very young birds and perhaps other animals, within the limited critical period of time, to follow and form a continuing filial attachment to the first large moving object seen.

impulsiveness A style of learning in which a child quickly selects a mode of action or an answer to a question and thereby often makes mistakes.

incubator An apparatus for the housing of premature or sick babies.

induced labor Uterine contractions started by the administration of drugs or by breaking the membranes surrounding the fetus and placenta.

infertility Inability to conceive or impregnate, diagnosed after a year of unprotected intercourse, and treatable in many cases.

information processing A theory that describes the flow of information into and out of memory; stresses quantitative mental capacities rather than qualitative advances.

intelligence quotient (IQ) Originally, an individual's intelligence defined as mental age, as determined by a standard test, divided by chronological age and multiplied by 100. Now determined by the standard deviation of the distribution of MA scores at a given age level and the deviation of the individual's score from the mean of this distribution.

intensive peer relations The expression of intense feelings and sharing of experiences and fantasies with just one or two other children. See extensive peer relations.

internal locus of control The belief that success and failure are within one's own personal control.

internal morality In Piaget's theory, the more advanced and mature form of moral reasoning in which the individual recognizes that rules are formulated through reasoning and discussion among equals.

interpropositional logic The ability to judge the truth of the logical relationship of propositions; a formal operation.

interval scale An arrangement of quantitative data on a scale in which division are equally spaced e.g., inches, pounds.

interventions Deliberate attempts to intercede in a person's life and development.

intrinsic motivation Inducement to do things because one wants to, not because someone else wants one to.

intuition In Piaget's theory, the preconceptual or prelogical thought of children from about 4 to 6 or 7 years of age, when children reason by guesses not logic.

invariants Unchanging properties of objects and events.

in vitro fertilization Literally ''in glass,'' laboratory fertilization of a human ovum.

juvenile delinquency Crimes and the antisocial acts considered wrong because they are committed by minors, like running away from home, promiscuity, and truancy.

Klinefelter's syndrome A disorder of males in which an extra X chromosome keeps the testes small at puberty, disrupts hormonal balance, and is likely to cause sterility and some breast development.

kwashiorkor Severe malnutrition of children 2 to 4 years old whose diet consists mostly of carbohydrates with very little protein. Symptoms are generalized swelling of the stomach, face, and legs; anemia; thinning hair, which changes color; and skin lesions.

labile Readily undergoing physical or physiological change.

labor The three-stage physiological process that results in the delivery and birth of an infant.

language play Rhyming, saying nonsense words, and playing with words.

lanugo A soft, fine hair that covers the fetus's body during the 5th and 6th months of prenatal development; some may persist on parts of the newborn's body for a few weeks after birth.

laparoscopy Examination of the abdominal cavity through a very small incision, now usually with the help of a fiber-optic illuminator.

late maturers Young people who undergo the physical changes of adolescence one or more years after the majority of their age-mates.

latency period In Freud's theory of psychosexual development, the years from age 7 to 11 during which the child has few sexual interests.

lateralization In the brain, the division of functions between the left and right hemispheres. The left hemisphere appears to control verbal skills, the right hemisphere visual skills and imagery.

learned helplessness An attitude of individuals that they simply cannot surmount failure, which tends to perpetuate it.

learning disability A problem that a child has in one or more of the basic processes necessary for using and understanding language and numbers.

life-span approach The school of psychology that studies human development from birth to death.

longitudinal research design A research method in which the same group of children is studied over an extended period of time to determine how they change with age.

macrosystem In the ecological view of development, the broad institutional patterns in a person's culture that affect his or her development.

magico-phenomenistic thinking In Piaget's theory, the infant's faulty linking of an inappropriate action and a desired end, which seems magical to the child because he or she does not really understand means and ends.

mainstreaming Placing handicapped children in school classes with nonhandicapped children.

marasmus Severe malnutrition of infants under 1 year of age who are deprived of necessary proteins and calories. They gain no weight, hardly grow, lose their muscles, and become emaciated.

masking The complete or partial obscuring of one sensory process with another.

maturation The developmental acquiring of skills by normal children through physiological growth, probably chiefly neural growth, rather than through learning.

mean A value intermediate between two extremes.

meconium Tarry waste that accumulates in the bowel during fetal life and is discharged shortly after birth.

meiosis A process of cell division unique to the gamete cells, leaving each sperm or ovum with 23 single chromosomes instead of 23 pairs.

menarche The first menstrual period; the establishment of menstruation.

mesoderm The middle of the three primary germ layers of the embryo from which the skeleton muscles, kidneys, and circulatory system develop.

mesosystem In the ecological view of development, the network of ties among major settings in a person's life, such as family, school, friends, church, and camp, which affect the person's development.

metabolism The chemical processes by which nutrients are broken down, releasing energy and wastes, and by which small molecules are built up into new living matter, by consuming energy.

metamemory The awareness of the phenomenon of memory and an understanding of how it works and how to aid it.

microanalysis In studies of social communications, a method that allows very close examination, such as stopping frames of films and videotapes or running them in slow motion.

microcephaly Abnormal smallness of head and brain area, usually causing mental retardation.

microsystem In the ecological view of development, the network of ties between a person and his or her immediate setting, such as a school or office.

mild mental retardation An IQ score of 55 to 69 and few, if any, physical disabilities.

mitosis The usual process of cell division in which the chromosomes split and duplicate within the nucleus, then separate, with one member of each duplicate going to one of the two daughter cells formed through division of the cytoplasm.

moderate mental retardation An IQ score of 40 to 55, usually accompanied by physical disabilities and neurological dysfunctions.

monozygotic (MZ) twins Birth partners who have developed from a single fertilized egg and thus have the same genotype.

Moro (embracing) reflex The newborn's normal reflexive response to a loud sound or a sudden drop of head and neck: the infant flings arms and legs out, fans its hands, and then convulsively brings arms toward the middle of the body.

morula A solid ball of 12 to 16 cells formed 60 hours after fertilization through several cell divisions; resembles a mulberry.

motherese The special language form used by adults when speaking to immature speakers. It consists of short simple sentences, frequent repetition and emphasis on the here and now.

mutation A sudden permanent change in hereditary material, physical in a chromosome, biochemical in a gene.

myelin A fatty covering on the axons of nerve cells, which increases the speed of nerve impulses.

myelination The accretion of myelin, a soft, white, somewhat fatty substance that coats the axon of a nerve cell and insulates it and increases the speed of impulses traveling along it.

natural childbirth A system to lessen pain during labor and birth that avoids general anesthesia and prepares parents for the birth of their child. They are given instructions on the mechanics of labor and birth as well as exercises to strengthen the mother's abdominal muscles and to encourage her proper breathing during labor.

naturalistic observation A research method in which records of people's or animals' spontaneous behavior are made in the natural setting with minimal intrusion by the observer.

nature In developmental psychology, the genetic and physiological factors that can affect development of the individual.

need for achievement An individual's motivation to strive for excellence.

negative identity A negative self-concept and low self-esteem.

neobehaviorist More recent versions of behaviorist theory.

neo-Freudian theories More recent versions of Freud's theory of psychosexual development. They emphasize the social and cultural factors in the development of personality.

neonatology A specialization in medicine directed to the medical care of the infant during the newborn period.

neo-Piagetian theories More recent versions of Piaget's theory of cognitive development in childhood.

neuroglia Delicate, branching connective tissue that fills the spaces between neurons, supporting and binding them together.

neurons Nerve cells.

neurotransmitters Chemicals in the brain that carry a nerve impulse across the synapse between neurons or keep it from crossing.

Nissl substance Material surrounding neurons that often appears just when a new function emerges.

norm A single value or a range of values constituting

the empirically established average or standard performance on a test under specified conditions.

nursery school A preschool that prepares children for kindergarten, usually with periods of group activities and shorter hours than day care. See day-care center.

nurture In developmental psychology, the factors in the environment that can affect development of the individual.

object permanence The understanding that objects continue to exist, even though they are out of sight or disappear from view; develops gradually between 6 and 18 months of age. A term used by Piaget.

Oedipal conflict In Freud's theory, the erotic attachment little boys in the phallic stage have for mother and their fear that father will find them out. These feelings are usually repressed.

ontogeny The development of the individual.

oocytes Immature egg cells.

open class A class in which choice of activities is flexible and decisions about where to be and what to do are often made by children, individually and in small groups, rather than by the teacher.

open classroom A school room in which spatial arrangements are flexible and physical equipment, including desks and walls, are moveable.

operant conditioning A learning process described by B. F. Skinner in which the individual responds again in a way rewarded in the past or refrains from activity earlier punished.

operant learning A form of training in which reward and punishment are used to shape behavior.

operation In Piaget's theory, a basic and logical mental manipulation and transformation of information.

oral stage In Freud's theory, the psychosexual stage from birth to 12 months, during which the mouth of the infant is the source of sustenance and pleasure, and his or her interest is in sucking.

organization In Piaget's theory, the process of combining and integrating perceptions and thoughts that continues throughout a lifetime. In information processing theory cognitive strategy for memorizing, grouping items into more general classes, clusters, or chunks.

ossification The process of bone formation in which, beginning in the center of each prospective bone, cartilage cells are replaced by bone cells.

otitis media Middle ear infection.

ova Human egg cells.

ovary The typically paired female reproductive organ that releases ova and in vertebrates female sex hormones; in the adult human female an oval, flattened body suspended from a ligament.

overextension Children's generalized use of a given word for several objects that share a particular characteristic but have others that are dissimilar, such as ''fly'' for flies, specks of dust, all small insects, crumbs of bread.

overregularize To extend the rules for the inflections denoting past tense and plural to verbs with irregular past tenses and nouns with irregular plurals.

ovulate To release a maturing ovum from the ovary into a fallopian tube; it occurs once about every 28 days from puberty until menopause.

ovum transfer A procedure for treating infertility whereby an ovum is surgically removed from a woman's ovary, fertilized in vitro, and then reintroduced into her own or a surrogate mother's uterus for gestation.

oxytoxin A hormone secreted together with vasopressin by the posterior lobe of the pituitary; stimulates both the uterine muscles to contract, initiating the birth process, and the breasts to eject milk. Also synthesized and used in obstetrics to induce labor and control postnatal hemorrage.

paired comparison A method of testing infant memory by showing the baby a new stimulus either to the right or left and then an old stimulus on the opposite side.

palmar grasp A newborn's normal reflexive response when a finger or thin object is pressed into the palm; the muscles in the hand flex so tightly that those in the upper arm and forearm flex too, and the infant can briefly suspend his or her weight.

parallel play Play in which two children are side by side using similar toys in similar ways, but their activities are not related.

parasomnias Sleep disorders.

parity The number of children previously borne by a mother; can affect the course of a child's prenatal development, birth, and infancy.

pelvic inflammatory disease (PID) Sexually transmitted infection of the female's reproductive organs; may cause infertility.

permissive parent A parent who gives children as much freedom as possible and allows them to do virtually what they want. The permissive parent does not state or enforce rules and gives children few responsibilities.

personal fable Adolescents' belief in their personal uniqueness and indestructibility.

pessary Any vaginal contraceptive.

personality The unique and consistent way in which an individual behaves and approaches the world. The complex of traits distinguishing one person from all others.

phallic stage In Freud's theory of psychosexual development, the period in which the genital area gives physiological pleasure and is of interest to the preschool child.

phenotype All the observable characteristics of the individual that depend on how the environment has affected expression of the genotype.

phenylketonuria (PKU) An inherited inability to produce a liver enzyme that metabolizes phenylalanine, which is contained in most protein foods; the buildup of phenylalanine and phenylpyruvic acid in body fluids damages the brain and causes restlessness and agitation. A special diet will prevent much of the retardation.

phocomelia The condition of having extremely short limbs so that feet and hands arise close to the trunk; the principal deformity of children whose mothers took the tranquilizer thalidomide in the 1960s.

phoneme The smallest unit of sound that signals a difference in meaning in a particular language.

phonic method A method of teaching children to read in which they are instructed to sound out words letter by letter.

phylogeny The evolution of a race or genetically related group as distinguished from the development of the individual.

placebo An inert substance given to a naive subject who believes it to be medication; used to distinguish effects with a physiological cause from those with a psychological cause.

placenta The disk-shaped structure rich in blood vessels by which the circulation of the embryo and then the fetus interlocks with that of the mother, allowing food and oxygen to diffuse into the conceptus and carrying away its body wastes.

pneumograph A device for recording chest movements during respiration.

polygenic trait A characteristic that is produced by the equal and cumulative effects of several genes, for example, skin color, body shape, intelligence, and memory.

postconventional moral reasoning Kohlberg's highest level of moral reasoning in which the person chooses and follows universal principles, realizing that some of the rules of society can be broken.

postterm babies Infants born later than normal, more than 293 days after the first day of the mother's last menstrual period.

practice effects Distortions of the behavior of subjects in long-term research by their becoming used to testing. The results of the research may be affected.

preconventional moral reasoning Kohlberg's first level of moral reasoning in which the child obeys rules to avoid punishment and to secure a fair exchange with others.

preoperational period In Piaget's theory, the second stage in the development of logical thinking, lasting from approximately 2 to 7 years of age, in which the child begins to employ mental symbols, to engage in symbolic play, and to use words. Thought remains egocentric in nature, and the child focuses on the striking states and conditions of objects and events, ignoring others. The child cannot think by operations, cannot logically manipulate information.

preterm babies Infants born earlier than normal, in fewer than 259 days after the first day of the mother's last menstrual period.

primary (biological) drive A physiological need of the individual, such as for food or sleep.

primitive streak A thickening caused by the growth of ectodermal cells; gives rise to the mesoderm and ultimately to the brain, the spinal cord, all the nerves and sensory organs, and the skin.

private speech The words young children address to themselves and that probably help them organize and understand their behavior.

profound mental retardation The condition of having no testable IQ and severe physical disabilities.

prosocial Cooperative, helpful, and socially integrative.

proximodistal development A pattern of physical growth and motor development progressing from the spine toward the extremities; in human beings, followed prenatally and throughout childhood.

pseudodialogue A conversation between mother and infant in which the mother pauses for an imagined response from her baby.

pseudoimitation Repetition of another's action by infants of 4 months, who are limited to imitating movements that they have made only shortly before. A term used by Piaget.

psychometrics A branch of psychology measuring mental abilities, traits, and processes; the study of mental testing.

psychosexual development The development of human sexual wishes and behavior in stages from infancy to maturity.

psychosocial development The social, cultural, and sexual aspects of development, first described by Erik Erikson.

psychosocial moratorium In Erikson's life-cycle theory, a period of time in adolescence for establishing identity, for finding a role, the work, the attitude, and the sense of social connectedness that will allow a person to assume a place in adult society.

puberty The period when the reproductive system matures and the secondary sex characteristics develop.

punishment In operant learning theory, the unpleasant consequences that get people and other animals to decrease behavior.

pyloric stenosis A condition of newborns, usually males, in which the opening from the stomach to the intestines closes, preventing digestion of food. Pyloric stenosis is corrected surgically.

quickening The first motion of a fetus in the uterus felt by the mother, usually between the 4th and 5th month.

reaction range The extent to which the expression of a genotype in a phenotype is affected by the environment.

recall A form of memory in which one must retrieve information seen or heard before without prompts from the external environment.

recessive gene In a pattern of genetic inheritance, a gene that must be paired with an identical one in order to determine a trait.

recognition Perception that an object, item, or image

is one that has been seen or heard before; the simplest form of memory.

reflection A cognitive style characterized by the weighing of all possible alternatives before an answer to a question is chosen.

reflex An unlearned, involuntary response of a part of the body to an external stimulus.

rehearsal A cognitive strategy for remembering that consists of repeating information until it is fixed in memory.

reinforcement In operant conditioning, an instance in which a response is followed by favorable consequence, increasing the likelihood that the response will be made again.

reliability In psychometrics, the consistency of a test as a measuring device; for example, if all the items on a test do a good job of predicting the total score.

replicability Repeatability of research results if a study is done again.

representative sample A group of subjects who accurately represent the composition of the entire population in which a researcher is interested.

restraining effect The maternal influences that keep a fetus with a genotype for large size small enough to develop in and be born from the uterus of a small mother.

retina The part of the eye that transforms light into nerve signals to the brain.

reversibility In Piaget's theory, the principle that one manipulation of an object can be reversed by applying the opposite.

rhythm method A method of preventing pregnancy that relies on abstinence from sexual intercourse during a female's fertile periods.

ribonucleic acid (RNA) A complex chemical substance that is able to use the information in DNA molecules to assemble proteins.

ribosomes The part of cells containing RNA and producing proteins necessary for the growth and survival of cells.

Ritalin A stimulant that is administered to hyperactive children and enables them to focus longer on tasks.

ritual play Repetitive, rhythmic exchanges or turns, found in preschoolers' play.

robust Strong (research results).

rooming in Procedure in which a newborn infant remains in the mother's hospital or birthing center room during the daytime, from soon after birth until they go home.

rooting reflex A newborn's normal reflexive response to a nipple on its cheek; the infant turns its head and starts to suck.

rubella (German measles) A mild form of measles; if contracted by a woman during the embryonic period of her pregnancy, may cause blindness, deafness, heart malformations, and mental retardation in her child.

saccadic eye movements (saccades) Small sideways movements of the eyes from one point of fixation to another. Saccadic eye movements move the eyes to objects of focus during visual scanning and reading.

scheme In Piaget's theory, a basic unit of knowledge, which may be an observable pattern of action or an image of an object.

schizophrenia The most common and severe psychosis, which may show itself in adolescence. The symptoms are jumbled thoughts and speech, flat or inappropriate emotions, hallucinations and delusions, loss of contact with reality.

scientific method A method for generating hypotheses and empirically testing them; extraneous factors are systematically eliminated, and factors under study are rigorously controlled by the investigator.

scoliosis Lateral curvature of the spine.

secondary sex characteristics Bodily and physiological signs of maleness and femaleness, other than the sex organs, which emerge during pubescence and indicate physical maturity—breast development, pubic and facial hair, voice changes.

secure attachment A relationship of an infant to his or her caregiver in which there is a good balance between exploration and proximity seeking.

self-concept The individual's sense of his or her identity as a person, beginning with the infant's discovery of parts of the body and then between 1 and 2 years of age the child's recognition of selfhood, of differentiation from others. Later self-concepts include the qualities and traits that individuals think are characteristic of themselves.

self-esteem One's high or low opinion of oneself.

self-righting tendency A regulative mechanism promoting normal prenatal development, overcoming all but the most adverse circumstances.

sensitive period An interval of time during which a very young animal is supposedly predisposed to learn particular behavior, according to ethologists.

sensorimotor period In Piaget's theory, the period of cognitive growth from birth to approximately 2 years of age during which knowledge is acquired through sensory perceptions and motor skills. Babies show their intelligence through ingenious actions and ways of handling objects.

seriation The process of arranging similar objects in a series according to the one quantified way in which they vary (e.g., arranging sticks from long to short). Multiple seriation is the process of arranging similar objects in a series according to the two or more quantified ways in which they vary (e.g., arranging glasses in columns from short to tall and in rows from narrow to wide).

set goal The degree of proximity to mother required by a particular child. The child's natural predisposition to seek proximity is modified by what his or her past experiences with mother have been.

severe mental retardation The condition of having an IQ score between 25 and 39 and related physical disabilities.

sex constancy The understanding that one cannot change sex at will or over time. Children only gradually acquire a notion of sex constancy that is based on their immutable anatomy.

sex-linked trait A trait inherited through genes located on the sex chromosomes.

sexual scripts Social norms about how people are to act sexually and about when and with whom to do sexual things; sexual scripts differ for adolescent boys and girls.

sexually transmitted disease (STD) Any of a number of diseases passed from one person to another during intimate contact.

shape constancy The tendency for an object viewed from different angles, which distort the retinal images, to be perceived as having a constant shape.

short-term memory Storage of information for a few seconds to a minute.

sickle-cell anemia An inherited blood abnormality in which the defective hemoglobin molecules crystallize and stick together to form elongated bundles of rods when oxygen level is low. The red blood cells sickle, causing blockage in capillary beds and bringing fever and pain to chest, abdomen, and joints.

sign According to Piaget, a shared, conventional symbol, including words, that children can use only after they have gone through stages of thinking in personal symbols.

sight–word method A method of teaching children to read in which they are taught to recognize whole words rather than to sound out the letters and blend them together.

sleep enuresis Bed wetting.

sleep terrors A sleep disturbance of children that involves loud crying, racing pulse, but little memory for the episode.

small for dates Babies who are born at full term but who have low birth weights.

social conventions Rules of conduct, attitude, or behavior in a society, culture, or subculture, such as table manners, a style of dress, a form of address.

social referencing The act of seeking cues from others about how to behave in unfamiliar situations.

social understanding The capacity to understand and communicate with the people in one's social world, to interpret their emotions and intentions, and to apply social rules and norms.

sociobiology The school of thought that posits a genetic basis to social behavior.

speeded labor Uterine contractions that are sped up by the administration of drugs.

sperm (spermatozoa) Male gametes or reproductive cells.

standard deviation A statistical index of the variability within a distribution. It is the square root of the average of the squared deviation from the mean.

statistical significance The magnitude of difference that has little probability, of occurring by chance alone and therefore should be accepted as real.

stepping reflex Reflex in which the young infant seems to walk.

storm and stress Translation of the German phrase, *Sturm und Drang*, used by early psychologists to characterize the presumed disruptions and extremism of adolescence. Now widely regarded as a stereotyped view, it survives nevertheless.

stranger anxiety The baby's wariness of unfamiliar people, beginning when he or she is 4 to 6 months old and peaking at the end of the first year.

strange situation A standard laboratory method for assessing the attachment of children 12 to 18 months old to their mother. The child is observed in a playroom with mother and a stranger, alone with the stranger, reunited with mother, alone in the room, then with the stranger again, then reunited with mother.

structured class A traditional class in which children spend most of their time on lessons, usually in the ''basics,'' the three R's. They are generally in their seats at desks or tables arranged in neat rows, receiving instruction from the teacher. Subject matter is from a set curriculum established for the class as a whole.

structured observation Research conducted with subjects in situations set up by a researcher.

sucking reflex A newborn's reflexive response to anything that touches its lips; the infant immediately starts to suck.

sudden infant death syndrome (SIDS) The sudden and unexplained death of apparently healthy babies who are usually between 2 and 4 months old. They stop breathing during sleep.

superego In Freud's theory, the conscience that develops through identification with the parent. The imposition of civilization and culture as filtered through parents' rules and the regulations of adult society.

surrogate mother In animal experiments, an artificial mother (e.g., one made of wire or cloth) to test the infant's reactions to having only some of its needs of mother fulfilled. In human beings, a woman who agrees by contract to bear a child for a biological father and an adoptive mother and to give them the infant after birth.

symbol A sound, written word, object, action, or drawing that stands for or signifies something else.

symbolic play The pretending and make-believe of young children.

synapse The very small gap between the axon terminals of one neuron and a dendrite or cell body of another across which the nerve impulse passes.

syntax Rules of a specific language by which words, and morphemes, are combined to form larger units such as clauses and sentences.

syphilis A sexually transmitted disease caused by a spirochete; found in males and females. The first symptom is a hard sore in the genital region. Untreated, syphilis has a clinical course of three stages continued over many years.

Tay-Sachs disease A recessive-gene disorder of fat metabolism causing severe mental retardation, muscular weakness, eventual blindness, and death, usually in the 3rd year. Found for the most part in Jewish families of Northeastern European ancestry.

telegraphic sentences The two-word and three-word sentences of young children, which contain only the most necessary words.

temperament A basic and apparently largely inherited behavior pattern of an infant or older person; the natural disposition of an individual.

teratogen An external agent that may cross the barrier of the placenta and harm the developing embryo or fetus.

teratology The study of serious malformations and deviations from the normal in animals and plants. Now applied to human beings with the goal of understanding the causes of abnormalities and anticipating risks in prenatal development.

terrible twos An age at which children test their autonomy in the world; their bad behavior consists of negativism and temper tantrums, their good of growing independence and mastery of their surroundings.

testis The typically paired male reproductive organ, which is located in the scrotum and in which sperm develop after puberty.

test-tube baby A baby born as a result of in vitro fertilization.

tonic neck reflex The newborn's normal reflexive response when placed on its back; the infant turns its head to one side and assumes a fencing position, extends arm and leg on this side, bends opposite limbs, and arches body away from the direction faced.

totipotent The ability of a cell formed during the first 60 hours of cell division after fertilization to develop into a complete person if separated from the zygote.

toxemia (of pregnancy) A disorder that usually has its onset in the last trimester; symptoms are persistent nausea and vomiting or, in preeclampsia, hypertension, sudden and rapid increase in weight through retention of water in the tissues, and albumin in the urine.

transductive reasoning In Piaget's theory, preoperational children's logic in which they reason from the particular to the particular without generalization.

transitive inference The mathematical notion that if A equals (or is greater than) B and B equals (or is greater than) C, it follows that A equals (or is greater than) C. Children begin to be able to make transitive inferences toward the end of the concrete operational period if they have visual aids. An abstract transitive inference is a formal operation.

Turner's syndrome A disorder of females in which absence of an X chromosome keeps stature short, ovaries rudimentary, and prevents secondary sexual characteristics from developing.

tympanum The eardrum.

Type A Behavior pattern of people who act hurriedly, aggressively, intensely, and competitively.

Type B Behavior pattern of people who act more slowly than Type A people and are relatively free of pressure.

ultrasound A wave phenomenon of the same physical nature as sound but with frequencies above the range of human hearing. Can be used to picture a fairly detailed outline of the fetus.

umbilical cord The organ connecting fetus to pregnant mother through which nutrients, waste, and other substances are transferred between their bloodstreams.

underextension Children's tendency to use a word too narrowly, such as applying the word ''cat'' only to the family cat and not to cats in the alley, on television, or in picture books.

uterus An organ in female mammals, resembling, when not pregnant, a flattened pear in size and shape; contains and nourishes the young during development previous to birth.

validity The ability of a test or other instrument to measure what it is supposed to measure.

vernix A white, pasty substance made up of the fetus's shed dead-skin cells and fatty substances from oil glands; serves as a protective coating.

villus On the surface of the chorion, a rootlike extension that may grow into the lining of the uterine wall during implantation and rupture the small blood vessels it meets.

visual cliff A laboratory structure for testing infants' depth perceptions; it consists of a glass-topped table with a middle runway, on one side of which there appears to be a drop.

Wernicke's area The part of the brain that coordinates seeing and hearing.

withdrawal An ineffective method of preventing pregnancy that relies on the male withdrawing from the female's vagina before ejaculating.

X chromosome A sex chromosome that, when combined with another X chromosome, carries the genetic information necessary for the development of a female.

XYY syndrome A condition of males in which an extra Y chromosome causes unusual tallness, facial acne at adolescence, and mental dullness. The syndrome has sometimes been associated with antisocial behavior.

Y chromosome A sex chromosome that, when combined with an X chromosome, carries the genetic information necessary for the development of a male.

zygote A single cell formed through the union of two gametes, a sperm and an ovum; in time the human zygote will develop into a human being.

References

ABER, L. The transition from attachment to autonomy concerns in early development: The influence of stage-specific parenting competencies. *Infant Behavior and Development*, 1986, *9* (Special Issue: Abstracts of papers presented at the Fifth International Conference on Infant Studies), 16.

ABIKOFF, H., GITTELMAN-KLEIN, R., AND KLEIN, D. F. Classroom observation code for hyperactive children: A replication of validity. *Journal of Consulting and Clinical Psychology*, 1980, *48*, 555–565.

ABRAMOVITCH, R., CORTER, C., PEPLER, D., AND STANHOPE, L. Sibling and peer interaction: A final follow-up and a comparison. *Child Development*, 1986, *57*, 217–229.

ABRAMOVITCH, R., PEPLER, D., AND CORTER, C. Patterns of sibling interaction among preschool-age children. In M. Lamb and B. Sutton-Smith (Eds.), *Sibling relationships: Their nature and significance across the lifespan*. Hillsdale, N.J.: Lawrence Erlbaum Associates, 1982.

ABRAVANEL, E., AND GINGOLD, H. Learning via observation during the second year of life. *Developmental Psychology*, 1985, *21*, 614–623.

ABRAVANEL, E., AND SIGAFOOS, A. Exploring the presence of imitation during early infancy. *Child Development*, 1984, *55*, 381–392.

ACREDOLO, C., ADAMS, A., AND SCHMID, J. On the understanding of the relationships between speed, duration, and distance. *Child Development*, 1984, *55*, 2151–2159.

ACREDOLO, L. P., AND HAKE, J. L. Infant perception. In B. B. Wolman and G. Strickler (Eds.), *Handbook of developmental psychology*. Englewood Cliffs, N.J.: Prentice-Hall, 1982.

ADAMS, G., AND COHEN, A. Children's physical and interpersonal characteristics that affect student-teacher interaction. *Journal of Experimental Education*, 1974, *43*, 1–5.

ADAMS, G. R., AND JONES, R. M. Female adolescents' identity development: Age comparisons and perceived child-rearing experience. *Developmental Psychology*, 1983, *19*, 249–256.

ADAMS, J. F. Earlier menarche, greater height and weight: A stimulation-stress factor hypothesis. *Genetic Psychology Monographs*, 1981, *104*, 3–22.

ADAMS, R. E., AND PASSMAN, R. H. Effects of visual and auditory aspects of mothers and strangers on the play and exploration of children. *Developmental Psychology*, 1979, *15*, 269–274.

ADAMS, R. J., AND MAURER, D. *A demonstration of color perception in the newborn*. Paper presented at the meetings of the Society for Research in Child Development, Detroit, April 1983.

ADAMS, R. J., AND MAURER, D. *The use of habituation to study newborns' color vision*. Paper presented at the Fourth International Conference on Infant Studies, New York, April 1984.

ADAMS, R. S., AND BIDDLE, B. J. *An analysis of classroom activities: A final report* (ERIC Document: EDO 15537). Columbia: Missouri University, 1967.

ADELSON, J. The political imagination of the young adolescent. In J. Kagan and R. Coles (Eds.), *12 to 16: Early adolescence*. New York: Norton, 1972.

ADELSON, J. The development of ideology in adolescence. In S. E. Dragastin and G. H. Elder Jr. (Eds.), *Adolescence in the life cycle*. Washington D.C.: Hemisphere, 1975.

ADELSON, J. Rites of passage. *American Educator*, Summer 1982, p. 6 ff.

ADELSON, J., GREEN, B., AND O'NEIL, R. P. The growth of the idea of law in adolescence. *Developmental Psychology*, 1969, *1*, 327–332.

ADKINS, D. C., PAYNE, F. D., AND BALLIF, B. Motivation factor scores and response set scores for ten ethnic-cultural groups of preschool children. *American Educational Research Journal*, 1972, *9*, 557–572.

AHLGREN, A. Sex differences in the correlates of cooperative and competitive school attitudes. *Developmental Psychology*, 1983, *19*, 881–888.

AHRENTZEN, S. The environmental and social context of distraction in the classroom. In A. E. Osterberg, C. P. Tiernan, and R. A. Findlay (Eds.), *Design research interactions*. Ames, Iowa: Environmental Design Research Association, 1981.

AIELLO, J. R., NICOSIA, G., AND THOMPSON, D. E. Physiological, social, and behavioral consequences of crowding on children and adolescents. *Child Development*, 1979, *50*, 195–202.

AINSLIE, R. C., AND ANDERSON, C. W. Day care children's relationship to their mothers and caregivers: An inquiry into the conditions for the development of attachment. In R. C. Ainslie (Ed.), *The child and the day care setting*. New York: Praeger, 1984.

AINSWORTH, M. D. S. *Infancy in Uganda: Infant care and the growth of love*. Baltimore: Johns Hopkins University Press, 1967.

AINSWORTH, M. D. S. The development of infant-mother attachment. In B. M. Caldwell and H. N. Ricciuti (Eds.), *Review of child development research*, Volume 3. Chicago: University of Chicago Press, 1973.

AINSWORTH, M. D. S., BLEHAR, M., WATERS, E., AND WALL, S. *Patterns of attachment: Observations in the strange situation and at home*. Hillsdale, N.J.: Lawrence Erlbaum Associates, 1978.

ALAN GUTTMACHER INSTITUTE. *Eleven million teenagers*. New York: Alan Guttmacher Institute, 1976.

ALAN GUTTMACHER INSTITUTE. *Teenage pregnancy: The problem that hasn't gone away*. New York: Alan Guttmacher Institute, 1981.

ALLAND, A., JR. *Playing with form*. New York: Columbia University Press, 1983.

ALLEN, J. *Visual acuity development in human infants up to 6 months of age*. Unpublished doctoral dissertation, University of Washington, 1978.

ALTUS, W. D. Birth order and its sequelae. *Science*, 1966, *151*, 44–49.

AMBROSE, J. A. The development of the smiling response in early infancy. In B. M. Foss (Ed.), *Determinants of infant behavior*. New York: Wiley, 1961.

ANASTASI, A. *Psychological testing* (2nd ed.). New York: Macmillan, 1976.

ANDERSON, D. R., AND LEVIN S. R. Young children's attention to *Sesame Street*. *Child Development*. 1976, *47*, 806–811.

ANDERSON, G. C. *Crying in newborn infants: Physiology and developmental implications*. Paper presented at the International Conference on Infant Studies, New York, April 1984.

ANDERSON, J. G., AND JOHNSON, W. H. Stability and change among three generations of Mexican-Americans: Factors affecting achievement. *American Educational Research Journal*. 1971, *8*, 285–309.

ANDRES, D., AND WALTERS, R. H. Modification of delay of punishment effects through cognitive restructuring. In *Proceedings of the 78th Annual Convention of the American Psychological Association*, 1970.

ANDREWS, L. B. Yours, mine, and theirs. *Psychology Today*, December 1984, 20–29.

ANDREWS, S. R., BLUMENTHAL, J. B., JOHNSON, D. L., KAHN, A. J., FERGUSON, C. J., LASATER, T. M., MALONE, P. E., AND WALLACE, D. B. The skills of mothering: A study of Parent Child Development Centers. *Monographs of the Society for Research in Child Development*, 1982, *47* (6, Serial No. 198).

ANGLE, C. R., AND MCINTIRE, M. S. Paper presented at the International Conference on Heavy Metals in the Environment, Toronto, 1975.

ANGLE, C. R., MCINTIRE, M. S., AND VEST, G. Blood lead of Omaha school children—topographic correlation with industry, traffic and housing. *Nebraska Medical Journal*, 1975, *60*, 97–102.

ANGLIN, J. M. *The growth of word meaning*. Research Monograph 63. Cambridge, Mass.: MIT Press, 1970.

ANGLIN, J. M. The child's first terms of reference. In S. Ehrlich and E. Tulving (Eds.), *Bulletin de Psychologie* (Special Issue on Semantic Memory), 1975.

ANGLIN, J. M. *Word, object, and conceptual development*. New York: Norton, 1977.

ANNIS, L. F. *The child before birth*. Ithaca, N.Y.: Cornell University Press, 1978.

APGAR, V., AND BECK, J. *Is my baby all right?* New York: Pocket Books, 1974.

APPEL, Y. H. Developmental differences in children's perception of maternal socialization behavior. *Child Development*, 1977, *48*, 1689–1693.

APPLETON, T., CLIFTON, R., AND GOLDBERG, S. The development of behavioral competence in infancy. In F. D. Horowitz (Ed.), *Review of child development research*, Volume 4. Chicago: University of Chicago Press, 1975.

ARCHER, S. L. Identity and the choice of social roles. In. A. S. Waterman (Ed.), *Identity in adolescence: Processes and contents. New Directions for child development*, No. 30. San Francisco: Jossey-Bass, 1985.

AREND, R., GOVE, F. L., AND SROUFE, L. A. Continuity of individual adaptation from infancy to kindergarten: A predictive study of ego-resiliency and curiosity in preschoolers. *Child Development*, 1979, *50*, 950–959.

ARIES, P. *Centuries of childhood*. New York: Random House, 1962.

ARMENTROUT, J. A. Sociometric classroom popularity and children's reports of parental child-rearing behaviors. *Psychological Reports*, 1972, 30, 261–262.

ARMITAGE, S. E., BALDWIN, B. A., AND VINCE, N. A. The fetal sound environment of sheep. *Science*, 1980, *208*, 1173–1174.

ASCIONE, F., AND CHAMBERS, J. Video game behavior. *Psychology Today*, (Sept) 1985, 19, p. 16.

ASHER, S., AND RENSHAW, P. Children without friends: Social knowledge and social skill training. In S. R. Asher and J. M. Gottman (Eds.), *The development of children's friendships*. New York: Cambridge University Press, 1981.

ASHER, S. T. Topic interest and children's reading comprehension. In R. J. Spiro, B. C. Bruce, and W. F. Brewer (Eds.), *Theoretical issues in reading comprehension*. Hillsdale, N.J.: Lawrence Erlbaum Associates, 1980.

ASHMEAD, D. H., AND PERLMUTTER, M. Infant memory in everyday life. In M. Perlmutter (Ed.), *New directions in child development: Children's memory*. San Francisco: Jossey-Bass, 1980.

ASLIN, R. N., PISONI, D. B., AND JUSCZYK, P. W. Auditory development and speech perception in infancy. In P. H. Mussen (Ed.), *Handbook of child psychology*, Volume 2. New York: Wiley, 1983.

ASLIN, R. N., AND SINNOTT, J. M. *Frequency discrimination of pure tones in human infants*. Paper presented at the International Conference on Infant Studies, New York, April 1984.

AXELROD, J. Neurotransmitters. *Scientific American*, June 1974, *230*, 59–71.

AXIA, G., AND BARONI, M. R. Linguistic politeness at different age levels. *Child Development*, 1985, *56*, 918–927.

AYMAN-NOLLEY, S. Influences of peer relationships on cooperation and competition in children. Unpublished doctoral dissertation. University of Chicago, 1985.

BABAD, Y. E., ALEXANDER, I. E., AND BABAD, E. Y. Returning the smile of the stranger: Developmental patterns and socialization factors. *Monographs of the Society for Research in Child Development*, 1983, *48* (5, Serial No. 203).

BACH, M. J., AND UNDERWOOD, B. J. Developmental changes in memory attributes. *Journal of Educational Psychology*, 1970, *61*, 292–296.

BACHMAN, J. G. *The American high school student: A profile based on survey data*. Paper presented in Berkeley, June 1982.

BACHMAN, J. G., AND O'MALLEY, P. M. Self-esteem in young men: A longitudinal analysis of the impact of educational and occupational attainment. *Journal of Personality and Social Psychology*, 1977, *35*, 365–380.

BAER, P. E., AND GOLDFARB, G. E. A developmental study of verbal conditioning in children. *Psychological Reports*, 1962, *10*, 175–181.

BAILEY, D. A. Exercise, fitness and physical education for the growing child. *Canadian Journal of Public Health*, 1973, *64*, 421–430.

BAILLARGEON, R. *Reasoning about hidden obstacles: Object permanence in the six-month-old infant*. Paper presented at the International Conference on Infant Studies, New York, April 1984.

BAILLARGEON, R. Young infants' representation of the properties of hidden objects. *Infant Behavior and Development*, 1986, *9* (Special Issue: Abstracts of papers presented at the Fifth International Conference on Infant Studies), 15.

BAIN, B. Verbal regulation of cognitive processes. A replication of Luria's procedures with bilingual and unilingual infants. *Child Development*, 1976, *47*, 543–546.

BAKAN, D. *The duality of human existence*. Chicago: Rand McNally, 1966.

BAKER, A. J. L., AND ABER, L. Reconceptualizing security of attachment in toddlers: Theoretical and methodological issues. *Infant Behavior and Development*, 1986, *9* (Special Issue: Abstracts of papers presented at the Fifth International Conference on Infant Studies), 16.

BAKWIN, H. Sleep-walking in twins. *Lancet*, 1970, *2*, 446–447.

BAKWIN, H. Car-sickness in twins. *Developmental Medicine and Child Neurology*, 1971, *13*, 310–312. (a)

BAKWIN, H. Constipation in twins. *American Journal of Diseases of Children*. 1971, *121*, 179–181. (b)

BAKWIN, H. Nail-biting in twins. *Developmental Medicine and Child Neurology*, 1971, *13*, 304–307. (c)

BAKWIN, H. Enuresis in twins. *American Journal of Diseases of Children*, 1971, *121*, 222–225. (d)

BALLENSKI, C. B., AND COOK, A. S. Mothers' perceptions of their competence in managing selected parenting tasks. *Family Relations*, 1982, *31*, 489–494.

BANDURA, A. The stormy decade: Fact or fiction? *Psychology in the Schools*, 1964, *1*, 224–231.

BANDURA, A. *Principles of behavior modification*. New York: Holt, Rinehart & Winston, 1969. (a)

BANDURA, A. Social-learning theory of identificatory process. In D. A. Goslin (Ed.), *Handbook of socialization theory and research*. Chicago: Rand McNally, 1969. (b)

BANDURA, A. Self-referent thought: A developmental analysis of self-efficacy. In J. H. Flavell and L. Ross (Eds.), *Social cognitive development: Frontiers and possible futures*. Cambridge, England: Cambridge University Press, 1981.

BANDURA, A., AND HUSTON, A. C. Identification as a process of incidental learning. *Journal of Abnormal and Social Psychology*, 1961, *63*, 311–318.

BANDURA, A., ROSS, D. M., AND ROSS, S. A. Transmission of aggression through imitation of aggressive models. *Journal of Abnormal and Social Psychology*, 1961, *63*, 575–582.

BANDURA, A., ROSS, D. M., AND ROSS, S. A. Imitation of film-mediated aggressive models. *Journal of Abnormal and Social Psychology*, 1963, *66*, 3–11.

BANE, M. J., AND JENCKS, C. Five myths about your I.Q. *Harper's Magazine*, February 1973, 28–40.

BANK, S., AND KAHN, M. D. Sisterhood–brotherhood is powerful: Sibling subsystems and family therapy. *Family Process*, 1975, *14*, 311–337.

BANKS, M. S., AND SALAPATEK, P. Infant pattern vision: A new approach based on the contrast sensitivity function. *Journal of Experimental Child Psychology*, 1981, *31*, 1–45.

BANKS, M. S., AND SALAPATEK, P. Infant visual perception. In P. H. Mussen (Ed.), *Handbook of child psychology*, Volume 2. New York: Wiley, 1983.

BARDWICK, J. M. *Psychology of women: A study of biocultural conflicts*.

New York: Harper & Row, 1971.

BARDWICK, J. M., AND DOUVAN, E. Ambivalence: The socialization of women. In V. Gornick and B. K. Moran (Eds.), *Women in sexist society*. New York: Basic Books, 1971.

BARENBOIM, C. Developmental changes in the interpersonal cognitive system from middle childhood to adolescence. *Child Development*, 1977, 48, 1467–1474.

BARENBOIM, C. The development of person perception in childhood and adolescence: From behavioral comparisons to psychological constructs to psychological comparisons. *Child Development*, 1981, 52, 129–144.

BARGLOW, P., VAUGHN, B. E., AND MOLITOR, N. Effects of maternal absence due to employment on the quality of infant–mother attachment in a low risk sample. *Child Development*, in press.

BARNETT, M. A., HOWARD, J. A., MELTON, E. M., AND DINO, G. A. Effect of inducing sadness about self or other on helping behavior in high- and low-empathic children. *Child Development*, 1982, 53, 920–923.

BARR, R., AND DREEBAN, R., WITH WIRATCHAI, N. *How schools work*. Chicago: University of Chicago Press, 1983.

BARRERA, M. E., AND MAURER, D. *The perception of facial expressions by the three-month-old*. Paper presented at the biennial meeting of the Society for Research in Child Development, San Francisco, March 1979.

BARRETT, D. E., AND RADKE-YARROW, M. Prosocial behavior, social inferential ability, and assertiveness in children. *Child Development*, 1977, 48, 475–481.

BARRETT, D. E., RADKE-YARROW, M., AND KLEIN, R. E. Chronic malnutrition and child behavior: Effects of early caloric supplementation on social and emotional functioning at school age. *Developmental Psychology*, 1982, 18, 541–556.

BARRETT, F. M. Sexual experience, birth control usage, and sex education of unmarried Canadian university students: Changes between 1968 and 1978. *Archives of Sexual Behavior*, 1980, 9, 367–390.

BARRY, H., BACON, M. K., AND CHILD, I. L. A cross-cultural survey of some sex differences in socialization. *Journal of Abnormal and Social Psychology*, 1957, 55, 327–332.

BARRY, H., AND PAXSON, L. M. Infancy and early childhood: Cross-cultural codes. *Ethnology*, 1971, 10, 467–508.

BARTLETT, J. C., AND SANTROCK, J. W. Affect-dependent episodic memory in young children. *Child Development*, 1979, 50, 513–518.

BASKETT, L. M. Ordinal position differences in children's family interactions. *Developmental Psychology*, 1984, 20, 1026–1031.

BASKETT, L.M., AND JOHNSON, S. M. The young child's interactions with parents versus siblings: A behavioral analysis. *Child Development*, 1982, 53, 643–650.

BATES, E. *Language and context: The acquisition of pragmatics*. New York: Academic Press, 1976.

BATES, E., MACWHINNEY, B., BASELLI, C., DEVESCOVI, A., NATALE, F., AND VENZA, V. A cross-linguistic study of the development of sentence interpretation strategies. *Child Development*, 1984, 55, 341–354.

BATES, J. E. Detailed progress report on "Difficult infants and their mothers." Unpublished report, Indiana University, 1980. (a)

BATES, J. E. The concept of difficult temperament. *Merrill-Palmer Quarterly*, 1980, 25, 299–319. (b)

BATES, J. E., AND BAYLES, K. Objective and subjective components in mothers' perceptions of their children from age 6 months to 3 years. *Merrill-Palmer Quarterly*, 1984, 30, 111–130.

BATES, J. E., FREELAND, C. A., AND LOUNSBURY, M. L. Measurement of infant difficultness. *Child Development*, 1979, 50, 794–803.

BAUER, D. H. An exploratory study of developmental changes in children's fears. *Journal of Child Psychology and Psychiatry*, 1976, 17, 69–74.

BAUMRIND, D. Current patterns of parental authority. *Developmental Psychology Monographs*, 1971, 4 (1, Part 2).

BAUMRIND, D. Early socialization and adolescent competence. In S. E. Dragastin and G. H. Elder (Eds.), *Adolescence in the life cycle*. New York: Wiley, 1975.

BAUMRIND, D. *Sex related socialization effects*. Paper presented at the biennial meeting of the Society for Research in Child Development, San Francisco, March 1979.

BAUMRIND, D., AND BLACK, A. E. Socialization practices associated with dimensions of competence in preschool boys and girls. *Child Development*, 1967, 38, 291–327.

BAY, E. Ontogeny of stable speech areas in the human brain. In E. H. Lenneberg and E. Lenneberg (Eds.), *Foundations of language development*, Volume 2. New York: Academic Press, 1975.

BAYER, L. M., AND BAYLEY, N. *Growth diagnosis* (2nd ed.). Chicago: University of Chicago Press, 1976. (First edition 1959.)

BAYLEY, N. Mental growth during the first three years: A developmental study of 61 children by repeated tests. *Genetic Psychology Monographs*, 1933, 14, 1–92.

BAYLEY, N. Learning in adulthood: The role of intelligence. In H. J. Klausmeier and C. W. Harris (Eds.), *Analysis of concept learning*. New York: Academic Press, 1966.

BAYLEY, N. Behavioral correlates of mental growth: Birth to thirty-six years. *American Psychologist*, 1968, 23, 1–17.

BAYLEY, N. The development of motor abilities during the first three years. In M. C. Jones, N. Bayley, J. W. McFarlane, and M. P. Honzik (Eds.), *The course of human development*. Waltham, Mass.: Xerox College Publishing, 1971.

BECK, I. L., PERFETTI, C., AND MCKEOWN, M. D. Effects of long-term vocabulary instruction on lexical access and reading comprehension. *Journal of Educational Psychology*, 1982, 74, 506–521.

BECKER, M. H. The health belief model and sick role behavior. In M. H. Becker (Ed.), *The health belief model and personal health behavior*. Thorofare, N.J.: Charles B. Slack, 1974.

BECKER, M. H., NATHANSON, C. A. DRACHMAN, R. H., AND KIRSCHT, J. P. Mothers' health beliefs and children's clinic visits: A prospective study. *Journal of Community Health*, 1977, 3, 125–135.

BECKER, W. C. Consequences of different kinds of parental discipline. In M. L. Hoffman and L. W. Hoffman (Eds.), *Review of child development research*, Volume 1. New York: Russell Sage Foundation, 1964.

BECKWITH, L. Relationships between infants' social behavior and their mothers' behavior. *Child Development*, 1972, 43, 397–411.

BECKWITH, L. Prediction of emotional and social behavior. In J. D. Osofsky (Ed.), *Handbook of infant development*. New York: Wiley, 1979.

BEE, H. L., DISBROW, M. A., JOHNSON-CROWLEY, N., AND BARNARD, K. *Parent-child interactions during teaching in abusing and non-abusing families*. Paper presented at the meeting of the Society for Research in Child Development, Boston, 1981.

BELL, A., WEINBERG, M., AND HAMMERSMITH, S. K. *Sexual preference*. Indianapolis: Indiana University Press (Alfred C. Kinsey Institute for Sex Research Publication), 1981.

BELL, S. M., AND AINSWORTH, M. D. S. Infant crying and maternal responsiveness. *Child Development*, 1972, 43, 1171–1190.

BELSKY, J. Experimenting with the family in the newborn period. *Child Development*, 1985, 56, 407–414.

BELSKY, J., GILSTRAP, B., AND ROVINE, M. The Pennsylvania Infant and Family Development Project, I: Stability and change in mother-infant and father-infant interaction in a family setting at one, three, and nine months. *Child Development*, 1984, 55, 692–705.

BELSKY, J., GOODE, M. K., AND MOST, R. K. Maternal stimulation and infant exploratory competence: Cross-sectional, correlational and experimental analyses. *Child Development*, 1980, 51, 1168–1178.

BELSKY, J., AND ISABELLA, R. Maternal, infant, and social-contextual determinants of attachment security. In J. Belsky and T. Nezworkski (Eds.), *Clinical implications of attachment*. Hillsdale, N.J.: Lawrence Erlbaum Associates, in press.

BELSKY, J., ROVINE, M., AND TAYLOR, D. The Pennsylvania Infant and Family Development Project, III: The origins of individual differences in infant–mother attachment: Maternal and infant contributions. *Child Development*, 1984, 55, 718–728.

BEM, S. L., MARTYNE, W., AND WATSON, C. Sex typing and androgyny: Further explorations of the expressive domain. *Journal of Personality and Social Psychology*, 1976, *34*, 1016–1023.

BENBOW, C. P., AND STANLEY, J. C. Sex differences in mathematical ability: Fact or artifact. *Science*, 1980, *210*, 1262.

BENN, R. K. *Factors associated with security of attachment in dual career families.* Paper presented at the biennial meetings of the Society for Research in Child Development, Toronto, 1985.

BENNETT, N. *Teaching styles and pupil progress.* London: Open Books, 1976.

BENNETT, W., AND GURIN, J. *The dieter's dilemma: Eating less and weighing more.* New York: Basic Books, 1982.

BEN-ZEEV, S. The influence of bilingualism on cognitive strategy and cognitive development. *Child Development*, 1977, *48*, 1009–1018.

BEREITER, C., AND SCARDAMALIA, M. From conversation to composition: The role of instruction in a developmental process. In R. Glaser (Ed.), *Advances in instructional psychology*, Volume 2. Hillsdale, N.J.: Lawrence Erlbaum Associates, 1982.

BERENBAUM, S. A., AND RESNICK, S. Somatic androgyny and cognitive abilities. *Developmental Psychology*, 1982, *18*, 418–423.

BERENDA, R. W. *The influence of the group on the judgments of children.* New York: King's Crown Press, 1950.

BERENTHAL, B., AND PROFFITT, D. The extraction of structure from motion: Implementation of basic processing constraints. *Infant Behavior and Development*, 1986, *9* (Special Issue: Abstracts of papers presented at the Fifth International Conference on Infant Studies), 36.

BERK, L. E. Private speech: Learning out loud. *Psychology Today*, May 1986, 34–42.

BERK, L. E., AND GARVIN, R. A. Development of private speech among low-income Appalachian children. *Developmental Psychology*, 1984, *20*, 771–786.

BERLIN, B., AND KAY, P. *Basic color terms: Their universality and evolution.* Berkeley: University of California Press, 1969.

BERLYNE, D. E. Novelty and curiosity as determinants of exploratory behavior. *British Journal of Psychology*, 1950, *41*, 68–80.

BERLYNE, D. E. Laughter, humor and play. In G. Lindzey and E. Aronson (Eds.), *Handbook of social psychology*, Volume 3. Boston: Addison-Wesley, 1969.

BERMAN, J. L., AND FORD, R. Intelligence quotients and intelligence loss in patients with phenylketonuria and some variant states. *Journal of Pediatrics*, 1970, *77*, 764–770.

BERMAN, P. W., AND GOODMAN, V. Age and sex differences in children's responses to babies: Effects of adults' caretaking requests and instructions. *Child Development*, 1984, *55*, 1071–1077.

BERNAL, J. Crying during the first 10 days of life and maternal responses. *Developmental Medicine and Child Neurology*, 1972, *14*, 362–372.

BERNAL, J., AND RICHARDS, M. P. M. *The effects of bottle and breast feeding on infant development.* Paper presented at the annual conference of the Society for Psychosomatic Research, London, November 1969.

BERNDT, T. J. *Children's conceptions of friendship and the behavior expected of friends.* Paper presented at the annual meeting of the American Psychological Association, Toronto, August 1978. (a)

BERNDT, T. J. *Developmental changes in conformity to parents and peers.* Paper presented at the annual meeting of the American Psychological Association, Toronto, August 1978. (b)

BERNDT, T. J. Developmental changes in conformity to peers and parents. *Developmental Psychology*, 1979, *15*, 608–616.

BERNDT, T. J. The features and effects of friendship in early adolescence. *Child Development*, 1982, *53*, 1447–1460.

BERNDT, T. J. Correlates and causes of sociometric status in childhood: A commentary on six current studies of popular, rejected, and neglected children. *Merrill-Palmer Quarterly*, 1983, *29*, 439–448.

BERNDT, T. J., AND BERNDT, E. G. Children's use of motives and intentionality in person perception and moral judgment. *Child Development*, 1975, *46*, 904–912.

BERNDT, T. J., AND BULLEIT, T. N. Effects of sibling relationships on preschoolers' behavior at home and at school. *Developmental Psychology*, 1985, *21*, 761–767.

BERNDT, T. J., AND HOYLE, S. G. Stability and change in childhood and adolescent friendships. *Developmental Psychology*, 1985, *21*, 1007–1015.

BERNSTEIN, A. C., AND COWAN, P. A. Children's concepts of how people get babies. *Child Development*, 1975, *46*, 77–91.

BERNSTEIN, R. M. The development of the self-system during adolescence. *Journal of Genetic Psychology*, 1980, *136*, 231–245.

BERSCHEID, E., WALSTER, E., AND BOHRENSTEDT, G. Body image. *Psychology Today*, July 1972, 57–66.

BERSCHEID, E., WALSTER, E., AND BOHRNSTEDT, G. Body image: The happy American body. *Psychology Today*, November 1973, 119–131.

BERSHAD, S., RUBINSTEIN, A., PATERNITI, J. R., LE, N., POLIACK, S. C., HELLER, B., GINSBERG, H. N., FLEISCHMAJER, R., AND BROWN, W. V. Changes in plasma lipids and lipoproteins during isotretinoin therapy for acne. *New England Journal of Medicine*, October 17, 1985, *313*, 981–985.

BERTENTHAL, B. I., AND FISCHER, K. W. Development of self-recognition in the infant. *Developmental Psychology*, 1978, *14*, 44–50.

BERTOFF, A. Tolstoy, Vygotsky, and the making of meaning. *College Composition and Communication*, 1978, *29*, 249–255.

BERTONCINI, J., AND MEHLER, J. Syllables as units in infant speech perception. *Infant Behavior and Development*, 1981, *4*, 247–260.

BERZONSKY, M. D. Inter and intraindividual differences in adolescent storm and stress: A life span developmental view. *Journal of Early Adolescence*, 1982, *2*, 211–217.

BEST, D. L., WILLIAMS, J. E., CLOUD, J. M., DAVIS, S. W., ROBERTSON, L. S., EDWARDS, J. R., GILES, H., AND FOWLES, J. Development of sex-trait stereotypes among young children in the United States, England, and Ireland. *Child Development*, 1977, *48*, 1375–1384.

BHATIA, V. P., KATIYAR, G. P., AND AGARWAL, K. N. Effect of intrauterine nutritional deprivation on neuromotor behaviour of the newborn. *Acta Paediatrica Scandinavica*, 1979, *68*, 561–566.

BIBRING, G. L., DWYER, T. F., HUNTINGTON, D. S., AND VALENSTEIN, A. F. A study of the psychological processes in pregnancy and of the earliest mother-child relationship. *Psychoanalytic Study of the Child*, 1961, *16*, 9–24.

BIGELOW, B. J. Children's friendship expectations: A cognitive-developmental study. *Child Development*, 1977, *48*, 246–250.

BIJOU, S. W., AND BAER, P. M. *Child development*, Volume 1. A systematic and empirical theory. New York: Appleton-Century-Crofts, 1961.

BILLER, H. B. The father and personality development: Paternal deprivation and sex-role development. In M. E. Lamb (Ed.), *The role of the father in child development*. New York: Wiley, 1976.

BIRCH, L. L., MARLIN, D. W., AND ROTTER, J. Eating as the "means" activity in a contingency: Effects on young children's food preference. *Child Development*, 1984, *55*, 431–439.

BIRNBAUM, J. A. *Life patterns, personality style and self esteem in gifted family oriented and career committed women.* Unpublished doctoral dissertation, University of Michigan, 1971.

BIXENSTINE, V. E., DE CORTE, M. S., AND BIXENSTINE, B. A. Conformity to peer-sponsored misconduct at four age levels. *Developmental Psychology*, 1976, *12*, 226–236.

BJORK, E. L., AND CUMMINGS, E. M. *The "A, not B" search error in Piaget's theory of object permanence: Fact or artifact?* Paper presented at the meeting of the Psychonomic Society, Phoenix, November 1979.

BJORKLUND, D. F., AND ZEMAN, B. R. Children's organization and metamemory awareness in their recall of familiar information. *Child Development*, 1982, *53*, 799–810.

BLACKBURNE-STOVER, G., BELENKY, M. F., AND GILLIGAN, C. Moral development and reconstructive memory: Recalling a decision to terminate an unplanned pregnancy. *Developmental Psychology*, 1982, *18*, 862–870.

BLACKSTOCK, E. G. Cerebral asymmetry and the development of infantile autism. *Journal of Autism and Childhood Schizophrenia*, 1978, *8*, 339–353.

BLECK, E. E. Cerebral palsy: In E. E. Bleck and D. A. Nagel (Eds.), *Physically handicapped children: A medical atlas for teachers*. New York: Grune and Stratton, 1982.

BLEWITT, P. Dog versus collie: Vocabulary in speech to young children. *Developmental Psychology*, 1983, *19*, 602–609.

BLIZZARD, R. M., THOMPSON, R. G., BAGHDASSARIAN, A., KOWARSKI, A., MIGEON, C. J., AND RODRIQUEZ, A. The interrelationship of steroids, growth hormone and other hormones on pubertal growth. In M. M. Grunch, G. D. Grave, and F. E. Mayer, (Eds.), *Control of the onset of puberty*. New York: John Wiley and Sons, 1974.

BLOCK, J. *Lives through time*. Berkeley: Bancroft Books, 1971.

BLOCK, J. H. Issues, problems, and pitfalls in assessing sex differences: A critical review of *The psychology of sex differences*. *Merrill-Palmer Quarterly*, 1976, *22*, 283–308.

BLOCK, J. H. Differential premises arising from differential socialization of the sexes: Some conjectures. *Child Development*, 1983, *54*, 1335–1354.

BLOOM, B. S. *Developing talent in young people*. New York: Ballantine Books, 1985.

BLOOM, K., RUSSELL, A., AND DAVIS, S. Conversational turn taking: Verbal quality of adult affects vocal quality of infant. *Infant Behavior and Development*, 1986, *9* (Special Issue: Abstracts of papers presented at the Fifth International Conference on Infant Studies), 39.

BLOOM, L. *Language development: Form and function in emerging grammars*. Cambridge, Mass.: MIT Press, 1970.

BLOOM, L., HOOD, L., AND LIGHTBOWN, P. Imitation in language development: If, when, and why. *Cognitive Psychology*, 1974, *6*, 380–428.

BLOS, P. *The young adolescent: Clinical studies*. New York: Free Press, 1974.

BLOTNER, R., AND BEARISON, D. J. Developmental consistencies in socio-moral knowledge: Justice reasoning and altruistic behavior. *Merrill-Palmer Quarterly*, 1984, *30*, 349–367.

BLURTON JONES, N. Categories of child–child interaction. In N. Blurton Jones (Ed.), *Ethological studies of child behaviour*. Cambridge, England: Cambridge University Press, 1972.

BOCCIA, M., AND CAMPOS, J. *Maternal emotional signalling: Its effect on infants' reaction to strangers*. Paper presented at the meeting of the Society for Research in Child Development, Detroit, April 1983.

BOGATZ, G. A., AND BALL, S. *The second year of Sesame Street: A continuing evaluation*. Princeton, N.J.: Educational Testing Service, 1971.

BOHANNON, J. N., III, AND MARQUIS, A. L. Children's control of adult speech. *Child Development*, 1977, *48*, 1002–1008.

BOLES, D. B. X-linkage of spatial ability: A critical review. *Child Development*, 1980, *51*, 625–635.

BONVILLIAN, J. D., AND NELSON, K. E. Exceptional cases of language acquisition. In K. E. Nelson (Ed.), *Children's language*, Volume 3. Hillsdale, N.J.: Lawrence Erlbaum Associates, 1982.

BORKE, H. Interpersonal perception of young children: Egocentrism or empathy? *Development Psychology*, 1971, *5*, 263–269.

BORKE, H. Piaget's mountains revisited: Changes in the egocentric landscape. *Developmental Psychology*, 1975, *11*, 240–243.

BORNSTEIN, M. H. Qualities of color vision in infancy. *Journal of Experimental Child Psychology*, 1975, *19*, 401–419.

BORNSTEIN, M. H. *Infant attention and caregiver stimulation*. Paper presented at the International Conference on Infant Studies, New York, April 1984.

BORNSTEIN, M. H. How infant and mother jointly contribute to developing cognitive competence in the child. *Proceedings of the Na-*

tional Academy of Sciences of the United States of America, 1985, *82*, 7470–7473.

BORNSTEIN, M. H. Human infant color vision and color perception. *Infant Behavior and Development*, 1985, *8*, 109–113. (b)

BORNSTEIN, M. H., AND SIGMAN, M. D. Continuity in mental development from infancy. *Child Development*, 1986, *57*, 251–274.

BOSKIND-LODAHL, M. Cinderella's stepsisters: A feminist perspective on anorexia nervosa and bulimia. *Signs*, 1976, *2*, 315–320.

BOWER, T. G. R., BROUGHTON, J. M., AND MOORE, M. K. Infant responses to approaching objects: An indicator of response to distal variables. *Perception and Psychophysics*, 1970, *9*, 193–196.

BOWER, T. G. R., AND WISHART, J. G. The effects of motor skill on object permanence. *Cognition*, 1972, *1*, 165–172.

BOWERMAN, C. E., AND KINCH, J. W. Changes in family and peer orientation of children between the fourth and tenth grades. *Social Forces*, 1956, *37*, 206–211.

BOWLBY, J. *Maternal care and mental health*. World Health Organization Monograph 2. Geneva: World Health Organization, 1951.

BOWLBY, J. *Attachment and loss*, Volume 1. *Attachment*. New York: Basic Books, 1969.

BOWLBY, J. *Attachment and loss*, Volume 2. *Separation*. New York: Basic Books, 1973.

BRACEY, G. W. Some reservations about minimum competency testing. In T. C. Hunt (Ed.), *Society, culture, and schools: The American approach*. Garrett Park, Md.: Garrett Park Press, 1979.

BRACKBILL, Y. Extinction of the smiling response in infants as a function of reinforcement schedule. *Child Development*, 1958, *29*, 115–124.

BRACKBILL, Y. Obstetrical medication and infant behavior. In J. D. Osofsky (Ed.), *Handbook of infant development*. New York: Wiley, 1979.

BRADLEY, R. H., AND CALDWELL, B. M. 174 children: A study of the relationship between home environment and cognitive development during the first 5 years. In A. W. Gottfried (Ed.), *Home environment and early cognitive development*. San Francisco: Academic Press, 1984.

BRADLEY, R. H., CALDWELL, B. M., AND ELARDO, R. Home environment, social status, and mental test performance. *Journal of Educational Psychology*, 1977, *69*, 697–701.

BRADLEY, R. H., AND CASEY, P. M. Home environments of low SES non-organic failure-to-thrive infants. *Merrill-Palmer Quarterly*, 1984, *30*, 393–402.

BRADLEY-JOHNSON, S., JOHNSON, C. M., SHANAHAN, R. M., RICKERT, V. C., AND TARDONA, D. R. Effects of token reinforcement on WISC-R performance of black and white, low socioeconomic second graders. *Behavioral Assessment*, 1984, *6*, 365–373.

BRADSHAW, D. L., CAMPOS, J. J., AND KLINNERT, M. D. Emotional expressions as determinants of infants' immediate and delayed responses to prohibitions. *Infant Behavior and Development*, 1986, *9* (Special Issue: Abstracts of papers presented at the Fifth International Conference on Infant Studies), 46.

BRADY, J. E., NEWCOMB, A. F., AND HARTUP, W. W. Context and companions' behavior as determinants of cooperation and competition in school-age children. *Journal of Experimental Child Psychology*, 1983, *36*, 396–412.

BRAINE, M. D. S., HEIMER, C. B., WORTIS, H., AND FREEDMAN, A. M. Factors associated with impairment of the early development of prematures. *Monographs of the Society for Research in Child Development*, 1966, *31* (4, Serial No. 106).

BRAINE, M. D. S., AND RUMAIN, B. Logical reasoning. In P. H. Mussen (Ed.), *Handbook of child psychology*, Volume 3. New York: Wiley, 1983.

BRAINERD, C. J. *Piaget's theory of intelligence*. Englewood Cliffs, N.J.: Prentice-Hall, 1978.

BRAINERD, C. J. Varieties of strategy training in Piagetian concept learning. In M. Pressley and J. L. Levin (Eds.), *Cognitive strategy research: Educational applications*. New York: Springer-Verlag,

1983.

BRANIGAN, G. Some reasons why successive single word utterances are not. *Journal of Child Language,* 1979, *6,* 443–458.

BRANSFORD, J. D., AND MCCARRELL, N. S. A sketch of a cognitive approach to comprehension: Some thoughts about what it means to comprehend. In W. B. Weimer and D. S. Palermo (Eds.), *Cognition and symbolic processes.* Hillsdale, N.J.: Lawrence Erlbaum Associates, 1974.

BRASK, B. H. The need for hospital beds for psychotic children. *Ugeskrift for Laeger,* 1967, *129,* 1559–1570.

BRAZELTON, T. B. Psychophysiologic reactions in the neonate: II. Effects of maternal medication on the neonate and his behavior. *Journal of Pediatrics,* 1961, *58,* 513–518.

BRAZELTON, T. B. *Infants and mothers.* New York: Delacorte Press/ Seymour Lawrence, 1969.

BRAZELTON, T. B., TRONICK, E., ADAMSON, L., ALS, H., AND WISE, S. Early mother–infant reciprocity. In *Parent-infant interaction,* Ciba Foundation Symposium 33. Amsterdam: Associated Scientific Publishers, 1975.

BRENNAN, W. M., AMES, E. W., AND MOORE, R. W. Age differences in infants' attention to patterns of different complexities. *Science,* 1965, *151,* 1354–1356.

BRENT, L. Radiations and other physical agents. In J. G. Wilson and F. C. Fraser (Eds.), *Handbook of teratology.* New York: Plenum, 1977.

BRETHERTON, I. Making friends with one-year-olds: An experimental study of infant-stranger interaction. *Merrill-Palmer Quarterly,* 1978, *24,* 29–52.

BRICKMAN, A. S., MCMANUS, M., GRAPETINE, W. L., AND ALESSI, N. Neuropsychological assessment of seriously delinquent adolescents. *Journal of the American Academy of Child Psychiatry,* 1984, *23,* 453–457.

BRIDGES, K. M. B. *The social and emotional development of the pre-school child.* London: Routledge, 1931.

BRITTAIN, C. Adolescent choices and parent-peer cross-pressures. *American Sociological Review,* 1963, *28,* 385–391.

BRITTAIN, C. Age and sex of siblings and conformity toward parents versus peers in adolescence. *Child Development,* 1966, *37,* 709–714.

Brody, E. B., and Brody, N. *Intelligence: Nature, determinants and consequences.* New York: Academic Press, 1976.

BRODY, G. H., STONEMAN, Z., MACKINNON, C. E., AND MACKINNON, R. Role relationships and behavior between preschool-aged and school-aged sibling pairs. *Development Psychology,* 1985, *21,* 124–129.

BRODY, J. E. TV violence cited as bad influence. *New York Times,* December 7, 1975, p. 20.

BRODY, J. E. Therapy helps teen-age girls having anorexia nervosa. *New York Times,* July 14, 1982, Section 4, p. 20.

BRODY, J. E. Heart attacks and behavior: Early signs are found. *New York Times,* February 14, 1984, Section C, p. 1.

BRODZINSKY, D. M. The role of conceptual tempo and stimulus characteristics in children's humor development. *Developmental Psychology,* 1975, *2,* 843–850.

BRONFENBRENNER, U., ALVAREZ, W. F., AND HENDERSON, C. R., JR. *Working and watching: Maternal employment status and parents' perceptions of their three-year old children.* Unpublished manuscript, Cornell University, 1983.

BRONFENBRENNER, U., AND CROUTER, A. C. Work and family through time and space. In S. Kamerman and C. D. Hayes (Eds.), *Families that work: Children in a changing world.* Washington, D. C.: National Academy Press, 1982.

BRONSON, G. W. Infants' reactions to unfamiliar persons and novel objects. *Monographs of the Society for Research in Child Development,* 1972, *37* (3, Serial No. 148).

BRONSON, G. W. Aversive reactions to strangers: A dual process interpretation. *Child Development,* 1978, *49,* 495–499.

BRONSON, W. C. Central orientation: A study of behavior organization from childhood to adolescence. *Child Development,* 1966, *37,*

125–155.

BRONSON, W. C. Mother-toddler interaction: A perspective on studying the development of competence. *Merrill-Palmer Quarterly,* 1974, *20,* 275–301.

BROOK, J. S., WHITEMAN, M., AND GORDON, A. S. Stages of drug use in adolescence: Personality, peer, and family correlates. *Developmental Psychology,* 1983, *19,* 269–277.

BROOK, J. S., WHITEMAN, M., GORDON, A. S., AND BROOK, D. W. Identification with paternal attributes and its relationship to the son's personality and drug use. *Child Development,* 1984, *20,* 1111–1119.

BROOKS, J., AND LEWIS, M. Infants' responses to strangers: Midget, adult, and child. *Child Development,* 1976, *47,* 323–332.

BROPHY, J. E. Teacher praise: A functional analysis. *Review Educational Research,* 1981, *51,* 1, 5–12.

BROPHY, J. E., AND EVERTSON, C. M. *Process-product correlations in the Texas Teacher Effectiveness Study: Final report (Research Report 74-4).* Austin, Tex.: Research and Development Center for Teacher Education, 1974.

BROPHY, J. E., AND EVERTSON, C. M. *Learning from teaching: A developmental perspective.* Boston: Allyn & Bacon, 1976.

BROPHY, J. E., AND GOOD, T. L. *Teacher-student relationships: Causes and consequences.* New York: Holt, Rinehart and Winston, 1974.

BROUGHTON, J. Development of concepts of self, mind, reality, and knowledge. *New Directions for Child Development,* 1978, *1,* 75–100.

BROUGHTON, R. Sleep disorders: Disorders of arousal. *Science,* 1968, *159,* 1070–1078.

BROUGHTON, R., AND GAUSTAUT, H. Recent sleep research in enuresis nocturia, sleep walking, sleep terrors, and confusional arousals. In P. Levin and W. Loella (Eds.), *Sleep 1974.* Basel: Karger, 1975.

BROWN, A. L. The development of memory: Knowing, knowing about knowing, and knowing how to know. In H. W. Reese (Ed.), *Advances in child development and behavior,* Volume 10. New York: Academic Press, 1975.

BROWN, A. L., BRANSFORD, J. D., FERRARA, R. A., AND CAMPIONE, J. C. Learning, remembering, and understanding. In P. H. Mussen (Ed.), *Handbook of child psychology,* Volume 3, New York: Wiley, 1983.

BROWN, A. L., AND DAY, J. D. Macrorules for summarizing texts: The development of expertise. *Journal of Verbal Learning and Verbal Behavior,* 1983, *22*(1), 1–14.

BROWN, A. L., DAY, J. D., JONES, R. S. The development of plans for summarizing texts. *Child Development,* 1983, *54,* 968–979.

BROWN, A. L., AND PALINCSAR, A. S. Reciprocal teaching of comprehension strategies: A natural history of one program for enhancing learning. In J. Borkowski and J. D. Day (Eds.), *Intelligence and cognition in special children: Comparative studies of giftedness, mental retardation, and learning disabilities.* New York: Ablex, in press.

BROWN, A. L., AND SMILEY, S. S. Rating the importance of structural units of prose passages: A problem of metacognitive development. *Child Development,* 1977, *48,* 1–8.

BROWN, A. L., SMILEY, S. S., DAY, J. D., TOWNSEND, M. A., AND LAWTON, S. C. Intrusion of a thematic idea in children's comprehension and retention of stories. *Child Development,* 1977, *48,* 1454–1466.

BROWN, E. Personal communication, University of Chicago, 1981.

BROWN, H., ADAMS, R. G., AND KELLAM, S. G. A longitudinal study of teenage motherhood and symptoms of distress: Woodlawn Community Epidemiological Project. In R. Simmons (Ed.), *Research in community and mental health,* Volume 2. Greenwich, Conn.: JAI Press, 1981.

BROWN, J., BAKEMAN, R., SNYDER, P., FREDRICKSON, W., MORGAN, S., AND HEPLER, R. Interactions of black inner-city mothers with their newborn infants. *Child Development,* 1975, *46,* 677–686.

BROWN, R. How shall a thing be called? *Psychological Review,* 1958, *65,* 14–21.

BROWN, R. *A first language: The early stages.* Cambridge, Mass.: Harvard University Press, 1973.

BROWN, R., AND HANLON, C. Derivational complexity and order of acquisition in child speech. In J. R. Hayes (Ed.), *Cognition and the development of language.* New York: Wiley, 1970.

BROZEK, J. Nutrition, malnutrition, and behavior. In M. R. Rosenzweig and L. W. Porter (Eds.), *Annual Review of Psychology,* 1978, *29,* 157–177.

BRUCEFORS, A., JOHANNESSON, I., KARLBERG, P., KLACKENBERG-LARSSON, I., LICHENSTEIN, H., AND SVENBERG, I. Trends in development of abilities related to somatic growth. *Human Development,* 1974, *17,* 152–159.

BRUCH, H. Obesity in adolescence. In H. Caplan and F. Lebovici (Eds.), *Adolescence: Psychosocial perspectives.* New York: Basic Books, 1969.

BRUNER, J. S. The course of cognitive growth. *American Psychologist,* 1964, *19,* 1–15.

BRUNER, J. S. *Beyond the information given: Studies in the psychology of knowing.* New York: Norton, 1972.

BRUNER, J. S. From communication to language: A psychological perspective. In I. Markova (Ed.), *The social context of language.* New York: Wiley, 1978.

BRUNER, J. S. The acquisition of pragmatic commitments. In R. M. Golinkoff (Ed.), *The transition from prelinguistic to linguistic communication.* Hillsdale, N.J.: Lawrence Erlbaum Associates, 1983.

BRUNK, M. A., AND HENGGELER, S. W. Child influences on adult controls: An experimental investigation. *Developmental Psychology,* 1984, *20,* 1074–1081.

BRYAN, J. H. Children's cooperation and helping behaviors. In E. M. Hetherington (Ed.), *Review of child development research,* Volume 5. Chicago: University of Chicago Press, 1975.

BRYANT, B. K. Locus of control related to teacher–child interperceptual experiences. *Child Development,* 1974, *45,* 157–164.

BRYANT, B. K. Sibling relationships in middle childhood. In M. Lamb and B. Sutton-Smith (Eds.), *Sibling relationships: Their nature and significance across the lifespan.* Hillsdale, N.J.: Lawrence Erlbaum Associates, 1982.

BRYANT, B. K. The neighborhood walk: Sources of support in middle childhood. *Monographs of the Society for Research in Child Development,* 1985, *50* (3, Serial No. 210).

BRYANT, P., AND BRADLEY, L. *Children's reading problems.* Oxford: Basil Blackwell, 1985.

BUCKHALT, J. A., MAHONEY, G. J., AND PARIS, S. C. Efficiency at self-generated elaborations by EMR and nonretarded children. *American Journal of Mental Deficiency,* 1976, *81,* 93–96.

BUCKY, S. F., AND BANTA, T. J. Racial factors in test performance. *Developmental Psychology,* 1972, *6,* 7–13

BUGENTAL, D. B., CAPORAEL, L., AND SHENNUM, W. A. Experimentally produced child uncontrollability: Effects on the potency of adult communication patterns. *Child Development,* 1980, *51,* 520–528.

BUGENTAL, D. B., AND SHENNUM, W. A. *Adult attributions as moderators of the effects of shy vs. assertive children.* Paper presented at the meeting of the Society for Research in Child Development, Boston, April 1981.

BUGENTAL, D. B., AND SHENNUM, W. A. "Difficult" children as elicitors and targets of adult communication patterns: An attributional-behavioral transactional analysis. *Monographs of the Society for Research in Child Development,* 1984, *49* (1, Serial No. 205).

BÜHLER, C. *The child and his family.* London: Harper & Bros., 1939.

BULLOCK, M. Animism in childhood thinking: A new look at an old question. *Developmental Psychology,* 1985, *21,* 217–225.

BULLOUGH, V. L. Age at menarche: A misunderstanding. *Science,* 1981, *213,* 365–366.

BURTON, R. V. Generality of honesty reconsidered. *Psychological Review,* 1963, *70,* 481–499.

BURTON, R. V. Honesty and dishonesty. In T. Lickona (Ed.), *Moral development and behavior: Theory, research and social issues.* New York:

Holt, Rinehart & Winston, 1976.

BURTON, W. *Helps to education.* Boston: Crosby and Nichols, 1863.

BUSS, D. M. Predicting parent-child interactions from children's activity level. *Developmental Psychology,* 1981, *17,* 59–65.

BUSS, R. R., YUSSEN, S. R., MATHEWS, S. R., II, MILLER, G. E., AND REMBOLD, K. L. Development of children's use of a story schema to retrieve information. *Developmental Psychology,* 1983, *19,* 22–28.

BUTLER, N. R., AND GOLDSTEIN, H. Smoking in pregnancy and subsequent child development. *British Medical Journal,* 1973, *4,* 573–575.

BUTLER, N. R., GOLDSTEIN, H., AND ROSS, E. M. Cigarette smoking in pregnancy: Its influence on birth weight and perinatal mortality. *British Medical Journal,* 1972, *2,* 127–130.

BUTTERFIELD, E. C., AND BELMONT, J. M. Assessing and improving the executive cognitive functions of mentally retarded people. In I. Bialer and M. Sternlicht (Eds.), *Psychological issues in mentally retarded people.* Chicago: Aldine, 1977.

BUTTERFIELD, P. M. Women "at risk" for parenting disorder perceive emotions in infant pictures differently. *Infant Behavior and Development,* 1986, *9,* (Special Issue: Abstracts of papers presented at the Fifth International Conference on Infant Studies), 56.

BUTTERWORTH, G. *Infancy and epistemology: An evaluation of Piaget's theory.* Brighton, England: Harvester, 1981.

BUTTERWORTH, G. E., AND CICCHETTI, D. Visual calibration of posture in normal and motor retarded Down's Syndrome infants. *Perception,* 1979, *7,* 513–525.

BUTTERWORTH, G. E., AND HICKS, L. Visual proprioception and postural stability in infancy: A developmental study. *Perception,* 1977, *6,* 255–262.

CALDWELL, B. M., HERSHER, L., LIPTON, E. L., RICHMOND, J. B., STERN, G. A., EDDY, E., DRACHMAN, R., AND ROTHMAN, A. Mother-infant interaction in monomatric and polymatric families. *American Journal of Orthopsychiatry,* 1963, *33,* 653–664.

CAMERON, R. Problem-solving inefficiency and conceptual tempo: A task analysis of underlying factors. *Child Development,* 1984, *55,* 2031–2041.

CAMPBELL, S. B., AND PAULAUKAS, S. Peer relations in hyperactive children. *Journal of Child Psychology and Psychiatry,* 1979, *20,* 233–246.

CAMPOS, J. J., EMDE, R., GAENSBAUER, T., AND SORCE, J. Cardiac and behavioral responses in human infants to strangers: Effects of mother's absence and of experimental sequence. *Developmental Psychology,* 1973, *11,* 589–601.

CAMPOS, J. J., LANGER, A., AND KROWITZ, A. Cardiac responses on the visual cliff in prelocomotor human infants. *Science,* 1970, *170,* 196–197.

CAMPOS, J. J., AND STENBERG, C. R. Perception, appraisal and emotion: The onset of social referencing. In M. E. Lamb and L. R. Sherrod (Eds.), *Infant social cognition.* Hillsdale, N. J.: Lawrence Erlbaum Asociates, 1981.

CAMRAS, L. A. Facial expressions used by children in a conflict situation. *Child Development,* 1977, *48,* 1431–1435.

CANDEE, D., SHEENAN, T. J., COOK, C. D., HUSTED, S. D. R., AND BARGEN, M. Moral reasoning and decisions in dilemmas of neonatal care. *Pediatric Research,* 9182, *16,* 846–850.

CANNING, H., AND MAYER, J. Obesity: Its possible effect on college acceptance. *New England Journal of Medicine,* 1966, *275,* 1172–1174.

CANTOR, P. These teenagers feel that they have no options. *People Weekly,* February 18, 1985, 84–87.

CAPLAN, P. J., MACPHERSON, G. M., AND TOBIN, P. Do sex-related differences in spatial abilities exist? *American Psychologist,* 1985, *40,* 786–799.

CAPLOW, T., BAHR, H. M., CHADWICK, B. A., HILL, R., AND WILLIAMSON, M. H. *Middletown families.* Minneapolis: University of Minnesota Press, 1982.

CARD, J., AND WISE, L. Teenage mothers and teenage fathers: The impact of early childbearing on the parents' personal and professional lives. *Family Planning Perspectives*, 1978, *10*, 199–205.

CAREW, J. Experience and the development of intelligence in young children. *Monographs of the Society for Research in Child Development*, 1980, *45* (1–2, Serial No. 183).

CAREY, S. Semantic development: State of the art. In E. Wanner and L. R. Gleitman (Eds.), *Language acquisition: State of the art.* New York: Cambridge University Press, 1982.

CAREY, S. *Conceptual change in childhood.* Cambridge, Mass.: MIT Press, 1985. (a)

CAREY, S. Constraints on semantic development. In J. Mehler and R. Fox (Eds.), *Neonate cognition: Beyond the blooming buzzing confusion.* Hillsdale, N.J.: Lawrence Erlbaum Associates, 1985. (b)

CARON, A. J., CARON, R. F., CALDWELL, R., AND WEISS, S. Infant perception of the structural properties of the face. *Developmental Psychology*, 1973, *9*, 385–399.

CARON, R. F., CARON, A. J., AND MYERS, R. Do infants see emotional expressions in static faces? *Child Development*, 1985, *56*, 1552–1560.

CARON, R. F., AND MYERS, R. *Do infants perceive emotions in static faces?* Paper presented at the International Conference on Infant Studies, New York, April 1984.

CARPENTER, C. J. Activity structure and play: Implications for socialization. In M. B. Liss (Ed.), *Social and cognitive skills: Sex roles and children's play.* New York: Academic Press, 1983.

CARR, S. J., DABBS, J. M., JR., AND CARR, T. S. Mother-infant attachment: The importance of the mother's visual field. *Child Development*, 1975, *46*, 331–338.

CASE, R. Structures and strictures: Some functional limitations on the course of cognitive growth. *Cognitive Psychology*, 1974, *6*, 544–573.

CASE, R. *Intellectual development: Birth to adulthood.* Orlando, Fla.: Academic Press, 1985.

CASE, R., KURLAND, D. M., AND GOLDBERG, J. Operational efficiency and the growth of short-term memory span. *Journal of Experimental Child Psychology*, 1982, *33*, 386–404.

CASSIDY, J., AND MAIN, M. *Quality of attachment from infancy to early childhood: Security is stable but behavior changes.* Paper presented at the International Conference on Infant Studies, New York, April 1984.

CATTELL, J. M. Mental tests and measurements. *Mind*, 1890, *15*, 373.

CAVANAUGH, J. C., AND PERLMUTTER, M. Metamemory: A critical examination. *Child Development*, 1982, *53*, 11–28.

CAVANAUGH, P. J., AND DAVIDSON, M. L. The secondary circular reaction and response elicitation in the operant learning of six-month-old infants. *Developmental Psychology*, 1977, *13*, 371–376.

CECI, S. J., AND BRONFENBRENNER, U. "Don't forget to take the cupcakes out of the oven": Prospective memory, strategic time-monitoring, and context. *Child Development*, 1985, *56*, 152–164.

CECI, S. J., AND TISHMAN, J. Hyperactivity and incidental memory: Evidence for attentional diffusion. *Child Development*, 1984, *55*, 2192–2203.

CEDARBAUM, S. Personal communication, 1976. Cited by C. B. Kopp and A. H. Parmelee, Prenatal and perinatal influences on infant behavior. In J. D. Osofsky (Ed.), *Handbook of infant development.* New York: Wiley, 1979.

CHAFETZ, M. E. Alcoholism: Drug dependency problem No. 1. *Journal of Drug Issues*, 1974, *4*, 64–68.

CHAMBLISS, W. J. The saints and the roughnecks. In T. J. Cottle (Ed.), *Readings in adolescent psychology: Contemporary perspectives* New York: Harper & Row, 1977.

CHANDLER, M. J. Egocentrism and antisocial behavior: The assessment and training of social perspective-taking skills. *Developmental Psychology*, 1973, *9*, 326–332.

CHAPMAN, M., AND ZAHN-WAXLER, C. Young children's compliance and noncompliance to parental discipline in a natural setting. *International Journal of Behavior Development*, 1982, *5*, 8194.

CHARLESWORTH, R., AND HARTUP, W. W. Positive social reinforcement in the nursery school peer group. *Child Development*, 1967, *38*, 993–1002.

CHARLESWORTH, W. R., AND KREUTZER, M. Facial expressions of infants and children. In P. Ekman (Ed.), *Darwin and facial expression.* New York: Academic Press, 1973.

CHASE-LANSDALE, P. L. Effects of maternal employment on mother-infant and father-infant attachment. Unpublished doctoral dissertation, University of Michigan, 1981. *Dissertation Abstracts International*, 1982, *42*, 2562.

CHEN, E. Twins reared apart: A living lab. *New York Times Magazine*, December 9, 1979, p. 110.

CHESNICK, M., MENYUK, P., LIEBERGOTT, J., FERRIER, L., AND STRAND, K. *Who leads whom?* Paper presented at the meeting of the Society for Research in Child Development, Detroit, April 1983.

CHI, M. T. Short-term memory limitations in children: Capacity or processing deficits? *Memory and Cognition*, 1976, *4*, 559–572.

CHI, M. T. Knowledge structures and memory development. In R. S. Siegler (Ed.), *Children's thinking: What develops?* Hillsdale, N.J.: Lawrence Erlbaum Associates, 1978.

CHI, M. T. Changing conception of sources of memory development. *Human Development*, 1985, *28*, 50–56.

CHI, M. T., AND KOESKE, R. D. Network representation of a child's dinosaur knowledge. *Developmental Psychology*, 1983, *19*, 29–39.

CHILDERS, P., AND WIMMER, M. The concept of death in early childhood. *Child Development*, 1971, *42*, 1299–1301.

CHILMAN, C. *Adolescent sexuality in a changing American society: Social and psychological perspectives.* Washington, D.C.: Public Health Service, National Institute of Mental Health, 1979.

CHOMSKY, C. *The acquisition of syntax in children from 5 to 10.* Research Monograph 57. Cambridge, Mass.: MIT Press, 1969.

CHOMSKY, N. *Syntactic structures.* The Hague: Mouton, 1957.

CHOMSKY, N. *Aspects of the theory of syntax.* Cambridge, Mass.: MIT Press, 1965.

CHOMSKY, N. *Language and mind.* New York: Harcourt Brace Jovanovich, 1968.

CHOMSKY, N. *Reflections of language.* New York: Pantheon, 1975.

CHUGANI, H. T., AND PHELPS, M. E. Maturational changes in cerebral function in infants determined by FGG positron emission tomography. *Science*, February 1986, *231*, 840–843.

CIALDINI, R. B., AND KENRICK, D. T. Altruism as hedonism: A social development perspective on the relationship of negative mood state and helping. *Journal of Personality and Social Psychology*, 1976, *34*, 907–914.

CICIRELLI, V. G. Concept learning of young children as a function of sibling relationships to the teacher. *Child Development*, 1972, *43*, 282–287.

CICIRELLI, V. G. Effects of sibling structure and interaction on children's categorization style. *Developmental Psychology*, 1973, *9*, 132–139.

CICIRELLI, V. G. Children's school grades and sibling structure. *Psychological Reports*, 1977, *41*, 1055–1058.

CICIRELLI, V. G. Effects of sibling presence on mother-child interaction. *Developmental Psychology*, 1978, *14*, 315–316.

CLARK, E. On the acquisition of the meaning of *before* and *after*. *Journal of Verbal Learning and Verbal Behavior*, 1971, *10*, 266–275.

CLARK, E. First language acquisition. In J. Morton and J. C. Marshall (Eds.), *Psycholinguistics Series 1: Developmental and pathological.* London: Paul Elek, 1977.

CLARK, E. Meanings and concepts. In P. H. Mussen (Ed.), *Handbook of child psychology*, Volume 3. New York: Wiley, 1983.

CLARK, H., AND CLARK, E. *Psychology and language: An introduction to psycholinguistics.* New York: Harcourt Brace Jovanovich, 1977.

CLARK, M., AND LESLIE, C. Why kids get fat: A new study shows obesity is in the genes. *Newsweek*, February 3, 1986, p. 61.

CLARK, P. M., AND KRIGE, P. D. *A study of interaction between infant peers: An analysis of infant-infant interaction in twins.* Paper presented at the second Joint Congress of the South African Psychology Association and the Psychological Institute of South Africa, Potchefstroom, September 1979.

CLARKE, H. H., AND CLARKE, D. H. Social status and mental health of boys as related to their maturity, structural, and strength characteristics. *Research Quarterly*, 1961, 32, 326–334.

CLARKE-STEWART, A. *Child care in the family: A review of research and some propositions for policy.* New York: Academic Press, 1977.

CLARKE-STEWART, A. Predicting child development from day care forms and features: The Chicago Study. In D. Phillips (Ed.), *Predictors of quality childcare.* NAEYC Research Monograph Series 1, in press.

CLARKE-STEWART, A., FRIEDMAN, S., AND KOCH, J. *Child development: A topical approach.* New York: Wiley, 1985.

CLARKE-STEWART, K. A. Interactions between mothers and their young children: Characteristics and consequences. *Monographs of the Society for Research in Child Development*, 1973, 38 (6–7, Serial No. 153).

CLARKE-STEWART, K. A. And daddy makes three: The father's impact on mother and young child. *Child Development*, 1978, 49, 466–478. (a)

CLARKE-STEWART, K. A. Recasting the lone stranger. In J. Glick and K. A. Clarke-Stewart (Eds.), *The development of social understanding.* New York: Gardner Press, 1978. (b)

CLARKE-STEWART, K. A. The father's contribution to child development. In F. A. Pedersen (Ed.), *The father-infant relationship: Observational studies in a family context.* New York: Praeger Special Studies, 1980.

CLARKE-STEWART, K. A. *Daycare.* Cambridge, Mass.: Harvard University Press, 1982.

CLARKE-STEWART, K. A. Daycare: A new context for research and development. In M. Perlmutter (Ed.), *Parent-child interaction and parent-child relations in child development. Minnesota Symposia on Child Psychology*, Volume 17. Hillsdale, N.J.: Lawrence Erlbaum Associates, 1984.

CLARKE-STEWART, K. A., AND APFEL, N. Evaluating parental effects on child development. In L. S. Shulman (Ed.), *Review of research in education*, Volume 6, Itasca, Ill.: Peacock, 1979.

CLARKE-STEWART, K. A., AND FEIN, G. G. Early childhood programs. In P. H. Mussen (Ed.), *Handbook of child psychology*, Volume 2. New York: Wiley, 1983.

CLARKE-STEWART, K. A., AND HEVEY, C. M. Longitudinal relations in repeated observations of mother–child interaction from 1 to 2½ years. *Developmental Psychology*, 1981, 17, 127–145.

CLEMENTS, D. H., AND GULLO, D. F. Effects of computer programming on young children's cognition. *Journal of Educational Psychology*, 1984, 76, 1051–1058.

CLOWARD, R. Studies in tutoring. *Journal of Experimental Education*, 1976, 36, 14–25.

COHEN, L. B., AND STRAUSS, M. S. Concept acquisition in the human infant. *Child Development*, 1979, 50, 419–424.

COHEN, L. J., AND CAMPOS, J. J. Father, mother, and stranger as elicitors of attachment behaviors in infancy. *Developmental Psychology*, 1974, 10, 146–154.

COHEN, S., EVANS, G. W., KRANTZ, D. S., AND STOKOLS, D. Physiological, motivational, and cognitive effects of aircraft noise in children. *American Psychologist*, 1980, 35, 231–243.

COHEN, S., AND WEINSTEIN, N. D. Nonauditory effects of noise. In G. W. Evans (Ed.), *Environmental stress.* New York: Cambridge University Press, 1982.

COHN, J. F., AND TRONICK, E. Z. Three-month-old infants' reaction to simulated maternal depression. *Child Development*, 1983, 54, 185–193.

COIE, J. D., AND KUPERSMIDT, J. B. A behavioral analysis of emerging social status in boys' groups. *Child Development*, 1983, 54, 1400–1416.

COLBY, A., AND DAMON, W. Listening to a different voice: A review of Gilligan's *In a Different Voice. Merrill-Palmer Quarterly*, 1983, 29, 473–481.

COLBY, A. KOHLBERG, L., GIBBS, J., AND LIEBERMAN, M. A longitudinal study of moral judgment. *Monographs of the Society for Research in Child Development*, 1983, 48 (1, Serial No. 200).

COLE, M. How education affects the mind. *Human Nature*, 1978, 1,

50–58.

COLE, M., GAY, J., GLICK, J. A., AND SHARP, D. W. *The cultural context of learning and thinking: An exploration in experimental anthropology.* New York: Basic Books, 1971.

COLE, M., AND SCRIBNER, S. Cross-cultural studies of memory and cognition. In R. V., Kail, Jr., and J. W. Hagen (Eds.), *Perspectives on the development of memory and cognition.* Hillsdale, N.J.: Lawrence Erlbaum Associates, 1977.

COLEMAN, J. C. *The adolescent society.* Glencoe, Ill.: Free Press, 1961.

COLEMAN, J. C. *Relationships in adolescence.* London: Routledge, 1974.

COLEMAN, J. C. Friendship and the peer group in adolescence. In J. Adelson (Ed.), *Handbook of adolescent psychology.* New York: Wiley, 1980.

COLEMAN, J. S. *The adolescent society.* New York: Free Press, 1961.

COLEMAN, M. A report on the autistic syndromes. In M. Rutter and E. Schopler (Eds.), *Autism: A reappraisal of concepts and treatment.* New York: Plenum, 1978.

COLLINS, G. Changes in a marriage when a baby is born. *New York Times*, January 6, 1985, p. 12.

COLLINS, W. A. Social antecedents, cognitive processing, and comprehension of social portrayals on television. In E. T. Higgins, D. N. Ruble, and W. W. Hartup (Eds.), *Social cognition and social development: A sociocultural perspective.* Cambridge, England: Cambridge University Press, 1983.

COMMONS, M. L., RICHARDS, F. A., AND KUHN, D. Systematic and metasystematic reasoning: A case for levels of reasoning beyond Piaget's stage of formal operations. *Child Development*, 1982, 53, 1058–1069.

CONDON, W. S., AND SANDERS, L. W. Neonate movement is synchronized with adult speech: Interactional participation and language acquisition. *Science*, 1974, 183, 99–101.

CONDRY, J., AND CONDRY, S. Sex differences: A study of the eye of the beholder. *Child Development*, 1976, 46, 812–819.

CONDRY, J., AND SIMAN, M. L. Characteristics of peer–adult-oriented children. *Journal of Marriage and the Family*, 1974, 36, 543–554.

CONEL, J. L. *The postnatal development of the human cerebral cortex* (8 vols.) Cambridge, Mass.: Harvard University Press, 1939–1967.

CONNELL, J. P. *A model of the relationship among children's self-rated cognitions, affects and academic achievement.* Unpublished doctoral dissertation, University of Denver, 1981.

CONNERS, C. K. *Food additives and hyperactive children.* New York: Plenum, 1980.

CONNOLLY, K., AND SMITH, P. K. Reactions of pre-school children to a strange observer. In N. Blurton Jones (Ed.), *Ethological studies of child behaviour.* Cambridge, England: Cambridge University Press, 1972.

COOPER, C. R. *Collaboration in children: Dyadic interaction skills in problem solving.* Paper presented at the meeting of the Society for Research in Child Development, New Orleans, March 1977.

COOPER, C. R., AYERS-LOPEZ, S., AND MARQUIS, A. Children's discourse during peer learning in experimental and naturalistic situations. *Discourse Processes*, 1982, 5, 177–191.

COOPER, C. R., GROTEVANT, H. D., AND CONDON, S. M. Individuality and connectedness in the family as a context for adolescent identity formation and role-taking skill. *New Directions for Child Development*, 1983, 22, 43–59.

COOPERSMITH, S. *The antecedents of self-esteem.* San Francisco: W. H. Freeman, 1967.

CORDES, C. School debate too often ignores effect of culture. *APA Monitor*, 1984, 15, 10.

CORDES, C. Attention disorder crime link dispelled. *APA Monitor*, November 1985, 16, 16.

COREA, G. *The mother machine.* New York: Harper & Row, 1986.

CORTER, C., TREHUB, S., BOUKYDIS, C., FORD, L., CELHOFFER, L., AND MINDE, K. Nurses' judgments of the attractiveness of premature infants. *Infant Behavior and Development*, 1978, 1, 373–380.

COSGROVE, B. B., AND HENDERSON, B. E. Male genitourinary abnormalities and maternal diethylstilbestrol. *Journal of Urology*, 1977,

117, 220–222.

Cosgrove, J. M., and Patterson, C. J. Adequacy of young speakers' encoding in response to listener feedback. *Psychological Reports*, 1979, *45*, 15–18.

Costanzo, P. R., and Shaw, M. E. Conformity as a function of age level. *Child Development*, 1966, *37*, 967–975.

Craik, F. I. M., and Lockhart, R. S. Levels of processing: A framework for memory research. *Journal of Verbal Learning and Verbal Behavior*, 1972, *11*, 671–684.

Craik, F. I. M., and Rabinowitz, J. C. Age differences in the acquisition and use of verbal information. In H. Bouma and D. G. Bouwhuis (Eds.), *Attention and performance*, Volume 10. Hillsdale, N.J.: Lawrence Erlbaum Associates, 1984.

Crandall, V. C., Katkovsky, W., and Crandall, V. J. Children's beliefs in their control of reinforcements in intellectual academic achievement behaviors. *Child Development*, 1965, *36*, 91–109.

Crano, W. D. Causal analyses of the effects of the socioeconomic status and initial intellectual endowment on patterns of cognitive development and academic achievement. In D. R. Green (Ed.), *The aptitude-achievement distinction*. Monterey, Calif.: California Test Bureau, 1974.

Crano, W. D., Kenny, J., and Campbell, D. T. Does intelligence cause achievement? A cross-lagged panel analysis. *Journal of Educational Psychology*, 1972, *63*, 258–275.

Craven, P. Understanding the atypical child: How I learned to live with my handicapped daughter. *Well Being*, 1978, *36*, 36–42.

Cravioto, J., Birch, H. G., DeLicardie, E., Rosales, L., and Vega, L. The ecology of growth and development in a Mexican preindustrial community. Report I: Method and findings from birth to one month of age. *Monographs of the Society for Research in Child Development*, 1969, *34* (5, Serial No. 129).

Crawford, C. It was a living nightmare. *TV Guide*. March 2, 1985, 36–38.

Crockenberg, S. Infant irritability, mother responsiveness, and social support influences on the security of infant–mother attachment. *Child Development*, 1981, *52*, 857–869.

Crockenberg, S. Early mother and infant antecedents of Bayley Scale performance at 21 months. *Developmental Psychology*, 1983, *19*, 727–730.

Crockenberg, S. *Toddlers reactions to maternal anger*. Paper presented at the International Conference on Infant Studies, New York, April 1984.

Crockenberg, S. Are temperamental differences in babies associated with predictable differences in care giving? In J. V. Lerner and R. M. Lerner (Eds.), *New directions for child development: Temperament and social interaction during infancy and childhood*. San Francisco: Jossey-Bass, 1986.

Crockenberg, S., and Acredolo, C. Infant temperament ratings: A function of infants, or mothers, or both. *Infant Behavior and Development*, 1983, *6*, 61–72.

Csikszentmihalyi, M., and Larson, R. *Being adolescent: Conflict and growth in the teenage years*. New York: Basic Books, 1984.

Csikszentmihalyi, M., Larson, R., and Prescott, S. The ecology of adolescent activity and experience. *Journal of Youth and Adolescence*, 1977, *6*, 281–294.

Cummings, E. M., and Bjork, E. L. The search behavior of 12 to 14 month-old infants on a five-choice invisible displacement hiding task. *Infant Behavior and Development*, 1981, *4*, 47–60.

Cummings, E. M., Iannotti, R. J., and Zahn-Waxler, C. Influence of conflict between adults on the emotions and aggression of young children. *Developmental Psychology*, 1985, *21*, 495–507.

Cundick, B. P. Measures of intelligence on Southwest Indian students. *Journal of Social Psychology*, 1970, *81*, 319–337.

Cunningham, S. Bulimia's cycle shames patient, tests therapists. *APA Monitor*, January 1984, *15*, 16.

Curtiss, S. *Genie: A psycholinguistic study of a modern-day wild child*. New York: Academic Press, 1977.

Dale, N. *Early pretend play in the family*. Unpublished doctoral thesis, University of Cambridge, 1983.

Dale, P. *Language development: Structure and function* (2nd ed.). New York: Holt, Rinehart & Winston, 1976.

Damon, W. *The social world of the child*. San Francisco: Jossey-Bass, 1977.

Damon, W., and Hart, D. The development of self-understanding from infancy through adolescence. *Child Development*, 1982, *53*, 841–864.

Damon, W., and Killen, M. Peer interaction and the process of change in children's moral reasoning. *Merrill Palmer Quarterly*, 1982, *28*, 347–367.

Dan, A. J. *Patterns of behavioral and mood variation in men and women: Variability and the menstrual cycle*. Unpublished doctoral dissertation, University of Chicago (Committee on Human Development), 1976.

D'Angelo, R. *Families of sand: A report concerning the flight of adolescents from their families*. Columbus, Ohio: State University School of Social Work, 1974.

Daniels, D., and Plomin, R. Origins of individual differences in infant shyness. *Developmental Psychology*, 1985, *21*, 118–121.

Daniels, D., and Weingarten, K. *Sooner or later: The timing of parenthood in adult lives*. New York: Norton, 1982.

Darling, C. A. Parental influence on love, sexual behavior, and sexual satisfaction. Unpublished doctoral dissertation, Michigan State University, 1979.

Darling, C. A., Kallen, D. J., and Van Dusen, J. E. Sex in transition, 1900–1980. *Journal of Youth and Adolescence*, 1984, *13*, 385–399.

Dasen, P. Are cognitive processes universal? A contribution to cross-cultural Piagetian psychology. In N. Warren (Ed.), *Studies in cross-cultural psychology*, Volume 1. London: Academic Press, 1977.

Davidson, E. S., Yasuna, A., and Tower, A. The effects of television cartoons on sex role stereotyping in young girls. *Child Development*, 1979, *50*, 597–600.

Davidson, J. R. Post-partum mood change in Jamaican women: A description and discussion on its significance. *British Journal of Psychiatry*, 1972, *121*, 659–663.

Dawson, C. D. Cerebral lateralization in individuals diagnosed as autistic in early childhood. *Brain and Language*, 1982, *15*, 353–368.

Day, B., and Brice, R. Academic achievement, self-concept development, and behavior patterns of six-year-old children in open classrooms. *Elementary School Journal*, 1977, *78*, 132–139.

Day, R. H., and McKenzie, B. E. Perceptual shape constancy in early infancy. *Perception*, 1973, *2*, 315–320.

Day, R. H., and McKenzie, B. E. Infant perception of the invariant size of approaching and receding objects. *Developmental Psychology*, 1981, *17*, 670–677.

Dayton, G. O., Jr., Jones, M. H., Aiu, P., Rawson, R. A., Steele, B., and Rose, M. Developmental study of coordinated eye movements in the human infant: I. Visual acuity in the newborn human: A study based on induced optokinetic nystagmus recorded by electro-oculography. *Archives of Ophthalmology*, 1964, *71*, 865–870.

De Boysson-Bardies, B., Sagart, L., and Durand, C. Discernible differences in the babbling of infants according to target language. *Journal of Child Language*, 1984, *11*, 1–15.

Décarie, T. G. *The infant's reaction to strangers*. New York: International Universities Press, 1974.

Decker, S. N., and DeFries, J. C. Cognitive ability profiles in families of reading disabled children. *Developmental Medicine and Child Neurology*, 1981, *23*, 217–227.

Deeths, T. M., and Breeden, J. T. Poisoning in children—a statistical study of 1,057 cases. *Journal of Pediatrics*, 1971, *78*, 299.

DeFries, J. C., and Baker, L. A. Parental contributions to longitudinal stability of cognitive measures in the Colorado Family Reading Study. *Child Development*, 1983, *54*, 388–395.

Delefes, P., and Jackson, B. Teacher–pupil interaction as a function of location in the classroom. *Psychology in the Schools*, 1972, *9*, 119–123.

DELFINI, L., BERNAL, M., AND ROSEN, P. Comparison of deviant and normal boys in home settings. In E. J. Mash, L. A. Hamerlynck, and L. C. Handy (Eds.), *Behavior modification and families*, Volume 1. *Theory and research*. New York: Brunner/Mazel, 1976.

DELISSOVOY, V. Child care by adolescent parents. *Children Today*, 1973, *14*, 22.

DELOACHE, J. S. Naturalistic studies of memory for object location in very young children. *New directions for child development: Children's memory*, San Francisco: Jossey-Bass, 1980.

DELOACHE, J. S., AND BROWN, A. L. Very young children's memory for the location of objects in a large-scale environment. *Child Development*, 1983,.*54*, 888–897.

DELOACHE, J. S., CASSIDY, D. J., BROWN, A. L. Precursors of mnemonic strategies in very young children's memory. *Child Development*, 1985, *56*, 125–137.

Demographic yearbook 1983, 35th issue. New York: United Nations, Statistical Office, 1983.

DEMOS, E. V. Facial expressions of infants and toddlers: A descriptive analysis. In T. Field and A. Fogel (Eds.), *Emotion and early interaction*. Hillsdale, N.J.: Lawrence Erlbaum Associates, 1982.

DEMOS, J., AND DEMOS, V. Adolescence in historical perspective. *Journal of Marriage and the Family*, 1969, *31*, 632–638.

DEMPSTER, F. N., AND ROHWER, W. D., JR. Age differences and modality effects in immediate and final free recall. *Child Development*, 1983, *54*, 30–41.

DEMYER, M. K., BARTON, S., ALPERN, G. D., KIMBERLIN, C., ALLEN, J., YANG, E., AND STEELE, R. The measured intelligence of autistic children: A follow-up study. *Journal of Autism and Childhood Schizophrenia*, 1974, *4*, 42–60.

DENIER, C. A., AND SERBIN, L. A. *Play with male-preferred toys: Effects on visual-spatial performance*. Paper presented at the annual meeting of the American Psychological Association, Toronto, 1978.

DENNEY, N. W. A developmental study of free classification in children. *Child Development*, 1972, *43*, 1161–1170.

DENNIS, W. Infant development under conditions of restricted practice and of minimum social stimulation: A preliminary report. *Pedagogical Seminary*, 1938, *53*, 149–158.

DENNIS, W. Infant development under conditions of restricted practice and of minimum social stimulation. *Genetic Psychology Monographs*, 1941, *23*, 143–189.

DENNIS, W. Causes of retardation among institutional children: Iran. *Journal of Genetic Psychology*, 1960, *96*, 47–59.

DENNIS, W. *Children of the crèche*. New York: Appleton-Century-Crofts, 1973.

DEUTSCH, F. Female preschoolers' perceptions of affective responses and interpersonal behavior in videotaped episodes. *Developmental Psychology*, 1974, *10*, 733–740.

DEUTSCH, M. New vitality in follow-ups of Head Start youngsters. *The Brown University Human Development Letter*, June 1985, *1*, 6.

DEVEREAUX, E. C. The role of the peer group experience in moral development. In J. P. Hill (Ed.), *Minnesota Symposia on Child Psychology*, Volume 4. Minneapolis: University of Minnesota Press, 1970.

DE VILLIERS, J. G., AND DE VILLIERS, P. A. A cross-sectional study of the development of grammatical morphemes in child speech. *Journal of Psycholinguistic Research*, 1973, *2*, 267–278.

DE VILLIERS, P. A., AND DE VILLIERS, J. G. *Early language*. Cambridge, Mass.: Harvard University Press, 1979.

DEVRIES, H. A. *Physiology of exercise* (1st ed., 3rd ed.). Dubuque, Iowa: W. C. Brown, 1966, 1980.

DIAMOND, R., CAREY, S., AND BACK, K. J. Genetic influences on the development of spatial skills during early adolescence. *Cognition*, 1983, *13*, 167–185.

DIAZ, R. M. The intellectual power of bilingualism. *The Quarterly Newsletter of the Laboratory of Comparative Human Cognition*, January 1985, *7*, 16–22. (a)

DIAZ, R. M. Bilingual cognitive development: Addressing three gaps in current research. *Child Development* 1985, *56*, 1376–1388. (b)

DIAZ, R. M., AND BERNDT, T. J. Children's knowledge of a best friend: Fact or fancy? *Developmental Psychology*, 1982, *18*, 787–794.

DICK-READ, G. *Childbirth without fear: The principles and practices of natural childbirth*. New York: Harper & Row, 1933.

DIBBLE, U., AND STRAUS, M. Some social structure determinants of inconsistency between attitudes and behavior: The case of family violence. *Journal of Marriage and the Family*, 1980, *42*, 71–80.

DIENER, C. I., AND DWECK, C. S. An analysis of learned helplessness: Continuous changes in performance, strategy and achievement cognitions following failure. *Journal of Personality and Social Psychology*, 1978, *36*, 451–462.

DIENSTBIER, R. A., HILLMAN, D., LEHNHOFFM J., HILLMAN, J., AND VALKENAAR, M. C. An emotion-attribution approach to moral behavior: Interfacing cognitive and avoidance theories of moral development. *Psychological Review*, 1975, *82*, 299–315.

DIETZ, W. *Childhood obesity*. Paper presented at NIH workshop on childhood obesity, March 10, 1986; reprinted in *Science*, 1986, *232*, 20–21.

DODGE, K. A. Social cognition and children's aggressive behavior. *Child Development*, 1980, *51*, 162–170.

DODGE, K. A. Behavioral antecedents of peer social status. *Child Development*, 1983, *54*, 1386–1399.

DODGE, K. A., AND FRAME, C. L. Social cognitive biases and deficits in aggressive boys. *Child Development*, 1982, *53*, 620–635.

DODSON, J. C., KUSHIDA, E., WILLIAMSON, M., AND FRIEDMAN, E. G. Intellectual performance of 36 phenylketonuria patients and their nonaffected siblings. *Pediatrics*, 1976, *58*, 53–58.

DOLLARD, J., DOOB, L., MILLER, N. E., MOWRER, O. H., AND SEARS, R. R. *Frustration and aggression*. New Haven, Conn.: Yale University Press, 1939.

DOMAN, G. *How to teach your baby to read: The gentle revolution*. New York: Random House, 1964.

DOMAN, G. *Teach your baby math*. New York: Pocket Books, 1982.

DOMAN, G. *How to multiply your baby's intelligence*. New York: Doubleday, 1984.

DONALDSON, M. Children's reasoning. In M. Donaldson, R. Graine, and C. Pratt (Eds.), *Early childhood development and education: Readings in psychology*. Oxford: Basil Blackwell, 1983.

DONALDSON, M., AND BALFOUR, G. Less is more: A study of language comprehension in children. *British Journal of Psychology*, 1968, *59*, 461–472.

DONOVAN, B. *The cesarean birth experience: A practical, comprehensive, and reassuring guide for parents and professionals*. Boston: Beacon Press, 1977.

DONOVAN, W. L., AND LEAVITT, L. A. *Effects of experimentally manipulated attributions of infant cries of maternal learned helplessness*. Paper presented at the International Conference on Infant Studies, New York, April 1984.

DONOVAN, W. L., LEAVITT, L. A., AND BALLING, J. D. Maternal physiological response to infant signals. *Psychophysiology*, 1978, *15*, 68–74.

DORE, J. Conditions for the acquisition of speech acts. In I. Markova (Ed.), *The social context of language*. New York: Wiley, 1978.

DORR, A. *Children's reports of what they learn from daily viewing*. Paper presented at the biennial meeting of the Society for Research in Child Development, San Francisco, March 1979.

DOUGLAS, V. I. Higher mental processes in hyperactive children. In R. M. Knights and D. J. Bakker (Eds.), *Treatment of hyperactive and learning disordered children*. Baltimore, Md.: University Park Press, 1980.

DOUVAN, E., AND ADELSON, J. *The adolescent experience*. New York: Wiley, 1966.

DOUVAN, E., AND GOLD, M. Modal patterns in American adolescence. In L. W. Hoffman and M. L. Hoffman (Eds.), *Review of child development research*, Volume 2. New York: Russell Sage Foundation, 1966.

DOVE, A. Taking the chitling test. *Newsweek*, July 15, 1968, pp. 51–52.

DOYLE, A-B., CHAMPAGNE, M., AND SEGALOWITZ, N. Some issues on the assessment of linguistic consequences of early bilingualism.

In M. Paradis (Ed.), *Aspects of bilingualism.* Columbia, S.C.: Hornbeam Press, 1978.

DOYLE, W., HANCOCK, G., AND KIFER, E. Teachers' perceptions: Do they make a difference? Paper presented at the annual meeting of the American Educational Research Association, New York, April 1971.

DRAKE, C. T., AND McDOUGALL, D. Effects of the absence of a father and other male models on the development of boys' sex roles. *Developmental Psychology*, 1977, *13*, 537–538.

DREYER, P. H. Sexuality during adolescence. In B. J. Wolman (Ed.), *Handbook of developmental psychology.* Englewood Cliffs, N.J.: Prentice-Hall, 1982.

DREYFUS-BRISAC, C. Neurophysiological studies in human premature and full-term newborns. *Biological Psychiatry*, 1975, *10*, 485–496.

DUFFTY, P., AND BRYAN, M. H. Home apnea monitoring in "near-miss" sudden infant death syndrome (SIDS) and in siblings of SIDS victims. *Pediatrics*, 1982, *70*, 69–75.

DUKE, P. M., CARLSMITH, J. M., JENNINGS, D., MARTIN, J. A., DORNBUSCH, S. M., GROSS, R. T., AND SIEGEL-GORELICK, B. Educational correlates of early and late sexual maturation in adolescence. *Journal of Pediatrics*, 1982, *100*, 633–637.

DULIT, E. Adolescent thinking à la Piaget: The formal stage. *Journal of Youth & Adolescence*, 1972, *1*, 281–301.

DUNCAN, D., SCHUMAN, H., AND DUNCAN, B. *Social change in a metropolitan community.* New York: Russell Sage Foundation, 1973.

DUNN, J. Sibling relationships in early childhood. *Child Development*, 1983, *54*, 787–811.

DUNN, J., AND KENDRICK, C. Studying temperament and parent-child interaction: Comparison of interview and direct observation. *Developmental Medicine and Child Neurology*, 1980, *22*, 484–496.

DUNN, J., AND KENDRICK, C. The speech of two- and three-year-olds to infant siblings: "Baby talk" and the context of communication. *Journal of Child Language*, 1982, *9*, 579–595.(a)

DUNN, J., AND KENDRICK, C. *Siblings: Love, envy, and understanding.* Cambridge, Mass.: Harvard University Press, 1982.(b)

DUNN, J., KENDRICK, C., AND MACNAMEE, R. The reaction of first-born children to the birth of a sibling: Mothers' reports. *Journal of Child Psychology and Psychiatry*, 1981, *22*, 1–18.

DUNN, J. PLOMIN, R., AND DANIELS, D. Consistency and change in mother's behavior toward young siblings. *Child Development*, 1986, *57*, 348–356.

DUNPHY, D.C. The social structure of urban adolescent peer groups. *Sociometry*, 1963, *26*, 230–246.

DURKIN, D. *Children who read early.* New York: Teachers College, Columbia University, 1966.

DUSEK, J. B., AND FLAHERTY, J. F. The development of the self-concept during the adolescent years. *Monographs of the Society for Research in Child Development*, 1981, *46* (4, Serial No. 191).

DWECK, C. S. Children's interpretation and evaluative feedback: The effect of social cues on learned helplessness. *Merrill-Palmer Quarterly*, 1976, *22*, 105–109.

DWECK, C. S. Social-cognitive processes in children's friendships. In S. R. Asher and J. M. Gottman (Eds.), *The development of children's friendships.* New York: Cambridge University Press, 1981.

DWECK, C. S., AND BUSH, E. S. Sex differences in learned helplessness: I. Differential debilitation with peer and adult evaluators. *Developmental Psychology*, 1976, *12*, 147–156.

DWECK, C. S., DAVIDSON, W., NELSON, S., AND ENNA, B. Sex differences in learned helplessness: II. The contingencies of evaluation feedback in the classroom: III. An experimental analysis. *Developmental Psychology*, 1979, *14*, 268–276.

DWECK, C. S., AND GOETZ, F. E. Attributions and learned helplessness. In J. H. Harvey, W. Ickes, and R. F. Kidd (Eds.), *New directions in attribution research*, Volume 2. Hillsdale: N.J.: Lawrence Erlbaum Associates, 1977.

DWECK, C. S., AND LICHT, B. Learned helplessness and intellectual achievement. In J. Garber and M. Seligman (Eds.), *Human help-*

lessness. New York: Academic Press, 1980.

DWECK, C. S., AND REPPUCCI, N. D. Learned helplessness and reinforcement responsibility in children. *Journal of Personality and Social Psychology*, 1973, *25*, 109–116.

DWECK, C. S., AND WORTMAN, C. Achievement, text anxiety, and learned helplessness: Adaptive and maladaptive cognitions. In H. Krohne and L. Laux (Eds.), *Achievement, stress and anxiety.* Washington, D. C.: Hemisphere, 1980.

EASTERBROOKS, M. A., AND GOLDBERG, W. A. Toddler development in the family: Impact of father involvement and parenting characteristics. *Child Development*, 1984, *55*, 740–752.

EBBS, J. H., BROWN, A., TISDALL, F. F., MOYLE, W. J., AND BELL, M. The influence of improved prenatal nutrition upon the infant. *Journal of the Canadian Medical Association*, 1942, *46*, 6–8.

ECKERMAN, C. O., AND WHATLEY, J. L. Infants' reactions to unfamiliar adults varying in novelty. *Developmental Psychology*, 1975, *11*, 562–566.

EDELMAN, R. Cell-mediated immune function in malnutrition. In R. M. Suskind (Ed.), *Malnutrition and the immune response.* New York: Raven Press, 1977.

EDELMAN, R., SUSKIND, R., SIRISINHA, S. AND OLSON, R. E. Mechanisms of defective cutaneous hypersensitivity in children with protein-calorie malnutrition. *Lancet*, 1973, *1*, 506–508.

EDGERTON, R. B. *Mental retardation.* Cambridge, Mass.: Harvard University Press, 1979.

EDUCATION COMMISSION OF THE STATES, TASK FORCE ON EDUCATION FOR ECONOMIC GROWTH. *Action for excellence.* Denver, Colo.: Education Commission of the States, 1983.

EDWARDS, C. P. The comparative study of the development of moral judgment and reasoning. In R. H. Munroe, R. L. Munroe, and B. Whiting (Eds.), *Handbook of cross-cultural human development.* New York: Garland, 1981.

EDWARDS, J. R. Social class differences and the identity of sex in children's speech. *Journal of Child Language*, 1979, *6*, 121–127.

EGELAND, B. Training impulsive children in the use of more efficient scanning techniques. *Child Development*, 1974, *45*, 165–171.

EGELAND, B., AND FARBER, E. A. Infant-mother attachment: Factors related to its development and changes over time. *Child Development*, 1984, *55*, 753–771.

EGELAND, B., AND SROUFE, L. A. Attachment and early maltreatment. *Child Development*, 1981, *52*, 44–52.

EIBL-EIBESFELDT, I. The expressive behavior of the deaf- and blind-born. In M. von Cranach and I. Vine (Eds.), *Social communication and movement.* New York: Academic Press, 1973.

EIMAS, P. D., SIQUELAND, E. R., JUZCZYK, P., AND VIGORITO, J. Speech perception in early infancy. *Science*, 1971, *171*, 303–306.

EISENBERG, L. The fathers of autistic children. *American Journal of Orthopsychiatry*, 1957, *27*, 715–724.

EISENBERG, N., LENNON, R., AND ROTH, K. Prosocial development: A longitudinal study. *Developmental Psychology*, 1983, *19*, 846–855.

EISENBERG, N., LUNDY, T., SHELL, R., AND ROTH, K. Children's justifications for their adult and peer-directed complaint (prosocial and nonprosocial) behaviors. *Developmental Psychology*, 1985, *21*, 325–331.

EISENBERG, N., MURRAY, E., AND HITE, T. Children's reasoning regarding sex-typed toy choices. *Child Development*, 1982, *53*, 81–86.

EISENBERG, R. B. Auditory behavior in the human neonate: I. Methodologic problems and the logical design of research procedures. *Journal of Auditory Research*, 1965, *5*, 159–177.

EISENBERG, R. B. *Auditory competence in early life: The roots of communicative behavior.* Baltimore, Md.: University Park Press, 1976.

EISENBERG, R. B. Stimulus significance as a determinant of infant responses to sound. In E. B. Thoman (Ed.), *Origins of the infant's social responses.* Hillsdale, N.J.: Lawrence Erlbaum Associates, 1979.

EITZEN, D. S. Athletics in the status system of male adolescents: A replication of Coleman's *The adolescent society. Adolescence*, 1975, *10*, 267–276.

ELASHOFF, J. D., AND SNOW, R. E. *Pygmalion reconsidered; a case study in statistical inference: reconsideration of the Rosenthal-Jacobson data on teacher expectancy.* Worthington, Ohio: C.A. Jones Publishing Co., 1971.

ELIAS, J., AND GEBHARD, P. Sexuality and sexual learning in childhood. *Phi Beta Kappan*, 1969, 50, 401–405.

ELIAS, M. F. *Nursing and night walking in the first two years.* Paper presented at the International Conference on Infant Studies, New York, April 1984.

ELKIND, D. Egocentrism in adolescence. *Child Development*, 1967, 38, 1025–1034.

ELKIND, D. Perceptual development in children. In I. L. Janis (Ed.), *Current trends in psychology.* Los Altos, Calif.: Kaufmann, 1977.

ELKIND, D. *The child and society.* New York: Oxford University Press, 1979.

ELKIND, D. *The hurried child: Growing up too fast too soon.* Reading, Mass.: Addison-Wesley, 1981.

ELKIND, D. Egocentrism redux. *Developmental Review*, 1985, 5, 218–226.

ELKIND, D., AND BOWEN, R. Imaginary audience behavior in children and adolescents. *Developmental Psychology*, 1979, 15, 38–44.

ELLIOTT, J. Risk of cancer, dysplasia for DES daughters found ''very low.'' *Journal of American Medical Association*, 1979, 241, 1555.

ELLIS, S., AND ROGOFF, B. The strategies and efficacy of child versus adult teachers. *Child Development*, 1982, 53, 730–735.

ELLIS, S., ROGOFF, B., AND CROMER, C. C. Age segregation in children's social interactions. *Developmental Psychology*, 1981, 17, 399–407.

ELMER, E., AND GREGG, C. D. Developmental characteristics of the abused child. *Pediatrics*, 1967, 40, 596–602.

EMDE, R. N. Levels of meaning for infant emotions: A biosocial view. In W. A. Collins (Ed.), *Development of cognition, affect, and social relations. Minnesota Symposia on Child Psychology*, Volume 13. Hillsdale, N.J.: Lawrence Erlbaum Associates, 1980.

EMDE, R. N., GAENSBAUER, T., AND HARMON, R. Emotional expression in infancy: A biohavioral study. In *Psychological issues*, Monograph 37. New York: International Universities Press, 1976.

EMERY, D. G. *Teach your preschooler to read.* New York: Simon and Schuster, 1975.

EMMERICH, W., GOLDMAN, K. S., KIRSCH, B., AND SHARABANY, R. Evidence for a transitional phase in the development of gender constancy. *Child Development*, 1977, 48, 930–936.

ENRIGHT, R. D., LAPSLEY, D. K., AND LEVY, V. M. JR. Moral education strategies. In M. Pressley and J. R. Levin (Eds.), *Cognitive strategy research: Educational application.* New York: Springer-Verlag, 1983.

ENTWISLE, D. R., AND DOERING, S. G. *The first birth: A family turning point.* Baltimore, Md.: Johns Hopkins University Press, 1981.

EPSTEIN, L. *Childhood obesity.* Paper presented at NIH workshop on childhood obesity, March 10, 1986, reprinted in *Science*, 1986, 232, 20–21.

ERICSON, A., KALLEN, B., AND WESTERHOLM, P. Cigarette smoking as an etiologic factor in cleft lip and palate. *American Journal of Obstetrics and Gynecology*, 1979, 35, 348–351.

ERIKSON, E. H. *Identify: Youth and crisis.* New York: Norton, 1968.

ERLENMEYER-KIMLING, L., AND JARVIK, L. F. Genetics and intelligence: A review. *Science*, 1963, 142, 1477–1479.

ERON, L. D., HUESMANN, R., BRICE, P., FISCHER, P., AND MERMELSTEIN, R. Age trends in the development of aggression, sex typing, and related television habits. *Developmental Psychology*, 1983, 19, 71–77.

ERON, L. D., WALDER, L. O., AND LEFKOWITZ, M. M. *Learning of aggression in children.* Boston: Little, Brown, 1971.

ERVIN-TRIPP, S. Discourse agreement: How children answer questions. In J. R. Hayes (Ed.), *Cognition and the development of language.* New York: Wiley, 1970.

ESPENSCHADE, A. S., AND MELENEY, H. E. Motor performances of adolescent boys and girls today in comparison with those of twenty years ago. *Research Quarterly*, 1961, 32, 186–189.

ETAUGH, C. Effects of maternal employment on children: A review of recent research. *Merrill-Palmer Quarterly*, 1974, 20, 71–98.

ETZEL, B. C., AND GEWIRTZ, J. L. Experimental modification of care-taker-maintained high rate operant crying in a 6- and a 20-week-old infant: Extinction of crying with reinforcement of eye contact and smiling. *Journal of Experimental Child Psychology*, 1967, 5, 303–317.

EVANS, D. R., NEWCOMBE, R. G., AND CAMPBELL, H. Maternal smoking habits and congenital malformations: A population study. *British Medical Journal*, 1979, 2, 171–173.

EVANS, G., AND HALL, J. The older the sperm. *Ms.*, January 1975.

EVANS, M. Impact of classroom acitvities on beginning reading development. In T. H. Carr (Ed.), *The development of reading skills.* New Directions for Child Development, No. 27. San Francisco: Jossey-Bass, 1985.

EVANS, R. *Jean Piaget: The man and his ideas.* New York: E. P. Dutton, 1973.

FAGAN, J. F. Infants' delayed recognition memory and forgetting. *Journal of Experimental Child Psychology*, 1973, 16, 424–450.

FAGAN, J. F., AND SINGER, L. T. Infant recognition memory as a measure of intelligence. In L. P. Lipsitt and C. K. Rovee-Collier (Eds.), *Advances in infancy research*, Volume 2. Norwood, N.J.: Ablex, 1983.

FAGOT, B. I. The influence of sex of child on parental reactions to toddler children. *Child Development*, 1978, 49, 459–465.

FAGOT, B. I. The construction of gender during the child's first two years. *Infant Behavior and Development*, 1986, 9 (Special Issue: Abstracts of papers presented at the Fifth International Conference on Infant Studies), 116.

FAGOT, B. I., AND LEINBACH, M. D. Play styles in early childhood: Social consequences for boys and girls. In M. B. Liss (Ed.), *Social and cognitive skills: Sex roles and children's play.* New York: Academic Press, 1983.

FAGOT, B. I., AND LITTMAN, I. Relation of preschool sex-typing to intellectual performance in elementary school. *Psychological Reports*, 1976, 39, 699–704.

FAIRWEATHER, H. Sex differences in cognition: A function of maturation rate? *Science*, 1976, 192, 572–573.

FANTZ, R. L. The origins of form perception. *Scientific American*, 1961, 204, 66–72.

FANTZ, R. L. Pattern vision in newborn infants. *Science*, 1963, 140, 296–297.

FANTZ, R. L. Visual perception from birth as shown by pattern selectivity. *Annals of the New York Academy of Science*, 1965, 118, 793–814.

FANTZ, R. L., AND NEVIS, S. The predictive value of changes in visual preferences in early infancy. In J. Hallmuth (Ed.), *Exceptional infant*, Volume 1. Seattle: Special Child Publications, 1967.

FARBER, S. L. *Identical twins reared apart: A reanalysis.* New York: Basic Books, 1981.

FARKAS-BARGETON, E., AND DIEBLER, M. F. A topographical study of enzyme maturation in human cerebral neocortex: A histochemical and biochemical study. In M. A. B. Brazier and H. Petsche (Eds.), *Architectonics of the cerebral cortex.* New York: Raven Press, 1978.

FARNHAM-DIGGORY, S. *Learning disabilities.* Cambridge, Mass.: Harvard University Press, 1978.

FARNHAM-DIGGORY, S. Why reading? Because it's there. *Developmental Review*, 1984, 4, 62–71.

FARRAN, D. C., BURCHINAL, M., HUTAFF, S. E., AND RAMEY, C. T. Allegiances or attachments: Relationship among infants and their day care teachers. In R. C. Ainslie (Ed.), *The child and the day care setting.* New York: Praeger, 1984.

FAUST, M. S. Developmental maturity as a determinant in prestige of adolescent girls. *Child Development*, 1960, 31, 173–184.

FAUST, M. S. Somatic development of adolescent girls. *Monographs of the Society for Research in Child Development*, 1977, 42 (1, Serial No. 169).

FEATHER, N. T. Values in adolescence. In J. Adelson (Ed.), *Handbook of adolescent psychology.* New York: Wiley, 1980.

FEATHERMAN, D. Schooling and occupational careers. Constancy and change in worldly success. In O. Brim and J. Kagan (Eds.), *Constancy and change in human development.* Cambridge, Mass.:

Harvard University Press, 1980.

FEDERATION CECOS, SCHWARTZ, D., AND MAYAUX, M. J. Female fecundity as a function of age: Results of artificial insemination in 2193 nulliparous women with azoospermic husbands. *New England Journal of Medicine*, 1982, *306*, 404–406.

FEIN, G., JOHNSON, D., KOSSON, N., STORK, L., AND WASSERMAN, L. Sex stereotypes and preferences in the toy choices of 20-month-old boys and girls. *Developmental Psychology*, 1975, *11*, 527–528.

FEIN, G., AND ROBERTSON, A. R. *Cognitive and social dimensions of pretending in two-year-olds.* Detroit: Merrill-Palmer Institute, 1975.

FEIN, G., SCHWARTZ, P., JACOBSON, S., AND JACOBSON, J. Environmental toxins and behavioral development. *American Psychologist*, 1983, *38*, 1188–1197.

FEINGOLD, B. F. *Why your child is hyperactive.* New York: Random House, 1975.

FEINMAN, S., AND LEWIS, M. *Social referencing and second-order effects in ten-month-old infants.* Paper presented at the meeting of the Society for Research in Child Development, Boston, April 1981.

FEINMAN, S., AND LEWIS, M. Social referencing at ten months: A second-order effect on infants' responses to strangers. *Child Development*, 1983, *54*, 878–887.

FEIRING, S., LEWIS, M., AND STARR, M. D. Indirect effects and infants' reaction to strangers. *Developmental Psychology*, 1984, *20*, 485–491.

FELD, S. Longitudinal study of the origins of achievement strivings. *Journal of Personality and Social Psychology*, 1967, *7*, 408–414.

FELDMAN, S. S., AND INGHAM, M. E. Attachment behavior: A validation study in two age groups. *Child Development*, 1975, *46*, 319–330.

FERGUSON, C. A. Baby talk in six languages. *American Anthropologist*, 1964, *66*, 103–114.

FERNALD, A. *Four-month-olds prefer to listen to "motherese."* Paper presented at the meeting of the Society for Research in Child Development, Boston, April 1981.

FERNALD, A. *Acoustic determinants of infant preference for "motherese."* Unpublished doctoral dissertation, University of Oregon, 1982.

FERNALD, A. The perceptual and affective salience of mother's speech to infants. In I. Feagans, C. Garvey, and R. Golinkoff (Eds.), *The origins and growth of communication.* Norwood, N.J.: Ablex, 1984.

FERNALD, A. Four-month-old infants prefer to listen to motherese. *Infant Behavior and Development*, 1985, *8*, 181–195.

FERNALD, A., AND SIMON, T. Expanded intonation contours in mothers' speech to newborns. *Developmental Psychology*, 1984, *20*, 104–113.

FESHBACH, S. The catharsis hypothesis and some consequences of interaction with aggressive and neutral play objects. *Journal of Personality*, 1956, *24*, 449–462.

FESHBACH, S. Aggression. In P. H. Mussen (Ed.), *Carmichael's manual of child psychology*, Volume 2. New York: Wiley, 1970.

FIELD, T. Interaction behaviors of primary versus secondary caretaker fathers. *Developmental Psychology*, 1978, *14*, 183–184.

FIELD, T., DE STAFANO, L., AND KOEWLER, J. H., III. Fantasy play of toddlers and preschoolers. *Developmental Psychology*, 1982, *18*, 503–508.

FIELD, T., SANDBERG, D., GARCIA, R., VEGA-LAHR, N., GOLDSTEIN, S., AND GUY, L. Pregnancy problems, postpartum depression, and early mother-infant interactions. *Developmental Psychology*, 1985, *21*, 1152–1156.

FILLMORE, C. J. The case for case. In E. Bach and R. T. Harms (Eds.), *Universals of linguistic theory.* Nerw York: Holt, Rinehart & Winston, 1968.

FINCHER, J. *Human intelligence.* New York: G. P. Putnam & Sons, 1976.

FINE, P. R., AND DOBIN, D. D. *International Symposium on Recent Advances in the Assessment of the Health Effects of Environmental Pollution.* Paris: C.E.C., 1974.

FINE, P. R., THOMAS, C. W., SUBS, R. H., COHNBERG, R. E., AND FLASHNER, B. A. Pediatric blood lead levels. *Journal of the American Medical Association*, 1972, *221*, 1475–1479.

FISCHER, K. W. A theory of cognitive development: The control and construction of hierarchies of skills. *Psychological Review*, 1980, *87*, 477–531.

FISCHER, K. W., AND CANFIELD, R. L. The ambiguity of stage and structure in behavior: Person and environment in the development of psychological structures. In I. Levin (Ed.), *Stage and structure: Reopening the debate.* Norwood, N.J.: Ablex, 1986.

FISCHER, K. W., AND SILVERN, L. Stages and individual differences in cognitive development. *Annual Review of Psychology*, 1985, *36*, 613–648.

FIVUSH, R. Children's long-term memory for a novel event: An exploratory study. *Merrill-Palmer Quarterly*, 1984, *30*, 303–316.

FLAPAN, D. *Children's understanding of social interaction.* New York: Teachers College Press, Columbia University, 1968.

FLAVELL, J. H. Developmental studies of mediated memory. In H. W. Reese and L. P. Lipsitt (Eds.), *Advances in child development and behavior*, Volume 5. New York: Academic Press, 1970.

FLAVELL, J. H. *Cognitive development.* Englewood Cliffs, N.J.: Prentice-Hall, 1977.

FLAVELL, J. H. Stage-related properties of cognitive development. *Cognitive Psychology*, 1978, *2*, 421–453.

FLAVELL, J. H., BEACH, D. H., AND CHINSKY, J. M. Spontaneous verbal rehearsal in memory tasks as a function of age. *Child Development*, 1966, *37*, 283–299.

FLAVELL, J. H., BOTKIN, P. T., FRY, C. L., WRIGHT, J. W., AND JARVIS, P. E. *The development of role-taking and communication skills in children.* New York: Wiley, 1968.

FLAVELL, J. H., EVERETT, B. A., CROFT, K., AND FLAVELL, E. R. Young children's knowledge about visual perception: Further evidence for the Level 1–Level 2 distinction. *Developmental Psychology*, 1981, *17*, 99–103.

FLAVELL, J. H., FRIEDRICHS, A. G., AND HOYT, J. D. Developmental changes in memorization processes. *Cognitive Psychology*, 1970, *1*, 324–340.

FLAVELL, J. H., SHIPSTEAD, S. G., AND CROFT, K. Young children's knowledge about visual perception: Hiding objects from others. *Child Development*, 1978, *49*, 1208–1211.

FLEENER, D. E. *Experimental production of infant-maternal attachment behaviors.* Unpublished manuscript, Indiana University–Purdue University, 1973.

FLEMING, A. T. New frontiers in conception. *New York Times Magazine*, July 20, 1980.

FOGELMAN, K. Smoking in pregnancy and subsequent development of the child. *Child: Care, Health and Development*, 1980, *6*, 233–249.

FOLEY, M., AND JOHNSON, M. K. Confusions between memories for performed and imagined actions: A developmental comparison. *Child Development*, 1985, *56*, 1145–1155.

FOLGER, J. P., AND CHAPMAN, R. S. A pragmatic analysis of spontaneous imitations. *Journal of Child Language*, 1978, *5*, 25–38.

FOLSTEIN, S., AND RUTTER, M. Genetic influences and infantile autism. *Nature*, 1977, *265*, 726–728.

FOREHAND, G., RAGOSTA, M., AND ROCK, D. *Conditions and processes of effective school designation.* Final report, U.S. Office of Education, Department of Health, Education and Welfare. Princeton, N.J.: Educational Testing Service, 1976.

FORMAN, G. E., AND HILL, F. *Constructive play applying Piaget in the preschool.* Monterey, Calif.: Brooks/Cole, 1980.

FORREST, D. L., AND WALLER, T. G. *Meta-memory and meta-cognitive aspects of decoding in reading.* Paper presented at the meeting of the American Educational Research Association, Los Angeles, April 1981.

FORREST-PRESSLEY, D. L., AND WALLER, T. G. *Cognition, metacognition, and reading.* New York: Springer-Verlag, 1984.

FOUNDATION FOR CHILD DEVELOPMENT. *Summary of preliminary results: National survey of children.* New York: Author, 1976.

FOURCIN, A. J. Acoustic patterns and speech acquisition. In N. Waterson and C. Snow (Eds.), *The development of communication.* New York: Wiley, 1978.

Fox, H. E., Steinbrecher, M., Pessel, D., Inglis, J., Medvid, L., and Angel, E. Maternal ethanol ingestion and the occurrence of human fetal breathing movements. *American Journal of Obstetrics and Gynecology*, 1978, *132*, 354–358.

Fox, N., Kagan, J., and Weiskopf, S. The growth of memory during infancy. *Genetic Psychology Monographs*, 1979, *99*, 91–130.

Fraiberg, S. Blind infants and their mothers: An examination of the sign system. In M. Lewis and L. A. Rosenblum (Eds.), *The effect of the infant on its caregiver*. New York: Wiley, 1974.

Fraiberg, S. The development of human attachments in infants blind from birth. *Merrill-Palmer Quarterly*, 1975, *21*, 315–334.

Fraiberg, S. *Every child's birthright. In defense of mothering*. New York: Basic Books, 1977. (a)

Fraiberg, S. *Insights from the blind*. New York: Basic Books, 1977. (b)

Frankel, K. *Origins of mother-toddler problem solving interactions*. Paper presented at the International Conference on Infant Studies, New York, April 1984.

Frankenberg, W. K., and Dodds, J. B. The Denver Developmental Screening Test. *Journal of Pediatrics*, 1967, *71*, 181–191.

Franklin, R. D. Youth's expectancies about internal versus external control of reinforcement. *Dissertation Abstracts*, 1963, *24*, 1684.

Frazier, T. M., Davis, G. H., Goldstein, H., and Goldberg, I. Cigarette smoking: A prospective study. *American Journal of Obstetrics and Gynecology*, 1961, *81*, 988–996.

Freeman, N. H. *Strategies of representation in young children: Analysis of spatial skill and drawing processes*. London: Academic Press, 1980.

Freeman, N. H., Lloyd, S., and Sinha, C. G. Infant search tasks reveal early concepts of containment and canonical usage of objects. *Cognition*, 1980, *8*, 243–262.

Freeman, R., and Pearson, P. Counseling with parents. In J. Apley (Ed.), *Care of the handicapped child*. Clinics in Developmental Medicine, No. 67. London: William Heinemann Medical Books, 1978.

Fremgen, A., and Fay, D. Overextensions in production and comprehension: A methodological clarification. *Journal of Child Language*, 1980, *7*, 205–211.

French, D. C. Children's social interaction with older, younger, and same-age peers. *Journal of Personal Relationships*, in press.

Freud, A. Adolescence. In J. F. Rosenblith, W. Alinsmith, and J. P. William (Eds.), *The causes of behavior* (3rd ed.). Boston: Allyn & Bacon, 1972.

Freud, S. Three contributions to the sexual theory (translated by A. A. Brill). *Nervous and Mental Disease Monograph Series*, 7, 1910.

Freud, S. *An autobiographical study* (translated by J. Strachey). London: Hogarth, 1935.

Freud, S. *Instincts and their vicissitudes* (Volume 14 of the Standard Edition). London: Hogarth, 1968. (Originally published 1915)

Freud, S. *An outline of psychoanalysis* (translated by J. Strachey). New York: Norton, 1970.

Freudenberg, R. P., Driscoll, J. W., and Stern, G. S. Reactions of adult humans to cries of normal and abnormal infants. *Infant Behavior and Development*, 1978, *1*, 224–227.

Freuh, T., and McGhee, P. E. Traditional sex role development and amount of time spent watching television. *Developmental Psychology*, 1975, *11*, 109.

Friedlander, B. Z., Jacobs, A. C., David, B. B., and Wetstone, H. S. Time sampling analysis of infant's natural language environments—the home. *Child Development*, 1972, *43*, 730–740.

Friedman, C. J., Mahn, F., and Friedman, A. S. A profile of juvenile street gang members. *Adolescence*, 1975, *10*, 563–607.

Friedman, M., and Rosenman, R. *Type A behavior and your heart*. New York: Knopf, 1974.

Friedman, S. L., and Jacobs, B. S. Sex differences in neonates' behavioral responsiveness to repeated auditory stimulation. *Infant Behavior and Development*, 1981, *4*, 175–183.

Friedrich, L. K., and Stein, A. H. Aggressive and prosocial television programs and the natural behavior of preschool children. *Monographs of the Society for Research in Child Development*, 1973, *38* (4, Serial No. 151).

Friedrich, O. What do babies know? *Time*, August 15, 1983, pp. 52–59. Reprinted in *Annual Editions Human Development 86/87*. Guilford, Conn.: Dushkin, 1986, pp. 62–67.

Frisch, H. L. Sex stereotypes in adult–infant play. *Child Development*, 1977, *48*, 1671–1675.

Frodi, A. M., Bridges, L., Shonk, S., and Greene, L. Responsiveness to infant crying: Effects of perceived infant temperament. *Infant Behavior and Development*, 1986, *9* (Special Issue: Abstracts of papers presented at the Fifth International Conference on Infant Studies), 131.

Frodi, A. M., Lamb, M. E., Leavitt, L. A., and Donovan, W. L. Fathers' and mothers' responses to infant smiles and cries. *Infant Behavior and Development*, 1978, *1*, 187–198.

Furman, I. *The development of problem solving strategies: A neo-Piagetian analysis of children's performance in a balance task*. Unpublished doctoral dissertation, University of California, Berkeley, 1981.

Furman, W., and Bierman, K. L. Children's conceptions of friendship: A multimethod study of developmental changes. *Developmental Psychology*, 1984, *20*, 925–931.

Furman, W., Rahe, D. F., and Hartup, W. W. Rehabilitation of socially withdrawn preschool children through mixed-age and same-age socialization. *Child Development*, 1979, *50*, 915–922.

Furrow, D., Nelson, K., and Benedict, H. Mother's speech to children and syntactic development: Some simple relationships. *Journal of Child Language*, 1979, *6*, 423–442.

Furstenberg, F., Moore, K. A., Peterson, J. L. Sex education and sexual experience among adolescents. *American Journal of Public Health*, 1985, *75*, 1331–1332.

Furstenberg, F. F. *Unplanned parenthood*. New York: Free Press, 1976.

Furth, H. G. *Thinking without language: Psychological implications of deafness*. Englewood Cliffs, N.J.: Prentice-Hall, 1966.

Gadberry, S. Effects of restricting first graders' TV-viewing on leisure time use, IQ change, and cognitive style. *Journal of Applied Developmental Psychology*, 1980, *1*, 45–57.

Gagnon, J. H., and Simon, W. *Sexual conduct: The social origins of human sexuality*. Chicago: Aldine, 1973.

Gallatin, J. Political thinking in adolescence. In J. Adelson (Ed.), *Handbook of adolescent psychology*. New York: Wiley, 1980.

Galler, J. R., Ramsey, F., and Solimano, G. The influence of early malnutrition on subsequent behavioral development: III. Learning disabilities as a sequel to malnutrition. *Pediatric Research*, 1984, *18*, 309–313.

Gamer, E., Thomas, J., and Kendall, D. Determinants of friendship across the life span. In M. F. Rebelsky (Ed.), *Life: The continuous process*. New York: Knopf, 1975.

Ganchrow, J. R., Steiner, J. E., and Daher, M. Neonatal facial expressions in response to different qualities and intensities of gustatory stimuli. *Infant Behavior and Development* 1983, *6*, 189–200.

Garbarino, J. The impact of anticipated rewards on cross-age tutoring. *Journal of Personality and Social Psychology*, 1975, *32*, 421–428.

Garbarino, J., and Asp, C. *Successful schools and competent students*. Lexington, Mass.: Lexington Books, 1981.

Garbarino, J., Sebes, J., and Schellenbach, C. Families at risk for destructive parent–child relations in adolescence. *Child Development*, 1984, *55*, 174–183.

Gardner, H. *Frames of mind: The theory of multiple intelligences*. New York: Basic Books, 1983.

Gardner, J. A. *Sesame Street* and sex role stereotypes. *Women*, 1970, *1*, 42.

Gardner, L. Deprivation dwarfism. *Scientific American*, 1972, *227*, 76–82.

Garmezy, N., and Nuechterlein, K. H. Invulnerable children: The fact and fiction of competence and disadvantage. *American Journal of Orthopsychiatry*, 1972, *77*, 328–329.

Garnica, O. K. Some prosodic and paralinquistic features of speech directed to young children. In C. E. Snow and C. A. Ferguson (Eds.), *Talking to children: Language input and acquisition*.

Cambridge, England: Cambridge University Press, 1977.

GARVEY, C. Some properties of social play. *Merrill-Palmer Quarterly*, 1974, *20*, 163–180.

GARVEY, C. Requests and responses in children's speech. *Journal of Child Language*, 1975, *2*, 41–63.

GARVEY, C. *Children's talk*. Cambridge, Mass. Harvard University Press, 1984.

GARVEY, C., AND HOGAN, R. Social speech and social interaction: Egocentrism revisited. *Child Development*, 1973, *44*, 562–568.

GAYL, I. E., ROBERTS, J. O., AND WERNER, J. S. Linear systems analysis of infant visual pattern preferences. *Journal of Experimental Child Psychology*, 1983, *35*, 30–45.

GEFFEN, G., AND SEXTON, M. A. The development of auditory strategies of attention. *Developmental Psychology*, 1978, *14*, 11–17.

GELMAN, R. Conservation acquisition: A problem of learning to attend to relevant attributes. *Journal of Experimental Child Psychology*, 1969, *7*, 167–187.

GELMAN, R. The nature and development of early number concepts. In H. W. Reese (Ed.), *Advances in child development and behavior*. Volume 7. New York: Academic Press, 1972.

GELMAN, R., AND BAILLARGEON R. A review of some Piagetian concepts. In P. H. Mussen (Ed.), *Handbook of child psychology*, Volume 3, New York: Wiley, 1983.

GELMAN, R., MECK, E., AND MERKIN, S. Young children's numerical competence. *Cognitive Development*, 1986, *1*, 1–29.

GERBNER, G. Violence in television drama: Trends and symbolic functions. In G. A. Comstock and E. A. Rubenstein (Eds.), *Television and social behavior*, Volume 1, *Media content and control*. Washington, D.C.: U.S. Government Printing Office, 1972.

GERBNER, G., GROSS, L., ELERY, M., JACKSON-BEECK, M., JEFFRIES-FOX, S., AND SIGNORIELLI, N. *Violence profile #8: Trends in network television drama and viewer conceptions of social reality, 1967–1976*. Philadelphia: Annenberg School of Communications, University of Pennsylvania, 1977.

GESCHWIND, N. Specialization of the human brain. *Scientific American*, 1979, *241*, 180–201.

GESELL, A., AND AMATRUDA, C. *Developmental diagnosis*. New York: Paul B. Hoeber, 1941.

GETZELS, J. W., AND CSIKSZENTMIHALYI, M. *The creative vision: A longitudinal study of problem finding in art*. New York: Wiley, 1976.

GETZELS, J. W., AND JACKSON, P. W. *Creativity and intelligence*. New York: Wiley, 1962.

GEWIRTZ, J. L. The course of infant smiling in four childrearing environments in Israel. In B. M. Foss (Ed.), *Determinants of infant behavior*, Volume 3. New York: Wiley, 1965.

GEWIRTZ, J. L. Contingent maternal responding can increase infant nondistress crying, in press.

GEWIRTZ, J. L., AND BOYD, E. F. Does maternal responding imply reduced infant crying? A critique of the 1972 Bell and Ainsworth report. *Child Development*, 1977, *48*, 1200–1207.

GHATALA, E. S. Developmental changes in incidental memory as a function of meaningfulness and encoding condition. *Developmental Psychology*, 1984, *20*, 208–211.

GHISELLI, E. E. *The validity of occupational aptitude tests*. New York: Wiley, 1966.

GIACONIA, R. M., AND HEDGES, L. V. Identifying features of effective open communication. *Review of Educational Research*, 1982, *52*, 579–602.

GIBBONS, J. L., JOHNSON, M. O., McDONOUGH, P. M., AND REZNICK, J. S. Behavioral inhibition in infants and children. *Infant Behavior and Development*, 1986, *9* (Special Issue: Abstracts of papers presented at the Fifth International Conference on Infant Studies), 139.

GIBBS, J. C., ARNOLD, K. D., AND BURKHART, J. E. Sex differences in the expression of moral judgment. *Child Development*, 1984, *55*, 1040–1043.

GIBBS, J. C., CLARK, P. M., JOSEPH, J. A., GREEN, J. L., GOODRICK, T. S., AND MAKOWSKI, D. G. Relations between moral judgment, moral courage, and field independence. *Child Development*, 1986, *57*,

185–193.

GIBSON, E. J. *Principles of perceptual learning and development*. New York: Appleton-Century-Crofts, 1969.

GIBSON, E. J., AND SPELKE, E. S. The development of perception. In P. H. Mussen (Ed.), *Handbook of child psychology*, Volume 3. New York: Wiley, 1983.

GIBSON, E. J., AND WALK, R. D. The ''visual cliff.'' *Scientific American*, 1960, *202*, 64–71.

GIBSON, J. J. *The senses considered as perceptual systems*. Boston: Houghton-Mifflin, 1966.

GIL, D. G. Violence against children. *Journal of Marriage and the Family*, 1971, *33*, 637–648.

GILL, N. E., WHITE, M. A., AND ANDERSON, G. C. *Transitional newborn infants in a hospital nursery: Time and behavior between first oral cue and first sustained cry*. Paper presented at the International Conference on Infant Studies, New York, April 1984.

GILLBERG, C., RASSMUSSEN, P., AND WAHLSTROM, J. Minor neurodevelopmental disorders in children born to older mothers. *Developmental Medicine and Child Neurology*, 1982, *24*, 437–447.

GILLIGAN, C. *In a different voice: Psychological theory and women's development*. Cambridge, Mass.: Harvard University Press, 1982.

GLEASON, J. B. Do children imitate? *Proceedings of the International Conference on Oral Education of the Deaf*, 1967, *2*, 1441–1448.

GLEITMAN, L. R., NEWPORT, E. L., AND GLEITMAN, H. The current status of the motherese hypothesis. *Journal of Child Language*, 1984, *11*, 43–79.

GLEITMAN, L. R., AND WANNER, B. Language acquisition: The state of the state of the art. In E. Wanner and L. R. Gleitman (Eds.), *Language acquisition: The state of the art*. Cambridge, England: Cambridge University Press, 1982.

GLENN, S. M., AND CUNNINGHAM, C. C. What do babies listen to most? A developmental study of auditory preferences in nonhandicapped infants and infants with Down's syndrome. *Developmental Psychology*, 1983, *19*, 332–337.

GLIDEWELL, J. C., KANTOR, M. B., SMITH, L. M., AND STRINGER, L. A. Socialization and social structure in the classroom. In L. W. Hoffman and M. L. Hoffman (Eds.), *Review of child development research*, Volume 2. New York: Russell Sage Foundation, 1966.

GLOBERSON, T., WEINSTEIN, E., AND SHARABANY, R. Teasing out cognitive development from cognitive style: A training study. *Developmental Psychology*, 1985, *21*, 682–691.

GLOGER-TIPPELT, G. A process model of the pregnancy course. *Human Development*, 1983, *26*, 134–148.

GLUCKSBERG, S., KRAUSS, R. M., AND HIGGINS, E. T. The development of referential communication skills. In F. D. Horowitz, (Ed.), *Review of child development research*, Volume 4. Chicago: University of Chicago Press, 1975.

GNEPP, J. Children's social sensitivity: Inferring emotions from conflicting cues. *Developmental Psychology*, 1983, *19*, 805–814.

GODDARD, H. H. *The Kallikak family: A study in the heredity of feeblemindedness*. New York: Macmillan, 1912.

GOLD, M. AND REIMER, D. J. Changing patterns of delinquent behavior among Americans 13 through 16 years old: 1967–72. *Crime and Delinquency Literature*, 1975, *7*, 483–517.

GOLD, M., AND YANOF, D. S. Mothers, daughters, and girlfriends. *Journal of Personality and Social Psychology*, 1985, *49*, 654–659.

GOLDBERG, R. J. *Maternal time use and preschool performance*. Paper presented at the meeting of the Society for Research in Child Development, New Orleans, March 1977.

GOLDBERG, S., AND DiVITTO, B. A. *Born too soon: Preterm birth and early development*. San Francisco: W. H. Freeman, 1983.

GOLDBERG, S., LaCOMBE, S., LEVINSON, D., PARKER, R., ROSS, C., AND SOMMERS, F. *Thinking about the threat of nuclear war: Relevance to mental health*. Unpublished manuscript, 1985.

GOLDBERG, S., PERLMUTTER, M., AND MYERS, N. Recall of related and unrelated lists by two-year-olds. *Journal of Experimental Child Psychology*, 1974, *18*, 1–8.

GOLDBERG, W. A., AND EASTERBROOKS, M. A. Role of marital quality in toddler development. *Developmental Psychology*, 1984, *20*, 504–514.

GOLDBERG, W. A., MICHAELS, G. Y., AND LAMB, M. E. Husbands' and wives' adjustment to pregnancy and first parenthood. *Journal of Family Issues*, 1985, *6*, 483–503.

GOLDFARB, W. Effects of psychological deprivation in infancy and subsequent stimulation. *American Journal of Psychiatry*, 1945, *102*, 18–33.

GOLDIN, P. C. A review of children's reports of parent behaviors. *Psychological Bulletin*, 1969, *71*, 222–236.

GOLDIN-MEADOW, S., AND FELDMAN, H. The development of a language-like communication without a language model. *Science*, 1977, *197*, 401–403.

GOLDIN-MEADOW, S., AND MYLANDER, C. Gestural communication in deaf children: The effects and noneffects of parental input on early language development. *Monographs of the Society for Research in Child Development*, 1984, *49* (3–4, Serial No. 207).

GOLDMAN, B. D., AND ROSS, H. S. Social skills in action: An analysis of early peer games. In J. Glick and K. A. Clarke-Stewart (Eds.), *The development of social understanding*. New York: Gardner Press, 1978.

GOLDMAN, R., AND GOLDMAN, J. *Children's sexual thinking*. London: Routledge, 1982.

GOLDSMITH, H., BRADSHAW, D. L., AND RIESER-DANNER, L. A. Temperament as a potential developmental influence on attachment. In J. V. Lerner and R. M. Lerner (Eds.), *Temperament and social interaction during infancy and childhood*. New Directions for Child Development, No. 31. San Francisco: Jossey-Bass, 1986.

GOLDSMITH, H. H. Genetic influences on personality from infancy to adulthood. *Child Development*, 1983, *54*, 331–355.

GOLDSTEIN, H. Factors influencing the height of seven-year-old children: Results from the National Child Development Study. *Human Biology*, 1971, *43*, 92–111.

GOLEMAN, S. Studies of children as witnesses find surprising accuracy. *New York Times*, November 6, 1984, Section C, p. 4.

GOLOMB, C. *Young children's sculpture and drawing: A study in representation development*. Cambridge, Mass.: Harvard University Press, 1974.

GOODENOUGH, F. L. *Anger in young children*. Minneapolis: University of Minnesota Press, 1931.

GOODNOW, J. *Children's drawings*. Cambridge, Mass.: Harvard University Press, 1977.

GORDON, B. N. Maternal perception of child temperament and observed mother-child interaction. *Child Psychiatry and Human Development*, 1983, *13*, 153–167.

GORDON, R. E., AND GORDON, K. K. Social factors in prevention of postpartum emotional problems. *Obstetrics and Gynecology*, 1960, *15*, 433–438.

GORDON, R. E., KAPOSTINS, E. E., AND GORDON, K. K. Factors in postpartum emotional adjustment. *Obstetrics and Gynecology*, 1965, *25*, 158–166.

GOREN, C., SARTY, M., AND WU, P. Visual following and pattern discrimination of face-like stimuli by newborn infants. *Pediatrics*, 1975, *56*, 544–549.

GOTTESMAN, I. I. Heritability of personality: A demonstration. *Psychology Monographs*, 1963, *77*, No. 572.

GOTTFRIED, A. W., ROSE, S. A., AND BRIDGER, W. H. Crossmodal transfer in human infants. *Child Development*, 1977, *48*, 118–123.

GOTTMAN, J. M. How children become friends. *Monographs of the Society for Research in Child Development*, 1983, *48* (2, Serial No. 201).

GOTTMAN, J. M., GONSO, J., AND RASMUSSEN, B. Social interaction, social competence and friendship in children. *Child Development*, 1975, *46*, 709–718.

GOTTMAN, J. M., AND PARKHURST, J. T. *Developing may not always be improving: A developmental study of children's best friendships*. Paper presented at the meetings of the Society for Research in Child Development, New Orleans, March 1977.

GOTTMAN, J. M., AND PARKHURST, J. T. A developmental theory of friendship and acquaintanceship processes. In W. A. Collins (Ed.), *Development of cognition, affect, and social relations. The Minnesota Symposia on Child Psychology*, Volume 13. Hillsdale, N.J.: Lawrence Erlbaum Associates, 1980.

GRATCH, G., APPEL, K. J., EVANS, W. F., LeCOMPTE, G. K., AND WRIGHT, N. A. Piaget's Stage IV object concept error: Evidence of forgetting or object conception? *Child Development*, 1974, *15*, 71–77.

GRAY, S. W., RAMSEY, B. K., AND KLAUS, R. A. From 3 to 20: The Early Training Project. Baltimore, Md.: University Park Press, 1982.

GRAY, W. M., AND HUDSON, L. M. Formal operations and the imaginary audience. *Developmental Psychology*, 1984, *20*, 619–627.

GREEN, E. H. Group play and quarrelling among preschool children. *Child Development*, 1933, *4*, 302–307.

GREEN, R. *Sissy boys to gay men: A 15-year prospective study*. New Haven, Conn.: Yale University Press, in press.

GREEN, R., NEUBERG, D. S., AND FINCH, S. J. Sex-typed motor behaviors of ''feminine'' boys, conventionally masculine boys, and conventionally feminine girls. *Sex Roles*, 1983, *9*, 571–579.

GREENBERG, D. J. Accelerating visual complexity levels in the human infant. *Child Development*, 1971, *42*, 905–918.

GREENBERG, M., AND MORRIS, N. Engrossment: The newborn's impact upon the father. *American Journal of Orthopsychiatry*, 1974, *44*, 520–531.

GREENBERG, M., ROSENBERG, L., AND LIND, J. First mothers rooming-in with their newborns: Its impact upon the mother. *American Journal of Orthopsychiatry*, 1973, *43*, 783–788.

GREENBERGER, E. *Over-time data on the psychosocial maturity inventory: The South Carolina study*. Working papers (mimeo). Baltimore, Md.: Center for the Social Organization of Schools, The Johns Hopkins University, December 1974.

GREENBERGER, E. *Two three-year longitudinal studies of growth in psychosocial maturity* (mimeo). Baltimore, Md: Center for the Social Organization of Schools, The Johns Hopkins University, 1975.

GREENBERGER, E. Education and the acquisition of psychosocial maturity. In D. C. McClelland (Ed.), *The development of social maturity*. New York: Irvington, 1982.

GREENBERGER, E. Defining psychosocial maturity in adolescence. In P. Karoly and J. J. Steffen (Eds.), *Adolescent behavior disorders: Foundations and applications*. Lexington, Mass.: D. C. Heath, 1983. (a)

GREENBERGER, E. A researcher in the policy arena: The case of child labor. *American Psychologist*, 1983, *38*, 104–110. (b)

GREENBERGER, E., AND STEINBERG, L. *When teenagers work: The psychological and social costs of adolescent employment*. New York: Basic Books, 1986.

GREENFIELD, P. M. *Mind and media: The effects of T.V., video games, and computers*. Cambridge, Mass.: Harvard University Press, 1984.

GREENFIELD, P. M., AND SMITH, J. H. *The structure of communication in early language development*. New York: Academic Press, 1976.

GREENWOOD, K. *The development of communication with mother, father, and sibling*. Unpublished doctoral thesis, Cambridge University, 1983.

GREIF, E. B. *Sex differences in parent–child conversation: Who interrupts who?* Paper presented at the biennial meeting of the Society for Research in Child Development, San Francisco, March 1979.

GREIF, E. B., AND ULMAN, K. J. The psychological impact of menarche on early adolescent females: A review of the literature. *Child Development*, 1982, *53*, 1413–1430.

GRIFFITH, C. R. A comment upon the psychology of the audience. *Psychological Monographs*, 1921, *30*, 36–47.

GRIMM, E. R. Psychological investigation of habitual abortion. *Psychosomatic Medicine*, 1962, *24*, 369.

GROLLMAN, E. A. *Explaining death to children*. Boston: Beacon Press, 1967.

GROSSMAN, F. K., EICHLER, L. S., AND WINIKOFF, S. A. *Pregnancy, birth and parenthood*. San Francisco: Jossey-Bass, 1980.

GROSSMANN, K., THANE, K., AND GROSSMANN, K. E. Maternal tactual contact of the newborn after various postpartum conditions of mother–infant contact. *Developmental Psychology*. 1981, *17*, 159–

169.

Grunebaum, H., Weiss, H. J., Cohler, B., Hartman, C., and Gallant, D. *Mentally ill mothers and their children*. Chicago: University of Chicago Press, 1975.

Guarnaccia, V. J. *Pupil tutoring in elementary math instruction*. Unpublished doctoral dissertation, Columbia University, 1973.

Guerin, D., and Gottfried, A. W. Infant temperament as a predictor of preschool behavior problems. *Infant Behavior and Development*, 1986, 9 (Special Issue: Abstracts of papers presented at the Fifth International Conference on Infant Studies), 152.

Guilleminault, C., and Anders, T. Sleep disorders in children, Part II. *Advances in Pediatrics*, 1976, 22, 151–174.

Gump, P. Educational environments. In D. Stokols and I. Altman (Eds.), *Handbook of environmental psychology*. New York: Wiley, 1987.

Gumperz, J. J., and Tannen, D. Individual and social differences in language use. In C. J. Filmore, D. Kempler, and W. S. Y Wang (Eds.), *Individual differences in language ability and language behavior*. New York: Academic Press, 1979.

Gunnar, M. R., and Donahue, M. Sex differences in social responsiveness between six months and twelve months. *Child Development*, 1980, 51, 262–265.

Gunnar, M. R., and Stone, C. The effects of positive maternal affect on infant responses to pleasant, ambiguous, and fear-provoking toys. *Child Development*, 1984, 55, 1231–1236.

Gupta, S., Dhingra, D. C., Singh, M. V., and Anand, K. Impact of nutrition on intelligence. *Indian Pediatrika*, 1975, 12, 1079–1082.

Gustafson, G. E. Effects of the ability to locomote on infants' social and exploratory behaviors: An experimental study. *Developmental Psychology*, 1984, 20, 397–405.

Haan, N. Processes of moral development: Cognitive or social disequilibrium? *Development Psychology*, 1985, 21, 996–1006.

Haan, N., Aerts, E., and Cooper, B. A. B. *On moral grounds: The search for practical morality*. New York: New York University Press, 1985.

Haan, N., Smith, M. B., and Block, J. Moral reasoning of young adults: Political-social behavior, family background, and personality correlates. *Journal of Personality and Social Psychology*, 1968, 10, 183–201.

Haas, A. *Teenage sexuality: A survey of teenage sexual behavior*. New York: Macmillan, 1979.

Haddad, G. G., Walsh, E. M., Leistner, H. L., Grodin, W. K., and Mellins, R. B. Abnormal maturation of sleep states in infants with aborted sudden infant death syndrome. *Pediatric Research*, 1981, 15, 1055–1057.

Hagen, J. W., and Hale, G. H. The development of attention in children. In A. D. Pick (Ed.), *Minnesota Symposia on Child Psychology*, Volume 7. Minneapolis: University of Minnesota Press, 1973.

Hains, A. A., and Ryan, E. B. The development of social cognitive processes among juvenile delinquents and nondelinquent peers. *Child Development*, 1983, 54, 1536–1544.

Haith, M. M. The response of the human newborn to visual movement. *Journal of Experimental Child Psychology*, 1966, 3, 112–117.

Haith, M. M., Bergman, T., and Moore, M. J. Eye contact and face scanning in early infancy. *Science*, 1977, 198, 853–855.

Hakuta, J. *Children who grew up skilled in two languages do better on cognitive tests*. Paper presented at the annual meeting of the American Psychological Association, Los Angeles, August 1985.

Hales, D. J., Lozoff, B., Sosa, R., and Kennell, J. H. Defining the limits of the maternal sensitive period. *Developmental Medicine and Child Neurology*, 1977, 19, 454–461.

Hall, G. S. The contents of children's minds. *Princeton Review*, 1883, 59, 38–43.

Hall, G. S. *Adolescence*, Volume 1. New York: D. Appleton, 1904.

Hall, W. M. *Observational and interactive determinants of aggressive behavior in boys*. Unpublished doctoral dissertation, Indiana University, 1974.

Hall, W. S., Nagy, W. E., and Linn, R. *Spoken words: Effects of situation and social group on oral word usage and frequency*. Hillsdale, N.J.: Lawrence Erlbaum Associates, 1984.

Hallgren, B. Enuresis: A clinical and genetic study. *Neurologica Scandinavica et Acta Psychiatrica Neurologica*, 1957, 1–159.

Hallinan, M. T. Recent advances in sociometry. In S. R. Asher and J. M. Gottman (Eds.), *The development of children's friendships*. New York: Cambridge University Press, 1981.

Hamblin, J. A., and Hamblin, R. L. On teaching disadvantaged preschoolers to read: A successful experiment. *American Educational Research Journal*, 1972, 9, 2209–2216.

Hamburg, B. Early adolescence: A specific and stressful stage of the life cycle. In G. V. Coelho, D. A. Hamburg, and J. E. Adams (Eds.), *Coping and adaptation*. New York: Basic Books, 1974.

Haney, D. Q. Boys found more likely to fantasize than girls. *Los Angeles Times*, October 28, 1984, part 8, p. 10.

Hanson, J. W. Unpublished paper, 1977.

Harding, P. G. R. The metabolism of brown and white adipose tissue in the fetus and newborn. *Clinical Obstetrics and Gynecology*, 1971, 14, 685–709.

Hardwick, D., McIntyre, A., and Pick, A. The content and manipulation of cognitive maps in children and adults. *Monographs of the Society for Research in Child Development*, 1976, 41 (3, Serial No. 166).

Hardy, J. B., and Mellits, E. D. Does maternal smoking during pregnancy have a long-term effect on the child? *Lancet*, 1972, 2, 1332–1336.

Hardy-Brown, K., and Plomin, R., and DeFries, J. C. Genetic and environmental influences on the rate of communicative development in the first year of life. *Developmental Psychology*, 1981, 17, 704–717.

Harkness, S., and Super, C. M. The cultural context of gender segregation in children's peer groups. *Child Development*, 1985, 56, 219–224.

Harlow, H. F., and Griffin, G. Induced mental and social deficits in rhesus monkeys. In S. F. Osler and R. E. Cooke (Eds.), *The biosocial bases of mental retardation*. Baltimore, Md.: Johns Hopkins University Press, 1965.

Harlow, H. F., and Zimmerman, R. R. Affectional responses in the infant monkey. *Science*, 1959, 130, 431–432.

Harper, J. F., and Collins, J. K. The effects of early or late maturation on the prestige of the adolescent girl. *Australian and New Zealand Journal of Sociology*, 1972, 8, 83–88.

Harris, B. Whatever happened to little Albert? *American Psychologist*, 1979, 34, 151–160.

Harris, P. L. Perseverative search at a visibly empty place by young infants. *Journal of Experimental Child Psychology*, 1974, 18, 535–542.

Harris, P. L. Infant cognition. In P. H. Mussen (Ed.), *Handbook of child psychology*, Volume 2, New York: Wiley, 1983.

Harris, P. L., and Bassett, E. Transitive inference by four year old children. *Developmental Psychology*, 1975, 11, 875–876.

Harter, S. *Children's understanding of multiple emotions: A cognitive-developmental approach*. Address given at the Ninth Annual Piaget Society meeting, Philadelphia, 1979.

Harter, S. Developmental perspectives on the self-system. In P. H. Mussen (Ed.), *Handbook of child psychology*, Volume 4. New York: Wiley, 1983.

Harter, S., and Connell, J. P. A comparison of alternative models of the relationships between academic achievement, and children's perceptions of competence, control, and motivational orientation. In J. Nicholls (Ed.), *The development of achievement-related cognitions and behaviors*. Greenwich, Conn.: JAI Press, 1982.

Hartshorne, H., and May, M. A. *Studies in the nature of character*, Volume 1. *Studies in deceit*. New York: Macmillan, 1928.

Hartshorne, H., May, M. A., and Maller, J. B. *Studies in the nature of character*, Volume 2, *Studies in self-control*. New York: Macmillan, 1929.

Hartshorne, H., May, M. A., and Shuttleworth, F. K. *Studies in the nature of character*, Volume 3, *Studies in the organization of character*. New York: Macmillan, 1930.

HARTUP, W. W. Peer interaction and social organization. In P. H. Mussen (Ed.), *Carmichael's manual of child psychology*, Volume 2. New York: Wiley, 1970.

HARTUP, W. W. Aggression in childhood: Developmental perspectives. *American Psychologist*, 1974, *29*, 336–341.

HARTUP, W. W. Peer relations. In P. H. Mussen (Ed.), *Handbook of child psychology*, Volume 4. New York: Wiley, 1983.

HARTUP, W. W., AND SANCILIO, M. F. Children's friendships. In E. Schopler and G. B. Mesibov (Eds.), *Social behavior in autism*. New York: Plenum, in press.

HARVEY, D., PRINCE, J., BUNTON, J., PARKINSON, C., AND CAMPBELL, S. Abilities of children who were small-for-gestational-age babies. *Pediatrics*, 1982, *69*, 296–300.

HASHER, L., AND CLIFTON, D. A. A developmental study of attribute encoding in free recall. *Journal of Experimental Child Psychology*, 1974, *7*, 332–346.

HAUSER, S. T., POWERS, S. I., NOAM, G. G., JACOBSON, A. M., WEISS, B, AND FOLLANSBEE, D. J. Familial contexts of adolescent ego development. *Child Development*, 1984, *55*, 195–213.

HAUSKNECHT, R., AND HEILMAN, J. R. *Having a cesarean baby*. New York: E. P. Dutton, 1978.

HAWKINS, J., PEA, R. D., GLICK, J., AND SCRIBNER, S. "Merds that laugh don't like mushrooms": Evidence for deductive reasoning by preschoolers. *Developmental Psychology*, 1984, *20*, 584–594.

HAY, D. F., NASH, A., AND PEDERSEN, J. Responses of six-month-olds to the distress of their peers. *Child Development*, 1981, *52*, 1071–1075.

HAY, D. F., AND RHEINGOLD, H. L. The early appearance of some valued social behaviors. In D. L. Bridgeman (Ed.), *The nature of prosocial development: Interdisciplinary theories and strategies*. New York: Academic Press, 1983.

HAY, D. F., AND ROSS, H. S. The social nature of early conflict. *Child Development*, 1982, *53*, 105–113.

HEIDER, E. R. "Focal" color areas and the development of color names. *Developmental Psychology*, 1971, *4*, 447–455.

HEINICKE, C., DISKIN, S., RAMSEY-KLEE, D., AND OATES, D. *Pre-birth parent characteristics and family development in the first two years of life*. Unpublished manuscript, University of California at Los Angeles, Department of Psychiatry, 1983.

HEINICKE, C. M., AND WESTHEIMER, I. *Brief separations*. New York: International Universities Press, 1966.

HEINONEN, O. P., SLONE, D., AND SHAPIRO, S. *Birth defects and drugs in pregnancy*. Littleton, Mass.: Publishing Sciences Group, 1976.

HELLMAN, L. M., AND PRITCHARD, J. A. *Williams' obstetrics* (14th ed.). New York: Appleton-Century-Crofts, 1971.

HELSON, R., AND CRUTCHFIELD, R. S. Mathematicians: The creative researcher and the average Ph.D. *Journal of Consulting and Clinical Psychology*, 1970, *34*, 250–257.

HENKER, B., AND WHALEN, C. K. The changing faces of hyperactivity: Retrospect and prospect. In C. K. Whalen and B. Henker (Eds.), *Hyperactive children: The social ecology of identification and treatment*. New York: Academic Press, 1980.

HERMAN, J. F., AND ROTH, S. F. Children's incidental memory for spatial locations in a large-scale environment: Taking a tour down memory lane. *Merrill-Palmer Quarterly*, 1984, *30*, 87–102.

HERSHENSON, M. Visual discrimination in the human newborn. *Journal of Comparative Physiological Psychology*, 1964, *58*, 270–276.

HESS, R. D., HOLLOWAY, S. D., DICKSON, W. P., AND PRICE, G. G. Maternal variables as predictors of children's school readiness and later achievement in vocabulary and mathematics in sixth grade. *Child Development*, 1984, *55*, 1902–1912.

HESS, R. D., AND McDEVITT, T. M. Some cognitive consequences of maternal intervention techniques: A longitudinal study. *Child Development*, 1984, *55*, 2017–2030.

HESTON, L. L. The genetics of schizophrenic and schizoid disease. *Science*, 1970, *167*, 249–256.

HETHERINGTON, E. M., COX, M., AND COX, R. *Aftermath of divorce*. Paper presented at the meeting of the American Psychological Association, Washington, D.C., September 1976. (a)

HETHERINGTON, E. M., COX, M., AND COX, R. Divorced fathers. *Family Coordinator*, 1976, *25*, 417–428. (b)

HETHERINGTON, E. M., COX, M., AND COX, R. *Family interaction and the social, emotional, and cognitive development of children following divorce*. Paper presented at the symposium on "The family: Setting priorities." Sponsored by the Institute for Pediatric Service of the Johnson and Johnson Baby Company. Washington, D.C., May 17–20, 1978.

HETHERINGTON, E. M., COX, M., AND COX, R. Effects of divorce on parents and children. In M. Lamb (Ed.), *Nontraditional families*. Hillsdale, N.J.: Lawrence Erlbaum Associates, 1982.

HICKS, D. J. Imitation and retention of film-mediated aggressive peer and adult models. *Journal of Personality and Social Psychology*, 1965, *2*, 97–100.

HILL, C. R., AND STAFFORD, F. P. *Parental care of children: Time diary estimates of quantity predictability and variety*. Working paper series, Institute for Social Research, University of Michigan, Ann Arbor, 1978.

HILL, J. P. AND PALMQUIST, W. J. Social cognition and social relations in early adolescence. *International Journal of Behavioral Development*, 1978, *1*, 1–36.

HILL, K., AND SARASON, S. The relation of test anxiety and defensiveness to test and school performance over the elementary school years: A further longitudinal study. *Monographs of the Society for Research in Child Development*, 1966, *31* (2, Serial No. 104).

HILL, R. Drugs ingested by pregnant women. *Clinical Pharmacology therapeutics*, 1973, *14*, 654–659.

HILLINGER, C. Help on way for expectant fathers. *Los Angeles Times*, June 17, 1984, Part 8, p. 14.

HIMMELBERGER, D. V., BROWN, B. W., JR., AND COHEN, E. N. Cigarette smoking during pregnancy and the occurrence of spontaneous abortion and congenital abnormality. *American Journal of Epidemiology*, 1978, *108*, 470–479.

HINES, M., AND SHIPLEY, C. Prenatal exposure to diethylstilbesterol (DES) and the development of sexually dimorphic cognitive abilities and cerebral lateralization. *Developmental Psychology*, 1984, *20*, 81–94.

HINGSON, R., ALPERT, J. J., DAY, N., DOOLING, E., KAYNE, H., MORELOCK, S., OPPENHEIMER, E., AND ZUCKERMAN, B. Effects of maternal drinking and marijuana use on fetal growth and development. *Pediatrics*, 1982, *70*, 539–547.

HINSHAW, S. P., HENKER, B., AND WHALEN, C. K. Cognitive-behavioral and pharmacologic interventions for hyperactive boys: Comparative and combined effects. *Journal of Consulting and Clinical Psychology*, 1984, *52*, 739–749.

HIRSCH, J. Cell number and size as a determinant of subsequent obesity. In M. Winick (Ed.), *Childhood obesity*. New York: Wiley, 1975.

HIRSH-PASEK, K., GOLINKOFF, R. M., FLETCHER, A., BEAUBEIN, F., AND CAULEY, K. *In the beginning: One-word speakers comprehend word order*. Paper presented at the Boston Language Conference, October 1985.

HIRSCH-PASEK, K., NELSON, D. G., JUSCZYK, P. W., AND WRIGHT, K. *A moment of silence: How the prosodic cues in motherese might assist language learning*. Paper presented at the International Conference on Infant Studies, Los Angeles, April 1986.

HIRSCH-PASEK, K., AND TREIMAN, R. Doggerel: Motherese in a new context. *Journal of Child Language*, 1982, *9*, 229–237.

HIRSH-PASEK, K., TREIMAN, R., AND SCHNEIDERMAN, M. Brown and Hanlon revisited: Mothers' sensitivity to ungrammatical forms. *Journal of Child Language*, 1984, *11*, 81–88.

HOCHHAUSER, M. Educational implications of drug abuse. *Journal of Drug Addiction*, 1978, *8*, 69–76.

HOCK, E. Working and nonworking mothers and their infants: A comparative study of maternal caregiving characteristics and infant social behavior. *Merrill-Palmer Quarterly*, 1980, *26*, 79–101.

HOFF-GINSBERG, E. Function and structure in maternal speech: Their relation to the child's development of syntax. *Developmental Psychology*, 1986, *22*, 155–163.

HOFFMAN, L. W. Changes in family roles, socialization and sex differences. *American Psychologist*, 1977, *32*, 644–657.

HOFFMAN, L. W. Maternal employment: 1979. *American Psychologist*, 1979, *34*, 859–865.

HOFFMAN, L. W. The effects of maternal employment on the academic attitudes and performance of school-aged children. *School Psychology Review*, 1980, *9*, 319–336.

HOFFMAN, L. W. Maternal employment and the young child. In M. Perlmutter (Ed.), *Parent–child interaction and parent–child relations in child development. Minnesota Symposia on Child Psychology*, Volume 17. Hillsdale, N.J.: Lawrence Erlbaum Associates, 1984.

HOFFMAN, M. L. Moral development. In P. H. Mussen (Ed.), *Carmichael's manual of child psychology*, Volume 2. New York: Wiley, 1970.

HOFFMAN, M. L. Altruistic behavior and the parent–child relationship. *Journal of Personality and Social Psychology*, 1975, *31*, 937–943.

HOFFMAN, M. L. Sex differences in empathy and related behaviors. *Psychological Bulletin*, 1977, *84*, 712–722.

HOFFMAN-PLOTKIN, D., AND TWENTYMAN, C. T. A multimodal assessment of behavioral and cognitive deficits in abused and neglected preschoolers. *Child Development*, 1984, *55*, 794–802.

HOFSTAETTER, P. R. The changing composition of intelligence: A study of the t-technique. *Journal of Genetic Psychology*, 1954, *85*, 159–164.

HOLLAND, J. *Making vocational choice: A theory of careers.* Englewood Cliffs, N.J.: Prentice-Hall, 1973.

HOLLOS, M. Comprehension and use of social rules in pronoun selection by Hungarian children. In S. Ervin-Tripp and C. Mitchell-Kernan (Eds.), *Child discourse*. New York: Academic Press, 1977.

HOLMES, D. L., RUBLE, N., KOWALSKI, J., AND LAUESEN, B. *Predicting quality of attachment at one year from neonatal characteristics.* Paper presented at the International Conference on Infant Studies, New York, April 1984.

HOLT, J. H. *How children fail.* New York: Dell, 1964.

HOLTZMAN, W. H., DIAZ-GUERRERO, R., AND SWARTZ, J. D. *Personality development in two cultures: A cross-cultural longitudinal study of school children in Mexico and the United States.* Austin: University of Texas Press, 1975.

HOOD, B., AND WILLATTS, P. Reaching in the dark: Object permanence in five-month-old infants. *Infant Behavior and Development*, 1986, *9* (Special Issue: Abstracts of papers presented at the Fifth International Conference on Infant Studies), 173a.

HOROWITZ, A. B., AND HOROWITZ, V. A. *The effects of task-specific instructions on the encoding activities of children in recall and recognition tasks.* Paper presented at the biennial meeting of the Society for Research in Child Development, Denver, April 1975.

HORSLEY, S. Psychological management of the pre-natal period. In J. G. Howells (Ed.), *Modern perspectives in psycho-obstetrics.* Edinburgh: Oliver and Boyd, 1972.

HORWITZ, R. A. Psychological effects of the "open classroom." *Review of Educational Research*, 1979, *49*, 71–86.

HOUSEHOLDER, J., HATCHER, R., BURNS, W. J., AND CHASNOFF, I. Infants born to narcotic-addicted mothers. *Psychological Bulletin*, 1982, *92*, 453–468.

How children grow. General Clinical Research Centers Branch, Division of Research Resources. National Institute of Health (DHEW), Bethesda, Md., 1972.

HOWARD, J. Counseling: A developmental approach. In E. E. Bleck and D. A. Nagel (Eds.), *Physically handicapped children: A medical atlas for teachers.* New York: Grune and Stratton, 1982.

HOWARD, L., AND POLICH, J. P300 latency and memory span development. *Developmental Psychology*, 1985, *21*, 283–289.

HUDSON, J., AND NELSON, K. Effects of script structure on children's story recall. *Developmental Psychology*, 1983, *19*, 625–635.

HUESMANN, L. R., ERON, L. D., LEFKOWITZ, M. M., AND WALDER, L. O. Stability of aggression over time and generations. *Developmental Psychology.* 1984, *20*, 1120–1134.

HUESMANN, L. R., LAGERSPETZ, K., AND ERON, L. D. Intervening variables in the TV violence-aggression relation: Evidence from two countries. *Developmental Psychology*, 1984, *20*, 746–775.

HUGHEY, M. J., McELIN, T. W., AND YOUNG, T. Maternal and fetal outcome of Lamaze prepared patients. *Obstetrics and Gynecology*, 1978, *51*, 643–647.

HUNT, C. C. Interviewed by Peter Gorner, "The sleeping world of quiet mysteries and silent killers." *Chicago Tribune*, May 3, 1982, Section 3, p. 1.

HUNTER, F. T. Socializing procedures in parent–child and friendship relations during adolescence. *Developmental Psychology*, 1984, *201*, 1092–1099.

HUNTER, F. T., AND YOUNISS, J. Changes in functions of three relations during adolescence. *Developmental Psychology*, 1982, *18*, 806–811.

HUNTER, S., WOLF, T., SKLOV, M., WEBBER, L., AND BERENSON, G. *A-B coronary-prone behavior pattern and cardiovascular risk factor variables in children and adolescents: The Bogalusa Heart Study.* Paper presented at the American College of Cardiology, San Francisco, March 1981.

HUTTENLOCHER, J. The origins of language comprehension. In R. L. Solso (Ed.), *Theories in cognitive psychology.* Hillsdale, N.J.: Lawrence Erlbaum Associates, 1974.

HUTTENLOCHER, J., AND PRESSON, C. B. Mental rotation and the perspective problem. *Cognitive Psychology*, 1973, *4*, 277–299.

HUTTENLOCHER, P. Press release, The University of Chicago, July 1979.

HUTTUNEN, M. O., AND NISKANEN, P. Prenatal loss of father and psychiatric disorders. *Archives of General Psychiatry*, 1978, *35*, 429–431.

HYDE, J. S. How large are gender differences in aggression? A developmental meta-analysis. *Developmental Psychology*, 1984, *20*, 722–736.

HYMAN, I. A., AND CLARKE, J. *Corporal punishment in the schools.* Testimony presented on behalf of the American Psychological Association before the United States Senate Subcommittee on Juvenile Justice Committee on the Judiciary, October 17, 1984.

IANNOTTI, R. J. Naturalistic and structured assessments of prosocial behavior in preschool children: The influence of empathy and perspective taking. *Developmental Psychology*, 1985, *21*, 46–55.

ICKES, W., AND EARNES, R. D. Boys and girls together—and alienated: On enacting stereotyped sex roles in mixed-sex dyads. *Journal of Personality and Social Psychology*, 1978, *36*, 669–683.

INHELDER, B., AND PIAGET, J. *The growth of logical thinking from childhood to adolescence.* New York: Basic Books, 1958.

ISABELLA, R. A., WARD, M. J., AND BELSKY, J. Convergence of multiple sources of information on infant individuality: Neonatal behavior, infant behavior, and temperament reports. *Infant Behavior and Development*, 1985, *8*, 283–291.

ISEN, A. M., HORN, N., AND ROSENHAN, D. L. Effects of success and failure on children's generosity. *Journal of Personality and Social Psychology*, 1973, *27*, 239–247.

ISKRANT, A. P., AND JOLIET, P. Y. *Accidents and homicide.* Vital Health and Statistics Monographs, American Public Health Association. Cambridge, Mass.: Harvard University Press, 1968.

ISTOMINA, Z. M. The development of voluntary memory in preschool-age children. *Soviet Psychology*, 1975, *13*, 5–64.

IVERSON, L. L. The chemistry of the grain. *Scientific American*, 1979, *241*, 134–149.

IVEY, M. E., AND BARDWICK, J. M. Patterns of affective fluctuation in the menstrual cycle. *Psychosomatic Medicine*, 1968, *30*, 336–345.

IZARD, C. E. *The face of emotions.* New York: Appleton, 1971.

IZARD, C. E. *Human emotions.* New York: Plenum, 1977.

IZARD, C. E., HEMBREE, E. A., DOUGHERTY, L. M., AND SPIZZIRRI, C. C. Changes in facial expressions of 2- to 19-month-old infants following acute pain. *Developmental Psychology*, 1983, *19*, 418–426.

IZARD, C. E., HUEBNER, R. R., RISSER, D., McGINNES, G. C., AND DOUGHERTY, L. M. The young infant's ability to produce discrete emotion expressions. *Developmental Psychology*, 1980, *16*, 132–141.

JACKSON, P. W. *Life in classrooms.* New York: Holt, Rinehart & Winston, 1968.

JACOBS, J. *Adolescent suicide.* New York: Wiley, 1971.

JACOBSON, J. L., AND WILLE, D. E. The influence of attachment pattern on developmental changes in peer interaction from the toddler to the preschool period. *Child Development,* 1986, *57,* 338–347.

JACOBSON, J., AND WILLE, D. *The influence of attachment pattern on peer interaction at 2 and 3 years.* Paper presented at the International Conference on Infant Studies, New York, April 1986.

JACOBSON, S. W., FEIN, G. G., JACOBSON, J. L., SCHWARTZ, P. M., AND DOWLER, J. K. Neonatal correlates of prenatal exposure to smoking, caffeine, and alcohol. *Infant Behavior and Development,* 1984, *7,* 253–265.

JACOBSON, W. J., AND DORAN, R. L. Girls and science: The gap remains. *Psychology Today,* 1985, 14.

JAQUISH, G. A., AND SAVIN-WILLIAMS, R. C. Biological and ecological factors in the expression of adolescent self-esteem. *Journal of Youth and Adolescence,* 1981, *10,* 473–485.

JARVIE, G. J., LAHEY, B., GRAZIANO, W., AND FRAMER, E. Childhood obesity and social stigma: What we know and what we don't know. *Developmental Review,* 1983, *3,* 237–273.

JEFFREY, W. The developing brain and child development. In M. Whittrock (Ed.), *The brain and psychology.* New York: Academic Press, 1980.

JELLIFFE, D. B., AND JELLIFFE, E. F. P. Breast-feeding is desirable—and vital for the poor. *Chicago Tribune,* May 5/6, 1982, Section 7, p. 13.

JENCKS, C., SMITH, M., ACLAND, H., BANE, M. J., COHEN, D., GINTIS, H., HEYNS, B., AND MICHAELSON, S. *Inequality: A reassessment of the effect of family and schooling in America.* New York: Harper & Row, 1972.

JENSEN, A. R. How much can we boost IQ and scholastic achievement? *Harvard Educational Review,* 1969, *39,* 1–123.

JENSEN, A. R. *Educability and group differences.* New York: Harper & Row, 1973.

JENSEN, A. R. *Bias in mental testing.* New York: Free Press, 1980.

JENSEN, K. Differential reactions to taste and temperature stimuli in newborn infants. *Genetic Psychology Monographs,* 1932, *12,* 363–479.

JERSILD, A. T. Characteristics of teachers who are "liked best" and "disliked most." *Journal of Experimental Education,* 1940, *9,* 139–151.

JERSILD, A. T., AND HOLMES, F. B. *Children's fears.* Child Development Monograph 20. New York: Teachers College Press, Columbia University, 1935.

JERSILD, A. T., AND MARKEY, F. V. *Conflicts between preschool children.* Child Development Monograph 21. New York: Teachers College Press, Columbia University, 1935.

JERUCHIMOWICZ, J., AND HANS, S. L. Behavior of neonates exposed in utero to methadone as assessed on the Brazelton Scale. *Infant Behavior and Development,* 1985, *8,* 323–336.

JESSOR, R., COSTA, F., JESSOR, L., AND DONOVAN, J. E. Time of first intercourse: A prospective study. *Journal of Personality and Social Psychology,* 1983, *44,* 608–626.

JESSOR, R., AND JESSOR, S. L. The transition from virginity to non-virginity among youth: A social-psychological study over time. *Developmental Psychology,* 1975, *11,* 473–484.

JOFFE, J. M. *Prenatal determinants of behavior.* Oxford: Pergamon, 1969.

JOHNSON, D. B. Self-recognition in infants. *Infant Behavior and Development,* 1983, *6,* 211–222.

JOHNSON, S. M., WAHL, G., MARTIN, S., AND JOHANSSEN, S. How deviant is the normal child: A behavioral analysis of the preschool child and his family. In R. D. Rubin, J. P. Brady, and J. D. Henderson (Eds.), *Advances in behavior therapy,* Volume 4. New York: Academic Press, 1973.

JOHNSTON, L. D., O'MALLEY, P. M., AND BACHMAN, J. G. *Use of licit and illicit drugs by American high school students, 1975–1984.* National Institute of Drug Abuse, United States Department of Health and Human Services. Washington, D.C., 1985.

JONES, K. L., SMITH, D. W., ULLELAND, C. N., AND STREISSGUTH, A. P. Pattern of malformation in offspring of chronic alcoholic mothers. *Lancet,* 1973, *1,* 1267–1271.

JONES, L. V. White–black achievement differences. *American Psychologist,* 1984, *39,* 207–213.

JONES, M. C. The later careers of boys who were early or late maturing. *Child Development,* 1957, *28,* 113–128.

JONES, M. C. Personality correlates and antecedents of drinking patterns in adult males. *Journal of Consulting and Clinical Psychology,* 1968, *32,* 2–12.

JONES, M. C., AND BAYLEY, N. Physical maturing among boys as related to behavior. *Journal of Educational Psychology,* 1950, *41,* 129–148.

JONES, S. J., AND MOSS, H. A. Age, state, and maternal behavior associated with infant vocalizations. *Child Development,* 1971, *42,* 1039–1051.

JOOS, S. K., POLLITT, E., MUELLER, W. H., AND ALBRIGHT, D. L. The Bacon Chow Study: Maternal nutritional supplementation and infant behavioral development. *Child Development,* 1983, *54,* 669–676.

JUSCZYK, P. W. Perception of syllable-final stop consonants by 2-month-old infants. *Perception and Psychophysics,* 1977, *21,* 450–454.

JUSCZYK, P. W., ROSNER, B. S., CUTTING, J. E., FOARD, F., AND SMITH, L. B. Categorical perception of non-speech sounds by 2-month-old infants. *Perceptions and Psychophysics,* 1977, *21,* 50–54.

JUST, M. A., AND CARPENTER, P. A. A theory of reading: From eye fixations to comprehension. *Psychological Review,* 1980, *87,* 329–354.

JUSTICE, E. M. Categorization as a preferred memory strategy: Developmental changes during elementary school. *Developmental Psychology,* 1985, *21,* 1105–1110.

KAGAN, D. M., AND SQUIRES, R. L. Eating disorders among adolescents: patterns and prevalence. *Adolescence,* 1984, *19,* 15–29.

KAGAN, J. Impulsive and reflective children: Significance of conceptual tempo. In J. D. Krumboltz (Ed.), *Learning and the educational process.* Chicago: Rand McNally, 1965.

KAGAN, J. *Change and continuity in infancy.* New York: Wiley, 1971.

KAGAN, J., AND MOSS, H. A. *Birth to maturity.* New York: Wiley, 1962.

KAGAN, J., AND TULKIN, S. R. Social class differences in child rearing during the first year. In H. R. Schaffer (Ed.), *The origins of human social relations.* London: Academic Press, 1971.

KAGAN, S., AND MADSEN, M. C. Cooperation and competition of Mexican, Mexican-American, and Anglo-American children of two ages under four instructional sets. *Developmental Psychology,* 1971, *5,* 32–39.

KAHN, A., AND BLUM, D. Phenothiazines and Sudden Infant Death Syndrome. *Pediatrics,* 1982, *70,* 75–79.

KAIL, R., AND NIPPOLD, M. A. Unconstrained retrieval from semantic memory. *Child Development,* 1984, *55,* 944–951.

KALES, A., JACOBSON, A., PAULSON, M., KALES, J., AND WALTER, R. Somnambulism: Psychophysiological correlates, I. *Archives of General Psychiatry,* 1966, *14,* 586–594.

KALES, J. D., KALES, A., SOLDATOS, C. R., CHAMBERLIN, K., AND MARTIN, E. D. Sleepwalking and night terrors related to febrile illness. *American Journal of Psychiatry,* 1979, *136,* 1214–1215.

KAMIN, L. J. A positive interpretation of apparent "cumulative deficit." *Developmental Psychology,* 1978, *14,* 195–196.

KANNER, L. Problems of nosology and psychodynamics of early infantile autism. *American Journal of Orthopsychiatry,* 1949, *19,* 416–426.

KATZ, B., BAKER, G., AND MACNAMARA, J. What's in a name? On the child's acquisition of proper and common nouns. *Child Development,* 1974, *45,* 267–273.

KATZ, I., ROBERTS, S. O., AND ROBINSON, J. M. Effects of difficulty, race of administrator and instructions on Negro digit-symbol performance. *Journal of Personality and Social Psychology*, 1965, *70*, 53–59.

KATZ, R. B., SHANKWEILER, D., LIBERMAN, I. Y. Memory for item order and phonetic recoding in the beginning reader. *Journal of Experimental Child Psychology*, 1981, *32*, 474–484.

KAVANAUGH, R. D. Observations on the role of logically constrained sentences in the comprehension of "before" and "after." *Journal of Child Language*, 1979, *6*, 353–357.

KAVANAUGH, R. D., AND JIRKOVSKY, A. M. Parental speech to young children: A longitudinal analysis. *Merrill-Palmer Quarterly*, 1982, *28*, 297–311.

KAYE, K. Toward the origin of dialogue. In H. R. Schaffer (Ed.), *Studies in mother-infant interaction*. London: Academic Press, 1977.

KAYE, K. *The mental and social life of babies: How parents create persons*. Chicago: University of Chicago Press, 1982.

KAYE, K., AND MARCUS, J. Imitation over a series of trials without feedback: Age six months. *Infant Behavior and Development*, 1978, *1*, 141–155.

KEARSLEY, R. The newborn's response to auditory stimulation: A demonstration of orienting and defensive behavior. *Child Development*, 1973, *44*, 582–590.

KEATING, D. P., AND BOBBITT, B. L. Individual and developmental differences in cognitive-processing components of mental ability. *Child Development*, 1978, *49*, 155–167.

KEENAN, E. O. Making it last: Repetition in children's discourse. In S. Ervin-Tripp and C. Mitchell-Kernan (Eds.), *Child discourse*. New York: Academic Press, 1977.

KEENEY, T. J., CANIZZO, S. R., AND FLAVELL, J. H. Spontaneous and induced verbal rehearsal in a recall task. *Child Development*, 1967, *38*, 953–966.

KELLER, A., FORD, L. H., AND MEACHAM, J. A. Dimensions of self-concept in preschool children. *Developmental Psychology*, 1978, *14*, 483–489.

KELLER, H. *The story of my life*. New York: Doubleday, 1905.

KELLOGG, R. *Analyzing children's art*. Palo Alto, Calif.: Mayfield, 1970.

KEMPE, H. C., AND HELFER, R. E. (EDS.) *Helping the battered child and his family*. Philadelphia: Lippincott, 1972.

KENDRICK, C., AND DUNN, J. Caring for a second child: Effects on the interaction between mother and first-born. *Developmental Psychology*, 1980, *16*, 303–311.

KENNELL, J. H., JERAULD, R., WOLFE, H., CHESLER, D., KREGER, N. C., McALPINE, W., STEFFA, M., AND KLAUS, M. H. Maternal behavior one year after early and extended postpartum contact. *Developmental Medicine and Child Neurology*, 1974, *16*, 172–179.

KERASOTES, D., AND WALKER, C. E. Hyperactive behavior in children. In C. E. Walker and M. C. Roberts (Eds.), *Handbook of clinical child psychology*. New York: Wiley, 1983.

KESSEN, W. Research design in the study of developmental problems. In P. H. Mussen (Ed.), *Handbook of research methods in child development*. New York: Wiley, 1960.

KESSEN, W. *The child*. New York: Wiley, 1965.

KESSEN, W. (ED.) *Childhood in China*. New Haven, Conn.: Yale University Press, 1975.

KEYE, E. *The family guide to children's television*. New York: Random House, 1974.

KHAN, A. U., AND CATAIS, J. *Men and women in biological perspective: A review of the literature*. New York: Praeger, 1984.

KIDD, R. F., AND BERKOWITZ, L. Dissonance, self-concept, and helplessness. *Journal of Personality and Social Psychology*, 1976, *33*, 613–622.

KIMURA, D. The asymmetry of the human brain. *Scientific American*, 1975, 70–78.

KING, K., NEGUS, K., AND VANCE, J. C. Heat stress in motor vehicles: A problem in infancy. *Pediatrics*, 1981, *68*, 579–582.

KINLOCH, G. C. Parent-youth conflict at home: An investigation among university freshmen. *Journal of Orthopsychiatry*, 1970, *40*, 658–664.

KINSBOURNE, M. Minimal brain dysfunction as a neurodevelopmental lag. *Annals of the New York Academy of Sciences*, 1973, *205*, 268–273.

KLAUS, M. H., AND KENNELL, J. H. *Maternal–infant bonding*. St. Louis: C. V. Mosby, 1976.

KLAUS, M. H., AND KENNELL, J. H. *Hunting and gathering societies: An empirical basis for exploring biobehavioral processes in mothers and infants*. Paper presented at the International Conference on Infant Studies, New York, 1984.

KLAUS, M. H., KENNELL, J. H., PLUMB, N., AND ZUEHLKE, S. Human maternal behavior at first contact with her young. *Pediatrics*, 1970, *46*, 187–192.

KLAUS, R., AND GRAY, S. The Early Training Project for Disadvantaged Children: A report after five years. *Monographs of the Society for Research in Child Development*, 1968, *33* (4, Serial No. 120).

KLECK, R. E., RICHARDSON, S. A., AND RONALD, L. Physical appearance cues and interpersonal attraction in children. *Child Development*, 1974, *45*, 305–310.

KLEIMAN, G. M. *Brave new schools: How computers can change education*. Reston, Va.: Reston, 1984.

KLEIN, R. E., HABICHT, J. P., AND YARBROUGH, C. Effects of protein-calorie malnutrition on mental development. *Advances in Pediatrics*, 1971, *18*, 75–91.

KLEINER, K.A., AND FAGAN, J. F., III *Neonatal discrimination and limitation of facial expression: A failure to replicate*. Paper presented at the International Conference on Infant Studies, New York, April 1984.

KLIMA, E., AND BELLUGI, U. Syntactic regularities—the speech of children. In J. Lyons and R. J. Wales (Eds.), *Psycholinguistic papers*. Edinburgh: Edinburgh University Press, 1966.

KNOBLOCH, H., AND PASAMANICK, B. Prospective studies on the epidemiology of reproductive casualty: Methods, findings and some implications. *Merrill-Palmer Quarterly*, 1966, *12*, 27–43.

KNOPF, I. J. *Childhood psychopathology*. Englewood Cliffs, N.J.: Prentice-Hall, 1979.

KOBASIGAWA, A. Utilization of retrieval cues by children in recall. *Child Development*, 1974, *45*, 127–134.

KOBASIGAWA, A., RANSOM, C., AND HOLLAND, C. Children's knowledge about skimming. *Alberta Journal of Educational Research*, 1980, *26*, 169–181.

KOCH, H. L. Some emotional attitudes of the young child in relation to characteristics of his sibling. *Child Development*, 1956, *27*, 393–426.

KOCH, H. L. Some personality correlates of sex, sibling position and spacing among five and six year old children. *Genetic Psychological Monographs*, 1955, *52*, 3–50.

KOEPKE, J. E., HAMM, M., LEGERSTEE, M., AND RUSSELL, M. Methodological issues in studies of imitation: Reply to Meltzoff and Moore. *Infant Behavior and Development*, 1983, *6*, 113–116.(a)

KOEPKE, J. E., HAMM, M., LEGERSTEE, M., AND RUSSELL, M. Neonatal imitation: Two failures to replicate. *Infant Behavior and Development*, 1983, *6*, 97–102.(b)

KOHLBERG, L. Development of moral character and moral ideology. In L. W. Hoffman and M. L. Hoffman (Eds.), *Review of child development research*, Volume 1. New York: Russell Sage Foundation, 1964.

KOHLBERG, L. Stage and sequence: The cognitive-developmental approach to socialization. In D. A. Goslin (Ed.), *Handbook of socialization theory and research*. Chicago: Rand McNally, 1969.

KOHLBERG, L. Moral stages and moralization: Cognitive-developmental approach. In T. Lickona (Ed.), *Moral development and behavior: Theory, research, and social issues*. New York: Holt, Rinehart & Winston, 1976.

KOHLBERG, L., COLBY, A., GIBBS, J., AND SPEICHER-DUBIN, B. *Standard form scoring manual*. Cambridge, Mass.: Center for Moral Education, Harvard Graduate School of Education, 1978.

KOHLBERG, L., AND GILLIGAN, C. The adolescent as a philosopher: The discovery of the self in a postconventional world. *Daedalus*, 1971, *100*, 1051–1086.

KOHLBERG, L., YAEGER, J., AND HJERTHOLM, E. Private speech: Four studies and a review of theories. *Child Development*, 1968, *39*, 691–736.

KOLATA, G. Studying learning in the womb. *Science*, 1984, *225*, 302–303.

KOLATA, G. Blindness of prematurity unexplained. *Science*, January 1986, *231*, 20–22. (a)

KOLATA, G. Obese children: A growing problem. *Science*, April 1986, *232*, 20–21. (b)

KONOPKA, G. *Young girls: A portrait of adolescence*. Englewood Cliffs, N.J.: Prentice-Hall, 1976.

KOPP, C. B. Risk factors in development. In P. H. Mussen (Ed.), *Handbook of child psychology*, Volume 2. New York: Wiley, 1983.

KOPP, C. B., AND PARMELEE, A. H. Prenatal and perinatal influences on infant behavior. In J. D. Osofsky (Ed.), *Handbook of infant development*. New York: Wiley, 1979.

KORN, S. J. Continuities and discontinuities in difficult/easy temperament: Infancy to young adulthood. *Merrill-Palmer Quarterly*, 1984, *30*, 189–199.

KORNER, A. F. Visual alertness in neonates: Individual differences and their correlates. *Perceptual and Motor Skills*, 1970, *31*, 499–509.

KORNER, A. F. State as variable, as obstacle and as mediator of stimulation in infant research. *Merrill-Palmer Quarterly*, 1972, *18*, 77–94.

KORNER, A. F. Individual differences at birth: Implications of early experience and later development. In J. C. Westman (Ed.), *Individual differences in children*. New York: Wiley, 1973.

KORNER, A. F., AND THOMAN, E. G. Relative efficacy of contact and vestibular stimulation on soothing neonates. *Child Development*, 1972, *10*, 67–78.

KOTELCHUCK, M. The infant's relationship to the father: Experimental evidence. In M. E. Lamb (Ed.), *The role of the father in child development*. New York: Wiley, 1976.

KOTULAK, R. Baby removed from womb, returned in new surgery. *Chicago Tribune*, November 15, 1981, Section 1, pp. 1–12.

KREBS, D. Commentary and critique: Psychological and philosophical approaches to prosocial development. In D. Bridgeman (Ed.), *The nature of prosocial development: Interdisciplinary theories and strategies*. New York: Academic Press, 1983.

KREBS, R. L. *Some relations between moral judgment, attention, and resistance to temptation*. Unpublished doctoral dissertation, University of Chicago, 1967.

KREBS, R. L., AND KOHLBERG, L. *Moral judgment and ego controls as determinants of resistance to cheating*. Unpublished manuscript, Center for Moral Education, Harvard University, 1973.

KREUTZER, M. A., LEONARD, C., AND FLAVELL, J. H. An interview study of children's knowledge about memory. *Monographs of the Society for Research in Child Development*, 1975, *40*, (1, Serial No. 159).

KREUZ, I. E., AND ROSE, R. M. Assessment of aggressive behavior and plasma testosterone in a young criminal population. *Psychosomatic Medicine*, 1972, *34*, 321–332.

KROSNICK, J. A., AND JUDD, C. M. Transitions in social influence at adolescence: Who induces cigarette smoking? *Developmental Psychology*, 1982, *18*, 359–368.

KRUGMAN, S., WARD, R., AND KATZ, S. *Infectious diseases of children*. St. Louis: C. V. Mosby, 1977.

KUHL, P. K. Discrimination of speech by nonhuman animals: Basic auditory sensitivities conducive to the perception of speech-sound categories. *Journal of the Acoustical Society of America*, 1981, *70*, 340–349.

KUHL, P. K. Perception of auditory equivalence classes for speech in early infancy. *Infant Behavior and Development*, 1983, *6*, 263–285.

KUHN, D., NASH, S. C., AND BRUCKEN, L. Sex-role concepts of two- and three-year-olds. *Child Development*, 1978, *49*, 445–451.

LADD, G. W. Effectiveness of a social learning method for enhancing children's social interaction and peer acceptance. *Child Development*, 1981, *52*, 171–178.

LaFRENIERE, P. J., AND SROUFE, L. A. Profiles of peer competence in the preschool: Interrelations among measures, influence of social ecology, and relation to attachment history. *Developmental Psychology*, 1985, *21*, 56–69.

LaFRENIERE, P. J., STRAYER, F. F., AND GAUTHIER, R. The emergence of same-sex affiliative preferences among preschool peers: A developmental ethological perspective. *Child Development*, 1984, *55*, 1958–1965.

LAMB, M. E. Parent–infant interaction in 8-month-olds. *Child Psychiatry and Human Development*, 1976, *7*, 56–63.(a)

LAMB, M. E. Twelve-month-olds and their parents: Interaction in a laboratory playroom. *Developmental Psychology*, 1976, *12*, 237–244.(b)

LAMB, M. E. Father–infant and mother–infant interaction in the first year of life. *Child Development*, 1977, *48*, 167–181.

LAMB, M. E., FRODI, A. M., HWANG, C. P., FRODI, M., AND STEINBERG, J. Mother- and father-infant interaction involving play and holding in traditional and nontraditional Swedish families. *Developmental Psychology*, 1982, *18*, 215–221.

LAMB, M. E., THOMPSON, R. A., GARDNER, W., AND CHARNOV, E. L. *Infant–mother attachment: The origins and developmental significance of individual differences in strange situation behavior*. Hillsdale, N.J.: Lawrence Erlbaum Associates, 1985.

LAMBERT, W. The relation of bilingualism to intelligence. In W. Lambert (Ed.), *Language, psychology, and culture*. Stanford, Calif.: Stanford University Press, 1972.

LAMBERT, W., AND TAYLOR, D. *Parent's view on bilingual education*. Paper presented at the annual meeting of the American Psychological Association, Los Angeles, August 1985.

LAMMER, E. J., CHEN, D. T., HOAR, R. M., AGNISH, N. D., BENKE, P. J., BRAUN, J. T., CURRY, C. J., FERNHOFF, P. M., GRIX, A. W., LOTT, I. T., RICHARD, J. M., AND SUN, S. C. Retinoic acid embryopathy. *The New England Journal of Medicine*, October 3, 1985, *313*, 837–841.

LANDIS, T. Y. Interactions between text and prior knowledge in children's memory for prose. *Child Development*, 1982, *53*, 811–814.

LANGLOIS, J. H., AND DOWNS, A. C. Mothers, fathers and peers as socialization agents of sex-typed play behavior in young children. *Child Development*, 1980, *51*, 1227–1247.

LANGLOIS, J. H., AND STEPHAN, C. The effects of physical attractiveness and ethnicity on children's behavioral attributions and peer preferences. *Child Development*, 1977, *48*, 1694–1698.

LAPSLEY, D. K., AND MURPHY, M. N. Another look at the theoretical assumptions of adolescent egocentrism. *Developmental Review*, 1985, *5*, 201–217.

LARK-HOROVITZ, B., LEWIS, H., AND LUCA, M. *Understanding children's art for better teaching* (2nd ed.). Columbus, Ohio: Charles E. Merrill, 1973.

LARSON, R., CSIKSZENTMIHALYI, M., AND GRAEF, R. Mood variability and the psychosocial adjustment of adolescents. *Journal of Youth and Adolescence*. 1980, *9*, 469–490.

LASKY, R. E., SYRDAL-LASKY, A., AND KLEIN, R. E. VOT discrimination by four- and six-and-a-half-month-old infants from Spanish environments. *Journal of Experimental Child Psychology*, 1975, *20*, 215–225.

LAWRY, J. A., WELSH, M. C., AND JEFFREY, W. E. Cognitive tempo and complex problem solving. *Child Development*, 1983, *54*, 912–920.

LAZAR, I., DARLINGTON, R. B., MURRAY, H., ROYCE, J., AND SNIPPER, A. Lasting effects of early education. *Monographs of the Society for Research in Child Development*, 1982, *47* (2-3, Serial No. 195).

LEBOYER, F. *Birth without violence*. New York: Knopf, 1975.

LECOURS, A. R. Myelogenetic correlates of the development of speech and language. In E. H. Lenneberg and E. Lenneberg (Eds.), *Foundations of language development*. New York: Academic

Press, 1975.

LEE, D. N., AND ARONSON, E. Visual proprioceptive control of standing in human infants. *Perception and Psychophysics*, 1974, *15*, 529–532.

LEFKOWITZ, M. M. Smoking during pregnancy: Long-term effect on offspring. *Developmental Psychology*, 1981, *17*, 192–194.

LEFKOWITZ, M. M., ERON, L. D., WALDER, L. O., AND HUESMANN, L. R. *Growing up to be violent: A longitudinal study of the development of aggression*. Elmsford, N.Y.: Pergamon, 1977.

LEGG, C., SHERICK, I., AND WADLAND, W. Reaction of preschool children to the birth of a sibling. *Child Psychiatry and Human Development*, 1974, *5*, 3–39.

LEIFER, M. Psychological changes accompanying pregnancy and motherhood. *Genetic Psychology Monographs*, 1977, *95*, 55–96.

LEMLY, E. B., AND SCHWARZ, J. C. The reactions of two-year-olds to unfamiliar adults. Report to the Research Foundation (Grant No. 35-497), 1979.

LEMPERS, J. D., FLAVELL, E. R., AND FLAVELL, J. H. The development in very young children of tacit knowledge concerning visual perception. *Genetic Psychology Monographs*, 1977, *95*, 3–53.

LENNEBERG, E. H. *Biological foundations of language*. New York: Wiley, 1967.

LENNEY, L. M. *Mother–daughter communication about maturation and sexuality*. Unpublished master's thesis, University of California, Irvine, 1985.

LEPMAN, J. (ED.). *How children see our world*. New York: Avon, 1971.

LEPPER, M. R. Extrinsic reward and intrinsic motivation: Implications for the classroom. In J. M. Levine and M. C. Wang (Eds.), *Teacher and student perceptions: Implications for learning*. Hillsdale, N.J.: Lawrence Erlbaum Associates, 1983.

LEPPER, M. R. Micro computers in education: Motivational and social issues. *American Psychologist*, 1985, *40*, 1–18.

LEPPER, M. R., AND GREENE, D. Turning play into work: Effects of adult surveillance and extrinsic rewards on children's intrinsic motivation. *Journal of Personality and Social Psychology*, 1975, *31*, 479–486.

LEPPER, M. R., AND GREENE, D. Overjustification research and beyond: Toward a means-ends analysis of intrinsic and extrinsic motivation. In M. R. Lepper and D. Greene (Eds.), *The hidden costs of reward*. Hillsdale, N.J.: Lawrence Erlbaum Associates, 1978.

LEPPER, M. R., GREENE, D., AND NISBETT, R. E. Undermining children's intrinsic interest with extrinsic rewards: A test of the "overjustification" hypothesis. *Journal of Personality and Social Psychology*, 1973, *28*, 129–137.

LERNER, J. V. The import of temperament for psychosocial functioning: Tests of a goodness of fit model. *Merrill-Palmer Quarterly*, 1984, *30*, 177–188.

LERNER, R. M., KARSON, M., MEISELS, M., AND KNAPP, J. R. Actual and perceived attitudes of late adolescents and their parents: The phenomenon of the generation gap. *Journal of Genetic Psychology*, 1975, *126*, 195–207.

LERNER, R. M., AND LERNER, J. V. Effects of age, sex, and physical attractiveness on child–peer relations, academic performance, and elementary school adjustment. *Developmental Psychology*, 1977, *13*, 585–590.

LESSER, G. S., FIFER, G., AND CLARK, D. H. Mental abilities of children from different social-class and cultural groups. *Monographs of the Society for Research in Child Development*, 1965, *30* (4, Serial No. 102).

LESTER, B. M., ALS, H., AND BRAZELTON, T. B. Regional obstetric anesthesia and newborn behavior: A reanalysis toward synergistic effects. *Child Development*, 1982, *53*, 687–692.

LEVER, J. Sex differences in games children play. *Social Problems*, 1976, *23*, 478–487.

LEVIN, J. A., BORUTA, M. J., AND VASCONCELLOS, M. T. Microcomputer-based environments for writing. In A. C. Wilkinson (Ed.), *Classroom computers and cognitive science*. New York: Academic Press, 1983.

LEVIN, J. R. The mnemonic '80s: *Keywords in the classroom*. Theoretical paper No. 86, Wisconsin Research and Development Center for Individualized Schooling, Madison, 1980.

LEVIN, J. R. Pictorial strategies for school learning: Practical illustrations. In M. Pressley and J. R. Levin (Eds.), *Cognitive strategy research: Educational applications*. New York: Springer-Verlag, 1983.

LEVINE, M. H., AND SUTTON-SMITH, B. Effects of age, sex and task on visual behavior during dyadic interaction. *Developmental Psychology*, 1973, *9*, 400–405.

LEVINE, S. C. Hemispheric specialization and functional plasticity during development. *Journal of Children in Contemporary Society*, 1983, *16*, 77–98.

LEVINE, S. V. Radical departures. *Psychology Today*, August 1981, 20–27.

LEVITAN, M., AND MONTAGU, A. *Textbook of human genetics*. London: Oxford University Press, 1971.

LEVY, J. *Nature*, 1969, *224*, 614.

LEVY, R. *Tahitians*. Chicago: University of Chicago Press, 1973.

LEWIS, C. C. The effects of parental firm control: A reinterpretation of findings. *Psychological Bulletin*, 1981, *90*, 547–563.

LEWIS, M. Individual differences in the measurement of early cognitive growth. In J. Hellmuth (Ed.), *Exceptional infant*, Volume 2. *Studies in abnormalities*. New York: Brunner/Mazel, 1971.

LEWIS, M., AND BROOKS, J. Self, other and fear: Infants' reactions to people. In M. Lewis and L. A. Rosenblum (Eds.), *The origins of fear:* New York: Wiley, 1974.

LEWIS, M., AND BROOKS-GUNN, J. *Social cognition and the acquisition of self*. New York: Plenum, 1979.

LEWIS, M., FEIRING, C., McGUFFOG, C., AND JASKIR, J. Predicting psychopathology in six-year-olds from early social relations. *Child Development*, 1984, *55*, 123–136.

LEWIS, M., AND FREEDLE, R. Mother–infant dyad: The cradle of meaning. In P. Pliner, L. Krames, and T. Alloway (Eds.), *Communication and affect: Language and thought*. New York: Academic Press, 1973.

LEWIS, M., AND JASKIR, J. Infant intelligence and its relation to birth order and birth spacing. *Infant behavior and development*, 1983, *6*, 117–120.

LEWIS, M., AND MICHALSON, L. *Affect labelling by mothers during reunion with their one-year-old infants*. Unpublished manuscript, Educational Testing Service, 1981.

LEWIS, M., AND MICHALSON, L. The socialization of emotions. In T. Field and A. Fogel (Eds.), *Emotion and early interaction*. Hillsdale, N.J.: Lawrence Erlbaum Associates, 1982.

LEWIS, M., AND WEINRAUB, M. Sex of parent × sex of child: Socioemotional development. In R. C. Friedman, R. M. Richart, and R. L. Van de Wiele (Eds.), *Sex differences in behavior*. New York: Wiley, 1974.

LEWIS, M., YOUNG, G., BROOKS, J., AND MICHALSON, L. The beginning of friendship. In M. Lewis and L. A. Rosenblum (Eds.), *Friendship and peer relations*. New York: Wiley-Interscience, 1975.

LEWIS, R. A. Parents and peers: Socialization agents in the coital behavior of young adults. *The Journal of Sex Research*, 1973, *9*, 156–170.

LEY, R. G., AND KOEPKE, J. E. *Sex and age differences in the departures of young children from their mothers*. Paper presented at the meeting of the Society for Research in Child Development, Denver, April 1975.

LEY, R. G., AND KOEPKE, J. E. Attachment behavior outdoors: Naturalistic observations of sex and age differences in the separation behavior of young children. *Infant Behavior and Development*, 1982, *5*, 195–201.

LIBEN, L. S. Perspective-taking skills in young children: Seeing the world through rose-colored glasses. *Developmental Psychology*, 1978, *14*, 87–92.

LIBERMAN, I. Y., SHANKWEILER, D., FISCHER, F. W., AND CARTER, B. Explicit syllable and phoneme segmentation in the young child. *Journal of Experimental Child Psychology*, 1974, *18*, 201–212.

LICHT, B. G., AND DWECK, C. S. Determinants of academic achievement: The interaction of children's achievement orientations with skill area. *Developmental Psychology*, 1984, *20*, 628–636.

LIDZ, T. The adolescent and his family. In H. Caplan and F. Lebovici (Eds.), *Adolescence: Psychosocial perspectives*. New York: Basic Books, 1969.

LIEBERMAN, A. F. Preschoolers' competence with a peer: Relations with attachment and peer experience. *Child Development*, 1977, *48*, 1277–1287.

LIEBERMAN, P. *Intonation, perception, and language*. Cambridge, Mass.: MIT Press, 1967.

LIEBERT, R. M., AND POULOS, R. W. Television and personality development: The socializing effects of an entertainment medium. In A. Davids (Ed.), *Child personality and psychopathology: Current topics*, Volume 2. New York: Wiley, 1975.

LIFTON, P. D. *Individual differences in moral development: A matter of anatomy or socialization?* Paper presented at the annual conference of the American Psychological Association in Los Angeles, August 1985.

LIGHT, P., AND NIX, C. "Own view" versus "good view" in a perspective-taking task. *Child Development*, 1983, *54*, 480–483.

LINDGREN, G. Height, weight and menarche in Swedish urban school children in relation to socioeconomic and regional factors. *Annals of Human Biology*, 1976, *3*, 510–528.

LINDHOLM, K. J., AND PADILLA, A. M. Language mixing in bilingual children. *Journal of Child Language*, 1978, *5*, 327–335.

LINN, M. C., AND PETERSEN, A. C. Emergency and characterization of sex differences in spatial ability: A meta-analysis. *Child Development*, 1985, *56*, 1479–1498.

LINTON, T. *Effects of grade displacement between students tutored and student tutors*. Unpublished doctoral dissertation, University of Cincinnati, 1972.

LIPSITT, L. P., ENGEN, T., AND KAYE, H. Developmental changes in the olfactory threshold of the neonate. *Child Development*, 1963, *34*, 371–376.

LIPSITT, L. P., McCULLAGH, A. A., REILLY, B. M., SMITH, I. M., AND STURNER, W. Q. Perinatal indicators of sudden infant death syndrome: A study of 34 Rhode Island cases. *Journal of Applied Developmental Psychology*, 1981, *2*, 79–88.

LIPSITT, L. P., REILLY, B. M., BUTCHER, M. J., AND GREENWOOD, M. M. The stability and interrelationships of newborn sucking and heart rate. *Developmental Psychobiology*, 1976, *9*, 305–310.

LIST, J. A., COLLINS, W. A., AND WESTBY, S. D. Comprehension and inferences from traditional and nontraditional sex-role portrayals on television. *Child Development*, 1983, *54*, 1579–1587.

LITOVSKY, V. G., AND DUSEK, J. B. Perceptions of child rearing and self-concept development during the early adolescent years. *Journal of Youth and Adolescence*, 1985, *14*, 373–387.

LITTLE, L., AND HAAR, C. Terms of enlargement. *Family Weekly*, March 24, 1985, p. 15.

LIVESLEY, W. J., AND BROMLEY, D. B. *Person perception in childhood and adolescence*. London: Wiley, 1973.

LOCKYER, L., AND RUTTER, M. A five to fifteen year follow-up study of infantile psychosis: IV. Patterns of cognitive ability. *British Journal of Social and Clinical Psychology*, 1970, *9*, 152–163.

LONDERVILLE, S., AND MAIN, M. Security of attachment, compliance and maternal training methods in the second year of life. *Developmental Psychology*, 1981, *17*, 289–299.

LONEY, J., LANGHORNE, J. E., AND PATERNITE, C. E. An empirical basis for subgrouping the hyperkinetic/minimal brain dysfunction syndrome. *Journal of Abnormal Psychology*, 1978, *87*, 431–441.

LONGSTRETH, L. E. Revisiting Skeels' final study: A critique. *Developmental Psychology*, 1981, *17*, 620–625.

LoPICCOLO, J. Mothers and daughters: Perceived and real differences in sexual values. *The Journal of Sex Research*, 1973, *9*, 171–177.

LORENZ, K. *Studies in animal and human behavior*, Volume 1. Cambridge, Mass.: Harvard University Press, 1971.

LOUGEE, M. D., GRUENEICH, R., AND HARTUP, W. W. Social interaction in same- and mixed-age dyads of preschool children. *Child Development*, 1977, *48*, 1353–1361.

LOVIBOND, S. *Conditioning and enuresis*. New York: Macmillan, 1964.

LOWREY, G. H. *Growth and development of children* (6th ed; 7th ed.). Chicago: Yearbook Medical Publishers, 1973, 1978.

LUCARIELLO, J., AND NELSON, K. Slot-filler categories as memory organizers for young children. *Developmental Psychology*, 1985, *21*, 272–282.

LUCAS, T. C., AND UZGIRIS, I. C. Spatial factors in the development of the object concept. *Developmental Psychology*, 1977, *13*, 492–500.

LUDEKE, R. J. *Teaching behaviors of 11-year-old and 9-year-old girls in same-age and mixed-age dyads*. Unpublished doctoral dissertation, University of Minnesota, 1978.

LUEPTOW, L. B. *Adolescent sex role and social change*. New York: Columbia University Press, 1984.

LUKASEVITCH, A., AND GRAY, R. F. Open space, open education and pupil performance. *Elementary School Journal*, 1978, *79*, 108–114.

LUNZER, E. A. Problems of formal reasoning in test situation. In P. H. Mussen (Ed.), European research in cognitive development. *Monographs of the Society for Research in Child Development*, 1965, *30* (2 serial No. 100), 19–46.

LURIA, A. R. *The role of speech in the regulation of normal and abnormal behavior*. London: Pergamon, 1961.

LURIA, A. R. Speech development and the formation of mental processes. In M. Cole and I. Maltzman (Eds.), *Handbook of contemporary Soviet psychology*. New York: Basic Books, 1969.

LUTKENHAUS, P. *Mother-infant attachment at 12 months and its relations to 3 year old's readiness to build up a new relationship*. Paper presented at the International Conference on Infant Studies, New York, April 1984.

LYND, R. S., AND LYND, H. M. *Middletown*. New York: Harcourt, Brace, & Co., 1929.

LYTTON, H. The socialization of two-year-old boys: Ecological findings: *Journal of Child Psychology and Psychiatry*, 1976, *17*, 287–304.

MACCOBY, E. E. Selective auditory attention in children. In L. P. Lipsitt and C. C. Spiker (Eds.), *Advances in child development and behavior*, Volume 3. New York: Academic Press, 1967.

MACCOBY, E. E. Social groupings in childhood: Their relationship to prosocial and antisocial behavior in boys and girls. In D. Olweus, J. Block, and M. Radke-Yarrow (Eds.), *Development of antisocial and prosocial behavior*. Orlando, Fla.: Academic Press, 1986.

MACCOBY, E. E., DOERING, C. H., JACKLIN, C. N., AND KRAEMER, H. Concentrations of sex hormones in umbilical-cord blood: Their relation to sex and birth order of infants. *Child Development*, 1979, *50*, 632–642.

MACCOBY, E. E., AND FELDMAN, S. S. Mother-attachment and stranger-reactions in the third year of life. *Monographs of the Society for Research in Child Development*, 1972, *37* (1, Serial No. 146).

MACCOBY, E. E., AND JACKLIN, C. N. *The psychology of sex differences*. Stanford, Calif.: Stanford University Press, 1974.

MACCOBY, E. E., AND JACKLIN, C. N. Sex differences in aggression: A rejoinder and reprise. *Child Development*, 1980, *51*, 964–980.

MACCOBY, E. E., AND MARTIN, J. A. Socialization in the context of the family: Parent-child interaction. In P. H. Mussen (Ed.), *Handbook of child psychology*, Volume 4. New York: Wiley, 1983.

MACCOBY, E. E., SNOW, M. E., AND JACKLIN, C. N. Children's dispositions and mother-child interaction at 12 and 18 months: A short-term longitudinal study. *Developmental Psychology*, 1984, *20*, 459–472. (a)

MACCOBY, E. E., SNOW, M. E., AND JACKLIN, C. N. Continuities and discontinuities in early mother-child interaction: A longitudinal study at 12 and 18 months. In M. E. Lamb and A. L. Brown (Eds.), *Advances in developmental psychology*, Volume 3. Hillsdale, N.J.: Lawrence Erlbaum Associates, 1984.

MacELMAN, R. M., AND BURDEN, C. E. Society versus the wheelchair: The experiences of a handicapped child. In E. E. Bleck and D. A. Nagel (Eds.) *Physically handicapped children: A medical atlas for teachers*. New York: Grune & Stratton, 1982.

MACFARLANE, A. *The psychology of childbirth*. Cambridge, Mass.: Harvard University Press, 1977.

MACFARLANE, J. W., ALLEN, L., AND HONZIK, M. P. *A developmental study of the behavior problems of normal children between twenty-one months and fourteen years.* Berkeley: University of California Press, 1954.

MACKENZIE, B. Explaining race differences in IQ: The logics, the methodology, and the evidence. *American Psychologist*, 1984, *39*, 1214–1233.

MADDEN, J., O'HARA, J., AND LEVENSTEIN, P. 1984, Home again: Effects of the mother-child home program on mother and child. *Child Development*, 1984, *55*, 636–647.

MADSEN, M. C. Developmental and cross-cultural differences in the cooperative and competitive behavior of young children. *Journal of Cross-Cultural Psychology*, 1971, *2*, 365–371.

MAGENIS, R. E., OVERTON, K. M., CHAMBERLIN, J., BRADY, T., AND LOVRIEN, E. Parental origin of the extra chromosome in Down's syndrome. *Human Genetics*, 1977, *37*, 7–16.

MAGRAB, P. R., AND CALCAGNO, P. L. Psychological impact of chronic pediatric conditions. In P. R. Magrab (Ed.), *Psychological management of pediatric problems: Early life conditions and chronic diseases*, Volume 1. Baltimore, Md.: University Park Press, 1978.

MAHLER, M. S., PINE, F., AND BERGMAN, A. *The psychological birth of the human infant.* New York: Basic Books, 1975.

MAIN, M., AND GEORGE, C. Responses of abused and disadvantaged toddlers to distress in agemates: A study in the day care setting. *Developmental Psychology*, 1985, *21*, 407–412.

MAIN, M., AND GOLDWYN, R. Predicting rejection of her infant from mother's representation of her own experience: Implications for the abused–abusing intergenerational cycle. *Child Abuse & Neglect, The International Journal*, 1984, *8*, 203–217.

MAIN, M., AND WESTON, D. R. The quality of the toddler's relationship to mother and to father: Related to conflict behavior and the readiness to establish new relationships. *Child Development*, 1981, *52*, 932–940.

MALATESTA, C. Z., AND HAVILAND, J. M. Learning display rules: The socialization of emotion expression in infancy. *Child Development*, 1982, *53*, 991–1003.

MALL, J. A study of U.S. teen pregnancy rate. *Los Angeles Times*, March 17, 1985, Part 7, p. 27.

MALLICK, S. K., AND McCANDLESS, B. R. A study of catharsis of aggression. *Journal of Personality and Social Psychology*, 1966, *4*, 590–596.

MANDLER, J. M. Representation and recall in infancy. In M. Moscovitch (Ed.), *Infant memory.* New York: Plenum, 1981.

MANHEIMER, D. L., DEWEY, J., MELLINGER, G. D., AND CORSA, L. 50,000 child-years of accident injuries. *Pacific Health Reports*, 1966, *81*, 519–533.

MANHEIMER, D. L., AND MELLINGER, G. D. Personality characteristics of the child accident repeater. *Child Development*, 1967, *38*, 491–513.

MANIS, F. R., AND MORRISON, F. J. Processing of identity and position information in normal and disabled readers. *Journal of Experimental Child Psychology*, 1982, *33*, 74–86.

MANOSEVITZ, M., PRENTICE, N. M., AND WILSON, F. Individual and family correlates of imaginary companions in preschool children. *Developmental Psychology*, 1973, *8*, 72–79.

MARANTZ, S. A., AND MANSFIELD, A. F. Maternal employment and the development of sex-role stereotyping in five- to eleven-year-old girls. *Child Development*, 1977, *48*, 668–673.

MARATSOS, M. Some current issues in the study of the acquisition of grammar. In P. H. Mussen (Ed.), *Handbook of child psychology*, Volume 3. New York: Wiley, 1983.

MARCIA, J. E. *Determination and construct validity of ego identity status.* Unpublished doctoral dissertation, Ohio State University, 1964.

MARCIA, J. E. Development and validation of ego identity status. *Journal of Personality and Social Psychology*, 1966, *3*, 551–558.

MARCIA, J. E. Identity in adolescence. In J. Adelson (Ed.), *Handbook of adolescent psychology.* New York: Wiley, 1980.

MARINI, M., AND GREENBERGER, E. Sex differences in occupational aspirations and expectations. *Sociology of Work and Occupation*, 1978, *5*, 147–178.

MARINI, Z. *The development of social and physical cognition in childhood and adolescence.* Unpublished doctoral dissertation, University of Toronto (OISE), 1984.

MARK, R. *Memory and nerve cell connections.* Oxford: Clarendon Press, 1974.

MARKMAN, E. M. The facilitation of part-whole comparisons by use of the collective noun "family." *Child Development*, 1973, *44*, 837–840.

MARKMAN, E. M. Realizing that you don't understand: Elementary school children's awareness of inconsistencies. *Child Development*, 1979, *50*, 643–655.

MARKMAN, E. M. Comprehension monitoring. In W. P. Dickson (Ed.), *Children's oral communication skills.* New York: Academic Press, 1981.

MARSHALL, J. C. On the biology of language acquisition. In D. Caplan (Ed.), *Biological studies of mental processes.* Cambridge, Mass.: MIT Press, 1980.

MARTIN, J. A. A longitudinal study of the consequences of early mother–infant interaction: A microanalytic approach. *Monographs of the Society for Research in Child Development*, 1981, *46* (3, Serial No. 190).

MARTIN, R. M. Effects of familiar and complex stimuli on infant attention. *Developmental Psychology*, 1975, *11*, 178–185.

MARTIN, W. E. Singularity and stability of profiles of social behavior. In C. B. Stendler (Ed.), *Readings in child behavior and development.* New York: Harcourt, Brace & World, 1964.

MARTINEZ, C., AND CHAVEZ, A. Nutrition and development in infants of poor rural areas: I. Consumption of mother's milk by infants. *Nutrition Reports International*, 1971, *4*, 139–149.

MARVIN, R. S. An ethological-cognitive model of the attenuation of mother–child attachment behavior. In T. Alloway, P. Pliner, and L. Krames (Eds.), *Attachment behavior: Advances in the study of communication and affect*, Volume 3. New York: Plenum, 1977.

MARVIN, R. S., MOSSLER, D. G., AND GREENBERG, M. *The development of conceptual perspective-taking in preschool children in a "secret game."* Paper presented at the biennial meeting of the Society for Research in Child Development, Denver, March 1975.

MASLIN, C. A., AND BATES, J. E. *Precursors of anxious and·secure attachments: A multivariate model at age 6 months.* Paper presented at the biennial meeting of the Society for Research in Child Development, Detroit, 1983.

MASLIN, C. A., BRETHERTON, I., AND MORGAN, G. The influence of attachment security and maternal scaffolding on toddler mastery motivation. *Infant Behavior and Development*, 1986, *9* (Special Issue: Abstracts of papers presented at the Fifth International Conference on Infant Studies), 244.

MASUR, E. F., McINTYRE, C. W., AND FLAVELL, J. H. Developmental changes in apportionment of study time among items in a multitrial free-recall task. *Journal of Experimental Child Psychology*, 1973, *15*, 237–246.

MASUR, E. F., AND RITZ, E. G. Patterns of gestural, vocal, and verbal imitation performance in infancy. *Merrill-Palmer Quarterly*, 1984, *30*, 369–392.

MATARAZZO, J. D. *Wechsler's measurement and appraisal of adult intelligence* (5th ed.). Baltimore, Md.: Williams & Wilkins, 1972.

MATAS, L., AREND, R. A., AND SROUFE, L. A. Continuity of adaptation in the second year: The relationship between quality of attachment and later competence. *Child Development*, 1978, *49*, 547–556.

MATHENY, A. P., JR., AND DOLAN, A. B. Persons, situations and time: A genetic view of behavioral change in children. *Journal of Personality and Social Psychology*, 1975, *32*, 1106–1110.

MATHER, P. L., AND BLACK, K. N. Hereditary and environmental influences on preschool twins' language skills. *Developmental Psychology*, 1984, *20*, 303–308.

MATSUNAGA, E., AND SHIOTA, K. Search for maternal factors associated with malformed human embryos: A prospective study. *Teratology*, 1981, *21*, 323–331.

MATTSON, A. Long-term physical illness in childhood: A challenge to psychosocial adaptation. *Pediatrics*, 1972, *50*, 801–811.

MAURER, D., AND BARRERA, M. Infants' perception of natural and distorted arrangements of a schematic face. *Child Development*, 1981, *52*, 196–202.

MAURER, D., AND YOUNG, R. E. Newborn's following of natural and distorted arrangements of facial features. *Infant Behavior and Development*, 1983, *6*, 127–131.

MAYER, J. Obesity during childhood. In M. Winick (Ed.), *Childhood obesity*. New York: Wiley, 1975.

McANARNEY, E., AND GREYDANUS, D. Adolescent pregnancy—a multifaceted problem. *Pediatrics in Review*, 1979, *1*, 123–126.

McCABE, M. P. Toward a theory of adolescent dating. *Adolescence*, 1984, *19*, 150–170.

McCABE, M. P., AND COLLINS, J. K. Dating desires and experiences: A new approach to an old question. *Australian Journal of Sex, Marriage, and the Family*, 1981, *2*, 165–173.

McCABE, V. Abstract perceptual information for age level: A risk factor for maltreatment? *Child Development*, 1984, *55*, 267–276.

McCALL, R. B. Challenges to a science of developmental psychology. *Child Development*, 1977, *48*, 333–344.

McCALL, R. B. Environmental effects on intelligence: The forgotten realm of discontinuous nonshared within-family factors. *Child Development*, 1983, *54*, 408–415.

McCALL, R. B. Underachiever—wasted talent. *The Brown University Newsletter*. February 1986, *2*, 1–3.

McCALL, R. B., HOGARTY, P. S., AND HURLBURT, N. Transitions in infant sensorimotor development and the prediction of childhood IQ. *American Psychologist*, 1972, *27*, 728–741.

McCALL, R. B., PARKE, R. D., AND KAVANNAUGH, R. D. Imitation of live and televised models in children one to three years of age. *Monographs of the Society for Research in Child Development*, 1977, *42*, (5 Serial No. 173).

McCARTHY, J. D., AND HOGE, D. R. Analysis of age effects in longitudinal studies of adolescent self-esteem. *Developmental Psychology*, 1982, *18*, 372–379.

McCARTHY, J. D., AND HOGE, D. R. The analysis of self-esteem and delinquency. *American Journal of Sociology*, 1985, *90*, 396–410.

McCLEARN, G. E. Genetic influences on behavior and development. In P. H. Mussen (Ed.), *Carmichael's manual of child psychology*, Volume 1. New York: Wiley, 1970.

McCLELLAND, D. C. Testing for competence rather than for intelligence. *American Psychologist*, 1973, *28*, 1–14.

McCLELLAND, D. C., ATKINSON, J. R., CLARK, R. A., AND LOWELL, E. O. *The achievement motive*. New York: Appleton-Century-Crofts, 1953.

McCLOSKY, M., CARAMAZZA, A., AND GREEN, B. Curvilinear motion in the absence of external forces: Naive beliefs about the motion of objects. *Science*, 1980, *210*, 1139–1141.

McCOY, C. L., AND MASTERS, J. C. The development of children's strategies for the social control of emotion. *Child Development*, 1985, *56*, 1214–1222.

McDAVID, J. W., AND HARARI, H. Stereotyping in names and popularity in grade school children. *Child Development*, 1966, *37*, 453–459.

McDEVITT, S. C. *A longitudinal assessment of longitudinal stability in temperamental characteristics from infancy to early childhood*. Unpublished doctoral dissertation, Temple University, 1976.

McGHEE, P. E., AND CRANDALL, V. C. Beliefs in internal-external control of reinforcement and academic performance. *Child Development*, 1968, *39*, 91–102.

McGRAW, M. B. *Growth: A study of Johnny and Jimmy*. New York: Appleton-Century-Crofts, 1935.

McGRAW, M. B. Swimming behavior in the human infant. In Y. Brackbill and G. G. Thompson (Eds.), *Behavior in infancy and early childhood*. St. Louis, Mo.: C. V. Mosby, 1939/1967.

McGREW, W. C. Aspects of social development in nursery school children, with emphasis on introduction to the group. In N. Blurton Jones (Ed.), *Ethological studies of child behaviour*. London:

Cambridge University Press, 1972.

McINTIRE, M. L. The acquisition of American sign language hand configurations. *Sign Language Studies*, 1977, *16*, 247–266.

McINTIRE, M. S., AND ANGLE, C. R. *Proceedings of the International Symposium on Environmental Health Aspects of Lead, Amsterdam, 1972*. Luxembourg: C.E.C., 1973.

McKENNA, J. J. SIDS babies may need reminders to breath. *Psychology Today*, March 1985, 35.

McKENZIE, B., AND OVER, R. Do neonatal infants imitate?: A reply to Meltzoff and Moore. *Infant Behavior and Development*, 1983, *6*, 109–111. (a)

McKENZIE, B., AND OVER, R. Young infants fail to imitate facial and manual gestures. *Infant Behavior and Development*, 1983, *6*, 85–95. (b)

McLOUGHLIN, D., AND WHITFIELD, R. Adolescents and their experience of parental divorce. *Journal of Adolescence*, 1984, *7*, 155–170.

McNEILL, D. Developmental psycholinguistics. In F. Smith and G. A. Miller (Eds.), *The genesis of language: A psycholinguistic approach*. Cambridge: Mass. MIT Press, 1966.

MEACHAM, J. A. The development of memory abilities in the individual and in society. *Human Development*, 1972, *15*, 205–228.

MEAD, M. Coming of age in Samoa. In *From the South Seas: Studies of adolescence and sex in primitive societies*. New York: William Morrow, 1939. (Originally published 1928)

MEAD, M. Adolescence in primitive and modern society. In V. F. Calverton and S. D. Schmalhausen (Eds.), *The new generation*. New York: Arno Press and The New York Times, 1971. (Originally published 1930)

MECHANIC, D. The influence of mothers on their children's health attitudes and behavior. *Pediatrics*, 1964, *33*, 444–453.

MECKLENBURG, M. E., AND THOMPSON, P. G. The adolescent family life program as a prevention measure. *Public Health Reports*, 1983, *98*, 21–29.

MEDRICH, E. A., ROIZEN, J. A., RUBIN, V., AND BUCKLEY, S. *The serious business of growing up: A study of children's lives outside school*. Berkeley: University of California Press, 1982.

MEHLER, J., BERTONCINI, J., BARRIERE, M., AND JASSIK-GERSCHENFELD, D. Infant recognition of mother's voice. *Perception*, 1978, *7*, 491–497.

MELHUISH, E. C. Visual attention to mother's and stranger's faces and facial contrast in 1-month-old infants. *Developmental Psychology*, 1982, *18*, 229–231.

MELTON, G. B. Toward "personhood" for adolescents: Autonomy and privacy as values in public policy. *American Psychologist*, 1983, *38*, 99–103.

MELTZOFF, A. N. Immediate and deferred imitation in fourteen- and twenty-four-month-old infants. *Child Development*, 1985, *56*, 62–72.

MELTZOFF, A. N., AND MOORE, M. K. Imitation of facial and manual gestures by human neonates. *Science*, 1977, *198*, 75–78.

MELTZOFF, A. N., AND MOORE, M. K. Newborn infants imitate adult facial gestures. *Child Development*, 1983, *54*, 702–709.

MENDELSON, B. K., AND WHITE, D. R. Development of self-body-esteem in overweight youngsters. *Developmental Psychology*, 1985, *21*, 90–96.

MENG, Z., HENDERSON, C., CAMPOS, J., AND EMDE, R. N. *The effects of background emotional elicitation on subsequent problem solving in the toddler*. Unpublished manuscript, University of Denver, 1983.

MERCER, J. R. Socio-cultural factors in labeling mental retardates. *Peabody Journal of Education*, 1971, *48*, 188–203.

MERRICK, F. Personal communication to Jean Sorrells-Jones, 1978.

MERVIS, C. B. On the existence of prelinguistic categories: A case study. *Infant Behavior and Development*, 1985, *8*, 293–300.

MERVIS, C. B., AND MERVIS, C. A. Leopards are kitty-cats: Object labeling by mothers for their thirteen-month-olds. *Child Development*, 1982, *53*, 267–273.

MERVIS, J. Adolescent behavior: What we think we know. *APA Monitor*, April 1984, *15*, 24–25.

MESSER, S. B. The effect of an anxiety over intellectual performance on reflection-impulsivity in children. *Child Development*, 1970, *41*,

723–735.

MESSER, S. B. Reflection-impulsivity: A review. *Psychological Bulletin*, 1976, *83*, 1026–1052.

MEYER, W., AND THOMPSON, G. Sex differences in the distribution of teacher approval and disapproval among sixth-grade children. *Journal of Educational Psychology*, 1956, *47*, 385–396.

MILGRAM, R. M., MILGRAM, N. A., ROSENBLUM, G., AND RABKIN, L. Quantity and quality of creative thinking in children and adolescents. *Child Development*, 1978, *49*, 385–388.

MILLARD, R., AND SIMPSON, D. Enjoyment and productivity as a function of classroom setting location. *Perceptual and Motor Skills*, 1980, 50, 439–444.

MILLER, C. A. The declining health of American children: APHA report. *The Brown University Human Development Letter*, June 1986, *2*, 8.

MILLER, J. *The body in question.* New York: Random House, 1978.

MILLER, L. C. Fears and anxiety in children. In C. E. Walker and M. C. Roberts (Eds.), *Handbook of clinical child psychology.* New York: Wiley, 1983.

MILLER, P. Y., AND SIMON, W. Adolescent sexual behavior: Context and change. *Social Problems*, 1974, *22*, 58–76.

MILLER, P. Y., AND SIMON, W. The development of sexuality in adolescence. In J. Adelson (Ed.), *Handbook of adolescent psychology.* New York: Wiley, 1980.

MILLER, S. Child rearing in the kibbutz. In J. G. Howells (Ed.), *Modern perspectives in international child psychiatry.* Edinburgh: Oliver and Boyd, 1969.

MILLS, M., AND FUNNELL, E. Experience and cognitive processing. In S. Meadows (Ed.), *Developing thinking: Approaches to children's cognitive development.* New York: Methuen, 1983.

MILNE, A. A. *Now we are six.* New York: E. P. Dutton, 1927.

MILNE, C., SEEFELDT, V., AND REUSCHLEIN, P. Relationship between grade, sex, race, and motor performance in young children. *Research Quarterly*, 1976, *47*, 726–730.

MILSTEIN, R. M. *Visual and taste responsiveness in obese-tending infants.* Unpublished paper, Yale University, 1978.

MINDE, K. K., HACKETT, J. D., KILLOU, D., AND SILVER, S. How they grow up: 41 physically handicapped children and their families. *American Journal of Psychiatry*, 1972, *128*, 1544–1560.

MINNETT, A. M., VANDELL, D. L., AND SANTROCK, J. W. The effects of sibling status on sibling interaction: Influence of birth order, age spacing, sex of child, and sex of sibling. *Child Development*, 1983, *54*, 1064–1072.

MINTON, J. H. The impact of *Sesame Street* on readiness. *Sociology of Education*, 1972, *48*, 141–151.

MINUCHIN, P. Sex-role concepts and sex typing in childhood as a function of school and home environments. *Child Development*, 1965, *36*, 1033–1048.

MINUCHIN, P., BIBER, B., SHAPIRO, E., AND ZIMILES, H. *The psychological impact of school experience.* New York: Basic Books, 1969.

MINUCHIN, P. P., AND SHAPIRO, E. K. The school as a context for social development. In P. H. Mussen (Ed.), *Handbook of child psychology,* Volume 4, New York: Wiley, 1983.

MOELY, B. E., OLSON, F. A., HALWES, T. G., AND FLAVELL, J. H. Production deficiency in young children's clustered recall. *Developmental Psychology*, 1969, *1*, 26–34.

MOERK, E. L. *The mother of Eve: As a first language teacher.* Norwood, N.J.: Ablex, 1983.

MOFENSON, H. C., AND GREENSHER, J. Childhood accidents. In R. A. Hoekelman, S. Blatman, P. A. Brunell, S. B. Friedman, and H. H. Seidel (Eds.), *Principles of pediatrics.* New York: McGraw-Hill, 1978.

MOLFESE, D. Neural mechanisms underlying the processes of speech information in infants and adults: Suggestions of differences in development and structure from electrophysiological research. In V. Kirk (Ed.), *Neuropsychology of language, reading, and spelling.* New York: Academic Press, 1983.

MOLFESE, D. L., AND MOLFESE, V. J. Electrophysiological indices of auditory discrimination in newborn infants: The bases for pre-

dicting later language development? *Infant Behavior and Development*, 1985, *8*, 197–211.

MONEY, J., AND EHRHARDT, A. A. *Man and woman. Boy and girl.* Baltimore, Md.: Johns Hopkins University Press, 1972.

MONEY, J., HAMPSON, J. G., AND HAMPSON, J. L. Imprinting and the establishment of gender role. *AMA Archives of Neurological Psychiatry*, 1957, *77*, 333–336.

MONTAGU, A. *Prenatal Influences.* Springfield, Ill.: Charles C Thomas, 1962.

MONTEMAYOR, R. The relationship between parent–adolescent conflict and the amount of time adolescents spend alone and with parents and peers. *Child Development*, 1982, *53*, 1512–1519.

MONTEMAYOR, R. Parents and adolescents in conflict: All families some of the time and some families most of the time. *Journal of Early Adolescence*, 1983, *3*, 83–103.

MONTEMAYOR, R., AND EISEN, M. The development of self-conceptions from childhood to adolescence. *Developmental Psychology*, 1977, *13*, 314–319.

MONTHLY VITAL STATISTICS REPORT. *Final mortality statistics (1977)*, Nos. 79–1120. Hyattsville, Md.: National Center for Health Statistics. Health Education, and Welfare, 1979.

MOORE, B. S., UNDERWOOD, B., AND ROSENHAN, D. L. Affect and altruism. *Developmental Psychology*, 1973, *8*, 99–104.

MOORE, M. J., KAGAN, J., AND HAITH, M. M. Memory and motives. *Developmental Psychology*, 1978, *14*, 563–564.

MOORE, R. S., AND MOORE, D. N. *Better late than early.* New York: Reader's Digest Press, 1975.

MOORE, W. M. The secular trend in physical growth of urban North American Negro school children. *Monographs of the Society for Research in Child Development*, 1970, *35* (7, Serial No. 140).

MORA, J. O., AMEZQUITA, A., CASTRO, L., CHRISTIANSEN, N., CLEMENT-MURPHY, J., COBOS, L. F., CREMER, H. D., DRAGASTIN, S., ELIAS, M. F., FRANKLIN, D., HERRERA, M. G., ORTIZ, N., PARDO, F., DE TIANSEN, B., WAGNER, M., AND STARE, F. J. Nutrition, health and social factors related to intellectual performance. *World Review of Nutrition and Dietetics*, 1974, *19*, 205–236.

MORRISON, F. J. Reading disability: A problem in rule learning and work decoding. *Developmental Review*, 1984, *4*, 36–47.

MORRISON, F. J., HOLMES, D. L., AND HAITH, M. M. A developmental study of the effects of familiarity on short term visual memory. *Journal of Experimental Child Psychology*, 1974, *18*, 412–425.

MORRISON, F. J., AND LORD, C. Age differences in recall of categorized material: Organization or retrieval? *Journal of Genetic Psychology*, 1982, *141*, 233–241.

MORRISON, H., AND KUHN, D. Cognitive aspects of preschoolers' peer imitation in a play situation. *Child Development*, 1983, *54*, 1054–1063.

MORRISON, J. R., AND STEWART, M. A. A family study of the hyperactive child syndrome. *Biological Psychiatry*, 1971, *3*, 189–195.

MORRISON, J. R., AND STEWART, M. A. The psychiatric status of legal families of adopted hyperactive children. *Archives of General Psychiatry*, 1973, *28*, 888–891.

MORSE, C., SAHLER, O., AND FRIEDMAN, S. A three-year follow-up study of abused and neglected children. *American Journal of Diseases of Children*, 1970, *120*, 439–446.

MOSCOVITCH, M. *Infant memory.* New York: Plenum, 1981.

MOSKOWITZ, D. S., DREYER, A. S., AND KRONSBERG, S. Preschool children's field independence: Prediction from antecedent and concurrent maternal and child behavior. *Perceptual and Motor Skills*, 1981, *52*, 607–616.

MOSS, H. A., AND SUSMAN, E. J. Longitudinal study of personality development. In O. G. Brim and J. Kagan (Eds.), *Constancy and change in human development.* Cambridge, Mass.: Harvard University Press, 1980.

MOSSLER, D. G., MARVIN, R. S., AND GREENBERG, M. Conceptual perspective taking in two- to six-year-old children. *Developmental Psychology*, 1976, *12*, 85–86.

MUCH, N. C., AND SHWEDER, R. A. Speaking of rules: The analysis of culture in the breach. In W. Damon (Ed.), *New directions for child development: Moral development*. San Francisco: Jossey-Bass, 1978.

MUELLER, E. The maintenance of verbal exchanges between young children. *Child Development*, 1972, *43*, 930–938.

MUELLER, E., BLEIER, M., KRAKOW, J., HAGEDUS, K., AND COURNOYER, P. The development of peer verbal interaction among two-year-old boys. *Child Development*, 1977, *48*, 284–287.

MUELLER, E., AND BRENNER, J. The origins of social skills and interaction among playgroup toddlers. *Child Development*, 1977, *48*, 854–861.

MUELLER, E., HOLLIEN, H., AND MURRY, T. Perceptual responses to infant crying: Identification of cry types. *Journal of Child Language*, 1974, *1*, 89–95.

MUELLER, E., AND LUCAS, T. A developmental analysis of peer interaction among toddlers. In M. Lewis and L. A. Rosenblum (Eds.), *Friendship and peer relations*. New York: Wiley-Interscience, 1975.

MUELLER, E., AND VANDELL, D. Infant-infant interaction. In J. D. Osofsky (Ed.), *Handbook of infant development*. New York: Wiley, 1979.

MUIR, D., AND FIELD, J. Newborn infants' orientation to sound. *Child Development*, 1979, *50*, 431–436.

MUNROE, R. L., AND MUNROE, R. H. Male pregnancy symptoms and cross-sex identity in three societies. *Journal of Social Psychology*, 1971, *84*, 11–25.

MURPHY, L. B. *The widening world of childhood: Paths toward mastery*. New York: Basic Books, 1962.

MURRAY, D. M., JOHNSON, C. A., LUEPKER, R., AND MITTELMARK, M. The prevention of cigarette smoking in children: A comparison of four strategies. *Journal of Applied Social Psychology*, 1984, *14*, 274–288.

MUSSEN, P. H., AND BOUTERLINE-YOUNG, H. Relationships between rate of physical maturing and personality among boys of Italian descent. *Vita Humana*, 1964, *7*, 186–200.

MUSSEN, P. H., AND EISENBERG-BERG, N. *Roots of caring, sharing, and helping*. San Francisco: W. H. Freeman, 1977.

MUSSEN, P. H., AND JONES, M. C. Self conceptions, motivations, and interpersonal attitudes of late and early maturing boys. *Child Development*, 1957, *28*, 243–256.

MUSTE, M., AND SHARPE, D. Some influential factors in the determination of aggressive behavior in preschool children. *Child Development*, 1947, *18*, 11–28.

MYERS, B. J. *Child rearing across the generations: Grandmother, mothers, and toddlers*. Paper presented at the International Conference on Infant Studies, New York, April 1984.

MYERS, N. A., AND PERLMUTTER, M. Memory in the years from two to five. In P. A. Ornstein (Ed.), *Memory development in children*. Hillsdale, N.J.: Lawrence Erlbaum Associates, 1978.

MYLES-WORSLEY, M., CROMER, C. C., AND DODD, D. H. Children's preschool script reconstruction: Reliance on general knowledge as memory fades. *Developmental Psychology*, 1986, *22*, 22–30.

NADELMAN, L. Sex identity in American children: Memory, knowledge, and preference tests. *Developmental Psychology*, 1974, *10*, 413–417.

NAEYE, R. L. Relationship of cigarette smoking to congenital anomalies and perinatal death. *American Journal of Pathology*, 1978, *90*, 289–294.

NAEYE, R. L., AND PETERS, E. C. Working during pregnancy: Effects on the fetus. *Pediatrics*, 1982, *69*, 724–727.

NATIONAL ASSESSMENT OF EDUCATIONAL PROGRESS. *What students know and can do: Profiles of three age groups*. Denver, Colo.: Education Commission of the United States, 1977.

NATIONAL CENTER FOR EDUCATIONAL STATISTICS (NCES). A 1985 study cited in C. Cordes. Test Tilt: Boys outscore girls on both parts of SAT. *APA Monitor*, June 1986, *17*, 30–31.

NATIONAL CENTER FOR HEALTH STATISTICS. *Anthropometric and clinical findings: Preliminary findings of the first Health and Nutrition Examination Survey. United States, 1971–1972*. Washington, D.C.: DHEW, 1975.

NATIONAL COMMISSION ON EXCELLENCE IN EDUCATION. *A nation at risk: The imperative for educational reform*. Washington, D.C.: U.S. Department of Education, 1983. (a)

NATIONAL COMMISSION ON EXCELLENCE IN EDUCATION. *The third national mathematics assessment: Results, trends, and issues*. Denver, Colo.: Education Commission of the United States, 1983. (b)

NAUS, M. J., ORNSTEIN, P. A., AND HOVING, K. L. Developmental implications of multistore and depth-of-processing models of memory. In P. A. Ornstein (Ed.), *Memory development in children*. Hillsdale, N.J.: Lawrence Erlbaum Associates, 1978.

NEEDLEMAN, H. L., GEIGER, S. K., AND FRANK, R. Lead and IQ scores: A reanalysis. *Science*, 1985, *227*, 701–704.

NEEDLEMAN, H. L., GUNNOE, C., LEVITON, A., REED, R., PERESIE, H., MATHER, C., AND BARRETT, P. Deficits in psychologic and classroom performance of children with elevated dentine lead levels. *New England Journal of Medicine*, 1979, *300*, 689–695.

NEIMARK, E. D. Longitudinal development of formal operational thought. *Genetic Psychology Monographs*, 1975, *91*, 171–225.

NEIMARK, E. D. Adolescent thought: Transition to formal operations. In B. B. Wolman and G. Stricker (Eds.), *Handbook of developmental psychology*. Englewood Cliffs, N.J.: Prentice-Hall, 1982.

NEISSER, U. The control of information pickup in selective looking. In A. D. Pick (Ed.), *Perception and its development*. Hillsdale, N.J.: Lawrence Erlbaum Associates, 1979.

NELSON, K. Structure and strategy in learning to talk. *Monographs of the Society for Research in Child Development*, 1973, *38* (1-2, Serial No. 149).

NELSON, K. Concept, word, and sentence: Interrelations in acquisition and development. *Psychological Review*, 1974, *81*, 267–285.

NELSON, K., AND GRUENDEL, J. At morning it's lunchtime: A scriptal view of children's dialogues. *Discourse Processes*, 1979, *2*, 73–94.

NELSON, K. E. Toward a rare event: Cognitive comparison theory and syntax acquisition. In P. Dale and D. Ingram (Eds.), *Children's language: An international perspective*. Baltimore, Md.: University Park Press, 1980.

NELSON, K. E. Experimental gambits in the service of language acquisition theory. In S. Kuczaj (Ed.), *Language development: Syntax and semantics*. Hillsdale, N.J.: Lawrence Erlbaum Associates, 1981.

NELSON, K. E., DENNINGER, M. M., BONVILLIAN, J. D., KAPLAN, B. J., AND BAKER, N. Maternal input adjustments and non-adjustments as related to children's linguistic advances and to language acquisition theories. In A. D. Pellegrini and T. D. Yawkey (Eds.), *The development of oral and written languages: Readings in developmental and applied linguistics*. Norwood, N.J.: Ablex, 1983.

NELSON, K. E., AND KOSSLYN, S. M. Recognition of previously labeled or unlabeled pictures by 5-year-olds and adults. *Journal of Experimental Child Psychology*, 1976, *21*, 40–45.

NESSELROADE, J. R., AND BALTES, P. B. Adolescent personality development and historical change: 1970–1972. *Monographs of the Society for Research in Child Development*, 1974, *39* (1, Serial No. 154).

NEUMANN, C. G., AND ALPAUGH, M. Birthweight doubling time: A fresh look. *Courrier du Centre International de l'Enfance*, 1976, *26*, 507.

NEWBERGER, C. M., NEWBERGER, E. H., AND HARPER, G. P. The social ecology of malnutrition in childhood. In J. D. Lloyd-Still (Ed.), *Malnutrition and intellectual development*. Littleton, Mass.: Publishing Sciences Group, 1976.

NEWCOMB, A. F., AND BRADY, J. E. Mutuality in boys' friendship relations. *Child Development*, 1982, *53*, 392–395.

NEWCOMBE, N., AND BANDURA, M. M. Effect of age at puberty on spatial ability in girls: A question of mechanism. *Developmental Psychology*, 1983, *19*, 215–224.

NEWPORT, E. L. Motherese: The speech of mothers to young children. In J. J. Castellan, D. B. Pisoni, and G. R. Potts (Eds.), *Cognitive theory*, Volume 3. Hillsdale, N.J.: Lawrence Erlbaum Associates, 1976.

NEWSON, J. An intersubjective approach to the systematic description of mother–infant interaction. In H. R. Schaffer (Ed.), *Studies in mother–infant interaction*. London: Academic Press, 1977.

Newson, J., and Newson, E. *Four years old in an urban community*. Harmondsworth, England: Pelican Books, 1968.

Newson, J., and Newson, E. *Seven years in the home environment*. New York: Wiley, 1976.

Nicholls, J. G. Causal attributions and other achievement-related cognitions: Effects of task outcomes, attainment values, and sex. *Journal of Personality and Social Psychology*, 1975, *31*, 379–389.

Nilsen, D. M. The youngest workers: 14- and 15-year-olds. *Journal of Early Adolescence*, 1984, *4*, 189–197.

Nisan, M., and Kohlberg, L. Universality and variation in moral judgment: A longitudinal and cross-sectional study in Turkey. *Child Development*, 1982, *53*, 865–876.

Niswander, K. R., and Gordon, M. (Eds.). *The Collaborative Perinatal Study of the National Institute of Neurological Diseases and Stroke: The women and their pregnancies*. Washington, D.C.: U.S. Government Printing Office, 1972.

Nizel, A. E. Preventing dental caries: The nutritional factors. *Pediatric Clinics of North America*, 1977, *24*, 141–155.

Northern, J., and Downs, M. *Hearing in children*. Baltimore, Md.: Williams & Wilkins, 1974.

Nottelman, E., and Susman, E. *Passage through puberty*. Paper presented at the annual meeting of the American Association for the Advancement of Science, Los Angeles, 1985.

Nucci, L. P., and Nucci, M. S. Children's responses to moral and social conventional transgressions in free-play settings. *Child Development*, 1982, *53*, 1337–1342.

Nucci, L. P., and Turiel, E. Social interactions and the development of social concepts in pre-school children. *Child Development*, 1978, *49*, 400–408.

O'Brien, M., and Huston, A. C. Development of sex-typed play behavior in toddlers. *Developmental Psychology*, 1985, *21*, 866–871.

O'Bryan, K. G., and Boersma, F. J. Eye movements, perceptual activity, and conservation development. *Journal of Experimental Child Psychology*, 1971, *12*, 157–169.

O'Bryan, K. G., and MacArthur, R. S. Reversibility, intelligence, and creativity in nine-year-old boys. *Child Development*, 1969, *40*, 33–45.

O'Connor, M. J., and Brill, N. *Alcohol use in elderly primips: Relation to infant cognition and growth*. Paper presented at the International Conference on Infant Studies, New York, April 1984.

Oden, S., and Asher, S. R. Coaching children in social skills for friendship making. *Child Development*, 1977, *48*, 495–506.

Odom, R. D. A perceptual salience account of decalage relations and developmental change. In L. S. Siegel and C. J. Brainerd (Eds.), *Alternatives to Piaget: Critical essays on the theory*. New York: Academic Press, 1978.

Odom, R. D. Lane and Pearson's inattention to relevant information: A need for the theoretical specification of task information in developmental research. *Merrill-Palmer Quarterly*, 1982, *28*, 339–345.

Offer, D. *The psychological world of the teen-ager: A study of normal adolescent boys*. New York: Basic Books, 1969.

Offer, D. *The adolescent*. New York: Basic Books, 1981.

Offer, D., Ostrov, E., and Howard, K. J. *The adolescent: A psychological self-portrait*. New York: Basic Books, 1981.

O'Keefe, E. S. C., and Hyde, J. S. The development of occupational sex-role stereotypes: The effects of gender stability and age. *Sex Roles*, 1983, *9*, 481–492.

Oliver, C. M., and Oliver, G. M. Gentle birth: Its safety and its effect on neonatal behavior. *Journal of Obstetrical, Gynecological and Neonatal Nursing*, 1978.

Olson, D. R. From utterance to text: The bias of language in speech and writing. *Harvard Educational Review*, 1977, *47*, 257–281.

Olson, G. M., and Sherman, T. Attention, learning, and memory in infants. In P. H. Mussen (Ed.), *Handbook of child psychology*. New York: Wiley, 1983.

Olson, G. M., and Straus, M. S. The development of infant memory. In M. Moscovitch (Ed.), *Infant Memory: Its relation to normal and pathological memory in humans and other animals*. New York: Plenum, 1981.

Olson, S. L., Bates, J. E., and Bayles, K. Mother–infant interaction and the development of individual differences in children's cognitive competence. *Developmental Psychology*, 1984, *20*, 166–179.

Olweus, D. The stability of aggressive reaction patterns in human males: A review. *Psychological Bulletin*, 1979, *85*, 852–875.

Olweus, D. Familial and temperamental determinants of aggressive behavior in adolescent boys: A causal analysis. *Developmental Psychology*, 1980, *16*, 644–660.

O'Malley, P. M., and Bachman, J. G. Self-esteem: Change and stability between ages 13 and 23. *Developmental Psychology*, 1983, *19*, 257–268.

Oren, D. L. Cognitive advantages of bilingual children related to labeling ability. *Journal of Educational Research*, 1981, *74*, 164–169.

Ornstein, P. A., and Naus, M. J. Rehearsal processes in children's memory. In P. A. Ornstein (Ed.), *Memory development in children*. Hillsdale, N.J.: Lawrence Erlbaum Associates, 1978.

Ornstein, P. A., Naus, M. J., and Liberty, C. Rehearsal and organizational processes in children's memory. *Child Development*, 1975, *26*, 818–830.

Ornstein, P. A., Stone, B. P., Medlin, R. G., Naus, M. J. Retrieving for rehearsal: An analysis of active rehearsal in children's memory. *Developmental Psychology*, 1985, *21*, 633–641.

Ornstein, R. E. The split and whole brain. *Human Nature*, May, 1978, *1*, 76–83.

Osherson, D. N., and Markman, E. Language and the ability to evaluate contradictions and tautologies. *Cognition*, 1975, *3*, 213–226.

Oster, H., and Ewy, R. *Discrimination of sad vs. happy faces by 4-month-olds: When is a smile seen as a smile?* Unpublished manuscript, University of Pennsylvania, 1980.

Ostrea, E. M., Jr., and Chavez, C. J. Perinatal problems (excluding neonatal withdrawal) in maternal drug addiction: A study of 830 cases. *The Journal of Pediatrics*, 1979, *94*, 292–295.

O'Toole, P. Casualties in the classroom. *The New York Times Magazine*, December 10, 1978, pp. 59–90.

Ounsted, C., Oppenheimer, R., and Lindsay, J. Aspects of bonding failure: The psychopathology and psychotherapeutic treatment of families of battered children. *Developmental Medicine and Child Neurology*, 1974, *16*, 447–452.

Overcast, T. D., Murphy, M. D., Smiley, S. S., and Brown, A. L. The effects of instruction on recall and recognition of categorized lists in the elderly. *Bulletin of the Psychonomic Society*, 1975, *5*, 339–341.

Owen, F. W., Adams, P. A., Forrest, T., Stolz, L. M., and Fisher, S. Learning disorders in children: Sibling studies. *Monographs of the Society for Research in Child Development*, 1971, 36, (4, Serial no. 144).

Palardy, J. N. What teachers believe, what children achieve. *Elementary School Journal*, 1969, *69*, 370–374.

Paley, V. *Boys and girls: Superheroes in the doll corner*. Chicago: University of Chicago Press, 1984.

Palkovitz, R. Parental attitudes and fathers' interactions with their 5-month-old infants. *Developmental Psychology*, 1984, *20*, 1054–1060.

Pannabecker, B. J., Emde, R. N., Johnson, W., Stenberg, C., and Davis, M. *Maternal perceptions of infant emotions from birth to 18 months: A preliminary report*. Paper presented at the International Conference of Infant Studies, New Haven, April 1980.

Paoni, F. J. *Reciprocal effects of sixth-graders tutoring third-graders in reading*. Unpublished doctoral dissertation, Oregon State University, 1971.

Papousek, H. A method of studying conditioned food reflexes in young children up to the age of 6 months. *Pavlov Journal of Higher Nervous Activities*, 1959, *9*, 136–140.

Papousek, H. Conditioned head rotation reflexes in infants in the first months of life. *Acta Pediatrica*, 1961, *50*, 565–576.

PAPOUSEK, H. Experimental studies of appetitional behavior in human newborns and infants. In H. W. Stevenson, E. H. Press, and H. L. Rheingold (Eds.), *Early behavior*. New York: Wiley, 1967.

PAPOUSEK, H., AND PAPOUSEK, M. *Biological aspects of parent-infant communication in man*. Invited address at the International Conference on Infant Studies, Providence, R.I., March 1978.

PAPPAS, C. C. The relationship between language development and brain development. *Journal of Children in Contemporary Society*, 1983, *16*, 133–169.

PARIS, S. G., AND LINDAUER, B. K. The role of inference in children's comprehension and memory for sentences. *Cognitive Psychology*, 1976, *8*, 217–227.

PARIS, S. G., AND OKA, E. R. Children's reading strategies, metacognition, and motivation. *Developmental Review*, 1986, *6*, 25–56.

PARKE, R. D. Punishment in children: Effects, side effects, and alternative strategies. In H. Hom and P. Robinson (Eds.), *Psychological processes in early education*. New York: Academic Press, 1977.

PARKE, R. D. Children's home environments: Social and cognitive effects. In I. Altman and J. F. Wohlwill (Eds.), *Children and the environment*. Volume 3. *Human behavior and environment*. New York: Plenum, 1978.

PARKE, R. D., AND O'LEARY, S. Family interaction in the newborn period: Some findings, some observations, and some unresolved issues. In K. Riegel and J. Meacham (Eds.), *The developing individual in a changing world*, Volume 2. *Social and environmental issues*. The Hague: Mouton, 1976.

PARKE, R. D., AND SAWIN, D. *Infant characteristics and behavior as elicitors of maternal and paternal responsibility in the newborn period*. Paper presented at the meetings of the Society for Research in Child Development, Denver, Colo., April 1975.

PARKER, S., AND PARKER, H. Fathers and daughters: The broken bond. *Psychology Today*, March 1985, 10.

PARKINSON, C., WALLIS, S., AND HARVEY, D. School achievement and behavior of children who were small-for-dates at birth. *Developmental Medicine and Child Neurology*, 1981, *23*, 41–50.

PARPAL, M., AND MACCOBY, E. E. Maternal responsiveness and subsequent child compliance. *Child Development*, 1985, *56*, 1326–1334.

PARSONS, J. E., ADLER, T. F., AND KACZALA, C. M. Socialization of achievement attitudes and beliefs: Parental influences. *Child Development*, 1982, *53*, 310–321.

PARSONS, J. E., KACZALA, C. M., AND MEECE, J. L. Socialization of achievement attitudes and beliefs: Classroom influences. *Child Development*, 1982, *53*, 322–339.

PARTEN, M. B. Social play among preschool children. *Journal of Abnormal and Social Psychology*, 1933, *28*, 136–147. Reprinted in R. E. Herron and B. Sutton-Smith (Eds.), *Child's play*. New York: Wiley, 1971.

PASTOR, D. L. The quality of mother-infant attachment and its relationship to toddlers' initial sociability with peers. *Developmental Psychology*, 1981, *17*, 326–335.

PATTERSON, C. J., AND MASSAD, C. M. Facilitating referential communication among children: The listener as teacher. *Journal of Experimental Child Psychology*, 1980, *29*, 357–370.

PATTERSON, G. R. Mothers: The unacknowledged victims. *Monographs of the Society for Research in Child Development*, 1980, *45* (5, Serial No. 186).

PATTERSON, G. R. *Coercive family process*. Eugene, Ore.: Castalia Press, 1982.

PATTERSON, G. R., AND STOUTHAMER-LOEBER, M. The correlation of family management practices and delinquency. *Child Development*, 1984, *55*, 1299–1307.

PEDERSEN, F. A., CAIN, R., ZASLOW, M., AND ANDERSON, B. Variation in infant experience associated with alternative family role organization. In L. Laesa and I. Sigel (Eds.), *Families as learning environments for children*. New York: Plenum, 1983.

PEDERSEN, F. A., ZASLOW, M. J., CAIN, R. L., AND ANDERSON,

B. J. Cesarean childbirth: Psychological implications for mothers and fathers. *Infant Mental Health Journal*, 1981, *2*, 257–263.

PEEL, E. A. *The nature of adolescent judgment*. New York: Wiley, 1971.

PEERY, J. C., AND STERN, D. Gaze duration frequency distributions during mother-infant interaction. *Journal of Genetic Psychology*, 1976, *129*, 45–55.

PENNINGTON, B. F., AND SMITH, S. D. Genetic influences on learning disabilities and speech and language disorders. *Child Development*, 1983, *54*, 369–387.

PENNINGTON, B. F., WALLACH, L., AND WALLACH, M. A. Nonconservers' use and understanding of number and arithmetic. *Genetic Psychology Monographs*, 1980, *101*, 231–243.

PEPLER, D. *Naturalistic observations of teaching and modeling between siblings*. Paper presented at the biennial meeting of the Society for Research in Child Development, Boston, April 1981.

PEPLER, D., CORTER, C., AND ABRAMOVITCH, R. Social relations among children: Siblings and peers. In K. Rubin and H. Ross (Eds.), *Peer relationships and social skills in childhood*. New York: Springer-Verlag, 1982.

PERLMUTTER, M. Development of memory in the preschool years. In R. Greene and T. D. Yawkey (Eds.), *Childhood development*. Westport, Conn.: Technomic Publishing Co., 1980.

PERLMUTTER, M., AND LANGE, G. A developmental analysis of recall–recognition distinctions. In P. A. Ornstein (Ed.), *Memory development in children*. Hillsdale, N.J.: Lawrence Erlbaum Associates, 1978.

PERLMUTTER, M., AND MYERS, N. A. Development of recall in 2- to 4-year-old children. *Developmental Psychology*, 1979, *15*, 73–83.

PESKIN, H. Pubertal onset and ego functioning. *Journal of Abnormal Psychology*. 1967, *72*, 1–15.

PETERSON, P., AND WALBERG, H. (EDS.). *Research in teaching*. San Francisco: McCutchen, 1980.

PETTERSEN, L., YONAS, A., AND FISCH, R. O. The development of blinking in response to impending collision in preterm, full term, and post term infants. *Infant Behavior and Development*, 1980, *3*, 155–165.

PETZEL, S. R., AND CLINE, D. W. Adolescent suicide: Epidemiological and biological aspects. *Adolescent Psychiatry*, 1978, *6*, 239–266.

PEZDEK, K., AND HARTMAN, E. F. Children's television viewing: Attention and comprehension of auditory versus visual information. *Child Development*, 1983, *54*, 1015–1023.

PEZDEK, K., AND STEVENS, E. Children's memory for auditory and visual information on television. *Developmental Psychology*, 1984, *20*, 212–218.

PHILLIPS, D. The illusion of incompetence among academically competent children. *Child Development*, 1984, *55*, 2000–2016.

PIAGET, J. *The moral judgment of the child*. Glencoe, Ill.: Free Press, 1932.

PIAGET, J. *The origins of intelligence in children*. New York: International Universities Press, 1952.

PIAGET, J. *The language and thought of the child*. New York: Meridian Books, 1955. (Originally published 1926)

PIAGET, J. *Play, dreams and imitation*. New York: Norton, 1962. (Originally published 1951)

PIAGET, J. *The child's conception of number*. New York: Norton, 1965.

PIAGET, J. *The child's conception of time*. New York: Basic Books, 1969.

PIAGET, J. Piaget's theory. In P. H. Mussen (Ed.), *Carmichael's manual of child psychology*, Volume 1. New York: Wiley, 1970.

PIAGET, J. Intellectual evolution from adolescence to adulthood. *Human Development*, 1972, *15*, 1–12.

PIAGET, J. *The child's conception of the world*. Totowa, N.J.: Littlefield, Adams, 1975. (Originally published 1929)

PIAGET, J., AND INHELDER, B. *The psychology of the child*. New York: Basic Books, 1969.

PICK, A. D., CHRISTY, M. D., AND FRANKEL, G. W. A developmental study of visual selective attention. *Journal of Experimental Child Psychology*, 1972, *14*, 165–175.

PICK, A. D., AND FRANKEL, G. W. A developmental study of strategies of visual selectivity. *Child Development*, 1974, *45*, 1162–1165.

PIERCE, J. E.   *A study of 750 Portland, Oregon children during the first year*. Papers and Reports on Child Language Development, 8. Stanford, Calif.: Stanford University Press, 1974.

PIERS, M. W.   *Infanticide*. New York: Norton, 1978.

PINES, M.   Can a rock walk? *Psychology Today*, November 1983, 46–54.

PINES, M.   Winning ways. *Psychology Today*, December 1984, 57–65.

PIOTRKOWSKI, C., AND STARK, E.   Blue collar stress worse for boys. *Psychology Today*, June 1985, 15.

PITCHER, E. G., AND SCHULTZ, L. H.   *Boys and girls at play—the development of sex roles*. New York: Praeger, 1984.

PITT, B.   "Maternity blues." *British Journal of Psychiatry*, 1973, *122*, 431–433.

PITTMAN, T. S., BOGGIANO, A. K., AND RUBLE, D. N.   Intrinsic and extrinsic motivational orientations: Limiting conditions on the undermining and enhancing effects of reward on intrinsic motivation. In J. M. Levine and M. C. Wang (Eds.), *Teacher and student perceptions: Implications for learning*. Hillsdale, N.J.: Lawrence Erlbaum Associates, 1983.

PLECK, J., AND RUSTAD, M.   *Husbands' and wives' time in family and paid work in the 1975–1976 study of time use*. Unpublished manuscript, Wellesley College Center for Research on Women, 1980.

PLESS, I. B., AND ROGHMANN, K. J.   Chronic illness and its consequences: Observations based on three epidemiologic. surveys. *Journal of Pediatrics*. 1971, *79*, 351–359.

PLESS, I. B., AND SATTERWHITE, B. B.   Chronic illness. In R. J. Haggerty; K. J. Roghmann, and I. B. Pless (Eds.), *Child health and the community*. New York: Wiley, 1975.

PLOMIN, R.   Developmental behavioral genetics. *Child Development*, 1983, *54*, 253–259.

PLOMIN, R., LOEHLIN, J. C., AND DEFRIES, J. C.   Genetic and environmental components of "environmental" influences. *Developmental Psychology*, 1985, *21*, 391–402.

POLANI, P. E., LESSOF, M. H., AND BISHOP, P. M. F.   Colour-blindness in "ovarian agenesis" (gonadal dysplasia). *Lancet*, 1956, *2*, 118–119.

POLLOCK, L.   *Forgotten children: Parent-child relations from 1500 to 1900*. Cambridge, England: Cambridge University Press, 1983.

POULSON, C. L.   Differential reinforcement of other-than-vocalization as a control procedure in the conditioning of infant vocalization rate. *Journal of Experimental Child Psychology*, 1983, *36*, 471–489.

POWELL, G. F., BRASEL, J. A., RAITI, S., AND BLIZZARD, R. M.   Emotional deprivation and growth retardation stimulating idiopathic hypopituitarism: II. Endocrinologic evaluation of the syndrome. *New England Journal of Medicine*, 1967, *276*, 1279–1283.

POWER, T. G., AND PARKE, R. D.   Patterns of mother and father play with their 8-month-old infant: A multiple analyses approach. *Infant Behavior and Development*, 1983, *6*, 453–459.

PRATT, L.   Child rearing methods and children's health behavior. *Journal of Health and Social Behavior*, 1973, *14*, 61–69.

PRICE, G. G., HESS, R. D., AND DICKSON, W. P.   Processes by which verbal-educational abilities are affected when mothers encourage preschool children to verbalize. *Developmental Psychology*, 1981, *17*, 554–564.

PRICE, J., AND FESHBACH, S.   *Emotional adjustment correlates of television viewing in children*. Paper presented at the American Psychological Association, Washington, D.C., August 1982.

PRENTICE, N., AND FATHMAN, R.   Joking riddles: A developmental index of children's humor. *Developmental Psychology*, 1975, *2*, 210–216.

PRESSLEY, M., FORREST-PRESSLEY, D. L., ELLIOTT-FAUST, D., AND MILLER, G.   Children's use of cognitive strategies, how to teach strategies, and what to do if they can't be taught. In M. Pressley and C. J. Brainerd (Eds.), *Cognitive learning and memory in children*. New York: Springer-Verlag, 1985.

PUNTIL, J.   *Juvenile delinquency in Illinois: Highlights of the 1972 adolescent survey*. Chicago: Institute for Juvenile Research, Illinois Mental Health Institute, 1972.

PURPURA, D. P.   Morphogenesis of the visual cortex in preterm infants. In M. A. B. Brazier (Ed.), *Growth and brain development*. New York: Raven Press, 1975.

PUTALLAZ, M.   Predicting children's sociometric status from their behavior. *Child Development*, 1983, *54*, 1417–1426.

QUERLEU, D., AND RENARD, K.   Les perceptions auditives du foetus humain. *Medicine et Hygiene*, 1981, *39*, 2102–2110.

QUIGLEY, M. E., SHEEHAN, K. L., WILKES, M. M., AND YEN, S. S. C.   Effects of maternal smoking on circulating catecholamine levels and fetal heart rates. *American Journal of Obstetrics and Gynecology*, 1979, *133*, 685–690.

RADKE-YARROW, M., CUMMINGS, E. M., KUCZYNSKI, L., AND CHAPMAN, M.   Patterns of attachment in two- and three-year-olds in normal families and families with parental depression. *Child Development*, 1985, *56*, 884–893.

RAFMAN, S.   The infant's reaction to imitation of the mother's behavior by a stranger. In T. G. Decarie (Ed.), *The infant's reaction to strangers*. New York: International Universities Press, 1974.

RAMEY, C. T., AND CAMPBELL, F. A.   Compensatory education for disadvantaged children. *School Review*, 1979, *87*, 171–189.

RAMEY, C. T., AND HASKINS, R.   The modification of intelligence through early experience. *Intelligence*, 1981, *5*, 5–19.

RAO, S.   *The effect of instruction on pupil reading strategies*. Unpublished dissertation, University of Reading, 1982.

RATNER, H. H.   Memory demands and the development of young children's memory. *Child Development*, 1984, *55*, 2173–2191.

RATNER, N. B., AND PYE, C.   Higher pitch in BT is not universal: Acoustic evidence from Quiche Mayan. *Journal of Child Language*, 1984, *11*, 515–522.

RAWAT, A.   Alcohol harms fetus, study finds. *Chicago Tribune*, April 19, 1982, section 1, p. 13.

RAY, C. G.   Common infectious diseases. In D. W. Smith (Ed.), *Introduction to clinical pediatrics*. Philadelphia: W. B. Saunders, 1977.

REBELSKY, F., AND HANKS, C.   Fathers' verbal interaction with infants in the first three months of life. *Child Development*, 1971, *42*, 63–68.

REED, E.   Anomalies in development. In F. D. Horowitz (Ed.), *Review of child development research*, Volume 4. Chicago: University of Chicago Press, 1975.

REESE, H. W.   Imagery and associative memory. In R. V. Kail, Jr., and J. W. Hagen (Eds.), *Perspectives in the development of memory and cognition*. Hillsdale, N.J.: Lawrence Erlbaum Associates, 1977.

REID, J. F.   A study of thirteen beginners in reading. *Acta Psychologica*, 1958, *14*, 294–313.

REID, J. F.   Into print: Reading and language growth. In M. Donaldson, R. Grieve, and C. Pratt (Eds.), *Early childhood development and education: Readings in psychology*. Oxford: Basil Blackwell, 1983.

REINISCH, J. M.   Prenatal exposure to synthetic progestins increases potential for aggression in humans. *Science*, 1981, *211*, 1171–1173.

RENNINGER, K. A., AND WOZNIAK, R. H.   Effect of interest on attentional shift, recognition, and recall in young children. *Developmental Psychology*, 1985, *21*, 624–632.

RESCORLA, L. A.   Category development in early language. *Journal of Child Language*, 1981, *8*, 225–238.

REST, J. R.   Morality. In P. H. Mussen (Ed.), *Handbook of child psychology*, Volume 3. New York: Wiley, 1983.

REST, J. R., DAVISON, M. L., AND ROBBINS, S.   Age trends in judging moral issues: A review of cross-sectional, longitudinal, and sequential studies of the defining issues test. *Child Development*, 1978, *49*, 263–279.

REST, J. R., TURIEL, E., AND KOHLBERG, L.   Level of moral development as a determinant of preference and comprehension of moral judgments made by others. *Journal of Personality*, 1969, *37*, 225–252.

RESTAK, R.   Male, female brains: Are they different? *Boston Globe*, September 9, 1979, p. A1.

REVILL, S. I., AND DODGE, J. A.   Psychological determinants of infantile pyloric stenosis. *Archives of Disease in Childhood*, 1978, *53*, 66–68.

RHEINGOLD, H. L. Independent behavior of the human infant. In A. D. Pick (Ed.), *Minnesota Symposia on Child Psychology*, Volume 7. Minneapolis: University of Minnesota Press, 1973.

RHEINGOLD, H. L., AND COOK, K. V. The contents of boys' and girls' rooms as an index of parents' behavior. *Child Development*, 1975, *46*, 459–463.

RHEINGOLD, H. L., AND ECKERMAN, C. O. Departures from the mother. In H. R. Schaffer (Ed.), *The origins of human social relations*. London: Academic Press, 1971.

RHEINGOLD, H. L., AND ECKERMAN, C. O. Fear of the stranger: A critical examination. In H. W. Reese (Ed.), *Advances in child development and behavior*, Volume 8. New York: Academic Press, 1973.

RHEINGOLD, H. L., AND EMERY, G. N. The nurturant acts of very young children. In D. Olweus, J. Block, and M. Radke-Yarrow (Eds.), *Development of antisocial and prosocial behavior*. Orlando, Fla.: Academic Press, 1986.

RHEINGOLD, H. L., HAY, D. F., AND WEST, M. J. Sharing in the second year of life. *Child Development*, 1976, *47*, 1148–1158.

RHOLES, W. S., AND RUBLE, D. N. Children's understanding of dispositional characteristics of others. *Child Development*, 1984, *55*, 550–560.

RICCIUTI, H. N. Fear and the development of social attachments in the first year of life. In M. Lewis and L. A. Rosenblum (Eds.), *The origins of fear*. New York: Wiley, 1974.

RICE, M. The role of television in language acquisition. *Developmental Review*, 1983, *3*, 211–224.

RICHARDS, D. D., AND SIEGLER, R. S. The effects of task requirements on children's life judgments. *Child Development*, 1984, *55*, 1687–1696.

RICHARDSON, G. A., AND DAY, N. L. Alcohol use during pregnancy and neonatal outcome. *Infant Behavior and Development*, 1986, *9* (Special Issue: Abstracts of papers presented at the Fifth International Conference on Infant Studies), 301.

RICHARDSON, S. A., GOODMAN, N., AND HASTORF, A. H. Cultural uniformity in reaction to physical disabilities. *American Sociological Review*, 1961, *26*, 241–247.

RICHMAN, L., AND HARPER, D. School adjustment of children with observable disabilities. *Journal of Abnormal Child Psychology*, 1978, *6*, 11–18.

RICHMAN, N., STEVENSON, J., AND GRAHAM, P. J. *Pre-school to school: A behavioural study*. London: Academic Press, 1982.

RICHMOND-ABBOTT, M. Sex-role attitudes of mothers and children in divorced, single-parent families. *Journal of Divorce*, 1984, *8*, 61–81.

RIEGEL, K. F. The dialectics of human development. *American Psychologist*, 1976, *31*, 689–699.

RIESE, M. L. Temperament stability between the neonatal period and 24 months in full-term and preterm infants. *Infant Behavior and Development*, 1986, *9* (Special Issue: Abstracts of papers presented at the Fifth International Conference on Infant Studies), 305.

RITTER, K., KAPROVE, B. H., FITCH, J. P., AND FLAVELL, J. H. The development of retrieval strategies in young children. *Cognitive Psychology*, 1973, *5*, 310–321.

RIVARA, F. P. Epidemiology of childhood injuries. In *Preventing childhood injuries*. Columbus, Ohio: Ross Laboratories, January 1982.

RIVLIN, L., AND ROTHENBERG, M. The use of space in open classrooms. In H. Proshansky, W. Ittelson, and L. Rivlin (Eds.), *Environmental psychology: People and their physical settings* (2nd ed.). New York: Holt, Rinehart & Winston, 1976.

ROBERTS, C. J., AND LOWE, C. R. Where have all the conceptions gone? *Lancet*, March 1, 1975, *7905*, 498–499.

ROBERTS, G. C., BLOCK, J. H., AND BLOCK, J. Continuity and change in parents' child-rearing practices. *Child Development*, 1984, *55*, 586–597.

ROBERTS, R. J., AND PATTERSON, C. J. Perspective taking and referen-

tial communication: The question of correspondence reconsidered. *Child Development*, 1983, *54*, 993–1004.

ROBERTSON, J., AND ROBERTSON, J. Young children in brief separation: A fresh look. *Psychoanalytic Study of the Child*, 1971, *26*, 264–315.

ROBINSON, E. J. The child's understanding of inadequate messages and communication failure: A problem of ignorance or egocentrism. In W. P. Dickson (Ed.), *Children's oral communication skills*. New York: Academic Press, 1981.

ROBINSON, E. J., AND ROBINSON, W. P. Development in the understanding of causes of success and failure in verbal communication. *Cognition*, 1977, *5*, 363–378.

ROBSON, K. S., AND MOSS, H. A. Patterns and determinants of maternal attachment. *Journal of Pediatrics*, 1970, *77*, 976.

ROCHE, A. F. The adipocyte-number hypothesis. *Child Development*, 1981, *52*, 31–43.

ROE, K. V., AND ROE, A. *Vocal stimulation early in life and infant vocal responsiveness to mother vs. stranger: A curvilinear relationship*. Paper presented at the International Conference on Infant Studies, New York, April 1984.

ROEDELL, W. C., AND SLABY, R. C. The role of distal and proximal interaction in infant social preference formation. *Developmental Psychology*, 1977, *13*, 266–273.

ROFFWARG, H. P., MUZIO, J. N., AND DEMENT, W. C. Ontogenetic development of the human sleep-dream cycle. *Science*, 1966, *152*, 604–619.

ROGERS, C. R. Toward a theory of creativity. In H. H. Anderson (Ed.), *Creativity and its cultivation*. New York: Harper, 1959.

ROHNER, R. P. *They love me, they love me not: A world-wide study of the effects of parental acceptance and rejection*. New Haven, Conn.: Human Relations, Area File Press, 1975.

ROOPNARINE, J. L., AND FIELD, T. M. Peer-directed behaviors of infants and toddlers during nursery school play. *Infant Behavior and Development*, 1983, *6*, 133–138.

ROOPNARINE, J. L., AND JOHNSON, J. E. Socialization in a mixed age experimental program. *Developmental Psychology*, 1984, *20*, 828–832.

ROSCH, E. Cognitive representations of semantic categories. *Journal of Experimental Psychology*, 1975, *104*, 192–233.

ROSCH, E., MERVIS, C. B., GRAY, W. D., JOHNSON, D. M., AND BOYES-BRAEM, P. Basic objects in natural categories. *Cognitive Psychology*, 1976, *8*, 382–439.

ROSE, S. A., AND BLANK, M. The potency of context in children's cognition: An illustration through conservation. *Child Development*, 1969, *40*, 383–406.

ROSE, W. L. *A documentary history of slavery in North America*. Oxford: Oxford University Press, 1976.

ROSEN, B., AND D'ANDRADE, R. The psychosocial origins of achievement motivation. *Sociometry*, 1959, *22*, 185–218.

ROSENBERG, M. *Society and the adolescent self-image*. Princeton, N.J.: Princeton University Press, 1965.

ROSENBERG, M., AND SIMMONS, R. G. *Black and white self-esteem: The urban school child*. Washington, D.C.: American Sociological Association, 1971.

ROSENBLATT, P. C., AND CUNNINGHAM, M. R. Television watching and family tensions. *Journal of Marriage and the Family*, 1976, *38*, 105–110.

ROSENFELD, E. F. *The relationship of sex-typed toys to the development of competency and sex-role identification in children*. Paper presented at the meeting of the Society for Research in Child Development, Denver, 1975.

ROSENSTEIN, D., AND OSTER, H. *Facial expression as a method for exploring infants' taste responses*. Paper presented at the meeting of the Society for Research in Child Development, Boston, April 1981.

ROSENSTOCK, I. M., AND KIRSCHT, J. P. Practice implications. In M. H. Becker (Ed.), *The health belief model and personal health behavior*. Thorofare, N.J.: Charles B. Slack, 1974.

ROSENTHAL, D. *Genetic theory and abnormal behavior*. New York: Mc-

Graw-Hill, 1970.

ROSENTHAL, R. From unconscious experimentor bias to teacher expectancy effects. In J. B. Dusek (Ed.) *Teacher Expectancies*. Hillsdale, NJ: Lawrence Erlbaum Associates, 1985.

ROSENTHAL, R., BARATZ, S. S., AND HALL, C. M. Teacher behavior, teacher expectations, and gains in pupils' rated creativity. *Journal of Genetic Psychology*, 1974, *124*, 115–121.

ROSETT, H. L., WEINER, L., ZUCKERMAN, B., McKINLAY, S., AND EDELIN, K. C. Reduction of alcohol consumption during pregnancy with benefits to the newborn. *Alcoholism: Clinical and Experimental Research*, 1980, *4*, 178–184.

ROSNER, B. S., AND DOHERTY, N. E. The response of neonates to intra-uterine sounds. *Developmental Medicine and Child Neurology*, 1979, *21*, 723–729.

ROSS, D. M., AND ROSS, S. A. *Hyperactivity: Research, theory, and action* (1st ed.; 2nd ed.). New York: Wiley, 1976, 1982.

ROSS, H. S., AND GOLDMAN, B. D. Establishing new social relations in infancy. In T. Alloway, P. Pliner, and L. Krames (Eds.), *Attachment behavior: Advances in the study of communication and affect*, Volume 3. New York: Plenum, 1977.(a)

ROSS, H. S., AND GOLDMAN, B. D. Infants' sociability toward strangers. *Child Development*, 1977, *48*, 638–642.(b)

ROTBERG, I. Some legal and research considerations in establishing federal policy in bilingual education. *Harvard Educational Review*, 1982, *52*, 149–168.

ROTH, C. Factors affecting developmental changes in the speed of processing. *Journal of Experimental Child Psychology*, 1983, *35*, 509–528.

ROTH, F. Accelerating language learning in young children. *Journal of Child Language*, 1984, *11*, 89–107.

ROUTH, D. K., SCHROEDER, C. S., AND O'TUAMA, L. Development of activity level in children. *Developmental Psychology*, 1974, *10*, 163–168.

ROVEE-COLLIER, C. K., SULLIVAN, M. W., ENRIGHT, M. L., LUCAS, D., AND FAGEN, J. W. Reactivation of infant memory. *Science*, 1980, *208*, 1159–1161.

ROVET, J. Cognitive and neuropsychological test performance of persons with abnormalities of adolescent development: A test of Waber's hypothesis. *Child Development*, 1983, *54*, 941–950.

ROVET, J., AND NETLEY, C. The triple X chromosome in childhood: Recent empirical findings. *Child Development*, 1983, *54*, 831–845.

ROWLEY, V., AND KELLER, E. D. Changes in children's verbal behavior as a function of social approval and manifest anxiety. *Journal of Abnormal Social Psychology*, 1962, *65*, 53–57.

RUBIN, J. Boosting baby's brain. *Psychology Today*, March 1986, 16.

RUBIN, J. Z., PROVENZANO, F. J., AND LURIA, Z. The eye of the beholder: Parents' views on sex of newborns. *American Journal of Orthopsychiatry*, 1974, *44*, 512–519.

RUBIN, K. H., AND DANIELS-BEIRNESS, T. Concurrent and predictive correlates of sociometric status in kindergarten and grade 1 children. *Merrill-Palmer Quarterly*, 1983, *29*, 337–351.

RUBIN, K. H., FEIN, G. G., AND VANDENBERG, B. Play. In P. H. Mussen (Ed.), *Handbook of child psychology*, Volume 4, *Socialization, personality and social development*. New York: Wiley, 1983.

RUBIN, K. H., AND KRASNOR, L. R. Social-cognitive and social behavior perspectives on problem solving. In M. Perlmutter (Ed.), *Minnesota Symposia on Child Psychology*, Volume 18. Hillsdale, N.J.: Lawrence Erlbaum Associates, 1986.

RUBIN, K. H., WATSON, K. S., AND JAMBOR, T. W. Free-play behaviors in preschool and kindergarten children. *Child Development*, 1978, *49*, 534–536.

RUBIN, L. B. The empty nest: Beginnings or ending? In L. A. Bond and J. C. Rosen (Eds.), *Competence and coping during adulthood*. Hanover, N.H.: University Press of New England, 1980.

RUBIN, Z. *Children's friendships*. Cambridge, Mass.: Harvard University Press, 1980.

RUBLE, D. N., AND BROOKS, J. *Adolescent attitudes about menstruation*. Paper presented at the biennial meeting of the Society for Research in Child Development, New Orleans, March 1977.

RUBLE, D. N., AND BROOKS-GUNN, J. The experience of menarche. *Child Development*, 1982, *53*, 1557–1566.

RUFF, H. A. Components of attention during infants' manipulative exploration. *Child Development*, 1986, *57*, 105–114.

RUKE-DRAVINA, V. Modifications of speech addressed to young children in Latvian. In C. E. Snow and C. A. Ferguson (Eds.), *Talking to children: Language input and acquisition*. Cambridge, England: Cambridge University Press, 1977.

RUSHTON, J. P. Generosity in children: Immediate and long term effects of modeling, preaching, and moral judgment. *Journal of Personality and Social Psychology*, 1975, *31*, 459–466.

RUSHTON, J. P. *Can genes help helping?* Paper presented at the annual convention of the American Psychological Association, Toronto, August 1984.

RUSSELL, D. E. The prevalence and seriousness of incestuous abuse: Stepfathers vs. biological fathers. *Child Abuse & Neglect, The International Journal*, 1984, *8*, 15–22.

RUSSELL, M. J. Human olfactory communication. *Nature*, 1976, *260*, 520–522.

RUTTER, M. *The qualities of mothering: Maternal deprivation reassessed*. New York: Jason Aronson, 1974.

RUTTER, M. On confusion in the diagnosis of autism. *Journal of Autism and Childhood Schizophrenia*, 1978, *8*, 137–161.

RUTTER, M. *Changing youth in a changing society: Patterns of development and disorder*. Cambridge, Mass.: Harvard University Press, 1980.

RUTTER, M., MAUGHAN, B., MORTIMORE, P., AND OUSTON, J. *Fifteen thousand hours: Secondary schools and their effects on children*. Cambridge, Mass.: Harvard University Press, 1979.

RUTTER, M., TIZARD, J., AND WHITMORE, R. *Education, health, and behavior*. New York: Wiley, 1970.

RUTTER, M., YULE, W., AND GRAHAM, P. Enuresis and behavioral deviance: Some epidemiological considerations. In I. Kolvin, R. MacKeith and R. Meadows (Eds.), *Bladder control and enuresis*. Philadelphia: Lippincott, 1973.

SAARIO, T., JACKLIN, C. N., AND TITTLE, C. K. Sex role stereotyping in the public schools. *Harvard Educational Review*, 1973, *43*, 386–404.

SAARNI, C. *When not to show what you feel: Children's understanding of relations between emotional experience and expressive behavior*. Paper presented at the biennial meeting of the Society for Research in Child Development, San Francisco, March 1979.

SACHS, J. The adaptive significance of linguistic input to prelinguistic infants. In C. E. Snow and C. A. Ferguson (Eds.), *Talking to children: Language input and acquisition*. Cambridge, England: Cambridge University Press, 1977.

SACHS, J., AND JOHNSON, M. Language development in a hearing child of deaf parents. In W. Von Raffler Engel and Y. Le Brun (Eds.), *Baby talk and infant speech*, Neurolinguistics Series, Volume 5. Amsterdam: Swets and Zeitlinger, 1976.

SADDLER, J. M. *Assessment of children's intelligence*. Philadelphia: Saunders, 1974.

SADKER, M., AND SADKER, D. Sexism in the schoolroom of the 80's. *Psychology Today*, March 1985, 54–57.

SALAPATEK, P. Pattern perception in early infancy. In L. B. Cohen and P. Salapatek (Eds.), *Infant perception: From sensation to cognition*, Volume 1. *Basic visual processes*. New York: Academic Press, 1975.

SALK, L., LIPSITT, L. P., STURNER, W. Q., REILLY, B. M., AND LEVAT, R. H. Relationship of maternal and perinatal conditions to eventual adolescent suicide. *Lancet*, March 16, 1985, 624–627.

SALTER, A. Birth without violence: A medical controversy. *Nursing Research*, 1978, *27*, 84–88.

SALTZ, E., CAMPBELL, S., AND SKOTKO, D. Verbal control of behavior: The effects of shouting. *Developmental Psychology*, 1983, *19*, 461–464.

SALTZ, E., DIXON, D., AND JOHNSON, J. Training disadvantaged preschoolers on various fantasy activities: Effects on cognitive functioning and impulse control. *Child Development*, 1977, *48*, 367–

380.

SALZMAN, L. K. Allergy testing, psychological assessment and dietary treatment of the hyperactive child syndrome. *Medical Journal of Australia*, 1976, *2*, 248–251.

SAMEROFF, A. J. The components of sucking in the human newborn. *Journal of Experimental Child Psychology*, 1968, *6*, 607–623.

SAMEROFF, A. J., AND CAVANAUGH, P. J. Learning in infancy: A developmental perspective. In J. D. Osofsky (Ed.), *Handbook of infant development*. New York: Wiley, 1979.

SAMEROFF, A. J., SIEFER, R., AND ELIAS, P. K. Sociocultural variability in infant temperament ratings. *Child Development*, 1982, *53*, 164–173.

SAMEROFF, A. J., SEIFER, R., AND ZAX, M. Early development of children at risk for emotional disorder. *Monographs of the Society for Research in Child Development*, 1982, 47 (7, Serial No. 199).

SAMUEL, J., AND BRYANT, P. Asking only one question in the conversation experiment. *Journal of Child Psychology and Psychiatry*, 1984, *25*, 315–318.

SAMUELS, H. R. The effect of an older sibling on infant locomotor exploration of a new environment. *Child Development*, 1980, *51*, 607–609.

SANDER, L. Issues in early mother-infant interaction. *Journal of the American Academy of Clinical Psychiatry*, 1962, 141–166.

SANDERS, B., AND SOARES, M. P. Sexual maturation and spatial ability in college students. *Developmental Psychology*, 1986, *22*, 199–203.

SANTROCK, J. W. *Adolescence: An introduction*. Dubuque, Iowa: W. C. Brown, 1984.

SAPIR, E. *Language*. New York: Harcourt, Brace, 1921. (Reprinted 1958.)

SARASON, S. B. Individual psychology: An obstacle to comprehending adulthood. In L. A. Bond and J. C. Rosen (Eds.), *Competence and coping during adulthood*. Hanover, N.H.: University Press of New England, 1980.

SAVIN-WILLIAMS, R. C. *Dominance-submission behaviors and hierarchies in young adolescents at a summer camp: Predictors, styles and sex differences*. Unpublished doctoral dissertation, University of Chicago, 1977.

SAVIN-WILLIAMS, R. C., AND DEMO, D. H. Developmental change and stability in adolescent self-concept. *Developmental Psychology*, 1984, *20*, 1100–1110.

SAVITSKY, J. C., AND WATSON, M. J. Patterns of proxemic behavior among preschool children. *Representative Research in Social Psychology*, 1975, *6*, 109-113.

SAXBY, L., AND BRYDEN, M. P. Left-ear superiority in children for processing auditory emotional material. *Developmental Psychology*, 1984, *20*, 72–80.

SCAFIDI, F. A., FIELD, T. M., AND SCHANBERG, S. M. Effects of tactile/kinesthetic stimulation on the clinical course and sleep/wake behavior of preterm neonates. *Infant Behavior and Development*, 1986, *9*, 91–105.

SCANLON, J. *Self-reported health behavior and attitudes of youth 12–17 years*. Vital and Health Statistics, Series 11, 147. Washington, D.C.: U.S. Government Printing Office, 1975.

SCANLON, J. W., BROWN, W. V., WEISS, J. B., AND ALPER, M. H. Neurological responses of newborn infants after maternal epidural anesthesia. *Anesthesiology*, 1974, *40*, 121–128.

SCARR, S., AND McCARTNEY, K. How people make their own environments: A theory of genotype—environment effects. *Child Development*, 1983, *54*, 424–435.

SCARR, S., PAKSTIS, A. J., KATZ, S. H., AND BARKER, W. B. The absence of a relationship between degree of white ancestry and intellectual skills within a black population. *Human Genetics*, 1977, *39*, 69–86.

SCARR, S., AND WEINBERG, R. A. I.Q. test performance of black children adopted by white families. *American Psychologist*, 1981, *36*, 1159–1166.

SCARR, S., AND WEINBERG, R. A. The Minnesota Adoption Studies: Genetic differences and malleability. *Child Development*, 1983, *54*,

260–267.

SCARR-SALAPATEK, S. Genetics and the development of intelligence. In F. D. Horowitz (Ed.), *Review of child development research*, Volume 4. Chicago: University of Chicago Press, 1975.

SCHACTER, D. L., AND MOSCOVITCH, M. Infants, amnesics, and dissociable memory systems. In M. Moscovitch (Ed.), *Infant memory*. New York: Plenum, 1981.

SCHAEFER, E. S., AND BAYLEY, N. Maternal behavior, child behavior and their intercorrelations from infancy through adolescence. *Monographs of the Society for Research in Child Development*, 1963, *28* (3, Serial No. 87).

SCHAFFER, H. R. Acquiring the concept of the dialogue. In M. H. Bornstein and W. Kessen (Eds.), *Psychological development from infancy: Image to intention*. Hillsdale, N.J.: Lawrence Erlbaum Associates, 1978.

SCHAFFER, H. R., COLLIS, G. M., AND PARSONS, G. Vocal interchange and visual regard in verbal and preverbal children. In H. R. Schaffer (Ed.), *Studies in mother-infant interaction*. London: Academic Press, 1977.

SCHAFFER, H. R., AND CROOK, C. K. The role of the mother in early social development. In H. McGurk (Ed.), *Childhood social development*. London: Methuen, 1978.

SCHAFFER, H. R., AND EMERSON, P. E. The development of social attachments in infancy. *Monographs of the Society for Research in Child Development*, 1964, *29* (3, Serial No. 94).(a)

SCHAFFER, J. R., AND EMERSON, P. E. Patterns of response to physical contact in early human development. *Journal of Child Psychology and Psychiatry*, 1964, *5*, 1–13.(b)

SCHATTEN, G., AND SCHATTEN, H. The energetic egg. *The Sciences*, September/October 1983. Reprinted in *Annual Editions Human Development 85/86*, Guilford, Conn.: Duskin, 1985, pp. 42–45.

SCHAU, C. G., KAHN, L., DIEPOLD, J. H., AND CHERRY, F. The relationships of parental expectations and preschool children's verbal sex typing to their sex-typed toy play behavior. *Child Development*, 1980, *51*, 266–270.

SCHEINFELD, A. *Your heredity and environment*. Philadelphia/New York: Lippincott, 1965.

SCHERER, M. W., AND NAKAMURA, C. Y. A peer-survey schedule for children: A factor analytic comparison with manifest anxiety. *Behavior Research and Therapy*, 1968, *6*, 173–182.

SCHERZ, R. G. Fatal motor vehicle accidents of child passengers from birth through 4 years of age in Washington State. *Pediatrics*, 1981, *68*, 572–576.

SCHIEFFELIN, B. B., AND OCHS, E. A cultural perspective on the transition from prelinguistic to linguistic communication. In R. M. Golinkoff (Ed.), *The transition from prelinguistic to linguistic communication*. Hillsdale, N.J.: Lawrence Erlbaum Associates, 1983.

SCHIFF, W. Conservation of length redux: A perceptual-linguistic phenomenon. *Child Development*, 1983, *54*, 1497–1506.

SCHLESINGER, H. S., AND MEADOW, K. P. *Sound and sign: Childhood deafness and mental health*. Berkeley: University of California Press, 1972.

SCHLISSEL, L. *Women's diaries of the westward journey*. New York: Schocken Books, 1982, pp. 109–110.

SCHMECK, H. M., JR. Fetal defects discovered early by new method. *New York Times*, October 18, 1983, p. C1.

SCHNEIDER-ROSEN, K., AND CICCHETTI, D. The relationship between affect and cognition in maltreated infants: Quality of attachment and the development of visual self-recognition. *Child Development*, 1984, *55*, 648–658.

SCHOLNICK, E. K. *New trends in conceptual representation: Challenges to Piaget's theory?* Hillsdale, N.J.: Lawrence Erlbaum Associates, 1983.

SCHRAG, P., AND DIVOKY, D. *The myth of the hyperactive child*. New York: Pantheon, 1975.

SCHROEDER, C., TEPLIN, S., AND SCHROEDER, S. An overview of common medical problems encountered in schools. In C. R. Reynolds and T. B. Gutkin (Eds.), *The handbook of school psychology*. New

York: Wiley, 1982.

SCHUBERT, J. B., BRADLEY-JOHNSON, S., AND NUTTAL, J. Mother-infant communication and maternal employment. *Childhood Development*, 1980, *51*, 246–249.

SCHULTZ, E. W., HEUCHERT, C., AND STAMPF, S.M. *Pain and joy in school.* Champaign, Ill.: Research Press, 1973.

SCHWARTZ, P. Length of day-care attendance and attachment behavior in eighteen-month-old infants. *Child Development*, 1983, *54*, 1073–1078.

SCHWARZ, J. C. *Young children's fears: Modeling or cognition?* Paper presented at the biennial meeting of the Society for Research in Child Development, San Francisco, March 1979.

SCHWARZ, J. C. *Effects of group day care in the first two years.* Paper presented at SRCD, Detroit, April 1983.

SCOLLEN, R. *One child's language from one to two: The origins of construction.* Unpublished doctoral dissertation, 1974.

SEARCH INSTITUTE. Young adolescents and their parents. Reported in *Psychology Today*, July 1984, 8.

SEARS, R. R., RAU, L., AND ALPERT, R. *Identification and child rearing.* Stanford, Calif.: Stanford University Press, 1965.

SEARS, R. R., AND WISE, G. W. Relation of cup feeding in infancy to thumbsucking and the oral drive. *American Journal of Orthopsychiatry*, 1950, *20*, 123–138.

SEAVEY, C. A., KATZ, P. A., AND ZALK, S. R. Baby X, the effect of gender labels on adult responses to infants. *Sex Roles*, 1975, *1*, 61–73.

SECORD, D., AND PEEVERS, B. The development and attribution of person concepts. In T. Mischel (Ed.), *Understanding other persons.* Oxford: Basil Blackwell, 1974.

SEIDEN, R. H. *Suicide among youth: A review of the literature, 1900–1967.* Chevy Chase, Md.: National Clearing House for Mental Health Information, 1969.

SELMAN, R. L. *The growth of interpersonal understanding: Developmental and clinical analyses.* New York: Academic Press, 1980.

SELMAN, R. L. The child as a friendship philosopher. In S. R. Asher and J. M. Gottman (Eds.), *The development of children's friendships.* New York: Cambridge University Press, 1981.

SELMAN, R. L., SCHORIN, M. Z., STONE, C. R., AND PHELPS, E. A naturalistic study of children's social understanding. *Developmental Psychology*, 1983, *19*, 82–102.

SELMAN, R. L., AND SELMAN, A. Children's ideas about friendship: A new theory. *Psychology Today,* October 1979, 70–80.

SERBIN, L. A., AND CONNOR, J. M. Sex-typing of children's play preferences and patterns of cognitive performance. *Journal of Genetic Psychology*, 1979, *134*, 315–316.

SERBIN, L. A., CONNER, J. M., AND DENIER, C. *Modification of sex typed activity and interactive play patterns in the preschool classroom: A replication and extension.* Paper presented at the Annual Meeting of the Association for the Advancement of Behavior Therapy, Chicago, 1978.

SERBIN, L. A., O'LEARY, K. D., KENT, R. N., AND TONICK, I. J. A comparison of teacher responses to the preacademic and problem behavior of boys and girls. *Child Development*, 1973, *44*, 796–804.

SERBIN, L. A., TONICK, I. J., AND STERNGLANZ, S. H. Shaping cooperative cross-sex play. *Child Development*, 1977, *48*, 924–929.

SEXTON, M. A., AND GEFFEN, G. Development of three strategies of attention in dichotic monitoring. *Developmental Psychology*, 1979, *15*, 299–310.

SHANTZ, C. U. Children's understanding of social rules and the social context. In F. C. Serafica (Ed.), *Social-cognitive development in context.* New York: Guilford Press, 1982.

SHAPIRO, B. J., AND O'BRIEN, T. C. Logical thinking in children ages six through thirteen. *Child Development*, 1970, *41*, 823–829.

SHATZ, M. *The comprehension of indirect directives: Can you shut the door?* Paper presented at the summer meeting of the Linguistic Society of America, Amherst, Mass., July 1974.

SHATZ, M. Children's comprehension of their mother's question-directives. *Journal of Child Language*, 1978, *5*, 39–46.

SHAYER, M., KUCHEMAN, D. E., AND WYLAM, H. The distribution of Piagetian stages of thinking in British middle and secondary school children. *British Journal of Educational Psychology*, 1976, *46*, 164–173.

SHAYER, M., AND WYLAM, H. The distribution of Piagetian stages of thinking in British middle and secondary school children: II. 14 to 16 years old and sex differentials. *British Journal of Educational Psychology*, 1978, *48*, 62–70.

SHEPHERD-LOOK, D. L. Sex differentiation and the development of sex roles. In B. B. Wolman and G. Stricker (Eds.), *Handbook of developmental psychology.* Englewood Cliffs, N.J.: Prentice-Hall, 1982.

SHERESHEFSKY, P. M., AND YARROW, L. J. *Psychological aspects of a first pregnancy and early postnatal adaptation.* New York: Raven Press, 1973.

SHERIF, M., HARVEY, O. J., WHITE, B. J., HOOD, W. R., AND SHERIF, C. W. *Intergroup conflict and cooperation: The robbers' cave experiment.* Norman: University of Oklahoma Press, 1961.

SHERIF, M., AND SHERIF, C. W. *Reference groups.* New York: Harper & Row, 1964.

SHERMAN, J. A., AND BUSHELL, D. Behavior modification as an educational technique. In F. D. Horowitz (Ed.), *Review of child development research*, Volume 4. Chicago: University of Chicago Press, 1975.

SHINN, M. Father absence and children's cognitive development. *Psychology Bulletin*, 1978, *85*, 295–324.

SHIPLEY, E. F., SMITH, C. S., AND GLEITMAN, L. R. A study in the acquisition of language: Free responses to commands. *Language*, 1969, *45*, 322–342.

SHIRLEY, M. M. *The first two years: A study of twenty-five babies.* Minneapolis: University of Minnesota Press, 1933.

SIEGAL, L. S. Children's and adolescents' reactions to the association of Martin Luther King: A study of political socialization. *Developmental Psychology*, 1977, *13*, 284–285.

SIEGAL, M., AND BARCLAY, M. S. Children's evaluations of fathers' socialization behavior. *Developmental Psychology*, 1985, *21*, 1090–1096.

SIEGAL, M., AND COWEN, J. Appraisals of intervention: The mother's versus the culprit's behavior as determinants of children's evaluations of discipline techniques. *Child Development*, 1984, *55*, 1760–1766.

SIEGAL, M., AND RABLIN, J. Moral development as reflected by young children's evaluation of maternal discipline. *Merrill-Palmer Quarterly*, 1982, *28*, 499–509.

SIEGEL, B. Doubts haunt town in sex abuse case. *Los Angeles Times*, December 29, 1984, pp. 1–28.

SIEGEL, E., BAUMAN, K., SCHAEFER, E., SANDERS, M., AND INGRAM, D. Hospital and home support during infancy: Impact on maternal attachment, child abuse and neglect, and health care utilization. *Pediatrics*, 1980, *66*, 183–190.

SIEGEL, L. S. The relationship of language and thought in the preoperational child: A reconsideration of non-verbal alternatives to Piagetian tasks. In L. S. Siegel and C. J. Brainerd (Eds.), *Alternatives to Piaget: Critical essays on the theory.* New York: Academic Press, 1978.

SIEGEL, L. S., McCABE, A. E., BRAND, J., AND MATTHEWS, J. Evidence for the understanding of class inclusion in preschool children: Linguistic factors and training effects. *Child Development*, 1978, *49*, 688–693.

SIEGLER, R. S. Information processing approaches to development. In P. H. Mussen (Ed.), *Handbook of child psychology*, Volume 1. New York: Wiley, 1983. (a)

SIEGLER, R. S. Five generalizations about cognitive development. *American Psychologist*, 1983, *38*, 263–277. (b)

SIEGLER, R. S. *Children's thinking.* Englewood Cliffs, N.J.: Prentice-Hall, 1986.

SILBERMAN, M. L. Teachers' attitudes and actions toward their students. In M. L. Silberman (Ed.), *The experiment of schooling.* New

York: Holt, Rinehart & Winston, 1971.

SILVERMAN, I. W., AND STONE, J. M. Modifying cognitive functioning through participation in a problem solving group. *Journal of Educational Psychology*, 1972, *63*, 603–608.

SIMAN, M. L. Application of a new model of peer group influence to naturally existing adolescent friendship groups. *Child Development*, 1977, *48*, 270–274.

SIMMONS, R. G., ROSENBERG, F., AND ROSENBERG, M. Disturbance in the self-image at adolescence. *American Sociological Review*, 1973, *38*, 553–568.

SIMNER, M. L. Newborns' response to the cry of another infant. *Developmental Psychology*, 1971, *5*, 136–150.

SIMPSON, E. Moral development research. A case study of scientific cultural bias. *Human Development*, 1974, *17*, 81–105.

SINCLAIR-DE ZWART, H. *Acquisition du langage et développement de la pensée*. Paris: Dunod, 1967.

SINGER, J. B., AND FLAVELL, J. H. Development of knowledge about communication: Children's evaluations of explicitly ambiguous messages. *Child Development*, 1981, *52*, 1211–1215.

SINGER, J. L., SINGER, D. G., AND SHERROD, L. R. *Prosocial programs in the context of children's total pattern of TV viewing*. Paper presented at the biennial meeting of the Society for Research in Child Development, San Francisco, March 1979.

SINGER, L. M., BRODZINSKY, D. M., RAMSAY, D., STEIR, M., AND WATERS, E. Mother–infant attachment in adoptive families. *Child Development*, 1985, *56*, 1543–1551.

SIQUELAND, E. R., AND LIPSITT, L. P. Conditioned head-turning in human newborns. *Journal of Experimental Child Psychology*, 1966, *3*, 356–376.

SIRIGNANO, S. W. AND LACHMAN, M. E. Personality change during the transition to parenthood: The role of perceived infant temperament. *Developmental Psychology*, 1985, *21*, 558–567.

SIZER, T. *Horace's compromise: The dilemma of the American high school*. Boston: Houghton Mifflin, 1985.

SKARIN, K. Cognitive and contextual determinants of stranger fear in six- and eleven-month-old infants. *Child Development*, 1977, *48*, 537–544.

SKEELS, H. M. Adult status of children with contrasting early life experiences. *Monographs of the Society for Research in Child Development*, 1966, *31* (3, Serial No. 105).

SKINNER, B. G. *Verbal behavior*. New York: Appleton-Century-Crofts, 1957.

SKODAK, M., AND SKEELS, H. M. A final follow-up study of one hundred adopted children. *Journal of Genetic Psychology*, 1949, *75*, 85–125.

SLATER, A. M. Visual perception at birth. *Infant Behavior and Development*, 1986, *9* (Special Issue: Abstracts of papers presented at the Fifth International Conference on Infant Studies), 346.

SLAUGHTER, D. T. Early intervention and its effects on maternal and child development. *Monographs of the Society for Research in Child Development*, 1983, *48* (4, Serial No. 202).

SLOBIN, D. I. Imitation and grammatical development in children. In N. S. Endler, L. R. Boulter, and H. Osser (Eds.), *Contemporary issues in developmental psychology*. New York: Holt, 1968.

SLOBIN, D. I. *Psycholinguistics*. Glenview, Ill.: Scott, Foresman, 1971.

SLOBIN, D. I. Cognitive prerequisites for the development of grammar. In C. A. Ferguson and D. I. Slobin (Eds.), *Studies of child language development*. New York: Holt, Rinehart & Winston, 1973.

SLOBIN, D. I. On the nature of talk to children. In E. H. Lenneberg and E. Lenneberg (Eds.), *Foundations of language development*, Volume 1. New York: Academic Press, 1975.

SLOBIN, D. E., AND WELSH, G. A. Elicited imitation as a research tool in developmental psycholinguistics. In C. A. Ferguson and D. I. Slobin (Eds.), *Studies of child language development*. New York: Holt, Rinehart & Winston, 1973.

SMILEY, S. S., AND BROWN, A. L. Conceptual preference for thematic and taxonomic relations: A nonmonotonic age trend from pre-school to old age. *Journal of Experimental Child Psychology*, 1979, *28*, 249–257.

SMITH, C. B., ADAMSON, L. B., AND BAKEMAN, R. Interactional predictors of early language. *Infant Behavior and Development*, 1986, *9* (Special Issue: Abstracts of papers presented at the Fifth International Conference on Infant Studies), 347.

SMITH, H. K. The responses of good and poor readers when asked to read for different purposes. *Reading Research Quarterly*, 1967, *3*, 53–84.

SMITH, L. B., KEMLER, D. G., AND ARONFREED, J. Developmental trends in voluntary selective attention: Differential effects of source distinctiveness. *Journal of Experimental Child Psychology*, 1975, *20*, 352–365.

SMITH, M., DELVES, T., LANSDOWN, R., CLAYTON, B., AND GRAHAM, P. The effects of lead exposure on urban children: The Institute of Child Health/Southampton Study. *Developmental Medicine and Child Neurology*, 1983, *25*, 1–54.

SMITH, P. K., AND CONNOLLY, K. Patterns of play and social interaction in preschool children. In N. Blurton Jones (Ed.), *Ethological studies of child behaviour*. Cambridge, England: Cambridge University Press, 1972.

SNAREY, J. R., REIMER, J., AND KOHLBERG, L. Development of social-moral reasoning among kibbutz adolescents: A longitudinal cross-cultural study. *Developmental Psychology*, 1985, *21*, 3–17.

SNOW, C. E. Mother's speech to children learning language. *Child Development*, 1972, *43*, 549–564.

SOAR, R. S., AND SOAR, R. M. *An attempt to identify measures of teacher effectiveness from four studies*. Paper presented at the meetings of the American Educational Research Association, San Francisco, April 1976.

SOEWONDO, S., ABEDNEGO, B., PEKERTI, A., AND KARJADI, D. The effect of nutritional status on some aspects of intelligence. *Paediatrica Indonesiana*, 1971, *11*, 28–36.

SOLANTAUS, T., RIMPELA, M., AND TAIPALE, V. The threat of war in the minds of 12–18 year olds in Finland. *Lancet*, 1984, *8380*, 784–785.

SONNENSCHEIN, S., AND WHITEHURST, C. J. Training referential communication skills: The limits of success. *Journal of Experimental Child Psychology*, 1983, *35*, 426–436.

SONTAG, L. W. Effect of fetal activity on the nutritional state of the infant at birth. *American Journal of Diseases in Children*, 1940, *6*, 621–630.

SONTAG, L. W. War and the fetal maternal relationship. *Marriage and Family Living*, 1944, *6*, 1–5.

SONTAG, L. W., AND NEWBERY, H. Normal variations of fetal heart rate during pregnancy. *American Journal of Obstetrics and Gynecology*, 1940, *40*, 449–452.

SOPHIAN, C. Perseveration and infants' search: A comparison of two- and three-location tasks. *Developmental Psychology*, 1985, *21*, 187–194.

SORCE, J., EMDE, R. N., CAMPOS, J. J., AND KLINNERT, M. *Maternal emotional signaling: Its effect on the visual cliff behavior of one-year-olds*. Paper presented at the meeting of the Society for Research in Child Development, Boston, April 1981.

SORCE, J. F., EMDE, R. N., CAMPOS, J., AND KLINNERT, M. D. Maternal emotional signaling: Its effect on the visual cliff behavior of 1-year-olds. *Developmental Psychology*, 1985, *21*, 195–200.

SORENSEN, R. C. *Adolescent sexuality in contemporary America*. New York: World Publishing, 1973.

SORRELLS-JONES, J. *A comparison of the effects of Leboyer delivery and modern "routine" childbirth in a randomized sample*. Unpublished doctoral dissertation, University of Chicago, 1983.

SOSA, R., KENNELL, J., KLAUS, M., ROBERTSON, S., AND URRUTIA, J. The effect of a supportive companion on perinatal problems, length of labor, and mother–infant interaction. *New England Journal of Medicine*, 1980, *303* 597–600.

SOSTEK, A. M., SCANLON, J. W., AND ABRAMSON, D. C. Postpartum contact and maternal confidence and anxiety: A confirmation of short-term effects. *Infant Behavior and Development*, 1982, *5*, 323–329.

SPANIER, G. B. Formal and informal sex education as determinants of premarital sexual behavior. *Archives of Sexual Behavior*, 1976, *5*, 39–67.

SPARROU, S., AND ZIGLER, E. Evaluation of a patterning treatment for retarded children. *Pediatrics*, 1978, *62*, 137–149.

SPEARMAN, C. *The abilities of man.* New York: Macmillan, 1927.

SPELKE, E. Infants' intermodal perception of events. *Cognitive Psychology*, 1976, *8*, 553–560.

SPELKE, E. *Intermodal exploration by 4-month-old infants: Perception and knowledge of auditory-visual events.* Unpublished doctoral dissertation, Cornell University, 1978.

SPELKE, E. Exploring audible and visible events in infancy. In A. D. Pick (Ed.), *Perception and its development: A tribute to Eleanor J. Gibson.* Hillsdale, N.J.: Lawrence Erlbaum Associates, 1979.(a)

SPELKE, E. Perceiving bimodally specified events in infancy. *Developmental Psychology*, 1979, *15*, 626–636.(b)

SPELKE, E. S. Perceptual knowledge of objects in infancy. In J. Mehler, M. Garrett, and E. Walker (Eds.), *Perspectives on mental representation.* Hillsdale, N.J.: Lawrence Erlbaum Associates, 1982.

SPELKE, E. S., AND OWSLEY, C. J. Intermodal exploration and knowledge in infancy. *Infant Behavior and Development*, 1979, *2*, 13–27.

SPELT, D. K. The conditioning of the human fetus in utero. *Journal of Experimental Psychology*, 1948, *38*, 338–346.

SPENCE, J. T., AND HELMREICH, R. L. *Masculinity and femininity: Their psychological dimensions, correlates and antecedents.* Austin: University of Texas Press, 1978.

SPENCE, M. J., AND DECASPER, A. J. *Human fetuses perceive maternal speech.* Paper presented at the meeting of the International Conference on Infant Studies, Austin, Texas, March 1982.

SPIELBERGER, C. D. The effects of anxiety on complex learning and academic achievement. In C. D. Spielberger (Ed.), *Anxiety and behavior.* New York: Academic Press, 1966.

SPILTON, D., AND LEE, L. C. Some determinants of effective communication in four-year-olds. *Child Development*, 1977, *48*, 968–977.

SPINELLI, D. N., JENSEN, F. E., AND VIANA DI PRISCO, G. Early experience effect on dendritic branching in normally reared kittens. *Experimental Neurology*, 1980, *68*, 1–11.

SPINETTA, J. J., AND RIGLER, D. The child-abusing parent: A psychological review. *Psychological Bulletin*, 1972, *77*, 296–304.

SPIVACK, G. AND SHURE, M. B. *Social adjustment of young children: A cognitive approach to solving real-life problems.* San Francisco, Ca.: Jossey-Bass, 1974.

SPRAFKIN, C., SERKIN, L., DENIER, C., AND CONNOR, J. Sex differentiated play: Cognitive consequences and early interventions. In M. Liss (Ed.), *Social and cognitive skills: Sex roles and children's play.* New York: Academic Press, 1983.

SPRING, C., AND CAPPS, C. Encoding speed, rehearsal, and probed recall of dyslexic boys. *Journal of Educational Psychology*, 1974, *66*, 780–786.

SQUIRES, D., HUNT, W., AND SEGARS, J. *Effective schools and classrooms: A research based prospective* Alexandria, Va.: Association for Supervision and Curriculum Development, 1984.

SROUFE, L. A. Wariness of strangers and the study of infant development. *Child Development*, 1977, *48*, 731–746.

SROUFE, L. A. Socioemotional development. In J. D. Osofsky (Ed.), *Handbook of infant development.* New York: Wiley, 1979.

SROUFE, L. A. Infant-caregiver attachment and patterns of adaptation in preschool: The roots of maladaptation and competence. In M. Perlmutter (Ed.), *Development and policy concerning children with special needs. Minnesota Symposium in Child Psychology*, Volume 16. Hillsdale, N.J.: Lawrence Erlbaum Associates, 1983.

SROUFE, L. A., SCHORK, E., MOTTI, E., LAWROSKI, N., AND LaFRENIERE, P. The role of affect in emerging social competence. In C. Izard, J. Kagan, and R. Zajonc (Eds.), *Emotion, cognition and behavior.* New York: Plenum, 1984.

SROUFE, L. A., AND WATERS, E. Attachment as an organizational construct. *Child Development*, 1977, *48*, 1184–1199.

SROUFE, L. A., AND WUNSCH, J. P. The development of laughter in the first year of life. *Child Development*, 1972, *43*, 1326–1344.

STARK, E. Taking a beating. *Psychology Today*, April 1985, 16.

STARK, E. Mom and dad: The great American heroes. *Psychology Today*, May 1986, 12–13.

STAUB, E. A. *The development of prosocial behavior in children.* Morristown, N.J.: General Learning Press, 1975.

STEELE, B. F. *Working with abusive parents from a psychiatric point of view*, U.S. Department of Health, Education and Welfare Publication No. (OHD) 75-70. Washington, D.C.: U.S. Government Printing Office, 1975.

STEIN, A. H. Imitation of resistance to temptation. *Child Development*, 1967, *38*, 159–169.

STEIN, A. H., AND BAILEY, M. The socialization of achievement orientation in females. *Psychological Bulletin*, 1973, *80*, 345–366.

STEIN, A. H., AND FRIEDRICH, L. K. Impact of television on children and youth. In E. M. Hetherington (Ed.), *Review of child development research*, Volume 5. Chicago: University of Chicago Press, 1975.

STEIN, N., AND GLENN, C. An analysis of story comprehension in elementary school children. In R. O. Freedle (Ed.), *New directions in discourse processing.* Norwood, N.J.: Ablex, 1979.

STEINBERG, L. D. *Changes in family relations at puberty.* Paper presented at the biennial meeting of the Society for Research in Child Development, San Francisco, March 1979.

STEINBERG, L. D. Early temperamental antecedents of adult Type A behaviors. *Developmental Psychology*, 1985, *21*, 1171–1180.

STEINHAUSEN, H.-C. Psychological evaluation of treatment in phenylketonuria: Intellectual, motor and social development. *Neuropaediatrie*, 1974, *5*, 146–156.

STENBERG, C. *The development of anger facial expressions in infancy.* Unpublished doctoral dissertation, University of Denver, 1982.

STENBERG, C. R., CAMPOS, J. J., AND EMDE, R. N. The facial expression of anger in seven-month-old infants. *Child Development*, 1983, *54*, 178–184.

STERN, D. N. A micro-analysis of mother-infant interaction—Behavior regulating social contact between a mother and her 3½-month-old twins. *Journal of the American Academy of Child Psychiatry*, 1971, *10*, 501–517.

STERN, D. N. Mother and infant at play: The dyadic interaction involving facial, vocal and gaze behaviors. In M. Lewis and L. A. Rosenblum (Eds.), *The effect of the infant on its caregiver.* New York: Wiley, 1974.

STERN, D. N. *The first relationship: Infant and mother.* Cambridge, Mass.: Harvard University Press, 1977.

STERN, M., NORTHMAN, J. E., AND VAN SLYCK, M. R. Father absence and adolescent "problem behaviors": Alcohol consumption, drug use and sexual activity. *Adolescence*, 1984, *19*, 301–312.

STERNBERG, R. J. *Intelligence, information processing, and analogical reasoning: The componential analysis of human abilities.* Hillsdale, N.J.: Lawrence Erlbaum Associates, 1977.

STERNBERG, R. J. Stalking the IQ quark. *Psychology Today*, September 1979, 42–54.

STERNBERG, R. J. *Beyond I.Q.* Cambridge, England: Cambridge University Press, 1985.

STERNBERG, R. J., CONWAY, B. E., KETRON, J. L., AND BERNSTEIN, M. People's conceptions of intelligence. *Journal of Personality and Social Psychology: Attitudes and Social Cognition*, 1981, *41*, 37–55.

STERNBERG, R. J., AND NIGRO, G. Developmental patterns in the solution of verbal analogies. *Child Development*, 1980, *51*, 27–38.

STERNBERG, R. J., AND POWELL, J. S. The development of intelligence. In P. H. Mussen (Ed.), *Handbook of child psychology*, Volume 3. New York: Wiley, 1983.

STERNGLANZ, S. H., AND SERBIN, L. A. Sex role stereotyping in children's television programs. *Developmental Psychology*, 1974, *10*, 710–715.

STETSON, P. C. *Verbal transitivity in children.* Unpublished doctoral dissertation, University of Delaware, 1974.

STEVENSON, H. W. *Making the grade: School achievement in Japan, Taiwan, and the United States.* Presentation made at the Center for Advanced Study in the Behavioral Sciences, Stanford, April 1983, and published in its Annual Report, 1983.

STEVENSON, H. W., LEE, S., AND STIGLER, J. W. Mathematics achievement of Chinese, Japanese, and American children. *Science*, February 14, 1986, *231*, 693–699.

STEVENSON-HINDE, J., HINDE, R. A., AND SIMPSON, A. E. Behavior at home and friendly or hostile behavior in preschool. In D. Olweus, J. Block, and M. Radke-Yarrow (Eds.), *Development of antisocial and prosocial behavior.* New York: Academic Press, 1986.

STEWART, M. A. Is hyperactivity normal? and other unanswered questions. *School Review*, 1976, *85*, 31–42.

STEWART, R. B. Sibling attachment relationships: Child-infant interactions in the strange situation. *Developmental Psychology*, 1983, *19*, 192–199.

STEWART, R. B., AND MARVIN, R. S. Sibling relations: The role of conceptual perspective-taking in the ontogeny of sibling caregiving. *Child Development*, 1984, *55*, 1322–1332.

STIRES, L. The effect of classroom seating location on student grades and attitudes: Environment or self-selection? *Environment and Behavior*, 1980, *12*, 241–254.

STOCKDALE, D. F., GALEJS, I., AND WOLINS, L. Cooperative-competitive preferences and behavioral correlates as a function of sex and age of school-age children. *Psychological Reports*, 1983, *53*, 739–750.

STODDARD, R., AND TURIEL, E. Children's concepts of cross-gender activities. *Child Development*, 1985, *56*, 1241–1252.

STOLZ, H. R., AND STOLZ, L. M. *Somatic development of adolescent boys.* New York: Macmillan, 1951.

STONEMAN, Z., AND BRODY, G. H. Immediate and long-term recognition and generalization of advertised products as a function of age and presentation mode. *Developmental Psychology*, 1983, *19*, 56–61.

STOTT, D. H. The child's hazards in utero. In J. G. Howells (Ed.), *Modern perspectives in international child psychiatry.* New York: Brunner/Mazel, 1971.

STRAUSS, M. E., LESSEN-FIRESTONE, J., STARR, R., AND OSTREA, E. M., JR. Behavior of narcotics-addicted newborns. *Child Development*, 1975, *46*, 887–893.

STRAUSS, M. S., AND COHEN, L. B. *Infant immediate and delayed memory for perceptual dimensions.* Unpublished manuscript, University of Illinois, 1978.

STRAYER, J. A naturalistic study of empathic behaviors and their relation to affective states and perspective-taking skills in preschool children. *Child Development*, 1980, *51*, 815–822.

STREISSGUTH, A. P., BARR, H. M., AND MARTIN, D. C. Maternal alcohol use and neonatal habituation assessed with the Brazelton Scale. *Child Development*, 1983, *54*, 1109–1118.

STREISSGUTH, A. P., MARTIN, D. C., BARR, H. M., SANDMAN, B. M., KIRCHNER, G. L., AND DARBY, B. L. Intrauterine alcohol and nicotine exposure: Attention and reaction time in 4-year old children. *Developmental Psychology*, 1984, *20*, 533–541.

STUCKEY, M. F., McGHEE, P. E., AND BELL, N. J. Parent-child interaction: The influence of maternal employment. *Developmental Psychology*, 1982, *18*, 635–644.

STUNKARD, A. *Childhood obesity.* Paper presented at NIH workshop on childhood obesity, March 10, 1986. Reprinted in *Science*, 1986, *232*, 20–21.

SULLIVAN, J. W., AND HOROWITZ, F. D. The effects of intonation on infant attention: The role of the rising intonation contour. *Journal of Child Language*, 1983, *10*, 521–534.

SULLIVAN, K., AND SULLIVAN, A. Adolescent-parent separation. *Developmental Psychology*, 1980, *10*, 93–99.

SUOMI, S. J. Social interactions of monkeys reared in a nuclear family environment versus monkeys reared with mothers and peers.

Primates, 1974, *15*, 311–320.

SUOMI, S. J. Adult male-infant interactions among monkeys living in nuclear families. *Child Development*, 1977, *48*, 1255–1270.

SUPER, D. E. *The psychology of careers.* New York: Harper & Row, 1967.

SUPER, D. E., KOWALSKI, R., AND GOTKIN, E. *Floundering and trial after high school.* Unpublished manuscript, Columbia University, 1967.

SURBER, C. F., AND GZESH, S. M. Reversible operations in the balance scale task. *Journal of Experimental Child Psychology*, 1984, *38*, 254–274.

SUSKIND, R. M. Characteristics and causation of protein-calorie malnutrition in the infant and preschool child. In L. S. Greene (Ed.), *Malnutrition, behavior and social organization.* New York: Academic Press, 1977.

SUSSMAN, R. P. *Effects of novelty and training on the curiosity and exploration of young children in day care centers.* Unpublished doctoral dissertation, University of Chicago, 1979.

SUTTON-SMITH, B., AND ROSENBERG, B. G. Sixty years of historical change in the game preferences of American children. In R. E. Herron and B. Sutton-Smith (Eds.), *Child's play.* New York: Wiley, 1971.

SVEJDA, M., PANNABECKER, B., AND EMDE, R. N. Parent-to-infant attachment: A critique of the early ''bonding'' model. In R. N. Emde and R. J. Harmon (Eds.), *The development of attachment and affiliative systems: Psychological aspects.* New York: Plenum, 1982.

SWANN, W. B., JR., AND PITTMAN, T. S. Initiating play activity of children: The moderating influence of verbal cues on intrinsic motivation. *Child Development*, 1977, *48*, 1125–1132.

SWANSON, J. M., AND KINSBOURNE, M. Food dyes impair performance of hyperactive children in a laboratory learning test. *Science*, 1980, *207*, 1485–1487.

SWITSKY, H. N. Exploration, curiosity, and play in young children: Effects of stimulus complexity. *Developmental Psychology*, 1973, *10*, 321–329.

SWITSKY, H. N., HAYWOOD, H. C., AND ISETT, R. Exploration, curiosity and play in young children: Effects of stimulus complexity. *Developmental Psychology*, 1974, *10*, 321–329.

SYLVA, K., BRUNER, J. S., AND GENOVA, P. The role of play in problem-solving of children three to five years old. In J. S. Bruner, A. Jolly, and K. Sylva (Eds.), *Play: Its role in development and evolution.* London: Penguin, 1976.

SYLVA, K., ROY, C., AND PAINTER, M. *Childwatching at playgroup and nursery school.* London: Grant McIntyre Ltd., 1980.

SYLVESTER-BRADLEY, B., AND TREVARTHEN, C. Baby talk as an adaptation to the infant's communication. In N. Waterson and C. E. Snow (Eds.), *The development of communication.* New York: Wiley, 1978.

TAKAHASHI, K. Examining the strange-situation procedure with Japanese mothers and 12-month-old infants. *Developmental Psychology*, 1986, *22*, 265–270.

TANNER, J. M. *Growth at adolescence* (2nd ed.). Oxford: Blackwell Scientific Publications, 1962.

TANNER, J. M. The trend towards earlier physical maturation. In J. E. Meade and A. S. Parkes (Eds.), *Biological aspects of social problems.* Edinburgh: Oliver and Boyd, 1965.

TANNER, J. M. Physical growth. In P. H. Mussen (Ed.), *Carmichael's manual of child psychology*, Volume 1. New York: Wiley, 1970.

TANNER, J. M. Variability of growth and maturity in newborn infants. In M. Lewis and L. A. Rosenblum (Eds.), *The effect of the infant on its caregiver.* New York: Wiley, 1974.

TANNER, J. M. *Foetus into man: Physical growth from conception to maturity.* London: Open Books, 1978.

TANZ, C. *Studies in the acquisition of deictic terms.* Cambridge, England: Cambridge University Press, 1980.

TANZER, D., AND BLOCK, J. L. *Why natural childbirth?* New York: Schocken Books, 1976.

TAVORMINA, J. B., BOLL, H., DUNN, N. J., LUSCOMB, R. L., AND TAY-

LOR, J. R. *Psychosocial effects of raising a physically handicapped child on parents*. Paper presented at the meeting of the American Psychological Association Convention, San Francisco, September 1975.

TAYLOR, M. E. Sex role stereotypes in children's readers. *Elementary English*, 1973, 50, 1061–1064.

TAYLOR, P. M., TAYLER, F. H., CAMPBELL, S. B. G., MALONI, J., AND DICKEY, D. *Effects of extra contact on early maternal attitudes, perceptions, and behaviors*. Paper presented at the meetings of the Society for Research in Child Development, San Francisco, March 1979.

TEC, N. Some aspects of high school status and differential involvement with marihuana: A study of suburban teenagers. *Adolescence*, 1972, 6, 1–28.

TENNES, E. R., KISLEY, A., AND METCALF, D. The stimulus barrier in early infancy: An exploration of some formulations of John Benjamin. In R. Holt and E. Peterfreund (Eds.), *Psychoanalysis and contemporary science*, Volume 1. New York: Macmillan, 1972.

TERMAN, L. M. *Genetic studies of genius*, Volume 1, *Mental and physical traits of a thousand gifted children*. Stanford, Calif.: Stanford University Press, 1925.

TERMAN, L. M., AND ODEN, M. H. *Genetic studies of genus*, Volume 4, *The gifted group at midlife*. Stanford, Calif.: Stanford University Press, 1959.

TERR, L. C. A family study of child abuse. *American Journal of Psychiatry*, 1970, 127, 665–671.

THELEN, E., FISHER, D. M., AND RIDLEY-JOHNSON, R. The relationship between physical growth and a newborn reflex. *Infant Behavior and Development*, 1984, 7, 479–493.

THIRER, J., AND WRIGHT, S. D. Sport and social status for adolescent males and females. *Sociology of Sport Journal*, 1985, 2, 164–171.

THOMAS A., AND CHESS, S. *Temperament and development*. New York: Brunner/Mazel, 1977.

THOMAS, A., AND CHESS, S. *Correlation of early temperament with later behavioral functioning*. Paper presented at CIBA Foundation temperament conference, London, September 1981.

THOMAS, A., CHESS, S., AND BIRCH, H. G. *Temperament and behavior disorders in children*. New York: New York University Press, 1968.

THOMAS, J. L. *Tutoring strategies and effectiveness: A comparison of elementary age tutors and college age tutors*. Unpublished doctoral dissertation, University of Texas at Austin, 1970.

THOMPSON, M. G. *Life adjustment of women with anorexia nervosa and anorexic-like behavior*. Unpublished doctoral dissertation, University of Chicago, 1979.

THOMPSON, R. A., AND LAMB, M. E. Security of attachment and stranger sociability in infancy. *Development Psychology*, 1983, 19, 184–191.

THOMPSON, S. K. Gender labels and early sex role development. *Child Development*, 1975, 46, 339–347.

THOMPSON, S. K., AND BENTLER, P. M. The priority of cues in sex discrimination by children and adults. *Developmental Psychology*, 1971, 5, 181–185.

THOMSON, C. A., AND POLLITT, E. Effects of severe protein-calorie malnutrition on behavior in human populations. In L. S. Greene (Ed.), *Malnutrition, behavior and social organization*. New York: Academic Press, 1977.

THORESEN, C., EAGLESTON, J., KIRMIL-GRAY, K., AND BRACKE, P. *Type A children anxious, insecure*. Paper presented at the annual meeting of the American Psychological Association, Los Angeles, August 1985.

THORNBURG, D. H. Sources of sex education among early adolescents. *Journal of Early Adolescence*, 1981, 1, 174.

TIEGER, T. On the biological basis of sex differences in aggression. *Child Development*, 1980, 51, 943–963.

TIESZAN, H. R. Children's social behavior in a Korean preschool. *Journal of Korean Home Economics Association*, 1979, 17, 71–84.

TILDEN J. T., AND CHACON, M. Associated Press report on sudden infant death syndrome. *Chicago Tribune*, November 6, 1981, Section 1, p. 14.

TISHLER, C., McKENRY, P. C., AND MORGAN, K. C. Adolescent suicide attempts: Some significant factors. *Suicide and life-threatening behavior*, 1981, 11, 86–92.

TIZARD, B., CARMICHAEL, H., HUGHES, M., AND PINKERTON, G. Four year olds talking to mothers and teacher. In L. A. Hersoveval (Ed.), *Language and language disorders in childhood* (Supplement No. 2, *Journal of Child Psychology and Psychiatry*). London: Pergamon Press, 1980.

TIZARD, B., AND REES, J. A comparison of the effects of adoption, restoration to the natural mother, and continued institutionalization on the cognitive development of four-year-old children. *Child Development*, 1974, 45, 92–99.

TODD, C. M., AND PERLMUTTER, M. Reality recalled by preschool children. In M. Perlmutter (Ed.), *New directions in child development: Children's memory*. San Francisco: Jossey-Bass, 1980.

TORRES, A., FORREST, J. D., AND EISMAN, T. Telling parents: Clinic policies and adolescents' use of family planning and abortion services. *Family Planning Perspectives*, 1980, 12, 284–292.

TRACY, R. L., LAMB, M. E., AND AINSWORTH, M. D. S. Infant approach behavior as related to attachment. *Child Development*, 1976, 47, 571–578.

TRAUB, R. E., WEISS, J., AND FISHER, C. W. Studying openness in education: An Ontario example. *Journal of Research and Development in Education*, 1974, 8, 47–59.

TRAUSE, M. A., VOOS, D., RUDD, C., KLAUS, M., KENNELL, J., AND BOSLETT, M. Separation for childbirth: The effect on the sibling. *Child Psychiatry and Human Development*, 1981, 12, 32–39.

TRAUTNER, H. M. [Relationships between parental sytle of education and parent orientation in 10–14 year old girls.] *Zeitschrift für Entwicklungpsychologie und Padagogische Psychologie*, 1972, 4 (3), 116–182.

TREHUB, S. E. Infants' sensitivity to vowel and tonal contrasts. *Developmental Psychology*, 1973, 9, 91–96.

TREHUB, S. E., AND CURRAN, S. Habituation of infants' cardiac response to speech stimuli. *Child Development*, 1979, 50, 1247–1250.

TRETHOWAN, W. H., AND CONLON, M. F. The couvade syndrome. *British Journal of Psychiatry*, 1965, 111, 57–66.

TREVARTHEN, C. Descriptive analyses of infant communicative behavior. In H. R. Schaffer (Ed.), *Studies in mother-infant interaction*. London: Academic Press, 1977.

TREVARTHEN, C. Development of the cerebral mechanisms for language. In V. Kirk (Ed.), *Neuropsychology of language, reading and spelling*. New York: Academic Press, 1983.

TRICKETT, P. K. The interaction of cognitive styles and classroom environment in determining first-graders' behavior. *Journal of Applied Developmental Psychology*, 1983, 4, 43–64.

TULKIN, S. R., AND KONNER, M. J. Alternative conceptions of intellectual functioning. *Human Development*, 1973, 16, 32–52.

TUAYCHAROEN, P. The babbling of a Thai baby: Echoes and responses to the sounds made by adults. In N. Waterson and C. E. Snow (Eds.), *The development of communication*. New York: Wiley, 1978.

TUDIVER, J. *Parental influences on the sex role development of the preschool child*. Unpublished manuscript, University of Western Ontario, London, Ontario, 1979.

TURIEL, E. An experimental test of the sequentiality of developmental stages in the child's moral judgments. *Journal of Personality and Social Psychology*, 1966, 3, 611–618.

TURIEL, E. The development of social concepts. In D. DePalma and J. Foley (Eds.), *Moral development*. Hillsdale, N.J.: Lawrence Erlbaum Associates, 1975.

TURKINGTON, C. Pituitary defect seen in anorexia. *APA Monitor*, January 1984, 15, 17. (a)

TURKINGTON, C. Physical factors explored in dieting, Type A behavior. *APA Monitor*, February 1984, 15, 24. (b)

TURKINGTON, C. Parents found to ignore sex stereotypes. *APA Monitor*, April 1984, 15, 12. (c)

TURKINGTON, C. Psychologists help spot danger in crib. *APA Monitor*, December 1984, 15, 38. (d)

TURNURE, C. Response to voice of mother and stranger by babies in the first year. *Developmental Psychology*, 1971, *4*, 182–190.

TURNURE, J., BUIUM, N., AND THURLOW, M. The effectiveness of interrogatives for promoting verbal elaboration productivity in children. *Child Development*, 1976, *47*, 851–855.

TYNAN, W. D. Behavioral stability predicts morbidity and mortality in infants from a neonatal intensive care unit. *Infant Behavior and Development*, 1986, *9*, 71–79.

ULLIAN, D. Z. The development of conceptions of masculinity and feminity. In B. Lloyd and J. Archer (Eds.), *Exploring sex differences*. London: Academic Press, 1976.

U.S. DEPARTMENT OF COMMERCE. *Social indicators*, Volume 3. Washington, D.C.: Author, 1981.

U.S. DEPARTMENT OF HEALTH AND HUMAN SERVICES. *Health, United States, 1980*. DHHS Publication No. (PHS) 81-1232, 1980, p. 276.

U.S. DEPARTMENT OF HEALTH AND HUMAN SERVICES. *Health, United States, 1982*. DHHS Publication No. (PHS) 83-1232, 1982.

U.S. PUBLIC HEALTH SERVICE. *Alcohol and health: Second special report to the U.S. Congress*. Rockville, Md.: National Institute on Alcohol Abuse and Alcoholism, 1974.

UTECH, D. A., AND HOVING, K. L. Parents and peers as competing influences in the decisions of children of different ages. *Journal of Social Psychology*, 1969, *78*, 267–274.

VANDENBERG, S. G. The nature and nurture of intelligence. In D. C. Glass (Ed.), *Genetics*. New York: Rockefeller University Press/ Russell Sage Foundation, 1968.

VANDENBERG, S. G., AND KUSE, A. R. Spatial ability: A critical review of the sex-linked major gene hypothesis. In M. A. Wittig and A. C. Petersen (Eds.), *Sex related differences in cognitive functioning: Developmental issues*. New York: Academic Press, 1979.

VAUGHN, B., JOFFE, L., EGELAND, B., DIENARD, A., AND WATERS, E. *Relationships between neonatal behavioral organization and infant-mother attachment in an economically disadvantaged sample*. Paper presented at the meeting of the Society for Research in Child Development, San Francisco, March 1979.

VAUGHN, B. E., AND LANGLOIS, J. H. Physical attractiveness as a correlate of peer status and social competence in preschool children. *Developmental Psychology*, 1983, *19*, 561–567.

VENTURA, S. J. Teenage childbearing: United States 1966–1975. *Monthly Vital Statistics Reports: National Center for Health Statistics*, 1977, *26* (5) (supp.).

VOLTERRA, V., AND TAESCHNER, T. The acquisition and development of language by bilingual children. *Journal of Child Language*, 1978, *5*, 311–326.

VURPILLOT, E. The development of scanning strategies and their relation to visual differentiation. *Journal of Experimental Child Psychology*, 1968, *6*, 632–650.

WABER, D. P. Sex differences in cognition: A function of maturation rate? *Science*, 1976, *192*, 572–573.

WABER, D. P., MANN, M. B., MEROLA, J., AND MOYLAN, P. M. Physical maturation rate and cognitive performance in early adolescence: A longitudinal examination. *Developmental Psychology*, 1985, *21*, 668–681.

WACHS, T. D., AND GANDOUR, M. J. Temperament, environment, and six-month cognitive-intellectual development: A test of the Organismic specificity hypothesis. *International Journal of Behavioral Development*, 1983, *6*, 135–152.

WACHS, T. D., AND GRUEN, C. E. *Early experience and human development*. New York: Plenum, 1982.

WADDINGTON, C. H. *The strategy of the genes*. London: Allen & Unwin, 1957.

WAKE, F. R. Attitudes of parents towards the premarital sex behavior of their children and themselves. *Journal of Sex Research*, 1969, *5*, 170–177.

WALDROP, M. F., AND HALVERSON, C. F., JR. Intensive and extensive peer behavior: Longitudinal and cross-sectional analyses. *Child Development*, 1975, *46*, 19–26.

WALKER, E., AND EMORY, E. Commentary: Interpretive bias and behavioral genetic research. *Child Development*, 1985, *56*, 775–778.

WALKER, J. A., AND KERSHMAN, S. M. *The deaf-blind in social interaction*. Paper presented at the meeting of the Society for Research in Child Development, Boston, March 1981.

WALKER, L. J. The sequentiality of Kohlberg's stages of moral development. *Child Development*, 1982, *53*, 1330–1336.

WALKER, L. J. Sex differences in the development of moral reasoning: A critical review. *Child Development*, 1984, *55*, 677–691.

WALKER, L. J. Sex differences in the development of moral reasoning: A rejoinder to Baumrind. *Child Development*, 1986, *57*, 522–526.

WALLERSTEIN, J. S., AND KELLY, J. B. The effects of parental divorce: The adolescent experience. In E. J. Anthony and C. Koopernick (Eds.), *The child in his family: Children at psychiatric risk*, Volume 3. New York: Wiley, 1974.

WALLERSTEIN, J. S., AND KELLY, J. B. *Surviving the breakup*. New York: Basic Books, 1980.

WALSTER, E., ARONSON, V., ABRAHAM, D., AND ROLTMAN, L. Importance of physical attractiveness in dating behavior. *Journal of Personality and Social Psychology*, 1966, *4*, 508–516.

WALTERS, J., PEARCE, D., AND DAHMS, L. Affectional and aggressive behavior of preschool children. *Child Development*, 1957, *28*, 15–26.

WARD, I. L. Prenatal stress feminizes and demasculinizes the behavior of males. *Science*, 1972, *176*, 82–84.

WARE, J. C., AND ORR, W. C. Sleep disorders in children. In C. E. Walker and M. C. Roberts (Eds.), *Handbook of clinical child psychology*. New York: Wiley, 1983.

WARSHAK, R., AND SANTROCK, J. W. *The effects of father and mother custody on children's social development*. Paper presented at the meetings of the Society for Research in Child Development, San Francisco, March 1979.

WASSERMAN, G. A., ALLEN, R., AND SOLOMON, C. R. At-risk toddlers and their mothers: The special case of physical handicap. *Child Development*, 1985, *56*, 73–83.

WASZ-HOECKERT, O., LIND, J., VUORENKOSKI, V., PARTANEN, T., AND VALANNE, E. *The infant cry*. London: Heinemann Medical Books, 1968.

WATERMAN, A. Identity development from adolescence to adulthood: An extension of theory and a review of research. *Developmental Psychology*, 1982, *18*, 341–358.

WATERMAN, A. S. Identity in the context of adolescent psychology. In A. S. Waterman (Ed.), *Identity in adolescence: Processes and contents*. New Directions for Child Development, No. 30. San Francisco: Jossey-Bass 1985.

WATERMAN, G., GEARY, P., AND WATERMAN C. Longitudinal study of changes in ego identity status from the freshman to the senior year at college. *Developmental Psychology*, 1974, *10*, 387–392.

WATERS, E., AND DEANE, K. E. Defining and assessing individual differences in attachment relationships. *Monographs of the Society for Research in Child Development*, 1985, *50* (1-2, Serial No. 209), 41–45.

WATERS, E., HAY, D., AND RICHTERS, J. Infant-parent attachment and the origins of prosocial and antisocial behavior. In D. Olweus, J. Block, and M. Radke-Yarrow (Ed.), *Development of antisocial and prosocial behavior*. New York: Academic Press, 1986.

WATERS, E., MATAS, L., AND SROUFE, L. A. Infants' reactions to an approaching stranger: Description, validation, and functional significance of wariness. *Child Development*, 1975, *46*, 348–356.

WATERS, E., WIPPMAN, J., AND SROUFE, L. A. Attachment, positive affect, and competence in the peer group: Two studies in construct validation. *Child Development*, 1979, *50*, 821–829.

WATERSON, N. Growth of complexity in phonological development. In N. Waterson and C. E. Snow (Eds.), *The development of communication*. New York: Wiley, 1978.

WATSON, J. B. *Psychological care of infant and child*. New York: Norton, 1928.

WATSON, J. B., AND RAYNER, R. Conditioned emotional reactions. *Journal of Experimental Psychology*, 1920, *3*, 1–4.

WATSON, M. W. The development of social roles: A sequence of social-cognitive development. *New Directions for Child Development*, 1981, *12*, 33–41.

WAXLER, C. Z., AND RADKE-YARROW, M. An observational study of maternal models. *Developmental Psychology*, 1975, *11*, 485–494.

WEATHERLY, D. Self-perceived rate of physical maturation and personality in late adolescence. *Child Development*, 1964, *35*, 1197–1210.

WEBER, R. A., LEVITT, M. J., AND CLARK, M. C. Individual variation in attachment security and strange situation behavior: The role of maternal and infant temperament. *Child Development*, 1986, *57*, 56–65.

WEBSTER, R. L., STEINHARDT, M. H., AND SENTER, M. G. Changes in infants' vocalizations as a function of differential acoustic stimulation. *Developmental Psychology*, 1972, *7*, 39–43.

WECHSLER, D. *Manual for the Wechsler Intelligence Scale for children— Revised*. New York: Psychological Corporation, 1974.

WEIL, W. B. Infantile obesity. In M. Winick (Ed.), *Childhood obesity*. New York: Wiley, 1975.

WEIMAN, L. A. Stress patterns of early child language. *Journal of Child Language*, 1976, *3*, 283–286.

WEINER, B., AND HANDEL, S. J. A cognition-emotion-action sequence: Anticipated emotional consequences of causal attributions and reported communication strategy. *Developmental Psychology*, 1985, *21*, 102–107.

WEINRAUB, M., CLEMENS, L. P., SOCKLOFF, A., ETHRIDGE, T., GRACELY, E., AND MYERS, B. The development of sex role stereotypes in the third year: Relationships to gender labeling, gender identity, sex-typed toy preference, and family characteristics. *Child Development*, 1984, *55*. 1493–1503.

WEINRAUB, M., AND WOLF, B. M. Effects of stress and social supports on mother-child interactions in single- and two-parent families. *Child Development*, 1983, *54*, 1297-1311.

WEIR, C. Auditory frequency sensitivity of human newborns: Some data with improved acoustic and behavioral controls. *Perception and Psychophysics*, 1979, *26*, 287–294.

WEIR, R. H. *Language in the crib*. The Hague: Mouton, 1962.

WEISBERG, D. K. *Children of the night: A study of adolescent prostitution* Lexington, Mass.: Heath, 1985.

WEISBERG, P. Developmental differences in children's preferences for high- and low-arousing forms of contact stimulation. *Child Development*, 1975, *46*, 975–979.

WEISFELD, G. E., BLOCH, S. A., AND IVERS, J. W. Possible determinants of social dominance among adolescent girls. *Journal of Genetic Psychology*, 1984, *144*, 115–129.

WEISS, M. J., AND ZELAZO, P. R. *The cephalocaudal hypothesis: A comparison of infant leg kicks and arm flexions in water*. Paper presented at the International Conference on Infant Studies, New York, April 1984.

WEISS, R. J. Understanding moral thought: Effects on moral reasoning and decision making. *Developmental Psychology*, 1982, *18*, 852–861.

WEITHORN, L., AND CAMPBELL, S. Competency of minors to make crucial decisions reported in S. Cunningham. Court fails to settle abortion rights of minors. *APA Monitor*, March 1984, *15*, 7.

WEIZMANN, F., COHEN, L. B., AND PRATT, J. Novelty, familiarity and the development of infant attention. *Developmental Psychology*, 1971, *4*, 149–154.

WELLMAN, H. M. The early development of intentional memory behavior. *Human Development*, 1977, *20*, 86–101.(a)

WELLMAN, H. M. Preschoolers' understanding of memory-relevant variables. *Child Development*, 1977, *48*, 1720–1723. (b)

WELLMAN, H. M., AND LEMPERS, J. The naturalistic communication ability of two-year-olds. *Child Development*, 1977, *48*, 1052–1057.

WELLMAN, H. M., RITTER, K., AND FLAVELL, J. H. Deliberate memory behavior in the delayed reactions of very young children. *Developmental Psychology*, 1975, *11*, 780–787.

WELLS, G., AND RABAN, B. *Children learning to read*, SSRC Final Report No. HR 397/1. School of Education, University of Bristol, 1978.

WERNER, J. S., AND PERLMUTTER, M. Development of visual memory in infants. In H. W. Reese and L. P. Lipsitt (Eds.), *Advances in child development and behavior*, Volume 14. New York: Academic Press, 1980.

WERNER, J. S., AND SIQUELAND, E. R. Visual recognition memory in the preterm infant. *Infant Behavior and Development*, 1978, *1*, 79–94.

WERNER, E. E., AND SMITH, R. S. *Vulnerable but invincible: A longitudinal study of resilient children and youth*. New York: McGraw-Hill, 1982.

WERTS, C. Paternal influence on career choice. *Journal of Counseling Psychology*, 1968, *15*, 48–52.

WESTINGHOUSE AND OHIO UNIVERSITY. The impact of Head Start: An evaluation of the effects of Head Start on children's cognitive and affective development. In J. L. Frost (Ed.), *Revisiting early childhood education: Readings*. New York: Holt, Rinehart & Winston, 1973.

WESTON, D. R., AND RICHARDSON, E. *Children's world views: Working models and quality of attachment*. Poster presented at the biennial meeting of the Society for Research in Child Development, Toronto, Canada, April 1985.

WESTON, D. R., AND TURIEL, E. *Act-role relations: Children's concepts of social roles*. Unpublished manuscript, University of California at Berkeley, 1979.

WHALEN, C. K., AND HENKER, B. Hyperactivity and the attention deficit disorders: Expanding frontiers. *Pediatric Clinics of North America*, 1984, *31*, 397–427.

WHALEN, C. K., HENKER, B., AND DOTEMOTO, S. Teacher response to the methylphenidate (Ritalin) versus placebo status of hyperactive boys in the classroom. *Child Development*, 1981, *52*, 1005–1114.

WHISNANT, L., AND ZEGANS, L. A study of attitudes toward menarche among white middle-class American adolescent girls. *American Journal of Psychiatry*, 1975, *132*, 809–814.

WHITE, B. L. An experimental approach to the effects of experience on early human behavior. In J. P. Hill (Ed.), *Minnesota Symposia on Child Psychology*, Volume 1. Minneapolis: University of Minnesota Press, 1967.

WHITEHURST, G., AND VASTA, R. Is language acquired through imitation? *Journal of Psycholinguistic Research*, 1975, *4*, 37–59.

WHITEN, A. Assessing the effects of perinatal events on the success of the mother-infant relationship. In H. R. Schaffer (Ed.), *Studies in mother-infant interaction*. London: Academic Press, 1977.

WHITING, B. B., AND EDWARDS, C. P. A cross-cultural analysis of sex differences in the behavior of children age three through 11. In S. Chess and H. Thomas, (Eds.), *Annual progress in child psychiatry and child development, 1974*. New York: Brunner/Mazel, 1975.

WHITING, B. B., AND POPE-EDWARDS, C. (EDS.) *The effects of age, sex, and modernity on the behavior of mothers and children*. Report to the Ford Foundation, January 1977.

WIDEMAN, M. V., AND SINGER, J. E. The role of psychological mechanisms in preparation for childbirth. *American Psychologist*, 1984, *39*, 1357–1371.

WIDMAYER, S. M., AND FIELD, T. M. Effects of Brazelton demonstrations on early interactions of preterm infants and their teenage mothers. *Infant Behavior and Development*, 1980, *3*, 79–89.

WIENER, G. Psychologic correlates of premature birth: A review. *Journal of Nervous and Mental Diseases*, 1962, *134*, 129–144.

WIESENFELD, A. R., AND KLORMAN, R. The mother's psychophysiological reactions to contrasting affective expressions by her own and an unfamiliar infant. *Developmental Psychology*, 1978, *14*, 294–304.

WILEN, J. B., AND PETERSEN, A. C. *Young adolescents' responses to the timing of pubertal changes*. Paper presented at the annual meeting of the American Psychological Association, Montreal, September 1980.

WILKENING, F. Integrating velocity, time, and distance information: A developmental study. *Cognitive Psychology*, 1981, *13*, 231–247.

WILLATTS, P. Stages in the development of intentional search by young infants. *Developmental Psychology*, 1984, *20*, 389–396.

WILLIAMS, A. F. Children killed in falls from motor vehicles. *Pediatrics*, 1981, *68*, 576–578.

WILLIAMS, C. L., ARNOLD, C. B., AND WYNDER, E. L. Primary prevention of chronic disease beginning in childhood. *Preventive Medicine*, 1977, *6*, 344–357.

WILLIAMS, K. G., AND GOULET, L. R. The effects of cuing and constraint instructions on children's free recall performance. *Journal of Experimental Child Psychology*, 1975, *19*, 464–475.

WILLIAMS, R. L. Black pride, academic relevance and individual achievement. *Counseling Psychologist*, 1970, *2*, 321–325.

WILLIAMS, T. M. *The impact of television: A study of three Canadian communities*, ERIC Document ED 171 401. Vancouver: University of British Columbia 1977.

WILLIAMS, T. P., AND LILLIS, R. P. Changes in alcohol consumption by 18-year-olds following an increase in New York State's purchase age to 19. *Journal of Studies on Alcohol*, 1986, *47*, 290–296.

WILLIS, J., MORRIS, B., AND CROWDER, J. A remedial reading technique for disabled readers that employs students as behavioral engineers. *Psychology in the Schools*, 1972, *6*, 67–70.

WILMORE, J. H., AND McNAMARA, J. J. Prevalence of coronary heart disease risk factors in boys 8 to 12 years of age. *Journal of Pediatrics*, 1974, *84*, 527–533.

WILSON, J. G. Current status of teratology. In J. G. Wilson and F. C. Fraser (Eds.), *Handbook of teratology*. New York: Plenum, 1977.

WILSON, J. G., AND FRASER, F. C. (EDS.). *Handbook of teratology*. New York: Plenum, 1977.

WILSON, R. S. The Louisville Twin Study: Developmental synchronies in behavior. *Child Development*, 1983, *54*, 298–316.

WILSON, R. S. Risk and resilience in early mental development. *Developmental Psychology*, 1985, *21*, 795–805.

WILSON, R. S., AND HARPRING, E. B. Mental and motor development in infant twins. *Developmental Psychology*, 1972, *7*, 277–287.

WINDLE, M., AND LERNER, R. M. The "goodness of fit" model of temperament-context relations: Interaction or correlation? In J. V. Lerner and R. M. Lerner (Eds.), *New directions for child development: Temperament and social interaction during infancy and childhood*. San Francisco: Jossey-Bass, 1986.

WINICK, M. *Childhood obesity*. New York: Wiley, 1975.

WINTERBOTTEM, M. R. The relation of need for achievement to learning experiences in independence and mastery. In J. W. Atkinson (Ed.) *Motives in fantasy, action, and society*. New York: Van Nostrand, 1958.

WISH, M., DEUTSCH, M., AND KAPLAN, S. J. Perceived dimensions of interpersonal relations. *Journal of Personality and Social Psychology*, 1976, *33*, 409–420.

WITELSON, S. F. Sex and the single hemisphere: Specialization of the right hemisphere for spatial processing. *Science*, 1976, *193*, 425–426.

WITKIN, H. A., DYK, R. B., PATERSON, H. F., GOODENOUGH, D. R., AND KARP, S. A. *Psychological differentiation*. New York: Wiley, 1962.

WITKIN, H. A., MEDNICK, S. A., SCHULSINGER, F., BAKKESTROM, E., CHRISTIANSEN, K. O., GOODENOUGH, D. R., HIRSCHHORN, K., LUNDSTEEN, C., OWEN, D. R., PHILIP, J., RUBIN, D. B., AND STOCKING, M. Criminality in XYY and XXY men: The elevated crime rate of XYY males is not related to aggression. It may be related to low intelligence. *Science*, 1976, *193*, 547–555.

WOLF, D. P. Flexible texts: Computer editing in the study of writing. In E. L. Klein (Ed.), *Children and computers*. New Directions for Child Development, No. 28. San Francisco: Jossey-Bass, 1985.

WOLF, T. M., SKLOV, M. C., WENZL, P. A., HUNTER, S. M., AND BERENSON, G. S. Validation of a measure of Type A behavior pattern in children: Bogalusa Heart Study. *Child Development*, 1982, *53*, 126–135.

WOLFF, P. H. Observations on the early development of smiling. In B. M. Foss (Ed.), *Determinants of infant behavior*, Volume 2. New York: Wiley, 1963.

WOLFF, P. H. The natural history of crying and other vocalizations in early infancy. In B. M. Foss (Ed.), *The determinants of infant behaviour*, Volume 4. London: Methuen, 1969.

WOLSTENHOLME, G. E. W., AND O'CONNOR, M. *Endocrinology of the testis*. Boston: Little, Brown, 1967.

WOROBEY, J. *Temperament ratings in infancy: The salience of perceived difficulty*. Paper presented at the International Conference on Infant Studies. New York, April, 1984.

WRIGHT, L., SCHAEFER, A. B., AND SOLOMONS, G. *Encyclopedia of pediatric psychology*. Baltimore, Md.: University Park Press, 1979.

WRIGHT, P., MACLEOD, H. A., AND COOPER, M. J. Waking at night: The effect of early feeding experience. *Child: Care, Health and Development*, 1983, *9*, 309–319.

WUBBERHORST, J., GRADFORD, S., AND WILLIS, F. N. Trust in children as a function of race, sex and socio-economic group. *Psychological Reports*, 1971, *29*, 1183–1187.

WYNNE, E. A. Behind the discipline problem: Youth suicide as a measure of alienation. *Phi Delta Kappan*, 1978, *59*, 307–315.

YAKOVLEV, P. I., AND LECAURS, A. R. The myelogenetic cycles of regional maturation of the brain. In A. Minkowski (Ed.), *Regional development of the brain in early life*. Oxford: Basil Blackwell, 1967.

YALOM, I. D., LUNDE, D. T., MOOS, R. H., AND HAMBURG, D. A. "Postpartum blues" syndrome: A description and related variables. *Archives of General Psychiatry*, 1968, *18*, 16.

YANKELOVICH, D. *New rules: Searching for self-fulfillment in a world turned upside down*. New York: Random House, 1981.

YARROW, L. J., RUBENSTEIN, J. L., AND PEDERSEN, F. A. *Infant and environment: Early cognitive and motivational development*. Washington, D.C.: Hemisphere, 1975.

YEATES, K. O., MacPHEE, D., CAMPBELL, F. A., AND RAMEY, C. T. Maternal IQ and home environment as determinants of early childhood intellectual competence: A developmental analysis. *Developmental Psychology*, 1983, *19*, 731–739.

YERUSHALMY, J. The relationship of parents' smoking to outcome of pregnancy: Implications as to the problem of inferring causation from observed effects. *American Journal of Epidemiology*, 1971, *93*, 443–456.

YERUSHALMY, J. Infants with low birth weight born before their mothers started to smoke cigarettes. *American Journal of Obstetrics and Gynecology*, 1972, *112*, 277–284.

YOGMAN, M. W. *The goals and structure of face-to-face interaction between infants and fathers*. Paper presented at the biennial meeting of the Society for Research in Child Development, New Orleans, March 1977.

YOGMAN, M. W., COLE, P., ALS, H., AND LESTER, B. M. Behavior of newborns of diabetic mothers. *Infant Behavior and Development*, 1982, *5*, 331–340.

YONAS, A., AND PETTERSEN, L. *Responsiveness in newborns to optical information for collision*. Paper presented at the biennal meeting of the Society for Research in Child Development, San Francisco, March 1979.

YONAS, A., PETTERSEN, L., AND GRANRUD, C. E. Infants' sensitivity to familiar size as information for distance. *Child Development*, 1982, *53*, 1285–1290.

YOUNISS, J., AND VOLPE, J. A relational analysis of children's friendship. In W. Damon (Ed.), *New directions in child development: Social cognition*. San Francisco: Jossey-Bass, 1978.

YUSSEN, S. R., AND LEVY, U. Developmental changes in conscious knowledge about different retrieval problems. *Developmental Psychology*, 1977, *13*, 114–120.

ZAHN-WAXLER, C., FRIEDMAN, S. L., AND CUMMINGS, E. M. Children's emotions and behaviors in response to infants' cries. *Child Development*, 1983, *54*, 1522–1528.

ZAHN-WAXLER, C., IANNOTTI, R., AND CHAPMAN, M. Peers and prosocial development. In K. H. Rubin and H. S. Ross (Eds.), *Peer relationships and social skills in childhood*. New York: Springer-Verlag, 1982.

ZAHN-WAXLER, C., AND RADKE-YARROW, M. *A developmental analysis of children's responses to emotions in others*. Paper presented at the biennial meeting of the Society for Research in Child Development, San Francisco, March 1979.

ZAHN-WAXLER, C., RADKE-YARROW, M., AND BRADY-SMITH, J. Perspective-taking and prosocial behavior. *Developmental Psychology*, 1977, *13*, 87–88.

ZAHN-WAXLER, C., RADKE-YARROW, M., AND KING, R. A. Child rearing and children's prosocial initiations toward victims of distress. *Child Development*, 1979, *50*, 319–330.

ZAHN-WAXLER, C., RADKE-YARROW, M., AND KING, R. Early altruism and guilt. *Academic Psychology Bulletin*, 1983, *5*, 247–259.

ZARBATANY, L., HARTMANN, D. P., AND GELFAND, D. M. Why does children's generosity increase with age: Susceptibility to experimenter influence or altruism? *Child Development*, 1985, *56*, 746–756.

ZELAZO, P. R. From reflexive to instrumental behavior. In L. P. Lipsitt (Ed.), *Developmental psychobiology: The significance of infancy*. Hillsdale, N.J.: Lawrence Erlbaum Associates, 1976.

ZELAZO, P. R. The development of walking: New findings and old assumptions. *Journal of Motor Behavior*, 1983, *15*, 99–137.

ZELAZO, P. R., ZELAZO, N. A., AND KOLB, S. Walking in the newborn. *Science*, 1972, *176*, 314–315.

ZELLER, W. W. Adolescent attitudes and cutaneous health. *Journal of School Health*, March 1970, 115–120.

ZELNICK, M., AND KANTNER, J. F. Sexual activity, contraceptive use and pregnancy among metropolitan-area teenagers, 1971–1979. *Family Planning Perspectives*, 1978, *12*, 230–237.

ZELNICK, M., AND KIM, Y. J. Sex education and its association with teenage sexual activity, pregnancy, and contraception use. *Family Planning Perspectives*, 1982, *14*, 117–126.

ZELNIKER, T., AND JEFFREY, W. E. Reflective and impulsive children: Strategies of information processing underlying differences in problem solving. *Monographs of the Society for Research in Child Development*, 1976, *41* (5, Whole No. 168).

ZIGLER, E., LEVINE, J., AND GOULD, L. Cognitive challenge as a factor in children's human appreciation. *Journal of Personality and Social Psychology*, 1967, *6*, 332–336.

ZUCKER, K. J. *The development of search for mother during brief separation*. Unpublished doctoral dissertation, University of Toronto, 1982.

ZUCKER, R. A. *Sex role identity patterns and drinking behavior in adolescents*. Center for Alcohol Studies, Rutgers University, 1967.

ZUCKERMAN, D. Mom's jobs, kid's careers. *Psychology Today*, February 1985, 6.

ZUSSMAN, J. V. Situational determinants of parental behavior: Effects of competing cognitive activity. *Child Development*, 1980, *51*, 792–800.

Photo credits

Source notes

Chapter 1

Page 7, Figure 1.1   W. K. Frankenberg and J. B. Dodds. The Denver Developmental Screening Test. *Journal of Pediatrics*, 1967, *71*, 181–191.

Chapter 2

Page 48, Table 2.2   R. R. Sears, L. Rau, and R. Albert. *Identification and child rearing*. Stanford, Calif.: Stanford University Press, 1965.

Page 51, Table 2.4   J. Kagan and S. R. Tulkin. Social class differences in child rearing during the first year. In H. R. Schaffer (Ed.), *The origins of human social relations*. London: Academic Press, 1971.

Chapter 3

Page 68, Figure 3.2   I. I. Gottesman. Genetic aspects of intelligent behavior. In N. Ellis (Ed.), *The handbook of mental deficiency: Psychological theory and research*. New York: McGraw-Hill, 1963.

Page 69, Figure 3.4   Adapted from C. H. Waddington. *New patterns in genetics and development*. New York: Columbia University Press, 1962.

Page 72, Figure 3.5   D. Watson. *Molecular biology of the gene* (3rd ed.). Menlo Park, Calif.: Benjamin/Cummings Publishing Co., 1976. Reprinted by permission.

Page 77, Figure 3.8   H. H. Goddard. *The Kallikak family*. New York: Macmillan, 1912. Copyright 1940, by Henry H. Goddard.

Page 82, Figure 3.9   Adapted from L. Erlenmeyer-Kimling and L. F. Jarvik. Genetics and intelligence: A review. *Science*, 1963, *142*, 1477–1479. Copyright © 1963, by the American Association for the Advancement of Science.

Page 84, Figure 3.10   R. S. Wilson. Synchronies in mental development: An epigenetic perspective. *Science*, 1978, *202*, 939–948. Copyright © 1978, by the American Association for the Advancement of Science.

Page 87, Table 3.1   V. Apgar and J. Beck. *Is my baby all right?* New York: Pocket Books, 1974. K. L. Moore. *The developing human: Clinically oriented embryology* (3rd ed.). Philadelphia: W. B. Saunders, 1982.

Chapter 4

Page 99, Figure 4.1   C. Grobstein. External human fertilization. *Scientific American*, 1979, *240*(6), 57–68. Copyright © 1979, by Scientific American, Inc. All rights reserved.

Page 107, Figure 4.3   B. M. Patten. *Human embryology* (3rd ed.). New York: McGraw-Hill, 1968.

Page 112, Figure 4.4   C. Grobstein. External human fertilization. *Scientific American*, 1979, *240*(6), 57–68. Copyright © 1979, by Scientific American, Inc. All rights reserved. Neurons: Dr. Dominick P. Purpura, Albert Einstein College of Medicine, 1300 Morris Park Avenue, Bronx, N.Y. 10461

Page 119, Figure 4.6   D. H. Stott. The child's hazards in utero. In J. G. Howells (Ed.), *Modern perspectives in international child psychiatry*. Edinburgh: Oliver and Boyd, 1969. By permission of Longman Group Ltd., Division M, 1–3 Baxter's Place, Edinburgh, EH1 3AF.

Page 122, Figure 4.7   Adapted from N. Newton and C. Modahl. Pregnancy: The closest human relationship. *Human Nature*, 1978, *1*, March, 47.

Page 129, Table 4.2   Adapted from C. L. Blair and E. M. Salerno. *The expanding family: Childbearing*. Boston: Little, Brown, 1976. Copyright © 1976, by Carole L. Blaire and Elizabeth M. Salerno.

Page 130, Figure 4.8   J. G. Wilson. *Environment and birth defects*. New York: Academic Press, 1973. K. L. Moore. *The developing human: Clinically oriented embryology* (2nd ed.). Philadelphia: W. B. Saunders, 1977.

Chapter 5

Page 150, Table 5.1   V. Apgar. A proposal for a new method of evaluation of the newborn infant. *Current Research in Anesthesia and Analgesia*, 1953, *32*, 260–267.

Page 155, Figure 5.1   T. Hoppenbrouwers, M. Calub, K. Arakawa, and J. E. Hodgman. SIDS and environmental pollutants. *American Journal of Epidemiology*, 1981, *113*, 623–635.

Page 165, Figure 5.3   W. K. Berg, C. D. Adkinson, and B. L. Strock. Duration and periods of alertness in neonates. *Developmental Psychology*, 1973, *9*, 434. Copyright © 1973, by the American Psychological Association. Adapted by permission of the authors.

Page 166, Figure 5.4   H. P. Roffwarg, J. N. Muzio, and W. C. Dement. Ontogenetic development of the human sleepdream cycle. *Science*, 1966, *152* 604–609. Copyright © 1966, by the American Association for the Advancement of Science.

Page 175, Figure 5.7   R. N. Aslin. Development of smooth pursuits in human infants. In D. F. Fisher, R. A. Monty, and J. W. Senders (Eds.), *Eye movements: Cognition and visual perception*. Hillsdale, N.J.: Lawrence Erlbaum Associates, 1981.

Page 176, Figure 5.8   R. L. Fantz. Pattern discrimination and selective attention as determinants of perceptual development from birth. In A. H. Kidd and J. L. Rivoire (Eds.), *Perceptual development in children*. New York: International Universities Press, 1966.

Page 176, Figure 5.9   C. Goren. *Form perception, innate form preferences, and visually mediated head-turning in human neonates*. Unpublished doctoral dissertation, Committee on Human Development, University of Chicago, 1970.

Page 177, Figure 5.10   M. S. Banks and P. Salapatek. Infant visual perception. In P. Mussen (Ed.), *Handbook of child psychology*, Vol. 2. New York: Wiley, 1983. Copyright © 1983, by John Wiley & Sons.

Page 177, Figure 5.11   D. Maurer and P. Salapatek. Developmental changes in the scanning of faces by young infants. *Child Development*, 1976, *47*, 523–527.

Page 186, Figure 5.13   B. I. Bertenthal, J. J. Campos, and M. M. Haith. Development of visual organization: The perception of subjective contours. *Child Development*, 1980, *51*, 1072–1080.

Chapter 6

Page 212, Table 6.1   Sample items from Bayley Scales of Infant Development (Mental Scale Record form). Copyright © 1969, by The Psychological Corporation.

Page 215, Table 6.2   E. H. Lenneberg. *Biological foundations of language*. New York: Wiley, 1967. Copyright © 1967, by John Wiley & Sons.

Page 219, Figure 6.3   Adapted from H. Gleitman. *Psychology*. New York: Norton, 1981.

Chapter 7

Page 239, Figure 7.1   L. A. Sroufe. Socioemotional development. In J. D. Osofsky (Ed.), *Handbook of infant development*. New York: Wiley, 1979. Copyright © 1979, by John Wiley & Sons.

Page 242, Figure 7.2   E. Waters, L. Matas, and L. A. Sroufe. Infants' reactions to an approaching stranger: Description, validation, and functional significance of wariness. *Child Development*, 1975, *46*, 348–356.

Page 254, Table 7.2   A. Thomas and S. Chess. *Temperament and development*. New York: Brunner/Mazel, 1977.

Chapter 8

Page 279, Figure 8.1   G. A. Harrison, J. S. Weiner, J. M. Tanner, and N. A. Barnicot. *Human biology* (1st and 2nd eds.). Oxford: Oxford University Press, 1964, 1977.

Page 281, Figure 8.3   J. M. Tanner. *Foetus into man*. London: Open Books Publishing Ltd., 1978.

Page 282, Figure 8.4   H. V. Meredith. Research between 1960 and 1970 on the standing height of young children in different parts of the world. In H. W. Reese and L. P. Lipsitt (Eds.), *Advances in child development and behavior*, Volume 12. New York: Academic Press, 1978.

Page 283, Table 8.1   G. H. Lowrey. *Growth and development of children* (6th and 7th eds.). Chicago: Yearbook Medical Publishers, 1973, 1978.

Page 290, Figure 8.5   Courtesy Campbell Soup Company.

Page 293, Figure 8.6   A. R. Lecours. Myelogenetic correlates of the development of speech and language. In E. H. Lenneberg and E. Lenneberg (Eds.), *Foundations of language development*. New York: Academic Press, 1975.

Page 297, Figure 8.8   Centers for Disease Control, 1982.

Page 298, Figure 8.9   U.S. Department of Health and Human Services, 1982.

Chapter 9

Page 311, Figure 9.1   C. Golomb. *Young children's sculpture and drawing: A study in representation development*. Cambridge, Mass.: Harvard University Press, 1974. Reprinted by permission.

Page 317, Figure 9.2   Adapted from J. Piaget and B. Inhelder. *The child's conception of space*. London: Routledge and Kegan Paul, 1956; Atlantic Highlands, N.J.: Humanities Press, 1963.

Page 323, Figure 9.4   R. Gelman. The nature and development of early number concepts. In H. W. Reese (Ed.), *Advances in child development and behavior*, Volume 7. New York: Academic Press, 1972.

Page 327, Figure 9.6   Adapted from J. Bruner. The course of cognitive growth. *American Psychologist*, 1964, *19*, 6. Copyright © 1964, by the American Psychological Association. Adapted by permission of the author.

Page 330, Figure 9.7   Adapted from R. Gelman. Conservation acquisition: A problem of learning to attend to relevant attributes. *Journal of Experimental Child Psychology*, 1969, *7*, 174.

Page 332, Figure 9.8   E. Vurpillot. The development of scanning strategies and their relation to visual differentiation. *Journal of Experimental Child Psychology*, 1968, *6*, 632–650.

Page 353, Figure 9.9   S. W. Gray, B. K. Ramsey, and R. A. Klaus. *From 3 to 20: The Early Training Project*. Baltimore, Md.: University Park Press, 1982.

Chapter 10

Page 359, Figure 10.1   H. L. Rheingold, and C. O. Eckerman. Departures from the mother. In H. R. Schaffer (Ed.), *The origins of human social relations*. London: Academic Press, 1971.

Page 379, Table 10.1   E. Mueller and T. Lucas. A developmental analysis of peer interaction among toddlers. In M. Lewis and L. A. Rosenblum (Eds.), *Friendship and peer relations*. New York: Wiley, 1975. Copyright © 1975, by John Wiley & Sons.

Page 403, Figure 10.2   E. G. Pitcher, and L. H. Schultz. *Boys and girls at play—The development of sex roles*. South Hadley, Mass.: Bergin and Garvey Publishers, 1983.

Chapter 11

Page 423, Table 11.1   M. A. Stewart, B. T. Thach, and M. R. Freidin.

Accidental poisoning and the hyperactive child syndrome. *Diseases of the Nervous System*, 1970, *31*, 403–407. Copyright © 1970, by Physicians Postgraduate Press. Reprinted by permission.

Page 428, Table 11.2   E. Frye. A do-it-yourself learning disability terminology generator. Newark, Del.: International Reading Association, 1968. Copyright © 1968, by International Reading Association. Reprinted by permission.

Page 429, Figure 11.1   S. Farnham-Diggory. *Learning disabilities*. Cambridge, Mass.: Harvard University Press, 1978.

Chapter 12

Page 440, Table 12.1   L. Kohlberg. Stage and sequence: The cognitive-developmental approach to socialization. In D. A. Goslin (Ed.), *Handbook of socialization theory and research*. Boston: Houghton Mifflin, 1969.

Page 457, Figure 12.2   Sample items from the Wechsler Intelligence Scale for Children and the Wechsler Adult Intelligence Scale. Copyright © 1971, by the Psychological Corporation. All rights reserved. Reproduced by permission.

Page 462, Figure 12.4   J. W. Getzels and P. W. Jackson. *Creativity and intelligence*. New York: Wiley, 1962. Copyright © 1962, by John Wiley & Sons.

Page 464, Figure 12.5   Last item taken from the Culture Fair Intelligence Test, Scale 3, Form B. Copyright © 1950, 1961, by the Institute for Personality and Ability Testing, Inc. All rights reserved. Reproduced by permission of the copyright owner.

Page 466, Figure 12.6   J. Kagan. Impulsive and reflective children: Significance of conceptual tempo. In J. D. Krumboltz (Ed.), *Learning and the educational process*. Chicago: Rand-McNally, 1965.

Page 467, Figure 12.7   Reprinted from *La bambola di Guilietta* (Dinah's doll) (Hebrew translation) with permission from Editrice Piccoli S.p.A., Milan, Italy. T. Zelniker and W. E. Jeffrey. Reflective and impulsive children. *Monographs of the Society for Research in Child Development*, 1976, *41* (5, Whole No. 168).

Page 479, Figure 12.10   Prefix Program produced by the Minnesota Educational Computing Corporation. Copyright © 1980, by the Minnesota Educational Computing Corporation. Reprinted by permission. Pizza Program developed by Sharon Dugdale and David Kibbey at the University of Illinois. Copyright © 1973, by the University of Illinois. Reprinted by permission.

Chapter 13

Page 489, Figure 13.1   S. Ellis, B. Rogoff, and C. Cromer. Age segregation in children's social interactions. *Developmental Psychology*, 1981, *17*, 399–407. Copyright © 1981, by the American Psychological Association. Adapted by permission of the authors.

Page 497, Figure 13.2   S. Kagan and M. C. Madsen. Cooperation and competition of Mexican, Mexican-American, and Anglo-American children of two ages under four instructional sets. *Developmental Psychology*, 1971, *5*, 32–39. Copyright © 1971, by the American Psychological Association. Adapted by permission of the authors.

Page 501, Figure 13.3   L. D. Eron, L. R. Huesmann, P. Brice, P. Fischer, and R. Mermelstein. Age trends in the development of aggression, sex typing, and related television habits. *Developmental Psychology*, 1983, *19*, 71–77. Copyright © 1983, by the American Psychological Association. Adapted by permission of the authors.

Page 522, Table 13.1   A. Thomas, S. Chess, and H. G. Birch. *Temperament and behavior disorders in children*. New York: New York University Press, 1968.

Chapter 14

Page 531, Figure 14.2   J. M. Tanner and R. H. Whitehouse. Clinical longitudinal standards for height, weight, height velocity, weight velocity, and the stages of puberty. *Archives of Disease in Childhood*, 1976, *51*, 170–179. J. M. Tanner. *Fetus into man: Physical growth from conception to maturity*. Cambridge, Mass.: Harvard University Press, 1978.

Page 534, Figure 14.4   H. Gardner. *Developmental psychology: An introduction* (2nd ed.). Boston: Little, Brown, 1982. Pictures drawn for the study E. Koff, J. Rierdan, and E. Silverstone. Changes in the representation of body image as a function of menarcheal status. *Developmental Psychology*, 1978, *14*, 635–642. Used by permission of E. Koff.

Page 540, Figure 14.6   Adapted from The Alan Guttmacher Institute. *Teenage pregnancy: The problem that hasn't gone away*. New York, 1981. With permission of the publisher.

Page 543, Figure 14.7   Adapted from H. Brown, R. G. Adams, and S. G. Kellam. A longitudinal study of teenage motherhood and symptoms of distress. In R. G. Simmons (Ed.), *Research in community and mental health*, Volume 2. Greenwich, Conn.: JAI Press, 1981.

Page 544, Figure 14.8   Adapted from The Alan Guttmacher Institute. *Teenage pregnancy: The problem that hasn't gone away*. New York, 1981. With permission of the publisher.

Page 547, Figure 14.9   J. Mervis. Adolescent behavior: What we think we know. *APA Monitor*, April 1984, pp. 24–25. T. Morganthau, M. Miller, J. Huck, and J. DeQuine. Kids and cocaine. *Newsweek*, March 17, 1986, pp. 58–65.

Chapter 15

Page 555, Figure 15.1   B. Inhelder and J. Piaget. *The growth of logical thinking from childhood to adolescence*. New York: Basic Books, 1958.

Page 558, Table 15.1   Z. Marini. *The development of social and physical cognition in childhood and adolescence*. Unpublished doctoral dissertation, University of Toronto (OISE), 1984.

Page 577, Figure 15.4   A. Colby, L. Kohlberg, J. Gibbs, and M. Lieberman. A longitudinal study of moral judgment. *Monographs of the Society for Research in Child Development*, 1983, *48* (1, Serial No. 200).

Page 582, Figure 15.5   W. M. Gray and L. M. Hudson. Formal oper-

ations and the imaginary audience. *Developmental Psychology*, 1984, *20*, 619–627. Copyright © 1984, by the American Psychological Association. Adapted by permission of the authors.

Chapter 16

Page 589, Figure 16.1   M. Csikszentmihalyi and R. Larson. *Being adolescent: Conflict and growth in the teenage years*. New York: Basic Books, 1984. Copyright © 1984 by Basic Books, Inc., Publishers. Reprinted by permission of the publisher.

Page 591, Figure 16.2   R. G. Simmons, E. F. Van Cleave, D. A. Blyth, and D. M. Bush. Entry into early adolescence: The impact of school structure, puberty, and early dating on self-esteem. *American Sociological Review*, 1979, *44*, 956.

Page 596, Table 16.2   A. S. Waterman. Identity in the context of adolescent psychology. In A. S. Waterman (Ed.), *Identity in adolescence: Processes and contents*. New Directions for Child Development, 30. San Francisco: Jossey-Bass, 1985.

Page 604, Table 16.3   M. Csikszentmihalyi and R. Larson. *Being adolescent: Conflict and growth in the teenage years*. New York: Basic Books, 1984. Copyright © 1984 by Basic Books, Inc., Publishers. Reprinted by permission of the publisher.

Page 607, Figure 16.3   P. R. Costanzo and M. E. Shaw. Conformity as a function of age level. *Child Development*, 1966, *37*, 967–975. T. J. Berndt. Developmental changes in conformity to peers and parents. *Developmental Psychology*, 1979, *15*, 608–616. Copyright © 1979, by the American Psychological Association. Adapted by permission of the author.

Page 609, Figure 16.4   D. C. Dunphy. The social structure of urban adolescent peer groups. *Sociometry*, 1963, *26*, 236.

Page 613, Figure 16.5   G. Sykes. The future of crime. *Crime and Delinquency Issues: A Monograph Series*, 1980, ADM 80–212, 85.

Author Index

Subject Index